薛鳳生 著

薛鳳生文集

鳳凰出版社

圖書在版編目（CIP）數據

薛鳳生文集 / (美) 薛鳳生著 ; 楊亦鳴主編. -- 南京 : 鳳凰出版社, 2024.5
ISBN 978-7-5506-4029-0

Ⅰ. ①薛… Ⅱ. ①薛… ②楊… Ⅲ. ①漢語－語言學－文集 Ⅳ. ①H1-53

中國國家版本館CIP數據核字(2023)第225070號

書　　名	薛鳳生文集
著　　者	(美)薛鳳生 著　楊亦鳴 主編
責任編輯	孫　州
特約編輯	莫　培
裝幀設計	陳貴子
責任監製	程明嬌
出版發行	鳳凰出版社(原江蘇古籍出版社) 發行部電話025-83223462
出版社地址	江蘇省南京市中央路165號,郵編:210009
照　　排	南京凱建文化發展有限公司
印　　刷	江蘇蘇中印刷有限公司 江蘇省泰州市經濟開發區鮑徐鎮,郵編:225315
開　　本	652毫米×960毫米　1/16
印　　張	73.75
字　　數	1129千字
版　　次	2024年5月第1版
印　　次	2024年5月第1次印刷
標準書號	ISBN 978-7-5506-4029-0
定　　價	480.00圓(全三册)

(本書凡印裝錯誤可向承印廠調換,電話:0523-82099008)

《薛鳳生文集》編委會

薛鳳生先生

與趙元任、楊步偉伉儷等合影（後排左一爲薛鳳生）

與王力(中)、周祖謨(左)合影

1982年9月,與嚴學宭(左二)、邵榮芬(右二)、王顯(右三)、趙誠(左三)等在唐乾陵合影(右一爲薛鳳生)

與錢鍾書、楊絳夫婦及黎天睦(Tim Light)合影(左一爲薛鳳生)

薛鳳生、陳慕勤伉儷（右二人）與丁邦新、陳琪伉儷（左二人）。

1999 年 7 月 13 日，與楊亦鳴(左)在加州大學戴維斯分校 Peter J. Shields 圖書館前

薛鳳生、陳慕勤伉儷

目　錄

上　册

音韻理論

中　册

方言研究

唐詩格律

下　册

語法探索

語文建設

文學風雅

序

2015 年，老友薛鳳生教授歸於道山，歲月不居，瞬已八載。現在他畢生的著述即將結集由鳳凰出版社出版，薛鳳生教授夫人約我寫幾句話，我感到十分榮幸。

薛鳳生教授是江蘇徐州邳縣(今邳州市)人，早年畢業於臺灣大學，受業於臺静農先生、董同龢先生，後赴美留學，在印第安納大學獲得博士學位後，任教於俄亥俄州立大學。中美建交之後，薛鳳生教授致力於中美學術交流。從上世紀 80 年代開始，薛鳳生教授的著作即開始在國内學術界傳播。《北京音系解析》和《〈中原音韻〉音位系統》由北京語言學院出版社出版，《漢語音韻史十講》由華語教學出版社出版。後者，我亦曾爲之作序。

讀《薛鳳生文集》中的詩，頗能感受到薛鳳生教授對家鄉徐州的深情厚誼。1981 年，薛鳳生教授第一次回家鄉徐州，途經西雅圖，即賦詩一首："塵埃野馬蔽山崗，滄溟無涯映夕陽。鐵翼御風歸去也，浮雲盡處是吾鄉。"詩中飽含蒼凉之意、滄桑之感與期待之情。1996 年，薛鳳生教授再回徐州，並賦詩："天涯爲客久，長憶古彭城。喜看雄豪地，英才輩輩生。"詩中洋溢着豪邁之感與喜悦之情。十餘年間，家鄉欣欣向榮的發展變化以及遇見學術上的知音，是薛鳳生教授心境變化之根源。薛鳳生教授在家鄉江蘇師範大學(當時名爲徐州師範學院)與年輕有爲的楊亦鳴教授結成忘年之交，楊亦鳴教授 1992 年出版的大著《李氏音鑒音系研究》頗有創見，所創立的透視分離法對後來的音韻學專書和漢語語音史研究很有啓發，好友楊耐思先生多所擊賞。在音韻學方法論方面，楊亦鳴教授很贊同薛鳳生教授"嚴格的音位學説"視野下的音韻學研究，頗有"當路誰相假，知音世所希"之意。此後薛鳳生教授作爲江蘇師範大學兼聘教授在江蘇師範大學語言研究所設壇講學，還建立了"薛叙齋語言學獎勵基金"，獎掖後學，造福桑梓。從某種意義上來説，徐州可謂薛鳳生教授學術思想在中國的傳播中心，也是薛鳳生教授在生命最後時刻魂歸夢縈的地方。薛鳳生教授夫人薛陳慕勤教授説，在薛鳳生教授的最後歲月裏，他一口流利的英文全都忘記了，衹能説徐州話。

擺在讀者面前的這套《薛鳳生文集》，是由薛陳慕勤教授全權授權江蘇師範大學楊亦鳴教授負責編纂和出版的。我推想,由薛鳳生教授的學術知音和家鄉人負責其文集的出版,也是薛陳慕勤教授爲了卻薛鳳生教授的心願而做出的决定。如今,《薛鳳生文集》的編纂不僅由家鄉的學者總其成,而且由家鄉的出版社鳳凰出版社出版,應如其願了。

我與薛鳳生教授相識,是先見其文,後聞其聲。1980 年,王力先生在山東省語言學會成立大會的講話中,稱贊美國一位漢學家"很簡明地解决了等韻學中的内外轉問題"。這位漢學家就是薛鳳生教授。當時王先生和我,與薛鳳生教授都還不認識。1982 年 8 月,薛鳳生教授與王先生和我,在西安舉辦的中國音韻學研究會第二次學術年會上第一次見面。薛鳳生教授見到王先生時,尊稱其"太老師",王先生特别高興。1984 年,王先生在《我的治學經驗》一文中再次談及薛鳳生教授:"近兩年,漢藏語系學術會議,我看到美國的、法國的一些作者寄來的論文很好,很有價值。例如,關於内外轉問題,羅常培先生寫過文章,我看了不滿意。我也寫過這方面的文章,覺得也没有解决問題。兩年前看到美國漢學家的文章,我認爲他解决了問題。總之,有些好東西,用外文寫的,我們要看。"可見,薛鳳生教授有關"内外轉"的研究給王先生留下了深刻的印象。

我曾經説過,薛鳳生教授"研究漢語音韻,頗有自己的特色。最突出的就是重視理論分析,因而能高瞻遠矚;重視音位的方法,强調系統性,因而能切合古漢語音韻的實際"。其實,重讀《薛鳳生文集》中的音韻學論著,我越來越感受到,"内外轉"在中古漢語到《中原音韻》音系結構演變中發揮着决定性作用。可惜等韻學的這一傳統,我們到現在還没有完全搞清楚,甚至有點兒遺忘了。現在很少能見到討論"内外轉"及其應用的文章。看來,國内學術界亟待加强等韻學的研究。

薛鳳生教授一生,"情繫祖國,誼淳同道。學貫中西,業通古今",正可謂"謙謙君子,温文爾雅"。雖然他的學術成就主要體現在等韻學和《中原音韻》的研究上,但在其他方面也頗有建樹,如語法學等,但無論是做什麼研究,薛鳳生教授都一貫地堅守其治學的基本特色,那就是努力挖掘漢語的本體特色。這是特别值得我們學習的。《薛鳳生文集》的出版是音韻學界的一件大事,也是語言學界的一件大事。在此再次"希望大家重視薛先生提出的理論方法問題,並從中獲得有益的啓迪"。

唐作藩 2023年10月22日

音韻理論

傳統聲韻學與現代音韻學理論*

一、選題的原因

這次承大會主持人的邀請，我才有機會回來與聲韻學界的同好們交換研究心得，我非常高興而且感激。這有兩層原因。首先，對於各位代表，我多半早已聞名，但却一直無緣識荆、交换意見，這實在是一大憾事。其次，更重要的是，我很想聽聽各位的批評。我是先研讀現代音韻理論而後轉治漢語史的。老實説，在開始的時候，我也像某些人一樣，對傳統聲韻學多少有一些偏見，認爲是老古董，不科學。但是在經過多年的鑽研與思考之後，終於認識到古人實不我欺。他們的觀點與方法，都是大有道理的，而且在很大程度上是與現代音韻理論相契合的。因此，我的研究工作終於走上了"中西結合"的路子；也因此一直希望能有機會，把我的"一愚之得"介紹給各位同好，請各位做我的裁判，評一評我的做法是否多少也有一些道理。所以，當我看到這次大會的主題是"聲韻學之過去、現在與未來"時，就特别高興，並且選定了現在這個題目。

二、聲韻學研究之目的

首先我想説一説我對中國聲韻學的看法，即我研究的目標何在。當代歐美學者們所謂的聲韻學（phonology），是一個兼容並蓄的多元性術語，一方面涵蓋着一般性的實驗語音學（experimental phonetics），做音量與聲波的分析；另一方面也涵蓋着個别自然語言的特定音位系統（phonemic system）的分析，因此它的研究目標也是多元性的。約略言之，包括下列幾個方面：1. 口舌等

---

* 該文收入《漢語音韻史十講》時有删減，今補全，收入本文集。
本文原是在第二屆聲韻學學術研討會（高雄，1992 年）上的報告，曾刊登在該會論文集。

器官的發音功能；2. 聽覺神經的辨音功能；3. 語音的合成與辨認；4. 語音相互間的生理與聲學關係；5. 語音轉變的原因與規律；6. 自然語言的音位分析；7. 音位區別的共同基礎；8. 聲韻與語法及語義的關係等。貫穿着這許多目標的是一個基本願望，即希望瞭解人類的"語言機能"(linguistic capability)的本質，以及各種自然語言所含有的共性(linguistic universals)。但在實際的研究工作中，没有哪個人可以兼顧這許多不同的方面。個別的學者衹能按他的興趣與需要，選擇個別的研究目標。比如說，上述的 1、2、3、4 等項，基本上是物理學、心理學與認知科學(cognitive science)的問題；而 5、6、7、8 等項，則與人文科學的研究較有關係。當然在爲了上述任何一個目標做研究時所取得的成果，都可能對達成另一些目標具有重要的功用；但作爲個別的研究者，我們就必須集中精力，認清我們所做的研究是什麽性質、爲了什麽目的。就我個人來說，我的興趣是漢語史，以及漢語與中國文化之間的關係，而不是更抽象的"語言機能"。因此我偏重對漢語音系的分析，儘可能地利用一切理論的假設與方法，以達成這一目標；也正是由於這一目標的選定，我終於"歸真反樸"，走回了與傳統聲韻學相結合的道路。我認爲這才是"中國聲韻學"的目標。

三、聲韻學的發展過程

上面列舉的一些聲韻學研究的目標，當然不是同時出現的，而是經過了一段相當長的歷史過程漸次産生的。

3.1 大家都知道，早期西方語言學的發展跟中國差不多，都是從人文觀點出發的。由於社會發展的需要，許多民族都先後制定了書寫文字，然後由於文獻的積累，也就有了注釋文獻的需要，因而促成專業語文工作者的出現。與中國不同的是，西方各民族采用的多半是拼音文字。拼音文字當然有許多優點，但也有一個缺點：它常常使人産生一種錯覺，以爲拼音符號是直接代表發音方式的，是放諸四海而皆準的，從而在觀念上忽略了個別語言的特定音位系統。這對音韻理論的研究就形成了一種阻礙。所以聲韻學在西方雖然也有相當悠久的歷史，而且在十八世紀、十九世紀曾經大放異彩，確立了歷史比較語言學的地位；但在觀念上，仍然無法擺脱語音音值普遍性的錯覺。音位觀念的提出,竟遲至二十世紀初,而且需要經過布拉格學派(Prague School)諸學者及布龍菲爾德(Bloomfield)、沙皮爾(Sapir)等美國學者大力鼓吹後,才漸爲多數學者所接受。從此聲韻學理論才得到突破性的發展。先有雅柯布遜(Jakobson)等提出"區别性特徵"(distinctive feature)説,試圖爲各種不同的音位系統找出共同的聲學基礎;繼有哈萊(Halle)與喬姆斯基(Chomsky)等提出"孳生聲韻學"(generative phonology)説,意圖把聲韻學與語法及語義學等密切地聯繫起來。這些新説都擴大了聲韻學的領域,而且在確認了音位觀念之後,仍想找出語音的共通性,因爲他們的目標是瞭解人類的"語言機能"。

3.2 中國聲韻學的研究史,可以説比西方長得多,所積累的資料也比較豐富;在理論與方法上也甚有貢獻,但是其研究的動機與目標,是比較具體的。我曾經大膽概括地説過,中國聲韻學家的目標,是研究"聖人與詩人的語言";這就是説,他們對"販夫、走卒、婦人、孺子"的俚言俗語是毫無興趣的。所謂研究"聖人的語言",就是"解經";所謂研究"詩人的語言",就是爲詩文"正音"。古韻學家的目的是通過古韻更正確地詮釋先秦典籍,今韻學家的目的是訂正詩詞韻律的用字,即所謂"正語作詞"。這在當時都是有極重要的社會與政治意義的。衹有等韻學家,才把注意力指向聲韻的系統與理論,但這系統與理論也是依附今韻而存在的。然而這並不意味着中國聲韻學没有理論根據,或不曾作出理論與方法上的貢獻。事實恰恰相反,在研究聖人與詩人的語言時,他們使用了很巧妙的方法,而且具有堅實的理論根據。要認識這一點,我們必須先明瞭中國聲韻學資料的性質。大家都知道,中文不是拼音文字,有不少缺點,但也有一個好處,即每個字都直接代表音系中允許存在的一個音節①,擺脱了細微發音差異的糾纏。這就嚴格地確立了這種資料的音位性(phonemic nature)。後來的韻書都采用反切標音,這種方式自然也衹能是音位性的。另一方面,像《切韻》(或《廣韻》)及《中原音韻》等韻書,都采用了分調、分韻及分

① 關於中國文字的性質,有許多誤解。最常見的説法是,中文是"表意文字",可以就形以求義,不必經過讀音。這個説法是有問題的,因爲當一個符號直接代表事物時,它衹是一個"符號"(symble),還不能算是真正的"文字"(writing)。衹有當它直接代表某一語言中的某一特定讀音(語詞)時,才變成"文字"。(趙元任先生對此有極精審的論證,參看趙 1968,第 101 頁。)中文當然是"文字",也就是説,每個字都有一個特定的讀法,代表一個音系中的一個特定的音節。

隔小韻等分類法,所根據的原則,也衹能是音位性的對比(phonemic contrast)。等韻學家進一步歸納聲類(三十六字母等),以"五音""清濁"等觀念爲之定性;並以"開、合、等、攝"等概念歸納界定各種韻類。這些做法都是很了不起的成就。用這種方式,討論或説明漢語聲韻的形態、漢語史中的演變,以及漢語方言之間的差異,自然是合理、簡潔而且有效的。這類韻書也都全面、完整地記録下當時語音音節的對比,因而爲我們提供了寶貴的資料,使我們得以窺見各不同時期的完整音系。因此我常説,中國古代的聲韻學家,比西方學者早好幾個世紀就應用音位觀念了;而等韻學家所用的方法,與"區别性特徵"説精神上亦暗合①。

3.3 上述中國式的音韻理論與方法,雖然極有道理,却也有一個附帶的缺點。由於它表達的方式過分抽象,所以不易流傳,而且還往往引起不必要的穿鑿附會。早在宋代,就已經有人把它跟五行、術數及宫商角徵羽等扯到一起去了②,結果是越講越玄。西方學者自然也不能領會這些中國的老法子,否則就用不着等到二十世紀才提出音位學説了。從這個觀點看,高本漢等人爲中古漢語"擬音",實在是繞了個不必要的大圈子。由於他不瞭解《廣韻》等書的音位性,所以做了許多不够形態化的構擬③;後來的學者在改進他的構擬時,也

① "傳統音韻學是建立在音位系統上的。"我這個説法,仍有很多人不能理解,或不能完全接受。例如,北京大學的何九盈教授,在他的《古漢語音韻學述要》中,引用了一大段我論等韻性質的話(第 89、90 頁),但同時又説:"美國學者薛鳳生甚至把漢語等韻學和西方的音位學説相提並論。"他説"甚至",可見他認爲我説過頭了。這大概是由於我們對"音位性"一詞的理解不完全相同。

② 自邵雍的《皇極經世聲音唱和圖》起,學者就常把聲韻跟所謂"天聲地音"等術數的觀念牽强地配在一起,或以"天地龍虎"等湊成十二個數目(如清樊騰鳳的《五方元音》。參看趙 1957、李 1983 及耿 1992),引起不少糾葛,也加深了聲韻學的神秘性。這是很不幸的。但從另一角度看,他們這樣做,既有可理解的原因,也有相當大的用處(全看我們如何利用)。音位結構有一個通性,即總是簡約的、對稱的、系統化的。當古人研究他們自己的語言時,自然會隱約地感覺到這個對稱結構的存在,驚詫之餘,自然便以爲這是"天造地設"的神物,是與四時萬物相表裏的,因此作出了許多玄學性的臆測(參看薛 1987)。然而他們留下的著作,如果我們能善加利用,却是幫助我們理解各時代之音系的好資料。周祖謨先生的《宋代汴洛語音考》就是一個好例子(周 1943)。

③ "構擬"(reconstruction)是出自印歐語研究的一個術語,意思是,利用後代的相關語言及文獻,推論出歷史上某一個未曾記録下來的語言,如印歐語和漢藏語。根據這個定義,當我們爲《切韻》以來的某一韻書"擬音"時,實在不算"構擬",而是分析那些記録,爲其背後的音系作詮釋(interpretation)。在中國聲韻學裏,衹有釐定上古韻部可以勉强稱爲"構擬"。

衹能從音系的觀點，把不够系統化的地方逐漸改正過來，不可能是根據"實際語言"的①。

關於"音位分析"這一概念的定義，學者迄今仍有不同的看法。例如趙元任先生就有所謂"非唯一性"（non-uniqueness，參看趙 1934）的説法，認爲對於同一種語言的音位，由於分析者的目的不同，就可以得出不同的結論，無所謂誰是誰非，所以不必過分嚴格。我的想法則跟雅柯布遜較接近，認爲真正完善的分析應該是唯一的（參看 Jakobson 1951）。當然，分析出這個獨特的音系，不是容易的，但我們應該以此爲終極目標。我更進一步認爲，真正完善的音系，應是"語感"的最佳具體表現，也可以説，音位分析的目的就是描述説某一種語言的人群的共同語感，即他們對語音的直覺反應方式。分析時務求嚴格，因爲就這個目標説，鬆散的標音或擬音是没有多大意義的。

四、由國音符號看傳統音韻學

我曾試圖用上述的觀點及方法，分析北京話的音系。在這方面，哈特曼（Hartman 1944）、霍克特（Hockett 1947）和藤堂明保（Toodoo 1963）等，早已作出了相當大的貢獻。但從上述的高度理論觀點看，他們的分析則仍未盡完善，所以我更推進一步，提出了自己的看法（參看薛 1980 及薛 1986）。這個分析是以現代音韻理論爲根據的，但其結論與傳統音韻學的分類結果完全一致。這一點我當時尚未完全認清，而是數年後才豁然領悟的。我開始認識到，凡是他們分析欠妥的地方，都是由於背離了中國傳統聲韻學的原則。這當然也不能怪他們，因爲他們對這一傳統的認識仍嫌不足。但這個事實，足以説明傳統聲韻學的優越性。我不擬在此細評他們的缺失，衹想用下面這張表説明，我的分析與國音符號是若合符契的。我想大家都同意，注音符號是傳統聲韻學的産物，所以由此可以看出傳統聲韻學的道理。（參看薛 1986）

① 當然我們必須承認（而且感謝）高本漢先生爲中國聲韻學所作出的貢獻，是他首先全面地把中國聲韻學與歐洲的歷史比較語言學聯繫起來，跨出了中國聲韻學"國際化"的第一步。同時，由於他采用較具體的標音符號詮釋古音，這就在相當大的程度上，減輕了傳統聲韻學的神秘色彩。但我們也必須認識到，他的貢獻基本上都不是理論性的。

韻基	wɨ	øɨ yɨ ywɨ	ə		a	ɨy	ay	ɨw	aw	ɨn	an	ɨŋ	aŋ
十三轍	姑蘇	一七	梭坡	乜斜	發花	灰堆	懷來	油求	遙條	人辰	言前	東中	江陽
注音符號	ㄨ	(ø) ㄧㄩ	ㄛㄜ	ㄝ	ㄚ	ㄟ	ㄞ	ㄡ	ㄠ	ㄣ	ㄢ	ㄥ	ㄤ
兒化轍	ㄨㄦ	ㄟㄦ	ㄜㄦ		ㄚㄦ	ㄟㄦ	ㄞㄦ	ㄡㄦ	ㄠㄦ	ㄟㄦ	ㄞㄦ	ㄥㄦ	ㄤㄦ

ㄟㄦ 小人辰兒　　ㄞㄦ 小言前兒

4.1 傳統音韻學把漢語的音節分段(syllable segmentation)界定爲“聲母、韻頭、韻腹、韻尾”四個音段,這是非常高明的,是語感的一種反應。我的分析嚴格遵守這一原則。但從上表中可以看出,注音符號爲了實用的考慮,作了兩個變通的處理。第一,它把韻腹和韻尾合爲一體,作爲韻基,用一個符號代表;第二,當高元音單獨作“支、思”兩類字的韻母時,這個韻母就省而不寫了。這兩個變通本身都有相當的道理,但也顯然違背了音節分段的原則;因此從表面看,它與我的分析之間的相通處,就不够明顯了。但是大家都知道,注音符號初創時,還有一個符號“帀”,後來不用了。這個符號正代表那個省略了的韻母。假如我們恢復這個符號,並進一步指出,當“ㄧ、ㄨ、ㄩ”單獨作韻母時,也是省略了這個元音符號的緣故,就可理解在注音符號裏,“支、宜、五、玉”的韻母,實際上應爲“帀、丨帀、ㄨ帀、ㄩ帀”。這就説明了它們爲什麽是四呼相配的;也就可以理解,在注音符號的設計中,“ㄧ、ㄨ、ㄩ”是衹作韻頭(介音)用的;同時也就可以理解,爲什麽我們應該把“i、u、ü”這三個所謂“單獨元音”分析爲/yɨ、wɨ、ywɨ/了①。從音系的觀點看,這是必然的結論,傳統音韻學的奧妙也就不言而喻了。

4.2 從上表也可看出,在所有帶尾韻的音節裏,衹有兩個構成對比的元音

① 我此處所謂:注音符號中“ㄧ、ㄨ、ㄩ”作韻母時,實際上是“丨帀、ㄨ帀、ㄩ帀”的省略;並不是説,當初創製注音符號的人,果真這麽考慮過或宣示過,而是説,如果我們一貫堅守漢語音節分段的模式,這將是無可避免的結論;從而也就可以證明,注音符號系統(或傳統聲韻學)具有嚴格的音位性。又:把“單獨元音”[i、u 、ü]分别解析爲/yɨ、wɨ、ywɨ/三個音位複合體的做法,對不主張嚴格音位分析的人來説,當然是很難接受的(丁邦新就曾對我這麽説過)。但有些主張嚴格音位分析的人(如鄭錦全,參看鄭 1973),對這樣的分析法也不同意,這衹能説是見仁見智了。

音位。其中之一是低元音/a/,這是大家都同意的;但與它相對的究竟是高元音/ɨ/(帀),還是中元音/ə/(ㄜ)呢?這就衆説紛紜了,由於注音符號祇用一個符號代表韻基,而不分韻腹與韻尾,這就無法看出它選擇的到底是哪一個;但它用同一個韻基符號貫串四呼的方法,則是符合語感的,比那些混用高元音與中元音的做法高明多了。我認爲此處的對比是高元音對低元音,中元音祇出現在無尾韻裏。這可以由兒化後,"枝:ㄓ"與"針:ㄓㄣ"變爲同音得到證明。這説明"針"的主要元音與"枝"的主要元音是相同的,跟"摺:ㄓㄜ"的主要元音不同。這也説明我的分析與注音符號是一致的。

五、考定古音的目的

在分析當代語言時,尚可分辨細微發音方式;由於我們去古已遠,找不到發音人,細辨語音就不大可能了。嚴格地説,除了可以滿足我們的好奇心以外,猜測古人的發音方式,也是没有多大意義的;因爲我們真正需要知道的是某一時代的特定音系以及它的來龍去脈。

5.1 然而在相當長的一段時間裏,在西方早期學者如高本漢等的影響之下,許多人却傾全力於"構擬音值",而不作音系的分析。我們可以用下表爲例,稍作説明。

徐孝《重訂司馬温公等韻圖經》之擬音

徐圖攝名	陸擬	薛擬	徐圖攝名	陸擬	薛擬
通 (東中)	əŋ iŋ uŋ iuŋ	(y)(w)ɨŋ	祝 (姑蘇)	u、iu	(C)wɨ#
止 (一七)	ʅ ʅ 'ər' i y(ʉ,iʉ?)	(y)(w)ɨ#	拙 (乜斜)	ɛ iɛ uɛ iuɛ	(y)(w)e#
蟹 (懷來)	ai iai uai	$\binom{y}{w}$ ay	臻 (人辰)	ən in u(ə)n iun	(y)(w)ɨn

續表

<table>
<tr><th>徐圖攝名</th><th>陸擬</th><th>薛擬</th><th>徐圖攝名</th><th>陸擬</th><th>薛擬</th></tr>
<tr><td>壘
(灰堆)</td><td>ei(iei)
uei(yei)</td><td>(w)ɨy</td><td rowspan="2">山
(言前)</td><td rowspan="2">an
iɛn
uan
iuɛn</td><td rowspan="2">(y)(w)an</td></tr>
<tr><td>效
(遥條)</td><td>ɒu(?)
iɐu(?)</td><td>$\binom{y}{w}$ aw</td></tr>
<tr><td>果
(梭坡)</td><td>ɔ
iɔ
uɔ</td><td>(y)(w)o♯</td><td rowspan="2">宕
(江陽)</td><td rowspan="2">ɑŋ(‘ɒŋ’?)
iɑŋ
uɑŋ(uɒŋ?)
(liuɑŋ)</td><td rowspan="2">$\binom{y}{w}$ aŋ</td></tr>
<tr><td rowspan="2">假
(發花)</td><td rowspan="2">ɑ
iɑ
uɑ</td><td rowspan="2">$\binom{y}{w}$ a♯</td></tr>
<tr><td>流
(由求)</td><td>əu(?)
iəu(?)</td><td>$\binom{y}{w}$ ɨw</td></tr>
</table>

這張表所代表的，是陸志偉先生爲徐孝的《重訂司馬温公等韻圖經》所作的擬音（參看陸 1947）及我的重新分析（參看薛 1983，《徐孝的〈重訂韻圖〉：一次大膽的革新》）。陸氏爲每一攝（徐孝的“攝”實際是“韻”）擬出了許多韻母，往往含有幾個不同的元音，而在好幾個地方打上了問號，表示他尚不敢確定。顯然他花了很多精力與時間，而且極爲慎重；其治學的精神是至爲可佩的。然而我們不禁要問，既然一攝中有那麽多不同的元音，爲什麽那些字曾化入同“攝”（韻）呢？徐孝分作十三攝時，難道是毫無根據的嗎？如果有，那個根據是什麽？爲了回答這類問題，我爲徐圖作了新的“構擬”。這種做法代表一種截然不同的理念，絶不僅僅是使用不同的標音符號而已。首先我們假定，徐圖是當時那個語言的忠實而且完整的記録，因此可能據以推論出它背後的音系，而這個音系正可説明，爲什麽徐孝那樣分攝制圖。結果我爲每一“攝”推定出獨特的韻基，並且證明，徐圖與《十三轍》所依據的，實爲同一音系，即明末清初時，北京（金臺）話的忠實反映。

5.2 我認爲上面的“構擬”法，是考定古音詮釋古韻的正確做法。所以我也先後爲《中原音韻》及早期韻圖（主要以《韻鏡》爲依據）推證出它們所根據的音系。其理論根據與思維方式，與前文所言是完全一致的。

《中原音韻》音系之韻基

R01	Dōngzhōng	東鍾	-ɨŋ	R11	Xiāoháo	蕭豪	-ow
R02	Jiāngyáng	江陽	-oŋ	R12	Gēgē	歌戈	-o#
R03	Zhīsī	支思	(C)ɨ#	R13	Jiāmá	家麻	-a#
R04	Qíwēi	齊微	-ɨy	R14	Chēzhē	車遮	-e#
R05	Yúmú	魚模	-wɨ#	R15	GēngQīng	庚青	-eŋ
R06	Jiēlái	皆來	-ay	R16	Yóuhóu	尤侯	-ɨw
R07	Zhēnwén	真文	-ɨn	R17	Qīnxún	侵尋	-ɨm
R08	Hánshān	寒山	-an	R18	Jiānxián	監咸	-am
R09	Huánhuān	桓歡	-on	R19	Liánxiān	廉纖	-em
R10	Xiāntiān	先天	-en				

《中原音韻》音系中韻母之分布

韻尾	ø				y		w		n				m			ŋ		
元音 / 介音	ɨ	e	a	o	ɨ	a	ɨ	o	ɨ	e	a	o	ɨ	e	a	e	a	ɨ
ø(開)	支		沙	歌	賊	來	侯	豪	根		山		森		三	生	當	
y(齊)		車	家		齊	皆	尤	蕭	真	天	奸		侵	廉	咸	庚	江	
w(合)	模		花	戈	微	快	否	郭	文		晚	桓				轟	光	東
yw(撮)	魚	靴		岳					春	川						兄		鍾
韻目	支思 ⁞ 魚模	車遮	家麻	歌戈	齊微	皆來	尤侯	蕭豪	真文	先天	寒山	桓歡	侵尋	廉纖	監咸	庚青	江陽	東鍾

等韻十六攝所據之韻母系統

a) 内轉A類各攝

攝 / 等	通	止	遇	流	深
一	-wɨ{ŋ/k}	——	-wɨø	-ɨw	——
二	——	——	——	——	——
二	-ywi{ŋ/k}	y(w)iy	-ywiø	-yɨw	-yɨ{m/p}
四	——	——	——	——	——

b) 内轉B類各攝

等＼攝	果	曾	宕
一	-(w)ɔø	-(w)ɔ{ɲ/k̂}	-(w)ɔ{ŋ/k}
二	——	——	——
三	-ywɔø	-y(w)ɔ{ɲ/k̂}	-y(w)ɔ{ŋ/k}
四	——	——	——

c) 外轉A類各攝

等＼攝	梗	江	蟹	效	山	咸	假
一	——	——	-(w)ɔy	-ɔw	-(w)ɔ{n/t}	-ɔ{m/p}	——
二	-(w)a{ɲ/k̂}	-a{ŋ/k}	-(w)ay	-aw	-(w)a{n/t}	-a{m/p}	-(w)aø
三	-y(w)a{ɲ/k̂}	——	-y(w)ay	-yaw	-y(w)a{n/t}	-ya{m/p}	-y(w)aø
四	-(w)e{ɲ/k̂}	——	-(w)ey	-ew	-(w)e{n/t}	-e{m/p}	——

d) 外轉B類臻攝

一等	-(w)ɨ{n/t}
二等	[-ə{n/t}]?
三等	-y(w)ɨ{n/t}
四等	——

六、中國聲韻學的現代化

我希望上文的討論,已經足以充分説明傳統聲韻學的優點了。這門學問的理論基礎是,撇開細微的發音差異,直搏聲韻學的核心,即音節的對比、聲類的性質、韻類的關係、雙聲叠韻的依據，等等。這些都是漢語音系的特點，是語感的具體表徵。因此我們可以説，中國聲韻學一開始就走上了音系研究的路子。在這方面，比西方學者早了差不多一千年。可惜這個了不起的成就，迄今未能得到世界學術界的公認。爲什麽呢？語言的隔閡當然是一個原因，但更重要的原因，是研究的動機與目標。衹有充分瞭解中國音韻學目標的人，才能贊賞中國音韻學的優點。中國音韻學始終是人文科學的一部分，它可以（而且應該）采用數理邏輯等推理的方法，但它始終是與經史詩文等密切聯繫着的；而當代的西方聲韻學，則是研究人類"語言機能"的一部分。有些人不明白這種目標上的差别，往往把它們混爲一談，因而説傳統聲韻學保守落後，進而生硬地采用所謂"先進的理論與方法"來分析漢語，結果反而把傳統聲韻學所反映的系統打亂了。這對中國聲韻學來説，是既不幸又不公平的。當然，在認識與贊賞中國傳統音韻學的同時，我們也必須承認，它也有不足之處。這樣才能靈活地采用古今中外的綜合研究法，把中國音韻學"現代化"。下面就略舉數例，説明它的局限性，以及如何改進。

6.1 傳統聲韻學，在作共時的（synchronic）分析時，是相當高明的。這是静態的（static）描述。但在説到動態的（dynamic）歷時演變（diachronic change）時，就有所不足了。我個人認爲，傳統聲韻學把等韻時期和《中原音韻》時期的音系交代得相當清楚，但對兩者之間的傳承關係，就衹能作一些模棱籠統的説法了。例如：明清以來有一個説法，叫做"四等亡而四呼出"。這句話就有點兒似是而非。從音系的觀點看，其實四等未曾全亡，四呼也是早就存在的，不是那個時期才出現的。在我前文討論的基礎上，我們可以用兩個簡單的公式，把這個現象作更具體更明確的詮釋（參看《〈中原音韻〉的音位系統》）。

（1）a ⟶ e/y____

（2）o ⟶ a/C____［E，-back］

頭一個公式的意思是，在等韻時期以後不久，三等韻的韻腹/a/受到腭化韻頭的同化，前移而變同四等韻的韻腹/e/，因此三等與四等的差别也就"亡"了。第二個公式的意思是，在前述音變之後，帶尾韻一等開口字的韻腹/o/，受到"前音"（anterior）韻尾（即/-m，-p，-n，-t，-y/）的同化，也前移而變同二等韻的韻腹/a/，因此在相當程度上，原來一等與二等的差别也變得模糊了。這種表達方式,就清楚地説明了音變的原因、程度及相對的時序。

6.2 再就音變性質的表達説,傳統聲韻學也有其局限;往往衹能列舉(enumerate),而不能確指(specify)其本質。例如,《切韻》時期與等韻時期之間的脣音變化,由單列四母,分列爲"幫滂並明"(重脣)及"非敷奉微"(輕脣)兩列八母,傳統聲韻學也衹能列舉,很難表達音變的性質。用現代音韻學的方法,就可清楚地標明,這是貫串四個聲母的同一個變化。

(1) [C,+lab]⟶[+aff]/____[pal,+lab]

這個公式意爲:原來的四個脣音聲母(/p-, ph-,pɦ-, m-/),在受到韻頭中腭化([+pal])與脣化([+lab])兩個因素(即三等合口)的影響時,都變成塞擦音([+aff])了(參看杜 1981),即變爲'非敷奉微'(/pf-,pfh-,pfɦ-,mv-/)四母。未受這個影響時,自然仍爲重脣。另如等韻時期與《中原音韻》時期之間,舌上音(知徹澄/tr,trh-,trɦ-/)與正齒音(照穿牀/cr-,crh-,crɦ-/)合併了。我們也可以用下面這樣簡便的方法,標明其性質,即原來的塞音捲舌聲母變爲塞擦音捲舌聲母了。

(2) t⟶c/____r

這兩個例子都清楚地指明了音變的本質與方向。

6.3 方言的比較研究,對我們來説,是一個重要的課題,但是古人並不很重視它,因此傳統聲韻學也没給我們留下很好的方法。這對我們來説,也是它的一個缺點。用傳統聲韻學的方法討論方言,一般衹能説,某類聲母的字在這個方言中的現狀,或某攝某等的字在某方言中的分布,等等。要作更明確的解説,就有些困難了。在討論同祖方言之間的關係時,如果我們能先確定祖方言的音系,然後從音變的觀點説明這些方言的關係,就更確切簡明了。在前年"中研院"主辦的討論會裏,我曾宣讀一篇有關官話正音史的論文(即《方言重疊與標準漢語文白異讀之形成》)。大意是説,國語標準音有三個來源,即北京地區的幽燕方言、中原地區的汴洛方言以及南京地區的江淮方言。在這三個方言的演變史裏,曾經發生過下面幾個音變。

(1) ø⟶y/G ____ a(即二等喉牙音開口字的腭化)

(2) o⟶a/C ____ [E,-back](説明見 6.1.節,第二式)

(3) k̂⟶y ____ ♯(即梗曾兩攝的入聲字改讀"收噫")

(4) {o,a}⟶e/____ [C,+pal] (即梗曾兩攝各等的合韻)

(5) k⟶w/____ # (即通江宕三攝的入聲字改讀"收嗚")

然而在不同的方言裏,這些音變發生的時序並不相同,也不一定全都發生過,因此造成了一部分字匯的異讀。上面的順序,是它們在幽燕方言中發生的時序;在汴洛方言中,它們發生的時序爲:(4)—(1)—(2)—(3),而音變(5)却未曾發生;在江淮方言中,其時序則爲:(4)—(1)—(2),而(3)及(5)兩條音變都未曾發生。用這樣的方法,我們就可以深入地瞭解和説明這三個方言之間的關係了。

以上所舉各例,代表我結合中西聲韻學的研究方法,作爲我給傳統聲韻學的一點兒補充。

音系學的幾個基本觀點與漢語音韻史**

前言

過去幾年,我曾在不同的場合及在不同的程度上,談到我對漢語音韻史的一些看法,特別是1992年在高雄及1995年在臺北的那兩次報告,但是仍有幾個理論原則未曾説到,現在想藉此機會再多説幾句。這篇短文也許該題爲“漫談”,因爲我要談的都是些最基本的原則問題,因此也就懶得去注明原始出處了,亦所謂“得魚忘筌”也。

所謂“理論”,我覺得衹是原則性的“假説”(hypothesis),讓我們可以根據這理論解説宇宙或人世的某些現象。當然在解説時,必須采用某些方法或手段,諸如邏輯公式等。但那衹是技術性的問題,而非理論性的原則。在聲韻學這個領域,近代學者也提出過一些原則性的假説,其中一些容或尚有爭議。我覺得應該把漢語聲韻學的研究,跟某些原則性的假説結合起來,看能否給漢語史提供更精確的解釋,或者藉漢語研究之助,證明某個假説是錯誤的,從而讓我們有機會提出新的假説或“理論”,使我們的研究與我們認爲正確的理論保持一致,而不是故意視而不見,或避而不談,因爲那樣衹會讓我們繼續做已經習慣了的工作,各説各話,也就無從“交流”了。在下文中,我想列舉幾條這類基本觀點,讓我們看看,是否應該把它們與漢語聲韻學的研究結合起來。

一、音系學的幾個原則性的“假説”

(一) 音系是以“音位對比”(phonemic contrast)爲基礎的

生理上,人類的發音器官可以發出極多不同的聲音,窮“國際音標”之數,

** 原載《聲韻論集》第9輯,學生書局,2000年。

也不能完全記録下來;但不同的語言都以不同的組合方式,確立數目有限的"音位"(phoneme),排列成特定的"音系"(sound system)。這已是"老生常談"了。假如我們認可這一"理論",在研究某一歷史階段的漢語時,首先就確定我們的研究目標:是要作"音值的描述"呢,還是要作"音系的詮釋"呢?如果成功的話,前者可以使我們重聞古人的"談吐音聲",後者可以使我們認識當時的"音系及其流變",兩者都是很有意義的。在選定了目標以後,我們也得問自己:所用的方法可以達到那個目標嗎?有比這個更好的方法嗎?不確定研究的目標或不采用妥善的方法,將使我們游離於二者之間,無法達成任一目標。

(二)嚴格的音系衹能存在於特定的語言(或方言)中

這是"音位學説"(phonemics)衍生出來的另一觀念,所以在做"田野調查"(field work)時,往往要找一個特定的"發音人"(informant),先分析他的"獨言"(idiolect),然後擴及其"方言"或其"語言"。這個做法的理據是:真正精確的"音系",衹能存在於特定的語言或方言中;把不同的語言或方言雜糅在一起,就無所謂"音系"了。許多學者在做方言調查時,都采用這一做法,但在研究漢語音韻史時,尚未見有人遵循。其實在研究一部完整可靠的韻書例如《切韻》或《中原音韻》時,我們也應該把它當作最權威的"發音人",先假定該書是依據某一個特定的方言而作的,即把該書所記録的現象作爲最優先的證據,以推論其背後的音系。試以《切韻》爲例,"真""臻"分韻和重紐等現象,就必須在《切韻》本身的音系基礎上提出解釋,不能因爲類似慧琳《一切經音義》或顔師古《漢書音義》等書有或没有這類現象,便懷疑《切韻》記録的可靠性,或僅僅指出梵漢對音或外語借字是否區分或如何區分這類現象就算了。那些韻書當然是有參考價值的,但不是主要資料,因爲我們尚未證明它們所依據的是同一方言。至於域外借字,情況就更複雜了:是什麼時候借的?從哪一個方言區借的?借入的語言當時的音系是什麼樣子的?都得先確定。所以這類材料,衹能是補充性的,衹能幫助我們猜測音位的發音近似值(phonetic approximation)。

(三)在音系的結構層次裏,每個音節都有且衹有一個元音

漢語是典型的所謂單音節語(monosyllabic language),每個字都代表一個單音節,因此在研討漢語音系時,如何界定"音節"就特別重要了。音節指的是

語流中每個包含一個"音峰"(peak)的單位,而音峰是由元音擔任的,所以從音系的結構層次(structural tier)上説,每一個音節都衹有一個元音,其他的都是邊際成分(marginal elements);當然在發音層次(phonetic tier)上,這些成分可能有相應的變化。這是較晚出的"CV Phonology"所堅持的一條原則。如果我們的目標是論證音系,這條原則就極爲重要。在近代學者的研究中,就我所知,没有人把古代漢語的某一韻或某一字"構擬"爲没有元音的音節;這是與基本原則相符的,但是有些研究當代方言的人,却常在他們的"音系"中包括一些"輔音音節"。這當然是由於他們"聽不出來有元音",但就音系結構説,此誠爲前所未有,需要我們説明它們是由哪些音變衍生出來的,並且給它們在整體音系中找到適當的地位。另一方面,我們也得堅持説,一個音節衹有一個元音,雖然在發音層次上説,某些音節聽起來似乎有兩個元音(diphthong)或三個元音(triphthong);這就涉及"元音、半元音"的定義了,它們的區别究竟是絶對的音值呢,還是相對的地位呢?多年來研究漢語的學者似乎傾向於前者,堅持把作爲介音或韻尾的"元音性成分"寫作[i]與[u]。但也有些學者,例如George Trager,則認爲所謂"半元音",不是音值的問題,而是與其相鄰的"主元音"對比的問題。例如"毛"字可拼寫爲[mao]或[mau]或[maw],主元音[a]之後的[o]、[u]、[w]不能構成音位對比,所以相對於[a]來説,都算"半元音";趙元任先生也曾指出,主元音前後的元音符號,衹代表舌位移動的方向(direction of the tongue movement),不代表音值;這就與本條假設原則相符了。當然,用什麽符號代表次要的"元音性成分"並不重要,關鍵的問題是:這類"元音性成分"是否能跟與其相對應的"非元音性"的半元音,構成音位對比。高本漢在其中古擬音中,認爲四等韻有"元音性的"[i]與三等韻的"半元音性的"[i̯]構成對比,即同有區别字讀的功能。根據此處所提出的原則,我們認爲這是不可能的,也就迫使我們作一選擇:另提新的音節定義,或改擬四等韻的介音。

(四)特定的語言具有特定的"音節分段"(syllable segmentation)模式

這也是現代音韻理論的一條發現,因此音段模式的認定,就成爲討論某一音系的必要條件了。古代中國學者雖未明確地提出這個説法。但其做法却與此若合符契,即將漢語的所有音節都界定爲"聲母+韻母",再將韻母分爲"韻頭、韻腹、韻尾"三段。(我用[C][M]V[E]表達這一概念,而不用"CCVC",因爲前者更便於説明漢語音節的性質及其轉變。)分段的依據是個別語言的特性,與音值無直接關係;所以同一語音成分,在不同的語言中,可能須作不同的分段。(例如[ʦ],在英語中分爲兩段,在漢語中則爲單一的音段,即“精母”。)音段模式確定了以後,就可以在這個基礎上,明確地界定每個音節的屬性,音段之間的搭配關係,以及音變的性質與條件,等等。這當然要求嚴格分析,不許例外。研究漢語的西方學者也都知道中國的這個分段法;雖然有些人故作神秘地説,不一定要用這個老法子,結果還是沿用此法,未提出新法,却在少數個別地方不遵守此法。我覺得如果真要“提高理論水平”,恐怕還得回到老路上去,嚴格遵循。這樣既反映了漢語的特性,也符合音系分析的原則。

(五) 可以互押的音節含有相同的“韻基”(元音與後綴)

這條原則是一般語言都適用的,自然早已是盡人皆知了,問題是:在“構擬”古音時,能否遵守?討論《切韻》的“重紐”問題時,許多學者都特别强調同韻字必須擬爲含有相同的元音,認爲這條原則是不能放棄的。這是極有見地的看法,但是許多人在“構擬”《中原音韻》以下的近代音,甚至在分析當代北京音時,却把同韻互押的字標作含有不同的元音,這不成了“嚴格要求古人,寬鬆對待自己”了嗎?還是説“古人守規矩,後人不守規矩”呢?我也認爲這條原則是不能放棄的,否則就無“理論”可言了。當然,即使是最完整可靠的古代文獻,例如《切韻》,也可能摻雜少數例外現象(例如“重紐”),因此迫使我們在特殊情況下,把同韻的字擬爲不同的韻基,或把不同的韻擬爲含有相同的韻基。但對這類違反原則的做法,我們必須提出充分合理的解釋,以説明這樣做其實並不違反本條原則。

(六) 音段是音節分類的依據,其搭配受一定的制約

確定了音段模式以後,音段之間的搭配關係及音節的類别,就可以清楚地解説了。在漢語聲韻學的發展過程中,《切韻》的分韻及區别字讀,是建立在直覺認知上的,其法至簡,其理甚明。到等韻時代,才有較抽象的理論分析,因爲韻圖的設計是建立在音段搭配和音節分類上的。這就不是一般人僅憑直覺就可以瞭解的了,所以歷來誤解極多。王力先生曾説,等韻學就是中國的音韻理論學,這是極有見地的看法。韻圖設計中的許多做法,諸如“五音”與“四等”的搭配、開合分圖、圖分“内外”、三等獨列腭化韻、合數韻以爲一攝等,都必須也

衹能在音段的基礎上得到合理的解釋。明清時代的等韻學家，在音節分類方面又提出了“開、齊、合、撮”等四呼分類，以及“直音（直喉）、收噫（展輔）、收嗚（斂脣）、抵腭、穿鼻、閉口”等韻類的區分，這些也都得嚴守音段的分際，才能解釋得清楚。能在音系分析的基礎上爲這些等韻學的做法和術語提出邏輯性的解説，就是相對地“提高理論水平”了，否則就衹能列舉式地説“哪些字屬哪一類”，而不能明言其理。

（七）音變是有規律的

這更是已經“老掉牙”的説法了，問題是：在漢語史的研究中，你是如何表達這類規律的？當然，語音演變常有多方面的原因，任何規律都有例外，但全面考慮，規律性的音變無疑仍爲常態。可是規律的認定與表達，却並不那麽容易，用今天的眼光看，早期學者的做法也不够嚴密。這有兩層原因：其一，例外過多時，規律可能不明顯且令人懷疑；其二，音變的規律性最突出地表現在音系層面上；如果音系的分析不够嚴密，“規律”也就顯得不那麽規律了。舉例來説，“知”字在《中原音韻》裏屬“齊微”韻，即與“微”[wei]類字押韻；許多人都把“知”的韻母訂爲[i]；這就跟押韻原則不合了。所以我根據它們的來源（“收噫”的内轉“止攝”），把它們的韻母分别訂爲/wɨy 和/yɨy/，即同以/-ɨy/爲韻基，就合理地説明了爲什麽它們在《中原音韻》時代押。到《十三轍》時代（徐孝《等韻圖經》同），“知”字改入“一七”轍，與“支、魚、齊”等互押，其後更變爲“支”的同音字。這個演變過程是有規律的嗎？在未作嚴格音位分析之前，恐怕不易看出。有人把這個過程叫做韻母[i]在捲舌聲母之後的“舌尖元音化”，表面看來也不算錯，但却未能顯示出音變的規律性。我們都知道，《中原音韻》時代以後，發生過兩個普遍性的音變，其一爲“齊微”韻的分裂，即“齊”類字不再跟“微”類字（仍爲“收噫”）互押，而改與“支、思、魚”等（無韻尾音節）互押；這個音變與聲母無關，而是韻母/yɨy/丢掉了韻尾（異化作用，dissimilation），變成了/yɨ/。另一音變是，原能洪細兩配的“照”系聲母，不再跟細音韻母相配了，也就是説，捲舌聲母之後的腭化介音/y/消失了。這個音變遍及各韻，不限於任一特定韻母。這兩個音變影響到整個音系，非專爲“知”類字而設，但却使“知”字無可避免地變得與“支”同音了，也讓我們看出其演變的絶對規律性。在做漢語史研究時，我們當然要爲個别歷史階段作細密的“共時分析”（synchronic analysis),同時也要推論不同階段之間的"歷時演變"(diachronic changes),如何推證出規律的音變及其先後發生的時代,似乎是一個猶待進一步研究的任務。

二、中國聲韻學的特點

中國的傳統聲韻學有下列特點,由此可以看出其與現代音系學的共通性。

(一) 研究的目的:聲韻之學起自魏晉,盛於南北朝,是爲"今韻"之濫觴,其目的皆爲"正語作詞"(借用周德清語)。"正語"者,規範推廣"標準語"也;"作詞"者,爲詩文格律及押韻訂立共守之準則也。"古韻"研究之興晚在明清,其目的則爲"訓詁解經"。

(二) 研究的對象:由於其特定之目的,"古韻"研究自然以先秦文獻爲課題,而"今韻"則以各時代的標準語(或"官話")爲其研究之對象。元明以降,亦偶見方言韻書,如《泉州十五音》之類,然其目的亦爲釐定某一方言區共守之標準。

(三) 研究的重點:指明字讀(音節)之差別與相互間之關係,諸如"雙聲""叠韻"等。

(四) 表達的方式:以韻書之分聲分韻與反切,或以韻圖之分等分攝與排列,表達音韻之區别。由於此種較抽象之表達方式,漢語音韻資料成爲"完全音位性的"。

(五) 資料的連貫性:歷代之標準語(朝廷用語)具有高度的傳承關係。"今韻"既以各時代之標準語爲其研究對象,故對比不同時代的韻書,可以推論出標準漢語音韻史。

三、音系學與漢語音韻史研究的綜合

綜合上兩節的説明,可以看出傳統聲韻學與現代音系學有甚多共通之處:對以漢語歷代音系及其流變爲研究目標的人來説,上述的幾條基本觀點可以説是理論性分析的起點,應使自己的研究符合這些原則,或者批判某些原則而另提新的理論代替。也許有人會説這好像是"無限上綱"。的確是,但學術研究的"無限上綱",不是强迫別人接受某種理論,而是要以此爲手段,迫使自己檢驗某種理論的真僞或是否需要修正。這種態度跟 Chomsky 的想法是一致的;他曾一再説,認真的研究是:先提出某種"假説",盡力推衍下去,看能把我們帶到何方,以證明其真僞或須作何修正。近些年來流行的"孳生音韻學"(generative phonology),主張以"區別性特徵"(distinctive feature)爲手段,直接表達音系的模式及其轉變,因此撇開"音位"這個層次,也不多計較"互補分布"(complementary distribution)現象,從而更抽象地表現出音系的特性。但是"音位對比"這個概念是少不得的,而且傳統聲韻學特別重視"雙聲""叠韻"等現象,爲了解説這類現象,也不得不承認,有某種"潛在形式"(underlying form)的存在。我覺得所謂"潛在形式",其實就是"音位",在解説古代韻書的聲韻區別時,是需要明白標出的。

上文所列舉的基本觀點,雖是近代學者提出的,但是可以説中國古代的音韻學家早就遵循應用了,祇是没有明白地説出來而已。大半個世紀以前,高本漢先生用當時北歐流行的歷史比較研究法,構擬(reconstruct,原意爲"重建")《切韻》音,開風氣之先,影響至巨,迄今仍爲許多學者所沿用,可見中國學者是很能接受外來思想的;但這種方法的原有功用是"無中生有",即用後代有記録的語言,重建古代未曾記録下來的祖語。用這種方法構擬想象中的漢台語或漢藏語,當然可以,也祇能用這種方法。但在有研究有記録的漢語音韻時,有必要用這種方法嗎?"重建"出來的某一時代的語音,能比當時的人(如陸法言或周德清)所記録的更可靠嗎?如果回答是否定的,那麽我們研究的任務就該是:發掘論證某本可靠的韻書(例如《切韻》或《中原音韻》)所依據的音系;這就要采用音位學説了,因爲那些韻書的分聲分韻及反切,都是以音位對比爲依據的。音位學的最大特點是:音系是以個別民族語言的特性爲基礎的,而不是以"國際音標"式的音值標音爲依據的。所以在觀念上,這一學説跟中國傳統聲韻學的做法是不謀而合的,是相當"中國式"的。我們也許可以把這幾個基本觀點,看作暫定的"理論標尺",先檢驗它們是否正確,然後用那幾條我們認爲是正確的作爲準則,檢驗一下我們研究漢語時所作的結論,看看是否合乎這些標準。

也談幾個漢語音韻史的理論問題*

過去十多年,我常回國内來與海峽兩岸的同好們共同論學,這是我最感愉快的事。在與同好們交談時,常聽有人説,漢語音韻學的研究必須“提高理論水平”。這是很令我欽佩的,因此我也曾在不同的場合及在不同的程度上,談到我的一些看法,特别是 1992 年在高雄的一次報告。但是仍有幾個理論原則問題未曾説到,現在想藉此機會再多説幾句。常見有人用“漫談”或“淺談”作題目,大概意思是説,撰寫時未曾仔細查閲有關文獻,注明出處,衹是即興式地把某些想法説出來。假如這個猜想不錯,我這篇短文也該題爲“漫談”。由於我要談的都是些最基本的原則問題,因此也就懶得去一一注明原始出處了,亦所謂“得魚忘筌”也。

所謂“理論”,我覺得衹是些原則性的“假説”(hypothesis),如同牛頓的“萬有引力”、達爾文的“物競天擇”等等,讓我們可以根據這類原則解説宇宙或人類的某些現象。當然,在解説時必須采取某些方法或手段,諸如邏輯公式等。但那衹是技術性(technical)的問題,而非理論性(theoretical)的原則。在音韻學這個領域,近代西方學者也先後提出過一些原則性的假説,其中一些内容或尚有争議。我覺得所謂“提高理論水平”,具體地説,就是把漢語音韻學的研究跟某些原則性的假説結合起來,看能否給漢語史提供更精確的解釋;或者藉漢語研究之助,證明某個假説是錯誤的,從而讓我們有機會提出新的假説或“理論”。這當然不是很容易的,首先要求我們必須克服心理障礙。這使我想起“葉公好龍”來。近世的音韻理論也是魚龍混雜的。我們不能衹説喜歡或重視理論,而是要面對這些所謂的“理論”,拿出“赤膽屠龍”的勇氣來,批駁我們認爲是錯誤的“理論”;或是展現出恢宏的雅量,邀請“真龍”登堂入室,使我們的

---

* 原刊《語言研究》1996 年增刊號,收入《漢語音韻史十講》。

本文原爲提交中國音韻學會第四次國際學術研討會(1996 年 8 月,福州)的論文。

研究與我們認爲正確的理論保持一致;而不是采取"鴕鳥政策",視而不見或避而不談,因爲那樣衹會讓我們繼續做已經習慣了的工作,各説各話,也就無所謂"提高理論水平"了。在下文中,我想列舉幾條這類基本原則,讓我們看看,是否應該把它們與漢語音韻學的研究結合起來。

一、語言交際是以音位對比(phonemic contrast)爲基礎的

從生理上説,人類的發音器官可以發出極多不同的聲音,窮國際音標之數也不能完全記録下來。但是不同的語言都以不同的組合方式,確立數目有限的"音位"(phoneme),排列成特定的"音系"(sound system)。這已經是老生常談了。假如我們認可這一"理論",在研究某一歷史階段的漢語時,首先就得確定我們的研究目標:是要作"音值的描述"呢,還是要作"音系的詮釋"呢?如果成功的話,前者可以使我們重聞古人的"談吐音聲",後者可以使我們認識當時的"音系及其流變",兩者都是很有意義的。在選定了目標以後,我們也得問自己:所用的方法可以達到那個目標嗎?有比這個更好的方法嗎?不確定研究的目標,或不采用妥善的方法,將使我們游離於二者之間,無法達成任一目標。在衆多的"理論"中,這是一條"巨龍",將好之乎?將屠之乎?抑將故作不見乎?

二、特定的語言(或方言)具有特定的"音系"

這是由音位學説衍生出來的另一觀念,所以在做"田野調查"(field work)時,往往要找一個特定的發音人(informant),先求證其"獨言"(idiolect),然後擴及其"方言"或其"語言"。這個做法的理據是:真正精確的音系衹能存在於特定的語言或方言中,把不同的語言或方言雜糅在一起,就無所謂"音系"了。許多國内學者在做方言調查時,已經采用這一做法了;但在研究歷史音韻時,尚未見有人遵循。其實在研究一部相當完整可靠的文獻資料例如《切韻》或《中原音韻》時,我們也應該把它當作最權威的"發音人",先假定該書是依據某一個特定的方言而作的,即把該書所記録的現象作爲最優先的證據,以推論其

背後的音系。這類文獻的分聲、分韻與反切,都是以字讀差異爲根據的,這更給我們提供了音位分析的直接證據。試以《切韻》爲例,"真""臻"分韻和重紐等現象,是不容懷疑的,而且必須在《切韻》本身的音系基礎上提出解釋。不能因爲類似慧琳《一切經音義》或顔師古《漢書音義》等書有或没有這類現象,便懷疑《切韻》記録的可靠性;或是僅僅指出梵漢對音,或是韓、日、越語借字,是否區别或如何區别這類現象就算了。這些著作當然是有參考價值的,但不是主要資料,因爲我們尚未證明它們所依據的是同一方言。至於域外借字,情況就更複雜了:是什麽時候借的?從哪一個方言區借的?借入的語言當時的音系是什麽樣子的?都很難確定。所以這些零星的材料,衹能是補充性的,以及幫助我們猜測音位的發音近似值(phonetic approximation)。

三、一個音節必有且衹有一個元音

漢語是典型的所謂單音節語(monosyllabic language),每個字都代表一個單音節,因此在研討漢語音系時,如何界定"音節"就特别重要了。音節指的是,語流中每個包含一個"音峰"(peak)的單位,而音峰是由元音擔任的,所以在音韻的結構層次(structural tiers)上説,每一個音節都得有一個元音,其他的都是邊際成分(marginal elements);當然在發音層次上(phonetic tier)上,這些成分可能有相應的變化。這是較晚出的"CV phonology"所特别堅持的一條原則。如果我們的目標是論證音系,這條原則就極爲重要。在近代學者的研究中,就我所知,没有人把古代漢語的某一韻或某一字構擬爲没有元音的音節,這是與本條原則相符的。但是有些研究現代方言的人,却常在他們的"音系"中包括一些"輔音音節"。這當然是由於他們"聽不出來有元音",但就音系結構説,此誠爲前所未有,需要我們説明,它們是由哪些音變衍生出來的,並且給它們在整體音系中找到適當的地位。果能如此,就可以推翻此處的假説,建立新説;否則就得把這類音節重新詮釋爲含有某種元音。(不同的人常有不同的反應,例如"支、思"等字,高本漢認爲有舌尖元音,霍凱特就認爲没有元音。)

另一方面,我們也堅持説,一個音節衹有一個元音,雖然從發音層次上説,某些音節似乎有兩個元音(diphthong)或三個元音(triphthong)。這就牽涉到“元音”“半元音”的定義了,它們的區别究竟是絶對的音值呢,還是相對的地位呢?多年來研究漢語的學者似乎都傾向於前者,堅持把作爲介音和韻尾的“元音性成分”寫作[i]與[u]。但也有些學者,例如George Trager,則認爲“半元音”不是音值的問題,而是與其相鄰的“主元音”對比的問題。例如“毛”字可拼寫爲[mao]或[mau]或[maw],主元音[a]之後的[o]、[u]、[w]不能構成音位對比,所以相對於[a]來説,都算“半元音”;趙元任先生也曾指出,主元音前後的元音符號,衹代表舌位移動的方向(direction of the tongue movement),不代表音值;這就與本條假設的原則相符了。當然,用什麽符號代表次要的“元音性成分”並不重要,關鍵的問題是這類“元音性成分”是否能跟與其相對應的“非元音性”半元音構成對比。高本漢在其中古擬音中,認爲四等韻有“元音性的[i]”,與三等韻的“半元音性的[i̯]”構成對比,即同有區别字讀的功能。根據此處所提出的原則,我們認爲這是不可能的,也就迫使我們作一選擇:另提新的音節定義,或改擬四等韻的介音。

四、特定的語言具有特定的“音節分段”(syllable segmentation)模式

這也是現代音韻理論的一條發現,因此音段模式的認定,就成爲討論某一語言的必要條件了。古代中國學者雖未明確地提出這個説法,但其做法却與此若合符契,即將漢語所有的音節都界定爲“聲母+韻母”,再將韻母分爲“韻頭、韻腹、韻尾”三段。(我用“[C][M]V[E]”來表達這一概念,而不用“CCVC”,因爲前者更便於説明漢語音節的性質及其轉變。)分段的依據是個别語言的特性,與音值無直接關係;所以,同一語音成分,在不同的語言中,可能須作不同的分段。(例如[ʦ],在英語中分爲兩段,在漢語中則爲單一的音段,即“精母”。)音段模式確定了以後,就可以在這個基礎上明確地界定每個音節的屬性、音段之間的搭配關係,以及音變的性質與條件,等等。這當然要求嚴格分析,不許例外。研究漢語的西方學者也知道中國的這個分段法。雖然有些人故作神秘地説不一定要用這個老法子,結果還是沿用此法,未見提出新法,但却在個别地方不遵守此法。我覺得如果真要“提高理論水平”,恐怕還得

回到老路上去,嚴格遵循。這樣既反映了漢語的特性,也符合音系分析的原理。

五、互相押韻的音節都含有相同的"韻基"(即主要元音加上韻尾)

這條原則是一般語言都適用的,自然早是盡人皆知了,問題是能否遵守。在討論《切韻》的"重紐"問題時,邵榮芬(1982)特别强調同韻字必須擬爲含有相同的元音,放棄這條原則就談不上什麽構擬了。這是極有見地的看法。但是許多人在構擬《中原音韻》以下的近代音或分析當代北京音時,却把同韻互押的字標作含有不同的元音,這不成了"嚴格要求古人,寬鬆對待自己"了嗎?還是説"古人守規矩,後人不守規矩"呢?我也認爲這條原則是不能放棄的,否則就無"理論"可言了。當然,即使是最完整可靠的古代文獻,例如《切韻》,也可能摻雜少數例外現象(例如"重紐"),因此迫使我們在特殊情況下,把同韻的字擬爲含有不同的韻基,或把不同的韻擬爲含有相同的韻基。但對這類違反原則的做法,我們必須作出充分合理的解釋,以説明這樣做其實並不違反本條原則。

六、音段搭配的規律與音節分類的原理

確定了音段模式以後,音段之間的搭配關係及音節的類别,就可以清楚地解説了。在漢語音韻學的發展過程中,《切韻》的分韻及區别字讀,是建立在直覺認知上的,其法至簡,其理甚明。到等韻時代,才有較抽象的理論分析,因爲韻圖的設計是建立在音段搭配和音節分類上的。這就不是一般人僅憑直覺就可以瞭解的了,所以歷來誤解極多。王力先生曾説,等韻學就是中國的音韻理論學,這是極有見地的看法。韻圖設計中的許多做法,諸如"五音"與"四等"的搭配、開合分圖、圖分"内外"、三等獨列腭化韻、合數韻以爲一攝等,都必須也衹能在音段的基礎上得到合理的解釋。明清時代的等韻學家,在音節分類方面又提出了"開、齊、合、撮"等四呼分類,以及"直音(直喉)、收噫(展輔)、收嗚(斂脣)、抵腭、穿鼻、閉口"等韻類的區分,這些也都得嚴守音段的分際,才能解

釋得清楚。能在音系分析的基礎上爲這些等韻學的做法和術語提出邏輯性的解説,就是相對地"提高理論水平"了。否則就衹能勉强地説,哪些字屬於哪一類,而不能明言其理;或者含混籠統地説,問題不大,不必計較,這就很難討論"理論"問題了。

七、音變是有規律的

這更是已經"老掉牙"的説法了,問題是:在漢語史的研究中,你是如何表達這類規律的?當然,語音演變常有多方面的原因,任何規律都有例外。因此早期學者提出的"格裏姆定律"(Grimm's Law)、"維爾納定律"(Verner's Law)等,曾受到質疑。但全面考量,規律性的音變無疑仍爲常態。可是規律的認定與表達却並不那麽容易,用今天的眼光看,早期學者的做法也不够嚴密。這有兩層原因:其一,例外過多時,規律可能不明顯而且令人懷疑;其二,音變的規律性最突出地表現在音系層面上,如果音系的分析不够嚴密,"規律"也就顯得不那麽"規律"了。舉例來説,"知"字在《中原音韻》裏屬"齊微韻",即與"微[wei]"類字押韻。許多人都把"知"的韻母訂爲[i],這就跟押韻原則(前文第五條)不合了。如果我們根據它們的來源(收噫的内轉"止攝"),把它們的韻母分别訂爲/wɨy/和/yɨy/,即同以/ɨy/爲韻基,就合理地説明了爲什麽它們在當時互押。到《十三轍》時代(徐孝《等韻圖經》同),"知"字改入一七轍,與"支、魚、齊"等互押,其後更變爲"支"的同音字。這個演變過程是規律的嗎?在未作嚴格的音位分析之前,恐怕不容易看出來,有人把這個過程叫做韻母[i]在捲舌聲母之後的"舌尖元音化",表面看來也不算錯,但却未能顯示出音變的規律性。我們都知道,《中原音韻》時代以後,發生過兩個普遍性的音變,其一爲"齊微"韻的分裂,即"齊"類字不再跟"微"類字(仍爲"收噫")互押,而改與"支、思、魚"等(無韻尾音節)互押;這個音變與聲母無關,而是韻母/yɨy/丢掉了韻尾(異化作用,dissimilation),變成了/yɨ/。另一音變是,原來能洪細兩配的"照系"聲母不再跟細音韻母相配了,也就是説,捲舌聲母之後的腭化介音/y/消失了。這個音變遍及各韻,不限於任一特定韻類。這兩個音變影響到整個音系,絶非專爲"知"類字而設,但却使"知"類字無可避免地變得與"支"同音了,這讓我們看出其演變的絶對規律性。在做漢語史研究時,我們當然要爲個别的歷史階段作細密的"共時分析"(synchronic analysis),同時也要推論不同階段之間的"歷時演變"(diachronic changes),如何推證出規律的音變及其先後發生的時代,似乎是一個猶待進一步研究的任務。

以上所舉各項,是音系理論的最基本原則,對以音值爲目標的人來説,顯然不足,他們還得采用類似"合成語音"(synthetic speech)等聲學技術。但對以研究漢語歷代音系及其流變爲目標的人來説,這些原則却是理論性研究的起點。要"提高理論水平"就不能不考慮這些"理論",嚴格要求自己的研究符合這些理論原則,或者批判某些原則而另提出新的理論以代替之。也許有人會説這好像是"無限上綱"。的確是,但學術研究中的"無限上綱"不是强迫别人接受某種理論,而是要以"無限上綱"爲手段,迫使自己檢驗某種理論的真僞或是否需要修正。這種態度跟喬姆斯基(Chomsky)的想法是一致的,他曾一再説:認真的研究是先提出某種"假説",盡力推衍下去,看它能把我們帶到何方,以證明其真僞或須做何種修正。近幾十年來流行的"生成音韻學"(generative phonology),主張以區别性特徵(distinctive feature)爲手段,直接表達音系的模式及其轉變,因此,撇開"音位"這一個層次,也不多計較"互補分布"(complementary distribution)現象,從而更抽象地表現出音系的特性,但是"音位對比"(phonemic contrast)這個概念是少不得的;而且漢語音韻特别重視"雙聲""叠韻",爲瞭解説這類現象,也不得不承認,有某種"潛在形式"(underlying form)的存在。我覺得所謂"潛在形式"其實就是音位。在解説古代韻書的聲韻區别時,是需要明白標出的。

去年有位年輕朋友寫信對我説,現在有些所謂"著作",多屬編抄文獻,少有新意,他頗不以爲然,很想做些理論性的研究;尤其是看到許多理論都是外國人提出的,覺得中國人也該提出一些新理論。我回信贊揚他很有志氣,相信他的努力一定會有成果;但提醒他學術研究是不該分内外的,理論也是没有國籍的。語云:"東海有聖人焉,西海有聖人焉,其心同,其理同。"衹要是用誠實的態度、開闊的胸懷,摒除個人得失的考慮,客觀地面對研究的課題,不同的人通常都會得到類似的結論。其實在一定的意義上説,本文所列舉的理論原則,雖是近代西方學者提出的,但是中國古代的音韻學家早就遵循應用了,衹是没有明白地説出來而已。大半個世紀以前,高本漢先生用當時北歐流行的歷史比較研究法,構擬《切韻》音系,開風氣之先,影響至巨,迄今仍爲許多學者所沿用,可見中國學者是很能接受外來思想的。但這種方法的本來功用是"無中生有",即用後代有記録的語言,"重建"古代未曾記録下來的祖語。用這種方法構擬想象中的漢台語或漢藏語,當然可以,而且也衹能用這種方法。但在研究有豐富文獻記録的漢語音韻時,有必要用這種方法嗎?"重建"出來的某一時代的語音,能比當時的人(如陸法言或周德清)所記録的更可靠嗎?如果回答是否定的,那麽我們的研究任務就應該是發掘論證某本可靠的韻書(如《切韻》或《中原音韻》)所依據的音系。這就要采用音位學説了,因爲那些韻書的分聲、分韻及反切,都是以音位對比爲依據的。音位學説的最大特點是:音系是以個别民族語言的特性爲基礎的,而不是以"國際音標"式的音值標音爲依據的。所以在觀念上,這一學説跟中國傳統音韻學的做法是不謀而合的,是相當"中國式"的,甚至可以説,原來就是"中國的音韻理論"。要"提高理論水平",自然要先選定"理論標尺"。本文列舉的這幾條"理論原則",可以説是暫定的標尺。我們可以先檢驗它們是否正確,然後用那幾條我們認爲正確的作爲準則,檢驗一下我們的每一項研究理論,看看是否合乎這些標準。

構擬與詮釋:漢語音韻史研究的兩種對立觀點**

一、韻書的性質與功用

多數人都同意,古代韻書對漢語史的研究是非常重要的,這就要求我們先把韻書的性質與功用弄清楚。就其功用説,《切韻》以來的韻書(所謂"今韻")都有一個共同的目標,即"正語作詞"(周德清語):所謂"正語",即確立標準讀音;所謂"作詞",即使用這種標準語音創作詩詞。這在當時是非常重要的,所以編書的人都非常認真。因此就其性質説,韻書所記録下來的也必然是其編者所認爲的當時的標準話,是那種語言的完整而且忠實的記録。當然,並非所有的韻書都具有同等的價值,但像《切韻》《韻鏡》《集韻》《中原音韻》等傳世之作,性質都是這樣的,其可靠性(或曰"可信度")都是極高的。能正確地解讀這類韻書,也就是正確地認識了各時代的標準語。這些韻書的定音,是以"分聲、分韻、分類、反切"等方式表達的。對不諳音系學原理的人來説,這種表音方式自然顯得抽象難解,不如"國際音標"式的注音來得直截了當,但對會説那種話而且明白其道理的人來説,却是非常自然的,一點也不抽象;因爲這是一種"內部互注表音法",即在同一音系之内,利用不同字音的音位異同而互注的,完全符合説那種話的人的語感;但對後代的以及外國的人來説,要真正徹底地瞭解這些韻書,就必須先掌握音系學的基本原則,因爲這類韻書所標示的,是音位對比(phonemic contrast)。

二、音系學的基本原則

音位學説是 20 世紀 30 年代才有人提出來的,但真正受到注意,還有賴於

** 原刊《語言科學》2003 年第 5 期。

布拉格學派(Prague School)及一些美國學者的大力鼓吹;但迄今仍有一些人不以爲然,仍在堅持以"音值"標音。有了音位概念作爲基礎,音系學的研究才走上正途,有關音系的理論才得以建立。

在此,我衹想提出音系學的幾個最基本的原則,作爲漢語史研究的準則。

一、"音位對比"是語言交際的基礎。

二、特定的"音系"(sound system)衹存在於特定的語言(或方言)中。

三、特定的語言具有特定的"音節分段"(syllable segmentation)模式。

四、一個音節必有且衹有一個主要元音。

五、互押的音節都含有相同的主要元音及其後綴。

六、音節分類的依據是音段,其搭配是有規律的。

七、"音變"(sound change)是有規律的。

這些具有普遍性的原則,對研究任何語言都是重要的。由於中國的古代韻書本質上都是音位性的,要正確地瞭解這些韻書,上述的原則就更是特別重要的了。

三、語音材料與表達意義

所謂構擬,其原意本爲:利用有記録的相關語言與現代方言,"重建"(reconstruct)未曾記録下來的某種古代語言。由於西方的語言大多采用了所謂的"拼音文字",早在18世紀就有學者注意到,他們的語言,包括希臘文、拉丁文、波斯文、梵文等,有甚多相似之處,可能出自同源,因此引起他們重建其祖語的興趣,即所謂"印歐語"(Indo-European,原稱"雅利安語"Aryan)。這很顯然是一種語言的歷史考古學,因此對那些缺乏悠久歷史文化的新興"民族國家"(nation states)特別有吸引力。這是爲什麼歷史比較語言學在北歐及中歐特別受到重視的道理。在此之前,語文學者所從事的,多爲古典文獻的版本校勘與文字注釋,即所謂"語文學"(philology),跟東方學者研究中國古代典籍的方式是一樣的。歷史比較語言學則以遠古未曾記録下來的語言爲目標,研究的可以説是語言的"史前史"。這就擴大了研究的範圍,並且創立了一些新的研究方法。這對瞭解不同語言之間的親疏關係,建立所謂"語族"(language family,亦稱“語系”)都有很大的功用。利用這種方法,也許可以重建“遠古漢語”(Proto-Chinese)、漢藏語(Sino-Tibetan)、漢台語(Sino-Tai)等古代的語言。事實上,不少學者正在努力做這種工作。

四、構擬法與中國音韻學

中國音韻學的“今韻”,目的是“正語作詞”,其對象爲其當代的標準語,因此幾乎可以説是與構擬風馬牛不相及的。明清時代興起的“古韻”研究,倒真有點兒像是“重建”,但也衹是利用古籍中的韻語與諧聲,以及這類字後來在《切韻》中的歸屬,試圖“重建”上古漢語的“韻部”與“聲類”,其目的爲“訓詁解經”,與構擬的目標仍是大異其趣的。但爲什麽會有那麽多人要爲漢語“擬音”呢？我猜想可能有好幾個原因。其一,對西方學者來説,中國音韻學的注音法太抽象了,“好像代數式”,“不用音標怎麽能知道如何發音呢?”其二,構擬法流行的時候,音位學説尚未出現,所以當時擬音的人很難想象得到中國音韻學的“音系内部互注表音法”,自然就按照他們的習慣,從調查方言與比對譯音入手;其三,《切韻》的確是相當複雜,等韻圖也實在相當抽象,兩者也都去今已遠,所以連中國學者也多弄不太清楚了,看到國際音標式的注音那麽簡明,也就群起擬音了。迄今爲止,爲《切韻》構擬的音系,比較有名的已不下十來個,顯然這個數目還會繼續增加。爲什麽《切韻》會有那麽多“音系”呢？這就顯示出,由於構擬法與韻書有本質上的冲突,勉强地結合起來,就會無可避免地產生一些問題。我們可以舉一些例子來説明這個現象。爲了避免煩瑣,我將儘可能地不指明有關的個人,因爲這些多是構擬常見的問題。

構擬法常使人不自覺地忽視詮釋韻書的重要性。采用這種方式研究漢語史的人,雖然意識中也許没有否定古代韻書的想法,但是從嚴格的邏輯觀點説,這種做法實質上等於否定了古代韻書的可靠性。(否則何必“重建”呢?)我們説過,像《切韻》和《中原音韻》這類的韻書,都是當時學者爲了訂正其時的標準音所編的精心之作,忠實地記録下那個語言。這個特定的語言必然含有其特定的音系,需要我們來解析,不需要我們來重建(或構擬)。當然這個特定的語言衹可能是當時的一個“方言”(儘管是最有權威和流傳最廣的一個),因此可能有某些與之相關的資料,與記録語言的那本韻書不合,但這絶不足以證明該書是不可信的,因爲那些資料所反映的可能是别的方言。例如,漢語與其他語言之間的對譯,尤其是佛經中的某些譯語,有許多是《切韻》音所不能解釋的,就極可能是因爲譯者所使用的是不同的方言;過分重視那些對音資料,就會把我們引向另一個方向:以構擬音值爲主,碰到韻書中某些問題無法解釋時,就置之不顧。這大概是《切韻》有那麽多"音系"的緣故,變成了構擬者各行其是的狀態。("我的系統!")

既然不重視詮釋韻書,自然就無法解讀韻書所記録的某些現象,例如音節分段問題。音系的特性之一是音節分段,中國的傳統音韻學把漢語音節分割爲"聲母+韻頭+韻腹+韻尾"四個音段〔我用"(C)(M)V(E)"代表這個分段法,参看薛鳳生 1986〕。這就要求我們在這個基礎上,爲每一個漢語音節定性。這是漢語的一個顯著特色,所以一般的擬音都在很大程度上顯示出這一現象。但由於構擬者不接受嚴格的音位觀點,在他們認爲不可能(或"聽不出來")的地方,就經常忽視這一原則,也就因此不能給韻書傳統中的許多做法提出簡明合理的解説。下面略舉幾個例子,都是各家所構擬的"音系"中常見的現象。

一、同韻的字互押,故應含有相同的韻基(元音+後綴)。爲《切韻》擬音的人基本上都能遵守這條原則。(儘管所采的方式不盡合理,且常違反其他原則。)奇怪的是,當他們爲《中原音韻》之類的韻書擬音時,甚至在分析現代方言時,却常忽視這條原則。(例如"齊微"韻)

二、音節有"洪/細"之分,又有"開/齊/合/撮"四呼之説,雖然是韻頭的問題,但因擬音者不嚴守音節分段的原則,也就不能爲這些分類提出合理簡明的定義。

三、韻圖將一些相關的韻合爲一"攝",看得出來是韻尾的問題,亦因構擬的人不能嚴守分段的原則而無法清楚地界定其含義。

四、漢語的音節分段顯示,衹有韻腹是元音,其他各段都是次要成分;但構擬者常以音值爲由,堅持説韻頭(介音)也是元音,甚至還以介音有"元音性/非元音性"的對比爲説,解釋三等與四等或"重紐"的區分。(他們用[i]與[j]或[i̯]的差别來區分重紐,大概不是有方言調查或古代文獻的證據。)

上述問題對構擬音值的人來説,也許不算什麽大問題,因爲對他們來説,韻書祇是可以利用的"一種材料"。他們重視的是擬音,不是詮釋韻書。但是如果我們信任韻書,以詮釋韻書爲要務,這些"問題不大"的問題,就變成理論上最關鍵的重大問題了。要解决這類問題,就必須嚴守音系學的基本原則,而一旦采用了音系學的觀點,也都可以看出韻書與韻圖的編者是多麽正確地記録下他們的語言,連他們偶爾所做的一些變通處置(例如"重紐""寄韻")也都可以得到合情合理的解釋了。爲了節省篇幅,我祇想舉一個例子來説明這一現象。

在高本漢的《切韻》擬音中,"支、脂、之、微"四個韻列的韻母標音是:

支[jie̯],[jwie̯];脂之[ji],[jwi];微[je̯i],[jwe̯i]

這樣的構音勉强把這幾個韻列分開了(高氏不分"脂、之",據説是找不到現代方言的證據;至於"重紐",那時候他還不知道),但却無法解説以下幾個問題:

一、這四韻在《切韻》中相鄰,顯然同屬一類,高氏的擬音就會引起韻母分類的誤會,這在馬丁爲之做"音位化"時,就立刻顯出來了。由於在他的擬音中,"支、脂、之"都没有韻尾,馬丁就不得不把這幾韻移入無尾韻欄,變成跟"虞、魚"同類了。(參看 Martin 1953)董同龢、陸志韋、周法高都把"脂"改擬爲帶有韻尾[i](馬丁也把"脂"音位化爲/i*i/),這就幫助我們清楚地認識到,這幾韻原來一定都是"收噫"韻。他們這樣改擬,大概不是方言調查的結果,而是由音系的内部結構推測出來的,可見内部結構多麽重要。日本學者橋本萬太郎給"梗"攝的擬音是另一個例子,他把該攝的韻擬爲帶腭化韻尾,主要也是由"内部構擬"(internal reconstruction)看出來的。

二、陸法言已經説,在當時的某些方言中,"支脂(虞魚),共爲一韻"。唐初"支、脂、之"已准"同用",而"微"韻則仍須"獨用"。到等韻時代,這四個韻列全歸入"止"攝三等,成爲"重韻"。這顯然是音變的結果。這些音變的性質、過程及條件,都很難在高氏擬音的基礎上得到簡明合理的解説。

三、到《中原音韻》時代,這四組重韻的字分入兩個韻:一爲"支思",由齒音聲母("精、照"兩系)開口字組成;另一爲"齊微",包括其餘各類字。這個演變的過程及條件是什麼樣子的?前此的擬音也不足以提供合理的解釋,而許多給《中原音韻》擬音的人,甚至把"齊"類字的韻母擬爲[i],把"微"類字的韻母擬爲[uei],更是違背了押韻的原則,顯然無意於詮釋這本韻書何以如此分韻了。

四、《中原音韻》的"齊微"韻後來也分裂了,"微"類字組成《十三轍》的"灰堆"轍(徐孝的"壘攝"),"齊"類字(包括"知、池、世、日"等)則改與"支、思、魚"等合成"一七"轍(徐孝的"止攝"),"支、知"且變爲同音。這些現象也不是一般擬音所能合理解釋的。

以上這些音韻現象,俱見於不同時代的韻書與韻圖。綜觀前人的構擬,似乎很少人考慮這些問題,是他們志不在此呢,還是因爲他們的構擬無法解説就置之不論了呢?

五、音系解析與漢語史研究

假如我們對韻書先不抱懷疑的態度,而是把編者看作最好的發音人,即先充分肯定韻書的可靠性,假定某一韻書代表某一時代的特定方言,使用的是"音系内部互注表音法",那麽就可以用音位分析法,即嚴守音系學的基本原則,推論出其所據的音系。上節提出的那些問題,我認爲都是很重要的,而且是必須要解決的。在推論出相關時代的音系以後,那些問題也就可以得到適當的解決了。我給上述問題所作的解答是這樣的:

一、在堅守音節分段及互押的基礎上,我推測《切韻》音系必有也衹有七個元音音位/ɨ, e, ə, o, ɛ, a, ɔ/,以"高、中、低/前、央、後"的相對位置構成對比,但衹有一個高元音。由於"支、脂、之、微"都是三等韻,且與"蟹"攝諸韻相對應,故必皆爲含有"非低"元音的細音"收噫"韻,因爲其所含的韻母應爲:支/yey, ywey/、脂/yəy, ywəy/、之/yɨy/、微/yoy, ywoy/。這樣就可以清楚地標明何以這些韻同屬一類了。(這種詮釋方法最易受到的批評是"證據不足",即没有現代方言或古代有關文獻的支持。其實我們研究的是《切韻》所記録的特定方言,《切韻》本身才是我們建立其特定音系的第一手資料,優於其他任何"證據"。)

二、這些韻列的演變,更可以在這個分析的基礎上得到合理的解釋,即中元音/e,ə,o/受到半元音/y/(腭化介音與韻尾)的同化,上升變爲高元音/ɨ/,所以這四個韻列就合併了,成爲等韻"止"攝三等的"重韻"。如果想要更細密地解釋何以陸法言衹説"支脂(魚虞),共爲一韻",以及何以唐初"支、脂、之"可以同用,而"微"仍然獨用,也衹須點明在同樣的條件下,/e, ə/先升高,而後元音/o/則較晚。

三、這樣分析,同樣也能合理地解釋這類字在《中原音韻》裏的分布。影響到這類字的其實衹是一條音變,即開口字的韻母/yɨy/在齒音聲母的影響之下,丢掉了韻頭及韻尾(遂産生了一個前所未有的"支思"韻)。這個音變一定相當早,因爲其時"知、池"等字的聲母仍爲舌音,故未受影響(其聲母變爲齒音是後來的事),自然就進入了韻基爲/-ɨy/的"齊微"韻。("世"等原屬"蟹"攝,"日"等原爲入聲,故亦未受影響。)

四、"齊微"韻後來的分裂,也衹是一個音變問題,這在我們的分析裏也很容易看出來,即"齊"類細音開口字的韻母/yɨy/丢掉了韻尾,與"微"類字不再具有相同的韻基,也就不應同屬一韻了。按押韻原則説,"齊"類字變讀後,應改與"支、思、魚、模"等類字互押,因爲這幾類字構成了相配的"四呼",共以/ɨø/爲韻基。我們發現"支、齊、魚"三類字果然互押,同屬"一七"轍。奇怪的是,"模"類字單獨構成一個"姑蘇"轍。這是什麽道理,頗難解釋。我曾推測是由於兒化時"模"類字與另三類不一致,故分出爲獨韻,確否尚不敢説。其實這個問題早在《中原音韻》分立"支思"和"魚模"兩韻時,就已經出現了。至於"知"是如何變爲"支"的同音字的,由我們的分析看,也是必然的結果,因爲"知"的韻母在"齊微"分裂時丢掉了韻尾,其後由於捲舌聲母(舌上音先已變入照系)不再配細音(丢掉介音/y/),"知"自然也就讀同"支"了。

六、結語

漢語標準語的源頭,可以遠溯至周秦時代,但我們能看到的正式全面系統性的記録,則衹有晚到隋代的《切韻》。這大概是因爲在南北朝的長期分裂與戰亂之後,亟需重新確立標準語。這也就奠定了中國音韻學的特色,使用"内部互注表音法”,記録下《切韻》以來歷代的標準語,因此也就間接地顯示了漢語標準語的演變過程。

要想準確地解讀韻書所記録的各種現象,就必須接受音位觀念,嚴格遵守音系學的基本原則。表面看來,構擬法與解析法所得到的結果似乎差别不大,也許有人會説“又多了一個構擬”,但其所代表的觀念則完全不同,後者所追尋的,是音系學意義上的嚴格的音系。另一方面,我們也必須認識到,這些韻書所展現的,衹是個别時代的某一特定方言,即那個時代的標準語,所以我們不可能通過這個特定的方言,説清楚漢語與其他語言之間的一切互借或對譯,因爲那些互借與對譯有可能是根據别的漢語方言而産生的。要考定未曾記録下來的古代語言,例如漢藏語或漢台語,當然衹能用構擬法,但構擬時若能以後代語言的音系爲基礎,其構擬當更可信。同理,在研究兩種語言的互借關係時,先確認互借時各個語言的音系,將會得到更可靠的成果。這在研究漢語與韓語或漢語與日語間的借字時,尤爲重要,因爲歷史上漢語詞彙好像常常是大批的(因此也是“有系統地”)借入韓文或日文的(或曰“轉讀爲韓語或日語”的),與在一般的語言接觸中所常見的偶然性互借不同。

參考文獻

董同龢 《〈廣韻〉重紐試釋》,《史語所集刊》第十三本,1948 年,第 1—20 頁。
董同龢 《等韻門法通釋》,《史語所集刊》第十四本,1948 年,第 257—308 頁。
董同龢 《漢語音韻學》,文史哲書局,1968 年。
高本漢 《中國音韻學研究》(趙元任、李方桂、羅常培譯),商務印書館,1962 年。
耿振生 《明清等韻學通論》,語文出版社,1992 年。
李　榮 《切韻音系》,科學出版社,1956 年。
李新魁 《漢語等韻學》,中華書局,1983 年。
羅常培 《釋内外轉》,《史語所集刊》第四本,第二分,1933 年,第 206—226 頁。
邵榮芬 《切韻研究》,中國社會科學出版社,1982 年。
王　力 《漢語史稿》(上册),中華書局,1957 年。
王　力 《中國語言學史》,山西人民出版社,1981 年。

王　顯　《等韻學和古韻》,《音韻學研究》第三輯,中華書局,1994 年。

薛鳳生　《北京音系解析》,北京語言學院出版社,1986 年。

薛鳳生　《〈中原音韻〉音位系統》(魯國堯、侍建國譯),北京語言學院出版社,1990 年。

薛鳳生　《漢語音韻史十講》(耿振生、楊亦鳴編),華語教學出版社,1999 年。

趙蔭棠　《等韻源流》,商務印書館,1957 年。

周祖謨　《〈切韻〉的性質和它的音系基礎》,《語言學論叢》第五輯,第 39—70 頁。商務印書館,1963 年。

Chang Kun　1979　The Composite Nature of the Ch'ieh Yun, *Bulletin of the Institute of History and Philology* (BI-HP). Vol. 50, Part 2, 241 - 255.

Chao. Y. R.　1934　The Non-uniqueness of Phonemic Systems. *Bulletin of the Institute of History and Philology* (BIHP). Vol. 4, Part 4, 363 - 398.

Chao. Y. R.　1941　Distinctions within Ancient Chinese. *Harvard Journal of Asiatic studies*. 5, 203 - 233.

Hartman, Lawton M. II　1944　The Segmental Phonemes of the Peiping Dialect, *Language*, 20, 28 - 42.

Hashimoto, Mantaro　1970　Internal Evidence for Ancient Chinese Palatal Endings. *Language*. 46. 2. Part One, 336 - 365.

Hockett, Charless F.　1947　Peiping Phonology, *Journal of American Oriental Society*. 67. 253 - 267.

Hsueh, F. S.　1975　*Phonology of Old Mandarin*, The Hague.

Hsueh, F. S.　1980　The Phonemic Structure of Pekingese Finals and Their R-Suffixation, *Bulletin of the Institute of History and Philology* (BIHP). Vol. 51. Part 3, 491 - 514.

Hsueh, F. S　1986—1987　The Languages of the Sages and the Poets: Some Aspects of the Chinese Linguistic Tradition, *Inaugural Lectures*. College of Humanities, The Ohio State University, 29 - 35.

Martin. Samuel E.　1953　The Phonemes of Ancient Chinese. *Supplement to the Journal of the American Oriental Society*. No. 16.

中國音韻學的性質與目的

——從兩個"事件"説起**

前言:"事件"本末

關於漢語音韻史研究的理論與方法,近年曾發生兩次争論,或曰"事件"。其一爲美國的羅傑瑞(J. Norman)和柯蔚南(S. Coblin)兩位教授所提出的"A New Approach to Chinese Historical Linguistics"(朱慶之譯《漢語歷史語言學研究的新方法》,並見參考資料):他們指出,自高本漢以來,以《切韻》和韻圖爲依據的中古音研究是不正確的,因爲兩者都是年代不明和地域來源可疑的材料,是文人的雜凑,兩者之間的關係也難以確定,所以都不代表實際的語言。結論是:必須重新開始,采用一種"動態的歷史模式",以調查現代方言爲本,逐步上推,才能構擬出漢語自北方平原逐步逐代向南擴散的過程與層次。這種説法可謂徹底地否定了中國音韻學的基礎與傳統,而且可能誤導人以爲漢語音韻史是從高本漢開始的,這一説法遭受到蒲立本(E. G. Pulleyblank)教授的强烈反駁。他在他的"*Qieyun and Yunjing: the Essential Foundation for Chinese Historical Linguistics*"(劉愛菊譯《〈切韻〉和〈韻鏡〉:漢語歷史語言學的主要依據》)中説,上述兩種資料絶對代表實際的語言,是研究中古漢語的無價之寶,而《韻鏡》更是中國智慧發展史和世界語言學史上極突出的成就。他認爲他們不能瞭解這兩種資料的重要,是因爲他們不瞭解當代的音系學理論。這兩篇文章都已譯爲中文。多謝他們都寄了給我,否則我可能還看不到呢!我感到奇怪的是,尚未見到國内學者的反應。没有反應不會是默認吧?

另一個争議是所謂"梅祖麟事件"。我於 2002 年 9 月下旬應邀到徐州師範大學講學,適逢古漢語語法討論會在泉州舉行,得便應邀列席;甫見面,郭錫

** 原刊《古漢語研究》2003 年第 2 期。

良教授就問我對"梅祖麟事件"的看法。我已退休多年,"不聞世事",於此一無所知,自然没有什麽看法;他於是把梅氏的《有中國特色的漢語歷史音韻學》從網上印了一份給我,同時也把他的反駁文《歷史音韻學研究中的幾個問題》以及其他一些相關資料給了我;讀後自然難免吃驚,原來梅氏把乾嘉時代的古韻學家(除了段玉裁)、近代的"章黄學派"及其"支流"王力等,都狠狠地批判了!(這是我頭一次聽説王力先生是"章黄支流"!)年底回美,又看到陳新雄教授早已寄來的反駁文《梅祖麟〈有中國特色的漢語歷史音韻學〉講辭質疑》。看來這次由於梅氏公開點名叫陣,國内學者才有相當激烈的反應,但公開回應的似乎也衹有少數幾個人。

一、事件的性質

看過上述兩次"事件"的正反辯論以後,我自然也有些個人的想法。首先我有些感慨。學術研究本應以禮待人、以禮服人,何必惡言相向呢? 繼而一想,蒲立本、郭錫良、陳新雄等人的强烈反應,都是既合理又必要的,因此都是完全可以理解的。假如不作反應,豈不等於默認自己畢生所從事的工作都是没有意義的了嗎? 退一步説,個人的毁譽不必計較,但這豈非也等於默認中國的傳統音韻學一開頭兒就是錯誤的? 這就不得不力加辯正了;這也就是爲什麽我奇怪没有更多的人作出反應。(據聞郭文發表時也有些波折,這就更令人費解了!)本人索居海外,退休多年,本不擬表示什麽意見,但最後還是覺得不得不説説自己的看法。我覺得,就他們研究的目的説,羅、柯的説法也不無道理,可惜他們没有考慮到别人研究的目的。同樣的,梅文開頭兒批評某些人要建立有中國特色的理論與方法,也是有道理的,因爲真正的理論與方法,應該是放諸四海而皆準的,無所謂那個國家或那個語言的有特色的方法或理論。但他在其他部分所説的就很有問題了。蒲、郭、陳的文章已經把對方文中的特定問題,以及對他們本人或其師友的惡評詳細辯正,所以我在這兒將不談那些細節,衹想從"衡諸常理"的角度,原則性地討論一下《切韻》和《韻鏡》之類的韻圖是否分别代表實際的語言,以及中國學者所説的"上古音"與國外某些人所説的"上古音"所指是否相同。

二、中國音韻學的目的

我們研究漢語音韻,大概不會都是爲研究而研究吧?也就是説,我們大多都有某種特定的目的。中國音韻學有近兩千年的歷史,代有人在,試想他們的目的是什麽呢?十多年前,我曾作過一個演講,向美國的同事們介紹中國語言研究的傳統(薛 1987),在那個報告中,我特別指出,中國學者研究的是哲人和詩人的語言。也就是説,爲了正確地解讀先秦時代的經典著作,他們才研究“古韻”;爲了樹立詩文寫作時的公認標準,他們才辨析“今韻”。當然,“今韻”還有另一個重要功能,即幫助推廣“標準話”。在中國的歷史中,最晚從東周起,就有了標準語的觀念與應用,即所謂“雅言”,後來也叫“通語”,明清時又叫“官話”。當然“標準語”是因時而異的,但不同時代的標準話是有密切的傳承關係的。不用任何書面證據,我們就可想象到,遠自“雅言”時代起,除了“通語”以外,每個時代必然還有許多方言,由於中國音韻學家的目的既如上所述,他們自然就以研究標準語爲本;這就是除了元代以後的幾個例外,中國學者很少較完整地記録下任何方言的原因。

現代研究漢語音韻的人,尤其是國外的學者,其目的顯然不盡相同。約而言之,可以分爲三類。第一類,以研究中國文史爲目的者,自然以研究“標準話”的傳承爲主要任務;這種研究就與中國傳統音韻學比較接近,儘管所用的方法和理論可能很不相同。例如高本漢采用其時歐洲流行的“構擬法”研究中古及上古漢語。雖然用這種方法分析《切韻》與韻圖並不妥當(説見下節),倒也開出了一條新途徑;同時他對古代經典如《詩經》《左傳》等也作過深入的研究,是一位可敬的漢學家。第二類,以音韻理論爲目的者,研究各種漢語方言(包括標準普通話),意在解説漢語的某些現象,藉以介紹或修正某種理論,或試圖建立某種新理論;這種研究衹是試圖在漢語中找例子,似與中國傳統音韻學無關,但真正好的理論却對我們如何詮釋《切韻》之類的傳統音韻學的韻書至爲重要。第三類,以建立“語族”(language family,或稱“語系”)爲目的者,想爲漢語找出其族屬,及其與某些非漢語的關係;這種研究是中國的前輩學者未曾做過的,因此與他們的研究很不一樣。由於許多國外研究漢語的人未能充分考慮到中國傳統音韻學的目的,有時就會因誤會而妄加批評。

三、中國音韻學的性質

在上一節裏,我提到高本漢對漢語歷史語言學的貢獻,但也指出他無意中給中國音韻學造成些問題。首先,他使用的"新方法"有時會給人(尤其是外國學者)一種錯覺,以爲漢語歷史語言學是從他開始的;羅、柯的論文可能更會增强這種錯覺。其次,他很自然地采用當時北歐流行的"構擬法"來擬測《切韻》音,不接受稍後出現的"音位學"理論。這就造成了更嚴重的問題,因爲《切韻》與韻圖之類的中國音韻學資料,本質上都是音位性的(我很高興看到蒲立本在他的文内也抱持這一看法),而構擬法却是以音值爲目標的,代表一種不同的觀念,其功能是"重建"古代未記録下來的語言。高氏既承認《切韻》是實際語言的記録,却又要重建它,豈非矛盾? 所以嚴格遵守"構擬"原則的人,必然會對高氏的做法質疑:在這個意義上説,羅、柯對"高本漢派"的批判,是必然的現象,衹是來何遲耶? 但否定"高本漢派"的做法是一回事,否定《切韻》就不同了,因爲這等於全盤否定中國傳統音韻學。

在以前的幾篇論文中(薛 1999、2000),我曾一再强調,《切韻》和《韻鏡》一類的韻書,其分聲、分韻、分調、分類,都是建立在"音位對比"(phonemic contrast)這個現象上的,因此要正確地解讀這些韻書,以及不同時代的韻書之間的承傳關係,就必須采用"音位對比"及"區别性特徵"等觀念。然而現在竟然有人説《切韻》和《韻鏡》都不代表實際語言,没有嚴格意義上的自己的語音。乍聽之下,真令人吃驚;其實可以"免驚"。不是有很多人都認爲《切韻》是"混合體"嗎? 如果不把所謂"混合"的含義説清楚,衹籠統地説是"混合體",就必然會有這樣的結論,因爲音系是衹能存在於某一特定時段的特定語言(方言)中的。

四、《切韻》是否代表實際語言

我從未懷疑《切韻》是根據陸法言時代的標準話編寫的。我們可以提出兩個最基本的觀點來支持這個看法。第一,這本書的編纂,像一般"今韻"類的韻書一樣,志在"正音"(陸法言就是一位語文老師);編者自然會在個别地方參考别人的意見,但他絶無理由故意編一個混合體來爲難想學標準話的人。第二,即使他有意編一個"混合體",恐怕他也没有那個本事(我們也都没那本事),因爲語言内在的語音系統是自然形成的,不是某一個人或某幾個人能够爲之編造的;退一步説,即使編造出來,也不會爲群衆所接受(所謂"世界語"Esperanto即爲一例),而《切韻》是有體系的,也是説那種話的人群所接受的;難道《切韻》會是一個例外嗎?

羅、柯引用了好幾位前輩學者的説法來支持"混合體"之説,主要都是以《切韻》序爲依據;這未免太簡單化了。我們得承認,這些前輩在没有音位觀念的時代,確實説過了頭,既説《切韻》不代表一個單一的方言,又忙着爲之"構擬"一個單一的音系,這不是自相矛盾嗎?當然會貽人口實。從這個角度看,我們還真得承認,羅、柯的説法是合乎邏輯的;你提出這樣的前提,他們當然可以得出那樣的結論。(他們没這麼説,而是"英雄所見略同"。)但我覺得,除了羅常培("於當時的方音……無所不包")和陸志韋("代表六朝漢語的整個局面")説得實在太過以外,其他幾位在説該書"不代表一時一地之方言"的同時,都説得比較具體而含蓄。例如,張琨説:"綜合許多以前……韻書中所提出的系統。"王力説:"有很明顯的存古性質。"可見對他們來説,所謂"混合"衹是有條件有限度的現象,假如"混合體"是這個意思,我們當然可以接受,因爲那些前人編的韻書,都是不久前根據其時的"標準話"編寫的,由此而"混合"進去的少數不很規律的成分,也能爲我們如何解釋某些韻的"從分不從合"及某些韻内的"重紐"現象,提供有力的證明。當然,能否爲《切韻》推證出一個合理完整的音位系統,並在這個系統的基礎上解釋書中的少數例外現象,才是充分説明該書是否代表一個實際語言的最有力最可信的證據,因爲一個大雜拌兒是不可能含有一個整齊合理的音系的;另一方面,我們也不能忘記,《切韻》所記録的"標準話",衹是當時許多漢語方言之一,衹代表一個自足的音系,不可能靠它全面解釋其他方言或域外對音或佛經翻譯等五花八門的現象;要解決那些問題,就衹能靠羅、柯所倡議的重建不同時代的其他方言,並考證佛經翻譯時分别使用了哪些不同的方言。埋怨《切韻》幫不上忙是不公平的,全盤否定《切韻》就更不公平了！

另一個問題是：《切韻》既然含有一些存古和方言的成分，這到底是一種什麼樣性質和程度上的"混合"？陸法言説："因論南北是非，古今通塞，欲更捃選精切，除削疏緩。"問題是他所説的"南北""古今"指的是什麼？所謂"古今"，比較容易理解，即他參考了某些較早的韻書，據之作了某些與時音不符合的"除削疏緩"。上文已經説過，這些較早的韻書都是根據較早的標準音編寫的；從語言學的角度看，這些書也不算太"古"，衹比陸法言早上百十來年而已，所記録的是與陸法言時代前後相承的語言，兩者差别不大，因之作少許"存古"的更動，衹會造成一些所謂"從分不從合""重紐""又讀"等書面上的例外現象，但這絶不意味《切韻》所記録的不是"實際的語言"。舉例來説，民國初年爲了推廣"國語"而制定了一套"國音符號"；其時"十三轍"的"乜斜"轍（相當於《中原音韻》的"車遮"韻）和"梭坡"轍（相當於《中原音韻》的"歌戈"韻）在北方官話裏已經合轍，但在南方官話裏仍然分開，因此就起了争論，結果決定"從分不從合"，用ㄝ注"乜斜"轍的字，用ㄜ/ㄛ注"梭坡"轍的字。（這自然會造成些小問題，例如："乜斜"轍的"格核額墨"，在北京話裏跟"梭坡"轍的"閣合蛾莫"變成兩兩相對的同音字了。這些字很巧合地也都是脣牙喉音字，類似"重紐"字，參看Chao 1968：52。）這是否意味如此注音的《國音字匯》不代表"實際語言"呢？我猜會説國語的人都已有了答案。至於"南北"，則較易引起誤會。"北"指的應爲黄河流域的中原地區，是"標準話"的發源地，當地的話方言性差别大概不很大。"南"指的是"江東"；我同意多數人的看法，即當時該地仍爲"吴語"區；那麽所謂"金陵音"究竟是當地的土語呢，還是中原人士南渡時帶過去的"標準話"呢？我認爲衹能是後者，因爲這種金陵式的標準話，由於兩三百年的隔離，自然跟"洛下之音"有些不同的地方，但兩者必然仍很接近，因此某些金陵音的讀法才有可能綜合到《切韻》中去，當然這也會促成"從分不從合"以及"又讀"等情況，但這是否就表示《切韻》記録的不是"實際的語言"呢？（蒲立本用臺北式的"國語"與大陸上的"普通話"爲例説明金陵音與中州音之間的關係，頗恰當。千年之後，如有人認爲臺北式的"國語"指的是閩南話或客家話，也將是一個笑話。由此推論，《切韻》中的"金陵音"成分對研究"古吴語"有多大用處，也頗令人懷疑。）

五、何謂"上古音"?

所謂"上古音"的情況更爲複雜。我們説過,至少在東周,即以《詩經》爲代表的時代,就有了標準語;不用引證就可以想象得到,其時一定還有别的漢語方言,但中國學者研究古音的目的是"解經",自然就以測定那個上古標準音爲任務。可惜那時没有韻書,相關的文獻也不够多,因此除了《詩經》的韻字之外,還不得不借重"諧聲字",但這會産生音系理論上的矛盾,因爲真正的音系衹能存在於特定時段的特定語言中,而《詩經》時代已有的諧聲字,必爲其前千百年間陸續造出來的,而且是否出自同一方言區也是很難斷定的。我曾當面問過李方桂先生這個問題,他笑着説:"資料太少,再分就没法做了!"這是一個雖不合"理"(音系理論)却很合情("没法做了!")的回答,我完全理解。由此我悟出,李先生的《上古音研究》與中國早期音韻學者的研究性質相近,所以他很少用非漢語的資料;否則從"構擬派"的角度看,可以利用温州話之類的方言、雲貴川藏等地少數民族的語言,以及緬、泰、老、柬等國的語言,資料可謂用之不竭,怎麽會説"資料太少"呢?王力先生也早已看出了我們此處所説的矛盾,所以他説諧聲字是非常重要的資料,但當諧聲與詩韻有矛盾時,仍應以詩韻爲準(引見郭文與陳文)。這就給我們提供了一個很好的折中原則,假如由此推論説他不懂諧聲字的重要,就似别有用心了。(當然你也可以一口咬定説諧聲字同樣代表《詩經》時代,但那不是違背常識嗎?)

國外研究所謂"上古音"者,除了像高本漢和蒲立本等少數人以外,多半對中國的古典文籍没有太大興趣;他們的目的是建立一個包括漢語在内的語系,類似印歐語系那樣,自然用不着看那些"老古董",但對"構擬"以外的音韻理論感興趣的也不多;現在流行的説法是"漢藏語系",儘管不少學者對此尚持存疑的態度,例如精研藏語的張琨先生(引見郭文)。我們不妨先接受這種説法,然後試想這兩種同源語是什麽時候分開的;有人説是早在"三代"之前,即約在《詩經》時代之前兩千年以上。假如有人能爲這個分裂出來的"漢語"構擬出它在這個漫長時期中某一時段的音系,當然很好,但這個音系肯定與以《詩經》爲依據的中國前輩學者所説的"上古音"很不一樣,不可混爲一談。很可惜的是,做這種構擬的人很少説明他們構擬的那個語言屬於哪個時段(大概不可能是《詩經》時代吧?),却常用他們的構擬臧否中國學者的"上古音"研究,説不像他們那樣做就無法與藏語接軌了。在我看來,這顯示出兩個思維上的錯亂;其一,把較早的那個時代與《詩經》時代混爲一談;這不有點兒像拿《切韻》作證據批評若干年後的《中原音韻》不該那麽分韻嗎?其二,把"漢藏語同源"當做無須證明的大前題,據以批評别人的做法不足以支持那個大前題,因此不算是"主流",這不是太主觀了嗎?(郭錫良似乎對這個"主流"之説很不以爲然,其實何必計較?結成一幫自號主流的人是常有的。我到國内時,就曾聽到某些人説:"《切韻》是個混合體,我們已經有了共識,不再討論了。"這不也類似自封爲"主流"把學術問題政治化了嗎?)我覺得由於研究目的不盡相同,實在没有這樣做的必要,何不各自客觀地做自己的研究呢?

六、結束語

有些問題是不需要引經據典高談理論才能解决的,往往衹要"衡諸常理"就可以説清楚。《切韻》是否代表"實際的語言"就是這樣一個問題。中國很早就有使用"通語"的傳統,如何爲"通語"訂立一個明確的標準,在隋唐時期建立科舉制度以後,就變得更重要了。作爲一本"正音"的書,《切韻》怎麽可能是"前人注音匯編"的大雜拌兒?假如真是那樣,就不可能含有什麽"音系"了。《切韻》利用"聲、韻、調"的區别標示字音的不同;這種區别衹可能是説那種話的人的聽覺反映,即"音位對比",不可能是細微的音值差異。高本漢錯誤地采用"構擬法"解説那些區别,遂使《切韻》音系顯得複雜零亂,似乎證實了"混合體"之説;這就不能抱怨有人説《切韻》不代表實際的語言及没有自身的語音了,因爲有那樣的前提,就會有這樣的結論。再説等韻圖吧,創造者不以僅僅標示"聲、韻、調"的區别爲滿足,進而分析"聲、韻"内在的成分,並據此將之分類;這在觀念上是與"區别性特徵"的想法一致的;難怪連蒲立本都説這是中國智慧發展史上的一大貢獻;王力先生也曾説過"等韻"就是中國的音韻理論。這樣了不起的創製能是分析了那個"混合體"以後的圖嗎?我看絶不可能。好"讀書"的中國學者到現在還没有把《切韻》完全弄清楚,那個唐代的韻圖創製者會把它分析得一清二楚並據之設計出系統分明的韻圖嗎？因此我相信，他必定是以他熟知的某種語言（當時的"標準話"）爲依據的。這一點連高本漢都似乎隱約地看出來了，所以他説韻圖顯示出某些《切韻》以後的音變。

我極力指出《切韻》和《韻鏡》等都代表實際語言，目的是説，爲了中國標準語音韻史的研究，這兩類書都是極爲重要的，但如果研究者的目的不同，就可能不那麽重要了。據羅、柯説，他們要做的是"漢語方言史"，用的是"一個動態的模式"。這就得在調查方言的基礎上逐步向上構擬了；這才是"正統構擬派"的本色，能"無中生有"，不像高本漢那樣爲一個有詳實記録的語言"構擬"，無怪他們不以"高本漢派"的做法爲然了；他們不使用《切韻》和韻圖所提供的資料是完全可以理解的。希望不久能看到那樣的"閩語音韻史"或"吴語音韻史"。

有關"上古音"的争論，基本上也是這樣的。中國學者爲了正確地解讀先秦時代的典籍而研究《詩經》時代的"上古音"，對這個目的來説，已經證明是很有價值的。現代的學者如果也要做那個時代的"上古音"，自然會發現前人積累的成果是很有價值的；正如李方桂先生所説："我們現在研究上古音，衹能利用他們得到的材料，另外用一種方法去研究它。"這才是合理持平的説法（其實研究中古音也應抱持這種態度）。但是漫漫上古，時間實在太長，如果有人要研究《詩經》時代以前的某種漢語，最好先指出是哪個時段，並且也取個新名稱，諸如"遠古漢語"（Proto - Chinese）和"上上古音"（Old - Old - Chinese）等，以免與前人（包括李方桂、董同龢等）所説的"上古音"混淆不清。這是音系學理論最起碼的要求，同時也可藉此避免無謂的相互指責及惡言相向。

參考文獻：

Chao, Y. R. *A Grammar of Spoken Chinese*, Berkeley, 1968.

Hsueh, F. S. The Languages of the Sages and the Poets: Some Aspects of the Chinese Linguistics Tradition, *Inaugural Lectures 1986—1987*, College of Humanities, OSU, 1987, pp. 29 - 35.

Normen, Jerry and Coblin, South. A New Approach to Chinese Historical Linguistics, *Journal of the American Oriental Society*. 115. (1995) pp.

576－584.

Pulleyblank, Edwin G.　Qieyun and Yunjing: the Essential Foundation for Chinese Historical Linguistics, *Journal of the American Oriental Society* 118.2(1998), pp.200－216.

陳新雄　《梅祖麟〈有中國特色的漢語歷史音韻學〉講辭質疑》,《語言研究》2002年第1期。

郭錫良　《歷史音韻學研究中的幾個問題》,《古漢語研究》2002年第3期。

梅祖麟　《有中國特色的漢語歷史音韻學》,在香港語言學會2001年會上的報告(Journal of Chinese Linguistics Vol.30 No.2)。

薛鳳生　《漢語音韻史十講》,華語教學出版社,1999年。

薛鳳生　《構擬與詮釋:漢語音韻史研究的兩種對立觀點》,《2000年中國言語學國際學術大會發表論文集》,韓國中國語文研究會,第85—93頁。(此文又見於《語言學與應用語言學集刊》第一輯,徐州師範大學語言研究所編印。)

羅傑瑞、柯蔚南　朱慶之譯《漢語歷史語言學研究的新方法》,《漢語史研究集刊》第一輯(下),巴蜀書社,1998年。

有關官話音系研究的幾個理論問題**

前言

語音研究大致可以分爲三種不同的方式:(1) 觀察發音器官的部位及動態以説明音值;(2) 利用聲波儀及録音器之類的機件,測量語音的音波形態與音量;(3) 根據説話人或受話人的聽覺反應確認語音的辨義功能。20 世紀 50 年代末,我曾聽過董同龢先生的課,他就説過類似上述三種方式的話;不過他説的第三種方式是測試聽覺神經,並説這是最困難的。但我後來慢慢體會到,第三種方式並不那麼困難,衹要仔細辨認母語發音人的聽覺反應就够了。這三種方式互爲表裏,前兩種對需要作合成語音之類的新科技(例如計算機電話等),當然至爲重要;但對語言學來説,第三種方式乃關鍵之所在,因爲那是構成"音系"的基礎。

一、形成音系的基本原理

不同的語言都含有不同的音系(反過來説,不同的音系都會形成不同的語言);這是因爲古今中外的語言,都有其自然形成的組合與區分語音的特定方式。推證出其特定的方式,是認證其音系的必要條件,因爲其特定方式(即"音位對比"的方式)是構成音系的基礎,撇開"音位"觀念而奢談音系是没有多大意義的,也就是説,根據"音值"是無法推證出真正的"音系"的。這就牽涉到"音系"的定義了,對以"音值"爲依歸的人來説,衹要能分析或構擬出一個大致還算整齊的形式,就可以叫做"音系",因此常見不同的人爲同一個語言(或韻書)構擬出不同的"音系";但從嚴格的意義上説,所謂"音系"不僅僅是表面上

** 原載《近代官話語音研究》,耿振生主編,語文出版社,2007 年。

的整齊排列,更重要的是充分表達説同一語言的人群所共有的深層"語感"。也許有人會説,"音位"是近代人提出的一個觀念,是用來合併没有互爲區别功能的語音的方法,怎麽會是古代的呢?其實這是一個誤會,音位系統是構成語言的必要條件,古今一理,不是因爲近代人發現了才存在的。舉例來説,"水"的成分是"氫二氧一",這是近代科學家的發現,但這絶不是説,上古"水"的成分是跟現在不一樣的。

二、"音位"的定義

"音位"到底是什麽?對某些人來説,迄今似乎還是一個問題。這並不奇怪,因爲很多人早已習慣於"構擬音值",而"音位説"出現得相當晚,起初還很有争議,後來才漸爲多數學者所接受,但形成了兩種不同的説法。其一爲趙元任先生的"非唯一説",此説完全以"實用"爲目的,認爲歸納音位衹是一種追求簡便的方法,因此不同的人爲了不同的目的,可以歸納出不同的"音位標音法",而其結果是各有所長,其間無所謂孰優孰劣。另一看法可名之爲雅柯布森(R. Jakobson)的"唯一説"。與趙説比較,Jakobson之流則是完全從"理論"着眼,認爲如果某些人爲某一語言作出不同的音位分析,我們一定可以根據某些理論原則,指出哪一個比較好,最終求證出其最妥善的(也就是獨一無二的)音系。從這個理論的層次上説,"音位"衹不過是由"一束區别性特徵"(a bundle of distinctive features)合成的單位,兩者同以"音位對比"(phonemic contrast)爲依據,代表兩個不同的層次,没有冲突,如果有人想要更抽象地表達音系,當然也可以跳過音位層次,直接用區别性特徵表達;這是爲什麽後來又有了"不必計較音位"的説法。(在我討論漢語音韻史的著作裏,爲了避免過分抽象,以便較易與傳統音韻學接軌,采用的是音位與特徵符號混用的方法;例如:以"r"代表"捲舌特徵"[+Retr],以"h"代表"送氣特徵"[+Asp],因此將之附加於/c/[代表"精"母的一束特徵])時,就構成了另一個音位,即"穿"母/crh/;這兒雖然用了三個拉丁字母,但衹代表一個音位,不是三個音位。)

三、中國傳統音韻學的本質

宋代以前，古人並無建立"音韻理論"的想法，也沒有明確的"時有今古、地有南北"的觀念，衹憑對其母語的直覺"語感"，按照聲韻調的異同，爲"通語"(標準語)的字匯分組。(當然，他們有時也會受到説鄰近方言的人或稍前韻書的影響，因而作出某些對其時的通語來説没有必要的區分。)這種做法完全符合"音位對比"所代表的觀念(正如我們調查方言時，要根據發音人的感覺區别字音，從而論證該方言的音系)。同時，由於古代學者的目的都是爲當時的通語正音，故不同時代的韻書，常能反映出通語音系之歷時演變；此類演變自然也衹能在音位理論的基礎上得到既合理又明確的詮釋，然而"本土學者"的這種做法，在音位學説出現之前，很難爲外族學者所接受，甚至後代的本國學者往往也弄不清楚；所以自高本漢以來，都偏重擬定或標示"音值"；最能表現這種精神的，莫過於陸志韋先生的做法，例如他爲徐孝的《等韻圖經》所做的擬音，其目的顯然不在解説：是什麽樣的音系使得徐孝必須那樣分韻？其實從顯示音系的角度看，符號本身並不那麽重要。常見有人斤斤計較於該用哪個符號，甚至老師用過的符號學生就再也不敢改動了。我個人覺得這實在没有必要。采用符號時，重要的是其突顯"音系"的功能，例如現代漢語的"注音符號"(説明見下節)，或代表日語五十音的"假名"，都比拉丁化式的"拼音"更清楚地顯示出其所代表的音系，更不用説國際音標式的標音了。

四、音系學原理與"近代漢語官話"的音系

"近代漢語官話"，指的大概是《中原音韻》時代以後形成的北方官話和中原官話。作爲"通語"的代稱，"近代官話"的這個含義可以説是相當合理的。就"最標準"的官話來説，自《中原音韻》，經《等韻圖經》和《十三轍》，以迄於現代漢語的"注音符號"，這個語言的音系可以説已經相當明確了，唯一的"缺陷"是没有使用拉丁字母或國際音標，因此外國人看不大懂而已。我們可以拿"注音符號"來説明這個音系；這種標音方式顯然源自等韻學的做法(唯一不同的

是,不再使用反切法而采用類似日文“假名”的單一符號),即先列出聲母(“字母”),再以“丨,ㄨ,ㄩ”之有無來分别標示“四呼”,繼之以標示“押韻”的符號。這些區分都完全符合音位對比原則;設計者當然知道漢語的音節分段模式,但爲了明示押韻的重要,他們把韻腹和韻尾合併起來,用單一符號代表(即我所謂的“韻基”),這是完全可以理解的。從帶尾韻的區分,我們可以看出,同韻尾的不同韻基衹有兩個,即“ㄟ/ㄞ”(收噫)“ㄡ/ㄠ”(收嗚)、“ㄣ/ㄢ”(抵腭),“ㄥ/ㄤ”(穿鼻);這就明顯地告訴我們,造成這些區分的,衹不過是兩個不同的韻腹元音音位而已。再就無尾韻説,情況似乎比較複雜;首先是“ㄓ,ㄔ,ㄕ,ㄖ”和“ㄗ,ㄘ,ㄙ”七個聲母,竟然可以没有韻母而自成音節,而通常擔任韻頭角色的“丨,ㄨ,ㄩ”竟也代表韻母了。這種做法當然是違反音節構成原則昀,但假如我們認識到,高元音單獨作爲韻母時,衹能出現在上述聲母之後(即所謂“舌尖元音”);而在出現於韻頭之後時,也會因同化而變得與其韻頭非常近似,也就可以理解,注音符號是爲了實用而作出上述省略的。另四個出現在無尾韻中的元音符號是“ㄚ,ㄛ,ㄜ,ㄝ”。“ㄚ”代表的顯然是低元音。“ㄛ,ㄜ”代表兩個偏低偏後的“中元音”,前者衹出現在合口韻母裹,與後者互補,其間的差别是音值性的,實屬同一音位,看來“注音符號”的設計者也未能免俗,其實在歷來的韻書裹,這兩類字同屬一韻,例如:《等韻圖經》的“果攝”和《十三轍》的“梭坡轍”。“ㄝ”代表一個偏底偏前的中元音,這類字在早期官話裹獨立成韻,例如《中原音韻》的“車遮”韻和《等韻圖經》的“拙攝”,但在現在的北方話裹,已與“ㄛ,ㄜ”類的字互韻了,而且部分對應的字已變爲同音了,例如:格/閣、核/合、墨/莫、客/課、曰/約、薛/削,等等。可見當初的設計者仍然改不了韻書編者的老習慣,有時會保留些照顧方言或“存古”的成分,這會給論證音系造成些麻煩,但不是什麽大不了的問題,犯不着説什麽“不代表實際的語言”。綜合以上的討論,我們可以説,從研究音系的角度看,“注音符號”給我們提供了非常簡明且極珍貴的資料,其“四元音”音系是早期官話的形態,其“三元音”音系則爲由前者衍變出來的當代“標準普通話”。

官話區域相當遼闊,自然還有不少方言性的差别,就發音形態和個别詞彙説,那些方言與北京話的差别可能相當大;但就其音系結構説,則與北京話相去不遠。因此在研究明清時代的韻書時,可能誤導我們,以爲這個時段編的北方話韻書，都代表同一個方言，而在未“驗明正身”之前就混用那些資料；比較可靠的做法，應爲先就某本韻書求證其所代表的音系，然後才與其他韻書比較，以觀察其音系的異同。明清兩朝是中國音韻學説百家争鳴的時期，在等韻學的啓迪和邵雍的玄學思維旳影響之下，不少人都隱約地感覺到漢語深層的神秘規律，驚詫之餘，便認爲這是宇宙間的普遍真理，因而采用陰陽八卦和五行七音等説法各抒己見，想爲這個神秘的現象提出解釋。他們的思維很自然地是以自己的語感（亦即他們的母語）爲基礎的，同時爲了遷就他們采用的玄理，有時也會忽視音節分段和韻類區分等基本原則，所以在使用這類資料時，我們不能先驗式地認爲它們都代表北京地區的“官話”。

結語

中國的傳統音韻學，是建立在本民族語言的字音相互對比的基礎上的，因此要正確地解讀前人的韻書，推證出其所代表的音系，就必須采用“音位對比”的觀點。但自高本漢以來，研究者多以構擬“音值”爲事，人人都把自己的構擬叫做“音系”，似乎衹要把擬音排成某種陣式就可以稱爲“音系”了，遂使“音系”觀念含混不明；這就嚴重地破壞了中國音韻學的傳統，因此我們必須再次强調，一個語言衹能有一個真正的（也就是“唯一的”）音系，代表的是説那個語言的人群共有的“語感”；我們的任務是儘可能地求證出那個音系；也就是説，如果我們真要研究近代漢語“音系”或任何音系，就必須把重點從音值的描述，轉移到音位的認定；這種思維上的轉變。衹不過是一念之間而已。

參考文獻

王　力　《現代漢語語音分析中的幾個問題》，《中國語文》1979 年 4 月，第 281—286 頁。

王輔世　《北京話韻母的幾個問題》，《中國語文》1963 年 2 月，第 115—124 頁。

羅常培　《北京俗曲百種摘韻》，北京來薰閣重印本，1950 年。

耿振生　《明清等韻學通論》，語文出版社，1992 年。

魯國堯　《明代官話及其基礎方言問題》，《南京大學學報》1985 年第 4 期。

陸志韋 《記徐孝重訂司馬温公等韻圖經》,《燕京學報》第 32 期,第 167—196 頁。

張洵如 《北平音系小轍編》,臺北開明書局重印,1956 年。

薛鳳生 《北京音系解析》,北京語言學院出版社,1986 年。

——— 《〈中原音韻〉音位系統》(魯國堯、侍建國合譯),北京語言學院出版社,1990 年。

——— 《漢語音韻史十講》(耿振生、楊亦鳴主編),北京華語教學出版社,1999 年。

Chao, Y. R. "The Non-Uniqueness of Phonemic Solution of Phonetic Systems", *Bulletin of the Institute of History and Philology* (BIHP, Vol. 4, No. 4(1934), 363 - 398.

Hartman, Lawton M. III "The Segmental Phonemes of the Peiping Dialect", *Language* 20(1944), 28 - 42.

Hsueh, F. S. "The phonemic Structure of Pekingese Finals and their R-Suffixation", BIHP Vol. 51, Part 3(1980), 491 - 514.

R. Jakobson, C. Fane and M. Halle *Preliminaries to Speech Analysis*, The MIT Press, Boston, 1951.

Wang, John C. and Hsueh, F. S. "The Lin-ch'i Dialect and its Relation Io Mandarin", *Journal of American Orienial Society*, 93. 2 (1973), 136 - 145.

試論《切韻》音系的元音音位與“重紐、重韻”等現象*

1.《切韻》一書，顯然摻雜一些方言分歧與歷史陳迹，但就其整體而論，基本上應代表一個單一的音系，因此爲之作細密的研究分析，才有可能也才有意義[①]。本文試從嚴格的音位學觀點，推測該音系中的元音音位，並據以解説該書分韻的道理，以及所謂“重紐”“重韻”等現象。本文將絶對遵守兩條大前提作爲分析的基礎，即一、《切韻》音系的音節分段模式與等韻音系相同，分爲聲母、韻頭、韻腹、韻尾四段；二、互押之字必含有相同的韻基（韻腹與韻尾之合體），分韻亦以此爲標準。由於“收噫”韻數目特多，分配特殊，也最突出地顯示了“重紐”“重韻”等問題，本文將集中討論這一韻類，據以推測《切韻》音系的元音數目及其分布。初步的結論是：《切韻》音系含有七個元音音位，“重紐”爲《切韻》以前遺留下來的現象；“重韻”則爲《切韻》與等韻之間的音變造成的。兩種現象都可以在元音音系的基礎上得到合理的解釋。

2.《切韻》製作的原始目的是審定音切，以爲詩文創作之助，所采用的方法則爲：分辨四聲、建立大韻、區别小韻、標注反切。這些做法的依據，當然衹能是作者們對字讀區分的聽覺認知，不是發音方式的直接描述，换言之，是以音位對比（phonemic contrast）爲根據的。由於是“集體創作”，人多嘴雜，難免摻入一些與整體音系有違的音切，但這應該衹是少數個别現象。《切韻》序云

---

* 原刊《語言研究》1996 年第 1 期，收入《漢語音韻史十講》。

本文曾於 1995 年 5 月 20 日在臺北舉行的第四屆“國際”暨第十三屆聲韻學學術研討會宣讀。現改寫多處，發表於此，以就教於方家。宣讀時曾得到許多與會朋友的批評指正，特别是評議人陳新雄教授的質疑，使我認識到必須增寫 6.3 節那一大段（原 6.3 節改作 6.4），謹在此表示謝意。

① 有些學者特别强調《切韻》的“綜合性”，這就等於説，《切韻》不代表一個音系。果爾，嚴格地説，爲之“擬構音系”豈非自相矛盾而且徒勞無功？如果説這個“綜合體”中含有一個“主體”，就與本文的論旨相同了，因爲本文的目的就是要爲那個“主體”推論出一個完整的音系，然後根據這個音系，具體地推證出哪些成分是“綜合”進去的。

"南北是非,古今通塞",正如今人動輒即曰"古今中外",多屬文人修辭之語,不必過分認真。好在這類違規的個別現象,由於明清以來學者們的深入分析與整理,已經相當清楚。這給我們推論《切韻》音系的工作創造了良好的條件,那些比較有系統的存古或方言性的例外,更讓我們可以上推《切韻》前的音韻情況。但是傳統式的表達方法,往往過分晦澀,變成了一種"絶學",因此當近代西方學者用音標"構擬"時,便令人耳目一新,似乎揭開了千古之謎。然而經過幾十年來許多中外學者的努力,《切韻》音系的性質似乎仍然無法確定。原因何在呢?我猜想還是基本觀念的問題。如上所述,《切韻》所表達的是"音位對比",而"構擬派"學者所孜孜追求的却是"音值"(phonetic value)。每個"構擬"的人,都使用了許多正反顛倒、穿靴戴帽的音標符號,而各人使用這些符號時,又不一定都賦予相同的音值;觀念上自詡爲審定"音值",但又常采用一些連自己都不知道如何發音的符號,來區别《切韻》中的韻類[①]。這不是自相矛盾嗎?他們都把各自"構擬"的結果叫做"音系",但看到那些煩瑣的符號及其散亂的分布,我們實難瞭解其"系"何在。要解決這個問題,我們必須有一個觀念性的轉變,即用音位學的觀念來解釋《切韻》所提供給我們的那些"音位對比"現象,而以諸家"構擬"的音值符號作爲參考,因爲"構擬"最多衹能告訴我們一些發音的近似值(phonetic approximation),而不能準確地解釋音韻規律。

3. 采用音位學説爲《切韻》"擬音",以前已經有人做過,最爲人知的大概要算馬丁教授的"簡化"了(Martin 1953)[②]。他大致遵守上文所提音節分段及押韻標準兩條原則,衹在個别不得已的地方暫時放棄,所以能把高本漢的十五個元音"簡化"爲六個。他完全以高本漢的擬音爲依據,高氏没有注意到的問題(例如"重紐")或者無法決定的問題(例如"之、脂"分韻),他自然也就未加解説,這等於是在"構擬"這個新"傳統"裏打圈子,似乎跟對《切韻》本身的研究隔

---

① 例如高本漢無法區分"之、脂",就衹好在[i]上加撇[ί];又如李榮區别"重紐"時,在[i]之外增加了[j]作介音,衹説"音值怎麽不同很難説"。

② 趙元任先生當然早已注意到"音位分析法"了,但限於當時的一般看法,他也衹認爲是一種"方法"(參看趙 1934)。馬丁所作的"簡化"深受趙先生另一論文(趙 1941)的影響。蒲立本後來也用音位説分析《切韻》(Pulleyblank 1962),他對音節分段及押韻的看法跟我們頗不一樣。

了一層[①]。周法高先生很早就注意到馬丁的"音位化",並給予很高的評價。他説以前的學者(包括他自己)"對高氏的系統都有所修正,但是大體上都不出高氏的範圍,衹不過在一些小地方加以修正罷了。一九五三年,馬丁,對中古音的構擬才有了一個新的面目"(周 1984:1)。稍後又説:"現在擬構《切韻》音的時候,要從音位學的觀點把《切韻》音的元音系統加以簡化。"(周 1984:6)這幾句話充分顯示出周先生胸襟開闊,眼光遠大,不墨守個人的舊説,但求日新又新,有"今日之我與昨日之我戰鬥"的高尚風格,是普通人做不到的。當然,限於他的時代,他也未能正確地認識音位學的真義,所以他的研究(周 1954)仍未嚴格遵守音節分段這個基本原則,所得出的十個元音也很不平衡地分屬高低六個層次,違背了元音對稱分配(symmetrical distribution) 的原則。因此他與馬丁的研究雖然對我們都有很大的幫助,却仍有不足。這是由於他們對音位觀念的理解,仍然衹是"語音的簡化",停留在"寬式標音"(broad transcription)的階段。我們則認爲,真正嚴格精確的音位分析應以解釋説某種語言的人群對語音的聽覺反應爲目標,所得出的結論應該是其語感的具體描述。在下文中,我們將以這一觀點,重新推證《切韻》的元音音位。我們將參考前人的"擬音",儘可能地使用類似的符號,但必須指出,這些符號所代表的概念,是與前人不同的。

4. 在爲高本漢的"擬音"作音位化時,馬丁説他決定先從收舌根音韻尾的韻類開始,即出現在等韻的"通、江、宕、曾、梗"五攝中的韻類,因爲這些韻類的數目最多,如果能够區别它們的元音,也就能够區分其他韻類了(Martin 1953:28)。這個想法當然是合理的,但却是建立在"構擬"上頭的。如果"構擬"有問題,這也就有問題了。從這些韻類本身及其在韻圖中的分布看,它們並不太特殊,比别的韻類可能還簡單些。問題倒是:爲什麽會有五攝之多的韻類都以舌根音爲韻尾?這牽涉到"攝"的定義問題。"構擬派"的學者們大多認爲同攝的韻都帶有相同的韻尾。周先生就説:"同轉之内,又可根據韻尾的性

---

① 有些"構擬"派的學者,的確給人一種印象,好像他們的重點衹是互相批評如何標音,甚至有人説要把各家的"構擬"都看作不同的"方言",再據以構擬一個新的"音系"。這不成替古人設計方言了嗎?

質而分爲若干攝。"但是,正如他們對音節分段的態度一樣,遇到困難時,就輕易地把這個定義放棄了。比如,周先生接着説:"有時也根據元音的性質而分攝。"這裏的"有時"以及所謂"元音的性質"就不大容易理解。在這個問題上,我是"死硬派",堅持"基本原則",這就使我們對前人的構擬不能不懷疑了,所以我多年前就指出,"曾、梗"兩攝的韻尾實爲舌面音,衹有"通、江、宕"三攝是帶舌根韻尾的(薛 1985)。就韻類本身及其在韻圖中的分布看,真正複雜的是"收噫"韻,即分屬"止、蟹"兩攝的韻,所含韻目特多,其中四個竟衹有去聲;在韻圖中的分布也最特殊,"止"攝僅有三等韻,所含竟多達四列韻目。"蟹"攝更爲特殊,三等僅有"祭、廢"兩個去聲韻,而一、二兩等獨多"重韻"。另外所謂"重紐",在這兩攝裏也特別突出。這使我覺得,能够區別及解釋"收噫"韻的一套元音,也必足以區別及解釋其他韻類,所以我據此推測出一個七音位的元音系統,其相對位置如下表左方①;右方爲馬丁的元音表(Martin 1953: 35),以供比較。

	前	央	後	前	央	後
高		ɨ			*	
中	e	ə	o	e	ə	
低	ɛ	a	ɔ	ɛ	a	ɑ

跟馬丁不同的是,我們增加了一個元音,故能區分他未區分的韻類,同時也充分顯示元音音位趨向平衡與對稱的合理分布,另以/ɨ/代/*/,以/ɔ/代/ɑ/,那衹不過是個符號問題而已。至於這些元音在各韻類中的分配,我們將廣泛地參考前人的"構擬",儘可能地表現它們語音上的近似值,因此也將使我們的標音與馬丁大不相同,這可以由下文的分韻討論看出來,不煩一一舉出。另外,我得特别感謝周先生,他做了一大張詳盡的"諸家《切韻》擬音對照表"(周 1984:3—4)。這對我們實在太有用了,當然使用時必須小心點兒,因爲諸家所用的符號,相同的不一定代表相同的音值,不同的也不一定代表不同的

① 早在十年前,我對《切韻》的元音系統就有這樣的看法(薛 1985:50,注 9)。當時未能想得很透徹,故衹大略言之,其後即爲俗務所累,未暇繼續研究,及今思之,真有"流水十年間"之感。這次説得雖較詳細,也還是倉促成文,言其大概而已。廣徵文獻,斟酌百家,仍然是愧未能也。

音值。

4.1 “支、脂、之、微”四個韻列，同屬止攝三等。三等韻的特徵是有腭化介音（即高本漢的[i̯]，我寫作/y/），這是大家都同意的。另一方面，假如堅守“攝”的定義，我們也得承認它們都以/y/爲韻尾（即所謂“收噫”韻也）[①]，所以這四個韻列的區别就衹能是“元音的性質”了。它們後來變爲“重韻”，也就是説，在等韻時代合韻了，同以高元音/ɨ/爲韻腹（薛 1985）。這表示它們的元音本來近似，都非低元音，所以我推測它們的韻母形態應如下表所示：

	開	合
支紙寘	yey	ywey
脂旨至	yəy	ywəy
之止志	yɨy	
微尾未	yoy	ywoy

也就是説，它們的差異原爲分别含有不同的“非低”（[-lo]）元音，後來在腭化介音與韻尾的雙重影響下，中元音/e,ə,o/升高而變爲/ɨ/，所以就合而爲一了。我把“支、脂、之”類的元音分别定爲/e,ə,ɨ/是爲從衆（參看周表），把“微”類定爲/o/，則因這幾韻的字都是脣牙喉音，多爲合口，在唐初仍保持“獨用”，且與“廢”韻有關（“廢”寄於此圖），所以推測其韻腹應爲後元音。“支、脂”兩類同有“重紐”問題，容後文再論（見 5.3 節）。

4.2 蟹攝各韻同爲“收噫”，諸家構擬倒是没有異議的[②]。各韻在韻圖上的分布却顯得很奇特，三等韻特少，而一、二等獨多“重韻”，其情況恰與止攝相反，隱然有互補之勢。它們原有密切的關係，應是不容置疑的。（研究上古音的人已經指出這一點來，但我們在此不願以更不明確的上古音來證明中古音。）我推測，中元音/e,ə,o/出現在腭化音節（“三等韻”）中時，後來上升而與高元音合併，構成了止攝；但出現在非腭化音節（没有/y/作介音）中時，後來下降而與相對應的低元音合併，構成了蟹攝。《切韻》所表現的，是其未變之時；

---

① 這個定義，諸家於止攝多不嚴格遵守，例如高本漢把“支”類的韻母定爲[ie]，把“脂、之”類的韻母定爲[i,í]，所以馬丁就衹好把它們改放在無尾韻一行，即跟“魚、虞”同類了。參看 Martin 1953：25。

② 衹有李榮獨樹一幟，把“佳”類的韻母定爲[(u)ä]。

等韻所表現的,是其既變之後。根據這個設想,我們可以爲蟹攝諸韻定位如下,元音的選擇,仍是儘量從"構擬"諸家之衆的(見周表),特殊的地方,將稍加按語説明如下表。

		開		合
Ⅰ	泰	ɔ y		w ɔ y
	咍海代	o y	(灰賄隊)	w o y
Ⅱ	佳蟹卦	a y		w a y
	皆駭怪	ɛ y		w ɛ y
	夬	ə y		w ə y
Ⅲ	廢	y ɔ y		y w ɔ y
	祭	y ɛ y		y w ɛ y
Ⅳ	齊薺霽	e y		w e y

按:一、我也認爲"泰、廢"的元音應爲後低元音,即/ɔ/。(諸家"泰"都作[ɑ],"廢"則作[ɑ]或[ɐ]。)一等韻含後元音,故"咍、灰"等之元音應爲稍高之/o/。(我推測中元音/e,ə,o/至少各有兩個變體,即在腭化音節中較高,音值當爲[e,ə,o],在非腭化音節中較低,音值也許是[ɛ,ɐ,ɔ];低元音音位/ɛ,a,ɔ/的音值應爲[æ,a,ɑ]。)

二、"佳"類韻的牙喉音字,部分後來改讀如"麻"類字,應是受某一方言之影響(吴語?),這可間接證明其韻腹原即爲央低元音/a/,故在丢掉韻尾後,自然變爲"麻"類字。"夬、卦"同爲二等韻,早在唐代即已"同用",故訂"夬"之韻腹爲稍高之央元音/ə/。"皆"類韻之韻腹則從衆訂爲前低元音。

三、"祭"韻之元音暫從衆訂爲/ɛ/,"重紐"問題容後再論。

四、四等韻有無腭化介音,仍是一個聚訟的問題。陸志韋、李榮、蒲立本、邵榮芬皆持無此介音説。我從等韻的整體設計看,也認爲四等韻不應有此介音,其産生應爲等韻後(但相當早)的音變結果。

五、比對上列兩個韻母表,可以看出,我把"齊/支、夬/至、咍/微、泰/廢、怪/祭"等兩兩相對的韻組,擬定爲含有相同的韻基。這是與我們的第二條大前題相悖的,其所以然之故,容待下文説明(見6.3節)。

5. “重紐”現象，有系統地出現在“支、脂、祭、真(諄)、仙、宵、侵、鹽”諸韻類的脣牙喉聲母之下。其中“侵、鹽”諸韻衹在“影”母下有幾個字，大批的“重紐”字出現在“支、脂、祭、真、仙、宵”六類韻中(董同龢先生説：“十分之八九。”董 1948：1)，而其中“收噫”韻就占了三個。從諸家的構擬中可以看出，這幾個韻類所含的都是前元音，所以如能合理地解釋“收噫”韻的“重紐”，其他各韻的“重紐”也就可以合理地解釋了。

5.1　所謂“重紐”，自然是指這類字在韻圖中的分布而言的①。它們既出現於同一韻中，自然表示可以互押，也自然表示，在《切韻》音系中含有相同的元音，那麼它們的差別就似乎衹能是聲紐了。然而《切韻》的聲母却是類别清晰、系統分明的，實在不能作任意性的增添，所以其區别必然是韻母的問題。韻母的區别衹能表現在三個方面，即韻頭的不同或韻腹的不同或韻尾的不同。在我所知的構擬諸家中，未見有人以爲“重紐”是韻尾的問題，倒是有幾位認爲是韻頭的問題，例如陸志韋、李榮、蒲立本、邵榮芬等。但是就音節結構説，介音是區别音節的“開、合、洪、細”的，一般以[i̯, u](/y, w/)兩個“半元音”來表示，除此以外，介音還有什麽功能呢？任意增添介音符號，説不出它的“音值”是什麽②，更把它限用在極少數幾個韻類中，實難算是合理的舉措，所以合理的解釋應是元音的性質或韻尾的有無。反對這一推論的人所持的理由是，“重紐”字既屬同韻，便不該有不同的元音(邵 1982：123)。這一想法，就《切韻》音系而言，是完全正確的，但却忽略了一件事：《切韻》是一群人合議的產物，因此片面地作了一些對“南北是非、古今通塞”的妥協，“重紐”應該就是對較早的韻書或某一方言所作的妥協，也就是説，“重紐”所顯示的，絶對是真實的音韻現象；不過這是以前的事，到《切韻》時代，這一現象或許仍保留在某一方言(金陵音?)中，但對《切韻》所代表的標準音(洛生咏?)來説，則已經消失了，相對的

① 我認爲，所謂“重紐”完全是中古音的問題，所代表的音韻對比絶對可信，無須再加以證明，其解釋自然亦應以中古音系爲據。所謂上古音的“重紐”或某某方言的“重紐”，嚴格地説，命題即頗可商榷，這類研究也衹能證明“重紐是真的不是假的”而已，無助於解釋其在中古音系裏所以有别之故。

② 有趣的是，許多非常計較“音值”的人，碰到這類問題的時候，却常用一些難以捉摸的符號來强分音類。例如陸志韋以[i, ɪ]作介音分“重紐”，李榮與邵榮芬同以[i, j]作介音分“重紐”，[ɪ, j]作爲介音到底怎麽讀，在音系中的分配又何以如此局限，則自然很難説定。

“重紐”字也就變爲同音了,自然也就同韻了。

5.2 根據上述的觀點,我們先討論祭韻的“重紐”問題。上文説在《切韻》的音系裏,祭韻的韻母是/y(w)εy/,即以前低元音作爲韻腹,那麽它的兩類“重紐”字是何以互異的呢?據董先生説,列於四等的“重紐”字跟列於三等的舌齒音字爲一類,三等的“重紐”字則自成一類,但也有人持相反的意見(邵 1982:70—80)。我承認對這個問題没有什麽深入的研究,所以祇能推測,它們的韻母原來應分别爲/*y(w)ay/和/*y(w)εy/,即以央低元音與前低元音而互異。至於哪個代表哪一類,我就不敢亂猜了,但我深信,它們後來合而爲一,是下面這個公式所代表的音變造成的。

$$a \rightarrow \varepsilon / y(w)\_\_\_\_y \qquad (1)$$

就是説,央低元音受到前半元音/y/的兩面夾擊,因而前移變成了前低元音。這是符合語音同化的一般趨勢的。經此一變,“祭”韻的“重紐”問題,也就“俯仰之間,已爲陳迹”了。

5.3 “支、脂”兩類韻中的“重紐”,可能是韻尾的問題。除了陸志韋,諸家的構擬都把“支紙寘”訂爲直喉韻,即無韻尾。據董先生説(董 1948:13),它們源自上古的“佳”部與“歌”部。這給我們一個很大的啓示,我們可以推測,其中一類(大概是來自“佳”部的吧),韻尾早已由[g]變爲[i],故其韻母先變爲/*y(w)ey/;另一類(大概是來自“歌”部的吧),原本没有韻尾,故其韻母先變爲/*y(w)e/,到《切韻》音系裏才也變爲“收噫”,但在其時的某方言中,仍保持着舊讀,因而就變成同韻中的“重紐”字了。“脂旨至”的來源比較複雜,分别來自“之、幽、微、脂”等部,諸家對這幾韻的構擬相當不一致,在周先生所列的八家中(包括他自己),半數擬有韻尾,半數則無。既然如此,我們就更有理由把其中的“重紐”字一類訂爲有尾,即/*y(w) əy/,另一類訂爲無尾,即/*y(w)ə/。這種差異也是在後者變爲有韻尾以後才在《切韻》系中消失的。這兩類“重紐”的消失,可用下式概括地表示,改用“區别性特徵”寫公式,是爲了表現不同的音位所含的共同“特徵”,是它們同步演變的原因。

$$\varnothing \rightarrow y / y(w)[V,\text{-lo},\text{-hi},\text{-bk}]\_\_\_\_ \qquad (2)$$

此式意爲:假如三等無尾韻的元音既非低[-lo]又非高[-hi]也非後[-bk](即如

果是中元音/ə,e/),則增生韻尾/y/。此式同時涵蓋着“支、脂”兩個韻列,恰足解釋這兩類“重紐”。

6 要徹底瞭解《切韻》(或《廣韻》)及其所代表的音系,自然必須做大量細緻的考訂工作,這是我目前無法做到的,所以本文衹能以“收噫”韻爲範圍,在前人研究的基礎上,概括地推測其元音音位。對解釋别的韻類來説,可能不需要這麽多,那是因爲音變是逐漸擴散的,在《切韻》以前的許多變化中,其他韻類在不同的階段都比“收噫”韻更早受到影響,因而更早合併了某些元音。常有人説,漢語音韻自中古以來大爲簡化,韻類也因而重新組合,但簡化及組合的原理與過程是什麽呢?却未見有人具體清晰地説明過。在上文推論的基礎上,我們也許可以嘗試做一下這件工作。這可以分成《切韻》以前、《切韻》到等韻、等韻以後三個階段來説明。

6.1 要系統化地説明《切韻》以前的音變,當然必須等我們對其前期的音系有了更明確的認識以後才能做到,但由於“重紐”的啓示,我們最少可以知道有公式(1)及公式(2)所代表的音變。如果進一步研究,應該可以發現,公式(1)所代表的音變,對解釋“仙、宵、鹽”三個韻類中的“重紐”也是同樣適用的,因爲它們的元音應該都是前低元音。公式(2)對我們也有啓示作用,進一步的研究也許可以幫助我們瞭解,爲什麽“假”攝的三等韻甚少而四等則全空着。

6.2 《切韻》以後的音變,由於我們對等韻音系已經有了比較深入的瞭解(薛1985),現在就可以更具體更明確地推證出來了。下面這幾個公式,可以説明這些音變的性質及其發生的相對時序。

$$[V,\text{-lo},-\text{hi}]\rightarrow[+\text{hi}]/y(w)\_\_\_\_y \qquad (3)$$

這個公式的意思是,中元音/e,ə,o/由於受到半元音/y/影響,全都升高變爲高元音/ɨ/。這解釋了何以“支、脂、之、微”四個韻列在《等韻》裏都變成了“止”攝三等的“重韻”。如果細分,應該説/e,ə/先與/ɨ/合併,其後/o/才加入,因爲陸序已説“支脂、魚虞,共爲一韻”,而且“支、脂、之”早在唐初即已“同用”,但是“微”在當時還是“獨用”的。

$$\varepsilon\rightarrow a/\_\_\_\_y \qquad (4)$$

這個公式表示,“收噫”韻母的前低元音變爲央低元音。從語音同化的角度看,這個公式的寫法是有問題的,因爲真正的變化是/a/受到韻尾介音/y/的同化,前移變爲/ɛ/;但在這個音變以後,/a/與/ɛ/這兩個音位就失掉了對比性,用其中任一符號代表都可以,而從符號采用的觀點説,用/a/代表低元音比較合乎一般人的習慣。(這個公式也把“祭”韻的韻母由/y(w) ɛy/改寫爲/y(w)ay/。)經此一變,“佳、皆”兩類韻的區别就消失了,因此也就變成“重韻”了。另有一個小問題跟此式有關,可在此附帶指出。“佳”類韻的牙喉音字,有幾個後來改讀“麻”類,如“佳蛙卦”等,“皆”類則没有這種現象,所以這個改變必定發生在公式(4)所代表的“佳、皆”合韻之前,似乎應有這樣的公式 y→ ø/G(w)a____,來表示這類字先丢掉了韻尾,但這個改變並不是很有規律的,因爲同類(甚至同音)字如“街矮邂”等却未改變。我猜想這是方言借讀的問題,因此衹限於個别的字。

ɔ→a/y(w)____y (5)

此式意爲:三等“收噫”音節的後低元音變爲央低元音,所以“祭、廢”變爲“重韻”。這顯然也是語音同化造成的,即韻母/y(w) ɔy/的元音因半元音/y/的同化而前移。

[V,-lo,-hi]→[+lo]/____y (6)

此式意爲:中元音/e,ə,o/下降而與其相對應的低元音合併。即,/o,ɔ/合併,故“泰”與“代(隊)”成爲“重韻”;/ə,a/合併,故“夬”亦與“卦、怪”成爲“重韻”;由於原來的前低元音/ɛ/已變爲/a/(公式4),/e/遂無可與合併者,故“齊”等無“重韻”,但/e/却因此變爲前低元音了。所謂中元音下降,是從“音位重組”(phonemic restructuring)的觀點説的,因爲中元音與低元音既已合併,新元音系統就衹有高低兩層了,就發音的實際説(phonetically),其實也可能是低元音上升。前後低元音的音值都比較高可能就是這個緣故。另外還可以指出一個有趣的現象:由於腭化音節裏的中元音早已升高(公式3),腭化音節裏的低元音也都早已變成央低元音(公式4、5)。所以現在前後低元音就都不配腭化介音了,這就造成了韻圖的一般模式:三等腭化,一、二、四等全不腭化。

6.3　前人在討論《切韻》的分韻方式時,有所謂“從分不從合”的説法。這基本上是正確的,但却失之含混籠統,因爲這個説法必然會引發兩個問題:其一,哪些是“從分不從合”的韻? 其二,爲什麼衹有這幾韻是“從分不從合”的,而其他的韻却是“從合不從分”的呢? 就我所知,前人對此似乎未曾提出過具體的解説。在本文推論出的音系基礎上,以及在本文討論的範圍之内,我們現在可以嘗試着爲這兩個問題提出部分解答。前文曾説到,我們給“齊/支、夬/至、哈(灰)/微、泰/廢、怪/祭”等兩兩相對的韻類擬定出相同的韻基,顯然是違背押韻原則的(見 4.2 節第五項説明)。表面上看來,他們是以“洪、細”的區别分韻的,但這是很膚淺的看法,因爲押韻與否實與介音無涉。真正的解釋恐怕還是《切韻》的合議妥協性,即陸法言所説對“南北是非、古今通塞”的照顧。當時最具“標準”資格的“言”,大概不外洛陽、長安、鄴下、金陵等所謂“帝王都邑”的通語。前三者在地緣與歷史上都非常接近,應爲大同小異之方言。所謂“金陵音”也應爲晉室南渡後帶過去的洛下之音,不會是當時的金陵土話;經過約兩百年的分離,這種“金陵音”自然也就與洛下之音有了相當差距了,但基本上應該還是大同小異的。這幾種有標準資格的“官話”,自然是會交互影響的(也是陸法言等要特别多加考慮的);也就是説,先發生在某一方言中的某一音變,會漸次擴及其他幾個方言,因此不同的方言在受到同一音變的影響時,便有先後之别了。(類似的情況也發生在元明時代的官話方言中,請參閲薛 1992。)在討論“重紐”時,我們説過,就《切韻》所依據的方言來説“重紐”已經消失,也就是説,公式(1) (2)所代表的音變已先在這個方言中發生了,但尚未波及其他某一個或某幾個方言。同理,我們可以想象,《切韻》後造成“重韻”的那幾個音變,很可能已先在另一個或另幾個方言中發生了,但尚未波及《切韻》所依據的那個方言。换言之,在“重紐”問題上,《切韻》所依據的方言較其他方言超前,但在“重韻”問題上則比較滯後。更具體地説,“齊/支、夬/至、哈(灰)/微”等韻類之所以“從分不從合”,是因爲公式(3)所代表的音變在《切韻》所代表的方言中尚未發生,但在其他某一個或某幾個方言中已經發生了。試以“齊/支/脂”三類爲例,其結果是,對《切韻》所依據的方言説,“齊/支”不當分,而“支/脂”必須分,但對已受到音變(3)影響的方言説,“齊/支”必須分,而“支/脂”不當分;這自然就成了蕭、顔等“夜永酒闌”争論的焦點了,最後也就很自然地達成了“從分不從合”的妥協,而陸法言也衹好承認説,某些方言已經是“支脂(魚虞)共爲一韻”了。同理,“泰/廢”之從分,也是由於音變(5)在不同的方言裏已否發生的問題。“怪/祭”之從分,則與“重紐”有關,因爲“祭”韻字本分屬兩韻,後來在《切韻》所代表的方言裏,由於音變(1)而先行合併,但對未受到該音變影響的方言説,這兩類是不該合併的,結果妥協爲另立一韻但區分“重紐”字。我認爲上面的推論才是“從分不從合”的真正原因,同時也讓我們有機會較具體地指出,“綜合”進《切韻》的到底有哪些外來成分。

6.4　等韻時期以後,語音當然還是繼續演變着的。逐字逐韻地列舉這些變化,會令人覺得數不勝數,最多不過知其然而不知其所以然。但如從音變的角度觀察,就會發現,這些變化都是一脉相承、脉絡分明的,而且是勢所必然的(請參閱薛 1975、薛 1978、薛 1980、薛 1992 等)。試以“收噫”韻爲例,我們可以用四條規律概括下及《中原音韻》時期的演變:(一) ø→ y/____(w)e,即四等韻變細音;(二) a→e/y(w)____,即三等韻變四等,故“廢、祭”兩韻與“霽”合併;(三) ɔ→ a/C____E,即一等開口帶尾字變入二等,故“咍”等不再與“灰”等互押,而改與“佳、皆、夬”等類互押;(四) {ɔ,e}→ɨ/____y,即蟹攝一等合口及四等全部(含原三等)變入止攝,故“灰、齊、祭、廢”等全變入《中原音韻》的“齊微”韻。另一方面,由於“曾、梗”兩攝的入聲字也都改變了(薛 1978、薛 1992),如“黑、白”等字,“收噫”韻又收編了許多“新兵”。當然也有許多變走了,主要是止攝的“精、照”系開口字丢掉了韻頭及韻尾,因此另立門户,形成了一個嶄新的“支思”韻(薛 1980)。

參考資料

陳復華、何九盈　《古韻通曉》,中國社會科學出版社,1987 年。

陳新雄　《〈廣韻〉二百零六韻擬音之我見》,《語言研究》1994 年第 2 期,第 94—111 頁。

董同龢　《〈廣韻〉重紐試釋》,《歷史語言研究所集刊》1948 年第十三本,第 1—20 頁。

———　《漢語音韻學》,學生書局,1968 年。

高本漢　《中國音韻學研究》,(趙元任、羅常培、李方桂譯),臺北商務印書館重印,1940 年。

薛鳳生　《論入聲字之演化規律》,《屈萬里先生七秩榮慶論文集》,第 407—

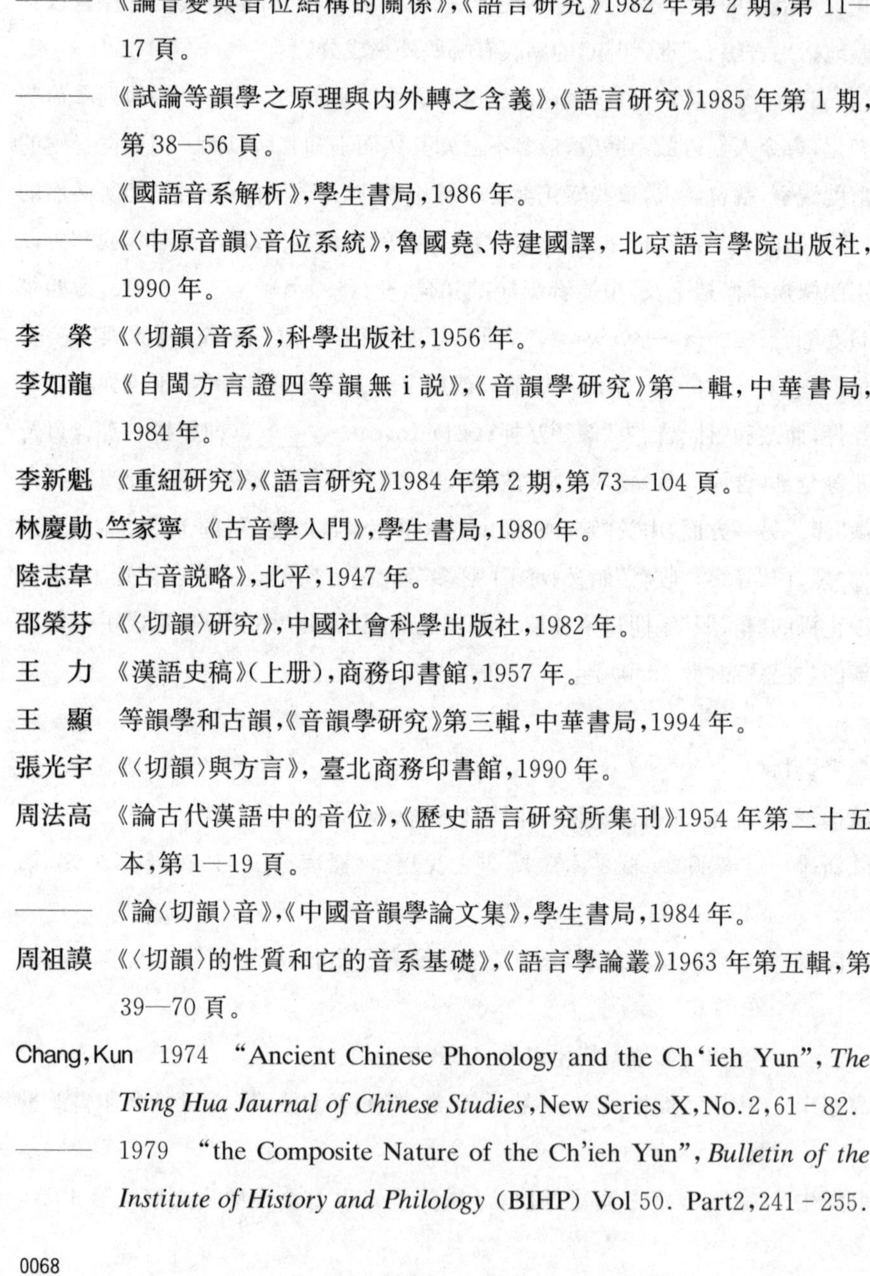

433 頁，聊經出版社，1978 年。

——《論支思韻的形成與演進》，《書目季刊》1980 年第 12 卷第 2 期，第 53—75 頁。

——《論音變與音位結構的關係》，《語言研究》1982 年第 2 期，第 11—17 頁。

——《試論等韻學之原理與内外轉之含義》，《語言研究》1985 年第 1 期，第 38—56 頁。

——《國語音系解析》，學生書局，1986 年。

——《〈中原音韻〉音位系統》，魯國堯、侍建國譯，北京語言學院出版社，1990 年。

李　榮　《〈切韻〉音系》，科學出版社，1956 年。

李如龍　《自閩方言證四等韻無 i 説》，《音韻學研究》第一輯，中華書局，1984年。

李新魁　《重紐研究》，《語言研究》1984 年第 2 期，第 73—104 頁。

林慶勛、竺家寧　《古音學入門》，學生書局，1980 年。

陸志韋　《古音説略》，北平，1947 年。

邵榮芬　《〈切韻〉研究》，中國社會科學出版社，1982 年。

王　力　《漢語史稿》（上册），商務印書館，1957 年。

王　顯　等韻學和古韻，《音韻學研究》第三輯，中華書局，1994 年。

張光宇　《〈切韻〉與方言》，臺北商務印書館，1990 年。

周法高　《論古代漢語中的音位》，《歷史語言研究所集刊》1954 年第二十五本，第 1—19 頁。

——《論〈切韻〉音》，《中國音韻學論文集》，學生書局，1984 年。

周祖謨　《〈切韻〉的性質和它的音系基礎》，《語言學論叢》1963 年第五輯，第 39—70 頁。

Chang, Kun　1974　"Ancient Chinese Phonology and the Ch'ieh Yun", *The Tsing Hua Jaurnal of Chinese Studies*, New Series X, No. 2, 61 - 82.

——　1979　"the Composite Nature of the Ch'ieh Yun", *Bulletin of the Institute of History and Philology* (BIHP) Vol 50. Part2, 241 - 255.

Chao. Y. R. 1941 "Distinctions within Ancient Chinese", *Harvard Journal of Asiatic Studies* 5,203 - 233.

Cheng, C-C. and Wang, W. S-Y 1971 "Phonological Change of Middle Chinese initials", *The Tsing Hua Journal of Chinese Studies*, New Series IX,No 10. 1& 2,216 - 270.

Hashimoto, Mantaro J 1970 "Internal Evidence for Ancient Chinese Palatal Endings" *Language*. 46.2. Part One, 336 - 365.

Hsueh. F. S. 1975 Phonology of Old Mandarin, The Hague.

——— 1987 "Historical Phonology and Dialect Study: Some Examples from the Pingdu Dialect", *Wang Li Memorial Volumes*, The Chinese Language Society of Hong Kong,221 - 243.

——— 1992 "On Dialectal Overlapping as a Cause for the Literary vs. Colloquial Contrast in Standard Chinese", *Chinese Languages and Dialects I*: Chinese Dialects, Symposium Series of the Institute of History and Philology, Academia Sinica No. 2,379 - 405.(又見耿振生譯《論標準漢語中的方言重叠與文白異讀現象》,《王力先生九十周年誕辰論文集》,1992 年。)

Karlgren, Bernhard 1954 "Compendium of Phonetics in Ancient and Archaic Chinese" *Bulletin of the Museum of Far Eastern Antiquities* 22,211 - 367.

Martin, Samuel E 1953 The Phonemes of Ancient Chinese, *supplement to the Journal of the American Oriental Society* 16.

Pulleyblank, E. G 1961 - 2 "The Consonantal System of Old Chinese", *Asia Major* 9,58 - 144,206 - 65.

Pulleyblank. E. G. 1984 *Middle Chinese: A Study in Historical Phonology*, Universiy of British Columbia Press, Vancouver.

Ting, Pang-hsin 1975 *Chinese Phonology of the Wei Chin Period: Reconstruction of the Finals as Reflected in Poetry*, Institute of History and Philology, Special Publications No. 65, Academia

Sinica.

Wang, John C. and Hsueh, F. S 1973 "The Lin-ch'i Dialect and its Relation to Mandarin", *Journal of the Ameican Oriental Society* 93.2, 136－145.

"梗、曾"兩攝的韻尾與《切韻》音系**

前言

分析《切韻》時,"梗、曾"兩攝所含各韻可以説是一大難題。這不僅是由於這些韻(尤其是"梗"攝諸韻)本身比較複雜,也由於歷來擬音的人都把它們的韻尾擬爲[ŋ,k],表面看來這似乎是順理成章的,因爲這些韻的字在現代漢語中都收舌根音;但這却造成許多不合音韻理論的問題,也使得認識嚴整的《切韻》音系成爲不可能之事了。本文將從多方面舉證説明這些韻的韻尾不是舌根音,實爲舌面音,從而在遵守理論原則的基礎上,討論該兩攝諸韻在整體音系中的形態,並揭示其演變過程。

一、幾個基本觀點

研究漢語音韻時,我認爲必須先掌握某些基本觀點,下述三條特别重要,但却常常被許多人忽略。

1.1 中國傳統音韻學的性質,完全是音位性的(phonemic),所采用的分聲調、分大韻、分小韻、注反切、立韻圖等方法,都是以字音之簡的音位對比(phonemic contrast)爲依據的,使用的是一種"音系内部互注表音法"(參看薛2000)。因此,充分認定及掌握這個原則,才能正確地瞭解古代的韻書。

1.2 古代的韻書,尤其是像《切韻》(含《唐韻》《廣韻》等)、《集韻》、《韻鏡》、《中原音韻》等,都出自深有造詣的音韻學家,他們的共同目的就是"正音",即訂正他們各自時代的標準音。這些音韻學家的態度是極認真的,因此他們編著的韻書也是相當可信的,也就是説,書中所提供的資料,多是符合其當時標

** 原載《音韻論叢》,齊魯書社,2004年。

準語的忠實記録,而當時標準語的音系自然也就隱含於其中了。(他們對某些個别字或某一類字,在這個音系内的讀法,容或有争議,但這不會影響到該音系的結構,他們絶無理由,也無必要,更無能力,另創一個"混合的音系"。)要瞭解其音系,最主要的就是仔細分析這些韻書記録下來的資料,如同化學分析一樣,由表面的資料分析出其所含的音位("元素")。由於各自時代的標準語音系已經隱含於其時的韻書中,自然也就不勞我們爲之"構擬"了,所以我們的工作衹是發掘出那個客觀存在的音系。(嚴格地説,用構擬法研究這些韻書,是先在觀念上懷疑這些韻書的可靠性,因而需要找些外在的資料加以證明,參看薛 2000。)

1.3 要發掘出這些韻書所代表的音系,必須嚴格遵守一般性的音系理論原則,包括前述的"音位對比"原則,也包括特定語言的特定"音節分段模式",還包括漢語音韻學傳統中特别重視的"押韻原則"(參看拙文《也談幾個漢語音韻史的理論問題》)。這類原則是音系分析的依據,忽視這些原則,就談不上什麽"音系"了。

二、先從聲母説起

傳統音韻學先將漢語音節分爲聲母與韻母兩部分,再將韻母分爲韻頭、韻腹、韻尾三部分。這種分段法是完全符合漢語特性的,充分反映了説漢語者的語感。在説明一個音節的屬性時,音韻學者也總是以這種分段法爲依據的。《切韻》的聲母系統,過去都以等韻圖的三十六字母爲代表,但由於清末及當代許多學者的深入研究,已經證明是與三十六字母不同的,足見《切韻》與"等韻"分别代表不同的音系。其間的差異主要有:

2.1《切韻》脣音不分輕重。(錢大昕:"古無輕脣音。")

2.2"照"系聲母字在《切韻》中分屬兩類:"莊、初、崇、生、俟"爲一類,"章、昌、船、書、常"爲一類。(陳澧的"系聯"充分證明了這一現象。)

2.3"日"母在《切韻》時代原爲鼻音,所以應屬"舌上音",與"知、徹、澄"相配。("日"母大約在公元 771 年以前不久才丢掉鼻音成分,參看李榮《切韻音系》,第 125—126 頁。這大概是"等韻"稱其爲"半齒"的緣故,性屬"章"系一類了。"等韻"另以"娘"配"知、徹、澄",純屬補空,"泥、娘"不分,亦早有定說。)

所以《切韻》的聲母系統應含下表中的八類:

脣音	舌頭	舌上	牙音
幫滂並明	端透定泥來	知徹澄日	見溪群疑

齒頭	正齒(A)	正齒(B)	喉音
精清從心邪	莊初崇生俟	章昌船書常	影曉匣喻

三、"梗、曾"兩攝的韻尾問題

在上節裏,我們不厭其煩地舉證及排列出《切韻》的聲母系統,目的在於説明,這個系統含有四種不同的塞音及其同部位的鼻音:"幫、端、知、見"及與之相對應的"明、泥、日、疑"。這個現象與我們認證"梗、曾"攝各韻的韻尾大有關係。首先指出中古音系可能含有腭化塞音與鼻音韻尾的,是日本學者橋本萬太郎(Hashimoto 1970),但他受限於"構擬"的傳統,很謹慎地認爲衹有"梗"攝的某些韻才帶這種韻尾;我們則認爲,"梗、曾"兩攝所有的韻都屬此類。下列諸現象支持我們這一看法。

3.1 音系有一特性,即其音位常有平衡對稱分配的趨勢。歐洲學者在構擬古印歐語時,有所謂"内部構擬"(internal reconstruction)之説,即基於此理。如上表所示,《切韻》既然有四類平行的塞/鼻音聲母,就極可能也有與之相對應的四類韻尾,但常見的構擬却衹有脣、牙及舌頭三類輔音韻尾,這就與音系的一般形態不相合了,因此我們可以假定"梗,曾"兩攝諸韻的韻尾有可能是舌上音。

3.2《切韻》的韻目序次、"等韻"的分攝,都是含有深意的;二者都似乎暗示説,"梗、曾"兩攝諸韻與"通、江、宕"三攝諸韻不同類。攝的含義與韻尾大有關係,同韻尾的韻一般分屬兩攝,如"深、咸""臻、山""止、蟹""流、效"等,或以特殊原因分屬三攝,如"遇、果、假";但常見的構擬却把"通、江、宕、梗、曾"五攝全擬爲收牙音。假如我們相信韻書與韻圖的安排是可信的,就必須爲之提出更合理的解釋,也就不能不對以前的擬音產生懷疑了。因此我們相信"梗、曾"

攝諸韻的韻尾應非牙音,而最可能的就是舌上音。

3.3 古音的形態都可以在其後代的方言中尋找到,這是構擬家奉爲圭臬的;認爲“梗、曾”攝諸韻的韻尾不可能是舌上音的理由,大概也不外於此。但有時候也不盡然,舌上音聲母後來都變了。首先是“日”母的鼻音成分消失了(“等韻”時期之前),因而變爲齒音(“半齒”),繼而“知、徹、澄”也變爲塞擦音(“等韻”時期之後),分别併入“照、穿、牀”等齒音聲母;因此聲母系統裏就没有舌上音了。在這種情況下,舌上音韻尾(姑且先假設其存在)自然也就難以獨存了,因此後代的方言中也就找不到了。這大概是構擬家不敢擬有此類韻尾的緣故,理由很簡單:找不到證據。但證據也可以是間接的(或曰“隱性的”)。“梗、曾”兩攝的陽聲韻後來合爲一韻,即《中原音韻》的“庚青”韻;在中原及北京地區,這一韻的韻尾顯然已變爲牙音(“舌根鼻音”)。但在南方官話中,却變爲舌頭音(“舌尖鼻音”),這可由皮黄戲的押韻傳統看出來。(皮黄戲是以“庚青”韻的字與“真文”韻的字互押的,參看周殿福 1980;但這一事實在現代南方官話中是看不出來的,因爲在那些方言中,作爲韻尾的[n]與[ŋ]後來也合併了。)問題是:爲什麽衹有“梗、曾”的陽聲字變讀,而變讀的時候,有時變[n]有時變[ŋ]呢?我覺得較合理的解釋應爲:這些字的韻尾原爲[n]與[ŋ]之間的舌上音,因此變讀時非前移即後移了。

3.4 另一個隱性的證據是入聲字的變讀。在南方官話裏,原屬“梗、曾”兩攝的入聲字跟其他各類入聲字一樣,都以收喉塞音的方式保持入聲,這就看不出來有何特别之處;但在北方官話裏則不然。構擬入聲的人很少以北方官話爲例,理由也很簡單:這些方言没有入聲。但原屬“梗、曾”攝的入聲字,在北京及中原官話裏都改讀爲“收噫”,而其他各類入聲字則没有這種現象,這就顯示這類入聲字原與其他入聲字不同,其韻尾很可能含有腭化成分,因此在丢掉了阻塞成分以後,剩下來的就是以/y/爲代表的腭化成分了。

3.5“音節分段模式”是音系分析的一個極重要原則。同時,受限於人類聽覺的制約,任何語言的音系都不可能有太多元音。假如“梗、曾”的韻尾與“通、江、宕”一樣,在遵守漢語音節四音段的原則之下,勢必需要增多元音;如果爲了保持元音數目在合理的範圍之内,也可以把韻腹擬爲複合元音,但這就打破了音節分段的模式;而如果這一做法衹限於“梗、曾”兩攝,也是極不合理的。

綜合上述原因，我相信“梗、曾”兩攝諸韻的韻尾一定是舌上音[ȵ]與[ȶ]（我以前寫作/ɲ,k̂/，現改作/ɲ,ȶ/）。當然更重要的理由是：衹有這樣的推論，才能最妥當地解釋《切韻》及“等韻”諸韻書給我們提供的資料，也衹有這樣的結論才能妥善地解釋這些韻類在後代的演變。

四、“梗、曾”兩攝各韻的韻母

“曾”攝衹含兩個韻列，即一等的“登等嶝德”與三等的“蒸拯證職”；“梗”攝比較複雜，一等全空着，二等含“庚耿敬陌”“耕耿諍麥”兩個韻列，而“庚梗敬陌”復見於三等，又與“清静勁昔”爲重韻，四等則僅有“青迥徑錫”一個韻列。“曾”攝屬“内轉”，“梗”攝屬“外轉”，但在“等韻”後期（《四聲等子》之前），兩攝已經“内外混等”了。（有關這些問題的討論，請參看拙作《等韻學之原理與内外轉之含義》，《語言研究》1985 年第 1 期。）這説明該兩攝性質相近，不僅韻尾相同，韻腹亦屬同類，皆爲低元音。《切韻》音系的元音系統是高低三層和前後三度的七個音位（請參看拙作《試論〈切韻〉音系的元音音位與“重紐、重韻”等現象》，《語言研究》1996 年第 1 期），如下表：

	前	央	後
高		ɨ	
低	e	ə	o
中	ɛ	a	ɔ

這是由分析“止、蟹”兩攝所得到的結論。該兩攝最複雜，顯示《切韻》音系必然有這麽多元音，但也顯示這個元音系統在《切韻》時期以前就在逐步簡化，因此其他韻類都早有了不同程度的簡化，惟獨“收噫”韻尚少簡化；從這個角度看，《切韻》也衹代表演變過程中的一個特定的階段。在漢語音節模式的基礎上，根據這個元音系統，並參照前人的構擬，就不難推證出“梗、曾”兩攝各韻的韻母了。

4.1 含低元音的攝，其一等韻的韻腹皆爲後元音，故“登等嶝”的韻母必爲

/ɔɲ/(開口)與/wɔɲ/(合口),“德”的韻母則爲/ɔȶ/(開)與/wɔȶ/(合)。三等韻皆含腭化介音(/y/),故相對的“蒸拯證”韻母應爲/yɔɲ/(開)與/ywɔɲ/(合),“職”的韻母應爲/yɔȶ/(開)與/ywɔȶ/(合)。前人擬音多以[ə]爲各韻的韻腹,大概是受官話方言的影響,或因誤認“内轉皆含高元音”(羅 1933)之故。

4.2 二等韻例以央低元音/a/爲韻腹,其有重韻者則以前低元音/ɛ/爲韻腹,因此把“庚梗敬”的韻母訂爲/aɲ/與/waɲ/,“陌”的韻母訂爲/aȶ/與/waȶ/;“耕耿諍”的韻母則訂爲/ɛɲ/與/wɛɲ/,“麥”的韻母爲/ɛȶ/與/wɛȶ/。這是與前人擬音完全一致的。(當然有人於[ɛ]之外,還用了諸如[ǎ,ä,ɐ]等。)

4.3 外轉三等與二等的差别衹在有無介音/y/,故“庚梗敬”中屬於三等的字,其韻母應爲/yaɲ/與/ywaɲ/,“陌”的三等字應以/yaȶ/與/ywaȶ/爲韻母。“清”列與二等的“耕”列相對應,故“清静勁”的韻母應爲/yɛɲ/與/ywɛɲ/,“昔”的韻母應爲/yɛȶ/與/ywɛȶ/。這也是與前人的擬音基本符合的。

4.4 四等韻的韻母,前人皆以[e]爲其韻腹,不同處衹在有無以[i]爲介音。我也認爲四等韻没有所謂“元音性的[i]”介音,對韻腹的看法則與他們完全相同,所以“青迥徑”的韻母應爲/eɲ/與/weɲ/,“錫”的韻母應爲/eȶ/與/weȶ/。

五、“梗、曾”兩攝諸韻與“等韻”音系的關係

多數人都認爲,“等韻”是幫助解讀《切韻》(或某本《切韻》系韻書)的工具,是根據某本韻書編制的。我的看法完全不同,我認爲“等韻”是其創製者根據其時的標準話設計出來的(薛 1999)。從這個觀點看,《切韻》與“等韻”之間,是一種傳承的關係,也就是説,“等韻”音系是在《切韻》音系的基礎上,經過一系列音變的産物;兩者之間的不同,除了上文提到的聲母差别,就是元音系統改變了;“等韻”的元音,已由《切韻》的七個元音音位,簡化爲高低兩層前後三度的四個音位。演變的過程我曾簡略地討論過(薛 1999),現在再專就“梗、曾”兩攝諸韻的演變稍作説明。

5.1 所謂“重韻”,當然是説原來在《切韻》中不同的韻,到“等韻”時期變爲同韻了。“曾”攝没有重韻,“梗”攝則有兩組,即二等的“庚”列字與“耕”列;三等的“庚”列字與“清”列;造成它們合韻的音變,表面看來似乎衹是韻腹元音

/a/與/ε/的合併,其實並非那麼簡單。考慮到整個音系,我們必須承認,這是兩個音變的結果。

頭一個音變是:

$$a \longrightarrow \varepsilon / y\_\_\_ \quad (1)$$

即央低元音受腭化介音的同化,變爲前低元音,這合乎音變的一般趨勢,所以"庚"列各韻的三等字就與"清"列各韻合流了。這個音變也是有文獻證據的,"庚三"類的字與"清"類韻的字在《切韻》裏已有互爲反切的現象,其他相關文獻中這個現象更多(參看邵 1982,83—86)。而且這個音變也絕非專爲"庚"類字而設;"祭、仙、宵"等韻類的"重紐"字變爲同音,應亦爲這個音變的結果,所以由音理的角度看,"庚三"類字與"清"類字的關係很像"重紐"。

另一個音變是:

$$a \longrightarrow \varepsilon / \_\_\_ (E, -back) \quad (2)$$

即央低元音受"非後"韻尾(即/m,p,n,t,ɲ,ŧ,y/等)的影響,變爲前低元音,所以"庚"列就與"耕"列成爲同韻了。這個音變也有很大的普遍性,促成了各攝二等"重韻"的合併,"庚、耕"的合併祇是其中之一而已,但其發生的時代應該比音變(1)稍晚。由於這兩個音變,/a/與/ε/的音位對比就消失了;就音變原理説,上述兩個音變當然是[a]變爲[ε],但與高及中元音相比,低元音的發音部位總是較靠中央,所以這個合併以後的音位,在"等韻"所代表的新音系中仍占着央低元音的位置,因此就符合應用説,仍以用/a/代表這個新音位爲宜,而原來的前中元音/e/就變成了新音系中的前低元音,因爲新音系祇有高低兩層對比,形成了"等韻"音系的/ɨ,e,a,ɔ/四個元音音位(請參閱薛 1999)。

5.2 所謂"内外混等",當然是"等韻"後期的現象,這也祇是音變造成的,即在含腭化介音/y/的音節中,後低元音/ɔ/受同化而前移,變爲央低元音/a/。

$$ɔ \longrightarrow a / y\_\_\_ (E, -back) \quad (3)$$

這個音變還受到另一個條件的制約,即韻尾不能是"後音"(/w,ŋ,k/),因爲我們發現"宕"攝三等字仍保有後低元音,反而是"江、效"兩攝的韻腹後來都變爲後低元音了,但這個音變却促成了"梗、曾"兩攝的"混等"。("果、假"亦然;

"江"攝則因元音後移而與"宕"攝合韻,但也被籠統地稱爲"混等"。)我們可以想象,這條音變很可能在"等韻"時期以前,甚至《切韻》時期以前,就已經在逐步發生作用了,因此到了"等韻"時期,除了"曾、果、宕"三攝以外,别的攝中都已經没有介音/y/與元音/ɔ/相配的韻了;因此"曾、果、宕"衹好各自獨立成攝,不能跟與其相對應的"梗、假、江"合成類似"山、咸、蟹、效"之類的典型外轉攝。

結語

多年前我即發現,"梗、曾"兩攝諸韻的韻尾必爲舌上音,並據以詮釋《切韻》與"等韻"的音系及其流變,但這一看法顯然未能爲多數學者所接受。我常聽到的批評是"没有證據"或"證據不足",大概是説,在漢語方言或中外對音裏找不到這種現象。這基本上是一個對古代韻書的態度問題。我們是懷疑韻書的可信性呢,還是相信韻書是可靠的忠實記録呢?假如是前者,自然就必須以方言及對音爲主,像歐美學者構擬古印歐語一樣,構擬("重建")某一時期的古代漢語,相關的韻書衹是一種"參考資料","構擬"能與相關韻書的記述符合,當然最好,否則也不必多計較。假如是後者,就必須以某本韻書爲主,而以其他相關的文獻及方言等爲參考資料,分析推論出那本曲書所代表的音系,而能否成功地爲該書推論出一個完整合理的音系,本身也就有力地證明了該書是否可靠。本文的主旨在説明,中古漢語的舌面音韻尾雖已消失,但韻書内部却給我們留下了許多明顯的證據,是最重要的第一手證據,同時方言中也有些"隱性的"證據。通過這些資料,輔之以音系學的理論原則,就可以推論出其存在及其所依附的音系。舌面音的認定,是《切韻》音系及"等韻"音系認證的一個關鍵,其認定也幫助我們瞭解,爲什麽"梗、曾"兩攝中的韻尤其是入聲韻,演變的過程大異於其他韻類。

參考文獻:

王　力　《漢語史稿》(上册),商務印書館,1957年。

李　榮　《切韻音系》,科學出版社,1956年。

邵榮芬　《切韻研究》,中國社會科學出版社,1982年。

周法高　《論〈切韻〉音》,《中國音韻學論文集》,學生書局,1994 年。

周殿福　《藝術語言發聲基礎》,中國社會科學出版社,1980 年。

高本漢　《中國音韻學研究》(趙元任、羅常培、李方桂譯),臺北商務印書館重印,1940 年。

董同龢　《廣韻重紐試譯》,《史語所集刊》第十三本,1948 年。

薛鳳生　《漢語音韻史十講》,華語教學出版社,1999 年。

———　《構擬與詮釋:漢語音韻史研究的兩種對立觀點》,韓國“中國語學國際學術會議”論文,高麗大學校,2000 年 12 月 20—22.第 85—93 頁。又見《語言學及應用語言學研究》,vol. 1,No. l. 學林出版社.2001 年 3 月第 1—8 頁。

羅常培　《釋内外轉》,《史語所集刊》第四本,1933 年,第 206—226 頁。

Hashimoto, M. J.:“Internal Evidence for Ancient Chinese Palatal Endings”, *Language* 46.2, Part I (1970),336 - 365.

Hsueh. F. S.:“On Dialectal Overlapping as a Cause for the Literary/Colloquial contrast in Standard Chinese”, *Chinese Languages And Linguistics: Chinese Dialects*, Taipei. 1992,379 - 405.

Martin. Samuel E.: The Phonemes of Ancient Chinese, Supplement to the *Journal of the American Oriental Society* 16(1953).

試論等韻學之原理與内外轉之含義*

一、等韻學的歷史地位

在漢語音韻學的研究中,等韻學是最值得大書特書的輝煌成就。它的重要性不僅在於爲中古漢語提供了許多極寶貴的資料,更重要的是它爲漢語音韻學的研究提供了極巧妙的新方法,所以有人説等韻學就是中國的理論音韻學,這是極有見地的看法①。事實上,有關漢語音韻的任何有意義的研究,不論是上古、中古或現代方言,也都離不開等韻學。在世界語言學史上,這也是我們可以爲之自豪的了不起的成就,衹可惜湮没太久,其重要性遂鮮爲世人所知。

1.1 要正確地理解等韻學的性質與重要性,我們必須首先確認音韻學研究的真正目標。對一般人來説,研究某一語言(或方言)的語音,當然是説明該語言(或方言)中某些字的讀法;研究古音,也就是想知道某一時代的古人究竟是怎麽説話的。早期的西方語言學在觀念上也是這樣的,因此着重在用特制的符號標注特殊的語音,所謂"國際音標"就是這一觀念的産物。在經過多年的實踐之後,學者們終於領悟到這不是語言學研究的真正目標。當然我們可以把人類所能發出的聲音作爲一種自然的物理現象來研究。這是聲學研究的

---

* 原刊《語言研究》1985 年第 1 期,收入《漢語音韻史十講》。
本文是爲中國音韻學研究會第三届年會寫的。本文之寫作由俄亥俄(原文爲"鄂亥鄂")州立大學(Ohio State University)以研究休假(Sabbatical Leave)的方式提供支持,並得到美中學術交流委員會(Committee on Scholarly Communication with the Pcople's Republic of China)的高级研究獎金(Advanced Research Fellowship)的資助,並此致謝!

① 1982 年夏,我在西安參加音韻學第二届年會時,許多朋友都告訴我説,多年來王力先生一再提醒音韻學界的朋友們多研究等韻,以加强理論基礎,還要大家多留意國外的等韻學研究。1979 年漢藏語言學會在巴黎召開時,我曾宣讀一篇題爲《内外轉新釋》的短文。現在這篇論文就是在那篇短文的基礎上擴充改寫而成的,算是響應王老的號召。另外,我的筆頭很不勤,這次終於改寫出來,還有賴於嚴學窘教授的一再催促,並此致謝。

一個部門,可以從研究聲波的形態着手,也可以從研究發音器官的部位及動態入手。但這類研究,不管如何精密細緻,仍不能表現出實際語言中語音所擔負的辨義功能,這是因爲在不同的語言(或方言)中,實質相同(或極相近)的語音,不一定擔負相同的辨義功能。一個語音所擔負的辨義功能,祇能由它在同一個音韻系統中與其他語音所起的對比作用來決定。這種聽覺上的對比,並不完全取决於客觀上的語音實質差異,而更表現在説話人的主觀認識上。語音實質的差異儘管千變萬化,但在個别語言(或方言)的應用裏,却總是自成簡約而整齊的體系。音韻學研究的對象,不是語音的物理現象,而是語音在語言中的應用,也就是語言中的音韻系統。在西方的語言學研究中,上述理論觀點到本世紀初才有人提出,即所謂音位(phoneme)學説,經過布拉格學派(Prague School)諸學者的宣揚,很久才漸次爲人接受;但是也有一些人,比如高本漢先生(Bernhard Karlgren),至死也不願接受這一觀點。另一方面,在接受這一觀點的學者當中,也有程度上的差别。有一些人認爲音位處理法有各種程度上的寬窄不同,即所謂 broad transcription 與 narrow transcription,也有人以爲這種處理法可以采用不同的方式而獲得類似的效果,趙元任先生的 non-uniqueness 學説(趙 1934)就代表這一想法。與這兩種看法不同的則有以 Roman Jakobson 爲代表的嚴格音位結構説(Jakobson 1951),根據這一看法,在對任何語言作最嚴格的分析時,祇能有一個最妥善的結論,這個結論就是該語言所獨具的音位結構。我個人對於漢語音韻的研究是采用最嚴格的音位結構説的。而且我更進一步認爲由嚴格分析而得出的獨特音位結構,就是説某種語言(或方言)的人群所共有的語感的具體表現(薛 1980)。

1.2 中國傳統音韻學的主旨是區别字音。起初使用的方法是分韻與標注反切,而不使用語音符號。到了等韻時代,更利用圖表與文字來表達不同字音間的韻類與聲類等關係,這種表達方法自然祇能是音位上的對比,而不是細微的語音描述,其基本精神與西方晚期的音韻理論是不謀而合的。我們也可以説,西方新起的音韻理論其實在中國古代早已廣泛應用了。反過來説,要想正確地瞭解中國音韻學,尤其是等韻學,我們必須采用(也祇能采用)嚴格的音位結構説。等韻學中的"五音、清、濁、等、攝、開、合"等觀念,與西方更晚出的"辨義音素"(distinctive features)説,精神上亦屬暗合,可惜等韻學的妙法,不爲西儒所知,否則近代語言學的發展也許會更快一些[①]。

二、等韻學的音韻基礎

由上文的討論,我們可以確知,中國傳統音韻學的本質完全是音位性的。任何一個音位系統,必然與一個特定的語言(或方言)有關。也可以説,脱離了實際語言的所謂音位系統是不可能存在的。前文已經指出等韻在傳統音韻學中的重要地位,它的本質究竟如何呢? 歷來的學者,不論是討論古韻或今韻,總要利用它立説,但多數人衹把它看作一種抽象的圖表,是爲了説明(或幫助讀者瞭解)某種韻書而作的,因此歷來很少有人想到要爲等韻擬音[②]。在這個問題上,我與前人的看法有本質上的不同,我認爲等韻圖是根據實際的語言設計出來的,是有它本身的獨立的生命的。

2.1 説等韻所依據的音系與《切韻》所代表的音系不同,並不是什麼新鮮的説法,連高本漢都説司馬光的《切韻指掌圖》表現了許多語音轉變以後的現象。問題是:改變以後的音系是什麼樣子的? 這個新的音系爲什麼可以作爲韻圖設計的基礎? 反過來説,爲什麼我們對等韻的瞭解必須建立在對這個新音系的瞭解上? 由於時代的變遷與方域的差異,《切韻》系的韻書也屢有改動,由《切韻》而《唐韻》而《廣韻》而《集韻》。同樣地,等韻圖也由最初的雛形(大概是中、晚唐時期吧),變爲較整齊的《韻鏡》與《七音略》,再變爲《四聲等子》與《切韻指掌圖》等,因此有些等韻學者常喜歡説:某本韻圖是根據某本韻書作的。嚴格地説,這種説法在觀念上是頗有商榷餘地的。首先,《切韻》一類的韻書極爲複雜,我們迄今尚未能分析清楚,因此很難想象韻圖的設計者當初是妥當地分析了《切韻》以後才製圖的。退一步説,假如他真的是分析了《切韻》以後才製圖的,那麼爲什麼他所設計的韻圖會與《切韻》有那麼多不符合的地方

① 當然,中國的音韻學研究是深受古印度聲明學的影響的。直接的文獻證明資料也許不易找到(羅常培先生曾爲文論及印度的影響),但這個事實幾乎是不需要證明的。有趣的是,近代西方語言學的興起也是受古印度語言學的影響的,歷史比較語言學受到梵文的啓示以後,才走上正途。

② 加拿大的漢學家蒲立本氏曾提出等韻圖自成音系,並爲之擬音,見 Pulleyblank1970。

呢？所以我覺得比較合理的説法應該是:“某本韻圖是根據某本韻書填字的。”爲什麽韻圖要根據已有的韻書填字呢？這與古代僞書作者的心理是大致相同的:爲了使自己的精心之作得以傳世,便不得不有所依托以合時俗之好。韻圖作者在分析了自己所熟知的語言之後,據以製爲圖表,本來可以按己意填字,不必藉助於别人的韻書,但是這種“胡僧妙法”,“儒者”往往不知,知道了也不重視,他們重視的是《切韻》之類的韻書。韻圖便以幫助他們瞭解韻書的姿態出現了。作者自然也就公開宣稱這些圖表是爲《切韻》而作的,因此也就想出許多辦法把《切韻》音系所有而等韻音系所無的語音現象儘可能地安排到韻圖裏去。

2.2 等韻的本質既如上述,那麽它所依據的音系究竟是什麽樣子的呢？這個問題當然不是三言兩語可以回答的。首先必須説明我們對漢語音節結構的看法。中國音韻學的傳統把音節分作聲母與韻母兩段,然後又把韻母(聲調除外)分作韻頭、韻腹與韻尾三段。多數研究漢語的西方學者,包括高本漢在内,也都遵循這種音節分段法,但也有少數例外①。我個人認爲,這一傳統音節分段法自《切韻》以迄於今都行之有效,在許多方面都是符合説漢語者的語感的,應該嚴格遵守。爲了方便,我采用(C)(M)V(E)這一簡單的公式來表達這一概念,明確地表示一個音節最多衹能有四段,在音節構成中,聲母C、韻頭M、韻尾E可以是零(即不出現),但韻腹V是不可少的。現在,我們就可在這個基礎上談等韻音系。

2.3 首先要談的是“攝”這一概念。早期韻圖如《韻鏡》及《七音略》衹有圖而無攝,分四十三圖,亦稱四十三轉。現存文獻中,《四聲等子》是最早標攝的,因此有人説《等子》首先併轉爲攝。其實這一説法並不全面,《等子》以前顯然已經有人利用攝的概念併轉了。這可以由兩方面看出來,其一,《等子》各攝除了標内或外,還標上號碼,但是這些號碼與《等子》中的攝次不同,顯然是根據

① 當然也許有少數人認爲這種音節分段法不必遵守。例如許多研究閩方言的人,常用“複合元音”作爲韻腹,外加韻尾。有些研究中古音的人也爲梗攝字擬出複合元音的韻腹。蒲立本認爲元音衹有兩個,另以複合元音及附加符號區别韻母(説見 Pulleyblank 1970 及 1972),自然也不符合這種音節分段法。他最近出版的 Middle Chinese (Vancouver 1984),我尚未看到,但猜想他的觀點未變。

前人的做法；其二，在其釋內、外轉例中，列舉十六攝，但却合併其中一部分而實得十三攝。如果攝的首創者是《等子》的作者，這種舉措就完全不可解了。另就音理説，攝所代表的概念，自始就存在於等韻所依據的音位結構中，它是把含有相同韻尾的許多韻按照特定的音韻關係組合起來的。《韻鏡》雖然没有標攝，但是它的圖次安排已經暗示這一概念了，《等子》各攝所標內、外之後的號碼，便源自韻鏡的圖次[①]。在給等韻（以及《切韻》）擬音時，凡是同攝的字當然都得擬作含有共同的韻尾，不容例外，否則便是誤解或忽視了攝的意義。

2.3.1 各攝所特有的韻尾，一般都相當容易確定，但也有需要特別討論的。讓我們先把各攝的韻尾列舉出來：

1. 遇、果、假：直音（-ø，無尾）

2. 止、蟹：收噫（/-y/，或作[i]）

3. 流、效：收嗚（/-w/，或作[u]）

4. 深、咸：收雙脣音（陽聲收/-m/；入聲收/-p/）

5. 臻、山：收舌尖音（陽聲收/-n/；入聲收/-t/）

6. 梗、曾：收舌面音（陽聲收/-ɲ/；入聲收/-k̂/）

7. 通、江、宕：收舌根音（陽聲收/-ŋ/；入聲收/-k/）

2.3.2 對於上列各攝的韻尾，絶大多數大家的看法都一致，需要討論的衹有止、梗、曾三攝。

a) 止攝所含皆爲收噫韻，這是"攝"的定義所嚴格要求的，但因其三等中有多達四組的重韻，而前人又無嚴格的音位觀念，因此在擬音時，往往忽略上述"攝"字的基本定義。比如高本漢即擬"支"爲[jie̯]，擬"脂、之"爲[ji]（Karlgren 1954），前者不收噫，而後兩者同以[i]爲主要元音，遂使韻尾不彰，而"攝"的定義亦因而遭到破壞，但亦未見有人爲"攝"字另定新義。我們認爲

① 李新魁教授也認爲"攝"的觀念早在《等子》以前已存在，並認爲《韻鏡》及《七音略》所標的"內外"就是以"攝"的觀念爲根據的。説見李 1982。

"攝"的定義是不容改動的,因此按嚴格的音位解析,止攝必爲收噫;

b) 梗、曾兩攝的韻尾,絶大多數人認爲是舌根音,即與通、江、宕同收[ŋ](陽聲)與[k](入聲),而把它們的區别放在韻腹上。有的人用許多不同的單元音區别這些韻,另一些人則認識到這種做法不合理,乃另立一些複合元音的韻腹,而置漢語的音節結構於不顧。對於這些做法,我們可以提出三個問題:其一,一個合理的音系真會有那麽多元音音位嗎?其二,真有必要打破漢語的音節結構嗎?其三,假如以韻尾立攝的定義是正確的話,爲什麽唯獨舌根音韻尾之下,允許有那麽多攝?(假如説這個定義不正確,那麽它的定義究竟是什麽?)按梗、曾兩攝所含諸韻在《切韻》的韻序中,以及等韻的圖次中,都與通、江、宕諸攝之韻不鄰,顯與後者差别甚大,我從音位觀點着眼,早就猜想梗、曾的韻尾與通、江、宕等的韻尾原不相同,及見日本學者橋本萬太郎所提梗攝韻尾原爲舌面音之説①,復證之以許多方言與域外借音的現象,乃知其不誤,因將梗、曾兩攝之韻尾確定爲/ɲ/(陽聲)與/k̂/(入聲)。

2.4 等韻圖的列字例分四等,許多韻圖(江攝是最突出的例外)也都是每等都有字的,但就其"辨例"的文字説明以及歷來學者們的研究看,一部分韻圖中列在二等或四等的字,性質實與三等字無異。由於聲母的特殊安排(爲節省篇幅),或由於"重紐"一類的問題,才把它們放在二等或四等。因此,假如我們純以韻母的性質爲準來看韻圖的列字,便可以把韻圖歸納爲兩種形式:

	甲　式	乙　式
一等	-(w)V_1(E)	-(w)V_1(E)
二等	……	-(w)V_2(E)
三等	-y(w)V_3(E)	-(w)V3(E)
四等	……	-(w)V_4(E)

① 橋本氏的説法見於 Hashimoto 1970。此處須作兩點補充説明:a)他是從所謂"内部構擬"(internal reconstruction)的結構觀點出發的,認爲聲母既有"明、泥、日、疑",則韻尾亦當有相對的四個鼻音音位,另以客家話等方言現象證實其説。b)他認爲梗攝中衹有部分韻類是收舌面韻尾的,另一部分及曾攝諸韻仍收古根韻尾,並認爲其中部分韻類原占江宕的四等位置。我的看法與他不同的地方是:我認爲梗曾都收舌面音,它們在等韻中的位置以及後來的同步演變都支持這一看法。又:橋本氏用/c/代表舌面塞音,我則采用董同龢先生論上古音時用的/k̂/來代表這個音位,雖衹是符號的差異,或可暗示該音與舌根音的關係更近些。

2.4.1 上表中加括號的/w/代表韻母的脣化(即合口,多數人寫作[u],我們爲表示它不是主要元音故寫作/w/),各等字的韻母都可能是脣化的或非脣化的,因此韻圖常常是開合相對的。所謂獨韻或獨攝衹表示該圖没有開合相對的字,絶不表示圖中的字既非合又非開。表中不帶括號的/y/表示腭化(傳統所謂的細音字,即因含有此一成分,高本漢等寫作[i])。凡是三等字皆爲腭化,凡是腭化的字也都屬三等。四等韻有無介音(即韻頭)是一個仍有争議的問題。高本漢認爲有一個"帶元音性的[i]"作介音,李榮(李 1956)認爲没有,我也認爲在《切韻》時代及等韻初期,四等韻的字没有這個介音。(從音位觀點看,所謂"帶元音性的"一詞即屬費解。)四等韻的字腭化是等韻後期的事。甲式韻圖衹能有一等性跟三等性的字,但個别韻圖却不一定兩種字都有,比如止攝就衹有三等韻。同樣地,乙式韻圖中一等性至四等性的字可能全有,但個别韻圖却不一定是四等具全的,比如梗攝無一等字,假攝無一、四等字,而江攝則僅有二等字,所以甲式與乙式在圖形上的關鍵性差别衹在有無真正的二等韻。説到此處,等韻傳統裏所謂的内轉即甲式、所謂外轉即乙式,也就不言自喻了。但在音理上,所謂内外轉還牽涉到一些别的問題,留到第三節中細論。

2.4.2 所謂"等",以及"某等性的字(或韻)"究竟是什麽意思呢?這個問題必須作音理上的實質回答,因此是等韻研究中最關鍵性的問題。參照前人的研究,尤其是我個人對漢語從等韻時期到早期官話之演變的研究(薛 1975),我得到一個結論,即等韻之"等"是以一個四音位的元音音系爲基礎而形成的(見下表)。

前	央	後
高	ɨ	
低 e	a	ɔ

	甲式	乙式
一等	-(w)ɨ(E)	-(w)ɔ(E)
二等	……	-(w)a(E)
三等	-y(w)ɨ(E)	-y(w)a(E)
四等	……	-(w)e(E)

把這個元音系統與甲、乙兩個圖式相對比，並參照宋元以來的韻部分合以及方言的差異，我們可以得出關於“等”的定義的一個初步假定，它包括了好幾個相當合理的假定，但須作如下的説明：

a）我們假定甲式韻圖裏，韻母的韻腹是一個高元音，而且一等性的字與三等性的字韻腹相同，差别祇在洪細。這是因爲大多數内轉攝中的字在現代方言中都含有高元音，這些圖裏列在一等與三等的字，或者在《切韻》裏原即同韻（如東韻），或者原雖不同韻，後來都互相押韻了（如侯與尤及幽），雖然它們的韻腹當初即使不相同，後來也都變爲相同的了。我們有理由相信早在等韻音系裏，這種轉變即已發生。

b）我們説乙式韻圖中的字都以低元音爲韻腹，因爲合乎這種圖形的都是等韻傳統中的所謂外轉，而外轉各韻的字，除了臻攝字，在現代方言中泰半都以低元音爲韻腹。在乙式圖的四個等裏，我們假定二等與三等同以低央元音/a/爲韻腹，而祇以洪細把它們分開。這有兩個原因：其一，早在《切韻》音系裏，就有一些韻（比如庚、麻）同時含有後來分屬二等與三等的字；反之，一等與二等之間，以及三等與四等之間，却没有這種現象。（四等齊韻有幾個三等字，全屬例外。）可見二等與三等的關係原較密切；其二，也是更重要的，二等韻的字在《切韻》音系中雖極複雜，在等韻音系中必已變得含有同一韻腹，否則就没有理由歸於同等了。三等韻字都是腭化音，而其他各等都非腭化，假如有些三等性的字在某種情況下失掉了腭化（即丢掉了韻頭中的/y/），那麽它們與其他三個等裏的字會有什麽樣的關係呢？答案是：它們跟二等無别了。這可由山攝三等輕脣音字的演變看出來。這類字（“翻、反、飯、萬”等）原爲腭化（三等）合口字，但後來都失掉了腭化，因此與二等“山”韻合併（在《中原音韻》中入“寒山”韻），而不與一等“桓”韻合併（不入“桓歡”韻），也不與四等“先”韻合併（不入“先天”攝）。我們認爲二等與三等的韻腹同是/a/的假定，很自然地説明了上述現象（薛 1975：50—58）。

c）我們作了一個元音分布的嚴格假定，即祇有央元音/ɨ，a/才可以出現在腭化韻母裏，後元音/ɔ/跟前元音/e/都不與韻頭中的/y/介音相配。這個嚴格的假定是由等韻音系中音位結構的特性推論出來的，在漢語音韻史的某一階段裏，這一現象也曾經出現過。就語音原理説，這一假定是合理的但不是必然的。四等韻在等韻後期孳生了一個/y/介音(變爲腭化),可見前低元音並非不可以出現在腭化韻母裏。同樣地,有許多迹象顯示,在《切韻》音系中,後低元音原來也是可以跟腭化介音相配的。這一點容待下文討論內、外轉時再詳細申説。

2.5 上表及文字説明所表達的是韻圖設計的間架,也可以説是漢語音韻由《切韻》音系演變到等韻音系後的一個概括。但是語音演變是一個漸進的漫長過程,因此有一些演變中殘留的過渡現象,這個概括性的設計就無法合理地容納進去,衹能用權宜的辦法處理,下文將討論的內、外轉問題即爲一例。另外爲了圖形的整齊及節省篇幅,韻圖的制作者也采用了一些變通的辦法,比如脣、舌、齒音兩組聲母的重叠。這些聲母在多數情形下都是兩兩互補的,因此可以合併起來節約篇幅,但有時却不盡然。以精系聲母爲例,它們是可以配腭化韻母的,但是由於圖例所限,精系三等字也衹好列入四等了。同樣地,《切韻》音系的莊系聲母(照系二等),在某些韻類裏也可以配腭化韻母(三等),但依例都列於二等(薛 1980)。最需要用變通辦法處理的,當然是許多音變所造成的《切韻》音系與等韻音系之間的差異。由於等韻的制作者想要解説《切韻》中的韻讀,便絞盡腦汁,用許多變通的辦法把這些差異勉强地安排到韻圖中去,這便造成了許多所謂"重紐、重韻、通、廣、偈、狹、寄韻"等問題。就等韻音系説,這些都是不必要的糾葛,但是這些令人頭痛的糾葛却可以提供給我們許多關於《切韻》音系的暗示。要解開這許多糾葛絶不是容易的,下一節裏我們將專論內外轉的含義。

三、內外轉的含義

現存五種較古老的等韻書中,除了《切韻指掌圖》,都在每圖上標示其爲內或外,另外又多在其門法辨例中,以文字説明內外轉的含義與十六攝的歸屬。例如《四聲等子》有"辨內外轉例"如下:

> 內轉者,脣、舌、牙、喉四音更無第二等字,唯齒音方具足;外轉者,五音四等都具足。今以深、曾、止、宕、果、遇、流、通括內轉六十七韻,江、山、梗、假、效、蟹、咸、臻括外轉一百三十九韻。

《經史正音切韻指南》的“内外門”説：

> 内外者，謂脣、牙、喉、舌、來、日下爲切，韻逢照一，内轉切三，外轉切二，故曰“内外”。如古雙切江、矣殊切熊字之類是也。

又另於“檢韻十六攝”下標出内八轉與外八轉，所標十六攝的歸屬與《等子》全同。

這種内、外兩分法似乎是頗具深意的，但除了幫助讀者死板地按圖找字以外，還有什麼意義呢？千百年來，這一直是一個謎。近代研究漢語音韻的學者，在許多門法中，也特别注意這一條，對於《等子》等書辨例中所作的解釋，自然也都不感滿意，其原因爲：

a）從音韻學的觀點看，衹把各圖分標爲内或外，而不説明它們在音韻性質方面的特點，可以説是没有多大意義的。

b）如果我們嚴格地按辨例中的文字定義審查各攝，我們就得説臻攝應屬内轉（脣、舌、牙、喉下無二等字，而齒音具足），同時也得説果、假、江等攝既非内轉也非外轉（四等不足）。

3.1 由於類似上述的原因，許多近代學者都曾經嘗試揭開内外轉的真正含義，其中最負盛名的是羅常培先生。他寫了一篇《釋内外轉》（羅 1933），以高本漢爲《切韻》所擬的音爲依據，提出一個新説法。他説内外轉的意思就是中古漢語裏高元音與低元音的對比，並以 Daniel Jones 的所謂 Carinal vowels 爲基礎，作圖示意。爲了使這一説法看起來順理成章，他就不得不先把臻攝由外轉搬到内轉，同時也把果攝及宕攝由内轉搬到外轉，並説這些改動是有根據的。羅先生畫了一張甚爲精緻的“各韻圖中之内外轉異同表”，衹要稍微檢查一下羅表，我們便可以看出，羅先生所謂的根據衹不過是《韻鏡》與《七韻略》的三四個頗爲鮮見的版本而已。我們很難理解爲什麼在大多數别的等韻書之前，羅先生對那幾個版本如此偏信，這不很像先有結論後找證據嗎？在下文裏，我將從多方面指出爲什麼羅先生的説法是不妥當的，並嘗試在等韻音系的基礎上提出一個音理性的不同解釋，但在此處我必須先説明，我的新説法得自羅先生的啓示。我們都知道等韻原本創自“胡僧”，後來流傳於僧尼之手，降至末流，等韻的真意已鮮爲人知，所謂通等韻的人也不過死記門法，按圖查字而已，變成諺語所謂的“小和尚念經，有口無心”了①。即使到近代，許多治等韻的學者也衹專注於文字與圖形的考證而不及音理。羅先生則不然，他把目光轉向音理，把研究的重點放在音韻對比上，即此一端，便足爲我們的楷模，我在此處對他的學説提出批評，衹是所謂的“《春秋》責賢”而已。

3.2 由於内外轉的含義一向未有善解，而羅先生又是第一個以音理立説的人，所以立刻便有很多人信以爲真，包括我自己在内。其實在他發表該説之後不久，董同龢先生即在給他的信中指出其不妥(董 1948)，而羅先生也回信承認了。在我以前發表的幾篇論文中，凡涉及等韻時，我都遵從羅先生的説法(如薛 1975、1978、1980 等文)，而且爲了落實這一新説，去掉它的含糊之處(比如，半高前元音[e]在羅先生的説法裏竟可兩屬)，我進一步提出：内外之分所反映的事實即前文已提到的四音位元音系統中的高低之分(見 2.4.2)。並據而把内外各攝兩兩相對的關係規律化，江、宕兩攝合併爲一，果、假亦以同理合併，如下表：

内	通 -ŋ/k	曾 -ɲ/k̂	臻 -n/t	深 -m/p	止 -y	流 -w	遇 -ø
外	江宕 -ŋ/k	梗 -ɲ/k̂	山 -n/t	咸 -m/p	蟹 -y	效 -w	果假 -ø

可是老實説，我自始就覺得這個説法仍相當有問題。近年來的研究終於使我相信：元音的高、低(或弇、侈)對比跟等韻的内外轉，實際上代表兩個截然不同的概念。因爲上述説法至少造成以下幾項困難：

a) 雖然我們知道羅先生的説法證據不足，但也不得不據以重新組合内、外各攝。

b) 按韻圖的常規，反切下字與其所切之字必須同等，即所謂“音和切”，二等照系字在某些圖裏可作同等字的反切下字或以同等字作它們的反切下字，

① 這種死背歌訣有口無心的現象，宋元以來似乎相當普遍，明人吕坤作《交泰韻》，在序文中講了一個類似笑話的故事(他自己是否真通聲律當然是另一個問題)。文繁無須備引，大意是：他有一次求教於一位號稱精於聲律的“天寧上座慕汭”。這位上座裝模作樣地説：“難言難言。”但説到實例時，竟衹會順口背誦一些口訣。在吕坤反詰辯駁他之後，才茫然若失地説：“平生苦心三十年，自謂深得七音三十六母之精、十三法門十六攝之妙，而公更簡徑明切！我學非耶?”引見趙蔭棠《等韻源流》，第 132 頁。

這是正常的;但在另一些圖裏,二等照系字却可能作三等字的反切下字(實際很少),或以三等字作它們的反切下字(例子較多),這是不正常的,如不標明,按理,就找不到字了。韻圖標作内或外,就是爲了幫助讀者解决這個問題,意思是説:在標"内"的圖上,二等照系字的反切下字,可能出現在三等裏。羅先生提出重新劃分各攝,自然就使得"内"與"外"這兩個標簽連原來的簡單功用都丢掉了。

c) 爲了使内、外各攝在元音高低的基礎上兩兩相對,我們不得不合併果攝與假攝以及江攝與宕攝,所根據的衹是所謂"互補分布"(Complementary distribution)。其實這種互補並不完全(果攝有幾個三等字,江攝與宕攝的齒音字冲突)。

d) 較晚出的等韻書如《四聲等子》,誠然將上述兩組韻攝合併了,而且還合併了曾、梗兩攝,名之曰"内外混等"(《指掌圖》合而不名,《指南》僅合果、假,乃圖序使然)。我們必須能爲這一現象提出合理的解説,但羅先生把果、宕搬入外轉,就無所謂"内外混等",也似乎自然不必解釋了。(當然音理上仍須解釋。另外,曾、梗仍分屬内、外,但也未見羅先生解釋。)

e) 就爲中古漢語擬音説,最嚴重的是:這一理論使我們把曾攝的韻腹誤認爲高元音(内轉),不僅將使中古音系的構擬發生錯誤,而且將使我們無法合理地解釋漢語自中古到現代的演變(見下文 3.4)。

3.3 上面提出的這些問題,終於使我感覺到,把内外轉與元音之高低等同看待的説法是不正確的。我們一旦放棄了這種看法以後,就不會感覺到有重新劃分各攝隸屬的必要,"内、外"這兩個符號的原始簡單功能也就恢復了,更重要的是:在我們給等韻音系(以及《切韻》音系)擬音時,就不必爲了某一韻的内外轉的歸屬而於元音的選擇有所顧慮。也就是説,衹要有充足的證據,某些内轉韻的韻腹可以擬爲低元音,同樣,外轉韻的韻腹也可以擬作高元音。我們在前文(2.4)中已經指出,所謂内外轉之分,衹是韻母在韻圖中的分布所表現出的甲式與乙式之分。約略檢查便可看出,屬於甲式(内轉)的韻多半以高元音爲韻腹,而乙式(外轉)各韻絶大多數以低元音爲韻腹,這説明我們在前文(2.4.2)中按四音位元音系統給韻圖所擬的結構形態是有相當道理的,它代表的是韻圖的基本音位結構。羅常培先生大概也是隱約地看到了這種結構才提出他的新説的。但是等韻音系的實況却不完全是這樣的。我們在前文(2.4.2.c)中已經指出,這個結構形態中,後元音/ɔ/跟前元音/e/都不與腭化介音相配,這可能是漢語由《切韻》音系演變到等韻音系的一個現象。在《切韻》時代,這一元音分布的限制並不存在,也就是説,那時一定有很多腭化韻母是以後元音爲韻腹的,後來腭化韻母中的後元音/ɔ/由於受到介音中/y/的同化,逐次前移而變爲央低元音/a/,可用公式表達如下:

$$ɔ \longrightarrow a / y\_\_\_ \qquad (1)$$

但是這個過程是漸進的、漫長的,到等韻初期還有一些殘留痕迹,我以爲内轉中的果、宕、曾三攝即屬此類,它們的韻母,不論是一等還是三等,都是以後低元音/ɔ/爲韻腹的,一直到等韻初期仍然如此。因此不能跟與它們相對的假、江、梗三攝各韻合爲一個完整的典型外轉攝,而後者也衹好把一等的位置空在那兒虚位以待了。因此就韻母的元音性質説,内轉實分兩類:

	内轉 A (通止遇流深)	内轉 B (果宕曾)
一等	-(w)ɨ(E)	-(w)ɔ(E)
二等	……	……
三等	-y(w)ɨ(E)	-y(w)ɔ(E)
四等	……	……

這兩類韻攝的圖式完全一樣,歸字找字的方式也就一致,所以便同屬"内轉"了。在這個理論的基礎上解釋"内外混等"也就順理成章了。在前述的同化作用最後終於影響到果、曾兩攝的三等字時,這些三等字就變得與跟它們相對應的外轉攝中的三等字没有區别,因此果與假、曾與梗就合攝了。宕與江的合攝雖亦名"内外混等",其實性質甚不相同。我們都知道,漢語中元音所受的影響主要來自韻尾,其次來自介音。宕攝的韻尾是/ŋ,k/,不大可能會讓介音中的/y/影響其元音向前移動。反之,江攝的韻尾也是/ŋ,k/,其韻腹爲央元音/a/,因此可能受韻尾的影響而後移變爲/ɔ/,因此就自然地跟宕攝合併了。

這一合併不是"混等",實爲合韻①:

$$a \longrightarrow ɔ/\_\_\_ ŋ,k \quad (2)$$

3.4 説果、宕兩攝字的韻腹原爲後低元音/ɔ/,大概不會有多少人反對,但説曾攝字的韻腹也是/ɔ/,可能就有人不以爲然了。羅先生就認爲它仍是"内轉"嘛！其實這也有不得不然的理由。其一,曾攝在混等之後與梗攝合攝,而梗攝毫無疑義是以低元音爲韻腹的,如果曾攝的韻腹不是低元音,這一合攝就不大可能;其二,在不少非官話的南方方言(如廣州話)裏,曾攝字的讀法仍爲低元音,可補證它們在古代本讀低元音。其三,曾攝照二系入聲字,諸如"色、測"等,在《中原音韻》裏出現在"皆來"韻中,迄今在北京口語中韻母仍讀/ay/,而曾攝的其他入聲字(如"力、食"等),則出現在"齊微"韻中,韻母當爲/ɨy/。如果我們遵守羅先生的説法,真的把曾攝韻腹定爲高元音,那就會得出一種極不可能的情況,即在一段語言學上説不算太長的時間裏(宋代到元代),這個高元音變成了低元音,然後又變了回去。與此相反,我們把曾攝的韻腹定爲後低元音/ɔ/,就"色、測"等字説,它們是三等字,故韻腹後來變爲/a/;由於是照二系字,故先丢掉腭化介音/y/而變爲二等字,所以後來三等字韻腹前移爲/e/而併入四等時,便没有影響到它們,而其他聲母的三等入聲字,則因變入四等,復變入蟹攝,終於隨蟹攝的三、四等字一同變入"齊微"韻了。這幾個有關的音變,都具有很大的普遍性,不是專爲曾攝字而造的特殊規則(薛 1978)。

3.5 臻攝的情況更棘手些。它被標作外轉,但就辨例的字面定義説,它完全有資格作爲内轉,因爲它的二等衹有齒音聲母字。然而它又非屬外轉不成,因爲那幾個二等齒音字與同圖三等字在《切韻》裏不同韻,而自成兩個獨立的韻——"臻"與"櫛",每韻衹含三個不同的音節而互爲反切。就音韻結構説,這

---

① 關於江宕合併的較詳細的討論,請參看薛 1982。在此擬作兩點補充説明:a) 低央元音受韻尾影響而後移爲/ɔ/的現象,不限於江攝(即不限於舌根音)。收嗚(/w/)的效攝,後來四個等合韻,而變成《中原音韻》的"蕭豪"的,其過程亦同。我以前把這一過程解釋爲前元音(/e/)與後元音(/ɔ/)同變作央元音/a/,現在我認識到這在音理上是欠妥的,應爲/e、a/同受後半元音韻尾/w/之影響而變爲/ɔ/。b)在漢語的元音系統由等韻以降的四音位系統變爲現代北京音的高中低三度元音制(薛 1980)以後,因爲衹有一個低元音音位,所以就没有前後之别了。因此,雖然"江陽"的(江宕合韻)及"蕭豪"韻(效攝各等合韻)的元音在發音的方式上未曾改變,在音位系統上説,又得改作/a/,説見薛 1982。

是一個很獨特的現象。我覺得這種現象在等韻音系裏是不應有的,它的出現衹能是去古未遠的早期等韻作者用極勉强的辦法儘可能地圖示《切韻》中的分韻現象而已。臻攝雖屬外轉,我們顯然也得把它的韻腹定爲高元音/ɨ/,連那幾個列在二等的齒音字,在等韻音系裏,也必已變成以/ɨ/爲韻腹的了。但它們在《切韻》音系裏,以及《切韻》之前,必然以不同的元音與臻攝中其他的字相區别,有人以許多隋唐時代早期的反切資料來證明這幾個小韻實與同圖三等字無别(龍 1983),但這衹能證明,即使在陸法言時代,許多方言裏已經没有這種區别了,不能證明特定的《切韻》音系裏没有,更不可能證明《切韻》以前也没有這種差别。陸法言既然特别爲這些字另立兩韻,等韻的創製者也不憚煩地把它們特别標出,必然是大有所謂的。這個問題音理上應如何解釋,我仍無絶對把握,但却有一個自覺頗爲合理的揣測。我們都知道《切韻》音系是很複雜的,即使承認它含有相當數量的方言混雜現象(Chang 1974、1979),我們或許仍然要爲它構擬一個比較複雜的元音系統,也就是説,它的元音音位不可能像等韻音系那樣衹有四個。如此看來,“臻、櫛”兩韻可能是原來字數相當多的兩個大韻的殘餘。我們可以假定這兩個大韻本來是以央元音/ə/作爲韻腹的,但在《切韻》之前,其中所有的字,除了照二系聲母(捲舌音)的幾個音節,都在某些條件下漸次地變入别的韻了。在《切韻》時代或稍前,這幾個因捲舌聲母而得以保持其元音不變的音節,押韻時自然特别突出地自成一格。如果它們所代表的字特别少,自然可以從權併入鄰韻(如“冬”韻的“湩、鴆”兩個上聲字寄入“腫”韻)。但它們偏偏每韻都有不少字,因此衹好讓他們分别自成一韻了。但是到了等韻時代,這幾個殘存音節的韻腹必然也已變爲高元音/ɨ/,因此必須與臻攝中别的韻一道納入同一韻圖,這張圖的音韻性質自然與 3.3 節中所説的“内轉 A”式完全相同,不過韻圖的作者是極其關心《切韻》的,他們因此把臻攝標爲外轉,以標明“臻、櫛”兩韻與同圖的三等韻原無反切上的關係。這對於韻圖的設計原理來説,自然是頗爲牽强的,但却含有可貴的歷史意蘊,使我們得以窺探更早期的元音系統。

結語

綜觀以上所論,我們可以藉用“内轉、外轉”這兩個不很恰當的術語,用下面四張表,把等韻十六攝的韻母音韻形態總結一下:表中虛線表示那個位置音理上可以有韻母,但實際上没有,或雖有但在他攝;實線則表示那個位置上不該有。

a) 内轉A式各攝

攝 / 等	通	止	遇	流	深
一	-wɨ{ŋ/k}	----	-wɨø	-ɨw	----
二	——	——	——	——	——
三	-ywɨ{ŋ/k}	-y(w)ɨy	-ywɨø	-yɨw	-yɨ{m/p}
四	——	——	——	——	——

b) 内轉B式各攝

攝 / 等	果	曾	宕
一	-(w)ɔø	-(w)ɔ{ɲ/k̂}	-(w)ɔ{ŋ/k}
二	——	——	——
三	-ywɔø	-y(w)ɔ{ɲ/k̂}	-y(w)ɔ{ŋ/k}
四	——	——	——

c) 外轉A式各攝

攝 / 等	梗	江	蟹	效	山	咸	假
一	----	----	-(w)ɔy	-ɔw	-(w)ɔ{n/t}	-ɔ{m/p}	----

續表

攝 等	梗	江	蟹	效	山	咸	假
二	-(w)a{ɲ/k}	-a{ŋ/k}	-(w)ay	-aw	-(w)a{n/t}	-a{m/p}	-(w)aø
三	-y(w)a{ɲ/k̂}	----	-y(w)ay	-yaw	-y(w)a{n/t}	-ya{m/p}	-y(w)aø
四	(w)e{ɲ/k̂}	----	-(w)ey	-ew	-(w)e{n/t}	-e{m/p}	----

d) 外轉B式臻攝

一等	-(w)ɨ{n/t}
二等	[-ə{n/t}]?
三等	-y(w)ɨ{n/t}
四等	——

按照音韻系統慣於趨向整齊的常理説,在所謂“内外混等”與臻攝轉内之後,韻腹爲高元音的攝跟韻腹爲低元音的攝應該形成如 3.2 節所示的兩兩相配的局面。在絶大多數的情況下,確是如此,即通對江宕、臻對山、深對咸、止對蟹、流對效、遇對果假,但梗、曾則無相對的高元音攝。其實在等韻初形成時,它們就没有相對的高元音韻,這是一個頗值得深思的現象。會不會是:在《切韻》音系裏原有一個與梗、曾相對的以高元音爲韻腹的韻,但在等韻形成以前,這個韻已經變走了呢?《切韻》裏有“東、冬”兩韻,唐詩押韻裏“東”韻仍爲“獨用”,晚至平水韻,“東、冬”仍然分韻。這表示它們的差别雖然在等韻音系裏早已消失,但這種差别在《切韻》裏以及在後來的一些方言音系裏,是確曾存在的,一般都把這種差異解釋爲韻腹的不同(高本漢:東[uŋ]、冬[uoŋ]),但這是否可以解釋爲韻尾的不同呢?這個問題當然祇有在調查研究以後才能作實證性的回答。音韻系統的演進,總是在平衡與不平衡的基礎上,作正反合式的變動,所以雖則變動的常勢是趨向整齊平衡,在個别的時代與方言裏,總會多少有一些不平衡的現象。這類現象祇有從嚴格的音位觀點上看得出來,因爲音韻的演變是以音位系統爲基礎的(參看薛 1982)。確認了這類現象以後,才

能據之在歷史音韻上作上推或下推的研究。我舉出"東、冬"之分,不過是作個别例子罷了。另外一個例子是收噫韻,它們在《切韻》與等韻中的分布極不平衡。例如止攝無一等韻,三等韻則有四組重韻,外加重紐問題;蟹攝則除了重韻、重紐問題以外,又有"祭、泰、夬、廢"這四個特殊的去聲韻,這使我隱約地感覺到,要想對《切韻》音系的元音系統有突破性的發現,恐怕必須從研究收噫韻入手。對於這兩個例子,我迄今還没有想通①,但仍大膽地在此作"野人之奏曝",向各位音韻學同好討教,以收拋磚引玉之效。

參考文獻

王　力　《漢語音韻學》,中華書局,1957 年。

　　　　《中國語言學史》,《中國語文》雜志社,1963 年。

李方桂　《上古音研究》,《清華學報》新九卷,第一、二期合刊(1971),第 1—61 頁。

① 《切韻》音系的元音音位系統究竟是什麼樣子的,迄今仍然説法不一,美國學者 Samuel E. Martin 根據高本漢的擬音嘗試作音位分析(Martin 1953),他得出六個元音音位,並以號碼標出其相對位置如下式:

前 央 後		前 央 後
*	高	1
e ə	中	6 2
ɛ a ɑ	低	5 3 4

我覺得他得出的這個元音音位系統尚有商榷餘地。首先,我們説過,韻書及韻圖本身是音位性的,可以直接用它們分韻或分圖的情形窺探音系的梗概,而用前人的擬音做參考。反之,便隔了一層。比方説,《切韻》中"脂、之"分韻當是音位性的差别,這是不必多説的。高本漢無法分辨它們,祇好都擬作[ji], Martin 據他的擬音以求音位,自然也就没有把它們分開的可能了。其次,元音音位系統總是趨向整齊平衡的,可以説是人類聽覺中對比選擇的具體表現,他提出的元音系統顯然不够平衡,其可靠性就令人懷疑。我猜想《切韻》音系的元音系統可能如下式,菱形之内的元音可以與腭化介音相配,而前、後低元音則否。

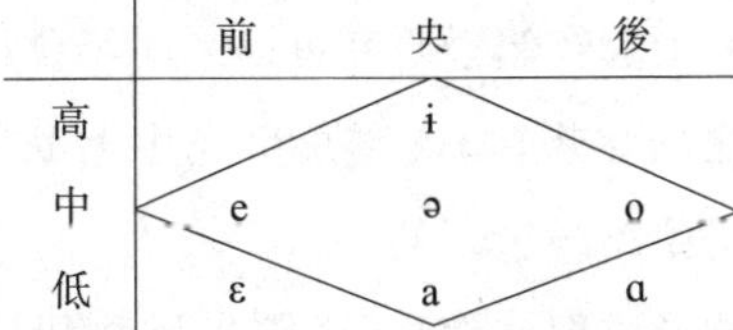

這樣就比較容易理解,爲什麽在等韻圖裏,三等的特别複雜,而一等及四等没有腭化。當然到目前爲止,這不過是一個大膽的假設而已,能否證實尚待對《切韻》本身作徹底的分析。

李　榮　《切韻音系》,科學出版社,1956 年。

李新魁　《韻鏡研究》,《語言研究》創刊號(1981),第 125—166 頁。

———　《論内外轉》,中國音韻學研究會第二屆年會,西安,1982 年。

周祖謨　《讀守温韻學殘卷後記》,《問學集》,中華書局,1966 年,第 501—506 頁。

———　《宋人等韻圖中“轉”字的來源》,《問學集》,中華書局,1966 年,第 507—510 頁。

邵榮芬　《切韻研究》,中國社會科學出版社。

俞光中　《説内外轉》,中國音韻學研究會第二屆年會,西安,1982 年。

陸志韋　《三四等與所謂喻化》,《燕京學報》第二十六期(1939),第 143—173 頁。

———　《釋中原音韻》,《燕京學報》第三十一期(1946),第 35—70 頁。

張世禄　《中國音韻學史》,泰興書局,1963 年影印本。

張　琨　《漢語方言中聲母韻母之間的關係》,《史語所集刊》第五十三本第一分(1982),第 57—77 頁。

許世瑛　《評羅、董兩先生釋内外轉之得失》,《淡江學報》1966 年第五期,第 1—15 頁。

董同龢　《廣韻重紐試釋》,《史語所集刊》第十三本(1948),第 1—20 頁。

———　《等韻門法通釋》,《史語所集刊》第十四本(1948),第 257—306 頁。

———　《〈切韻指掌圖〉中幾個問題》,《史語所集刊》第十七本(1948),第 195—212 頁。

———　《漢語音韻學》,學生書局,1968 年。

趙蔭棠　《中原音韻研究》,商務印書館,1936 年。

———　《等韻源流》,商務印書館,1957 年。

潘文國　《評四等洪細説》,華東師範大學油印本,1981 年。

———　《等韻辨説》,中國音韻學研究會第二屆年會,西安,1982 年。

薛鳳生　《論入聲字之演化規律》,《屈萬里先生七秩榮慶論文集》,聯經出版社,1978 年,第 407—433 頁。

———　《論支思韻的形成與演進》,《中國書目季刊》第 12 卷第 2 期(1980),第 53—75 頁。

——— 《論音變與音位結構的關係》,《語言研究》1982 年第 2 期,第 11—17 頁。

龍宇純 《從臻櫛兩韻性質的認定到韻圖二、四等字的擬音》,國際漢藏語言學會第十六届年會,Seattle, Washington, 1983。

羅常培 《釋内外轉》,《史語所集刊》第四本第二分(1933),第 206—226 頁。

——— 《知徹澄娘音值考》,《史語所集刊》第三本第一分,第 121—157 頁。

——— 《敦煌寫本守温韻學殘卷跋》,《史語所集刊》第三本第二分,第 251—262 頁。

Chang, Kun: Ancient Chinese Phonology and the Ch' ieh-yun, *Tsing Hua Journal of Chinese Studies*, New series X, No. 2(1974), 61 - 82.

——: The Composite Nature of the Ch' ieh-yun, *The Bulletin of the Institute of History and Philology*, Academia Sinica, Vol. 50, Part 2 (1979).

Chao, Yuen Ren: Distinctions within Ancient Chinese, *Harvard Journal of Asiatic Studies* 5 (1941), 203 - 233.

——: The Non-uniqueness of Phonemic Solution of Phonetic Systems, *Bulletin of the Institute of History and Philology*, Academia Sinica, Vol. 4, No. 4 (1934)363 - 398.

Halle, Morris: Phonology in Generative Grammar, *Word* 18 (1962), 54 - 72.

Hartman, Lawton M, Ⅲ: The Segmental Phonemes of the Peiping Dialect, *Language* 20 (1944), 28 - 42.

Hashimoto, Mantaro J.: Internal Evidence for Ancient Chinese Palatal Endings, *Language* 46. 2, Part 1 (1970), 336 - 365.

——: Phonology of Ancient Chinese, *Study of Languages and Cultures of Asia & Africa Monograph Series* No. 10, Vol. 1 (1978), Vol. 2 (1979), Tokyo, Japan.

Hsueh, F. S.: Phonology of Old Mandarin, Janua Linguarum Series Practica No. 179 (1975), The Hague, The Netherlands.

——: The Phonemic Structure of Pekingese Finals and their R-suffixation, *The Bulletin of the Institute of History and Philology*, Academia Sinica, Vol. 51, Part 3 (1980), 491 - 514.

——：Xu Xiao's Revised Rhyme-Tables：a Bold Renovation, Papers from the XIVth International Conference on Sino-Tibetan Languages and Linguistics, Xuesheng Book Co, Monographs in Modern Linguistics, Series B, No. 7 (1983), Taipei, Taiwan.

——：Historical Phonology and Dialect Study：Some Examples from the Pingdu Dialect, to appear in Papers Presented to *Wang Li on His Eightieth Birthday*, The Chinese Language Society of Hong Kong (scheduled for publication in 1984).

Jakobson, R. . G. Fant, and M. Halle：*Preliminaries to Speech Analysis: the Distinctive Features and their Correlates*, the M. I. T. Prese, Cambridge, Mass, 1951.

Karlgren, Bernhard：Compendium of Phonetics in Ancient and Archaic Chinese, *Bulletin of the Museum of Far Eastern Antiquities* 22 (1954), 211 - 367.

Martin, Samuel E. ：The Phonemes of Ancient Chinese, supplement to *the Journal of the American Oriental Society* 16 (1953).

Pulleyblank, E. G. ：Late Middle Chinese, *Asia Major* XV, 2 (1970), 197 - 239, and XVI, 1 - 2 (1971), 121 - 168.

——：The Analysis of Vowel Systems, *Acta Linguistica Hafniensia* (Copenhagen) Vol. XIV, No. 1 (1972), 39 - 62.

Stimson, Hugh M. ：*The Jongyuan In Yunn*, New Haven, Conn. 1966.

——：F. S. Hsueh'sPhonology of Old Mandarin (book review), *Language* Vol. 53, No. 4(1977), 940 - 944.

——：Old Mandarin Dialects, Old Pekingese, and the Rhymes of the Zhongyuan yinyun, *Proceedings of Symposium on Chinese Linguistics*, 1977 Linguistic Institute of the Linguistic Society of America, Xuesheng Book Co. (Taipei), 1978, 221 - 232.

Ting, Pang-hsin：F. S. Hsueh's Phonology of Old Mandarin, (book review), *Journal of American Criental Society* Vol. 100, No. 1 (1980), 94.

音韻學二題**

一、漫談漢語音韻學與音韻理論

多年來我從事漢語音韻的研究，采用的理論和方法與常見的做法不大一樣，因此有人説我的做法太怪。這使我覺得也許有必要多説幾句，藉以證明我的做法既與當代音韻學理論符合，也與漢語韻書分聲析韻時所呈現的道理是完全一致的。

1.1 研究漢語音韻的目的

研究漢語音韻的人，可能有不同的目的，因此各有偏得。約而言之，可舉出下列三類：

1）以音值爲本，尋求妥善的“拼音”方式。此法始於歐洲，以拉丁字母爲拼音符號。但不同的語言往往各有不同的“音值”，學者們就衹好增添新標音符號，集成了“國際音標”。然而爲了實用，拼音文字不可能使用太多及太罕見的拼音符號，因此就有了“從寬/從嚴”的説法。研究漢語的學者也多采用此法，但未見有人爲“寬/嚴”下過清楚的定義，似乎由各人視情況決定。這就可見各類拼音文字不一定真的都是“音值”性的。

2）研究語言的通性及其共有的規律。二十世紀中期，歐美學者提出了“一般語言學”（亦稱“理論語言學”）的概念，認爲不同的語言都有深層的共性，因而提出一些可用於各種語言的“規律”，例如“音位對比”“區别性特徵”，以及稍後對“音節模式”的肯定（在此之前“音節模式”不受重視）等等。這類規律自然也可以應用於漢語的研究，藉以證實其正確性或是否須要修正，當然更希望能發現新的規律。

3）專注於研究漢語的音系及其演變。這種研究一般都有兩個目的：分析

** 原刊《語言科學》2009 年第 4 期。

某一時期的漢語音系以及其來龍去脉。做這種研究的人,有的以"音值"爲根據,有的以"音位"爲根據。後者比較抽象,不十分計較所使用的標音符號,衹重視其相互的對比關係。

研究漢語音韻,當然不限於上述三種目的,但限於本文討論的範圍,姑且不再多説。這三類研究,雖然目的有别,做法却常有糾葛。有些人未認清他人的研究目的而亂加批評,或未認清自己的研究目的而使用不當的做法。

1.2 漢語音系研究與音位學的關係

研究漢語音韻者,當然各有自擇的目的。我選擇的是上述第三種(薛1990、1992)。説來也是一個巧合。我留美時(20世紀60年代)選讀的是所謂"一般語言學",在選修"音位學"時,驚奇地感覺到,其中的道理與"等韻學"的做法極爲相似。進一步思考,使我領悟到,《切韻》《中原音韻》之類的韻書,在分聲析韻等方面反映出來的道理,也都是"音位性"的。因此就采用這種理論分析《中原音韻》(薛1986、1990),而且嚴格遵守漢語音節四音段的傳統説法(我以"(C)(M)V(E)"表示這種分段模式;當時歐美學者都還不很重視音節模式),從此就改行做漢語音韻學研究了。下文簡略説明我研究漢語音系的看法與做法。

任何語言都有其特定不二的音系。要推論其音系,先要認識"音位對比"的重要性。"音位"已經是一個很普通的名詞了,但是不同的人對其含義仍有不同的認知。當初提出這個説法的人可能衹是説:爲一個語言標音時,不必過分堅持音值,因爲某些不同的音值可能衹是互補的"同位音",合併起來可以簡化其拼寫方式。但我認爲"音位"這個觀念絶不限於簡化拼音,同位音組合後固然是音位,没有同位音的個别"音值"也是"音位"。重要的是它們都有"對比"的功能,而這種對比才是構成音系的必要條件。如果不把一組同位音認作一個音位,就無法推證出任何語言的正確音系。

爲了説明這個簡單的道理,我們姑且以大家都熟悉的"漢語標準語"爲例。在通行的漢語拼音裹,顯然衹有一個低元音"a"。例如:

天 tian/貪 tan/臺 tai;加 jia/他 ta;江 jiang/剛 gang/高 gao

問題是,在這些不同的音節裹,"a"果真代表相同的音值嗎?善於區别音值的人,一定知道這不可能。不會説漢語的外國人更會讀出不同的聲音來。例如:你寫下你姓 Wang,美國人就會叫你“萬先生”;你説你姓“王”,他們才會叫你“Mr. Wong”。又如:Wade-Giles 式的漢語拼音把“天”字拼爲 tien,但“貪”字則拼爲 tan,顯然也不認爲那兩個音節的元音相同。爲什麽“漢語拼音”可以用單一的“a”代表好多個不同的“音值”呢?因爲那些不同的音值都是音位/a/的“同位音”,分别在不同的情況下出現,形成互補,所以不構成對比。把它們合而爲一,才能反映出説這種語言的人群所共有的語感(例如“天”“貪”互韻)。音位/a/的那些同位音是如何互補的呢?説起來很自然也很簡單。在没有韻尾的情况下,這個低元音自然是居中的“央低元音”[ʌ],例如“他”;但在有韻尾的時候,就會因受其“同化”而移動,例如“山該”之類的音節,因其韻尾爲前音,故其韻腹元音前移而變爲“前低元音”[æ]。同理,韻尾爲後音的音節,例如“高剛”等,其韻腹元音就會後移而變爲“後低元音”[ɑ]。韻頭對韻腹也有影響,例如,“天”是細音字,其韻腹元音就上移而變爲[ɛ]。這些音值性的變動,都未構成對比,故可合爲一個音位。漢語拼音衹用一個“a”代表這許多不同的音值,是很高明的做法。設計者可能没有想到音位問題,但漢語音系的潛在力量把他們帶上了這條路。(他們也許知道“音位”,但以爲衹是簡化拼寫而已。)

然而在如何拼寫高元音時,他們設定了[ï、i、u、ü、e、o]等六個高元音(又似乎把“ï”“i”合爲一音,也把“u”“ü”合而爲一),最後兩個又似乎介於高元音和中元音(例如“車 che”,“多 duo”)之間,這就完全違背了音位對比原則了。但這也難怪,因爲他們的目的是實用而非音系。爲了遷就外國人對符號及其讀音的習慣,也爲了印刷和打字的方便,他們的做法是完全可以理解的。但如果爲了本國人的語感,就必須遵守音系理論。從這個角度看,這種拼音法造成了下列四條理論性的難題:

一是互韻的字必有相同的韻基。這是構擬古音的人共守的原則,但“漢語拼音”却把“今 jin,真 zhen”和“留 liu,樓 lou”等兩兩互押的字拼成含有不同的韻基。爲什麽古人押韻的字必須含有相同的韻基,而我們自己説的話却不遵守這個原則呢?

二是漢語音節分爲“開、齊、合、撮”四類,即所謂“四呼”。這種分類的定義非常簡單,即“没有介音,或帶有三種介音中的某一種”。但常見的拼音方式都没有注意這個原則,因此常見的“四呼”定義都是:“開口呼没有介音,但雖然没有介音,如果元音是 i、u、ü,也不算開口。齊齒呼的介音是 i,但没有介音時,如果元音是 i,也是齊齒。……”這種定義真够囉唆的,但更不合理的是,竟然把“四呼”和元音扯在一起了,破壞了“四呼”的真實定義。

三是北方官話有一個特别現象,即“兒化韻”。例如:兒化後“真 zhen”與“枝 zhi”就變成爲同音(zheir)了,而且也就跟兒化後的“鷄 ji、今 jin、駒 jü、黑 hei”等互押了。這類例子非常多,可知這種現象必然有一定的音變規律,但在常見的拼音方式上是無法解説的。

四是音位的分布都是平衡對應的。尤其是元音的分布,通常都以“高低前後”爲基準而形成幾何式的圖型(這是聽覺神經的自然反映)。漢語拼音衹有一個低元音,但却有六個高元音。其中 i、ü、e 同屬前音,ï 獨爲央音,u、o 爲後音。這顯然不平衡,也跟低元音很不配稱。如果把此處的 e、o 劃歸中元音(即與“車 che”和“國 guo”的元音同類),就更不合理了,因爲違背了押韻原則(“金”“針”互韻,“留”“侯”互韻。)

要解決上述這些難題,就必須接受音位學的觀點。一旦采用了這種觀點與做法,我們就會發現,那些高元音其實都是同位音,應該合爲一個音位。更驚人的是,其組合的原理與過程,跟那些音值性低元音的組合幾乎完全相同。“支思”類的音節没有韻頭也没有韻尾,其韻腹顯然是“央高元音”;但“黑根”之類的音節,韻尾爲前音,因而韻腹也就變爲“前高元音”了;“侯紅”之類的音節,韻尾爲後音,其韻腹自然也後移而變爲“後高元音”。韻頭也有促使韻腹略微上移的作用,例如“今”與“真”互韻,“留”與“侯”互韻。唯一與低元音的同位音組合不同的是,在没有韻尾的情况下,高元音也會隨着韻頭前後移動,例如“衣”yi、“迂”yü、“屋”wu 等。這些現象自然使得那些音值性的高元音成爲同位音,因而也就合成一個音位了。這就順理成章地解決了上述那些理論性的問題①。

① 高元音音位化以後,上述四難題迎刃而解。兒化所引起的音變,根據北京“内城話”的讀法,可以用公式表達如下:

$$\begin{Bmatrix} \text{ø} \\ \text{n} \end{Bmatrix} \longrightarrow \text{y} / \quad \begin{Bmatrix} \text{ɨ} \\ \text{a} \end{Bmatrix} \_\_\_\_ \text{r}$$

*韻母爲/wɨ/(u)者除外。

(轉下頁)

1.3 結語

學術研究互相批評,本來是好事,是促成進步的必要條件。但有時却見意氣之爭而相互攻擊(甚至在網上匿名亂説),而非提出理論性的評説。這實在令人惋惜。這類争吵不必多説,我衹擬從"研究目的"的角度,稍述個人的看法。

一、近幾年有人提出,介音"i"應劃屬聲母(如 Duanmu 1990、2000 等,相關討論還可參見孫景濤[2006])。這是理論性的看法,不是音值問題。這將使聲母數目大增,而且必須説明聲母是單一的音位還是幾個音位的合體。但更重要的是,必須先説明這種分析法爲何比傳統的分法更好。另一新説法是介音"ü"應分爲"i、u"兩段。這個説法似乎跟等韻學的"開/合"與"洪/細"之分是一致的。但等韻的這個做法是標示分圖與分等的,而非分割介音。"四呼"之説起於明代,可見其時的音韻學者是把"撮口"和其他三呼視爲平等的。藉用"區别性特徵"的觀點看,也可以説"iu"代表兩個不同的成分,介音的區分取決於它們是否分别或同時出現。總而言之,爲漢語音韻提出新分析法是好事,但必須先説明,爲什麽某些傳統分析法是不好的,而不是盲目地遵循某些歐美學者的"新理論"①。

(接上頁)即韻腹爲高或低元音之音節,若其韻尾爲零或 n,兒化時皆改以 y(i)爲韻尾。又:根據這樣的分析,北京話衹有三個以"高中低"爲對比的元音音位/ɨ、e、a/。"十三轍"時代仍保留著"乜斜"和"梭坡"的對比,故有四個元音音位/ɨ、e、o、a/,是以"高中低前央後"爲對比的菱形分布。但高低兩個元音都無前後對比,/e、o/兩個前後元音都無高低對比,所以也可以把那兩個前後元音看作低元音。這就衹有"高低前央後"的對比了,因而省去了"中"作爲對比的角色。這是我以前分析《中原音韻》和"等韻圖"時,都將其元音分爲一高三低的緣故(1985、1990)。

① 雖然《切韻》類韻書都是音位性的,但那衹是語感的自然反映。所用的反切上下字,也是憑其"雙聲/叠韻"的語感隨意采字的。真正有意識的理論性的做法,始於"等韻"時代;竟然能於千餘年前,在不使用任何注音符號的情況下,用抽象的圖表顯示出當時標準漢語的音系。這是非常了不起的學術成就。Pulleyblank(2006)説,這是人類智慧發展史上的一大貢獻。約而言之,其貢獻有四:1) 首次列出音位,例如以三十六字母表明有多少個音位聲母;2) 標明音位的内涵成分,例如《韻鏡》僅以"五音、清濁"點明聲母的性質而不用代號;3) 以圖表顯示韻母的性質,例如分轉分等;4) 確定漢語音節的四段結構,例如以"洪細""開合"點明韻頭,以分"攝"點明韻尾的分類(韻腹是必有的音段,聲母已列於表端)。可嘆的是,這個了不起的成就,南宋以後就失傳了。有一次我跟王力先生談起這個問題,他説他早就認爲等韻學就是中國的音韻理論,所以常常勸告他的學生多多研究等韻。

二、在調查任何語言或方言時，自然必須以記録其音值爲起手。如果要爲那個語言設定拼音文字，采用“從寬”的做法，也是完全合理的，但那就不是音值問題了。在研究古代漢語時，猜測其音值更困難，也犯不着爲那個時代設立拼音文字。重要的是論證其音系。假如有相當可靠的韻書，例如《切韻》，就更有利於論證該時代的音系了，因爲那些韻書所反映的就是“音位對比”。然而有些人對音位的看法，迄今仍停留在“節省拼音符號”的階段，甚至有人説，要認定一個音位，必須先構擬其音值，即先構擬其同位音。這是一個很有勇氣的説法，但其實不然，也絶對做不到。説“做不到”，大概很多人都能理解，但爲什麽説“其實不然”呢？舉例來説，高本漢分析“支思”的韻母，説前者爲“舌尖後元音”，後者爲“舌尖前元音”。有人就用這個例子解説“音位”，這當然是對的，但説必須先有他的音值分類，然後才能定出音位，似乎忘記了七百年前周德清把“支思”合爲一韻了。他的語感告訴他這兩類字互押，而互押的字都含有相同的韻腹元音。其他韻書也是這樣的，所以我説它們都是音位性的，因此我們也衹能在音位對比的基礎上論證這些韻書所隱含的音系。用構擬的音值解讀這些韻書是不可能的①。

三、研究古代漢語，除了認清其音系，還有另一目的，即其歷時的演變。很早以前就有人説音變是有規律的，漢語的演變自然也不例外。但要想用嚴密的邏輯數理方式把漢語語音的演變表達出來，也不是容易的事。這要先推論出歷代韻書所隱含的音系才能做到。當然嚴格的音位系統衹能在有相當多的資料時才能推證出來，所以這種研究，恐怕最多衹能上推到《詩經》時代，即中國學者所説的“上古音”時代，再往上推就不管用了。研究“遠古漢語”(還能叫“漢語”嗎?)乃至“漢藏語”(假如漢語和藏語果真同源)，恐怕就衹能構擬了。

---

① 有些研究古代漢語的外國學者，在調查方言以構擬《切韻》時代的古音之後，雖然知道自己的構擬有許多與該類韻書不符合之處，也就滿足了，甚至説那些韻書是雜亂的、不可靠的或没有價值。有些中國學者也這麽做，也這麽説。但中國學者畢竟不能忘懷自家的傳統音韻學，所以常有人用自己或他人的擬音解説《切韻》及“等韻”，其結果自然是方枘圓鑿，無法合榫。最有名的例子，是羅常培先生爲“内外轉”所作的詮釋。他以高本漢的擬音爲根據，説“内外轉”是元音高低的分類。在董同龢先生和王力先生質疑之後，他也承認這個説法不妥。使我至爲敬佩的是，王力先生八十高齡時，還不忘一再公開宣稱，他對自己給這個問題所作的詮釋也不滿意。其人格之高尚，實在令人高山仰止。

好在構擬的原意本來就是“重建”(reconstruction),即將遠古無記録的語言發掘出來。這當然也是一種很有意義的考古。

二、再説“等韻”

研究漢語音韻的人都很重視等韻,構擬中古音或近古音,甚至上古音,都以某字某等爲説。但等韻究竟爲何物?却未見説清楚講明白。在尚未弄清楚其性質以前,就用來作證,豈非冒險?研究等韻的人當然也不少,但很少有人追問韻圖的基本道理是什麽。二十多年前,我曾寫過一篇説“内外轉”的論文(薛 1985),當時就覺得必須先説明其本質,而後才能説清楚“内外”的道理。大概所用的説法比較少見,能接受的人不多(王力先生似乎是唯一的例外[①]),使我覺得也許尋常閑談的方式比較好。近年來我對等韻中的某些問題,又有了些新看法,包括對“内外轉”説法的修正,因此想到寫此短文。韻圖多奥秘,且付笑談中!

2.1 “等韻圖”的起源與依據

“等韻圖”原稱“切韻圖”,但因“切韻”後來專指陸法言的《切韻》,爲免誤會而改稱。這種韻圖最早出現於晚唐,晚於陸氏《切韻》大約三百年,這是大家都知道的。是什麽人創始的呢?鄭樵在《七音略》序中説:“梵僧欲以其教傳之天下,故爲此書……華僧從而定之。”這個説法是可信的。按常理説,這個梵僧一定是個深通聲明學的專家,到中國以後,也必然學會了當時通用的漢語,但他絶不可能仔細分析過《切韻》而設圖,可能也没有那個功力(直到現在我們也都没那種能力)。所以他設計的韻圖,一定是以他學會的那種漢語爲根據的。他爲何不用拼音符號呢?(佛典的《悉曇章》已傳入中土。)這是因爲唐人慣用漢字,重視“反切”,雖有拼音法也不易爲時人接受,故衹好與“從而定之”的華僧一同設計“切韻圖”,並由華僧填字了。但唐人專重“切韻”,除此之外,别無他類韻書,故衹能按《切韻》類韻書填字。這就造成了很多認證其音韻體系的困難。

---

① 參見薛鳳生(1990)的魯譯序言和薛鳳生(1999)唐作藩先生的序言。

2.2“等韻圖”的外表與內涵

用圖表顯示字韻的異同,必然是也必須是非常嚴格的。例如:爲北京話畫一張音節對照表,用在別的方言上就不合轍。所以要查證等韻圖所依據的語言,就應當也祇能根據其圖式,並從而推算出其立圖的規則。韻圖以漢字爲各類聲母的代號,連零聲母(喻)都算在內;韻母則以圖形表示。那個梵僧顯然已經看出了漢語的韻母結構,所以標示出“開、合、洪、細”之別,顯示出與元音相配的介音,正如同聲母包括喻母,也很自然地把零介音(既“開”且“洪”)包括在內;無尾韻與帶尾韻的對比,自然也顯示出零韻尾的對比功能。這三種“零”大有功用,讓我們可以用一個最簡單的公式(C)(M)V(E)表達出漢語所有音節的結構模式。(近三四十年來,美歐學者才重視音節模式,所倡導的CV Phonology,性質頗似漢語的音節模式,但較煩瑣。)

早期韻圖分四十三“轉”而不言“攝”,但其排列的順序及“內/外”標示,已顯示出“攝”的觀念。這是韻圖所不可少的觀念,即以韻尾的異同分“攝”,所以後來韻圖都標明這種分類。形式上每圖皆分爲四等,依照《切韻》類韻書填字,有的是四個等皆填仍不够用,祇好另開一圖(例如外轉二十五及二十六轉“宵”韻字),有的則非各等都有字,最極端的是“江”攝,祇在二等有字。“轉”又分爲“內/外”兩類。意義何在?前人早有“內外轉之分在有無真二等”的說法,這是對的,但祇說出其區分,没說出其含義何在。其實這是一個巧合,因爲外轉各攝碰巧在二等都有字;假如四等也都有字,豈不也可以說“區分在有無真四等”?所以我說這祇是一個巧合,没有理論性。爲了說明“內/外”之分實有音韻性的含義,我近年才思考出其含義何在。簡言之,即“內轉者同轉同韻,外轉者同轉異韻”。(此處所謂同韻與否,皆以等韻音系爲據,非指《切韻》。又:所謂外轉同轉異韻,是指四等俱全或至少三個等皆有字而言。如果一等和四等皆爲空位,自然就不會有異韻了,例如江攝和假攝,說見下節。)

順便談談“等”的含意。常見的說法把“等”看作“等級”。例如江永曾說過:“一等洪大,二等次大,三四皆細,而四尤細。”說法過於籠統。我認爲“等”指的祇不過是按“列”分“類”而已,重點在區別韻母,尤其是韻腹;根據的是等韻時代的元音系統(不是《切韻》音系,否則就更複雜了)。製圖者先按低元音的分布列出四個“等”,其中惟有“三等”是細音,韻腹則與“二等”相同。這就是外轉的理論形態。内轉各韻類僅以洪細分成兩列,爲了省事不另設圖,衹利用外轉圖式中的一等與三等位置而已。餘見下節。

2.3“内/外”轉新説

仔細比對一下“内/外”兩種韻圖,可以看出其列字規格果然不同。外轉的四個等皆可列字,雖然實際上不一定都有字。内轉則衹可在一等和三等列字,但也不一定兩等都有字,特殊的是,在其齒音聲母下,二等與四等也可列字,但這些字皆與其三等字同類,衹因聲母不同而借位罷了。知道了“内/外”在圖形上的差别,就可瞭解爲什麼它們分稱“内/外”了。據説“轉”是佛經轉唱的術語。韻圖把細音字全列在三等,因此内轉各攝的一等與三等字元音相同,衹有“洪/細”之分,轉唱不出本韻,故爲“内”。外轉則不然,二等與三等雖然也衹是“洪/細”之别,但與一等及四等都有各自不同的元音,轉唱時必須换韻,故爲“外”。但這牽涉到“臻攝”,就其列字方式及《四聲等子》的“辨内外轉例”看,臻攝完全符合内轉的定義,但却被劃歸外轉,因而得有“内外轉各八攝”的説法。但把臻攝劃歸外轉的唯一理由是:列於二等的“臻”類韻字,在《切韻》裏不與三等的“真”類韻字互爲反切,成爲所謂“真二等”(嘗見擬上古音者每謂二等韻的字如何如何,不知他們認爲包括此類“真二等”否?如不包括,則顯然認爲臻攝與其他外轉攝不同)。其實這也是一個巧合。從音變的角度看,我們有理由相信,不管“臻”類字在《切韻》時代是什麼樣的,在等韻時代之前,必然已經變得與“真”類韻同韻了,所以才會列入同攝。再從另一個音變角度看《切韻》時代互爲對比的“莊/章”兩系聲母,在等韻時代之前就已合併了。這時因爲原來“洪/細”兩配的“莊”系聲母變爲衹配洪音韻母(即丢掉了介音 i,與三等字脱離關係),而“章”系聲母仍然衹配細音韻母,因此兩系變成互補而合爲“照”系。這就使得内轉各攝原來的所謂“假二等”字都丢掉了其原有的細音,也就都變成“真二等”了。我們當然不能説,因爲這個音變“内轉”各攝全都變成“外轉了”!但説臻攝實屬内轉應是合理的。這也完全符合上文爲“内/外”轉所下的新定義。

附帶説明:羅常培(1933)在論“内外轉”時,也把臻攝歸類爲内轉,但他是根據早期韻圖版本的差異重新分内外的,與我根據音變理論和韻圖形式説臻攝應屬内轉,是完全不同的。但他認爲“内轉各攝皆含高元音,外轉各攝皆含低元音”的説法,倒是很有意思的。這從《四聲等子》的“内外混等”中可以看出來。由於“江宕/果假/曾梗”三類内外混等,十六攝就變爲十三攝了,但無礙於内外之分。“曾梗”合併後顯然屬外轉(《等子》説是“鄰韻借用”),“果假”也應屬同類。但“江宕”則比較特别,已經合爲同韻(《等子》説是“江陽借形”),所以應屬内轉,成爲一個低元音内轉攝了。假如我們姑且撇開“江宕”攝不算,則其餘六個内轉攝(包括臻攝)皆含高元音,而與之對應的六個外轉攝恰巧也都是含低元音的。這個情况可謂正合羅先生的説法,可惜“内外混等”來得太晚。當然也可以説,羅先生頗有先知之明。

2.4“等韻”的貢獻與流傳

約而言之,等韻對漢語音韻學有兩大貢獻:其一是以高妙的韻圖記録下晚唐時期的漢語音系。這使我們可以有信心地推論由《切韻》時代到等韻時代經過哪些音變,以及從等韻時代到《中原音韻》時代又經過哪些音變。這對瞭解漢語音韻演變史是非常重要的。另一貢獻是開創了理論性的漢語音韻學。明顯地列出聲母音位,並且指出造成這些音位相互對比的内在特徵。較含蓄的是,用分圖、分等、分轉和分攝等方法,表示韻母的不同。這樣就確定了漢語的音節模式,奠定了漢語音韻學的基礎。即使到後代,在經過許多音變之後,原來的等韻圖形已不適用,這些理論原則仍是研究漢語音韻及漢語史的必要條件。明代學者把韻母分成“韻頭、韻腹、韻尾”三段,又用“開、齊、合、撮”分别指名四種不同的韻頭,即所謂“四呼”,根據的就是等韻的道理。

由於唐人獨重《切韻》及其反切,等韻出現之後,就變成了《切韻》的附庸(類似“索引”),埋没了其所紀録的漢語及其分析語音的理論。這對研究《切韻》或等韻本身都是不利的。頗爲難解的是,傳承等韻的華僧,後來也都把注意力全放在韻圖如何安排《切韻》中諸類字的反切上,死記硬背,還編了許多“門法”和歌訣,教小和尚背誦,全不知也全不在意等韻究竟爲何物。比較能反映出等韻性質的,衹有據説是出現在宋遼時期的《四聲等子》。該書以“攝”爲基礎,併四十三轉爲二十圖。看來似乎太大膽了,其實這正是等韻所隱含的基本道理。由於離初期等韻不遠(大約一百年吧),雖然已經有了幾個音變(例如“内外混等”),這兩個時期的音系還是相當接近的。能瞭解音變原理和《四聲等子》的圖式,也就可以認清等韻學的真相了。

清末民初,歐式"音值性語言學"傳入中國,高本漢先生也以"構擬"法研究古代漢語,中國學者群起從風,等韻學的基本原理幾乎無人注意了。(王力先生又是例外,一再説等韻學是中國的音韻學理論。)然而世事茫茫難意料,歐美學者在二十世紀三十年代先有"音位"説,五十年代又有音位性對比的"區别性特徵"説,七十年代更覺悟到"音節模式"的重要性。這些"新理論"的想法,都與等韻學的基本原理不謀而合。看來等韻學也許將會有復活的一天。

參考文獻

羅常培　《釋内外轉》《史語所集刊》第四本第二分册,1933 年,第 206—226 頁。

孫景濤　《介音在音節中的地位》,《語言科學》2006 年第 2 期,第 44—52 頁。

薛鳳生　《等韻學之原理與内外轉之含義》,《語言研究》1985 年第 1 期。又見薛鳳生(1999:24—45)。

薛鳳生　《北京音系解析》,北京語言學院出版社,1986 年。

薛鳳生　《〈中原音韻〉音位系統》,北京語言學院出版社,1990 年。

薛鳳生　《從等韻到〈中原音韻〉》,《語言學論叢》第 17 輯,商務印書館,1992 年。

薛鳳生　《漢語音韻史十講》,華語教學出版社,1999 年。

Duanmu, San　1990　*A Formal Study of Syllable, Tone, Stress and Domain in Chinese Languages*. Ph. D. dissertation. Cambridge, Mass: MIT.

Duanmu, San　2000　*The Phonology of Standard Chinese*. Oxford: Oxford University Press.

Pulleyblank, E. G.　1998　Qieyun and Yunjing: The essential foundation for Chinese Historical Linguistics. *The Journal of the American Oriental Society*, Vol. 118.

A Comparative Study of E. G. Pulleyblank and F. S. Hsueh's Theories on *Dengyun* (等韻) Phonology**

I. Introduction

A. General remarks on *dengyun* phonology

B. Outline of paper

C. The need for LMC & EMC

1. the source of *dengyun* rhyme tables

2. LMC leads to understanding of EMC

II. Vowel System of LMC

A. Hsueh's system

1. 4vowels—front/back distinction

2. syllable makeup—(C) (M) V (E)

B. Pulleyblank's system

1. 2 vowels—high/low distinction

2. system of palatalization

III. Inner/Outer Distinction

A. Pulleyblank's opinion

** 未刊稿，中文題爲《蒲立本與薛鳳生等韻音系理論之比較》，據作者打印稿編輯。

1. Luo Changpei's theory—high/low vowel
2. not necessary for reconstruction

B. Hsueh's analysis

1. purpose—locate retroflex sibilant initials
2.

C. Importance of distinction for reconstruction

IV. Conclusions

A. General evaluation of Pulleyblank

—strengths & weaknesses

B. General evaluation of Hsueh

—strengths & weaknesses

C. Final comments

Hsueh's vowel system:

	front	central	back
high		ɨ	
low	e	a	o

outer		inner A.		inner B.
Ⅰ	o	Ⅰ	ɨ	o
Ⅱ	a	Ⅱ	-	-
Ⅲ	a	Ⅲ	ɨ	o
Ⅳ	e	Ⅳ	-	-

Syllabic structure: (C) (M) V (E)

outer		inner A.		inner B.
Ⅰ	(W)o(E)	Ⅰ	(W)ɨ(E)	(W)o(E)

Ⅱ	(W)a(E)	Ⅱ	—	—
Ⅲ	y(W)a(E)	Ⅲ	y(W)ɨ(E)	y(W)o(E)
Ⅳ	(W)e(E)	Ⅳ	—	—

*labialization (*he*/*kai*) can occur in any grade

*palatalization [y] only occurs in grade Ⅲ

Pulleyblank's vowel system:

	front	central	back
high		e	
low		a	

outer		inner	
Ⅰ	a	Ⅰ	e
Ⅱ	a	Ⅱ	-
Ⅲ	a	Ⅲ	e
Ⅳ	a	Ⅳ	-

medial system: (initials)

	Kai			He		
Ⅰ	K	T	P*	Ku	Tu	Pu/P*
Ⅱ	Kj	Tr	P*	Kw	Trw	P*
Ⅲ	Kj	Tri	Pi	Ky	Try	Fjy
Ⅳ	Kji	Ti	Pji	Kjy	Ty	

*vacillation of labial initials between *hekou&kaikou**

*labialization [u, w] occurs in grade Ⅰ

*palatalization [y. i. j] occurs in grades Ⅱ, Ⅲ, & Ⅳ

從等韻到《中原音韻》*

我研究《中原音韻》是從六十年代開始的，在一九六八年曾寫了一篇較長的論文，後來交給了荷蘭海牙一個出版社，那是西方出版語言學著作的一個主要的出版社。等印出來已經到了一九七五年[①]。從一九七五年到現在，又過了好多年了，我對《中原音韻》的看法有了不少改變，但是我的新看法還没有寫成文章。今天藉這個機會，談一談我的新看法。

我研究《中原音韻》，主要是從歷史發展趨勢來研究它，看標準漢語發展到《中原音韻》這個環節出現了哪些新現象，到了現代又經過哪些音變。往上，聯繫到早期等韻時期的音韻系統；往下，聯繫到現代的北京話。

我分析《中原音韻》所用的方法和我分析現代北京話所用的方法是一樣的（參看薛 1986）。在分析現代北京話音位系統時用了四個原則：第一是音節分段的原則，即每一音節可分爲聲母、韻頭（介音）、韻腹（主要元音）、韻尾（收聲）這四部分。一個音節中可以没有聲母、韻頭、韻尾，但必須有韻腹。第二是押韻的原則。在任何語言中，嚴格地説，押韻的音節都含有相同的主要元音及後加成分，漢語也不例外，因此我們必須把相押的字解釋爲含有相同的韻腹和韻尾，即含有共同的"韻基"。第三是雙聲原則，凡是本地人認爲是雙聲的字，我們都必須把它們解釋爲含有相同的聲母。第四是音節分類的原則。傳統音韻學中有兩種分類法：其一是根據韻頭分出開合和洪細的不同，這是四呼分類；其二是根據韻尾分類，分出"收噫、收嗚、抵腭、穿鼻"等，這是韻類的分類。根據上面這四條原則所得到的分析結果，可以具體地表現出説任何一個漢語方言的人群的語感，所以它們不僅適用於分析現代北京話，也適用於分析古代的漢語，所以我們研究《中原音韻》的時候也應該遵守它們。

---

* 原刊《語言學論叢》第 17 輯，商務印書館，1992 年，收入《漢語音韻史十講》。

本文原是 1985 年 4 月 8 日在北京大學中文系所作的報告，由耿振生、郭力根據録音整理成文。

① 即 F. S. Hsueh：Phonology of Old Mandarin，The Hague，1975.

所謂等韻的語音系統，指的是早期的韻圖《韻鏡》《七音略》的語音系統。對這些材料，人們的看法是不一樣的，多數人説那些材料是根據一個抽象的設計，用來表示《切韻》或《唐韻》或《廣韻》的語音系統的，不是根據一個實際的語言而作的。我的看法與此不同，我認爲等韻本身代表一個獨立的音系，它是根據一個特定的語言設計的，這個特定語言大概是唐代的"普通話"。等韻作者是在製成圖表以後才根據《切韻》一類的韻書填字的，由於早期韻書的音系和唐代"普通話"的音系並不一樣，而韻圖的作者想把它們調和起來，即把《切韻》音系所有而等韻音系所無的音韻現象也想方設法地安排到韻圖中去，因此就造成了韻圖上的許多矛盾現象，出現了重紐、重韻等問題。我認爲等韻音系的元音系統含有一個高元音/ɨ/與三個分爲前/e/、央/a/、後/ɔ/的低元音。就韻母的性質説，韻圖的結構應如下表[①]：

攝 等	内轉甲式 （通止遇流深）	内轉乙式 （果曾宕）	外轉甲式 （梗江蟹效山咸假）	外轉乙式 （臻）
Ⅰ	-(w)ɨ(E)	-(w)ɔ(E)	-(w)ɔ(E)	-(w)ɨ(E)
Ⅱ	……	……	-(w)a(E)	-(w)ə(E)？
Ⅲ	-y(w)ɨ(E)	-y(w)ɔ(E)	-y(w)a(E)	-y(w)ɨ(E)
Ⅳ	……	……	-(w)e(E)	……

經過"内外混等"後，各攝的韻基形態應如下表：

遇-wiø	止-ɨy	流-ɨw	通-wɨ$\left\{\begin{matrix}\text{ŋ}\\ \text{k}\end{matrix}\right\}$		臻-ɨ$\left\{\begin{matrix}\text{n}\\ \text{t}\end{matrix}\right\}$	深-ɨ$\left\{\begin{matrix}\text{m}\\ \text{p}\end{matrix}\right\}$
果 假-$\left\{\begin{matrix}\text{ɔ}\\ \text{a}\end{matrix}\right\}$ø	蟹-$\left\{\begin{matrix}\text{ɔ}\\ \text{a}\\ \text{e}\end{matrix}\right\}$y	效-$\left\{\begin{matrix}\text{ɔ}\\ \text{a}\\ \text{e}\end{matrix}\right\}$w	江 宕-ɔ$\left\{\begin{matrix}\text{ŋ}\\ \text{k}\end{matrix}\right\}$	曾 梗e-$\left\{\begin{matrix}\text{ɔ}\\ \text{a}\\ \text{e}\end{matrix}\right\}$$\left\{\begin{matrix}\text{ɲ}\\ \hat{\text{k}}\end{matrix}\right\}$	山-$\left\{\begin{matrix}\text{ɔ}\\ \text{a}\\ \text{e}\end{matrix}\right\}$$\left\{\begin{matrix}\text{n}\\ \text{t}\end{matrix}\right\}$	咸-$\left\{\begin{matrix}\text{ɔ}\\ \text{a}\\ \text{e}\end{matrix}\right\}$$\left\{\begin{matrix}\text{m}\\ \text{p}\end{matrix}\right\}$

至於《中原音韻》，大家的看法没有什麽分歧，都相信它是根據當時一個實際語言而作的，這個語言是當時雜劇作家們所依據的一個方言，到底是哪個地方的方言，看法就各有不同了。我認爲，《中原音韻》所記録的那個方言是現代北京話中所謂"口語"的祖語。以前人們説，漢語發展到《中原音韻》時代起了一個大轉變，形成了所謂官話，《中原音韻》就反映了這種官話。我的看法和這

① 關於等韻音系的較詳細的討論，參看拙作《試論等韻學之原理與内外轉之含義》。

説法不大一樣,我認爲語言是自然發展的,是漸進的,而在什麽時候有一部韻書把它記下來,則是一種社會性的偶然現象。元朝時候的語言跟它以前一段時期的語言不可能是截然不同的,而是慢慢變過來的。因爲當時有一種新的文學形式發展起來了,所以有人編寫新韻書。有人説,周德清完全根據一個實際語言來寫《中原音韻》,不管以前的傳統(參看陸 1946)。其實也不盡然,他也考慮到古代一些情形。他在分韻部、分小韻、分聲調的時候是根據實際語言,而在安排韻部次第的時候,從東鍾韻到廉纖韻的安排跟《切韻》以來的韻書對韻部的安排大體是一致的,根據這一點,我覺得周德清對早期的音韻學有相當的瞭解。不過,除了韻部的安排以外,他更重視實際語言。

我們討論《中原音韻》,實際上就是看它的音系怎樣從等韻的音系轉變過來的。我們把《中原音韻》所代表的音韻系統與早期等韻的音韻系統相比較,就可以看出其間的轉變。今天衹講分韻方面的問題,由於時間關係,聲母問題就不講了。

根據韻尾的形態,《中原音韻》十九個韻部的情況如下:

韻尾收-ø 的韻部:支思、魚模、車遮、家麻、歌戈。

韻尾收-y 的韻部:齊微、皆來。

韻尾收-w 的韻部:尤侯、蕭豪。

韻尾收-n 的韻部:真文、先天、寒山、桓歡。

韻尾收-ŋ 的韻部:東鍾、庚青、江陽。

韻尾收-m 的韻部:侵尋、監咸、廉纖。

根據押韻的原則,收聲相同的不同韻部,其主要元音一定不一樣。從這個觀點看,既然收-n 的韻分成四個不同的韻部,就表明這個音系中音節的韻腹部分至少有四種不同的形態。我們給等韻音系定了四個主要元音:/ɨ、e、a、ɔ/,近代北方話十三轍也含有這四個元音,《中原音韻》處在兩個時代的中間,它的元音系統應該是相同的。

先天、寒山、桓歡這三韻的字在十三轍裏都屬言前轍。我們把這三個韻與等韻比較,可以看出它們都是由山攝演變出來的。寒山韻是原來的二等韻加上一等開口字,它們的韻腹是央低元音的可能性較大,所以我們説寒山韻的韻基是 an。桓歡韻是原來的一等合口字,一等韻的元音是 ɔ,我們很自然地認爲桓歡韻的韻基是 ɔn。先天韻是三、四等的合併,三等字裏輕脣音字轉到寒山韻了，其餘的三等字和四等字都不分了，聲母相同的已經成了同音字。這個演變的過程，我們猜是受到介音的影響：三等韻的主要元音由於受到同化作用的影響而向前移動，這時四等韻母已經産生了腭化介音，因此兩個等就合併了，我們把先天韻的韻基定爲en。

上述影響到韻母的音變，可以概括爲下列四條公式，它們的次序就代表這些音變發生的時代順序。

(1) y ⟶ ø/f____。(輕脣音字變爲洪音。)

(2) ø ⟶ y/____e。(四等韻字變爲細音。)

(3) a ⟶ e/y____。(三等與四等合韻。)

(4) ɔ ⟶ a/C____。(一等開口字變入二等。)

要是考慮到介音的關係，寒山韻本來是二等全部加上一等開口字。二等的喉牙音開口字這時已有了個腭化介音，所以寒山韻含有三個可能的韻母-an、-yan、-wan。二等喉牙音開口字的腭化可以概括爲：ø→y/C_a。這個音變必然發生在上述第三個音變之後與第四個音變之前，因爲這類字既未隨三等韻字進入先天韻，也未與變入寒山韻的一等喉牙音字相混。先天韻由三等字和四等字合併而成，這一韻中衹能有齊齒和撮口韻母，全是細音字，没有洪音字，韻母是-yen和-ywen。桓歡韻衹有一等合口字，韻母衹能是-wɔn。就介音的分配來説，我們也得認爲這三個韻部的主要元音必定不一樣。假如我們説寒山韻和桓歡韻有相同的韻基，那它們的合口字構成對比就不好解釋了。先天韻都是細音字，寒山韻也有細音字，其間差別也衹能是主要元音的差別。如果説這幾個韻部也和現代官話方言一樣，主要元音相同，衹是介音有差別，那就没有必要分成不同的韻部。周德清把它們分成三韻，顯然它們的韻基是不一樣的，它們必然含有不同的主要元音。

從等韻音系來推斷，我們説真文韻的韻基是ɨn。這一韻是從等韻的臻攝轉變過來的，我們知道臻攝的主要元音本來就是高元音，到了《中原音韻》時代，韻腹没發生什麽變化，還是高元音ɨ。

侵尋、監咸、廉纖這幾部是閉口韻。侵尋韻來自等韻的深攝，韻基是ɨm。深攝原衹有三等開口字，宋代以後産生了幾個一等字，如"怎"。個别方言中變出來幾個撮口字，如"尋"。這是極少的例外。監咸、廉纖的情況，跟寒山、桓歡、先天是完全一致的。這些韻來自咸攝,咸攝是獨攝,没有一等合口字,所以到《中原音韻》中没有相當於桓歡部的閉口韻部,也就是没有-ɔm 這樣一個韻基。咸攝的一等開口字併入了二等,成爲相當於寒山韻的監咸韻,它的二等開口喉牙音字也發生腭化現象,如同今天北方話裏“尴尬”本應念成 jiān jiè。二等開口喉牙音字的腭化現象是官話方言與非官話方言的重要差别之一。監咸韻正相當於寒山韻,它所包含的韻母是-am、-yam。廉纖韻是咸攝三等和四等的合併,和先天韻是相對的,韻基是 em。這一韻中也没有合口字,衹能有-yem 這一個韻母。

蕭豪韻是從效攝演變過來的。我以前認爲它的演變過程和山攝、咸攝是一致的,也就是説在某一個時期也含有三個不同的韻基。這個看法與押韻原則冲突,既然是有三個不同的韻基,爲什麽周德清把它們合在一起呢?爲什麽關漢卿、鄭光祖、白樸、馬致遠又把它們同押一韻呢?我當時爲瞭解釋疑母 ŋ 的存在,説《中原音韻》中的 ŋ 聲母存在於少數韻母之前,條件是未變入二等的一等開口字,即果攝與效攝的一等開口字。在其他情况下已經消失了。這樣,必須把蕭豪韻解釋成含有三個不同的韻基:ɔw、aw、ew,然後説韻母-ɔw 之前的疑母 ŋ 才得以保存,所以“傲”(疑母字)與“奥”(影母字)晚至《中原音韻》時代仍保持對立。這個解釋違背了押韻原則,但有助於解釋疑母的存在以及“高、交、嬌”的三重對立。我當時解釋説:在周德清記録的方言裏,-ɔw、-aw、-ew 的對立還存在,而在關漢卿、馬致遠等所用的方言裏已經没有這種差别了,也就是説周德清所記録的特定方言在演變上慢了一步,但他爲了表示那些大劇作家的押韻現象,還是把這類字放在一塊兒了。我這個説法後來受到耶魯大學的司徒修教授和臺灣大學的丁邦新教授的批評①,他們都指出我給蕭

① 司徒修所寫的書評即 Hugh M. Stimson:F. S. Hsueh's Phonology of Old Madarin,language Vol. 53,Part4 (1977). 丁邦新所寫的書評即 Panghsin Ting:F. S. Hsueh's Phonology of Old Madarin, Journal of American Oriental Society Vol. 100,No. Ⅰ(1980). 94. 他們兩位都意猶未盡,後來又分别各寫了一篇長文討論《中原音韻》的性質,即 Stimson:Old Mandarin Dialects,Old Pekinnese and the Rhymes of the Zhongyuan yinyun. in Cheng,Li,and Tang (ed):Proceedings of Symposium on Chinese Linguistics,1977, Linguistic Institute of the Linguistic Society of America,Taipei,1978,223 - 231. 丁邦新《與〈中原音韻〉相關的幾種方言現象》,刊於《“中央研究院”歷史語言研究所集刊》第五十二本第四分(1981),第 619—650 頁。

豪韻的構擬違背了自訂的押韻原則,而這個原則是不應違背的,所以蕭豪韻的韻基衹能是-aw,疑母問題是方言的影響。我對他們的批評非常感激,因爲他們迫使我重新思考這個問題。經過多年的思考之後,我現在的想法是,在《中原音韻》的音系裏,蕭豪韻確實衹應含有一個韻基,但這個韻基應是含有後元音的-ɔw,而不是含有央元音的-aw。這個説法既合音理,同時又對我們解釋疑母的存在更爲妥帖。效攝的一、二、三、四等原來含有三個不同的韻基,其後由於前、央兩個元音受韻尾-w 的同化影響向後移動,終於跟後元音 ɔ 合併起來了,$\left(\begin{Bmatrix}a\\e\end{Bmatrix}\longrightarrow ɔ/\_\_\_\_ w\right)$。因此蕭豪韻的韻基衹能是一個 ɔw。但在這個音變發生之前,疑母已經起了變化,概括地説,即除了外轉直音韻(果攝)與收嗚韻(效攝)的一等開口字,疑母完全消失。這個音變可以概括爲"$ŋ\rightarrow ø/\#\_\_\_\_x, x\neq ɔ(w)$"。這樣我們既能解釋少數疑母字存在的條件(包括歌戈韻裏"婀"與"我"的對比),又能解釋爲什麽效攝後來變成了一個韻。我覺得這解釋比從前的解釋要好些,而且更合音理。

江陽韻是江宕兩攝合併成的韻部。這類字直到現在仍自成韻部,一般都把它們的韻基寫作-ang,我以前也把《中原音韻》江陽韻的韻基擬作-aŋ。但後來覺得這個做法有點可疑,其一,這就等於説宕攝的字,包括一等合字,都變入江攝。就音理説,這是相當可疑的,因爲江宕兩攝同以舌根音爲韻尾,江攝的韻腹爲央低元音 a,宕攝的韻腹爲後低元音 ɔ,前者受韻尾的同化影響而變爲後者甚有可能,反之則不然。其二,這兩攝的入聲字後來都變入蕭豪或歌戈,這説明它們的韻腹是後元音 ɔ,也就是説,不惟宕攝的入聲字韻腹未變,而且江攝的入聲字也變同宕攝了。所以我現在相信江宕的"混等"實爲合韻,即江攝變同宕攝。這個音變的道理與前述效攝的合韻是一致的,因此江陽韻的韻基實爲 ɔŋ。這個讀法就音值説迄今未變,但由於音系結構的轉變,却必須寫作 aŋ 了①。

《中原音韻》裏衹有三個收舌根韻尾的韻,即東鍾、江陽、庚青,它們的韻腹

① 關於這個問題的理論性討論,請參看拙作《論音變與音位結構的關係》。這個問題實際上不限於江陽韻,蕭豪韻的韻基就音值説也仍爲/ɔw/,但由於音系的轉變,也必須改寫爲/aw/,這兩韻性質相近,因爲它們的韻尾含有共同的"區别特徵",即同屬"後音"[-anterior]。

應該是什麼形態呢？當初我既然毫不猶豫地認爲江陽韻的韻基是-aŋ，便進而根據結構對稱的觀點，把東鍾韻的韻腹定爲-ɔŋ，庚青韻的韻腹定爲-eŋ，因爲這樣我們就可以說，《中原音韻》的音系有一個特性：舌根韻尾衹配低元音。現在我的看法已經改變了，我認爲江陽韻的韻基應爲-ɔŋ，理由已在前文說明了。至於東鍾韻，我現在認爲它的韻腹衹能是-ɨŋ，因爲這一韻的字來自通攝，全屬合口，在現在的北京音系裏屬東中轍，韻腹仍爲高元音，說它們的韻腹由等韻時代的高元音變爲《中原音韻》時代的後低元音，然後又變爲現代的高元音，音理上顯然可疑，較合理的說法是它們的韻腹一直未變。把庚青韻的韻腹解釋爲-eŋ倒是完全合理的。這一韻的字是由梗曾兩攝變來的，原來的曾攝是後低元音一、三等字，梗攝是外轉二、三、四等字，由於"内外混等"的關係，它們合成一個標準的外轉攝，過去多數人都認爲梗曾兩攝的韻尾也是舌根音 ŋ 與 k，這就等韻音系說是可疑的，因爲收其他韻尾的字衹構成兩攝或至多三攝，而收舌根音的字竟構成五攝之多。在《切韻》及上古音裏，梗曾兩攝的字與江宕兩攝的字也有明顯的差異。等韻音系形成之後，江攝的韻腹因受韻尾的影響而後移併入宕攝，兩攝的入聲字在"口語"音裏都變爲收嗚（變入蕭豪），但梗曾兩攝字則相反，由"混等"而進一步合併爲含有前元音的庚青韻，其入聲字在"口語"音裏都改讀爲收噫（變入皆來或齊微），我們因此可以知道它們的韻尾原非舌根音，應爲舌面音 ɲ 與 k̂，在這個基礎上說舌根韻尾影響江攝的韻腹由 a 變 ɔ，舌面音韻尾影響梗曾兩攝的韻腹由 ɔ 及 a 前移而變爲 e$\left(\begin{Bmatrix}\text{ɔ}\\ \text{a}\end{Bmatrix}\rightarrow \text{e}/__\text{ɲ}\right)$就很順理成章了。同時說入聲字的舌根韻尾 k 變爲收嗚，而舌面韻尾 k̂ 變爲收噫，也是完全合乎音理的。經過韻腹的演變以後，庚青韻與江陽韻的對比，就主要由韻腹的差别來擔負了，韻尾的差别變爲次要，因此舌面鼻音也就消失了。這個韻尾在北方話和南方話裏的轉變不一樣，在北方官話裏變爲舌根音 ŋ，因此在《中原音韻》之後，這類字得以併入東鍾，形成十三轍的東中轍；但在南方官話裏，原來的梗曾陽聲字都變到真文韻裏了，所以在皮黄戲的押韻裏，原屬庚青韻的字却與真文韻字相押。這也間接證明原來梗曾兩攝是收舌面鼻音韻尾的，這個韻尾在很多方言如北京話裏後移爲 ŋ，在南方官話裏則前移而變爲 n，因爲它是舌尖鼻音與舌根鼻音之間的一個鼻音。

皆來韻和齊微韻都是收噫韻，皆來韻來自蟹攝，由於蟹攝也是一個類似山攝的標準外轉攝，我們猜想它的演變方式跟山攝、咸攝是一致的。把前文討論過的有關韻母的音變應用到蟹攝上，我們可以設想它後來也形成了三個類似桓歡、寒山、先天的韻部，即 wɔy、$\left(\begin{Bmatrix}\text{y}\\ \text{w}\end{Bmatrix}\right)$ay 與 y(w)ey，但在《中原音韻》裏，衹有皆來韻是來自蟹攝的。細審皆來韻的字，我們可以看出它們完全符合韻基爲-ay 的那一類，即它們包括了全部二等字及一等開口字，可能變爲 wɔy 的一等合口字以及可能變作 y(w)ey 的三、四等字，都出現在齊微韻裏。我認爲這表示蟹攝確曾跟山攝一樣經過同一個演變過程。不過由這個過程所形成的 ɔy 與 ey 兩個韻部稍後又變入齊微韻了$\left(\begin{Bmatrix}\text{ɔ}\\ \text{e}\end{Bmatrix}\longrightarrow \text{ɨ}/____\text{y}\right)$。由此可知，低元音前後三度對比的消失首先發生在收噫的韻裏，這在《中原音韻》以前相當久就出現了。到底早多少，我們不能確知，但《切韻指掌圖》已經給了我們一個暗示。因爲普通的韻圖都是一開一合相對應的。可是止攝和蟹攝的開合却併了起來，成了兩開對兩合，這種不合理的兩兩相對的現象，大概就是因爲當時上述的音變已經發生了:《切韻指掌圖》的作者既要照顧原來的等韻形式，又要考慮到“杯、回、西、鷄”之類字的實際讀法已屬齊微，所以就造成不合理的現象。《中原音韻》比較客觀，不管原來等韻的歸屬，而直接把那些字都歸入齊微韻，原來的齊微韻是止攝三等字，有開有合，韻母是-yiy、-wiy。

歌戈、家麻、車遮這三個韻是果攝和假攝混等以後再繼續演變成的。它們演變的方式基本上和山攝、咸攝及蟹攝是一致的。不過它的一等開口字並未變入二等，仍與一等合口字相押，共同構成了歌戈韻，所以前文這個音變的公式應改寫爲 ɔ⟶a/C____E。也就是説，這個音變衹發生在帶尾韻裏，果攝字除外。家麻韻是原來的假攝二等字，韻基是-aø，車遮韻是假攝三等字，加上極少數果攝三等字，如“瘸”等。這一韻使我們看到一個很有趣的現象。果假合併以後，它根本没有四等字，本來没有-eø 這個韻基，但是語音演變的一般趨勢却可以造成這麽一個韻基。車遮韻裏邊除入聲字，都是果假攝的三等字，這些字本來與家麻韻的字押韻，但後來不押了，變成了不同的韻。山咸等攝原來就有四等字，後來三等字變入四等，並没有增加韻母，衹是四等韻字數擴大了，可是果假攝原没有四等字,三等字變爲四等韻母,就增加了一個新的車遮韻,假攝、果攝的三等字本不太多,所以産生出的新的韻部裏,舒聲字數目有限,但是入聲字變入這一韻的字遠遠超過果假兩攝舒聲字,原因就是果假二攝本來没有四等字。

魚模韻是由遇攝變來的,原來就衹有合口字,含有兩個韻母——wɨø 與 ywɨø,到《中原音韻》時没有改變。支思韻是從止攝變來的,含有兩類,一類是精系開口字,一類是照系開口字。這兩類後來變成一個新的韻部,周德清是頭一個標出這個韻部的人,止攝字全屬三等,又都是收噫的,所以開口韻母是 yɨy。精系照系聲母可以説含有一個共同的"區別特徵",即同爲"齒音"(Sibilants),韻母 yɨy 即以此爲條件而丢掉了韻頭(y ⟶ ø/S____ɨy),這個變化發生在《中原音韻》之前,這在《切韻指掌圖》中看得很清楚,它把原來的三等開口精系字放到一等去了,一等自然是没有 y 介音的,照系聲母本屬兩類,即莊系及章系聲母,莊系聲母原來也配細音韻母,但後來變爲衹配洪音韻母了,與章系形成互補,因此就併爲等韻音系的照系聲母了。我相信止攝照系開口字與精系字同時丢掉韻頭,《切韻指掌圖》没有改動它們的位置,衹是因爲找不到别的地方安置它們罷了。這個新形成的韻母 øɨy 後來又丢掉了韻尾(y ⟶ ø/Cɨ____),形成了一個更爲特殊的韻母 øɨø,這類字自然也就不會再與其他止攝字相押了,這就産生了一個前所未有的新韻,即支思韻。由於這類字以前押韻時衹與齊微韻字發生關係,從來不與魚模韻字發生關係,它們跟魚模韻的音值差别也許比較大,所以周德清把它們分立爲不同的韻。

《中原音韻》的音系是由等韻音系遞變出來的,其間有關韻母的主要音變我們已在前面約略地討論過了。這些音變出現的次序是至爲重要的,因爲這代表它們在時代上發生的順序,有些所謂"破音字",如耕字"口語音"讀 jing(/kyɨŋ/),"讀書音"讀 geng(/kɨŋ/),就是由於在兩個方言中相同的音變發生的順序不同而造成的。現在我們可以根據"口語音",按照我們能推斷出來的順序,再把這些音變系統化地排列出來。

(1) y→ø/f____ (輕脣音字變讀爲洪音)

(2) ø→y/____e (四等韻字變讀爲細音)

(3) a→e/y____ (三等韻字變入四等)

(4) $\varnothing \rightarrow y/G\_\_\_a$ (二等開口喉牙音字變讀爲細音)

(5) $k \rightarrow w/v\_\_\_$ (舌根韻尾入聲字改讀收嗚)

(6) $\hat{k} \rightarrow y/v\_\_\_$ (舌面韻尾入聲字改讀收噫)

(7) $ɔ \rightarrow a/C\_\_\_E$ (帶尾韻一等開口字變入二等)

$E \neq w、ŋ$ (但效攝、宕攝一等開口字除外)

(8) $ŋ \rightarrow \varnothing/\#\_\_\_x$ (疑母在一般情况下消失)

$x \neq ɔ(w)$ (但尚保留在果效一等開口韻母之前)

(9) $a \rightarrow ɔ/\_\_\_ŋ$ (江宕合韻)

(10) $\begin{Bmatrix} ɔ \\ a \end{Bmatrix} \rightarrow e/\_\_\_ɲ$ (梗曾由混等進而合韻)

(11) $y \rightarrow \varnothing/S\_\_\_ɨy$ (止攝齒音開口字變讀爲洪音)

(12) $y \rightarrow \varnothing/Ci\_\_\_$ (原止攝齒音開口字變洪音後又失掉韻尾,形成支思韻)

(13) $\begin{Bmatrix} ɔ \\ e \end{Bmatrix} \rightarrow ɨ/\_\_\_y$ (蟹攝一等合口及三、四等字,包括由梗曾等攝變來之入聲字,變入齊微韻)

(14) $w \rightarrow \varnothing/wɨ\_\_\_$ (由通攝變入流攝之入聲字,以及原流攝之脣音字,變入魚模韻)

關於入聲字,許多人説《中原音韻》中有入聲字,也有許多人説没有,我的看法是:《中原音韻》所代表的那個特定的方言的音系没有入聲字了。這個特定方言可以説是現代北京話中"口語"音的祖語。周德清是根據實際口語記録的。《中原音韻》中,原來江宕攝的入聲字全部出現在蕭豪韻裏,衹有少數選收在歌戈韻裏。根據讀書音,江宕攝的入聲字應該都出現在歌戈韻,但根據"口語音"則應該出現在蕭豪韻。原來梗曾攝的入聲字根據"口語音"應該出現在皆來或齊微韻(改讀收噫),這與它們在《中原音韻》中的分配是完全一致的。根據"讀書音",梗曾兩攝合韻後,其中的入聲字都應分入車遮韻,但實際上《中原音韻》的車遮韻没有把它們收進去。因此,我們看得出,《中原音韻》所依據的是"口語音",而且當時這個方言確實已經没有入聲了,因爲這些入聲字既改讀爲收噫(皆來、齊微),或改讀爲收嗚(蕭豪、尤侯),後面就不可能再有入聲韻尾了。不過當時的讀書音倒可能有入聲,那個入聲的讀法應該是一個喉塞音韻尾，其後當這個韻尾消失時，這類入聲字就很自然地進入了車遮、歌戈、魚模等直喉韻部①。

① 關於入聲字的較詳細的討論，請參看拙作《論入聲字的演化規律》，刊於《屈萬里先生七秩榮慶論文集》，聯經出版社，1978 年，第 407—433 頁。

論音變與音位結構的關係*

"語言學"的定義,一般認爲是"對於語言的科學研究"(the scientific study of language)。這種科學的研究,不論中外,都發端於對語言歷史演變的研究,尤其是語音史的研究,也就是所謂"歷史語言學"(historical linguistics)。語音史的研究是建立在一條最基本的信念上的,那就是:"音變是有規律的"(sound changes are regular)。因此歷史語言學家的任務也就是如何發現及確認音變的規律。然而總觀歷來的漢語歷史音韻學著作,我們難免會感到美中不足,因爲我們看到的往往不是系統化的規律,而衹是一些對某類音律的片斷與模棱兩可的解説,或是實例的排比。這樣,我們就看不出音律的本質以及音律之間的交互關係,自然,更看不出歷史演變的逐步情況了。造成這種現象的原因當然是這種工作的艱難困苦,這包括了歷史文獻的數量龐大與性質複雜,以及歷代方言的雜出紛陳,但我覺得,另一原因也許是理論認識的不足與方法選擇的不當。音位學(phonemics)的確立在西洋語言學上是較晚近的事,而歷史語言學的研究與發展則早得多。因此,早期大師的著作以及後來的"仿古"之作,用音位學的理論與方法來評斷,便難免顯得不盡完善。所謂"音變是有規律的"這一事實,在語音(phonetics)基礎上,當然也可以粗略地看出來,但總不够清晰嚴密。這是什麼原因呢?我個人的看法是:音韻系統的轉變,不是個别語音的問題,而是音位對比(phonemic contrast)的轉變。因此,"音變是有規律的"這一説法也衹有在音位結構的基礎上才可以清楚地顯示出來,並從而得到有力的支持。真正有規律的不是個别的發音改變(phonetic change),而是由偶然發生的發音改變所引起的音韻系統中的音位轉化(phonemic alternation)。在多數情況下,轉化的音位是受到發音改變的直接影響的,因而使我們直覺上

---

* 原刊《語言研究》1982 年第 2 期,收入《漢語音韻史十講》。
本文原是提交第十三届國際漢藏語言學術探討会(北京,1982 年)的報告。

感到音位的轉化與發音的改變似乎完全是一回事。但是,有時候在特定的情況下,没有直接受到發音改變之影響的音位也可能會轉化,而直接受到影響的却不一定會轉化。在漢語史的研究中,我們發現有以下幾種現象,可以説明語音改變與音位轉化在本質上是截然不同的。

(一)音位結構轉化了,但跟這一轉化有關的音變之性質却不明朗。

這一現象可以用莊組聲母與章組聲母之合併作爲例子來説明。我們都知道,等韻時期的漢語衹有五個正齒聲母,即“照、穿、牀、審、禪”。但是前賢對《切韻》一書中反切上下字的研究已經證明,切韻時期的漢語具有兩組與照系相對應的聲母,即“莊、初、崇、生、俟”與“章、昌、船、書、常”。這兩組聲母都可以與細音韻母(三等韻)相配,因此形成了兩套不同的對比音位。高本漢等把它們分别擬定爲[tṣ,tṣʻ,dẓʻ,ṣ,(ẓ)]與[tś,tśʻ,dźʻ,ś,ź](參看 Karlgren1954,李榮 1952,董 1968)。我則用音位與區别特徵(distinctive feature)的混合表示法把它們標爲/cr,crh,crɦ,sr,srɦ/與/cj,cjh,cjɦ,sj,sjɦ/。(“r,j,h,ɦ”分别代表捲舌、腭化、送氣、全濁等區别特徵,參看薛 1975:27—30 與 1980。)在這個基礎上,莊、章兩組聲母合併的道理,便可以用下面兩個簡明的公式表示出來。

$$y \longrightarrow ø / r\_\_\_ \qquad (1)$$

$$j \longrightarrow r \qquad (2)$$

頭一個公式的含義是:跟莊組聲母相配的細音韻母,在切韻之後丢掉了介音中的“y”而變爲洪音。第二個公式則表示章組腭化聲母變爲捲舌,因此跟莊組混同了。就音位理論説,這種表示法是絶對合理的,因爲章組聲母衹配細音韻母(三等韻),而莊組在發生了公式(1)所代表的音變之後,就衹配洪音韻母了。這兩組聲母因此變成了互補的音位變體(allophones in complementary distribution),等韻學家們自然也就把它們看作同類而名之爲照系了。然而就字匯説,原來因莊、章兩組聲母而分讀的字却並没有混淆。因此有人用“照二”與“照三”這兩個術語代表莊組與章組字之分。我們要在此處提出的問題是:莊、章兩組併爲照系時,章組聲母的“發音方式”有無改變?歷史文獻顯然不能幫助我們解答這個問題。當然,章組聲母後來都變爲捲舌了,但在莊、章合併的當時,這個變化却不是“必要條件”,因此也不能説這個變化當時就肯定發生了。就音位理論説，莊、章成爲互補音以後就該合併。章組聲母當時有無發音上的改變是不相干的，也是我們無法知道的。

（二）音變確已發生，但有關的音位對比則未變。

等韻三十六字母中，包括兩組脣音聲母，即所謂重脣“幫、滂、並、明”與輕脣“非、敷、奉、微”。然而在《切韻》中，由《切韻》上下字的分析研究可以看出，輕、重脣音的區别是不存在的。顯然《切韻》時期的漢語衹有一套脣音聲母。性質都是所謂“重脣”，但是在《切韻》成書以後，等韻形成之前，發生了一種音變，使原來的一組脣音聲母分裂爲輕、重兩組。分裂的條件是什麼？目前似仍有争論，但多數人（包括我本人）都認爲是“三等合口韻母”（參看陸 1946），也就是説，合口的三等脣音字聲母由重變輕。這一音變的發生是絶對不容置疑的，但是却没有引起音位對比的改動。原來異讀的脣音字自然也没有混淆。各本韻圖書仍把輕脣音的字排在三等，而且除《切韻指掌圖》以外，也都把“非、敷、奉、微”虚列在“幫、滂、並、明”之下。這種安排没有造成問題，就是因爲音位對比没有改動。

輕脣音的字後來都由細音變爲洪音。這種韻母的改變是與聲母的發音改變同時還是稍後？我們很難測定。就音理説，我們衹能把它假定爲稍後，但幾乎同時，因此在標寫這類字的時候，我們可以不作任何改動，也可以省略介音中的“y”，同時在聲母中增加“緩放”（delayed release）成分，即把“非、敷、奉、微”標爲/pf，pfh，bv，mv/。音位對比的改動是到“非、敷、奉”混同的時候才發生的。

與上例類似的是日母的發音變化，這一聲母原是腭化鼻音，但早在唐代就丢掉了鼻音成分（參看李榮 1952：119）。到了宋代，又隨着章系聲母由腭化音變爲捲舌音（參看薛 1975：43—44）。但是雖然先後經過兩次音變，作爲一個獨立的音位，却始終保持着它與其他聲母的對比。

（三）發音方式由 A 變 B，但音位轉化却須解釋爲由 B 變 A。

這種現象是極爲特殊而且少見的。但在特定的情况下，却有此可能。我們可以用《中原音韻》中寒山、桓歡、先天三韻的合併來説明這一現象。這三韻裏的字來自等韻時代的山攝。山攝是一個四等俱全的外轉攝。各等的韻母形態是：一等 ɔn/wɔn，二等 an/wan，三等 yan/ywan，四等 yen/ywen（參看薛

1978、1985)。等韻時期之後,經過下列幾條語音演變,山攝陽聲字終於重新組合成中原音韻的桓歡、寒山及先天三韻(參看薛 1975:56—57)。

1. 輕脣音字由細變洪,亦即失掉介音中的“y”。

$$y \longrightarrow \varnothing / B\_\_\_ w \tag{3}$$

這是一條通則,當然也影響到了山攝的三等合口脣音字,諸如“翻、煩、反、飯、晚”等,使得它們的韻母變得跟二等合口韻母相同了。

其後,三、四等合韻時,它們便自然不受影響。因此,它們出現在寒山韻而不入先天韻。

2. 三等韻變入四等,也就是説三等韻的主要元音/a/受到介音中“y”的同化而前移變成/e/了。

$$a \longrightarrow e / y(w)\_\_\_ \tag{4}$$

這也是一條通則。因爲發生的時代較公式(3)晚,所以没有影響到“煩、反、晚”等原三等字,但却使仙與先、蹇與繭、彦與硯等分別異讀的字變成同音了,所以先天韻中三、四等字完全混合。

3. 喉牙音二等開口字由洪變細,也就是説原無介音(介音爲 ø)的二等喉牙字孳生了一個“y”作爲介音。

$$\varnothing \longrightarrow y / G\_\_\_ a \tag{5}$$

這也是一條通則,波及山攝的結果是:“奸、簡、雁、閑、眼”等都變成了細音。但是,它們的主要元音没變,所以都出現在寒山韻裏。

4. 除了果、宕、效三攝以外,一等開口字變入二等,也就是説,在韻尾含有“齦前”音素時([+anterior]即 y,m,p,n,t/等),一等開口字的主要元音/ɔ/受同化而前移變爲/a/。

$$\begin{gathered} ɔ \longrightarrow a / C\_\_\_ E \\ E \neq ŋ、k、w \end{gathered} \tag{6}$$

這還是一條通則。對山攝來説,原與桓韻“通用”的寒韻字,至此便轉而與山、删相押了,因此一同組成了寒山韻。

由以上的推論,可以得知這三個韻的音韻性質及所能含有的韻母,即桓歡：wɔn，寒山：an/wan/yan，先天：yen/ywen。這三個韻到了明末就合爲一轍兒了，即十三轍兒的言前轍兒。我曾經用下列公式表示它們的合併：

$$\begin{Bmatrix} ɔ \\ e \end{Bmatrix} \longrightarrow a/\_\_\_ n \qquad (7)$$

就音位標音法說，這個公式是既簡明又合理的，但就音變的原理說，却難免令人懷疑。這個公式其實是兩個小公式的合併，即 ɔ→a/____n 跟 e→a/____n。頭一個没有問題，後元音受舌尖鼻音韻尾的影響而前移是合乎音變原理的。第二個就顯得可怪了，舌尖鼻音韻尾之前的元音怎麽會後移呢？再就實際情況說，先天韻字數甚多，全是細音，而寒山韻中的細音字衹有因公式(5)而變來的幾個喉牙音字。後者變入前者較合理，否則就成了多數變入少數了。在這件事上，洋人的感覺(non-native speaker's feeling)倒可以給我們一點啓示。曾經有一位美國學者滿懷不解地對我説："干與奸的元音完全不同，怎麽可以押韻呢?"更具體的例子是：在 Wade Giles 拼音法裏，"間"與"先、天"等的韻母都作"ien"，可見就發音說，是"間"的韻母受了介音與韻尾的雙重影響，由[ian]變爲[ien](a→e/i____n)而不是"先、天"等的韻母由[ien]變爲[ian]。但是寒山與先天兩韻的差異主要是細音字的對立。當寒山韻的幾個細音字變入先天以後，這兩韻就構成互補了，說現代漢語的人也就覺得它們完全可以押韻了。現代漢語音位中衹有一個低元音，不分前後，因此就發音來説，雖然是[ian]變爲[ien]，我們仍得用公式(7)來代表這一歷史性的音位轉變。

(四) 未受音變直接影響的音位有時亦須作音位轉化的新解釋。

這種現象也是相當少見的，因此也不容易令人接受。但在特定的情況下確有此必要的。我們可以拿等韻中江、宕兩攝的合併與演進爲例來説明這一現象。差不多三年前，漢藏學會在巴黎召開時，我提出了一篇論文，題爲"内外轉新釋"(薛 1979)。我在該文中説，多年來我一直服膺羅常培先生的説法(羅 1933)，但近年却有點動摇，我的新看法是：内外轉之分跟主要元音的高低之分確有很多巧合。但二者所代表的觀點與本質則截然不同。由於韻圖中列在二等的齒音字(照二，即原莊組)在切韻時期的漢語中可能是細音也可能是洪音，所以韻圖也必須分成"内、外"兩類，以便讓讀者們能够正確地分別對待這類齒音字。其目的不過如此而已。因此，根據我提出的四度元音説，我把韻圖的音位結構表示如下表：

	内轉 A （通、止、遇、流、深）	内轉 B （果、宕、曾）	外轉 （江、蟹、山、效、假、咸、梗）
一等	-(w)ɨ(E)	-(w)ɔ(E)	-(w)ɔ(E)
二等	——	——	-(w)a(E)
三等	-y(w)ɨ(E)	-y(w)ɔ(E)	-y(w)a(E)
四等	——	——	-y(w)e(E)

（臻攝的音位形態跟内轉 A 式完全相同。但是由於列在二等的幾個原莊組字在切韻中獨立成韻[臻、櫛]，所以也被勉强地標作“外”，但其性質與其他外轉攝完全不同。）

在這個説法的基礎上，我給“内外混等”提出了一個簡明的解説：

$$ɔ \longrightarrow a / y\_\_\_ \qquad (8)$$

這個公式的意思是：細音韻母裏的後低元音/ɔ/，由於受到介音“y”的同化作用，前移而變成/a/。换句話説，“果、曾、宕”三攝中的三等字，因此變得跟外轉三等字相同了，所以果與假、曾與梗、宕與江也就合併了。當時我覺得這個説法極有道理。現在我仍覺得這個説法相當有道理，但需要作一點修改。這個公式適用於果攝及曾攝是絶無問題的，但就音理説，用於宕攝則頗有問題。我們知道，漢語中元音所受的影響主要來自韻尾，其次來自介音。宕攝的韻尾是舌根音/ŋ/跟/k/，不大可能會讓介音中的“y”影響元音向前移動。更大的問題是：這一説法不能合理地解釋江、宕兩攝入聲字的演變。這些入聲字同時出現在中原音韻的蕭豪與歌戈韻裏。前者代表它們在“口語”中的演變，即韻尾/k/變爲/w/，不論其元音是/ɔ/或是/a/，它們都得進入蕭豪韻，這是容易理解的（參看薛 1975：107—110 及薛 1978）。後者代表它們在“讀音”中的演變，即韻尾消失。這就涉及主要元音的性質了。假如宕攝真受到公式(8)的影響，那麽除了它的一等入聲字（元音未變）應入歌戈以外，它的三等入聲字及江攝的入聲字都應該分入家麻韻，因爲它們的元音爲/a/而韻尾消失了。但事實不然，這些入聲字不入家麻而入歌戈。十多年前，當我研究《中原音韻》的時候，這是最使我苦惱的問題之一。當時我衹好勉强地作結論説：舌根鼻音之前的後元音前移(ɔ→a/____ŋ),而舌根塞音之前的央元音後移(a→ɔ/____k)。換句話説,宕攝的陽聲字變入江攝,而江攝的入聲字則變入宕攝(參看薛 1975:107—110,128)。這雖成功地標示了江、宕兩攝字在《中原音韻》中的分配,但却未能正確地標明音變的原理。多年來我一直不感滿意,却也無可奈何,直到最近,由於比較正確地理解了發音改變與音位轉化之間的關係,才找到了合理近情的解釋。我現在相信,不是宕攝受到公式(8)的影響,而是江攝的元音受到韻尾的影響而後移,

a→ɔ/____ŋ,k　　(9)

經此一變,江、宕當然也就"内外混等"了。但它們的混等跟果與假及曾與梗的混等,性質與方式都不相同。在另一方面説,因爲是江攝變入宕攝,所以合併後形成的江陽韻,應以後低元音爲韻腹。這一事實,就發音方式説,直到現在也没有改變。(所以"王"字的讀音,對美國人來説,像是[wong]而不是[wang]。)然而《中原音韻》以後,漢語的音韻系統發生了變化,低元音減少而漸次失掉了元音音位的前後對比(參看薛 1976、1978),跟舌根韻尾相配的低元音衹剩下一個後元音。因此,雖然這個後低元音在發音方式上不曾改變,在音位結構的轉化上,我們也不得不説這個/ɔ/又變成了/a/。

在兩年前印出的一篇討論入聲字的論文裏(薛 1978),我曾經説過這樣一段話:"中國的傳統音韻學,在顯示語音中的音位對比關係方面,是極爲高明的,但這個優點衹有從現代的語音理論觀點上才可以看得出來。把傳統的音韻學與最近的語音理論結合起來,我們才可以測定出不同時代的音韻系統,並從而清楚地指出不同時代之間的演變。本文的方法與理論就是建立在這二者結合的基礎上的。"這一看法我到現在還没有改變,因此抄録在這兒作爲本文的結尾。

PHONOLOGY OF OLD MANDARIN***

PREFACE

Compared with most studies on the history of Chinese phonology done by modern scholars, this little book represents a different approach. It adopts a strict phonemic interpretation and tries to explain a long section of the history of the language by a set of diachronic rules arranged in a specific order. The fundamental spirit of this approach is, however, not quite new. It may be regarded as a humble but conscious effort to follow as closely as possible that part of the Chinese tradition of phonological study high-lighted by the 'Rime Tables' of the T'ang-Sung period. For many centuries, this tradition has not been fully understood, if not completely forgotten. With the help of the theories of modern phonemics and generative phonology, it is now possible for us to understand and appreciate this tradition better, and we can see now that it is, after all, still an ideal, if not the best, approach for the study of the Chinese language. In this sense, the present work is the most conservative of all.

I believe historical linguistics makes the best sense only when it is strictly phonemic and the best way to understand the history of a language is to select some key stages of the language and then trace back stage by stage from the modern to the ancient. The key stage immediately before Modern Pekinese, it seems to me, is Old Mandarin as represented by the rime book *Chūng-yüán*

*** 中文題爲《古官話音系》,原由荷蘭海牙 Mouton 出版社出版,1975 年。

Yīn-yùn compiled by Chōu Té-ch'īng in the early fourteenth century. Since Modern Pekinese has been reasonably well analyzed in phonemic terms, it is now possible to move back to Old Mandarin with a two-fold objective in mind: to gain a thorough understanding of the phonology of that period and to build up a solid foundation for the study of the earlier periods.

The fundamental assumption underlying the present work is that the above-mentioned rime book has preserved all the contrasts among the phonologically possible syllables of the language of its day by grouping the numerous characters into independent homonym groups. So by making use of our knowledge of Ancient Chinese, the Rime Table Period, and modern Mandarin dialects, we should be able to construct a phonemic system which will explain in a logical and systematic manner all the contrasts contained in that book.

Since the phonological structure of one dialect or language is no proof for that of another, the system established here is strictly based upon *Chūng-yüán Yīn-yùn*. This means that *Chūng-yüán Yīn-yùn* always receives the primary consideration while other sources are consulted only occasionally when some phenomena in *Chūng-yüán Yīn-yùn* cannot be readily explained in formal terms. I believe the reconstructed system presented in this book is basically sound, not merely because it has practically solved all the puzzles in *Chūng-yüán Yīn-yùn* in a logical manner, but also because it is so neat and symmetric that it makes it possible to draw reasonable and economical rules to show the development from Ancient Chinese to Old Mandarin and from Old Mandarin to Modern Pekinese.

In formulating diachronic rules of this kind, I have decided to use individual 'phonemes' and other similar but larger cover symbols, instead of distinctive features, though it has been quite convincingly demonstrated that the latter approach has certain advantages over the former (Halle 1962). This decision is motivated mainly by two considerations. First, our knowledge about Ancient Chinese is as yet hardly solid enough to let us relate it in terms of features. Second, but more importantly, it is my hope that the format employed in this study may make it more readily accessible to scholars of all trainings, though I am aware of the risk that this just might please nobody. At any rate, the disadvantages of this 'phoneme' approach, if there are indeed any in this particular case, may have been greatly compensated by the special treatment we have given to such features as aspiration, retroflexion, etc. (see 3.2.2). Some day, when we have learned enough about Ancient Chinese, it will surely be a simple matter to rewrite these rules in terms of features, if one wants to. After all, there is really not too much difference in fundamentals, I believe, between a truly strict phonological analysis in terms of phonemes and one in terms of features.

It may be noted at this juncture that all through the present work primary attention has been persistently given to determining what actually happened in the historical development of the language rather than theorizing on why such changes should have taken place. Too often have we found theorizations proposed ardently for some phonological changes only to discover later that they did not exist or are yet to be proven. I do not mean to say by this that theoretical explanation is not desirable, but that it can be done only after the facts have been established and my concern here is mainly to establish those facts in the most explicit terms as we possibly can.

During a period of more than six hundred years since *Chūng-yüán Yīn-yǜn* was compiled, a large number of researches on the book have been made. I have mentioned only a few which are useful to me in one way or another. If it seems that I have been unusually critical of the few authors I quoted, let it be known that I actually have high opinions of, and have been benefited by, their work. The fact that I argue against them is evidence enough for this.

This work is a revised version of my dissertation written in the

Department of Linguistics at Indiana University with Dr. Fred W. Householder serving as the chairman of the advisory committee. To him and all the others on the committee, I wish to take this opportunity to express my sincere gratitude for the time they spent in reading the manuscript, the numerous valuable suggestions they made to me, and the help they gave me in many other ways. I also want to express my thanks to Dr. Y. R. Chao who most kindly read the manuscript and suggested some corrections. Of course, I alone shall be fully responsible for whatever flaws will be found in the book.

February, 1972

Columbus, Ohio

LIST OF ABBREVIATIONS

AC	Ancient Chinese, also known as Middle Chinese, as represented by *Ch'ièh-yǜn* 切韻.
B	Labial initials(Cf. 3.2).
C	The initial consonant of a syllable (Cf. 7.2a).
CYYY	The rime book *Chūng-yüán Yīn-yǜn* 中原音韻.
D	Dental initials (Cf. 3.2).
Ds	Dental sibilant initials(Cf. 3.2).
E	The ending of a syllable (Cf. 3.1).
F	The final of a syllable(Cf. 3.5.1).
Fr	Fricatives (Cf. 3.2).
G	Guttural initials (Cf. 3.2. For the use of the term 'guttural' instead of 'velar', see Note 2 to Chapter 3).
I	The initial of a syllable (Cf. 3.1).
M	The medial of a syllable (Cf. 3.1).
MP	Modern Pekinese.
P	Palatal stop initials (Cf. 3.2).
Pj	Palatal sibilant initials (Cf. 3.2).
Pr	Retroflex initials (Cf. 3.2).
R	Resonants(Cf. 3.2).
RC	The rime classes of the rime tables, i.e., shè 攝.
RG	Rimes in CYYY, followed by a numeral to specify any of the rimes (Cf. 2.8).
RIL	Martin Joos (ed.): *Readings in Linguistics* (New York, 1963).
RTP	The Rime Table period, roughly around A. D. 1000, particularly as represented by *Ch'ièh-yǜn Chǐh-nán* 切韻指南 in Lǐ Júng's

	revised version (Cf. 1. 3).
S	Stops(Cf. 3. 2).
TG	Tone groups in CYYY, followed by a numeral to specify any of the groups (Cf. 2. 8).
V	The nucleus of a syllable (Cf. 3. 1).
V_n	The nuclear vowel of the rimes of the inner series(Cf. 3. 6. 2).
V_w	The nuclear vowels of the rimes of the outer series(Cf. 7 . 2d).
V_1	The nuclear vowel of the first division of the outer series (Cf. 3. 6. 2).
V_2	The nuclear vowel of the second division of the outer series.
V_3	The nuclear vowel of the third division of the outer series.
V_4	The nuclear vowel of the fourth division of the outer series.
X, Y, Z	Variables in the phonological rules.
ZGYW	*Zhongguo Yuwen* 中國語文 (Chinese Language and Writing), Peking, monthly.

CHAPTER ONE INTRODUCTION

The history of the Chinese language has generally been divided into three principal periods, though the names given to them have not been agreed on by all modern scholars. The earliest period, represented mainly by the Book of Odes (Shīh-chīng 詩經 d. 6th cent. B. C.), has been called 'Archaic Chinese' or 'Old Chinese'; the second period, represented by the rime book *Ch'ièh-yǜn* (切韻 A. D. 601), has been called 'Ancient Chinese' or 'Middle Chinese'①; the third period, from the rime book *Chūng-yüán Yīn-yǜn* (中原音韻 A. D. 1324) up to the present, is widely known as 'Mandarin', though the term 'New Chinese' also seems to be acceptable. Each of these principal periods can, of course, be further divided into sub-periods, for example, Mandarin can be divided into three stages: Old Mandarin, represented by *Chūng-yüán Yīn-yǜn*; Middle Mandarin, represented by one of the rime books of the Míng dynasty (Pì Kǔng-ch'én's *Yǜn-lüèh Huì-t'ūng* 畢拱辰:韻略匯通 seems to be a possible choice); and New Mandarin or Modern Pekinese. What I propose to do here is to make a new interpretation of the phonology of Old Mandarin, so as to show as systematically as possible the development from Ancient Chinese to this period and the development from this period to Modern Pekinese. But before we begin to study the Old Mandarin phonology, some introductory remarks must be made on the background of Chinese phonological study, so as to put our topic in the proper historical perspective. This is what will be done in this chapter, though as briefly as possible. In addition, I will try to outline, in the most sketchy

① The first term in each case was first used by Bernhard Karlgren; the second in each case which seems to have become more and more popular has been proposed by E. G. Pulleyblank.

terms, the work I propose to do.

1.1 Phonological study in China has a long history. The first breakthrough is the invention of the method of indicating the pronunciation of one graph by means of two different graphs. This method, dated as early as the second century A. D. and known to posterity as *fǎn-ch'ièh* 反切, was probably the result of the newly acquired knowledge of Sanskrit phonology, though no direct evidence can be found. Before this, the so-called *chíh-yīn* 直音 and *shēng-hsǜn* 聲訓 had been used. The former means to indicate the pronunciation of one graph by another graph with the same or a very similar pronunciation; the latter means the graph used to indicate the pronunciation must also show or hint the meaning of the graph in question①.

1.2 In the *fǎn-ch'ièh* method, an analysis of a monosyllable represented by a graph into an 'initial' and a 'final' was first made. Then another graph which had the same initial, be it a consonant or a zero element, was chosen to be the first part of a notational compound, and a third graph which had the same final, namely, everything after the initial in the syllable, was chosen to form the second part of the compound. Before the seventh century A. D., there existed already quite a number of rime books making use of this new technique of notation, but the most famous one is *Ch'ièh-yǜn* 切韻, a summing-up work compiled by Lù Fǎ-yán 陸法言 in A. D. 601. This book, however, is known to us only through two later editions, slightly modified but essentially intact. The first is a Táng edition by Wáng Jén-Hsǜ 王仁昫 called *K'ān-miù Pǔ-ch'üēh Ch'ièh-yǜn* 刊謬補缺切韻; the second, more widely known through the ages, is a Sùng edition by Ch'én P'éng-nién 陳彭年 and others called (*Tà Sùng Ch'úng-hsiū*) *Kuǎng-yǜn* (大宋重修)廣韻. These rime books all classify the graphs into four tonal categories (*shēng* 聲) and group them within each tonal category into a number of rimes (*yǜn* 韻). The

① Cf. Chāng (1963), Chapter 3, and Wáng (1967), Chapter 1.

Sung edition has altogether 206 rimes, the T'áng edition has 195, while the original has only 193①.

1.3 The next stage of Chinese phonological study saw two important events. First, thirty-six initials were established, each represented by a fixed graph; then, rime tables were made in which, besides the contrast of *K'āi-k'ǒu* 開口(open-mouth i. e., unrounded) vs. *hó-k'ǒu* 合口(close-mouth, i. e., rounded), four divisions were set up. The rime tables were so designed that each phonologically possible syllable in the Chinese of that period would have one proper place within a certain table in a certain tonal category under a certain initial type and in a certain division. We now have quite a few books of rime tables. Besides *Yǜn-chìng* 韻鏡 which was printed in the Sùng dynasty but seems to be of T'áng origin and shows a relatively closer relation to the original *Ch'ièh-yǜn*, there are *Szù-shēng Těng-tzǔ* 四聲等子 and *Ch'ièh-yǜn Chǐh-chǎng T'ú* 切韻指掌圖, both of the Sùng dynasty, and (*Chīng-shǐh Chèng-yīn*) *Ch'ièh-yǜn Chǐh-nán* (經史正音)切韻指南 by Liu Chièn 劉鑑 of the Yüán dynasty. The last three further grouped together tables with corresponding rounded and unrounded finals into classes of rimes, called *shè* 攝. They all show some drastic deviations from the original *Ch'ièh-yǜn*②. Although *Ch'ièh-yǜn Chǐh-nán* was compiled in the Yüán dynasty, even later than *Chūng yüàn* Yīn-yǜn(CYYY), we know for sure that it originated from books of the same nature of a much earlier period and represents probably the standard language around the tenth century.③ In later discussions, whenever I mention the rime tables, it should be understood that I refer to this book, especially in its revised form made by Lǐ Júng 李榮④, unless I specify otherwise.

---

① For more details, see Tǔng (1954), Chapter 4,38-44, and Martin (1953),1-2.

② See Tǔng (1954), Chapter 5,67-88.

③ See Tung(1954), Chapter 5,67.

④ Lǐ Júng (1956), particularly, the 'Tān Tzù Yīn Piǎo' 單字音表.

1.4 A great deal of work has been done on the phonology of Ancient Chinese (AC) as represented by the book of *Ch'ièh-yǜn*, notably, Bernhard Karlgren's *Études surla phonologie chinoise*, Y. R. Chao's "Distinctions within Ancient Chinese", Tŭng T'úng-hó's *Chūng-kuó Yǚ-yīn Shĭn* 中國語音史 and Lĭ Júng's *Ch'ièh-yǜn Yīn-hsì* 切韻音系, to name just a few[①]. A remarkable effort has also been made to draw out the phonemic system of the age in Samuel E. Martin's *The Phonemes of Ancient Chinese*. All these scholars have their eye on the phonology of Ancient Chinese while making use of the rime tables of the Sung dynasty as a framework for their reconstruction, though they freely admit that the rime tables often show phonological features of their own day. Curiously, as far as I know, no effort has been made specially to interpret the phonological system underlying any one of the books of rime tables, namely, the phonological system of the period about four centuries after *Ch'ièh-yǜn* was compiled[②]. It is true that surprisingly brilliant work has been done on the phonology of Ancient Chinese, but there still remain some problems to be solved, for example, the rimes marked off from each other merely by a prime, the dentilabialization of the labial initials under certain conditions, and the real meaning of the contrast between the *nèi-chuăn* 内轉 (inner series) and the *wài-chuăn* 外轉 (outer series)[③]. Moreover, I am somewhat less than completely satisfied with the vowel system set up in Martin's phonemicization. It does not look very neat and symmetrical. All these point to the fact that more work will have to be done before we can have a precise and conclusive understanding of the phonology of AC, but all that can be done has perhaps already been done

---

① For all the works cited here, see bibliography.

② Three years after the original version of the present work was completed (Dissertation, Indiana University, 1968), I was happy to read Pulleyblank's "Late Middle Chinese" (Pulleyblank 1970) in which he made a special effort to reconstruct a phonological system for the rime tables.

③ For problems mentioned here, see Martin (1953), 37-41.

in the present line of research, that is, by concentrating on *Ch'ièh-yǜn*. But isn't a new approach possible?

1.5 One way to reconstruct the phonology of AC, if we did not have any written documents to rely on, would perhaps be to start from the numerous modern dialects (or languages). We might first try to reconstruct a parent language for each modern dialect group, for example, Old Cantonese from the various modern Cantonese dialects. When this was done, we might push one more step backward by reconstructing the language of a still earlier period from the already reconstructed languages. This, however, is entirely unnecessary, because we do have a number of valuable written documents—the rime books and the rime tables. Insofar as these books have maintained all the necessary distinctions of the language of the period which they meant to represent, we may feel confident that underlying each of them is the phonemic structure of the language of the period which the book was compiled to represent. It follows that in a synchronic study based on one of these books, it will be relatively easier to sketch first a somewhat loose phonemic structure than to figure out the phonetic value of the graphs in the book. The best we can do about the phonetic value or values of a phoneme in the system is to make the most reasonable guess we can concerning its origin in the previous periods and its behavior in its later development. Of course, it is impossible to set up the phonemic system of a historical period without referring to that of modern times, for the simple reason that we have to start from what we know for sure. It is also obvious that the closer the period we are going to study is to our time, the more confident we can be in decoding its phonemic system. I thus feel that a different approach in the study of the history of Chinese phonology would be to pick out some key stages and then trace back stage by stage from the modern to the ancient. This does not mean that, in the study of a later stage, we cannot make use of whatever knowledge we may have of the earlier stages. Indeed, we have to. It simply means that by knowing a certain period better, we will be better equipped to tackle some of the problems of its preceding period, which otherwise may not be possible to solve. After AC, we probably have to deal with two intermediate stages before we reach Modern Pekinese. One is roughly of the tenth century, the rime table period (RTP), as represented by one of the books of rime tables; the other is of the fourteenth century, represented by *Chūng-yüán Yīn-yùn* (CYYY).

1.6 To help solve the problems of the earlier periods is, of course, only one of the many reasons, linguistic and non-linguistic, why we should study the later periods. By studying each of the important stages in the development of the phonology of the language, we hope some day we may fill up all the gaps and thus eventually have a more complete and systematic explanation of the development of the language. On the other hand, each period has its own literature, and in order to understand the literature of a period, we certainly should try to understand its language as well as possible. My work on the phonology of Old Mandarin as represented by CYYY can be roughly outlined as follows:

(*a*) A phonological background of CYYY, namely, an outline of the phonology of AC and the rime table period (RTP), will be set up, based upon both the traditional studies and the researches of modern scholars.

(*b*) A strict phonemic reconstruction of CYYY will be made by means of our knowledge about Modern Pekinese (MP) and other dialects as well as our knowledge about AC and RTP. This reconstructed system must be able to account for all he contrasts shown in that book.

(*c*) If the reconstructed system is accurate, it must then show a close relation to RTP, and consequently, we should be able to draw a set of rules to show the development. Since no analysis of RTP in modern phonemic terms is available yet, we may expect to run into some difficulties in writing explicit rules, but I shall try my best with the rime tables which seem to me to be already a highly refined structural analysis, though they are, as Karlgren puts it, but a set of algebraic formulas[①].

(*d*) I shall also try to say something about the development from CYYY to MP, though real meaningful formulation of this development will have to wait until more precise analysis of the latter has been done.

① Karlgren (1948), 4.

CHAPTER TWO　SOME REMARKS ON CYYY

A few paragraphs are needed here as an introduction to the book under study. However, I shall no go into the details for which Chào Yìn-t'ang (1936), Hattori and Tōdō (1958), and Stimson (1966), three comprehensive works on this subject, must be consulted (see bibliography).

2.1 The rime book*Chūng-yüán Yīn-yǔn* (CYYY) 中原音韻, meaning literally pronunciations and rimes of the central plains, was compiled by Chou Té-ch'īng 周德清 in 1324. It was an answer to the need for a standard reference book for versification in its own time when a new form of poetic literature suddenly rose into prominence. This new form of poetry, strictly vernacular, is known to us as *ch'ǚ* of the Yüán dynasty 元曲 and most probably is based upon the language then spoken around Peking, capital of the Yüán dynasty but called Tà-dū 大都 in those days. For this reason and others I do not have to mention here, we believe the book is a faithful recording of the language of its day. It represents a stage of the Chinese language when a number of drastic changes which mark the distinction between Ancient Chinese (AC) and Mandarin took place. It is thus a very important book, both linguistically and otherwise.

2.2 The book is unique in its organization in the following respects:

2.2.1 Unlike the rime books of earlier periods which first classify their entries into tonal categories and then into rimes within each tonal category, this book first classifies its entries into rimes and then into tonal groups within each rime. So the term 'rime' (*yǔn* 韻) used in CYYY has a different meaning from that which it has when it is used in connection with the earlier rime books such as *Ch'ièh-yǔn*. Roughly speaking, one rime in CYYY would be phonologically equivalent to four corresponding *Ch'ièh-yǔn* rimes with different tones; in reality, it is often even larger, because many of the rimes in *Ch'ièh-yǜn* had coalesced by this time. This new arrangement, of course, reflects the fact that in the *ch'ǚ* poetry of the Yüān dynasty, tonal difference was no longer as prominent a feature in riming as it had been in the *shīh* poetry of the former ages. There are only nineteen rimes, but as we shall see later, one of them, however, contains as many as three nuclear vowels.

2. 2. 2 In the rime books of earlier times there were four tonal categories, namely, *p'íng-shēng* 平聲, the even tone, *shǎng-shēng* 上聲, the rising tone, *ch'ǜ-shēng* 去聲, the going tone, and *jù-shēng* 入聲, the entering tone. CYYY keeps all the labels, but makes the following changes:

(*a*) The even tone group within each rime was now divided into two, one was labeled *yīn* 陰, the other, *yáng* 陽, two terms which cannot be readily translated but will be discussed later (see 3. 5. 3).

(*b*) The entering tone graphs were now divided into three tonal sub-groups each of which was then attached to one of the other three tonal groups within a rime, under the remark '*jù-shēng tsò* X-shēng', 入聲作 X 聲 'the entering tone as the X tone' (X here stands for *p'íng*, *shǎng*, or *ch'ǜ*). The sub-group attached to the even tone group was specified to be of the *yáng* type. Moreover, in the earlier rime books and rime tables, the so-called entering tone groups which contain syllables ending in one of the three stop consonants /p, t, k/, were all matched respectively with rimes ending in /m, n, ŋ/, but in CYYY, the sub-groups of the entering tone were attached only to the rimes of open syllables, that is, syllables without a consonant ending of any sort. This rime book is the first which makes this type of redistribution of the former entering tone graphs, and scholars up to the present day have been disputing whether or not the entering tone syllables had lost their consonant endings and thus lost their distinction as a special group in the language of CYYY. This will be one of the most important questions I am going to try to answer.

(*c*) In its fourth rime, after the tonal sub-group 'entering tone as even tone', there is another tonal sub-group called '*ch'ǜ-shēng tsò p'íng-shēng*, *yáng*', 去聲作平聲, 陽 'going tone as even tone of the *yáng* type'. This sub-group has but one graph 鼻 *pí*. Many efforts have been made to give it an explanation and as yet no agreement has been reached[①]. It seems to me that the establishment of this unique sub-group does not tell us anything meaningful phonologically. It does remind us, however, that no matter how objective an attitude Chōu Té-ch'īng might have held when he compiled this book, he was occasionally influenced by the phonological tradition.

2.2.3 Within each tone group or sub-group of a rime, graphs of identical pronunciation (homophones) are grouped together into homonym groups. These homonym groups are separated from one another simply by a small circle. Within each homonym group, unlike rime books of earlier times, the graphs are not defined, and above all, there is no *fǎn-ch'ièh* notation to indicate their reading. This lack of further information about the homonym groups presents some difficulty when we try to figure out their initials, but our knowledge of the previous periods and that of the modern dialects helps us solve this problem in all but a few exceptional cases.

2.3 The book has always been treasured as a standard reference in writing the *ch'ǚ* poems, but not until as late as the twenties of the present century did scholars begin to realize its immense linguistic value. Since that time, an enormous amount of work has been done, and much has been learned, but continuous efforts are still needed. Among the numerous writings dealing with CYYY, the following ones seem to be the more important and hence have to be given a few brief comments.

(*a*) Ishiyama Fukuji 石山福治: *Kōtei chūgen on'in* 考定中原音韻 (Tokyo, 1925). This book is the first attempt to make a comprehensive study

---

① See Lù(1946), 59, and Chào and Tsēng (1962), 324.

of CYYY in modern linguistic terms. The author gives all the homonym groups a reconstructed phonetic notation, but like all pioneers, he is not very successful in this effort, and there remains much to be desired. The book has thus been overshadowed by later works.

(*b*) Chào Yìn-t'áng 趙蔭棠: *Chūng-yüán Yīn-yǜn Yén-chiū* 中原音韻研究 (Shanghai, 1936). This book has two parts. The first part is an excellent exposition of the historical background of CYYY and other rime books written afterwards and related to it. Part two contains a reprint of the original text and two chapters of discussion on phonological changes, which are only a number of impressionistic observations. The reprint of the text is, however, very good. Instead of separating the homonym groups by a circle as in the original text, Chào numbered them within each rime. Chào also gave each homonym group a phonetic notation, which, though "far more consistent [than Ishiyama's]"①, is far from being satisfactory. For one thing, in order to keep the basic principle that within each tone group the homonym groups must be different from one another, he sometimes added new initials at will, and sometimes he did not even live up to this principle②.

(*c*) Lù Chìh-wéi 陸志韋: "Shìh Chūng-yüán Yīn-yǜn" 釋中原音韻 in Yēnchīng Hsüéh-pào 燕京學報 31 (1946), 35–70. In my opinion, this article is probably the most inspiring of all the works dealing with CYYY. The whole treatment is cast in an old-fashioned quasi-phonetic frame, but the author is very consistent in his arguments and makes a number of interesting, though not necessarily correct, points. In my discussions on CYYY later on, I will refer to this article and refute some of the points in it. If I appear to criticize him too often, it should be taken as evidence that I have a very high

① Stimson (1966), 10.

② Chào Yìn-t'áng (1936). For example, Chào establishes four more guttural initials [c, c', ȵ, ç] in addition to [k, k', ŋ, x] (p. 101) particularly for Rime Group 11; in Rime Group 15, he gives the same transcription to Homonym Groups 10 and 27.

opinion of his work.

(*d*) Hattari Shirō 服部四郎 and Tōdō Akiyasu 藤堂明保：*Chūgen On'in no Kenkyū* 中原音韻の研究（Tokyo，1958）. This book is the result of very careful textual criticism and is therefore very reliable for many of the details which are in doubt. It numbers all the homonym groups from the beginning straight down to the end，with no regard even to rime distinction.

(*e*) Stimson，Hugh M：“Phonology of the Chūng-yüán Yīn-yǜn”，in *Ts'ing-hua Journal of Chinese Studies* 清華學報 n. s. 3，No. 1（1962），Taipei，114 - 158. This article is the second part of the author's dissertation，but is the most important part for us，because it is this part that deals directly with CYYY. The article is significant in that it is the first attempt to work out the phonemic system of CYYY，but unfortunately，the author chose to build his phonemicization upon Chào Yìn-t'áng's phonetic reconstruction which，as I have said，is by no means well done. That “it contains an alarming number of misprints in the transcription” is only a minor flaw，when compared with its inconsistency in reconstruction. It thus simply cannot be “the logical starting point in a phonemic analysis”①. For this purpose，we must go back to the original text.

(*f*) Stimson，Hugh M.：The *Jongyuan in yunn*（New Haven，1966）. This book has a long introduction in which the part dealing with CYYY is essentially a summary of the above-mentioned article，though the author makes some revisions in notation. The bulk of the book is a glossary of all the graphs found in CYYY，based upon Hattari and Tōdō's edition，but rearranged and renumbered，with phonemic transcriptions for Middle Chinese（i. e.，Ancient Chinese），Old Mandarin（i. e.，CYYY），and Modern Pekinese.

2.4 In the beginning of his well-known article，Lù Chìh-wéi asserts

① Stimson（1962a），115.

without explanation that the method with which Chōu Té-ch'īng compiled CYYY is "purely inductive", that he simply collected the rime words together from the *ch'ǔ* poems of his day and classified them into nineteen rimes, that his 'teachers' are not the rime books and rime tables before him, but the famous playwrights of his time whom he mentioned in his book①. Later he says that in his discussion of CYYY he will not mention the rime tables, because "actually it will be much more convenient in the discussion of the phonological development to link Chōu's book directly with *Kuǎng-yǜn*"②. Curiously, this kind of statement has been accepted by practically all the modern students of CYYY, or at least no one, as far as I know, has refuted him. In what follows, I am going to prove that this is wrong, and more importantly, I am going to show the close relation between the rime table period (RTP) and CYYY. The fact that this has been overlooked probably explains why no tolerably satisfactory conclusion has been reached on this subject, in spite of the tremendous effort that has been spent.

2.4.1 There are altogether some 5876 graphs in CYYY. It seems to me incredible to claim that every one of these graphs had been used as a rime word at least once by one or another of the playwrights before Chōu Té-ch'īng, though frankly, I have not done any research in this regard. Moreover, as a reference work for versification, it would not be very useful if it should confine its entries only to those which had been used before, and Chōu certainly knew this. Chào Yìn-t'áng also says that Chōu's book is "induced from the theatrical writings of his predecessors", but he adds that Chōu "combined (some of the rimes of) *Kuǎng-yǜn*, improved *Kuǎng-yǜn*"③. I do not know exactly what Chào means by this, but if he means that Chōu used *Kuǎng-yǜn* as an important reference work when compiling

① Lù(1946), 35.

② Lù(1946), 36.

③ Chào Yìn-t'áng (1936), 7.

CYYY, he is certainly right.

2.4.2 To say that Chōu wrote his book merely by collecting and classifying the rime words from the works of the playwrights before him is to give him too much and too little credit at the same time. We give him too much credit if we say that he had analyzed the riming scales of all the works written before him, a job not yet completely done even today. On the other hand, we give him too little credit when we say or imply that he was so over-cautious that he did not even dare to add a few words of his own which he was sure could be included in a certain rime. To be sure, he must have given special consideration to the riming habits of the famous writers before him. After all, they all wrote in the language he recorded, and this surely gave prestige to his work, but he must also have been bold enough to go beyond that and to make some generalizations by using his own knowledge of the language. At least in one case where the riming habits of Kuān Hàn-ch'īng 關漢卿, the most famous playwright and one of those Chōu claimed to follow, has been analyzed, we are told there are quite a basketful of rime words which are 'exceptions' according to CYYY!①

2.4.3 The correspondence between the order of the rimes of CYYY and that of the rimes of *Kuǎng-yǜn* is too clear to be ignored, and yet it has been almost consistently overlooked. Since the rimes of *Kuǎng-yǜn* were later further grouped into sixteen rime classes (RC) called she, and the term 'rime' as used in CYYY means roughly the same thing as rime class of the rime tables, we may conveniently show the correspondence in the following manner:

RC of the rime tables			Rimes of CYYY	
(1) T'ūng	通	——	(1) Tūng-chūng	東鍾
(2) Chiāng	江	——	(2) Chiāng-yáng	江陽

① Liào (1963).

(3) Chĭh	止	(3) Chīh-szū	支思
		(4) Ch'í-wéi	齊微
(4) Yǜ	遇	(5) Yǘ-mú	魚模
(5) Hsièh	蟹	(6) Chiēh-lái	皆來
(6) Chēn	臻	(7) Chēn-wén	真文
(7) Shān	山	(8) Hán-shān	寒山
		(9) Huán-huān	桓歡
		(10) Hsiēn-tiēn	先天
(8) Hsiào	效	(11) Hsiāo-háo	蕭豪
(9) Kuǒ	果	(12) Kē-kē	歌戈
(10) Chiǎ	假	(13) Chiā-má	家麻
		(13) Ch'ē-chē	車遮
(11) Tàng	宕	(2Chiāng-yáng)	
(12) Kĕng	梗	(15) Kēng-ch'īng	庚青
(13) Tsēng	曾		
(14) Liú	流	(16) Yóu-hóu	尤侯
(15) Shēn	深	(17) Ch'īn-hsǘn	侵尋
(16) Hsién	咸	(18) Chiēn-hsién	監咸
		(19) Lién-hsiēn	廉纖

The correspondence is of course not completely neat in the following respects:

RC11 had merged completely with RC2, and together they formed Rime 2 in CYYY. The same is true with RC12 and RC13. There are still other minor regroupings.

The entering tone graphs were all taken out from the rime classes to which they formerly belonged, and redistributed among the rimes with no nasal cnding.

It should be remembered that there may be as many as four divisions in a rime class, while there is no such thing in a rime of CYYY. In fact, the split of some of the rime classes into two or more rimes is just a matter of different development of the divisions, as we shall see later (see 5.6).

Unless we want to say there is some intrinsic value in the order of the rimes of *Kuǎng-yùn*, we must admit that Chōu did this merely by following the tradition. Lù Chìh-wéi obviously does not believe there could be any intrinsic value in that order, for he rearranged the rimes in his article, and so does Stimson. It might be argued that Chōu was following not just *Kuǎng-yùn* but also some of the books of rime tables, though there is no direct evidence for it. The correspondence between CYYY and *Kuǎng-yùn* is already sufficient to prove that Chōu depended heavily on the phonological studies of the past.

2.5 By proving that Chōu did not just collect and classify the rime words of the playwrights before him but rather depended heavily on his own knowledge of the language as well as the phonological studies of the past. I mean to say that Chōu is a far better phonologist than he has so far been credited with being. Another thing which often looms unnecessarily large in the mind of the students of CYYY is that Chōu was born in a southern province instead of Peking. In fact, it has been used as a kind of *deus ex machina*. Whenever they are frustrated by some seemingly inexplicable features in the book, they charge Chōu for letting his native pronunciation enter the book?① This charge seems to me quite unreasonable, if not entirely groundless. Though Chōu was not born in the north, we cannot logically deny, indeed we must assume, that he knew the standard language of his day very well. Furthermore, Chōu's sole purpose for compiling the book is to teach people how to rime, and his book has ever since been accepted as a standard for that It is very hard for us to imagine that he did not know the language well enough and that he made many mistakes in his book because of

① For example, Chào Yìn-t'áng (1936), 2, and Lù (1946), 55.

that. As a logical starting point, we will assume that Chōu is right all through the book. This does not mean that Chōu or his book, as we have it now, is infallible. It simply means that we have to start with this assumption. Perhaps toward the end of our study we may claim that he is mistaken in some rare and minor cases, when we have strong internal evidence from his book to support such charges.

2.6 Lù Chìh-wéi once criticized another scholar as illogical, who tried to prove that actually there was no entering tone in CYYY by quoting a book written four hundred years after it①. I think this principle must be pushed much further. After assuming that CYYY indeed reflects the language of its day faithfully, I will confine my analysis to the limits of the book itself. By this I mean I will try my best to explain all the phonological phenomena in the book as they are, even if other documents such as Chuó Ts'úng- chīh's *Chūng-chōu Yüèh-fǔ Yīn-yǜn Lèi-piēn* 卓從之:中州樂府音韻類編 and the hPhags-pa script, both of which are supposed to represent the same language as CYYY, may seem to be "more reasonable" in some respects. CYYY will receive the primary stress while others will be used only when some facts in the former cannot be accounted for in formal terms. I hope that, by applying this principle vigorously, the phonological structure we finally arrive at will be able to answer for us many of the questions in dispute, such as whether there is still an entering tone in CYYY, and whether it represents an earlier stage of Modern Pekinese.

2.7 The normal method of making a phonemic analysis of a living language is to begin with phonetic transcriptions made of the language. Practically, all those who have done something about CYYY have followed this procedure in trying to give the book a quasi-phonetic reconstruction by using evidence found in modern dialects and other rime books, though few of

① Lù (1946), 57.

these scholars have attempted to make a refined phonemic analysis. My approach is somewhat different (see 1.5). I feel that in the case of our study the steps of this procedure must be reversed. We must try to outline a rough phonemic system first and to figure out the phonetic value or values of the rather abstract phonemes later. The reason is, as I said before, that the book supplies us with all the necessary hints about the phonemic system it represents by giving us presumably all the attested contrasting syllables (i.e., homonym groups) in nineteen rimes, but does not say anything about their phonetic reality①. In the following chapters, when I reconstruct the phonemic system of the book, I shall roughly take the following steps in this order:

(*a*) Setting up a tentative hypothetical system after an overall check of the book.

(*b*) Modifying and revising this hypothetical system so that it may maintain a maximum number of contrasts among the homonym groups, ideally, all of them.

(*c*) Straightening out this hypothetical system in structural terms.

(*d*) Trying to deduce the allophones of the phonemes in this system by all means and from all the known facts.

Of course, these steps are not clearly distinct from each other, but rather interwoven. For example, what we know about the later steps must influence us, consciously or unconsciously, in setting up the hypothetical system of the first step, but logically, if we need an order of some sort, it should be something like the above. What I put down in the following discussions is, of course, not all the troubles I have gone through, but the

① In his article of 1962a, Stimson calls his work "an attempt to apply the methods of phonemic analysis to hints of phonetic facts supplied in ... CYYY." (114). Later, in the second note to the article (155), he says: "The data supplied by the CYYY are at best mere hints." I differ with him.

result of innumerable trials and failures.

2.8 CYYY has been thoroughly numbered several times. Chào Yìn-t'áng numbered the homonym groups within each rime successively, paying no attention to the tone groups. Hattari and Tōdō numbered them from the beginning straight down to the end, without even bothering about the rimes. Stimson did still differently. He completely rearranged the entries of the book and then numbered each graph successively, instead of the homonym groups. I am reluctant to add one more numerical system, but for quick reference and in order to save the trouble of mentioning tediously the rime and the tone of a certain graph or homonym group in question, I have set up a reference number for each homonym group. Each number in my system will consist of seven digits to be understood in the following manner:

(*a*) The first two digits represent the number of a rime (RG) as it stands in CYYY. For example, a number like 03XXXXX means that the homonym group represented by this number belongs to the third rime (RG03) namely, *Chīh-szū* 支思. 15XXXXX means *Kēng-ch'īng* 庚青(RG15).

(*b*) The next two digits represent the tone group (TG); 01 for the even tone of the yin type (TG01); 02 for the even tone of the yang type (TG02); 03 for the rising tone (TG03); 04 for the going tone (TG04). When the tone group is one of those 'entering tone as X-tone' tones, 5 will be used to replace the zero. For example, 53 means 'entering tone as rising tone' (TG53). The unique tone group of 'going tone as the even tone of the *yáng* type' may also be represented by TG42, though it is really of very little significance.

(*c*) The last three digits represent the number of a homonym group in a certain rime as numbered by Chào Yìn-t'áng. For example, 0101001 means the homonym group of the two graphs 東 and 冬, in TG01 of RG01. 1654087 means then homonym group No. 87 of TG54 in RG16, namely, the graph 六.

The number might need only six digits, if Chào had numbered the homonym groups in each tone group separately, but since he did not, we have to settle for one more digit, because his book is easily accessible, and a new edition is not in sight yet.

CHAPTER THREE
THE PHONOLOGICAL BACKGROUND OF CYYY

In this chapter we shall set up the foundation necessary for future discussions on CYYY. We shall begin with a brief discussion of the syllabic structure of the Chinese language, and then attempt to give, in as concise a manner as possible, the initial and tonal systems of Ancient Chinese. For reasons to be discussed later, the system of finals of the rime tables will be given, instead of that of AC. The changes of the initials and the finals from the earlier periods to CYYY, however, will not be discussed here, because their complexity requires that they be treated in separate chapters; but since the changes involving the tones, the medials, and the endings are relatively simple, they will be cleared up here.

3. 1 Chinese Syllabic Patterns

Samuel E. Martin in his The Phonemes of Ancient Chinese abstracted Karlgren's interpretation of the AC syllable as follows:

$$\frac{T}{(C)(V)(V)V(V,C)}$$

This he later reinterpreted in phonemic terms in the following form which he said is "more parallel to that of Mandarin and other modern dialects"①,

① Martin (1953), 20-23. This interpretation of the syllabic structure follows essentially the Chinese traditional analysis in which a syllable is divided into an 'initial' (*shēng-mǔ* 聲母) and a 'final' (*yǜn-mǔ* 韻母) with the latter further analyzed into three segmental (轉下頁)

$$\frac{T}{(C)(SV)(SV)V(C,SV)} \text{ i.e. } \frac{1,2,3,4}{(C)(y)(w)V(C,y,w)}$$

The fact that both AC and all the modern dialects have the same syllabic form forces us to believe that the syllabic structure of the language represented by CYYY is also the same, because it is impossible to imagine that it could be otherwise. I, therefore, assume without trying to prove that each homonym group in CYYY stands for a monosyllable of a pattern conforming to the above formula. It may be noted that, in both AC and the various modern dialects, the SV which fills the pre-nuclear and the post-nuclear slots can be phonemically interpreted as /y/ and /w/. In this sense, they can be called the constants in the formula, while C, V, and T are, in different degrees, variables. Traditionally, a syllable is first analyzed into two parts: the 'initial' represented in the formula by the initial consonant, and the 'final' which is the rest of the syllable including the tone. The final is then further analyzed into three parts besides the tone, namely, the 'medial' represented here by either of the two semi-vowels or both with /y/ always preceding /w/, the 'nucleus' which is represented by a vowel and is the only obligatory element of all the segmental phonemes in the above formula, and the 'ending' which may be either a semi-vowel or a consonant. I will discuss these elements following this analysis.

$$I \frac{T}{(M)V(E)}$$

(接上頁) components, the 'medial' (*chièh-yīn* 介音 or *yǜn-t'óu* 韻頭), the 'nucleus' (*yǜn-fù* 韻腹), and the 'ending' (*yǜn-wěi* 韻尾). The interpretation of the so-called *ts'uō-k'ǒu* medial (撮口 i. e. [ü]) as a compound of /yw/ with the two elements in this order is, to some extent, a modern invention (Hartman 1944, 118), but in terms of distinctive features, this interpretation does not seem to be as important now as it was thought before. Even the order of the two elements which is so crucial in the 'phoneme' representation loses much of its meaning in the 'feature' representation. Cf., among other writings, Yüán (1960) and Hsueh (1973).

3.2 The Initial System of AC

There are thirty-six initials(including the zero initial) in AC, which are listed in the chart①.

3.2.1 In the chart, I have labeled both the stops and the affricates with 'S', because I feel their difference is basically phonetic, while phonemically the two types of consonants behave in an identical manner when they are combined with /h/ or /ɦ/②. The chart is essentially the result of Martin's phonemicization which is based upon Karlgren's reconstruction and Y. R. Chao's revision③. However, I have made here some modifications which can be discussed right away. There might be some phonetic reasons to make these revisions, but I would rather be satisfied to say that the only rationale for them is that they will make it possible for us to account for the development from AC to CYYY in a much more general and economical fashion.

		S (Stops)			Fr (Fricatives)		R (Resonants)	
(Labials)	B	p	ph	pɦ			m	
(Dental stops)	D	t	th	tɦ			n	l
(Dental sibilants)	Ds	c	ch	cɦ	s	sɦ		
(Palatal stops)	P	tj	tjh	tjɦ				
(Palatal retroflexes)	Pr	cr	crh	crɦ	sr	srɦ		

① I use the term 'guttural' (abbreviated 'G') in the chart, instead of the commonly used 'velar'. There might well be good phonetic reasons for this choice, but as far as the present study is concerned, the only serious justification is that since Karlgren first used this term and later Y. R. Chao accepted it, it has become part of the tradition in the study of the Chinese language. Also following Chao, I use the term 'sibilant' here (Y. R. Chao 1948, 19).

② The original symbol is ḣ́, but for ease of understanding, it is changed to ɦ. ɦ in other places, also represents the orginal symbol ḣ́.

③ Martin (1953), 17-18.

續表

		S (Stops)			Fr (Fricatives)		R (Resonants)	
(Palatal sibilants)	Pj	cj	cj	cjɦ	sj	sjɦ	nj	
(Gutturals)	G	k	kh	kɦ	x	xɦ	ŋ	
		q						ø

I replace the initial /h/ with /x/ and add /x/ before the initial /ɦ/. This revision puts the two initials more in line with the other initials in the columns where they appear respectively. Aside from the possibility that phonetically these two initials in AC are probably velar fricatives, instead of glottal, the compelling reason for this revision is that we can now treat /h/ as purely a symbol for aspiration and /ɦ/, a symbol for voicing. This will allow us to say, when we try to account for the process of devoicing, that /ɦ/ simply disappeared, without specifying somewhat awkwardly that /ɦ/ became /h/ when it served as an initial by itself, and otherwise disappeared. It must be added promptly that this is a consideration for diachronic study. As for a purely synchronic description, /x/ can surely be spared.

(b) The glottal stop /q/ now occupies a new row in the column of the voiceless unaspirated stops. This is necessary when we want to account for the changes in tones, because /q/ behaves like the other initials in this column (see 3. 5. 2). It may not seem to be very good to add a new row just for this one initial, but otherwise we would have to add one more column, as Martin does.

(c) Karlgren's initial [ńź] certainly looks unique. Martin re-interprets it as /nɦ/ which still looks to me quite peculiar, because /n/ is then the only resonant which could be combined with /ɦ/. Purely for diachronic study, it would be better to represent this initial by /nj/, as will become evident in later discussion (see 4. 5. 4). This is supported by the analysis made by Lǐ

Júng who uses [ń] for this initial, that is, a palatal nasal of some sort[①]. If we are bold enough, we can simply use /j/ alone to represent this initial, because I feel the essential character of this initial is palatalization, though it may be colored by nasalization, but this would compel us to say that /j/ is a voiced consonant, which is obviously incompatible with other facts. I, therefore, will accept /nj/, though I am still not quite satisfied with it.

I add /srɦ/ to the chart, following Tǔng T'úng-hó's analysis. It must be admitted that this initial is quite marginal in AC, and later development has made it even more insignificant (see 4. 5 4. 5. 3), but the fact that it existed in AC requests us to include it, and its inclusion clearly gives a feeling of more symmetry to the whole picture.

(e) I replace his /ng/ with /ŋ/. This is purely a graphic matter, but /ŋ/ seems to suit my purpose better.

3. 2. 2 The above chart can be further simplified into a chart of the individual consonant phonemes as follows:

		B	D	Ds	G	
Non-resonants	S	p	t	c	k	q
	Fr			s	x	
Resonants	N	m	n		ŋ	
	L		l			
					(j), (r), (h), (ɦ)	

① Lǐ Júng (1956), 125 - 126. Actually Maspero fist proposed [ñ] (= [ń]) for the initial in question (Henri Maspero, "Le dialecte de Tch'ang-ngan sous les T'ang", *BEFEO* 20 (1920), 34). This proposal was later refuted by Karlgren who replaced it with [ńź] (Karlgren 1954, 230). Lǐ Júng made a careful study of the Chinese graphs used to transcribe the Sanskrit syllabic 'ña' before the T'ang dynasty, and found that, before 724, several graphs with the initial in question were always used for this purpose, but after that date, a graph with the initial /n/ was used. He thus confirmed Maspero's proposal and concluded that this initial did not lose its nasal quality until 771.

Of these individual phonemes, the four in parentheses are categorically different from the others. Strictly speaking, they are not phonemes in the ordinary sense, but four distinctive features (or series generating elements) each of which involves some special type or types of phonemes. Their characters can be defined in the following manner:

/j/: palatalization, occurring with dental stops, sibilants, and nasals.

/r/: retroflexion, occurring with dental sibilants.

/h/: aspiration, occurring with stops except /q/.

/ɦ/: voicing, occurring with non-resonants except /q/.

In my discussions later, however, I will treat them as if they were really phonemes.

3.2.3 The thirty-six initials given in 3.2 are not identical to the thirty-six initials of the rime tables. Although we do not know enough about the later, the following points seem to be clear:

(a) The labials are split into two series, the bilabials and the labiodentals, though this split is probably allophonic in nature.

(b) The two palatal series Pr and Pj in AC are represented by one series of initials in the rime tables[①]. This may imply that the two contrasting series in AC had become allophones of one series of phonemes, though we cannot be sure before further analysis has been made.

(c) The voiced guttural fricative /xɦ/ has disappeared before finals of the third division, though otherwise remaining.

Ideally, we should start with an initial chart of RTP, if we had one. However, the initial systems of AC and RTP do not seem to have too many

① The five initials in the rime tables represented by the five graphs 照穿牀審禪 combine with the finals of both the second and the third divisions. Students of AC have found it necessary to split them into two series, 章昌船書常 which combine only with the finals of the third division, namely, the Pj series in our system, and 莊初崇生俟 which combine mainly with finals of the second division, but also with those of the third division, namely, the Pr series here.

drastic differences, so it may not be a bad idea to account for the initial system of CYYY by beginning with that of AC.

3.3 The Medials

I have stated that in the syllable structure of the Chinese language, the two semivowels, /y/ and /w/ in medial position can be called constants in a historical sense. By this I do not mean that syllables have always remained the same in having or lacking /y/ and/or /w/ in their medial position. In fact, many of them have had their medial changed systematically, but this change is limited to the loss of the /y/ or /w/ which they used to have, or the acquisition of one of them which they did not have before, under certain circumstances. Thus the inventory of the medial position has always been limited to these two semi-vowels. As a result of the loss of the AC /j/ in a rather early stage (see 4.5), the medial /y/ and /w/ in CYYY may now be interpreted as symbols for palatalization and labialization respectively. Their appearance or disappearance must thus be closely connected with the shifts of the initials and the nuclear vowels, and consequently, it can be most effectively discussed together with those shifts.

3.4 The Endings

The ending slot has a larger inventory. Besides the two semi-vowels and the three nasals /m, n, ŋ/, the three stops /p, t, k/ also occur in this slot in AC. Syllables ending in the stops are traditionally regarded as one unique 'tonal' group called the 'entering tone'. We do not know why it is so, though I suspect that the practice might well indicate that each of the stops in this position actually appears phonetically in an unreleased form. This allophonic form serves as a check to the whole syllable and makes it sound rather abrupt when compared with syllables of other types. This, however, is hard to prove, though it may sound reasonable. The /y/ and /w/ occurring in the ending slot must also be phonetically different from the /y/ and the /w/ occurring in the medial slot, for when they occur in the ending slot, they obviously exert a much stronger effect on the syllable as a whole than when they occur in the medial slot, as is reflected by the fact that syllables with different endings always form different rimes, while syllables with different medials are very often put together in one rime. Whatever the difference may be, it is so subtle that it will be even harder to prove. Since the so-called entering tone in AC has been split into three sub-groups in CYYY, it has long been a controversy whether the entering tone still exists in CYYY, in other words, whether /p, t, k/ or perhaps a new item, say, a glottal stop, can still appear in the ending position. This is a very crucial and complicated problem which will have to be treated in a separate chapter (see Chapter Six). The semi-vowels and the nasals clearly still occur in that position in CYYY, with a minor change which can be expressed explicitly by the following formula①:

$$B + X + m \rightarrow B + X + n \qquad (1)$$

This means that, due to dissimilation, ending /m/ in syllables with labial initials had been changed to /n/ before CYYY②. Consequently, these syllables now appear in rimes with ending /n/, for example, 0703074 品

---

① In writing rules like this one, I adopt the notational conventions of modern generative grammar, particularly as they are defined in Koutsoudas (1966), 1-39, but confer also 7.1 for the few deviations I have made. Though my approach is heavily influenced by this modern development of linguistic science, I do not, however, consider my present work generative in a strict sense. I borrow these conventions only because I feel they provide us a precise and yet concise means to express what we may want to say. The domain of the rewriting rules is limited to the syllable. In other words, the initial string is # syllable #, though it is only implied here.

② Lù Chìh-wéi seems to be the first one who pointed out the change in this kind of strictly formal terms (see Lù 1946, 39).

(AC /ᶜ phiəm/, MP /phyěn/), 1003053 貶 (AC /ᶜ piɛm/, MP /pyǎn/), 0802026 凡(AC /꜀ pɦiuam/, MP /fwán/) and 0804067 泛(AC /phiuamᵓ/, MP /fwàn/)①.

3.5 The Tones

Before we move on to the discussion of the initial system of CYYY, it is better to deal first with the changes of tones from AC to CYYY, because they are completely conditioned by the AC initial system. From AC to CYYY, there clearly occurred a devoicing process of the initial system, accompanied by a process of splitting and regrouping of the tonemes. It is not unreasonable to imagine that some of the four tonemes in AC might have had two or more allotones. These allotones were in complementary distribution in that each occurred in syllables with a certain type of initial. For example, we may say the even tone had a high register allotone which occurred only in syllables with voiced initials, and a low register allotone which occurred otherwise. So far as the contrast between voicing and voicelessness in the initial system was maintained, allotonic difference was nothing but a redundant feature, but as soon as the process of devoicing was completed, the formerly overshadowed allotonic difference rose up to replace it and thus became a distinctive feature. This, however, can hardly be ever proved, as

---

① From now on, I shall give each example graph its AC reading and MP reading. The AC reading is based on Martin's phonemicization (Martin 1953, 18 and 38), with a few slight modifications on the initial system discussed in 3.2. The small half circle at one corner of the transcription is the symbol for the tonal category to which the graph belongs, as it is traditionally marked (i.e., at the lower left corner it means the even tone; at the upper left corner it means the rising tone; at the upper right corner it means the going tone. The entering tone is already marked by the terminal stop). The MP reading is based on my own revision of both Hartman (1944) and Hockett (1947), as is outlined in 7.5.1 to 7.5.3. Confer also Note ③ in page 173.

the phonetic value of a tone of the past is about the most difficult thing to determine①. Phonemically, we can only say that part of the functional load of the vl. /vd. contrast in the initials is taken over by the tonal contrast. But for a formal account of the phonological changes, we may pretend that the above hypothesis is correct by treating the splitting and regrouping of the AC tones as an event separate from and prior to the devoicing of the initials.

3. 5. 1 Following the traditional practice where the tone of a syllable is always indicated by the second or lower element of the *fǎn-ch'ièh* compound, I choose to interpret a toneme as part of the complex called 'final', though it has been said that phonetically the tone of a syllable spreads over the voiced part of the syllable, i. e, starting from the initial, when it is voiced②. Consequently, I shall indicate a toneme by a superscript attached to F, the abbreviation of 'final', in the form of F^t. In this way, we can formulate the changes of the tones from AC to CYYY as follows:

$$F^{even} \longrightarrow \begin{Bmatrix} F^{02} / \begin{Bmatrix} \text{ɦ} \\ R \end{Bmatrix} \_\_\_ \\ F^{01} \end{Bmatrix} \tag{2}$$

$$F^{rising} \longrightarrow \begin{Bmatrix} F^{04} / \text{ɦ}\_\_\_ \\ F^{03} \end{Bmatrix} \tag{3}$$

$$F^{going} \longrightarrow F^{04} \tag{4}$$

$$F^{entering} \longrightarrow \begin{Bmatrix} F^{52} / \text{ɦ}\_\_\_ \\ F^{54} / R\_\_\_ \\ F^{53} \end{Bmatrix} \tag{5}$$

① Cf. Martin(1953), 10 - 11. This uncertain or relative character of the tones was vividly illustrated by the words of Lù Fǎ-yén who, in his preface to *Ch'ièh-yǜn*, said: "The going tone of Ch'ín and Lǔng sounds like the entering tone(of the standard language), while the even tone of *Liáng* and *Yì* sounds like the going tone."

② Cf. Y.R. Chao (1968), 25. Actually, I am still too cautious in treating the tone of a syllable as spreading over the entire 'final'. A much simpler alternative is perhaps to say that it is associated with the nuclear vowel only (at least phonemically). Our analysis of the syllable certainly permits us to do so.

3.5.2 The first three formulas need no further explanation, as the same processes have also been witnessed in MP. A few rather rare irregular graphs like 1201014 麽 (AC /꜀muɑ/, MP /mwé/) can simply be treated as exceptions. The change of the entering tone, on the other hand, requires careful study. The author of CYYY tells us explicitly that this AC tone has been split into three sub-groups, represented here by 52,53,54, because they can 'used as' 02,03, and 04 respectively. The real nature of these three new 'tones', however, involves too many problems to be discussed here (see Chapter Six), but I can raise one important point, viz, the split of the entering tone into three in CYYY is a relatively later development, while the splitting and regrouping of the other three AC tones must have taken place much earlier. The proof for this is the disappearance of the glottal stop initial /q/. When the first three AC tones underwent the process of splitting and regrouping, the glottal stop must have been still there, functioning as a conditioning factor, so that syllables of the even tone with this initial were all entered into TG01 in CYYY, instead of TG02, as should have been the case, if the glottal stop had already been lost. But when the split of the entering tone took place, the glottal stop had obviously dropped out, for syllables formerly having this initial were now entered into TG54, instead of TG53, with but two exceptions, 0453107 一(AC /qi*t/, MP /yɨ/)[①] and 0553102 屋 (AC /q*k/, MP /wɨ/), 沃(AC /qu*k/, MP /wè/ or /wɨ/). Thus, between Rule 4 and Rule 5, there should be added a rule specifying that syllables with the glottal stop initial had by this stage lost their initial and consequently joined the zero initial group under the column of resonants.

$$q \rightarrow \varnothing \qquad (6)$$

① 0453107 一 can hardly be called an exception, because the graph is also found in 0454147 where it will be regarded as regular according to my interpretation. Its entrance into TG53 might be the result of a sandhi pronunciation according to some morphophonemic rule unknown to us.

However, the split of the AC entering tone cannot be too late either. It must have taken place before the process of devoicing of the initial system, because voicing is one of the conditioning features for the tonal split.

3.5.3 As has been said before, all the tones can only be studied in phonemic terms, but for TG01 and TG02, I would like to venture a conjecture. The fact that the word 陰 *yīn* 'dark; cloudy; female' was associated with TG01 may indicate that it was low, while TG02, described as 陽 *yáng* 'bright; sunny; male' was high. I, therefore, think that contrary to MP, TG01 in CYYY is perhaps a low register tone and TG02, a high register. This speculation is supported by many modern Northern Mandarin dialects other than MP, though evidence from modern dialects, strictly speaking does not mean too much in this case.

3.6 The RTP System of Finals

The shift of the initial system from AC to CYYY is, to a very great extent, determined by the system of finals. However, to account for this shift, we cannot start with the AC system of finals, though we can do so with the AC system of initials. The reason is that, during the period of almost one millennium from AC to CYYY, the vowel system had undergone a much more drastic change than the consonant system. We must, therefore, start with the system of finals as shown in the rime tables of *Ch'ièh-yǜn Chǐh-nán* (see 1.3), if we wish to draw eventually some meaningful rules of correspondence. Since no phonemicization in modern linguistic terms has been made for RTP, I will have to refer to them in purely abstract structural terms, that is, by referring to the categories in them as they are traditionally labelled.

3.6.1 Of the three books of rime tables, *Szù-shēng Těng-tzǔ*, *Ch'ièh-yǜn Chǐh-nán*, and *Ch'ièh-yǜn Chǐh-chǎng T'ú*, the last shows the largest number of deviations from *Ch'ièh-yǜn*, and can therefore be assumed to represent the stage of the Chinese language closest to that of CYYY. The basic form of the rime tables is, however, the same in all these books. First, the rimes of *Ch'ièh-yǜn* are further grouped into some classes of rimes called '*shè*'①, and then, within each rime class, if appropriate, the contrast between the rounded and unrounded is set up, according to whether or not the syllables involved have the semi-vowel /w/ in the medial position. Syllables are then each entered into one of the four tonal categories, in one of the four divisions (*těng* 等), under one of the thirty-six initials. Not all the rime classes have for divisions. Some have only one or two, .the first and / or the third. The inter-relation of the four divisions is still not very clear, in spite of the tremendous amount of work that has been done in this regard. It seems safe to say that, with a few exception those rime classes which have only the first and/or the third divisions have probably some high level vowel as their nucleus, while those which may have all the four divisions, particularly the second division, must have some vowels of the lower levels as their nuclei. This contrast of high vs. low among the nuclear vowels may perhaps account for the traditional practice of classifying the rimes into two type the inner series (*nèi-chuǎn* 内轉) and the outer series (*wài-chuǎn* 外轉)②. There is some confusion about the affinities of the rime classes to the series. The following is Ló Ch'áng-p'éi's version of this contrast which I

---

① *Szù-shēng Těng-tzǔ*, and *Ch'ièh-yǜn Chǐh-nán* both have sixteen rime classes. *Ch'ièh-yǜn Chǐh-chǎng T'ú* does not use the term '*shè*', but the idea is implied there, with, however, only thirteen of such classes. Cf. Martin (1953), 2-3.

② Cf. Ló(1933), 206-226.

adopt here as a base for future discussion[①].

Outer series		Inner series	
kuǒ	果	yǜ	遇
chiǎ	假	chǐh	止
hsièh	蟹	líú	流
hsiào	效	shēn	深
hsién	咸	chēn	臻
shān	山	tsēng	曾
tàng	宕	t'ūng	通
chiāng	江		
kěng	梗		

3. 6. 2 If we use 'C' for the initial, 'E' for the ending, 'V' subscribed with 'n' for the nuclear vowel of the inner series, and 'V' subscribed with a numeral for the nuclear vowels of the outer series of a certain division, we can summarize the structure of the rime tables in the following manner:

Division	Outer series	Inner Series
1	C (w) V_1(E)	C (w) V_n(E)
2	C (w) V_2(E)	—
3	(C)y (w) V_3(E)	(C) y (w) V_n(E)
4	(C) y (w)V_4(E)	—

This means that, as far as the finals of the inner series are concerned,

---

① Ló(1933). This version is later adopted by Y. R. Chao (1941,204) and Martin (1953,3). Actually, this version was first proposed by a Japanese scholar, Ōya Tōru 大矢透, but it was Ló who produced some strong arguments in its support. It should be noted here that the classification in *Szù- shēng Těng -tzǔ* and *Ch'ièh-yǜn Chǐh-nán* is different. They both have the Chēn-shè in the outer series, and have the *kuǒ-shè* and the *Tàng-shè* in the inner series. It seems to me that the difference between Ló's version and that of the two books might well indicate some aspect of the development from AC to RTP, though I am far from being certain. For the purpose of our study of CYYY, Ló's version is somewhat more suitable, when slightly modified (see 7. 2d).

the distinction between the first and the third divisions lies not, we believe, in the quality of the nuclear vowel, but rather in whether or not there is /y/ in the medial position. With regard to the outer series, the distinction among the four divisions lies not just in this fact, but also in the quality of the nuclear vowels, though we do not know how many there were or what they were (but see 5. 6. 1).

3. 6. 3 The third division of the rime tables is the most complicated one. We are told that, besides those which actually appear there, many entries which should have been included in this division were instead put into the second or the fourth division.

To accommodate this problem, Karlgren sets up two types, α and β, for the rimes of the third division. Lǐ Júng goes further in setting up three types, with one of them having two sub-types. Although much more research will have to be done before we can have a clear understanding of this matter, I believe this is a problem of AC, not of RTP. It is a difficulty which is bound to rise when people try to explain the phonological structure of one period by that of another, four or five hundred years later. In other words, I believe the rime tables truly represent the state of the language of the day when they were designed, not that of AC. Those third-division graphs they put into the second and the fourth divisions might have changed from what they used to be, though in AC they were of a similar kind to those now appearing in the third division①. Another peculiar phenomenon we observe in the arrangements of the rime tables is that, sometimes within the same rime class, of the same tone, and in the same division of both the rounded and the unrounded types, two or three AC rimes may be listed together, for example, in the *Hsièh-shè*, the *Hsién-shè*, and the *Chǐh-shè*. If we take the arrangements of the rime tables seriously, as I think we should, the only

---

① This point will be elaborated a bit further when I discuss the finals of CYYY in 5. 6 – 5. 7.

reasonable conclusion we can come to is that in RTP those AC rimes must have coalesced into one. The reason is very simple. So far there has been no way to predict the direction of phonological changes. In this regard, the compiler of the rime tables was certainly no better prophet than we are. What he stated must needs be what he was able to observe. In the following discussion on the initials and the finals of CYYY, I shall assume the above arguments to be true.

CHAPTER FOUR THE INITIAL SYSTEM OF CYYY

This chapter will be devoted exclusively to discussions of the changes of the initial system from AC to CYYY. In order for these discussions to be intelligible, the chart of initials in 3. 2 and the structure of syllables in terms of the rime tables as is given in 3. 6. 2 must be kept constantly in mind.

4. 1 The Process of Devoicing

The most prominent change from the initial system of AC to that of CYYY is the process of devoicing of the non-resonants. Martin's reinterpretation of the voiced stops and fricatives as voiceless followed by /ɦ/, aided by the slight modifications I have made, makes it possible for us to account for this process in a neat and economical manner as follows:

$$ɦ \longrightarrow \begin{Bmatrix} h/s \_\_\_ F^{02} \\ \varnothing \end{Bmatrix} \qquad (7)$$

This single rule immediately redistributes both the columns of voiced stops and fricatives into their voiceless counterparts. Note that the condition for /ɦ/ to become /h/ is ' S—F^{02} '. This means syllables undergoing this change must be of TG02, not just 'the second tone', because it has been observed that the voiced stop initials of syllables of TG52 have become unaspirated voiceless stops. The result of this shift from AC to CYYY is so clear as to make it unnecessary to give any example to illustrate it. With the disappearance of /ɦ/, the contrast between /h/ and /x/ is made meaningless; consequently, we can put them together as one phoneme by the following rule,

$$x \longrightarrow h \tag{8}$$

The process of devoicing affects consonants of all points of articulation. After having dealt with it, we can now turn to the more specific changes which affect some special types of consonants only. In what follows, I shall discuss the initials in groups according to their points of articulation.

4.2 The Labials (B)

Among the labial initials, the process of dentilabialization had been noticed long before CYYY. In the rime tables, four labiodentals are listed: 非 fēi, 敷 fū, 奉 fèng, and 微 wéi. They appear only with finals of the rounded type in the third division, in complementary distribution with 幫 pāng, 滂 p'āng, 並 pìng, and 明 míng, respectively. It has been said that these initials may be a kind of labial affricate, something like [pf, pf', bv', mv][1]. But in view of their distribution, I feel it is safe to say that they are only allophonic in nature, no matter what their phonetic value may be. It is a different story in CYYY. We notice that in CYYY the first three of these four initials have merged completely, for example, 0404111 吠 (AC /pɦiuaiᑐ/, MP /fwèy/), 沸(AC /piuəiᑐ/, MP /fwèy), 費 (AC /phiuəiᑐ/, MP /fwèy/); 0504113 付 (AC /piu*ᑐ/, MP /fwɨ/), 赴 (AC /phiu*ᑐ/, MP /fwɨ/), 父 (AC /ᑕ pɦiu*/, MP /fwɨ/), and 0804067 販(AC /piuanᑐ/, MP /fwàn/), 泛 (AC /phiuamᑐ/, MP /fwàn/), 范 (AC /ᑕ pɦiuam/, MP /fwàn/). This is also true in MP, as is evident from the MP readings given to these graphs. We can therefore postulate in CYYY an initial /f/ which is the result of the coalescence of the first three labials under certain conditions. The last one, however, still maintains its distinction and contrasts particularly with syllables of the rounded type with zero initial, for example, 0202032 亡

---

[1] Lù(1946),41.

(AC /$_c$ miuɑŋ/, MP /wáŋ/) vs. 0202048 王 (AC /$_c$ iuɑŋ/, MP /wáŋ/); 0404108 未 (AC /miuəiᵓ/, MP /wèy) vs. 0404109 胃 (AC /iuəiᵓ/, MP /wèy/); 0503060 武 (AC /^{c} miu*/, MP /wɨ̌/) vs. 0503065 五 (AC /^{c} ŋu*/, MP /wɨ̌/)①, though in MP, every contrasting pair here has merged into one reading. Like others, I will also represent this initial with /v/②.

4.2.1 In MP, phonemically speaking, labials must be followed either by /y/ or /w/, but not by both, that is, syllables with a labial initial must assume one of these two forms, BwV(E) and ByV(E), though phonetically the medial /w/ is not very much noticeable when the nuclear vowel is of a low level③. The same phenomenon is also very clear in CYYY, perhaps even more so④. This fact can perhaps help us to determine the formal condition or

---

① In 0402026, two graphs of this initial 微薇 are grouped together with two graphs of zero initial 維惟. This case must be treated as an exception, for there is one group, 0402034, which can only be reconstructed with zero initial.

② Lù Chìh-wéi has a long discussion on the phonetic value of this element, which, however, does not seem to be very convincing to me (see Lù 1946, 41 - 42).

③ A glance at Tǔng's chart (Tǔng 1954, Chart One, between p. 14 and p. 15) will make this clear. In the chart, labials combine only with two 'hó-k'ǒu' finals, [u] (/wɨ/) and [uo] (/we/). The Pinyin system of Romanization goes even farther in writing [uo] as [o] whenever it combines with a labial initial, for example, [pō] (*/pē/) for 玻/pwē/. It is, however, unreasonable to write /pwɨ̀/ (布[pù]) as */pɨ̀/, because the syllable rimes with /swɨ̀/(素[sù]) but not with /sɨ̀/ (四 [sɿ]). If, adopting a different approach, we reinterpret all the syllables with labial initials but no medial as syllables with medial /w/, we can make a very general claim as we do here. Indeed, practically all of these syllables were said to be '*hó-k'ǒu*' in *Ch'ièh-yǔn Chǐh-chǎng T'ú*. Moreover, we are here confronted with the principle of economy. In my thinking, there are two different levels of economy in phonology. One is the economy in actual transcription; the other is that of the overall phonemic structure. By the former, medial /w/ after labials can certainly be omitted, for it is partially predictable (i. e., in all cases when labials are not followed immediately by /y/), but in view of the latter as well as the prevailing riming habit, it is better to say that there is a /w/ after the labial.

④ A small number of graphs of unrounded type of the *Chǐh-shè* with labial initials curiously do not have the final /yɨy/ in CYYY, as they are supposed to have (see 5.12.5). Instead, they appear together with the first division graphs of the rounded type from the *Hsièh-shè*, and hence must be reconstructed as having a final /wɨy/ (see 5.12.5). If my reasoning is correct, the corresponding syllables of these graphs of the *Chǐh-shè* must first (轉下頁)

conditions of dentilabialization from AC to RTP, which has remained a problem to be solved①. We may assume that sometime between these two periods, labials began to behave in this new pattern. The result is that syllables with zero medial now had a /w/ added after the labial initials, and those with medial /yw/ lost the /y/. But before the /y/ was lost, the initials were changed from bilabial to labiodental②. These processes can be summed up by the following rules:

$$B+V(E) \longrightarrow B+w+V(E) \qquad (9)$$

$$\begin{bmatrix} p\left(\begin{Bmatrix} h \\ \text{ɦ} \end{Bmatrix}\right) \\ m \end{bmatrix} \rightarrow \begin{bmatrix} f \\ v \end{bmatrix} / \underline{\quad} y+w \qquad (10)$$

$$y \longrightarrow \text{ø} / \begin{Bmatrix} f \\ v \end{Bmatrix} \underline{\quad} \qquad (11)$$

4.2.2 Some amendments concerning Rule 10 must be made immediately. We find that, in CYYY as well as in MP, initial /m/ in syllables which had a final of the third division of the *T'ūng-shè* remains as /m/ instead of changing to /v/, for example, 0104065 夢 (AC /mi*ŋ$^{\supset}$/, MP /mwèŋ/) and 0554132 目(AC /mi*k/, MP /mwɨ/). We therefore must add one rule to account for this exception③:

(接上頁) have lost the medial /y/. Then their inclusion together with graphs with medial /w/ indicates that, as a result of the loss of the medial /y/, they had acquired automatically the medial /w/ before CYYY.

① Cf. Martin (1953) 40.

② In my opinion, medial /y/ in syllables of the type BywV(E) was still there, when the labial initials were changed to labiodentals, for graphs representing these syllables were still listed in the third division in the rime tables, while in CYYY. the medial /y/ must have been lost, for graphs of this type were grouped into the same rimes as the second division graphs (see 5.6.1b).

③ These graphs must be reconstructed with initial /m/, for they appear in the homonym groups which also include graphs of the first division, and they also have initial /m/ in MP. Here we also assume that the two series of rimes in the *T'ūng-shè* had coalesced by RTP (see 3.6.3); hence, the two graphs cited here should now have /yw/ in the (轉下頁)

$$y \longrightarrow \phi \,/\, m \,\_\_\_\, w + V_{tu} \begin{Bmatrix} ŋ \\ k \end{Bmatrix} \qquad (12)$$

V_{tu} = Nucleus of the *T'ūng-shè*

This is about the best we can do for the moment, since we have no idea what the nuclear vowel of the *T'ūng-shè* might have been at the time of dentilabialization. It must be added here that, when the order of the rules is taken into consideration, Rule 12 will have to be put before Rule 10, with the latter possibly simplified.

4.2.3 A very difficult problem in the application of Rule 10 is the peculiar development of the syllables with labial initials in the *Liú-shè*. The *Liú-shè* includes two types of finals in AC, the *Yóu-hóu* (尤侯) type and the *Yōu* (幽) type. The former occurs in both the first and third divisions, while the latter occurs only in the third division. We find that the third division syllables of the *Yóu-hóu* type with labial initials except /m/ are affected by the process of dentilabialization while those of the *Yōu* type are not, for example, 0502036 浮 (AC /$_{\text{c}}$pɦi*u/, MP /fwɨ/) and 0504113 富 (AC

(接上頁) medial position. The problem here also involves the third division words with initial /m/ in the *Liú-shè* such as 0502026 謀 and 1602027 矛牟 etc. (See Note ① in page 225). Our explanation is based upon the fact that all these words appear in the third division of the rime tables and consequently have been given a reconstructed reading with medial /y/ by most scholars. It may be interesting to mention here an alternative solution proposed by Pulleyblank (1970, 128) based mainly upon the Sino-Korean and the Sino-Japanese readings of these words. Briefly paraphrased, his solution says that (*a*) at the time of *Ch'ièh-yǜn*, all the words in the rimes to which words like 夢目謀 belong were *hó-k'ǒu*, having medial /u/ but no medial /i/, (*b*) in the early T'áng period, medial /u/ in these rimes became /iu/ except in syllables with initial /m/, (*c*) medial /iu/ in these rimes then lost its /u/ except in syllables with labial initials; consequently, when the process of dentilabialization took place, labial initials except /m/ in words of these rimes became fricative. Needless to say, this solution presupposes that the rime tables were wrong in entering words like and in the third division. In making use of Sino-Korean and Sino-Japanese, it is also presupposed that (*a*) we know the time when the borrowing was made, (*b*) at the time of borrowing, the Korean or the Japanese phonological system must permit phonemically both [mu-] and [mü-], while the former instead of the latter was persistently used to read such Chinese words like 夢 and 目.

/pi*u⊃/, MP /fwɨ/), 婦(AC /⊂ pɦi*u/, MP /fwɨ/) of the *Yóu-hóu* type, but 1601018 (彪 AC /⊂ piəu/, MP /pyāw/) of the *Yōu* type. This fact suggests that the process of dentilabialization might have taken place before the coalescence of the two types of finals. Lǐ Júng's reconstruction of the *Yóu-hóu* type as [(i)u] and the *Yōu* type as [iěu][1] seems to be the only one which is potentially good enough to explain this phenomenon. If, however, we could prove that the *Yóu-hóu* type is phonemically something like /(y)wɨw/ and the *Yōu* type, /yɨw/, which later coalesced with the former one when it lost the /w/ in the medial position, we would be able to treat this as part of a general phenomenon and consequently apply the above rules to it. The fact that many, though not all, graphs of the *Yóu-hóu* type with labial initials were entered into RG05 in CYYY, after the initials had been dentilabialized, powerfully hints that this assumption is not impossible. It is also phonetically convincing to have /wɨw/ changed to /wɨ/[2].

With what has been said so far, we can come to the conclusion that there are five labial initials in CYYY, namely, /p, ph, f, v, m/.

4.3 The Dentals (D)

Except for the devoicing of /tɦ/, dental stops and resonants have practically no change either in form or in behavior. We have thus four initials of this series in CYYY: /t, th, n, l/.

---

① Lǐ Júng' (1956), 145 - 150.

② Syllables with final /yɨ/ in MP are found to have the final /yɨy/ in CYYY (see 5.12.6). Thus, we have one case where /yɨy/ became /yɨ/. Similarly. it is not unreasonable to say that /wɨw/ became /wɨ/ before CYYY, if this helps us to understand the peculiar phenomenon mentioned here.

4.4 The Dental Sibilants (Ds)

After the process of devoicing, the dental sibilant series (Ds) has now only three initials, namely, /c, ch, s/. These three initials, for a period before CYYY, showed a very peculiar behavior which will be discussed later (see 5.12).

4.5 The Three Palatal Series (P, Pr, Pj)

The three palatal series of AC (P, Pr, Pj) had fallen completely together by the time of CYYY, and remained so in MP. If we want to account for this fact in MP by skipping CYYY, we can do it by two simple rules as follows:

$$t \longrightarrow c / \_\_\_ j$$

$$j \longrightarrow r$$

However, when we take CYYY into consideration, we shall find that the process of this great coalescence is a far more complex one and that it took a long time before it was completed. In AC, the Pj series combined only with finals of the third division; the P series combined with finals of both the second and the third divisions; while the Pr series combined primarily with finals of the second division, but also with those of the third division so far as the rime groups of the α type are concerned. The fact that the three series all combined with finals of the third division makes it clear that they were in contrast. In CYYY, syllables with Pr initials and those with Pj initials are still in contrast, for cxample, 0501007 梳 (AC /꜀ srɨ*/, MP /srwɨ/) vs. 0501015 書 (AC /꜀ sji*/, MP /srwɨ/), 0701015 真 (AC /꜀ cji*n/, MP /crēn/) vs. 0701020 臻 (AC /꜀ cri*n′/, MP /crēn/), and 1701004 深 (AC

/꜀sjiəm/, MP /srēn/) vs. 1701006 森 (AC /꜀sriəm/, MP /sēn/), but the contrast can now be explained easily by the presence or absence of /y/ in the medial position①. In other words, Pr and Pj can now be treated as two series of allophones of one single series of phonemes, with Pj initials combining only with finals having medial /y/, and Pr, otherwise. Syllables with P initials, depending upon whether their finals are of the second division or the third division, are now grouped together with those of the Pr initials and those of the Pj initials respectively, for example, 0201008 莊(AC /꜀criɑŋ/, MP /crwāŋ/)椿 (AC /꜀tjɛŋ/, MP /crwāŋ/), 1501012 (AC 鐺 /꜀crhaŋ/, MP /crhēŋ/) 撐(AC /꜀tjhaŋ/, MP /crhēŋ/), and 0701015 真 (AC /꜀cji*n/, MP /crēn/)珍 (AC /꜀tji*n/ MP /crēn/), 1003056 闡 (AC /꜂cjhiɛn/, MP /crhǎn/) 蕆(AC /꜂tjhiɛn/, MP /crhǎn/). There is not even one exception to the above observations, but some supplementary rules must be added promptly. In RG01, the graph 崇 a word with initial /crɦ/ in AC and a third division final /i*ŋ/, is grouped together with graphs of the same final but with P and Pj initials into one homonym group 0102027. This is rather due to the loss of medial /y/ in this final after all palatal initials (see 5. 5. 1). In RG03, we find that graphs with corresponding Pr and Pj initials fell

① Many signs make me believe that medial /y/ after Pr initials had been lost long before the compilation of CYYY. Some of them can be given here:

(a) Graphs with Pr initials were listed only in the second division, regardless of their AC origin.

(b) The third division graphs with Pr initials in the *Tàng-shè* all appear together in CYYY with those of the second division of the *Chiāng-shè*, for example, 0201004, 0201026.

(c) The graph W, one of the third division with initial /crh/ in the *Shān-shè*, is now found in RG08 (0802030) instead of RG10 where it should have been, if it had maintained its medial /y/ (see 5. 6. lc).

(d) The *Shēn-shè* has only third division graphs, that is, only those with medial /y/. But in RG17 of CYYY, which is derived from the Shēn-shè, we find graphs like 1703029 怎 and 1704044 唔 which were created after *Ch'ièh-yǜn* and must have a final without medial /y/ in CYYY. This of course, indicates that the new final without medial /y/ must have already been in existent at the time of the creation of these new graphs.

together, for example, 0301003, 0301004, and 0303014. Their coalescence is rather because of the loss of the medial /y/ in this type of final after Pj initials (see 5.12). However, graphs with the same final (the unrounded type of the *Chĭh-shè*), but with P initials do not, with one exception 0303011 徵 (AC /ᶜ tji*i′/, MP /crɨ̆/), appear in RG03. They appear rather in RG04, for example, 0401024, 0402043, 0403066, and 0404132. Lù Chìh-wéi has given us a very keen observation in this regard. From the facts given above, he concludes that the retroflexion of 0301001 支 (AC /꜀ cjiə/, MP /crɨ̄/) (hence, all the graphs of the same final with Pj initials) took place much earlier than that of 0401024 知 (AC /꜀ tjiə/, MP /crɨ̄/) (hence, all those with P initials)[①]. Indeed, this is the only logical way to explain this peculiar distributional aspect of the two palatal series in question.

4.5.1 The problem here involves the form of the unrounded finals of the AC rimes in *Chĭh-shè*, which will be discussed later (see 5.12). I believe that, by RTP, all the four finals had merged together and can be represented in phonemic terms by /yɨy/ where /ɨ/ stands for a high central vowel. Assuming this is true, we can now sum up our discussion as follows:

(a) After Pr initials, all finals with /y/ in the medial position lost the /y/. probably happened before RTP, for graphs of this kind all appear in the second division.

(b) Pr and Pj initials thus turned out to be in complementary distribution and became consequently allophones of one single series of phonemes represented by 照穿牀審禪 (Cf. Note ① in page 160).

(c) After each of the Pj initials had phonemically joined its corresponding Pr initial, the medial /y/ in the final /yɨy/ which occured after the former Pj initials was also lost. Thus, we find that graphs of Pr initials

① Lù (1946), 43. We accept Lù's interpretation only in a loose sense. Strictly speaking, we shall say that P and Pj went through the process of retroflexion simultaneously, and that they merge only when the P initials were affricated later.

fell together with graphs of Pj initials in RG03 of CYYY, but not in other rimes.

(d) When the above processes had been completed, the P initials also joined the newly formed retroflexed series, but the final /yɨy/ after the former P initials still maintained the medial /y/ at the time of CYYY. Consequently, graphs representing the syllables with this final and the former P initials were entered into RG04, instead of RG03.

4.5.2 We can now formulate the above points in more precise terms as follows. Note that the relative order of these rules must be preserved.

$$y \longrightarrow ø/Pr\underline{\quad} \qquad (13)$$

$$j \longrightarrow r \qquad (14)$$

$$y \longrightarrow ø/Pr\underline{\quad}ɨ+y \qquad (15)$$

$$t \longrightarrow c/\underline{\quad}r \qquad (16)$$

The following diagram is perhaps also needed here, so as to make the coalescing processes of the three AC palatal series even clearer. 'X' stands here for anything in a final after medial /y/, if there is one.

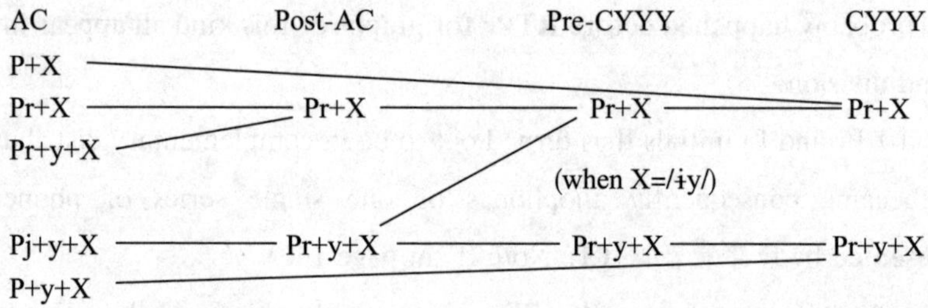

4.5.3 By Rule 14 in 4.5.2, the initial /nj/ is now changed to /nr/. However, it has been noticed that before A. D. 724 graphs with this initial were always chosen to transcribe the Sanskrit syllabic 'ña', while after A. D. 771, a graph with initial /n/ was used for this purpose (see Note ① in page 159). This fact indicates that as early as 771 initial /nj/ had probably already lost its nasal quality. Consequently, for CYYY, we must rewrite /nr/ as /r/, as it has been done for its MP counterpart①. Here we are confronted with the same dilemma as we might have been, if we had used only /j/ for this initial in AC, instead of /nj/ (see 3.2.1c). Obviously, we have to admit that /r/ is a voiced consonant, but what about those initials with /r/ as one element? Fortunately, the contrast between voicing and voicelessness no longer seems to be a conditioning feature in the phonological development from CYYY to MP, and so we can safely ignore this problem.

$$n \longrightarrow \emptyset / \_\_ r \qquad (17)$$

We now have only four retroflex initials in CYYY, namely, /cr, crh, sr, r/.

4.6 The Gutturals (G)

The two guttural series (for the use of the term 'guttural', see Note ① in page 157) also went through some drastic changes which can be handled in the following discussions.

4.6.1 As we have seen, the devoicing process eliminated two of these initials, /kɦ/ and /xɦ/, and made it possible to rewrite /x/ as /h/ (see 4.1). But before the devoicing process took place, initial /xɦ/ had already shown some change. All the books of rime tables, including the earliest ones, *Yǜn-chìng* 韻鏡 and *Ch'ī-yīn-lüèh* 七音略, do not have any graphs under this initial in the third division, but they all have graphs with zero initial in both the third and the fourth divisions. Modern researches have shown that the so-called zero initial in syllables of the third division is clearly distinct from that

---

① Both Hartman and Hockett (see bibliography) establish a phoneme /r/ in MP, but there is a difference beween their /r/ and mine here for CYYY. Theirs is treated as a 'medial' (semi-vowel), while mine is still an 'initial' (consonant).

of the fourth division, as far as *Ch'ièh-yǜn* is concerned. The 'zero initial' of the syllables of the third division is thus in complementary distribution with initial /xɦ/; hence, Y. R. Chao and others all conclude that the former is actually part of the latter in AC①. If we accept this interpretation, we certainly have to add a rule to specify this fact before we apply the rule of devoicing.

$$\text{x}\text{ɦ} \longrightarrow \text{ø}/\_\_\text{y(w)}\begin{Bmatrix}V_n\\V_3\end{Bmatrix} \qquad (18)$$

4. 6. 2 Syllables of the unrounded type in the second division with guttural initials and their counterparts in the first division generally still form minimal pairs in CYYY, for example, 0601001 皆 (AC /꜀kai/, MP /cyē/) vs. 0601002 該(AC /꜀kəi/, MP /kāy/), 0601006 哀(AC /꜀qəi/, MP /āy/) vs. 0601008 挨 (AC /꜀qai/, MP /āy/), 0802020 寒(AC /꜀xɦan/, MP /hán/) vs. 0802024 閑(AC /꜀xɦan/, MP /syán/) etc. With regard to initial/ŋ/ the contrast is not so clear, but that is rather due to the changes of the initial /ŋ/ in a relatively later period, as we shall see very soon (see 4. 6. 4). These contrasts are generally still maintained in MP where those of the second division now have /y/ in the medial position. It is then logical for us to hypothesize that the distinction in CYYY is also maintained by the same device, as indeed was shown in the h̲Pags-pa script②. We can then write a rule as follows,

$$G + V_2(E) \longrightarrow G + y + V_2(E) \qquad (19)$$

---

① Y. R. Chao (1941), 211 - 212. Cf. also Tǔng (1954), 55, and Lǐ Júng (1956), 76. It may be added here that interestingly the clumsy form of Rule 18 seems to have confirmed Lǐ Júng's conclusion (1956) that at the time of *Ch'ièh-yǜn*, rimes of the fourth division did not have medial /y/. In such a case, the rule can be simplified as: xɦ→ø/_y. The acquisition of medial /y/ by the fourth division rimes will then be interpreted as a later development (but before RTP).

② Cf. Lù (1946), 49, 54, and 55.

When we try out this rule in CYYY, we find it works so surprisingly well that it admits practically no exceptions. Lù Chìh-wéi apparently has also noticed this phenomenon, though he has not put it in such strictly formal terms as I do here, and he shows some uncertainty in his discussions of RG11 and RG15, where he either blames the 'dialectal nature' of the book or frankly admits that he does not understand①. Chào Yìn-t'áng, on the other hand, seems to be unaware of this all. The result is that he is terribly inconsistent in this regard, and, in some cases, even is forced to be absurd. The following facts can perhaps illustrate this.

(a) After having established four gutttural initials, [k, k', ŋ, x], for both the first and the second divisions, he added: "But for the second division, sometimes [c, c', ȵ, ç] are used", without any further specification②.

(b) By adding four more initials, he can thus transcribe the finals without [i] as a medial, but in RG13 he still transcribes some syllables of the second division with [i] as medial, for example, 1301007, 1302016, and 1303030.

(c) It is accepted by all, including Chào himself, that graphs of one homonym group by definition must have the same and identical reading. However, in quite a few cases, where there appears to be a mixture of second division graphs and third division graphs, Chào gives each homonym group two different readings, for example, 1501001, 1501015, 1503054, etc., instead of trying to account for their coalescence. In a few cases where the same mixture is found, Chào somehow gives each just one reading, for example, 1502040. Stimson has noticed Chào's 'inconsistency' in this case, and consequently revised Chào's transcription by giving the group two

① Lù (1946), 48 and 55.

② Chào Yìn-t'áng (1936), 101.

readings[1]. This revision unfortunately only makes Chào consistently inconsistent.

All these difficulties which seem to puzzle Chào so much actually can be solved easily by applying vigorously the rule I gave above, as we shall see in the discussions of the vowel system (see 5. 7. 1 and 5. 10).

4. 6. 3 We have clear evidence that by the time of CYYY, initial /q/ had lost its phonemic status, if indeed it still existed phonetically as it does in some modern Northern Mandarin dialects where all syllables with zero medial and zero initial may have either a [q]-like or an [ŋ]-like on glide, regardless of their origin[2]. However, the disappearance of /q/ as an initial is rather a relatively late development. As I have pointed out, when the even tone of AC split into two, initial /q/ was obviously still there, functioning as a determining factor (see 3. 5. 2). Furthermore, it will be more economical and logical to say that /q/ was also still there as a determining factor, when syllables of the second division with guttural initials and zero medial took an additional /y/ in their medial position, as we discussed in the last section.

4. 6. 4 The existence or non-existence of /ŋ/ as an initial in CYYY has long been a controversy, and it indeed presents a very difficult problem. The situation in MP is that graphs formerly with this initial have all merged with those of zero initial except a few of the unrounded type of the third and the fourth divisions which have now /n/ as their initial, for example, 倪(AC /꜀ŋiei/, MP /nyɨ/), 牛(AC /꜀ŋi*u/, MP /nyéw/), 蘖(AC /ŋiɛt/, MP /nyè/), 虐(AC /ŋiɑk/, MP /nywè/), and 凝(AC /꜀ŋiəŋ/, MP /nyéŋ/)[3]. In CYYY, we find that graphs with this former initial, for the most part,

① Stimson (1962a), 132.

② Cf. Lù (1946), 46, and Hsueh (1973).

③ Cf. Tǔng 1954, Chart 4, between p. 110 and p. 111. Tǔng's chart shows that only some of those of the third division turn out to be with initial /n/, but actually there are also some fourth division graphs, for example, 倪 and 臬.

have also fallen together with those with former initial /q/ or zero initial, but in the following cases, they seem to form a three-way contrast with those having initial /n/ or zero initial (including /q/).

(a) 0203052 養 (AC /ᶜ iaŋ/, MP /yǎŋ/) 鞅 (AC /ᶜ qiaŋ/, MP /yǎŋ/) vs. 0203071 仰 (AC /ᶜ ŋiaŋ/, MP /yǎŋ/).

(b) 0204081 漾 (AC /iaŋᵓ/, MP /yàŋ/) 怏 (AC /qiaŋᵓ/, MP /yàŋ/) vs. 0204102 仰 (AC /ŋiaŋᵓ/, MP (——) vs. 0204101 釀 (AC /niaŋᵓ/, MP /nyàŋ/).

(c) 1104147 奥 (AC /qauᵓ/, MP /àw/) vs. 1104125 傲 (AC /ŋauᵓ/, MP /àw/) vs. 1104146 鬧 (AC /nɛuᵓ/, MP /nàw/).

(d) 1203046 婀 (AC /ᶜ qa/, MP /ě/) vs. 1203048 我 (AC /ᶜ ŋa/, MP /wě/) vs. 1203042 娜 (AC /ᶜ na/, MP /nwě/).

(e) 1254083 岳 (AC /ŋɛk/, MP /ywè/) 約 (AC /qiak/, MP /ywē/) 藥 (AC /iak/, MP /ywè/) vs. 125409 虐 (AC /ŋiak/, MP /nywè/).

(f) 1154153 岳 (AC /ŋɛk/, MP /yàw/) 約 (AC / qiak /, MP /yāw/) 藥 (AC /iak/, MP /yàw/) vs. 1154160 虐 (AC /ŋiak /, MP /nyàw/).

(g) 1454057 拽 (AC /iɛt/, MP /yè/) 謁 (AC /qiat/, MP /yè/) vs. 1454058 業 (AC /ŋiap/, MP /yè/) vs. 1454055 捏 (AC /niet/, MP /nyē/).

The situation is further complicated by the fact that in some cases, for example, (e) and (f) given above, graphs with initial /ŋ/ but different finals in AC now apparently have the same final but are still separated from each other, presumably because of the initials. Moreover, in at least two cases, 1003049 讞 (AC /ᶜ ŋiɛn/, MP /nyǎn/) and 1454055 臬 (AC /ŋiet/, MP /nyè/), we find graphs with initial /ŋ/ in AC now appear together with graphs of initial /n/. The facts given above show that, by the time of CYYY, initial /ŋ/, under different conditions, had either remained the same, or become /n/, or disappeared. What are these conditions? or rather, are there really formal conditions for these changes? My answer is yes.

4.6.4.1 Confronted with this problem, scholars of CYYY have shown drastically different reactions. Chào Yìn-t'áng's solution, as can be expected, is to add one more initial. He asserts that /ŋ/ did not change with regard to 1104125, 1203048, but changed to [ɲ] with regard to 0203071, 0204102, 1154160 and 1254090, merged with /n/ in 1003049 and 1454055, disappeared in all the other cases, though he gives no conditions for these divergent changes[①]. Lù Chìh-wéi adopts an even more peculiar attitude. He seems to say that initial /ŋ/ has either disappeared, as in most cases, or remained the same in a few cases, without any other possibility. As to why it should remain in the few cases mentioned above, he frankly admits he does not know[②]. Tǔng T'úng-hó chooses to believe that /ŋ/ as an initial does not exist in CYYY by saying that the small circle between 0204101 and 0204102 and the one between 1454057 and 1454058 were probably added mistakenly by later editors of the book. In this way, he can now say that the initial of has changed from /ŋ/ to /n/, though he does not specify the condition or conditions of this change either. He does not mention cases (*e*) and (*f*), presumably because he believes the initial of 虐 has also changed from /ŋ/ to /n/, as indeed it has in MP. As to cases (*c*) and (*d*), he attributes the contrasts either to irregular development or the author's carelessness[③]. I feel that both Chào's and Lù's approaches are not serious efforts to solve the problem. By adding new initials in an ad hoc manner, or by saying vaguely that no change has taken place, we can certainly maintain all the contrasts, often more than required, and thus we will lose any chance of making a meaningful and systematic account of the phonological development. Tǔng's approach seems to me the most plausible, though he tried rather too hard to explain away initial /ŋ/ and did not try at all to explain how it has changed to /n/ in a limited number of cases.

---

① Chào Yìn-t'áng (1936), 95－96.

② Lù (1946), 45－46

③ Tǔng (1954), 26－27.

4.6.4.2 It is quite reasonable to suspect that two contiguous homonym groups might actually be one, that is, the small circle between them might be added, consciously or unconsciously, by some later editors under the influence of their own dialects, if we can deduce a rule to support our suspicion. Tŭng's assertion that the circle between 0204101 and 0204102 is mistakenly added can indeed be accepted as correct, if we follow this line of argument. The two graphs 虐瘧 are pronounced /nywè/ in MP. If we hypothesize that their initial in CYYY is also /n/, the two minimal pairs (*e*) and (*f*) will be logically maintained. A quick check shows us that these two graphs belong to the third division of the *Tàng-shè*. The initial of their counterpart in the rising tone and the going tone can be reasonably assumed to have developed in the same direction, that is, from /ŋ/ to /n/. This will require us to say that 0204101 and 0204102 should have been put together, and the problems involved in the two cases (*a*) and (*b*) can now be easily and reasonably solved. Hence, we need a rule as follows,

$$\text{ŋ} \longrightarrow \text{n}/\_\_\_\text{y} + V_{ta} \qquad (20)$$

V_{ta} = Nuclear vowel of the *Tàng-shè*.

4.6.4.3 The process of change represented by Rule 20 must have taken place long before CYYY, for it was not affected by another process also recorded in CYYY which requires initial /ŋ/ before /y/ to be eliminated,

$$\text{ŋ} \longrightarrow \text{ø}/\_\_\_\text{y} \qquad (21)$$

No examples are needed here to illustrate the loss of /ŋ/ in this case. There are a great many. However, it should perhaps promptly be added that this process must have begun to function not earlier than that represented by Rule 19 which specifies that unrounded second division syllables with guttural initials all acquire a medial /y/. This is the only logical way to explain why graphs of the second division of the *Chiāng-shè* and those of the third division in the *Tàng-shè* both with initial /ŋ/ are now still in contrast, though they have now the same final, as we have seen in cases (*e*) and (*f*). Naturally, we reconstruct the syllable represented by the graph with zero initial in CYYY.

The kind of argument in the last section forces us to regard 1454057 and 1454058 also as one homonym group, because otherwise the two graphs 業鄴 would be the only exceptions to Rule 21, while their counterparts in other tones all conform to it, for example, 1902018 嚴(AC /꜀ ŋiam/, MP /yán/). We have more evidence here to support this belief, if more is needed. The graph 額 (AC /ŋak/, MP /é/) in the same homonym group as that of 業 belongs to the second division of the *Kěng-shè*. By the time of CYYY, it must have taken a medial /y/, according to Rule 19. Indeed, this is probably why it can be entered into RG14 (see 6.4.1.3). Like other graphs of its kind, it must have lost its initial /ŋ/.

4.6.4.4 1003049 and 1454055 present a unique problem. Both consist mainly of graphs with initial /n/ in AC, and hence can be assumed to have the same initial in CYYY. However, we find one graph 讞 in the former and three 囓臬蘖 in the latter, which have initial /ŋ/ in AC. So far they have not been discussed by anyone. Presumably, they have been treated as irregular, due to borrowing. But the fact that they all belong to either the third or the fourth division of the *Shān-shè* seems to me to be something worth noticing, even though it seems no rule can be written, because their counterparts in other tones, such as 1002031 妍(AC /꜀ ŋien/, MP /yán/) and 1004073 彦 (AC /ŋiɛn꜄/, MP /yàn/), are obviously all with zero initial.

4.6.4.5 There are now left to us only two pairs to handle, namely, (*c*) and (*d*) given above. Judging strictly by the internal evidence in the book, I have come to the conclusion that initial /ŋ/ does still exist in 1104125 and 1203048 and only in these. This means that the functional load of this initial has become lighter and lighter, and seems in CYYY to be on the verge of passing out. In order to understand this, we have to know first the great shift of the vowel system from RTP to CYYY. I shall discuss this great shift in the next chapter. Suffice it to say here that the nuclear vowel of the first division of the outer series has, for the most part, become the same as that of the second division. This process can be best expressed by the following rule,

$$C + V_1 + E \longrightarrow C + V_2 + E \qquad (22)$$
$$E \neq w$$

To translate this formula into verbal terms, it means that, except in cases where it is preceded by /w/ and/or followed by /w/ or syllable boundary, V_1 has become V_2 (see 5.6 and 5.10.2). A careful study will show that the graphs of the four homonym groups involved here, 1104125, 1104147, 1203046, and 1203048, all belong to the first division and remain so while other first division graphs have changed, according to the above rule. It is then very logical to say that, after the vowel shift, initial /ŋ/ exists only in cases where it occurs immediately before the remaining V_1, whatever it is at that time. Thus, we can now write a rule to account for this fact,

$$\text{ŋ} \longrightarrow \left\{ \begin{matrix} \text{ŋ}/\_\_\_ V_1 \\ \varnothing \end{matrix} \right\} / \#\_\_\_ \qquad (23)$$

It seems to me that this explains quite satisfactorily why we have in CYYY two pairs of contrast (*c*) and (*d*), while in other cases, first division graphs with initial /q/ and those with /ŋ/ have been grouped together, for example, 0804053 案 (AC /qɑnᵓ/, MP /àn/) 岸 (AC /ŋɑnᵓ/, MP /àn/) and 0604064 艾 (AC /ŋɑiᵓ/, MP /ày/) 愛 (AC /qəiᵓ/, MP /ày/). The process represented by this rule must begin to function after Rule 20, and since it is much more general in its claim, Rule 21 is no longer needed.

4.7 Summing Up

We have just finished discussing the changes of the initial system from

AC to CYYY. To sum up, we can list the initials of CYYY in the form of a new chart as follows,

	S		Fr	R	
B	p	Ph	f	m	v
D	t	th		n	l
Ds	c	ch	s		
Pr	cr	crh	sr		r
G	k	kh	h	ŋ	ø

This chart can be further condensd into a chart of the consonant phonemes like the following,

		B	D	Ds	G
Non-resonants	S	P	t	c	k
	Fr	f		s	h
Resonants	N	m	n		ŋ
	L	v	l	r	

As I said before (see 4.5.3), /r/ still presents some problems to us. Exactly what kind of a phoneme it is, I am not quite sure. Quite certainly, it is now different from whatever it stood for in AC. Since it never occurred as an initial by itself in AC, I have chosen to say that it is, along with /j/, /h/ and /ɦ/, actually a distinctive feature. But as it does occur as an initial by itself in CYYY, such an interpretation no longer holds. Perhaps, like /h/ in CYYY which stands for both the velar fricative [x] and aspiration, /r/ now stands for both retroflexion, when it combines with other consonants, and a voiced and retroflexed fricative, when it functions as an initial alone. Both the treatment of /h/ and that of /r/ are now possible, because the contrast vd./vl. no longer exists as a determining feature in the Chinese language after CYYY.

CHAPTER FIVE THE VOWEL SYSTEM OF CYYY

After having dealt with the initials, the medials, and the endings, we are now ready to tackle the toughest problem in the study of CYYY, viz., the reconstruction of its vowel system. Since the status of the so-called 'entering tone' in CYYY has long been in dispute and cannot be readily discussed here, I shall base my study of the nuclear vowels of CYYY exclusively on the homonym groups of the non-entering tones, lest the use of those of the entering tone should make the discussion on the vowel system also disputable. This, of course, does not mean that we shall ignore the entering tone graphs for good, but that we want to build up a system upon undisputed ground and then to test it by applying it to all the graphs, including those with the entering tone which I shall deal with in the next chapter in great detail. From now on, whenever I say 'the graphs of a certain rime' it should be understood to mean all the graphs of that group except those with entering tone, unless it is unequivocally specified otherwise.

5.1 The Working Rules

As it has been noted, the term 'rime' (yǜn 韻) used in CYYY is drastically different from the same term used in *Ch'ièh-yǜn*, but is rather closer in reality to the term '*shè*' which is used for the classes of rimes in some of the rime tables (see 2.2). From this fact, we can draw a loose presumption that one rime in CYYY may possibly contain syllables with different nuclear vowels while two or more rimes having the same ending are most unlikaly to share the same nuclear vowel. Two working rules based upon this presumption can then be written down as follows:

(*a*) Only one nuclear vowel will be allowed for each rime unless two or more must be postulated for the sake of maintaining all the required contrasts.

(*b*) Different rimes sharing the same ending must have different nuclear vowels.

5.2 The Rime Groups with Nasal Endings

Of the nineteen rimes in CYYY, ten have nasal endings. It follows that if we can figure out a satisfactory system of nuclear vowels for these ten, the other nine will be automatically taken care of. Three of these ten rimes with nasal endings, RG01, RG02, and RG15, have the velar nasal /ŋ/ as their ending in AC and MP, and thus must have the same ending in CYYY. The other seven now all end in /n/ in MP, but three of them, RG17, RG18, and RG19, end in /m/ in AC as well as in many modern non-Mandarin dialects, for example, Cantonese. Since these three are kept apart from the rest in CYYY, the most logical conclusion we can draw is that they must still have /m/ as their ending at that time. We are now left with four rimes which then must have /n/ as their ending, namely, RG07, RG08, RG09, and RG10. By working rule (*b*) given above, we can now reasonably assume that there should be at least four nuclear vowels in CYYY. But this obviously cannot be simply assumed. It can only be taken as a starting point for further investigation and eventual proof.

5.3 RG07, RG08, RG09, and RG10

Among the four rimes ending in /n/, RG07, the *Chēn-wén* 真文, presents us with no great difficulty. It is developed from the *Chēn-shè* of the previous period, which is one of the inner series and must then have a high vowel as its nucleus①. In MP, graphs of RG07 still have phonetically very high vowels, though phonemically they can be analyzed as having the middle vowel as their nucleus②. Consequently, we have to postulate a high vowel as the nucleus for RG07, and since it seems to be the only rime of this type with a high vowel, we can further designate this vowel as central and represent it with /ɨ/. The real challenge comes from the other three groups, RG08, RG09, and RG10. Graphs of these three groups now all represent syllables having the low vowel /a/ as their nucleus in MP③. Could this also be the case in CYYY? The question may sound rather ridiculous, but not so, if we remember that, occasionally though rarely, two rimes may be different merely in their medial. There are quite a few examples of this in *Ch'ièh-yǜn*, but as I said before, the term 'rime' used in CYYY has a much broader coverage than used before, it is then highly unlikely that two rimes in CYYY would be different only in the medial, especially when a low vowel has to be postulated as the nucleus. Again, this cannot be simply assumed. To be convincing, we must give a close check to the distribution of the medials in the three rime groups in question.

5. 3. 1 Graphs of RG09 are all of the rounded type in the rime tables, and all represent syllables with medial /w/ in MP. Consequently, they must represent syllables with medial /w/ in CYYY, too④. For the same reason, we know that RG08 contains both syllables with zero medial and those with medial /w/, plus a few with medial /y/, which are from the second division with guttural initials in the rime tables (see 4. 6. 2), for example, 0801005 姦 (AC /꜀kɛn/, MP /cyān/) and 0802024 閑(AC /꜀xɦan/, MP /syán/). RG10

① Cf. Martin(1953),38.

② See 7. 5. 1 to 7. 5. 3, but confer also Hartman (1944) and Hockett (1947). Stimson, however, chooses to believe that it should be the high vowel (see Stimson 1966, 15).

③ Cf. both Hartman (1944) and Hockett (1947).

④ Professor Tǔng T'úng-hó however, transcribes them as having a final with zero medial (Tǔng 1954, 30 [on]), perhaps under the influence of the hPhags-pa script (Cf. Lù 1946, 51).

consists of syllables either with /y/ alone or with the compound /yw/ in the medial position, for they are all from the third and the fourth divisions. The situation can then be clearly demonstrated by the following table:

RG \ F	-øVn	-yVn	-wVn	-ywVn
RG08	×	×	×	
RG09			×	
RG10		×		×

5. 3. 2 The above chart shows that RG08 must have a different nuclear vowel from that of RG09. Minimal pairs like 0801007 關（AC /$_{\subset}$kuɛn/, MP /kwān/）vs. 0901001 官（AC /$_{\subset}$kuɑn/, MP /kwān/）, and 0801010 彎（AC /$_{\subset}$quɛn/, MP /wān/）vs. 0901006 剜（AC /$_{\subset}$quɑn/, MP /wān/）, must be in contrast for having different nuclear vowels. It also shows that RG08 and RG10 have different vowels, for both have entries with medial /y/ and thus form minimal pairs like 0801005 姦（AC /$_{\subset}$kɛn/, MP /cyān/）vs. 1001003 堅（AC /$_{\subset}$kien/, MP /cyān/）, and 0804064 間（AC /kan$^{\supset}$/, MP /cyàn/）vs. 1004069 見（AC /kien$^{\supset}$/, MP /cyàn/）. RG09 and RG10 seem to be in complementary distribution so far as the medials are concerned, and consequently we could postulate a single nuclear vowel for both of them and still maintain all the contrasts in them. However, this cannot be true, though it is seemingly possible, because in no rime book, not even in *Ch'ièh-yǜn*, have graphs representing syllables with the same nucleus and the same ending but different in having /yw/ or /w/ alone in the medial position ever been classified into different rimes. The fact that homonym groups like 0901003 歡（AC /$_{\subset}$xuɑn/, MP /hwān/）and 1001007 喧（AC /$_{\subset}$xiuan/, MP /sywān/）do not appear in the same rime may thus be taken as evidence that they have different nuclear vowels.

5.4 A Tentative Vowel System

We have now proved that there are four nuclear vowels in CYYY. One of the four is high and may be represented by /ɨ/. The other three are all low and can be assumed to be phonemically on the same level, for lack of any reason to be otherwise. The nuclear vowel of RG10 has been unanimously accepted as a low front vowel and thus can be represented by /e/①. That of RG09 is in all probability a low back vowel and can be represented by /o/②. This leaves the low central vowel for RG08, and indeed all previous studies postulate [a] as its nucleus③. We therefore shall represent this nuclear vowel by /a/. We have thus arrived at a very neat patterning of vowel phonemes, with two levels in height (compact/diffuse) and three degrees in depth (grave/acute and flat/plain) as follows:

	Front	Central	Back
High		ɨ	
Low	e	a	o

As to the phonetic realization of these phonemes, we can do nothing yet at this stage, though we may already suspect that /e/ and /o/ may be relatively higher than /a/.

① Lù (1946), 50 [ɛ]; Chào Yìn-t'áng (1936), 129 [ɛ]; Tǔng (1954), 30 [e].

② Lù (1946), 50 [ɔ]; Tǔng (1954), 30[o]. Chào Yìn-t'áng, following his teacher Ch'ién Hsüán-t'úng 錢玄同, chooses [œ] for this group (p. 128). but he has been criticized by Lù for doing so (Lu 1946, 51).

③ Lù (1946), 49; Tǔng (1954), 29; but Chào Yìn-t'áng (1936), followed by Stimson (1962a) postulates two vowels for this group, [ɑ] (Stimson, /o/) for graphs of the first division origin, and [a] for those of the second.

5.5 RG01, RG02, and RG15

The three rimes in CYYY which have the velar nasal /ŋ/ as their ending, namely, RG01, RG02, and RG15, can now be readily handled here. Graphs of RG02 now have the low vowel /a/ as their nuclear vowel in MP. They belong to the two rime classes *Chiāng-shè* and *Tàng-shè* in the rime tables. Naturally, we believe the nucleus of RG02 is /a/, the low central vowel in the above chart. A similar consideration leads us to postulate /e/, the front low vowel, as the nucleus of RG15 which is the combination of the *Kěng-shè* and the *Tsēng-shè* of the previous period①. RG01 is now left with two alternatives to choose from. Its nuclear vowel may be said to be the high vowel /ɨ/ or the low back vowel /o/. Both are descriptively adequate; therefore, we are here compelled to make a choice which will be supported only by its explanatory power. I choose /o/ for this group on the following grounds:

(*a*) Structurally, /o/ is better, because in this way, we can make a generalization by saying that ending /ŋ/ occurs only after low (compact) vowels.

(*b*) Most of the graphs of RG15 representing syllables with /w/ in the medial position are also found in RG01, but not vice versa (see 5.7.2). It seems to me that this fact can be more reasonably explained if we say the nuclear vowels of RG15 and RG01 are on the same bar.

(*c*) By postulating a low vowel for RG01 which is developed from the *T'ūng-shè*, we can now claim that all the rimes of the 'inner series' with

① That words of RG15 have the low front vowel /e/ as their nucleus by the time of CYYY is beyond any doubt. It is, however, rather difficult to account for the historical development of the *Kěng-shè* and the *Tsēng-shè* and their eventual coalescence. For a brief discussion on this problem, see 6.4.1. Cf., also, Hashimoto (1970).

ending /ŋ/ have, without exception, joined the 'outer series' by the time of CYYY, since the *Tsēng-shè* has fallen together with the *Kĕng-shè* to form RG15 which has /e/ as its nuclear vowel.

It must be promptly added that the decision here cannot be reached on a phonetic ground. In the first place, we have no way to know precisely what phonetic value this nuclear vowel might have. Secondly, even if it might have been phonetically relatively high, we still can assign it to the low back vowel phoneme /o/. Indeed, I believe it is phonetically high. It might well be [o], for one of the two vowels postulated by Karlgren for the rimes of the *T'ūng-shè* is [o][1]. If this is the case, we can now say that the phoneme /o/ has two allophones at least, [o] before /ŋ/ and [ɔ] before /n/.

5. 5. 1 One phenomenon we notice in RG01 which came from the *T'ūng-shè* is that the contrast between the graphs of the third division with Pr initials and those with Pj and P initials in AC no longer exists. For example, in 0102027, we find the graph 崇(AC /꜀ crɦi*ŋ/, MP /crhwéŋ/) appearing together with 蟲(AC /꜀ tjɦi*ŋ/, MP /crhwéŋ/) and 鱅(AC /꜀ sjɦiu*ŋ/, MP /ywéŋ/). This is the only example we have, because third division graphs with Pr initials in the *T'ūng-shè* are rare, and 崇 happens to be the only one included in RG01. In accordance with the rules given in 4. 5. 2, we must conclude that the syllable represented by the graph 崇 first lost the /y/ in the medial position, then syllables with corresponding Pj and P initials fell together, and finally they also lost their medial /y/, and thus turned out to be the same as 崇[2]. Since we have decided that the nuclear vowel of RG01 is /o/, we can add the following formula behind those in 4. 5. 2; Pr in this rule comes, of course, from the combination of Pj and P.

---

① Karlgren (1948), 523 - 525.

② The matter discussed here is somewhat complicated by the fact that 崇 is the only word of its kind included in RG01. The conclusion is, however, probably right. For a more detailed discussion, see Hsueh (1971).

$$y \longrightarrow \varnothing / Pr\_\_\_ w + o + \eta \quad (24)$$

It is perhaps needless to add here that this process of change took place very late. It was later not only than the coalescence of the three palatal series, but, as we shall see (6.4.2.1 - 6.4.2.2), even later than the redistribution of the graphs which formerly had the entering tone. This is why in the above rule we do not include /k/ in the terminal position.

5.5.2 The loss of /y/ in the medial position is also observed among some of the graphs in RG01 with guttural initials (for the use of 'guttural', see Note ① in page 157). For example, 公 (AC /꜀ k*ŋ/, MP /kwēŋ/) and 弓 (AC /꜀ ki*ŋ/, MP /kwēŋ/) appear together in 0101014. But, on the other hand, we also notice many minimal pairs which must be in contrast merely by the presence or absence of this medial /y/, for example, 0101007 空 (AC /꜀ kh*ŋ /, MP /khwēŋ/) vs. 0101013 穹 (AC /꜀ khi*ŋ /, MP /chywēŋ/), and 0101015 烘 (AC /꜀ x*ŋ /, MP /hwēŋ/) vs. 0101016 胸 (AC /꜀ xiu*ŋ/, MP /sywēŋ/). We are therefore helpless in this situation to find a formal conditioning factor. The best we can offer is perhaps a random remark that there is a tendency for the final /ywoŋ/ to become /woŋ /.

5.6 The CYYY Vowel System and That of RTP

RG08, RG09, RG10 are all from the *Shān-shè* of the previous period. A comparison of the *Shān-shè* with the three rimes shows a remarkably regular pattern of development. We find graphs of the third division and those of the fourth division have merged completely in RG10, for example, 1001012 軒 (AC /꜀ xian/, MP /sywān/) 祆 (AC /꜀ xien/, MP /syān/), 1002023 連 (AC /꜀ liɛn/, MP /lyán/) 憐 (AC /꜀ lien/, MP /lyán/), and 1004069 見 (AC /kien꜄/, MP /cyàn/) 建 (AC /kian꜄/, MP /cyàn/). Graphs of the first division with medial /w/ remain distinct in forming RG09, but those with zero medial have been grouped together with the graphs of the second division in forming RG08. However, only one example, 0802021 蘭 (AC /$_{\subset}$lɑn/, MP /lán/) 斕 (AC /$_{\subset}$lan/, MP /lán/), can be given to show the coalescence of any first division graphs and second division graphs into one homonym group. There are several reasons why we do not have more homonym groups like this. First, graphs of the first division with labial initials now all have phonemically medial /w/ (see 4. 2. 1) and therefore are all entered in RG09, instead of merging with those of the second division which are now in RG08. Secondly, while graphs of the first division with non-labial initials and zero medial are entered in RG08, they still form homonym groups by themselves, either because they have different initials (dentals for those of the first division and palatals for those of the second division, except /l/ and /n/), or because, in the case of the guttural initials, those of the second division have by now acquired an additional /y/ in the medial position (see 4. 6. 2). Despite the lack of more examples of this kind, we still cannot, as Chào Yìn-t'áng and Stimson do①, set up two nuclear vowels for RG08. The fact that graphs of this group rime together in contrast to those of RG09 and RG10 is evidence that they have the same nucleus. With this in mind, we can now formulate the shift of the nuclear vowels of the *Shān-shè* from RTP to CYYY.

$$V_1 \longrightarrow \begin{Bmatrix} o/w\_\_\_ \\ a \end{Bmatrix} \tag{25}$$

$$V_2 \longrightarrow a \tag{26}$$

$$\begin{Bmatrix} V_3 \\ V_4 \end{Bmatrix} \longrightarrow e \tag{27}$$

5. 6. 1 It must be noted here that these changes of vowels took place after four changes involving the initials which have been discussed before. To put

① Chào Yìn. t'áng (1936), 127; Stimson (1962a), 142 and 144.

them in a proper perspective, we may list them here:

(*a*) The time the labial initials acquired the special character of being followed by /w/ when not by /y/ must have been earlier than that of the vowel shift (see Rule 9 in 4. 2. 1).

(*b*) The process of dentilabialization also took place earlier, as is evident from the fact that graphs of the rounded type of the third division are now found in RG08, instead of RG10, for example, 0801012 番 (AC /꜀phiuan/, MP /fwān/), 0802026 煩 (AC /꜀pɦiuan/, MP /fwán/), and 0803034 晚 (AC /꜂miuan/, MP /wǎn/). See Rule 10 in 4. 2. 1.

(*c*) Syllables with AC Pr initials must have lost the /y/ in the medial position (see Rule 13 in 4. 5) before the vowel shift, too. The result is that graphs representing these syllables in the third division of the *Shān-shè* are entered in RG08, instead of RG10, for example, 0801008 拴 (AC /꜀sriuɛn/, MP /srwān/), 0801018 跧 (AC /꜀criuɛn/, MP /crwān/), and 0802030 潺 (AC /꜀crɦiɛn/, MP /crhán/).

(*d*) Graphs of the second division with guttural initials got the medial /y/ earlier than the vowel shift, too. See Rule 19 in 4. 6. 2.

It may be interesting to add here that what happened to the third division syllables with B and Pr initials after their dentilabialization or retroflexion strongly hints that V_2 and V_3 may be the same vowel. Evidence like this makes me feel that the design of the Rime Tables was probably based on the same vowel system as that of CYYY, namely, a system of four vowels, with the high vowel for the inner series and the three low vowels for the outer series. If this is true, the only difference between the second division syllables and their third division counterparts is then the presence of medial /y/ in the latter. Thus, when third division syllables of the outer series lost their medial /y/, they would become automatically second division syllables. Those of the inner series would then become first division syllables, but would be entered into either the first division or the second division, depending upon their initials (as is partially witnessed in *Ch'ièh-yǜn Chǐh-chăng T'ú*). Viewed in this light, it would seem that the departure of Old Mandarin from Ancient Chinese might not be so drastic as most scholars seem to believe.

5. 6. 2 A very natural extension of the conclusion arrived at in the last section can now be made. We may hypothesize at this point that, with the eminent exception of the rimes with /ŋ/ as syllable ending which have been discussed already (see 5. 5), rimes in CYYY developed from the inner series have now the high vowel /ɨ/ as their nucleus, regardless of the distinction in divisions, but those developed from the outer series have now one of the three low vowels as their nucleus, specified by the three rules and the preconditions given in the last section. These rules can be restated in the following order:

$$\text{ø} \longrightarrow \text{w/B\_\_\_V} \quad (9)$$

$$\text{y} \longrightarrow \text{ø/Pr\_\_\_} \quad (13)$$

$$\text{y} \longrightarrow \text{ø/m\_\_\_}V_{tu} \quad (12)$$

V_{tu} = Nucleus of the *T'ūng-shè*.

$$\begin{bmatrix} \text{P}\left(\begin{Bmatrix}\text{h}\\ \text{ɦ}\end{Bmatrix}\right) \\ \text{m} \end{bmatrix} \longrightarrow \begin{bmatrix}\text{f}\\ \text{v}\end{bmatrix}\text{/\_\_\_y+w} \quad (10)$$

$$\text{y} \longrightarrow \text{ø/}\begin{Bmatrix}\text{f}\\ \text{v}\end{Bmatrix}\text{\_\_\_} \quad (11)$$

$$V_3 \longrightarrow \begin{Bmatrix} V_2\text{/C(w)\_\_\_} \\ V_4 \end{Bmatrix} \quad (28)$$

$$\text{ø} \longrightarrow \text{y/G\_\_\_}V_2 \quad (19)$$

$$V_n \longrightarrow \text{ɨ} \quad (29)$$

$$V_1 \longrightarrow \begin{Bmatrix} \text{o/w\_\_\_} \\ \text{a} \end{Bmatrix} \quad (25)$$

$$V_2 \longrightarrow \text{a} \quad (26)$$

$$V_4 \longrightarrow e \tag{27}$$

5.7 The Exceptional Course of Syllables with Ending /ŋ/

The exceptional course of development of the rimes with ending /ŋ/ from the general vowel shift described above has been observed, though we cannot as yet offer any sufficient explanation for it. However, this observed exception now helps us explain in a very satisfactory manner two unusual phenomena in RG15 which have haunted all the students of CYYY.

5.7.1 We have mentioned (4.6.2c), without explaining, that there are a small number of homonym groups which show a mixture of second division and third division graphs. These homonym groups are all found in RG15, for example, 1501001 京(AC /꜀ kiaŋ/, MP /cyēŋ)/) 庚(AC /꜀ kaŋ/, MP /kēŋ/), and 1504092 杏(AC /꜂ xɦiaŋ/, MP /syèŋ/) 興(AC /xiəŋ꜄/, MP /syèŋ/). Now, with our new knowledge of the vowel shift, we can easily understand why these homonym groups all concentrate in that rime. It has been noted that RG15 is the combination of the *Kĕng-shè* and the *Tsēng-shè*, which in their peculiar development have in CYYY the front low vowel /e/ as their common nucleus (see 5.5). Since the second division graphs of the unrounded type with G initials had acquired the medial /y/ (4.6.2), a natural consequence in RG15 is, of course, the coalescence of the second division graphs with those of the third and the fourth division graphs of this type, because they have now the same nuclear vowel and everything else. In MP, we find most of the second division graphs of this type do not have medial /y/ and thus still maintain their distinction from those of the third and the fourth divisions. This fact is perhaps, as Stimson has pointed out, "evidence of an avuncular relationship between the dialect recorded there and MP"①. If

① Stimson (1962a), 132. Cf., also, Hsueh (1971).

so, we would have to say that in the dialect from which MP came directly, the coalescence of the *Kěng-shè* and the *Tsēng-shè* in sharing the same nucleus /e/ must have taken place before the change represented by Rule 19, with the consequence that the rule did not apply to syllables of the second division in the *Kěng-shè*.

5.7.2 A small number of graphs are found both in RG01 and RG15, for example, 轟（AC /$_{\text{c}}$ xueŋ/, MP /hwēŋ/) in 0101015 and 1501010, 兄（AC /$_{\text{c}}$ xiuaŋ/, MP /sywēŋ/) in 0101016 and 1501026. A close check reveals that they are all from the *Kěng-shè* and the *Tséng-shè*, and are all of the rounded type. According to the rules we have set up so far, they are expected to occur in RG15 with the final /weŋ/ or /yweŋ/. When they appear in RG01, we find they are grouped together respectively with graphs from the *T'ūng-shè* which should be reconstructed with the final /woŋ/ or /ywoŋ/, but these graphs from the *T'ūng-shè* do not occur in RG15①. This phenomenon shows that there is a one way development from /(y)weŋ/ to /(y)woŋ/. I can suggest here tentatively that the change of the front low vowel /e/ to the back low vowel /o/ is under the influence of the medial /w/. This suggestion is supported by two facts. First, the final /weŋ/ is unique in that it is the only one where /w/, functioning alone as the medial, occurs before the front low vowel /e/; its very uniqueness may be the cause of its change. Secondly, while practically all graphs standing for the syllables with the final /weŋ/ are also found in RG01, only some of the graphs representing syllables with the final /yweŋ/ also occur in RG01, showing that the /y/ here may exert some force to hold back this trend, though the general development has made it almost irreversible. It is true that further development after CYYY seems to have made RG01 and RG15 contrast only in having or lacking /w/ in the

① For obvious reasons, I do not accept Stimson's assertion "that Chōu Té-ch'īng confused 甖 with 甕". (Stimson 1962a, 134.).

medial position（*hó-k'ǒu* vs. *k'āi-k'ǒu*），but so far as these graphs still appear in RG15，we have to preserve the finals /weŋ/ and /yweŋ/.① When they appear in RG01，we shall say that their nucleus has changed to /o/. In other words，we believe the age of CYYY is a transitional period for this kind of graphs，each of which then had two readings.

5.8 RG17，RG18，and RG19

We may now test our hypothesis of the vowel shift by applying it first to the rimes with ending /m/，viz.，RG17 developed from the *Shēn-shè*，and RG18 and RG19 which are both from the *Hsién-shè*. Naturally，we postulate /ɨ/ as the nuclear vowel for RG17，and we find this postulation works perfectly well. For RG19，we postulate /e/ as its nuclear vowel，because graphs of this group are either from the third or the fourth division of the *Hsién-shè*. Graphs of these two divisions with the same initials have also fallen into the same homonym groups，for example，1902014 黏（AC /꜀niɛm/，MP /nyán/）拈（AC /꜀niem/，MP /nyán/），and 1904035 欠（AC /khiam꜃/，MP /chyàn/）歉（AC /꜂khiem/，MP /chyàn/）. RG18 must then have /a/ as its nucleus. We have here again only one example to show the coalescence of the graphs of the first and the second divisions into one homonym group，1802017 南（AC /꜀nəm/，MP /nán/）諵（AC /꜀nam/，MP /nán/）. For the same reasons given in discussing RG08（5.6），examples of this kind may occur only to syllables with initial /l/ or /n/，but unfortunately，the only other possible example，臉 AC /꜂lam/，MP /lyǎn/）a second division graph which might have been entered into 1803027 together

① Stimson discussed this problem in great detail in his article of 1962（Stimson 1962a，133－137），but the solution he presented there is not convincing. In his book of 1966，however，he seems to have ignored the problem completely by postulating /ɨŋ)/ and /iɨŋ)/ as the finals of RG15，and /uɨŋ/ and /iuɨŋ/ for RG01（Stimson 1966，22）.

with its counterpart in the first division 覽(AC /ᶜ lam/, MP /lǎn/), is now found in 1903025, obviously due to some irregular development①. There is no rime with /o/ as its nuclear vowel and /m/ as its ending, because there are no first division graphs with medial /w/ in the *Hsién-shè*. First division graphs with labial initials should have */wom/ as their final, according to Rule 9. There are only two of them, 姏 (AC /꜀ mam/, MP /mwán/) and 媏 (AC /ᶜ mam/, MP—), which are, however, not included in CYYY. But even if they had been, they would not have formed a separate rime or been entered in RG18, because the process of dissimilation (Rule I in 3.4) would have certainly made it necessary to enter them in RG09.

5.9 RG12, RG13, and RG14

We can now move forward with more confidence in our hypothesis of the vowel shift. The three rimes, RG12, RG13, and RG14, are developed from the *Kuǒ-shè* and the *Chiǎ-shè*, both with zero ending. Though the *Kuǒ-shè* and the *Chiǎ-shè* are treated as two separate classes in *Ch'ièh-yǜn Chǐh-nán*, they are actually in complementary distribution so far as the divisions are concerned②; therefore, in *Ch'ièh-yǜn Chǐh-chǎng T'ú* they are treated by implication as one single rime class③ Consequently, according to our hypothesis, we now postulate /e/ as the nuclear vowel for RG14, /a/ for

---

① The graph 臉 is noted as 力減 in Li Júng's book (Lǐ Júng 1956, 70) which is based upon an old edition of *Ch'ièh-yǜn*(王仁昫本) but in *Chí-yǜn*, it is noted as 居奄切, that is, with initial /k/.

② Actually, it is not so clear-cut. There does exist one contrasting pair, namely, 虵/꜀ iɑ/vs. 耶/꜀ iɛ/, but since it was so marginal, it must have been wiped out quickly in later development (see Lǐ Júng 1956, 46 and 48.)

③ See *Ch'ièh-yǜn Chih-chǎng T'ú*, Tables 11 and 12. The few third division graphs of the *Kuǒ-shè* are now simply listed as belonging to the rime 麻. one of the *Chiǎ-shè*. Also cf. Martin (1953), 3 and 38.

RG13, and /o/ for RG12. This works perfectly well so far as RG13 and RG14 are concerned, but with regard to RG12, we find we have to slightly modify the conditioning part of Rule 25. Instead of saying that only those first division graphs which stand for the syllables with medial /w/ remain distinct in having /o/ as their nucleus, we now have to say that all the first division graphs of the corresponding syllables with medial /w/ and/or with zero ending remain distinct in having /o/ as their nucleus, because we find that no first division graphs are entered in RG13, while in RG12, in addition to graphs representing syllables with medial /w/, such as 1201002 科（AC /꜀khuɑ/, MP /khē/）and 1201004 戈（AC /꜀kuɑ/, MP /kē/）, there are many with zero medial, such as 1201001 歌（AC /꜀kɑ/, MP /kē/）and 1201003 軻（AC /꜀khɑ/, MP /khē/）. Thus, we must revise Rule 25 as follows:

$$V_1 \longrightarrow \left\{ \begin{array}{l} o/ \left\{ \begin{array}{l} w\_\_\_ \\ \_\_\_\# \end{array} \right\} \\ a \end{array} \right\} \qquad (30)$$

In reality, this revision is needed only for syllables with guttural initials, because all those with non-guttural initials and zero medial had by the time of CYYY, apparently, already acquired medial /w/, and subsequently merged with those originally with medial /w/, for example, 1201005 娑（AC /꜀sɑ/, MP /swē/）莎（AC /꜀suɑ/, MP /swē/）, 1202015 羅（AC /꜀lɑ/, MP /lwé/）螺/AC /꜀luɑ/, MP /lwé/）, and 1204067 馱（AC /tɑ꜄/, MP /twè/）惰（AC /tuɑ꜄/, MP /twè/）. A rule like the following, therefore, is needed,

$$C + V_1 + \# \longrightarrow C + w + V_1 + \# \qquad (31)$$

$$C \neq G$$

There is, of course, a problem of order in time. We do not know at this point which of the two processes represented by the two rules above took place first. Either of the two possible orders seems to be descriptively satisfactory, and both rules will be needed anyway. Another problem which must be mentioned here concerns RG13. We find there a small number of graphs which had their origin not in the *Chiă-shè* but in the *Hsièh-shě*, for example, 1301001 佳 (AC /$_{c}$kɛi′/, MP /cyā/) and 1304063 話 (AC /xɦuɛi$^{\supset}$/, MP /hwà/). According to the general development, we would expect to see them in RG06, but insofar as they appear here, we must postulate that they did not have /y/ in the terminal slot. These graphs all belong to the second division, and with no exception, they all have guttural initials. These two facts make me suspicious that the peculiar occurrence of these graphs in RG13 might perhaps be explained by some conditioning feature which, however, is not likely to be known to us within the limit of our present knowledge.

5.10 RG11

RG11 has always been a major challenge to the students of CYYY. We find in this rime a number of three way contrasts among graphs with labial and guttural initials, for example:

1101009 包 (AC /$_{c}$pɛu/, MP /pwāw/) vs. 1101028 褒 (AC /$_{c}$pɑu/, MP /pwāw/) vs. 1101007 標(AC /$_{c}$piɛu/, MP /pyāw/).

1101011 高 (AC /$_{c}$kɑu/, MP /kāw/) vs. 1101008 交 (AC /$_{c}$kɛu/, MP /cyāw/) vs. 1101005 嬌 (AC /$_{c}$kiɛu/, MP /cyāw/).

1101026 蒿(AC /$_{c}$xɑu/, MP /hāw/) vs. 1101022 哮 (AC /$_{c}$xɛu/, MP /syāw/ vs. 1101003 囂 (AC /$_{c}$xiɛu/, MP /syāw/).

1104147 奥 (AC /qɑu$^{\supset}$/, MP /àw/) vs. 110413 拗 (AC /qɛu$^{\supset}$/, MP /àw/) vs. 1104130 要 (AC /qiɛu$^{\supset}$/, MP /yàw/).

Confronted with these problems, scholars in the past all reacted with uncertainty. Chào Yìn-t'áng blames the book for not representing here the true state of the language of its day, but rather that of an earlier period①. T'ŭng T'úng-hó uses several southern non-Mandarin dialects to support these contrasts②. Lù Chìh-wéi, in my opinion, does the best job. By adopting a somewhat structural approach, he comes to the conclusion that there should be at least three nuclear vowels, though he readily confesses that he is not sure of what he is doing③.

5.10.1 When we apply our hypothesis of vowel shift to this rime group, we notice immediately that these three-way contrasts no longer present any problem at all. They rather turn out to be the natural and inevitable consequence of the phonological structure of the language of that period. It is true that we will come to roughly the same conclusion as Lù does, but there is a great difference. While his is more or less the result of guesswork, ours is a necessity dictated by the overall phonemic structure we set up for the language of that time. As we know, RG11 comes from the *Hsiào-shè* which contains graphs of all the four divisions. Moreover, these graphs are all of the unrounded type④. Consequently, according to our vowel shift rules, syllables of the first division should have /aw/ as their final, except those with labial initials which should have, instead, /wow/; syllables of the second division should also have /aw/, except those with labial initials which should have /waw/ and those with guttural initials which should have /yaw/; and graphs of the third and the fourth divisions should have fallen together in having /yew/ as their final. In this fashion, all the three-way contrasts in this rime as exemplified by those cited above are maintained and explained in the most reasonable manner I can imagine.

---

① See Chào Yìn-t'áng (1936), 129－131.

② Tŭng (1954), 30－31.

③ Lù (1946), 54－55.

④ Practically, all the books of rime tables label this rime class 'tú' i. e., either *k'āi* 開 (unrounded) or *hó* 合 (rounded) alone. This class has been unanimously interpreted as unrounded by modern scholars.

5.10.2 Plausible though the above solution may seem to be, it is not yet completely satisfactory, because it fails to cope with one fact observed in this rime. One strange phenomenon in RG11 is that we find here a peculiar minimal pair of contrast, namely, 1104147 奥 (AC /qɑuᵓ/, MP /àw/) vs. 1104125 傲 (AC /ŋɑuᵓ/, MP /àw/), which turns Case (*d*) in 5.10 into a four way contrast, a situation the proposed solution cannot explain. In our discussion of the AC initial /ŋ/ (4.6.4.-4.6.4.5), mainly for the existence of two minimal pairs, 1203046 vs. 1203048 and the one just mentioned, we have been forced to say that initial /ŋ/ still exists in CYYY, though rather marginally. By admitting this, we are then obliged to figure out the formal condition for the marginal existence of this initial. Since the two homonym groups with initial /ŋ/ involved here both belong to the first division, I have thought it reasonable to say that nucleus V_1 remains unchanged in these two cases, while in others it has changed to V_2. Thus, we can say that initial /ŋ/ remains unchanged only when it immediately precedes the remaining V_1. So far as 1203048 is concerned, Rule 30 in 5.9 has already taken care of it, because the rule assigns to it nucleus /o/, an equivalent to V_1 in the previous period, but the rule must now be revised once more in order to account for 1104125, that is, we have to say that, before ending /w/, V_1 should also be represented by /o/ in CYYY. We can do this by adding a new condition to the rule in the following manner:

$$V_1 \longrightarrow \left\{\begin{array}{l} o/\left\{\begin{array}{l} w\underline{\hspace{2em}} \\ \underline{\hspace{2em}}\left\{\begin{array}{l}\#\\ w\end{array}\right\}\end{array}\right\} \\ a \end{array}\right\} \qquad (32)$$

but this new rule, heavily loaded with conditions, looks rather clumsy. Instead of saying under what conditions V_1 is to be represented by /o/, it may be simpler to say under what conditions it has changed to V_2, i.e., to be represented by /a/. Thus we can replace Rule 32 with Rule 22 given before in

4.6.4.5：

$$C + V_1 + E \longrightarrow C + V_2 + E \qquad (22)$$

$$E \neq w$$

Rule 22, of course, must be supplemented by another rewriting rule as follows:

$$V_1 \longrightarrow o \qquad (33)$$

It may seem undesirable to replace Rule 32, clumsy though it is, with two rules, but it is true only because we have found it necessary to state the nuclear vowels of RTP in purely abstract terms, otherwise, Rule 33, together with Rule 26 and Rule 27, would probably be unneeded.

5.10.3 If we accept Rule 22, as I think we should, we must now write /ow/ as the final for all the first division graphs with non-labial initials in RG11. In other words, we have to maintain the distinction between the first division and the second division. In view of the fact that graphs of these two divisions now appear in one rime, it might look rather arbitrary to maintain the distinction for the sake of a single minimal pair, 1104147 vs. 1104125. This is why many people have found it tempting to disregard the pair in question by treating it as a mistake on the part of the compiler of the book①. However, our discussion on this point so far should have been persuasive enough to support this distinction. To make our argument even stronger, we may make a close check to see if there are any homonym groups where graphs of these two types appear together. As it has been noted before (5.6 and 5.8), this can occur only to graphs corresponding to syllables with /l/ or /n/ as their initial. It happens that there is no second division graph under initial /l/ in the *Hsiào-shè*, but there are quite a few under initial /n/ in both divisions. If our hypothesis is correct, we shall then expect to see in CYYY

① For example, Ting (1954), 26-27.

the first division graphs of this type still in contrast with those of the second. Unfortunately, the situation here is a little bit confusing. We find they appear together in TG02, namely, 1102038 猱(AC /$_{c}$ nɑu/, MP /náw/) 鐃(AC /$_{c}$ nɛu/, MP /náw/), but remain in contrast in TG03, namely, 1103074 腦 (AC /^{c} nɑu/, MP /nǎw/) vs. 1103094 撓 (AC /^{c} nɛu/, MP /nǎw/). I take the contrast between 1103074 and 1103094 to be a strong proof for the soundness of our hypothesis, for the two homonym groups are so far apart that there seems to be little ground for saying that they were separated by mistake, especially when we can offer a reasonable explanation for their separation. As to 1102038, I feel it can be easily explained away. On several occasions so far, we have said that two contiguous homonym groups might actually be one which was divided mistakenly by some editor of a later period from a different dialectal area, who did not understand Chōu Té-ch'īng well enough. The reverse of this argument should also hold, that is, a certain homonym group might be actually two contiguous groups in the original version of the book, combined by mistake only in a later period, if and only if we can propose a theory to support this argument. I believe 1102038 is exactly such an example. The first graph of this homonym group 猱 must have formed one homonym group by itself, while the rest formed another. Since the two groups occurred in succession and their distinction soon disappeared after CYYY, they were mistakenly written into one①.

5.10.4 There should be no doubt now about our solution for this rime, but to some people, the contrast between the two finals /yaw/ and /yew/ may seem rather strange. As a general rule, I do not like to rely on external evidence, unless there is no other way, since the phonemic structure of one dialect or language is no proof of another. But in case anyone thinks such

① The problem discussed here has been consistently overlooked, deliberately or not, by all scholars of CYYY except Hugh Stimson whose conclusion is, however, exactly the opposite to mine (see Stimson 1962a. 138–139).

evidence is necessary to support the contrast we set up here, we are not in want of it. First of all, as Lù Chìh-wéi has mentioned repeatedly①, the h̲Phags-pa script show clearly that the second division graphs with guttural initials had by this time acquired medial /y/. Thus, we can not ignore this fact and assign to the second division graphs with guttural initials a final without medial /y/ so as to give those of the third division and the fourth division one with it. Secondly, in a rime book compiled later than CYYY, *Húng-wǔ Chèng-yǔn* 洪武正韻, graphs of RG11 of CYYY appear in two separate sets, showing clearly that graphs of the first two divisions and those of the third and the fourth divisions must have different nuclear vowels. This fact has forced Tǔng T'ǔng-hó to admit that the final of the third and the fourth division graphs in that book is "probably [ieu]"②, just in line with our conclusion. One serious and legitimate question can be raised here. If RG11 indeed contains three different nuclear vowels, then why is it not split into three rimes, in the same manner as RG08, RG09, and RG10 are from the *Shān-shè*? Quite a number of answers can be suggested, but none of them will be completely satisfactory in the sense of being provable. To me, the most reasonable conjecture is that Chōu Té-ch'īng was recording here a peculiar form of Mandarin dialect of his day which still maintained the contrast among the three low vowels in syllables with /w/ as their ending, while in the dialect (or dialects) in which most of the great playwrights wrote the contrast had already disappeared. In other words, Chōu was faithful in recording the dialect he learned to speak but compromised in establishing only one rime category here, under the influence of the prevailing riming practice of the

① Cf. Lù (1946), 49, 51, 54, and 55.
② Tǔng (1954), 35.

great writers①.

5.10.5 One supplementary point to our solution for this rime must be added here. Theoretically, graphs of the first division with labial initials should all contrast with their counterparts in the second division. However, in this rime we find it is true only when the initial is /p/ in AC, for example, 1101028 vs. 1101009 given above, 1103070 寳(AC /ᶜ pɑu/, MP /pwǎw/) vs. 1103088 飽(AC /ᶜ pɛu/, MP /pwǎw/), and 1104122 報(AC /pɑuᵓ/, MP /pwàw/) vs. 1104121 豹(AC /pɛuᵓ/, MP /pwàw).

As to the other labial initials, the contrast seems to be no longer maintained. As a result, we have now homonym groups containing both the first and the second division graphs, for example, 1102047 袍(AC /꜀ pɦɑu/, MP /phwáw/)庖(AC /꜀ pɦɛu, MP /phwáw/), and 1102037 毛(AC /꜀ mɑu/, MP /mwáw/) 茅(AC /꜀ mɛu/, MP /mwáw/). (There is no first division graph with initial /ph/). I can offer no explanation as to why graphs with initial /p/ alone could maintain this contrast while others could not, but the whole phenomenon can perhaps be taken as evidence that the contrast in question is on the verge of disappearing.

---

① The problem discussed here involves the shift of the vowel system of RTP (and CYYY) to that of Modern Pekinese. Though a detailed discussion on this matter cannot be given here, it may be interesting to note that the shift went through many stages (roughly from middle T'áng to late Míng) before it was completed. The first step took place before CYYY when the contrast among the three low vowels was lost in syllables with ending /y/, as a consequence of the change of /e/ and /o/ to /ɨ/ (see 5.11 and 5.12.2). The second step is the coalescence of the three low vowels in syllables with ending /w/ discussed here. The same coalescence in syllables with ending /n/ and the merger of /e/ and /o/ before ending /ŋ/ were implied in *Yùn-lueh Hui-t'ùng*(韻略匯通, 1642). It is quite clear that the shift was a very gradual one, with each step affecting only a limited number of words. Moreover, it seems safe to say that each step must have started in one dialect (or sub-dialect) and then spread to others, as was the merger of the low vowels before ending /w/.

5.11 RG06

Our hypothesis also works extremely well with RG06, though this fact may have been some what obscured by some further changes after the vowel shift. This rime comes from the *Hsièh-shè* which, like the *Hsiào-shè*, is one of the outer series and contains graphs of all the four divisions. Naturally, we expect to see three different types of finals in CYYY coming from it:

(i) /woy/: for the first division graphs of the rounded type.

(ii) $/\left(\begin{Bmatrix}\text{w}\\ \text{y}\end{Bmatrix}\right)$ ay/: for the first division graphs of the unrounded type and all the second division graphs.

(iii) /y(w)ey/: for graphs of both the third and the fourth divisions.

Most of the graphs of RG06 are from the sources described in (ii) above, and should therefore be transcribed with finals indicated there, for example, 0601001 街(AC /꜀ kɛi/, MP /cyē/) will be /kyay/, 0601002 該(AC /꜀ kəi/, MP /kāy/) will be /kay/, and 0601015 乖(AC /꜀ kuai/, MP /kwāy/) will be /kway/. However, three peculiar phenomena connected with this rime must be promptly pointed out here:

(*a*) The other two types of finals do not exist in CYYY. This is so, because graphs which, according to our hypothesis, might have such finals now all appear in RG04, for example, 0401001 鷄(AC /꜀ kiei/, MP /cyɨ/), 0402032 齊(AC /꜀ cɦiei/, MP /chyɨ́/). 0403070 賄(AC /꜂ xuəi/, MP /hwèy/), and 0404116 祭(AC /ciɛi꜄/, MP /cyɨ̀/). Evidently, this is due to some new changes which can be more easily dealt with later in the discussion of RG04 (see 5.12.2).

(*b*) There are a few graphs in RG06, such as 0601009 衰(AC /꜀ sriu*i/, MP /srwāy). 0603042 揣(AC /꜂ crhiuə/, MP /crhwǎy/), and 0604083 帥(AC /sriu*i꜄/, MP /srwày), which are not from the *Hsièh-shè*, but from the *Chĭh-shè*. They will also be discussed later (see 5. 12. 3).

(*c*) We have noted in 5. 9 that some graphs of the *Hsièh-shè* with guttural initials turn out to be in RG13 rather than in RG06 where they are expected to go. Unless further research on *Ch'ièh-yǜn* and on the rime tables in particular can shed some new light in this regard, we shall not be able to see the conditioning factor, if any, for the seemingly irregular development of the syllables represented by those graphs.

5. 12 RG03, RG04, and RG05

RG03, RG04, and RG05 must be discussed together for the best effect. With the exception of the graphs in RG04 which came from the *Hsièh-shè* (5. 11a), the first two groups here are from the *Chĭh-shè*, while the last one is from the *Yǜ-shè*. According to our hypothesis, all the three rimes here must have the high vowel /ɨ/ as their nuclear vowel, because both the *Chĭh-shè* and the *Yǜ-shè* belong to the inner series. Furthermore, our presumption that the rimes of AC found together in the same division of the same rime class must have coalesced by the time when the rime tables were compiled (3. 6. 3) requests us to say that all the sylables of the *Yǜ-shè* must have /w/ in the medial position and all the syllables of the *Chĭh-shè* must have ending /y/ by this time. Consequently, we believe the sole feature that differentiates the *Yǜ-shè* from the *Chĭh-shè* is the absence of the syllabic ending /y/. Thus for RG05, there should be two finals, /wɨ/ for the first division graphs and those of the third division with B and the AC Pr initials, for cxample, /swɨ/ for 0501003 蘇(AC /$_c$ su*/, MP /swɨ̄/), /srwɨ/ for 0501007 梳(AC /$_c$ sri*/, MP /srwɨ̄/, and /ywɨ/ for the rest of the third division graphs, for example, /kywɨ/ for 0501001 居(AC /$_c$ ki*/, MP /cywɨ̄/) and /crywɨ/ for 0501002 諸(AC /$_c$ cji*/, MP /crwɨ̄/). The development of the *Chĭh-shè* is much more complex. I believe it must have the two finals /i*i/ (our /yɨy/) and /iu*i/ (our /ywɨy/) in RTP as were still maintained in *Ch'ièh-yǜn chǐh-nán*. The process of losing the medial /y/ after certain initials soon came into operation. It was at first restricted to syllables of all kinds with AC Pr initials (Rule 13 in 4.5), then it began to afect the unrounded of the *Chǐh-shè* with Ds initials, and finally syllables of the unrounded type of the *Chǐh-shè* with Pj initials (Rule 15 in 4.5) were also affected. We know that syllables with Ds initials were affected before those with Pj initials, for in *Ch'ièh-yǜn Chǐh-chǎng T'ú*, we find graphs representing syllables of the former kind such as 玆(AC /꜀ci*i'/, MP /cɨ/) and 斯(AC /꜀siə/, MP /sɨ/) were moved up from the fourth division to the first division[①], while those with Pj initials still appear in the third division (Table 18), though in CYYY they have joined those with Pr initials in the second division, for example, 0301003 眵 (AC /꜀cjhiə/, MP /crhɨ/) 差 (AC /꜀crhiə/, MP /crhɨ/, and 0301004 詩(AC /꜀sji*'/, MP /srɨ/) 師 (AC /꜀sri*i/, MP /srɨ/). There is no reason, however, to believe that ending /y/ in syllables of this kind was also lost so early; the corresponding graphs cited above still appear in the same table as other graphs of the *Chǐh-shè*. Thus we have now a new final /ɨy/ which occurs only after Ds and Pr (including Pj) initials. If ending /y/ had been maintained in this final by the time of CYYY, graphs with this final should have then rimed with other graphs of the *Chǐh-shè* and formed together a single rime. But instead they form a separate rime, RG03, in CYYY, contrasting with the rest of the *Chǐh-shè* graphs which form RG04. This leads to a logical conclusion that the ending in the new final /ɨy/ was also lost before CYYY, and there for the first time emerged the unique final /ɨ/ in the Chinese language.

The following rules can be given as a summing up of the above discussion:

$$y \longrightarrow \emptyset / Pr\_\_\_ \qquad (13)$$

① See Table 18 of the book. Also cf. Chào Yìn-t'áng (1936), 108.

$$j \longrightarrow r \quad (14)$$

$$y \longrightarrow \text{ø}/Ds\_\_\_ ɨ + y \quad (34)$$

$$y \longrightarrow \text{ø}/Pr\_\_\_ ɨ + y \quad (15)$$

$$y \longrightarrow \text{ø}/C + ɨ\_\_\_ \quad (35)$$

5. 12. 1 The process of depalatalization must have stopped operating some time before the P initials fell together with the Pr (including Pj) initials (Rule 16 in 4. 5), for graphs of the *Chǐh-shè* with P initials appear in RG04 rather than in RG03(see 4. 5). This fact indicates that the graphs involved here still maintained their final /yɨy/, and as such, they were not affected by Rule 35. For the same reason, we believe this process of depalatalization must also have stopped working before the merging of a large number of *Hsièh-shè* graphs with those of the *Chǐh-shè*, which will be discussed immediately.

5. 12. 2 We have said in our discussion of RG06 that three types of finals are expcted to develop from the *Hsièh-shè*, but two of these, /woy/ and /y(w)ey/, actually do not exist in CYYY. Graphs which could have had such finals now all turn out to be included in RG04 (5. 11a). Since now we know RG04 has the high vowel /ɨ/ as is nucleus, this phenomenon can be very easily registered here by the fllowing rule.

$$\begin{Bmatrix} o \\ e \end{Bmatrix} \longrightarrow ɨ/\_\_\_\_\_ y \quad (36)$$

In so doing, we have already made a presumption yet to be proved, that is, we have taken for granted that the *Hsièh shè* developed at first in the same line as other rime classes in the outer series and only after this shift of vowels had been completed did it make a unique turn of its own in having its /o/ and /e/ raised up to /ɨ/. I belive this presumption is true, not only because it explains the development of the *Hsièh-shè* in the most satisfactory manner, but also because we have evidence in CYYY that these *Hsièh-shè* graphs joined those of the *Chǐh-shè* rather late, – later than the loss of medial /y/ in the sllables with final /yɨy/ and Pj initials. We have noticed that graphs with Pj nitials in the *Chĭh-shè* have merged with those with Pr initials and together wound up in RG03 (5.12). If the *Hsièh-shè* graphs had indeed joined those of the *Chĭh-shè* very early, then the *Hsièh-shè* graphs with Pj initials must have also fallen together with those of the *Chĭh-shè* with the same initials and subsequently they should also have been affected by the process of depalatalization and should have been included in RG03, together with the latter. But such is not the case. The few graphs with Pj initials in the *Hsièh-shè* now turn out to be in RG04 and thus have to be transcribed with the final /yɨy/, for example, 0404132 制(AC /cjiɛiᑐ/, MP /crɨ/), 0404133 世(AC /sjiɛiᑐ/, MP /srɨ/) and 逝(AC /sjɦiɛiᑐ/, MP /srɨ/). Unfortunately, evidence from *Ch'ièh-yùn Chĭh-chăng T'ú* seems to contradict this presumption. We find in that book the graphs of the *Hsièh-shè* involved here are already listed on the same tables (Tables 18 and 19) with those of the *Chĭh-shè*, while the *Chĭh-shè* graphs with Pj initials are still listed in the third division. This seems to break down our reasoning, because it hints that the shift of the *Hsièh-shè* graphs in question took place a long time ago, even before the vowel shift. However, I still believe we should rely on what we have figured out in CYYY, not just because our main concern is CYYY to which *Ch'ièh-yùn Chĭh-chăng T'ú* may not be directly related, but also because the former may be taken as a real and unprejudiced recording of the language of its day while the latter is certainly a modified form of the books of its kind before it and thus is likely to be a mixture of obsolete features and new ones. The peculiar arrangement of the last four tables which contain the graphs under study bere certainly arouses our suspicion①.

① The arrangement of the rime tables in *Ch'ièh-yùn Chĭh-chăng T'ú* is like this: the first six are 'single' (tú 獨) that is each is either rounded or unrounded, without a counterpart: the next ten form successively five rounded/unrounded pairs; the last four, strangely. form one unit, with two unrounded ones versus two rounded ones.

5. 12. 3 The shift of some of the *Hsièh-shè* graphs to join those of the *Chǐh-shè* does not seem to be a one-way traffic, because we also find some, though rather few, *Chǐh-shè* graphs in RG06 which comes mainly from the *Hsièh-shè* (5. 11b). The few graphs involved here are all of the rounded type with AC Pr initials; hence, their change can be described in the following manner:

$$\text{Pr} + \text{w} + \text{ɨ} + \text{y} \longrightarrow \text{Pr} + \text{w} + \text{a} + \text{y} \tag{37}$$

This change, we know for sure, must have taken place after the depalatalization of the graphs with Pr initials but before the depalatalization of those with Pj initials (5. 12. 4), for graphs having formerly the same final /ywɨy/ but with Pj initials are now found in RG04, that is, having the same nucleus as before, for ecxample, 0401016 吹 (AC /꜀cjhiuə/, MP /crhwēy/), 0402047 誰 (AC /꜀sjɦiu*i/, MP /srwéy/ and /sréy/), and 0404128 睡 (AC /sjɦiuə꜄/, MP /srwèy/)①.

5. 12. 4 There are many homonym groups in RG04 which contain both graphs of the first division and those of the third and the fourth divisions, for example, 0401008 灰 (AC /꜀xuəi/, MP /hwēy/,. 輝 (AC /꜀xiuəi/, MP /hwēy); 0402030 雷 (AC /꜀luəi/, MP /léy/), 纍 (AC /꜀liu*i/, MP /léy/); 0404123 最 (AC /cuɑi꜄/, MP /cwèy/, 醉 (AC /ciu*i꜄/, MP /cwèy/); 0404112 會 (AC /xɦuɑi꜄/, MP /hwèy/), 慧 (AC xɦuei꜄/, MP /hwèy/). This phenomenon shows indisputably that the third and the fourth division graphs involved here had lost their medial /y/ before CYYY. We thus need a rule as follows:

$$\text{y} \longrightarrow \text{ø}/\_\_\_\text{w} + \text{ɨ} + \text{y} \tag{38}$$

---

① The above rule should probably be revised as ɨ→a/(C)w_y, so as to show that the change is strictly confined to a speciftce final rather than having anything to do with the initial. This revision is possible beause before the change specied by Rule 38 in 5. 12. 4 and the change represented by Rule 36 in 5. 12. 2 the final /wɨy/ could only occur after Pr initials.

Again, we have presumed here in so doing that the loss of the /y/ in this case took place after Rule 36, because it is more economical to assume so.[①] It certainly must have taken place after Rule 37, because otherwise those with Pj initials would have been the same as those with Pr initials and as such, should have shown the same development, but in fact this is not true, as we have noted in the last section.

5.12.5 In RG04, we also find some homonym groups which include graphs of the first and the third divisions, all with labial initials, for example, 0401009 杯 (AC /꜀ puəi/, MP /pwēy/), 悲 (AC /꜀ pi * i/, MP /pwēy/); 0401017 胚 (AC /꜀ phuəi/, MP /phwēy/), 披 AC /꜀ phiə/, MP /phyɨ/ and /phwēy/); 0402029 枚 (AC /꜀ muəi/, MP /mwéy/), 眉 (AC /꜀ mi*i/, MP /mwéy/). This phenomenon is indeed very strange. So far as the first division graphs are concerned, there is no difficulty. Since they are all of the rounded type from the *Hsièh-shè*, we naturally reconstruct for them a final /wɨy/. The third division graphs, however, provide quite a challenge. They could not have been of the rounded type, because in that case they would have /f/ or /v/ as their initial (see 4.2.1). Therefore, their final must have been /yɨy/. If we could somehow say that medial /y/ was lost in this final after labial initials, the problem would be solved, because our theory that labials must be followed by /w/ when not by /y/ (sce 4.2.1) would automatically add medial /w/ there and make the occurrence of the graphs in question only natural. This, however, we cannot do, because there

---

① Otherwise, we would have to revise Rule 38 as follows:

$$y \longrightarrow \emptyset / \_\_\_ w \begin{Bmatrix} e \\ ɨ \end{Bmatrix} y$$

A more general claim may be made by writing the formula as:

$$y \longrightarrow \emptyset / \_\_\_ w + V + y$$

for both /-oy/ and /-ay/ are never preceded by /yw/. anyway. I prefer the rule as it is to the more general one, because it seems to be historically more precise.

are also many graphs of this kind which do not behave in this way, for example, 0402045 疲 (AC /꜀ pɦiə/, MP /phyɨ́/) and 0402046 彌 (AC /꜀ miə/, MP /myɨ́/). Within the limit of our present knowledge, I can see no other way than to treat these graphs as the result of irregular development①.

5.12.6 We have seen that the graphs of RG03 stood for sylables which had in RTP the final /yɨy/ which later, due to depalatalization, was changed to /ɨy/ and finally to/ɨ/in CYYY (5.12). So far, there has been no direct evidence to prove this last step, but it is necessary for two reasons. First, as I have said in 5.12, if ending /y/ in these graphs had not disappeared by the time of CYYY, there would have been no reason to separate them from the rest of the *Chĭh-shè* graphs by establishing a special rime category for them. Secondly, as we shall see later, some of the entering tone graphs will have to be transcribed with the final /ɨy/ and these graphs all appear in RG04, confirming our reasoning that graphs with final /ɨy/ should not form a separate rime, for example, 0452058 劾(AC /xɦək/, MP /hé/) and 0452059

---

① Statisticly, slightly fewer *Chĭh-shè* graphs of the unrounded type of the third division turn out to be /Byɨy/ in CYYY. This may justily the inclusion of the fllowing rule for CYYY:

$$/Byɨy/ \longrightarrow (*/Bɨy/) \longrightarrow /Bwɨy/$$

It is quite possible that former syllables of the type /Byɨy/ lost their medial /y/ in some dialects. as is suggested by the above rule (I believe we ought to be able to find some dialects in which syllables of the form /Byɨy/ or /Bɨy/ are no longer possible), while in some other dialects they remained unchanged by the time of CYYY. In other words, what we see in CYYY as well as MP is perhaps a mixture of these two types of dialects as far as words of this kind are concerned. Morcover, the problem here seemingly involves the so-called initial doublets (*ch'úng-niŭ* 重紐) in Ancient Chinese which I have not touched on. While there is no doubt about the phonological distinction of these doublets in AC, I believe by RTP the contrast had probably been shifted to the final, i.e., the distinction between every *ch'úng-niŭ* pair was replaced by some feature in the final. The h̠Phags-pa scriptions seem to suggest that those of the *ch'úng-niŭ* pairs listed in the fourth division of the rime tables had become indeed fourth division words (Cf. Hashimoto 1965. 211). lending some support to my assumption expressed in 3.6.3. However, whatever the contrast between each of the *ch'úng-niŭ* pair might have been, in the language of CYYY, it had clearly disappeared. Consequenly, it cannot help us solve the problem we have here. For detailed discussions on the *ch'úng-niŭ* problem, see Hashimoto (1965), 207-220, and Tung (1948a).

贼(AC /cɦək/, MP /céy/) (see 6.4.1.1).

RG04 is now left with only two finals, namely, /yɨy/ and /wɨy/ (excluding the one coming from the entering tone which will be discussed separately). No objection is likely to be raised against the second one, but can't the first one be rewritten as /yɨ/?① Graphs with this final are now in MP all pronounced with [-i] which Hartman has analyzed into /-yɨ/. In view of this fact and for the sake of economy, /yɨ/ seems indeed preferable to /yɨy/. After all, they are both descriptively satisfactory in CYYY. Stimson has noticed this problem and concluded after an elaborate discussion that /ie/ (our /yɨ/) is"not only acceptable ... but preferable to /iei/ (our /yɨy) from the phonological point of view②. I do not feel his argument is convincing, and it seems to me, from the phonological point of view, we must conclude exactly the other way. The reasons are:

(*a*) Historically, the existence of ending /y/ in this case is beyond any doubt. In fact, it is the sole feature which differentiates some of the graphs of the *Chǐh-shè* from those of the *Yǜ-shè*③. Unless we have some compelling reason to write it off, we have to assume it is still there in CYYY, otherwise, we would be recording a change which we cannot prove.

(*b*) It is true that riming may sometimes be nothing but an arbitrary practice, but generally it is not. Our study of CYYY is mainly based upon this practice. So logically we must start with the presumption that all the graphs of one rime share not just the same nucleus but also the same ending, if there is one. We can abandon this presumption, as we have done in our discussion of RG11, but only in some rare cases where all evidence agrees. In the case of RG04, we certainly do not feel this obligation. On the contrary, by maintaining /yɨy/, we shall be able to establish /ɨy/ as the unique rime

---

① Hartman writes them /ji/ (Hartman 1944, 118).

② Stimson (1962a), 130.

③ Cf. Martin (1953), 38. The contrast is: /i*/ vs. /i*i/.

feature for RG04.

(*c*) Most important of all, the overall phonological structure makes it much more desirable to represent the final in question by /yɨy/. We have established four nuclear vowels on two levels for CYYY. All the four can and do combine with endings. In fact, we have seen the combination /ɨy/ in the final /wɨy/. The general patterning naturally requires us to establish a final like /yɨy/, if there had been syllables in AC which would develop in this direction. Indeed, this "would leave a single blank in a distribution chart for the potential position /yɨ/①, but this is inherently unavoidable. There are other blanks, too, simply because no words exist to fill them up. The situation in MP is entirely different. As has been seen in Hartman's analysis, three nuclear vowels on three levels have been established there. One of the characteristics of the high vowel is that it never combines with any ending. The final /yɨy/ in CYYY turns out to have the high vowel as its nucleus in MP and no longer rimes smoothly with the final /wɨy/ which has now in MP the middle vowel as its nucleus. Consequently, ending /y/ in the CYYY final /yɨy/ must be written off in MP so as to register this new development②.

Thus we can see now it is by no means an arbitrary decision in either CYYY or MP whether to represent the final in question by one form or the other. It may be noted here in passing that the decision to choose /yɨy/ over /yɨ/ may present us with a tough problem when we deal with the entering tone graphs. We shall discuss it when we come to it (see 6. 4. 4. 2).

---

① Stimson 1962a, 130.

② This claim is based upon my own analysis of MP which is roughly outlined in 7. 5. 1 – 7. 5. 3. It is more or less a revision of Hartman's analysis but I differ from Hartman here in that he allows the two nasal endings to occur after the high vowel when it is preceded by the semi-vowel /j/ (our /y/). See Hartman (1944), 119.

5. 13 RG16

RG16 is now the only rime to be discussed, but after what has been said so far, the nature of this group has become too clear to need any detailed discussion. The finals of this rime are, of course, /ɨw/, /yɨw/, and /wɨw/, with /ɨw/ as the rime feature. The final /wɨw/ is rather rare. It occurs only after labial initials, for example, 1602026 裒 (AC /꜀ pɦəu/, MP /phwéw) will be /phwɨw/, and 1603055 否 (AC /꜂ pi*u/, MP /fwěw/) will be /fwɨw/ in CYYY. This may sound like a circular argument. Indeed, if not for the rule that labials must be followed by /w/ when not by /y/ (Rule 9), we would not have to establish a final with medial /w/ in RG16. The same thing can perhaps be said about RG11, too. But the total phonological picture makes us believe this rule of labials is sound, and as we shall see, it also helps to explain the peculiar development of the graphs with labial initials in the *Liú-shè* whence comes RG16.

5. 13. 1 As we have noted (4. 2. 3), the *Liú-shè* has two types of AC rimes in the third division, the *Yóu* rimes (尤有宥) and the *Yōu* rimes (幽黝幼). These two types later merged, except the graphs with labial initials. From the later development of these graphs with labial initials, we can reasonably suspect that, before the coalescence, syllables of the *Yóu* rimes had /w/ in their medial position while those of the *Yōu* rimes did not. In other words, they perhaps differed in *hó-k'ǒu* Vs. *k'āi-k'ǒu* (rounded/unrounded). Consequently, syllables of the *Yóu* rimes with labial initials were later dentilabialized①, while those of the *Yōu* rimes were not (4. 2. 3).

① Those with initial /m/ present a difficult problem. While 謀 (AC /꜀ mi*u/, MP /mwéw/ appears in 0502026 and hence must be transcribed /mwɨ́/. most of its homophones in AC, 矛牟 etc., appear in 1602027 and can be transeribed either as /myɨ́w/ or as /mwɨ́w/. Though 繆 (AC /꜀ mi*u/ and /꜀ miəu/, MP /mwéw/) could have the reading /myɨ́w/ in (轉下頁)

In CYYY, all but a few of the graphs with labial initials in *Liú-shè* appear in RG05, instead of RG16 where they are expected, for example, 0502036 浮 (AC /꜀ pɦi*u/, MP /fwɨ/), 0503069 否 (AC /꜂ pi*u/, MP /fwěw/), 0503070 母 (AC /꜂ məu/, MP /mwɨ̌/) and 0504113 富 (AC /pi*u꜄/, MP /fwɨ̀/). This change, in my thinking, may be regarded as the result of the combined effect of the medial /w/ and the ending /w/ in the following process:

$$w \longrightarrow \text{ø}/w + \text{ɨ}\_\_\_ \qquad (39)$$

but the few exceptions to this rule, for example, 1602026 抔 (AC /꜀ pɦəu/, MP /phwéw/), 1603052 剖 (AC /꜂ phəu/, MP /phwěw/) and 1604085 貿 (AC /məu꜄/, MP /mwàw/), force us to maintain /wɨw/ as one of the finals in RG16, and as far as I can see, the only way to explain why they were not affected by the same change is interdialectal borrowing[①].

5. 13. 2 Another problem involving RG16 concerns graphs with Pr initials in AC. There seems to be a tendency for them to merge with those of the first division with Ds initials, for example, 1601004 鄒 (AC /꜀ cri*u/, MP /cēw/) 緅 (AC /꜀ cəu/, MP /cēw/) and 1604075 輳 (AC /chəu꜄/, MP /chèw/甃 (AC /cri*u꜄/, MP /crèw/). In at least one case, former homophones with initial /sr/ are split into two homonym groups, namely, 1601003 搜 (AC

(接上頁) CYYY and the variant reading of 矛 AC /꜀ mi*u/, MP /mwáw/) as /myáw/ in MP (as in 丈八蛇矛) indicates that it could have the reading /myɨw/ in CYYY, I still feel /mwɨw/ should be chosen for 1602027. If this is true, we may say that graphs with initial /m/ in the *Yóu* rimes are just like those or the *T'ūng-shè* in merely losing /y/ in the medial position sometime before the process of dentilabialization (4. 2. 2).

① It seems reasonable to me to say that in the dialect represented by CYYY whence came Colloqual Pekinese, Rule 39 took place, while in the dialect whence came Literary Pekinese it did not. Note that the few words which have to be reconstructed with the final /wɨw/ would not belong to what we might call the basice vocabulary of a language. They are thus more likely to be influenced by other dialects. Moreover, even 謀 and 某 which belong to RG05 in CYYY have now the final /wew/ in Literary Pekinese.

/$_{\text{c}}$sri*u/, MP /sēw/) vs. 1601017 溲(AC /$_{\text{c}}$sri*u/, MP /sēw). Chào Yìn-t'áng transcribes the former as [sou] and the latter as [ʂou] with no explanation. This is to me basically an arbitrary decision, because in MP they have the same reading, though evidence from a rime book of the Sùng dynasty, *Chí-yǜn* (集韻), may somewhat justify what he does. The tendency is by no means overwhelming. We therefore must still keep the contrast between the two types of initials involved bere.

5.14 Summing Up

With the eminent exception of graphs of the entering tone, we have now finished discussing all the rimes in CYYY. A chart to show all the attested finals is in line here. After this, a table of rime features may be added, and a comprehensive chart of all the atested syllables, i.e., combinations of initials and finals, with reference to the homonym groups they represent in CYYY, is also in need as a summing up of the work we have done so far.

5.14.1 The following is a chart of all the attested finals. Numerals in the chart show the number of the rimes these finals belong to.

E	-ø				-y		-w				-n				-m			-ŋ		
V / M	ɨ	e	a	o	ɨ	a	ɨ	e	a	o	ɨ	e	a	o	ɨ	e	a	e	a	o
ø	03		13	12		06	16		11	11	07		08		17		18	15	02	
y		14	13		04	06	16	11	11		07	10	08		17	19	18	15	02	
w	05		13	12	04	06	16		11	11	07		08	09				15	02	01
yw	05	14									07	10						15	?	01

A question mark, instead of '02', is filled into the slot for */ywaŋ/. This is because I am rather suspicious of the contrasting pair 0204099 晃 (AC /^{c}xɦuaŋ/, MP /hwàŋ/) Vs. 0204100 況 (AC /xiuɑŋ$^{\supset}$/, MP /kwàŋ/. If we should accept this, we would have to establish the contrast between /waŋ/

and /ywaŋ/, and homonym groups 0201023, 0202048, 0202049, 0203063, and 0204091, would have to be all reconstructed with the final */ywaŋ/. I am suspicious of the contrasting pair which makes this necessary for two reasons: first, the two homonym groups appear contiguously and thus might actually belong to one group; second, as we noted before (5. 5. 1 and 5. 5. 2), there is a tendency for final /ywoŋ/ to become /woŋ/; similarly, it is also likely that /ywaŋ/ tends to become /waŋ/.

5. 14. 2 It is my belief that riming reveals a great deal about the feeling of the native speakers with regard to the unique phonological structure of their own language. It follows that an adequate phonemic analysis of any language must be able to display clearly the phonological justification for the riming practice of its native speakers. It is generally agreed that Chinese words can rime only when they share the same nuclear vowel and the same syllable ending (if there is one). Our analysis of CYYY obviously can live up to this challenge, though there exist two seemingly incompatible cases. First, RG11 occupies three columns in the chart given above (i. e., having three nuclear vowels). The reason why this is necessary has been explained in 5. 10. 4. Thus, as far as the Yüan playwrights who rimed words of this group indiscriminately are concerned, there is actually no violation to the requirement for riming stated above. Second, RG05 differs from RG03 only for the presence of /w/ in the medial position. This is, of course, contradictory to the requirement for riming, but it is quite understandable. As we have said before (5. 12), the final /ɨ/, coming from former /yɨy/, was the result of a rather late development in the history of the Chinese language. In fact, CYYY is the first book which established a separate rime for words with this final. The tradition of riming and the very unique nature of this final must thus have had a strong impact on the mind of the poets and the compilers of rime books. Indeed, the numerous compilers of rime books after Chōu Té-ch'īng never seemed to be quite certain about the four finals:

/ɨ/, /yɨ/, /wɨ/, and /ywɨ/. Some establish a rime for each of them, some put all the four in one rime, while others waver between the two extremes①. We may now list the rime features of the nineteen rimes of CYYY. Since syllable ending plays a determining role in riming, we shall mark zero ending with 'ø'.

RG01	-oŋ	RG11	-{o, a, e}w
RG02	-aŋ		
RG03	(C)ɨø	RG12	-oø
RG04	-ɨy	RG13	-aø
RG05	-wɨø	RG14	-eø
RG06	-ay	RG15	-eŋ
RG07	-ɨn	RG16	-ɨw
RG08	-an	RG17	-ɨm
RG09	-on	RG18	-am
RG10	-en	RG19	-em

5.14.3 Two charts are given here to show all the attested syllables in CYYY regardless of the tones. The first chart contains what traditionally are called the *yīn-shēng*（陰聲）rimes, i.e., those without nasal sylabic ending; the second chart, the *yáng-shēng*（陽聲）rimes, i. e., those with nasal syllabic ending. Each syllable will be repesented by a graph which in most cases will be chosen from TG01. Following the charts, an appendix of all the homonym groups in CYYY will be given, arranged in the four tones correspondingly and in the order of the columns in the two charts.

① Cf. the contrastive chart of rimes of various rime books in Chào Yìn-t'áng (1957), between p. 258 and p. 259.

RG	03	05		12		13			14		04		06			16			11					
I \ F	ɨ	wɨ	ywɨ	o	wo	a	ya	wa	ye	ywe	yɨy	wɨy	ay	yay	way	ɨw	yɨw	wɨw	ow	wow	aw	yaw	waw	yew
p		逋			波			巴			篦	杯			擺		彪			褒			包	標
ph		蒲			坡			葩			批	醅			排			抔					抛	飄
f		膚										非						否					缶	
v		無										微												
m		模			麽			麻			迷	梅			埋		繆	貿					毛	苗
t		都			多	大			爹		低	堆	䨹			兜			刀					刁
th		徒			他						梯	頹	台			偷			掏					挑
l		盧	驢		羅				倈		黎	雷	來			樓	劉		牢					寮
n		奴	女		那	拏					泥	餒	能			羺	扭		腦		撓			裊
c	髭	租	疽		左	咱			嗟		躋	觜	哉			鄒	啾		遭					蕉
ch	雌	粗	蛆		磋				且		妻	崔	猜			傷	秋		操					鍬
s	斯	蘇	須		莎				些		西	雖	腮			搜	修		騷					蕭
cr	支	阻	諸			查		撾	遮		知	追	齋			皺	周				嘲			昭
crh	眵	初	樞			叉			車		癡	吹	釵		揣	篘	抽				抄			超
sr	施	梳	書			沙		耍	奢		世	誰	篩		衰	溲	收				梢			燒
r	兒		如						惹			蕤					柔							饒
k		孤	居	歌	戈		家	瓜			機	歸	該	皆	乖	鈎	鳩		高			交		嬌
kh		枯	區	軻	科			誇		瘸	溪	魁	開	揩	快	摳	丘		考			敲		喬
h		呼	虛	呵	和		蝦	花		靴	希	灰	孩	鞋	懷	齁	休		蒿			哮		梟
ŋ				哦															傲					
ø		嗚	迂	阿	窩		鴉	蛙	耶		衣	威	哀	挨	歪	謳	憂		奧			坳		邀

RG	01		02			15				07				09	08			10		17		18		19
I \ F	woŋ	ywoŋ	aŋ	yaŋ	waŋ	eŋ	yeŋ	weŋ	yweŋ	ɨn	yɨn	wɨn	ywɨn	won	an	yan	wan	yen	ywen	ɨm	yɨm	am	yam	yem
p	崩				邦		冰	崩			賓	奔		般			班	邊						
ph	烹				滂		平	烹			貧	噴		潘			攀	篇						
f	風				方							分					番							
v					忘							文					晚							
m	蒙				忙		明	盲			民	門		瞞			蠻	眠						
t	東		當			登	丁					敦		端	丹			顛				擔		掂
th	通		湯			滕	汀			吞		暾		湍	灘			天		唔		貪		添
l	籠	龍	郎	粮		楞	靈				鄰	論	倫	鸞	蘭			連	聯	啉	林	婪		廉
n	農	濃	囊	娘		能	寧				紉	嫩		暖	難			年			賃	南		黏
c	宗	蹤	臟	漿		曾	精				津	尊	遵	鑽	趲			煎	鐫	怎	駸	簪		尖
ch	匆	從	倉	槍		層	青				親	村	逡	攛	餐			千	痊		侵	參		僉
s	鬆	松	桑	湘		僧	星				新	孫	詢	酸	珊			先	宣		心	三		纖
cr	鍾			章	莊	箏	征			臻	真		諄		赸		跧	氈	專	簪	針	詀		瞻
crh	冲			昌	瘡	鐺	稱			襯	嗔		春		潺		篡		川	岑	琛	攙		襜
sr				商	雙	生	聲			莘	申		瞬		山		拴	羶		森	深	杉		苫
r	戎			穰			仍				人		閏					然	軟		壬			髯
k	工	拱	岡	姜	光	亘	京	觥	肩	根	巾	鯤	君	官	干	姦	關	堅	鵑		金	甘	監	兼
kh	空	穹	康	腔	曠		輕		瓊	哏	勤	坤	群	寬	刊	慳		牽	圈		欽	堪	嵌	謙
h	烘	凶	杭	香	荒	亨	馨	轟	兄	痕	欣	昏	薰	歡	寒	閑	還	軒	喧		歆	憨	咸	杴
ŋ																								
ø	翁	邕	昂	央	汪	罌	英	泓	縈	恩	因	温	氳	剜	安	殷	彎	烟	淵		音	庵	巖	淹

APPENDIX TO 5.14.3

The appendix here is designed to disperse whatever remaining doubt there may still exist about the system we have established. It will do so by assigning to each homonym group with a non-entering tone a phonemic transcription deduced from the rules we set up earlier and by providing a reasonable explanation for all the controversial ones. For easy identifcation, each homonym group will be represented by a graph along with its number.

Basic form	TG01	TG02	TG03	TG04
/cɨ/	0301002 髭	—	0303015 子	0304023 字
/chɨ/	0301006 雌	0302008 慈	0303013 此	0304022 次
/sɨ/	0301005 斯	0302010 詞	0303016 死	0304021 似
/crɨ/	0301001 支	—	0303011 紙	0304024 志
/crhɨ/	0301003 眵	—	0303017 齒	0304026 翅(A) 0304027 厠
/srɨ/	0301004 施	0302009 時	0303014 史	0304020 是
/rɨ/ (B)	—	0302007 兒	0303012 爾	0304025 二
/pwɨ/	0501004 逋	—	0503067 補	0504121 布
/phwɨ/	—	0502037 蒲	0503068 普	0504126 鋪
/fwɨ/	0501018 膚	0502036 扶	0503069 甫	0504113 赴
/vwɨ/	—	0502025 無	0503060 武	0504115 務
/mwɨ/	—	0502026 模	0503070 母	0504117 暮
/twɨ/	0501021 都	—	0503063 堵	0504112 杜
/thwɨ/	—	0502027 徒	0503061 土	0504124 兔
/lwɨ/	—	0502029 盧	0503062 魯	0504118 路
/nwɨ/	—	0502028 奴	0503073 弩	0504125 怒
/cwɨ/	0501022 租	—	0503059 祖	0504123 做
/chwɨ/	0501006 粗	0502039 徂	—	0504122 醋
/swɨ/	0501003 蘇	—	—	0504116 素
/crwɨ/	—	—	0503056 阻	0504130 助

續表

Basic form	TG01	TG02	TG03	TG04
/crhwɨ/	0501020 初	0502032 鋤	0503071 楚	—
/srwɨ/	0501007 梳	—	0503058 數	0504109 數
/kwɨ/	0501011 孤	—	0503064 古	0504119 故
/khwɨ/	0501012 枯	—	0503076 苦	—
/hwɨ/	0501019 呼	0502038 胡	0503066 虎	0504114 户
/wɨ/	0501014 鳴	0502031 吾	0503065 五	0504120 誤
/lywɨ/	—	0502023 驢	0503052 吕	0504104 慮
/nywɨ/	—	—	0503078 女	—
/cywɨ/	0501010 疽	—	0503077 咀	0504129 聚
/chywɨ/	0501009 蛆	—	0503075 取	0504107 趣
/sywɨ/	0501017 須	0502040 徐	0503079 嶼	0504110 絮
/crywi/	0501002 諸	—	0503053 主	0504108 注
/crhywɨ/	0501005 樞	0502035 除	0503057 杵	0504127 處
/srywɨ/	0501015 書	0502033 殊	0503055 鼠	0504106 恕
/rywɨ/	—	0502024 如	0503054 汝	0504111 孺
/kywɨ/	0501001 居	—	0503072 舉	0504105 鋸
/khywɨ/	0501016 區	0502034 渠	0503080 傴	0504128 去
/hywɨ/	0501008 虚	—	0503074 許	—
/ywɨ/	0501013 迂	0502030 魚	0503051 語	0504103 御
/ko/	1201001 歌	—	1203040 哿	1204075 箇
/kho/	1201003 軻	—	1203044 可	1204082 嗑
/ho/	1201012 呵	1202019 何	1203043 荷	1204065 賀
/ŋo/	—	1202022 哦	1203048 我	1204076 餓
/o/	1201008 阿	—	1203046 婀	—
/pwo/	1201011 波	—	1203047 跛	1204071 簸
/phwo/	1201010 坡	1202023 婆	1203045 頗	1204081 破
/mwo/	1201014 麼	1202016 摩	1203053 嬤	1204072 磨
/two/	1201013 多	—	1203041 朵	1204067 舵
/thwo/	1201007 他	1202020 驼	1203050 妥	1204080 唾
/lwo/	—	1202015 羅	1203039 裸	1204070 邏

續表

Basic form	TG01	TG02	TG03	TG04
/nwo/	—	1202017 那	1203042 娜	1204074 懦
/cwo/	—	—	1203049 左	1204066 佐
/chwo/	1201006 磋	1202021 矬	1203054 脞	1204068 銼
/swo/	1201005 莎	—	1203037 鎖	1204077 些
/kwo/	1201004 戈	—	1203038 果	1204078 過
/khwo/	1201002 科	—	1203052 顆	1204079 課
/hwo/	—	1202018 和	1203051 火	1204069 禍
/wo/	1201009 窩	1202024 訛	—	1204073 卧
/ta/	—	—	1303038 打	1304068 大
/na/	—	1302020 拏	—	1304064 那
/ca/	—	1302021 咱	—	—
/cra/	1301005 查	—	1303037 鮓	1304060 詐
/crha/	1301008 叉	1302019 茶	1303034 詫	1304058 汊
/sra/	1301004 沙	—	1303031 洒	1304067 厜
/kya/	1301001 家	—	1303032 賈	1304054 駕
/hya/	1301010 蝦	1302017 遐	—	1304061 下
/ya/	1301007 鴉	1302016 牙	1303030 雅	1304057 亞
/pwa/	1301002 巴	—	1303035 把	1304065 罷
/phwa/	1301011 葩	1302018 爬	—	1304059 怕
/mwa/	—	1302014 麻	1303029 馬	1304069 駡
/crwa/	1301006 撾	—	—	—
/srwa/	—	—	1303039 耍	—
/kwa/	1301013 瓜	—	1303033 寡	1304066 卦
/khwa/	1301009 誇	—	—	1304056 跨
/hwa/	1301012 花	1302015 譁	—	{1304062 化(C) 1304063 話
/wa/	1301003 蛙	—	1303036 瓦	1304055 凹
/tye/	1401005 爹	—	—	—
/lye/	—	1402011 倈	—	—
/cye/	1401001 嗟	—	1403028 姐	1404052 借

續表

Basic form	TG01	TG02	TG03	TG04
/chye/	—	—	1403029 且	1404053 趄
/sye/	1401007 些	1402009 邪	1403024 寫	1404049 謝
/crye/	1401004 遮	—	1403023 者	1404051 柘
/crhye/	1401003 車	—	1403027 撦	1404054 偖
/srye/	1401002 奢	1402010 蛇	1403025 捨	1404048 舍
/rye/	—	—	1403026 惹	—
/ye/	—	1402008 耶	1403022 野	1404050 夜
/khywe/	—	1402012 瘸	—	—
/hywe/	1401006 靴	—	—	—
/pyɨy/	0401023 篦	—	0403071 比	0404126 閉
/pbyɨy/	0401021 批	0402045 脾	0403068 否	—
/myɨy/	—	0402046 迷	0403077 米	0404127 謎
/tyɨy/	0401005 低	—	0403074 底	0404118 帝
/thyɨy/	0401025 梯	0402039 啼	0403083 體	0404117 替
/lyɨy/	—	0402027 黎	0403072 禮	0404120 利
/nyɨy/	—	0402028 泥	0403078 你	0404139 膩
/cyɨy/	0401003 躋	—	0403073 擠	0404116 霽
/chyɨy/	0401006 妻	0402032 齊	—	0404121 砌
/syɨy/	0401007 西	—	0403075 洗	0404122 細
/cryɨy/	0401024 知	—	—	0404132 置
/crhyɨy/	0401019 癡	0402043 池	0403066 恥	—
/sryɨy/	—	—	—	0404133 世
/kyɨy/	0401001 機	—	0403065 幾	0404125 計
/khyɨy/	0401013 溪	0402036 奇	0403076 啓	0404115 氣
/hyɨy/	0401014 希	0402037 奚	0403080 喜	0404137 戲
/yɨy/	0401015 衣	0402038 移	{0403063 倚 0403061 迆(D)	04040414 異
/pwɨy/	0401009 杯	—	0403079 彼	0404119 背
/phwɨy/	0401017 醅	0402041 培	—	0404135 配
/fwɨy/	0401012 非	0402035 肥	—	0404111 吠

續表

Basic form	TG01	TG02	TG03	TG04
/vwɨy/	—	0402026 微	0403062 尾	0404108 未
/mwɨy/	—	0402029 梅	0403064 浼	0404136 妹
/twɨy/	0401022 堆	—	—	0404124 對
/thwɨy/	—	0402044 頹	0403084 腿	0404129 退
/lwɨy/	—	0402030 雷	0403082 壘	0404134 淚
/nwɨy/	—	—	0403089 餒	0404142 內
/cwɨy/	—	—	0403086 觜	0404123 罪
/chwɨy/	0401020 崔	0402048 摧	—	0404113 翠
/swɨy/	0401004 雖	0402031 隋	0403087 髓	0404130 歲
/crwɨy/	0401010 追	—	—	0404131 墜
/crhwɨy/	0401016 吹	0402040 垂	0403067 捶	—
/srwɨy/	—	0402047 誰	0403088 水	0404128 睡
/rwɨy/	—	0402049 蕤	0403085 蕋	0404140 芮
/kwɨy/	0401002 歸	—	0403069 鬼	0404110 貴
/khwɨy/	0401018 魁	0402042 葵	—	0404138 簣
/hwɨy/	0401008 灰	0402033 回	0403070 悔	0404112 會
/wɨy/	0401011 威	0402034 圍	0403081 委	0404109 胃
/tay/	—	—	0603034 靆	0604068 帶
/thay/	0601005 台	0602028 臺	—	0604062 態
/lay/	—	0602018 來	—	0604074 賴
/nay/	—	0602029 能	0603039 奶	0604066 奈
/cay/	0601003 哉	—	0603036 宰	0604072 在
/chay/	0601007 猜	0602027 才	0603037 彩	0604076 菜
/say/	0601010 腮	—	—	0604078 賽
/cray/	0601014 齋	—	—	0604061 寨
/crhay/	0601004 釵	0602025 柴	—	—
/sray/	0601016 篩	—	—	0604077 曬
/kay/	0601002 該	—	0603048 改	0604063 蓋
/khay/	0601012 開	—	0603041 凱	0604081 慨
/hay/	—	0602024 孩	0603033 海	0604067 害

續表

Basic form	TG01	TG02	TG03	TG04
/ay/	0601006 哀	0602023 騃	0603038 靄	0604064 艾
/kyay/	0601001 皆	—	0603045 解	0604069 戒
/khyay/	0601013 揩	—	0603046 楷	0604084 溘(E)
/hyay/	—	0602019 鞋	0603035 蟹	0604060 懈
/yay	0601008 挨	0602026 崖	0603044 矮	0604065 捱
/pway/	—	—	0603043 擺	0604075 拜
/phway—	—	0602020 排	—	0604082 派
/mway/	—	0602022 埋	0603047 買	0604073 賣
/crhway/	0601017 揣	—	0603042 揣	—
/srway/	0601009 衰	—	—	0604083 帥
/kway/	0601015 乖	—	0603040 拐	0604079 怪
/khway/	—	—	—	0604071 快
/hway/	—	0602021 懷	—	0604080 壞
/way/	10601011 歪	—	—	0604070 外
/tɨw/	1601008 兜	—	1603044 斗	1604073 豆
/thɨw/	1601015 偷	1602033 頭	—	1604084 透
/lɨw/	—	1602028 樓	1603047 摟	1604077 漏
/nɨw/	—	—	—	1604082 耨
/cɨw/	1601004 鄹	—	1603054 走	1604083 奏
/chɨw/	—	—	1603058 傷	1604075 湊
/sɨw/	1601003 捜	—	1603043 叟	1604067 嗽
/crɨw/	—	—	—	1604068 皺
/crhɨw/	1601016 篘	1602034 愁	1603059 瞅	1604081 僽
/srɨw/	1601017 溲	—	—	1604080 瘦
/kɨw/	1601007 鉤	—	1603045 狗	1604074 搆
/khɨw/	1601021 摳	—	1603057 口	1604070 扣
/hɨw/	1601020 齁	1602023 侯	1603053 吼	1604071 后
/ɨw/	1601006 謳	—	1603046 藕	—
/pyɨw/	1601018 彪	—	—	—
/myɨw/	—	—	—	1604077 謬

續表

Basic form	TG01	TG02	TG03	TG04
/lyiw/	—	1602024 劉	1603038 柳	1604069 溜
/nyiw/	—	—	1603039 扭	—
/cyiw/	1601001 啾	—	1603050 酒	1604072 就
/chyiw/	1601009 秋	1602032 酋	—	—
/syiw/	1601011 脩	1602029 囚	—	1604066 秀
/cryiw/	1601013 周	—	1603048 肘	1604063 晝
/crhyiw/	1601012 抽	1602030 紬	1603040 丑	1604078 臭
/sryiw/	1601019 收	—	1603042 首	1604065 受
/ryiw/	—	1602025 柔	1603056 揉	—
/kyiw/	1601002 鳩	—	1603041 九	1604064 臼
/khyiw/	1601014 丘	1602031 求	1603051 抝	—
/hyiw/	1601005 休	—	1603049 朽	1604079 嗅
/yiw/	1601010 憂	1602022 尤	1603037 有	1604062 又
/phwiw/	—	1602026 抔	1603052 剖	—
/fwiw/	—	—	1603055 否	—
/mwiw/	—	1602027 矛	—	1604085 貿
/tow/	1101012 刀	—	1103078 倒	1104129 道
/thow/	1101020 掏	102048 桃	1103091 討	—
/low/	—	1102039 牢	1103073 老	1104143 涝
/now/	—	1102038 猱(F)	1103074 腦	—
/cow/	1101014 遭	—	1103077 早	1104123 皂
/chow/	1101032 操	1102049 曹	1103092 草	1104133 糙
/sow/	1101013 騷	—	1103075 掃	1104144 噪
/kow/	1101011 高	—	1103079 杲	1104142 告
/khow/	—	—	1103081 考	—
/how/	1101026 蒿	1102033 豪	1103093 好	1104128 號
/ŋow/	—	1102044 嗷	—	1104125 傲
/ow/	1101015 鏖	—	1103080 襖	1104147 奥
/pwow/	1101028 褒	—	1103070 保	1104122 抱
/naw/	—	1102038 鐃(F)	1103094 撓	1104146 鬧

續表

Basic form	TG01	TG02	TG03	TG04
/craw/	1101010 嘲	—	1103089 爪	1104138 罩
/crhaw/	1101024 抄	1102051 巢	1103090 炒	1104148 鈔
/sraw/	1101004 梢	—	1103096 稍	1104151 哨
/kyaw/	1101008 交	—	1103072 狡	1104137 窖
/khyaw/	1101023 敲	—	1103086 巧	—
/hyaw/	1101022 哮	1102046 肴	—	—
/yaw/	1101025 坳	—	1103095 齩	1104139 拗
/pwaw/	1101009 包	—	1103088 飽	1104121 豹
/phwaw/	1101019 拋	1102047 袍	1103097 剖(G)	1104141 砲
/fwaw/	—	—	1103098 缶(G)	1104152 覆(G)
/mwaw/	—	1102037 毛	1103071 卯	1104140 貌
/pyew/	1101007 標	—	1103085 表	1104135 俵
/phyew/	1101018 飄	1102050 瓢	1103076 殍	—
/myew/	—	1102036 苗	103068 眇	1104145 妙
/tyew/	1101002 刁	—	—	1104120 釣
/thyew/	1101029 挑	1102040 迢	1103082 挑	1104119 糶
/lyew/	—	1102034 寮	1103065 了	1104124 料
/nyew/	—	—	1103064 裊	1104150 溺
/cyew/	1101006 蕉	—	—	1104132 醮
/chyew/	1101031 鍬	1102043 樵	1103069 悄	1104134 俏
/syew/	1101001 蕭	—	1103062 小	1104118 笑
/cryew/	1101016 昭	—	1103083 沼	1104126 趙
/crhyew/	1101030 超	1102041 潮	—	—
/sryew/	1101027 燒	—	1103084 少	1104127 少
/ryew/	—	1102035 饒	1103067 遶	—
/kyew/	1101005 嬌	—	1103063 皎	1104131 叫
/khyew/	—	1102045 喬	—	1104149 竅
/hyew/	1101003 梟	—	1103087 曉	1104136 孝
/yew/	1101017 邀	1102042 遥	1103066 杳	1104130 曜
/pwoŋ/	0101018 崩	—	0103053 唪	0104069 迸

續表

Basic form	TG01	TG02	TG03	TG04
/phwog/	0101019 烹	0102034 蓬	—	—
/fwoŋ/	0101009 風	0102028 馮	0103049 捧	0104055 鳳
/mwoŋ/	—	0102032 蒙	0103047 蠓	0104065 夢
/twoŋ/	0101001 東	—	0103036 董	0104054 洞
/thwoŋ/	0101003 通	0102020 同	0103039 桶	0104062 痛
/lwoŋ/	—	0102024 籠	0103042 攏	0104058 弄
/nwoŋ/	—	0102025 農	0103052 噥	—
/cwoŋ/	0101008 宗	—	0103048 總	0104068 粽
/chwoŋ/	0101011 匆	0102029 叢	—	—
/swoŋ/	0101010 鬆	—	—	0104057 宋
/kwoŋ/	0101014 工	—	—	0104056 貢
/khwoŋ/	0101007 空	—	0103038 孔	0104059 控
/hwoŋ/	0101015 烘	0102033 紅	0103040 汞	0104067 哄
/woŋ/	0101017 翁	—	—	0104061 甕
/lywoŋ/	—	0102022 龍	0103041 隴	—
/nywoŋ/	—	0102026 濃	—	—
/cywoŋ/	0101012 蹤	—	—	0104064 縱
/chywoŋ/	—	0102035 從	—	—
/sywoŋ/	10101004 松	—	0103044 聳	0104060 訟
/crywoŋ/	0101002 鍾	—	0103037 腫	0104063 衆
/crhywoŋ/	0101005 冲	0102027 蟲	0103050 寵	0104070 銃
/rywoŋ/	—	0102021 戎	0103051 冗	—
/kywoŋ/	—	—	0103045 拱	—
/khywoŋ/	0101013 穹	0102023 窮	—	—
/hywoŋ/	0101016 兇	0102030 熊	0103043 洶	—
/ywoŋ/	101006 邕	0102031 容	0103046 勇	0104066 用
/taŋ/	0201012 當	—	0203067 黨	0204093 蕩
/thaŋ/	0201020 湯	0202040 唐	0203066 倘	0204111 湯
/laŋ/	—	0202033 郎	0203069 朗	0204094 浪
/naŋ/	—	0202050 囊	—	—

續表

Basic form	TG01	TG02	TG03	TG04
/caŋ/	0201027 臟	—	0203074 髒	0204095 葬
/chaŋ/	0201025 倉	0202044 藏	—	0204106 愴
/saŋ/	0201003 桑	—	0203064 嗓	0204103 喪
/kaŋ/	0201009 岡	—	—	0204110 鋼
/khaŋ/	0201010 康	—	—	0204099 炕
/haŋ/	—	0202034 杭	0203073 沆	0204105 行
/aŋ/	—	0202035 昂	—	204108 盎
/lyaŋ/	—	0202030 粮	0203054 兩	0204080 亮
/nyaŋ/	—	0202046 娘	0203071 仰	0204101 釀
/cyaŋ/	0201007 漿	—	0203053 蔣	0204087 匠
/chyaŋ/	0201022 槍	0202042 墻	0203076 搶	0204109 戧
/syaŋ/	0201021 湘	0202041 詳	0203055 想	0204079 象
/cryaŋ/	0201005 章	—	0203068 掌	0204085 帳
/crhyaŋ/	0201019 昌	0202039 長	0203059 敞	0204088 唱
/sryaŋ/	0201006 商	—	0203077 賞	0204083 上
/ryaŋ/	—	0202031 穰	0203060 壤	0204084 讓
/kyaŋ/	0201001 姜	—	0203051 講	0204078 絳
/khyaŋ/	0201016 腔	0202045 强	0203075 强	—
/hyaŋ/	0201014 香	0202047 降	0203058 響	0204086 巷
/yaŋ/	0201017 央	0202028 陽	0203052 養	0204081 養
/pwaŋ/	0201002 邦	—	0203065 榜	0204096 謗
/phwaŋ/	0201015 滂	0202037 旁	—	0204104 胖
/fwaŋ/	0201018 方	0202038 房	0203061 倣	0204092 放
/vwaŋ/	—	0202032 忘	0203062 罔	0204090 望
/mwaŋ/	—	0202029 忙	0203056 蟒	—
/crwaŋ/	0201008 莊	—	—	0204082 狀
/crhwaŋ/	0201026 瘡	0202036 牀	—	0204089 創
/srwaŋ/	0201004 雙	—	0203057 爽	—
/kwaŋ/	0201011 光	—	0203072 廣	0204107 誑
/khwaŋ/	0201023 匡	0202049 狂	—	0204098 曠

續表

Basic form	TG01	TG02	TG03	TG04
/hwaŋ/	0201013 荒	0202043 黄	0203070 謊	{0204099 晃(H) {0204100 况
/waŋ/	0201024 汪	0202048 王	0203063 枉	0204091 旺
/teŋ/	1501009 登	—	1503072 等	1504079 鄧
/theŋ/	—	1502036 滕	—	—
/leŋ/	—	1502033 楞	1503069 冷	—
/neŋ/	—	1502035 能	—	—
/ceŋ/	1501011 曾	—	—	1504095 贈
/cheŋ/	—	1502034 層	—	—
/seŋ/	1501024 僧	—	—	—
/creŋ/	1501004 箏	—	—	1504082 諍
/crheŋ/	1501012 鐺	1502048 橙	—	1504100 撑
/sreŋ/	1501003 生	—	1503059 省	—
/keŋ/	—	—	—	1504101 亘
/heŋ/	1501025 亨(I)	1502037 莖	—	—
/eŋ/	1501023 罌(I)	—	—	—
/pyeŋ/	1501008 冰	—	1503056 丙	1504085 病
/phyeŋ/	—	1502029 平	—	1504089 娉
/myeŋ/	—	1502030 明	1503064 茗	1504078 命
/tyeŋ/	1501005 丁	—	1503067 頂	1504094 定
/thyeŋ/	1501019 汀	1502043 亭	1503068 艇	1504096 聽
/lyeŋ/	—	1502031 靈	I1503066 領	1504086 令
/nyeŋ/	—	1502050 寧	—	1504090 佞
/cyeŋ/	1501002 精	—	1503070 井	1504091 净
/chyeŋ/	1501017 青	1502041 情	1503071 請	1504081 清
/syeŋ/	1501020 星	1502053 餳	1503058 醒	1504088 性
/cryeŋ/	1501007 征	—	1503063 整	1504083 正
/crhyeŋ/	1501013 稱	1502044 澄	1503065 逞	1504093 秤
/sryeŋ/	1501018 聲	1502052 繩	—	1504086 聖
/ryeŋ/	—	1502051 仍	—	—

續表

Basic form	TG01	TG02	TG03	TG04
/kyeŋ/	1501001 京	—	1503054 景	1504075 敬
/khyeŋ/	1501015 輕	1502039 擎	1503055 頃	1504077 慶
/hyeŋ/	1501016 馨	1502040 行	1503074 涬	1504092 杏
/yeŋ/	1501014 英	1502038 盈	1503058 影	1504076 映
/pweŋ/	1501021 崩	—	—	1504097 迸
/phweŋ/	1501028 烹	1502032 朋	—	—
/mweŋ/	—	1502046 盲	1503062 艋	1504098 孟
/kweŋ/	1501022 觥	—	1503060 礦	—
/hweŋ/	1501010 轟	1502047 横	—	1504099 横
/weŋ/	1501027 泓	—	—	—
/kyweŋ/	1501006 扃	—	1503061 囧	—
/khyweŋ/	—	1502043 瓊	—	—
/hyweŋ/	1501026 兄	1502045 熒	—	1504080 迥
/yweŋ/	—	1502049 榮	1503073 永	1504084 咏
/thɨn/	0701008 吞	—	—	—
/crɨn/	0701020 臻	—	—	—
/crhɨn/	—	—	—	0704098 襯
/srɨn/	0701021 莘	—	—	—
/kɨn/	0701012 根	—	—	—
/khɨn/	0701035 哏	—	0703062 肯	—
/hɨn/	—	0702059 痕	0703075 狠	0704117 恨
/ɨn/	0701003 恩	—	—	—
/pyɨn/	0701017 賓	—	—	0704092 鬢
/phyɨn/	—	0702038 貧	0703074 牝(J) 10703076 不	—
/myɨn/	—	0702039 民	0703065 閔	—
/lyɨn/	—	0702037 鄰	—	0704091 吝
/nyɨn/	—	0702060 紉	—	—
/cyɨn/	0701036 津	—	0703087 儘	0704095 進
/chyɨn/	0701031 親	0702050 秦	—	—

續表

Basic form	TG01	TG02	TG03	TG04
/syɨn/	0701016 新	—	—	0704089 信
/cryɨn/	0701015 真	—	0703061 軫	0704088 震
/crhyɨn/	0701005 嗔	0702049 陳	—	0704121 趂
/sryɨn/	0701004 申	0702057 神	0703073 哂	0704092 慎
/ryɨn/	—	0702040 人	0703077 忍	0704090 刃
/kyɨn/	0701029 巾	—	0703063 緊	0704097 近
/khyɨn/	—	0702043 勤	—	—
/hyɨn/	0701013 欣	—	—	0704113 釁
/yɨn/	0701003 因	0702047 銀	0703064 隱	0704099 印
/pwɨn/	0701028 奔	—	0703070 本	0704108 逩
/phwɨn/	0701034 噴	0702048 盆	—	0704112 噴
/fwɨn/	0701001 分	0702054 墳	0703083 粉	0704096 忿
/vwɨn/	—	0702046 文	0703067 吻	0704105 問
/mwɨn/	—	0702044 門	—	0704107 悶
/twɨn/	0701027 敦	—	0703078 盾	0704106 頓
/thwɨn/	0701009 暾	0702056 屯	—	0704119 褪
/lwɨn/	—	0702045 論	—	0704114 論
/nwɨn/	—	—	—	0704118 嫩
/cwɨn/	0701026 尊	—	0703079 撙	—
/chwɨn/	0701030 村	0702058 存	0703082 忖	0704116 寸
/swɨn/	0701025 孫	—	0703080 損	0704101 遜
/kwɨn/	0701023 鯤	—	0703085 衮	—
/khwɨn/	0701018 坤	—	0703071 閫	0704111 困
/hwɨn/	0701002 昏	0702055 魂	—	0704115 混
/wɨn/	0701024 温	—	0703084 穩	0704120 揾
/lywɨn/	—	0702041 倫	—	—
/cywɨn/	0701032 遵	—	—	0704102 俊
/chywɨn/	0701011 逡	—	—	—
/sywɨn/	0701007 詢	0702052 巡	0703068 筍	0704100 峻
/crywɨn/	0701010 諄	—	0703066 准	—

續表

Basic form	TG01	TG02	TG03	TG04
/crhywɨn/	0701006 春	0702051 脣	0703081 蠢	—
/srywɨn/	—	—	0703086 瞬	0704103 舜
/rywɨn/	—	—	—	0704104 閏
/kywɨn/	0701019 君	—	0703072 窘	0704110 郡
/kbywɨn/	—	0702042 群	—	—
/hywɨn/	0701022 薰	—	—	0704109 訓
/ywɨn/	0701014 氳	0702053 云	0703069 允	0704094 運
/pwon/	0901002 般	—	—	0904037 半
/phwon/	0901004 潘	0902017 盤	—	0904035 判
/mwon/	—	0902013 瞞	0903023 滿	0904031 漫
/twon/	0901005 端	—	0903028 短	0904033 斷
/thwon/	0901010 湍	0902016 團	0903026 疃	0904040 彖
/lwon/	—	0902012 鸞	0903027 卵	0904039 亂
/nwon/	—	—	0903024 暖	0904041 愞
/cwon/	0901009 鑽	0902018 攢	0903020 纂	0904038 鑽
/chwon/	0901011 攛	—	—	0904032 竄
/swon/	0901007 酸	—	—	0904034 算
/kwon/	0901001 官	—	0903019 館	0904036 貫
/khwon/	0901008 寬	—	0903021 款	—
/hwon/	0901003 歡	0902014 桓	0903022 瀚	0904029 喚
/won/	0901006 剜	0902015 丸	0903025 椀	0904030 玩
/tan/	0801002 丹	—	0803038 癉	0804050 旦
/than/	0801011 灘	0802025 壇	0803040 坦	0804052 嘆
/lan/	—	0802021 蘭	0803043 懶	0804071 爛
/nan/	—	0802027 難	0803046 赧	0804074 難
/can/	—	—	0803044 趲	0804062 贊
/chan/	0801017 餐	0802023 殘	—	0804055 粲
/san/	0801013 珊	—	0803033 散	0804073 散
/cran/	0801016 赸	—	0803047 盞	0804056 棧
/crhan/	—	0802030 潺	0803037 産	—

續表

Basic form	TG01	TG02	TG03	TG04
/sran/	0801001 山	—	—	0804065 訕
/kan/	0801003 干	—	0803039 趕	0804054 幹
/khan/	0801006 刊	—	0803042 侃	0804070 看
/han/	—	0802020 寒	0803041 罕	0804049 旱
/an/	0801004 安	—	—	0804053 案
/kyan/	0801005 姦	—	0803036 簡	0804064 澗
/khyan/	0801015 慳	—	—	—
/hyan/	—	0802024 閑	—	0804068 限
/yan/	0801019 殷	0802029 顏	0803048 眼	0804069 雁
/pwan/	0801009 班	—	0803035 板	0804066 辦
/phwan/	0801014 攀	—	—	0804057 盼
/fwan/	0801012 番	0802026 煩	0803032 反	0804067 飯
/vwan/	—	—	0803034 晚	0804051 萬
/mwan/	—	0802028 蠻	—	0804060 慢
/crwan/	0801018 跧	—	—	0804058 譔
/crhwan/	—	—	—	0804072 篡
/srwan/	0801008 拴	—	—	0804059 渲
/kwan/	0801007 關	—	—	0804061 慣
/hwan/	—	0802022 還	0803045 綰	0804063 患
/wan/	0801010 彎	0802031 頑	—	0804075 腕
/pyen/	1001006 邊	—	1003053 貶	1004077 變
/phyen/	1001015 篇	1002038 駢	1003066 諞	1004076 片
/myen/	—	1002024 眠	1003054 沔	1004075 面
/tyen/	1001004 顛	—	1003057 典	1004072 電
/thyen/	1001021 天	1002028 田	1003046 腆	—
/lyen/	—	1002023 連	1003050 輦	1004086 練
/nyen/	—	1002040 年	1003049 撚	—
/cyen/	1001002 煎	—	1003048 翦	1004081 箭
/chyen/	1001011 千	1002027 前	1003060 淺	—
/syen/	1001001 先	1002041 涎	1003045 鮮	1004078 線

續表

Basic form	TG01	TG02	TG03	TG04
/cryen/	1001008 氈	—	1003061 展	1004084 戰
/crhyen/	—	1002026 廛	1003056 闡	—
/sryen/	1001009 羶	—	—	1004080 扇
/ryen/	—	1002025 然	—	—
/kyen/	1001003 堅	—	1003047 蹇	1004069 見
/khyen/	1001014 牽	1002032 乾	1003062 遣	1004085 譴
/hyen/	1001012 軒	1002029 賢	1003058 顯	1004070 獻
/yen/	1001013 烟	1002031 延	1003043 兖	1004073 硯
/lywen/	—	1002039 聯	1003051 臠	1004089 戀
/cywen/	1001022 鐫	—	—	—
/chywen/	1001017 痊	1002034 全	1003063 吮	—
/sywen/	1001018 宣	1002035 旋	1003065 選	1004082 鏇
/crywen/	1001010 專	—	1003052 轉	1004083 傳
/crhywen/	1001019 川	1002036 船	1003055 喘	1004079 釧
/rywen/	—	—	1003064 軟	—
/kywen/	1001005 鵑	—	1003044 卷	1004074 眷
/khywen/	1001020 圈	1002037 拳	1003059 犬	1004068 勸
/hywen/	1001007 喧	1002030 玄	—	1004071 楦
/ywen/	1001016 淵	1002033 元	1003042 遠	1004067 院
/thɨm/	—	—	—	1704044 唔
/lɨm/	—	—	—	1704043 啉
/cɨm/	—	—	1703029 怎	—
/crɨm/	1701004 簪	—	—	1704041 譖
/crhɨm/	—	1702018 岑	1703025 磣	1704040 讖
/srɨm/	1701006 森	—	—	1704039 滲
/lyɨm/	—	1702013 林	1703021 廩	1704038 臨
/nyɨm/	—	—	1703028 您	1704042 賃
/cyɨm/	1701003 駸	—	—	1704037 浸
/chyɨm/	1701011 侵	—	1703030 寢	1704036 沁
/syɨm/	1701009 心	1702015 尋	—	—

續表

Basic form	TG01	TG02	TG03	TG04
/cryɨm/	1701001 針	—	1703026 枕	1704031 朕
/crhyɨm/	1701007 琛	1702019 沉	—	—
/sryɨm/	1701004 深	1702020 忱	1703023 審	1704032 甚
/ryɨn/	—	1702014 壬	1703022 稔	1704033 任
/kyɨm/	1701002 金	—	1703024 錦	1704034 禁
/khyɨm/	1701010 欽	1702017 琴	—	—
/hyɨm/	1701012 歆	—	—	—
/yɨm/	1701008 音	1702016 吟	1703027 飲	1704035 蔭
/tam/	1801002 擔	—	1803028 膽	1804045 淡
/tham/	1801008 貪	1802020 覃	1803032 毯	1804054 探
/lam/	—	1802019 婪	1803027 覧	1804047 濫
/nam/	—	1802017 南	1803041 腩	—
/cam/	1801011 簪	1802025 喒	1803036 昝	1804051 暫
/cham/	1801009 參	1802021 蠶	1803029 慘	1804056 慘
/sam/	1801005 三	—	1803038 糁	1804053 三
/cram/	1801014 詀	—	1803040 斬	1804049 站
/crham/	1801016 攙	1802023 讒	—	1804057 懺
/sram/	1801007 杉	—	—	(1804058)訕(K)
/kam/	1801006 甘	—	1803026 感	1804043 紺
/kham/	1801004 堪	—	1803034 坎(L) 1803035 砍	1804042 勘(M) 1804048 闞
/ham/	1801010 憨	1802022 含	1803031 喊	1804044 憾
/am/	1801001 菴	—	1803030 揞	1804052 暗
/kyam/	1801003 監	—	1803033 鹻	1804050 鑑
/khyam/	1801012 嵌(M) 1801013 鵮	—	—	—
/hyam/	—	1802018 咸	—	1804046 艦
/yam/	1801015 渰	1802024 巌	1803037 俺(N) 1803039 黯	1804055 渰
/tyem/	1901009 掂	—	1903031 點	1904036 店
/thyem/	1901012 添	1902019 甜	1903028 忝	—

續表

Basic form	TG01	TG02	TG03	TG04
/lyem/	—	1902013 廉	1903025 斂	1904037 斂
/nyem/	—	1902014 黏	—	1904038 念
/cyem/	1901008 尖	—	—	1904040 漸
/chyem/	1901005 僉	1902021 潛	—	1904041 茜
/syem/	1901004 纖	1902015 撏	—	—
/cryem/	1901001 瞻	—	1903030 颭	1904043 占
/crhyem/	1901006 襜	1902017 蟾	1903032 諂	1904044 韂
/sryem/	1901010 苫	—	1903027 閃	1904034 贍
/ryem/	—	1902020 髯	1903026 染	1904042 染
/kyem/	1901002 兼	—	1903024 撿	1904039 劍
/khyem/	1901011 謙	1902016 鈐	—	1904035 欠
/hyem/	1901007 忺	1902022 嫌	1903029 險	—
/yem/	1901003 淹	1902018 鹽	1903023 掩	1904033 豔

Aditional Remarks：

（A）The graph 翅（0304026）should have been included in 0304020，if it had developed regularly. As it is now，we have to transcribe it as /crhɨ/ in CYYY，for that is how it reads in MP. In so doing，we are forced to say 0304026 and 0304027 should be one group. In other words，the small circle between them was added by mistake.

（B）This series of graphs can be transcribed as either /rɨ/ or simply /ɨ/. Both forms will set them apart satisfactorily. In MP，they are all pronounced with zero initial，though strongly colored by an [r]-like sound. If we are bold enough，we can suggest that，at a certain point of time，/rɨ/ became /ɨr/. （Nicolas Trigault's *Hsī-jú Er-mù Tzū* transcribes these words with [ul]. Cf. Lù 1947b.）This metathetical change then made the post-nuclear 'r' phonemically unimportant，So far as individual syllables are concerned（Tŭng T'úng-hó treated them simply as [ï]，i. e.，/ɨ/ with zero initial and zero ending. See Tŭng（1954），Chart I，between p. 14 and p. 15）. We might perhaps suggest that this is how suffix ‘r’ in Mandarin first came into existence. If so, post-nuclear ‘r’ would be very important on the morphophonemic level. The question is, however, when /rɨ/ became /ɨr/, before or after CYYY. Though external evidence cannot give us a sure answer to this question, we find it will be more plausible and economical to account for the relationship among the Mandarin dialects when we postulate that the change took place after CYYY (Cf. Hsueh 1971). It may be also relevant to mention here that Hsǘ Hsiào's *Ch'úng-tìng Szū-mǎ Wēn-kūng Těng-yǜn T'ú-chīng* (徐孝:重訂司馬温公等韻圖經 1606. Cf. Lù 1947a) seems to be the first book to list these words under the initial *yǐng* 影, i. e., zero initial at Hsǘ's time.

(C) 1304063 話 (AC /xhuɛiᵓ/, MP /hwà/) must be reconstructed with the reading /hwa/ in CYYY (see 5.9). This forces us to say that it belongs to the same homonym group with 1304062 化 etc.; in other words, we believe the small circle between them was added mistakenly by somebody after Chōu Té-ch'īng.

(D) According to Chào Yìn-t'áng's study, the two groups here should be combined, for in other rime books, graphs of 0403061 either appeared together with those of 0403063, or were not included at all. See Chào Yìn-t'áng (1936), 173, Note 3.

(E) 0604084 consists of only one graph with two AC readings 瀣 (AC /xɦəiᵓ/ and /xɦaiᵓ/, MP /syè/) which, therefore, can be transcribed as /hay/ or /hyay/, but the first would conflict with 0604067, the second with 0604060. I tentatively let it fill the gap here for no better reason than that it is possible.

(F) See 5.10.3 for the reasons why 1102038 has to be split into two groups, with 猱 alone as one and the rest of the graphs as the other.

(G) The three graphs here, together with 茂 (1104140), are peculiar in that they are not from the *Hsiào-shè* from which RG11 is developed, but from the *Liú-shè*. Hence, they are expected to appear in RG16 (剖 does appear there, too), or in RG05, if they have been affected by the change of /wɨw/ to /wɨ/ discussed in 5.13.1 (Rule 39). Their ocurrence in RGI1 thus shows that in a third dialect (see Note 38 in page 224), the final /wɨw/ had its nuclear vowel lowered to /a/. It seems that even after CYYY, the influence of this dialect on Pekinese still continued, for both 矛 (1602027) and 貿 (1604085) have now the final /waw/ in MP. Even 彪 (1601018) now reads /pyāw/. It would be descriptively as satisfactory to say that /ɨ/ in this case becomes /o/, instead of /a/. I decided to adopt /a/, because the final /wow/ seems to be steadily losing ground.

(H) See discussions in 5.14.1.

(I) According to Rule 19, the graph 亨 (AC /꜀xaŋ/, MP /hēŋ/) should appear in 1501016, and the graph 罌 (AC /꜀qeŋ/, MP /yēŋ/) should be in 1501014. Since they both appear separately, the only reasonable explanation is that they are exceptions to the rule, whatever the cause may be. Stimson's explanation (Stimson 1962a, 134－135) cannot be accepted.

(J) 0703076 is peculiar in that the only graph it contains has been in dispute. I merely follow Chào Yìn-t'áng here, without trying to join the controversy (see Chào Yìn-t'áng 1936, 207, Note 1).

(K) This homonym group was added here mistakenly. See Chào Yìn-t'áng (1936), 293, Note 7.

(L) 1803034 坎 and 1803035 砍 must have been separated by mistake. The latter is a graph created after *Ch'ièh-yǜn* 切韻 and is said to have the same reading as the former according to several other rime books. They still read the same in MP.

(M) One of our most fundamental presumptions is that different AC rimes which appear together in the same division of the same rime class (*shè*) must have merged by RTP, that is, long before CYYY (3.6.3). Two contrasting pairs are found in RG18 which seem to contradict this presumption, namely, 1804042 勘(AC /khəm$^{\supset}$/, MP /khàn/) vs. 1804048 闞(AC /khɑm$^{\supset}$/, MP /khàn/), and 1801012 嵌(AC /$_{\subset}$ khɛm/, MP /chyān/) vs. 1801013 鵮(AC /$_{\subset}$ kham/, MP /chyān/. Since the homonym groups of the second pair appear contiguously, the contrast can perhaps be dismissed by saying that the two groups are divided mistakenly. Thus, the first pair is the only example to contradict our presumption However, this presumption is really too important to be denied just for one exception. I, therefore, admit here that, for once, Chōu Té-ch'īng made a mistake which might have very serious consequence.

(N) There should be no objection to transcribing the graph 黯(AC /$^{\subset}$qam/, MP /ǎn/ and /yǎn/) as /yam/ in CYYY, but the graph 俺(AC /qiam$^{\supset}$/, MP /ǎn/) is very troublesome. According to our rules, we would expect to see the graph in TG04 of RG19, but instead, it appears now in TG03 of RG18. Furthermore, we are not sure at all that this graph in CYYY still represents the same morpheme as it did in AC. As it is now, we can transcribe it either as /yam/ or as /am/. Evidence from other rime books (see Chào Yìn-t'áng 1936, 293, Note 5) makes the former preferable.

CHAPTER SIX
ON THE SO-CALLED ENTERING TONE IN CYYY

The question whether the entering tone still exists in CYYY has been long in dispute and up to this moment no satisfactory answer has been found. This is seemingly a yes-or-no question, but in reality it is far more than that. Whatever the answer may be, it must be backed up by a detailed and systematic description of the development of the syllables of this kind from AC to CYYY. But unfortunately, practically all participants in this debate have overlooked this deeper aspect of the question. They seem to be interested only in providing a straightforward answer, and then, if they care enough, adding some ad hoc transcription for the graphs involved. Moreover, the arguments they present to support their case are, for the most part, extrinsic, in the sense that these arguments do not bear any direct relation to the phonological structure under study, though they may be reasonable or even persuasive.① This is, I believe, why the dispute has not been settled until now. Arguments extrinsic in nature yield only probability, not logical necessity. In order to solve this seemingly insoluble problem of the entering tone, we, therefore, have to present both extrinsic and intrinsic arguments. This is what will be done in this chapter. With what we have done up to now, we are very well prepared to attack this problem, and we hope we can solve it once and for all. We shall do this by following three steps. First, we shall go over briefly some of the extrinsic aspects of this problem, reevaluating, by using common sense as a measure, evidence from sources other than CYYY as well as the remarks made by the author of CYYY himself. The conclusion we come to here will obviously not convince

① Chào and Tsēng (1962) and Lǐ Hsīn-k'uéi (1963) can be given here as two typical examples.

everybody, but it may perhaps convince most of the people. Secondly, we shall try, from a structural point of view, to exhaust all the intrinsic aspects of this problem, to see what the entering tone must be and must not be within the framework of Chinese phonology, if it really still exists in CYYY. The conclusion we arrive at in this part should be acceptable to anybody who believes in structuralism. Finally, we shall propose a systematic solution to the problem. This solution will explain in very precise terms how the syllables with the entering tone developed from AC to CYYY and why they were redistributed the way they were. Nobody would be able to make us give up our solution, unless he could propose a better one.

6.1 Extrinsic Evidence

The dispute about the entering tone in CYYY arises mainly from two facts. First, though the former entering tone graphs have been divided into three tonal groups and included in the rime without nasal ending, they still form independent tonal groups, separate from the non-entering tone graphs. Second, Chōu Té-ch'īng seems very uncertain in this matter. In his preface to the book (*Hsǜ* 序) and "Rules for Correct Composition" (*Chèng-yǚ Tsò-tz'ú Ch'ǐ-lì* 正語作詞起例) he said in several places that there was no entering tone any longer, so the former entering tone graphs had been grouped into the other three tones, but in other places, he said that the reason why these graphs were redistributed into the other three tones was only to make riming easier, though in reality, they still existed in actual speech①. It follows that if we can find some good explanation or explanations for the two facts above, we shall be in a better position to solve the problem.

① It is amusing to read the arguments of the many scholars on this matter, both pro and con. They all quote Chōu, but believe only what they choose to believe. This demonstrates vividly the futility of relying merely on what Chōu said about the entering tone.

6. 1. 1 The tonal status of the former entering tone words in modern Mandarin dialects varies a great deal, often conditioned by the initials. We can show this by the dialects in the following chart, which are by no means exhaustive and hence should be taken only as examples[①]. Each square block in the chart represents a graph (hence, a monosyllable) with its tone marked by a small semi-circle at one corner in the traditional way, i. e, lower left: even tone, upper left: rising tone, upper right: going tone, and lower right: entering tone. Whenever a tone has to be split into the *yīn* type and the *yáng* type, the semi-circle will be underlined for the *yáng* type while remain unmarked for the *yīn* type.

AC Initials / Dialects	Cɦ-	R-	C(h)-
Nanking	□꜆	□꜆	□꜆
Chunking, K'unming etc.	꜁□	꜁□	꜁□
Tsingtao	꜁□	□꜄	꜂□
Tsinan	꜁□	□꜄	꜀□
Chengchow Sian	꜁□	꜁□	꜀□
Lanchow	꜁□	□꜄	□꜄
Peking	꜁□	□꜄	꜀□ ꜁□ ꜂□ □꜄

Furthermore, we are told that even among the Northern Mandarin dialects, there are still some which have maintained or partially maintained the entering tone[②]. Now let us use a little imagination. If we push back seven

---

① The chart is based upon the information given in Lǐ Júng (1963), 84. For MP, see also Stimson (1962b).

② Lù Chìh-wéi gives Shansi dialect as an example (Lù Chih-wéi 1946, 58). Lǐ Júng says that there are some dialects which have only partially maintained the entering tone, but he does not give the names of these dialects (Li Júng 1963, 84). For a clear example, see Wang and Hsueh (1973).

or eight hundred years from the present, wouldn't the tonal status have varied even more from dialect to dialect? I believe that, when the entering tone was in the process of disappearing the situation must have been quite chaotic. It was chaotic not in the sense that there was no rule for the new development, but in the sense that different dialects had different rules①. Indeed, many dialects must have been divided into sub-dialects just for this reason. The result might well be that people of two neighbouring towns or areas agreed with each other on everything in their speech except the former entering tone syllables. In one area, the entering tone might still be kept, while in the other it was already gone. To add to the confusion, the tradition-minded educated people might insist that they still had the entering tone in their speech while in reality they did not. Admittedly, the above situation is somewhat imaginary, but against the Chinese phonological background, it is absolutely possible or even probable. It reminds us of one thing. viz., that when we say there is or there is not an entering tone in CYYY, we are talking about the speech of a relatively small dialectal or sub-dialectal area, wherever it might be. We are not talking about Northern Mandarin even in the narrowest sense of the term.

6. 1. 2 There is strong evidence to prove that the change of the entering tone started long before CYYY. We can cite at random three events to support this point here.

(*a*) In *Ch'ièh-yǜn Chǐh-chǎng T'ú*, entering tone graphs are matched both to the rimes with nasal endings and to the rimes with no ending or semi-vowel endings. Sometimes, the same entering tone graph may appear in three tables. For example 則(AC /cək/, MP /cé/)appears in Tables 4, 9, and 18. This fact shows that the compiler was not sure of himself and consequently was adopting a double or even a triple standard in this matter.

① For a forceful illustration, see Hsueh (1971).

(*b*) According to Hsià Ch'éng-t'áo's research, the redistribution of the entering tone graphs among the other three tones was found also in the *Tz'ú* poetry of the Sùng dynasty①.

(*c*) Another scholar, T'áng Yuèh, concludes in his research that the entering tone was completely lost around the year 1190②.

It must be admitted that these facts do not necessarily prove that CYYY does not have an entering tone, because it might be argued that the language of CYYY may not be a later reflex of the dialect or dialects these scholars studied, but the strongly suggest that CYYY may not have an entering tone.

6.1.3 The sole aim of the author in compiling CYYY is to teach people how to versify correctly. It follows that the book was primarily directed to non-native speakers of the dialect of CYYY and was of rather limited use to its native speakers. For people from other dialectal areas to imitate this new form of poetry, the most annoying thing was, quite understandably, the entering tone graphs. In order to achieve the maximum effect, it is only natural for the compiler to sort out these troublesome graphs. In this way, he certainly served better the need of the careful imitators and brought the problem to the attention of the sloppy imitators whom he was so eager to correct. Thus, the separation of the AC entering tone graphs from the graphs of the other tones does not necessarily mean that they still preserve the entering tone in the language represented by CYYY. This is all the more believable when we remember that scholars of later periods, even today, often mark out the former entering tone graphs.

6.1.4 Chōu Té-ch'ing's uncertainty about the status of these graphs is

① Hsià Ch'éng-t'áo: "Yáng-shǎng tsò ch'ǜ jù p'ài sān-shēng shuō", Kuó-wén Yüèh-k'ān (夏承燾:"陽上作去入派三聲説"國文月刊)68(1948), quoted in Chào and Tsēng (1962), 321.

② Táng Yüèh: "Jù-shēng Pièn-ch'ien yü Tz'ú-ch'ü Fā-tá te Kuān-hsì", Tūng-fāng Tsá-chìh (唐鉞:"入聲變遷與詞曲發達的關係"東方雜志)23.1(1926), quoted in Chào and Tsēng (1962), 321.

quite understandable. Given the situation he was in, he really deserves all our sympathy and should only be admired for what he had done. He was, after all, not a native speaker of the language he recorded, no matter what competence he had acquired in it When this 'standard' language happened to consist of several sub-dialects so far as the entering tone graphs were concerned, and one sub-form seemed to be as prestigious as another, he must have been quite confused. When even the 'educated' native speakers insisted that there was an entering tone, it certainly took more courage than he had to deny it. The result is that he played it safe. On the one hand, he noted unequivocally that all the great writers rimed the entering tone graphs with the non-entering tone graphs, but on the other, he conceded that there was indeed an entering tone in actual speech. At this point, we must treat Chōu only as an informant, though an excellent one. This means that we can accept his observations about the individual words but not his opinion about the general character of the language he was trying to record. The plain fact is that the so-called entering tone graphs were, as far as versification was concerned, no longer differentiable from the others in Old Mandarin.

6.1.5 Chōu Té-ch'ing's assertion that the entering tone did exist in actual speech though it was of no relevance in riming simply cannot be accepted. Writers of vernacular literature use the language of the people as the medium of their artistic creation. They have to work within the limit of this medium, that is, they have no freedom to change or modify this medium beyond creating a few new terms. The reason is very simple. If they do, they will be rejected by the people. To rime the entering tone syllables and the non-entering tone syllables together is thus impossible, if those entering tone syllables are actually of the entering tone①.

---

① This argument has been used by several scholars before. Cf. Chào and Tsēng (1962), 322-323.

6.2 Intrinsic Evidence

We have given several extrinsic arguments to support our belief that there was not an entering tone in CYYY. More can be added, but they will not be logically decisive, no matter how reasonable they are. I am going to present some intrinsic reasons here which I hope will be more convincing.

6.2.1 We all know that the so-called entering tone in AC actually consists of syllables with the three stops /p, t, k/ as their ending. It has been suggested that at a certain stage these three endings merged into one, perhaps a glottal stop, and this glottal stop, or whatever it is, still existed at the time of CYYY, marking off the entering tone syllables from the others①. This is structurally impossible for CYYY. We have noted that the syllabic pattern in AC as well as in MP is (C)(M)V(E) (see 3.1). We have every reason to believe that the pattern remained the same in CYYY. If the ending stops had indeed merged into a new element, this element must necessarily occupy the terminal slot. It certainly cannot be something in addition to it②. In CYYY, we find the former entering graphs were assigned not only to the rimes with zero ending, but also to the rimes with semi-vowel endings, viz., RG04, RG06, RG11 and RG16. This single fact tells us that the so-called entering tone graphs cannot really have the entering tone. Furthermore, the entering tone graphs now appearing in the rimes with semi-vowel endings are of a special type, namely, they are those which formerly had the ending /k/. This is why I have suggested that it is also impossible to say that the three stop endings merged into one in some earlier stage of the language of CYYY, because in that way any entering tone graph could join any of the four rimes

① Stimson(1962a), 153 - 154.

② Stimson actually did so by adding /q/ to syllables with semi-vowel endings in his book of 1966.

above. The fact observed above would not be possible.

6.2.2 Although Lù Chìh-wéi had hardly a clear idea about structuralism when he wrote his well-known article, astonishingly he was aware of the above dilemma for those who insist that CYYY still maintains the entering tone, including himself①. However, the remedy he proposed for this dilemma is rather a strange one. Dragunov, in his study of the h̲Phags-pa script, holds the view that there is no entering tone in 'Ancient Mandarin' (i.e., Old Mandarin). He made a rather keen observation by saying that after [ɑ] or [e], ending [k] seems to have left some traces which he transcribed as [u] or [i]②. The graphs involved here are just those included in the rimes with semi-vowel endings in CYYY. Lù Chìh-wéi said that he did not agree with Dragunov on the matter of the entering tone, because the two symbols Dragunov used "were actually [w] and [j] in the h̲Phags-pa script". Then, "in order to avoid misunderstanding", he replaced them with [ʎ] and [ɥ] respectively③. What this amounts to is that he replaces the three AC stop endings with three new elements in an ad hoc manner. [ʔ] for those entering tone graphs included in the rimes with zero ending, [ʎ] for those included in the rimes with ending /w/, and [ɥ] for those included in the rimes with ending /y/. Now, do these three new elements, if they did exist, have any phonemic status? If not, can we accept this argument?

6.2.3 It may be argued that the entering tone graphs now found in the rimes with semi-vowel endings no longer belonged to the entering tone by that time, but those found in the rimes with zero ending still had a glottal stop or something like that as their ending and were thus genuine entering tone graphs. This seems to be an argument just for argument's sake, so nobody, as

---

① See Lù (1946), 61. However, he seems to have forgotten this problem later by reluctantly suggesting a final [iə̣uʔ] (p. 66) for the entering tone graphs in RG16.

② Quoted in Lù (1946). 62.

③ Lù (1946), 62.

far as I know, has ever brought it up. But we must admit that the situation suggested by this argument is theoretically possible though it is highly unlikely. I think it is unlikely for two reasons. In the first place, it rather seems unusual that the alveolar stop and the bilabial stop had merged into a glottal stop while the velar stop had disappeared. Secondly, we have proved that the glottal stop as an initial had disappeared before CYYY; it does seem a little strange to me that we have to restore it as an ending. It should be conceded that these two reasons are not very strong, so the possibility of the situation suggested above should not be ruled out completely It just might be true that this partial preservation of the entering tone had influenced Chōu Té-ch'īng to mark off even those graphs which no longer belonged to this category.

6.2.4 We have seen that the former entering tone syllables were divided into three tonal groups conditioned by their initials (see 3.5.1) in CYYY. Those with unvoiced initials were all assigned to TG53 which corresponds to the third tone in MP. But in MP, the distribution of these syllables of TG53 is quite irregular. They are found in any of the four tones and no conditioning feature has been found so far. Observing this fact, Lù Chìh-wéi says: "Just because the entering tone words with unvoiced initials could be altogether assigned to the rising tone, so we know that they could not be words truly with the rising tone"①. I fail to see his logic. In fact, this is quite possible, as it has been observed in the Tsingtao dialect (6.1.1) which we know for sure does not have an entering tone. Commenting on the same fact, Stimson writes: "The fact that it is only in this group (TG53) where such a degree of irregularity obtains clearly supports the CYYY triple jù-shēng distinction. This fact supports equally clearly the CYYYˇ-q/ˇ(or ˊ,ˇ,ˋ) distinction."② The

① Lù (1946), 59.

② Stimson(1962a)153.

first part of this remark is quite right. In fact, nobody has ever questioned that. The second part, however, does not bear any logical necessity. Lǜ's and Stimson's reasoning makes some sense only when we accept the proposition that MP came directly from the language represented by CYYY, but both of them deny it①. Furthermore, even if we should accept this proposition, their conclusion could not be taken as logically inevitable. As we have seen in the chart of 6. 1. 1, the other two types of the former entering tone syllables are quite regular among practically all the modern Northern Mandarin dialects, but those with unvoiced initials are different in different dialects. We have reason to believe that the situation of the past must be more or less the same. Thus, the irregularity of syllables corresponding to the CYYY TG53 graphs in MP might well be the result of extensive borrowing from surrounding dialects or sub-dialects if indeed MP came directly from CYYY. Recent research has shown that, in Kūan Hàn-ch'īng's works, the tonal distribution of the former entering tone graphs with voiceless initials is very close to that in MP. About seventy per cent of this type of graphs were not used as graphs of the rising tone, that is, they do not conform with CYYY②. If Kūan's language is the earlier Pekinese, then the only conclusion we can come to in the light of the above fact is that CYYY must represent a different dialect, though it must be very closely related to the former, for in all other respects they are practically the same. It also tells us that the irregularity of the former entering tone syllables with voiceless initials in MP is a phenomenon dated as early as the days before CYYY. The fact can by no means be taken as evidence to support the existence of the entering tone in CYYY.

6. 2. 5 A very unique phenomenon in CYYY is that Chōu Té-ch'īng established a tonal category "ch'ǜ-shēng tsò p'ing-shēng" (going tone as even

---

① Lǜ(1946)67; Stimson(1962a)132.

② Liào (1963),273.

tone, TG42). It consists of only a single graph. This category, by common sense, must be dismissed immediately. There simply cannot be a tonal group with just one syllable. Lù Chìh-wéi explains that Chōu did so because the graph 鼻(AC /pɦi*iᑐ,/ MP /pyɨ́/) was in Chōu's time still a going tone graph (TG04). Lù goes on saying that what Chōu did here shows that he was extremely careful in his work, so when he said "entering tone as X tone", the graphs involved must also still have the entering tone①. I do not know how Lù knew that 鼻 was still a going tone graph in Chōu's time. If so, it should have been included in TG04 of RG04, too. But it is not found there. The lesson I read from the above fact is just contrary to his. It shows that Chōu was again making a special effort here to remind the readers of his book, particularly the non-native speakers of this dialect among them, that the former going tone word 鼻 now belonged to the even tone of the *yáng* type.

6.2.6 Dr. Y. R. Chao says in his "Introduction on pronunciation" in Mathews's Chinese-English Dictionary②:

Words with the entering tone in Ancient Chinese which ended in -k often have a literary and a colloquial pronunciation. They occur with the following finals:

Literary	-e			-o		-u		-üeh
Colloquial	-ai,	-ei	-ai,	-ao,	-ei	-iu,	-ou	-iao
	色	賊	百	落	北	六	軸	角

Some of the graphs he cites here and many others of this kind appear twice in different rimes in CYYY, for example, 落(AC /lɑk/, MP /lwè/ and /làw/) in 1154156 an 1254087, 軸(AC /tjɦi*k/, MP /créw/) in 0552046 and 1652035. The most straight forward and reasonable explanation for this phenomenon in CYYY, more extensive than in MP, is naturally that these

① Lù (1946), 59.

② Y. R. Chao (1943), x.

graphs, just as in MP, also had two different readings each, one, literary, the other, colloquial①. By admitting that there were two social strata in the pronunciation of the entering tone graphs, it is now theoretically possible to hypothesize that in the literary pronunciation, these graphs were truly of the entering tone, with perhaps a glottal stop ending (see 7. 3. 2), because the literary readings were always those in the rimes with zero ending. Moreover we can draw very neat rules to show the development of the literary reading from RTP through CYYY to MP which conform to the vowel system we set in the last chapter(see discussion in 6. 4. 1. 2). Since some of the inevitable consequences dictated by these rules were not recorded in CYYY(see 7. 3. 5), I still believe that there is no entering tone in CYYY, though we may admit that in the same period as that of CYYY, the literary pronunciation indeed preserved the entering tone in the form of a terminal glottal stop.

6. 3 Some General Remarks

We have extensively discussed the various aspects of the entering tone question which all energetically point to the fact that there is no entering tone in CYYY. The question is answered but the problem remains unless we can propose a systematic description of the distribution of these graphs in CYYY, which is at the same time potentially good enough to explain their development to MP. What follows is an endeavor in this direction. But before we go into detailed discussions, some points of a more or less general nature must be treated first.

6. 3. 1 As has been noted, some entering tone graphs may be found in two rimes, for example, those of RG11 appear also in RG12. I interpret this

① Strangely. there are people who do not agree. They seem to believe that the different readings show the pronunciations in different dialects somehow arbitrarily collected together in this book. See Lù (1946), 65, and Chào and Tsēng (1962), 319.

phenomenon as the result of two different lines of development, the literary and the colloquial. It may be more precise to say that the literary development was a phenomenon in a different sub-dialect closely related to that where the colloquial development took place. As I have said, the literary pronunciation might have for a while preserved the entering tone in the form of a glottal stop, but in the dialect of CYYY, I believe, the literary pronunciation minus the glottal stop must have been accepted by the public along with the colloquial, though in a rather unbalanced manner that is. some but not all, as we shall see later (6.4.1.2). However, in the course of time when this dialect which was regarded as the standard speech kept spreading over a larger and larger area, understandably, it is the more prestigious literary pronunciation that prevailed over the colloquial except for some most commonly used words ('the core vocabulary'). Consequently, for many graphs involved here it is the literary pronunciation that has been preserved in MP, instead of the colloquial. When Lù Chìh-wéi tries to prove the existence of the entering tone in CYYY, he cites as one proof the fact that the MP reading of some of the entering tone graphs included in a certain rime may be drastically different from those with a non-entering tone in the same rime①. Obviously, he has overlooked the point discussed here.

6.3.2 When we tried to construct the vowel system, we found that those rime classes (shè) with ending /ŋ/ were exceptions to the rules of the vowel shift (see 5.6.2) In studying the entering tone graphs of these rime classes, we are now confronted with an even greater difficulty, because the entering tone graphs of a rime class of this kind often appear in two or even three rimes in CYYY, for example, those of the *Kěng-shè* can be found in RG04 (e.g., 0452050 石 AC /sjɦiɛk/, MP /srí/), RG06 (e.g., 0652030 白 AC /pɦak/, MP /pwáy/), and RG14 (e.g., 145303 客 AC /khak/, MP /khè/).

① Lù (1946), 59-60.

This fact suggests that the change of the entering tone might well have taken place before the vowel shift in the other tones, at least in the dialect of CYYY and for graphs of this kind.

6. 3. 3 Dragunov's remark in his study of the hPhags-pa script that the AC ending /k/ left some traces after [ɑ] or [e], which seem to be [u] or [i], also suits CYYY (see Note ③ in page 257). Of course, we are not satisfied with this imprecise description. To say that something seems to be either this or that when it occurs after either one condition or another is to say very little. I, therefore, will start with a much stricter assumption that, in the colloquial pronunciation, ending /k/ had always left some 'traces' where it was found before. Furthermore, these traces can only be /w/ or /y/, each conditioned by some formal features. The question is then: under what condition or conditions did the ending /k/ become /w/ and under what different condition or conditions did it become /y/? It seems we can only give an ad hoc answer to this question, that is, when the corresponding graphs of the syllables with the former ending /k/ appear in the rimes with ending /w/, /k/ became /w/, but when they appear in the rimes with ending /y/, it became /y/. As a matter of fact, this is virtually what is said or implied in all the earlier researches. But we have noticed that the entering tone graphs now appearing in the rimes with ending /y/ (i. e., RG04 and RG06) all came from the *Tsēng-shè* and the *Kĕng-shè*, while those now appearing in the rimes with ending /w/ (i. e., RG11 and RG16) all came from the *Chiāng-shè*, the *Tàng-shè*, and the *T'ūng-shè*. It will be better to state the conditions for the change of /k/ in this way though it is still ad hoc. We have one clue to this puzzle in the traditional binary division of the rimes: inner series vs. outer series. Ló Ch'áng-p'éi's version which we have adopted (3. 6. 1) does not give us any help in this regard; but the version in *Ch'ièh-yǜn Chĭh-nán* and *Ch'ièh-yǜn Chĭh-chăng T'u* (Cf. Note ② in page 167) which has the *Tàng-shè* in the inner series gives us some hint. If, following

this version, we could prove that when the *Tsēng-shè* joined the *Kěng-shè*, it moved out of the inner series to the outer, but when the *Chiāng-shè* joined the *Tàng-shè*, it moved out of the outer series, the dilemma we are in would be solved. We could then simply say that ending /k/ became /y/ in the outer series but became /w/ otherwise①.

6.4 The Redistribution of the Former Entering Tone Graphs

We can now move ahead to discuss the entering tone graphs per se. Instead of beginning with the rimes of CYYY into which they have been distributed, we are going to start from the rime classes of the rime tables. This means that we are going to start with what these graphs are supposed to be in AC or RTP and then subject them to the system we set up earlier so as to see what they 'should' have become in the later period when they either lost their ending or had it changed to a different form. If what we think they should be is confirmed by what they are in CYYY, we shall naturally be greatly encouraged, but even if it is not, we shall still not lose confidence in our system. Instead, we shall try to find some explanations, also in formal terms, within this framework.

---

① There, of course, remains the task of interpreting this inner/outer contrast in phonological terms. Our uncertainty here shows that Ló's version can by no means be taken as ultimate. Actually, the problem is much more complicated. I believe that, within the framework of the binary contrast of inner series vs. outer series, only two rime classes with the same syllabic ending are permitted, one in the inner series, the other in the outer series. The only problem with this interpretation is that there are too many rime classes with velar endings (see 6.4.3 and 7.2d). The solution I propose for this problem is to treat both the *Chiāng-shè* and the *Tàng-shè* as exceptions to the syllabic patterns of the rime tables given in 3.6.2. In other words, they have exceptional nuclear vowels which are perhaps residues from the AC vowel system in its evolution to the RTP vowel system, i.e., the phoemic status of these vowels had been lost in all cases except in the position before the velars. Hashimoto, on the other hand, tries to solve this problem by proposing a pair of palatals, /ɲ/ and /c/ as syllabic endings for the *Kěng-shè*. See Hashimoto (1970).

6.4.1 Those of *Kĕng-shè* and *Tsēng-shè*

We may begin with the seemingly most difficult part, namely, the entering tone graphs of the *Tsēng-shè* and the *Kĕng-shè*. These graphs in CYYY are now found mainly in RG04 and RG06, but a few with guttural initials are also found in RG14. In *Ch'ièh-yùn Chǐh-chăng T'ú*, the *Kĕng-shè* and the *Tsēng-shè* are combined into one①. I take this as evidence that the *Tsēng-shè* had moved out of the inner series and joined the *Kĕng-shè* in the outer series to form a single rime class with all four divisions sometime before they merged completely in forming RG15 of CYYY. Then, at a certain point, the syllabic forms of this newly formed rime class must have been as follows:

Division	Syllabic Form
1.	C(w)V_1ŋ
2.	C(w)V_2ŋ
3.	(C)y(w)V_3ŋ
4.	(C)y(w)V_4ŋ

Their counterparts in the entering tone must then be:

1.	C(w)V_1k
2.	C(w)V_2k
3.	(C)y(w)V_3k
4.	(C)y(w)V_4k

Now, if ending /k/ in these forms had been replaced by /y/, what would have happened? Wouldn't it be that syllables of this kind became entirely indistinguishable from those of the *Hsièh-shè*? The answer is an emphatic yes. Then, we should expect to see their corresponding graphs in CYYY to be distributed in exactly the same way as were those of the *Hsièh-shè* (see 5.11 and 5.12.2). Except in one minor aspect we find that this is

① Tables 15 and 16. Cf. also Y.R.Chao (1941), 204, and Martin (1953), 3.

just the way it is, namely, all those of the second division plus a few of the third division with AC Pr initials are in RG06, and all the rest, in RG04. The problem is now solved. All that we have to do is to add a simple rule in a proper place, probably before Rule 28 (see 5.6.2).

$$k \longrightarrow y/V_g\_\_\_\_\_ \qquad (42)$$

V_g = nuclear vowels of the *Kĕng-shè* and the *Tsēng-shè*.

The condition to the rule may seem awkward, but there is nothing we can do at this point. The problem involves the *T'ūng-shè* and the *Tàng-shè* (including the *Chiāng-shè*), so we shall say something more about it later (see 6.4.3). A few minor points have to be added here.

6.4.1.1 The minor aspect just mentioned concerns our vowel shift rules. We have said that first division syllables of the unrounded type all had their nucleus V_1 changed to V_2 except when it was followed by /w/ or nothing (Rule 22 in 4.6.4.5 and 5.10.2). Following that rule, we would expect to see the entering tone graphs of the unrounded type in the first division of the *Tsēng-shè* all be included in RG06, but in fact there are only two, 0653053 刻 (AC /khək/, MP /khè/) and 0653059 則 (AC /cək/, MP /cé/). Others of this kind turn out to be in RG04, for example. 0452058 劾 (AC /xhək/, MP /hé/) and 0452059 賊 (AC /cɦək/, MP /céy/). One even appears in RG03 namely, 0353019 塞 (AC /sək/, MP /sè/). A recent research on the riming habits of Kuān Hàn-ch'īng has shown that not only Kuān but also several other great writers of that period actually rimed the graph 刻 with graphs of RG04①. Since most of these graphs are included in RG04, they will have to be transcribed with the final /ɨy/. We have cited this fact as one reason why we can only transcribe the graphs of RG03 with the final /ɨ/ (see 5.12.6). More on the distribution of these graphs will be said later (see 6.4.5.2).

① Liào (1963), 274.

6.4.1.2 With the exception of a handful of most commonly used graphs, such as 白(AC /pɦak/, MP /pwáy/ 'white') and 北(AC /pək/, MP /pwěy/ 'north'), practically all the entering tone graphs of the first two divisions in the two rime classes discussed here have /e/ or /we/ as their final in MP, regardless of their division origin. This reading is, of course, the literary, and the whole phenomenon is actually very easy to explain. This line of development seems to be quite different. When the two rime classes had merged completely in having merely the front low vowel /e/ as their nucleus, the ending /k/ was undoubtedly still preserved. Then when the /k/ dropped out (or became a glottal stop), all the syllables involved here had the nucleus /e/ as they still do in MP; hence for the literary pronunciation, we need only add a rule specifying the change of the ending, somewhere after the vowel shift, but before we say that the nucleus of the third and the fourth division changed to /ɨ/(see 7.3.3).

$$k \longrightarrow q \qquad (43)$$

The strange thing is that this literary pronunciation is not included in CYYY. If it were, the corresponding graphs would then all appear in RG14. This fact may perhaps be taken as evidence to support the strictly colloquial nature of CYYY.

6.4.1.3 Three of these graphs do reappear in RG14, namely, 1453033 客(AC /khak/, MP /khè/), 1453035 嚇(AC /xak/, MP /hè/) and 1454058 额(AC /ŋak/, MP /é/); but their appearance here does not seem to be the result of the literary pronunciation. Note that they are all of the unrounded type with guttural initials, and therefore are subject to the change specified by Rule 19(4.6.2). When they appear in RG06 we have to transcribe them with the final /yay/, but when they appear in RG14, they must be transcribed with the final /ye/. The interesting thing here is that the final /yay/ in CYYY have become /ye/ in MP, except when it is a syllable by itself (e. g. ,崖 MP /yay/). We can see now that the process /yay/→/ye/ started as early as CYYY, but was first confined to the former entering tone syllables (including the one with zero initial), and only later spread all over except the syllable with zero initial, perhaps as a result of analogical change. Incidentally, the literary pronunciation of these graphs obviously was not affected by Rule 19, confirming our suspicion expressed in 5. 7. 1.

6. 4. 2 Those of *T'ūng-shè*

We have decided mainly on the basis of structuralism that the nuclear vowel of RG01 is /o/ (5. 5), and we know that graphs of this rime are practically all from the *T'ūng-shè*. With this knowledge in mind, our first and spontaneous reaction about the status of the entering tone graphs of the *T'ūng-shè* in CYYY is, of course, that their colloquial pronunciation should have finals like*/(y)wow/ and should therefore be included in RG11. This, we know, is not what we find. Entering tone graphs of this type now appear rather in RG05, with a handful of them also found in RG16①. How, then, should this fact be explained? There seem to be two possible explanations. First, we have noted that /o/ as the nuclear vowel of the *T'ūng-shè* is phonetically considerably higher than in other cases (5. 5). When ending /k/ changed to /w/ (6. 3. 3), the resulting [ow] must have been closer to /ɨw/ than to /ow/and was therefore identified with the former. Second, in formal terms, we can say that the process k→w took place before the nuclear vowel of the *T'ūng-shè* changed from /ɨ/ (Martin's /*/) to /o/; hence, the resulting finals should be */(y)wɨw/ and the graphs they represent should be in RG16. The two explanations are both reasonable, though only the latter suits our purpose. Consequently, we add a rule somewhere before the one which specifies that the nuclear vowel of the *T'ūng-shè* has changed to /o/:

---

① Only ten graphs in six homonym groups. The two graphs 肉 and 六, however, appear only in RG16.

$$k \longrightarrow w / V_{tu}\_\_\_\_ \qquad (44)$$

V_{tu} = the nuclear vowel of the *T'ūng-shè*.

Needless to say, this rule eventually will have to be combined with Rule 42, if it is permitted by other considerations.

6.4.2.1 We are now pressed to explain immediately why then most of these entering tone graphs appear only in RG05, instead of RG16. This is seemingly a very tricky question, but actually it can be answered very easily, if our memory does not fail us. Rule 39 in 5.13.1 says that the form /wɨw/ has changed to /wɨ/. After the entering tone syllables of the *T'ūng-shè* assumed the new finals */(y)wɨw/, they were then naturally affected by this rule with the consequence that their corresponding graphs must be included in RG05. We may be asked then that if this is true, why then should a few of them also appear in RG16? The question can be ignored by saying that they are exceptions due to borrowing, since they are so few, but in view of the two facts that they are all of the third division and that with but two exceptions, 1653061 宿(AC /si*k/, MP /swɨ/) and 1654087 六(AC /li*k/, MP /lyèw/), they all had either P or Pj initials in AC, I think we are obliged to provide a better answer. In 5.13.1, I made a venturesome guess that the distinction between the Yóu rimes and the Yōu rimes in AC might be the contrast between /ywiw/ and /yiw/. They merged only when the former lost the /w/ in the medial position. The change suggested there remains to be proved, but we can now borrow the idea to explain the few entering tone graphs in RG16. We can add an 'optional' rule after the merging of P and Pj initials with Pr, and before Rule 39, to specify that the final /ywɨw/ either remains the same or changes to /yɨw/, when it occurs after Pr①.

---

① To say that this rule is 'optional' is only a loose way to put it. Most probably, it represents a change in the colloquial speech which took place before the one represented by Rule 39. The reading with the final /ywɨ/ for graphs of this kind may thus be regarded as the result of simply losing their stop ending in the literary speech.

$$w \longrightarrow \emptyset / Pr + y \_\_\_ ɨ + w \quad (45)$$

6.4.2.2 The above proposition that the entering tone graphs of the *T'ūng-shè* first joined RG16 and then moved to RG05 obviously escaped the observation of Dragunov. This explains his over-caution in saying that only in some cases did ending /k/ leave some traces. Lù Chìh-wéi certainly did not notice this either, for he asserted that RG03 and RG16 should not have included any entering tone graphs and the few which appeared there were the result of "riming by convenience"①. We have proved that this remark about RG16 is incorrect, and we shall prove that it is also wrong in the case of RG03(see 6.4.4.1). Perhaps we should not blame them for this failure. With their methodology, I feel there is no possible way to detect this phenomenon of the deep structure. After all the finals/(y)wɨw/ must have had a very brief life, and they did not leave any trace in CYYY. Even long before CYYY we are told, graphs of this kind rimed only with those of RG05②. One more excuse for them is that this colloquial pronunciation resulting from the two-step evolution happened to be identical with the literary pronunciation resulting simply from the loss of the /k/. Since everybody is satisfied with this happy accident (or, is it unhappy?) nobody cares to give it some second thoughts. At first, I myself also took the inclusion of these graphs in RG05 to be the only possible direct result. and tried to explain the appearance of the few in RG16 as the result of metathesis (/ywɨ/→/yɨw/after Pr). Not until I found it was impossible did I turn back for a new interpretation. It is impossible, because in that way the graphs

① Lù (1946),61 and 66. The phrase is a loose translation of mine for the Chinese terms t'ūng-yā 通押 and hsiéh-yǜn 叶韻.

② Liào (1963),274. The phenomenon here can perhaps be better understood in the light of what has recently been called ' rule opacity'. Since the result of Rule 44 was almost immediately obscured by Rule 39, it is naturally very difficult to see the processes of change through the surface structure.

with Pj initials from the *Chēn-shè* in RG05 like 0553091 出(AC /cjhiu*t/, MP /Crhwɨ/) should have also been included in RG16, while in reality, those appearing in RG16 are exclusively from the *T'ūng-shè*.

6. 4. 3 Those of *Tàng-shè* and *Chiāng-shè*

In *Ch'ièh-yǜn Chǐh-nán*, the *Chiāng-shè* and the *Tàng-shè* are independent of each other, but in *Ch'ièh-yǜn Chǐh-chǎng T'ú*, they are combined into one (Tables 13 and 14). We may take this as a sign that they had merged by that time and later formed together RG02 in CYYY. The problem is how they merged. Did they merge completely in having one and the same nuclear vowel, or did they merely form a new rime class while still maintaining the distinction of divisions as in the case of the *Tsēng-shè* and the *Kěng-shè*? I think the former must be the truth. The reason is that structurally speaking, within the outer series, if there is one rime class having all the four divisions, there cannot possibly be another rime class sharing the same ending with it. Since the combination of the *Tsēng-shè* and the *Kěng-shè* happens to be such a rime class with four divisions (see 6. 4. 1), the combination of the *Chiāng-shè* and the *Tàng-shè* cannot be the same. Here the version of the outer/inner series in *Ch'ièh-yǜn Chǐh-nán* which has the *Tàng-shè* in the inner series (see 6. 3. 3) hints a possible solution. Frankly, I do not know yet how this version should be interpreted, but it strongly suggests that when the *Chiāng-shè* and the *Tàng-shè* joined each other, they merged completely in having only one nuclear vowel, and this vowel is probably low and back①, The non-entering tone graphs of these two rime classes now appear in RG02 which we have interpreted as having the nuclear vowel /a/. A reasonable extension of this is to say that their counterparts in the entering tone should have now /(y)(w)aw/ as their final in the colloquial

① Karlgren, followed by Tǔng T'úng-hó and Lǐ júng, represents the vowel of the *Chiāng-shè*. by [à]([ɔ]), but Martin uses /ɛ/, the low front vowel in his system. That of the *Tàng-shè* has been unanimously reconstructed [ɑ].

pronunciation and therefore should appear in RG11. We find this is just right. All the former entering tone graphs in RG11 are from these two rime classes, except two, 1153155 末沫(AC /muɑt/, MP /mwè/) which are from the *Shān-shè*. However, the literary pronunciation of these graphs forces us to give this postulation some second thoughts. When /k/ dropped out, we naturally expect to see these graphs appear in RG13, since in the literary pronunciation they should have /(y)(w)a/ as their final. But the fact is that not even one of them is found there. Instead, they appear rather in RG12, and therefore should have /(y)(w)o/ as their final. The two explanations given for the change of the entering tone syllables of the *T'ūng-shè* (6.4.2) also fit here. But if such is the case how can the colloquial pronunciation have /(y)(w)aw/ while the literary has /(y)(w)o/? Happily, we find that if we postulate /(y)(w)ow/ for the colloquial pronunciation the result will be just as good as before, for the graphs involved will still have to be assigned to RG11 where they do appear. What we have to do now is only to modify slightly the condition to Rule 44 in 6.4.2 so as to include the *Chiāng-shè* and the *Tàng-shè*.

6.4.3.1 The whole phonological picture of CYYY has shown that it is a rather unnatural thing to have the back semi-vowel /w/ alone serving as the medial before the front vowel /e/, or to have the front semi-vowel /y/ appear immediately before the back vowel /o/. In fact, we have cited this as a reason to explain why the final /weŋ/, unique in this respect, tends to become /woŋ/ (see 5.7.2). The conclusion we arrived at in the last section now yields a final /yow/ which is hardly acceptable in this light. We, therefore, suggest here that we rewrite it either as /yew/ or as /yaw/ Neither is supported by any overt evidence, but neither can be refuted on any formal ground. Since in MP these graphs have the final /yaw/, we shall choose it, and we believe it just might be so even in the time of CYYY.

6.4.3.2 The above decision is actually based upon a working rule observed all this time but so far not yet overtly stated. The rule is that we try to push the phonological phenomena in MP as far back as we can, until we meet some signs which clearly indicate that it is no longer possible to maintain them. Following this rule we have transcribed the non-entering tone graphs having AC Pr initials in the *Chiāng-shè* and the *Tàng-shè* with the final /waŋ/, instead of /aŋ/ which is supported by *Ch'ièh-yǜn* and is descriptively as satisfactory in CYYY as the former①. Now, our conclusion in 6. 4. 3 about the literary pronunciation of the entering tone graphs yields one final /yo/ which is just as unacceptable as /yow/ for the same reason given in the last section. How should it be rewritten then? The MP readings of these graphs suggest that there should be an additional /w/ in the medial position, for example, 1252032 學(AC /xɦɛk/, MP /sywé/), and 1254089 略(AC /liɑk/, MP /lywè/). A careful check of the graphs involved shows that this is descriptively adequate, though there is no direct evidence to support it. In the light of the working rule stated above, we then accept the final /ywo/ which is new, because it does not exist for the non-entering tone graphs.

$$X+y+o+\# \longrightarrow X+y+w+o+\# \qquad (46)$$

6. 4. 3. 3 We further notice that not only the graphs which might have the final */yo/ but many of those which are supposed to have the final /o/ in CYYY also have an additional /w/ in the medial position in MP, for example, 1252033 鑿(AC /cɦɑk/, MP /cwé/) and 1254085 諾(AC /nɑk/, MP /nwè/) Could it be that the final /o/ had also acquired medial /w/ by the time of CYYY? The question can be answered only by checking whether the final /o/ was still in contrast with /wo/ in that period. Apparently it

---

① See the second chart in 5. 14. 3 where the three graphs 莊瘡雙 are entered under the final /waŋ/, though they can be moved to their counterpart slots under /an/. *Szù-shēng Těng-tzǔ* actually has these graphs in the table for the rounded finals, as does *Chièh-yǜn Chǐh-chǎng T'ú*, though the arrangement is a bit confusing. Cf. also Lǐ Júng (1956)130 - 131.

was, for we find the following five pairs of contrast which can only be maintained by this means.

(*a*) 1252029 薄(AC /pɦɑk/, MP /pwé/) vs. 1252026 跋(AC /pɦuɑt/, MP /pwá/)

(*b*) 1252030 鐸(AC /tɦɑk/, MP /twé/) vs. 1252034 奪(AC /tɦuɑt/, MP /twé/)

(*c*) 1252025 鶴(AC /xɦɑk/, MP /hè/) vs. 1252028 鑊(AC /xɦuɑk/, MP /hwè/)

(*d*) 1253055 閣(AC /kɑk/, MP /ké/) vs. 1253058 聒(AC /kuɑt/, MP /kwā/)

(*e*) 1253059 渴(AC /khɑt/, MP /khě/) vs. 1253060 闊(AC /khuɑt/, MP /khwè/)

It seems that the question raised above has been given a negative answer, but not so when we take a close look at the five contrasting pairs. The last three are all with guttural initials and hence can be easily specified as exceptional to the change. The first pair must be a mistake, because the graphs involved have a labial initial and therefore cannot maintain the rounded/unrounded contrast (Rule 9). The mixture of these two types of graphs in both 1253057 and 1254084 also strengthens our belief in this. Thus, the second pair is now the only one blocking our way to make a sweeping generalization that the final /o/ became /wo/ except after guttural initials. I believe we should ignore this pair in favor of the following rule:

$$C + o + \# \longrightarrow C + w + o + \# \quad (47)$$

$$C \neq G$$

In view of the limited number of the graphs involved in RG12, and because of the exceptional pair, some people may still have doubt about the above rule. If so they may be referred to Rule 31 in 5. 9 which is actually the same thing. We said then that we did not know when the change specified by that rule took place. Now we know it must be after the vowel shift. In fact, it must be after the disappearance of the entering tone, because otherwise all the entering tone graphs of the first division in the *Shān-shè* and the *Hsién-shè* would have been entered into RG12(see 6. 4. 5. 2)

6. 4. 3. 4 Practically all the entering tone graphs of the *Chiāng-shè* and the *Tàng-shè* which are now found in RG12 also appear in RG11, but the reverse is not true. What is mysterious is that while graphs of both TG52 and TG54 of RG11 almost all appear also in RG12, only one of the several dozen (17 homonym groups) in TG53 of the former is found in the latter, namely, 閣(1153113 and 1253055). It is every-body's guess how this could happen. I suggest that this confirms my belief that CYYY is strictly colloquial in nature (see 6. 4. 1. 2). It included only those literary readings which had been accepted (borrowed) into the colloquial speech. So far as borrowing is concerned, there is no prediction. Incidentally, the occurrence of the two graphs 末 and 沫 in 1154155 is quite interesting in one respect. They belong to the first division of the *Shān-shè* and hence should have the final /wo/ only (see 6. 4. 5. They do appear in 1254084). But since there were so many graphs which could be pronounced with both the final /ow/ and /wo/, some people might be influenced to think that those with the final /wo/ only could also be read with the final /ow/. The recurrence of these two graphs in RG11 might well come from this effort of over-correction. In other words, it is the result of hyper-urbanism.

6. 4. 4 Those of *Chēn-shè* and *Shēn-shè*

We have just finished discussing all the most difficult problems in the entering tone. What is left is now very easy to handle. The literary/colloquial distinction ends with those syllables which formerly had /k/ as their ending. Those with /p/ or /t/ as their ending simply lost it. A natural consequence of the dropping out of these two endings is that syllables formerly differentiated from each other in this way must have then become homophones. This means that the entering tone graphs of the *Chēn-shè* and those of the *Shēn-shè* must have joined each other in forming a single group and hence should have developed along the same line. The same thing should also be true of the entering tone graphs of the *Shān-shè* and those of the *Hsién-shè*. Let us talk about the former first. We know that the nucleus of both the *Chēn-shè* and the *Shēn-shè* is /ɨ/, so when the entering tone graphs in them lost their ending and thus joined together, there should have emerged four finals:

/ɨ/ for all the unrounded of the first division plus those of the third with AC Pr initials.

/yɨ/ for all the unrounded of the third division minus those with AC Pr initials.

/wɨ/ for all the rounded of the first division plus those of the third with AC B and Pr initials.

/ywɨ/ for all the rounded of the third division minus those with AC B and Pr initials.

It seems to me there should be no question about how graphs representing syllables with these finals should have been distributed in CYYY.

6.4.4.1 Those with the final /ɨ/ should, of course, be entered into RG03. We find there only three entering tone graphs. One of them 塞 is an exception(6.4.1.1) The other two confirm our theory. Both 澀 and 瑟 are third division graphs of the unrounded type with initial /sr/ in AC. The former belongs to the *Shēn-shè* and the latter, to the *Chēn-shè*. The fact that graphs with this final are so rare often makes people suspicious. For example, Lù Chìh-wéi asserts that these graphs should all belong to RG04 while RG03 should not have any entering tone graphs (see Note 27). Now we can see that the place where they appear is the only possible place for them to go. That graphs of this kind are so few is unavoidable, because the *Shēn-shè* does not have first division graphs of any kind while the *Chēn-shè* has virtually no entering tone graphs of the unrounded type in the first division, and the third division graphs with Pr initials in both are very limited in number. It just happens that 澀 and 瑟 are the only two included in CYYY.

6.4.4.2 The graphs which are supposed to have the final */yɨ/ are almost all found in RG04, a logical place for them to go[①]. But here we come to the tough problem which we mentioned in 5.12.6. We discussed there in great detail why we should choose /yɨy/ over /yɨ/ as a final, though descriptively one is as good as the other Now, how shall we accomodate that decision with the present situation? In formal terms, this problem can be easily solved by saying the /p/ and /t/ as endings became /y/ after /yɨ/, otherwise, they simply disappeared.

$$\begin{Bmatrix} p \\ t \end{Bmatrix} \longrightarrow \begin{Bmatrix} y/y + ɨ\_\_\_ \\ ø \end{Bmatrix} /V\_\_\_ \qquad (48)$$

This treatment does not seem quite desirable for two reasons. First, we might have been able to write a very simple rule to the effect that post-nuclear /p/and /t/ were dropped unconditionally, but now we cannot. Second, which is much more serious than the first, we are saying here that we must add to the combination /yɨ/ the ending /y/ which we know will have to be dropped after CYYY. However, the three reasons we gave in 5.12.6 seem to me more than strong enough to outbalance the two objections raised above. I, therefore, decide to accept this seemingly redundant treatment.

6.4.4.3 The graphs which, according to our proposition, had /wɨ/ or /ywɨ/ as their final should be included in RG05 as indeed they had been. The graph 入(AC /njiəp/, MP /rwɨ/) in 0554135 is, of course, an exception. It should be in RG04 where it does appear (0454143). In RG12, there are also three graphs which, according to our rules, should be in RG05 namely 1252027 佛(AC /pɦiuət/, MP /fwé/) and 1252029 勃渤(AC /pɦuət/, MP /pwé/). I can offer no explanation for their exceptional course of

① The only exception is 褶(AC /sɦiəp/, MP /syɨ́/) which appears in 1453043.

development. It perhaps gives us some comfort to notice that the graph 佛 does appear in RG05, too (0552042).

6.4.5 Those of *Shān-shè* and *Hsién-shè*

When the post-nuclear /t/ and /p/ were lost, the distinction between the entering tone syllables of the *Shān-shè* and those of the *Hsién-shè* was also lost. Three types of finals should have then emerged for the graphs representing these syllables, in accordance with our vowel shift rules which we assume functioned earlier.

/wo/ for those of the rounded type of the first division which should then be included in RG12.

$/\left(\left\{\begin{matrix}y\\w\end{matrix}\right\}\right)a/$ for (a) all those of the second division and (b) those of the first division of the unrounded type, plus (c) those of the third division with AC Pr initials and (d) those of the rounded type of the third division with labial initials. They should be included in RG13.

/y(w)e/ for all those of the third and the fourth divisions minus those mentioned above. Graphs of this kind should be found in RG14.

The result is almost perfect as we shall see from the following discussions

6.4.5.1 Those supposedly having /y(w)e/ as their final are all found in RG14. The graph 俠 (AC /xɦiep/, MP /syá/) in 1452013 somehow also appears in RG13 (1352024). Those which are supposed to have the final /wo/ appear, without any exception, in RG12, as is expected.

6.4.5.2 All but a few of those which should have $/\left(\left\{\begin{matrix}y\\w\end{matrix}\right\}\right)a/$ as their final do appear in RG13. The few exceptional graphs are all of the unrounded type of the first division with guttural initials. They appear rather in RG12 where they obviously help to maintain the rounded/unrounded contrast, for example, 1252025 合 (AC /xɦɑp/, MP /hé/) vs. 1252028 活 (AC /xɦuɑt/, MP /hwé/), 1253055 葛 (AC /kɑt/, MP /kě/) vs. 1253058 聒 (AC /kuɑt/, MP /kwā/) and the last pair in 6.4.3.3. This is perhaps a very simple matter to scholars of the past. All that they have to do is to add a few words about the peculiar development of the first division graphs of this kind. (Actually none of them did.) But to us who always have the whole structural picture in mind. this simple matter presents a very serious problem. It almost throws us out of balance. Apparently, we must revise our vowel shift rules, at least partially. We can no longer say in that rather devastating manner that all the first division graphs of the unrounded type had their nucleus V_1 changed to V_2, except when it was followed by /w/ or nothing (Rule 22 in 4.6.4.5). Is it possible, some may ask to say that Rule 22 began to function only after the loss of the post-nuclear /t/ and /p/? The answer is no, because if that were true, all the entering tone graphs of the first division in the *Shān-shè* and the *Hsién-shè* should have been included in RG12, but in reality all of them except the few with guttural initials are now in RG13, indicating that when Rule 22 was functioning, the post-nuclear /t/ and /p/ must still have existed as a determining feature. Neither can we say that first division graphs of the unrounded type with guttural initials did not have their nucleus changed, because we have found that graphs of this description with the non-entering tones did join those of the second division to form a single rime in CYYY, for example 干(AC /$_c$ kɑn/, MP /kān/) appears in RG08 instead of RG09(0801003). So what we can say is only that the entering tone syllables of the unrounded type in the first division with guttural initials did not have their nucleus changed; in other words when V is preceded by a guttural initial and followed by /t/ or /p/, it does not change either. We can express this by writing a new rule or by adding another condition to Rule 22. I think the simplest way is to add one more condition, though the condition needed is rather clumsy, because it is actually a conditioned condition

$$C + V_1 + E \longrightarrow C + V_2 + E \qquad (49)$$

1. $E \neq w$
2. When $C = G$, $E \neq S$.

I use the symbol 'S' here, not just because I think it is simpler than $\left\{\begin{matrix}t\\p\end{matrix}\right\}$, but because I want to include the post-nuclear /k/, too. Its inclusion helps us solve at least partly the dilemma mentioned in 6.4.1.1. We found then that most of the entering tone graphs of the unrounded type in the first division of the *Tsēng-shè* defied our vowel shift rule by appearing in RG04, instead of RG06. With the new condition added to the rule, we can say now that it is just right for those with guttural initials to appear there, though we are still at a loss to explain the three homonym groups with non-guttural initials, namely, 0452059 賊(AC /cɦək/, MP /céy/), 0453101 德得(AC /tək/, MP /té/) and 0454148 勒肋(AC /lək/, MP /lè/). It is perhaps interesting to note here that Kuān Hàn-ch'īng actually rimed the graph 得 with those of RG06![①] In view of this, and that he rimed 刻(0653053) with graphs of RG04 (see 6.4.1.1), we can almost claim that he is on our side.

6.4.5.3 The modification of the vowel shift rule leads us to another dilemma. We have chosen to explain the marginal existence of the AC initial /ŋ/ in CYYY by saying that it was kept only when it occurred immediately before the remaining V_1 (Rule 23 in 4.6.4.5). Now, since we have seen that the entering tone graph of the unrounded type in the first division with guttural initials also maintained V_1, we then naturally expect to see the graphs with initial /ŋ/ and those with zero initial (/q/ in AC) still in contrast. Actually, when we proposed that /(y)(w)ow/ rather than /(y)(w)aw/ should be adopted as the final for the entering tone graphs of the *Chiāng-shè* and the *Tàng-shè* in RG11(6.4.3), this problem already popped up by itself though we did not mention it then. However, the contrast in reality does not exist. We find that graphs like 咢(AC /ŋɑk/, MP /è/) and 惡(AC /qɑk/, MP /è/) were grouped together both in 1154157 and in

---

① Liào (1963), 274.

1254088. How should this fact be explained then? One way to do it is to assert that these two kinds of graphs were put into one homonym group by mistake. This is not unreasonable but it lacks other evidence to support it, and hence amounts to evading the problem under discussion. A better way, and a logical one, is to put more restrictions on the existence of the initial /ŋ/. We can do this by revising Rule 23 in the following manner:

$$\text{ŋ} \longrightarrow \left\{ \begin{array}{l} \text{ŋ}/\_\_\_ V_1 (\text{w}) \\ \text{ø} \end{array} \right\} / \#\_\_\_ \qquad (50)$$

By adding the optional /w/ after V_1, we are now saying that initial /ŋ/ was not preserved before any V_1, but only before the V_1 followed by either /w/ or nothing. If we can manage to put this rule somewhere before the one or the ones which specify the change of the post-nuclear stops, it will not apply to syllables with a final like /V_1k/. Graphs representing syllables with this kind of a final but different in having /ŋ/ or zero as their initial would have fallen together as they are found in CYYY.

6.5 Summing Up

We have finished our discussion of all the entering tone graphs. It seems to me that the result is quite satisfactory. To sum up, we can again draw a chart of the finals derived from the entering tone syllables. All of these finals except the two marked with asterisk, /ɨy/ and /ywo/, are identical with their counterparts in the non-entering tones:

E	-ø				-y		-w		
V / M	ɨ	e	a	o	ɨ	a	ɨ	a	o
ø	03		13	12	*04	06			11
y		14	13		04	06	16	11	
w	05		13	12	04	06			11
yw	05	14		*12					

RG	03	05		12			13			14		04			06			16	11		
F / I	ɨ	wɨ	ywɨ	o	wo	ywo	a	ya	wa	ye	ywe	ɨy	yɨy	wɨy	ay	yay	way	yɨw	ow	wow	yaw
p		僕			跋				拔	別			逼	筆			白			薄	
ph		暴			潑					瞥			匹				拍				
f		復			佛				乏											縛	
v		物							襪												
m		木			沐				抹	滅			覓	密			麥			末	
t		獨			奪		達			叠		德	荻						鐸		
th		禿			脱		塔			鐵			滌						拓		
l		禄	録		落	畧	臘			列	劣	勒	立					六	落		畧
n		訥			諾	虐	納			揑			匿		搦				諾		虐
c		族	足		鑿		雜			捷	絶	賊	疾		則				鑿		爵
ch		簇	促		撮		笈			切			七						錯		鵲
s	塞	速	俗				颯			屑	雪		夕					宿	索		削
cr			逐		濁	著	閘			哲	拙		直		宅			逐	濁		著
crh		觸	出				察			撤	啜		尺		策				戳		綽
sr	澀	淑	贖			杓	殺		刷	折	説		實		色		摔	熟	朔		杓
r			辱			若				熱	爇		日					肉			弱
k		谷	局	葛	聒			甲	刮	傑	蹶		及	國		革	摑		閣	郭	角
kh		哭	曲	渴	闊			恰		怯	闕		乞			客					
h		鵠		合	活	學		狎	滑	協	血	劾	吸	惑		嚇	畫		鶴	鑊	學
ø		屋	玉	蕚		岳		壓		拽	月		一			額			蕚		岳

6. 5. 1 The following table is given to show the rime classes from which these finals originated:

Finals	Belonging to	Originated from
/ɨ/	RG03	Chēn, Shēn
/wɨ/, /ywɨ/	RG05	Chēn, T'ūng
/ye/, /ywe/	RG14	Shān, Hsién, Kĕng
/a/, /ya/, /wa/	RG13	Shān, Hsién
/o/, /wo/, /ywo/	RG12	Chiāng, Tàng, Shān, Hsién
/ɨy/, /yɨy/, /wɨy/	RG04	Chēn, Shēn, Tsēng, Kĕng
/ay/, /yay/, /way/	RG06	Kĕng, Tsēng
/yɨw/	RG16	T'ūng
/ow/, /wow/, /yaw/	RG11	Chiāng, Tàng

6. 5. 2 Following is a chart of the combinations of the initials and the finals, with each attested one represented by a graph. An appendix will also be added to show the corresponding homonym groups in the three tones.

ON THE SO-CALLED ENTERING TONE IN CYYY

APPENDIX TO 6. 5

Basicform	TG52	TG53	TG54
/sɨ/	—	0353019 塞	—
/srɨ/	—	0353018 澀	—
/pwɨ/	0552048 僕	0553084 卜	—
/phwɨ/	—	0553094 暴	—
/fwɨ/	0552042 復	0553083 福	—
/vwɨ/	—	—	0554134 物
/mwɨ/	—	—	0554132 木
/twɨ/	0552041 獨	0553093 督	—
/thwɨ/	—	0553099 禿	—
/lwɨ/	—	—	0554131 禄

續表

Basicform	TG52	TG53	TG54
/nwɨ/	—	—	0554137 訥
/cwɨ/	0552047 族	0553100 卒(A) 0553101 甓	— —
/chwɨ/	—	0553096 簇	—
/swɨ/	—	0553082 速	—
/crhwɨ/	—	0553095 觸(B)	—
/srwɨ/	0552050 淑(B)	—	—
/kwɨ/	—	0553081 谷	—
/khwɨ/	—	0553090 哭	—
/hwɨ/	0552043 鵠	0553086 忽	—
/wɨ/	—	0553102 屋	—
/lywɨ/	—	—	0554133 録
/cywɨ/	—	0553097 足	—
/chywɨ/	—	0553098 促	—
/sywɨ/	0552045 俗	0553088 宿	—
/crywɨ/	0552046 逐	0553087 竹	—
/crhywɨ/	—	0553091 出(B)	—
/srywɨ/	0552044 贖(B)	0553092 叔	—
/rywɨ/	—	—	0554135 辱
/kywɨ/	0552049 局	0553085 菊	—
/khywɨ/	—	0553089 曲	—
/ywɨ/	—	—	0554136 玉
/ko/	—	1253055 葛	—
/kho/	—	1253058 渴	—
/ho/	1252025 合	—	—
/o/	—	—	1254088 萼
/pwo/	1252029 薄(C) 1252026 跋	1253056 鉢	— —
/phwo/	—	1253057 撥	—
/fwo/	1252027 佛	—	—
/mwo/	—	1253064 抹	1254084 沫

續表

Basicform	TG52	TG53	TG54
/two/	{1252030 鐸(C) 1252034 奪	1253062 掇	— —
/thwo/	—	1253063 脱	—
/lwo/	—	—	1254087 落
/nwo/	—	—	1254085 諾
/cwo/	1252033 鑿	—	—
/chwo/	—	1253061 撮	—
/crwo/	1252031 濁	—	—
/kwo/	—	1253058 聒	—
/khwo/	—	1253060 闊	—
/hwo/	1252028 活	—	—
/lywo/	—	—	1254089 畧
/nywo/	—	—	1254090 虐
/crywo/	1252035 著	—	—
/srywo/	1252036 杓	—	—
/rywo/	—	—	1254086 若
/hywo/	1252032 學	—	—
/ywo/	—	—	1254083 岳
/ta/	1352022 達	1353047 答	—
/tha/	—	1353040 塔	
/la/	—	—	1354070 臘
/na/	—	—	1354071 納
/ca/	1352027 雜	1353043 咂	—
/cha/	—	1353049 笈	—
/sa/	—	1353048 颯	—
/cra/	1352028 閘	1353042 劄	—
/crha/	—	1353044 察	—
/sra/	—	1353041 殺	—
/pwa/	1352026 拔	1353052 八	—
/fwa/	1352025 乏	1353045 法	—

續表

Basicform	TG52	TG53	TG54
/wa/	—	—	1354074 襪
/mwa/	—	—	1354073 抹
/srwa/	—	—	1354075 刷
/kwa/	—	1353050 刮	—
/hwa/	1352023 滑	—	—
/kya/	—	1353046 甲	—
/khya/	—	1353053 恰	—
/hya/	1352024 狎	1353051 瞎	—
/lya/	—	—	1354072 壓
/pye/	1452019 别	1453040 鼈	—
/phye/	—	1453039 瞥	—
/mye/	—	—	1454056 滅
/tye/	1452015 叠	—	—
/thye/	—	1453038 鐵	—
/lye/	—	—	1454059 列
/nye/	—	—	1454055 捏
/cye/	1452018 捷	1453034 節	—
/chye/	—	1453031 切	—
/sye/	—	1453030 屑	—
/crye/	—	1453043 哲	—
/crhye/	—	1453042 撤	—
/srye/	1452017 折	1453044 設	—
/rye/	—	—	1454061 熱
/kye/	1452014 傑	1453032 結	—
/khye/	—	1453033 怯	—
/hye/	1452013 恊	—	—
/ye/	—	—	1454057 拽(D)
			1454058 業
/lywe/	—	—	1454063 劣
/cywe/	1452020 絶	—	—

續表

Basicform	TG52	TG53	TG54
/sywe/	1452021 蒦	1453046 雪	—
/crywe/	—	1453041 拙	—
/crhywe/	—	1453045 啜	—
/srywe/	—	1453047 說	—
/rywe/	—	—	1454062 爇
/kywe/	1452016 鐝	1453037 玦	—
/khywe/	—	1453036 闕	—
/hywe/	—	1453035 血	—
/ywe/	—	—	1454060 月
/tɨy/	—	0453101 德	—
/lɨy/	—	—	0454148 勒
/cɨy/	0452059 賊	—	—
/hɨy/	0452058 劾	0453106 黑	—
/pyɨy/	0452057 逼	0453097 必	—
/phyɨy/	—	0453092 匹	—
/myɨy/	—	—	0454144 覓
/tyɨy/	0452054 荻	0453100 的	—
/thyɨy/	—	0453102 滌	—
/lyɨy/	—	—	0454146 立
/nyɨy/	—	—	0454150 匿
/cyɨy/	0452052 疾	0453096 唧	—
/chyɨy/		0453091 七	—
/syɨy/	0452053 夕	0453098 息	—
/cryɨy/	0452051 直	0453090 汁	—
/crhyɨy/	—	0453099 尺	—
/sryɨy/	0452050 實	0453095 失	—
/ryɨy/	—	—	0454143 日
/kyɨy/	0452055 及	0453093 吉	0454149 劇
/khyɨy/	—	0453104 乞	—
/hyɨy/	—	0453103 吸	—

續表

Basicform	TG52	TG53	TG54
/yɨy/	—	0453107 一	0454147 逸
/pwɨy/	—	0453094 筆	—
/mwɨy/	—	—	0454145 密
/kwɨy/	—	0453105 國	—
/hwɨy/	0452056 惑	—	—
/nay/	—	—	0654087 搦
/cay/	—	0653059 則	—
/cray/	0652031 宅	0653054 責	—
/crhay/	—	0653050 策	—
/sray/	—	0653055 色	—
/kyay/	—	0653052 革	—
/khyay/	—	0653053 客	—
/hyay/	—	0653058 嚇	—
/yay/	—	—	0654086 額
/pway/	0652030 白	0653051 伯	—
/phway/	—	0653049 拍	—
/mway/	—	—	0654085 麥
/srway/	—	0653057 摔	—
/kway/	—	0653056 摑	—
/hway/	0652032 畫	—	—
/lyiw/	—	—	1654087 六
/syiw/	—	1653061 宿	—
/cryiw/	1652035 逐	1653060 竹	—
/sryiw/	1652036 熟	—	—
/ryiw/	—	—	1654086 肉
/tow/	1152053 鐸	—	—
/thow/	—	1153104 拓	—
/low/	—	—	1154156 落
/now/	—	—	1154154 諾
/cow/	1152058 鑿	1153111 柞	—

續表

Basicform	TG52	TG53	TG54
/chow/	—	1153112 錯	—
/sow/	—	1153105 索	—
/crow/	1152052 濁	1153100 捉	—
/crhow/	—	1153117 戳	—
/srow/	—	1153107 朔	—
/kow/	—	1153113 閣	—
/how/	1152057 鶴	1153114 壑	—
/ow/	—	—	1154157 咢
/pwow/	1152054 薄	1153108 剝	—
/fwow/	1152056 縛	—	—
/mwow/	—	—	1154155 末
/kwow/	—	1153106 郭	—
/hwow/	1152059 鑊	—	—
/lyaw/	—	—	1154159 畧
/nyaw/	—	—	1154160 虐
/cyaw/	—	1153109 爵	—
/chyaw/	—	1153103 鵲	—
/syaw/	—	1153110 削	—
/cryaw/	1152060 著	1153101 斫	—
/crhyaw/	—	1153115 綽	—
/sryaw/	1152061 杓	1153102 爍	—
/ryaw/	—	—	1154158 弱
/kyaw/	—	1153099 角	—
/hyaw/	1152055 學	1153116 謔	—
/yaw/	—	—	1154153 岳

Additional remarks：

（A）0553101 蹙（AC /ci*k/，MP /chwɨ/）should have been included in 0553097 with the reading /cywɨ/，if it had been regular. After CYYY，syllables with the final /ywɨ/ and non-guttural initials except /n/ and /l/ all lost the /y/ in medial position. Thus we can interpret the peculiar occurrence of the above graph by saying that it had lost the /y/ even by the time of CYYY. This interpretation forces us to say that the small circle between 0553100 and 0553101 was entered by mistake. Chào Yìn-t'áng asserts that it should have been included in 0553098 without saying why（Chào Yìn-t'áng 1936，187，Note 3）.

（B）0553095 should have been put together with 0553091 with the reading /crhywɨ/，and 0552050 should have been put together with 0552044 with the reading /srywɨ/. Since in the development after CYYY，medial /y/ after Pr initials was lost，we can interpret the separation here by saying that even by CYYY，one in each pair had lost the /y/，but there is no way to tell which one lost it first. Here，I accept what Chào Yìn-t'áng did，assuming that he must have some reason for doing so，though he did not give any.

（C）See 6.4.3.3.

（D）See 4.5.4.3.

CHAPTER SEVEN CONCLUSION

We have reconstructed a fairly adequate phonological system for CYYY. More properly, this work of reconstruction should be called reinterpretation, because the system has always been underlying there, waiting to be dug out, so to speak. If our approach has given anyone the illusion that this system depends on that of AC or RTP, it must be dismissed immediately. The system certainly has its own life. Its existence does not depend upon any other system. What we have been doing is only to make the best use of our knowledge of AC, RTP, and MP in reading the signs of this system contained in CYYY. In so doing, we have also shown fragmentarily some aspects of the development from AC to CYYY. We are going to do more in this respect by arranging the rules of the development in a proper order. It is hoped that this 'proper' order will also make sense historically. We shall also try to say something briefly about the development from CYYY to MP, and thus provide an answer to the question whether CYYY represents Old Pekinese.

7.1 Some Remarks on the Diachronic Rules

In writing the rules of the phonological development, we have adopted the conventions used in modern generative grammar, especially the so-called 'operators' and 'abbreviators', though no claim is made here that the present work is strictly generative in nature (see Note ① in page 162). In some cases, we have not followed those conventions strictly. The few deviations can be stated as follows:

(*a*) Generally, we have accepted the linear treatment in writing the rules, but in one case at least, we allow an exception. We analyze a syllable into three parts the initial (I), the final (F), and the tone (T), with the tone as a supra-segmental element above the final in the form $I\frac{T}{F}$ (see 3.1). Later, whenever we deal with the tone, we shall represent it by a superscript attached to F (see 3.5.1).

(*b*) The distinction between the 'phrase structure rules' and the 'transformational rules' does not seem to be crucial in our formulating. To be sure, we have to start with defining the syllables (the first eight rules in 7.2), before we begin to state the changes, but frequently, in form, rules of the second part may not be quite different from those of the first part. For one thing, new elements can be introduced anytime when needed. The reason is that we are only trying to show the relationship between two independent phonological systems. In this sense, the 'new elements' introduced in the rules of changes are not really new.

(*c*) For the same reason given above, we shall permit rules in the form A→A. The same symbol may be used for a certain phoneme in AC and one in CYYY, but in relation to other phonemes of each system its status in one system is certainly different from that in the other.

(*d*) It may be better to state the phonological changes in terms of distinctive features, but we cannot do so at present due to many limits; for one thing, our knowledge of AC and RTP is hardly precise enough for us to do so. Instead, we shall formulate these changes in terms of individual phonemes and types of phonemes. Admittedly, this makes our rules somewhat less than precise in some cases. For example, each initial will belong to two large categories at the same time. When we use the symbol R, the initial /nj/ is included, but when we use the symbol Pj, the same initial is also included. We shall be satisfied so far as no misunderstanding is likely to arise. Besides, it seems to me that this method is not without its own advantages. For one thing, it may serve as a bridge between scholars of the 'old school' and those of the 'new school'.

(*e*) We do not plan to formulate the details about the combination of the initials and the finals. It is a rather complicated matter which we would like to state in a note①. This is another source of imprecision because both the in-put and the out-put of these rules will be unnecessarily increased. Again, we feel content to say that the in-put for these rules is limited to what existed in AC.

7.2 The Colloquial Development

Since there were two different lines of development, the literary and the colloquial we have to deal with them separately. We are going to arrange the rules to show the colloquial pronunciation first, because we believe that is what CYYY stands for. Some remarks have to be added before we start.

(*a*) Following the traditional approach, we have labeled the syllabic initial with 'I' (see 3.1 and 7.1a), but in formulating the rules, we have instead used 'C' which we treated as an optional part of a syllable (see 3.6.2). To be consistent, only 'C' will be used for the slot 'initial' in the following set of rules. Since zero initial had only a marginal existence (before /y/ only) in both AC and RTP, and since syllables with zero initial behaved in the same way as those with guttural initials in their historical development, we shall treat it as a member under 'G' (as well as 'R'). Consequently 'C' will be used as a cover symbol for all initials including zero, i.e, it will always appear as an obligatory part. There are also many minor revisions, but I shall not mention them one by one, because they are

---

① See the note after Rule N8 in 7.2. Dr. Fred W. Householder says: "In some parts of the smaller special grammars, various kinds of charts, tables or mazes may be simpler and more economical (than formulas), however." (Householder 1959, 233, Note 4) I believe our case here is one good example.

all self-explanatory.

(*b*) We shall try to arrange the rules in the most proper order historically. Ideally, beyond the syllable-defining rules (up to N8), each additional rule which specifies some change would represent a different stage of the language. This seems to be too strong a claim to make, so we would only say that the order is justified because descriptively it works very well, and we believe it reflects to a rather high degree the real diachronic development. Beyond this working criterion, there are still some rules which can be moved up and down within certain limits. In cases like these, we shall consider evidence from books other than CYYY, whenever available; otherwise, we simply use our own judgment.

(*c*) None of these rules is recursive. One possible exception can perhaps be allowed. for Rule 9 (N9), but even this is not necessary (see 5.12.5)

(*d*) Syllables with the ending /ŋ/ have persistently troubled us at every turn. Mainly for these syllables, we now have to slightly revise Ló Ch'áng-p'éi's version of the inner/outer contrast among the rime classes, which we have adopted (3.6.1). This revision is to us mainly a matter of necessity, so we shall not try to justify it for any other reason (but see Note ① in page 264).

i. We accept the theory that the *Kuŏ-shè* and the *Chiă-shè* have joined each other in forming a single rime class while still maintaining the distinction of divisions.

ii. We assume that the *Tsēng-shè* has moved out from the inner series to the outer series. Graphs of its first division now have V_1 as the nucleus. Those of the third division have joined their counterparts of the *Kěng-shè* in having V_3 as the nucleus. This means that we believe the *Tsēng-shè* and the *Kěng-shè* have joined each other in forming a single rime class of the outer series (see 6.4.1), while maintaining the distinction of the divisions. Thus, the *T'ūng-shè* is now the only rime class with ending /ŋ/ in the inner series, so we can say that its nucleus is V_n.

iii. The *Chiāng-shè* and the *Tàng-shè* must now be treated as exceptions in that they do not belong to either the outer series or the inner series. This is structurally necessary (see 6. 4. 3), We know that these two rime classes later merged completely in having one and the same nucleus, but we cannot start with this presumption. Instead, we have to say that when our rules first began to function, these two rime classes were still distinct from each other. The reason is that Rule 19 (N26) in 4. 6. 2 affected only the *Chiāng-shè*. So we shall say that, aside from the inner nuclear vowel (V_n) and the outer nuclear vowels ($V_w = V_1$, V_2, V_3, V_4), there were still two additional ones: V_{ch} for the *Chiāng-shè* and V_{ta} for the *Tàng-shè*. We may suggest that the obvious unbalance here might well be the feature which later triggered the rearrangement of all the syllables with ending /ŋ/ or /k/ to fit the inner/outer contrast among the nuclear vowels (cf. 7. 3. 1).

(*e*) 'X, Y, Z' will stand in the rules as variables, unless specified otherwise. '#' will be used for syllable boundary, but only when absolutely needed.

With the above remarks as a foundation, we may now begin to list the rules. For possible later reference, each rule will be given a number preceded by N, meaning its number in this new order. A cross-reference showing where the rules first appeared or were discussed will also be added after them. I have no illusion that this set of rules is so comprehensive that every change in the development from AC to CYYY has been registered, but I believe all the major events have been recorded perspectively. It will not be difficult to find many individual graphs which are exceptions to some of the changes specified by these rules. Such exceptions, or counter-examples, are of very little significance to us, unless "they suggest a different general framework or the formulation of deeper rules"[①].

---

① Chomsky and Halle (1968), IX

#Syllable#

N1 Syllable → C $\frac{T}{F}$ (3.1)

N2 F → (M)V(E) (3.1)

N3 T=even, rising, going, entering (3.5.1)

N4 C → (3.2)

	S($\begin{Bmatrix} h \\ ɦ \end{Bmatrix}$)			Fr(ɦ)		R	
B	p	ph	pɦ			m	
D	t	th	tɦ			n	
Ds	c	ch	cɦ	s	sɦ		
P	tj	tjh	tjɦ				
Pr	cr	crh	crɦ	sr	srɦ		
Pj	cj	cjh	cjɦ	sj	sjɦ	nj	
G	k	kh	kɦ	x	xɦ	ŋ	
	q						ø

N5 M → (y)(w) (3.3)

N6 E → y, w, m, n, ŋ, p, t, k (3.4)

N7 $V \rightarrow \begin{Bmatrix} V_{ch}, V_{ta}, V_n, V_w / \_\_\_ \begin{Bmatrix} k \\ ŋ \end{Bmatrix} \\ V_n \\ V_w \end{Bmatrix}$ (7.2d)

N8 $V_w \rightarrow V_1, V_2, V_3, V_4$ (7.2d iii)

Note: possible syllable patterns in RTP.

Division	Outer series	Inner series	Exceptions
1	C(w)V_1(E)	C(w)V_n(E)	C(w)V_{ta}+(E)
2	C(w)V_2(E)	—	C+V_{ch}+E
3	C+y(w)V_3(E)	C+y(w)V_n(E)	C+y(w)V_{ta+}(E)
4	C+y(w)V_4(E)	—	—

(3.6.2 & 7.2d)

Additional remarks:

(1) Pj occurs only before finals of the third division.

(2) P and Pr occur only before finals of the second and the third divisions.

(3) Ds and D, except /n/ and /l/, do not occur before finals of th second division.

(4) Zero initials occurs only before finals of the third and the fourth division.

(5) The rest of the initials may occur anywhere.

N9 $\text{ø} \rightarrow \text{w/B\_\_\_V}$ (4. 2. 1)

N10 $\text{xɦ} \rightarrow \text{ø/\_\_\_y(w)} \left\{\begin{array}{l} V_n \\ V_3 \\ V_{ta} \end{array}\right\}$ (4. 6. 1)

N11 $\text{y} \rightarrow \text{ø/Pr\_\_\_}$ (4. 5. 2)

N12 $\text{j} \rightarrow \text{r}$ (4. 5. 2)

N13 $\text{n} \rightarrow \text{ø/\_\_\_r}$ (4. 5. 3)

N14 $F^{even} \rightarrow \left\{\begin{array}{l} F^{02} / \left\{\begin{array}{l} \text{ɦ} \\ R \end{array}\right\} \text{\_\_\_} \\ F^{01} \end{array}\right.$ (3. 5. 1)

N15 $F^{rising} \rightarrow \left\{\begin{array}{l} F^{04} / \text{ɦ\_\_\_} \\ F^{03} \end{array}\right\}$ (3. 5. 1)

N16 $F^{going} \rightarrow F^{04}$ (3. 5. 1)

N17 $\text{q} \rightarrow \text{ø}$ (3. 5. 2)

N18 $F^{entering} \rightarrow \left\{\begin{array}{l} F^{52} / \text{ɦ\_\_\_} \\ F^{54} / \text{R\_\_\_} \\ F^{53} \end{array}\right\}$ (3. 5. 1)

N19 $\text{ɦ} \rightarrow \left\{\begin{array}{l} \text{h/s—}F^{02} \\ \text{ø} \end{array}\right\}$ (4. 1)

N20 $\text{x} \rightarrow \text{h}$ (4. 1)

N21 $\text{y} \rightarrow \text{ø /m\_\_\_w}+V_n \left\{\begin{array}{l} \text{w} \\ \text{k} \\ \text{ŋ} \end{array}\right\}$ (4. 2. 2 & 5. 13. 1)

N22 $\begin{bmatrix} \text{p(h)} \\ \text{m} \end{bmatrix} \rightarrow \begin{bmatrix} \text{f} \\ \text{v} \end{bmatrix} \text{/\_\_\_y+w}$ (4. 2. 1)

N23 $\text{y} \rightarrow \text{ø} / \left\{\begin{array}{l} \text{f} \\ \text{v} \end{array}\right\} \text{\_\_\_}$ (4. 2. 1)

N24 $\text{w} \rightarrow \text{ø /y\_\_\_}V_n + \text{w}$ (5. 13. 1)

N25 $V_3 \rightarrow \left\{\begin{array}{l} V_2\text{/C(w)\_\_\_} \\ V_4 \end{array}\right\}$ (5. 6. 1 & 5. 6. 2)

N26 $\text{ø} \rightarrow \text{y/G\_\_\_} \left\{\begin{array}{l} V_2 \\ V_{ch} \end{array}\right\}$ (4. 6. 2 & 7. 2d)

N27 $V_1 \rightarrow V_2 / C\_\_\_E$ (5.10.2 & 6.4.5.2)

Conditions: i) $E \neq W$;

ii) if $C = G$, the $E \neq p, t, k$

N28 $\eta \rightarrow n / \_\_\_ y + V_{ta}$ (4.6.4.2)

N29 $\eta \rightarrow \begin{Bmatrix} \eta / \_\_\_ V_1(w) \\ \varnothing \end{Bmatrix} / \# \_\_\_$ (4.6.4.5 & 6.4.5.3)

N30 $k \rightarrow \begin{Bmatrix} y / V_w \_\_\_ \\ w \end{Bmatrix} / V\_\_\_$ (6.4.1,64.2 & 6.4.3)

N31 $\begin{Bmatrix} V_1 \\ V_2 \end{Bmatrix} \rightarrow V_4 / \_\_\_ \eta$ (5.7.1 & 6.4.1)

N32 $\begin{Bmatrix} V_{ta} \\ V_{ch} \end{Bmatrix} \rightarrow \begin{Bmatrix} V_2 / \_\_\_ \eta \\ V_1 \end{Bmatrix}$ (6.4.3)

N33 $V_n \rightarrow V_1 / \_\_\_ \eta$ (5.5 & 6.4.2)

N34 $V_1 \rightarrow o$ (5.6 & 5.10.2)

N35 $V_2 \rightarrow a$ (5.6)

N36 $V_4 \rightarrow e$ (5.6 & 5.6.2)

N37 $V_n \rightarrow ɨ$ (5.6.2)

N38 $y \rightarrow \varnothing / \begin{Bmatrix} Ds \\ Pr \end{Bmatrix} \_\_\_ ɨ + y$ (4.5.2 & 5.12)

N39 $y \rightarrow \varnothing / C + ɨ \_\_\_$ (5.12)

N40 $t \rightarrow c / \_\_\_ r$ (4.5.2)

N41 $\begin{Bmatrix} p \\ t \end{Bmatrix} \rightarrow \begin{Bmatrix} y / y + ɨ \_\_\_ \\ \varnothing \end{Bmatrix} / V\_\_\_$ (6.4.4.2)

N42 $o \rightarrow a / y \_\_\_ w$ (6.4.3.1)

N43 $\varnothing \rightarrow w / C \_\_\_ o \#$ (5.9 & 6.4.3.3)

Condition: $C \neq G$.

N44 $w \rightarrow \varnothing / Pr + y \_\_\_ ɨ + w$ (6.4.2.1)

Note: optional.

N45 $w \rightarrow \varnothing / w + ɨ \_\_\_$ (5.13.1 & 6.4.2.1)

N46 $ɨ \rightarrow a / C + w \_\_\_ y$ (5.12.3)

N47 $\begin{Bmatrix} o \\ e \end{Bmatrix} \rightarrow ɨ / \_\_\_ y$ (5.12.2 & 6.4.1)

N48 y → ø/___w + ɨ + y (5. 12. 4)

N49 ø → w/Pr___a + ŋ (6. 4. 3. 2)

N50 e → o/w___ŋ (5. 7. 2)

Note: optional.

N51 y → ø/___w + a + ŋ (5. 14. 1)

N52 y → ø/Pr___w + o + ŋ (5. 5. 1)

N53 B + X + m → B + X + n (3. 4)

7. 3 The Literary Development

The divergence between the literary pronunciation and the colloquial pronunciation exists mainly in two phonological aspects, the readjustment of the syllables with ending /ŋ/ or /k/ to fit the inner/outer contrast among the nuclear vowels and the change of the entering tone; otherwise, the literary and the colloquial are virtually identical. It follows that if we can replace some of the rules in the development of the colloquial pronunciation with some new rules which specify the changes in the two aspects mentioned above, we can leave the rest untouched and thus get a new set of rules which represents the development of the literary pronunciation. This is what we are going to try to do here.

7. 3. 1 We have noticed that graphs of the second and the third divisions in the *Kěng-shè* with G initials had merged in CYYY, but in MP, those of the second division are still different from those of the third division in having no medial /y/ (see 4. 6. 2c). I have explained this phenomenon by saying that in the dialect from which MP came directly, the complete coalescence of the *Kěng-shè* and the *Tsēng-shè* in sharing the same nucleus /e/ took place before the change specified by Rule 19 (in 4. 6. 2) while in the dialect of CYYY, the coalescence took place after that rule (see 5. 7. 1). If we accept this thesis as we must, we then do not have to establish in an ad

hoc manner two nuclear vowels in addition to V_n and V_w, as we did for the colloquial development (7.2). We can simply say that the *Chiāng-shè*, the *Tàng-shè* and the *Kěng-shè* combination had joined together in forming a new rime class as follows:

$$\textit{Tàng} \qquad (y)(w)V_1\begin{Bmatrix} k \\ ŋ \end{Bmatrix}$$

$$\textit{Chiāng} \qquad V_2\begin{Bmatrix} k \\ ŋ \end{Bmatrix}$$

$$\textit{Kěng- Tsēng} \qquad (y)(w)V_4\begin{Bmatrix} k \\ ŋ \end{Bmatrix}$$

This new rime class is slightly different from the others in that V_1 here can take medial /y/, and V_4, can occur with zero medial or medial /w/ alone. Starting with this presumption, we can now revise the following rules without changing their order. We may add 'L' after each number to show that the rules in question belong to the literary development.

N7L. $V \rightarrow \begin{Bmatrix} V_n \\ V_w \end{Bmatrix}$

N10L. $xɦ \rightarrow ø/\_\_\_ y(w) \begin{Bmatrix} V_n \\ V_1 \\ V_3 \end{Bmatrix}$

N26L. $ø \rightarrow y/G\_\_\_V_2$

N28L. $ŋ \rightarrow n/\_\_\_y + V_1$

N31 and N32 can now be replaced by the two following rules:

N31L. $V_1 \rightarrow V_2/\_\_\_ŋ$

N32L. $V_2 \rightarrow V_1/\_\_\_k$

These two rules specify that when the *Chiāng-shè* and the *Tàng-shè* merged, they did so in a rather peculiar way, because the non-entering tone syllables of the *Tàng-shè* joined their counterparts of the *Chiāng-shè* in having V_2 as their nucleus, but the entering tone syllables of the *Chiāng-shè* joined their counterparts of the *Tàng-shè* in having V_1 as their nucleus. The second rule is possible because in the development of the literary pronunciation, N30 should be eliminated.

7. 3. 2 Our discussions in Chapter Six have made it clear that the literary pronunciation differs most drastically from the colloquial pronunciation with regard to the former entering tone, especially those syllables with ending /k/. Instead of having the post-nuclear /k/ changed to /y/ or /w/ as in the colloquial pronunciation, the literary pronunciation simply dropped it, together with the post-nuclear /p/ and /t/. The question to answer now is whether, in the earlier stages of the literary development, the three post-nuclear stops were dropped completely without leaving any trace, or rather were replaced by a new element, perhaps a glottal stop, which still marked off the entering tone syllables as a special group. I think the latter possibility is more likely. There is only one case to support this belief, because in all the other cases, the later development has made the existence or non-existence of this new ending rather irrelevant. This single case involves the entering tone graphs of the *Chēn-shè* and the *Shēn-shè* with AC Pr initials, particularly, the two graphs 澀 and 瑟 appearing in RG03 of CYYY. We have said that in the colloquial pronunciation they had /ɨ/ as their final (6. 4. 4. 1). In the literary pronunciation, these graphs should also have had /ɨ/ as their final, if the former post-nuclear stops had really dropped out without leaving a trace. This would have made them entirely indistinguishable from those non-entering tone graphs included in RG03, and thus there would have been no reason for them to follow a separate line of development after the period of CYYY. However, both 澀 and 瑟 now read /sè/ in MP, that is, with the middle vowel as their final, different from all the non-entering tone graphs of RG03, which have the high vowel /ɨ/ as their final in MP. A logical hypothesis is that in the literary pronunciation these two graphs must represent a syllable with a final different from that of the non-entering tone syllables of RG03, and this final can be represented by /ɨq/ where /q/ stands

for the new element coming from the former post-nuclear stops and functioning as a conditioning feature in the development of syllables with this final. A natural extension of this hypothesis is, of course, that all the entering tone syllables had /q/ as their ending in the early stage of the literary development.

7.3.3 The above hypothesis is by no means contradictory to our conclusion that there is no entering tone in CYYY, because when the literary readings of these entering tone graphs were borrowed into the colloquial, the ending /q/ must have automatically dropped out, and as such they were subject to the later changes in the development of the colloquial pronunciation (e.g., N43). What we have to do now in formulating the development of the entering tone syllables in the literary pronunciation is to eliminate N30 and N41, and then add a new rule which says that all the post-nuclear stops should be replaced by /q/. But before we add this new rule, we need another one. We find that the entering tone graphs of the third and the fourth divisions in the *Kĕng-shè* and the *Tsēng-shè*, namely, those with /y/ in the medial position, have now in MP the final /yɨ/ or /ywɨ/, instead of /ye/ or /ywe/, as they should have had, if they had at one time the final /yeq/ or /yweq/, for example, 錫(AC /siek/, MP /syɨ̄/), 極(AC /kɦiək/, MP /cyɨ́/), and 域(AC /xɦiuək/, MP /ywɨ̀/). Their counterparts in the *Shān-shè* and the *Hsién-shè*, namely, those with ending /t/ or /p/, have, however, the final /ye/ or /ywe/ in MP, for example, 屑(AC /siet/, MP /syè/), 牒(AC /tɦiep/, MP /tyé/) and 越(AC /xɦiuat/, MP /ywè/). This fact indicates, it seems to me, that before the three post-nuclear stops were replaced by /q/, the two finals /yek/ and /ywek/ had been changed to /yɨk/ and /ywɨk/ respectively. So after we have eliminated N30 and N41, we have to add the two following rules after N40 in this order:

N41La. e → ɨ/y(w)k____

$$\text{N41Lb.} \quad \begin{Bmatrix} p \\ t \\ k \end{Bmatrix} \rightarrow q/V\_\_\_$$

7.3.4 Our interpretation of the development of the entering tone graphs in the literary pronunciation yields two finals /oq/ and /yoq/ which we have said should be rewritten with /w/ in the medial position except when the former occurs after guttural initials (see 6.4.3.2 and 6.4.3.3). N43 should thus be revised as follows for the literary development:

$$\text{N43L.} \quad X + o(q) \rightarrow X + w + o(q)$$
$$X \neq \begin{Bmatrix} G \\ Y + w \end{Bmatrix}$$

7.3.5 The following chart shows the entering tone finals in the literary pronunciation, marked with the rime classes from which they originated. The numerals represent the rimes into which they were borrowed at the time of CYYY. The two in parentheses are the only ones which were not borrowed into the colloquial pronunciation, i.e., not included in CYYY.

E	-q			
V \ M	ɨ	e	a	o
ø	Chēn, Shēn 03	Tsēng, Kěng (14)	Shān, Hsién 13	Chiāng, Tàng, Shān, Hsién 12
y	Chēn, Shēn Tsēng, Kěng 04	Shān, Hsién 14	Shān, Hsién 13	
w	Chēn, T'ūng 05	Tsēng, Kěng (14)	Shān, Hsién 13	Chiāng, Tàng, Shān 12
yw	Chēn, T'ūng 05	Shān 14		Chiāng, Tàng, 12

7.4 The Relationship Between CYYY and MP

The question whether MP is the modern reflex of the dialect represented by CYYY can now be easily answered, though by this time the question must have lost much of its tincture of curiosity. In a strict sense, the answer is obviously no, because the following phenomena in MP cannot be explained by what we see in CYYY.

(*a*) The irregular distribution of all the former entering tone graphs with voiceless initials (6.2.4).

(*b*) The development of the second division syllables of the unrounded type of the *Kěng-shè* (5.7.1).

(*c*) The development of both the first and the second division syllables of the entering tone in the *Tsēng-shè* and the *Kěng-shè* (6.4.1.2).

(*d*) The development of the former entering tone graphs included in RG03 of CYYY (7.3.2).

These are only the major ones. We have set up a system of development which we call the literary pronunciation. Since all the above phenomena except the first one can be well explained there, we are now obliged to say that MP came from this literary system rather than from the colloquial system represented by CYYY. As we said before, the two systems must represent two closely related sub-dialects, and the inter-borrowing between these two sub-dialects must have already been extensive even before CYYY. So in a slightly looser sense, we can indeed say that MP was developed from CYYY. After all, the basic phonological structure of the literary system is almost identical to that of the colloquial system, except that the former maintained for a while the entering tone in the form of an ending /q/. Moreover, as the two systems may possibly represent the speeches of two social strata, we may perhaps call them two 'co-existing systems', if we can use this term. It should be added here promptly that the question whether MP was developed from the dialect represented by CYYY is by no means equivalent to the question whether CYYY represents Old Pekinese, i. e., whether the dialect of CYYY was formerly spoken in and around the city of Peking. It is not entirely inconceivable that neither the literary development nor the colloquial development represents the dialect formerly spoken in Peking; in other words, MP is derived from the dialect of some other place, which later spread to Peking and replaced the dialect spoken there before. But I seriously doubt that this can be the truth. Lǐ Hsīn-k'uéi says that, according to his research, the phonological system of the Lòyáng（洛陽）dialect is much closer to that of CYYY than that of MP is①. I have serious reservations on this assertion. If he or anyone else could show us that the phonological system of Lòyáng or any place other than Peking is much closer to the colloquial system we have set up than that of MP is, we would accept the proposition that CYYY indeed does not represent Old Pekinese; otherwise, we shall assume that both the literary system and the colloquial system represent Old Pekinese. CYYY is based upon the colloquial system with heavy borrowing from the literary, while MP is derived from the literary system but with heavy borrowing from the colloquial.

7.5 The Development from CYYY to MP

The development from CYYY to MP is beyond the domain of the present work, but something can be added here to show the great potential of our system in this regard. To do this, we shall have to set up an analysis of our own for MP, because none of the existing ones seem to be adequate for our purpose. Since it involves too many problems, we cannot discuss this new

① Lǐ Hsīn-k'uéi (1963), 279.

analysis here beyond giving some of its main aspects in the most sketchy manner. I shall describe it barely enough for us to add some rules to show the major changes from CYYY to MP.

7. 5. 1 The system of initials in this new analysis is practically the same as that in Hartman's and Hockett's analyses, though it will look more like Hockett's graphically. The greatest difference is that we shall treat /r/ as an initial feature, instead of as a semi-vowel. Consequently, it will be treated as an initial or part of an initial①. When it combines with the symbol of aspiration /h/, it will appear before the latter (/crh/, instead of /chr/). It will be noticed that this system is almost the same as the one we set up for CYYY (4. 7), except that it does not have /ŋ/ and /v/.

7. 5. 2 We accept Hartman's analysis that there are three vowels, /i, e, a/, but we shall write the first one as /ɨ/, hoping to avoid any possible misunderstanding. However, we do not accept Hartman's analysis that /n/ and /ŋ/ can occur after the high vowel②. In all those cases, we shall say that they are preceded by the middle vowel. In this way we can make a sweeping generalization in saying that only the middle and the low vowels can be followed by an ending. This will justify the writing off of the ending /y/ of the CYYY final /yɨy/ in its development to MP (see 5. 12. 6)③.

7. 5. 3 Both Hartman and Hockett discuss extensively the problem concerning the syllables with the ending /r/, and Hockett alone also discusses the syllables with the ending /m/. We feel these problems belong to the morphophonemic level. There are also other possible syllable endings of this kind: for example, the noun suffix 'tz' (our /c/) and the auxiliary noun 'g'

---

① Cf. Sùng Yüán-chiā (1965), 171 - 172.

② Hartman (1944), 119.

③ Stimson probably has also realized this possibility, for he has the high and the low vowels combine with endings but not the middle vowel (Stimson 1966, 15 - 16). The choice, however, does not seem to be right to me. Cf. Hsueh (1973).

(our /k/), as they are used in Y. R. Chao's *Mandarin Primer*①. All these can and should be treated by a small set of morphophonemic rules, so that the basic phonological analysis will not have to be unnecessarily complicated②.

7.5.4 With the above remarks on MP in mind, we can now write some rules to show the major changes from the literary system of the Yüán dynasty to MP. I shall not add any explanation nor shall I give any example to illustrate these rules. Obviously, much research will have to be done before we can have a comprehensive set of rules arranged in the most proper order.

(1) $\eta \rightarrow \emptyset / \# \_\_\_$

(2) $\begin{Bmatrix} e \\ o \end{Bmatrix} \rightarrow a / \_\_\_ w$

(3) $m \rightarrow n / V \_\_\_$

(4) $o \rightarrow e / \_\_\_ \eta$

(5) $\begin{Bmatrix} e \\ o \end{Bmatrix} \rightarrow a / \_\_\_ n$

(6) $ɨ \rightarrow e / C \_\_\_ q$

(7) $q \rightarrow \emptyset$

(8) $y \rightarrow \emptyset / y + ɨ \_\_\_$

(9) $\# r + ɨ \# \rightarrow \# ɨ + r \#$

(10) $v \rightarrow \emptyset$

---

① Y. R. Chao (1948), 40 and 46. For example, "ig yiiz" (p. 46). Upon reading this section, Dr. Chao said to this author that he used "tz" and "g" only as abbreviations for the syllables they stand for, not as syllable endings. This seems to have undermined our argument here, but not quite if we remember that, to the Chinese native speakers, [m] in such expressions as [t'ām] 'they' is *not a syllable ending*, either, but a *syllable*. It becomes a single consonant (hence, *a syllable ending*) only 'phonetically, i.e., to the non-native speakers' ears. Similarly, the reason why the noun suffix 子 and the auxiliary noun 個 can be represented by 'tz' and 'g' respectively is, I believe, that to the non-native speakers they sound rather like single consonants phonetically. (Certainly, it cannot be for the purpose of saving one space in printing).

② We might perhaps be accused of what has been called "Pike's heresy", but this does not seem to be a serious fault any longer. Cf. Postal (1968).

(11) $y \rightarrow ø / Pr\_\_\_$

(12) $o \rightarrow e / \_\_\_ \#$

(13) $ɨ \rightarrow e / \_\_\_ E$

Condition: $E \neq r$.

(14) $y \rightarrow ø / C\_\_\_ w + e + ŋ$

Condition: $C \neq G$.

(15) $\begin{Bmatrix} k \\ kh \\ h \end{Bmatrix} \rightarrow \begin{Bmatrix} c \\ ch \\ s \end{Bmatrix} / \_\_\_ y$

SELECTED BIBLIOGRAPHY

Works included here are limited to those which have been referred to at least once in the present work.

Chāng Shìh-lù 張世祿：

1963 *Chūng-kuó Yīn-yǜn-hsüéh Shǐh* 中國音韻學史［History of the Chinese Phonological Study］(reprint)(Hong Kong).

Chao，Yuen Ren：

1941 "Distinctions within Ancient Chinese"，*Harvard Journal of Asiatic Studies* 5，203－233.

1943 "Introduction on Pronunciation"，*Mathews' Chinese-English Dictionary*，rev. American edition (Cambridge，Mass.，1965)，IX－XXI.

1948 *Mandarin Primer: An Intensive Course in Spoken Chinese* (Cambridge，Mass.).

1968 *A Grammar of Spoken Chinese* (Berkeley，Calif.).

Chào Yìn-t'áng 趙蔭棠：

1936 *Chūng-yüān Yīn-yǜn Yén-chiū* 中原音韻研究［A Study of CYYY］(Shanghai).

1957 *Těng-yǜn Yüán-liú* 等韻源流［The Historical Development of the Rime Tables］(Peking).

Chào Hsiá-ch'iū 趙遐秋 and Tsēng Ch'ìng-juì 曾慶瑞：

1962 "Chūng-yüán Yīn-yǜn Yīn-hsì te Chī-ch'ǔ hó Jù-p'ai-sān-shēng te Hsìng-chíh"，中原音韻音系的基礎和"入派三聲"的性質［The foundation of the phonological system of CYYY and the nature of the redistribution of the entering tone graphs in the other three tones)，*ZGYW*，July，312－324.

Chomsky，Noam and Morris，Halle：

1968 *The Sound Pattern of English*（New York）.

Chōu Tsŭ-mó 周祖謨：

1960 Kuǎng-yǜn Chiào-pěn 廣韻校本［A Critical Edition of Kuǎng-yǜn］（Peking）.

Halle，Morris：

1962 "Phonology in Generative Grammar"，*Word* 18，54－72. Also in Jerry A. Fodor and Jerrold J. Katz（ed.），*The Structure of Language*（New Jersey，1964），334－352.

Hartman，Lawton M.，III：

1944 "The Segmental Phonemes of the Peiping Dialect"，*Language* 20，28－42. Also in Martin Joos'（ed.），*Readings in Linguistics*，116－123.（Reference will be made to *RIL*）.

Hashimoto，Mantaro Joseph：

1965 "Phonology of Ancient Chinese"，Ph.D. dissertation（The Ohio State University）.

1970 "Internal Evidence for Ancient Chinese Palatal Endings"，*Language* 46.2，Part 1，336－365.

Hattori Shiro 服部四郎 and Tōdō Akiyasu 藤堂明保：

1958 *Chūgen On'in no Kenkyū* 中原音韻の研究［A Study of CYYY］（Tokyo）.

Hockett，Charles F.：

1947 "Peiping Phonology"，*Journal of the American Oriental Sociery* 67，253－267. Also in *RIL*，217－228.

Householder，Fred W.：

1959 "On Linguistic Primes"，*Word* 15，231－239.

Hsueh，F. S.：

1973 "The P'íng-tù Dialect as a Variant of Mandarin"，*Tsinghua Journal of Chinese Studies* 清華學報 n. s. X，1，74－89.

1971 "The Impact of Dialect Study on Historical Linguistics: Some Examples from the P'ing-tù Dialect", paper presented at the Fourth International Conference on Sino-Tibetan Linguistics (Oct., 1971, Bloomington, Indiana).

Ishiyama Fukuji 石山福治:

1925 *Kōtei Chūgen On'in* 考定中原音韻[A Critical Study of CYYY] (Tokyo).

Jakobson, Roman and Morris, Halle:

1956 *Fundamentals of Language* (The Hague).

Karlgren, Bernhard:

1948 Chūng-kuó Yīn-yùn-hsüéh Yén-chiū 中國音韻學研究. Authorized Chinese translation of Bernhard Karlgren's *Érudes sur la phonologie chinoise*, Leiden, 1915 - 26, by Y. R. Chao, F. K. Li, and Ló Ch'áng-p'ei (Shanghai).

1954 "Compendium of Phonetics in Ancient and Archaic Chinese", *Bulletin of the Museum of Far Eastern Antiquities* 22, 211 - 367.

Koutsoudas, Andreas:

1966 *Writing Transformational Grammar: An Introduction* (New York).

Lǐ Hsīn-k'uéi 李新魁:

1963 "Kuān-yǘ CYYY Yīn-hsì te Chī-ch'ǔ hó Jù-p'ài-sān-shēng te Hsìng-chíh" 關於《中原音韻》音系的基礎和"入派三聲"的性質[Comments on Chào and Tsēng 1962], *ZGYW*, 4, 275 - 281.

Lǐ Júng 李榮:

1956 *Ch'ièh-yǜn Yīn-hsì* 切韻音系[The Phonological System of *Ch'ièh-yǜn*) (Peking 1952), rev. edition.

1963 *Hàn-yü Fāng-yén Tiào-ch'á Shǒu-ts'è* 漢語方言調查手册[A Manual for the Investigation of the Chinese Dialects] (Peking).

Liào Hsǜn-yīng 廖珣英:

1963 "Kuān Hàn-ch'īng Hsì-ch'ǚ te Yùng-yǜn" 關漢卿戲曲的用韻[The

riming habits in the plays by Kuān Hàn-ch'īng), *ZGYW*, 4, 267 - 274.

Ló Ch'áng-p'éi 羅常培:

1933 "Shìh Nèi wài Chuǎn"釋内外轉[On the meaning of the inner and the outer series] *Bulletin of the Institute of History and Philology*, Academia Sinica, IV, 2, 206 - 226.

Lù Chìh-wéi 陸志韋:

1946 "*Shìh Chūng-yüán Yīn-yǜn*" 釋中原音韻[On CYYY], *Yēnchīng Hsüéh-pào* 燕京學報 31, 35 - 70.

1947a "*Chì Hsǘ Hsiào Ch'úng-tìng Szū-mǎ Wēn-kūng Těng-yǜn T'ú-chīng*" 記徐孝重訂司馬温公等韻圖經[Remarks on Hsu Hsiao's Rime Tables], *Yēnchīng Hsüéh-pào* 32,167 - 196.

1947b "*Chīn-ní-kó Hsī-jú Er-mù Tzū Suǒ-chì-te Yīn*"金尼閣《西儒耳目資》所記的音[The Sound Pattern Revealed in Nicolas Trigault's HJEMT], *Yēnchīng Hsüéh-pào* 33, 115 - 128.

Lúng Yü-shún 龍宇純:

1960 *Yǜn-chìng Chiào-chù* 韻鏡校注[A Critical Edition of *Yǜn-chìng*] (Taipei).

Martin, Samuel E.:

1953 *The Phonemes of Ancient Chinese*, supplement to Journal of the American Oriental Society 16.

Postal, Paul M.:

1968 *Aspects of Phonological Theory* (New York).

Pulleyblank, E. G.:

1970 "Late Middle Chinese", *Asia Major* XV, 2, 197 - 239, and XVI (1971), 1 - 2, 121 - 168.

Stimson, Hugh M.:

1962a "Phonology of the *Chūng-yüán Yīn-yǜn*", *Tsinghua Journal of Chinese Studies* 清華學報. New Series, 3, 114 - 159.

1962b "Ancient Chinese -p, -t, -k Endings in the Peking Dialect", *Language* 38, 376 - 384.

1966 *The Jongyuan In Yunn* (New Haven, Conn).

Sùng Yüán-chiā 宋元嘉:

1965 "*P'ing Ha-t'e-men hó Huo-k'ai-t'e tuèi Pĕi-chīng Yǔ-yīn te Fēn-hsī*" 評哈忒門和霍凱特對北京語音的分析[Critical Comments on Hartman's and Hockett's *Analyses of the Phonology of the Peking Dialect*), *ZGYW* 3, 167 - 178.

Tīng Shēng-shù 丁聲樹:

1958 Kŭ-chīn Tzù-yīn Tuèi-chào Shŏu ts'è 古今字音對照手册[A Manual of the Corresponding Readings of Chinese Characters in AC and MP] (Peking).

Tŭng T'úng-hó 董同龢:

1948a "*Kuăng-yǜn Ch'úng-niŭ Shìh-shìh*" 廣韻重紐試釋[A Tentative Interpretation of the Initial Doublets in *Kuăng-yǜn*], *Bulletin of the Institute of History and Philology*, Academia Sinica 13, 1 - 20.

1948b "*Tĕng-yǚn Mén-fă T'ūng-shìh*" 等韻門法通釋[A Comprehensive Interpretation of the 'keys' to the Rime Tables), *Bulletin of the Institute of History and Philology*, Academia Sinica 14, 257 - 306.

1954 *Chūng-kuó Yǚ-yīn Shĭh* 中國語音史[History of Chinese Phonology] (Taipei).

Wáng Lì 王力:

1967 *Chūng-kuó yǚ-yén-hsüéh Shĭh* 中國語言學史[History of the Chinese Linguistic Studies) (Peking).

Wang, John C. and Hsueh, F. S.:

1973 "The Lín-ch'í Dialect and its Relation to Mandarin", in *Journal of the American Oriental Sociery* 93, 2, 136 145.

Yüán Chiā-huá 袁家驊:

1960 *Hanyu Fangyan Gaiyao* 漢語方言概要(Peking).

古官話音系***

譯者弁言

薛鳳生(1931—2015)先生是享譽海内外的漢語音韻學家,在漢語等韻學、北音學(《中原音韻》)等研究上有獨到的見解。他認爲等韻學就是漢語傳統的音韻學理論,其中暗含着區别性特徵和對立互補等音位學觀念,而這一點在理論上的真正構建要到二十世紀初美國的結構主義描寫語言學才完成。薛鳳生先生認爲"所有韻書(不僅《中原音韻》)在語音上没有告訴我們任何東西,它們僅僅展示了一個潛在的音位系統的'代數'結構。"我們研究這些韻書的音系,就是要對"潛在的音位系統的'代數'結構"進行"詮釋",而不是"構擬"。薛鳳生先生治學特點是采用嚴格的結構主義音位觀念,關照漢語的音系結構,揭示中國音韻學研究傳統的理論價值,從動態的音系結構轉變視角,用一套按照特定順序排列的歷時規則,詮釋中古漢語—韻圖時期—《中原音韻》—現代北京話音系的演變過程。

1979 年,薛鳳生先生在第十二屆國際漢藏語學術會議(巴黎)上宣讀有關内外轉的論文"A New Interpretation of the Inner vs Outer Contrast in the Rhyme Tables and Its Implication on Middle Chinese Phonology"(後來這篇文章由劉樂寧譯爲中文發表在陝西語言會編《語言研究與教學》1982 年第四號,增訂稿發表於《語言研究》1985 年第 1 期,篇名爲《等韻學之原理與内外轉之含義》)。1980 年,王力先生在山東省語言學會成立大會上的講話中,稱贊美國一位漢學家"很簡明地解決了等韻學中的内外轉問題",這位漢學家就是

*** 《古官話音系》係薛鳳生教授 Phonology of Old Mandarin(Monton,1975)重譯中文本,首次收入本文集。

薛鳳生先生。(唐作藩 1999,《漢語音韻史十講·序》)後來,王力先生又在《我的治學經驗》一文中又提及此事:"近兩年,漢藏語系學術會議,我看到美國的、法國的一些作者寄來的論文很好,很有價值。例如,關於内外轉問題,羅常培先生寫過文章,我看了不滿意。我也寫過這方面的文章,覺得也没有解决問題。兩年前看到美國漢學家的文章,我認爲他解决了問題。總之,有些好東西,用外文寫的,我們要看。"(《高教戰綫》1984 年第 8 期)。

在薛鳳生先生看來,"内外轉"是傳統音韻學理論的精髓,它體現著漢語元音音位系統的深層結構特徵。如果仔細閱讀"Phonology of Old Mandarin"(Mouton,1975)一書,我們就能深刻體會到"内外轉"在中古漢語到《中原音韻》音系結構轉變過程中的巨大影響。正如薛鳳生先生所言:"For many centuries, this tradition has not been fully understood, if not completed forgotten."(幾個世紀以來,漢語音韻學的傳統,即便没有被完全遺忘,但也没有被完全理解)。看來,"内外轉"大有深意,等待着繼續挖掘,繼續研究。

"Phonology of Old Mandarin"一書曾於 1990 年,由魯國堯、侍建國譯爲中文,名爲《〈中原音韻〉音位系統》,在北京語言學院出版社出版。這個譯本將原著中作者依據馬丁(1953)的分析給每一個例字標注的中古漢語擬音删除,换成"攝、呼、等、調、韻、聲"中古音韻地位。這一點,對全面理解原著,有一定的影響。此外,這個譯本,有一些失校和失譯的地方,影響閱讀。例如,將著名音韻學家董同龢先生的名字寫成"董同和"。此外,原著本身存在的一些校勘問題,譯本也没有指出來,如原著 89 頁 1003052"輯",當爲"轉",譯本 101 頁照舊;原著 47 頁 1204090,當爲 1254090,譯本 42 頁也照舊。這些衹有完全理解原文,認真核對英文原文和《中原音韻》的原文,才能看出來。

爲了使"Phonology of Old Mandarin"這本書的精神得到真正的領悟,爲了推進漢語等韻學的深入開展,爲了中國音韻學研究的傳統得以發揚光大,我們在得到薛陳慕勤先生的授權編纂《薛鳳生文集》之際,决定重譯這本書。本次重譯最大的目的是保持原書的全貌。

爲了方便讀者,本次重譯,我們將原著所有的注釋和作者在第一個譯本中的"追注"全都改爲脚注。根據需要,適當增加"譯注",幫助讀者增進對原著的理解。此外,原著中以"XXXXXXX"七個數字代表的同音字組,在無例字的情况下，此次重譯將直接補出《中原音韻》該同音字組的全部例字。

在翻譯過程中，參閲了趙蔭棠《中原音韻研究》，服部四郎、藤堂明保《中原音韻の研究・校本編》、訥菴本《中原音韻》、楊耐思《中原音韻音系》、李新魁《中原音韻音系研究》、寧繼福《中原音韻表稿》，以及張玉來、耿軍《中原音韻校本：附中州樂府音韻類編校本》等著作，未在参考文獻中著録，特此聲明！

薛鳳生先生於 2015 年 9 月 6 日離開了我們，"斯人已去，佳音猶存！"我們重譯 Phonology of Old Mandarin，編纂《薛鳳生文集》，緬懷薛鳳生先生。

前　言

與現代學者對漢語音韻史的大多數研究相比，這本小書代表了一種不同的方法。它采用嚴格的音位解釋，試圖用一套按特定順序排列的歷時規則來解釋一長段漢語（語音）的演變史。然而，這種方法的基本精神並不十分新穎。它没有什麽特别之處，但却有意識地努力並儘可能密切地追隨由唐宋時期"韻圖"所凸顯的中國音韻學研究傳統的那一部分。幾個世紀以來，這一傳統即便没有被完全遺忘，但也没有被完全理解。在現代音位學（Phonemics）和生成音系學（Generative phonology）理論的幫助下，我們現在有可能更好地理解並欣賞這一傳統，並且可以看到，對於漢語研究來説，它即便不完美，但仍然是理想的方法。從這個意義上説，本書再保守不過了。

我認爲歷史語言學衹有在下列情況下才顯得最有意義：理解一種語言歷史的最好方法是采用嚴格的音位理論，選擇這種語言的一些關鍵階段，然後從現代到古代一步一步地回溯。在我看來，現代北京話之前的關鍵階段似乎是以 14 世紀初周德清編纂的以《中原音韻》爲代表的早期官話。由於現代北京話已經用音位理論得到了很好的分析，我們現在有可能帶着雙重目標回溯到早期官話的研究：對那個時期的音系有一個徹底的瞭解，並爲更早時期的研究奠定堅實的基礎。

本書的基本假設是，《中原音韻》通過將衆多的漢字分成互相獨立的同音字組，從而記録了當時語言音節之間可能存在的所有音系對比。因此，利用中古漢語、韻圖和現代官話方言的知識，我們應該能够構建一個音位系統，合乎邏輯地、系統地解釋《中原音韻》中所包含的所有（音系）對比。

因爲一種方言或語言的音位結構並不能證明另一種方言或語言的音位結構，所以本書所構建的系統是嚴格基於《中原音韻》的。這意味着《中原音韻》總是作爲研究的首要材料得到重視，其他材料衹是偶爾在《中原音韻》中的一些現象不能很容易地用嚴格的規則合理地解釋時才被參考。我認爲這本書所重建的體系基本上是可靠的，不僅因爲它以邏輯的方式實際地解决了《中原音韻》中的所有難題,而且因爲它是如此的整齊對稱,以致於有可能制定出合理而經濟的規則來展示從中古漢語到早期官話,從早期官話到現代北京話的演變。

在標示這類歷史規則時,我決定使用單個的"音位"和其他類似但更大的概括性符號,而不使用區别性特徵,儘管已經相當令人信服地證明,後一種方法比前者有一定的優勢(參看 Halle 1962)。這一決定的動機主要出於兩個方面考慮。首先,我們關於中古漢語的知識還不够扎實,還不足以用(區别性)特徵來闡釋。其次,更重要的是,我希望本研究中采用的格式更容易被(所有不同背景的)學者理解,儘管我意識到這樣做可能存在不能讓任何人滿意的風險。不管怎麽説,這種"音位"方法的缺點,如果在這種特殊情况下確實存在的話,可能已經被我們對諸如"送氣""捲舌"等特徵的特殊處理大大彌補了(見 3.2.2)。總有一天,當我們對中古漢語有充分瞭解的時候,如果願意的話,用區别性特徵來改寫這些規則肯定是一件很簡單的事情。總之,我相信,使用"音位"或使用"區别性特徵"來表達真正嚴格的分析,在本質上真的没有太大的區别。

在這個關鍵時刻,可以注意到,本書的寫作,主要注意力一直集中在確定語言在歷史發展中實際發生了什麽,而不是理論性闡釋爲什麽會發生這種變化。我們經常發現,人們竭力爲某些語音變化的産生提出理論性闡釋,但後來却發現這些變化並不存在或尚未得到證明。我的意思並不是説理論解釋是不可取的,而是説衹有在事實被確立之後才能進行理論解釋。我在這裏主要關心的是儘可能用最明確的術語來確立這些事實。

自《中原音韻》成書以來的六百多年間,人們對這本書進行了大量的研究。我衹提及在某些方面對我有所幫助的一些著作。如果説,我似乎對我所引用的少數幾位作者持異乎尋常的批評態度的話,那就必須澄清,其實我對他們的作品評價很高,並從中受益。與之争論便足以爲證。

這本小書是我在印第安那大學語言學系撰寫的博士論文的修訂版,當時由豪斯侯德爾(Fred W. Householder)博士擔任指導委員會主任。我謹借此機會向豪斯侯德爾博士和委員會的所有其他成員表示衷心的感謝,感謝他們花時間閲讀我的手稿,提出了許多寶貴意見,在許多其他方面給予幫助。我還要感謝趙元任博士,他非常熱心地閱讀了書稿,並提出了一些修改意見。當然,書中任何錯誤概由我個人負責。

1972年2月

於俄亥俄州哥倫布市

縮略語列表

AC	古漢語,也稱中古漢語,以《切韻》爲代表
B	脣音聲母(參 3.2)
C	音節前的聲母輔音(參 7.2a)
CYYY	《中原音韻》
D	齒音(參 3.2)
Ds	齒呲音(參 3.2)
E	韻尾(參 3.1)
F	韻母(參 3.5.1)
Fr	擦音(參 3.2)
G	喉音聲母(參 3.2)
I	聲母(參 3.1)
L	流音(參 3.2)
M	介音(參 3.2)
N	鼻音(參 3.2)
P	腭塞音聲母(參 3.2)
Pj	腭呲音聲母(參 3.2)
Pr	捲舌音聲母(參 3.2)
R	響音(參 3.2)
S	塞音(含塞擦音)(參 3.2)
T	聲調(參 3.1)
V	韻腹(參 3.1)
V_n	内轉韻的主元音(參 3.6.2)
V_w	外轉韻的主元音(參 7.2d)
V_1	外轉一等的主元音(參 3.6.2)
V_2	外轉二等的主元音(參 3.6.2)

V_3	外轉三等的主元音(參 3.6.2)
V_4	外轉四等的主元音(參 3.6.2)
X、Y、Z	語音規則的變項

第一章 緒 論

漢語的歷史一般分爲三個主要時期,儘管各個時期的名稱都還沒有得到現代學者的同意。最早的一個時期,主要以《詩經》(公元前 6 世紀)爲代表,稱爲"上古漢語"(Archiaic Chinese)或"古漢語"(Old Chinese);第二個時期,以《切韻》(公元 601 年)爲代表,稱爲"古代漢語"(Ancient Chinese)或"中古漢語"①;第三個時期,從《中原音韻》(公元 1324 年)至今,一般稱爲"官話",儘管"新漢語"一詞似乎也可以接受。當然,這些主要時期中的每一個都還可以進一步劃分爲不同階段,例如,官話可以分爲三個階段:一是以《中原音韻》爲代表的早期官話;二是以明代某本韻書(畢拱辰《韻略匯通》似可入選)爲代表的中期官話;三是現代官話或現代北京話。筆者在這裏要做的是對早期官話的音韻作一個全新的闡釋,以便儘可能系統地展示從中古漢語到早期官話,以及從早期官話到現代北京話的發展。但在我們開始研究早期官話音韻之前,必須對漢語音韻學研究的背景做一些介紹,以便將我們的話題置於適當的歷史視角中。這就是本章的要旨。此外,我們儘量以最簡略的語言概述要做的工作的大致輪廓。

1.1 中國音韻學研究歷史悠久。第一次突破是發明了用兩個字給另一個字注音的方法。這種方法最早可追溯到公元二世紀,後人稱之爲反切,它可能是新獲得的梵語音韻學知識東傳的結果,儘管没有找到直接的證據。反切之前的注音方法就是所謂的直音和聲訓。前者是用同音字或音近字給某字注音,後者要求注音的字必須也顯示或暗示被注音字的意義②。

1.2 在反切方法中,首先是將由一個漢字代表的單音節分成"聲母"和"韻母"兩部分。然後,選擇另一個與之具有相同聲母(無論是輔音還是零聲母)的漢字,作爲反切上字,再選擇與之具有相同韻母(即音節中聲母之後的所有内

---

① 第一個術語是由高本漢(Bernhard Karlgren)首先使用的;第二個似乎越來越流行的術語是由蒲立本(E. G. ,Pulleyblank)首先使用的。

② 參張世禄(1963),第 3 章。王力(1967)第 1 章。

容)的第三個漢字,作爲反切下字。七世紀前,已經有相當多的韻書使用了這種新的注音法,但最著名的是《切韻》,這是一部由陸法言在公元 601 年編寫的具有總結性的韻書。(這本書久已失傳)我們衹能通過它後來的兩個修訂本瞭解這本書(的原貌),後來的版本略有修改,但基本上是完整的。第一個版本是唐《王仁昫刊謬補缺切韻》;第二種版本更爲人所熟知,它就是由陳彭年等人編纂的《大宋重修廣韻》。這些韻書都將漢字先按四聲分類,每個聲調下再分若干個韻。宋代的《廣韻》共 206 韻,唐代的《王仁昫刊謬補缺切韻》共 195 韻,而原書(《切韻》)則衹有 193 韻①。

1.3 下一階段的漢語音韻學研究發生了兩個重要事件。首先,確立了三十六個聲母,每一個聲母有一個固定的代表漢字;然後是創製韻圖,其中除了開口(不圓脣)和合口(圓脣)的對立外,還有四"等"之别。這些韻圖是這樣設計的,當時漢語中每一個可能的音節,都在某圖某聲調某字母某等下,有一個恰當的位置。這些韻圖尚存數種。《韻鏡》刊行於宋代,但起源於唐代,它與《切韻》的關係最近。除此之外,還有宋代的《四聲等子》《切韻指掌圖》,以及元代劉鑑的《經史正音切韻指南》。後三種韻圖進一步將包含相應的開口與合口韻母的圖分組合併,稱爲"攝"。這些韻圖與《切韻》差異較大②。雖然《切韻指南》編纂於元代,甚至比《中原音韻》還要晚,但我們可以肯定的是,《切韻指南》起源於一個更早的時期的同類韻書,可能代表十世紀左右的標準語③。下文提及韻圖時,除非另作説明,總是指這本書,尤其是李榮所校訂過的版本④⑤。

1.4 對以《切韻》爲代表的中古漢語語音,已經做了大量的工作。主要有高本漢的《中國音韻學研究》,趙元任的《中古漢語的區别》,董同龢的《中國語音史》和李榮的《切韻音系》,僅舉這幾例⑥。馬丁的《中古漢語的音位》也做出了值得稱道的努力,重建了中古漢語時期的音位系統。以上這些學者在研究

① 詳參董同龢(1954)第 4 章,第 38—44 頁,以及馬丁(Martin,1953),第 1—2 頁。

② 參董同龢(1954)第 5 章,第 67—88 頁。

③ 參董同龢(1954)第 5 章,第 67 頁。

④ 參李榮(1956)《切韻音系》,特别是"單字音表"。

⑤ [譯注]李榮(1956)《切韻音系》之"單字音表"依據的是唐《王仁昫刊謬補缺切韻》,不是《經史正音切韻指南》,原文存疑。

⑥ 此處引用的成果,見書目選録。

中古漢語的音系時，都利用宋代的韻圖作爲他們重建的框架，儘管他們也坦率地承認，這些韻圖經常顯示出它們各自時代的音韻特徵。奇怪的是，據我所知，没有人特别努力地去解釋任何一本韻圖所藴含的語音系統，即《切韻》編纂後大約四個世紀的語音系統[①]。在中古漢語音系方面，確實取得了驚人的成就，但仍有一些問題有待解决，例如：一些韻實質上没有區别開來[②]，輕脣化的具體條件，以及内外轉對立的真正含義等[③]。此外，我對馬丁所構建的音位化體系中的元音系統不太滿意，它看起來不是很整齊和對稱。所有這些都表明，在我們對中古漢語的音系有一個精確無争議的結論之前，還需要做更多的工作，但是對於《切韻》音系的研究來説，所有可以做的事情可能已經在目前的研究中完成了。然而，難道就不可能有一種新的研究方法或途徑嗎？

1.5 如果我們没有任何書面文獻爲依據，重建中古漢語音系的一種方法可能是從衆多的現代方言（或語言）開始。我們可能首先嘗試爲每個現代方言群重建一個母語，例如，從各種現代粵方言中重建古粵語。當這項工作完成後，我們可以通過從已經重建的語言重建更早時期的語言，然後再推進。不過，這是完全没有必要的，因爲我們確實有許多有價值的書面文獻——韻書和韻圖。衹要這些書保留了它們所要表現的那個時代的語言的所有必要的區别特徵，我們就可以確信，這些書中的每一本都藴含着它們各自編纂時代語言的音位結構。由此可見，在對其中某本書的共時研究中，先大略勾勒出它的音位結構，要比弄清書中每個字音值相對容易些。對於系統中音位的音值，我們所能做的就是對它在前幾個時期的來源，以及它在後來發展中的音系行爲，做出最合理的推測。當然，要建立一個某個歷史時期的音位系統，不能不參考現代的音位系統，原因很簡單，我們必須從確知的東西出發。顯然，我們要研究的時代越接近我們的所處的時代，我們就越有信心去揭示它的音位系統。因此

① 本書原稿（博士畢業論文，印第安那大學，1968 年）完成三年後，我很高興地讀到蒲立本的《晚期中古漢語》（1970 年），他在書中特别努力地重建了韻圖時期（語言）的音位系統。

② ［譯注］比如止攝"脂"韻開口，馬丁音位化爲 i*i，"之"韻衹有開口，音位化爲 i*i′，爲了與"脂"區别，衹是在"之"韻的擬音上加上一個"′"符號而已。詳見馬丁（1953）第 38 頁。馬丁這麽做的根據其實是高本漢對脂韻之韻没有區别。薛鳳生（2003）《構擬與詮釋：漢語音韻史研究的兩種對立觀點》，《語言科學》第 5 期，有詳細地分析和討論。

③ 更多的問題，請參馬丁（1953），第 37—41 頁。

我覺得,研究漢語音韻學史的另一種方法,應該是挑出一些關鍵階段,然後由今及古一步一步追溯。這並不是説,在對較後期的研究中,我們不能利用我們可能擁有的任何有關較早時期語言的知識。事實上,我們不得不這樣做。這僅僅意味着,對一個確定時期的瞭解越清晰,我們將更能準備好解決前一時期的一些問題,否則這些問題可能無法解決。從中古漢語到現代北京話,我們可能還要處理好兩個中間階段。一個大致是十世紀,即韻圖時期,以某種韻圖爲代表;另一個是十四世紀,以《中原音韻》爲代表。

1.6 當然,幫助解決較早時期的問題,衹是我們爲什麼要研究較晚時期的衆多原因之一,無論是語言學方面的還是非語言學方面的。通過研究語言音系發展的每一個重要階段,我們希望有一天我們可以填補所有的空白,從而最終對語言的發展有一個更完整、更系統的解釋。另一方面,每個時期都有它自己特有的文學,爲了理解一個時期的文學,我們當然應該儘可能地去理解它的語言。我對以《中原音韻》爲代表的早期官話的研究大致可以概括如下:

(a) 在傳統研究和現代學者研究的基礎上,勾勒出《中原音韻》的音系背景,即中古漢語音系和韻圖時期音系的輪廓。

(b) 利用我們對現代北京話和其他方言的知識,以及對中古漢語和韻圖時期的知識,對《中原音韻》進行嚴格的音位重建。這個重建的系統必須能够解釋書中所顯示的所有對比。

(c) 如果這重建的系統是正確的,那麼它必須顯示出與韻圖時期的密切關係,這樣,我們應該能够用一套規則來展示從韻圖時期到《中原音韻》的發展。由於目前没有對韻圖時期語言的音位分析可資利用,我們在寫出明確的規則時可能會遇到一些困難,但我將盡我最大的努力使用韻圖。儘管高本漢曾認爲,韻圖不過是一套代數公式①,但在我看來它們已經是一種經過高度精細結構分析的作品。

(d) 儘管有關從《中原音韻》到現代北京話這一發展階段的真正有意義的演變公式的完全確定還必須等到對現代北京話作出更精確的分析之後,我也將試着談談從《中原音韻》到現代北京話的發展。

---

① 高本漢(1948),第4頁。

第二章 《中原音韻》評介

此處應該用幾段話來介紹一下接下來要研究的這本書——《中原音韻》。不過,我不準備細説了,因爲有趙蔭棠(1936)、服部四郎和藤堂明保(1958)以及司徒修(1966)這三本關於這一主題的綜合性著作(見書目選録)可資參考。

2.1《中原音韻》字面上的意思就是中原地區的音和韻,是 1324 年由周德清編著的。當一種新的詩歌文學形式突然興起時,就需要有標準參考書,《中原音韻》就是適應這種需求而問世的。這種新的詩歌形式,是地道的通俗文學,也就是我們熟悉的元曲,它最有可能是以當時元朝首都北京(但在當時被稱爲“大都”)周圍的口語爲基礎。出於這個原因,以及其他我不必在這裏提及的原因,我們相信這本書是對當時語言的忠實記録。從中古漢語到現代普通話之間發生了一系列劇烈的變化,《中原音韻》代表期間的一個階段,既區别於中古漢語,也區别於現代普通話。因此,無論在語言學上還是其他方面,《中原音韻》都是一本非常重要的書。

2.2 這本書在結構上有獨樹之處,表現如下:

2.2.1 與早期的韻書以調統韻(先按聲調分類,然後再在每個聲調下分韻)不同,本書是以韻統調(即先分韻,然後在每韻内分聲調)。因此,《中原音韻》的“韻”與早期韻書如《切韻》的“韻”有不同的含義。粗略地説,《中原音韻》中的一個“韻”在音系上相當於《切韻》中四個相應的不同聲調“韻”;實際上,它(的範圍)往往更大,因爲《切韻》中的許多韻在《中原音韻》時代已經合併了。當然,這種新的安排反映了一個事實,元曲用韻與前代詩韻不同,聲調的不同不再是主要的因素。《中原音韻》衹有十九韻,但我們將在後面看到,其中有一韻包含的主要元音多達三個。

2.2.2 在早期的韻書中,有四種聲調,即平上去入。《中原音韻》保留了這些名稱,但做了以下改變:

(a) 每一韻内平聲一分爲二,一個被標記爲“陰”,另一個被標記爲“陽”,這兩個術語不容易翻譯,將在後面討論(見 3.5.3)。

(b) 入聲字分作三個小類，附在一韻中其他三個聲調中的任何一個聲調之後，標作“入聲作×聲”(×在這裏代表平、上或去)。附在平聲下的入聲小類被指定爲陽調類(即平聲陽)。此外，在早期的韻書和韻圖中，所謂入聲實指以/p、t、k/三個塞音之一收尾的音節，分別與以/m、n、ŋ/收尾的音節相匹配[①]，但在《中原音韻》中，這些入聲小類衹附在開口韻(即没有任何輔音韻尾的音節)之後。《中原音韻》是第一本對以前的入聲字進行這種重新分配的書，學者們直到今天都還在争論入聲音節是否失去了輔音韻尾，也即在《中原音韻》所代表語言中作爲入聲特殊一類是否失去了它的區别性特徵。這將是我努力回答的最重要的問題之一。

(c) 在它的第四韻(即齊微韻)中，在聲調小類“入調作平聲”之後，還有另一個小類叫做“去聲作平聲”。這個聲調小類衹有一個“鼻”字。人們做了很多努力來解釋它，但到目前爲止還没有取得共識[②③]。在我看來，這個獨特的小類的建立並没有告訴我們任何音系上的意義。然而，它確實提醒我們，無論周德清在編纂這本書時抱着多麽客觀的態度，他偶爾也會受到傳統音韻學的影響。

2.2.3 在每一個韻的聲調分類或聲調小類下，字音相同的字匯聚成同音字組。這些同音字組之間由一個小圓圈“○”隔開。與早期韻圖不同，這些同音字組内部没有釋義，更没有反切標示其讀音。關於這些同音字組，由於缺乏更進一步的信息，當我們試圖去解讀它們的聲母時，便出現了一些困難。不過，除了一些特殊情况外，有關以前時期和現代方言的知識都可以幫助我們解决這個問題。

2.3 這本書一直被視爲作曲時的標準參考韻書而備受重視，但直到本世

---

① 【追注】我原來遵循一般的看法，也認爲中古漢語的入聲韻尾衹有/p、t、k/三個塞音，後來看法改變了，認爲還有一個舌面塞音/k̂/的入聲韻尾，與收舌面鼻音/ɲ/的陽聲韻尾相配，詳細的説明請參閲薛鳳生(1985)。

② 參陸志韋(1946)，第59頁；趙遐秋、曾慶瑞(1962)，第324頁。

③ [譯注]陸志韋、楊耐思(1987)《訥菴本〈中原音韻〉校勘記》云：“‘去聲作平聲’收‘鼻’字，瞿本、嘯本並同。全書去聲作平聲陽衹此一例。案玄應《一切經音義》‘鼻’與‘毗(毘)’每互用。例如‘阿鼻至或言阿毗至’(見《阿毗達磨俱舍論》)，‘阿毘達磨或言阿鼻達磨’(見《阿毗曇婆沙論》)，‘毗舍或云鼻奢’(見《立世阿毗曇論》)。佛經‘鼻’字此等處本作平聲讀，周氏不必開此一例。”[譯者案]這一點，在傳統韻書中没有記録，周德清想必也未見到。

紀二十年代,學者們才開始意識到它在語言學上巨大的價值。從那時起,出版了大量的研究著作,本人由此獲益良多,但仍需繼續努力研究。在衆多研究《中原音韻》的著作中,以下幾種似乎更爲重要,因此有必要略作評論①。

(a) 石山福治(Ishiyama Fukuji):《考定中原音韻》(Kōtei chūgen on'in)(東京,1925)。這本書第一次嘗試從現代語言學的角度全面研究《中原音韻》。作者給所有的同音字組都構擬了音值,但和所有先驅者一樣,他在這方面的努力並不是很成功,還有很多地方需要改進。因此,這本書被後來的著作超越。

(b) 趙蔭棠:《中原音韻研究》(上海,1936)。本書分兩部分。第一部分對《中原音韻》的歷史背景以及後來與之相關的其他韻書作了很好的闡述。第二部分包含了對原文的重印和兩章關於音韻變化的討論,這些討論衹是一些印象式的觀察。不過,該書對原文的重印還是很好的。趙蔭棠没有像原文那樣用一個圈“○”來分隔同音同音字組,而是在每韻内對它們進行編號。趙蔭棠也給每個同音字組作了一個語音標注,雖然(較石山福治的擬音)更具一貫性”②,但遠不能令人滿意。舉一個例子,爲了維護每個聲調内的同音字組必須彼此有别的基本原則,他有時會隨意添加新的聲母,有時甚至連這個原則也不能遵守③。

(c) 陸志韋:《釋中原音韻》(《燕京學報》1946 年第 31 期,第 35—70 頁)。在我看來,這篇文章可能是所有關於《中原音韻》的著作中最令人鼓舞的。整個論述都是在舊式的語音框架内進行的,但作者的論述非常一致,提出了一些有趣的觀點,雖然不一定正確。在後面關於《中原音韻》的討論中,我將引用這篇文章並反駁其中的一些觀點。如果我對他的批評顯得過於頻繁的話,那恰恰應該作爲證據證明我對他的研究有很高的評價。

(d) 服部四郎(Hattari Shirō)和藤堂明保(Tōdō Akiyasu)《中原音韻的研

---

① 【追注】近年來國内的學者對《中原音韻》作了許多認真與細緻的研究,提供了許多珍貴的資料,真是可喜的現象,比較突出的有,楊耐思(1981)《中原音韻音系》,李新魁(1983)《〈中原音韻〉音系研究》,寧繼福(1985)《中原音韻表稿》等。邵榮芬(1981)《中原雅音研究》亦與此有關。這些均極有參考價值,可與本書參照閱讀。

② 參司徒修(1966)第 10 頁。

③ 例如,爲了蕭豪韻,趙蔭棠(1936)特别在[k、k‘、ŋ、x]外新增四個舌面中音聲母[c、c‘、ȵ、ç];在庚青韻,如法施之於第 10 個和第 27 個同音字組。

究》(Chūgen on'in no Kenkyū)(東京,1958)。這本書對《中原音韻》的文本進行了非常細緻的校勘,因此對於考察其中許多有疑問的細節是非常可靠的。它從頭到尾對所有的同音字組進行了編號,没有考慮到每個韻之間的區别。

(e) 司徒修:《〈中原音韻〉的音系》,《清華學報》(臺北),1962年,新3卷,第1期,第114—158頁。這篇論文是作者長篇博士學位論文的第二部分,但對我們來説最爲重要,因爲它直接研究《中原音韻》。這篇文章的意義在於它首次嘗試構建《中原音韻》的音位系統,但很遺憾,作者以(我前面所提及的)趙蔭棠對《中原音韻》的語音構擬爲基礎進行音位化,這是不可能有好的結果的。司徒修曾指出"趙氏書中存在數量驚人的音標印刷錯誤",但與趙蔭棠擬音的前後不一致相比,這衹能算是一個小缺點。因此趙蔭棠《中原音韻研究》根本不能作爲"音位分析的邏輯起點"[①]。爲了達到(音位分析)這個目的,我們必須回到(《中原音韻》)原文本身。

(f) 司徒修:《中原音韻》(紐黑文,1966)。這本書有一個很長的緒論,其中處理《中原音韻》的部分,雖然在符號上做了一些修改,但本質上是對上述這篇文章的總結。本書的主體部分是在服部四郎和藤堂明保校勘的基礎上,對《中原音韻》所收録的字進行重新排列和重新編號,並附有中古漢語、早期官話(即《中原音韻》)和現代北京話的標音。

2.4 陸志韋在他那篇著名的文章的開頭,不加解釋地斷言,周德清編纂《中原音韻》的方法是"純粹的歸納法",他衹是簡單地將他那個時代的元曲韻字收集在一起,並將它們分爲十九個韻,他的"老師"不是他面前的韻書和韻圖,而是他在書中提到的那個時代的著名劇作家[②]。後來他説,在他討論《中原音韻》時,他不會提到韻圖,因爲"實際上,在討論語音發展時,直接將周書與《廣韻》聯繫起來要方便得多"[③]。奇怪的是,這種處理方式幾乎被後來所有研究《中原音韻》的現代學者所接受,至少據我所知,無人反駁過。接下來,我將證明這是錯誤的,更重要的是,我將展示韻圖時期(語言)與《中原音韻》之間的密切關係。這一點被忽視,或許可以解釋爲什麽付出了如此巨大的努力,但在

---

① 參司徒修(1962a)第115頁。

② 陸志韋(1946),第35頁。

③ 陸志韋(1946),第36頁。

《中原音韻》研究這個課題上仍然没有得出差强人意的結論。

2.4.1《中原音韻》共收 5876 個字①。儘管坦率地説,我在這方面没有做過任何統計,但在我看來,如果説其中每一個字都曾被周德清之前的某位劇作家用作韻脚字,這似乎令人難以置信。再者,作爲韻書,如果它的收字衹局限於以前用過的,那麼它的使用價值必然降低,周德清當然知道這一點。趙蔭棠也説周德清這本書是"他從前輩戲劇作品中歸納出來的",但他補充説周書"歸併《廣韻》,改革《廣韻》"。我不知道趙蔭棠的話到底是什麼意思,但如果他的意思是周德清在編寫《中原音韻》時將《廣韻》作爲重要的參考,那他當然是對的。

2.4.2 如果説周德清僅僅通過從他之前的劇作家的作品中收集韻字並加以分類而寫出了這本書,那就既譽之過甚,又貶之過甚了。(一方面)如果我們説他分析了之前所有作品的用韻情况,這就是譽之過甚,因爲這項工作直到今天也没有完全完成。另一方面,如果我們説(或暗示)他過於謹慎,以至於他甚至不敢在韻書中添加幾個字,而這些字他確有把握可以放在某一韻中,這就是貶之過甚。可以肯定的是,周德清一定特别重視前輩作家的用韻習慣。畢竟,這些作家都是用周德清所記録的語言來創作的,這當然給他的著作帶來聲望,但他也一定足够大膽,超越了這個範圍,利用自己所掌握的有關這種語言的知識,使之規則化。對陸志韋和趙蔭棠之説,至少有一個反證:周德清最推崇的劇作家關漢卿作品的用韻已被分析過了,其中有好些韻字,依照《中原音韻》的標準來看都是例外②。

2.4.3《中原音韻》與《廣韻》韻目順序之間的對應關係非常明顯,不容忽視,但這一點却偏偏一直被忽視。由於《廣韻》的韻後來被進一步歸併爲十六個大類,稱爲"攝",《中原音韻》中使用的術語"韻"與韻圖中的"攝"大致相當,

---

① [譯注]《中原音韻》各版本收字不同。作者認爲《中原音韻》收字 5876 個字,乃據趙蔭棠説。寧繼福(1985)《中原音韻表稿》指出訥菴本《中原音韻》收字 5866 個,《中原音韻表稿》單字音表共收單字 5869 個字,其中比訥菴本多出的 3 個字乃據其他版本增補。張玉來、耿軍(2013)《中原音韻校本(附中州樂府音韻類編校本)》認爲《中原音韻》共 1627 個同音字組,5867 個單字。司徒修(1966)《中原音韻》共收單字 5865 個。服部四郎、藤堂明保(1958)認爲《中原音韻》共 1626 個同音字組。

② 參廖珣英(1963)。

順便以如下這種方式顯示其對應關係：

韻圖的“攝”	《中原音韻》的“韻”
(1) 通	(1) 東鍾
(2) 江	(2) 江陽
(3) 止	(3) 支思
	(4) 齊微
(4) 遇	(5) 魚模
(5) 蟹	(6) 皆來
(6) 臻	(7) 真文
(7) 山	(8) 寒山
	(9) 桓歡
	(10) 先天
(8) 效	(11) 蕭豪
(9) 果	(12) 歌戈
(10) 假	(13) 家麻
	(14) 車遮
(11) 宕……	(2) 江陽
(12) 梗 (13) 曾	(15) 庚青
(14) 流	(16) 尤侯
(15) 深	(17) 侵尋
(16) 咸	(18) 監咸
	(19) 廉纖

這種對應關係在以下幾個方面當然不是完全整齊的：

(a) 宕攝和江攝完全合併，它們一起在《中原音韻》中形成了江陽韻。梗攝和曾攝也是如此(合併爲庚青韻)。還有其他一些較小的重組。

(b) 入聲字完全從其之前所屬的韻攝中分離出來，在陰聲韻(不帶鼻音韻尾的韻)中重新分配。

(c) 應該記住，在韻圖中一個韻攝所包含的“等”可能多達四個，而在《中原音韻》的一個韻内没有等的區别。事實上，一些韻攝分爲兩個或更多的韻正是等的差異所導致的不同演變，我們將在後面討論(見 5.6)。

除非《廣韻》的韻目次序有某種内在的價值，否則我們必須承認周德清這樣做衹是遵循了傳統。陸志韋顯然不相信這種(韻目)次序會有任何内在的價值，因爲他在文章中重新排列了韻目，司徒修也是如此。有人可能會説，周德清不僅遵循了《廣韻》，而且還遵循了某些韻圖，儘管没有直接的證據(證明這一點)。《中原音韻》和《廣韻》之間的對應關係已經足以證明周德清在很大程度上對過去的音韻研究頗爲倚重。

2.5 通過證明周德清不僅僅收集前輩劇作家的韻字並進行歸類，而且在很大程度上依賴於他自己的語言知識以及過去的音韻研究成果。我的意思是説,周德清作爲一個音韻學家,他的高明遠超迄今爲止所獲得的贊譽。另一件事在《中原音韻》研究者的心目中常常被無形地不必要的誇大,即周德清出生在南方而不是北京。事實上,它已經被用作一種解圍的手段。每當學者們對《中原音韻》一書中一些看似莫名其妙的特點感到沮喪時,他們就會指責周德清把他的方音摻入到書中。[①] 這個指責在我看來,即使不是毫無根據,也是相當不合理的。雖然周德清不是出生在北方,但我們不能從邏輯上否認,實際上我們必須假設,他非常瞭解他那個時代的標準語。此外,周德清編寫這本書的唯一目的是教人們如何正確押韻,他的書後來在這方面一直被視爲標準。我們很難想象他對這種語言不够瞭解,因此在書中犯了許多錯誤。作爲一個合乎邏輯的起點,我們將假設,從《中原音韻》全書所論來看,周德清是正確的。但這並不意味着,就像我們現在看到的那樣,周德清或他的書是絶對無誤的。這僅意味着我們必須從這個假設開始。也許研究到最後,當我們從他的書中得到强有力的内部證據來支持這些指責時,我們可以聲稱,在一些罕見的和次要的情況下,周德清有失誤的地方。

2.6 陸志韋曾批評另一位學者不符合邏輯,因爲這個學者試圖引用《中原音韻》成書四百年後寫的一本書,來證明《中原音韻》没有入聲[②]。我認爲這個原則必須進一步加以運用。在假設《中原音韻》確實忠實地反映了當時的語言之後,我將把我的分析限制在這本書本身的範圍内。我的意思是我將盡力解釋《中原音韻》中所有的語音現象,即使另外一些文獻,如被認爲表現了與《中原音韻》相同語言的卓從之《中州樂府音韻類編》和八思巴字文獻等,在某些方面似乎"更爲合理"。《中原音韻》本身始終將得到優先考慮,衹有當其中的某些現象不能用正常的理論解釋時,才使用其他材料。我希望,通過大力運用這一原則,我們最終得出的音韻結構將可以回答那些對我們來説有争議的難題,例如《中原音韻》中是否還有入聲,《中原音韻》是否代表現代北京話的早期階段,等等。

2.7 對一種現存語言進行音位分析,一般的方法是從對該語言的記音開

① 例如趙蔭棠(1936),第 2 頁,陸志韋(1946),第 55 頁。

② 陸志韋(1946)第 57 頁。

始。實際上,儘管有少數學者試圖對《中原音韻》進行精細的音位分析,但絕大多數學者都遵循上述程序,試圖利用在現代方言和其他韻書中發現的證據對《中原音韻》進行準語音性重建。我的方法有些不同(見 1.5)。我覺得在我們的研究中,這個程序的步驟必須顛倒過來。我們必須首先設法勾勒出一個大致的音位系統,然後再推論出其音值,或相當抽象的音位的音值。原因是,正如我前面所説的,這本書通過展示全書十九韻中所有被證實的對立音節(即同音字組),從而爲我們提供了關於它所代表的音位系統的所有必要綫索,儘管對它的實際讀音没有做任何説明①。在接下來的章節中,當我重建這本書的音位系統時,將大致依次采取以下步驟:

(a) 在對該書進行全面考察之後,建立一個嘗試性的假設系統。

(b) 修改和改進這個假設的系統,以便使它可以保持大多數同音字組之間的對立,最理想的結果是能保持全部同音字組之間的對立。

(c) 從結構上理順這個假設的系統。

(d) 努力通過一切手段,從所有已知的事實出發,推斷出這個系統中音位的變體。

當然,這些步驟彼此之間並不是涇渭分明,而是相互交織的。比如,在建立第一步的假設系統時,我們對後面步驟的瞭解一定會有意無意地影響到我們,但從邏輯上講,如果我們需要某種順序,它應該是類似於上述的東西。當然,在下面的討論中所寫下的,並不是我所經歷的所有麻煩,而是無數次嘗試和失敗的結果。

2.8《中原音韻》(的韻譜)已經過多次徹底編號。趙蔭棠將每個韻内的同音字組依次編號,不注意顯示聲調的不同。服部四郎和藤堂明保對全書(同音字組)進行了自始至終的編號,甚至没有考慮到韻的界限問題。司徒修的做法與上述不同,他將《中原音韻》韻譜中的每個字依次編號,不涉及同音字組的編

① 司徒修(1962a)稱他的工作是試圖把音位分析的方法運用到《中原音韻》所提供的有關語音事實的衆多綫索中去(第 114 頁),後來在該文的第二個附注中(第 155 頁),他説:"《中原音韻》提供的材料充其量不過是綫索而已。"在這一點上,我不同意他的觀點。對我來説,所有韻書(不僅《中原音韻》)在語音上没有告訴我們任何東西,它們僅僅展示了一個潛在的音位系統的"代數"結構。

號。我實在不願意再給《中原音韻》韻譜進行一次數字編號,但爲了快速引用,也爲了在討論問題時省去每提及一個特定的字或同音字組必提及其所在的韻與調的煩瑣,我爲每一個同音字組都設置了一個檢索編號。在我的系統中,每一個編號將由 7 個數組成,按以下方式理解:

(a) 前兩位數表示《中原音韻》的"韻"。例如,像 03×××××這個編號,表示它所代表的同音字組屬於第三韻,即"支思韻"。15×××××這個編號,表示它所代表的同音字組屬於第十五韻,即"庚青韻"。

(b) 其後的兩位數代表聲調類别:01 爲平聲陰,02 爲平聲陽,03 爲上聲,04 爲去聲。當聲調小類是"入聲作某聲"之一時,5 將占據零的位置。例如,53 表示"入聲作上聲"。"去聲作平聲陽"這一獨特的聲調組,雖然它的意義不大,也可以用 42 來表示。

(c) 末三位數字是趙蔭棠給某韻中的一個同音字組的編號。例如,0101001 表示第一韻(即東鍾韻)中第一個同音字組,包含"東""冬"兩個字。1654087 即第十六韻(尤侯韻)裹"入聲作去聲"的第 87 個同音字組,衹包含一個"六"字。

如果趙蔭棠給每個調類中的同音字組分開編號的話,我們這個檢索編號衹需要 6 位數就够了,但由於他没有做,我們不得不多用一個數字。這是由於趙書比較容易見到,而又没有新的版本出現的緣故。

第三章 《中原音韻》的音系背景

在本章中，我們將爲將來討論《中原音韻》奠定必要的基礎。我們將首先簡要地討論漢語的音節結構，然後儘量簡明扼要地給出中古漢語的聲母系統和聲調系統。由於某些原因（稍後討論），將給出韻圖的韻母系統，而不是中古漢語（《切韻》）的韻母系統。然而，從較早時期到《中原音韻》的聲母和韻母的變化，這裏將不討論，因爲這個問題比較複雜，需要設專章討論；但由於涉及聲調、介音、韻尾的變化相對簡單，所以就在這裏解決。

3.1 漢語音節模式

馬丁（Samuel E. Martin）在其《中古漢語的音位》一文中將高本漢對中古漢語音節的解釋概括如下：

$$\frac{\mathrm{T}}{(\mathrm{C})(\mathrm{V})(\mathrm{V})\mathrm{V}(\mathrm{V},\mathrm{C})}$$

後來他用音位術語將這種模式重新解釋爲如下形式，他説這種形式“更與普通話和其他現代方言相符”[①]：

$$\frac{\mathrm{T}}{(\mathrm{C})(\mathrm{SV})(\mathrm{SV})\mathrm{V}(\mathrm{C},\mathrm{SV})} \quad \text{即} \quad \frac{1,2,3,4}{(\mathrm{C})(\mathrm{y})(\mathrm{w})\mathrm{V}(\mathrm{C},\mathrm{y},\mathrm{w})}$$

中古漢語和所有現代方言都有相同的音節形式，這一事實迫使我們相信，《中原音韻》所代表的語言的音節結構也是如此，因爲不可能想象它會是其他什麽

① 馬丁（1953：20—23）。這種對音節結構的解釋基本上遵循了對漢語的傳統分析方法，其中一個音節分爲“聲母”和“聲母”，後者進一步將韻母分爲三個部分，“介音”（或“韻頭”），“韻腹”和“韻尾”。將撮口介音（即 ü）解釋爲/yw/這兩個成分的複合體，在某種程度上説，是一項現代的發明（哈特門 1944：118），但從區別性特徵角度看，這種解釋似乎並不像以前想象的那麽重要了。甚至這兩個成分的順序，在“音位”表述上雖至關重要，但在“特徵”表述上就變得無關緊要了。參袁家驊（1960）和薛鳳生（1973）等論著。

樣子。因此,我假設《中原音韻》中的每個同音字組都代表一個符合上述公式的單音節模式,(這一點)無需努力證明便可以肯定。值得注意的是,在中古漢語和各種現代方言中,出現在韻腹前和韻腹後的半元音(SV)在音位上都可以解釋爲/y/和/w/。從這個意義上説,它們在公式中可以看作"常數",而 C、V 和 T,在不同程度上都是"變數"。傳統上,一個音節首先被分析成兩部分:聲母(公式中由輔音表示),韻母(包括聲調在内的音節其餘部分)。然後,除了聲調之外,韻母進一步分析爲三個部分,即"介音"(由兩個半元音音中的一個或兩個代表,/y/總是在/w/之前)、"韻腹"(由元音代表,是上述公式中所有音段音位成分中必不可少的成分)、"韻尾"(可以是一個半元音或輔音)。我將按照這樣的分析討論這些成分。

$$I\,\frac{T}{(M)V(E)}$$

3.2 中古漢語的聲母系統

中古漢語中有 36 個聲母(包括零聲母在内)。如下表所示[①]:

	塞音 S			擦音 Fr		響音 R	
脣　音　B	p	ph	pɦ			m	
齒　音　D	t	th	tɦ			n	l
齒咝音　Ds	c	ch	cɦ	s	sɦ		
腭塞音　P	tj	tjh	tjɦ				
腭捲舌音 Pr	cr	crh	crɦ	sr	srɦ		
腭咝音　Pj	cj	cjh	cjɦ	sj	sjɦ	nj	
喉　音　G	k	kh	kɦ	x	xɦ	ŋ	
	q						ø

① 我在表中使用"喉音",而不使用常用的"舌根音"。這樣選擇可能有語音上的理由。如果考慮到當代的研究著作的話,唯一可靠的理由應該是高本漢首次使用這個術語,後來被趙元任接受,於是它就成爲漢語研究傳統的一部分。此外,我也追隨趙元任先生,在這裏使用"咝音"這個術語。(趙元任 1948:19)

3.2.1 在上表中，我用“S”標記了塞音和塞擦音，因爲我覺得它們的區別基本上是語音上的，而在音位上，這兩種類型的輔音與/h/或/ɦ/結合時表現出相同的方式。這個表本質上是馬丁音位化的結果，而馬丁的音位化是以高本漢的構擬和趙元任的修正爲基礎的[1]。不過，我在這裏做了一些修改，可以馬上討論(爲什麽這麽修改)。進行這些修改可能有一些語音上的原因，但我更願意説，進行這些修改的唯一理由是，它們將使我們能够以更普遍和更經濟的方式解釋從中古漢語到《中原音韻》的發展。

(a) 我用/x/代替了/h/，並在/ɦ/之前加上/x/。這一修改使得這兩個聲母在各自出現的列中與其他聲母更加一致。除了從語音上看，中古漢語中的這兩個聲母可能是舌根擦音，而不是喉擦音之外，這樣修改的令人信服的原因是，我們現在可以把/h/當作一個純粹送氣符號，把/ɦ/看作一個濁音符號。這將允許我們在解釋濁音清化的過程時簡單地説，/ɦ/消失了，而不必再尷尬地説，當/ɦ/本身作爲一個聲母時，它變成了/h/，在其他情況下消失了。必須立即補充的是，這種處理方式出於歷時研究的考慮。至於對共時的描述來説，/x/當然可以省略[2]。

(b) 喉塞音/q/現在在不送氣清塞音一列中獨占一格。當我們想要解釋聲調的變化時，這是必要的，因爲/q/的表現與這一列中其他聲母一樣(見3.5.2)。僅僅爲這個聲母添加新的横行似乎不是很好，但如果不這樣的話，我們就必須得像馬丁那樣再添加一新的縱列。

(c) 高本漢的聲母[ńź]看起來確實很獨特。馬丁將其重新解釋爲/nɦ/，這在我看來仍然很奇怪，因爲/n/是唯一可以與/ɦ/組合的響音。如果純粹爲了歷時研究的話，用/nj/來表示這個聲母會更好，其優越性在後面的討論中會變得明顯(見4.5.4)。這一點得到了李榮分析的支持，他使用[ń]來表示這個

---

① 馬丁(1953)第17—18頁。

② 【追注】現在看來，這一申明有些過於謹慎，理論上亦無必要。當時我過於執著，把每一個符號都看作一個音位，才覺得有必要如此聲明。後來我的看法改變了，我覺得聲母表中的“h、ɦ、r、j”等都不是音位，而是代表區別性特徵的符號，因此本節所討論的修正就更有道理了。

聲母,即某種形式的腭化鼻音①。如果我們足够大膽,我們可以簡單地使用/j/單獨來代表這個聲母,因爲我覺得這個聲母的本質特徵是腭化,雖然它可能帶有鼻化色彩,但這將迫使我們説/j/是一個濁音聲母,這顯然與其他事實相悖。這樣的話,我將接受/nj/這個表示法,儘管我對它仍然不太滿意。

(d) 根據董同龢的分析,我在圖表中添加了/srɦ/。必須承認,這個聲母在中古漢語裏是微不足道的,後來的發展使它變得更加没有意義(見 4.5—4.5.3),但它在中古漢語中存在的事實要求我們把它列在表内。它的存在,也使整張表看起來有對稱感。

(e) 我把馬丁的/ng/换成了/ŋ/。這純粹是一個書寫問題,但/ŋ/似乎更符合我的目的。

3.2.2 上表可以進一步簡化爲單輔音音位表,如下所示:

	喉音 G	脣音 B	齒音 D	齒咝音 Ds	喉音 G	
非響音	塞音 S	p	t	c	k	q
	擦音 Fr			s	x	
響音	鼻音 N	m	n		ŋ	
	流音 L		l			
						(j)、(r)、(h)、(ɦ)

在這些單輔音音位中,帶括弧的四個與其他完全不同。嚴格地説,它們不是普通意義上的音位,而是四組區别性特徵(或四組生成要素),每一組都涉及一些特殊類型的音位。它們的特徵可以用以下方式來定義:

/j/:腭化,與齒塞音、咝音和鼻音伴生。

/r/:捲舌,與齒咝音伴生。

/h/:送氣,與除/q/之外的塞音伴生。

---

① 李榮(1956),第 125—126 頁。實際上馬伯樂首先提議用[ñ](=[ń])表示日母(H·馬伯樂《唐代長安方音》,河内《遠東法文學報》BEFFO,1920 年第 20 期,第 34 頁)這個主張後來遭到高本漢的反駁,高本漢以[ńź]代之(高本漢 1954,230)。李榮仔細地研究了唐代以前梵語音節"ña"的漢字對音,發現公元 742 年以前,總是用日母字來譯"ña",此後便改用泥母[n]的字。最後李榮確認了馬伯樂的主張,並且得出結論:公元 771 年以前,這個聲母始終保存着鼻音性質。

/ɦ/：濁化，與除/q/之外的非響音伴生。

不過，在後面的討論中，我權且把它們當作真正的音位來對待。

3.2.3　3.2所列出的36個聲母與韻圖的36個聲母是不相同的。雖然我們對後者的瞭解還不够，但以下幾點似乎是清楚的：

(a) 脣音分裂爲兩個系列，重脣音和輕脣音，儘管這種分裂在本質上可能是同位音(即音位變體)。

(b) 中古漢語的兩組腭輔音(Pr和Pj)在韻圖中由一組字母表示①。這可能意味着中古漢語中這對立的兩組聲母已經成爲一組音位的兩組變體，儘管在進一步分析之前我們不能確定。

(c) 喉濁擦音/xɦ/在三等韻母前消失了，儘管一、二、四等韻母前還保存着。

理想情況下，如果我們有一張韻圖時期(語言)的聲母表的話，我們應以此爲起點。然而，中古漢語和韻圖時期(語言)的聲母系統似乎没有太大的差別，因此從中古漢語的聲母系統開始解釋《中原音韻》的聲母系統可能不是一個行不通的主張。

3.3　介音

我説過，在漢語的音節結構中，介音位置的/y/和/w/這兩個半元音，在歷史意義上可以算是"常數"。我這樣説，並不意味着，在漢語音節的介音位置上，可以是/y/或/w/或/yw/，也可以是零形式，但總保持相同的狀態。事實上，很多音節的介音已經系統地改變了，但這種變化僅限於失去了原有的介音/y/或/w/，或者在某些情況下增生了介音/y/或/w/。因此，能出現在介音位置上的僅限於這兩個半元音。由於中古漢語的/j/在《中原音韻》前就丢失了(見4.5)，因此《中原音韻》中的介音/y/和/w/分别可以解釋爲腭化或脣化的符號。它們的出現或消失必然與聲母和主元音位移變化密切相關，因此與這些變化一起討論最爲有效。

① 韻圖中用"照穿牀審禪"五個字母代表的五個聲母，既與二等也與三等韻母相拼。中古漢語的研究者發現，必須把它們分爲兩組："章昌船書常"，衹和三等韻母相拼，即我們體系中的腭噝音；"莊初崇生俟"，主要和二等韻母相拼，但是也和三等相拼，即這裏的腭捲舌音。

3.4 韻尾

韻尾的庫藏比較大(也就是説可以出現在韻尾位置上的音位數量比較多)。除了兩個半元音和三個鼻音/m、n、ŋ/外,/p、t、k/這三個塞音也能出現在中古漢語的韻尾位置上。傳統上,以塞音結尾的音節被看作一個獨立的調類,叫做入聲。我們不知道爲什麽會這樣,我想這種做法可能很好地表明,這個位置上的每個塞音實際上都是以非除阻形式出現的。這種非除阻的語音形式對整個音節來説都是一種抑制,從而使得這類整個音節與其他類型的音節相比,聽起來相當突兀。然而,這一觀點儘管聽起來可能很合理,但很難證明。處於韻尾位置上的與處於介音位置上的/y/和/w/,在語音上是不同的,因爲當它們處在韻尾位置上時,要比處在介音上時,對整個音節的影響更大。帶有不同韻尾的音節總是形成不同的韻,而帶有不同介音的音節却可以劃歸同一個韻,這一事實可以作爲佐證。無論這種差異是什麽,它都是如此微妙,難以證明。由於中古漢語中所謂的入聲在《中原音韻》中已經分裂爲三個聲調小類,所以在《中原音韻》中是否還存在入聲,换句話説,就是/p、t、k/或者一個新的音,比如喉塞音,是否還可以出現在韻尾位置,一直是個聚訟的話題。這是一個非常關鍵和非常複雜的問題,我們將設專章討論(見第六章)。在《中原音韻》中,半元音和鼻音顯然仍然出現在那個位置,衹是有一個小小的變化,可以用下面的公式明確地表達出來①:

$$B+X+m \rightarrow B+X+n \tag{1}$$

這意味着,由於異化作用,在《中原音韻》前,在帶有脣音聲母的音節中,韻

① 在書寫這樣的規則時,我采用了現代生成語法學的標寫方式,特别是按照庫蘇達氏(Koutsoudas1966:1—39)所規定的那樣,至於我所做的少數修改,可參7.1。雖然我的研究方法受到現代語言科學最新理論的重大影響,但我並不認爲我這本書是嚴格意義上的生成語言學式的。我使用這些表達法則,衹是因爲我感到它們爲我們提供了一個準確而簡明的手段,去表達我們想要説的東西。這些轉寫規則的使用範圍限於"音節",换言之,這些規則的"起首式"(initial string)是#音節#,雖然我們在這裏並未言明。

尾/m/變成了/n/[①]。因此,這些音節現在出現在韻尾爲/n/的韻中,例如,0703074"品"(中古:深開三上寢滂 AC /ᶜ phiəm/, MP /phyěn/),1003053"貶"(中古:咸開三上琰幫 AC /ᶜ piɛm/, MP /pyǎn/),0802026"凡"(中古:咸合三平凡並 AC /꜀ pɦiuam/, MP /fwán/)和 0804067"泛"(中古:咸合三去梵滂 AC /phiuamᵓ/, MP /fwàn/)[②③]。

3.5 聲調

在我們繼續討論《中原音韻》的聲母系統之前,最好先處理一下從中古漢語到《中原音韻》的聲調變化,因爲這些變化完全受中古漢語聲母系統的制約。從中古漢語到《中原音韻》,聲母系統明顯發生了濁音清化,並伴隨着調位的分裂和重組過程。不是没有理由去假設中古漢語中的某些調位可能有兩個或更多的變體。這些調位變體都出現在帶有一定類型的聲母的音節中,呈互補分布狀態。比如,我們可以説平聲有兩個調位變體:一個是高調域變體,衹出現在以濁聲母起首的音節中;另一個是低調域變體,出現在其他音節中[④]。衹要

① 用這樣嚴格的方式指出這種變化,陸志韋似爲第一人(見陸志韋 1946:39)。

② 從現在起,我將給每一個漢字注出中古漢語讀音和現代北京音。中古漢語讀音基本上取自馬丁的音位化標音(馬丁 1953,18 和 38),但在聲母系統裏有若干小的修正,已在 3.2 討論過。在每一個中古漢語標音的某個角落上有一個小半圓,這是此標音所代表的漢字所屬的聲調類别的符號,因爲在傳統上就是如此標記的(即꜀□,在左下角表示平聲;ᶜ□,在左上角表示上聲;□ᵓ,在右上角表示去聲。入聲已經由韻尾塞音標示出來了)。現代北京音以我自己對哈特門(1944)和霍凱特(1947)的修正方案爲依據,7.5.1—7.5.3 將作概略介紹,也請參看第四章的注釋 4。

③ [譯注]薛鳳生(1999)《中原音韻音位系統》第 29 頁"譯注 1"曾提到"著者校閲時考慮到,馬丁的漢語中古音的音位化標音國内知之者不多,建議采用丁聲樹編録、李榮参訂的《古今字音對照手册》的辦法,爲中古音依次注出'攝、呼、等、調、韻、聲'六者。譯者據《手册》注出中古音,但將其'非敷奉微'改爲'幫滂並明'。《手册》未收的字則查檢《廣韻》,據反切注音。與《手册》不同者或依據《集韻》者特别加注説明。括弧内的'現代'指現代北京音。"爲保持薛鳳生英文原著内容的完整性,此次翻譯將在忠實於原文的基礎上,爲其中例字增加中古音"攝、呼、等、調、韻、聲"標注。標注格式爲:"品"(中古:深開三上寢滂 AC /ᶜ phiəm/, MP /phyěn/)其中,AC 爲馬丁音位化標音,MP 爲現代北京音。

④ [譯注]一般來説,在現代漢語方言中,高調位與清聲母伴隨,而低調位與濁聲母伴隨,也即"陰高陽低",但這不是絶對的。

維持聲母系統中濁音與清音的對比，調位變體的差異就衹能算是羨餘特徵，不過一旦濁音清化過程完成，以前被掩蓋的調位差異就會凸顯並代替音節中聲母的清濁對比差異，進而成爲一個區別性特徵。然而，這一點幾乎是無法證明的，因爲前代的調值大概是最難確定的①。在音位上，我們衹能説聲母清/濁對立所負載的部分功能被聲調的對立所取代。但是，爲了給音韻變化做形式上的説明，我們可以聲稱上述假設是正確的，即認爲中古漢語聲調的分裂和重組不與聲母濁音清化的過程同步，而是早於濁音清化的過程。

3.5.1 按照一個音節的聲調總是由反切下字決定的傳統辦法，我選擇將聲調解釋爲韻的一部分，儘管有人説，從語音上講，聲調覆蓋至音節的濁音起首部分，也即，當聲母是濁音時，聲調從聲母開始（覆蓋整個音節）②。因此，我用 F 表示韻母，以上標的形式表示調位，如 F^t。這樣，我們可以用公式來表述中古漢語到《中原音韻》的聲調變化：

$$F^{平} \rightarrow \begin{Bmatrix} F^{02} / \begin{Bmatrix} ɦ \\ R \end{Bmatrix}\_\_\_ \\ F^{01} \end{Bmatrix} \tag{2}$$

$$F^{上} \rightarrow \begin{Bmatrix} F^{04} / ɦ\_\_\_ \\ F^{03} \end{Bmatrix} \tag{3}$$

$$F^{去} \rightarrow F^{04} \tag{4}$$

$$F^{入} \rightarrow \begin{Bmatrix} F^{52} / ɦ\_\_\_ \\ F^{54} / R\_\_\_ \\ F^{53} \end{Bmatrix} \tag{5}$$

3.5.2 前三個公式無需進一步解釋，因爲同樣的過程在現代北京話中也發生了。一些非常罕見的不規則字，如 1201014"麽"（中古：果合一平戈明 AC /꜀ muɑ/，MP /mwé/）③可以簡單地視爲例外。不過入聲調的變化，則需要仔細研究。《中原音韻》的作者明確地告訴我們，中古漢語的入聲調被分成

① 參見馬丁(1953:10—11)。陸法言生動地描述了聲調的這種不定的和相對的特點，其《切韻序》云："秦隴則去聲爲入，梁益則平聲似去。"

② 參見趙元任(1968:25)。我把聲調視作覆蓋整個"韻母"，顯得過於拘謹。一個更簡單的變通辦法或許是説，它僅與主元音關聯（至少在音位上），我們對音節的分析確實允許我們這樣做。

③ ［譯注］"麽"，《王仁昫刊謬補缺切韻》（以下稱"王三"）哿韻莫可反；《廣韻》果韻亡果切；《集韻》果韻母果切，戈韻眉波切，支韻忙皮切，皆細小義，此取《集韻》戈韻眉波切音。

三個聲調小類,在這裏用 52(入聲作平聲陽)、53(入聲作上聲)、54(入聲作去聲)表示,因爲它們可以分別“作”02(平聲)、03(上聲)和 04(去聲)用。然而,這三個新“聲調”的真正性質涉及太多問題,故在這裏不作討論(見第六章),但我可以提出一個重要的觀點,即,在《中原音韻》中,入聲一分爲三是相對較晚的發展,而其他三個中古漢語聲調(平聲、上聲和去聲)的分裂和重組一定發生得更早。喉塞音聲母/q/的消失可以作爲這一點的證據。當前三個中古漢語聲調經歷分裂和重組的過程時,喉塞音一定還作爲一個條件存在,所以中古漢語帶有這個喉塞音聲母的平聲字在《中原音韻》中都進入了平聲陰,而不是平聲陽。如果喉塞音早已丢失了,情況就應該恰恰相反。但是,當入聲調發生分裂時,喉塞音顯然已經脱落,因爲以前有這個聲母的音節現在分配到入聲作去聲,而不是入聲作上聲,衹有兩個例外,0453107“一”(中古:臻開三入質影 AC /qi*t/, MP /yɨ/)[①][②]和 0553102“屋”(中古:通合一入屋影 AC /q*k/, MP /wɨ/),“沃”(中古:通合一入沃影 AC /qu*k/, MP /wè/或/wɨ/)。因此,在規則(4)和規則(5)之間,應該增加一條規則,規定帶喉塞音聲母的音節在這個階段已經失去了它們的聲母,因此加入了響音縱列的零聲母組。

$$q \rightarrow \varnothing \tag{6}$$

---

① 0453107“一”幾乎不能算作例外,因該字又出現在 0454147,按照我們的解釋,那應該是規則的,其所以進入“入聲作上聲”,可能是由某種我們尚未瞭解的連讀變調所形成的結果。

② [譯注]與其他全清聲母入聲字不同,在《中原音韻》中,除了“一屋沃”三字外,其他影母入聲字與次濁聲母入聲字一道歸入“入聲作去聲”,這是《中原音韻》的基本規律。薛鳳生在該書中認爲零聲母的性質與鼻音、邊音等一樣屬於響音,因此零聲母入聲字就應該與次濁入聲字一道歸入“入聲作去聲”,這是合乎規律的演變。這實際上是説,在薛鳳生看來,影母字的性質在歷史上有個變化的過程,當影母字的聲母爲/q/時,它屬於全清,當/q/脱落之後,即當 q→ø 發生之後,影母字歸入次濁,參 3.2“中古漢語聲母表”。或許“一屋沃”這三個入聲字出現兩屬的情況,正是 q→ø 音變發生過程不是一蹴而就的明證。陸志韋、楊耐思(1978)《訥菴本〈中原音韻〉校勘記》指出“‘一’小韻祇此一字,在韻末。瞿本、嘯本並同。卓書不收。案《中原音韻》系統,凡古‘影’母字除這韻的‘一’及魚模韻的‘屋沃’二字外,一律歸‘入聲作去聲’。這韻‘入聲作去聲’的‘逸’小韻也收了‘一’字。‘入聲作上聲’的‘一’在韻末,或後加。”(第 210 頁)同時還指出“‘屋’小韻有‘屋沃兀’三字,瞿本、嘯本並同。案古‘影’母入聲字,《中原音韻》除此處‘屋沃’二字及齊微韻‘一’字外,一律歸‘入聲作去聲’。‘兀’本疑母字,也該歸入‘入聲作去聲’。卓書‘入聲作上聲’不收此小韻,而‘屋’字正收在‘入聲作去聲’。本書這小韻在韻末,或後加。”(第 212 頁)

然而,中古漢語入聲的分裂也不會太遲。它一定發生在聲母系統濁音清化之前,因爲濁音是聲調分裂的條件之一。

3.5.3 如前所述,所有的聲調都衹能從音位的角度來研究,但對於平聲陰和平聲陽,我想做一個猜想。事實上,“陰”表示“陰暗的、多雲的、女性”,可能暗示與此有關的“平聲陰”調值低,而“陽”表示“明亮的;晴朗的;男性”,則暗示與此有關的“平聲陽”調值高。因此,我認爲與現代北京話相反,《中原音韻》中的“平聲陰”可能屬低調域,“平聲陽”則可能屬於高調域。這一推測得到了除現代北京話以外的許多現代北方官話方言的支持,儘管嚴格意義上説,現代方言的證據在證明這一點上價值不是太大①。

3.6 韻圖時期的韻母系統

從中古漢語到《中原音韻》聲母系統的變化,在很大程度上是由韻母系統決定的。然而,爲瞭解釋這種變化,我們不能從中古漢語的韻母系統開始,但我們可以從中古漢語的聲母系統開始。原因是,從中古漢語到《中原音韻》近一千年的時間裏,元音系統經歷了比輔音系統更劇烈的變化。因此,如果我們希望最終制定出一些有意義的對應規則的話,就必須從以《切韻指南》(見1.3)爲代表的韻圖的韻母系統開始。由於韻圖時期的音系還没有人用現代音位學術語進行音位化分析,所以我將不得不用純粹抽象的結構術語來稱説它們,也就是説,按照它們傳統上的名稱來指稱它們的類别②。

---

① [譯注]根據《漢語方音字匯》的記録,濟南話陰平 213,陽平 42;合肥話陰平 212,陽平 55;揚州話陰平 21,陽平 34。又根據《普通話基礎方言基本詞彙》(語音卷),天津話陰平 21,陽平 35;鄭州話陰平 24,陽平 42,這些方言都屬於北方官話方言中陰低陽高的類型,不過這並不能説明《中原音韻》也是如此。不僅僅北京話是陰高陽低的類型,根據《漢語方音字匯》,武漢話陰平 55,陽平 213;成都話陰平 44,陽平 21。又根據《普通話基礎方言基本詞彙》(語音卷),齊齊哈爾話陰平 44,陽平 24;哈爾濱話陰平 44,陽平 24,重慶話陰平 55,陽平 31,也都是屬於與北京相同的類型。正如作者所言,這段話屬於“猜想”。

② 【追注】本書寫成之後,我繼續上推,終於構擬出了等韻圖所依據的近古漢語音系,請參薛鳳生(1985)《試論等韻學之原理與内外轉之含義》。假如以這一新構擬爲基礎,本書本節關於韻母的討論可以相對地大爲簡化了,並且將更爲明晰合理,但就基本理論説,此處所論與後來的改訂在精神上仍是一貫的。

3.6.1 在《四聲等子》《切韻指南》和《切韻指掌圖》三本韻圖中,《切韻指掌圖》與《切韻》的距離最大,因此可以認爲它代表了與《中原音韻》最接近的那個時期的漢語。然而,在所有這些書中,韻圖的基本形式都是一樣的。首先,將《切韻》的韻進一步歸納爲"攝"[①]。然後,在每個攝中,如果合適的話,根據在介音位置上是否有半元音/w/,建立合口與開口的對比。然後,每個音節都能安排在某調、某等、某字母下。並不是所有的攝都四等俱全。有些攝衹有一等或三等,有些攝則兼俱一等和三等。儘管在這方面已經做了大量的研究,但這四個等之間的相互關係仍然不是很清楚。似乎可以肯定地説,除了少數例外,那些衹有一等或三等,或兼俱一等和三等的韻攝可能以高元音爲韻腹,而那些四等俱全,特别是有二等的韻攝,一定以低元音爲韻腹。主元音的高低對比也許可以解釋爲何將韻攝分爲内轉和外轉兩個系列[②][③]。在哪些韻攝歸内轉,哪些韻攝歸外轉方面,還有混亂的現象,下表是經羅常培修正後的内外轉表,我以此作爲進一步討論的基礎[④]。

外轉:果、假、蟹、效、咸、山、宕、江、梗

内轉:遇、止、流、深、臻、曾、通

3.6.2 如果我們用"C"表示聲母,"E"表示結尾,"V"的下標 n 表示内轉諸攝的主元音,"V"的下標數字表示外轉攝某等的主元音,我們可以用以下方式概況韻圖的結構:

---

① 《四聲等子》和《切韻指南》都有十六攝,《切韻指掌圖》不用"攝"這個名稱,但有"攝"的觀念(有十三攝),參馬丁(1953:2—3)。

② 參加羅常培(1933:206—226)。

③ 【追注】本書寫作時,我完全接受羅常培先生對内外轉的解釋,但我後來的研究證明他的説法是錯誤的,元音的高低與韻攝的内外實際代表兩個毫不相干的概念,衹在形式上貌似偶合而已,詳細的辯證見薛鳳生(1985)。

④ 羅常培(1933)。這種修正以後爲趙元任(1941:204)和馬丁(1953:3)所接受。實際上首先提出這種看法的是日本學者大矢透,但羅常培在采用這種看法的時候,又提出一些更有力的辯證。應該指出,《四聲等子》和《切韻指南》在韻的分類上有區别。二者都將臻攝入外轉,果攝、宕攝入内轉。我猜想,羅常培的修正與這兩本韻圖的差異有可能顯示出從中古漢語至韻圖的發展的若干方面,雖然我還不能肯定這一點。將羅常培的修正再作少許改動(見 7.2d),對於我研究《中原音韻》的目的來説,就比較適合。

等	外轉	内轉
1	$C(w)V_1(E)$	$C(w)V_n(E)$
2	$C(w)V_2(E)$	——
3	$Cy(w)V_3(E)$	$Cy(w)V_n(E)$
4	$Cy(w)V_4(E)$	——

這意味着,就内轉的韻母而言,我們認爲,一等和三等的區别不在於主元音,而在於介音位置是否有/y/。至於外轉,四等之間的區别不僅在於介音,也在於主元音的性質。雖然我們不知道這其中有多少不同,也不知道它們分别是什麽(但參見 5.6.1)。

3.6.3 韻圖的三等最爲複雜。我們知道,除了那些已列在三等位置的以外,還有那些本應列在三等位置的字,却分别列在二等和四等位置。

爲瞭解釋這個問題,高本漢將三等分爲 α 和 β 兩種類型。李榮更進一步,分爲三類,其中一類又分爲兩個小類①。雖然在我們清楚地瞭解這個問題之前還需要做更多的研究,但我認爲這是中古漢語的問題,而不是韻圖時期的問題。當人們試圖用當時的音系結構去解釋四五百年前的音系結構時,這個問題必然會出現。换句話説,我相信韻圖真正代表的是其設計時的語言狀態,而不是中古漢語的語言狀態。那些放在二等位置和四等位置上的三等字,儘管在中古漢語裏與目前出現在三等位置上的三等字在性質上是類似的②,但現在其性質可能已經改變了。我們在韻圖的排列中觀察到的另一個奇特的現象是,有時在同攝、同調、同等、同開合的情况下,中古漢語的兩個或三個韻可能列在一起,例如在蟹攝、咸攝和止攝中就有這樣的現象。如果我們認真思考韻

① [譯注]李榮(1956)將三等分爲子、丑、寅三類。其中子類爲純三等韻,在韻圖上全都列在三等位置,最多有 11 個聲母。丑類最多有 33 個聲母,其中齒音有 5 個聲母列在二等,5 個聲母列在四等,以母也列在四等,這樣列在二等和四等位置的聲母共 11 個,列在三等位置的共 22 個。寅類最多 42 個聲母,其在韻圖上的分布是在丑類的基礎上,四等位置再增加脣、牙、喉 10 個聲母(與三等相應位置的脣、牙、喉音聲母字,並爲"重紐"),但由於寅類在二等位置上的聲母爲 4 個(比丑類少一個"俟"母),故最多 42 個聲母。高本漢將三、四等分爲 α、β、γ 三類,其中 α 是指三等丑類和寅類,β 是指三等子類,γ 是指四等韻。高本漢不區别"重紐",所以不區别丑類和寅類。

② 在 5.6—5.7 討論《中原音韻》的韻母時,這觀點將作進一步的闡述。

圖的排列,我們應該衹能得出唯一合理的結論是,在韻圖時期,這些中古漢語的韻必然合而爲一。原因很簡單,迄今爲止,還没有辦法預測語音變化的方向。在這方面,韻圖的編纂者當然不比我們更聰明。他所記録的,必然是他能够觀察到的(事實)。在下面有關《中原音韻》聲母和韻母的討論中,我將假設上述論點是正確的。

第四章 《中原音韻》的聲母系統

本章將專門討論從中古漢語到《中原音韻》聲母系統的變化。爲了使這些討論易於理解,必須時刻記住 3.2 中的聲母表和 3.6.2 中根據韻圖給出的音節結構。

4.1 濁音清化的過程

從中古漢語的聲母系統到《中原音韻》的聲母系統,最突出的變化是非響音的濁音清化過程。馬丁將濁塞音和濁擦音重新解釋爲清音後附/ɦ/,再加上我所做的輕微修改,使我們能夠以一種整齊而經濟的方式解釋這一過程,如下所示:

$$ɦ \rightarrow \left\{ \begin{array}{l} h/s \underline{\qquad\qquad} F^{02} \\ ø \end{array} \right\} \tag{7}$$

這個規則將濁塞音和濁擦音重新分配到相應的清塞音和清擦音中去。注意/ɦ/變成/h/的條件是“$S\underline{\quad\quad}F^{02}$”。這意味着經歷這種變化的音節一定是“平聲陽”,而不能是單純的“第二聲”,因爲可以觀察到,(在《中原音韻》中)“入聲作平聲”音節的濁塞音聲母已經變成了不送氣的清塞音。從中古漢語到《中原音韻》的這種演變的結果是如此明顯,以至於沒有必要給出任何例子來説明它。隨着/ɦ/的消失,/h/和/x/之間的對比變得毫無意義,因此,我們可以通過以下規則將它們組合成一個音位。

$$x \rightarrow h \tag{8}$$

濁音清化過程影響到所有發音部位的輔音。在處理完它之後,我們現在可以轉向更具體的變化,它衹影響一些特殊類型的輔音。在下文中,我將根據發音部位對它們進行分組討論。

4.2 脣音(B,幫組)

在脣音聲母中,脣齒化的過程在《中原音韻》之前很早就已被注意到。在韻圖中有"非、敷、奉、微"四個脣齒音聲母。它們衹出現在三等合口韻中,並在分布上與幫滂並明互補。有研究認爲這種聲母可能是一種脣塞擦音,有點像[pf、pf'、bv'、mv][①]。但是鑒於非敷奉微這些聲母的分布,我覺得可以肯定地説,不管它們的音值到底是什麼,它們在本質上衹是幫滂並明的音位變體而已。在《中原音韻》中情況完全不同。我們注意到,在《中原音韻》中,這四個聲母的前三個已經完全合併,例如,0404111"吠"(中古:蟹合三去廢並 AC /pɦiuaiᵓ/, MP /fwèy/)、"沸"(中古:止合三去未幫 AC /piuəiᵓ/, MP /fwèy/)、"費"(中古:止合三去未滂 AC /phiuəiᵓ/, MP /fwèy/);0504113"付"(中古:遇合三去遇幫 AC /piu*ᵓ/, MP /fwɨ/),"赴"(中古:遇合三去御滂 AC /phiu*ᵓ/, MP /fwɨ/)、"父"(中古:遇合三上麌並 AC /ᶜpɦiu*/[②], MP /fwɨ/)和 0804067"販"(中古:山合三去願幫 AC /piuanᵓ/, MP /fwàn/)、"泛"(中古:咸合三去梵滂 AC /phiuamᵓ/, MP /fwàn/)、"范"(中古:咸合三上范並 AC /ᶜpɦuam/, MP /fwàn/)。從每一個例字標注的現代北京話讀音來看,中古非敷奉三個聲母在現代北京話中也合而爲一了。因此,我們可以在《中原音韻》中假設一個聲母爲/f/,這是前三個脣齒音聲母(非敷奉)在一定條件下合併的結果。然而,最後一個(微母)仍然保持着它的特徵,特別是與零聲母合口音節形成對立,例如,0202032"亡"(中古:宕合三平陽明 AC /꜀miuɑŋ/, MP /wáŋ/)與 0202048"王"(中古:宕合三平陽云 AC /꜀iuɑŋ/, MP /wáŋ/);0404108"未"(中古:止合三去未明 AC /miuəiᵓ/, MP /wèy)與 0404109"胃"(中古:止合三去未云 AC /iuəiᵓ/, MP /wèy/);0503060"武"(中古:遇合三上麌明 AC /ᶜmiu*/, MP /wɨ/)與 0503065"五"(中古:遇合三上姥疑 AC

---

① 陸志韋(1946:41)。

② [譯注]英文原文"父"的馬丁擬音爲"pɦiu*ᵓ",聲調標爲"去聲",誤,當爲"上聲"。

/ᶜ ŋu*/, MP /wɨ̌/)[①][②],但在現代北京話中,上述《中原音韻》中每一對讀音不同的例字都變成了同音字。與其他人一樣,我也將用/v/來表示這個聲母[③]。

4.2.1 在音位層面上,在現代北京話中,脣音聲母後面必須後接介音/y/或/w/,但不能後接介音/yw/,也就是説,帶有脣音聲母的音節在形式上必然是 BwV(E)和 ByV(E)二者之一,儘管語音上看,當主元音是低元音時,介音/w/不太顯著[④]。同樣的情況,在《中原音韻》中表現得也相當清楚,或許更加明顯[⑤]。這個事實也許可以幫助我們確定從中古漢語到韻圖時期脣齒化發生的條件,這仍然是一個有待解決的問題[⑥]。我們可以假設,在中古漢語到韻圖時期之間的某個階段,脣音聲母開始以這種新的模式出現。結果,介音爲零的音節現在在脣音聲母後面增生一個介音/w/,而介音爲/yw/的音節則失去了

---

① 在 0402026 中,微母的兩個字"微薇"和零聲母的兩個字"維惟"放在一起,這種情況應視作例外,因另一組 0402034,衹能用零聲母來構擬。

② [譯注]卓從之《中州樂府音韻類編》"微薇"與"維惟"分處兩個不同的小韻,"微薇"在"陽"調類下,而以母字"維惟"與云母字"闈違爲"及疑母字"危嵬巍桅"在"陰陽"調類下同一個小韻中。在《中原音韻》中,疑母字除了在蕭豪、歌戈、先天、江陽韻中還有殘存讀 ŋ 聲母外(因爲在這些韻中,疑母字與泥母字及影母字形成三向對立,參 4.6.4),在其他韻中,已經與影母、云母合併,變成了零聲母。這樣,0402034"圍闈韋幃違嵬巍危桅爲"這一小韻,衹能是零聲母,因爲"圍闈韋幃違爲"爲云母字,"嵬巍危桅"爲疑母字。

③ 陸志韋對這個成分的音值有較長的討論,看來似乎説服力不强。

④ 衹消看一下董同龢(1954:14—15)表一,就會弄清楚這一點。在那個表中,脣音衹和兩個合口韻母[u](/wɨ/與[uo]/we/)結合,漢語拼音方案更進一步,當[uo]與脣音聲母結合時,被寫作[o],例如以[pō](*/pē/)代表"玻"/pwē/。但是把/pwɨ/(布[pù]寫作*/pɨ/)就没有道理了,因爲這個音節和/swɨ/(素[sù])押韻,不和/sɨ/(四[sɿ])押韻。如果我們采用另一種研究方法,把所有具有脣音聲母而似乎不帶介音的音節,解釋爲具有脣音聲母且帶介音/w/的音節,我們就能像在這兒所作的一樣,提出這樣一個一般的原則。其實所有這些音節在《切韻指掌圖》裏都出現在合口圖裏。另一方面,我們還面對着經濟原則問題。我認爲,在音韻學裏有兩個不同層次的經濟原則:一是實際書寫上的經濟原則,一是總的音位結構的經濟原則。對於前者,脣音後的介音/w/確實可以省略,因爲它能部分地被預測到(即"在脣音不直接後附/y/的所有情況下"),但如考慮到後者,加上通行的押韻習慣,最好還是説脣音後有一個介音/w/。

⑤ 很奇怪,在《中原音韻》裏,少數止攝開口脣音字的韻母按理説應該是/yɨy/,但事實上却不是。(見 5.12.5),事實上,這些止攝開口脣音字在《中原音韻》裏跟來自蟹攝的合口一等字一同出現,因此它們的韻母必須構擬成/wɨy/(見 5.12.5)。如果我此處所説的理由是正確的話,止攝的這些字必屬首先失落介音/y/,它們和帶介音/w/的音節混同這件事正可説明,作爲失落介音/y/的一個結果,它們在《中原音韻》前自動獲得了介音/w/,即變成合口字。

⑥ 參見馬丁(1953:40)。

/y/。但在/y/丟失之前,這些聲母從雙脣音變成了脣齒音[①]。這些過程可以用以下幾個規則來表示:

$$B+V(E)\rightarrow B+W+V(E) \qquad (9)$$

$$\begin{bmatrix} P\left(\begin{Bmatrix} h \\ ɦ \end{Bmatrix}\right) \\ m \end{bmatrix} \rightarrow \begin{bmatrix} f \\ v \end{bmatrix} / \_\_\_\_ y+w \qquad (10)$$

$$y\rightarrow ø/\begin{Bmatrix} f \\ v \end{Bmatrix}\_\_\_\_\_\_ \qquad (11)$$

4.2.2 必須馬上對於規則(10)作若干修訂。在《中原音韻》和現代北京話中,通攝三等脣音明母字仍然保持原來的讀音/m/,並沒有變成/v/。例如,0104065"夢"(中古:通合三去送明 AC /mi*ŋᑐ/, MP /mwèŋ/)和0554132"目"(中古:通合三入屋明 AC /mi*k/, MP /mwɨ̀/)。因此,我們必須添加一條規則來解釋這個例外[②]:

$$y\rightarrow ø/m\_\_\_\_\_\_ w+V_{tu}\begin{Bmatrix} ŋ \\ k \end{Bmatrix} \qquad (12)$$

V_{tu}=通攝的主元音

這是我們目前能得到的最好的結果,因爲我們不知道通攝的主元音在脣齒化

---

① 我認爲,當雙脣聲母變成脣齒聲母時,在ByWV(E)這種類型的音節裏介音/y/可能仍然存在,所以代表這些音節的字在韻圖裏仍然被放在三等位置上。在《中原音韻》裏,介音/y/必然已經失落,因爲這種類型的字和二等字出現在同一韻裏(見5.6.1b)。

② 這些字的聲母必須構擬爲/m/,因爲在它們所屬的同音字組裏還有一等字,而且這些字在現代北京話中的聲母也是/m/。我們在此也假設通攝裏這兩個韻系(即東韻系與鍾韻系)到韻圖時期已經合併(見3.6.3),因此上引兩字的介音應爲/yw/。同樣的問題也涉及流攝三等明母字,如0502026"謀"、1602027"矛牟"等(見第五章5.13.1注①)我們的解釋基於以下事實:這些字都出現在韻圖的三等位置,因此大多數學者構擬的讀音都有/y/介音。蒲立本(1970:128)提出的另一個解釋頗令人感興趣,他主要依據的是朝鮮漢字音和日本漢字音。現簡要概述他的結論:(a)在《切韻》時代,"夢目謀"等字所在的韻都是合口韻,有/u/介音,但没有/i/介音;(b)到唐初,這些韻中除了聲母爲/m/的音節外,其他音節的介音都由/u/變成了/iu/;(c)其後除了脣音外,這些韻中的介音/iu/失落了其中的/u/。所以當脣齒化過程發生時,除了這些韻中的/m/外,脣音聲母統統變成了擦音。不用説,這種解釋先須假定,韻圖把"夢目"置於三等是錯誤的。在利用朝鮮漢字音和日本漢字音時,也要預先假定:(a)我們知道借用的時間;(b)在借用的時代,朝鮮語或日語的音韻系統在音位上必須容許既有[mu-]又有[mü-],並且前者而非後者一直被用來讀漢語的"夢目"等字。

時可能是什麽。這裏必須補充一點,當考慮到規則的順序時,規則(12)將不得不放在規則(10)之前,後者可能會被簡化。

4.2.3 在規則(10)的應用中,有一個非常困難的問題,就是流攝中脣音聲母演變的特殊性。流攝在中古漢語中包括兩類韻母:尤侯型(有一等和三等)和幽型(衹有三等)。我們發現除了/m/聲母外,尤侯型三等脣音字受到脣齒化的影響,而幽型三等脣音字則没有。例如,0502036"浮"(中古:流開三平尤並 AC /꜀pɦi*u, MP /fwɨ́/)和 0504113"富"(中古:流開三去宥幫 AC /pi*uᵓ/, MP /fwɨ̀/),"婦"(中古:流開三上有並 AC /꜂pɦi*u/, MP /fwɨ̀/)等字發生了脣齒化,屬"尤侯型",但 1601018"彪"(中古:流開三平幽幫 AC /꜀piəu/ MP /pyāw/)字没有發生脣齒化,屬"幽型"。這一事實表明,齒音化的過程可能發生在兩類韻母合併之前。李榮對尤侯型構擬爲[(i)u],而將幽類型構擬爲[iĕu][1],似乎是唯一可能足以解釋這一現象的構擬。然而,如果我們能够證明尤侯型在音位上類似於/(y)wɨw/,而幽型則類似於/yɨw/,當尤侯型失去介音位置上的/w/時,即與幽型合併,我們將能够將流攝脣音字的脣齒化過程視爲普遍現象的一部分,並因此將上述規則應用於它。事實上,許多(但並非全部)尤侯型脣音聲母字經歷脣齒化過程之後出現在《中原音韻》的"魚模"韻中,這有力地暗示了這種假設並非不可能。/wɨw/演變爲/wɨ/在語音上也是令人信服的[2]。

綜上所述,我們可以得出結論,在《中原音韻》中有五個脣音聲母,分别是/p, ph, f, v, m/。

4.3 齒音(D,端組)

除了/tɦ/清化外,齒塞音和齒響音在形式和行爲上都没有變化。因此,在《中原音韻》中這一組有四個聲母:/t, th, n, l/。

---

① 李榮(1956:145—150)。

② 現代北京話裏韻母是/yɨ/的音節,在《中原音韻》裏韻母是/yɨy/(見 5.12.6)。這樣,就有/yɨy/變成/yɨ/的情況。與之類似,在《中原音韻》前/wɨw/變成/wɨ/,並非毫無理由,如果這能有助於我們理解這兒提到的特殊現象的話。

4.4　齒噝音(Ds,精組)

經過濁音清化之後,齒噝音(Ds)到現在衹剩下三個聲母,即/c, ch, s/。在《中原音韻》之前的一段時間,這三個聲母在音系行爲上表現得非常特殊,這一點將在後面討論(見 5.12)。

4.5　三組腭聲母(P,知組;Pr,莊組;Pj,章組)

中古漢語三組腭聲母(P,知組;Pr,莊組;Pj,章組)在《中原音韻》裏已完全合併,在現代北京話中依然保持這個狀況。如果要跳過《中原音韻》來解釋現代北京話的這個事實的話,我們可以使用下面兩個簡單的規則:

1. t→c/＿＿＿＿j

2. j→r

然而,當考慮到《中原音韻》時,我們會發現這個大合併的過程要複雜得多,而且經歷了很長時間才完成。在中古漢語裏,腭噝音(章組)聲母衹與三等韻相拼,腭塞音(知組)聲母兼與二等和三等韻相拼,而捲舌音(莊組)聲母主要和二等韻相拼,但也與 α 型三等韻相拼①。這三個聲母都與三等韻相拼的事實清楚地表明它們是對立的。在《中原音韻》中,莊組字與章組字仍然是對立的,例如,0501007“梳”(中古:遇合三平魚生 AC /꜀sr*/, MP /srwɨ/)與 0501015“書”(中古:遇合三平魚書 AC /꜀sji*/, MP /srwɨ/)、0701015“真”(中古:臻開三平真章 AC /꜀cji*n/, MP /crēn/)與 1701020“臻”(中古:臻開三平臻莊 AC /꜀cri*n′/, MP /crēn/)、1701004“深”(中古:深開三平侵書 AC /꜀sjiəm/, MP /srēn/)與 1701006“森”(中古:深開三平侵生 AC /꜀sriəm/, MP /sēn/),

---

① [譯注]所謂 α 型三等韻,是指高本漢對三等的分類,相當於李榮(1956)的丑類和寅類。

但是這種對立現在可以很容易地用介音位置上是否有/y/來解釋①。换句話説,莊和章現在可以解釋爲一個音位的兩個變體,章衹與帶有/y/介音的韻母相拼,莊則不與帶有/y/介音的韻母相拼。知組聲母字則以與之相拼的是二等韻母還是三等韻母爲條件,分别於莊組聲母字和章組聲母字相混,例如0201008"莊"(中古:宕開三平陽莊 AC /꜀criɑŋ/, MP /crwāŋ/)"椿"(中古:江開二平江知 AC /꜀tjɛŋ/, MP /crwāŋ/),1501012"鐺"(中古:梗開二平庚初 AC /꜀crhaŋ/, MP /crhēŋ/)"撑"(中古:梗開二平庚徹 AC /꜀tjhaŋ/, MP /crhēŋ/),和0701015"真"(中古:臻開三平真章 AC /꜀cji*n/ MP /crēn/)"珍"(中古:臻開三平真知 AC /꜀tji*n/ MP /crēn/),1003056"闡"(中古:山開三上獮昌 AC /꜂cjhiɛn/, MP /crhǎn/)"蕆"(中古:山開三上獮徹 AC /꜂tjhiɛn/, MP /crhǎn/)。儘管以上觀察没有一個例外,但必須及時補充一些補充規則。在東鍾韻中,"崇"字在中古漢語中的聲母是/crɦ/,韻母是三等韻/i*ŋ/,但它與知組和章組三等韻字共處0102027"重蟲牖鱅崇"這個同音字組中。這應該是三組腭聲母音節中/y/介音丢失的結果(見5.5.1)。相應地,在支思韻中我們也發現莊組字和章組字出現在同一個同音字組中,如0301003"眵嗤差"、0301004"施詩師獅尸屍鳲蓍"和0303014"史駛使弛豕矢始屎菌"。這樣的合併應該是由於章組字的/y/介音丢失的結果(見5.12)。然而,具有相同韻母(止攝開口三等)的知組字,除了0303011"徵"(中古:止開三上止知 AC /꜂tji*i'/, MP /crɨ/)出現在支思韻外,其他字出現在齊微韻中,例如,0401024"知蜘"、0402043"池馳遲墀篪持"、0403066"耻侈"和0404132"製制置滯雉稚致彘治智幟熾質"。陸志韋敏鋭地觀察到上述事實,他認爲0301001"支"(中古:止開三平支章 AC /꜀cjiə/, MP /crɨ/)(所有同韻母的章組字)比0401024"知"(中古:

① 很多迹象使我相信,莊組聲母後的介音/y/在《中原音韻》編纂前早已失落,僅述其中幾點:(a)不管中古來源如何,莊組聲母字衹列在二等。(b)在《中原音韻》中,所有宕攝莊組三等字與江攝莊組二等字混同,如0201004"雙艭霜孀鸘驦"和0201026"牕瘡"。(c)"潺"爲山攝三等"崇"母字,在《中原音韻》中出現在"寒山"韻(0802030),如果它還保持着/y/介音,應該出現在"先天"韻(見5.6.1C)(d)深攝衹有三等字,即全都有/y/介音。但在《中原音韻》的侵尋韻(源於深攝),我們發現有1703029"怎"和1704044"唔"等這些《切韻》後新造的字,它們在《中原音韻》中必然没有/y/介音。這當然表明,在這些新字産生的時候,無/y/介音的新韻母已經存在。

止開三平支知 AC /꜀tjiə/, MP /crɨ̄/)(所有同韻母的知組字)更早發生捲舌化[①]。的確,這是解釋這兩組腭聲母特殊分布唯一合乎邏輯的方法。

4.5.1 這裏的問題涉及中古止攝各韻開口韻母的形式,稍後將討論(見5.12)。我相信,在韻圖中,止攝開口這四組韻母都已合併,在音位上可以用/yɨy/這個韻母來表達,其中/ɨ/代表央高元音。假設這是真的,我們現在可以把上述討論作如下總結:

(a) 在莊組聲母後,所有介音位置上有/y/的韻母都失去了/y/。這可能發生在韻圖時期之前,因爲這些字都出現在二等位置上。

(b) 莊組和章組聲母由此呈互補分布狀態,從而成爲"照穿牀審禪"這一組聲母的兩組音位變體。

(c) 當章組的每一個聲母在音位上與相應的莊組聲母合併之後,其後隨韻母/yɨy/的/y/介音也跟着丢失了。由此莊組聲母與章組聲母在《中原音韻》的支思韻合併,但在其他韻則不是這樣。

(d) 上述過程完成之後,知組聲母也加入新形成的捲舌音行列,但在《中原音韻》中原知組聲母後的這個韻母/yɨy/依然保持着/y/介音。結果,代表原知組聲母與/yɨy/韻母相拼的音節全都出現在《中原音韻》的"齊微"韻,而不是"支思"韻。

4.5.2 我們現在可以用如下幾個公式以更精確的方式概況上述過程,但這些公式的次序必須保持不變:

$$y \rightarrow \emptyset / Pr\_\_\_\_ \quad (13)$$

$$j \rightarrow r \quad (14)$$

$$y \rightarrow \emptyset / Pr\_\_\_\_ ɨy \quad (15)$$

$$t \rightarrow c / \_\_\_\_ r \quad (16)$$

下表或許也是需要的,它可以使中古漢語這三組腭聲母的合併過程顯得更清晰,"X"代表韻母中介音之後的所有成分,如果有的話。

---

① 陸志韋(1946:3)。我們衹是在不太嚴格的意義上接受陸志韋的解釋。嚴格地説,知組和章組應該同時經歷了捲舌過程,知組聲母變成塞擦音以後它們才合併。

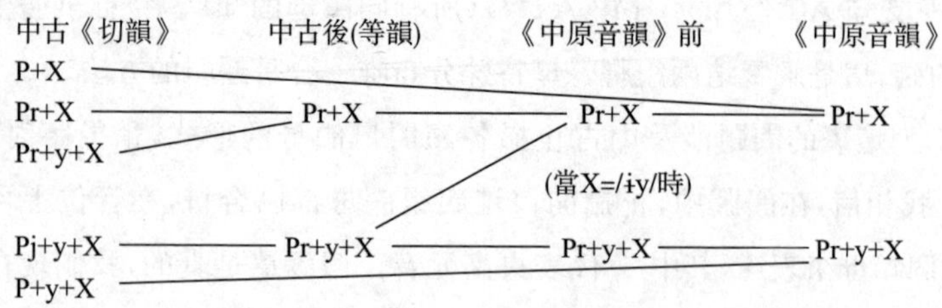

4.5.3 根據 4.5.2 中的規則(14),日母/nj/變成了/nr/。然而,前文提到過,在公元 724 年之前,帶有這個聲母的字總是用來對譯梵語"ña"音節,而在公元 771 年之後,泥母/n/字取而代之(見 3.2.1c 注釋①)。這一事實表明,早在 771 年,日母/nj/可能已經失去了鼻音性質。因此,就像在現代北京話中將日母字的聲母修訂爲/r/一樣,我們也必須將《中原音韻》的日母/nr/修改爲/r/①。如果我們放棄/nj/,而衹使用/j/代表中古漢語的日母,就會陷入兩難境地(見 3.2.1c)。顯然,我們必須承認/r/是一個濁輔音,但是那些含有/r/的聲母算是什麽呢? 幸運的是,在從《中原音韻》到現代北京話的語音發展過程中,濁音和清音之間的對比似乎不再是一個條件限制特徵,所以我們可以安全地忽略這個問題。

$$n \rightarrow \emptyset / \underline{\qquad\quad} r \tag{17}$$

現在在《中原音韻》中衹有四個捲舌聲母,即/cr、crh、sr、r/。

4.6 喉音(G,包括牙音)

兩組喉音聲母(關於爲什麽使用"喉音"這個術語,見 3.2 注釋 2)也經歷了一些劇烈的變化,下面就討論這個問題。

4.6.1 正如我們所看到的,濁音清化使/kɦ/(群母)和/xɦ/(匣母)這兩個聲母消失了,並使/x/改寫爲/h/成爲可能(見 4.1)。但濁音清化發生之前,

① 哈特門和霍凱特(見書目選録)這兩位爲現代北京話設置了一個/r/音位,但他們的/r/與我給《中原音韻》設置的/r/不同。哈特門和霍凱特將現代北京話中的/r/看作半元音,而我仍將《中原音韻》中的/r/看作聲母(輔音)。

/xɦ/(匣母)已經顯示出一些變化。所有的韻圖,包括最早的《韻鏡》和《七音略》,這個聲母的三等位置上都没有列字,但在零聲母的三等和四等位置上都有列字。現代研究表明,就《切韻》而言,零聲母的三等(即喻三)與零聲母的四等(即喻四)是截然不同的。因此,零聲母三等就與/xɦ/(匣母)處於互補分布狀態;因此,趙元任和其他人認爲,在中古漢語中,前者實際上是後者的一部分(喻三歸匣)[①]。如果接受這種解釋,在運用濁音清化規則之前,必須增加一條規則以闡明以上事實:

$$\text{x}\text{ɦ} \rightarrow \text{ø} / \underline{\quad\quad} \text{y(w)} \begin{Bmatrix} V_n \\ V_3 \end{Bmatrix} \tag{18}$$

4.6.2 在《中原音韻》裏,喉音聲母二等開口字與其相應的一等開口字仍然形成最小對比對,例如0601001"皆"(中古:蟹開二平皆見AC /꜀kai/, MP /cyē/)對0601002"該"(中古:蟹開一平咍見AC /꜀kəi/, MP /kāy/)、0601006"哀"(中古:蟹開一平咍影AC /꜀qəi/, MP /āy/)對0601008"挨"(中古:蟹開二平皆影AC /꜀qai/, MP /āy/)、0802020"寒"(中古:山開一平寒匣AC /꜀xɦɑn/, MP /hán/)對0802024"閑"(中古:山開二平山匣AC /꜀xɦan/, MP /syán/)等。疑母/ŋ/的對比就不那麼明顯了,但這是由於疑母/ŋ/在一個相對較晚的時期的變化所致,我們很快就會討論到這一點(見4.6.4)。這些對立一般情況下在現代北京話中還保持着,其方式爲原二等字有了/y/介音。因此可以合乎邏輯地假設這些對立在《中原音韻》中必然以同樣的方式保持着,因爲八思巴字也以同樣的方式顯示着這種區别[②]。我們寫出下面這個規則:

$$G + V_2(E) \rightarrow G + y + V_2(E) \tag{19}$$

當我們在《中原音韻》中嘗試應用這個規則時,我們發現它十分管用,没有例外。陸志韋顯然也注意到了這一現象,儘管他没有像我在這裏用嚴格的形

---

① 趙元任(1941:211—212),也參見董同龢(1954:55)和李榮(1956:76)。可以再多説一句,有趣的是,規則(18)的臃腫形式似乎可以證明李榮有關《切韻》四等韻無/y/介音説是正確的。在這種情況下,這個規則就可以簡化爲 xɦ→ø/____y。四等韻的/y/是後來產生的(但必須在韻圖時期之前)。

② 參見陸志韋(1946:49,54—55)。

式來表述,而且他在討論蕭豪韻和庚青韻時又顯得有些猶豫,他要麽指責這是這本書所體現的"方言成分",要麽坦率地承認他不理解[①]。另一方面,趙蔭棠似乎根本没有覺察到這一點。結果他在處理這個問題時前後十分不一致,有時甚至有點荒謬。以下事實可以説明這一點。

(a) 他在給一等和二等字設置了四個喉音聲母[k、kh、ŋ、x]後,又補充道:"但二等有時用[c、c'、ȵ、ç]",没有進一步説明。

(b) 通過增加這四個聲母,他在給二等字擬音時就可以省略[i]介音。但在家麻韻中,他給某些二等字擬音時仍使用[i]介音,例如 1301007"鵶丫呀"、1302016"牙芽衙涯衙笁"和 1303030"雅瘂"這三個同音字組中的二等字[②]。

(c) 根據定義,同音字組中的字必同音,這是包括趙蔭棠本人在内的所有人都同意的。然而,在相當多的情况下,當出現二等字與三等字混並時,趙蔭棠没有去試圖解釋它們的合併,反而給每個同音字組標注了兩個不同的讀音,例如 1501001"京麐庚鶊賡更粳羹畊驚荆經兢矜涇"、1501015"輕坑卿誙硜甖傾鏗"、1503054"景儆璟橄骾鯁綆梗警境頸耿哽"等[③]。但對另外一些包含二等和三等混併的同音字組,他衹標注了一個讀音,例如 1502040"行形刑邢桁衡鉶珩硎"[④]。司徒修注意到趙蔭棠在處理這些問題時的前後"不一致"做法,於是修改了趙蔭棠的標音,也給這個同音字組標注了兩個讀音[⑤]。遺憾的是,司徒修這種修改衹會使趙蔭棠的做法始終不一致。

所有這些似乎令趙蔭棠陷入如此困惑的難題,通過積極應用我在上面給出的規則,實際上都很容易得到解决,這一點我們會在元音系統的討論中看到(見 5.7.1 和 5.10)。

4.6.3 我們有明確的證據表明,到《中原音韻》時期,聲母/q/已經失去了

---

① 陸志韋(1946:48,55)。

② [譯注]趙蔭棠(1936)給這三個同音字組標注的讀音都是[ia],分别出現在第 251、252、253 頁。

③ [譯注]趙蔭棠(1936)給 1501001"京"標注了[ceŋ]和[tɕiŋ]兩個讀音(第 265 頁),給 1501015"輕"標注了[c'eŋ]和[tɕ'iŋ](第 266 頁),給 1503054"景"標注了[ceŋ]和[tɕiŋ]兩個讀音(第 270 頁)。

④ [譯注]趙蔭棠(1936)給 1502040"行"標注了一個讀音[ɕiŋ]。

⑤ 司徒修(1962a:132)。

音位地位，即便在某些現代北方官話方言中，不管來源如何，所有零聲母零介音的音節在語音上往往可能存在像/q/或/ŋ/一樣的輔音。但是作爲聲母，/q/的消失是相當晚的變化。正如我所指出的，當中古漢語的平聲一分爲二時，聲母/q/作爲一個決定因素顯然仍是存在的(見 3.5.2)。此外，正如我們在上一節討論的那樣，當原來没有介音的喉音聲母二等字在介音位置上産生/y/介音時，/q/也仍然作爲一個決定因素存在，這樣解釋將顯得更經濟、更合乎邏輯。

4.6.4 在《中原音韻》中疑母(/ŋ/聲母)是否還存在，一直有争議，這確實是一個非常棘手的問題。在現代北京話中的情况是，原疑母字大多與零聲母字合併了，但少數開口三、四等字的聲母變爲/n/，例如："倪"(中古：蟹開四平齊疑 AC /꜀ŋiei/，MP /nyɨ́/)，"牛"(中古：流開三平尤疑 AC /꜀ŋi*u/，MP /nyéw/)，"孽"(中古：山開三入薛疑 AC /ŋiɛt/，MP /nyè/)，"虐"(中古：宕開三入藥疑 AC /ŋiɑk/，MP /nywè/)，"凝"(中古：曾開三平蒸疑 AC /꜀ŋiəŋ/，MP /nyéŋ/)[①]。在《中原音韻》中，我們發現，在大多數情况下，原疑母字與原影母(/q/聲母字)或原喻母字(零聲母字)共處一個同音字組，但在下列情况下，它們似乎與那些原泥母字(/n/聲母字)或原喻母字(零聲母字(也包括原影母字，即/q/聲母字))，形成了三向對立。

(a) 0203052"養"(中古：宕開三上養以 AC /꜂iɑŋ/，MP /yǎŋ/)、"鞅"(中古：宕開三上養影 AC /꜂qiɑŋ/，MP /yǎŋ/[②])對 0203071"仰"(中古：宕開三上養疑 AC /꜂ŋiɑŋ/，MP /yǎŋ/)。

(b) 0204081"漾"(中古：宕開三去漾以 AC /iɑŋ꜄/，MP /yàŋ/)"怏"(中古：宕開三去漾影 AC /qiɑŋ꜄/，MP /yàŋ/)對 0204102"仰"(中古：宕開三去漾疑 AC /ŋiɑŋ꜄/，MP(——)對 0204101"釀"(中古：宕開三去漾泥 AC /niɑŋ꜄/，MP /nyàŋ/)。

(c) 1104147"奥"(中古：效開一去号影 AC /qɑu꜄/，MP /àw/)對 1104125

---

① 參見董同龢(1954：110—111)表 4。董表衹顯示少數幾個疑母三等字轉成泥聲母字，但實際上還有一些四等字也如此，如"倪臬"。

② [譯注]"鞅"在《國音常用字匯》第 252—253 頁中讀[ㄧㄤ yeang]上聲，又讀[ㄧㄤ iang]陰平。在《新華字典》(第 12 版 APP)中"鞅"有陰平和去聲兩讀，並在陰平一讀中注明，"舊讀上聲"，但紙本中没有此標注。

"傲"(中古:效開一去号疑 AC /ŋɑuᵓ/, MP /àw/)對 1104146"鬧"(中古:效開二去效泥[①] AC /nɛuᵓ/, MP /nàw/)。

(d) 1203046"妸"(中古:果開一上哿影 AC /ᶜ qɑ/, MP /ě/)對 1203048 "我"(中古:果開一上哿疑 AC /ᶜ ŋɑ/, MP /wě/)對 1203042"娜"(中古:果開一上哿泥 AC /ᶜ nɑ/, MP /nwě/[②])。

(e) 1254083"岳"(中古:江開二入覺疑 AC /ŋɛk/, MP /ywè/)"約"(中古:宕開三入藥影 AC /qiɑk/, MP /ywè/)"藥"(中古:宕開三入藥以 AC /iɑk/, MP / ywè/)對 125409"虐"(中古:宕開三入藥疑 AC /ŋiɑk/, MP /nywè/)。

(f) 1154153"岳"(中古:江開二入覺疑 AC /ŋɛk/, MP /yàw/)"約"(中古:宕開三入藥影 AC /qiɑk/, MP /yāw/)"藥"(中古:宕開三入藥以 AC /iɑk/, MP / yàw/)對 1154160"虐"(中古:宕開三入藥疑 AC /ŋiɑk/, MP /nyàw/)。

(g) 1454057"拽"(中古:山開三入薛以 AC /iɛt/, MP /yè/)"謁"(中古:山開三入月影 AC /qiat/, MP /yè/)對 1454058"業"(中古:咸開三入業疑 AC /ŋiap/, MP /yè/)對 454055"揑"(中古:山開四入屑泥 AC /niet/, MP /nyē/)。

這種情況在下列事實中顯得更加複雜,例如,上舉的(e)和(f)中,例字裏有中古漢語聲母都爲原疑母但韻母不同的字,現在這些字韻母變得相同,但仍互相區别,究其原因當在聲母。而且至少在 003049"讞"(中古:山開三上獮疑 AC /꜀ ŋiɛn/, MP /nyǎn/)和 1454055"臬"(中古:山開四入屑疑 AC /ŋiet/, MP /nyè/)這兩例中,我們發現中古漢語/ŋ/聲母字(疑母字)與/n/聲母字(泥母字)一道出現。上述事實表明,到《中原音韻》時代,在不同的條件下,/ŋ/聲母(疑母)要麼保持不變,要麼變成/n/,要麼消失。這些條件是什麼呢?或者更確切地説,這些變化真的有形式條件嗎?我的答案是肯定的。

4.6.4.1 面對這個問題,《中原音韻》的研究者表現出截然不同的反應。

---

① [譯注]"鬧"字"王三"未收,《廣韻》"奴教切","奴"爲泥母,而"教"爲二等韻;《集韻》"女教切","鬧"字當爲二等"娘"母字,但由於作者采用李榮先生的觀點,認爲中古漢語没有"娘"母,故這裏將"鬧"字標爲泥母。

② [譯注]"娜"字,現在北京話中讀陽平。

趙蔭棠的解決辦法,可以想見,就是增加一個聲母。他認爲/ŋ/聲母(疑母)在1104125“傲奡鏊”、1203048“我”這兩個同音字組中仍然保持,但在0203071“仰”、0204102“仰”、1154160“虐瘧”和1254090[①]“虐瘧”中變成了/ɲ/,在1003049“撚輾碾讞”和1454055“捏聶躡鑷囓臬蘖”中與/n/合併,在所有其他情況下都消失了,儘管他没有指出導致這些不同變化的條件是什麽?[②] 陸志韋采取了一種更奇特的態度。他似乎是在説,/ŋ/聲母(疑母)在大多數情況下消失了,在少數情況下保持不變,别無其他可能的變化。至於爲什麽/ŋ/聲母(疑母)會在上面提到的少數情況下保持不變,陸志韋坦率地承認他不知道[③]。董同龢選擇相信在《中原音韻》中疑母消失了,這是由於他認爲0204101“釀”和0204102“仰”這兩個同音字組之間的小圓圈“○”以及1454057“拽噎謁葉熚”和1454058“業鄴額”這兩個同音字組之間的小圓圈“○”可能是後來的編者誤加的。這樣,董同龢就可以説,“仰”的聲母已經從/ŋ/變成了/n/,儘管他也没有具體説明這種變化的條件。董同龢没有提到(e)和(f)這兩種情况,大概是因爲他認爲“虐”的聲母就像在現代北京話中一樣,也從/ŋ/變成了/n/。至於(c)和(d)這兩種情况,董同龢將這種對比歸因於不規律的發展或作者的粗心大意[④]。我認爲由趙蔭棠和陸志韋解決問題的方法來看,他們都不是在認真努力地解決問題。通過隨意添加新的聲母,或者含糊地説没有發生變化,我們當然可以維持所有的對比,甚至一些“不必要”的“對比”,這樣我們就失去了對音系發展進行有意義的和系統的説明的任何機會。董同龢的方法在我看來是最合理的,儘管他過於努力試圖將/ŋ/聲母(疑母)問題全部解決掉,但對少數例子中疑母爲何由/ŋ/變成/n/根本没有努力去解釋。

4.6.4.2 兩個相鄰的同音字組實際上有可能是一個,也就是説,相鄰的同音字組之間的小圓圈“○”可能是後來的一些編輯在他們自己方言的影響下有意或無意地加上去的,如果我們能推導出一個規則來支持這樣的懷疑的話,這

---

① [譯注]原文編碼爲“1204090”,誤,應爲“1254090”。因爲第十二韻“歌戈”衹有90個同音字組。最後一個同音字是“入聲作去聲”,是故此編碼的第3、4兩位應該是54。

② 趙蔭棠(1936:95—96)。

③ 陸志韋(1946:45—46)。

④ 董同龢(1954:26—27)。

樣的懷疑就確有道理了。如果我們遵循這一論證思路,董同龢認爲 0204101“釀”和 0204102“仰”之間的小圓圈“○”是誤加的觀點,確實可以被認爲是正確的。“虐瘧”這兩個字在現代北京話中讀作/nywè/。如果我們假設這兩個字的聲母在《中原音韻》中也是/n/,則(e)和(f)這兩個最小對比對在邏輯上就可以繼續保持了。稍加考察,我們就可以發現這兩個字都是宕攝三等(入聲字),與之相應的上聲字和去聲字的聲母,可以合理地假設向同一個方向發展,即從/ŋ/變成/n/。這就需要我們承認 0204101“釀”和 0204102“仰”這兩個同音字組本來就應該是一個(也就是説,它們之間的小圓圈“○”是誤加的),這樣(a)和(b)這兩例所涉及的問題,現在就可以輕鬆合理地解決了。因此,我們需要這樣一個規則:

$$ŋ \rightarrow n/\_\_\_\_ y+V_{ta} \qquad (20)$$

V_{ta}=宕攝的主元音。

4.6.4.3 規則(20)所代表的變化過程必須發生在《中原音韻》之前很久,因爲(與此相關的字)不受《中原音韻》記録的另一個音變過程的影響,這個音變過程要求/ŋ/聲母在/y/介音前完全消失。

$$ŋ \rightarrow ø/\_\_\_\_ y \qquad (21)$$

關於這一點,無需再舉例説明了,這樣的例子有很多。然而,也許應該立即補充的是,這個音變過程開始起作用必須不能早於規則(19)所代表的音變過程,這個音變過程就是喉音聲母開口二等字增生了一個/y/介音。這是解釋以下事實唯一合乎邏輯的方式,即爲什麼江攝疑母二等字和宕攝疑母三等字在《中原音韻》裏仍然對立,雖然此時它們的韻母已變得相同,就像我們在(e)和(f)這兩組中所看到的那樣。自然地,在《中原音韻》裏,我們必須將“岳”所代表的音節構擬成零聲母音節。

上節所論迫使我們也將 1454057“拽噎謁葉燁”和 1454058“業鄴額”視爲一個同音字組,否則“業鄴”都將成爲規則(21)的唯一例外,而與之相應的舒聲字都符合這條規則,例如 1902018“嚴”(中古:咸開三平嚴疑 AC /꜀ŋiam/, MP /yán/)。如果需要的話,我們在這裏有更多的證據來支持這一推測。“額”(中古:梗開二入陌疑 AC /ŋak/, MP /é/),與“業”共處一個同音字組,它是梗攝二等字，根據規則(19)，到《中原音韻》時，它必須獲得一個介音/y/。事實上，這可能就是它被歸入車遮韻的原因(見 6.4.1.3)。與其他同類型的字一樣，它一定(已因受規則 21 的影響)丟失了/ŋ/聲母。

4.6.4.4 1003049“撚輾碾讞”和 1454055“揑聶躡鑷囓臬蘖”帶來的問題很奇特。這兩個同音字組主要由中古漢語的泥母字組成，因此可以假設在《中原音韻》中它們的聲母依然是/n/。然而我們發現，前一個同音字組中的“讞”字和後一個同音字組中的“嚙臬蘖”字，都是中古漢語的疑母字。到目前爲止還沒有人討論過這兩個同音字組的問題。據推測，由於借用的關係，它們已經被視爲不規則。但事實上，它們都是山攝三等或四等(入聲字)，這在我看來是值得注意的，即便如此，還不能把將上述情況寫成什麽規則，因爲與其相應的舒聲字，如 1002031“妍”(中古：山開四平先疑 AC /$_c$ ŋien/, MP /yán/)和 1004073“彥”(中古：山開三去綫疑 AC /ŋiɛn^ɔ/, MP /yàn/)，顯然都是零聲母。

4.6.4.5 現在祇剩下(c)和(d)這兩組需要處理了。嚴格根據《中原音韻》的內部證據判斷，我們得出一個結論，即在 1104125“傲奡鰲”和 1203048“我”這兩個同音字組中，/ŋ/作爲聲母仍然存在。這意味着這個聲母的功能負荷已經變得越來越輕，在《中原音韻》中似乎已處於消失的邊緣。爲了理解這一點，我們首先必須知道從韻圖時期到《中原音韻》元音系統的大“位移”。我將在下一章討論這個大“位移”。這裏祇要説一句，位移的結果是外轉一等的主元音大部分與二等主元音合併。這個過程可以用下列公式充分表達：

$$C+V_1+E \rightarrow C+V_2+E \quad (22)$$

$$E \neq w$$

如果用語言來表述這個公式所表達的意思的話，就是説在有尾韻中除了收嗚韻之外，外轉開口一等字的主元音都變成了二等字的主元音(參見 5.6 和 5.10.2)。仔細研究就會發現，1104125“傲奡鰲”、1104147“奥懊澳”、1203046“痾”和 1203048“我”這四個同音字組中的字，雖然全都屬於一等字，但其(主元音)依然保持原來的性質，而其他一等字(的主元音)則根據上述規則發生了變化。那麽，非常合乎邏輯地説，在元音位移變化之後，聲母/ŋ/祇存在於殘存的一等字的主元音之前，不管這個主元音當時是什麽。因此，我們現在可以寫出一個規則來解釋這一事實：

$$\eta \rightarrow \left\{ \begin{array}{l} \eta / \_\_ V_1 \\ \varnothing \end{array} \right\} / \# \_\_ \quad (23)$$

在我看來，這非常令人滿意地解釋了爲什麼我們在《中原音韻》中有(c)和(d)這樣的對比對，而在其他情況下，影母一等字和疑母一等字已經變爲同音字，例如，0804053"案"(中古：山開一去翰影 AC /qɑnᵓ/，MP /àn/)、"岸"(中古：山開一去翰疑 AC /ŋɑnᵓ/，MP /àn/)和 0604064"艾"(中古：蟹開一去泰疑 AC /ŋɑiᵓ/，MP /ày/)"愛"(中古：蟹開一去代影 AC /qəiᵓ/，MP /ày/)。這條規則所代表的音變過程必須在規則(20)之後開始起作用，而且由於它的適用範圍具有更大的普遍性，因此不再需要規則(21)了。

4.7 結語

到此，我們剛剛把中古漢語到《中原音韻》聲母系統的變化討論完。綜上所述，我們可以將《中原音韻》的聲母系統用下面這個新表來表示：

	塞音(S)		擦音(Fr)	響音(R)	
脣　音(B)	p	ph	f	m	v
齒　音(D)	t	th		n	l
齒呲音(Ds)	c	ch	s		
腭捲舌音(Pr)	cr	crh	sr		r
喉　音(G)	k	kh	h	ŋ	ø

此表可以進一步簡化爲下面這個輔音音位表：

		脣音 B	齒音 D	齒呲音 Ds	喉音 G
非響音	塞音(S)	p	t	c	k
	擦音(Fr)	f		s	x
響　音	鼻音(N)	m	n		ŋ
	流音(L)	v	l	r	

正如我之前所説的(見 4.5.3)，/r/仍然會給我們帶來一些麻煩。它到底是一

種什麽様的音位,我不是很確定。可以肯定的是,它現在和它在中古漢語中的意思已經不一樣了。因爲它在中古漢語中從來没有單獨作爲一個聲母出現過,所以我曾認爲它和/j/、/h/和/ɦ/一樣,實際上是一個區别性特徵。但由於它在《中原音韻》中確實作爲聲母出現,因此這種解釋就不再成立了。也許,這個/r/就像《中原音韻》中的/h/,既代表舌根擦音[x],又代表送氣一樣,當它與其他輔音結合時,代表捲舌,當它單獨作爲聲母時,又代表捲舌濁擦音。現在對/h/和/r/的處理就是完全可能的了,因爲在《中原音韻》之後的漢語裏清濁對立已經不再是(語音演變的)决定性因素了。

第五章 《中原音韻》的元音系統

在討論完聲母、介音和韻尾之後，我們現在準備解決《中原音韻》研究中最棘手的問題，即元音系統的重建。由於《中原音韻》中所謂的"入聲"的性質長期以來一直存在爭議，在這裏無法進行討論，因此我將衹根據舒聲同音字組（材料）來研究《中原音韻》的主元音，以免因使用入聲同音字組（材料）給元音系統的討論帶來爭議。當然，這並不意味着我們將永遠忽略入聲字，而是説我們要在無可爭議的基礎上建立一個系統，然後通過將其應用於所有的字來測試它，包括那些我將在下一章詳細討論的入聲韻字。從現在起，每當我説"某韻字"時，它應該被理解爲該韻除了入聲之外的所有舒聲字，除非另有明確説明。

5.1 作業規則

如前所述，《中原音韻》使用的術語"韻"與《切韻》使用的"韻"截然不同，實際上它更接近於一些韻圖中的"攝"（見 2.2）。基於這一事實，我們可以得出一個不太嚴格的假設，《中原音韻》中的一個韻可能包含不同主元音的音節，而兩個或兩個以上具有相同韻尾的韻最不可能具有相同的主元音。基於這一假設我們可以確立下面兩個作業原則①：

(a) 一個韻衹允許有一個主元音，除非必須假設有兩個或兩個以上的主元音才能解釋此韻中所有的（字音）對立。

---

① 【追注】撰寫本書時，我對"韻"的嚴格定義尚無十分把握，因此含糊地説，《中原音韻》之"韻"有點像等韻的"攝"，後來發現這個説法是不對的。這兩個術語代表兩個截然不同的概念。就"韻"的嚴格定義説，一韻之内的字衹能含有一個主元音，這是理論所嚴格要求的，當然實際上有些韻書却未能完全遵守，這是因爲有些編者可能考慮到別的需要而做出妥協，因此未嚴格據實分韻，這就會給我們在作理論解釋時造成困難，此處第一條作業原則裏的"除非"云云，就是爲了解決類實際的困難而説的。關於這個理論問題，可參閲薛鳳生（1986）《北京音系解析》第一章和第二章。

(b) 不同的韻若有相同的韻尾,其主元音一定不同。

5.2 《中原音韻》裏的陽聲韻

在《中原音韻》的19個韻中,以鼻音收尾的陽聲韻有10個。由此可見,如果我們可以爲這十個陽聲韻設計出一個令人滿意的主元音系統,其他九個韻的問題將迎刃而解。在這十個陽聲韻中,東鍾、江陽和庚青這三個在中古漢語和現代北京話中的韻尾都是/ŋ/,因此在《中原音韻》它們的韻尾也必然是/ŋ/。其他七個陽聲韻在現代北京話中的韻尾都是/n/,但其中侵尋,監咸和廉纖三個,在中古漢語以及許多現代非官話方言中以/m/爲韻尾,例如廣東話。由於這三個陽聲韻在《中原音韻》中與其他分開,我們可以得出的最合乎邏輯的結論是,它們的韻尾仍然是/m/。現在,剩下的真文、寒山、桓歡和先天這四韻的韻尾就必須是/n/了。根據前文中作業規則(b),我們現在可以合理地假設《中原音韻》中應該至少有四個主元音。顯然,我們不能簡單地做如此假設,這衹能作爲一個進一步調試和最後驗證的起點而已。

5.3 真文韻、寒山韻、桓歡韻、先天韻

在韻尾爲/n/的四個抵腭韻中,真文韻對我們來説没有太大的困難。它是由前一時期的臻攝發展而來的,臻攝屬於内轉,因此它們的主元音必然是高元音①。在現代北京話中,真文韻的字儘管在音位上可以分析爲以中元音韻腹,但在語音層面它們的韻腹元音的舌位仍然是很高的②③。因此,我們必須將真文韻的韻腹元音假設爲高元音,又因爲它似乎是這四韻中唯一一個高元音韻,我們可以進一步指定這個元音爲央高元音,並用/ɨ/來表示它。真正的挑戰來

① 參馬丁(1953:38)。

② 見7.5.1至7.5.3,也參看哈特門(1944)和霍凱特(1947)。但司徒修認爲應該是高元音。(見司徒修1966:15)。

③ 【追注】爲了遷就多數教學者的研究,我當時采用了這一説法。其後的研究使我相信,在現代北京話中這類字的韻腹其實是高元音/ɨ/(參薛鳳生1986,第1—2章)。這一發現更有力地支持我們此處爲真文韻所作的構擬。

自其他三個韻：寒山、桓歡和先天。這三韻的字在現代北京話中都以低元音/a/爲韻腹[①]。在《中原音韻》中也會是這種情況嗎？這個問題聽起來可能相當荒謬，但事實並非如此，如果我們還記得有些韻書也許衹根據介音的不同，將本屬一韻的字分作兩韻，這種現象雖然罕見但畢竟偶爾出現。在《切韻》中有很多這樣的例子，但正如我之前所説，《中原音韻》中使用的術語"韻"比之前的内涵更廣泛，因此《中原音韻》中兩個韻之間的區别不太可能僅僅是介音的不同，特别是當韻腹必須假設爲低元音時。同樣，這也不能簡單地作如此假設。爲了令人信服，我們必須對這三韻中的介音分布情況作嚴密地檢查。

5.3.1"桓歡"韻的字在韻圖中都是合口，在現代北京話中也都是有介音/w/，因此它們在《中原音韻》中也必須是代表帶有介音/w/的音節[②]。出於同樣的原因，我們知道"寒山"韻包含了零介音音節和/w/介音音節，還有一些從韻圖喉音二等變來的帶有/y/介音的音節（見4.6.2），例如0801005"姦"（中古：山開二平删見AC /꜀ kɛn/，MP /cyān/）和0802024"閑"（中古：山開二平山匣AC /꜀ xɦan/，MP /syán/）。構成"先天"韻的音節，要麼僅帶有介音/y/，要麼帶有複合介音/yw/，因爲它們都來自三等和四等。這種情況可以通過下表清楚地展示出來：

韻母 / 韻類	-øVn	-yVn	-wVn	-ywVn
寒山	x	x	x	
桓歡			x	
先天		x		x

5.3.2 由上表可知，寒山韻的主元音必須與桓歡韻的主元音不同。像0801007"關"（中古：山合二平删見AC /꜀ kuɛn/，MP /kwān/）與0901001"官"（中古：山合一平桓見AC /꜀ kuɑn/，MP /kwān/），以及0801010"彎"（中古：山合二平删影AC /꜀ quɛn/，MP /wān/）和"剜"（中古：山合一平桓影AC

① 參哈特門(1944)和霍凱特(1947)。

② 董同龢教授(1954:30)把它們標注爲帶有零介音的韻母[on]，可能是受八思巴字的影響，參陸志韋(1946:51)。

/꜀quɑn/, MP /wān/),這些構成最小對比對的字之間的差異,必須是二者所俱不同主元音之間的差異。此表還顯示,寒山韻和先天韻有不同的元音,因爲它們都包含介音爲/y/的字,因此形成最小對比對,如0801005"姦"(中古:山開二平删見AC /꜀kɛn/, MP /cyān/)與1001003"堅"(中古:山開四平先見AC /꜀kien/, MP /cyān/),以及0804064"間"(中古:山開二去襉見AC /kanᵓ/ MP /cyàn/)和1004069"見"(中古:山開四去霰見AC /kienᵓ/ MP /cyàn/)。從介音角度看,桓歡韻和先天韻似乎是互補分布的,因此我們可以在保持它們之間對比的前提下假設它們含有相同的主元音。這麼處理,儘管看起來好像可以,但事實上是不可能的。因爲不管哪本韻書,即便是在《切韻》中,都没有將韻基相同而僅介音爲/yw/與/w/之别的字歸入不同的韻。因此,像0901003"歡"(中古:山合一平桓曉AC /꜀xuɑn/, MP /hwān/)和1001007"暄"(中古:山合三平元曉AC /꜀xiuan/, MP /sywān/)這樣的同音字組不在同一韻中出現的事實,可以作爲它們具有不同主元音的證據。

5.4 一個實驗性的元音系統

我們現在已經證明了《中原音韻》中有四個主要元音。其中有一個是高元音,可以用/ɨ/來表示。其他三個都是低元音,在没有任何理由作其他解釋的情況下,可以假設它們在音位上處於同一級上。先天韻的主元音被公認爲是低前元音,因此可以用/e/表示[①]。桓歡韻的元音很可能是一個低後元音,可以用/o/表示[②]。這就爲寒山韻留下了央低元音,事實上,之前所有的研究都假設它的韻腹元音是[a][③],因此,我們將用音位/a/來表示這個主元音。這樣,我們就得到了一個非常整齊的元音音位模式,高度上分爲兩級(集聚性/分散性),深度分爲三度(鈍音性/鋭音性和降音性/平音性),如下表所示:

---

① 陸志韋(1946:50)[ɛ];趙蔭棠(1936:129)[ɛ];董同龢(1954:30)[e]。

② 陸志韋(1946:50)[ɔ];董同龢(1954:30)[o]。趙蔭棠(1936:128)從其師錢玄同,爲這一組選擇了[œ],但受到陸志韋的批評,(參陸志韋1946:51)。

③ 陸志韋(1946:49)、董同龢(1954:29)。但趙蔭棠(1936)以及後來的司徒修(1962a)假設這一韻有兩個元音,來自一等的是/ɑ/(司徒修/o/),來自二等的是/a/。

	前	央	後
高		ɨ	
低	e	a	o

至於這些音位在表層的語音實現(也即這些音位的具體音值),在這個階段我們還不能做什麼,儘管我們可以猜想/e/和/o/可能比/a/相對高一點。

5.5 東鍾韻、江陽韻、庚青韻

現在可以很容易地處理東鍾、江陽和庚青這三個韻尾爲舌根鼻音/ŋ/的穿鼻韻。江陽韻的字在現代北京話中以低元音/a/作爲韻腹,它們在韻圖中屬於江攝和宕攝。自然,我們認爲江陽韻的韻腹是/a/,即上表中的央低元音。基於類似的考慮,我們假設庚青韻的韻腹爲前低元音/e/,它是由之前梗攝字和曾攝字組成的①。剩下的東鍾韻現在有兩個選擇,它的主元音可以說是央高元音/ɨ/,或者後低元音/o/②。兩種選擇都有足够的理由,因此我們衹能根據它的解釋力作出選擇。我爲這一韻選擇/o/,是基於以下理由:

(a) 在結構上,/o/更好,因爲這樣,我們就可以概括地説,韻尾/ŋ/衹出現在低(集聚性)元音之後。

(b) 大多數庚青韻合口字也出現在東鍾韻裏,反之則不然(見5.7.2)。如果我們説庚青韻和東鍾韻的主元音在同一個層次上,上述這個現象便可以更合理地得到解釋。

(c) 假設東鍾韻的韻腹是一個低元音,我們現在可以斷言,到《中原音韻》時期,所有韻尾爲/ŋ/的"内轉"韻都毫無例外地轉入到"外轉",因爲曾攝和梗

---

① 在《中原音韻》時期,庚青韻的字韻腹應爲前低元音/e/,這是毫無疑問的。然而,要解釋梗攝和曾攝的歷史發展以及它們最終的合併是相當困難的。關於這個問題的簡要説明,請見6.4.1。也可參見橋本萬太郎(1970)。

② 【追注】在這個問題上,我的看法已經完全改變了。由於我們對等韻中内外轉的含義有了正確的瞭解(參考薛鳳生 1985),而且對語音演變的性質與趨勢也有了更清楚的認識(參看薛鳳生 1982),此處(b)和(c)兩個論點便不攻自破了,我現在認爲,東鍾韻的韻腹衹能是高元音,而江陽韻的韻腹則必爲後低元音。這樣,作爲穿鼻韻韻腹的元音構成了一個正三角形的分配形式,結構上仍是合理的(參看薛鳳生 1986,第七章)。

攝一道形成了以/e/爲主元音的庚青韻。

必須立刻補充一點，這裏的決定不能在語音的基礎上實現。首先，我們没有辦法確切地知道這個主元音可能具有什麽樣的音值。其次，即使它可能在語音上相對較高，但我們仍然可以將其分配給後低元音音位/o/。其實，我相信它在語音上是高的，很可能是[o]，因爲高本漢爲通攝構擬的兩個元音之一便是[o]。如果是這樣的話，我們現在可以説，音位/o/至少有兩個變體，在/ŋ/之前是[o]，在/n/之前是[ɔ]。

5.5.1 我們在來自通攝的東鍾韻裏發現一個現象，即原中古漢語中知莊章三組字之間的對立在《中原音韻》不復存在。例如，在 0102027“重蟲慵鱅崇”這個同音字組裏，我們發現“崇”（中古：通合三平東崇 AC /꜀crɦ*ŋ/ MP /crhwéŋ/）和“蟲”（中古：通合三平東澄 AC /꜀tjɦ*ŋ/ MP /crhwéŋ/）和“鱅”（中古：通合三平鍾禪 AC /꜀sjɦiu*ŋ/，MP /ywéŋ/①）這三個字同時出現在此處。我們衹能找到這一個例子，因爲通攝中捲舌（莊組）聲母三等字很罕見，而東鍾韻中恰好衹有這一個“崇”字。根據 4.5.2 給出的規則，我們應該推論：“崇”所代表的音節首先失去了介音“/y/”，然後與之對應的腭噝音（章組）聲母和腭塞音（知組）聲母音節合併，最後它們也失去了介音“/y/”，從而與“崇”聲母音節共處一個同音字組。既然我們已經確定東鍾韻的主元音是/o/，我們可以在 4.5.2 所提出的規則後面加上下面的公式：這個公式中的捲舌聲母（Pr），當然是章（Pj）和知（P）合併後的結果。

$$y \rightarrow \emptyset / Pr\_\_\_\_\_ w + o + \eta \qquad (24)$$

或許不必解釋就知道，這個變化過程發生得很晚。它不僅晚於三組腭聲母的合併，而且正如我們將看到的（6.4.2.1—6.4.2.2），它甚至晚於以入聲字的重新分配。這就是爲什麽在上述規則中，我們没有將/k/寫在韻尾位置上的理由。

5.5.2 /y/介音的失落現象，在東鍾韻一些牙喉音聲母（“喉音”的使用見3.2注釋①）字中也能看到。例如，“公”（中古：通合一平東見 AC /꜀k*ŋ/，

① ［譯注］今讀[yŋ]陰平。其實，此字在《廣韻》中的反切分别是“餘封切”“蜀庸切”，均爲“魚名”，此取後者。

MP /kwēŋ/)和“弓”(中古:通合三平東見 AC /꜀ki*ŋ/, MP /kwēŋ/)”一起在0101014“工功攻公蚣弓躬恭宫龔供肱觥”這個同音字組中出現。但是,另一方面,我們也注意到許多最小對比對,它們之間的區别衹能由介音/y/的存在與否來顯示,例如,0101007“空”(中古:通合一平東溪 AC /꜀kh*ŋ/, MP /khwēŋ/)對0101013“穹”(中古:通合三平東溪 AC /꜀khi*ŋ/, MP /chywēŋ/)和0101015“烘”(中古:通合一平東曉 AC /꜀x*ŋ/, MP /hwēŋ/)對0101016“胸”(中古:通合三平鍾曉 AC /꜀xiu*ŋ/, MP /sywēŋ/)。因此,在這種情況下,我們無法給出一個形式化的制約條件。我們所能提供的最好的辦法,也許就是隨便説一句:韻母/ywoŋ/有變成/woŋ/的趨勢。

5.6 《中原音韻》和韻圖時期的元音系統

寒山、桓歡、先天均源自之前山攝。將山攝與三個韻進行對比,可以發現一個非常有規律的演變模式。我們發現三等字和四等字在先天韻中已經完全合併,例如1001012“軒”(中古:山開三平元曉 AC /꜀xian/, MP /sywān/)“祆”(中古:山開四平先曉 AC /꜀xien/, MP /syān/),1002023“連”(中古:山開三平仙來 AC /꜀liɛn/, MP /lyán/)“憐”(中古:山開四平先來 AC /꜀lien/, MP /lyán/)和1004069“見”(中古:山開四去霰見 AC /kien꜄/, MP /cyàn/)“建”(中古:山開三去願見 AC /kian꜄/, MP /cyàn/)。一等合口字單獨構成桓歡韻,一等開口字與二等字共同構成寒山韻。然而,衹能給出一個例子0802021“蘭”(中古:山開一平寒來 AC /꜀lɑn/, MP /lán/)“斕”(中古:山開二平山來 AC /꜀lan/, MP /lán/)來展示一等字和二等字合併成一個同音字組。有幾個原因可以解釋爲什麼我們找不到更多類似的例子。首先,脣音聲母一等字在音位上都有/w/介音(見4.2.1),因此都出現在桓歡韻,而不是與出現在寒山韻裏的二等字合併。其次,雖然在寒山韻裏出現了非脣音聲母開口一等字,但它們仍自成同音字組,或者是因爲它們與二等字的聲母不同(齒音配一等,腭音配二等,/l/和/n/除外),或者是因爲,在喉音聲母的情況下,由於二等字在介音位置上出現了新增生的/y/(因此即便一二等字聲母和韻基都相同,但字音仍不同)。(見4.6.2)。儘管缺乏更多這樣的例子,我們仍然不能像趙蔭棠和司徒修那樣①,爲寒山韻構擬兩個主元音。寒山韻的字互相押韻,且不與桓歡韻和先天韻的字押韻,證明寒山韻的字必然含有相同的主元音。我們現在可以用公式來表達山攝的主元音從韻圖時期到《中原音韻》的位移變化。

$$V_1 \rightarrow \begin{Bmatrix} o/w\_\_\_ \\ a \end{Bmatrix} \tag{25}$$

$$V_2 \rightarrow a \tag{26}$$

$$\begin{Bmatrix} V_3 \\ V_4 \end{Bmatrix} \rightarrow e \tag{27}$$

5.6.1 這裏必須指出,元音的這些位移變化一定發生在前面討論過的四個涉及聲母的變化之後。爲了將它們置於適當的位置,我們現在將那四個變化列在下面:

(a) 原無介音的脣音聲母字,增生/w/介音,這個變化肯定早於元音位移變化的時間(見4.2.1中的規則9)。

(b) 脣齒化的過程也發生得更早,這一點可以從以下事實中看出:三等合口字現在出現在寒山韻而不是先天韻中,例如,0801012"番"(中古:山合三平元滂 AC /꜀phiuan/, MP /fwān/)、0802026"煩"(中古:山合三平元並 AC /꜀pɦiuan/, MP /fwán/)、0803034"晚"(中古:山合三上阮明 AC /꜂miuan/, MP /wǎn/)。參見4.2.1中的規則(10)。

(c) 中古漢語捲舌(莊組)聲母音節必須在元音位移變化變化之前失去/y/介音(見4.5中的規則13)。結果山攝的這些三等莊組字進入寒山韻而不是先天韻。例如,0801008"拴"(中古:山合三平仙生 AC /꜀sriuɛn/, MP /srwān/)②,0801018"跧"(中古:山合三平仙莊 AC /꜀criuɛn/, MP

---

① 趙蔭棠(1936:127);司徒修(1962a:142,144)。

② [譯注]0801008這個同音字組共有兩個字"櫁拴"。服部四郎、藤堂明保(1958:124—125):"廣韻櫁に作る"。"1. 廣韻栓は山員切、拴は此緣切。この項栓に作るべし。2. この字廣韻になし。"作者給"拴"字標注的馬丁音位化的讀音爲/꜀sriuɛn/,這顯示作者認爲"拴"爲"仙"韻生母字。但事實上"拴"字,《廣韻》此緣切,《集韻》逡緣切,皆仙韻清母字,音韻地位不合。在《集韻》中"櫁栓"在二等"删"韻中同處一個小韻,"數還切"。但"栓"還有另外一個仙韻的讀音,在《廣韻》爲"山員切",《集韻》爲"所員切",但此時"栓"不與"櫁"共處一個小韻。如果由於《集韻》删韻"櫁栓"共處一個小韻,而認爲《中原音韻》0801008"櫁拴"這個 (轉下頁)

/crwān/)①,和 0802030“潺”(中古:山開三平仙崇 AC /$_{\text{c}}$crɦɛn/ MP /crhán/)②。

(d) 喉音聲母開口二等字增生/y/介音的時間也早於上述元音的變化。參見 4.6.2 中的規則(19)。

一個有趣的現象可以在此提出來,即脣音聲母三等字和捲舌(莊組)聲母三等字分别經歷脣齒化和捲舌化之後所發生的變化,强烈暗示了外轉二等和三等的主元音可能相同。這樣的證據,使我覺得韻圖所依據的元音系統可能與《中原音韻》的元音系統是一樣的,即一個四元音的系統,高元音爲内轉,三個低元音爲外轉。如果這是真的,那麽二等音節與三等音節之間的唯一區别就是三等有/y/介音。因此,當外轉三等音節失去了/y/介音時,它們將自動變成二等音節。同樣,内轉三等音節失去/y/時,便自動變爲一等音節,但根據它們的聲母,這些音節將分别被置於一等位置和二等位置(《切韻指掌圖》的部分現象可以證實這一點)。從這個角度來看,從中古漢語到早期官話之間的變化並不像大多數學者所認爲的那樣劇烈。

5.6.2 現在可以對上一節得出的結論作一個很自然的拓展。我們可以假設,除了已經討論過的穿鼻韻之外(見 5.5),《中原音韻》中源自内轉的韻,無論是幾等,其元音都是高元音;源自外轉的韻,其主元音則是三個低元音之一。這一點,由上一節給出的三個規則及先决條件具體指定。這些規則可以按以下順序重述:

$$ø \rightarrow w/B\_\_\_\_V \tag{9}$$

$$y \rightarrow ø/Pr\_\_\_\_ \tag{13}$$

$$y \rightarrow ø/m\_\_\_\_V_{tu} \tag{12}$$

V_{tu}=通攝的主元音

(接上頁)同音字組中的“拴”字本應該是“栓”,則“栓”在這裏不適合作爲“仙”韻字來處理,而應該作爲“删”韻字。因爲作者此處是舉例説明莊組三等字失去/y/介音之後進入“寒山”韻,而不是先天韻。司徒修(1966)認爲“拴”字另外一個寫法是“栓”。

① [譯注]服部四郎、藤堂明保(1958:125)“跧の反切を示す。”

② [譯注]服部四郎、藤堂明保(1958:128)指出“潺”,《廣韻》有“士山”和“士連”兩個反切,作者采用的是後者。

$$\left\{\begin{matrix} p\left(\begin{Bmatrix} h \\ ɦ \end{Bmatrix}\right) \\ m \end{matrix}\right\} \rightarrow \begin{Bmatrix} f \\ v \end{Bmatrix} / \_\_\_ y+w \quad (10)$$

$$y \rightarrow ø / \begin{Bmatrix} f \\ v \end{Bmatrix} \_\_\_\_ \quad (11)$$

$$V_3 \rightarrow \begin{Bmatrix} V_2 / C(w) \_\_\_ \\ V_4 \end{Bmatrix} \quad (28)$$

$$ø \rightarrow y / G \_\_\_ V_2 \quad (19)$$

$$V_n \rightarrow ɨ \quad (29)$$

$$V_1 \rightarrow \begin{Bmatrix} o / w \_\_\_ \\ a \end{Bmatrix} \quad (25)$$

$$V_2 \rightarrow a \quad (26)$$

$$V_4 \rightarrow e \quad (27)$$

5.7 穿鼻韻的特殊演變過程

我們已經觀察到前文所描述的穿鼻韻字元音的特殊發展過程,儘管還不能對此提供充分的解釋。然而,庚青韻中的兩個奇異現象却因此得到非常滿意的解釋,這一點曾使所有研究《中原音韻》的學者感到疑惑不解①。

5.7.1 我們已經提到有一小部分同音字組顯示了二等和三等的合併,但沒有解釋(見 4.6.2c)。這些同音字組都出現在庚青韻中,例如 1501001"京"(中古:梗開三平庚見 AC /꜀kiaŋ/, MP /cyēŋ)/)"庚"(中古:梗開二平庚見

① 【追注】由於我們現在對等韻的性質有了更深入更正確的瞭解,本節關於穿鼻韻之演變的討論就必須重寫了。概括地説,我們現在知道,梗曾兩攝在等韻及其以前的時代是收舌面音韻尾的,故能與收舌根音韻尾的江宕等攝形成對立。在韻圖的結構裏,尤其是在促成"内外混等"的音變之後,它們的形態與分布也跟其他所謂"外轉"攝毫無差别(參看薛鳳生 1985),但在後來的演變中,舌根音韻尾影響韻腹元音前移,故梗曾合併成庚青韻。這樣一來,兩韻的音位差别改由韻腹元音擔任,韻尾的差别也就變爲次要而終於消失了。從這個新的理論觀點看穿鼻韻的演變,就可以看出它們仍是遵循元音演變的一般規律的,並不特殊,本節所討論的"奇異現象"也就可以得到更合理的解釋了。

AC /꜀kaŋ/, MP /kēŋ/)和 1504092“杏”(中古:梗開二上梗匣 AC /꜂xɦaŋ/[①], MP /syèŋ/)“興”(中古:曾開三去證曉 AC /xiəŋ꜄/, MP /syèŋ/)。現在,運用關於元音位移變化的新見解,就可以很容易地解釋爲什麼這些同音字組都集中在這一韻裹了。已經聲明,庚青韻是梗攝和曾攝合併的結果,它們在經歷特殊的演變之後,在《中原音韻》中以前低元音/e/爲主元音(見 5.5)。由於二等開口牙喉音字增生了/y/介音(4.6.2),結果當然就是,在庚青韻中,二等與三、四等合併了,因爲現在它們的主元相同,其他部分也相同。在現代北京話中,我們發現大多數這種類型的二等字没有介音/y/,因此仍然保持着與三、四等之間的區别。正如司徒修所指出的,這個事實也許就是“(中原音韻)所記録的方言和現代北京話之間作爲一種叔侄關係的證據”[②]。若果真如此,我們就不得不説,在現代北京話的直系祖語中,梗攝和曾攝合併後共同以/e/爲韻腹一定發生在規則(19)所代表的音變之前,結果規則(19)自然就没有影響到梗攝二等字。

5.7.2 少數字同時出現在東鍾韻和庚青韻中,如 0101015“烘叿轟薨”和 1501010“轟薨”這兩個同音字組裹的“轟”(中古:梗合二平耕曉 AC /꜀xueŋ/, MP /hwēŋ/),以及 0101016“凶兇胷洶兄”和 1501026“兄”這兩個同音字組裹的“兄”(中古:梗合三平庚曉 AC /꜀xiuaŋ/, MP /sywēŋ/)。仔細檢查就會發現,它們都來自梗攝和曾攝,而且都是合口字。根據目前我們制定的規則,在庚青韻中,它們出現的形式是/weŋ/或/yweŋ/。當它們出現在東鍾韻時,我們發現它們分别與通攝字共處一個同音字組,這些通攝字的韻母應該構擬爲/woŋ/或/ywoŋ/,但這些通攝字却不出現在庚青韻中[③]。這種現象表明,從/(y)weŋ/到/(y)woŋ/是單向的。我揣測,前低元音/e/到後低元音/o/的變化是受到了介音/w/的影響。這一看法得到兩個事實的支持。首先,韻母/weŋ/很特别,因爲衹在這個韻母裹/w/單獨作爲介音出現在前低元音前,正是這一點導致發生了(從/(y)weŋ/到/(y)woŋ/的)音變。其次,雖然實際上所有

---

① [譯注]原文標爲去聲,“誤”,當爲“上聲”。

② 司徒修(1962a:132),也可參薛鳳生(1971)。

③ 很顯然,我們不能接受司徒修的説法,即“周德清混淆了‘甖’和‘甕’”(司徒修 1962a:134)。

/weŋ/韻母字都出現東鍾韻，但衹有部分/yweŋ/韻母字也同時出現在東鍾韻，這説明，介音位置上的/y/對這個音變有某阻礙作用，儘管全面的發展使得這一趨勢不可逆轉。的確，《中原音韻》之後的進一步發展似乎使東鍾韻和庚青韻之間的對比衹體現在介音/w/的有和無上（合口對開口）。但衹要這些字仍然出現在庚青韻中，我們必須保留韻母/weŋ/和/yweŋ/①。如果它們出現在東鍾韻中，我們就可以説它們的主元音變成了/o/。换句話説，我們認爲《中原音韻》時期是這類字的過渡時期，那時它們每個字都有兩個讀音。

5.8 侵尋韻、監咸韻、廉纖韻

現在，可以通過首先將我們有關元音位移變化的假設運用到韻尾爲/m/的閉口韻（即源自深攝的“侵尋”韻，源自咸攝的“監咸”韻和“廉纖”韻）上，進而來驗證它。自然地，我們假設/ɨ/是侵尋韻的主元音，且我們發現這個假設非常有效。對於廉纖韻，我們假設/e/是它的主元音，因爲該韻字來自咸攝三、四等字。這兩等聲母相同的字都出現在同一個同音字組，例如1902014“黏”（中古：咸開三平鹽泥 AC /꜀ niɛm/，MP /nyán/）“拈”（中古：咸開四平添泥 AC /꜀ niem/，MP /nyán/）；1904035“欠”（中古：咸開三去釅溪 AC /khiamᵓ/，MP /chyàn/）“歉”（中古：咸開四上忝溪 AC /꜂ khiem/，MP /chyàn/）。監咸韻必須以/a/爲韻腹。我們在這裏也衹有一個例子來證明一等字和二等字合併成一個同音字組，1802017“南”（中古：咸開一平覃泥 AC /꜀ nəm/，MP /nán/）“諵”（中古：咸開二平咸泥 AC /꜀ nam/，MP /nán/）。同討論寒山韻（5.6）時理由一樣，這種例子可能衹出現在以/l/或/n/開頭的音節上，但不幸的是，唯

① 司徒修（1962a：133—137）詳細地討論了這個問題，但是他提出的結論不能令人信服。司徒修（1966：22）好像完全忽視了這個問題，而假定/ɨŋ/和/iɨŋ/爲庚青韻的韻母，/uɨŋ/和/iuɨŋ/爲東鍾韻的韻母。

一可能出現的例子"臉"(中古:咸開二上豏來 AC /ᶜ lam/, MP /lyǎn/)①②與"覽"(中古:咸開一上敢來 AC /ᶜ lɑm/, MP /lǎn/),它們應該出現在 1803027"覽攬欖爦"這個同音字組中。但這個二等字却出現 1903025"斂臉"這個同音字組中,顯然是由於一些不規則的變化造成的。由於咸攝一等没有合口字,因此《中原音韻》的穿鼻韻中没有主元音是/o/的韻③。根據規則(9),脣音聲母咸攝一等字的韻母應該是*/wom/,這類字衹有兩個,即姏(中古:咸開一平談明 AC /꜀ mɑm/, MP /mwán/)和"媎"(中古:咸開一上敢明 AC /ᶜ mɑm/, MP——),但《中原音韻》不收這兩個字。然而,即便是收了,它們既不會另成一韻,也不會進入"監咸"韻,因爲閉口韻脣音聲母字的異化過程(3.4 中的規則 1)肯定會迫使它們進入"桓歡"韻。

5.9 歌戈韻、家麻韻、車遮韻

我們現在可以更有信心地將我們有關元音位移變化的假設再向前推進了。歌戈、家麻和車遮這三韻從果攝和假攝發展而來,屬無尾韻。雖然《切韻指南》將果攝和假攝劃爲兩個獨立的類,但就"等"而言,它們實際上處於互補

---

① 李榮(1956:70)注爲"力減反",這是根據《王仁昫刊謬補缺切韻》,但《集韻》裏標爲居奄切,即聲母是/k/。

② [譯注]訥菴本《中原音韻》中,"臉"在 1903024"撿鐮臉"和 1903025"斂臉"這兩個同音字組中同時出現。趙蔭棠本第一個同音字組爲"撿鐮瞼"。《中原音韻》"正語作詞起例"第 21 條中有"撿有蹇",第 25 條"略舉釋疑字樣"對"臉"字的讀音進行了解釋,"桃腮杏臉,則呼爲檢;若呼美臉兒,當呼爲斂字音。"由此可見,趙蔭棠本不確。因爲如果前者爲"瞼",後者爲"臉"的話,就没有必要再在"略舉釋疑字樣"作解釋了。再者,應該注意的是 1903024 這個同音字組的首字究竟是"撿"還是"檢"的問題。關於這一點,《中原音韻》内部有矛盾,"正語作詞起例"第 21 條和第 25 條是互斥的。《廣韻》居儼切下有"檢"字,注云"俗作撿"。這一點,服部四郎、藤堂明保(1958)和寧繼福(1985)都注意到了。但似乎都没有注意到"正語作詞起例"第 21 條和第 25 條之間的矛盾。如果 1903024 這個同音字組同時包含"撿"和"檢",則這個矛盾就不存在了。《中原音韻問奇集》相應的同音字組是四個字"撿瞼檢臉"同時出現,同時把"鐮"放在"斂臉"這個同音字組,以"X"爲標記,表示"舊本所無,皆係增入"。

③ [譯注]也就是説,没有與"桓歡"韻相當的閉口韻。

分布狀態①②。因此,《切韻指掌圖》暗示它們被視爲一個攝。因此,根據我們的假設,車遮韻的主元音應是/e/,家麻韻爲/a/,歌戈韻爲/o/。就家麻和車遮而言,這非常有效,但就歌戈而言,我們發現我們必須稍微修改一下規則(25)的制約條件。不是合口一等字才能保持一等且主元音爲/o/,我們現在不得不説,所有的合口一等字,以及無尾韻的一等字,都仍保持一等且主元音爲/o/。因爲我們發現在家麻韻中没有一等字,而在歌戈韻中,除了合口一等字外,例如1201002“科”(中古:果合一平戈溪 AC /꜀khuɑ/, MP /khē/)和1201004“戈”(中古:果合一平戈見 AC /꜀kuɑ/, MP /kē/),還有很多開口一等字,比如1201001“歌”(中古:果開一平歌見 AC /꜀kɑ/, MP /kē/)和1201003“軻”(中古:果開一平歌溪 AC /꜀kha/, MP /khē/)。因此,我們必須將第25條規則修改如下:

$$V_1 \rightarrow \begin{Bmatrix} o/ \begin{Bmatrix} w\_\_\_ \\ \_\_\_\# \end{Bmatrix} \\ a \end{Bmatrix} \qquad (30)$$

實際上,這個修改衹對喉音聲母字來説才是必須的,因爲到《中原音韻》時,所有非喉音聲母開口字顯然已經增生了/w/介音,並隨後與原合口字合併了,例如,1201005“娑”(中古:果開一平歌心 AC /꜀sɑ/, MP /swē/)“莎”(中古:果合一平戈心 AC /꜀suɑ/, MP /swē/),1202015“羅”(中古:果開一平歌來 AC /꜀lɑ/, MP /lwé/)“螺”(中古:果合一平戈來 AC /꜀luɑ/, MP /lwé/),1204067 馱(中古:果開一去箇定 AC /tɦɑ꜄/③, MP /twè/)“惰”(中古:果合一去過定 AC /tɦuɑ꜄/④, MP /twè/)。因此,下面這個規則是必須的:

$$C + V_1 + \# \rightarrow C + w + V_1 + \# \qquad (31)$$
$$C \neq G$$

① 實際上,二者之間的界限並不是十分清楚。確實存在一個對立“虵”/꜀ia/對“耶”/꜀iɛ/,但由於分布如此有限,在以後的發展中一定很快消失了(見李榮 1956:46,48)。

② 【追注】現在我們知道這個説法是錯誤的了。雖然果攝三等字很少,性質上與假攝三等字是衝突的,衹就聲母的不同而説它們可以互補是没有意義的。果假二攝衹在“内外混等”以後才形成韻圖形式上的互補,成爲一個“外轉”攝。詳細的討論請參閱薛鳳生(1985)。

③ [譯注]英文原文爲/tɑ꜄/,誤,當爲/tɦɑ꜄/。

④ [譯注]英文原文爲/tuɑ꜄/,誤,當爲/tɦuɑ꜄/。

當然,這裏有一個時間順序的問題。在這一點上,我們不知道上述兩個規則所代表的音變哪一個先發生。在兩種可能的順序中無論哪一種在描述上都能得到滿意的結果。不過,無論如何,這兩種規則都是需要的。這裏必須提到另一個與家麻韻有關的問題。我們發現家麻韻裏的少數字源自蟹攝而非假攝,例如 1301001“佳”(中古:蟹開二平佳見 AC /꜀kɛi′/, MP /cyā/)和 1304063“話”(中古:蟹合二去夬匣 AC /xɦuɛiᵓ/, MP /hwà/)。根據一般的發展,我們預計會在皆來韻中看到它們,但就它們出現在家麻韻而言,我們必須假設它們失去了韻尾/y/。這些字都是喉音聲母二等字,無一例外。這兩個事實使我猜測,這些字何以例外地出現在家麻韻中,也許可以用某種制約條件來解釋。然而,限於目前的認識,我們不太可能知道這個制約條件應該是什麼。

5.10 蕭豪韻

蕭豪韻一直是《中原音韻》研究者面臨的主要難題。我們發現,在這一韻的脣音和喉音聲母字中,存在三向對立,例如:

(a) 1101028“褒”(中古:效開一平豪幫 AC /꜀pɑu/, MP /pwāw/)對 1101009“包”(中古:效開二平肴幫 AC /꜀pɛu/, MP /pwāw/)對 1101007“標”(中古:效開三平宵幫 AC /꜀piɛu/, MP /pyāw/)①。

(b) 1101011“高”(中古:效開一平豪見 AC /꜀kɑu/, MP /kāw/)對 1101008“交”(中古:效開二平肴見 AC /꜀kɛu/, MP /cyāw/)對 1101005“嬌”(中古:效開三平宵見:AC /꜀kiɛu/, MP /cyāw/)。

(c) 1101026“蒿”(中古:效開一平豪曉 AC /꜀xɑu/, MP /hāw/)對 1101022“哮”(中古:效開二平肴曉 AC /꜀xɛu/, MP /syāw/)對 1101003“囂”(中古:效開三平宵曉 AC /꜀xiɛu/, MP /syāw/)。

(d) 1104147“奧”(中古:效開一去号影:AC /qɑuᵓ/, MP /àw/)對 110413“拗”(中古:效開二去效影 AC /qɛuᵓ/, MP /àw/)對 1104130“要”(中古:效開

① [譯注](a)的三向對立,原文爲包、褒、標,由於下面的(b)、(c)、(d)全都是一等字、二等字與三等字排列次序,故這裏將一等“褒”字排在二等“包”字前面。

三去号影 AC /qiɛu⊃/, MP /yàw/)。

面對這些問題,以往學者的反應都是猶豫不決。趙蔭棠指責這本書在此處没有反映出當時語言的真實狀況,而反映的是更早時期語言的狀態[①]。董同龢使用了幾種非官話南方方言來説明這些對立[②]。在我看來,陸志韋在處理這個問題上做得最好。通過采用在一定程度上帶有結構意味的方法,他得出結論,認爲至少需要三個主元音來處理這些三向對立,儘管他欣然地承認對此没有什麽把握[③]。

5.10.1 當我們將元音位移變化的假設應用到這一韻時,我們立即注意到,這些三向對立不再構成任何問題。相反,它們是那個時期語言的音系結構的自然的和不可避免的演變結果。的確,我們將得出一個與陸志韋大致相同的結論,但兩者有很大的區别。他的結論或多或少是猜測的結果,我們的結論是由我們爲當時語言所建立的整體音位結構所決定的必然結果。我們知道,蕭豪韻來自四等俱全的效攝,而且都是開口字[④]。因此,根據我們的元音位移變化規則,一等字應該以/ow/[⑤]爲韻母,但脣音聲母字除外,它們的韻母應該是/wow/。二等字韻母也應該是/aw/,但脣音字應該/waw/,喉音字應該是/yaw/。三、四等字必然已合併,且韻母爲/yew/。這樣,被上述例證證實的三向對立便以我所能想象的到的最合理的方式給解釋了。

5.10.2 儘管上面的解决方案看上去似乎是合理的,但它還不能完全令人滿意,因爲它不能解釋這個韻中存在的另一個奇怪現象。我們發現在蕭豪韻中有這樣一個最小對比對,即 1104147“奥”(中古:效開一去号影:AC /qɑu⊃/, MP /àw/)與 1104125“傲”(中古:效開一去号疑 AC /ŋɑu⊃,MP /àw/),這使5.10 中的(d)組變成了四向對比,這是上述方案無法解釋的。在我們討論中古漢語/ŋ/聲母(即疑母)時(4.6.4—4.6.4.5),主要是因爲存在兩個最小對比對,一個是 1203046“婀”與 1203048“我”,另一個就是剛才提到的那個

① 見趙蔭棠(1936:129—131)。

② 見董同龢(1954:30—31)。

③ 見陸志韋(1946:54—55)。

④ 實際上,所有韻圖都將這一攝標爲“獨”,即全都是“開”,或全都是“合”。現代學者無一例外地都把這一攝解釋爲開口。

⑤ [譯注]英文原文爲/aw/,誤,當爲/ow/。

(1104147“奥懊澳”與 1104125“傲鼻鳌”),我們不得不説,在《中原音韻》中仍然存在疑母,儘管其分布相當有限。既然承認這一點,我們就必須找出這個聲母分布如此邊緣的形式條件。由於這裏涉及的兩個同音字組中的疑母字都是一等字,所以我認爲有理由説,在這兩個同音字組中,外轉一等主元音保持不變,而在其他情況下,則已變成了外轉二等的主元音了。因此,我們可以説,當出現在殘存的外轉一等主元音之前時,/ŋ/聲母才保持不變。就 1203048 這個同音字組而言,5.9 中的規則(30)已將其妥善處理,因爲按照規則,它的韻腹衹能是/o/,相當於從前外轉一等字的主元音。但現在必須再次修改規則以解釋 1104125 這個同音字組,也就是説,我們不得不説,在/w/韻尾前,外轉一等的主元音在《中原音韻》也必須由/o/來表示。我們衹要在規則中添加一個新的制約條件就可以做到這一點:

$$V_1 \rightarrow \left\{ \begin{array}{l} o/\left\{ \begin{array}{l} w\underline{\qquad} \\ \underline{\qquad}\left\{ \begin{array}{l} \# \\ w \end{array} \right\} \end{array} \right\} \\ a \end{array} \right\} \qquad (32)$$

但是這個新規則,限制條件太多,看起來相當臃腫。與其説在什麼條件下外轉一等主元音保持不變,即用/o/表示,還不如直接説在什麼條件下外轉一等主元音變成了外轉二等主元音,即用/a/表示,這樣我們就可以用 4.6.4.5 中給出的規則(22)來代替規則(32):

$$C+V_1+E \rightarrow C+V_2+E \qquad (22)$$
$$E \neq w$$

當然,規則(22)還必須補充另一條重寫規則,如下所示:

$$V_1 \rightarrow o \qquad (33)$$

規則(32)雖然笨拙,但用兩條規則代替它,似乎不可取。這是事實,但這衹是因爲我們發現有必要用純粹抽象的術語來表示韻圖時期的主元音,否則(如果一開始就使用音位符號的話),規則(33)以及規則(26)和規則(27)可能就不需要了。

5.10.3 我想如果我們接受規則(22)的話,我們現在必須將蕭豪韻中所有非脣音聲母一等字的韻母寫作/ow/。换句話説,我們必須保持一等與二等之間的區别。從這些一等字與二等字同時出現在蕭豪韻的事實看,僅爲了解釋1104147與1104125這一個最小對比就認爲一等字與二等字全都有别的做法看起來相當武斷。這就是爲什麽很多研究者試圖忽略這個最小對比,認爲它是本書編纂者周德清的一個錯誤①。然而,到目前爲止,我們對這一點的討論應該有足够的説服力來支持這種區分了。爲了使我們的論證更加有説服力,我們可以仔細檢查一下,看看是否有這兩種類型的字同時出現的同音字組。如前所述(5.6和5.8),這種現象衹會發生在來母或泥母字上。碰巧在效攝中,來母没有二等,但在泥母下,一等和二等都有不少字。如果我們的假設是正確的,那麽我們將有可能在《中原音韻》中看到這種類型的一等字仍與二等字保持對立。不幸的是,這裏的情况有點令人困惑。我們發現在"平聲陽"中,它們合併了,即1102038"猱"(中古:效開一平豪泥AC /꜀nɑu/, MP /náw/)"鐃"(中古:效開二平肴泥AC /꜀nɛu/, MP /náw/),但在"上聲"中仍然仍然保持對立,即1103074"腦"(中古:效開一上晧泥AC /꜂nɑu/, MP /nǎw/)對1103094"撓"(中古:效開二上巧泥AC /꜂nɛu/, MP /nǎw/)。我認爲1103074和1103094之間的對比是證明我們假設的合理性的有力證據,因爲這兩個同音同音字組相距如此之遠,以至於似乎没有什麽理由説它們是被錯誤地分開的,特别是當我們可以爲它們的分離提供合理的解釋時。至於1102038"猱獶鐃呶怓撓譊",我覺得很容易解釋。到目前爲止,我們已經好幾次説過,兩個相鄰的同音字組實際上可能是一個,是後來某個來自不同方言地區的人錯誤地將它們分作兩組,因爲他對周德清理解得不够充分。反之,也應該成立。也就是説,某一同音字組實際上可能是原書中兩個相鄰的同音字組,衹是在後來才被錯誤地合併了,但我們必須能够提出一個理論來支持這一論點。我相信1102038正是這樣一個例子。這個同音字組中的"猱"字肯定自成一個同音字組,而其餘的字形成另一個同音字組。由於這兩個同音字組相繼出現,加之它們的區别在《中原音韻》之後又很快就消失了,所以它們被錯誤地寫成了一個

① 例如董同龢(1954:26—27)。

同音字組[①]。

5.10.4 我們給這個韻的解決方案,現在應該没有疑問了,但是對一些人來説,/yaw/和/yew/這兩個韻母之間的對比可能會顯得相當奇怪。作爲一個通則,我不喜歡依賴外部證據,除非别無他法。因爲一種方言或語言的音位結構並不能證明另一種方言或語言的音位結構。但是,如果有人認爲需要這樣的證據來支持我們在這裏提出的對比,那我們倒也不是没有。首先,正如陸志韋反復提到的那樣[②],八思巴字清楚地顯示,喉音聲母二等字此時已經增生了/y/介音。因此,我們不能忽視這一事實,爲了衹給三、四等字構擬帶有/y/介音的韻母,而不給喉音聲母二等字構擬/y/介音。其次,在《中原音韻》之後的韻書《洪武正韻》中,《中原音韻》的蕭豪韻字分爲兩個韻,清楚地顯示,一二等和三、四等必定有不同的主元音。這一事實迫使董同龢不得不承認,《洪武正韻》三、四等字的主元音"大概是[ieu]"[③],這正好符合我們的結論。這裏可以提出一個嚴肅而合理的問題。如果蕭豪韻確實包含三個不同的主元音,那麼爲什麼它不像源自山攝的寒山、桓歡和先天一樣分爲三個韻呢?我們可以提出相當多的答案,但從可驗證性來看,没有一個答案是完全令人滿意的。在我看來,最合理的猜想是周德清在這裏記録的是他那個時代的一種特殊的官話方言,這種方言仍然保留着/w/尾韻中的三個低元音之間的對比,而在大多數著名劇作家賴以寫作的方言(或方言)中,這種對比已經消失了。换句話説,周德清忠實地記録了他已學會説的那種方言,但在分韻時,却受到那些大作家用韻的影響,采取了折衷的辦法,把這三類字合成一韻了[④]。

---

① 這兒討論的問題始終都被《中原音韻》的研究者自覺或不自覺地忽視了。司徒修是唯一的例外,但他的結論正好與我相反(見司徒修 1962:138—139)。

② 參陸志韋(1946),第 49、51、54—55 頁。

③ 董同龢(1954:35)。

④ 此處討論的問題牽涉到從韻圖時期(經《中原音韻》),到現代北京話的元音系統的變化。儘管不能在此詳細討論,但大致可以説,這一變化過程在完成之前曾經歷了許多階段(大致從中唐到明末)。第一步發生在《中原音韻》之前,那是在/y/尾韻中,三個低元音的對立消失了。結果/e/和/o/變作/ɨ/(見 5.11 和 5.12)。第二步是這裏討論的/w/尾韻中三個低元音的合併。/n/尾韻中低元音的合併,以及/ŋ/尾韻中/e/和/o/的合併,都可以在畢拱辰(1642)《韻略匯通》裏看出端倪。顯然,這些變化是個非常緩慢和漸進的過程,每一步衹影響到數量有限的某一類字。此外,我們也可以穩妥地説,變化的每一步必定從某一方言(或次方言)開始,然後擴散到其他方言,正如/w/尾韻中低元音的合併那樣。

5.10.5 關於這個韻的解決方案，這裏必須再補充一點。從理論上講，脣音聲母一等字都應該與相應的二等字對立。然而，在蕭豪韻中，我們發現，衹有當聲母爲中古漢語的幫母時，這種對立才出現，例如，上面給出的 1101028“褒”對 1101009“包胞苞”，1103070“寶”（中古：效開一上晧幫 AC /ᶜ pɑu/, MP /pwǎw/）對 1103088“飽”（中古：效開二上巧幫 AC /ᶜ pɛu/, MP /pwǎw/），1104122“報”（中古：效開一去号幫 AC /pɑuᵓ/, MP /pwàw/）對 1104121“豹”（中古：效開二去效幫 AC /pɛuᵓ/, MP /pwàw）。至於其他脣音聲母字，這種對比似乎已不復存在。因此，我們現在有了包含一等和二等的同音字組，例如，1102047“袍”（中古：效開一平豪並 AC /꜀ pɦɑu/, MP /phwáw/）“庖”（中古：效開二平肴並 AC /꜀ pɦɛu/, MP /phwáw/）和 1102037“毛”（中古：效開一平豪明 AC /꜀ mɑu/, MP /mwáw/）“茅”（中古：效開二平肴明 AC /꜀ mɛu/, MP /mwáw/）。（效攝滂母無一等字）。我無法解釋爲什麽僅幫母字能保持這種對比，而其他字則不能，但整個現象或許可以作爲證據，證明所討論的對比正處於消失的邊緣。

5.11 皆來韻

我們的假設也非常適用於皆來韻，儘管這個事實可能有點被元音位移變化後的一些進一步變化所遮掩。這一韻源自蟹攝，像效攝一樣，是外轉攝之一，且四等俱全。自然，我們期待在《中原音韻》中會看到源自蟹攝的三種不同類型的韻母：

(i) /woy/：合口一等字的韻母。

(ii) /($\begin{Bmatrix}w\\y\end{Bmatrix}$)ay/：開口一等字和全部二等字的韻母。

(iii) /y(w)ey/：三、四等字的韻母。

皆來韻的大多數字都源自上述第二種情況，因此它們的韻母應該像上面所標示的那樣，例如，0601001“街”（中古蟹開二平佳見 AC /꜀ kɛi/, MP /cyē/）將是/kyay/，0601002“該”（中古：蟹開一平咍見 AC /꜀ kəi/, MP /kāy/）將是/kay/，0601015“乖”（中古：蟹合二平皆見 AC /꜀ kuai/, MP /kwāy/）將是

/kway/。然而,在此必須立即指出與此韻有關的三個奇特現象:

(a) 其他兩種韻母在《中原音韻》中不存在。之所以如此,是因爲根據我們的假設,可能具有這樣韻母的字都出現在齊微韻中了,例如,0401001"鷄"(中古:蟹開四平齊見 AC /꜀kiei/, MP /cyī/),0402032"齊"(中古:蟹開四平齊從 AC /꜀cɦiei/, MP /chyí/)。0403070"賄"(中古:蟹合一上賄曉 AC /꜂xuəi/, MP /hwèi/),0404116"祭"(中古:蟹開三去祭精 AC /ciɛiᵓ/, MP /cyì/)。顯然,這是由於一些新的變化所致,這些變化在稍後討論齊微韻時將比較容易解釋(見 5. 12. 2)。

(b) 皆來韻中有一些源自止攝而不是蟹攝的字,如 0601009"衰"(中古:止合三平脂生 AC /꜀sriu*i/, MP /srwāy),0603042"揣"(中古:止合三上紙初 AC /꜂crhiuə/, MP /crhwǎy/),0604083"帥"(中古:止合三去至生 AC /sriu*iᵓ/, MP /srwày),這也將在後面討論(見 5. 12. 3)。

(c) 我們已在 5. 9 中注意到,一些喉音聲母蟹攝字出現在家麻韻中,而没有按照我們預測的那樣出現在皆來韻。如果某種制約因素導致這些字如此演變的話,除非對《切韻》的進一步研究,尤其是對韻圖的進一步研究,能在這方面提供一些新的啓示,否則我們將無法找出制約因素。

5. 12　支思韻、齊微韻、魚模韻

爲獲得最佳效果,支思韻、齊微韻和魚模韻必須同時討論。除了齊微韻中的部分字來自蟹攝外(5. 11a),齊微韻的其他字以及支思韻字均來自止攝,而魚模韻來自遇攝。根據我們的假設,這三個韻的主元音必須都是高元音/ɨ/,因爲止攝和遇攝都是内轉。此外,我們推測出現在韻圖同攝同等位置上的中古漢語不同的韻在韻圖時期一定已經完全合併(3. 6. 3),這要求我們必須相信,此時所有的遇攝字在介音位置上都有/w/,所有的止攝字在韻尾位置上都有/y/。因此,我們認爲遇攝和止攝的唯一區别就是韻尾位置是否有/y/。這樣魚模韻應該有兩個韻母,即/wɨ/和/ywɨ/。一等字、脣音聲母三等字以及中古漢語捲舌(莊組)聲母三等字的韻母是/wɨ/,例如,0501003"蘇"(中古:遇合一平模心 AC /꜀su*/, MP /swī/)爲/swɨ/,0501007"梳"(中古:遇合三平魚生

AC /꜀sri*/, MP /srwɨ̄/)爲/srwɨ/;其他三等字的韻母是/ywɨ/,例如,0501001“居”(中古:遇合三平魚見 AC /꜀ki*/, MP /cywɨ̄/)爲/kywɨ/,0501002“諸”(中古:遇合三平魚章 AC /꜀cji*/, MP /crwɨ̄/)爲/crywɨ/。止攝的演變要複雜得多。我認爲在韻圖時期止攝一定有兩個韻母/i*i/(相當於我們的/yɨy/)和/iu*i/(相當於我們的/ywɨy/),直到《切韻指南》依然保持這種狀態。不久某些聲母字開始失去/y/介音。這個過程開始祇涉及中古漢語的捲舌(莊組)聲母字(4.5 中的規則 13),接着影響到止攝齒唑音(精組)聲母開口字,最後止攝腭唑音(章組)聲母開口字也受到影響(4.5 中的規則 15)。我們知道齒唑音(精組)聲母字受影響要比腭唑音(章組)聲母字早,因爲在《切韻指掌圖》中,我們發現,止攝開口齒唑音(精組)聲母字,如“茲”(中古:止開三平之精 AC /꜀ci*i′/, MP /cɨ̄/)和“斯”(中古:止開三平支心 AC /꜀siə/, MP /sɨ̄/),從四等位置移至一等位置,而腭唑音(章組)聲母字依然出現在三等(第十八圖),儘管在《中原音韻》中,它們與二等位置上的捲舌(莊組)聲母字合併了[①],如0301003“眵”(中古:止開三平支昌 AC /꜀cjhiə/, MP /crhɨ̄/),“差”(中古:止開三平支初 AC /꜀crhiə/, MP /crhɨ̄/)和 0301004“詩”(中古:止開三平之書 AC /꜀sji*i′/, MP /srɨ̄/),“師”(中古:止開三平脂生 AC /꜀sri*i/, MP /srɨ̄/)。然而,我們没有理由相信,在這類字的/y/韻尾也那麽早就消失了,因爲上述各例字仍然與止攝其他字同在一張圖中。因此,現在出現了一個新的韻母/ɨy/,它祇出現在齒唑音(精組)聲母和捲舌(莊組,也包括章組)聲母之後。如果到《中原音韻》時韻尾/y/仍然在保持在這個韻母中,韻母爲/ɨy/的字應該與止攝其他字互相押韻,共同組成一個新韻。事實上,它們在《中原音韻》自成一韻,形成一個獨立的支思韻,與進入齊微韻的其他止攝字形成對立。從這個事實出發,祇能推導出一個合乎邏輯的結論,即在《中原音韻》之前,新韻母/ɨy/的韻尾/y/也丢失了,於是在漢語中第一次出現了/ɨ/這個獨特的韻母。下列規

① [譯注]在《切韻指掌圖》中,止攝莊組三等字“差”和“師”出現在二等位置,章組三等字“眵”和“詩”出現在三等位置。作者的意思是説,三等位置上的章組字與二等位置上的莊組字在《中原音韻》中分别出現在同一個同音字組中,變成了同音字。並不是説“差”和“師”是捲舌聲母(莊組)二等字。或者也可以理解爲,此時由於這些莊組三等字由於失去了/y/介音,自然變成了相應的二等字。

則可以作爲對上述討論的總結：

$$y \rightarrow \emptyset / Pr\_\_\_ \quad (13)$$

$$j \rightarrow r \quad (14)$$

$$y \rightarrow \emptyset / Ds\_\_\_ \text{ɨ}y \quad (34)$$

$$y \rightarrow \emptyset / Pr\_\_\_ \text{ɨ}y \quad (15)$$

$$y \rightarrow \emptyset / C+\text{ɨ}\_\_\_ \quad (35)$$

5.12.1 在腭塞音(知組)聲母與捲舌音(莊組,也包括腭呲音章組)聲母合併(4.5 規則 16)之前,腭化介音/y/消失過程必須停止一段時間,因爲止攝中的腭塞音(知組)聲母字出現在齊微韻而不是支思韻(見 4.5)。這一事實表明,這些止攝腭塞音(知組)聲母字的韻母仍然是/yɨy/,因此不受規則(35)的影響。同理,我們認爲在大量的蟹攝字與止攝字合併之前,腭化介音/y/丟失的過程也必須停止工作,這將立即討論。

5.12.2 我們在討論皆來韻時説過,根據規則推測出來的源自蟹攝的三類韻母中的/woy/和/y(w)ey/這兩種韻母實際上在《中原音韻》並中不存在。本來按照規則應該具有這類韻母的字現在都現在齊微韻中了(5.11a)。既然現在我們知道齊微韻的主元音爲高元音/ɨ/,這個現象可以很容易地通過下面的規則在這裏記録下來：

$$\begin{Bmatrix} o \\ e \end{Bmatrix} \rightarrow \text{ɨ} / \_\_\_ y \quad (36)$$

這樣做,我們實際上已經預先做了一個有待證明的假設。也就是説,我們認爲,毋庸置疑,蟹攝從一開始就與其他外轉攝一道沿着相同的演變路徑演變,衹是在元音位移變化過程完成之後,蟹攝的元音進一步發生了獨特的變化,即/o/和/e/高化爲/ɨ/。我相信這個假設是正確的,不僅因爲它以最令人滿意的方式解釋了蟹攝的發展,而且還因爲我們在《中原音韻》中發現了相關證據,由《中原音韻》來看,蟹攝併入止攝發生地相當晚,比腭呲音(章組)聲母後/yɨy/韻母中的/y/介音的丟失還要晚。我們已經注意到,止攝腭呲音(章組)聲母字已經與捲舌音(莊組)聲母字合併,一起出現在支思韻中(5.12)。如果蟹攝字確實很早就併入了止攝,那麼蟹攝的腭呲音(章組)聲母字必須也與止攝腭齒音(章組)聲母字合併,隨後它們應該共同受到腭化介音消失過程的影響,並且最終一起出現在支思韻中。但事實並非如此。蟹攝中爲數不多的幾個腭齒音(章組)聲母字出現在齊微韻中,因此它們的韻母必依然是/yɨy/,例如,0404132“制”(中古:蟹開三去祭章 AC /cjiɛiᵓ/, MP /crɨ̀/),0404133“世”(中古:蟹開三去祭書 AC /sjiɛiᵓ/, MP /srɨ̀/)和“逝”(中古:蟹開三去祭禪 AC /sjɦɛiᵓ/, MP /srɨ̀/)。遺憾的是,來自《切韻指掌圖》的證據似乎與這種假設相矛盾。我們發現在《切韻指掌圖》中,蟹攝字已經與止攝字共同出現在同一圖中(圖 18 和圖 19),而止攝腭齒音(章組)聲母字依然列在三等位置上。這似乎打斷了我們的推理,因爲它暗示了蟹攝字併入止攝發生在很久以前,甚至在元音位移變化之前。然而,我仍然相信我們應該依賴我們依據《中原音韻》所作的理論推測,不僅因爲我們主要關注的是《中原音韻》,而《切韻指掌圖》可能與它没有直接關係,還因爲《中原音韻》可以認爲是對當時語言的真實的、無偏見的記録,而《切韻指掌圖》肯定是對之前同類韻圖的修訂形式,因此可能是融合不同時代語言新舊特徵的混合體。《切韻指掌圖》中的最後四張圖,其中包含了我們剛才討論所涉及的幾個字,以奇特的方式組織,不能不引起我們的懷疑①。

5.12.3 一些蟹攝字併入止攝,但這種流動並不意味着兩攝字之間的流動是單向的,因爲我們在主要源自蟹攝的皆來韻中也發現了一些止攝字,雖然數量極少(5.11b)。所涉及的這幾個字都是中古漢語的捲舌(莊組)聲母合口字。因此,它們的變化可以用以下方式來描述:

$$Pr+w+ɨ+y \rightarrow Pr+w+a+y \tag{37}$$

可以肯定的是,這種變化一定發生在捲舌(莊組)聲母字失去腭化介音/y/之後,腭齒音(章組)聲母字失去腭化介音/y/之前(5.12.4),因爲在齊微韻中發現了韻母爲/ywɨy/的腭齒音(章組)聲母字,這表明它們的主元音没有變,例如,0401016“吹”(中古:止合三平支昌 AC /꜀cjhiuə/, MP /crhwēy/),0402047

① 《切韻指掌圖》是這樣組織韻圖的:前六圖是“獨”,就是説每張圖不是合口,就是開口,没有對應的部分。其後的十張圖,形成五個兩兩開合相對的格局。最後四張圖,不可思議地列爲一組,兩開對兩合。

"誰"(中古:止合三平脂禪 AC /꜀sjɦiu*i/, MP /srwéy/和/srwéy/),0404128"睡"(中古:止合三去寘禪 AC /sjɦiuə꜄/, MP /srwèy/)①。

5.12.4 齊微韻中有許多同音字組,它們既包含一等字也包含三、四等字,如0401008"灰"(中古:蟹合一平灰曉 AC /꜀xuəi/, MP /hwēy/)"輝"(中古:止合三平微曉 AC /꜀xiuəi/, MP /hwēy);0402030"雷"(中古:蟹合一平灰來 AC /꜀luəi/, MP /léy/),"纍"(中古:止合三平脂來 AC /꜀liu*i/, MP /léy/);0404123"最"(中古:蟹合三去泰精 AC /cuɑi꜄/, MP /cwèy/)"醉"(中古:止合三去至精 AC /ciu*i꜄/, MP /cwèy/);0404112"會"(中古:蟹合一去泰匣 AC /xɦuɑi꜄/, MP /hwèy/)"慧"(中古:蟹合四去霽匣 AC /xɦiei꜄/, MP /hwèy/)。這一現象無可爭辯地表明,這裏所涉及的三、四等字在《中原音韻》之前已經失去了/y/介音。因此,我們需要這樣一條規則:

$$y \rightarrow \varnothing / \underline{\quad} w + ɨ + y \tag{38}$$

我們這樣做,是再次做了一個有待證明的假設,即/y/介音的丟失發生在規則(36)之後,因爲這樣假設更經濟②。這種現象當然肯定是發生在規則(37)之後,否則那些腭㗇音(章組)聲母字的就會和捲舌(莊組)聲母字的一樣,並由此顯示出相同的發展,但事實並非如此,這一點在上一節已經指出了。

5.12.5 在齊微韻中,我們還發現了一些同音字組,它們包含脣音聲母一等和三等字,如0401009"杯"(中古:蟹合一平灰幫 AC /꜀puəi/, MP /pwēy/),"悲"(中古:止開三平脂幫 AC /꜀pi*i/, MP /pwēy/);0401017"胚"(中古:蟹合一平灰滂 AC /꜀phuəi/, MP /phwēy/)"披"(中古:止開三平支滂 AC /꜀phiə/, MP /phyɨ/和/phwēy/);0402029"枚"(中古:蟹合一平灰明 AC /꜀muəi/, MP /mwéy/),"眉"(中古:止開三平脂明 AC /꜀mi*i/, MP

---

① 上述規則可能應該修改爲:ɨ→a/(C)w___y,以表明這種變化嚴格限於一個特定的韻母,而與聲母没有任何關係。因爲在5.12.4中規則(38)和5.12.2中規則(36)所代表的兩種變化之前,韻母/wɨy/衹能出現在捲舌(莊組)聲母之後,所以這一修訂是可能的。

② 否則,規則(38)就不得不這樣修改:$y \rightarrow \varnothing / \underline{\quad} w \begin{Bmatrix} e \\ ɨ \end{Bmatrix} y$。一個更普遍性的寫法是把這個公式改寫爲:$y \rightarrow \varnothing / \underline{\quad} w + V + y$。因爲/-oy/和/-ay/從不在/yw/之後出現。我傾向於用規則(38)的形式而不用較普遍的寫法,因爲從歷史的角度來看,它更爲精確。

/mwéy/)。這種現象確實很奇怪。就一等字而言,没有什麽困難。由於它們都是來自蟹攝的合口字,我們很自然地爲它們重建一個韻母/wɨy/。然而,三等字就帶來了相當大的挑戰。它們原來不可能是合口的,因爲在這種情况下,它們的聲母應該是/f/或/v/(見 4.2.1)。因此,它們的韻母必然是/yɨy/。如果我們能以某種方式説,在這個韻母中,介音/y/在脣音聲母後消失了,問題就解决了。因爲我們認爲,脣音聲母後的介音位置上,要麽是/y/,要麽是/w/(見 4.2.1)。既然/y/丢失了,脣音聲母介音位置會自動增生介音/w/,這樣它們與一等字合併就再正常不過了。然而,我們不能這樣做,因爲還有許多同類字不是這樣表現的,例如,0402045"疲"(中古:止開三平支並 AC /꜀ pɦiə/, MP /phyɨ́/)和 0402046"彌"(中古:止開三平支明 AC /꜀ miə/, MP /myɨ́/)。限於我們目前的認識,除了將這些字看作不規則演變外,找不到其他辦法①。

5.12.6 我們已經看到,支思韻字所代表的音節,在韻圖時期的韻母曾是/yɨy/,後來,由於腭化介音的丢失,這個韻母變成/ɨy/,最後在《中原音韻》中變成了/ɨ/(5.12)。到目前爲止,還没有直接的證據來證明這最後一步,但它是必要的,原因有二。首先,正如我在 5.12 節中所説的,如果這些字的韻尾/y/在《中原音韻》中没有消失,那麽就没有理由讓它們自成一韻,進而與其他止攝字分開。其次,正如我們稍後將看到的,按照演變的一般規則,某些入聲字的韻母必須構擬爲/ɨy/,這些字都出現在齊微韻中,這證實了我們的推理,即韻母爲/ɨy/的字不應該自成一韻,例如,0452058"劾"AC(中古:曾開一入德匣 AC /xɦək/, MP /hé/)和 0452059"賊"(中古:曾開一入德從 AC /cɦək/, MP

① 統計起來,止攝開口三等字在《中原音韻》變成/Byɨy/這類音節的爲數較少些,因此説《中原音韻》曾受/Byɨy/→(*/Bɨy/)→/Bwɨy/這個規則的影響,也不是没有道理的。原來形式爲/Byɨy/的音節,可能在某些方言裏丢失了/y/介音,如上述規則所示(我相信一定能找到這樣的方言,即不再有/Byɨy/或/Byɨ/這樣的音節了),而在另一些方言中,到《中原音韻》時代,它們仍保持不變。換句話説,就這類字來説,我們在《中原音韻》以及現代北京話中所見到的可能是這兩類方言的混合。此外,這個問題涉及尚未探討的中古漢語的所謂"重紐"。儘管中古漢語重紐一定表示語音上的區别,但我還是認爲,到韻圖時期,對立可能已經轉化到韻母,即每對重紐的區别被韻母的某個特徵所取代。八思巴字似乎暗示了列在韻圖四等的重紐字確實已經變成四等字(參看橋本萬太郎 1965:211),這爲 3.6.3 的假設提供了某種證據。然而,不管每對重紐之間的對立可能是什麽,在《中原音韻》的語言裏,它們已經完全消失了。因此,重紐問題無助於解决我們這裏的問題。對重紐的詳細討論見橋本萬太郎(1965:207—220),以及董同龢(1948a)。

/céy/)(見 6.4.1.1)。

齊微韻現在衹剩下兩個韻母,即/yɨy/和/wɨy/(不包括來自入聲的一個/ɨy/,將在下一章單獨討論)。對第二個韻母的形態,可能不會有人提出異議,但也許有人會問,第一個就不能改寫爲/yɨ/嗎?這個韻母在現代北京話中的發音是[-i],哈特門把它分析成/-yɨ/①。鑒於這一事實,且爲了簡約起見,/-yɨ/似乎確實比/yɨy/要好。畢竟(如果僅僅是爲了區别不同的字音),這兩種寫法在《中原音韻》中都是令人滿意的。司徒修注意到了這個問題,經過一番詳盡的討論後得出結論:/ie/(我們寫作/yɨ/)"不僅可以接受……而且從音韻學的角度來看,比/iei/(我們寫作/yɨy/)更可取"②。我不覺得他的論點有説服力,而且在我看來,從音韻學的觀點來看,我們必須得出完全相反的結論。原因是:

(a) 在音韻史上,這類字的韻尾爲/y/是毋庸置疑的。事實上,這是止攝的某些字區别於遇攝的唯一特徵。除非我們有令人信服的理由將這個韻尾去掉,否則我們必須假設它在《中原音韻》仍然存在,要不然,我們將記録一個我們無法證明的變化。

(b) 的確,押韻有時可能衹是帶有某種"武斷"性質的實踐而已,但一般情况下並非如此。我們對《中原音韻》的研究主要是基於這種押韻的實踐。所以從邏輯上講,我們必須從一個假設開始,同韻的字不僅韻腹要相同,如果有韻尾的話,韻尾也必須相同。我們可以放棄這種假設,就像我們在討論蕭豪韻時所做的那樣,但衹有在所有證據都與這個假設衝突的罕見情况下,才能放棄。就齊微韻而言,我們當然没有放棄這種假設的必要。相反,因爲/yɨy/韻母的保留,我們才能够將/ɨy/作爲齊微韻的唯一韻類特徵③。

(c) 最重要的是,用/yɨy/來表示這個韻母,在整體的音系結構上更加可取。我們已經爲《中原音韻》構建了一個分高低兩層的四元音系統。這四個元音都能够也確實與韻尾結合。事實上,我們已經在/wɨy/韻母中看到了/ɨy/這樣的組合。如果中古漢語中存在朝這個方向發展的音節,按照一般的模式,自然需要建立一個像/yɨy/的韻母。的確,這"將在一張(韻母)分布圖上留下唯

① 哈特門(1944:118)將它們標爲/ji/。

② 司徒修(1962a:130)。

③ 參看馬丁(1953:38)。這個對立是/i*/對/i*i/。

一的空白”[①],這個空白就是/ɨy/韻母的潛在位置,但這是不可避免的。還有其他的空白,衹是因爲無字可填而已。現代北京話的情況則完全不同。從哈特門的分析中可以看出,三個主元音分居高中低三個層次。高元音的一個特點是,它從不與任何尾音結合[②]。《中原音韻》中韻母爲/yɨy/的字在現代北京話中都以高元音爲韻腹,不再與韻母爲/wɨy/的字和諧地押韻了。因此,爲了顯示這個新變化,《中原音韻》/yɨy/韻母中的韻尾/y/在現代北京話中必須取消[③]。

因此,我們現在可以看到,無論在《中原音韻》還是在現代北京話中,選擇一種或其他形式來表示齊微韻中的這個韻母,絶不可能是隨便的。這裏可以順便指出,在/yɨy/和/yɨ/這兩種形式中選擇/yɨy/,可能會在處理入聲字時,給我們帶來一個棘手的問題。我們將在面對那個問題的時候再討論它(參見6.4.4.2)。

5.13 尤侯韻

現在衹剩下尤侯韻需要討論了,但經過到目前爲止的討論,這一韻的性質已經非常清楚,毋庸詳論。這一韻的韻母當然分别是/ɨw/、/yɨw/和/wɨw/,且以/ɨw/爲韻類的區别特徵。/wɨw/韻母比較少見,它衹出現在脣音聲母之後,例如,在《中原音韻》中,1602026“裒”(中古:流開一平侯並 AC /꜀ pɦəu/, MP /phwéw/)應該是/phwɨw/,而 1603055“否”(中古:流開三上有幫 AC /꜂ pi*u/, MP /fwěw/)則應該是/fwɨw/。這聽起來有點像循環論證。事實上,如果不

① 司徒修(1962a:130)。

② 這個觀點的基礎是我對現代北京話的分析。我對現代北京音系的看法將在 7.5.1—7.5.3 粗略談到。它或多或少是哈特門的分析的修改,但這裏我與哈特門有所不同,即在有介音/j/(我寫作/y/)的情況下,它允許高元音後面出現鼻音韻尾。見哈特門(1944:119)。

③ 【追注】這條我原以爲極重要的證據,現在看來並不重要,也不可靠。其實,爲了證明這類字的韻母應爲/yɨy/而非/yɨ/,前兩條證據已經够强了。由於我們現在對北京話音系有了更正確的瞭解(參看薛鳳生 1986,第二章),這裏的第三條證據應該寫爲“因爲這類字與‘微’/wɨy/、‘賊’/cɨy/、‘灰’/hwɨy/等一同出現在齊微韻,所以它們的韻母衹能是/yɨy/。《中原音韻》以後,這類字不再跟‘微’‘賊’‘灰’等押韻,而改與‘支’‘思’‘魚’等押韻,屬於十三轍的一七轍,或徐孝所謂的‘止攝’,這衹能解釋爲它們在《中原音韻》以後才丢掉韻尾/y/。”(參看薛鳳生 1986,第七章)。

是因爲脣音聲母後的介音不是/y/便是/w/這個規則（規則 9），我們就不必爲尤侯韻構擬介音爲/w/的韻母。蕭豪韻的情況也許也是如此。但是整體的音系結構使我們相信有關脣音的這個規則是正確的，正如我們將看到的，它也有助於解釋流攝脣音聲母字的獨特變化。

5.13.1 如前所述（4.2.3），流攝在中古漢語中有兩個三等韻，“尤”（尤有宥）和“幽”（幽黝幼）。除了脣音聲母字外，這兩個韻後來合併了。從這些脣音聲母字在後來的發展，我們可以合理地推測，在合併之前，尤韻字在介音位置上有/w/，而幽韻字則没有。换句話説，它們可能在是否屬於合口或開口（圓脣或非圓脣）上有所不同。因此，尤韻脣音聲母字後來輕脣化了[1]，而幽韻字則没有（4.2.3）。在《中原音韻》中，除了少數幾個例外，流攝脣音聲母字都出現在魚模韻，而不是像所預期的那樣出現在尤侯韻。例如，0502036“浮”（中古：流開三平尤並 AC /꜀ pɦi*u/, MP /fwɨ́/），0503069“否”（中古：流開三上有幫 AC /꜂ pi*u/, MP /fwěw/），0503070“母”（中古：流開一上厚明 AC /꜂ məu/, MP /mwɨ̌/）和 0504113“富”（中古：流開三去宥幫 AC /pi*u꜃/, MP /fwɨ̀/）。這種變化，在我看來，是在介音和韻尾都是/w/的情况下，因異化而丢失/w/韻尾的結果：

$$w \rightarrow \varnothing / w + ɨ \_\_\_ \qquad (39)$$

但這條規則的少數例外，例如 1602026“抔”（中古：流開一平侯並 AC /꜀ phəu/, MP /phwéw/），1603052“剖”（中古：流開一上厚滂 AC /꜂ phəu/, MP /phwěw/）和 1604085“貿”（中古：流開一去侯明 AC /məu꜃/, MP /mwàw/），迫使我們保留/wɨw/作爲尤侯韻的韻母之一，據我所見，解釋它們爲什麽没有

① 這一韻的明母字是個難題。當“謀”（中古：流開三平尤明 AC /꜀ mi*u/, MP /mwéw/）出現在 0502060“模謨摸謀”這個同音字組且應該標寫爲/mwɨ/時，它在中古漢語裏的多數同音字，如“矛牟”等却出現在 1602027“繆矛眸鍪蝵牟麰侔”這個同音字組裏，這樣它就應該標寫爲/myɨw/或/mwɨw/。儘管“繆”（中古：流開三平尤明，流開三平幽明 AC /꜀ mi*u/，/꜀ miəu/, MP /mwéw/）在《中原音韻》裏可以讀作/myɨw/，而且“矛”（中古：流開三平尤明 AC /꜀ mi*u/, MP /mwáw/）在現代北京話裏也可以讀作/myáw/（如“丈八蛇矛”），這表明它在《中原音韻》裏也能讀作/myɨw/，但我還是認爲 1602027 這個同音字組的讀音應該選擇/mwɨw/。如果這一點正確的話，我們就可以説，就像通攝一樣，尤韻明母字在脣齒化過程前，先失去了/y/介音，故未輕脣化。

受到相同變化的影響的唯一方法就是方言間的借用①。

5.13.2 另外一個問題與尤侯韻的捲舌(莊組)聲母字有關,它們似乎有與齒噝音(精組)聲母一等字合併的趨勢,例如,1601004"鄹"(中古:流開三平尤莊 AC /꜀cri*u/, MP /cēw/)、"緅"(中古:流開一平侯精 AC /꜀cəu/, MP /cēw/)和 1604075"輳"(中古:流開一去候清 AC /chəu꜄/, MP /chèw/)、"甃"(中古:流開三去宥莊 AC /cri*u꜄/, MP /crèw/)。至少還有這樣一種情況,同是生母字,竟分爲兩個同音字組,分别是 1601003"搜"(中古:流三開平尤生 AC /꜀sri*u/, MP /sēw/)和 1601017"溲"(中古:流開三平尤生 AC /꜀sri*u/, MP /sēw/)。趙蔭棠將前者標爲[sou],後者標爲[ʂou],没有任何解釋。儘管來自宋代《集韻》的證據可以在某種程度上證明他的觀點②,但對我來説,這基本上是一個武斷的決定,因爲在現代北京話中,它們是同音字。這種莊組聲母字與精組聲母字合併的趨勢絶非勢不可擋,因此我們仍不得不保持它們之間的對立。

5.14 結語

除了入聲字這個明顯的例外,我們現在已經將《中原音韻》所有的韻都討論完了。這裏將已經證實的韻母排列成表。在此之後,可能會添加一個韻母特徵表,以及所有被證實音節的聲韻調配合表,即在《中原音韻》中聲母和韻母

① 在我看來,似乎有理由可以説,在《中原音韻》所代表的那個方言裏,也即作爲現代北京話所謂"口語音"的祖語裏,規則(39)所代表的音變曾經發生,而在作爲現代北京話所謂的"讀書音"的祖語裏,該音變却未發生。值得注意的是,那幾個必須構擬爲/wɨw/韻母的字都不是常用字,也即不屬於"基本詞彙"。所以它們很可能受其他方言的影響。此外,即便是作爲《中原音韻》魚模韻的"謀"和"某",在現代北京話裏,其讀書音的韻母也是/wew/了。

② [譯注]《集韻》"搜溲"作爲平聲字,同時有一等和三等的讀音,一等爲心母"蘇遭切",三等爲生母"疏鳩切",且都在一個小韻中。這衹能説明流攝三等莊組字和流攝一等精組字很早就有同音的現象,但不能作爲"搜"和"溲"在《中原音韻》中分居兩個同音字組的證據。在《中原音韻》"正語作詞起例"第 21 條"諸方語病"尤侯韻中有"溲有搜",這説明,在周德清看來,"搜"和"溲"在《中原音韻》中必不同音。"搜"≠"溲"作爲"同音分裂"現象,在正在發生的音變過程中,是正常的現象之一。其過程大致是 ʂ、ʂ→ʂ、s→s、s,《中原音韻》就處在這個過程中間,因此才會出現這種現象。

的組合,以及它們所代表的同音字組,作爲我們迄今爲止所做工作的總結。

5.14.1 以下是所有已證實存在的韻母的表。表中的數字表示這些韻母所屬的韻的編號。

韻尾	-ø				-y		-w				-n				-m			-ŋ		
韻腹 / 介音	ɨ	e	a	o	ɨ	a	ɨ	e	a	o	ɨ	e	a	o	ɨ	e	a	e	a	o
ø	03		13	12		06	16		11	11	07		08		17		18	15	02	
y		14	13		04	06	16	11	11		07	10	08		17	19	18	15	02	
w	05		13	12	04	06	16		11	11	07		08	09				15	02	01
yw	05	14									07	10						15	?	01

在*/ywaŋ/的位置上,以"?"代替"02"。這是因爲我對 0204099"晃"(中古:宕合一上蕩匣 AC /ᶜ xɦuɑŋ/, MP /hwàŋ/)與 0204100"况"(中古:宕合三去漾曉 AC /xiuɑŋᵓ/, MP /kwàŋ/)之間的對立有點懷疑。如果我們要接受這一對立,我們就必須建立/waŋ/和/ywaŋ/之間的對比,而 0201023"匡筐眶"、0202048"王"、0202049"狂"、0203063"枉往"和 0204091"旺王"這些同音字組,就必須全部用*/ywaŋ/這個韻母來重建。我之所以懷疑這一對比,有兩個原因:首先,這兩個同音字組是連續出現的,因此可能實際上屬於一個;其次,正如我們之前提到的(5.5.1 和 5.5.2)韻母/ywoŋ/有變成/woŋ/的趨勢一樣,/ywaŋ/也有變成/waŋ/的趨勢。

5.14.2 我相信,押韻在很大程度上揭示了母語者對本族語言獨特的音系結構的感知。由此可見,對任何一種語言進行充分的音位分析,都必須能够清楚地顯示出母語者的押韻實踐在音系上的依據。一般來説,兩個(或兩個以上的)字祇具有相同的主元音和韻尾(如果有韻尾的話),才能互相押韻。我們對《中原音韻》的分析顯然可以滿足這一要求,儘管存在兩種與這一要求看似不匹配的情况。首先,蕭豪韻在上面給出的表中占據了三列(即有三個主元音)。必須這樣做的理由已在 5.10.4 中解釋過了。由此可見,就元曲作家對這一韻字不加區别地押韻而言,事實上不存在與上述押韻原則有什麽相悖之處。第二,魚模韻與支思韻的區别僅僅在於介音位置上是否有/w/。這當然與押韻的要求是矛盾的,但却是可以理解的。我們在前面(5.12)已經説過,韻母/ɨ/,

是由韻母/yɨy/變化而來的，它在漢語音韻史上出現得相當晚。事實上，《中原音韻》是將具有這一韻母的字獨立成韻的第一本韻書。因此，押韻傳統和該韻母的獨特性質一定對詩人和韻書編纂者的思想産生了强烈的影響。事實上，周德清之後的衆多韻書編纂者就如何處理/ɨ/、/yɨ/、/wɨ/和/ywɨ/這四個韻母從來没有拿定過主意。有的分爲四韻，有的合爲一韻，還有的則在兩個極端之間摇擺不定[①]。我們現在可以列出《中原音韻》十九個韻的韻類特徵。由於韻尾在押韻時有決定作用，我們用"ø"把零韻尾也標示出來。

(01) 東鍾——oŋ
(02) 江陽——aŋ
(03) 支思——(C)ɨø
(04) 齊微——ɨy
(05) 魚模——wɨø
(06) 皆來——ay
(07) 真文——ɨn
(08) 寒山——an
(09) 桓歡——on
(10) 先天——en
(11) 蕭豪——{o, a, e}w
(12) 歌戈——oø
(13) 家麻——aø
(14) 車遮——eø
(15) 庚青——eŋ
(16) 尤侯——ɨw
(17) 侵尋——ɨm
(18) 監咸——am
(19) 廉纖——em

5.14.3 下面兩個表(見下頁)，顯示了《中原音韻》中所有經過驗證的音節(先不考慮聲調)。第一個表包含傳統上的"陰聲韻"(没有鼻音韻尾)，第二個表，是"陽聲韻"(有鼻音韻尾)。一個字代表一個音節，這些字大多選自"平聲陰"這個聲調。表後，附有一個包含所有《中原音韻》同音字組的附録，以四聲和這兩個表中的縱列(即聲母)的次序排列。

5.14.3 之附録

製作這個附録，是旨在消除對我們所建立的體系可能仍然存在的任何疑問。爲實現這一目標，我們將爲每個舒聲同音字組分配一個從我們先前建立的規則中推斷出來的音位標音，並爲所有有争議的同音字組提供合理的解釋。爲了便於識别，每個同音字組除編號外再附上一個代表字。

① 参看趙蔭棠(1957:258—259)所列不同韻書的韻類對比表。

韻類	03	05		12		13			14		04		06			16			11						
聲母＼韻母	ɨ	wɨ	ywɨ	o	wo	a	ya	wa	ye	ywe	yɨy	wɨy	ay	yay	way	ɨw	yɨw	wɨw	ow	wow	aw	yaw	waw	yew
p		逋			波			巴			篦	杯			擺		彪			褒			包	標
ph		蒲			坡			葩			批	醅			排			抔					拋	飄
f		膚										非						否					缶	
v		無										微												
m		模			麼			麻			迷	梅			埋		繆	貿					毛	苗
t		都			多	大			爹		低	堆	韃			兜			刀					刁
th		徒			他						梯	頹	台			偷			掏					挑
l		盧	驢		羅				倈		黎	雷	來			樓	劉		牢					寮
n		奴	女		那	拏					泥	餒	能			耨	扭		腦		撓			裊
c	髭	租	疽		左	咱			嗟		躋	觜	哉			鄹	啾		遭					蕉
ch	雌	粗	蛆		磋				且		妻	崔	猜			㑳	秋		操					鍬
s	斯	蘇	須		莎				些		西	雖	腮			捜	修		騷					蕭
cr	支	阻	諸			查		撾	遮		知	追	齋			皺	周				嘲			昭
crh	眵	初	樞			叉			車		癡	吹	釵		揣	篘	抽				抄			超
sr	施	梳	書			沙		耍	奢		世	誰	篩		衰	溲	收				梢			燒
r	兒		如						惹			蕤					柔							饒
k		孤	居	歌	戈		家	瓜			機	歸	該	皆	乖	鉤	鳩		高			交		嬌
kh		枯	區	軻	科			誇		瘸	溪	魁	開	揩	快	摳	丘		考			敲		喬
h		呼	虛	呵	和		蝦	花		靴	希	灰	孩	鞋	懷	齁	休		蒿			哮		梟
ŋ				哦															傲					
ø		嗚	迂	阿	窩		鴉	蛙	耶		衣	威	哀	挨	歪	謳	憂		奧			坳		邀

續表

韻類	01		02			15				07				09	08			10		17		18		19
韻母 聲母	woŋ	ywoŋ	aŋ	yaŋ	waŋ	eŋ	yeŋ	weŋ	yweŋ	ɨn	yɨn	wɨn	ywɨn	won	an	yan	wan	yen	ywen	ɨm	yɨm	am	yam	yem
p	崩				邦		冰	崩			賓	奔		般			班	邊						
ph	烹				滂		平	烹			貧	噴		潘			攀	篇						
f	風				方							分					番							
v					忘							文					晚							
m	蒙				忙		明	盲			民	門		瞞			蠻	眠						
t	東		當			登	丁					敦		端	丹			顛				擔		掂
th	通		湯			滕	汀			呑		暾		湍	灘			天		唔		貪		添
l	籠	龍	郎	粮		楞	靈				鄰	論	倫	鸞	蘭			連	聯	啉	林	婪		廉
n	農	濃	囊	娘		能	寧				紉	嫩		暖	難			年			賃	南		黏
c	宗	蹤	臧	漿		曾	精				津	尊	遵	鑽	趲			煎	鎸	怎	駸	簪		尖
ch	匆	從	倉	槍		層	青				親	村	逡	攛	餐			千	痊		侵	參		僉
s	鬆	松	桑	湘		僧	星				新	孫	詢	酸	珊			先	宣		心	三		纖
cr	鍾			章	莊	箏	征			臻	真		諄		赸		跧	氈	專	簪	針	詀		瞻
crh	冲			昌	瘡	鐺	稱			襯	嗔		春		潺		篡		川	岑	琛	攙		襜
sr				商	雙	生	聲			莘	申		瞬		山		拴	羶		森	深	杉		苫
r	戎			穰			仍				人		閏					然	軟		壬			髯
k	二	拱	岡	姜	光	亘	京	觥	扃	根	巾	鯤	君	官	干	姦	關	堅	鵑		金	甘	監	兼
kh	空	穹	康	腔	曠		輕		瓊	哏	勤	坤	群	寬	刊	慳		牽	圈		欽	堪	嵌	謙
h	烘	凶	杭	香	荒	亨	馨	轟	兄	痕	欣	昏	薰	歡	寒	閑	還	軒	喧		歆	憨	咸	忺
ŋ																								
ø	翁	邕	昂	央	汪	甖	英	泓	滎	恩	因	温	氳	剜	安	殷	彎	烟	淵		音	菴	巖	淹

基本形式	平聲陰	平聲陽	上聲	去聲
/cɨ/	0301002 髭	—	0303015 子	0304023 字
/chɨ/	0301006 雌	0302008 慈	0303013 此	0304022 次
/sɨ/	0301005 斯	0302010 詞	0303016 死	0304021 似
/crɨ/	0301001 支	—	0303011 紙	0304024 志
/crhɨ/	0301003 眵	—	0303017 齒	{0304026 翅(A) {0304027 廁
/srɨ/	0301004 施	0302009 時	0303014 史	0304020 是
/rɨ/(B)	—	0302007 兒	0303012 爾	0304025 二
/pwɨ/	0501004 逋	—	0503067 補	0504121 布
/phwɨ/	—	0502037 蒲	0503068 普	0504126 鋪
/fwɨ/	0501018 膚	0502036 扶	0503069 甫	0504113 赴
/vwɨ/	—	0502025 無	0503060 武	0504115 務
/mwɨ/	—	0502026 模	0503070 母	0504117 暮
/twɨ/	0501021 都	—	0503063 堵	0504112 杜
/thwɨ/	—	0502027 徒	0503061 土	0504124 兔
/lwɨ/	—	0502029 盧	0503062 魯	0504118 路
/nwɨ/	—	0502028 奴	0503073 弩	0504125 怒
/cwɨ/	0501022 租	—	0503059 祖	0504123 做
/chwɨ/	0501006 粗	0502039 徂	—	0504122 醋
/swɨ/	0501003 蘇	—	—	0504116 素
/crwɨ/	—	—	0503056 阻	0504130 助
/crhwɨ/	0501020 初	0502032 鋤	0503071 楚	—
/srwɨ/	0501007 梳	—	0503058 數	0504109 數
/kwɨ/	0501011 孤	—	0503064 古	0504119 故
/khwɨ/	0501012 枯	—	0503076 苦	—
/hwɨ/	0501019 呼	0502038 胡	0503066 虎	0504114 户
/wɨ/	0501014 鳴	0502031 吾	0503065 五	0504120 誤
/lywɨ/	—	0502023 驢	0503052 吕	0504104 慮
/nywɨ/	—	—	0503078 女	—
/cywɨ/	0501010 疽	—	0503077 咀	0504129 聚
/chywɨ/	0501009 蛆	—	0503075 取	0504107 趣

續表

基本形式	平聲陰	平聲陽	上聲	去聲
/sywɨ/	0501017 須	0502040 徐	0503079 嶼	0504110 絮
/crywɨ/	0501002 諸	—	0503053 主	0504108 注
/crhywɨ/	0501005 樞	0502035 除	0503057 杵	0504127 處
/srywɨ/	0501015 書	0502033 殊	0503055 鼠	0504106 恕
/rywɨ/	—	0502024 如	0503054 汝	0504111 孺
/kywɨ/	0501001 居	—	0503072 舉	0504105 鋸
/khywɨ/	0501016 區	0502034 渠	0503080 傴	0504128 去
/hywɨ/	0501008 虚	—	0503074 許	—
/ywɨ/	0501013 迂	0502030 魚	0503051 語	0504103 御
/ko/	1201001 歌	—	1203040 哿	1204075 箇
/kho/	1201003 軻	—	1203044 可	1204082 嗑
/ho/	1201012 呵	1202019 何	1203043 荷	1204065 賀
/ŋo/	—	1202022 哦	1203048 我	1204076 餓
/o/	1201008 阿	—	1203046 婀①	—
/pwo/	1201011 波	—	1203047 跛	1204071 簸
/phwo/	1201010 坡	1202023 婆	1203045 頗	1204081 破
/mwo/	1201014 麽	1202016 摩	1203053 嬤	1204072 磨
/two/	1201013 多	—	1203041 朵	1204067 舵
/thwo/	1201007 他	1202020 駝	1203050 妥	1204080 唾
/lwo/	—	1202015 羅	1203039 裸	1204070 邏
/nwo/	—	1202017 那	1203042 娜	1204074 懦
/cwo/	—	—	1203049 左	1204066 佐
/chwo/	1201006 蹉	1202021 矬	1203054 脞	1204068 銼
/swo/	1201005 莎	—	1203037 鎖	1204077 些
/kwo/	1201004 戈	—	1203038 果	1204078 過
/khwo/	1201002 科	—	1203052 顆	1204079 課
/hwo/	—	1202018 和	1203051 火	1204069 禍
/wo/	1201009 窩	1202024 訛	—	1204073 卧

① 原文爲“何”,誤,當爲“婀”。

續表

基本形式	平聲陰	平聲陽	上聲	去聲
/ta/	—	—	1303c38 打	1304068 大
/na/	—	1302020 拏	—	1304064 那
/ca/	—	1302021 咱	—	—
/cra/	1301005 查	—	1303037 鮓	1304060 詐
/crha/	1301008 叉	1302019 茶	1303034 詫	1304058 汊
/sra/	1301004 沙	—	1303031 洒	1304067 厏
/kya/	1301001 家	—	1303032 賈	1304054 駕
/hya/	1301010 蝦	1302017 遐	—	1304061 下
/ya/	1301007 鴉	1302016 牙	1303030 雅	1304057 亞
/pwa/	1301002 巴	—	1303035 把	1304065 罷
/phwa/	1301011 葩	1302018 爬	—	1304059 怕
/mwa/	—	1302014 麻	1303029 馬	1304069 罵
/crwa/	1301006 撾	—	—	—
/srwa/	—	—	1303039 耍	—
/kwa/	1301013 瓜	—	1303033 寡	1304066 卦
/khwa/	1301009 誇	—	—	1304056 跨
/hwa/	1301012 花	1302015 譁	—	1304062 化(C) 1304063 話
/wa/	1301003 蛙	—	1303036 瓦	1304055 凹
/tye/	1401005 爹	—	—	—
/lye/	—	1402011 俫①	—	—
/cye/	1401001 嗟	—	1403028 姐	1404052 借
/chye/	—	—	1403029 且	1404053 趄
/sye/	1401007 些	1402009 邪	1403024 寫	1404049 謝
/crye/	1401004 遮	—	1403023 者	1404051 柘
/crhye/	1401003 車	—	1403027 撦	1404054 偖
/srye/	1401002 奢	1402010 蛇	1403025 捨	1404048 舍
/rye/	—	—	1403026 惹	—

① 原文爲“徠”,誤,當爲“俫”。

續表

基本形式	平聲陰	平聲陽	上聲	去聲
/ye/	—	1402008 耶	1403022 野	1404050 夜
/khywe/	—	1402012 瘸	—	—
/hywe/	1401006 靴	—	—	—
/pyɨy/	0401023 篦	—	0403071 比	0404126 閉
/phyɨy/	0401021 批	0402045 脾	0403068 否	—
/myɨy/	—	0402046 迷	0403077 米	0404127 謎
/tyɨy/	0401005 低	—	0403074 底	0404118 帝
/thyɨy/	0401025 梯	0402039 啼	0403083 體	0404117 替
/lyɨy/	—	0402027 黎	0403072 禮	0404120 利
/nyɨy/	—	0402028 泥	0403078 你	0404139 膩
/cyɨy/	0401003 躋	—	0403073 擠	0404116 霽
/chyɨy/	0401006 妻	0402032 齊	—	0404121 砌
/syɨy/	0401007 西	—	0403075 洗	0404122 細
/cryɨy/	0401024 知	—	—	0404132 置
/crhyɨy/	0401019 癡	0402043 池	0403066 恥	—
/sryɨy/	—	—	—	0404133 世
/kyɨy/	0401001 機	—	0403065 幾	0404125 計
/khyɨy/	0401013 溪	0402036 奇	0403076 啓	0404115 氣
/hyɨy/	0401014 希	0402037 奚	0403080 喜	0404137 戲
/yɨy/	0401015 衣	0402038 移	{0403063 倚 {0403061 迤 (D)	0404114 異
/pwɨy/	0401009 杯	—	0403079 彼	0404119 背
/phwɨy/	0401017 醅	0402041 培	—	0404135 配
/fwɨy/	0401012 非	0402035 肥	—	0404111 吠
/vwɨy/	—	0402026 微	0403062 尾	0404018 未
/mwɨy/	—	0402029 梅	0403064 浼	0404136 妹
/twɨy/	0401022 堆	—	—	0404124 對
/thwɨy/	—	0402044 頹	0403084 腿	0404129 退
/lwɨy/	—	0402030 雷	0403082 壘	0404134 淚
/nwɨy/	—	—	0403089 餒	0404142 内

續表

基本形式	平聲陰	平聲陽	上聲	去聲
/cwɨy/	—	—	0403086 觜	0404123 罪
/chwɨy/	0401020 崔	0402048 摧	—	0404113 翠
/swɨy/	0401004 雖	0402031 隋	0403087 髓	0404130 歲
/crwɨy/	0401010 追	—	—	0404131 墜
/crhwɨy/	0401016 吹	0402040 垂	0403067 捶	—
/srwɨy/	—	0402047 誰	0403088 水	0404128 睡
/rwɨy/	—	0402049 蕤	0403085 蕊	0404140 芮
/kwɨy/	0401002 歸	—	0403069 鬼	0404110 貴
/khwɨy/	0401018 魁	0402042 葵	—	0404138 簣
/hwɨy/	0401008 灰	0402033 回	0403070 悔	0404112 會
/wɨy/	0401011 威	0402034 圍	0403081 委	0404109 胃
/tay/	—	—	0603034 逮	0604068 帶
/thay/	0601005 台	0602028 臺	—	0604062 態
/lay/	—	0602018 來	—	0604074 賴
/nay/	—	0602029 能	0603039 奶	0604066 奈
/cay/	0601003 哉	—	0603036 宰	0604072 在
/chay/	0601007 猜	0602027 才	0603037 彩	0604076 菜
/say/	0601010 腮	—	—	0604078 賽
/cray/	0601014 齋	—	—	0604061 寨
/erhay/	0601004 釵	0602025 柴	—	—
/sray/	0601016 篩	—	—	0604077 曬
/kay/	0601002 該	—	0603048 改	0604063 蓋
/khay/	0601012 開	—	0603041 凱	0604081 慨
/hay/	—	0602024 孩	0603033 海	0604067 害
/ay/	0601006 哀	0602023 騃	0603038 靄	0604064 艾
/kyay/	0601001 皆	—	0603045 解	0604069 戒
/khyay/	0601013 揩	—	0603046 楷	0604084 溘(E)
/hyay/	—	0602019 鞋	0603035 蟹	0604060 懈
/yay/	0601008 挨	0602026 崖	0603044 矮	0604065 捱

續表

基本形式	平聲陰	平聲陽	上聲	去聲
/pway/	—	—	0603043 擺	0603043 拜①
/phway/	—	0602020 排	—	0604082 派
/mway/	—	0602022 埋	0603047 買	0603073 賣
/crhway/	0601017 揣	—	0603042 揣	—
/srway/	0601009 衰	—	—	0604083 帥
/kway/	0601015 乖	—	0603040 拐	0604079 怪
/khway/	—	—	—	0604071 快
/hway/	—	0602021 懷	—	0604080 壞
/way/	0601011 歪	—	—	0604070 外
/tɨw/	1601008 兜	—	1603044 斗	1604073 豆
/thɨw/	1601015 偷	1602033 頭	—	1604084 透
/lɨw/	—	1602028 樓	1603047 摟	1604077 漏
/nɨw/	—	—	—	1604082 耨
/cɨw/	1601004 鄒	—	1603054 走	1604083 奏
/chɨw/	—	—	1603058 傷	1604075 湊
/sɨw/	601003 搜	—	1603043 叟	1604067 嗽
/crɨw/	—	—	—	1604068 皺
/crhɨw/	1601016 篘	1602034 愁	1603059 瞅	1604081 僽
/srɨw/	1601017 溲	—	—	1604080 瘦
/kɨw/	1601007 鉤	—	1603045 狗	1604074 搆
/khɨw/	1601021 摳	—	1603057 口	1604070 扣
/hɨw/	1601020 齁	1602023 候	1603053 吼	1604071 后
/ɨw/	1601006 謳	—	1603046 藕	—
/pyɨw/	1601018 彪	—	—	—
/myɨw/	—	—	—	1604077 謬
/lyɨw/	—	1602024 劉	1603038 柳	1604069 溜
/nyɨw/	—	—	1603039 扭	—
/cyɨw/	1601001 啾	—	1603050 酒	1604072 就

① 原文爲"幫",誤,當爲"拜"。

續表

基本形式	平聲陰	平聲陽	上聲	去聲
/chyɨw/	1601009 秋	1602032 酋	—	—
/syɨw/	1601011 修	1602029 囚	—	1604066 秀
/cryɨw/	1601013 周	—	1603048 肘	1604063 晝
/crhyɨw/	1601012 抽	1602030 紬	1603040 丑	1604078 臭
/sryɨw/	1601019 收	—	1603042 首	1604065 受
/ryɨw/	—	1602025 柔	1603056 揉	—
/kyɨw/	1601002 鳩	—	1603041 九	1604064 臼
/khyɨw/	1601014 丘	1602031 求	1603051 扻	—
/hyɨw/	1601005 休	—	1603049 朽	1604079 嗅
/yɨw/	1601010 憂	1602022 尤	1603037 有	1604062 又
/phwɨw/	—	1602026 抔	1603052 剖	—
/fwɨw/	—	—	1603055 否	—
/mwɨw/	—	1602027 矛	—	1604085 貿
/tow/	1101012 刀	—	1103078 倒	1104129 道
/thow/	1101020 掏	1102048 桃	1103091 討	—
/low/	—	1102039 牢	1103073 老	1104143 澇
/now/	—	1102038 猱(F)	1103074 腦	—
/cow/	1101014 遭	—	1103077 早	1104123 皂
/chow/	1101032 操	1102049 曹	1103092 草	1104133 糙
/sow/	1101013 騷	—	1103075 掃	1104144 噪
/kow/	1101011 高	—	1103079 杲	1104142 告
/khow/	—	—	1103081 考	—
/how/	1101026 蒿	1102033 豪	1103093 好	1104128 號
/ŋow/	—	1102044 敖	—	1104125 傲
/ow/	1101015 鏖	—	1103080 襖	1104147 奥
/pwow/	1101028 褒	—	1103070 保	1104122 抱
/naw/	—	1102038 鐃(F)	1103094 撓	1104146 鬧
/craw/	1101010 嘲	—	1103089 爪	1104138 罩
/crhaw/	1101024 抄	1102051 巢	1103090 炒	1104148 鈔
/sraw/	1101004 梢	—	1103096 稍	1104151 哨

續表

基本形式	平聲陰	平聲陽	上聲	去聲
/kyaw/	1101008 交	—	1103072 狡	1104137 窖
/khyaw/	1101023 敲	—	1103086 巧	—
/hyaw/	1101022 哮	1102046 肴	—	—
/yaw/	1101025 坳	—	1103095 齩	1104139 拗
/pwaw/	1101009 包	—	1103088 飽	1104121 豹
/phwaw/	1101019 抛	1102047 袍	1103097 剖(G)	1104141 炮
/fwaw/	—	—	1103098 缶(G)	1104152 覆(G)
/mwaw/	—	1102037 毛	1103071 卯	1104140 貌
/pyew/	1101007 標	—	1103085 表	1104135 俵
/phyew/	1101018 飄	1102050 瓢	1103076 殍	—
/myew/	—	1102036 苗	1103068 眇	1104145 妙
/tyew/	1101002 刁	—	—	1104120 釣
/thyew/	1101029 挑	1102040 迢	1103082 挑	1104119 糶
/lyew/	—	1102034 寮	1103065 了	1104124 料
/nyew/	—	—	1103064 裊	1104150 溺
/cyew/	1101006 蕉	—	—	1104132 醮
/chyew/	1101031 鍬	1102043 樵	1103069 悄	1104134 俏
/syew/	1101001 蕭	—	1103062 小	1104118 笑
/cryew/	1101016 昭	—	1103083 沼	1104126 趙
/crhyew/	1101030 超	1102041 潮	—	—
/sryew/	1101027 燒	—	1103084 少	1104127 少
/ryew/	—	1102035 饒	1103067 遶	—
/kyew/	1101005 嬌	—	1103063 皎	1104131 叫
/khyew/	—	1102045 喬	—	1104149 竅
/hyew/	1101003 梟	—	1103087 曉	1104136 孝
/yew/	1101017 邀	1102042 遥	1103066 杳①	1104130 曜
/pwoŋ/	0101018 崩	—	0103053 琫	0104069 迸
/phwoŋ/	0101019 烹	0102034 蓬	—	—

① 原文爲“杳”，誤，當爲“杳”。

續表

基本形式	平聲陰	平聲陽	上聲	去聲
/fwoŋ/	0101009 風	0102028 馮	0103049 捧	0104055 鳳
/mwoŋ/	—	0102032 蒙	0103047 蠓	0104065 夢
/twoŋ/	0101001 東	—	0103036 董	0104054 洞
/thwoŋ/	0101003 通	0102020 同	0103039 桶	0104062 痛
/lwoŋ/	—	0102024 籠	0103042 攏	0104058 弄
/nwoŋ/	—	0102025 農	0103052 噥	—
/cwoŋ/	0101008 宗	—	0103048 總	0104068 綜
/chwoŋ/	0101011 匆	0102029 叢	—	—
/swoŋ/	0101010 鬆	—		0104057 宋
/kwoŋ/	0101014 工	—	—	0104056 貢
/khwoŋ/	0101007 空	—	0103038 孔	0104059 控
/hwoŋ/	0101015 烘	0102033 紅	0103040 汞	0104067 哄
/woŋ/	0101017 翁	—	—	0104061 甕
/lywoŋ/	—	0102022 龍	0103041 隴	—
/nywoŋ/	—	0102026 濃	—	—
/cywoŋ/	0101012 蹤	—	—	0104064 縱
/chywoŋ/	—	0102035 從	—	—
/sywoŋ/	0101004 松	—	0103044 聳	0104060 訟
/crywoŋ/	0101002 鍾	—	0103037 腫	0104063 衆
/crhywoŋ/	0101005 冲	0102027 蟲	0103050 寵	0104070 銃
/rywoy/	—	0102021 戎	0103051 冗	—
/kywoŋ/	—	—	0103045 拱	—
/khywoŋ/	0101013 穹	0102023 窮	—	—
/hywoŋ/	0101016 凶	0102030 熊	0103043 洶	—
/ywoŋ/	0101006 邕	0102031 容	0103046 勇	0104066 用
/taŋ/	0201012 當	—	0203067 黨	0204093 蕩
/thaŋ/	0201020 湯	0202040 唐	0203066 倘	0204111 湯
/laŋ/	—	0202033 郎	0203069 朗	0204094 浪
/naŋ/	—	0202050 囊	—	—
/caŋ/	0201027 臟	—	0203074 髒	0204095 葬

續表

基本形式	平聲陰	平聲陽	上聲	去聲
/chaŋ/	0201025 倉	0202044 藏	—	0204106 愴
/saŋ/	0201003 桑	—	0203064 嗓	0204103 喪
/kaŋ/	0201009 岡	—	—	0204110 鋼
/khaŋ/	0201010 康	—	—	0204099 炕
/haŋ/	—	0202034 杭	0203073 沆	0204105 行
/aŋ/	—	0202035 昂	—	0204108 盎
/1yaŋ/	—	0202030 粮	0203054 兩	0204080 亮
/nyaŋ/	—	0202046 娘	0203071 仰	0204101 釀
/cyaŋ/	0201007 漿	—	0203053 蔣	0204087 匠
/chyaŋ/	0201022 槍	0202042 墻	0203076 搶	0204109 戧
/syaŋ/	0201021 湘	0202041 詳	0203055 想	0204079 象
/cryaŋ/	0201005 章	—	0203068 掌	0204085 帳
/crhyaŋ/	0201019 昌	0202030 長	0203059 敞	0204088 唱
/sryaŋ/	0201006 商	—	0203077 賞	0204083 上
/ryaŋ/	—	0202031 穰	0203060 壤	0204084 讓
/kyaŋ/	0201001 姜	—	0203051 講	0204078 絳
/khyaŋ/	0201016 腔	0204045 强	0203075 强	—
/hyaŋ/	0201014 香	0202047 降	0203058 響	0204086 巷
/yaŋ/	0201017 央	0202028 陽	0203052 養	0204081 養
/pwaŋ/	0201002 邦	—	0203065 榜	0204096 謗
/phwaŋ/	0201015 滂	0202037 旁	—	0204104 胖
/fwaŋ/	0201018 方	0202038 房	0203061 倣	0204092 放
/vwaŋ/	—	0202032 忘	0203062 罔	0204090 望
/mwaŋ/	—	0202029 忙	0203056 蟒	—
/crwaŋ/	0201008 莊	—	—	0204082 狀
/crhwaŋ/	0201026 瘡	0202036 牀	—	0204089 創
/srwaŋ/	0201004 雙	—	0203057 爽	—
/kwaŋ/	0201011 光	—	0203072 廣	0204107 誑
/khwaŋ/	0201023 匡	0202049 狂	—	0204098 曠

續表

基本形式	平聲陰	平聲陽	上聲	去聲
/hwaŋ/	0201013 荒	0202043 黄	0203070 謊	{0204099 晃(H) 0204100 况
/waŋ/	0201024 汪	0202048 王	0203063 枉	0204091 旺
/teŋ/	1501009 登	—	1503972 等	1504079 鄧
/theŋ/	—	1502036 滕	—	—
/leŋ/	—	1502033 愣	1503069 冷	—
/neŋ/	—	1502035 能	—	—
/ceŋ/	1501011 曾	—	—	1504095 贈
/cheŋ/	—	1502034 層	—	—
/seŋ/	1501024 僧	—	—	—
/creŋ/	1501004 筝	—	—	1504082 諍
/crheŋ/	1501012 鐺	1502048 橙	—	1504100 撑
/sreŋ/	1501003 生	—	1503059 省	—
/keŋ/	—	—	—	1504101 亘
/heŋ/	1501025 亨(I)	1502037 莖	—	—
/eŋ/	1501023 罌(I)	—	—	—
/pyeŋ/	1501008 冰	—	1503056 丙	1504085 病
/phyeŋ/	—	1502029 平	—	1504089 娉
/myeŋ/	—	1502030 明	1503064 茗	1504078 命
/tyeŋ/	1501005 丁	—	1503067 頂	1504094 定
/thyeŋ/	1501019 汀	1502043 亭	1503068 艇	1504096 聽
/lyeŋ/	—	1502031 靈	1503066 領	1504068 令
/nyeŋ/	—	1502030 寧	—	1504090 佞
/cyeŋ/	1501002 精	—	1503070 井	1504091 净
/chyeŋ/	1501017 青	1502041 情	1503071 請	1504081 清
/syeŋ/	1501020 星	1502053 餳	1503058 醒	1504088 性
/cryeŋ/	1501007 征	—	1503063 整	1504083 正
/crhyeŋ/	1501013 稱	1502044 澄	1503065 逞	1504093 秤
/sryeŋ/	1501018 聲	1502052 繩	—	1504086 聖
/ryeŋ/	—	1502051 仍	—	—

續表

基本形式	平聲陰	平聲陽	上聲	去聲
/kyeŋ/	1501001 京	—	1503054 景	1504075 敬
/khyeŋ/	1501015 輕	1502039 擎	1503055 頃	1504077 慶
/hyeŋ/	1501016 馨	1502040 行	1503074 涬	1504092 杏
/yeŋ/	1501014 英	1502038 盈	1503058 影	1504076 暎
/pweŋ/	1501021 崩	—	—	1504097 迸
/phweŋ/	1501028 烹	1502032 朋	—	—
/mweŋ/	—	1502046 盲	1503062 艋	1504098 孟
/kweŋ/	1501022 觥	—	1503060 礦	—
/hweŋ/	1501010 轟	1502047 横	—	1504099 横
/weŋ/	1501027 泓	—	—	—
/kyweŋ/	1501006 扃	—	1503061 冏	—
/khyweŋ/	—	1502043 瓊	—	—
/hyweŋ/	1501026 兄	1502045 熒	—	1504080 迥
/yweŋ/	—	1502049 榮	1503073 永	1504084 咏
/thɨn/	0701008 吞	—	—	—
/crɨn/	0701020 臻	—	—	—
/crhɨn/	—	—	—	0704098 櫬
/srɨn/	0701021 莘	—	—	—
/kɨn/	0701012 根	—	—	—
/khɨn/	0701035 哏	—	0703062 肯	—
/hɨn/	—	0702059 痕	0703075 狠	0704117 恨
/ɨn/	0701003 恩	—	—	—
/pyɨn/	0701017 賓	—	—	0704092 鬢
/phyɨn/	—	0702038 貧	0703074 牝(J) 0703076 不	—
/myɨn/	—	0702039 民	0703065 閔	—
/lyɨn/	—	0702037 鄰	—	0704091 吝
/nyɨn/	—	0702060 紉	—	—
/cyɨn/	0701036 津	—	0703087 儘	0704095 進
/chyɨn/	0701031 親	0702050 秦	—	—

續表

基本形式	平聲陰	平聲陽	上聲	去聲
/syɨn/	0701016 新	—	—	0704089 信
/cryɨn/	0701015 真	—	0703061 軫	0704088 震
/crhyɨn/	0701005 嗔	0702049 陳	—	0704121 趂
/sryɨn/	0701004 申	0702057 神	0703073 哂	0704092 慎
/ryɨn/	—	0702040 人	0703077 忍	0704090 刃
/kyɨn/	0701029 巾	—	0703063 緊	0704097 近
/khyɨn/	—	0702043 勤	—	—
/hyɨn/	0701013 欣	—	—	0704113 釁
/yɨn/	0701003 因	0702047 銀	0703064 隱	0704099 印
/pwɨn/	0701028 奔	—	0703070 本	0704108 逩
/phwɨn/	0701034 噴	0702048 盆	—	0704112 噴
/fwɨn/	0701001 分	0702054 墳	0703083 粉	0704096 忿
/vwɨn/	—	0702046 文	0703067 吻	0704105 問
/mwɨn/	—	0702044 門	—	0704107 悶
/twɨn/	0701027 敦	—	0703078 盾	0704106 頓
/thwɨn/	0701009 暾	0702056 屯	—	0704119 褪
/lwɨn/	—	0702045 論	—	0704114 論
/nwɨn/	—	—	—	0704118 嫩
/cwɨn/	0701026 尊	—	0703079 撙	—
/chwɨn/	0701030 村	0702058 存	0703028 忖	0704116 寸
/swɨn/	0701025 孫	—	0703080 損	0704101 遜
/kwɨn/	0701023 鯤	—	0703085 袞	—
/khwɨn/	0701018 坤	—	0703071 閫	0704111 困
/hwɨn/	0701002 昏	0702055 魂	—	0704115 混
/wɨn/	0701024 温	—	0703084 穩	0704120 搵
/lywɨn/	—	0702041 倫	—	—
/cywɨn/	0701032 遵	—	—	07041024 俊
/chywɨn/	0701011 逡	—	—	—
/sywɨn/	0701007 詢	0702052 巡	0703068 筍	0704100 峻
/crywɨn/	0701010 諄	—	0703066 準	—

續表

基本形式	平聲陰	平聲陽	上聲	去聲
/crhywɨn/	0701006 春	0702051 脣	0703081 蠢	—
/srywɨn/	—	—	0703086 瞬	0704103 舜
/rywɨn/	—	—	—	0704104 閏
/kywɨn/	0701019 君	—	0703072 窘	0704110 郡
/khywɨn/	—	0702042 群	—	—
/hywɨn/	0701022 薰	—	—	0704109 訓
/ywɨn/	0701014 氳	0702053 云	0703069 允	0704094 運
/pwon/	0901002 般	—	—	0904037 半
/phwon/	0901004 潘	0902017 盤	—	0904035 判
/mwon/	—	0902013 瞞	0903023 滿	0904031 漫
/twon/	0901005 端	—	0903028 短	0904033 斷
/thwon/	0901010 湍	0902016 團	0903026 疃	0904040 彖
/lwon/	—	0902012 鸞	0903027 卵	0904039 亂
/nwon/	—	—	0903024 暖	0904041 愞
/cwon/	0901009 鑽	0902018 攢	0903020 纂	0904038 鑽
/chwon/	0901011 攛	—	—	0904032 竄
/swon/	0901007 酸	—	—	0904034 算
/kwon/	0901001 官	—	0903019 館	0904036 貫
/khwon/	0901008 寬	—	0903021 款	—
/hwon/	0901003 歡	0902014 桓	0903022 澣	0904029 喚
/won/	0901006 剜	0902015 丸	0903025 椀	0904030 玩
/tan/	0801002 丹	—	0803038 癉	0804050 旦
/than/	0801011 灘	0802025 壇	0803040 坦	0804052 嘆
/lan/	—	0802021 蘭	0803043 懶	0804071 爛
/nan/	—	0802027 難	0803046 赧	0804074 難
/can/	—	—	0803044 趲	0804062 贊
/chan/	0801017 餐	0802023 殘	—	0804055 粲
/san/	0801013 珊	—	0803033 散	0804073 散
/cran/	0801016 虥	—	0803047 盞	0804056 棧
/crhan/	—	0802030 潺	0803037 産	—

續表

基本形式	平聲陰	平聲陽	上聲	去聲
/sran/	0801001 山	—	—	0804065 訕
/kan/	0801003 干	—	0803039 趕	0804054 幹
/khan/	0801006 刊	—	0803042 侃	0804070 看
/han/	—	0802020 寒	0803041 罕	0804049 旱
/an/	0801004 安	—	—	0804053 案
/kyan/	0801005 姦	—	0803036 簡	0804064 澗
/khyan/	0801015 慳	—	—	—
/hyan/	—	0802024 閑	—	0804068 限
/yan/	0801019 殷	0802029 顏	0803048 眼	0804069 雁
/pwan/	0801009 班	—	0803035 板	0804066 辦
/phwan/	0801014 攀	—	—	0804057 盼
/fwan/	0801012 番	0802026 煩	0803032 反	0804067 飯
/vwan/	—	—	0803034 晚	0804051 萬
/mwan/	—	0802028 蠻	—	0804060 慢
/crwan/	0801018 跧	—	—	0804058 譔
/crhwan/	—	—	—	0804072 篡
/srwan/	0801008 拴	—	—	0804059 涫
/kwan/	0801007 關	—	—	0804061 慣
/hwan/	—	0802022 還	0803045 綰	0804063 患
/wan/	0801010 彎	0802031 頑	—	0804075 腕
/pyen/	1001006 邊	—	1003053 貶	1004077 變
/phyen/	1001015 篇	1002038 駢	1003066 諞	1004076 片
/myen/	—	1002024 眠	1003054 沔	1004075 面
/tyen/	1001004 顛	—	1003057 典	1004072 電
/thyen/	1001021 天	1002028 田	1003046 腆	—
/lyen/	—	1002023 連	1003050 輦	1004086 練
/nyen/	—	1002040 年	1003049 撚	—
/cyen/	1001002 煎	—	1003048 剪	1004081 箭
/chyen/	1001011 千	1002027 前	1003060 淺	—
/syen/	1001001 先	1002041 涎	1003045 鮮	1004078 綫

續表

基本形式	平聲陰	平聲陽	上聲	去聲
/cryen/	1001008 氈	—	1003061 展	1004084 戰
/crhyen/	—	1002026 廛	1003056 闡	—
/sryen/	1001009 羶	—	—	1004080 扇
/ryen/	—	1002025 然	—	—
/kyen/	1001003 堅	—	1003047 蹇	1004069 見
/khyen/	1001014 牽	1002032 乾	1003062 遣	1004085 譴
/hyen/	1001012 軒	1002029 賢	1003058 顯	1004070 獻
/yen/	1001013 烟	1002031 延	1003043 兖	1004073 硯
/lywen/	—	1002039 聯	1003051 臠	1004089 戀
/cywen/	1001022 鐫	—	—	—
/chywen/	1001017 痊	1002034 全	1003063 吮	—
/sywen/	1001018 宣	1002035 旋	1003065 選	1004082 鏇
/crywen/	1001010 專	—	1003052 轉①	1004083 傳
/crhywen/	1001019 川	1002036 船	1003055 喘	1004079 釧
/rywen/	—	—	1003064 軟	—
/kywen/	1001005 鵑	—	1003044 卷	1004074 眷
/khywen/	1001020 圈	1002037 拳	1003059 犬	1004071 勸
/hywen/	1001007 喧	1002030 玄	—	1004071 韗
/ywen/	1001016 淵	1002033 元	1003042 遠	1004067 院
/thɨm/	—	—	—	1704044 唔
/lɨm/	—	—	—	1704043 啉
/cɨm/	—	—	1703029 怎	—
/crɨm/	1701004 簪	—	—	1704041 譖
/crhɨm/	—	1702018 岑	1703025 磣	1704040 讖
/srɨm/	1701006 森	—	—	1704039 滲
/lyɨm/	—	1702013 林	1703021 廩	1704038 臨
/nyɨm/	—	—	1703028 您	1704042 賃
/cyɨm/	1701003 駸	—	—	1704037 浸

① 原文爲“輯”,誤,當爲“轉”。

續表

基本形式	平聲陰	平聲陽	上聲	去聲
/chyɨm/	1701011 侵	—	1703030 寢	1704036 沁
/syɨm/	1701009 心	1702015 尋	—	—
/cryɨm/	1701001 針	—	1703026 枕	1704031 朕
/crhyɨm/	1701007 琛	1702019 沉	—	—
/sryɨm/	1701004 深	1702020 忱	1703023 審	1704032 甚
/ryɨm/	—	1702014 壬	1703022 稔	1704033 任
/kyɨm/	1701002 金	—	1703024 錦	1704034 禁
/khyɨm/	1701010 欽	1702017 琴	—	—
/hyɨm/	1701012 歆	—	—	—
/yɨm/	1701008 音	1702016 吟	1703027 飲	1704035 蔭
/tam/	1801002 擔	—	1803028 膽	1804045 淡
/tham/	1801008 貪	1802020 覃	1803032 毯	1804054 探
/lam/	—	1802019 婪	1803027 覽	1804047 濫
/nam/	—	1802017 南	1803041 腩	—
/cam/	1801011 簪	1802025 喒①	1803036 昝	1804051 暫
/cham/	1801009 參	1802021 蠶	1803029 慘	1804056 慘
/sam/	1801005 三	—	1803038 糝	1804053 三
/cram/	1801014 詀	—	1803040 斬	1804049 站
/crham/	1801016 攙	1802023 讒	—	1804057 懺
/sram/	1801007 杉	—	—	(1804058)訕(K)
/kam/	1801006 甘	—	1803026 感	1804043 紺
/kham/	1801004 堪	—	1803034 坎(L) 1803035 砍	1804042 勘(M) 1804048 闞
/ham/	1801010 憨	1802022 含	1803031 喊	1804044 憾
/am/	1801001 庵	—	1803030 揞	1804052 暗
/kyam/	1801003 監	—	1803033 鹻	1804050 鑒
/khyam/	1801012 嵌(M) 1801013 鵮	—	—	—
/hyam/	—	1802018 咸	—	1804046 檻

① 原文爲“喒”,誤,當爲“喒”。

續表

基本形式	平聲陰	平聲陽	上聲	去聲
/yam/	1801015 湁	1802024 巖	{1803037 俺(N) 1803039 黯	1803055 湁
/tyem/	1901009 掂	—	1903031 點	1904036 店
/thyem/	1901012 添	1902019 甜	1903028 忝	—
/lyem/	—	1902013 廉	1903025 斂	1904037 斂
/nyem/	—	1902014 黏	—	1904038 念
/cyem/	1901008 尖	—	—	1904040 漸
/chyem/	1901005 僉	1902021 潛	—	1904041 茜
/syem/	1901004 纖	1902015 撏	—	—
/cryem/	1901001 瞻	—	1903030 颭	1904043 占
/crhyen/	1901006 襜	1902017 蟾	1903032 諂	1904044 韂
/sryem/	1901010 苫	—	1903027 閃	1904034 贍
/ryem/	—	1902020 髯	1903026 染	1901042 染
/kyen/	1901002 兼	—	1903024 撿	1904039 劍
/khyem/	1901011 謙	1902016 鈐	—	1904035 欠
/hyem/	1901007 忺	1902022 嫌	1903029 險	—
/yam/	1901003 淹	1902018 鹽	1903023 掩	1904033 艷

附注:

(A) 如果"翅"(0304026)的變化是規則的話,那它應該出現在 0304020"是氏市柿侍士仕使示謚蒔恃事施嗜豉試弑筮視噬"這個同音字組中。如果像現在這樣,我們在《中原音韻》中必須將其標爲/crhɨ/,因爲這就是它在現代北京話中的讀法。這樣一來,我們就不得不説 0304026"翅"和 0304027"廁"應該合併爲一個同音字組。也就是説,它們之間的小圓圈"○"是誤加的。

(B) 這一系列字可以標爲成/rɨ/,或者簡單地標爲/ɨ/。這兩種形式都能令人滿意地將其與其他音節區分開來。在現代北京話中,這些字儘管帶有[r]音色彩,但它們都是零聲母字。如果我們足够大膽,我們可以認爲,在某個時間點,/rɨ/變成了/ir/。(金尼閣《西儒耳目資》用[ul]來標示這些字。參看陸志韋 1947b)。

$$\# r + ɨ \# \rightarrow \# ɨ + r \# \quad (40)$$[①]

就單個音節而言，這種換位（metathetical change）使得元音後的“r”在音位上顯得不重要了（董同龢將它們簡單地視爲[ï]，即零聲母和零韻尾的/ɨ/。參見董同龢 1954，第 14 頁和第 15 頁之間的表 1）。我們也許可以説，這就是“r”作爲後綴如何首次出現在官話方言裏的原因。如果是這樣的話，後綴“r”在形態音位上將是非常重要的。然而，問題是，什麼時候/rɨ/變成/ɨr/，在《中原音韻》之前還是之後。雖然外部證據不能給這個問題提供一個確切的答案，但我們發現，當我們假設這種變化發生在《中原音韻》之後時，解釋官話方言之間的關係將更加合理和經濟（參看薛鳳生 1971）。還有一點在這裏應該提及，徐孝（1606）《重訂司馬温公等韻圖經》（參陸志韋 1947a），似乎是將這些字放在“影”母下（即當時的零聲母）的第一本書。

（C）1304063“話”（中古：蟹合二去夬匣 AC /xɦuɛiᑐ/[②]，MP /hwà/）在《中原音韻》中必須標爲/hwa/（見 5.9）。這就迫使我們説它和 1304062“化”等應該屬於同一個同音字組；换句話説，我們認爲它們之間的小圓圈“○”是有人在周德清之後錯誤添加的[③]。

（D）根據趙蔭棠的研究，這兩個同音字組應該合併，因爲在其他韻書中，0403061“迤旖”這組字要麽與 0403063“倚椅錡扆偯蟻矣已以苡顗擬艤”在同音小韻内出現，要麽根本未收録。見趙蔭棠（1936：173）注三[④]。

（E）0604084 這個同音字組衹有一個“瀣”（中古：蟹開一去代匣、蟹開二去怪匣 AC /xɦəiᑐ/和/xɦaiᑐ/，MP /syè/）字，它在中古漢語裏有兩個讀音，所

---

① ［譯注］原文並未將此音變用公式（40）表達出來，但却在 7.5.4 將其用公式（9）來表述，且本章正文的公式到（39）結束，而第六章的公式則從（42）開始，因此本章附注中涉及的兩個音變就需要用公式表達出來，序號分别是（40）和（41）。公式（41）見注釋 G。

② ［譯注］“話”爲匣母字，原文標爲/xhuɛiᑐ/，誤，當爲/xɦuɛiᑐ/。

③ ［譯注］1304062“化畫華鱯”和 1304063“話”在趙蔭棠（1936：256）《中原音韻研究》中是兩個相連的同音字組。但在訥菴本《中原音韻》中則爲一個同音字組“化畫華鱯樺話”。這印證了作者的觀點。

④ ［譯注］趙蔭棠（1936：173）注釋原文爲“61 與 63 當合併。若分之，是一音兩見，與周氏條理不合。且卓氏《中州韻》上聲以尾亹爲首，無迤旖二字；《瓊林雅韻》亦以尾亹爲首。有迤旖二字，與倚椅在一圈之内。由是可知迤旖與倚椅當讀爲一音也。《中原音韻問奇集》將迤作爲因已切，倚作爲銀已切，是乃强爲區别，不足爲據。”

以可以標爲/hay/或/hyay/，但第一個會與0604067“害亥妎”衝突，第二個與0604060“懈械薤解獬”衝突。我暫時讓它來填補這裏的空白，没有更好的理由，衹是因爲它是可能的。

(F) 1102038“猱獶鐃呶怓撓譊”這個同音字組必須分成兩個的原因見5.10.3，“猱”單獨爲一組，其餘的字爲另一組。

(G) 這裏的三個字，加上“茂”(1104140“貌冒帽毷眊茂”)，很特别，因爲它們不是來自蕭豪韻的源頭效攝，而是來自流攝。因此，它們應該出現在尤侯韻中(“剖”字確實重見於該韻)，如果它們受到5.13.1(規則39)中討論的/wɨw/到/wɨ/的音變影響的話，則應該出現在魚模韻。因此，它們在蕭豪韻中的出現表明，在第三種方言中(見本章注釋38)，韻母/wɨw/的主元音降爲/a/。

$$ɨ \rightarrow a / w\_\_\_ w \qquad (41)$$

即使在《中原音韻》之後，這種方言對北京話的影響似乎仍在繼續，因爲無論是“矛”(1602027)還是“貿”(1604085)在現代北京話中的韻母都是/waw/。就連“彪”(1601018)現在也讀作/pyāw/。我們也可以説，在這種情況下/ɨ/變成了/o/，而不是/a/，這在描述上同樣是令人滿意的。我決定采用/a/，因爲韻母/wow/似乎正在逐漸衰退。

(H) 見5.14.1的討論。

(I) 根據規則(19)，“亨”(中古:梗開二平庚曉AC /꜀xaŋ/，MP /hēŋ/)應出現在1501016“馨興”這個同音字組中，“甖”(中古:梗開二平耕影AC /꜀qeŋ/，MP /yēŋ/)應出現在1501014“英瑛鷹應膺櫻嬰嚶膺鸚纓瓔縈”這個同音字組中。既然它們都是分開出現的，那麼唯一合理的解釋就是，不管原因是什麼，它們都是規則的例外。司徒修的解釋(司徒修1962a，134－135)不能被接受。

(J) 0703076“不”的奇特之處在於，它僅有一個字，一直存在争議。我在這兒衹是采用趙蔭棠的做法，無意加入争論(見趙蔭棠1936，207，注1)[①]。

---

① [譯注]趙蔭棠注釋原文爲：木原板漫漶，卓氏本作“不”，《嘯餘》本及《問奇》本仍之，《嘯餘》本《中州韻》削之；或仍或削，俱爲不識此字之表現。石山福治對於此字雖加懷疑，但没有進一步的解决，故仍注pu音。案“不”字乃“朩”字之誤也。《五音集韻》震韻滂母有此字，注云：“《説文》曰：分枲皮也。”因此之故，我才標寫p‘in。不過它的位置與牝品在一圈之内。卓氏本“不”與“品”本相鄰。[譯者案]丁聲樹先生曾對此字有過考證。朱琰《陶説·陶冶圖(轉下頁)

(K) 這個同音字組是誤加的。參見趙蔭棠(1936:293)注 7 ①。

(L) 1803034"坎"和 1803035"砍"一定是誤分了。"砍"是《切韻》後産生的字,根據其他幾本韻書,"砍"與"坎"是同音字。它們在現代北京話中仍然是同音字。

(M) 我們最基本的假設之一是,中古漢語同攝同等不同的韻,到韻圖時期,也就是説在《中原音韻》前很久,已經合併了(3.6.3)。在監咸韻中發現了兩個對比,似乎與這一假設相矛盾,即 1804042"勘"(中古:咸開一去勘溪 AC /khəm⊃/, MP /khàn/)對 1804048"闞"(中古:咸開一去闞溪 AC /khɑm⊃/, MP /khàn/)和 1801012"嵌"(中古:咸開二平銜溪 AC /⊂khɛm/, MP /chyān/)對 1801013"鵮"(中古:咸開二平咸溪 AC /⊂kham/, MP /chyān/)。由於第二對同音字組是連續出現的,也許可以認爲這兩個組被錯誤地劃分了,從而忽略了這種對比。這樣,第一對就成爲唯一與我們的假設相矛盾的例子。然而,這個假設真的太重要了,不能因爲一個例外而否定它。因此,我承認(僅此一次),周德清犯了一個可能造成非常嚴重後果的錯誤。

(N) 在《中原音韻》裏將"黯"(中古:咸開二上豏影 AC /⊂qam/, MP /ǎn/和/yǎn/)中標爲/yam/應該没有異議,但是"俺"(中古:咸開三去豔影 AC /qiam⊃/, MP /ǎn/)字非常麻煩。根據我們的規則,我們希望它在廉纖韻的去聲中出現,但是現在它在監咸韻的上聲裏出現了。此外,我們不確定《中原音韻》"俺"是否與中古漢語的"俺"字代表相同的語素(即含義是否相同)。現在,我們可以將其標爲/yam/或/am/。來自其他韻書的證據(見趙蔭棠 1936,第 293 頁,注 5)表明,/yam/似乎更可取②。

(接上頁)説》有"白不",注有"敦上聲,凡造瓷泥土皆從此名,蓋景德土也。"朱琰《陶説·陶冶圖説》:"石産江南徽州祁門縣坪里、谷口二山……土人藉溪流設輪作碓,舂細淘净,制如土磚,名曰白不。"下注云:"敦上聲。凡造瓷泥土皆從此名,蓋景德土音也。"(《翠琅玕館叢書》本,卷六十五)又紐秀《觚賸》云:"粵人以截土作墪爲不"。(《筆記小説大觀》本)現代客家方言裏仍有"不"字,讀上聲(見《客話七言雜字》)。引自楊耐思(1981:123—124)《中原音韻音系》。

① [譯注]趙蔭棠(1936:293)注 7 原文爲:"訕字依《嘯餘》本補,非閉口音。"訥菴本《中原音韻》無"訕"字。

② [譯注]趙蔭棠(1936:293)注五原文爲:俺本去聲影三,依規則黨標爲 iam,與今音之讀爲 ɑn 者相差太遠。考卓氏本俺在糝下與黯相鄰,我們由此可知俺與黯有在一圈之内的可能,如此則兩字俱可讀爲 ɑm,與今音相差不多。

第六章　關於《中原音韻》的所謂入聲問題

《中原音韻》是否還存在入聲,是個聚訟已久的問題,至今也没有令人滿意的答案。這表面上看起來是個衹要回答"是"或"否"的一般問題,但實際上遠不止於此。無論答案是什麽,它都必須以對這類音節從中古漢語到《中原音韻》的演變的詳細而系統的描述作爲後盾。但遺憾的是,幾乎所有參與這場辯論的人都忽略了這個問題更深層次方面的意義。他們似乎衹對提供一個直截了當的答案感興趣,然後,如果他們足够關心的話,還會爲所涉及的字添加一些特别的標音。此外,他們爲支持自己的論點而提出的論據大都是外部的。也就是説,這些論據儘管可能是合理的,甚至是有説服力的,但與《中原音韻》的音系結構没有任何直接關係[①]。我相信,這就是爲什麽這個問題到現在還没有解决的根本原因。本質上外部的論證衹能説明有某種可能性,而不能説明有邏輯上的必然性。因此,爲了解决這個似乎無法解决的入聲問題,我們必須同時提出外部的和内部的論證。這就是本章要做的。以我們目前所做的工作,我們已經爲攻克這個問題做好了充分的準備,我們希望能够一勞永逸地解决這個問題。我們將分三個步驟來解决這個問題。首先,我們將簡要地回顧一下有關這個問題的幾個外部證據,以常識作爲衡量標準,重新評估《中原音韻》之外的這些證據以及《中原音韻》作者周德清本人對此所作的評論。我們在這個時候所得出的結論顯然不能使每個人都信服,但它也許可以使大多數人信服。其次,我們將嘗試從結構的角度,窮盡分析這個問題所有内在的方面,看看如果入聲在《中原音韻》中真的還存在的話,那麽在漢語音系的框架内,它究竟應該是什麽樣子的,或者説一定不可能是什麽樣子的。我們在這一部分得出的結論,應該是任何相信結構主義的人都能接受的。最後,我們將對這個問題提出一個系統的解决方案。這個解决方案將用非常精確的術語解釋入聲音節怎樣從中古漢語發展到《中原音韻》,以及爲什麽《中原音韻》采用現

① 趙遐秋、曾慶瑞(1962)和李新魁(1963)可以看作兩個典型的例子。

在的方式對這些入聲字進行重新分配。没有人能讓我們放棄我們的解決方案,除非他能提出一個更好的方案。

6.1 外部證據

關於《中原音韻》入聲字的争議主要源於兩個事實。第一,儘管從前的入聲字分别派入三個聲調,收在無鼻音韻尾的陰聲韻類的下面①,但仍自成一個獨立小類,與其他非入聲字分開。第二,周德清對入聲字的態度似乎很不確定。在《中原音韻》的"序"和"正語作詞起例"中,周德清在好幾個地方説,"音韻無入聲,派入平上去三聲",但在别處他又説"入聲派入平上去三聲者,以廣其押韻,爲作詞而設耳。然呼吸言語之間還有入聲之别"②。由此可見,如果能對周德清上述兩種不同的説法提供更好的解釋,那麽我們就爲更好地解決《中原音韻》的所謂入聲問題奠定了堅實的基礎。

6.1.1 受聲母條件制約,在現代各官話方言中,原入聲字的聲調狀況彼此差别很大。下表所列方言可以説明這一點,這不是窮盡性的,僅舉例説明而已③。

中古漢語聲母 / 方言	Cɦ-	R-	C(h)-
南京	□꜆	□꜆	□꜆
重慶 昆明等	꜁□	꜁□	꜁□
青島	꜁□	□꜄	꜂□
濟南	꜁□	□꜄	꜀□
鄭州 西安	꜁□	꜀□	꜀□

---

① [譯注]周德清在自序中説"入聲派入平上去三聲,如'鞞'字,次本韻後,使黑白分明,以别本聲外來,庶使學者。有才者本韻自足矣。"

② 讀一讀諸多學者對這一點的論述很有意思。不管是贊成的,還是反對的,都引用周德清的話,但各取所需,衹相信自己選擇相信的。這生動地表明,衹根據周德清有關入聲的説法是無效的。

③ 此表根據李榮(1963:84)所提供的材料而作。關於北京話,也可參司徒修(1962b)。

續表

中古漢語聲母 / 方言	Cɦ-	R-	C(h)-
蘭州	⊆□	□⊃	□⊃
北京	⊆□	□⊃	⊂□⊆□⊂□ □⊃

表中的每個小方框“□”代表一個字(也即一個音節),其聲調以傳統的“圈發”方式標注,即在一個角落用一個小半圓標記,左下角:平聲,左上角:上聲,右上角:去聲,右下角:入聲。當一個聲調必須分爲陰類和陽類時,小半圓下加横綫表示陽調,無標記表示陰調。此外,我們得知,即便是在北方官話方言區内,仍有一些全部保留或部分保留入聲的方言①。現在讓我們發揮一點想象力。如果前推七八百年,各方言的聲調狀況豈不是差别更大嗎?我相信,當入聲處在消失的過程中時,情况一定是相當混亂的。這種混亂不是説没有新的發展規律,而是説不同的方言有不同的規律②。事實上,很多原本單一的方言一定就是因爲這個原因才分成若干次方言的。結果很可能是,兩個相鄰城鎮或地區的人所講的話中,除了入聲音節之外,其他完全相同。入聲在一個地區可能還保留着,而在另一個地區則已經消失了。更令人困惑的是,思想傳統的受過教育的人可能會堅持説,他們的講話中仍然有入聲,而實際上他們没有。誠然,上述情况多少帶有點想象的色彩,但從漢語的音系背景來看,這是絶對有可能,甚至可能是真的。這讓我們想起了一件事。也就是説,當我們説《中原音韻》中有或没有入聲時,我們是在談論一個相對較小的方言或次方言,不管它可能在哪裏。我們不是在談論北方官話,即便是狹義上的北方官話,也不是我們在這裏要探討的對象。

6.1.2 有强有力的證據證明,入聲的變化早在《中原音韻》之前就開始了。這裏我們可以隨便舉出以下三點來支持這個觀點。

(a) 在《切韻指掌圖》中,入聲字既與陽聲韻相配,也與陰聲韻相配。有

① 陸志韋以山西方言爲例(陸志韋 1946:58)。李榮説某些方言僅部分保留入聲,但他没有説是哪些方言(李榮 1963:84)。王靖宇、薛鳳生(1973)《臨淇方言及其與官話方言的關係》一文可以作爲一個明確的個例。

② 薛鳳生(1971)可以作爲一個有力的例證。

時,同一個入聲字可能會出現在三個圖中。例如,“則”(中古:曾開一入德精 AC /cək/, MP /cé/)字出現在圖四、圖九和圖十八中。這一現象表明,編纂者自己也不確定如何處理,結果采用了雙重甚至三重標準。

(b) 根據夏承燾的研究,在宋詞用韻中也發現了“入派三聲”現象[①]。

(c) 另一位學者唐钺,在他的研究中指出,入聲在 1190 年前後已完全消失了[②]。

必須承認,這些現象並不一定能證明《中原音韻》没有入聲,因爲可能有人認爲,《中原音韻》的語言可能不是這些學者所研究的方言,或者不是從這些學者所研究的那些方言演變過來的,但這些現象强烈暗示,《中原音韻》可能没有入聲。

6.1.3 周德清編纂《中原音韻》的唯一目的是教人們如何正確地用韻。因此,這本書主要是針對母語不是《中原音韻》所代表的那種方言的人而編寫的,而對於母語是《中原音韻》所代表的那種方言的人來説,作用相當有限。對於來自其他方言區,且想模仿作曲(這種新的詩歌形式)的人來説,最令人煩惱的,就是入聲字,這一點完全可以想象得到。爲了達到最大的效果,編纂者自然要把這些麻煩的入聲字整理出來。這當然更好地滿足了那些細心的模仿者的需要,也可以引起那些粗心的且急需糾正的模仿者的注意。因此,將中古漢語入聲字與其他聲調字分開並不一定意味着這些入聲字在《中原音韻》所代表的方言中仍然保留着入聲調。當我們想到後來的學者,甚至是今天的學者,經常會把中古漢語的入聲字標注出來時,就更加相信這一點了。

6.1.4 周德清不確定該如何對待這些入聲字,是可以理解的。考慮到他當時的處境,他確實應該得到我們所有人的同情,對他的所作所爲我們衹能表示欽佩。不管他掌握了怎樣的語言能力,他所記録的語言畢竟不是他的母語,當這種當時的“標準語”恰好由於入聲字的原因分爲幾個次方言,而每一種次方言的地位又是如此相當時,周德清一定感到很困惑。甚至當遇到當地操這

① 據夏承燾(1948)《陽上作去入派三聲説》,《國文月刊》第 68 期。引自趙遐秋、曾慶瑞(1962:321)。

② 據唐鉞(1926)《入聲變遷與詞曲發達的關係》,《東方雜志》第 23 卷第 1 號。引自趙遐秋、曾慶瑞(1962:321)。

種“標準語”且受過教育的讀書人堅持認爲仍有入聲時,就需要付出比否定它更多的勇氣。結果是他小心翼翼地行事。一方面,他毫不含糊地指出,所有偉大元曲作家都將入聲字與非入聲字一起押韻,但另一方面,他又承認,在實際講話中確實存在入聲。在這一點上,我們僅僅衹能把周德清當作一個“發音人”,儘管他是一個非常可靠的發音人。這意味着我們可以接受他對單個字音的觀察,但不能接受他對他所努力記録的語言的總體特徵的看法。顯而易見的事實是,在早期官話中,就韻文而言,所謂的入聲字與其他聲調字不再有區別了。

6.1.5 周德清認爲入聲確實存在於當時的實際言語中,儘管它與押韻没有關係,這個看法根本不能被接受。通俗文學的作者以人民的語言作爲自己藝術創作的工具,也就是説,他們衹能在這個工具允許的範圍内創作,除了能增添幾個新詞外,不可能隨心所欲地改動或修飾這個工具。原因很簡單,如果他們這樣做,他們的作品將遭到人民的抵制。因此,如果入聲音節在實際語言中仍然是真的入聲音節,那麽入聲音節與非入聲音節在一起押韻將是不可能的[①]。

6.2 内部證據

我們已經給出了好幾個外部的證據來論證我們關於《中原音韻》没有入聲的觀點。還可以提供更多的論據,但無論這些證據多麽合理,它們在邏輯上都不會是决定性的。我將在這裏提出一些内部的證據,我希望這些證據會更有説服力。

6.2.1 我們都知道,中古漢語中的所謂的入聲,實際上是由以/p、t、k/爲韻尾的音節組成的。有人提出,在某個階段,這三個韻尾合併成一個,也許是一個喉塞音,而這個喉塞音,或者不管它是什麽,在《中原音韻》時代仍然存在,以此爲標記將入聲音節與非入聲音節區别開來[②]。對於《中原音韻》來説,這

① 前有好幾位學者采用這一觀點。參看趙遐秋、曾慶瑞(1962:322—323)。

② 司徒修(1962a:153—154)。

在結構上是不可能的。我們注意到,中古漢語和現代北京話的音節模式都是(C)(M)V(E)(見3.1)。我們有充分的理由相信,這種模式在《中原音韻》中保持不變。如果韻尾塞音變成了一個新的成分,那麼這個新的成分必然依然占據韻尾的位置,它不可能占據音節中除韻尾外的其他位置①。在《中原音韻》中,我們發現,以前的入聲字,不僅出現在韻尾爲零韻尾的韻中,也出現在韻尾爲半元音的韻中,即齊微韻、皆來韻、蕭豪韻和尤侯韻中,這個簡單的事實告訴我們,所謂的入聲字不可能真正有入聲調。此外,現在出現在韻尾爲半元音的韻中的入聲字屬於一種特殊類型,以前這些入聲字的韻尾都是/k/。這就是爲什麼我説這三個塞音韻尾在《中原音韻》所代表的語言的早期階段也不可能合併爲一個的理由,若果真如此,任何一個入聲字都有可能進入齊微、皆來、蕭豪和尤侯這四韻中的任何一個。這顯然與事實不符。

6.2.2 雖然陸志韋在寫《釋中原音韻》這篇著名文章時,對結構主義幾乎没有明確的認識,但令人驚訝的是,他意識到上述那個令所有堅持《中原音韻》仍然保留入聲的人(包括他自己)陷入困境的問題②。然而他爲這個困境提出的補救辦法却是相當奇怪的。龍果夫在其對八思巴字的研究中,認爲"早期官話"没有入聲。他做了一個相當敏鋭的觀察,他説在[ɑ]或[e]之後,韻尾[k]似乎留下了一些痕迹,他將其標爲[u]或[i]③,這裹所涉及的字恰好就是《中原音韻》中韻尾爲半元音的韻裹的那些入聲字。陸志韋表示,在入聲這個問題上,他不同意龍果夫的説法,因爲龍果夫使用的兩個符號"實際上在八思巴字中分别是[w]和[j]"。然後,"爲了避免其他方面的誤會起見",他又分别用[ʎ]和[ɥ]代替了它們④,這相當於他以一種特殊的方式用三個新成分替换了三個中古漢語韻尾。在零韻尾韻裹的入聲字是[ʔ],在/w/韻尾韻裹的入聲字是[ʎ],在/y/韻尾韻裹的入聲字是[ɥ]。現在我們要問,如果這三個新成分確實存在,它們有音位地位嗎?如果没有,我們能接受這種説法嗎?

---

① 司徒修(1966)果真爲帶有半元音韻尾的音節加了/q/。

② 見陸志韋(1946:61)。但他後來又爲尤侯韻的入聲字勉强假定了一個韻母[iəuʔ](66頁),似乎把這個問題忘記了。

③ 引自陸志韋(1946:62)。

④ [譯注]陸志韋使用的這兩個符號分别是[ɦ]和[ɥ],分别對應於英文原文中的[ʎ]和[ɥ]。

6.2.3 也許有人會說，現在在半元音韻尾韻的入聲字，在那時已經不屬於入聲了，但在零韻尾韻中的入聲字，仍然有喉塞音或類似的東西作爲韻尾，因此是真正的入聲字。這似乎衹是爲了辨論而辨論，所以據我所知，還没有人提出過這樣的觀點。但是我們必須承認，這一論點所假設的情形儘管在事實上不太可能，但在理論上却是可能的。我認爲它不太可能的原因有兩個：首先，說舌尖塞音和雙唇塞音合併成了一個喉塞音，而舌根塞音却消失了，這似乎有點不太尋常。其次，我們已經證明喉塞音作爲一個聲母在《中原音韻》之前就已經消失了。現在我們又將它作爲一個韻尾來恢復它，這確實有關奇怪。應該承認，這兩個原因都不是十分有力，所以不應該完全排除上面假設的情形。也許這種入聲的部分保留現象影響了周德清，使他將已不再是入聲的字連同那些還是入聲的字一起被標記出來，單獨設爲一類。

6.2.4 我們已經看到，在《中原音韻》中，從前的入聲字根據聲母（見3.5.1）派入三個聲調。清音聲母入聲字都派入到"入聲作上聲"這一類，相當於現代北京話的第三聲（"上聲"）。但在現代北京話中，這些"入聲作上聲"的字，今讀陰平、陽平、上聲和去聲的都有，非常不規則，目前還没有發現導致其如此分布的制約條件。鑒於這一事實，陸志韋說："就因爲清音入聲能完全派入上聲，所以知道他們不能是真正的上聲"[①]。我看不出他的邏輯。事實上，這是很有可能的，正如我們在青島方言（6.1.1）中觀察到的那樣，我們肯定青島方言没有入聲。面對同樣的現象，司徒修作如此評論：事實是，衹有這一組（入聲作上聲）入聲字在現代北京話中出現了如此程度的不規則性變化，這使得《中原音韻》"入派三聲"得到了清晰地證明。這一事實同樣清晰地證明了"入聲作上聲"與"上聲"（或平聲陽、上聲、去聲）之間的區别[②]。這句話的第一部分是非常正確的。事實上，從來没有人質疑過這一點。然而，第二部分並没有任何邏輯上的必要性。衹有當我們接受現代北京話是《中原音韻》所代表的方言的直系後裔時，陸志韋和司徒修的推理才稍有意義，但他們都否認了這一點[③]，而且，即使我們應該接受這個主張，他們的結論也不是邏輯上的必然結

① 陸志韋（1946：59）。

② 司徒修（1962a：153）。

③ 陸志韋（1946：67）；司徒修（1962a：132）。

果。正如我們在6.1.1的表中看到的那樣,從前入聲音節的另外兩種類型在幾乎所有的現代北方官話方言中都是相當有規律的,清音入聲音節在不同的方言中有不同的表現。我們有理由相信,過去的情況一定也是如此。因此,如果現代北京話確實直接來自《中原音韻》,那麼現代北京話中與《中原音韻》"入聲作上聲"字相對應的音節的不規則性很可能是大量借用周圍方言或次方言的結果。最近的研究表明,在關漢卿的作品中,從前清音入聲字聲調的分布情況與現代北京話非常接近。這種類型的字約有百分之七十沒有用作上聲字,也就是説,它們與《中原音韻》不一致[①]。如果關漢卿的語言是早期的北京話,那麼根據上述事實,我們可以得出的唯一結論是,《中原音韻》一定代表一種不同的方言,然而它必須與關漢卿的語言關係非常密切,因爲在所有其他方面,它們實際上是一樣的。這還告訴我們,在現代北京話中,清音入聲字在現代北京話中的不規律演變現象早在《中原音韻》之前就存在了。這一事實絶不能作爲《中原音韻》有入聲的證據。

6.2.5《中原音韻》還有一個非常獨特的現象,就是周德清建立了"去聲作平聲陽"這個調類。它衹由一個"鼻"字構成。根據常識,必須立即排除這一類。根本不可能存在衹有一個音節的調類。陸志韋解釋説,周德清這樣做是因爲"鼻"(中古:止開三去至並 AC /pɦi*iᵓ/, MP /pyɨ/)字在當時仍然是一個去聲字。陸志韋接着説,周德清這樣做,説明他的工作是非常細緻的,所以當他説"入聲作×聲"時,所涉及的字也一定還是入聲[②]。不知道陸志韋是怎麼知道,在周德清的時代,"鼻"字仍然是一個入聲字。如果有,應該也包含在齊微韻的去聲中。但在那裏並没有發現。我從上述事實中得到的推論正好與陸志韋的相反。這表明周德清在這裏再次特別努力地提醒讀者,特別是母語非這種方言的讀者,"鼻"字從前讀"去聲",現在讀"平聲陽"了[③]。

---

① 廖珣英(1963:273)。

② 陸志韋(1946:59)。

③ [譯注]今南昌話中,"鼻"爲陽入字,讀[piʔ²]。很可能在周德清的母語中,"鼻"字也是個全濁入聲字。但在傳統韻書中,"鼻"爲去聲字,如《廣韻》爲並母"毗至切"。按照語音演變規律,全濁聲母去聲"鼻"字是不可能變爲"平聲陽"的,但是全濁入聲字在《中原音韻》中幾乎全都變成了"入聲作平聲陽"。周德清通過整理,發現了這個語音演變規律,於是在此處提供讀者"鼻"字已經讀作"平聲陽"了。但由於鼻字在傳統韻書中都是全濁去聲,因此他衹能據此(轉下頁)

6.2.6 趙元任在他給《馬修斯漢英詞典》(Mathew's Chinese-English Dictionary)寫的"讀音導論"中説[①]：

原來以-k收尾的中古漢語入聲字通常有文白異讀。它們以下面韻母形式同時出現：

讀書音	-e	-o	-u	-üeh
口語音	-ai,-ei	-ai,-ao,-ei	-iu,-ou	-iao
	色 賊	百 落 北	六 軸	角

他舉的這些字和其他許多類似的字在《中原音韻》的不同韻裏出現了兩次，例如，1154156"落絡烙洛酪樂珞"和1254087"落洛絡酪樂烙"這兩個同音字組中的"落"(中古：宕開一入鐸來 AC /lɑk/, MP /lwè/和/làw/)，0552046"逐軸"和1652035"軸逐"這兩個同音字組中的"軸"(中古：通合三入屋澄 AC /tjɦi*k/, MP /créw/)。這種現象在《中原音韻》中的分布比在現代北京話中更廣泛，對這種現象最直接、最合理的解釋自然是，就像在現代北京話中一樣，這些字也有文白異讀，一種是讀書音，另一種是口語音[②]。如果承認入聲字的這兩種不同的讀音反映了不同社會階層的讀音，那麽在理論上就有可能假設，這些入聲字的讀書音，就是真正的入聲，可能帶有一個喉塞音(見7.3.2)，因爲讀書音總是出現在零韻尾韻中。此外，我們可以寫出非常簡潔的規則來顯示讀書音從韻圖時期，經《中原音韻》，到現代北京話的發展，這些規則符合我們在第五章構建的元音系統(見6.4.1.2的討論)。由於一些規則應産生的結果並没有記録在《中原音韻》中(見7.3.5)，我仍然認爲《中原音韻》中没有入聲，儘管我們可以承認，與《中原音韻》同時期的代表"讀書音"的方言裏，入聲音節確實還存在着喉塞音韻尾。

(接上頁)設置了一個"去聲作平聲陽"這個特殊的類别。這是個權宜之計。因爲如果周德清根據他自己的母語方言將"鼻"字歸爲全濁入聲字的話，雖然在體例上將顯得得整齊，但就影響了作爲"標準語"韻書的嚴肅性與權威性。因爲在文獻上，"鼻"作爲入聲字，是没有出處的，至少周德清當時是没有看到的。

① 趙元任(1943：X)。

② 奇怪的是竟有人不同意這一看法。他們似乎認爲，不同的讀法是因爲某些不同方言的讀法毫無道理地混收在這本書裏。例如陸志韋(1946：65)和趙遐秋、曾慶瑞(1962：319)。

6.3 有關入聲的普遍性問題

我們已經廣泛地討論了與入聲有關的各個方面的問題，這些問題都有力地説明了《中原音韻》没有入聲。《中原音韻》有無入聲這個疑問雖然回答了，但問題仍然存在，除非我們能够對《中原音韻》中入聲字的分布狀况做出系統的描寫，並且這些入聲字到現代北京話的發展也必須在這個描寫的基礎上得到充分合理的解釋。下面就朝着這個方向努力。但是，在我們進行詳細討論之前，必須首先處理一些或多或少帶有普遍性的問題。

6.3.1 如前所述，有些入聲字可能出現在兩個韻裏，例如蕭豪韻的入聲字也出現在歌戈韻中。我把這種現象解釋爲兩種不同發展路綫的結果：讀書音和口語音。更準確地説，在與口語音密切相關的另一個次方言中，發生了讀書音的演變現象。也就是説，讀書音和口語音分别代表兩個不同而又密切相關的次方言。正如我所説的，讀書音代表的這個次方言可能在一段時間内以喉塞音的形式保留了入聲，但在《中原音韻》這個代表口語音的方言中，我相信，與“口語音”一起爲大衆所接受的“讀書音”一定是失去了喉塞音的“讀書音”，儘管這些被接受的“讀書音”分布並不平衡，也就是説，衹有部分“讀書音”被接受了，而不是全部。這一點，我們將在後面看到(6.4.1.2)。然而，可以理解的是，隨着時間的推移，當這種被視爲標準語的方言在越來越大的地區傳播時，除了一些最常用的字(“核心詞彙”)之外，更具權威性的“讀書音”覆蓋了“口語音”。因此，這裏所討論的很多入聲字在現代北京話中衹保留了“讀書音”，“口語音”消失了。當陸志韋試圖證明《中原音韻》存在入聲時，他引用了一個事實作爲證據，某一韻中的入聲字在現代北京話中的讀音可能根本不同於該韻非入聲字的讀音①。顯然，陸志韋忽略了這裏所討論的這一點。

6.3.2 當我們試圖構建元音系統時，我們發現，那些/ŋ/韻尾“攝”是元音位移變化規則的例外(見5.6.2)。在研究這些攝的入聲字時，我們遇到了更大的困難，因爲這類入聲字在《中原音韻》兩個甚至三個韻中出現，例如梗攝的

① 陸志韋(1946:59—60)。

入聲字可以在齊微韻中出現，例如 0452050“石”（中古：梗開三入昔禪 AC /sjɦiɛk/，MP /srɨ́/），也可以在皆來韻中出現，例如 0652030“白”（中古：梗開二入陌並 AC /pɦak/，MP /pwáy/），還可以在車遮韻中出現，例如 145303“客”（中古：梗開二入陌溪 AC /khak/，MP /khè/）。這一事實表明，入聲字的變化很可能發生在其他聲調字（即其相應的舒聲字）的元音位移變化之前，至少對《中原音韻》所代表的方言的這類入聲字來説是這樣的①。

6.3.3 龍果夫在研究八思巴字時指出，中古漢語的/k/韻尾在[ɑ]或[e]後面留下一些痕迹，似乎是[u]或[i]，這一點同樣適用於《中原音韻》（見 6.2.2 注③）。當然，我們對這種不精確的描述並不滿意。説某音在某一個條件下或另一個條件下出現時，它可能變成這個，也可能變成那個，這等於什麽也没有説。因此，我將從一個更嚴格的假設開始，即在口語音中，韻尾/k/雖然消失了但總會在它之前出現的位置上留下一些“痕迹”。而且，這些痕迹衹能是/w/或/y/，每一個都受到一些形式特徵的限制。那麽問題來了：韻尾/k/是在什麽條件下變成/w/的，又是在什麽不同的條件下變成/y/的？對於這個問題，我們似乎衹能給出一個特别的答案，即當從前帶有/k/韻尾的入聲在出現在/w/韻尾韻時，/k/就變成了/w/，但出現在/y/韻尾韻時，它就變成了/y/。事實上，所有早期的研究都是直接或間接地這麽説的。但是我們已經注意到，現在出現在/y/韻尾韻（即齊微和皆來）中的入聲字都來自曾攝和梗攝，而出現在/w/韻尾韻（即蕭豪和尤侯）中的入聲字都來自江攝、宕攝和通攝。用這個方法來處理韻尾/k/的變化，儘管仍然顯得很特别，但似乎要好一點。對於這個謎題，我們可以從傳統上將韻分爲内轉和外轉的二分現象中找到綫索。在這方面，我們之前采用的羅常培的説法（3.6.1）並没有給我們任何幫助；但是《切韻指南》和《切韻指掌圖》（參見 3.6.1 注釋②）將宕攝作爲内轉的分法給了我們一些提示。如果按照這個分法，我們可以證明當曾攝併入梗攝時，是由内轉外，但是當江攝併入宕攝時，則是由外轉内，我們所處的困境就比較好解决了。

① 【追注】在撰寫本書時，由於我對梗曾兩攝的性質認識不足，誤以爲它們也收舌根音，所以才不得不含混地説它們是元音位移變化的例外。現在我們對梗曾江宕等攝的性質有了更清楚更可靠的認識，因此知道它們並不例外，也因此可以看出本節與下一節的一些説法並不妥當。詳細的討論見於薛鳳生（1985）。

然後,我們可以簡單地説,韻尾/k/在外轉中變成了/y/,但在内轉中變成了/w/[①]。

6.4 入聲字的再分配

討論完有關入聲的普遍性問題之後,現在我們可以繼續討論入聲字本身了。我們不準備從入聲字在《中原音韻》中的分布入手,而準備從韻圖的攝開始我們的討論。這意味着,我們的討論將從這些入聲字在中古漢語或韻圖時期語言中的形態開始,然後將它們置於我們之前構建的系統中,以便觀察它們在後來失去韻尾或變成其他形式之後,"應該"是什麽樣子。如果我們爲它們推論出的應有的形態被它們在《中原音韻》中的實際形態證實,我們自然會受到鼓舞,但即便好像没有得到證實,我們也不會對我們構建的系統失去信心。相反,我們應該在這個框架内,用同樣嚴格的方式,解釋那些看起來未被證實的現象。

6.4.1 梗曾攝入聲字。我們先從看起來最困難的部分,即梗曾攝入聲字,開始我們的討論。在《中原音韻》中,梗曾攝入聲字主要出現在齊微韻和皆來韻中。但在車遮韻中也發現了一些喉音聲母入聲字。在《切韻指掌圖》中,梗攝和曾攝合併爲一個攝[②],我認爲這證明,在形成《中原音韻》的庚青韻之前,曾攝由内轉移入外轉,併入梗攝,形成了一個四等俱全的外轉攝。這樣,在某一時間點上,這個新形成的外轉攝的音節形式一定如下:

---

① 當然,我們還得用音位術語闡明内外轉對立的真正内涵。我們這兒的疑問説明,羅常培的説法决不能算是定論。實際上,問題要複雜得多。我認爲在内轉和外轉的二重對立框架内,同韻尾的攝衹可能有兩個,一個在内轉,一個在外轉。這一解釋唯一困難是,帶舌根音韻尾的攝太多了(見 6.4.3 和 7.2d)。我對這個難題的解答是把江攝和宕攝當作 3.6.2 所提出的韻圖音節模式的例外。就是説,它們有異常的主元音,可能是中古漢語元音系統向韻圖時期的元音系統演變時留下的殘餘,即這些元音的音位地位在别的地方都消失了,但在舌根音前却仍存在。另一方面,爲了解决這個問題,橋本萬太郎則提出了有一對腭音/ɲ/和/c/作爲梗攝的韻尾。見橋本萬太郎(1970)。

② 圖 15 和圖 16。參見趙元任(1941:204)和馬丁(1953:3)。

等	音節形式
1	$C(w)V_1ŋ$
2	$C(w)V_2ŋ$
3	$Cy(w)V_3ŋ$
4	$Cy(w)V_4ŋ$

與之相對應的入聲則是

1	$C(w)V_1k$
2	$C(w)V_2k$
3	$Cy(w)V_3k$
4	$Cy(w)V_4k$

現在,如果把這些形式中的/k/韻尾换成/y/,會發生什麽呢?難道這類音節不就和蟹攝的音節完全無法區分了嗎?答案是肯定的。然後,我們應該看到這些入聲字在《中原音韻》中的分布方式已與蟹攝字的分布方式完全相同(參見5.11和5.12.2)。除了一個小的方面的例外,我們發現情况確實如此。也即,所有的二等字和幾個捲舌(莊組)聲母三等字都出現在皆來韻,其餘的都在齊微韻。現在,問題解决了。我們所要做的就是在適當的地方添加一個簡單的規則,可能在規則(28)之前(見5.6.2)。

$$k \rightarrow y / V_g\_\_\_\_ \quad (42)$$

V_g=梗攝和曾攝的主元音

這個規則的制約條件看起來可能有些尷尬,但在這一點上我們無能爲力。這個問題涉及通攝和宕攝(包括江攝),所以我們將在後面進一步討論(見6.4.3)。下面先講幾個小問題。

6.4.1.1 剛才提到的那個小方面的例外與我們的元音位移變化規則有關。我們已經説過,除了/w/韻尾或零韻尾字外,(4.6.4.5和5.10.2中的規則22),外轉開口一等字的主元音變成了二等字的主元音。按照這個規則,我們期望看到曾攝開口一等入聲字都出現在皆來韻中,但實際上衹有兩個,0653053"刻"(中古:曾開一入德溪 AC /khək/, MP /khè/)和0653059"則"(中古:曾開一入德精 AC /cək/, MP /cé/),其他這類字都出現在齊微韻中。例如:0452058"刻"(中古:曾開一入德匣 AC /xɦək/, MP /hé/)和0452059"賊"(中古:曾開一入德從 AC /cɦək/, MP /céy/)。還有一個甚至出現在支思韻中,即0353019"塞"(中古:曾開一入德心 AC /sək/, MP /sè/)。最近一項有關關漢卿用韻的研究表明,不僅關漢卿,與其同時期的幾位大作家實際上也都用"刻"字與齊微韻字押韻①。由於這些字大部分都出現在齊微韻中,因此它們的韻母必須用/ɨy/來標示。爲了説明支思韻的韻母衹能標爲/ɨ/,我們曾引用過這個現象(見5.12.6)。關於這些字的分布,後面詳談(見6.4.5.2)。

6.4.1.2 除了少數幾個最常用的字,如"白"(中古:梗開二入陌並 AC /pɦak/, MP /pwáy/"白色")和"北"(中古:曾開一入德幫 AC /pək/, MP /pwěy/"北方")外,不管是曾攝一等入聲字,還是梗攝二等入聲字,在現代北京話中的韻母都是/e/或/we/。當然,這種讀法是讀書音,整個現象其實也是很容易解釋的。這條發展路綫似乎是很不一樣的。當兩攝完全合併,其主元音爲前低元音/e/時,韻尾/k/毫無疑問還保留着。後來,當/k/失落(或變成喉塞音)時,所有這類音節的主元音還是/e/,就像在現代北京話中一樣。因此,對於讀書音,我們衹需要在元音位移變化之後的某個地方加上一條規定韻尾變化的規則,但這個規則必須加在梗攝和曾攝合併之後,三等和四等字的韻腹變爲/ɨ/之前(見7.3.3)。

$$k \rightarrow q \qquad (43)$$

奇怪的是,這種讀書音,《中原音韻》没有記録。如果記録的話,那麽相應的字將全部出現在車遮韻中。這一事實或許可以作爲證據,證明《中原音韻》是嚴格地以當時代表"口語音"的某種方言爲基礎的。

6.4.1.3 在車遮韻中確實出現了三個這類入聲字,即1453033"客"(中古:梗開二入陌溪 AC /khak/, MP /khè/)、1453035"嚇"(中古:梗開二入陌曉 AC /xak/, MP /hè/)和1454058"額"(中古:梗開二入陌疑 AC /ŋak/, MP /é/);但它們之所以在這裏出現,似乎並不是讀書音所致。請注意,它們都是喉音聲母開口二等字,因此它們的變化必然受4.6.2所論之規則(19)的影響。當它們出現在皆來韻中時②,它們的韻母必須標爲/yay/,但當它們出現在車

① 廖珣英(1963:274)。

② [譯注]皆來韻中,這三個入聲字出現的同音字組分别是0653053"客刻",0653058"嚇",0654086"額厄客輻"。

遮中,它們的韻母必須標爲/ye/。有趣的是,絶大多數情況下,《中原音韻》中的/yay/韻母在現代北京話中已變成了/ye/韻母,除了極個别陽平音節字(例如,"崖"MP /yáy/[①])仍代表這個韻母之外。我們現在可以看到,/yay/→/ye/這個過程早在《中原音韻》就開始了,但最初僅限於以前的入聲音節(其中包括一個零聲母音節),後來才擴散到除了零聲母音節之外的所有音節,這可能是類推變化的結果。順便提一下,這些字的讀書音顯然没有受到規則(19)的影響,這證實了我們在5.7.1看法。

6.4.2 通攝入聲字。我們主要根據結構學説確定了東鍾韻的主元音是/o/(5.5),我們知道此韻字幾乎都來自通攝。有了這些知識,我們對《中原音韻》中通攝入聲字最初的、本能的反應,當然是它們的口語音應該有*/(y)wow/之類的韻母,因此應該出現在蕭豪韻中。我們知道,事實並非如此。這類入聲字現在出現在魚模韻中,其中一些也出現在尤侯韻中[②][③]。那麽,應該如何解釋這個事實呢?似乎有兩種可能的解釋。首先,我們已經注意到/o/作爲通攝的主元音在語音上比其他情况下要高得多(5.5)。當韻尾/k/變爲/w/時(6.3.3),由此産生的[ow]一定更接近/ɨw/而不是/ow/,因此被確認爲/ɨw/。其次,如果采用嚴格的表達方式,我們可以説k→w的過程發生在通攝的主元音從/ɨ/(馬丁的/*/)變爲/o/之前;因此所産生的韻母應該是*/(y)wɨw/,它們所代表的字自然就應該出現在尤侯韻。兩種解釋都是合理的,儘管衹有後者符合我們的目的。因此,我們可以在那條指明通攝主元音向/o/變化的規則前面某個地方,再加上一條規則[④]:

$$k \rightarrow w / V_{tu} \_\_\_ \qquad (44)$$

① 這裏涉及的就是幾個蟹攝開口二等牙喉音字。"崖"字在現代北京話中讀[ia]陽平,現代北京話已經不存在[iai]韻母。在《國音常用字匯》中"涯"讀"ㄧㄚ ya"陽平,"厓崖睚"讀"ㄧㄞ yai"陽平,且yai這個韻母,衹有這三個字,且都讀陽平。

② 衹有6個同音字組,共10個字。其中"肉"和"六"兩字衹在尤侯韻出現。

③ [譯注]這6個同音字組分别是1652035"軸逐"、1652036"孰"、1653060"竹燭粥"、1653061"宿"、1654086"肉褥"、1654087"六"。

④ 【追注】由於我們現在對通攝的性質有了更好的認識(參看薛鳳生1985),知道它的韻腹始終都是高元音/ɨ/,所以本節的討論可以大爲簡化了,但規則(44)所代表的音變是肯定的,不能忽視。

V_{tu}＝通攝主元音

毋庸解釋,如果其他方面允許,這條規則最終必須與規則(42)合併。

6.4.2.1 我們現在迫切需要立即解釋爲什麽大多數這類入聲字衹出現在魚模韻,而不是尤侯韻。這似乎是一個非常棘手的問題,如果我們的記憶没有讓我們失望的話,實際上它可以很容易地回答。5.13.1 這一節中的規則(39)説韻母/wɨw/已經變成/wɨ/。在通攝的入聲字的韻母變成新韻母*/(y)wɨw/後,它們自然受到這一規則的影響,結果這些字衹能出現在魚模韻中了。有人可能會問,如果這是真的,爲什麽還有一些字出現在尤侯韻呢?這個問題可以忽略,因爲它們的數量如此之少,可能是由於借用而形成的例外。但是,考慮到下面兩個事實,即一方面它們都是三等字;另一方面,除了 1653061"宿"(中古:通合三入屋心 AC /si*k/, MP /swɨ/)和 1654087"六"(中古:通合三入屋來 AC /li*k/, MP /lyèw/)這兩個例外,它們都是中古漢語的腭塞音(知組)聲母和腭呲音(章組)聲母字。我想我們應該爲這個問題提供更好的答案。在 5.13.1 這一節中,我大膽地猜測中古漢語尤韻和幽韻之間的區别可能是/ywɨw/和/yɨw/之間的對比。衹有當前者失去/w/介音時,它們才會合併。這個假設雖然有待證明,但我們現在可以借來解釋爲何少數入聲字出現在尤侯韻。我們可以在表示腭塞音(知組)聲母、腭呲音(章組)聲母和捲舌音(莊組)聲母合併的規則之後,在規則(39)之前,添加一個"可選擇性"規則,來説明當韻母/ywɨw/出現在捲舌聲母之後時,可能保持不變,也可能變成/yɨw/,因此這些字出現了兩讀①②。

$$w \rightarrow \varnothing / Pr + y \underline{\quad\quad} ɨ + w \qquad (45)$$

① 説這條規則是可選擇性的(optional),衹是一種不嚴格的説法。很可能它代表了"口語音"方言中的一種相當普遍的變化(不限於捲舌音),這變化發生在規則(39)所代表的變化之前。因此,韻母是/ywɨ/的讀法可以看作完全是它們在"讀書音"方言中僅僅失落閉塞韻尾的結果。

② [譯注]這個可選擇性規則實際上是説在捲舌聲母後韻母/ywɨw/要麽丢失介音/w/,要麽不變,但介音/y/却保持着。這與捲舌音聲母音節逐漸丢失/y/介音的變化不同。此外,在音韻史上,江宕攝開口知二莊組字確曾出現過/w/介音增生現象,但發生在/y/介音失落之後,且與江宕攝的韻腹爲後低圓脣元音有密切關係。因"增生"而出現的/w/介音是否存在問題,與此處因"失落"而出現的/w/介音是否存在問題,還是有區别的。因此用這個可選擇性規則來解釋這一點,還需要再深入研究。同時,這種現象本身也需要再深入研究。

6.4.2.2 上述有關通攝的入聲字先變入尤侯韻再轉入到魚模韻的觀點，顯然没有被龍果夫注意到。這就解釋了龍果夫爲何過分謹慎地説，衹有在某些情況下，/k/韻尾才會留下一些痕迹。陸志韋顯然也没有注意到這一點，因爲他斷言支思韻和尤侯韻不應該有任何入聲字，而出現在支思韻和尤侯韻的少數幾個入聲字則是"通押"或"叶韻"的結果①。我們已經證明了陸志韋關於尤侯韻入聲字的看法是不正確的，我們在下文將證明他有關支思韻入聲字的看法也是錯誤的(見 6.4.4.1)。也許我們不應該因爲他們的這個失誤而過分指責他們。以他們的方法論，我覺得根本没有辦法觀察到這種深層結構中的現象。其實，/ywɨw/這個韻母存在的時間可能很短，而且在《中原音韻》中没有留下任何痕迹。據説，在《中原音韻》之前很久，這類字就衹與魚模韻字押韻了②。另一個值得諒解的理由是，這個經過兩步演變而形成"口語音"恰好與直接丢失/k/韻尾而産生的"讀書音"相同。既然每個人都對這個令人高興的巧合(也許應該説是"不幸"吧)感到滿意，就没有人願意再去認真研究它了。起初，我自己也認爲魚模韻中這些入聲字是唯一可能直接演變的結果。並試圖將尤侯韻中少數幾個入聲字看作捲舌聲母之後因"换位"(/ywɨ/→/yɨw/Pr____)而産生的結果。直到我發現這是不可能的，我才回過頭來尋求新的解釋。爲什麽説"這是不可能的"呢？因爲果真如此，則魚模韻中的腭噝音(章組)聲母入聲字，如 0553091"出"(中古：臻合三入術昌 AC /cjhiu*t/, MP /crhwɨ̄/)，也應該出現在尤侯韻中，而實際上，那些出現在尤侯韻中的入聲字全部來自通攝。

6.4.3 江宕攝入聲字。在《切韻指南》中，江攝和宕攝，彼此獨立，但在《切韻指掌圖》中，它們合而爲一(圖十三和圖十四)。我們可以認爲這是它們在那個時候業已合併的迹象，後來在《中原音韻》形成了江陽韻。問題是它們是如何合併的。它們是完全合併爲一個韻且共享一個主元音，還是僅僅像曾攝和梗攝那樣合爲一個新的類似"攝"的韻類，但仍然保持着"等"的區别。我認爲

① 陸志韋(1946)第 61、66 頁。

② 廖珣英(1963:274)。用最近的所謂"規則的不透明性"理論來解釋這種現象，或許能更好地理解。由於規則(44)的結果幾乎立即被規則(39)完全遮蔽(obscured)，所以通過表層結構來看這一變化過程自然很困難了。

前者一定是正確的。原因在於,從結構上講,在外轉中,如果一個攝四等俱全,那麼就不可能存在另外一個與其韻尾相同的外轉攝。由於曾攝和梗攝的組合恰好是這樣一個四等俱全的類似"外轉攝"的韻類(見 6.4.1),所以江攝和宕攝的組合不可能也是如此。宕攝在《切韻指南》中歸在"内轉"(參見 6.3.3),這暗示了一個可能的綫索。坦率地説,我還不知道應該如何解釋這個内外轉的分類,但它充分説明,當江攝和宕攝合併時,它們完全合併爲一個韻了,而且它的主元音是後低元音①。這兩攝的舒聲字出現在江陽韻,我們已把它的主元音解釋爲/a/。由此合理推論,這兩攝入聲字的口語音韻母當是/(y)(w)aw/,因此應該出現在蕭豪韻中。我們發現事實恰好就是這樣。除 1153155"末""沫"(中古:山合一入末明 AC /muɑt/, MP /mwè/)這兩個來自山攝外,蕭豪韻中入聲字全都來自江攝和宕攝。然而,這些字的讀書音迫使我們對這一假設進行一些重新思考。當/k/韻尾失落後,我們自然會期望在家麻韻中看到這些字,因爲在讀書音中,它們的韻母應該是/(y)(w)a/。但事實上,家麻韻中連一個這樣的字也没有。相反,它們出現在歌戈韻中,因此它們的韻母應該是/(y)(w)o/。對通攝(6.4.2)入聲字的變化給出的兩個解釋也適用於此。但如果是這樣的話,爲什麼口語音韻母是/(y)(w)aw/而讀書音韻母是/(y)(w)o/呢?令人高興的是,我們發現,如果我們假設口語音韻母爲/(y)(w)ow/,結果將和前面的一樣好,因爲所涉及的字仍然必須分配給它們確實出現的蕭豪韻。我們現在要做的衹是稍微修改一下 6.4.2 規則(44)的條件,以便也將江攝和宕攝包括在内②。

6.4.3.1《中原音韻》的整個音韻結構表明,在前元音/e/前出現單獨作介音的後半元音/w/,或者在後元音/o/前出現單獨作介音的前半元音/y/,都是相當不自然的。事實上,我們在第五章已經引用過這一點來解釋爲什麼在這方面獨一無二的韻母/weŋ/往往會變成/woŋ/(見 5.7.2)。從這個角度看,上

① 董同龢和李榮都追隨高本漢,把江攝的主元音擬作[ȧ]([ɔ]),但馬丁則用他自己的系統裹的前低元音/ɛ/。宕攝的元音大家無一例外地擬作[ɑ]。

② 【追注】此外對江宕兩攝入聲字的討論,雖然基本上是正確的,但不够簡明,推理上也不够嚴密。這是因爲我當初對江宕兩攝的性質尚不能完全掌握,現在我們知道江宕的所謂"混等"實爲合韻,形成一個以後低元音爲韻腹的江陽韻,其入聲字自然也是以後低元音爲韻腹。詳細的討論參看薛鳳生(1982)和薛鳳生(1985)。

一節結論中的/yow/這個韻母就過分特殊而令人難以接受。因此,我們在此建議將其改寫爲/yew/或/yaw/,這兩者都没有任何明顯的證據支持,但也都不能以任何形式上的理由加以駁斥。由於在現代北京話中這些字的韻母都是/yaw/,我們就選擇它,我們相信即使在《中原音韻》時代它們的韻母也可能就是這樣。

6.4.3.2 上述決定實際上是基於我們在任何時候都一直遵守的作業原則,不過這個原則到目前爲止還没有公開聲明。這個作業原則就是,我們儘可能將現代北京話中的語音現象向上推,直到我們發現某些迹象能指明不再可能再將這些語音現象向上推爲止。按照這一作業原則,我們將江宕攝捲舌音(莊組)聲母入聲字的韻母標爲/waŋ/,而不是/aŋ/,儘管後者有《切韻》的支持,且從描寫《中原音韻》江陽韻的效果來看,/aŋ/與/waŋ/都一樣令人滿意[①]。根據上一節給出的原因,6.4.3 關於入聲字的讀書音的結論中産生的/yo/這個韻母,與/yow/韻母一樣不可接受。那麽該如何改寫這個韻母呢?這些字在現代北京話的讀音表明,介音位置上還應該有一個/w/,例如,1252032“學”(中古:江開二入覺匣 AC /xɦɛk/, MP /sywé/)和 1254089“略”(中古:宕開三入覺來 AC /liɑk/, MP /lywè/)。仔細檢查所涉及的字,可以發現在介音位置上增加/w/描述上也是足够好的,儘管没有直接證據證明在《中原音韻》中就是這樣[②]。根據上述作業原則,我們接受韻母/ywo/,它是個新韻母,因爲它在

---

① 見 5.14.3 第二表,其中“莊、瘡、雙”三字列在韻母/waŋ/下,儘管也可以把它們移到/aŋ/下對應的位置。《四聲等子》雖然在安排上有些混亂,實際上已把這些字列在合口圖中。《切韻指掌圖》亦然。參見李榮(1956:130—131)。

② [譯注]薛鳳生(1999:133)給《重訂司馬温公等韻圖經》果攝的擬音是/(y)(w)o/。但在《重訂司馬温公等韻圖經》中,江宕攝入聲字都出現在開口圖細音位置上,如果這些字的韻母形態早在《中原音韻》時代就是/ywo/,那麽它們應該出現在合口圖中。其實這是周德清在《中原音韻》中將入聲字與舒聲字分開排列造成的結果。如果像《重訂司馬温公等韻圖經》那樣將入聲字與舒聲字一起排列,那麽這些入聲字到底是否與那些舒聲字完全同音,就顯現出來了。同時也就可以給我們的研究提供更多的音韻信息。王力(1957:155)《漢語史稿》曾指出:“藥韻的非知照系字和覺韻的喉音字轉入車遮,則比較晚得多。發生的時代還没有能够考證出來;大約不會早於十八世紀。在《圓音正考》裏,‘覺’‘决’還不同音。到底先變撮口呼然後改變主要元音呢,還是先改變主要元音然後改變韻頭呢?我們以爲前者比較近理。因爲韻頭帶動主要元音的情形在漢語發展史中是比較常見的。”我們同意王力先生的意見,同時也認爲在《中原音韻》中,此類入聲字的韻母形態還是/yo/,至於在現代北京話中它們變爲撮口呼,那是後來增生的/w/介音的結果。我們研究音韻史,應該嚴格區分本來如此與後來變得如此之間的區别。

舒聲音節中不存在。

$$X+y+o+\#\rightarrow X+y+w+o+\# \quad (46)$$

6.4.3.3 我們進一步注意到,不僅原來韻母應該是*/yo/的這些入聲字到現代北京話介音位置上有附加的/w/,而且許多在《中原音韻》中韻母被認爲是/o/的入聲字也是如此,例如,1252033“鑿”(中古:宕開一入鐸從 AC /cɦɑk/, MP /cwé/)和 1254085“諾”(中古:宕開一入鐸泥 AC /nɑk/, MP /nwè/)。是否在《中原音韻》時,韻母/o/前也增生了/w/介音呢?這個問題祇能在檢查當時/o/是否仍然與/wo/形成對比之後才能回答。事實上這種對比是存在的,因爲我們發現下面的五對對比祇有通過這種方法才能保持。

(a) 1252029“薄”(中古:宕開一入鐸並 AC /pɦɑk/, MP /pwé/)對 1252026“跋”(中古:山合一入末並 AC /pɦuɑt/, MP /pwá/)

(b) 1252030“鐸”(中古:宕開一入鐸定 AC /tɦɑk/, MP /twé/)對 1252034 奪(中古:山合一入末定 AC /tɦuɑt/, MP /twé/)

(c) 1252025“鶴”(中古:宕開一入鐸匣 AC /xɦɑk/, MP /hè/)對 1252028 “鑊”(中古:宕合一入鐸匣 AC /xɦuɑk/, MP /hwè/)

(d) 1253055“閣”(中古:宕開一入鐸見 AC /kɑk/, MP /ké/)對 1253058 “聒”(中古:山合一入末見 AC /kuɑt/, MP /kwā/)

(e) 1253059“渴”(中古:山開一入曷溪 AC /khɑt/, MP /kě/)對 1253060 “闊”(中古:山合一入末溪 AC /khuɑt/, MP /khwè/)

似乎上面提出的問題已經得到了否定的答案,但當我們仔細觀察這五對對比對時,就知道其實不然。後三個都有喉音聲母字,因此可以將它們看作例外。第一對一定是錯誤的,因爲所涉及的字是脣音聲母字,因此不可能有開口與合口之間的對比(規則 9)。1253057“潑粕鏺”和 1254084“幕末沫莫寞”中這兩種類型字的混合也加强了我們對此的信念。因此,現在祇有第二對阻礙我們做出一套總括性的音變規則,即除了在喉音聲母後面,韻母/o/都變成了/wo/。爲了下面的規則,我們認爲應該忽略這對對比:

$$C+o+\#\rightarrow C+w+o+\# \quad (47)$$

$$C\neq G$$

因爲歌戈韻中這類字數量有限,而且還有一個例外,所以可能有人對規則(47)産生懷疑。如果是這樣的話,他們可以參考一下 5.9 這一節中的規則(31),它和規則(47)其實是同一個規則。我們當時説,我們不知道規則(31)所代表的音變是什麽時候發生的。現在我們知道它一定發生在元音位移變化之後。實際上,必須是在入聲消失之後。否則,山攝和咸攝一等入聲字全都將出現在歌戈韻中(見 6.4.5.2)。

6.4.3.4 歌戈韻裏出現的江宕攝入聲字也幾乎都出現在蕭豪韻中,但反之則不然。令人不解的是,當蕭豪韻中"入聲作平聲陽"和"入聲作去聲"這兩類入聲字幾乎都出現在歌戈韻時,而"入聲作上聲"這 17 個同音字組中,却衹有一個出現在歌戈韻,即"閣"(1153113 和 1253055)。没有人確切知道爲什麽會出現這種狀況,衹能猜測。我認爲這證實了我的看法,即《中原音韻》在本質上是以"口語音"作爲嚴格的記録標準的。(見 6.4.1.2)。它衹收録那些被"口語音"方言認可(或借入)的"讀書音"。就借用而言,無法預測哪些字該借,哪些字不該借。順便説一下,1154155"末幕漠寞莫沫"中出現的"末、沫"這兩個字在某些方面是很有意思的。它們屬於山攝的一等字,因此它們的韻母衹能是/wo/(見 6.4.5,它們確實出現在 1254084"幕末沫莫寞"中)。但由於有很多字,其韻母可以是/ow/,也可以是/wo/,有些人可能會受到影響,認爲那些韻母衹能是/wo/的字,其韻母也可以是/ow/。歌戈韻中這兩個字的重現很可能就是"矯枉過正"的結果。换句話説,就是錯誤類推的結果。

6.4.4 深臻攝入聲字。我們剛討論完有關入聲的最困難問題,剩下的問題就都好處理了。"讀書音"和"口語音"的區别衹限於以前韻尾爲/k/的音節。那些韻尾爲/p/或/t/的音節僅僅是簡單地失去了韻尾而已。這兩種韻尾消失的必然結果是,原來僅因韻尾有别而讀音不同的字現在變成了同音字。這意味着臻攝和深攝入聲字必然合併爲一類,向同一個方向發展。山攝和咸攝也應該是如此。這裏先談談臻攝和深攝入聲字。我們知道臻攝和深攝的主元音都是/ɨ/,所以當它們的入聲字失去了韻尾而合併時,應該出現四個韻母:

/ɨ/,所有開口一等和捲古音(莊組)聲母開口三等字。

/yɨ/,捲舌音(莊組)聲母字之外的其他開口三等字。

/wɨ/,合口一等字、脣音聲母及捲舌音(莊組)聲母合口三等字。

/ywɨ/,除了脣音聲母及捲舌音(莊組)聲母字之外的合口三等字。

在我看來,要描述與上述韻母相應的字在《中原音韻》中是如何分布的,應該是没有問題的。

6.4.4.1 韻母爲/ɨ/的臻攝和深臻入聲字當然應收録在支思韻。我們發現這一韻衹有三個入聲字。其中一個"塞"字是例外(6.4.1.1),另外兩個證實了我們的看法。"澀"屬深攝,"瑟"屬臻攝,在中古漢語裏都是開口三等生母字。由於變爲此韻母的入聲字數量極少,因此常常遭到質疑。例如,陸志韋曾斷言這些字都應該屬於齊微韻,且支思韻不應該有任何入聲字(見 6.4.2.2 注釋1)。現在我們可以看到,它們出現的地方是它們唯一應該出現的地方。這類字數量如此之少,是不可避免的,因爲深攝無一等字,而臻攝事實上没有開口一等入聲字,這兩攝捲舌音(莊組)聲母三等入聲字數量也非常有限。碰巧,《中原音韻》就衹收録了"澀"和"瑟"這兩個入聲字。

6.4.4.2 韻母應該是*/yɨ/的字幾乎都在齊微韻,這是它們應該出現的地方[①]。但是在這裏我們遇到了我們在 5.12.6 中提到的難題。我們在那裏非常詳細地討論了爲什麼我們最終應該選擇/yɨy/而不是/yɨ/作爲這一韻在韻類上的區别性特徵,儘管兩者在描述魚模韻字上效果一樣好。現在,我們如何根據目前的情況作出這個决定呢?在形式上,這個問題可以很容易解决,衹消説/p/和/t/作爲韻尾在/yɨ/之後變成/y/,在其他情況下,它們就消失了。

$$\begin{Bmatrix} \mathrm{p} \\ \mathrm{t} \end{Bmatrix} \rightarrow \begin{Bmatrix} \mathrm{y/y+ɨ}\,\underline{\qquad} \\ \varnothing \end{Bmatrix} /\mathrm{V}\,\underline{\qquad} \tag{48}$$

這種處理方式似乎不太可取,原因有二。首先,我們本來能够寫出一個非常簡單的規則,大意是説主元音後的/p/和/t/被無條件删除了,但現在我們做不到。第二,這比第一點嚴重得多,我們在這裏要説的是,我們必須給/yɨ/韻母加上/y/韻尾,儘管我們知道它在《中原音韻》之後必須立刻被删除。然而,在我看來,我們在 5.12.6 中給出的三個理由似乎已經足够强大,足以抵消上面提出的兩個反對意見。因此,我决定接受這種看似多餘的處理方法。

---

① 唯一的例外是"褶"(中古:深開三入緝邪 AC /sɦiəp/, MP /syɨ́/)字,出現在 1453043 這個同音字組。

6.4.4.3 根據我們的看法,韻母爲/wɨ/或/ywɨ/的入聲字應該出現在魚模韻,這些字也確實出現魚模裏了。當然,0554135“入”(中古:深開三入緝日 AC /njiəp/, MP /rwɨ/)是一個例外。它應該在齊微韻中出現,實際上也確實出現這一韻(0454143)。在歌戈韻中還有三個字,根據我們的規則,應該在魚模韻中,即 1252027“佛”(中古:臻合三入物並 AC /pɦiuət/, MP /fwé/)和 1252029“勃渤”(中古:臻合一入没並 AC /pɦuət/, MP /pwé/)。對於它們的例外演變過程,我無法給出任何解釋。由於“佛”字也出現在魚模韻(0552042)中,這也許能使我們感到一些安慰。

6.4.5 山咸攝入聲字。當/p/和/t/失落之後,山攝和咸攝的入聲音節之間的區别也就消失了。由於我們假設的元音位移變化規則已經影響到山攝和咸攝,因此當/p/和/t/失落之後,其相應的入聲字應該形成三類韻母:

/wo/,合口一等字,應該出現在歌戈韻。

/($\left\{\begin{matrix}y\\w\end{matrix}\right\}$)a/,(a) 所有二等字、(b) 開口一等字、(c) 捲舌音(莊組)聲母三等字,(d) 脣音聲母合口三等字。它們應該出現在家麻韻。

/y(w)e/,其他三、四等字。這類字應該出現在車遮韻。

我們將從下面的討論中看到,這個結果幾乎是完美的。

6.4.5.1 以/y(w)e/爲韻母的入聲字都在車遮韻中找到。“俠”(中古:咸開四入怗匣 AC /xɦiep/, MP /syá/)也不知爲何出現在家麻韻(1352024)中。那些韻母應該是/wo/的入聲字,正如預期的那樣,全都出現在歌戈韻中,毫無例外。

6.4.5.2 除了極個别例外,韻母應該是/($\left\{\begin{matrix}y\\w\end{matrix}\right\}$)a/的入聲字,都出現在家麻韻。

這幾個例外都是喉音聲母開口一等入聲字。它們出現在歌戈韻中,很明顯它們以開口的形式保持着與喉音聲母合口一等入聲字之間的對立,例如,1252028“合”(中古:咸開一入合匣 AC /xɦɑp/, MP /hé/)對 1252028“活”(中古:山合一入末匣 AC /xɦuɑp/, MP /hwé/),1253055“葛”(中古:山開一入曷見 AC /kɑt/, MP /kě/)對 1253058“聒”(AC /kuɑt/, MP /kwā/),還有在

6.4.3.3 中提到的最後一對，即 1253059“渴”（中古：山開一入曷溪 AC /khɑt/，MP /kě/）對 1253060“闊”（中古：山合一入末溪 AC /khuɑt/，MP /khwè/）。這對於過去的學者來説，可能是一件非常簡單的事情。他們所要做的，就是對這一類字的奇特發展再加幾句説明就算了（實際上連這個也都没有人做過）。但對我們這些總是從整個音系結構角度考慮問題的人來説，這個簡單的現象却提出了一個非常嚴重的問題。它幾乎使我們的信心有所動摇。顯然，我們必須修改我們的元音位移變化規則，至少部分修改。我們不能再用絶對的口氣説，除/w/韻尾字和零韻尾字外，所有開口一等字的主元音都變成了二等字的主元音（4.6.4.5 中的規則 22）。有人可能會問，規則（22）是在失去韻尾/t/和/p/之後才開始發揮作用的嗎？答案是否定的，因爲如果這是真的，那麽山咸攝入聲字全都應該出現在歌戈韻中，但實際上，除了喉音聲母字外，它們都出現在家麻韻中，這表明當規則（22）起作用時，韻尾/t/和/p/必須仍然作爲一個決定性特徵存在[①]。我們也不能説喉音聲母開口一等字的主元音没有變化，因爲我們已經在《中原音韻》中發現，山咸攝舒聲開口一等字的主元音確實併入了二等，例如，“干”（中古：山開一平寒見 AC /꜀kɑn/，MP /kān/）出現在“寒山韻”（0801003），而不是“桓歡韻”。因此，我們衹能説，一等開口喉音聲母入聲字的主元音没有變化；换句話説，當一等字的主元音出現在喉音聲母後韻尾/t/或/p/之前時，它也没有變。我們可以通過寫一條新規則或

---

① ［譯注］著者當時未考慮到，在北方官話音韻史上，外轉一等主元音變爲外轉二等主元音，也就是説外轉一二等合併，其實不是一次完成的，每次都涉及一類字。這裏牽涉的主要問題就是入聲字與相應的舒聲字是否一直同步演變。從整體上看，四等俱全的外轉攝一二等韻的合併，分爲三個步驟。第一步是開口一等舌齒音字先與二等合併，這時舒聲字與入聲字同步演變，結果舒聲字則分别出現在“寒山”和“監咸”韻中。第一步完成之後，山咸攝入聲字的塞音韻尾/p/和/t/直接丢失了，未留下任何痕迹，結果這些入聲字自然進入《中原音韻》的家麻韻。第二步是開口一等牙喉音字步舌齒字後塵與二等合併，但此時其相應的入聲字由於已變爲無尾韻，故未受到影響，是故這些字未與舒聲牙喉音字同步演變，結果在《中原音韻》中山攝和咸攝一等開口舒聲牙喉音字繼續分别出現在“寒山”和“監咸”韻中，而入聲字則出現在歌戈韻中（因爲它們的主元音依然是一等的主元音）。山攝留下合口桓韻字組成“桓歡”韻，咸攝一等没有合口字，故没有形成類似“桓歡”韻的韻類，當然山攝一等合口入聲字也必然出現在“歌戈”韻中，因爲它們的主元音依然保持一等。這就是《中原音韻》外轉攝一二等字的音韻格局。《中原音韻》之後，外轉一等舒聲合口字繼續與二等合併，但仍然没有影響到入聲字，這是第三步。但正如著者所言，/ŋ/韻尾字一直是個難題。這可能是由於無論是曾梗攝，還是江宕攝，都不是真正意義上四等俱全的外轉攝。這幾攝的演變還有待更深入地研究。

在規則(22)中再添加一個條件來表達這一點。我認爲最簡單的方法是再增加一個條件,儘管這個條件顯得相當笨拙,因爲它實際上是一個自帶條件的條件。

$$C+V_1+E\rightarrow C+V_2+E \qquad (49)$$

1. $E\neq w$

2. 若 $C=G$,則 $E\neq S$

我在這裏使用符號"S"表示塞音,不僅僅是因爲我認爲它比$\begin{Bmatrix}t\\p\end{Bmatrix}$更簡單,還因爲我想把韻尾/k/也包括進來。把/k/包括進來之後,至少可以幫助我們部分解決 6.4.1.1 中提到的難題。在那裏我們發現,大部分曾攝開口一等入聲字没有按照我們提出的元音位移變化規則進行變化,因此它們出現在齊微韻中,而不是皆來韻中。隨着規則(49)添加了新的限制條件,我們現在可以説那些喉音聲母字出現在齊微韻是符合規律的,儘管我們現在仍然無法解釋三個非喉音聲母同音字組,即 0452059"賊"(中古:曾開一入德從 AC /cɦək/, MP /céy/),0453101"德得"(中古:曾開一入德端 AC /tək/, MP /té/)和 0454148 "勒肋"(中古:曾開一入德來 AC /lək/, MP /lè/)。有趣而又值得注意的是,實際上,在關漢卿的作品中,"得"字與皆來韻字是互相押韻的[①]。考慮到這一點,再加上,皆來韻的"刻"(0653053)與齊微韻字在關漢卿的作品中也互相押韻這個現象(見 6.4.1.1),我們幾乎可以説關漢卿是站在我們這一邊的。

6.4.5.3 對元音位移變化規則的修改又使我們陷入另一個困境。我們曾説過,在《中原音韻》中,中古漢語的/ŋ/聲母,衹在殘餘的一等元音前才被保留(4.6.4.5 規則 23)。現在,由於我們已經看到,喉音聲母開口一等字的主元音也没有變化,我們自然就可以預測/ŋ/聲母字與零聲母(中古漢語的影母 q)字之間仍然保持對立。實際上,當我們放棄/(y)(w)aw/而選擇/(y)(w)ow/爲蕭豪韻中江宕攝入聲字的韻母時(6.4.3),這個問題就已經自動顯現出來了,儘管我們當時没有提到這一點。然而,這類對比在現實中是不存在的。我們發現像"萼"(中古:宕開一入鐸疑 AC /ŋɑk/, MP /è/)和"惡"(中古:宕開一入鐸影 AC /qɑk/, MP /è/)這樣的字同時出現在 1154157"萼鶚鰐惡愕"和

---

① 廖珣英(1963:274)。

1254088"萼鶚鰐惡堊鄂"這兩個同音字組中。那麼該如何解釋這一事實呢?一種解釋方法是斷言這兩個字被錯誤地放到了一個同音字組中。這雖然可行,但缺乏旁證,因此等於是在迴避問題。一個更好的、合乎邏輯的方法是對/ŋ/聲母的存在進行更多的條件限制,我們可以通過以下方式修改規則(23)來實現此目的:

$$\text{ŋ} \rightarrow \left\{ \begin{array}{l} \text{ŋ}/\_\_\_ V_1(w) \\ \text{ø} \end{array} \right\} / \# \_\_\_ \qquad (50)$$

通過在一等主元音之後添加可選的韻尾/w/,我們現在要說的是,/ŋ/聲母並不是在所有的一等主元音之前都保留,而衹有當一等主元後接/w/韻尾或零韻尾時,它才保留。如果能設法將這條規則放在那一條或幾條涉及入聲韻尾變化規則之前,它就不再適用於帶塞音韻尾的入聲音節了。因此,韻母爲此類韻母,衹因聲母分別爲/ŋ/聲母和零聲母,而在讀音上存在差異的兩類字,將變成同音字,就像它們在《中原音韻》中所表現的一樣。

6.5 結語

我們已經完成了對所有入聲字的討論。依我看,結果是相當令人滿意的。綜上所述,我們可以再用一張表,列出所有源自入聲音節的韻母。除了帶有星號的/ɨy/和/ywo/這兩個韻母外,所有這些韻母都與舒聲音節中的韻母完全一致:

韻尾	-ø				-y		-w		
介音 \ 韻腹	ɨ	e	a	o	ɨ	a	ɨ	a	o
ø	03		13	12	*04	06			11
y		14	13		04	06	16	11	
w	05		13	12	04	06			11
yw	05	14		*12					

6.5.1 下表説明産生這些韻母的韻攝:

韻類	03	05		12			13			14		04			06			16	11		
聲母＼韻母	ɨ	wɨ	ywɨ	o	wo	ywo	a	ya	wa	ye	ywe	ɨy	yɨy	wɨy	ay	yay	way	yɨw	ow	wow	yaw
p		僕			跋				拔	別			逼	筆			白			薄	
ph		暴			潑					瞥			匹				拍				
f		復			佛				乏											縛	
v		物							襪												
m		木			沫				抹	滅			覓	密			麥			末	
t		獨			奪		達			叠		德	荻						鐸		
th		禿			脱		塔			鐵			滌						拓		
l		禄	録		落	略	臘			列	劣	勒	立					六	落		畧
n		訥			諾	虐	納			捏			匿		搦				諾		虐
c		族	足		鑿		雜			捷	絶	賊	疾		則				鑿		爵
ch		簇	促		撮		笈			切			七						錯		鵲
s	塞	速	俗				颯			屑	蒦		夕					宿	索		削
cr			逐		濁	著	閘			哲	拙		直		宅			逐	濁		著
crh		觸	出				察			撤	啜		尺		策				戳		綽
sr	澀	淑	贖			杓	殺		刷	折	説		實		色		摔	熟	朔		杓
r			辱			若				熱	爇		日					肉			弱
k		穀	局	葛	聒			甲	刮	傑	蹶		及	國		革	摑		閣	郭	角
kh		哭	曲	渴	闊			恰		怯	闕		乞			客					
h		鵠		合	活	學		狎	滑	協	血	劾	吸	惑		嚇	畫		鶴	鑊	學
ø		屋	玉	蕚		岳		壓		拽	月		一			額			蕚		岳

韻　　母	歸屬韻類	起源韻攝
/ɨ/	支思	臻、深
/wɨ/,/ywɨ/	魚模	臻、通
/ye/,/ywe/	車遮	山、咸、梗
/a/,/ya/,/wa/	家麻	山、咸
/o/,/wo/,/ywo/	歌戈	江、宕、山、咸
/ɨy/,/yɨy/,/wɨy/	齊微	臻、深、曾、梗
/ay/,/yay/,/way/	皆來	梗、曾
/yɨw/	尤侯	通
/ow/,/wow/,/yaw/	蕭豪	江、宕

6.5.2 下面是聲韻配合表,每一個被證實的音節都用一個漢字表示。還將增加一個附録,以顯示與三個聲調對應的同音字組。

6.5 附録

基本形式	入聲作平聲	入聲作上聲	入聲作去聲
/sɨ/	—	0353019 塞	—
/srɨ/	—	0353018 澀	—
/pwɨ/	0552048 僕	0553048 卜	—
/phwɨ/	—	0553094 暴	—
/fwɨ/	0552042 復	0553083 福	—
/vwɨ/	—	—	0554134 物
/mwɨ/	—	—	0554132 木
/twɨ/	0552041 獨	0553093 督	
/thwɨ/	—	0553099 禿	—
/lwɨ/	—	—	0554131 禄
/nwɨ/	—	—	0554137 訥
/cwɨ/	055204 族	{0553100 卒(A) {0553101 蹙	— —
/chwɨ/	—	0553096 簇	—
/swɨ/	—	0553082 速	—

續表

基本形式	入聲作平聲	入聲作上聲	入聲作去聲
/crhwɨ/	—	0553095 觸(B)	—
/srwɨ/	0552050 淑(B)	—	—
/kwɨ/	—	0553081 谷	—
/khwɨ/	—	0553090 哭	—
/hwɨ/	0552043 鵠	0553086 忽	—
/wɨ/	—	0553102 屋	—
/lywɨ/	—	—	0554133 録
/cywɨ/	—	0553097 足	—
/chywɨ/	—	0553098 促	—
/sywɨ/	0552045 俗	0553088 宿	—
/crywɨ/	0552046 逐	0553087 竹	—
/crhywɨ/	—	0553091 出(B)	—
/srywɨ/	0552044 贖(B)	0553092 叔	—
/rywɨ/	—	—	0554135 辱
/kywɨ/	0552049 局	0553085 菊	—
/khywɨ/	—	0553089 曲	—
/ywɨ/	—	—	0554136 玉
/ko/	—	1253055 葛	—
/kho/	—	1253058 渴	—
/ho/	1252025 合	—	—
/o/	—	—	1254088 萼
/pwo/	1252029 薄(C) 1252026 跋	1253056 缽	—
/phwo/	—	1253057 潑	—
/fwo/	1252027 佛	—	—
/mwo/	—	1253064 抹	1254084 沫
/two/	1252030 鐸(C) 1252034 奪	1253062 掇	—
/thwo/	—	1253063 脱	—
/lwo/	—	—	1254087 落
/nwo/	—	—	1254085 諾

續表

基本形式	入聲作平聲	入聲作上聲	入聲作去聲
/cwo/	1252033 鑿	—	—
/chow/	—	1253061 撮	—
/crwo/	1252031 濁	—	—
/kwo/	—	1253058 聒	—
/khwo/	—	1253060 闊	—
/hwo/	1252028 活	—	—
/lywo/	—	—	1254089 畧
/nywo/	—	—	1254090 虐
/crywo/	1252035 著	—	—
/srywo/	1252036 杓	—	—
/rywo/	—	—	1254086 若
/hywo/	1252032 學	—	—
/ywo/	—	—	1254083 岳
/ta/	1352022 達	1353047 答	—
/tha/	—	1353040 塔	—
/1a/	—	—	1354070 臘
/na/	—	—	1354071 納
/ca/	1352027 雜	1353043 咂	—
/cha/	—	1353049 笈	—
/sa/	—	1353048 颯	—
/cra/	1352028 閘	1353042 劄	—
/crha/	—	1353044 察	—
/sra/	—	1353041 殺	—
/pwa/	1352026 拔	1353052 八	—
/fwa/	1352025 乏	1353045 法	—
/vwa/	—	—	1354074 襪
/mwa/	—	—	1354073 抹
/srwa/	—	—	1354075 刷
/kwa/	—	1353050 刮	—
/hwa/	1352023 滑	—	—

續表

基本形式	入聲作平聲	入聲作上聲	入聲作去聲
/kya/	—	1353046 甲	—
/khya/	—	1353053 恰	—
/hya/	1352024 狎	1353051 瞎	—
/ya/	—	—	1354072 壓
/pye/	1452019 别	1453040 鱉	—
/phye/	—	1453039 瞥	—
/mye/	—	—	1454056 滅
/tye/	1452015 叠	—	—
/thye/	—	1453038 鐵	—
/lye/	—	—	1454059 列
/nye/	—	—	1454055 捏
/cye/	1452018 捷	1453034 節	—
/chye/	—	1453031 切	—
/sye/	—	1453030 屑	—
/crye/	—	1453043 哲	—
/crhye/	—	1453042 撤	—
/syre/	1452017 折	1453044 設	—
/rye/	—	—	1454061 熱
/kye/	1452014 傑	1453032 結	—
/khye/	—	1453033 怯	—
/hye/	1452013 協	—	—
/ye/	—	—	1454057 拽(D) 1454058 業
/lywe/	—	—	1454063 劣
/cywe/	1452020 絶	—	—
/sywe/	1452021 踅	1453046 雪	—
/crywe/	—	1453041 拙	—
/crhywe/	—	1453045 啜	—
/srywe/	—	1453047 説	—
/rywe/	—	—	1454062 爇

續表

基本形式	入聲作平聲	入聲作上聲	入聲作去聲
/kywe/	1452016 瘚	1453037 玦	—
/khywe/	—	1453036 闕	—
/hywe/	—	1453035 血	—
/ywe/	—	—	1454060 月
/tɨy/	—	0453101 德	—
/lɨy/	—	—	0454148 勒
/cɨy/	0452059 賊	—	—
/hɨy/	0452058 劾	0453106 黑	—
/pyɨy/	0452057 逼	0453097 必	—
/phyɨy/	—	0453092 匹	—
/myɨy/	—	—	0454144 覔
/tyɨy/	0452054 荻	0453100 的	—
/thyɨy/	—	0453102 滌	—
/lyɨy/	—	—	0454146 立
/nyɨy/	—	—	0454150 匿
/cyɨy/	0452052 疾	0453096 唧	—
/chyɨy/	—	0453091 七	—
/syɨy/	0452053 夕	0453098 息	—
/cryɨy/	0452051 直	0453090 汁	—
/crhyɨy/	—	0453099 尺	—
/sryɨy/	0452050 實	0453095 失	—
/ryɨy/	—	—	0454143 日
/kyɨy/	0452055 及	0453093 吉	0454149 劇
/khyɨy/	—	0453104 乞	—
/hyɨy/	—	0453103 吸	—
/yɨy/	—	0453107 一	0454147 逸
/pwɨy/	—	0453094 筆	—
/mwɨy/	—	—	0454145 密
/kwɨy/	—	0453105 國	—
/hwɨy/	0452056 惑	—	—

續表

基本形式	入聲作平聲	入聲作上聲	入聲作去聲
/nay/	—	—	0654087 搦
/cay/	—	0653059 則	—
/cray/	0652031 宅	0653054 責	—
/crhay/	—	0653050 策	—
/sray/	—	0653055 色	—
/kyay/	—	0653052 革	—
/khyay/	—	0653053 客	—
/hyay/	—	0653058 嚇	—
/yay/	—	—	0654086 額
/pway/	0652030 白	0653051 伯	—
/phway/	—	0653049 拍	—
/mway/	—	—	0654085 麥
/srway/	—	0653057 摔	—
/kway/	—	0653056 摑	—
/hway/	0652032 畫	—	—
/lyɨw/	—	—	1654087 六
/syɨw/	—	1653061 宿	—
/cryɨw/	1652035 逐	1653060 竹	—
/sryɨw/	1652036 熟	—	—
/ryɨw/	—	—	1654086 肉
/tow/	1152053 鐸	—	—
/thow/	—	1153104 拓	—
/low/	—	—	1154156 落
/now/	—	—	1154154 諾
/cow/	1152058 鑿	1153111 柞	—
/chow/	—	1153112 錯	—
/sow/	—	1153105 索	—
/crow/	1152052 濁	1153100 捉	—
/crhow/	—	1153117 戳	—
/srow/	—	1153107 朔	—

續表

基本形式	入聲作平聲	入聲作上聲	入聲作去聲
/kow/	—	1153113 閣	—
/how/	1152057 鶴	1153114 壑	—
/ow/	—	—	1154157 萼
/pwow/	1152054 薄	1153108 剥	—
/fwow/	1152056 縛	—	—
/mwow/	—	—	1154155 末
/kwow/	—	1153106 郭	—
/lwow/	1152059 鑊	—	—
/lyaw/	—	—	1154159 略
/nyaw/	—	—	1154160 虐
/cyaw/	—	1153109 爵	—
/chyaw/	—	1153103 鵲	—
/syaw/	—	1153110 削	—
/cryaw/	1152060 著	1153101 斫	—
/crhyaw/	—	1153115 綽	—
/sryaw/	1152061 杓	1153102 爍	—
/ryaw/	—	—	1154158 弱
/kyaw/	—	1153099 角	—
/hyaw/	1152055 學	1153116 謔	—
/yaw/	—	—	1154153 岳

附注：

(A) 如果按照規則變化，0553101"蹙"（中古：通合三入屋精 AC /ci*k/，MP /chwɨ/）應該出現在 0553097"足"中，讀音爲/cywɨ/。在《中原音韻》之後，除了/n/和/l/之外，韻母爲/ywɨ/的非喉音聲母音節都失去了介音位置上的/y/。因此，我們可以把這個字的特殊演變現象歸因於它在《中原音韻》之前就已經失去了/y/介音。這種解釋迫使我們説，0553100"卒"和 0553101"蹙"之間的小圓圈"○"是後人誤加的。趙蔭棠認爲這個字應該出現在 0553098"促"這個同音字組中，而没有説明原因（趙蔭棠 1936，187 頁，注 3）[①]。

① ［譯注］趙蔭棠（1936：187）注 3 原文爲："蹙與促宜合併。原本分者，係傳寫之誤。"

(B) 如果按照規則變化,0553095“觸束”應與 0553091“出黜畜”合併爲一個同音字組,讀爲/crhywɨ/,0552050“淑蜀孰熟塾”也應 0552044“贖屬述秫術术”合併爲一個同音字組,讀爲/srywɨ/。由於在《中原音韻》之後的發展中,捲舌音聲母之後的介音/y/丢失了,這裏的分立似可勉强解釋爲,在《中原音韻》前,其中一個已經先丢失/y/介音,但無法知道究竟是哪個先丢失。這裏我們采用趙蔭棠的做法,雖然他没有説明理由,但我猜想他總該有點兒道理吧。

(C) 見 6.4.3.3 的討論。

(D) 見 4.5.4.3 的討論。

第七章　結　論

我們已經爲《中原音韻》構擬了一個相當完善的音位系統。更恰當地説，這種構擬應該稱爲“詮釋”，因爲這個系統一直潛藏在《中原音韻》的韻譜裏，等待着被“發現”。如果我們的方法給任何人造成一種錯覺，認爲這個系統依賴於中古漢語或韻圖的音位系統而存在的，那麽我們必須馬上對此進行澄清。這個系統當然有它自己的生命，它的存在不依賴於任何其他系統。我們所做的衹是充分利用我們對中古漢語、韻圖和現代北京話的知識來解讀隱藏在《中原音韻》中的與這個系統有關的各種綫索。在這個過程中，我們也零碎地展示了從中古漢語到《中原音韻》演變的某些方面。我們將在這方面做更多的工作，把演變的規則安排得井然有序。希望這個“合理”的順序同樣具有歷史意義。我們也想簡述《中原音韻》到現代北京話的發展，這樣也許能够爲《中原音韻》是否代表老北京話這個問題提供一個答案。

7.1　關於歷時性規則

在書寫語音演變的規則時，我們采用了現代生成語法中使用的慣例，特别是所謂的“操作成分”和“縮寫符號”，但我無意宣稱目前的工作具有嚴格意義上的生成性(見 3.4 注釋①)。在某些情況下，我們並没有嚴格地遵循這些慣例。幾點不同之處陳述如下：

(a) 一般來説，我們以綫性方式來書寫規則，但至少在一種情況下，破了個例。我們把一個音節分成三個部分：聲母(I)，韻母(F)和聲調(T)，在 $I\frac{T}{F}$ 這個表達式中，聲調是韻母 F 之上的超段音成分(見 3.1)。之後，每當我們處理聲調時，我們將用附在 F 上的上標來表示它(見 3.5.1)

(b) “短語結構規則”和“轉換規則”之間的區别在我們的公式中似乎並不重要。當然，在講述變化之前，我們必須先對音節(7.2 中的前八條規則)進行定義，但從形式上看，第二部分（讀書音系統）的規則與第一部分（口語音系統）的規則之間的差異並不是那麼大。例如，祇要需要，新成分可隨時出現。原因在於，我們祇想展示兩個獨立的語音系統之間的關係。從這個意義上說，變化規則中引入的“新成分”並不是真正的“新”的成分。

(c) 基於同樣的理由，我們將允許 A→A 形式的規則。同一個符號可以代表中古漢語中的某個音位，也可以代表《中原音韻》中的某個音位，但這個符號在系統中與其他音位之間的關係，肯定與這個符號在另一個系統中與其他音位之間的關係有區别。

(d) 用區别性特徵來描述音位的變化可能會更好，但由於許多限制，我們目前不能這樣做；比如，我們對中古漢語和韻圖時期語言的瞭解的精確程度還不足以支撑我們這樣做。因此，我們將用單個音位或音位類型符號來表達音位變化。誠然，這使得我們的規則在某些情況下不够精確。例如，每個聲母將同時屬於兩個大類。當我們使用表示響音的符號 R 時，/nj/聲母（日母）包括在内，但當我們使用表示腭龇音的符號 Pj 時，/nj/聲母（日母）也包括在内。祇要不存在引發誤解的可能，我們就滿意了。此外，在我看來，這種方法在某些方面也有優勢。比如，它可以作爲“老派”學者和“新派”學者之間的橋樑。

(e) 我們不打算用公式詳細地描述聲母和韻母結合的細節。這是一個相當複雜的問題，我們將以附注的形式加以説明①。這是我們的規則在某些情況下表達不够精確的另一個原因，因爲規則的“輸入項”和“輸出項”都將因此而不必要地增大。此外，可以確切地説，這些規則的所有輸入項都限制在中古漢語已經存在的内容。

7.2 口語音的演變

由於“讀書音”和“口語音”分别代表兩種不同的發展路徑，我們必須分别處理。我們將首先用規則來顯示口語音的形成，因爲我們相信這就是《中原音

① 見 7.2 規則 N8 之後的注釋。豪斯侯德爾先生説：“用各種圖、表形式來表示較小的特殊語法的某些部分可能比用公式來表示更簡潔、更經濟。”（豪斯侯德爾 1959，第 233 頁注釋 4）。我認爲這裏的情況是個好例子。

韻》所代表的發音。但在開始之前,先做幾點補充説明。

(a) 按照傳統的習慣,我們用"I"(initial)表示音節的聲母(見 3.1 和 7.1a),但在製定規則時,我們换作"C"(Consonant),並將其視爲音節的可選部分(見 3.6.2)。爲了保持一致,在下面的規則中,我們將衹用"C"來表示聲母。由於零聲母在中古漢語和韻圖時期的語言中的分布非常有限(僅出現在/y/介音前),而且由於零聲母音節和喉音聲母音節在歷史發展過程中步調一致,因此,就像我們把零聲母作爲"響音聲母"的成員之一那樣,也將零聲母看作"喉音聲母"的成員之一。因此"C"將被用作包括零聲母在内的代表所有聲母的總括性符號,也就是説,它將始終作爲必要成分出現。還有很多小的改動,我就不一一解釋了,因爲它們都是不釋自明的。

(b) 我們儘量用從歷時角度看最適當的順序把這些規則排列出來。理想情況下,在定義音節的規則(N1 直到 N8)之後,每增加一條規定某種音變的規則將代表語言進入不同的發展階段。這個説法也許太嚴格了,可能無法證實。但由於音變規則在這樣的順序下運作良好且恰如其分地描述了這個語言的發展歷程,所以我們衹能説這個順序是合理的,我們相信它在相當高的程度上反映了這種語言真實的歷史發展過程。在這個作業標準之外,還有一些規則的順序可以在一定的範圍内上下移動。在這種情況下,衹要能找到,我們就將考慮來自《中原音韻》以外的其他相關書籍的證據。否則,就衹能靠我們自己的直覺判斷了。

(c) 這些規則都不能循環使用(recursive)。也許規則 9(N9)可以看作唯一可能的例外,但似乎也是不必要的(見 5.12.5)

(d) /ŋ/韻尾的音節一直困擾着我們。主要就是因爲這些音節,我們現在不得不對我們已采用的羅常培内外轉説(3.6.1)稍加修改。對我們來説,這個修改不得不進行,因此就不再爲我們的修改提出任何其他理由了(但可參考 6.3.3 注釋 1)。

(i) 我們接受這樣一種觀點:果攝和假攝合併爲一個外轉攝,同時仍然保持着"等"的區别。

(ii) 我們假設曾攝由内轉變入外轉。其一等字的主元音現在變成外轉一等字的主元音。三等字與梗攝三等合併,其主元音也變成外轉三等字的主元音。這意味着，我們相信曾攝和梗攝已經合併，形成一個外轉攝（見6.4.1），但仍保持"等"的區别。因此，通攝現在是内轉中唯一以/ŋ/韻尾韻了，因此我們可以説它的主元音是内轉的主元音。

(iii) 江攝和宕攝現在必須被視爲例外，因爲它們既不屬於外轉，也不屬於内轉。從結構上説，這是不得已的（見6.4.3），我們知道這兩個攝後來完全合併爲一個擁有共同主元音的韻類了，但我們不能從這個假設開始。相反，我們不得不説，當我們的規則最初開始起作用時，這兩個攝仍然彼此有别。原因是4.6.2中的規則（19即N26）衹影響江攝。所以我們説，除了内轉主元音（V_n）和外轉主元音（$V_w = V_1$、V_2、V_3、V_4）外，仍有兩個附加的主元音：江攝主元音（V_{ch}）和宕攝主元音（V_{ta}）。我們可以假設，這種明顯的不平衡很可能就是後來觸發所有$\begin{Bmatrix} ŋ \\ k \end{Bmatrix}$韻尾音節重新排列的因素，以（便使這些音節在經過重新排列後在主元音上）符合内外轉主元音對立的模式特徵（參見7.3.1）。

(e) 除非另有説明，"X, Y, Z"將在規則中表示變項，"＃"將用作音節邊界符號，但僅在絶對需要時使用。

有了上面的幾點作爲基礎，我們現在可以列出音變規則了。爲了以後作爲參考，每條規則將被賦予一個以N開頭的新編號，表示它在這個新順序中的位置，再在其後面加上一個交叉參考信息，説明該規則在何處首次出現，或最初在哪裏討論過。我從未幻想過這些規則可以包羅萬象，可以從中發現中古漢語到《中原音韻》發展過程中的每一個變化，但我相信所有的主要變化都已在恰當的位置反映出來了。不難發現，有許多單個的字，對於這些規則所描述的音變來説，可能是例外。可是，這些例外或反例對我們來説意義不大，除非"它們暗示着一個不同的、更具普遍性的理論框架，或者能幫助我們寫出含義更深刻的規則"①。

＃音節＃ (3.1)

N1 音節→C $\dfrac{T}{F}$ (3.1)

① 喬姆斯基和哈萊（1968：Ⅸ）。

N2　F→(M)V(E)　(3.1)

N3　T→平,上,去,入　(3.5.1)

N4　C→　(3.2)

	S$\left(\begin{Bmatrix}h\\ ɦ\end{Bmatrix}\right)$塞音			Fr(ɦ)擦音		R 響音	
B 脣音	p	ph	pɦ			m	
D 齒音	t	th	tɦ			n	l
Ds 齒咝音	c	ch	cɦ	s	sɦ		
P 腭塞音	tj	tjh	tjɦ				
Pr 腭捲舌音	cr	crh	crɦ	sr	srɦ		
Pj 腭咝音	cj	cjh	cjɦ	sj	sjɦ	nj	
G 喉音	k	kh	kɦ	x	xɦ	ŋ	
	q						ø

N5　M→(y)(w)　(3.3)

N6　E→y,w,m,n,ŋ,p,t,k　(3.4)

N7　$V\rightarrow\begin{cases}V_{ch},V_{ta},V_n,V_w/\_\_\_\begin{Bmatrix}k\\ ŋ\end{Bmatrix}\\ V_n\\ V_w\end{cases}$　(7.2d)

N8　$V_w\rightarrow V_1,V_2,V_3,V_4$　(7.2diii)

注:韻圖時期音節的可能模式

等	外　轉	内　轉	例　外
1	C(w)V_1(E)	C(w)V_n(E)	C(w)V_{ta}+E
2	C(w)V_2(E)	—	C+V_{ch}+E
3	C+y(w)V_3(E)	C+y(w)V_n(E)	C+y(w)V_{ta}+E
4	C+y(w)V_4(E)	—	—

(3.6.2 及 7.2d)

附注:

(1) 腭咝音(Pj 章組)聲母衹出現在三等韻母前。

(2) 腭塞音(P 知組)聲母與捲舌音(Pr 莊組)聲母衹出現在二、三等韻母前。

(3) 除了/n/和/l/,齒音(D 端組)和齒咝音(Ds 精組)聲母不出現在二等韻母前。

(4) 零聲母衹出現在三、四等韻母前。

(5) 其他聲母可出現在任何地方。

N9　ø→w/B___V　(4.2.1)

N10　$xɦ\rightarrow ø/\_\_\_y(w)\begin{Bmatrix}V_n\\ V_3\\ V_{ta}\end{Bmatrix}$　(4.6.1)

N11　$y \to ø / Pr\ \_\_\_$　(4.5.2)

N12　$j \to r$　(4.5.2)

N13　$n \to ø / \_\_\_\ r$　(4.5.3)

N14　$F^{平} \to \left\{ \begin{matrix} F^{02} / \left\{ \begin{matrix} ɦ \\ R \end{matrix} \right\} \_\_\_ \\ F^{01} \end{matrix} \right\}$　(3.5.1)

N15　$F^{上} \to \left\{ \begin{matrix} F^{04} / ɦ \_\_\_ \\ F^{03} \end{matrix} \right\}$　(3.5.1)

N16　$F^{去} \to F^{04}$　(3.5.1)

N17　$q \to ø$　(3.5.2)

N18　$F^{入} \to \left\{ \begin{matrix} F^{52} / ɦ \_\_\_ \\ F^{54} / R \_\_\_ \\ F^{53} \end{matrix} \right\}$　(3.5.1)

N19　$ɦ \to \left\{ \begin{matrix} h / S \_\_\_\_\_ F^{02} \\ ø \end{matrix} \right\}$　(4.1)

N20　$x \to h$　(4.1)

N21　$y \to ø / m \_\_\_ w + V_n \left\{ \begin{matrix} w \\ k \\ ŋ \end{matrix} \right\}$　(4.2.2 及 5.13.1)

N22　$\begin{bmatrix} p(h) \\ m \end{bmatrix} \to \begin{bmatrix} f \\ v \end{bmatrix} / \_\_\_ y + w$　(4.2.1)

N23　$y \to ø / \left\{ \begin{matrix} f \\ v \end{matrix} \right\} \_\_\_$　(4.2.1)

N24　$w \to ø / y \_\_\_ V_n + w$　(5.13.1)

N25　$V_3 \to \left\{ \begin{matrix} V_2 / C(w) \_\_\_ \\ V_4 \end{matrix} \right\}$　(5.6.1 及 5.6.2)

N26　$ø \to y / G \_\_\_ \left\{ \begin{matrix} V_2 \\ V_{ch} \end{matrix} \right\}$　(4.6.2 及 7.2d)

N27　$V_1 \to V_2 / C \_\_\_ E$　(5.10.2 及 6.4.5.2)

條件:i) $E \neq w$

ii) 如 $C = G$,則 $E \neq p, t, k$

N28　$ŋ \to n / \_\_\_ y + V_{ta}$　(4.6.4.2)

N29　$ŋ \to \left\{ \begin{matrix} ŋ / \_\_\_ V_1(w) \\ ø \end{matrix} \right\} / \#$　(4.6.4.5 及 6.4.5.3)

N30 $k \rightarrow \begin{Bmatrix} y/V_w \_\_\_ \\ w \end{Bmatrix} /V\_\_\_$ (6.4.1.6,6.4.2及6.4.3)

N31 $\begin{Bmatrix} V_1 \\ V_2 \end{Bmatrix} \rightarrow V_4/\_\_\_ŋ$ (5.7.1及6.4.1)

N32 $\begin{Bmatrix} V_{ta} \\ V_{ch} \end{Bmatrix} \rightarrow \begin{Bmatrix} V_2/\_\_\_ŋ \\ V_1 \end{Bmatrix}$ (6.4.3)

N33 $V_n \rightarrow V_1/\_\_\_ŋ$ (5.5及6.4.2)

N34 $V_1 \rightarrow o$ (5.6及5.10.2)

N35 $V_2 \rightarrow a$ (5.6)

N36 $V_4 \rightarrow e$ (5.6及5.6.2)

N37 $V_n \rightarrow ɨ$ (5.6.2)

N38 $y \rightarrow ø/ \begin{Bmatrix} Ds \\ Pr \end{Bmatrix} /\_\_\_ɨ+y$ (4.5.2及5.12)

N39 $y \rightarrow ø/\ C+ɨ\_\_\_$ (5.12)

N40 $t \rightarrow c/\_\_\_r$ (4.5.2)

N41 $\begin{Bmatrix} p \\ t \end{Bmatrix} \rightarrow \begin{Bmatrix} y/y+ɨ\_\_\_ \\ ø \end{Bmatrix} V\_\_\_$ (6.4.4.2)

N42 $o \rightarrow a/y\_\_\_w$ (6.4.3.1)

N43 $ø \rightarrow w/C\_\_\_o\#$ (5.9及6.4.3.3)

條件:$C \neq G$

N44 $w \rightarrow ø/Pr+y\_\_\_ɨ+w$ (6.4.2.1)

注:任選的

N45 $w \rightarrow ø/w+ɨ\_\_\_$ (5.13.1及6.4.2.1)

N46 $ɨ \rightarrow a/C+w\_\_\_y$ (5.12.3)

N47 $\begin{Bmatrix} o \\ e \end{Bmatrix} \rightarrow ɨ/\_\_\_y$ (5.12.2及6.4.1)

N48 $y \rightarrow ø/\_\_\_w+ɨ+y$ (5.12.4)

N49 $ø \rightarrow w/Pr\_\_\_a+ŋ$ (6.4.3.2)

N50 $e \rightarrow o/w\_\_\_ŋ$ (5.7.2)

注:任選的

N51 $y \rightarrow ø/\_\_\_w+a+ŋ$ (5.14.1)

N52 $y \rightarrow ø/Pr\_\_\_w+o+ŋ$ (5.5.1)

N53 B+X+m→B+X+n (3.4)

7.3 讀書音的演變

讀書音和口語音主要在兩個方面存在音系差異：即/ŋ/韻尾或/k/韻尾音節以適應主元音的内外轉對比模式而作的重新調整和入聲的變化；在其他方面，讀書音和口語音在本質上的是相同的。由此可見，如果我們能够寫出幾條描述讀書音在上述兩個方面發生特殊變化的某些新規則，來代替口語音演變中的相應的規則，我們就可以在不修改其他規則的情況，得到一套代表讀書音演變的新規則。這就是我們在這裏要努力完成的工作。

7.3.1 我們注意到，在《中原音韻》中，梗攝喉音聲母二三等字已經合併，但在現代北京話“讀書音”中，二等字依然與三等字有别，原因在於二等字没有/y/介音(見 4.6.2c)。我已經解釋過這種現象，我們認爲，在現代北京話的祖語裏，梗攝和曾攝完全合併爲一個含有主元音/e/的韻，這發生在規則(19)規定的變化之前(見 4.6.2)，而在《中原音韻》所代表的方言中，這一合併發生在規則(19)所代表的變化之後(見 5.7.1)。如果我們必須接受這個論點，那麽我們就不必像我們在口語音發展中所做的那樣，在 V_n 和 V_w 之外以特别的方式建立兩個主元音(7.2)。我們可以簡單地説，江宕攝和曾梗攝共同組成了一個新的外轉攝，如下所示：

宕 $(y)(w)V_1\begin{Bmatrix}k\\ ŋ\end{Bmatrix}$

江 $V_2\begin{Bmatrix}k\\ ŋ\end{Bmatrix}$

梗—曾 $(y)(w)V_4\begin{Bmatrix}k\\ ŋ\end{Bmatrix}$

這個新攝與其他外轉攝略有不同，這裏的一等主元音前可以有/y/介音，四等主元前可以没有介音或衹有/w/介音。從這個假設開始，我們現在可以在不改變順序的情況下修改下面的規則。我們在每個規則的新編號後面加上“L”，以表明這些規則是描寫讀書音發展的。

$$\text{N7L.}\qquad V \rightarrow \begin{Bmatrix} V_n \\ V_w \end{Bmatrix}$$

$$\text{N10L.}\qquad x\text{ɦ} \rightarrow /\_\_\_ y(w) \begin{Bmatrix} V_n \\ V_1 \\ V_3 \end{Bmatrix}$$

$$\text{N26L.}\qquad \varnothing \rightarrow y/G\_\_\_V_2$$

$$\text{N28l.}\qquad \text{ŋ} \rightarrow n/\_\_\_y+V_1$$

N31 和 N32 現在可以用以下兩條規則替换：

$$\text{N31L.}\qquad V_1 \rightarrow V_2/\_\_\_\text{ŋ}$$

$$\text{N32L.}\qquad V_2 \rightarrow V_1/\_\_\_k$$

這兩條規則表明，當江攝和宕攝合併時，它們以一種相當奇特的方式進行，因爲它們舒聲音節合併的方向是，宕攝併入江攝，以外轉二等主元音爲韻腹，而入聲音節合併的方向恰好相反，是江攝併入宕攝，以外轉一等主元音爲韻腹。第二條規則是可以這些寫的，因爲在讀書音的發展中，N30 應該删除①。

7.3.2 我們在第六章的討論已經清楚地表明，從前的入聲音節，特别是那些/k/韻尾音節，其讀書音與口語音差别最大。讀書音没有像口語音那樣把/k/改讀成/y/或/w/，而是與/p/和/t/一起直接脱落了。現在要回答的問題是，在讀書音的早期階段，這三個韻尾塞音是完全脱落且没有留下任何任何痕迹，還是由一個可能是喉塞音的新元素所代替，它仍然是入聲音節作爲特殊一類的特徵標記。我認爲後者的可能性更大。祇有一個比較明顯的例證支持這個看法。因爲在其他情况下，後來的發展已經使這種新韻尾的存在與否變得相當無關緊要。這僅有的例證是關於深臻攝原中古漢語捲舌音(莊組)聲母入聲字，尤其是出現在《中原音韻》"支思韻"裏的"澀"和"瑟"。我們已經説過，在口語音中，它們的韻母是/ɨ/(6.4.4.1)。在讀書音中，如果之前的韻尾塞音確實不留痕迹地脱落了，那麼這些字的韻母也應該是/ɨ/。這將使它們與支思韻中舒聲字完全無法區分，因此没有理由讓它們在《中原音韻》之後沿着不同的

① 【追注】這裏的公式及解釋，雖然勉强地標明了江宕合併後有關字匯在《中原音韻》裏的分配，其實不合音理而有點强詞奪理。我們現在對等韻的性質有了正確的認識，所以此處討論的難題就不成問題了。請參看薛鳳生(1982)和薛鳳生(1985)。

路綫發展。然而,“澀”和“瑟”在現代北京話中讀/sè/,即以中元音/e/爲韻母,而支思韻的舒聲字在現代北京話中都以高元音/ɨ/作爲韻母。一個合乎邏輯的假設是,在讀書音中,這兩個字必須代表一個音節,其韻母與支思韻的舒聲字韻母不同,這個韻母可以用/ɨq/來表示,其中/q/代表代替中古漢語三個塞音韻尾(/p/、/t/、/k/)的新元素。在/ɨq/韻母後來的發展過程中,/q/作爲制約條件發揮著作用。當然,這一假設的自然延伸是,在讀書音發展的早期階段,所有入聲音節都以/q/作爲韻尾。

7.3.3 上述假設與我們的結論“《中原音韻》没有入聲”並不矛盾,因爲當這些入音字的讀書音被借用到口語音中時,韻尾/q/必須有自動脱落,因此它們受到後來口語音發展變化的影響(例如,N43)。我們現在用公式表達入聲音節讀書音的發展,就要把N30和N41去掉,然後加上一條新規則,即所有的韻尾塞音都應該由/q/代替。但在加入這條新規則之前,我們還需要再加一條。我們發現梗攝和曾攝三、四等入聲字,也就是那些有介音/y/的入聲字,在現代北京話中韻母是/yɨ/或/ywɨ/,而不是/ye/或/ywe/。如果這些入聲字的韻母曾經是/yeq/或/yweq/的話,那麽它們在現代北京話中韻母應該是/ye/或/ywe/,但事實却不是這樣,例如,“錫”(中古:梗開四入錫心 AC /siek/, MP /syī/),“檵”(中古:曾開三入職群 AC /kɦiək/, MP /cyɨ́/)和“域”(中古:曾合三入職云 AC /xɦiuək/, MP /ywɨ̀/)。與之對應的山咸攝入聲字,即以/t/或/p/爲韻尾的入聲字,在現代北京話中的韻母都是/ye/或/ywe/,例如“屑”(中古:山開四入屑心 AC /siet/, MP /syè/),“牒”(中古:咸開四入帖定 AC /tɦiep/, MP /tyé/)和“越”(中古:山合三入月云 AC /xɦiuat/, MP /ywè/)。在我看來,這一事實表明,在三個韻尾塞音被/q/取代之前,韻母/yek/和/ywek/已經分别變成/yɨk/和/ywɨk/。所以在我們删除了N30和N41之後,我們必須在N40之後按這個順序添加以下兩個規則:

N41La. $e \rightarrow ɨ/y(w)\_\_\_k$

N41Lb. $\begin{Bmatrix} p \\ t \\ k \end{Bmatrix} \rightarrow q/V\_\_\_$

7.3.4 我們對讀書音中入聲字發展的解釋,産生了兩個韻母/oq/和

/yoq/,我們已經説過,這兩個韻母介音位置上應該添加/w/,但/oq/韻母前爲喉音聲母時例外,(見6.4.3.2和6.4.3.3)。因此,就讀書音的發展來説,N43應該作如下修訂:

$$\text{N43L.} \qquad X+o(q)\rightarrow X+w+o(q)$$

$$X\neq\begin{Bmatrix}G\\Y+w\end{Bmatrix}$$

7.3.5 下表顯示了讀書音中的入聲韻母,並標出了它們起源的韻攝。數字表示在《中原音韻》中它們被借入哪一韻。括號中的兩個韻母表示僅有的没有被借入口語音的韻母,换句話説,就是《中原音韻》未收録這類字音。

韻尾	-q			
韻腹／介音	ɨ	e	a	o
ø	臻、深 03	曾、梗 (14)	山、咸 13	江、宕、山、咸 12
y	臻、深、曾、梗 04	山、咸 14	山、咸 13	
w	臻、通 05	曾、梗 (14)	山、咸 13	江、宕、山 12
yw	臻、通 05	山 14		江、宕 12

7.4 《中原音韻》與現代北京話的關係

現代北京話是不是《中原音韻》所代表的方言在現代的反映?這個問題現在很容易回答,儘管這個問題現在肯定没有原來那麽好奇了。從嚴格意義上説,答案顯然是否定的,因爲現代北京話中的以下現象不能用我們在《中原音韻》中看到的現象來解釋。

(a) 原清音入聲字的不規則分布(6.2.4)。

(b) 梗攝開口二等音節的演變。(5.7.1)

(c) 曾梗一二等入聲字的演變(6.4.1.2)。

(d)《中原音韻》支思韻中入聲字的演變。(7.3.2)

這些僅是主要的幾點。我們已經建立了一個讀書音系統。既然以上現象(除了第一條)都可以在這個系統中得到圓滿的解釋,我們現在不得不説,現代北京話來自這個讀書音系統,而不是來自《中原音韻》所代表的口語音系統。如前所述,這兩個系統必然代表着兩個密切相關的次方言,而這兩個次方言之間的相互借用在《中原音韻》之前就已經很廣泛了。所以寬泛一點説,我們確實可以認爲現代北京話是由《中原音韻》發展而來的。畢竟,讀書音系統和口語音系統在音系的基本結構上幾乎是相同的,衹是讀書音在一段時間内以/q/韻尾的形式保持了入聲。而且,由於這兩種系統可能代表了兩個社會階層的言語,我們或許可以稱它們爲"共存系統"(co-existing systems),如果我們可以使用這個術語的話。這裏應該立即補充一點,現代北京話是否從《中原音韻》所代表的方言發展而來這個問題,絶不等同於《中原音韻》是否代表老北京話,即《中原音韻》所代表的方言以前是否在北京城内及周邊地區使用。要説讀書音和口語音都不代表從前的北京方言,换句話説,現代北京話起源於其他地區,後來擴散到北京,代替了原來的北京方言,這並不是一個完全不可想象的觀點。但我覺得這恐怕不太符合事實。李新魁説,根據他的研究,洛陽方言的語音系統比現代北京話的語音系統更接近《中原音韻》[①]。我對這種説法持慎重的保留意見。如果他或任何人能向我們證明洛陽或北京以外的任何地方的語音系統比現代北京話的語音系統更接近我們所建立的口語音系統,我們就會接受《中原音韻》確實不代表老北京話這個觀點;否則,我們就會假設讀書音系統和口語音系統都代表老北京話。《中原音韻》以口語音系統爲基礎,大量借用讀書音,而現代北京話則來源於讀書音系統,但大量借用口語音。

7.5 從《中原音韻》到現代北京話的演變

從中原音韻到現代北京話的演變不在本書的討論範圍之内,但在這裏可以多説幾句,以顯示我們的系統在這方面有巨大的潛力。要做到這一點,我們必須建立我們自己對現代北京話分析,因爲現有的分析似乎都與我們的研究

① 李新魁(1963:279)。

目的不符。由於它牽扯的問題太多,故無法在這裏詳細討論這個新的分析,衹能以最粗略的方式列出一些要點。對這些要點的描述衹勉强够我們建立幾條規則,從而粗略地説明《中原音韻》到現代北京話的主要變化①。

7.5.1 在我的這個新分析中,聲母系統實際上與哈特門和霍凱特的分析相同,儘管從符號使用來看,也許更像霍凱特一點。最大的區别在於,我們將把/r/作爲聲母特徵,而不是半元音。因此,它將被視爲聲母或聲母的一部分②③。當/r/與送氣符號/h/組合時,它將出現在/h/的前面,而不是後面(是/crh/,而不是/chr/)。請注意,除了没有/ŋ/和/v/這兩個聲母,這個系統與我們爲《中原音韻》構建的系統(4.7)幾乎一樣。

7.5.2 我們接受哈特門的分析,現代北京話有三個元音,即/i, e, a/,但我們將第一個寫成/ɨ/,由此希望避免任何可能的誤解。然而,我們不接受哈特門關於/n/和/ŋ/可以出現在高元音之後的觀點④。在所有這些情況下,我們可以説它們前面都是中元音。這樣,我們就可以籠統地概括説,衹有中元音和低元音後面可以有韻尾。這將幫助我們證明,《中原音韻》的韻母/yɨy/在向現代北京話發展的過程中,韻尾/y/脱落是合理的(參見5.12.6)⑤。

7.5.3 哈特門和霍凱特都廣泛討論了/r/韻尾音節的問題,霍凱特自己又單獨討論了/m/韻尾音節。我們覺得這些問題屬於語素音位層面(morphophonemic)。這種音節韻尾,可能還有别的:如趙元任在《漢語入門》(Mandarin Primer)中使用的名詞後綴"tz"(我們的/c/)和助名詞"g"(我們的/k/)⑥,所有

---

① 【追注】我給現代北京話所作的最新分析見薛鳳生(1986),第二、三、四章。請注意,我的看法與以前寫本書時又有了一些不同了,但基本精神是一致的。該書的第七章比較詳細地討論了《中原音韻》到現代北京話的演變,亦可參考。

② 參宋元嘉(1965:171—172)。

③ [譯注]"宋元嘉"乃李榮先生筆名。

④ 哈特門(1944:119)。

⑤ 司徒修可能也注意到這個可能性,因爲他讓韻尾衹同高元音和低元音組合,而不同中元音組合(司徒修:1966:15—16)。我認爲這樣選擇不恰當,參薛鳳生(1973)。

⑥ 趙元任,(1948:40,46),如"ig yiitz"(46頁),在讀這一節時,趙先生對本書作者説,他衹是將"tz"和"g"作爲音節的縮寫,不是作韻尾。這似乎徹底摧毁了我們討論的基礎,但其實並不如此嚴重。我們知道對母語爲漢語的人來説,[m]在[t'ām]"他們"中也不是韻尾,而是一個音節。衹是在"語音上",即在非母語者聽來,它變爲一個單獨的輔音(因此,是個韻尾)。同樣,我認爲名詞後綴"子"和助名詞"個"可以分别寫成"tz"和"g"的理由,是因爲"tz"和"g"在非母語者聽來語音上更像單獨的輔音。(當然,這絶不可能是爲了在印刷時簡省一格。)

這些都可以而且應該用一套語素音位規則來處理,這樣基本的音位分析就不會不必要地過分複雜了。

7.5.4 有以上有關現代北京話的幾點討論作基礎,我們現在可以寫一些規則來顯示從元代讀書音系統到現代北京話的主要變化。我不打算作任何解釋,也不打算舉任何例子來説明這些規則。顯然,在我們能够以最適當的順序排列出一套全面的規則之前,還需要做大量的研究工作。

(1) ŋ→ø/#____ (疑母的消失)

(2) $\begin{Bmatrix}e\\o\end{Bmatrix}\rightarrow a/\_\_\_\_w$ (效攝的合韻)

(3) m→n/V____ (閉口韻的消失)

(4) o→e/____ŋ (東鍾與庚青的合韻)

(5) $\begin{Bmatrix}e\\o\end{Bmatrix}\rightarrow /a\_\_\_\_n$ (山攝的合韻)

(6) ɨ→e/C____q (入聲開口字高元音降爲中元音)

(7) q→ø (入聲的消失)

(8) y→ø/y+ɨ____ (齊、微分韻)

(9) #r+ɨ#→#ɨ+r# (兒尾的出現)

(10) v→ø (微母的消失)

(11) y→ø/Pr____ (捲舌聲母不配細音——“上口字”的一類)

(12) o→e/____# (歌戈與車遮的合韻)

(13) ɨ→e/____E (帶尾韻高元音降爲中元音)
條件:E≠r

(14) y→ø/C____w+o+ŋ (東鍾韻内撮口字變合口——另一類“上口字”)
條件:C≠G

(15) $\begin{bmatrix}k\\kh\\h\end{bmatrix}\rightarrow\begin{bmatrix}c\\ch\\s\end{bmatrix}/\_\_\_\_y$ (尖團不分)

書目選録(限於本書直接引用者)

第一部分以姓氏的漢字(包括日語漢字)拼音字母爲序。

丁聲樹　1958 《古今字音對照手册》,北京。

董同龢　1948a 《廣韻重紐試釋》,中央研究院歷史語言研究所《集刊》十三本,第1—20頁。

1948b 《等韻門法通釋》,中央研究院歷史語言研究所《集刊》十四本,第257—306頁。

1954 《中國語音史》,臺北。

服部四郎和藤堂明保　1958 《中原音韻の研究》,東京。

高本漢　1948 《中國音韻學研究》,商務印書館。

李　榮　1956 《切韻音系》,商務印書館。

1963 《漢語方言調查手册》,科學出版社。

1965 《評哈忒門和霍凱特對北京語音的分析》,《中國語文》第3期,第167—178頁。[譯者案]署名"宋元嘉"。收入《語文論衡》,北京,1985年,第148—159頁。

李新魁　1963 《關於〈中原音韻〉音系的基礎和"入派三聲"的性質》,《中國語文》,第4期,第275—281頁。

廖珣英　1963 《關漢卿戲曲的用韻》,《中國語文》第4期,第267—274頁。

龍宇純　1960 《韻鏡校注》,藝文印書館。

陸志韋　1946 《釋中原音韻》,《燕京學報》第31期,第35—70頁。

1947a 《記徐孝重訂司馬温公等韻圖經》,《燕京學報》第32期,第167—196頁。

1947b 《金尼閣〈西儒耳目資〉所記的音》,《燕京學報》第33期,第115—128頁。

羅常培　1933 《釋内外轉》,中央研究院歷史語言研究所《集刊》第四本第二分,第206—226頁。

石山福治　1925　《考定中原音韻》,東洋文庫。

王　力　1967　《中國語言學史》。

袁家驊　1960　《漢語方言概要》,語文出版社。

張世祿　1963　《中國音韻學史》,泰興書局。

趙遐秋和曾慶瑞　1962　《〈中原音韻〉音系的基礎和"入派三聲"的性質》,《中國語文》第4期,第312—324頁。

趙蔭棠　1936　《中原音韻研究》,商務印書館。

　　1957　《等韻源流》,商務印書館。

周祖謨　1960　《廣韻校本》,中華書局。

第二部分以西文字母爲序。

Chao, Yuen Ren 趙元任：

1941 "Distinctions within Ancient Chinese", *Harvard Journal of Asiatic Studies* 5, 203 - 233.

1943 "Introduction on Pronunciation", Mathews' Chinese-English Dictionary, rev. American edition (Cambridge, Mass., 1965), Ⅸ - ⅩⅪ.

1948 *Mandarin Primer: An Intensive Course in Spoken Chinese* (Cambridge, Mass.)

1968 *A Grammar of Spoken Chinese* (Berkeley, Calif.)

Chomsky, Noam and Morris, Halle. 喬姆斯基和哈萊：

1968 *The Sound pattern of English* (New York).

Halle, Morris 哈萊：

1962 "Phonology in Generative Grammar", *Word* 18, 54 - 72. Also in Jerry A. Fodor and Jerrold J. katz (ed.), *The Structure of Language* (New Jersey, 1964), 334 - 352.

Hartman, Lawton M., III 哈特門：

1944 "The Segmental Phonemes of the Peiping Dialect", *Language* 20, 28 - 42. Also in Martin Joos' (ed.), *Readings in Linguistics*, 116 - 123. (Reference will be made to *RIL*).

Hashimoto,Mantaro Joseph 橋本萬太郎：

1965 "Phonology of Ancient Chinese", Ph. D. dissertation (The Ohio state University).

1970 "Internal Evidence for Ancient Chinese Palatal Endings", *Language* 46. 2, Part 1, 336 - 365.

Hockett, Charles F 霍凱特：

1947 "Peiping Phonology", *Journal of the American Oriental Society* 67, 253 - 267. Also in RIL, 217 - 228.

Householder, Fred w. 豪斯侯德爾：

1959 "On Linguistic Primes", *Word* 15, 231 - 239.

Hsueh, F, S. 薛鳳生：

1973 "TheP'ing -tù Dialect as a Variant of Mandarin",《清華學報》新十卷第一期,74—89 頁。

1971 "The Impact of Dialect Study on Historical Linguistics: Some Examples from theP'íng-tù Dialect", Paper Presented at the Fourth International Conference on Sino-Tibetan Linguistics (oct, 1971, Bloomington Indiana).

Jakobson, Roman and Morris, Halle 雅可布遜和哈萊：

1956 *Fundamentals of Language* (The Hague).

karlgren, Bernhard 高本漢：

1954 "Compendium of phonetics in Ancient and Archaic Chinese", *Bulletin of the Museum of Far Eastern Antiquities* 22, 211 - 367.

Koutsoudas, Andreas 庫蘇達氏：

1966 *Writing Transformational Grammar. An Introduction* (New York).

Martin, Samuel E. 馬丁：

1953 The Phonemes of Ancient Chinese, *Supplement to Journal of the American Oriental Society* 16.

Postal, Paul M. 波斯特爾：

1968 *Aspects of Phonological Theory* (New York).

Pulleyblank, E. G. 蒲立本：

1970 "Late Middle Chinese", *Asia Major* XV, 2, 197 - 239, and XV1 (1971), 1 - 2, 121 - 168.

Stimson, Hugh M. 司徒修：

1962a "Phonology of the *Chūng-yüán Yīn-yǜn*," Tsinghua Journal of Chinese studies 清華學報 n. s. x, 1, 74 - 89.

1962b "Ancient Chinese-p, -t, -k Endings in the Peking Dialect", *Language* 38, 376 - 384.

1966 *The Jongyuan In Yunn* (New Haven, Conn.).

Wang, John C. 王靖宇 and Hsueh, F. S. 薛鳳生：

1973 "The Lin-ch'i Dialect and its Relation to Mandarin", in *Journal of the American Oriental Society* 93, 2, 136 - 145.

書目增補

薛鳳生 1978 《論入聲字之演化規律》

1980 《論支思韻的形成與演進》

1982 《論音變與音位結構的關係》

1985 《試論等韻學之原理與内外轉之含義》

1986 《北京音系解析》

楊耐思 1981 《中原音韻音系》,中國社會科學出版社。

寧繼福 1985 《中原音韻表稿》,吉林文史出版社。

周德清 1978 《中原音韻》(訥菴本,附陸志韋、楊耐思校勘記),中華書局。

薛鳳生文集

薛鳳生 著

鳳凰出版社

論支思韻的形成與演進*

在我國的許多方言中,所謂“官話”自然是最主要的。這固然是因爲説這種話的人數目最多、居地最廣,但同時也有政治文化的歷史背景。比方説,晚近七八百年間的主要文學創作活動就差不多全是在這個大方言區裏進行的。然而所謂官話究竟是什麼呢?很顯然並不指任何個别地區所説的話,而是泛指一大群“次方言”(subdialects)。這一大群次方言之間,自然都有不少差異,但更重要的是,它們都具有某些共通的性質。這些共通性質就是它們被認爲同屬一大方言區的原因,也就是它們與非官話方言有别之處。這種共通性究竟有什麼?是什麼?前人尚少論列,有之也嫌過於寬泛及簡略①。數年前,我曾與斯坦福大學的王靖宇教授合寫了一篇論文,討論河南省北部林縣(編者注:今河南省林州市)臨淇方言的語音結構(參看 Wang and Hsueh 1971)。在該文中我們自然要回答這一問題:“臨淇話是不是一種官話方言?”直覺上我們當然推測它是一種官話,“是北方話嘛!”但是顯而易見地,以地理的緣故來確定語言的隸屬是不合理的。正確的看法自然是應從語言本身的特性着眼。這就引起了另一問題:什麼是官話?换句話説,官話的性質是什麼?衹有在回答了這個問題以後我們才能合理地及確定地説某一地方的話是不是官話的一種。當時我們草擬了十條“測驗條例”,也就是十條官話方言的共通性。現在姑且把它們譯述出來,作爲本文討論“支思”韻的發端。這十個條例牽涉頗廣,當時未能詳論。可以附帶説明的是,它們的次序是按照歷史演進的順序排列的,它們的重要性大概也是從第一條以後向下遞減。换句話説,爲了確定某一

---

* 原刊《書目季刊》1980 年第 14 卷第 2 期,收入《漢語音韻史十講》。
本文原是提交第八届國際漢藏語言學術研討會(1975 年,加州伯克利)的論文,題爲 The Emergence and the Development of the Chih-Szu Rhyme in the History of the Chinese Language.

① 例如袁家驊在《漢語方言概要》裏(第 23 頁)説,北方話内部的一致性非常强,但衹列出以下幾個共同點:(1) 全獨聲母清化;(2) 平分陰陽、全濁上聲變去聲;(3) 輔音韻尾少,没有-p、-t、-k 和-m。

地方的話算不算一種官話,也許前五條或六條就够了。

(甲)全濁上聲字之改讀去聲。

(乙)平聲分陰陽及全濁聲母之清化。

(丙)二等韻喉牙音聲母字之腭化。

(丁)梗、曾兩攝各韻陽聲字之合韻。

(戊)“支思”韻之形成。

(己)閉口韻之轉爲抵腭。

(庚)入聲之消失。

(辛)知、照系聲母後腭化介音之完全消失。

(壬)兒化韻之出現。

(癸)尖團音之混合。

1. 上述十條共通性包括了支思韻及兒化韻,因爲我覺得它們似乎普遍地存在於所有的官話方言裏。本文的主旨在討論支思韻的形成及演進。兒化韻雖與此關係密切,但由於時間及篇幅所限,也衹好留待將來再另文論述了(參看薛 1986,第六章)。由於這十則條例所代表的語言現象在漢語史裏是比較晚近的產物,也就是近代“北音”跟“唐韻”或“古韻”不合之處,所以很多人對此常有誤解,甚至以爲這是受了外族語言影響的結果,非我中華所有,天真地建議應該抛棄。比如一代大儒章太炎先生就曾經説過(章炳麟,1915):

> “若夫金元虜語,侏離而不馴者,斯乃財及幽并冀豫之間,自淮漢以南亡是,方域未廣,曷爲不可替哉?”

他所謂的“金元虜語”,“支思”跟“兒化”韻這兩種現象大概一定在内,尤其是後者,即使到今天,連説這種話的人有時也弄不清楚①。其實所有學過外國語的人都知道,支思韻跟兒化韻這兩種現象都是漢語所特有的。本文將從語音結構及歷史演進的觀點詳論支思韻從古到今的發展。所謂“今”,當然指作爲現代標準音的北京話。在這個討論裏我們將可看出,現代北京話支思韻的内涵是宋代以來許多不同層次的語音演變的結果。

---

① 何容在他的“《北平音系小轍編》再版題記”裏説到一位“東北朋友”對他嘆息:“什麼國語喲!就是(兒)啊,(兒)啊!”至爲傳神。文見張洵如,1956:8。

2. 本文所謂的支思韻，自然是指普通話裏"兹、次、思、支、尺、師、日"這一類所謂"咬齒呼"的字而説的。它們互相押韻而不常跟他類字押韻。因爲這一類字自成韻部的記録最早見於元朝周德清的《中原音韻》名爲"支思"韻，所以我們在此便姑且借用這一名目。其實《中原音韻》以後的明清韻書裏，這一類字不一定自成韻部，韻目名稱自然也很不一致，而且在今天的普通話裏，這一類字的數目也比《中原音韻》的"支思"韻多得多。趙元任先生曾用現代北京話裏"尸"[ʂʅ]這一音節寫了一篇有趣的短文(聲調的差别不計)，現在姑且把這篇短文轉録在這兒，下加黑點的字在《中原音韻》裏不屬於支思，如此便可看出現代北京話裏的支思韻跟《中原音韻》裏的支思韻内容很不一樣了(趙元任，1959：143)。

石室詩士施氏，嗜獅，誓食十獅。氏時時適市視獅。十時，氏適市，適十獅適市。是時，氏視是十獅，恃十石矢勢，使是十獅逝世。氏拾是十獅尸，適石室。石室濕，氏使侍試拭石室，氏始試食是十獅尸。食時，始識是十獅尸，實十石獅尸。是時，氏始識是實事實。試釋是事。

在本文的結論裏，我們將説明何以這一類字在《中原音韻》裏字數有限但必須自成一韻，而在其後的韻書裏，字數大增但却不一定要獨立成韻。

2.1 "支、思"等字，在以《切韻》爲代表的中古音裏，並無特殊之處，它們跟"其、悲、爲"一類字一同出現於支、脂、之各韻中(舉平以賅上去)。這些韻在稍後的等韻圖裏是被看作一類的，所以《四聲等子》和《切韻指南》等書便把它們混爲一體，名爲止攝。韻圖的所謂"攝"最早見於《四聲等子》，其前的等韻書如《韻鏡》及《七音略》並無這一名目，因此很多前輩學者便説這是語音簡化的結果(參看董同龢，1968：113、128)。我個人的意見跟他們頗有出入。各種等韻書的韻圖組織是基本一致的，我認爲這表示它們是根據同一元音系統設計出來的。這個元音系統自晚唐以迄於清初的"十三轍兒"並未改變(當然在其他方面，漢語在這段時間裏轉變甚多)。支、脂、之、微各韻合併爲止攝正表示這些個在《切韻》時代不同的韻部在等韻時代已經合併了。《韻鏡》等書把支、脂、之、微各韻分列在不同的韻圖上衹是想勉强地把《切韻》時代的不同表現出來，其實就韻圖所代表的語音系統來説，這種表面的區别是徒勞無益的①。這個元音系統共包含四個元音，一高三低，如下表：

(/e/或作[ɛ]，/o/或作[ɑ])：

	前	央	後
高		ɨ	
低	e	a	o

等韻學家根據這個語音現象設計韻圖，把含有高元音的韻攝叫做"内轉"，把含有低元音的韻攝稱爲"外轉"，再加上介音/j/與/w/所代表的"洪細"與"開合"等現象，以及韻尾(E)的差異，等韻的基本結構便可以用下面兩個抽象的公式表現出來了(參看薛 1975，3.6 節)：

	内轉	外轉
一等	(w)ɨ(E)	(w)o(E)
二等	……	(w)a(E)
三等	j(w)ɨ(E)	j(w)a(E)
四等	……	(w)e(E)

四等韻是否有介音/j/是一個聚訟已久的問題。李榮以爲在《切韻》時代没有(李榮，1956)，我覺得很對，並且以爲在等韻初形成時，四等韻仍無這個介音，但在等韻形成不久以後，四等韻即孳生了介音/j/，再經過相當時間，三等韻的韻腹/a/由於受到介音/j/的影響，前移而變爲/e/，因此三等與四等便合流了。止攝屬於所謂内轉，根據羅常培先生的解釋，這表示止攝各韻都含有某種高元音②。我個人的解釋比羅先生更嚴格。我認爲這一攝的字都具有同一個高元音/ɨ/(或作[ï])作爲主要元音，同時都具有前半元音/j/作爲韻尾(參看薛 1975：5.12 節)，這就是它們爲什麽同屬一攝的道理。止攝衹有三等字，前文早已指出這是由於止攝字都含有腭化介音/j/(或作[i̯])的緣故，另外加上開合的區别，那麽止攝就衹可能含有/jɨj/和/jwɨj/兩個不同的韻母了。《中原音韻》

① 韻圖由於形式所限，無法列出同音字，但如多畫數張圖，同音字自然也就有了地方了。這當然不表示它們不是同音。"支、脂、之"數韻之分圖或即可如此解釋。

② 羅常培，1933。我對羅先生的解釋還不能説没有疑問，在此無法細論，姑且以他的説法爲準。(編者按：新説請參看薛 1985)。

裹支思韻的字,除了“入聲作上聲”的“澀、瑟、塞”三個字以外,全數來自止攝。我們現在就可以拿上面對止攝的説明作爲基礎,進一步説明支思韻的形成。

2.2 雖然支思這一韻目最早出現在《中原音韻》裹,但在比《中原音韻》更早的一些資料裹已經有些蛛絲馬迹可尋了。其一,《切韻指掌圖》把原列四等的止攝精系字“兹、雌、慈、思、詞”等(舉平以賅上去)改列於一等(第十八圖)。其二,吴才老的《韻補》裹,支韻日母“入”字後,破例列出“資、次、斯、私、兹”等字。其三,由朱熹《詩集傳》的叶韻,許世瑛先生已經看出,在止攝精系聲母開口字作爲韻脚時,朱子總是加注叶韻反切的。由此可見在朱子的語音裹,這些字已經變讀爲“舌尖前高元音”了(許世瑛,1971)。以上這幾種現象可以作如下的解釋:

(一)《切韻指掌圖》把“兹、雌”等字改列一等字而不另立一圖,最合理的解釋是:這些字所代表的音節在《切韻指掌圖》成書以前不久失掉了它們的介音/j/。《韻補》對“資、次”等字的特別處理也可以同樣解釋。假如我們用Ds代表精系聲母,上述的轉變就可以用下面的公式簡明地表達出來:

$$j \longrightarrow \emptyset / Ds\_\_\_ ɨj \qquad (1)$$

(二)上面的解釋不足以説明爲什麽在《詩集傳》裹朱子爲這一類字加注叶韻反切,因爲假如這一類字的韻母是/ɨj/,那麽它們跟止攝其他的字互押是再自然不過了(兩字互押的條件自然是它們的主要元音跟韻尾完全相同)。果真如此,就不勞朱子爲它們另立叶韻反切了。所以我相信許先生的推斷是完全正確的。在朱子的口中,這些字必然已經變爲“咬齒呼”了,换句話説,它們不僅失掉了/j/介音,連韻尾/j/也丢掉了,因此變成了一個很奇特的韻母,跟别的止攝字不叶了。下式代表這一轉變,C代表輔音,也就是聲母:

$$j \longrightarrow \emptyset / Cɨ\_\_\_ \qquad (2)$$

理論上我們可以説《切韻指掌圖》所代表的音系跟朱子的語音也許有時與地的差異,因此在這一方面不合,所以《切韻指掌圖》没有爲“兹、雌”的等字另立一圖。這是極嚴格的解釋,也許跟事實不盡相符。説不定《切韻指掌圖》對“兹、雌”等字的處理也表示它們已經變爲咬齒呼了。其所以未立新圖,大概是一則由於字數太少,再則由於韻圖傳統所限,不是《切韻指掌圖》的作者敢於過事更張的。與此相關的另一問題是止攝開口字的音韻形態。也許有人説它們的韻母應該是/jɨ/([i])而不是/jɨj/。這樣在前述第一公式標明"兹、雌"等字失去/j/介音的時候,它們自然就變爲咬齒呼了,用不着再説它們以後又丢掉了韻尾,這一説法誠然不無道理。實則在現代的北京話裏,我們就是把"西、尼"類字的韻母分析爲/jɨ/的。但是就等韻時代的漢語來説,這一假設不足以解釋爲什麽止攝的開合口兩類字同屬一攝,因爲"吹、推"等字的韻母在等韻時代是/jwɨj/而不是/jwɨ/,否則它們便跟遇攝三等字無别了。所以我以爲從音韻結構(phonological structure)的觀點説,我們必須認定止攝開口字的韻母是/jɨj/,但是就語音實踐(phonetic realization)來説,/jɨj/所代表的音跟/jɨ/所代表的音已在可分與不可分之間了。因此在形式上我們必須説精系咬齒呼的字是由兩個步驟形成的,但實際上這兩個步驟可能密不可分。

2.3 假如上節的結論是正確的話,我們現在可以進一步證明止攝開口字之改讀咬齒呼並不限於精系字,更不始於精系字。等韻書通用的三十六字母裏,正齒五母"照、穿、牀、審、禪"依列衹配二等及三等韻。自陳澧首倡系聯反切上下字以來,語言學家都已承認《切韻》音裏有兩套截然不紊的聲母相當於三十六字母的正齒音。這兩套聲母已被分别命名爲"莊、初、崇、生、俟"和"章、昌、船、書、常"[①]。在韻圖中,二等"照"系字的聲母相當於"莊"組,三等"照"系字的聲母相當於"章"組,因此這兩套《切韻》音的聲母又被稱爲"照二"系和"照三"系。我對韻圖的看法是,最早的韻圖大概是中晚唐時期的語言學家(也許是鄭樵所説的胡僧)根據當時的語音設計出來的。當時的語音跟《切韻》所代表的隋代語音自然已有相當差異,但是因爲相去尚不甚遠,所以還可以勉强拿韻圖來解析《切韻》。莊、章兩組《切韻》聲母合併爲三十六個字母的照系聲母便是《切韻》與等韻之間的音變之一。但是莊、章兩組聲母合併的條件是什麽呢?原來在《切韻》裏,章系聲母衹跟三等韻母相配,而莊系聲母則兼配二等及三等韻母。二等跟三等韻母的最大差異當然是三等有腭化介音/j/而二等没有。在這種情形下,解釋莊、章兩系聲母合併的最合理説法,當然是假定莊系

① 前人皆謂"莊"系僅有"莊、初、崇、生"四母,至董先生始證實"俟"母之存在,"禪"母也就改稱"常"了。參看董同龢,1968:147。

聲母後的介音/j/在韻圖形成之前就脱落了。這樣莊系和章系聲母就變成互補的同位音(allophones)了。等韻學家自然也就把它們視同一體而以"照、穿、牀、審、禪"代表它們了。原來含有介音/j/的莊系字,因爲現在已失落了介音,就被置於二等位置,尤以本無二等韻的内轉各圖爲然。原來就没有介音/j/的莊系字自然居於二等。表面上看,照二系跟照三系恰好相對於《切韻》的莊、章兩系,但在骨子裏,它們兩者之間的關係是不同的。爲明晰起見,我們可用 Pr 代表原莊系聲母,以上的討論便可用下式代表了:

$$j \longrightarrow \emptyset / Pr\_\_\_ \qquad (3)$$

這個公式所代表的音變自然比公式(1)和公式(2)所代表的音變發生得更早,而且影響普及,不限於止攝,但跟我們目前的討論直接有關的倒衹限於止攝的照二系開口字,因爲這一音變的必然結果是使得它們也變爲咬齒呼了。這類字爲數不多,包括"師、史、事"等。因爲在韻圖裏原莊系字依例都列於二等,它們的位置便很少有人注意,不像"兹、雌"等字,一經《切韻指掌圖》改動位置,大家就都看出來了。但是這類字很早就變爲咬齒呼是不容置疑的。我從音韻結構的觀點上數年前就有此推論(薛 1975:5.12 節),但一直未能找到書面的例證,比及看到許世瑛先生討論朱熹叶韻的論文,才喜獲一條確證。朱子在《曹風・下泉》"念彼京師"句下及《小雅・節南山》"不宜空吾師"句下,都注了"叶霜夷反",可見在他的口語裏"師"已變爲咬齒呼,跟"維、迷"等字不能押韻了①。

以上兩節的討論得出三條音變規律,它們的時序應是:(3)—(1)—(2),可以説是支思韻形成的第一階段,最遲在兩宋之交就該已經完成了。

2.4 止攝照三系(包括日母)開口字的轉爲咬齒呼跟照二系比起來自然晚

① 關於"師"字的讀音,許先生的説法跟我不一樣。許先生説在朱子的語音中,衹有精系止攝開口字的韻母變爲"舌尖前高元音","師"字在《廣韻》裏爲"疏夷切",屬審母二等,本不該變,因爲"霜"是心母字,由朱子把"師"字改叶爲"霜夷反",可知在朱子口中"師"字的聲母已由審母變爲心了,因此它的韻母才會變爲"舌尖前高元音"(許世英,1971:10—11 及 15)。按:"霜"字在《廣韻》中爲"色莊切",聲母仍爲審母二等,許先生説是心母,不知何據。我猜想許先生大概是在不自覺中上了高本漢的當,先認定"舌尖前高元音"跟"舌尖後高元音"不同類,就覺得它們不能互押,因此設想朱子口中衹可能有"舌尖前高元音"了。其實它們在音位同屬一音,衹不過音值稍異而已。"支"與"思"互韻也是由來已久的。

得多了。韻圖把它們列於三等固爲明證,但即使晚到朱熹時代它們仍然未變。許世瑛先生已經指出,朱子在這一類字下是不注叶韻反切的。比如在《小雅·楚茨》第五章裏,"私"字下注"叶息夷反","尸"字下則没有注,這當然是審母三等的"尸"字尚未變讀的證明了(許世瑛,1971:11)。這類例子尚多,比如,《檜風·隰有萇楚》第一章"隰有萇楚,猗儺其枝,夭之沃沃,樂子之無知"裏頭,"枝"字是照母三等字,自然也不用注叶韻("知"字是舌上音,變讀爲咬齒呼更晚,朱子當然更不會加注了,詳見下文討論)。再往下推,成書在宋元之交的《韻會舉要》也衹顯示出照二系字的變讀而照三系字仍似未變(參看廖珣英,1963:271)。可見南宋亡時,咬齒呼還衹限於止攝精、莊兩系的開口字。但止攝照三系開口字的變讀無疑是在《中原音韻》以前的,支思韻獨立便是鐵證,"支"字就是照母三等字。元曲作家的作品裏,凡用支思韻的,也是照系二、三等字不分的。例如張可久的《訪梅孤山》(中華書局,《全元散曲》上,831):

> 蒼苔封了歲寒枝(照三),翠袖閒來日暮時(禪三),黄昏説盡平生事(牀二),西湖林處士(牀二),想當年鶴骨松姿,花下孤山寺,水邊新月兒,慰我相思。

如此説來,照三系字的改讀當是元朝初年的事。但是我們不能忘記,一種音變被接受爲正宗,總要經過一段相當長的時間,所以《韻會舉要》没有標示照三系字的改變,並不足以證明南宋末年北京地區的語音裏它們尚未改讀。這一演變也可以用公式標明如下:

$$j \longrightarrow \varnothing / Pr\_\_\_ ɨj \qquad (4)$$

這個公式裏的 Pr 所代表的不限於原莊系聲母,而是包括章系聲母的,因爲莊、章兩系早已合併爲照系了,我們現在便可以用同一符號代表後者了。這個公式的意思是説,在《中原音韻》之前某一時代,止攝照三系的開口字也丢掉了介音/j/。這一音變衹限於止攝,所以在《中原音韻》裏原止攝的照二系跟照三系字已經混同了,而其他各攝的照二系跟照三系字仍然保持着洪細的分别。我們在上文説過,一個音節要變成咬齒呼必須丢掉介音跟韻尾,剩下一個孤零零的高元音/ɨ/作韻母,所以公式(4)本身尚不足以表示止攝照三系開口字已經變爲咬齒呼。我們必須把它放在公式(2)之前。但這樣就等於説止攝的照二、照三及精系字雖然丢掉介音/j/不在同時,變爲“咬齒呼”却在同時了。這在解釋《中原音韻》的音系來説是最合理的,所以我以前便采用這種説法(薛1975)。但是這一説法的困難是不能解釋爲什麽朱子在《詩集傳》裏爲精系及照二系字加注叶韻反切而不爲照三系字加注。如要綜合解釋朱子的叶韻及《中原音韻》,我們就得説公式(2)所代表的音變先後發生了兩次,前述四條公式的歷史順序就得假定爲:

(3)——(1)——(2)——(4)——(2)。

我們在前文討論韻母/jɨj/跟/jɨ/的關係時所説的話,自然也適用在這個地方(參看2.2節),此處不必贅述。另外《中原音韻》的支思韻裏還收了三個由入聲字變來的字,將留待下文討論入聲字的演變時一並説明。

以上關於《中原音韻》中支思韻的討論,主要是説明止攝照三系開口字如何變化爲咬齒呼。這一時期可以稱爲支思韻形成的第二期。前後兩期的變化所影響到的主要是止攝字,第一期限於照二系及精系兩類開口字,第二期則包括了止攝、照三系開口字以及臻、深兩攝的照二系入聲開口字(參看下文2.7節),但是因爲照二系字爲數甚少,所以就受到影響的字彙説,前後兩期可謂旗鼓相當。

2.5 在《中原音韻》裏,“知、池、世、日”等現讀咬齒呼的字都不出現在支思韻裏,而出現在齊微韻中,這一現象自然表示在當時這些字尚未變爲咬齒呼。這些字實則可以分爲三類:其一爲原屬止攝的知系(舌上音)開口字,其二爲原屬蟹攝的三等知、照兩系開口字,其三爲散見於臻、深、梗、曾各攝的知、照兩系入聲開口字。在本節裏我們先討論第一類,後兩類則留待下文再詳細申論。

舌上音四母中,娘母跟我們此處討論的問題無關,姑置不論。知、徹、澄三者所代表的聲母原爲捲舌塞音[①],它們以清濁跟送氣與否而三分。我們可以用音位標寫法把它們分别寫作:/tr,trh,trɦ/。照系五母在音韻結構上説則爲

① 根據高本漢的擬測,“知、徹、澄”代表腭化塞音[t̂,t̂‘,d̂‘]。羅常培以梵語漢對音證明它們應爲捲舌塞音[ṭ,ṭ‘,ḍ‘](羅常培,1931),我覺得羅先生的説法比較可信。

捲舌的塞擦音跟擦音，可以標寫爲：/cr，crh，crɦ，sr，srɦ/[1]。要想説明止攝知系開口字如何變爲咬齒呼，第一步要解决的問題當然是知、照兩系聲母是怎樣合併的。更具體一點兒説，捲舌塞音聲母如何變爲捲舌塞擦音的。這一點表面上是很容易的，我們衹要説在捲舌成分（/r/）前頭塞音變爲塞擦音就成了，如下式：

$$t \longrightarrow c / \underline{\quad} r \qquad (5)$$

問題當然不是這麽簡單，我們還必須把時代的因素考慮在内。知系聲母之變爲照系究竟在什麽時候呢？很顯然，在等韻時代這一轉變尚未發生，但在《中原音韻》時代無疑已經完成了。所以《中原音韻》的聲母系統正如今天的北京話，衹有四個捲舌音：/cr，crh，sr，r/[2]，概括了以前知、莊、章（包括日母）三系的字。但就歷史演變説，知系之轉入照系雖在《中原音韻》成書之前，却不會早得太多。我們説過，止攝照三系開口字之失去介音/j/（公式4）大概在宋末元初，我們可以斷言知系聲母之變入照系（公式5）必然還要晚一些。理由是：假如知系變照系在前，那麽止攝原知系開口字便也符合了公式（4）所標明的音變條件，因此在照三系字變爲咬齒呼的同時，它們就也該變爲咬齒呼了。事實當然不是這樣的。"知、痴、耻、治"等字都出現在齊微韻裏，表示它們没有受到公式（4）的影響，因爲其時它們的聲母仍爲塞音。雖然它們的聲母後來變爲塞擦音（公式5），但因公式（4）所代表的音變已成過去，它們的韻母/jɨj/便没有受到影響，一直保持到《中原音韻》時代，所以它們就被收入齊微韻了。它們進一步變爲咬齒呼自然要等到它們失掉介音與韻尾以後才能實現。這將留待我們討論過另兩類後期咬齒呼字以後再一並闡述。

2.6 由等韻時代到現代的北京話，漢語演進的歷史在元音系統方面主要是由高低四個元音變爲高中低三個元音（參看下文3.2及3.3）。簡化的方式是前後低元音的上移合併於高元音/ɨ/，或集中合併於央低元音/a/。簡化的過程則是逐步的，每一次衹涉及某一類韻尾的字，到現代的北京話裏才算全部

---

① 關於知、照兩系聲母的標音法，請參看薛，1975：3.2節。我在這兒是以/c/代替[ʦ]，以/r/代表捲舌成分，/h/代表送氣成分，/ɦ/代表濁音成分。

② 看薛1975：4.5.2跟4.7節。這四個聲母在《中原音韻》時代尚爲洪、細兩配，在配細音時它們的音值大概跟配洪音時多少有些差異。

完成,但在西南官話裏,無韻尾的音節迄今仍保持着前後低元音的對比。以成都話爲例,"格"與"閣"、"缺"與"却"就是以此區别的(袁家驊,1960: 27)。前文已經提到,等韻學裏所謂内轉跟外轉是以主要元音的高低爲區分條件的,所以此處所説的元音系統的改變跟外轉最有關係。演變的第一步始自韻尾爲/j/的蟹攝字。這早在《切韻指掌圖》裏已露端倪。該書第十七至第二十圖以兩開兩合相配,已甚可怪;第十八跟第十九圖更是止、蟹兩攝字混列。《中原音韻》表現得更明顯。原蟹攝字除了全部二等字及一等開口字共同構成皆來韻以外,一等合口字及三、四等字都出現在齊微韻裏,换句話説,都跟原止攝字合流了。蟹攝一等合口字的韻母是/woj/,三、四等合併後(參看 2.1),開口韻母爲/jej/,合口韻母爲/jwej/,所以這一轉變可以用下式表示(薛 1975:5.11、5.12):

$$\begin{Bmatrix} o \\ e \end{Bmatrix} \longrightarrow ɨ / \_\_\_ j \qquad (6)$$

跟本文直接有關的是蟹攝三等知、照開口字,諸如"滯、世、哲"等。它們都見於《中原音韻》的齊微韻,可見它們的韻母在止攝照三系開口字變咬齒呼的時候仍然是/jej/,所以未受公式(4)的影響,變爲/jɨj/是稍後的事。至於這一轉變跟知系聲母變照系(公式 5)孰先孰後,這從語音結構上倒是看不出來的,因爲不管孰先孰後,都可以適當地解釋有關各字的演變,結果是一樣的。《切韻指掌圖》最後四圖的安排似乎暗示蟹攝字轉入止攝發生在知系聲母變照系之前。我們姑且把公式(6)放在公式(5)之前,但這並非定論。

2.7 由入聲字的演變看,《中原音韻》所代表的是現代北京話裏的所謂口語音,而不是作爲主流的讀書音。例如"色"讀/sraj/(見於皆來)而不讀/se/(不見於車遮),"雀"讀/chjaw/(見於蕭豪)而不讀/chjwo/(不見於歌戈)。當然這兩種音系除了在入聲字及梗、曾兩攝字的演變上有相當差異外,其他各方面基本上是一致的,而且即使在《中原音韻》時代,兩方面的異讀字已經大量互借了(薛 1975:6.2 跟 6.4 節)。在《中原音韻》所代表的口語音裏,入聲無疑已經消失了,但在其同時的讀書音裏,我們必須假定入聲尚存,否則有些語音現象便無法解釋了(薛 1975:7.3 節)。《中原音韻》中"入派三聲"的情形所顯示出的入聲變化可以簡述如下:

(一) 收韻尾/k̂/及/k/的入聲字首先發生變化,/k̂/變爲/j/(梗、曾兩攝的入聲字)①,/k/變作/w/(通、江、宕三攝的入聲字)。與本文直接有關的是前者的三等字,所以我們可以用下式代表這一變化(參看薛 1975:6.4 節):

$$/\hat{k}/\longrightarrow j/V\_\_\_ \qquad (7)$$

在這一變化以後,梗攝的三、四等開口入聲字的韻母就變成了/jej/了,因此便自然地歸屬於蟹攝了。我們在上節裏説過,這類韻母後來主要元音升高,因此轉入止攝,有關各字自然就非收進齊微韻不可了,包括像"隻、擲、尺、石"一類的知、照系字。在解釋歷史演進時,我們衹要把公式(7)置於公式(6)之前就可以了。

(二)韻尾爲/p/或/t/的入聲字稍後也失去了它們的韻尾,因此便根據它們的主要元音的性質分配到各開尾韻裏去了。跟本文的論題有關的是内轉臻、深兩攝的入聲開口字。這類知、照系聲母字可以分爲兩類:(1)原來的莊系聲母字,它們的介音/j/在等韻初形成時就丢掉了(公式3),現在又丢掉了韻尾/p/或/t/,自然就剩下一個孤零零的/ɨ/作爲它們的韻母了,换句話説,這些字也變成咬齒呼了。這類字數目甚少且多僻字,但在語音演變的規律上説,它們在《中原音韻》之前已變爲咬齒呼是不容置疑的。《中原音韻》的支思韻裏衹收了三個入聲字。臻攝的"瑟"跟深攝的"澀"都是這一類字,收入支思韻是順理成章的事。"塞"字是曾攝心母字,出現在支思韻裏自然是例外了(應入齊微,作/sɨj/)。"瑟、澀"兩字在今天的北京話裏不屬咬齒呼而讀作/se/,那自然是順着讀書音發展的結果②。(2)第二類是這兩攝的三等開口入聲字。它們的韻母原來是/jɨt/跟/jɨp/,當韻尾/p/跟/t/消失以後,這兩個韻母自然就合而爲一變成/jɨ/了。在《中原音韻》裏這類字都出現在齊微韻中,包括"姪、質、十、濕"等,表示它們的韻母在當時應該是/jɨj/,所以我們必須用下式表達上述對

① 我在這兒是采用日本漢學家橋本萬太郎的説法而稍加修訂(參看 Hashimoto,1970)。前此研究中古音的人都以爲梗、曾、通、江、宕等攝的韻尾一律是舌根音,陽聲爲/ŋ/,入聲爲/k/,橋本氏把梗韻的韻尾擬作舌面音,陽聲爲/ɳ/,入聲爲/c/。我覺得這一説法甚好,且應擴大。即梗、曾兩攝的韻尾同爲舌面音。這一説法的好處甚多,其中之一便是很合理地解釋了爲什麽梗、曾的入聲字韻尾變/j/而通、江、宕的入聲字韻尾變/w/(參看薛 1975:6.4.2 節)。因爲我已用符號"c"代表塞擦音"ʦ",所以在本文裏便用"k̂"代替橋本氏的"c"了。(董同龢先生在他的《上古音韻表稿》裏曾用"k̂"作聲母。)

② 陸志韋説支思韻不當有入聲,"瑟、澀"兩字應入齊微韻(陸志韋 1946:61 及 66)。顯然是他未看出我們這兒討論的道理。

入聲字的討論：

$$\begin{Bmatrix} p \\ t \end{Bmatrix} \longrightarrow \begin{Bmatrix} j/j\text{ɨ}\_\_\_ \\ ø \end{Bmatrix} \tag{8}$$

换句話説，在韻尾位置的/p/跟/t/衹有在/jɨ/之後變爲/j/，在其他情形下都變爲零了。我們必須承認，説/p/跟/t/在/jɨ/之後變爲/j/似乎是一件多餘的事，但在音韻結構上説，這却是不得不然的。我們曾經説過，在《中原音韻》之前，韻母/jɨj/在語音實踐上可能跟/jɨ/已在可分與不可分之間了（參看 2.2 節）。上述臻、深兩攝三等開口入聲字之演變似乎可以作這一説法的佐證。當它們失去韻尾/p/跟/t/時，剩下的/jɨ/也就很自然地被認作/jɨj/了。

以上各節所論及的音變，在時間的順序上大致應該假定爲：

(7)—(8)—(6)—(5)

這些變化都是在《中原音韻》以前發生的，但衹有臻、深兩攝照二系入聲開口字變爲咬齒呼，其他各類字的轉化是以後的事。

2.8 從《中原音韻》時代到今天的北京話，這六七百年間漢語語音的演變自然不少，最重要的是上文提到的元音系統的改變（參看 2.6 節）。這種改變的步驟之一是原齊微韻開口字失落韻尾。我們説過，在《中原音韻》以前，就音韻結構説，這類字的韻母必須假定爲/jɨj/，但在其後的演變中，這類字的韻母顯然失掉了韻尾/j/。

$$j \longrightarrow ø/j\text{ɨ}\_\_\_\_ \tag{9}$$

這一轉變在明代蘭茂的《韻略易通》裏尚看不出來①，但在稍後的徐孝《重訂司馬温公等韻圖經》裏便很明顯了。他把這類字跟“魚”類字相配，作爲他的止攝開合口三等，另把“模”類字獨立爲祝攝②。明末畢拱辰的《韻略匯通》更把這類字放在“居魚”韻裏，即與原遇攝三等字（撮口韻母/jwɨ/）同韻③。假如這類

① 《韻略易通》分韻略同《中原音韻》，其西微韻相當於《中原音韻》的齊微韻，可證其開口字尚未失掉韻尾。

② 參看陸志韋，1947。徐書三、四兩圖以“資、支、鷄”等作爲止攝開口，而以“珠、居”等作爲其相對的合口；另以“孤、初、夫”等爲第五圖，名爲“祝攝第五獨韻篇”。

③ 《韻略易通》分《中原音韻》之齊微韻爲兩類，一類獨立爲灰微韻，另一類則併入居魚類，即以/jɨ/與/jwɨ/爲一韻，處理的方式跟徐孝是一致的。

字的韻尾/j/尚未消失,徐氏跟畢氏的舉措便不可解了。沈乘麐的《韻學驪珠》裏相對於《中原音韻》的齊微韻的爲機微和灰回,前者不注"直音",後者下注"收噫",更是明顯地指出它們所以分韻之故了①。

2.9《中原音韻》以後咬齒呼增加新字是另一音變的結果。這一轉變就是照系聲母完全捲舌化,衹配洪音不再兼配細音了。可以用公式表示如下:

$$j \longrightarrow ø/Pr\_\_\_ \quad (10)$$

此處所謂的照系聲母(Pr)當然包括以前的知系聲母,因爲在《中原音韻》之前它們就加入照系了〔參看 2.5 節,公式(5)〕。這一音變的影響遍及各攝的三等開合口字,但跟本文有關的自然衹限於《中原音韻》齊微韻内的知、照系開口字。這些字的來源我們已在前文逐一討論過了。公式(10)所代表的音變必須假定爲發生在公式(9)所代表的音變之後,否則就很難解釋何以有關各字會變爲咬齒呼了②。這一點在明清韻書裏也可以找到書面的證據。比方説,《韻略匯通》成書在明末,書内顯示原知、照系聲母還是洪細兩配的。所以這一轉變最早也不過是明清初年的事,實在是去今未遠的。在這一牽涉至廣的音變之前,應該還有一個小的轉變,即是"兒、耳、二"等字的讀音。這些字在《中原音韻》時讀爲/rɨ/,但在今天的北京話裏則讀爲/ɨr/③。我們必須假定這一"音易位"(metathesis)發生在公式(10)所代表的音變之前,因爲不如此便不足以解釋"二"與"日"等字之讀音了,同時這一"易位"也給兒化韻的韻尾找到了歷史來

---

① 參看汪經昌,1965。另據趙蔭棠,1936:50,沈書名爲《曲韻驪珠》,未詳孰是。又曲韻韻書多有以"微"字爲開口者,大概因爲在所謂"南音"中,其讀音近"vi"。參看羅常培"曲韻韻目對照表",引見張世禄,1963:253。

② 曾攝入聲字韻尾/k̂/變爲/j/以後(參看 2.7 節),其一等入聲字如"賊、黑"等之韻母,即變爲/ɨj/,因此這類字也就出現在《中原音韻》的齊微韻裏了。在《中原音韻》以後,假如捲舌聲母後介音/j/之消失(公式 10)在先,"知、世"等字之韻母就跟"賊、黑"等字之韻母相同了,因此也就不會受到公式(9)的影響了。這當然與事實不符。

③ 研究漢語的西方學者,多以爲"兒、耳"等字的北京音讀爲/er/([ər])(例如 Hartman 1944、Hockett 1947 以及各式羅馬拼音),這是不對的(理由複雜,非數言可盡,將來當另文陳述)。董先生以爲是/ɨ/(參看董同龢,1968:22。董表作[ɤ],自然比較合適),我以爲或當作/ɨr/。在等韻時代以後,經過公式(4)及公式(2)所代表的音變,"兒"等之讀音自然該是/rɨ/,恰好説明爲什麼它們出現在《中原音韻》的"支思"韻裏。我以爲這兩個音位的"易位"發生在《中原音韻》之後,但它們的易位也不會太晚,因爲徐孝在他的《等韻圖經》裏已經把"兒、爾、二"等字置於影母之下了。參看陸志韋,1947。

源。可以附帶指出的是,在《中原音韻》以前,咬齒呼的形成是韻母/jɨj/先失介音後失韻尾的結果,但在《中原音韻》以後,"知、尺、世、日"等咬齒呼字的形成則是先失韻尾後失介音的結果。其次在《中原音韻》以前,止攝精系開口字變爲咬齒呼,但在《中原音韻》以後,齊微韻内的精系開口字諸如"祭、齊、夕"等,在同樣的條件下倒不變咬齒呼了,反而與見系細音字合流,弄成現在北京話中的所謂"尖團不分"了。語音音變之機深不可測,遠不是我們目前的知識能够解釋的。

3.作爲本文的結束,我們可以用一張表來説明咬齒呼的各種不同來源及歷史演進的軌迹。另外我們將討論爲什麼這類字在《中原音韻》時代必須獨立成韻而在其後却不一定要獨立。

3.1下表十八個字都是三等開口字,每一個都代表等韻時代的一個不同的聲系或韻攝。外轉三等的主要元音原爲/a/,等韻形成以後不久就變爲/e/了(參看2.1節),所以表中就直接寫作/e/。"直、姪、滯"三字的聲母是全濁音。因爲聲母由濁化清的現象跟本文的論題無關,所以未列入公式,我們把濁音符號/ɦ/略去就算了。另外莊、章兩系聲母的合併(公式3)是等韻形成以前的事,我們也不在表内標出。"澀、瑟"二字的今讀我們已經討論過(見2.7節)。"入"字的今讀是不合規格的,這一不規則的讀法在《中原音韻》裏已經有了,收在魚模韻的"入聲作去聲"裏,但是規則的讀法也同時出現在齊微韻裏。這十八個字的中古切音,以及所代表的韻攝與聲系可以簡單地條列於下。

師:疏夷切,代表内轉止攝(脂韻)莊系聲母字。

思:息兹切,代表内轉止攝(之韻)精系聲母字。

支:章移切,代表内轉止攝(支韻)章系聲母字。

知:陟離切,代表内轉止攝(支韻)知系聲母字。

兒:汝移切,代表内轉止攝(支韻)日母字。

直:除力切,代表内轉曾攝(職韻)知系入聲字。

織:之翼切,代表内轉曾攝(職韻)章系入聲字。

擲:直炙切,代表外轉梗攝(昔韻)知系入聲字。

尺:昌石切,代表外轉梗攝(昔韻)章系入聲字。

瑟:所櫛切,代表内轉臻攝(櫛韻)莊系入聲字。

質:之日切,代表内轉臻攝(質韻)章系入聲字。

等韻期音讀 / 語音演進律	止攝					曾攝		梗攝		臻攝				深攝			蟹攝		
	師	思	支	知	兒	直	織	擲	尺	瑟	質	姪	日	澀	濕	人	滯	世	
	srɨj	sjɨj	crjɨj	trjɨj	rjɨj	trɦjɨk̂	crjɨk̂	trɦjek̂	crhjek̂	srɨt	crjɨt	trɦjɨt	rjɨt	srɨp	srjɨp	rjɨp	trɦjej	srjei	韻鏡時代
j→ø/Ds__ɨj		sɨj																	
j→ø/Cɨ__	srɨ	sɨ																	朱熹時代
j→ø/Pr__ɨj			crɨj		rɨj														
j→ø/Cɨ__			crɨ		rɨ														
k̂→j/V__						trjɨj	crjɨj	trjej	crhej										
{P, t}→{j/jɨ__, ø}										srɨ	crjɨj	trjɨj	rjɨj	srɨ	srjɨj	rjɨj			
{e, o}→ɨ/__j						trjɨj		trjɨj	crhjɨj								trjɨj	srjɨj	
t→c/__r				crjɨj		crjɨj		crjɨj				crjɨj				(rjwɨ)	crjɨj	srjɨ	周德清時代
j→ø/jɨ__				crjɨ		crjɨ	crjɨ	crjɨ	crhjɨ		crjɨ	crjɨ	rjɨ		srjɨ	rjɨ	crjɨ		
rɨ→ɨr					ɨr														徐孝時代
j→ø/Pr__				crɨ		crɨ	crɨ	crɨ	crhɨ		crɨ	crɨ	rɨ		srɨ	rɨ(rwɨ)	crɨ	srɨ	
20世紀北京音	srɨ	sɨ	crɨ	crɨ	ɨr	crɨ	crɨ	crɨ	crhɨ	(se)	crɨ	crɨ	rɨ	(se)	srɨ	(rwɨ)	crɨ	srɨ	

姪:直一切,代表内轉臻攝(質韻)知系入聲字。

日:人質切,代表内轉臻攝(質韻)日母入聲字。

澀:色立切,代表内轉深攝(緝韻)莊系入聲字。

濕:失入切,代表内轉深攝(緝韻)章系入聲字。

入:人執切,代表内轉深攝(緝韻)日母入聲字。

滯:直例切,代表外轉蟹攝(祭韻)知系聲母字。

世:舒制切,代表外轉蟹攝(祭韻)章系聲母字。

3.2 語音的演變是否會造成新的韻部,完全要看新形成的韻母在整個音韻系統裏所占的地位。支思韻的獨立自成一韻始自《中原音韻》,但在其後的明清韻書裏,它又不一定自成韻部,這在我們明白了各個時代的不同音韻結構以後,就不會感到茫然不解了。現在先就《中原音韻》説起。這本韻書無疑地是當時某種北方官話的實録,這種方言跟大多數元曲作家所使用的語音是相同的或極爲相近的。它一共包含十九個韻部。我個人對於分韻的解釋是極嚴格的。我覺得同一韻部裏的字都必須具有相同的主要元音跟韻尾,這就是它們爲什麽可以互押的基礎,合起來可以稱爲"韻基"。反過來説,不同韻部的字必須具有不同的主要元音或不同的韻尾,或二者都不相同。根據這個原則我爲《中原音韻》建立的元音系統祇有四個主要元音,它們相互之間的關係如下表(參看上文 2.1 節及薛 1975:5.4 節):

	前	央	後
高		ɨ	
低	e	a	o

另外加上决定四呼隸屬的前後兩個半元音,再加上區别韻類的六個韻尾(包括零韻尾),《中原音韻》裏可能有的韻母在十九韻部中的分配便可以用下表清晰地表現出來了①:

---

① 參看薛 1975:5.14 及 6.5 節。嚴格地説,《中原音韻》的蕭豪韻應含有/-ew,-aw,-ow/三個不同的"韻基",但這三個韻基在與其同時的别的北方話裏,顯然已合併爲一個韻基了。我的解釋是,周德清遵從多數元曲作家的習慣,把有關各字合爲一韻,但在處理個别字音時,却遵守他所熟知的那個北方話。在這種北方話裏,上述的差别依然存在,因此他便很忠實地把"奥"跟"傲"等字分開了。(編者按:據薛 1992,應當是/aw/改作/ɔw/,/oŋ/改作/ɨŋ/,/aŋ/改作/ɔŋ/)。

韻尾	ø				j		w		n				m			ŋ		
介音 元音	ɨ	e	a	o	ɨ	a	ɨ	a	i	e	a	o	ɨ	e	a	e	a	o
ø(開)	支		沙	歌	賊	來	侯	豪	根		山		森		三	生	當	
j(齊)		車	家		齊	皆	尤	蕭	真	天	奸		侵	廉	咸	庚	江	
w(合)	模		花	戈	微	快	否	郭	文		晚	桓				轟	光	東
jw(撮)	魚	靴		岳					春	川						兄		鍾
韻目	支思 魚模	車遮	家麻	歌戈	齊微	皆來	尤侯	蕭豪	真文	先天	寒山	桓歡	侵尋	廉纖	監咸	庚青	江陽	東鍾

由上表可以看出，支思韻跟魚模韻同占一欄，這就嚴格的押韻條件説是不合原則的，因爲它們的主要元音跟韻尾都相同，理當同屬一韻，其他各欄便是明證。它們之間的差異是介音，即以廣義的開合爲條件而分韻。在一般情形下，介音跟聲母一樣，與押韻無關，所以支思跟魚模分韻是相當不尋常的。但是這却不是不可理解的。這可以從兩方面來瞭解。其一，就歷史演進説，咬齒呼在當時還算是剛形成不太久。這一類字向來衹跟由止攝變來的齊微韻字相押，而跟源自遇攝的魚模韻字從不押韻，這對當時人的心理必有相當影響。他們甚或還會下意識地遷就那些尚無咬齒呼的方言地區的人呢！其二，就音值説，支思韻的韻母/ɨ/([ɿ]跟[ʅ])跟魚模韻的韻母/wɨ/([u])和/jwɨ/([y])在音質上相差頗大，連説這種話的人(native speakers)也聽得出來，因此就破例不把它們一同押韻了。

在另一方面，支思韻的字跟齊微韻的字雖然同源於止攝，但在前者變爲咬齒呼以後，就沒有再跟後者押韻的道理了，因爲它們不再具有共同的韻基了。這從上表裏可以清楚地看出來。所以它們分屬兩韻乃語音變化後不得不然的現象。元曲作家遵守這種音變的自然後果，周德清也就據實記録下來，這都是毫不足怪的。

3.3《中原音韻》以後的情形跟以前大不相同。原齊微韻的開口字失掉了韻尾/j/(公式 9)，含有低元音的帶尾韻漸次歸併，因此韻目大減，到了清朝初年便形成了北方官話地區的十三轍兒了。其音韻結構如下表(參看薛 1983 及薛 1986:22)：

韻尾	ø				j		w		n		ŋ	
介音＼元音	ɨ	e	a	o	ɨ	a	ɨ	a	ɨ	a	ɨ	a
ø(開)	支	格	大	歌	黑	來	侯	豪	跟	山	生	唐
j(齊)	一	切	加			厓	油	遥	因	言	京	江
w(合)	古	拙	花	果	灰	懷			文	晚	東	王
jw(撮)	玉	月		岳					君	全	兄	
韻	一 ┆ 姑	乜	發	梭	灰	懷	油	遥	人	言	東	江
目	七 ┆ 蘇	斜	花	坡	堆	來	求	條	辰	前	中	陽

"十三轍兒"以後,官話的元音系統起了基本的變化,新的高、中、低三度元音取代了以前的高低兩度及前、央、後三度的四個元音,因此現代北京話的音韻結構就變成下式了①:

韻尾	ø			j		w		n		ŋ	
介音＼元音	ɨ	e	a	e	a	e	a	e	a	e	a
ø(開)	支	歌	大	黑	來	鬥	豪	痕	山	登	唐
j(齊)	一	切	加		(厓)	酒	要	因	奸	英	江
w(合)	古	果	花	灰	外			文	寬	東	王
jw(撮)	玉	月						君	宣	永	

跟《中華新韻》相比,我們可以大膽地説,十三轍兒的分韻是接近現代標準漢語的音韻系統的,真所謂天籟。它代表着説這種話的人對語音的感受(native intuition),而所謂《中華新韻》不過是文人學士們根據他們所謂的"音值"與"傳統"而造作出來的。由上兩表可以看出,十三轍兒跟今天的北京話也有不合之處。其一,十三轍兒的"梭坡"跟"乜斜"兩韻,衹相當於今北京話的

① 北京話的高、中、低三度元音説,首見於 Hartman 1994,其後復有 Hockett(1947)所倡之高、低二元音説。我在此處采用 Hartman 之説而加以更訂,因爲我覺得他文中有好些地方在理論的解説上是不充分的(explanatorlly inadequate)。至於 Hockett 的二度元音説,表面上雖似有理而其爲驚世駭俗,實則連在語音的基本描述上也嫌不够充分(descriptively inadequate)。這個問題牽涉甚多,非數言可盡,衹好留待將來另文討論了。(編者按:據薛 1980 及薛 1986 第二章,帶尾韻之元音應爲高與低之對比,故/e/當改爲/ɨ/。)

“歌”欄，這就現在的北京話説當然是不合押韻原則的，但其中另有道理。我們在上文已經提到（參看2.6節），由等韻時代的元音系統演變到現在北京話的元音系統，前央後三個低元音的對比是逐步消失的，始自“收噫”韻（蟹攝）而終於“直音”韻（果、假攝）。所以《中原音韻》裏歌戈和車遮兩韻的合韻是很晚的事。康熙年間（1670前後）阿摩利諦等所撰的《三教經書文字根本》還把這兩類字分韻，乾隆九年（1744）都四德的《黄鍾通韻》才把它們合成一韻（參看趙蔭棠，1957:258之後的“明清等韻化濁入清系統韻母表”）。在其他官話方言中，這一合韻現象可能發生的更晚，甚或像現在的西南官話一樣，迄今尚未完成呢！（參看2.6節）所以故老相傳的十三轍兒保持這兩類字的分立是毫不足怪的。其二，“支”欄下十三轍兒分作一七跟姑蘇兩韻，這一點跟本文的論題直接相關。我們已經説過，按押韻的原理，這一欄的四個韻母都應該可以押韻。《中原音韻》時代，支思韻（韻母/ɨ/）初形成，受到傳統及音質的雙重影響，這類字尚不跟魚模韻（韻母/wɨ/跟/jwɨ/）的字押韻，但這究竟是跟押韻原理不合的。等到齊微韻的開口字失去了韻尾/j/（公式9），這一類字就變成四呼俱全了。以審音爲事的等韻學家們面臨着這個問題的時候，就難免見仁見智，徘徊於“傳統”與“音理”之間，各是其是，各非其非。明清韻書的韻部分合在其他各類字大體上都是一致的，有不一致的地方也很容易拿語音演變的規律來解釋，唯獨對一這類字處置各異（參看趙蔭棠，1957:258後的韻母表）。一方面有人把這一類四個韻母的字合爲一韻，如喬中和《元韻譜》的“卜”佸跟阿摩利諦等《三教經書文字根本》的“及”攝，另一方面則有人把這四個韻母的字干脆分成四韻，如《山東十五音》的“支、齊、姑、虞”跟華長忠《韻籟》的“玆、基、沽、居”。在這兩極端之間，一切可能的配合幾乎是應有盡有，甚至有復古到把“灰、微”一類字也拉進來（如樊騰鳳的《五方元音》），或細分到把同是開口的“支、玆”兩韻不同聲母的字分開（如趙紹箕的《拙庵韻悟》）。但大體説來，最占優勢的分法是把開（/ɨ/）、齊（/jɨ/）、撮（/jwɨ/）三個韻母的字合爲一韻，而把合（/wɨ/）這一個韻母個别分開，包括徐孝的《等韻圖經》、馬自援的《等音》、林本裕的《聲位》、都四德的《黄鍾通韻》及龍爲霖的《本韻一得》等。這是什麽道理，我也説不出來，衹能瞎猜是因爲韻母/wɨ/的音質特殊了。十三轍兒的一七和姑蘇兩轍兒跟這四個韻母的關係究竟如何呢？我起初以爲是由於傳統的影響而以廣義的開合分韻，即韻母爲/ɨ，jɨ/的字屬一七，韻母爲/wɨ，jwɨ/的字屬姑蘇。張洵如在他的《説轍兒》裏也是如此解釋的[①]。但後來看到羅常培的《北京俗曲百種摘韻》(羅常培，1950)，始知不然。他以研究古韻的方法，把北方俗曲的入韻字歸納出來，結果證明十三轍兒大有道理。一七轍兒裏包含了/ɨ，jɨ，jwɨ/三個韻母的字，比如平聲的“衣、尸、居”同屬一七轍兒(羅常培，1950：35)。换句話説，它是跟前述最占優勢的一派相合的。我們雖然無法確知這樣分韻的道理，但在明白了近代漢語的音韻結構以後，也就明白了爲什麽“衣、尸、居”可以互韻了，同時也明白了爲什麽支思韻在《中原音韻》時代非跟齊微韻分立不可，而在其後咬齒呼字大量增加却又不一定要跟“齊”類字分立了。

本文初稿於一九七二年，一擱就是四五年，有許多應該查證的前賢作品，當時未及徵引，其後也未能遍查。更因索居海外，國内時賢的論著也很少有機會看到(在此我要特别感謝許世英先生寄贈抽印本，想不到就在這數年間，許先生也老成凋謝了!)，因此疏漏之處一定很多。但我以爲本文的理論基礎大體上應無太多問題。將來如能歸納宋元人的用韻及遍查宋元明清各代的韻書，一定可以印證我們此處由音理上所推出的一些結論。某些音變公式也許要作少許更動，但就整體説，現在的順序也應該是大致不差的。時光易逝，董先生作古不覺已是十年，每念及此，便不由得想到陸法言的話：“疑惑之所，質問無從……生死路殊，空懷可作之嘆!”謹以此文，略表懷念之意。

一九七二年初稿，一九七六年重訂
寫於美國哥倫布市俄亥俄州立大學

① 該文附載於張氏的《小轍編》之末。有關一七和姑蘇兩轍的原文爲：“國音將《中原》的支思分别爲ㄖ、ㄙ和ㄦ：ㄦ就是十三道轍兒的小轍兒；十三道轍兒不但ㄖ、ㄙ未分，還又把ㄧ合來做了主體”(第七頁)。又：“《中原音韻》的魚模，《五方元音》的虎，就是姑蘇轍兒，全部不分ㄨ、ㄩ(第十頁)。”

On the Redistribution of the Rusheng Words in *Qieyun Zhizhang Tu* **

1. Introduction
2. The Design of the Rhyme Tables
3. Differences in Rusheng Distribution betweenYùnjìng and Qièyùn Zhǐzhǎng Tú
4. Phonological Changes Implied by Zhǐzhǎng Tú
5. Conclusion

1. INTRODUCTION

For a very long period of time in the history of phonological study in China，the rhyme-table book Qièyùn Zhǐzhǎng Tú(ZZT 切韻指掌圖) played a very prominent and influential role. Mistakenly attributed to Sīmǎ Guāng (司馬光)，a highly respected statesman and scholar of the Northern Song dynasty (460—1127)，Zhǐzhǎng Tú was thought to be the earliest book of rhyme tables before the return of Yùnjìng (YJ，韻鏡) to China from Japan in the Ching dynasty. But even after that，it continues to command great respect among many scholars as the typical form of rhyme tables. Several special studies on the book by modern scholars such as Zhào Yīntáng (1934) and Dǒng Tónghé (1948a) have helped removing many of the misunderstandings about this book. It is now quite clear that，far from being

** 未刊稿，中文題爲《〈切韻指掌圖〉中入聲字的再分配》，據作者打印稿編輯。
本文與 S. Z. Chou 合作，曾在第 16 屆國際漢藏語言暨語言學會議上宣讀。

the earliest book of its kind, Zhǐzhǎng Tú was obviously compiled not only after Yùnjìng and Qīyīnlüè(七音略), but even after Sìshēng Děngzǐ (DZ,四聲等子). Though the authorship and background of Děngzǐ is also unknown, most people believe, and we agree with them, that it was compiled in the Northern Song dynasty by somebody in the North. On the other hand, many people believe now that Zhǐzhǎng Tú was compiled in the Southern Song dynasty (1127—1278) by somebody in the South, perhaps the Jiāngxī (江西) area, and some very impressive documentary evidence has been presented to support this belief. While we agree with them on this conclusion, we feel external evidence alone is not enough. To answer the question about the authorship and the date of this book, and more importantly, to provide logical explanations for the differences between this book and other books of its kind, particularly Yùnjìng, we have to adopt an internal (i. e., phonological) approach. Only after we have grasped the underlying sound system can we clearly see the motivations of the compiler, whoever he might be, in making all those revisions he did. In this paper, we shall concentrate on the most fascinating aspect of this book, namely, the redistribution of the rùshēng (入聲,entering tone) words. Other issues will be discussed only when they are related to this issue.

2. THE DESIGN OF THE RHYME TABLES

In order to discuss in a sensible way the redistribution of the rùshēng words in Zhǐzhǎng Tú, we must start with presenting our view on the Děngyùn(等韻) tradition. First of all, we believe the rhyme tables were not the result of arbitrary design, but were based upon the sound system of a real language (Cf. Hsueh 1978). This sound system was probably that of the "standard" Chinese speech of the late Tang and early Song period. It was derived from the earlier Qièyùn (QY 切韻) sound system, but differed in quite a few ways. For this reason, the rhyme tables designed on the basis of the later sound system are capable of maintaining most of the phonemic contrasts in the older system, but incapable in quite a few cases, such as the so-called Chóngniŭ (重紐) and Chóngyùn (重韻) problems. One way to gloss over these problems is to draw extra tables, and that is exactly what was done in Yùnjìng which has as many as 43 tables, and seemingly has no Chóngyùn problem. This leads to another conviction in our view of the rhyme-table tradition. Although the term shè(攝, rhyme-class) appears only in Děngzǐ but not in Yùnjìng and Qīyīnlüè, we believe the phonological reality it represents is a built-in feature for the rhyme tables and the concept existed for Yùnjìng's author, too (see Hsueh 1980a:55, also Cf. Li 1981 and 1982).

2.1. THE ORIGIN OF THE TERM SHE

Actually, Děngzǐ is not the first book using the term Shè. Two things give away this fact. First, it numbers each Shè according to some older arrangement rather than its own order. Second, in its note on the inner/outer contrast it lists 16 graphs as labels for the rhyme classes, but in its tables, it combined some of them, the so-called inner/outer mixtures. Quite obviously, Děngzǐ cannot be the first book to make use of this concept. This fact lends strong support to our belief mentioned above. The following chart shows the relationship between the 43 tables of Yùnjìng and the 16 rhyme-classes, as well as the coalescence of some of them in Děngzǐ and Zhǐzhǎng Tú.

Chart I

韻鏡	攝	等子	指掌圖
東$_{(1)}$冬$_{(2)}$	通 内一	通$_{(1)}$	公$_{(2)}$
魚$_{(11)}$模$_{(12)}$	遇 内三	遇$_{(4)}$	孤$_{(3)}$
支$_{(4,5)}$脂$_{(6,7)}$之$_{(8)}$微$_{(9,10)}$	止 内二	止$_{(7)}$	基$_{(18)}$傀$_{(19)}$
灰$_{(14)}$齊$_{(13,14)}$ 哈$_{(13)}$皆$_{(13,14)}$佳$_{(15,6)}$	蟹 外二	蟹$_{(6)}$	該$_{(17)}$乖$_{(20)}$
痕$_{(17)}$魂$_{(18)}$欣$_{(19)}$文$_{(20)}$	臻 外三	臻$_{(8)}$	根$_{(9)}$昆$_{(10)}$

續表

韻鏡	攝	等子	指掌圖
山$_{(21,22)}$寒$_{(23)}$桓$_{(24)}$	山 外四	山$_{(9)}$	干$_{(7)}$官$_{(8)}$
豪$_{(25)}$宵$_{(26)}$	效 外五	效$_{(2)}$	高$_{(1)}$
歌$_{(27)}$戈$_{(28)}$	果 内四	果$_{(10)}$内外混	歌$_{(11)}$戈$_{(12)}$
麻$_{(29,30)}$	假 外六		
江$_{(3)}$	江 外一	宕$_{(3)}$内外混	剛$_{(13)}$光$_{(14)}$
唐$_{(31,32)}$	宕 内五		
庚$_{(33,34)}$耕$_{(35,36)}$	梗 外(二)(八)?①	曾$_{(11)}$内外混	揯$_{(16)}$觥$_{(15)}$
登$_{(42,43)}$	曾 内八		
侯$_{(37)}$	流 内六	流$_{(5)}$	鈎$_{(4)}$
侵$_{(38)}$	深 内七	深$_{(13)}$	金$_{(6)}$
覃$_{(39)}$談$_{(40)}$凡$_{(41)}$	咸 外八	咸$_{(12)}$	甘$_{(5)}$

2.2. THE PHONEMIC STRUCTURE OF THE RHYME TABLES

The phonemic structure of the rhyme tables can now be formulated on the basis of the rhyme classes (see Hsueh 1979 and 1982). Here, we strictly adhere to the time-honoured canonic form of Chinese syllable, namely, (C)(M)V(E), because we see no advantage in changing to a different pattern. To do that would only serve to undercut the common ground for communication (Cf. Hsueh 1975:26-27).

Chart II

The Design of the Rhyme Tables(Cf. Hsueh 1982:14)

	Inner-A	Inner-B	Outer -A	Outer-B
	通止遇流深	果曾宕	梗江蟹效山咸假	臻
I	-(w)ɨ(E)	-(w)ɔ(E)	-(w)ɔ(E)	-(w)ɨ(E)

① In DZ, both xiánshè and gěngshè were marked as outer No. 8(外八). In the HéKǒu Table of Zēng-Gěng, Gěngshè was marked as Outer No. 2(外二). Since there is no rhyme-class marked as Outer No. 7(外七), we think that Gěngshè is probably Outer No. 7.

續表

	Inner-A	Inner-B	Outer -A	Outer-B
II	——	——	-(w)a(E)	[-(w)a(E)]?
III	-y(w)ɨ(E)	-y(w)ɔ(E)	-y(w)a(E)	-y(w)ɨ(E)
IV	——	——	-y(w)e(E)	——

2.3 THE SYLLABLE FINALS OF THE RHYME-CLASSES

The specific forms of all the syllable finals in the 16 rhyme-classes can be shown as follows.

Chart III

Syllable Finals of the Rhyme-classes(Shè)(Cf. Hsueh 1978:410)

Inner	(y)wɨ{ŋ/k} 通	(y)(w)ɔ{ŋ/k} 宕	(y)(w)ɔ{ɲ/k̂} 曾	——	——	(y)ɨ{m/p} 深	y(w)ɨy 止	(y)ɨw 流	(y)wɨ 遇	(y)(w)ɔ 果
Outer	——	江 a{ŋ/k}	梗 (y)(w){a/e}{ɲ/k̂}	臻 (y)(w)ɨ{n/t}	山 (y)(w){ɔ/a/e}{n/t}	咸 (y){ɔ/a/e}{m/p}	蟹 (y)(w){ɔ/a/e}y	效 (y){ɔ/a/e}w	——	假 (y)(w)a

3. DIFFERENCES IN RUSHENG DISTRIBUTION BETWEEN YUNJING AND ZHIZHANG TU

The most noticeable distinction of Zhǐzhǎng Tú is the double, triple or even quadruple distribution of the rùshēng words. Being different from the earliest Děngyùn book, Yùnjìng, which assigned rùshēng to yángshēng groups only. Zhǐzhǎng Tú assigned rùshēng words to yángshēng rhymes as well as to yīnshēng rhymes. A comparison in rùshēng distribution between Yùnjìng and Zhǐzhǎng Tú is given in the following chart:

Chart IV

Differences in Rusheng distribution between Yùnjìng and Zhǐzhǎng Tú

入聲韻尾	原攝	呼	入聲例字	韻鏡 韻目/轉次	四聲等子 陽聲	四聲等子 陰聲 收噫 /-y/	四聲等子 陰聲 零尾 /-ø/	四聲等子 陰聲 收嗚 /-w/	切韻指掌圖 陽聲	切韻指掌圖 陰聲 收噫 /-y/	切韻指掌圖 陰聲 零尾 /-ø/	切韻指掌圖 陰聲 收嗚 /-w/
-t	山	-ø-	葛	山寒/21,23	山攝	蟹攝	假開		干 姦(7) 堅	該 皆(17)	歌 嘉(11) 迦	
			戛									
		-y-	揭									
		-w-	括	山桓/22,24			假合		官 關(8) 涓	乖(20)	戈 瓜(12) 瘸	
			劀									
		-(y)w-	厥									
	臻	-w-	骨	文魂/20,18	臻攝	止合			昆 君(10)	傀 歸(19)		鳩 鉤(4)
		-yw-	亥									
		-y-	訖	欣諄/19,17					斤 根(9)	基 鷄(18)		
		-ø-										
-k̂	曾	-ø-	裓	登 /42	曾梗 内外混等				搄 京(16)			
		-y-	殛	蒸 /42		止開						
		-(y)w-	國	登 /43					肱(15)			
	梗	-ø-	格	庚耕/34,35					庚 經(16)			
		-y-	激			止開						
		-(y)w-	虢	庚耕/34,35					虢(15)			
-k	宕	-ø-	各	唐 /31,32	江宕 内外混等		果開	效攝	剛 薑(13)			高 嬌(1)
		-y-	脚									
		-(y)w-	郭				果合		光 江(14)			
	江		覺	江 /3								交
	通		谷	東冬/1,2	通攝		遇攝	流攝	公(2)		孤(3)	
-p	咸		閤	覃談凡/39,40,41					甘(5)			
	深		急	侵 /38					金(6)			

As can be seen from the above chart, among the original different types of rùshēng words included in the nine yángshēng rhyme-classes, those of the Gěng, Xián and Shēn still match with their yángshēng counterparts only. those of the Dàng, Jiāng and Tōng show double distribution, those of the Shān and Zhēn show triple distribution, and that of the Zēngshè reveal quadruple distribution. However, by the time of the ZZT, Jiāng and Dàng, as well as Zēng and Gěng, had merged. So there were actually only seven types of rùshēng words.

The differences between these two books have two implications. First, the author of ZZT seems to feel that each rhyme should have four tones. Since there were only seven rùshēng groups and the total number of rhyme groups, including both yīn and yáng, was thirteen by the period represented by Zhǐzhǎng Tú, he made this kind of multiple distribution to satisfy his own feeling. Second, the endings of the previous rùshēng words had been reduced to a neutralized consonantal check on the main vowel① after the period represented by YJ, and this change made it possible, or even more natural, to match the rùshēng words with the yīnshēng groups, sometimes with one type of rùshēng words matching several different types of yīnshēng rhymes. Therefore, consciously or unconsciously, the author of ZZT made his peculiar double, triple, or even quadruple distribution.

Questions like the following may be raised: Did all the rùshēng endings actualy merge in the dialect represented by ZZT? What kind of dialect, Southern or Northern, does ZZT represent? Does the redistribution of the rùshēng words in ZZT reflect only real sound changes, or sometimes its author's arbitrary decision? The following detailed discussion. table by table, hopefully may answer these questions.

---

① We represent it with/-q/, but do not mean that the residue of rushing endings contains the back feature as a glottal stop does.

4. THE PHONOLOGICAL CHANGES REFLECTED BY THE RUSHENG REDISTRIBUTION IN ZZT

4.1. FOLLOWING THE OLD PRACTICE WITH MINOR CHANGES

Following the old practice, ZZT matched each rùshēng group with its original yángshēng counterpart. However, ZZT made some minor changes.

4.1.1. THE RELOCATION OF THE WORD WITH LABIAL INITIALS

In all the paired Tables except 15/16 and 17/20, the words with labial initials were altogether entered into the Hékǒu(合口, rounded) Tables. This seems to imply that all the Kāikǒu (開口, unrounded) words with labial initials had become Hékǒu. Generally speaking, this is not unreasonable except for those of the third and fourth divisions which didn't undergo the dentolabialization sound change (Cf. Hsueh 1975: 38 - 39). However, the few exceptions show the uncertainty of the author about the nature of words with labial initials.

4.1.2. THE RELOCATION OF THE JIANG RHYME

ZZT entered all the words of Jiāngshè into Table 14, where the Hékǒu words of Dàngshè were. This arrangement may mistakenly give one the impression that all the words within the Jiāngshè were labialized in the dialect represented by ZZT. Two things can help clear this illusion. First, we can find no dialect in which all the Jiāngshè words are labialized. Second, the double entry of the rùshēng words of Jiāngshè (i.e. Jué 覺 rhyme) in both the Kāikǒu (table 13) and the Hékǒu (Table 14) reflected the uncertainty of ZZT's author between Kāi and Hé (Cf. also Dǒng 1948a: 205 & 209). It may be taken as a result of the conservative view of the author who was unwilling to mix those two formerly seperated rhyme-classes (the words of Jiāngshè and the words of Dàngshè), though they had really merged. Since there were several words of Dàngshè occupping the slots of the second division under the sibilant initials in Tables 13, he put Jiāngshè into Table 14, where the corresponding slots are empty. It also shows the author's tendency of filling, as many blanks in the Tables as possible. However, the ambiguous status of the Jué rhyme in ZZT reveals that, during the period of ZZT, Jiāng and Dàng were probably not as distinct as the Tables seem to imply.

4.1.3. THE DENG(登)RHYME AND GENG(庚 耕)RHYMES IN TABLE 15

In Table 15, the Hékǒu words of the Dēng rhyme which used to be in the first division exchanged their positions with the Hékǒu words of the Gēng rhymes which used to be in the second division. This seems to imply that not only the Zēng and Gěng rhyme-classes had joined, but words of all four divisions in this new Zēng-Gěng rhyme-class had merged into a new rhyme, namely, the later Gēngqīng rhyme in Zhōngyuán Yīnyùn(ZYYY 中原音韻) (Cf. Hsueh 1978:418), This switch was possible, because the Hékǒu Table happened to have no words under the dental stop and sibilant initials. Since the Kāikóu Table (Table 15) did have words under these initials, the switch was not possible, and so he did not make it.

4.2. THE REDISTRIBUTION OF THE RUSHENG WORDS IN EACH RHYME-CLASS

4.2.1. THE RUSHENG WORDS OF THE SHAN RHYME-CLASS

The rùshēng words of the Shānshè (i. e., those from Tables 21,22,23,24 in YJ), such as 括滑厥缺葛札揭結, show triple distribution. They were matched with the Guǒ-jiǎ in Table 11 and 12, the Xièshè in Table 17 and 20, as well as the Shānshè in Table 7 and 8 (their original counterpart), since most of these words later entered Gēgē rhyme (e. g. 葛括 the first division words), Jiāmá rhyme (e. g. 札滑 the second division words) and Chēzhē rhyme (e. g. 厥缺揭結 the third and fourth division words) in ZYYY, it is very reasonable for them to appear in Table 11 and 12 in ZZT. The fact that

Guǒ and Jiǎ are zero ending rhyme-classes seems to imply the disappearing of the rùshēng ending/-t/in the dialect represented by ZZT. If it is true, then how can we explain the inclusion of some of the above-mentioned words(e.g. 葛札滑, in the first or second division of Shānshè) in Table 17 and 20, which contain the words with a palatal semi-vowel/-y/as their ending (該齋懷 in the first and second division of Xièshè)? To hypothesize that the ending changed from/-t/to/-y/is also unreasonable. It is thus more reasonable to assume that the rùshēng ending/-t/in this dialect did not entirely disappear but only became a neutralized consonantal check on the vowel, together with/p,k,k̂/, as has been observed in some modern dialect (e.g. Chou's native tongue, the Nanking dialect).

4.2.2. THE RUSHENG WORDS OF THE ZHEN RHYME-CLASS

Zhǐzhǎng Tú matched the rùshēng words of the Zhēnshè(Mo 没 Wu 物 Qi 迄, rhymes in Tables 17, 18, 19 and 20 of YJ) with the words of the Zhǐshè and the Xièshè (Tables 18 and 19) in addition to their former yángshēng counterpart (tables 9 and 10). Furthermore, the Kāikǒu words among them also matched with the Liúshè (table 4). The fact that they can match with both Liúshè, a rhyme-class with/-w/as ending, and Zhǐshè (including those words coming from the Xièshè), a rhyme-class with/-y/as ending, indicates that they must have acquired a neutralized rùshēng ending, as has been discussed in the above sections. This shows that the sound system underlying ZZT is definitely different from that of DZ and that of ZYYY, where these rùshēng words show no relation to the Liúshè at all. ZZT seems to have a sound system similar to the modern southern dialects in the lower Yangtze valley.

4.2.3. THE RUSHENG WORDS OF ZENG-GENG RHYME-CLASS

ZZT's distribution of the first division rùshēng words of the Kāikóu type from Zēngshè,(e.g. the Dé rhyme), is seemingly confusing. They appear in the following four Tables involving six different rhyme-classes.

Chart V

Dé rhyme：/-ɨk̂/①

Table 4 /-ɨw/鉤（the words of Liúshè）

Table 9 /-ɨn/根（the words of Zhēnshè）

Table 16 /-ɨn/揯（the words of Zēng-Gěng）

Table 18 /-ɨy/基（the words of Zhǐ-Xiè）

The entering of the Dé rhyme into Table 16 requires no discussion，as it is nothing but a blind obedience to the old practice. Its inclusion in the other three Tables（Table 4 鉤/-ɨw/，Table 9 根/-ɨn/and Table 18 基/-ɨy/）reminds us of its close similarity to the rùshéng words of the Zhēnshè（see 4.2.2.）.

Chart VI

Zēngshè	zhēnshè	liúshè	zhǐshè
德/-ɨk/	根/-ɨn/	鉤/-ɨw/	基/-ɨy/
Zhēnshè			
訖/-yɨt/	斤/-yɨn/	鳩/-yɨw/	基/-yɨy/
吉		樛	鷄

The comaprative chart above implies the following：

a) The entry of the Dé rhyme to the first division slots of Zhēnshè may be the result of an arbitary decision of the author of ZZT. Since the first division slots for rùshēng in Zhēnshè contain only a few words which were no longer in common use. The author used the Dé rhyme to fill the blank, instead.

b) This distribution gives us a clue about the disappearing of contrast between the palatal ending/-k̂/and the dental ending/-t/.

① The main vowel of Zēng-Gěng was originally low and back. It moved front and became higher under the assimilation of its palatal ending/-k̂/and/-ɲ/（Cf. Hsueh 1978：418－419）. According to the fact that the words of Zēng-Gěng can match with the words from the thyme-class with high vowel as their main vowel in ZZT，we assume that the main vowel of the Zēng-Gěng rhyme-class had changed in the dialect represented by ZZT.

c) Arbitrary or not, the author's decision can only be made under one condition: Dé shares the same or at least a similar vowel with the rhymes it matches. Zhēnshè, Liúshè and Zhǐshè all possess a high vowel while the main vowel of Zēngshè was originally low and back. If the main vowel of Zēngshè had not changed, it would have been impossible for the Dé rhyme to join the Zhēnshè, Liúshè and Zhǐshè. This means that the development of the rùshēng words in the dialect underlying ZZT is similar to that of the literary pronunciation but quite different from the colloquial pronunciation recorded in ZYYY (Cf. Hsueh 1975: 123-133).

d) This kind of distribution was probably made under the influence of some southern dialect. In many areas along the lower Yangtze river, words from Zēng-Gěng rhyme-class and words from Zhēn rhyme-class have lost contrast. (Cf. Jiāng 1960 and Zhōu 1980)

4.2.4. THE RUSHENG WORDS OF THE JIANG-DANG RHYME-CLASS

The distribution of the rùshēng words from Jiāng and Dàng (e.g. 各覺脚郭) is less problematic. Aside from matching their original non-rùshēng counterpart (Table 13 and 14), they were also entered in Table 1 to match the words of the Xiào rhyme-class (e.g. 高交嬌) Sìshēng Děngzǐ shows the same distribution as ZZT. In ZYYY, these words were all entered in the Xiāoháo rhyme. This seems to mean that in the dialect of ZZT, the velar stop/-k/ending had also changed to the the semi-vowel/-w/(Cf. Hsueh 1975: 106-108). However, it may be only a coincidence. In some lower Yangtze valley dialects, in which the rùshēng ending was reduced to a neutralized stop, the rùshēng words from Jiāng and Dàng rhyme-class can also match the Xiào rhyme-class words. ① This fact makes another hypothesis possible, that is, if the ending of the above-mentioned rùshēng words did not change to the

① Cf. Jiāng 1960. As a native speaker of Nanking dialect, Chōu has the same feeling.

semi-vowel/-w/but was only reduced to a neutralized stop, these words can still match the words of Xiào rhyme-class.

4.2.5. THE RUSHENG WORDS OF THE TONG RHYME-CLASS

The rùshēng words from the Tōng rhyme-class has double distribution, in Table 2 with their original Yángshēng counterpart and in Table 3 with the words of the Yù rhyme-class. This phenomenon seems to indicate that the rùshēng ending /-k/ of these words disappeared or at least was reduced to a neutralized stop.

4.2.6. THE RUSHENG WORDS OF XIAN AND SHEN RHYME-CLASSES

The rùshēng words from Xiānshè and the rùshēng words from Shēnshè match their Yángshēng counterpart only as they did before (Table 5 and Table 6). The fact that the rùshēng words of these two rhyme-classes did not mix with those of other rhyme-classes seems to imply that by the period represented by ZZT, the labial stop ending /-p/ remained unchanged. However it is not inconceivable that the rùshēng words of these two rhyme-classes had also been affected by the same sound change as the other rùshēng endings, but the author of ZZT did not use them to match the non-rùshēng words of other rhyme-classes, only because the rhyme-classes they can possibly enter were already occupied by the rùshēng words from Shānshè and Zhēnshè. The author was only trying arbitrarily to be consistent in using words which formerly belong to the same rhyme.

5. CONCLUSION

Our study makes us believe that Zhǐzhǎng Tú is a revised and rearranged version of Děngzǐ. It was most probably compiled by a native speaker of a certain southern dialect of Southern Song dynasty. This unknown compiler, possibly a Buddist monk from the Jiangxi area as Professor Dǒng and his friend Mr. Zhāng speculated (Cf. Dǒng 1948a), must be a very enthusiastic Děngyùn scholar, though his training, and hence, his understanding, of this subject was apparently not as high as we might have hoped. We can imagine that, upon obtaining a copy of rhyme-table book, perhaps Děngzǐ, he was only too eager to revise it according to his own speech and he must have shared a common feeling with the people who had only a limited understanding of the Shēng and the Děng in thinking that all four tones and all four divisions should have words. This can perhaps explain his tendency in filling up as many slots as he possibly could, sometimes mistakenly. He also showed a lack of understanding of the Děngyùn theory by moving graphs representing purely palatalized syllables with labial initials to the Hékǒu tables and by entering the Jiāng series of rhymes into the rounded table of the Dàng rhyme class. The revisions he made are of three kinds:

a) Those which reveal important intermediate stages of sound changes in the development of the "standard" Chinese, in line with what can be inferred from Děngzǐ and Zhōngyuán Yīnyùn.

b) Those which show deviations (for which the book has been criticized by some as being "incorrect" or "improper"). We believe revisions of this kind probably reflect some dialectal features of the compiler's speech which might even be verified by studying some modern southern dialect.

c) Those which reveal the compiler's lack of genuine understanding of Děngyùn theory.

It is rather difficult to evaluate the historical role the book has played. In the absence of a better book of its kind, it has been quite instrumental in many people's learning of the Děngyùn tradition, because it by and large preserves the basic design of rhyme tables. But its prominent false authorship may have helped it acquiring some undue prestige and thus overshadowing better books of its kind, such as Déngzǐ and Qīyīnlüè. Considering the misleading features of the book caused by its compiler's imappropriate revisions, we tend to feel the importance of the book may have been overrated.

Reference in English

Chang, Kun(1974): "Ancient Chinese Phonology and the Ch'ieh-yun", The Tsinghua Journal of Chinese Studies, n. s. No. 2 (1974). 61 - 82.

Hashimoto, Mantaro J. (1979): Phonology of Ancient Chinese. Study of Languages & Cultures of Asia & Africa Monograph Series No. 11. Tokyo, 1979.

Hsueh, F. S. (1975): Phonology of Old Mandarin, The Hague, 1975.

——(1976): "Seven Centuries of Rhyming in Chinese Poetry: a Linguistic Interpretation", Paper presented at the ACTFL-CLTA annual meeting, New Orleans, 1976.

——(1979): "A New Interpretation of the Inner/Outer Contrast in the Rhyme Tables and its Implication on Middle Chinese Phonology", Paper presented at the 12th International Conference on Sino-Tibetan Linguistics, Paris, 1979.

——(1980b): "The Phonemic Structure of Pekingese Finals and their R-suffixation". The Bulletin of the Institute of History and Philology. Academia Sinica, Vol. 51, part 3 (1980), 491 - 514.

——(1983): "Xu Xiao's Revised Rhyme-tables: a Bold Renovation", in Chu, Coblin and Tsao (ed.). Papers from the 14th International Conference on Sino-Tibetan Languages and Linguistics, Taipei, 1983 (Gainesville, 1981), 153 - 170.

Pulleyblank, E. G(1970): "Late Middle Chinese", Asia Major XV. 2, (1970) 197 - 239, and XVI, 1 - 2(1971), 121 - 168.

Stimson, Hugh M. (1966): The Jongyuan In Yunn, New Haven, 1966.

——(1977): "Review of Hsueh's Phonology of Old Mandarin", Language 53 (1977), part 4, 941 - 944.

Wang, William S-Y (1969): "Competing Changes as a Cause of Residue", Language, 45(1969), 9 - 25.

Reference in Chinese

Dong(1948a)董同龢:《〈切韻指掌圖〉中的幾個問題》,《史語所集刊》,14(1948),257—306

Dong(1948b)——:《等韻門法通釋》,《史語所集刊》,17(1948).195—212

Dong(1968)——:《漢語音韻學》,臺北,1968

Jiang(1960)江蘇省和上海市方言調查組:《江蘇省和上海市方言概況》,南京,1960

Li(1981)李新魁:《韻鏡研究》,《語言研究》No.0(1981),125—166

Li(1981)——:《論内外轉》,《中國音韻學研究會一九八二年討論會論文》,西安,1982

Long(1960)龍宇純:《韻鏡校注》:臺北, 1960

Luo(1933)羅常培:《釋内外轉》,《史語所集刊》,第四本第二分,209—226. also in Luo(1963),《羅常培語言研究論文集》,北京, 1963,87—103

Luo(1935)——:《通志・七音略研究》,《史語所集刊》,第五本第四分 521—535. also in Luo(1963),《羅常培語言研究論文集》,北京, 1963.104—116

Luo(1947)陸志韋:《記徐孝重訂司馬温公等韻圖經》,《燕京學報》,32 (1947),167—196

Wang(1967)王力:《中國語言學史》,北京。

Xue(Hsueh)(1978)薛鳳生:《論入聲字之演化規律》;《屈萬里先生七秩榮慶論文集》。

Xue(Hsueh)(1980a)——:《論支思韻的形成與演進》,《書目季刊》Vol.14,No.2. 1980,53—75

Xue(Hsueh)(1982)——:《論音變與音位結構的關係》,《語言研究》,No.2(1982).11—17

Zhang(1937)張洵如:《北平音系十三轍》,魏建功校,中國大辭典編纂處,1937

Zhao(1934)趙蔭棠:《〈切韻指掌圖〉撰述年代考》,《輔仁學志》,四卷二期

(1934), 1—4. Also in Zhao(1957)

Zhao(1936)——:《中原音韻研究》,上海。

Zhao(1957)——:《等韻源流》,上海。

Zhou(1980)周殿福:《藝術語言發聲基礎》,北京。

論入聲字之演化規律**

1. 在古籍的研讀中,尤其是在古典詩詞的分析與創作中,所謂"入聲字"常是一個最令人困惑的問題。這個問題的產生,自然是由語音演化造成的,結果使得原來的入聲字在現代標準音裏不再是入聲了,因此與原來的舒聲字没有分别了。這對研析古典詩詞是很不利的,因爲原本工整的格律與韻脚,如此一來就變得支離破碎了。在另一方面説,由於演化過程的錯綜複雜,許多原來衹有一種讀法的入聲字,現在竟有了兩種甚或三種不同的讀法。這對學習標準話的人,固然是一個令人迷惘的問題,對研究漢語史的人來説,如何在理論上解釋説明這些現象,更是一大難題。歷來研究這個問題並發表專文的人相當不少(參看附目),但迄今未得定論,反而由於衆説紛紜,相互抵牾,令人覺得越説越亂,似乎毫無規律可言,這實在是一個很不幸的錯誤印象。

1.1 語音的演化都是有規律的。這些規律有時候簡直嚴格到令人吃驚的地步,但要發現這些規律却也不是很容易的事。這有許多原因。其一,語音的演變是以音位系統爲基礎的,除非我們能把某一時期的音位系統發掘出來,我們就無法清楚地看出該時期演變到下一時期的語音規律。其二,在演變的過程中,由於地區的隔離或社會層次的差别,一種語言往往會分裂成數種不同的方音,雖然在個别的方音中,語音的演化仍是極有規律的,但方音間的歧異雜出紛陳,如不能分别看待,就會給人一種漫無規則的感覺。其三,由於各種複雜的社會活動,各種歧出的方音又會漸趨統一,這時某一方音就變成了新的標準語,但它同時也無可避免地會自其他方音吸收相當多的詞彙和音讀,因此某些字便似有多種不同的標準讀音,這對於音變規律的認定當然是極不利的。

1.2 以上所説的幾種原因,也就是爲什麽入聲字問題糾纏不清的道理。要合理地解決這個問題,我們自然必須認清問題的本質,用抽絲剥繭的辦法,

---

** 原載《屈萬里先生七秩榮慶論文集》,聯經出版事業有限公司,1978 年。

把真相顯露出來。這就是本文的目的。爲了避免無謂的糾葛,也爲了使得篇幅不致太長,我們對前人的討論,除有必要外,將不作批評。對此問題有興趣的人,衹要把本文與前人的論著比對一下,自然就可以看出其間的差異了。

1.3 俗謂"平、上、去、入"四聲爲沈約所發明,這當然是不足信的。漢語中聲調的存在,應自上古已然。但上古時期聲調之形態與分配究竟如何呢?這是學者們迄今尚在熱烈討論的問題[①]。我們對入聲的性質,自中古起才算有較確切的瞭解。本文討論入聲字的演化,也將以中古爲起點。中古漢語以《切韻》所代表的音系爲準。爲中古擬音最有名的是高本漢[②]。他的做法偏重於追尋他所認爲可靠的音值,因此對音類及音位系統的確立比較疏忽,但對於聲調,他却嚴守着四聲的分類。他對四聲的看法是:平、上、去三聲是音調(pitch)的差異(也就是現在習謂的 tonemes),但入聲則是具有塞音韻尾的,也就是説,以成段音位(segmental phonemes)與其他三聲相別,音調有無差異倒在其次了。這一説法一向爲大家所接受,但近來又有人提出新説。加拿大的漢學家蒲立本氏最近就主張:上聲意指有喉塞音/ʔ/作爲韻尾,去聲有舌根擦音/h/(或 ɦ)作爲韻尾,入聲則有塞音韻尾[③]。根據此説,四聲在音位上的區別就全在成段音位了,音調衹是附帶成分(redundant features)。這一説的好處是較合理地解釋了平仄的對立,因爲如此一來,就衹有平聲才是真正的舒聲(unchecked syllables)了,其他三聲都有塞音或擦音韻尾,性質相近,因而合稱仄聲(check-ed syllables)。這一新説能否成立,恐怕尚待進一步的證明,因此我們在本文裏將仍遵舊説,好在新舊兩説對入聲的看法倒是相同的。

2. 切韻的音位系統,許多學者都曾在高本漢擬音的基礎上嘗試推求過,但切韻的內容過分繁雜,並且有方言混雜的現象[④],因此一個整齊合理而又可以解釋一切分韻現象的元音系統,迄今尚難推出。起於中晚唐的等韻學,在中國語言學史上是最值得大書特書的發明。在表面上,韻圖是爲着解讀切韻而作的,因此研究切韻(甚至上古音)的人,都以韻圖爲瞭解韻部關係的工具,但

---

① 關於上古聲調問題研究的近況,最好參看丁邦新教授的綜合報告。Ting 1975, PP.38—44。

② 參看高本漢 1962,pp.454—455。

③ 參看 Pulleyblank 1977。

④ 張琨教授即主此説,參看 Chang 1974。

却很少有人注意到等韻本身的獨立生命。我覺得像韻圖這樣的發明,必然是有實際的音系作爲根據的。以現存最早的等韻書如《韻鏡》及《七音略》爲例,我相信這必然是中唐以後的人(也許是鄭樵所説的胡僧吧),在精當地分析了當日的標準音以後;才設計出來的一套極具巧思的圖表。在這些圖表上,凡是當日標準音可能有的音節,都有一個(而且也衹有一個)特定的位置。用這些圖表去瞭解《切韻》,當然可以得到許多啓示,而且大部分地方也都符合,但是由於二者之間的音變,尤其是元音音位的併合與移轉,格格不入的地方也不少,因而就産生了許多諸如"重紐"與"重韻"問題;又有些地方,爲了節省篇幅,也受到權宜的改動,所謂"借位"即是一例。在此我們不能詳論等韻與《切韻》的差異,衹能把等韻的音位結構作一簡介,作爲討論入聲演化的基礎。

2.1 個人近年研讀的結果,使我深信韻圖的基本形態是建立在當日元音音位的相對關係上的。我們都知道,漢語音節的傳統分析法是聲母加韻母,韻母則含有韻頭(介音),韻腹(主要元音)、及韻尾(收聲)。我用(C)(M)V(E)來代表這些觀念,這一公式裏的"V"在等韻時期代表着下面的元音音位:

	前	央	後
高		ɨ	
低	e	a	o

等韻中所謂的"内轉"與"外轉",大致就是以元音的高低爲區分的①,連同四等的觀念,就可以用下列二式清楚地表達出來。介音部分的/w/表示開合之

① 關於内外轉的定義,傳統的説法是:有二等字的攝屬外轉,包括"江蟹臻山效咸梗"八攝,没有二等字(齒音除外)的攝屬内轉,包括"通止遇果宕流深曾"八攝。分法有自相矛盾的地方(臻攝除齒音外無二等字),但更成問題的是:純以圖式立説而不談語音的本質。因此歷來有許多學者不感滿意。日人大矢透首倡新説,謂内外乃指元音之高低對比。羅常培先生作"釋内外轉"(羅 1933),亦主此説,因移臻入内移果宕入外,成外九内七之分。(他們没有音位的觀念,因此對他們説,元音之高低對比衹是一種約略的概念,我提出高低四度元音説以後,這對比觀念才算確定。)我前此一直相信羅先生的説法,最近却有些動摇。我現在覺得傳統的定義可能是對的。(儘管這個定義没有多少語音上的意義。)果爾則元音之高低對比與内外轉之分雖在表面上有相當的巧合,在本質上却是兩個截然不同的觀念。此點容後另文詳論,爲方便計,我們姑且利用這一巧合,權借"内外"兩詞代表元音之高低。各攝的分屬問題,請參看第 522 頁注②。

分,/y/在内轉裏區别一等與三等,在外轉裏則區别二等與三等①。

	内 轉 攝	外 轉 攝
一等	(w)ɨ(E)	(w)o(E)
二等	……	(w)a(E)
三等	y(w)ɨ(E)	y(w)a(E)
四等	……	y(w)e(E)

2.2 等韻中“攝”的觀念,是以韻尾(E)爲準的。比對各本韻圖的形式,並參照近人的研究結果,各攝的隸屬與韻基形態應如下式②,配鼻音韻尾的塞音即爲入聲韻尾,介音部分有括號的表示“獨”攝,即無相對的開合圖者。

内:通(y)wɨ$\begin{Bmatrix}\text{ŋ}\\ \text{k}\end{Bmatrix}$,曾 ɨ$\begin{Bmatrix}\text{ɲ}\\ \hat{\text{k}}\end{Bmatrix}$,臻 ɨ$\begin{Bmatrix}\text{n}\\ \text{t}\end{Bmatrix}$,深(y)ɨ$\begin{Bmatrix}\text{m}\\ \text{p}\end{Bmatrix}$,止 ɨy,流(y)ɨw,遇(y)wɨø

外:$\begin{matrix}\text{宕}\\ \text{江}\end{matrix}\begin{Bmatrix}\text{o}\\ \text{a}\end{Bmatrix}\begin{Bmatrix}\text{ŋ}\\ \text{k}\end{Bmatrix}$,梗$\begin{Bmatrix}\text{a}\\ \text{e}\end{Bmatrix}\begin{Bmatrix}\text{ɲ}\\ \hat{\text{k}}\end{Bmatrix}$,山$\begin{Bmatrix}\text{o}\\ \text{a}\\ \text{e}\end{Bmatrix}\begin{Bmatrix}\text{n}\\ \text{t}\end{Bmatrix}$,咸(y)$\begin{Bmatrix}\text{o}\\ \text{a}\\ \text{e}\end{Bmatrix}\begin{Bmatrix}\text{m}\\ \text{p}\end{Bmatrix}$蟹$\begin{Bmatrix}\text{o}\\ \text{a}\\ \text{e}\end{Bmatrix}$y,效(y)$\begin{Bmatrix}\text{o}\\ \text{a}\\ \text{e}\end{Bmatrix}$w,$\begin{matrix}\text{果}\\ \text{假}\end{matrix}\begin{Bmatrix}\text{o}\\ \text{a}\end{Bmatrix}$ø

2.3 聲母跟入聲字的轉化並無直接關係,但爲了明確地標出這些字如何變爲今讀,却也必須列出。雖然我們有時用複合符號,但每一聲母都是一個單位。“ɦ”表示“全濁”,“h”表示“次清”(即“送氣”),“r”表示“捲舌”。

---

① 自高本漢以來,大家都認爲四等韻有介音(i),但根據李榮的研究(李 1956),四等韻在《切韻》時代無此介音。就純粹的音位對比説,四等韻介音/y/亦似多餘,但四等字後來都變細音則是不容置疑的。我們在此假定,在三等合口脣音字變輕脣以後不久,四等韻即産生介音/y/,也就是説四等字在等韻時代已變爲細音。

② 《四聲等子》及《切韻指掌圖》都把果與假、江與宕、梗與曾合成一圖,前書更把它們稱爲“内外混等”。在這樣的安排下,前二組尚有相對的内轉攝(即遇與通),最後一組則没有,因此我們在此接受前二組的混等,但仍遵守梗與曾的外内之分。(另一種辦法則爲:把梗曾也作混等處理,而把通攝中的東類與冬類的差别解釋爲舌根與舌面韻尾的對比,衹不過東與冬之别在韻圖形成之前就已消失了。這樣的好處是可以把三組内外混等都解釋爲同一音變〔o-a/y__〕的結果。)在音理上説,果與假、江與宕之所以分圖分轉,應是早期音系的殘留現象。在切韻時代,後低元音/o/,即(ȧ),可以出現於介音/y/之後,因此果假的三等字構成對比,故必須分作兩圖,前者且因無二等字而被歸入内轉;後來/y/後之/o/因同化作用前移而變作/a/,因此便内外混等了。宕攝韻腹與果攝同,江攝的韻腹原爲較高的元音,變低是較晚的事,可能因此未被合爲一圖,但宕三韻腹轉變之後,便不得混等了。至於把梗曾的韻尾訂爲舌面音,則是采用橋本萬太郎的説法(Hashimoto 1970),詳情請參看第 524 頁注②。

	阻音(S)			擦音(F)		振音(R)	
脣音(B)	p 幫 pf 非	ph 滂 pfh 敷	pɦ 並 pfɦ 奉			m 明 mv 微	
舌音(D)	t 端 tr 知	th 透 trh 徹	tɦ 定 trɦ 澄			n 泥 (娘)	l 來
齒音(Ds)	c 精 cr 照	ch 清 crh 穿	cɦ 從 crɦ 牀	s 心 sr 審	sɦ 邪 srɦ 禪		r 日
喉牙音(G)	k 見 q 影	kh 溪	kɦ 群	x 曉	xɦ 匣	ŋ 疑	ø 喻

3. 入聲字的改讀,顯然在宋代就已發端了。這可以從宋代的詞曲作品中看出[①],也可以從晚出的等韻書看出來。《指掌圖》及《四聲等子》都把入聲字拿來作陰陽兩配甚至三配,便露出端倪了。到了元代,周德清在《中原音韻》裏把入聲字派進其他三聲,更是入聲字已經改讀的明證。然而改變的方式如何呢? 這却人言人殊。一般説來,每一時代都有一種標準話,即朝廷用語,或稱"官話"。我們通常總傾向於把不同時代的標準話連串起來,看作一條直綫的發展。這種求整齊的心理原是無可厚非的,從實用的觀點説,也是必須如此做的。然而我們不可忘記,語音的演化雖然有其本身的嚴格規律,不同時代裏標準話的確定,則是由許多非語言性的(non-linguistic)社會因素促成的。兩個銜接時代的標準話,因此不一定具有直屬的"父子"關係,却可能衹是"叔侄"的關係,二者之間的音變規律也就難免有不協調的地方。同時,所謂一個時代的"標準話",本身就可能有一些方音性的差異,因此同一時代的兩個作者所紀録的"標準話",就可能有少許差異。這是我們應用歷史資料時必須注意的,我們衹應就個别的資料作事實的論斷,用不着去評斷誰是誰非。等韻以後的情況大致就是上述的樣子。由於某些音變,尤其是入聲字的改讀,原來的標準話分裂成了許多方音(或稱"次方言"subdialects),其中之一在元代顯然取得了相當標準的地位,這可由元曲作家的用韻、八思巴字的標音,以及《中原音韻》的入聲字分派趨勢看得出來。這種話經過繼續的演變,遺留下來的痕迹就是北京話中的所謂"(口)語音",如讀"藥"爲"要"(而不讀"月")、讀"額"爲"葉"(而不讀"鵝")等。當時顯然另有一種方音,與上述作爲標準話的"口語音"在音位系

① 參看唐鉞 1926 及夏承燾 1948 與 1958。

統上幾不可分,但在入聲字的改讀上,却與"口語"大相徑庭,經過繼續的演變,這種話就是北京話的所謂"讀(書)音"了,如證"藥"爲"月"、讀"額"爲"鵝"等。這種話在元代雖不如"口語音"那麼"標準"但顯然也甚具影響力,因此周德清在説明入聲改讀時,便常模棱兩可,而且把部分入聲字的兩種讀法都一併收入了。降及明清"讀書音"取代了"口語音"的標準地位,民國以後,由於"國語統一運動",公布了標準常用字彙,"讀書音"更取得了壓倒性的優勢,但有一部分常見的字彙,諸如"黑、白、賊、北、六、肉"等,仍以"語音"讀法爲標準。除了上述兩種具有標準性的方音以外,北方官話裏另有一種方音,分布在以徐州爲中心的黄淮平原地區。這種方音的音位系統與前者相同,但入聲字的演化則另有一套規律①,拿來與前二種方音的入聲演變相比對,既饒興味且富啓示,因此在本文裏,我們將以這三種方音爲代表,討論入聲字的三種不同演變。

3.1 入聲演化以原屬"通,江,宕,梗、曾"五攝的入聲字最爲錯綜複雜。在高本漢的擬音裏,這幾攝都以[ŋ](陽)與[k](入聲)爲韻尾,這對解釋當時的韻類説,已有許多問題,對解釋語音的演變説,困難更多。日本學者橋本萬太郎提出把梗攝的韻尾改擬爲舌面音/ɲ/與/c/(我們改用/k̂/),恰可解决這些困難②。我認爲這一改擬應包括曾攝,傳統上梗曾總是相提並論的,説明這兩攝必有語音上的關聯,後世的演變也説明這兩攝字具有共同的韻尾。在這個基礎上,我提出下列兩個音變規律,用以説明入聲字在"口語"方音中的轉變。

$$*\hat{k} \rightarrow y / V\_\_\_ \qquad 〔1〕$$

$$k \rightarrow w / V\_\_\_ \qquad 〔2〕$$

3.1.1 第一條公式的意思是:梗曾兩攝的入聲字,韻尾/k̂/一律變爲/y/;第二條的意思則是:通、江、宕三攝的入聲字,韻尾一律由/k/變爲/w/。就語音的性質説,舌面音變爲前半元音而舌根音變爲後半元音,是極合理的。我們

① 關於這種方音,我在此是以自己的土話(下邳土山鎮)爲準的。據個人的粗略觀察,整個黄淮地區在這方面都差不多。屈先生説的話(山東魚臺)似亦屬此類,故特將這種方音收入本文,以爲屈先生壽。

② 見 Hashimoto 1970,橋本氏根據越南語即日語的漢字音讀,以及客家話等方言,得出這樣的結論,並指出四組鼻音與塞音韻尾與聲母之間的對稱關係。由於我們已用/c/代表精母,避免誤會,我采用了董同龢先生討論上古音所采用的[k̂]作爲梗曾的入聲韻尾。

説梗曾的入聲字變爲“收噫”,因爲這類字後來都與止攝及蟹攝的字合流,分别變入《中原音韻》的“齊微”韻及“皆來”韻,如“黑、白、色、澤”等。説江、宕兩攝的入聲字變爲“收嗚”,也許比較容易接受,因爲很多人都知道這類字與效攝合流,變入中原的“蕭豪”韻,但説通攝的入聲字也變爲“收嗚”,很多人便要懷疑了,因爲這類字絶大多數不出現在《中原音韻》的“尤侯”韻裏。其實這一演變也是不容置疑的,衹不過這一現象已被另一後起的音變遮蓋住了罷了(參看3.1.4公式〔8〕)。

3.1.2 經此一變以後,這幾類入聲字在“口語”方音中,就不再是入聲了,其後的變化自然也都得隨着一般舒聲字的通則。問題是:(1)這種變化發生在什麽時候?(2)在此之前,這類入聲字經過什麽變化?(3)在此之後,又有那些變化通則影響到這類以前的入聲字?要回答頭一個問題,我們可以采用兩種途徑。其一,由歷史文獻中找出前人的明説或暗示。但由於文獻的繁雜與抵牾,這衹能給我們一個概括含混的答案。據此我們衹能説這種變化大概發生在宋金時代。另一方法是先尋出某些音變的規律,然後從而推論這些規律間必有的先後關係,也就是在歷史上發生的早晚關係。這樣得出的答案自然要客觀可靠得多,同時以上三個問題也就分不開了。

3.1.3 直接影響到這類入聲字的早期音變,至少有下述三種:

3.1.3.1《切韻》時代的莊系及章系聲母合併爲等韻時代的照系聲母。莊系聲母原可配細音韻母,因而與章系對立,後來莊系聲母字失掉細音,對立消失,因此就合併了。對入聲字説,梗、曾兩攝的莊系字如“縮、色、測”等,至此便丢掉了介音中的/y/,後來曾攝的“色、測”等變入皆來韻,其韻腹由高變低,就是以此爲條件的。

$$i \rightarrow ɑ / r \underline{\quad\quad} \hat{k} \qquad 〔3〕$$

3.1.3.2 由於腭化介音/y/的同化作用(assimilation),央元音/a/向前移位而變成了前元音/e/,三、四等韻的差别就因而消失了。

$$a \rightarrow e / y(w) \underline{\quad\quad} \qquad (4)$$

這是漢語史上的一大變革,原不同音的字如“連”與“憐”,“硯”與“彦”等,也統變爲同音了,而自南宋時起也就有人注意到,一個新韻類(/-eø/,即後來的“車遮”)也就出現了。入聲字在這個變化裏自然也不例外,但是這個變化與入聲的消失孰先孰後,純就音理説却不易證明。因爲一般都以爲入聲的消失不太早,所以我們把這個變化放在前面。

3.1.3.3 第三個可能發生在韻尾/k,k̂/改變以前的變化,是二等喉牙音字的細音化。

$$ø \rightarrow y/G\_\_\_\_ a \qquad 〔5〕$$

這一變化使得諸如“交、江、家,番、間、耕”等字,都變成了細音字。合於這一條件的入聲字,如“角、學、瞎、隔、嚇”等,自然也都隨之而變了。但是這些字並没有跟原來的三等字混同,因爲原三等字已因公式〔4〕轉入四等了。梗曾兩攝跟江宕兩攝先後發生了所謂“内外混等”的現象,後來更進而合爲單一的韻類,即《中原音韻》的“庚青”與“江陽”。這兩個變化在“口語”方音及“讀音”方音中都發生過,但時間的先後顯然不同(見下文討論)。在“口語”方音中,二等喉牙音字變作細音顯然在梗曾合併之前,因此“耕、更、坑、硬、客”等原二等字才得變爲細音。我們假定公式(5)所代表的音變早於入聲的消失,部分也是這個緣故。

3.1.4 在韻尾/k,k̂/改變之後,“口語”方音裏原通攝入聲字即變同流攝字,江宕的入聲即變同效攝字,曾攝的入聲字即變同止攝字(莊系字除外,見公式〔3〕,梗攝的入聲字也就變同蟹攝字了)。自此以後,這些所謂入聲字就得隨着舒聲字一同變化。自宋迄今影響到它們的,計有下述幾種音變規律。

3.1.4.1 舌上音“知、徹、澄”三母塞擦化,因而併入照系聲母。原不同讀音的入聲字,如“竹”與“粥”,“摘”與“責”,便因而變成同音了。

$$t \rightarrow c/\_\_\_\_ r \qquad 〔6〕$$

3.1.4.2 變入流攝的原通攝三等入聲字(莊系除外),由於異化作用(dissimilation),由合口變開口。

$$w \rightarrow ø/y\_\_\_\_ ɨw \qquad 〔7〕$$

這就是“口語”方音中“六、肉、宿、粥、熟”等字今讀的來源。“縮、謖”等字已失掉介音中的/y/,故不在此例。

3.1.4.3 流攝的一等重脣字及三等輕脣字,在音理上説都是合口音[①]。在"口語"方音中,也由於異化作用,失掉了韻尾/w/,因而讀同遇攝字,如"部、母、不,浮、謀"等,皆是其例。

$$w \to ø / wɨ\_\_\_\_ \qquad 〔8〕$$

由通攝一等入聲及部分三等入聲變入流攝的字,都符合這個音變條件,自然不能例外,因此都出現在《中原音韻》的"魚模"韻裏,"尤模"韻的入聲字反而寥寥無幾。大概由於這個緣故,有些人硬説尤侯韻不該有入聲字,因此也就無法看出舌根塞音韻尾一律變後半元音的一大通則[②]。

3.1.4.4 在"收噫"韻裏,前後低元音上升而變成高元音,蟹攝的一等合口字如"雷、灰、對、内"等[③],及全部四等字(包括由三等變入者,見公式〔4〕),都變同止攝字,因而共同組成了《中原音韻》的"齊微"韻。

$$\begin{Bmatrix} o \\ e \end{Bmatrix} \to ɨ / \_\_\_\_ y \qquad 〔9〕$$

梗攝的三等及四等入聲字,在韻尾變/y/以後,正符合這條音變的條件,因此"擲、石、覔、戟、昔"等字,也就都出現在齊微韻裏了。

3.1.4.5 效攝原是一個四等具備的大韻類,但降及元代,其中各韻合而爲一,形成了《中原音韻》的"蕭豪"韻,可用下式表示這一音變[④]。

$$\begin{Bmatrix} o \\ e \end{Bmatrix} \to a / \_\_\_\_ w \qquad 〔10〕$$

等韻之後一直到清代中葉,漢語的元音系統未曾改變,但前後低元音却在特定的情形下,在不同的時代裏,分别合併於央元音。公式〔9〕所代表的是第一步"收噫"韻的轉變,公式〔10〕則代表第二步"收嗚"韻的轉變,其後别的韻類也循

---

① 關於洪音脣音字的性質問題,我的看法是:理論上它們都是合口。參看薛 1975,第 38—39 頁及薛 1977。

② 參看陸志韋 1946,第 66 頁。

③ 我們在此衹提一等合口字,因爲這個音變發生時,一等開口字已因前此的另一音變改讀二等了(參看 4.3 節的 公式〔24〕)。因該音變與梗攝入聲字無直接關係,故未先討論。

④ 嚴格地説,蕭豪韻歸字現象顯示,在《中原音韻》所代表的那種"口語"這一音變當時尚未完成。參看薛 1975,第 62—66 頁。

此途徑漸次合併，終於形成了現代漢語的高中低三度元音①。在公式〔10〕所代表的音變發生時，由入聲變來的字當然也受到影響，因此"角"與"脚"、"岳"與"藥"、"濁"與"著"等也都變成同音了。（"博"與"剥"應同，但在《中原音韻》裏却分屬平、上。）

3.1.4.6 明代中葉以後，原齊微韻的字分爲不再互韻的兩類。在徐孝的等韻圖經裏，"齊"類字被拿來與"支、思"及"魚、如"兩類字相配，畢拱辰的韻略匯通把"齊"類字歸入"居魚"韻，十三轍也把"齊、支、魚"三類字合爲"一七"轍②，"微"類字則獨立成韻，即十三轍的"灰堆"轍。這種分裂是由下式所代表的音變造成的。

$$y \rightarrow ø / y\text{ɨ}\_\_\_\_ \qquad 〔11〕$$

原入齊微韻的入聲字如"國、賊"等未受影響，但"石、直、激、昔"等便因此變爲"直音"。入聲字在"口語"方音中的這一轉變，在明清兩代的韻書中是看不出來的，因爲其時"讀書音"已取得作爲標準的地位，像易通及匯通等書，又都把入聲字分出强配陽聲。

3.1.4.7 大約從清代早期起，北京話裏捲舌聲母不再配細音韻母，也就是説，丢掉了介音中的/y/。

$$y \rightarrow ø / r\_\_\_\_ \qquad 〔12〕$$

入聲字如"直、擲、尺、釋"等，先因公式〔11〕所代表的音變而失掉韻尾，至此復失掉介音，因此就變同"支、思"了。

3.1.4.8 在現代標準話裏，原屬皆來韻的細音字都改讀成車遮韻，用十三轍的術語説，即由"懷來"變大"乜斜"，比如"街、解、鞋"等字，這種變化可用下式表達：

$$ay \rightarrow e / y\_\_\_\_ \qquad 〔13〕$$

這些字的介音，都是由公式〔5〕所代表的音變産生的。梗攝二等入聲字如"客、隔、額、嚇"等的韻母，當然也受到影響而變成/ye/了。老北京人把"來客了"

① 關於元音音位的轉變步驟，參看薛 1976。

② 十三轍中一七轍的内涵以及與姑蘇轍的關係，一直有許多誤解（例如張洵如 1937 及 1956）。經羅常培先生作了歸納研究以後，這個問題才得到解決（參看羅 1950）。

説得像“來妾了”，把“隔壁”説成“接壁”，等等，就是這個緣故。在《中原音韻》裏，這類入聲字自然都出現在皆來韻裏，但“客、額、嚇”三個字却同時出現在車遮韻裏，而且顯然都是細音，這似乎表示我們此處討論的音變，先發端於入聲字，到清代中葉以後才波及其他。

3.1.5 另一近代音變，即“尖團混合”，自然也涉及入聲字，但對本文的主旨不很重要，就略而不論了。綜合以上的討論，我們可以用下面的例字列一簡表，以標明入聲字在“口語”方音中的演化規律與程序，見下頁。

木:莫卜切;代表通一入聲如“獨、哭、速、禄”等。

六:力竹切;代表通三入聲如“粥、熟、肉、竹”等。

角:古岳切;代表江喉牙入聲如“岳、覺、學,確”等。

捉:側角切;代表江非喉牙入聲如“濁、剥、朔、犖”等。

各:古落切;代表宕一入聲如“莫、鐸、錯、落”等。

藥:以灼切;代表宕三入聲如“著、脚、杓、弱”等。

黑:呼北切;代表曾一入聲如“北、得、賊、國”等。

色:所力切;代表曾照二入聲如“測、仄,嗇、骰”等。

敇:恥力切;代表曾三知照系入聲如“直、陟、食、織”等。

力:林直切;代表曾三其他入聲如“逼、殛、息、憶”等。

摘:陟革切;代表梗二知照系入聲如“窄、宅、策,擇”等。

客:苦格切;代表梗二喉牙入聲如“革、隔、嚇、額”等。

麥:莫獲切;代表梗二其他入聲如“白、百、摑、脉”等。

尺:昌石切;代表梗三知照系入聲如“擲、石、隻、釋”等。

錫:先積切;代表梗三其他及梗四入聲如“狄、覔、昔、績”等。

3.2 所謂“讀書音”，可以説是與“口語音”同源而稍異趣，二者的不同主要在入聲字方面。在“口語”方音裏，入聲消失甚早，但在“讀音”方音裏，真正的入聲可能保留到明末。造成二者之歧異的原因，一部分是各有一些不同的音變規律，另一部分則是共有的音變規律發生在不同的時間與順序中。以下我們便分層討論通、江、宕、梗、曾五攝入聲字在“讀音”中的演化。

3.2.1 “讀音”演變最突出的地方，是梗曾兩攝由混等而混一，可以用下式來代表:

演化律＼例字	木	六	捉	角	各	藥	黑	色	敕	力	麥	客	摘	尺	錫	
	mwɨk	lywɨk	crak	kak	kok	yak	xɨk̂	srik̂	trhyik̂	lyik̂	mak̂	khak̂	trak̂	crhyak̂	syek̂	
ɨ→a/r___k̂								srak̂								
a→e/y(w)___						yek								crhyek̂		
ø→y/G___a				kyak								khyak̂				
k̂→y/V___							xɨy	sray	trhyɨy	lyɨy	may	khyay	tray	crhyey	syey	
k→w/V___	mwɨw	lywɨw	craw	kyaw	kow	yew										
t→c/___r									crhyɨy				cray			
w→ø/y___ɨw		lyɨw														
w→ø/wɨ___	mwɨ															
{o, e}→ɨ/___y														crhyɨy	syɨy	
{o, e}→a/___w					kaw	yaw										
	魚模	尤侯	蕭豪	蕭豪	蕭豪	蕭豪	齊微	皆來	齊微	齊微	皆來	皆來	皆來	齊微	齊微	中原音韻
y→ø/yɨ___									crhyɨ	lyɨ				crhyɨ	syɨ	
y→ø/r___									crhɨ					crhɨ		
ay→e/y___												khye				
	姑蘇	油求	遥條	遥條	遥條	遥條	灰堆	懷來	一七	一七	懷來	乜斜	懷來	一七	一七	十三轍
華氏音標	mu	liu	chạo	chiao	kao	yao	hêi	shai	ch'ih	li	mai	ch'ieh	chai	ch'ih	hsi	
注音符號	ㄇㄨ	ㄌㄧㄡ	ㄓㄠ	ㄐㄧㄠ	ㄍㄠ	ㄧㄠ	ㄏㄟ	ㄕㄞ	ㄔ	ㄌㄧ	ㄇㄞ	ㄑㄧㄝ	ㄓㄞ	ㄔ	ㄒㄧ	

$$\begin{Bmatrix} \text{ɨ} \\ \text{a} \end{Bmatrix} \rightarrow \text{e}/\underline{\quad} \begin{Bmatrix} \hat{\text{k}} \\ \text{ɲ} \end{Bmatrix} \qquad 〔14〕$$

這一演變在"口語"裏也發生了,不過發生時已經没有收/k̂/的字了(即晚於公式〔1〕),同時二等開口喉牙音字也早變成細音了(公式〔5〕),因此"麥"讀"賣","耕"讀"京"。但在"讀音"裏,這個演變比公式〔5〕所代表的音變還要早,而入聲字其時尚未變成舒聲,故"耕、客"等不變細音,而二等入聲字不入皆來,却終於變同車遮了。

3.2.2"讀音"的另一突出演變是江宕兩攝也由混等而混一。梗曾的韻尾是舌面音,因此影響韻腹前移,江宕兩攝的韻尾是舌根音,因而使得韻腹後移;就音理説,這是很合情理的。

$$\text{a} \rightarrow \text{o}/\underline{\quad} \begin{Bmatrix} \text{k} \\ \text{ŋ} \end{Bmatrix} \qquad 〔15〕$$

我們説江宕併爲一等韻,主要是因爲二者的入聲字併爲一韻而終變同果攝一等字。"岳"與"約"、"濁"與"著"、"落"與"犖"等也都變成同音了。江宕的混一顯然發生在公式〔5〕所代表的音變之後,因爲即使在"讀書"音裏,江攝的喉牙音字也都變成細音了。在《中原音韻》裏,這類入聲字被收入歌戈韻,但衹是一部分,而蕭豪韻則把這類入聲字全部收入。我們説《中原音韻》是當時"口語"的紀録,這是主要原因之一。顯然"讀音"在當時也頗有影響力,因此説"口語"的人也就借入了一部分這類入聲字的"讀音"讀法,周德清也就據實録入《中原音韻》了。但我相信借讀時韻尾塞音(其時當已變/q/,見公式〔18〕)一定是被丢掉的,因爲衹有如此才能跟歌戈韻的字押韻。

3.2.3 經過上述兩類韻攝的混一,舌面音韻尾與舌根音韻尾便失去了對比的意義,自然合併了①。

$$\begin{Bmatrix} \hat{\text{k}} \\ \text{ɲ} \end{Bmatrix} \rightarrow \begin{Bmatrix} \text{k} \\ \text{ŋ} \end{Bmatrix} \qquad 〔16〕$$

---

① 在這個公式裏,爲求劃一,我們仍用音位符號,因此表面上看來似有兩個獨立的變化,其實二者衹是一回事,即"舌面音變舌根音"可見在這樣的細微地方,音素(distinctive features)表示法比較妥當,因爲我們可以説 $\begin{bmatrix} \text{C} \\ +\text{pal} \end{bmatrix}$ 變成 $\begin{bmatrix} -\text{pal} \\ +\text{vcl} \end{bmatrix}$ 了。公式〔14〕中的限制條件其實也衹是個(+pal),其他如公式〔15〕等皆仿此。

就入聲字說,後來韻尾/k/更進而與韻尾/p/(深咸入聲)及韻尾/t/(臻山入聲)合而爲一,成爲一種喉塞音韻尾/q/。我們說在“讀音”中真正的入聲可能保留到明末,就是指此而言。

$$\begin{Bmatrix} p \\ t \\ k \end{Bmatrix} \rightarrow q/V\_\_\_ \qquad 〔17〕$$

明清韻書多仍把入聲字分出以配陽聲,但不同韻的入聲字常有混雜的現象(例如匯通的互見),就是這個道理。降及清代,連這個喉塞音韻尾也終將消失了。

$$q \rightarrow \emptyset/V\_\_\_ \qquad 〔18〕$$

3.2.4 曾攝照二系入聲字如“色、測”等,先已失掉介音/y/(參看 3.1.3),迨韻腹變/e/後(公式〔14〕),更與梗攝照二系字合併,後來便同以無介音/y/爲條件失掉聲母中的捲舌成分而變同精系了。這一變化顯然發生得不太早。梗攝二等知系字如“摘、宅”等,聲母也變爲精系,因此我們相信,這個變化必然發生在公式〔6〕所代表的音變之後。雖然這一變化衹涉及梗曾的入聲字,其發生時間却不一定是在塞音韻尾合併之前(公式〔17〕),因爲衹有梗曾兩攝的入聲字才會變出/eq/這樣的韻母(參看下文討論)。同時爲了較合理地解釋另一些現象,把這個音變定得晚些也比較有利(參看 4.4)。

$$r \rightarrow \emptyset/\_\_\_eq \qquad 〔19〕$$

3.2.5 梗曾的三、四等入聲字,即使在“讀音”中也没有變入乜斜轍,而是一律讀入一七轍。山咸兩攝的三、四等入聲字(即收/p,t/者,如“結、舌、薛、攝”等),則全讀入乜斜轍,這表示在塞音韻尾合併之前(公式〔17〕),收/k/的入聲字(由收/$\hat{k}$/變來),先有如下的變化。

$$e \rightarrow ɨ/y(w)\_\_\_k \qquad 〔20〕$$

這類字在失掉韻尾/q/以後(公式(18)),開口字韻母變作/yɨ/,其時它們的“口語”讀法也已由/yɨy/變作/yɨ/(公式〔11〕),因此兩種讀法便很巧合地復歸於一了。同樣的巧合也發生在通攝的入聲字裏,在“讀音”中,它們的韻母由/(y)wɨq/變作/(y)wɨ/(公式〔18〕),在“口語”中則由/(y)wɨw/變成/(y)wɨ/

(公式〔8〕),因而也殊途同歸了。(公式〔8〕所代表的音變,在"讀音"中似未發生,故"謀、浮、剖"等仍屬油求轍。)

3.2.6 江宕的入聲字,除了"郭、廓、霍"等字外[①],本來都是開口字,但在"讀音"的今讀裏,除了一等喉牙音如"各,恪、惡"等字外,都已一律改讀合口,連二等及三等喉牙音字也不例外。其實這一變化不限於入聲字,原爲舒聲的果攝一等開口字如"多、左、羅"等,也都變爲合口了,而其一等喉牙音字如"歌、可、何"等,也在例外,可見這個變化是起於後元音/o/的同化作用,從而亦可推知其發生時間不會太早,應在公式〔15〕及下文公式〔24〕所代表的音變之後,更可能在入聲韻尾合併之後[②]。

$$\emptyset \rightarrow w / \begin{Bmatrix} y \\ c \end{Bmatrix} \_\_\_ o(q) \qquad C \neq G$$ 〔21〕

3.2.7 前文已經提到,等韻時期的四個元音一直到清代中葉才變成現代標準音的高中低三個元音音位(參看3.1.4.5),這個演變的最後一步是韻腹爲/e/的直音韻(即乜斜轍)跟韻腹爲/o/的直音韻(即梭坡轍)合併。前後元音的這一次合併跟以前各次不同(參看公式〔9〕及〔10〕),既未併入高央元音,也未併入低央元音,而是形成了一個中央元音/ə/。

$$\begin{Bmatrix} o \\ e \end{Bmatrix} \rightarrow ə$$ 〔22〕

這個音變在"讀音"及"口語"兩種方音中都發生了,但在"口語"中與入聲字無直接關係,所以等到現在才提出來討論。我們説這個音變不早於清代中葉,因爲清初形成的十三轍所表現的還是未變以前的狀態。因爲梭坡及乜斜兩轍的字在今天的北京話裏已經合併,有些人不瞭解這兩轍分開的道理,便硬説是洪細的對立,這是不對的。其實未變以前的狀況迄今仍保留在南

① 在八思巴字裏,"郭"標作/kwaw/。有人以爲/waw/這樣的韻母是不可能的,可見是多餘的顧慮。這一事實也説明了公式〔2〕在"口語"中是毫無例外的。

② 在這個公式裏,我把(q)附入作條件之一,因爲我推測這個變化應在"讀音"失掉入聲之前。在"口語"中,則在入聲消失之後,故應以[#]代"(q)"。同時"口語"中没有/yo/這樣的韻母,所以也不需要限制條件中的/y/。

演化律 \ 例字	木	六	捉	角	各	藥	黑	色	敕	力	麥	客	摘	尺	錫	
	mwɨk	lywɨk	crak	kak	kok	yak	xɨk̂	srik̂	trhyik̂	lyik̂	mak̂	khak̂	trak̂	crhyak̂	syek̂	
$\begin{Bmatrix}\text{ɨ}\\ a\end{Bmatrix}\to e/\_\begin{Bmatrix}\hat{k}\\ \text{ɲ}\end{Bmatrix}$							xek̂	srek̂	trhyek̂	lyek̂	mek̂	khek̂	trek̂	crhyek̂		
ø→y/G___a				kyak												
$a\to o/\_\_\_\begin{Bmatrix}k\\ \text{ŋ}\end{Bmatrix}$			crok	kyok		yok										
$\begin{Bmatrix}k\\ \text{ɲ}\end{Bmatrix}\to\begin{Bmatrix}k\\ \text{ŋ}\end{Bmatrix}$							xek	srek	trhyek	lyek	mek	khek	trek	crhyek	syek	
e→ɨ/y(w)___k									trhyɨk	lyɨk				crhyɨk	syɨk	
t→c/___r									crhyɨk				crek			
p, t, k→q/V__	mwɨq	lywɨq	croq	kyoq	koq	yoq	xeq	sreq	crhyɨq	lyɨq	meq	kheq	creq	crhyɨq	syɨq	
$ø\to w/\begin{Bmatrix}y\\ c\end{Bmatrix}\_o(q)$ C≠G			crwoq	kywoq		ywoq										相當於《中原音韻》時代
r→ø/___eq								seq					ceq			
q→ø/V___	mwɨ	(lwɨ) lywɨ	crwo	kywo	ko	ywo	xe	se	crhyɨ	lyɨ	me	khe	ce	crhyɨ	syɨ	
y→ø/r									crhɨ					crhɨ		相當於十三轍時代
$\begin{Bmatrix}o\\ e\end{Bmatrix}\to\text{ə}$			crwə	kywə	kə	ywə	xə	sə			mə	khə	cə			
華氏音標	mu	(lu) lü	cho chuo	chüeh	ko kê	yüeh	hê	sê	ch'ih	li	mo mê	ko kê	cê	ch'ih	hsi	
注音符號	ㄇㄨ	ㄌㄨ	ㄓㄨㄛ	ㄐㄩㄝ	ㄍㄜ	ㄩㄝ	ㄏㄜ	ㄙㄜ	ㄔ	ㄌㄧ	ㄇㄛ	ㄎㄜ	ㄗㄜ	ㄔ	ㄒㄧ	

方官話裏[①]。

3.2.8 許多發生在"口語"中的音變，如公式〔4〕、〔5〕、〔6〕、〔9〕、〔10〕、〔11〕、〔12〕、〔13〕等所代表者，以及"尖團音"的混同，也都在"讀音"裏發生過，可見這兩種"方音"的關係至爲密切。綜合以上的討論，我們可以仍用原來的一套例字，列表説明"讀音"的特有變化，表中祇列直接有關的音變公式，見上頁。

3.3 我們要討論的第三種入聲演化方式，發生在以徐州爲中心的黄淮地區。就音位系統説，這種方音跟上述兩種完全一樣，因此這種方音的押韻方式與十三轍完全符合，《徐州十三韻》及《滕縣十三韻》便是歷史見證，但就個别字彙的讀法説，這種方音就顯然不同了，這尤其反映在入聲字的讀法上。

3.3.1 這種方音裏，梗曾的混一(公式〔14〕)也發生了，而且發生的時間也像在"讀音"中那麽早，即在公式〔1〕及〔5〕所代表的音變之前，這是與"口語"不同的地方，但是這類入聲字的韻尾/k̂/，後來却像"口語"一樣變/y/了。因此像"或、國、賊、麥、客、白、昔、石"等字，就先變同蟹攝四等字(即韻基變爲/ey/)，然後更進而變向齊微韻了(即韻基變爲/ɨy/，公式〔9〕)。通江宕三攝的入聲字在這種方音值的演化，則是緊隨着"讀音"傳統的，但"讀音" 中公式〔19〕所代表的音變(照二化精)，則未曾發生在這種方音裏，也無從發生，因爲符合限制條件的字音已不存在。"口語"中公式〔8〕所代表的音變，則發生過，但與入聲字無涉。

3.3.2 至於韻尾/p,t,k/在這種方音裏是否也先合併爲/q/(公式〔17〕)然後過了很久才丢掉(公式〔18〕)，這是我們無法推知的，祇好假定它們也走"讀音"的路綫。除了公式〔13〕所代表的音變以外，其他音變也都在這種方音裏發生過，因此就不再討論了。我們現在也仍用同一套例字，列表説明這類入聲字在這種方音裏的演化。在這種方音裏與入聲字無直接關係的音變規律，亦不列入，見下頁。

4. 臻山深咸四攝的入聲字，在自唐迄今的演化中比較簡單得多，而日在

① 對北京人説，注音符號さこせ之分實在是多餘的。趙元任先生曾多次提到這個問題。參看趙1968，第52頁。

例字 演化律	木	六	捉	角	各	樂	黑	色	敕	力	麥	客	摘	尺	錫	
	mwɨk	lywɨk	crak	kak	kok	yak	xɨk̂	srik̂	trhyik̂	lyik̂	mak̂	khak̂	trak̂	crhyak̂	syek̂	
{ɨ, a}→e/__{k̂, ɲ}							xek̂	srek̂	trhyek̂	lyek̂	mek̂	khek̂	trek̂	crhyek̂		
ø→y/G____a				kyak												
a→o/____{k, ŋ}			crok	kyok		yok										
k̂→y/V____							xey	srey	trhyey	lyey	mey	khey	trey	crhyey	syey	
t→c/____r									crhyey				crey			
{o, e}→ɨ/____y							xɨy	srɨy	crhyɨy	lyɨy	mɨy	khɨy	crɨy	crhyɨy	syɨy	
p, t, k→q/V__	mwɨq	lywɨq	croq	kyoq	koq	yoq										
ø→w/{y, c}_o(q) C≠G			crwoq	kywoq		ywoq										
y→ø/yɨ____									crhyɨ	lyɨ				crhyɨ	syɨ	徐州十三韻滕縣十三韻
q→ø/V____	mwɨ	(lyɨw) lywɨ	crwo	kywo	ko	ywo										
y→ø/r									crhɨ					crhɨ		
{o, e}→ə			crwə	kywə	kə	ywə										
華氏音標	mu	(liu) lü	cho chuo	chüeh	ko kê	yüeh	hêi	shêi	ch'ih	li	mêi	k'êi	chêi	ch'ih	hsi	
注音符號	ㄇㄨ	ㄌㄧㄡ	ㄓㄨㄛ	ㄐㄩㄝ	ㄍㄜ	ㄩㄝ	ㄏㄟ	ㄕㄟ	ㄔ	ㄌㄧ	ㄇㄟ	ㄎㄟ	ㄓㄟ	ㄔ	ㄒㄧ	

上述三種方音博統中,除了幾個内轉照二系字以外(見下文4.4),也顯得相當一致,因此没有分開討論的必要。像以上兩章所討論的多數音變一樣,許多影響到這類入聲字的音變,也都是具有一般性的。這些音變産生了許多無可避免的後果,入聲字的改讀衹不過是其中的一小部分而已。

4.1 這類入聲字變爲舒聲的原因當然是韻尾/p、t/的消失。在討論“讀音”時,我們用公式〔17〕及〔18〕表示這種變化,意思是説韻尾/p、t/與/k/一同變爲喉塞音/q/,然後經過相當年代,/q/也終於消失了。因爲没有任何反證,所以我們相信同樣的變化也發生在黄淮方音中。在“口語”方音裏/k̂、k/先已轉變,剩下的/p,t/是直接消失的呢?還是先合併爲/q/然後才消失的呢?這在音理上是頗難推知的,我們衹好假定這種方音也走同樣的道路,也許在“口語”中公式〔18〕發生的時間比另兩種方音要早一些。《中原音韻》的作者周德清在談論入聲有無的問題時,常有自相矛盾的地方①,因此後世的學者常常各據一詞,聚訟紛紜。其實《中原音韻》本身(即“口語”)有無入聲,與《中原音韻》時代有無入聲,本質上是兩回事。周書記録的是“口語”,但他在言談時心理上難免受到“讀音”一派的影響。我們在測定《中原音韻》的音位系統時,應該以他分韻歸字的“做法”爲準繩,不能以他模棱兩可的“説法”爲依據。他的做法顯示其時入聲在“口語”中已不存在了,但這並不排除其前不久韻尾/p,t/先合併爲/q/而後失掉的可能。臻深兩攝的三等開口入聲字(即韻母爲/yɨt/及/yɨp/者,如“日、疾、十、泣”等),都出現在齊微韻裏。爲了解釋這種現象,我們得説在/yɨ/的後面,韻尾/p,t/變爲/y/,但較合理的説法則是/p,t/合併爲/q/以後才有這一轉變。其後不久,餘下的/q/才消失。

$$q \rightarrow y / yi\_\_\_\_ \qquad 〔23〕$$

對“讀音”方音而言,這條公式則是不必要的。

4.2 在韻尾/p、t/合併之前,某些一般性的音變自然也影響到這類入聲字的音讀。我們已對論過的有三、四等的合韻(公式〔4〕),二等喉牙音的細音化

① 周德清在他的凡例上一則説:“音韻無入聲,派入平上去三聲,前輩佳作中間備載明白。”但又説“然呼吸言語之間,還有入聲之别”。唐鉞甚至説,入聲之失乃由於唱戲(見唐1926)。似乎是説要是不唱戲入聲就保留下來了。

(公式〔5〕),知照兩系聲母的合併(公式〔6〕)等。但尚有一項未曾討論過,即三等合口脣音字的輕脣化。脣音之分輕重,在等韻時期已然,亦即遠在入聲字改讀之前。因爲這個變化没有影響到通江宕梗曾各攝入聲字的歸韻,所以我們未早討論。這個音變以介音/yw/(即"三等合口")爲條件,在這種情形下,雙脣音即變爲脣齒塞擦音而失掉介音中的/y/①。因爲這一變化發生在三、四等合韻(公式〔4〕)之前,所以三等合口脣音字就因條件不合而没有變入四等,反而很自然地跟二等字同歸一韻了。在《中原音韻》裏,"番、反、飯、晚"等字入寒山而不入先天,就是這個道理。基於同理,山咸兩攝的脣音三等合口入聲字如"乏、法、發、襪"等,也祇能歸入家麻而不會歸入車遮。脣音分輕重可能跟莊章合併爲照系一樣早,因此我們也不列入公式,祇把介音中的/y/省去就算了。

4.3 另一項影響更廣泛的音變是一二等的合韻。這一演變發生的時間顯然相當晚。在音理上,我們推論其時間當在韻尾/p, t, k/合併爲/q/之後,但在/q/消失之前,因爲/q/是這個音變的條件之一。

$$o \rightarrow a / C\_\_\_E \quad \text{若 } C = G \text{ 則 } E \neq q \qquad 〔24〕$$

這一公式的意思是:外轉一等元音變同二等元音,但附有如下幾個限制條件。

(一) 合口字不變。(故公式中聲母"C"後無/w/。)《中原音韻》的桓歡韻全爲山攝一等合口字,相應的開口字如"寒、干"等,則入寒山韻,就是這個道理。

(二) 韻尾爲零的音節不變。(故公式中韻尾"E"不帶括號。)果攝一等字全入《中原音韻》的歌戈韻,即一等開口字没有進入家麻韻,也就是這個道理。

(三) 喉牙音的入聲字不變。(故公式有附注。)若非入聲,喉牙音字也變,故"干"入寒山,"該"入皆來;若非喉牙音,入聲字也變,故"達、拉"入家麻而不入歌戈;既非喉牙音又非入聲自然得變,故"才"入皆來、"難"入寒山;但若既是

---

① 從音素觀點説,這祇是脣音在$\begin{pmatrix}+\text{pal}\\+\text{lab}\end{pmatrix}$之前變爲塞擦(+aff)而已。用音位符號則不易表明其關鍵所在。

喉牙音又是入聲，則不變，故“割、合”入歌戈而不入家麻[①]。

4.4 韻尾爲/p,t/的入聲字，在本文論及的三種方音中，似乎衹有内轉照二系字（即已失掉介音中之/y/者），顯出分歧的變化。這類字爲數極少，且多僻字，因此常遭忽略或誤解，我們姑且用“瑟、澀”這兩個常用字爲代表，試論這類字的演化。

（一）這兩個字出現在《中原音韻》的支思韻裏。就“口語”的演化規律説，這是天經地義的。這類字既先失去介音/y/，其後韻尾消失，就形成了一個前所未有的韻母/ɨ/，自然該聲入支思韻。有些人不明此理，且見支思韻衹有三個入聲字（“塞”且爲例外），便説支思韻不該有入聲字，這當然是誤解[②]。

（二）在“讀音”中，這兩個字讀/sə/，即與梗曾照二系入聲字同轍（如“色”等）。我們已用公式〔19〕標示後者的非捲舌化，現在這兩個字的變讀似應歸入，但其實可疑，因爲把該公式改爲 $r \rightarrow \emptyset / \_\_\_ \begin{Bmatrix} ɨ \\ e \end{Bmatrix} q$ 在音理上説是相當勉强的；在另一方面説，非入聲的深攝照二系字如“岑、森”等，多數也已變爲精系聲母了，而通攝的“縮”、遇攝的“阻、所”、及流攝的“鄒、搜”等，也顯出同樣的變讀。這一切都表示，在“讀音”傳統中，照二化精是一個相當廣泛而有趣的現象，但這一音變的語音條件尚難確定，須作進一步的研究，我們姑且存而不論，以待後賢。

（三）在黄淮方音中，“瑟、澀”讀/srɨy/，也跟梗曾的照二系入聲相同（“色”亦讀/srɨy/），我們衹能假定這是模擬變化（analogical change）的結果。

4.5 韻尾/q/消失後，這類入聲字自然也得隨着一般舒聲字移轉。通過公式〔12〕及〔22〕所代表的音變，終於變爲今讀。我們選出下面十五個代表字爲例，也用一張表來説明它們的演化過程。爲了簡明，省去公式〔23〕，其他無直接關係的音變也都省去，見下頁。

---

① “割”之類的字，在膠東平度方言裏讀作/ka/，表示在那種方言裏，公式〔24〕没有第三條限制（參看薛 1973，這是很有趣的。同時由於第二及第三兩個限制，以及公式〔5〕的影響，/ka, kha, ha/二個音節在北京話裏變成有聲無字了，這是演化的巧合。有人因此説這三個音節在北京音系裏是不存在的，這就太過分了。我們可以預言，利用這三個音節的新詞彙，將會不斷産生。）

② 參看陸志韋 1946，第 66 頁。

例字／演化律	瑟	質	必	禿	澀	濕	急	欱	辣	掇	甲	劄	髮	劫	貼	
	srɨt	cryɨt	pyɨt	thwɨt	srɨp	sryɨp	kyɨp	xop	lot	twot	kap	trap	fwat	kyap	thyep	
a→e/y(w)														kyep		
ø→y/G___a											kyap					
t→c/___r												crap				
p,t,k→q/V__	srɨq	cryɨq	pyɨq	thwɨq	srɨq	sryɨq	kyɨq	xoq	loq	twoq	kyaq	craq	fwaq	kyeq	thyeq	
o→a/C___E 若C=G則E≠q									laq							
q→ø/V___	srɨ	cryɨ	pyɨ	thwɨ	srɨ	sryɨ	kyɨ	xo	la	two	kya	cra	fwa	kye	thye	中原音韻
y→ø/r		crɨ				srɨ										
$\left\{\begin{matrix}o\\e\end{matrix}\right\}\to ə$								xə		twə				kyə	thyə	
華氏音標	(shih) sê	chih	pi	t'u	(shih) sê	shih	chi	ho hê	la	to tuo	chia	cha	fa	chieh	t'ieh	
注音符號	ㄙㄜ	ㄓ	ㄅㄧ	ㄊㄨ	ㄙㄜ	ㄕ	ㄐㄧ	ㄏㄜ	ㄌㄚ	ㄉㄨㄛ	ㄐㄧㄚ	ㄓㄚ	ㄈㄚ	ㄐㄧㄝ	ㄊㄧㄝ	

瑟:所櫛切;代表臻攝照二系字。

質:之日切;代表臻三知照開口字如“秩、失、實、日”等。

必:卑吉切;代表臻三其他開口字如“一、七、吉、密”等。

秃:他谷切;代表臻攝合口字如“律、骨、卒、出”等。

澀:色立切;代表深攝照二系字。

濕:失入切;代表深三知照系字如“十、執、入、汁”等。

急:居立切;代表深三其他字如“立、揖、集、吸”等。

欱(喝):呼合切;代表山咸一等開口喉牙音字如“葛、渴、合、盍”等。

辣:盧達切;代表山咸一等其他開口字如“達、捺、拉、雜”等。

掇:丁活切;代表山(咸)一等合口字如“末、奪、括、豁”等。

甲:古狎切;代表山咸二等喉牙音開口字如“瞎、軋、夾、恰”等。

劄:竹洽切;代表山咸其他二等字如“插、刮、滑、刷”等。

髮:方伐切;代表山咸輕脣音字如“發、韈、法、乏”等。

劫:居怯切;代表山咸其他三等字如“熱、説、越、業”等。

帖:他協切;代表山咸四等字如“血、結、協、蝶”等。

5. 入聲字變爲舒聲以後,自然不得不各有一個特定的聲調。聲調的轉化是以聲母中的成分爲條件的。像平聲字分成陰陽兩類,就是以聲母中的濁音成分爲條件的。入聲字歸調的有系統記録,最早見於《中原音韻》,即所謂“入派三聲”,也是以聲母成分爲分派條件的。在不同的方音中,入聲字的歸調也有不同的方式,我們仍拿本文討論的三種方音爲例,略論如下。

5.1“口語”的入聲歸調,可以拿《中原音韻》的“入派三聲”爲代表。我們發現在該書中:屬於“入聲作平聲、陽”的都是全濁聲母字(即聲母中含/ɦ/者),如“直及獨白學斜”;屬於“入聲作去聲”的都是次濁聲母字,(我們用“R”作這類聲母的代表符號,即有共振性的 resonants,包括鼻音、邊音、顫音及零聲母。)如“日立木欲虐納肉”等等;屬於“入聲作上聲”的則是其他各類聲母字(全清與次清),如“瑟汁七骨百則脚”等等。我們如用“F^{r}”代表入聲韻母,上述的歸調現象,即可用下面的公式標示出來。“2,3,4”等即表示現代話的第二聲(陽平)、第三聲(上聲)、第四聲(去聲)。

$$F^r \rightarrow \begin{cases} F^2 / \text{ɦ}\_\_\_ \\ F^4 / R\_\_\_ \\ F^3 \end{cases} \qquad [25]$$

需要附帶説明的是:這一音變必然發生在影母消失之後,因爲影母字已被視同喻母字(零聲母,屬"R"類)而讀爲去聲了,如"乙郁厄惡鴨"等。(但平分陰陽時則不然,影母字皆入陰平。)

5.2 黄淮方音中的入聲歸調比較簡單,可用下式標明。

$$F^r \rightarrow \begin{cases} F^2 / \text{ɦ}\_\_\_ \\ F^1 \end{cases}$$

這就是説,全濁聲母入聲字在這種音裏也變陽平,但其他各類聲母字(包括次濁"R"),全都變作陰平了。

5.3 "讀音"的入聲歸調,如以現代標準讀法爲憑,則顯得較爲雜亂。基本上這一式跟"口語"的方式極接近,即全濁聲母字變陽平、次濁聲母字變去聲。但清音聲母字却並不全變上聲,讀入任何一聲的都有相當數目。這是一個很奇特的現象。我覺得這絶不表示在"讀音"中入聲歸調是没有規律的,我相信"讀音"的歸調方式跟"口語"的方式當初是完全相同的,後來由於官話方言的相互影響,才把第三類的字弄亂了。全濁入聲字的歸調,官話方言完全相同,次濁入聲字的歸調,大多數也跟"口語"相同,唯獨清音聲母入聲字(第三類)的歸調,官話方言各行其是。濟南徐州等地作第一聲,成都昆明等地作第二聲,青島及北京("口語")第三聲,蘭州等地作第四聲①。當各地人士群集北京的時候,北京人要保持頭兩類字的讀法是容易的,要保持第三類字的原來讀法就不容易了。另外需要附帶一提的是:全濁聲母入聲字變陽平以後,聲母由濁化清時,没留下任何痕迹(即變全清)。這與舒聲字變陽平不同,後者在化清時留下送氣成分(即變次清)。有些入聲字可從今讀判别出來,"陽平不送氣者"即其一例。

6. 入聲既以成段音位與其他三聲相别,在歷史的演化中,也就造成了許多成段音位上的差異,因此也就造成了複雜的歸韻問題;同時由於入聲字變爲

---

① 参看李榮 1963,第 84 頁及袁家驊 1960,第 28—30 頁。

舒聲,也就有了歸調的問題。在這兩個問題上,本文已經找出了入聲字演化的來龍去脉,另有一些細節就不再討論了。

6.1 我們的分析使我們更加相信,語音的演化是有嚴格的規律的。但有些規律並不明顯;要找出這些規律,就得把許多雜亂的表面現象作個別的定性分析,使它們各歸本位。這就是爲什麼我們必須分別建立"口語"演化律、"讀音"演化律、或其他方音演化律的道理。近年國外有不少學者研究入聲字問題,大概由於不明白上述的道理,常把已經標準化的"口語"讀法(如"白"讀/pay/,"藥"讀/yaw/)及"讀音"讀法(如"客"讀/khə/,"錯"讀/chwə/),雜糅並列,並想據而推求演化的規律,結果當然找不出合理的答案。這是忽略事實空談理論的必然結果。

6.2 我們説過,任何時期標準話的確立,都是許多非語言性的社會因素造成的。"標準"一旦形成以後,不同的方言,尤其是音系原極接近的方音,便有復歸統一的趨勢,因此個別字彙的借讀現象是免不了的。漢語自唐代到現代標準音的演化,一般説來相當規律。我們可以説,北方話的主流在過去千餘年的演化中,雖有一些小波折,但就總體説,一種聚合統一的趨勢,一直是演化的一股巨大力量。入聲字的改讀造成了不少分歧的方音,算是最大的波折,其時適當金元之交,社會政治的紊亂,可能是"口語"未取得"絶對標準"地位的原因,所以到明代便被"讀音"取代了。明清長期大一統的局面,對標準的確立與延續是極有利的,因此不同的方音便又走上同一條演化的道路,因而縮小了它們之間的差距,像公式〔24〕—〔21〕—〔11〕—〔12〕—〔22〕—〔13〕等所代表的音變,都以相同的次序發生在上述三種不同的方音中,便是最好的證據。

6.3 關於入聲字,又常有人提出類似如下的籠統問題:"入聲在元代到底消失了没有?"要回答這樣的問題,我們必須反問,"你問的是哪一種元代方言?"(當時的"口語"已無入聲,"讀音"則有。)同時也得問:"你問的是哪一類入聲?"(我相信即使在"口語"裏,收/p,t/的入聲字變成舒聲的時間也比較晚些。)在另一方面説,現代標準音讀裏,當然有一些字讀法跟我們發掘出來的音律不合,但這並不足以證明這些音律是錯誤的。在人文科學的研究裏,任何理論都免不了有例外,但正如兩位有名的美國語言學家所説①,在提出反例(counterexamples)時,我們必須可以用這些反例推翻原有的理論而代之以新的理論,或將原有的理論作更合理更妥善的修正,否則反例本身是毫無意義的。

6.4 最後我想重複一提的是:本文討論到的多數音變,都非專爲入聲字而設,而是具有一般性的,波及入聲字僅是它們必然效果的一小部分而已。在理論上説,公式的順序應該代表各别時代的語音狀況(這可由韻書的研究加以證實),也可能代表現代方音中的不同形態(比方説,公式〔13〕尚不適用於黄淮方音,而公式〔22〕所代表的音變,在南方官話裏也尚未發生。參看第 535 頁注①)。還是我們與前人在方法與理論上不同的地方。我國的傳統音韻學,在顯示語音中的音位對比關係方面,是極爲高明的,但這個優點衹有從現在的語音理論觀點上才可以看得出來。把傳統的音韻學與最近的語音理論結合起來,我們才可以測定出不同時代的音位系統,並從而清楚地指出不同時代之間的演變。本文的理論就是建立在這二者結合的基礎上的。

參考文獻

上田金次郎　《中古漢語の入聲變遷と北京語の破音の現象》,《中國語學》,1956 年 7 月份,pp.9—18,及 8 月份,pp.16—19。

王　力　《從元音的性質説到中國語的聲調》,《清華學報》第 10 卷第 1 期(1935),pp.157—183。

方　毅　《國音沿革》,臺北商務印書館 1961 年。

平山久雄　《北京話における清入聲舒聲化の條件について》,《中國語學》,1961 年 10 月份(pp.9—12)及 12 月份,pp.6—10。

有坂秀世　《入聲韻尾消失の過程》,《音聲學會報》41 (1936),pp.5—7。

李　榮　《切韻音系》,科學出版社,1956 年。

——　《漢語方言調查手册》,科學出版社,1963 年。

周法高　《説平仄》,《史語所集刊》,第十三本(1948),pp.153—162。

① 參看 Chomsky and Halle 1968, ix.

胡 適 《入聲考》,《胡適文存》,臺北遠東,1953, pp. 311—352。

唐 鉞 《入聲演化和詞曲發達的關係》,《國故新探》,商務印書館,1926, pp. 45—77。

夏承燾 《陽上作去入派三聲説》,《國文月刊》第 68 期(1948),pp. 14—16。

—— 《唐宋詞聲調淺説》,《語文學習》,1958 年 6 月,pp. 18—21。

袁家驊 《漢語方言概要》,文字改革出版社,1960 年。

高本漢 《中國音韻學研究》,臺北商務印書館重印,1962 年。

張世禄 《從日本譯音研究入聲韻尾的變化》,《中山大學語言歷史研究所周刊》第 99 期(1929),pp. 1—11。

—— 《中國音韻學史》,香港泰興重印,1963 年。

張洵如 《北平音系十三轍》,中國大辭典編纂處出版,1937 年。

—— 《北平音系小轍編》,臺北開明書店,1956 年。

陳寅恪 《四聲三問》,《清華學報》第 9 卷第 2 期(1934), pp. 275—288。

陸志韋 《釋中原音韻》,《燕京學報》第 31 期(1946),pp. 35—70。

—— 《記徐孝重訂司馬温公等韻圖經》,《燕京學報》第 32 期(1947),pp. 167—196。

—— 《國語入聲演變小注》,《燕京學報》第 34 期(1948), pp. 21—28, 315。

董同龢 《等韻門法通釋》,《史語所集刊》第十四本(1948),pp. 257—306。

—— 《漢語音韻學》,臺北學生書局,1968 年。

趙蔭棠 《中原音韻研究》,上海商務印書館,1936 年。

—— 《等韻源流》,上海商務印書館,1957 年。

龍宇純 韻鏡校注,臺北藝文印書館,1860 年。

龍果夫 《八思巴字與古漢語》(唐虞譯,羅常培校訂),科學出版社,1959 年。

魏建功 《説轍兒》,《國語周刊》第 103、104 期。

羅常培 《釋内外轉》,《中央研究院歷史語言研究所集刊》第四本第二分(1933), pp. 206—226。

—— 《北京俗曲百種摘韻》,來薰閣重校本,1950 年。

—— 《京劇中的幾個音韻問題》,《羅常培語言學論文集》,中華書局,

1963 年，pp. 157—176。

Chang，Kun："Ancient Chinese Phonology and the Ch'ieh-yün，" *Tsing Hua Journal of Chinese Studies*，series，No. 10(1974)，pp. 61 - 82.

Chao，Yuen Ren：*A Grammar of Spoken Chinese*，Berkeley，California，1968.

Chomsky，Noam and Halle，Morris：*The Sound Pattern of English*，New York，1968.

Forrest，R. A. D.："The Ju-sheng Tone in Pekingese，" *Bulletin of the School of Oriental and African Studies* 13 (1949—51)，pp. 343 - 373.

Hsueh，F. S："The P'ing-tu Dialect as a Variant of Mandarin，" *Tsing Hua Journal of Chinese Studies*，new series，No. 10.1 (1973)，pp. 74 - 89.

——*Phonology of Old Mandarin*，The Hague，1975.

——"Seven Centuries of Rhyming in Chinese Poetry：a linguistic interpretation，" paper presented at the annual meeting of the Chinese Language Teachers Association，New Orleans，1976.

——"Pekingese Phonology Revisited，"paper presented at the Symposium on Chinese Linguistics，Honolulu，1977.

Pulleyblank，E. G.："The Nature of the Middle Chinese，Tones and Their Development to Early Mandarin，" paper prepared at the 10th International Conference on Sino-Tibetan Languages and Linguistics，Washington，1977.

Stimson，Hugh M.："Phonology of the Chung-Yüan Yin-Yün，" *Tsing Hua Journal of Chinese Studies*，new series，No. 3 (1962)，pp. 114 - 159.

——"Ancient Chinese -p，-t，-k Endings in the Peking Dialect，" *Language* 38 (1962)，pp. 376 - 384.

Ting，Pang-hsin：Chinese Phonology of the Wei-Chin Period：*Reconstruction of the Finals as Reflected in Poetry*，Taipei，1975.

Wang，John C. and Hsueh，F. S.："The Lin-ch'i Dialect and its Relation to Mandarin，" *Journal of American Oriental Society* 93.2 (1973)，pp. 136 - 145.

On Dialectal Overlapping as a Cause for the Literary/Colloquial Contrast in Standard Chinese **

0. Abstract

One problem in Modern Standard Chinese is the phenomenon that a sizable number of words have double or even triple readings known as the *literary* vs. *colloquial* readings, without, however, any basic distinction in meaning. How to systematically and logically explain this phenomenon has remained quite a challenge. This paper tries to demonstrate that this seemingly confusing phenomenon is merely a logical and inevitable result of dialectal overlapping. However, its main purpose will be to propose a few theoretical and methodological hypotheses for the study of the interactions among closely related dialects. Basically, it argues that after the standard speech of the Tang dynasty spread into different geographical areas, different sound changes occurred in different areas and different Mandarin dialects thus appeared. A sound change that started in one area naturally had a tendency to spread into another area, and that often helped create an interesting situation, namely, what occurred *first* in Dialect A became *second* to what occurred first in Dialect B, and vice versa. The relative timing consequently might generate different readings in different dialects for those words which could have been affected by both the sound changes involved. Then, due to social, demographical, and political interactions, the

** 中文題爲《方音重疊與標準語文白異讀之形成》，原載《中國境內語言暨語言學》第 1 輯，"中央研究院"歷史語言研究所，1992 年。

closely related dialects were 'synthesized' into a new form of standard speech for the elite class, in which two or more different dialectal readings of the same word were all accepted but labelled as either 讀音 *duyin* 'pronunciation for reading' or 語音 *yuyin* 'pronunciation for speaking'. This form of 'standard speech' prevailed from probably the middle of the Ming dynasty to the immediate pre-modern time.

1. Introduction.

2. The unique nature of the literary/colloquial contrast in Modern Standard Chinese.

3. The merging of the rhymes in the Geng-Zeng and in the Jiang-Dang rhymeclasses that restructured the syllabe-ending system.

4. The palatalization of syllables with a central low vowel and velar initials.

5. The replacement of two types of consonant endings with semivowels.

6. Sociolinguistic factors for the overlapping of the Mandarin dialects and the formation of the standard speech.

1. About ten years ago, in honour of the late Professor Ch'u Wan-li, I wrote a paper on the evolution of the entering-tone words (Hsueh 1978). In that paper, I focused my discussion on the formation of the literary and colloquial readings of the entering-tone words, without fully recognizing the important role of many sociolinguistic factors, particularly the political and cultural ones. Reconsideration of the issues involved has led me to believe that many of the sound change rules discussed there have far broader implications than I realized then. In this paper, I will elaborate on these implications in light of more recent discoveries, both by myself and by others. I will also demonstrate that basically three prominent types of sound changes were involved here, as far as the literary/colloquial contrast is concerned. The first is the coalescence of the rhymes 曾攝 *Zeng-she*. and 梗攝 *Geng-she* into a single rhyme, and the coalescence of 江攝 *Jiang-she* and 宕攝 *Dang-she* into a single rhyme, which probably started in the Loyang-

Kaifeng area but eventually spread to both Nanking and Peking. The second is the palatalization of unrounded syllables with a central low vowel and a velar initial. (In terms of the 等韻 *Dengyun*, "palatalization of the second-division unrounded words with velar initials".) This change probably first occurred in the Peking area before the above-mentioned change from the Loyang-Kaifeng area reached there, but eventually it spread as far as the Nanking area. The third is the replacement of the stop consonant ending with the front semivowel for the entering-tone syllables in both the *Zeng-she* and the *Geng-she*, and the replacement of the ending stop consonant with the back semivowel for the entering-tone syllables in the *Jiang-she* and the *Dang-she*, as well as the 通攝 *Tong-she*, which probably also started from the Peking area before the change from the Loyang-Kaifeng area reached there. However, even though the latter did not spread southwards very far, the former did spread (as far south as Bangpu but short of Nanking) into areas which had been affected by the changes mentioned above. As a result of this intricate situation, quite a number of words acquired different readings in different dialects. Subsequent social and political changes, as well as population movements, primarily during the Ming dynasty, created a new form of standard speech which adopted the Nanking readings for the words affected by the changes mentioned above, in preference to their native Peking readings (some of which were only accepted at random and were called colloquial or 'vulgar' readings.)

2. The phenomenon known as literary/colloquial contrast in reading is a fairly common one among Chinese dialects. For some non-Mandarin dialects such as Amoy, the contrast may almost represent two coexisting sound systems. This is because, at a certain historical period, native speakers of such dialects tried to read the literary works according to the pronunciation of the then standard Chinese, but inevitably with a local accent. This practice often froze in the course of time, giving a large number of words two parallel

readings, the colloquial vs. the literary. For dialects which are more closely related to, and hence share many common readings with, the 'standard speech', such a contrast may involve only a small portion of their vocabulary. In the sense given above, one may wonder why Pekingese, the 'standard form' of Chinese speech, also has a similar phenomenon. The answer is that this 'standard form' of speech was not considered to be 'the standard' by the educated or elite class, especially during the Ming dynasty but even up to very recent times. Hence, more 'elegant' forms of pronunciation had to be adopted into this dialect as 'literary' readings. Fortunately, the dialect or dialects from which the literary readings were adopted are closely related to, and generally share the same basic sound system with, Pekingese. So the number of words that have acquired double or triple readings are relatively small. Moreover, they are mostly former entering-tone words of two different types, namely, those of the *Geng-Zeng* classes of rhymes and those of the *Tong-Jiang-Dang* classes of rhymes. The seventeen types of words in Appendix One represent roughly all possible cases of the literary/colloquial contrast in Pekingese.

3. All the 切韻 *Qieyun* rhymes that were included in the *Zeng-she* and the *Geng-she* of the *Dengyun* books later coalesced, except those with entering-tones, into a single rhyme. This was first recorded as the 庚青 *Geng-Qing* rhyme in the 中原音韻 *Zhongyuan Yinyun* (1324) by 周德清 Zhou Deqing of the Yuan dynasty. However, their coalescence started obviously much earlier than Zhou Deqing's time and the process was a rather complex one. According to Zhou Zumo (1943), words of all rhymes with nasal endings in the *Geng-she* already rhymed together in the Loyang dialect as early as the middle of the Tang dynasty (as reflected in 元結 Yuan Jie's and 元稹 Yuan Zhen's poems), but those of the *Zeng-she* joined the former only during the Song dynasty. In a similar fashion, words of all rhymes with nasal endings in the *Jiang-she* and the *Dang-she* also, according to Zhou Zumo,

rhymed together in the Loyang dialect by the middle of the Tang dynasty, and they were all put into the same rhyme (江陽 *Jiang-yang*) in Zhou Deqing's Zhongyuan Yinyun. How can we most logically explain these phenomena?

3.1. It seems to me that both cases of coalescence mentioned above are probably the result of assimilation. On the basis of my phonemicization of the *Dengyun* sound system (Hsueh 1985), I have proposed to explain the coalescence of the *Jiang-she* and the *Dang-she* with the following sound change rule:

$$a \longrightarrow o / \_\_\_ [C, +velar] \quad (1)$$

This rule means that the central low vowel /a/ became the back low vowel /o/ under the assimilating force of the velar ending /k/ or /ŋ/; namely, the distinction between the *Jiang-she* and the *Dang-she* simply disappeared after this sound change.

3.2 On the same basis, the coalescence of the *Geng-she* and the *Zeng-she* can be logically summarized with the following rule:

$$o, a \longrightarrow e / \_\_\_ [C, +palatal] \quad (2)$$

This rule means that both the back and the central low vowels become the front low vowel /e/ under the assimilating influence of the palatal ending /k̂/ or /ɲ/.① There are, however, two problems. First, most scholars do not yet agree with the proposal that these two rhyme-classes have palatal endings

① Scholars all know that the *Geng-she* and the *Zeng-she* are different from the other rhyme-classes with a velar ending (*Tong*, *Jiang*, *Dang*), but they do not agree as to what the difference is. I tend to agree with Hashimoto who proposed that the syllable ending of the former was probably palatal (Hashimoto 1978—79), because the puzzle as to why there were so many rhyme-classes with the velar ending alone (if that hypothesis were right) would be solved, and, more importantly, it would explain the development of the language more logically and systematically. Note that i use /k̂/ as the symbol for the entering-tone syllable ending, instead of Hashimoto's /c/, but what is really crucial is the concept behind the symbols, not the symbols per se.

(See, for example, Chou 1983 and Ting 1987.) They still believe that rhymes of both the two classes have a velar ending and, hence, try to differentiate them from the rhymes of the *Tong-Jiang-Dang* classes with a large number of 'front-vowel' symbols (thus, making systematic phonemicization impossible), or with some diphthongs, instead of single vowels, as syllable nuclei (thus, breaking the pattern of the traditional Chinese syllable segmentation). For these scholars, a different explanation for the *Geng-Zeng* coalescence would have to be found. Second, and perhaps more seriously for us, Zhou Zumo's study reveals that the rhymes in the *Geng-she* coalesced first, long before the rhymes of the *Zeng-she* joined them in the Song dynasty. Therefore, we must revise the above rule as follows to reflect this historical fact:

$$a \longrightarrow e / \_\_\_ [C, +\text{palatal}] \qquad (2')$$

and claim that this sound change took place as early as the middle of the Tang dynasty, and repeated itself once more early in the Song dynasty, after two other general sound changes had turned the vowel of the syllables of the *Zeng-she* from /o/ to /a/. (They are: $o \longrightarrow a/y\ (w)\_\_\_ (E)$, and $o \longrightarrow a/C\_\_\_E$, where E=[-back] for both rules; see Hsueh 1985 for a detailed discussion). The revision above may seem to be rather cumbersome, but it reflects the historical reality more faithfully and makes the rule simpler and phonetically more believable.

3.3 The inevitable consequences of the changes discussed above are clearly noticeable in all Mandarin dialects. Indeed, we can say that these sound changes marked the beginning of a new era of the Chinese language which was eventually labelled Mandarin Chinese. What is important for us to keep in mind is that these changes started from the Loyang area and probably spread quickly to the Kaifeng area. From Kaifeng, the new capital after the Tang dynasty, these changes acquired a new momentum and spread out even more quickly. Eventually, they covered the whole territory where Mandarin Chinese is now spoken, including Peking and Nanking. However, it would hardly require any special imagination or proof to see that this diffusion must have been a gradual process, like a ripple on a pond, in terms of time and space. Therefore, before these sound changes reached areas beyond the Loyang-Kaifeng district, other sound changes could have already occurred in those places and altered the shape of some syllables in such a way that those syllables could no longer be affected by either or both of these changes, as we shall soon illustrate.

4. Another major phonological feature which helps to mark off the Mandarin dialects from other Chinese dialects is the acquisition of the medial /y/ by a special type of syllable. It involves a large number of words in many rhymes. In terms of *Dengyun* phonology, this is known as the palatalization of the second-division unrounded words under velar initials. On the basis of my phonemicization of the *Dengyun* system, this can again be formulated into a strict rule of sound change as follows (Cf. Hsueh 1982 and 1985):

$$\emptyset \longrightarrow y / G \_\_\_ a \qquad (3)$$

This is a very powerful rule which changes all the velar-initial syllables with the central low vowel /a/ as the nucleus and without a medial, regardless of the form of their ending. In general, this is quite true in all Mandarin dialects, but there are apparently some exceptions. For example, the word 客 /khak̂/ "guest" is pronounced *ke* /khə/ and the word 耕 /kaɲ/ "to plow" is pronounced *geng* /kɨŋ/ in Modern Pekingese. Other examples headed by these two in Appendix One apparently have also changed in the same manner as they have. However, native Pekingese speakers often pronounce these words in a different way. For example, "guest" is *qie* /khyə/ to them, and "to plow" is *jing* /kyɨŋ/ to them. These alternative readings represent exactly what is meant by the literary/colloquial contrast.

4.1 The seemingly exceptional cases mentioned above are all of the unrounded type and belong to the second division of the *Geng-she*. Their colloquial readings indicate that they went through the change symbolized by Rule (3), while their literary forms seem to say that they did not. Are they really exceptions to the sound change rule, or rather, residues from an earlier time? (Cf. Wang 1969.) Probably neither. A more logical explanation could be that when the change represented by Rule (3) was operating in the Loyang-Kaifeng area, the words in question were perhaps no longer qualified to receive input for that rule. In other words, they had been disqualified by an earlier change represented by Rule (2') in 2.2, which we know occurred in the Loyang dialect of middle Tang. Following the same reasoning, we have to say that, when Rule (3) took effect in the "colloquial dialect", wherever it was spoken, the words in question were not yet affected by Rule (2'). Naturally, we want to know when and where the change represented by Rule (3) first started. Since it is such a prominent and prevailing feature for Mandarin Chinese, one might be tempted to say that perhaps it also started in the Loyang-Kaifeng area, but that would force us to say that this change spread out faster than, and hence overtook, the change symbolized by Rule (2'), reaching the "colloquial dialect" area before the latter did, a possible but not probable situation. It more likely started in the "colloquial dialect" before the wave of influence of Rule (2') reached there and its own wave of influence reached the Loyang-Kaifeng area after Rule (2') had taken effect there. We cannot say for sure where the "colloquial dialect" was spoken at that time, except that it must have been somewhere to the north of Loyang and Kaifeng. Peking is a good candidate, but places like Zhengding and Baoding are also possible. Lu Zhiwei, quoted by Shao Rongfen (1981:93), once speculated that the *Zhongyuan Yinyun* was based upon a dialect of the central Hebei area. I do not quite agree with him on that, but it is certainly not illogical to speculate that the Pekingese of the Yuan dynasty, which Zhou Deqing happened to use as the basis for his book, originally came from somewhere to the south of Peking. One thing we know for sure is that Rule (3), which started in the "colloquial dialect", spread in all directions. In the north (all the way to north Manchuria), it was always one step ahead of Rule (2'), but to the south (as far as the Nanking area), the reverse is true.

4.2. Words of the *Jiang-she* all belong to the second division. Those under velar initials obviously went through the change represented by Rule (3) in almost all Mandarin dialects. For example, 江 /kaŋ/ "river" now reads *jiang* /kyaŋ/ and 角 /kak/ "horn" now reads *jue* /kywə/ or *jiao* /kyaw/. (These two different readings also represent an example of the literary/ colloquial contrast, but they are the result of a different type of sound change which will be discussed in Section 5.) This seemingly straightforward matter has nevertheless one important implication. As we have pointed out, the vowel of the *Jiang-she* rhymes shifted from the central low position to the back low position and thus joined the *Dang-she* rhymes as early as the middle of the Tang dynasty (see the discussion in Section 3 and 3.1). Clearly, the change represented by Rule (3) occurred quite early in the history of the Chinese language. When it spread into the Loyang-Kaifeng area, the change represented by Rule (1) obviously had not yet occurred. Therefore, the chronology of the changes discussed so far should be:

Rule (2') — Rule (3) — Rule(1)

for the Loyang-Kaifeng area, or "Central Mandarin". Their order of occurrence in the Peking area, or "Northern Mandarin", should be:

Rule (3) — Rule (2') — Rule(1)

5. The sound changes that generated the largest number of cases of literary/colloquial contrast are those that affected two types of entering-tone words, namely, those of the *Geng-Zeng* rhyme-classes and those of the

Tong-Jiang-Dang rhyme-classes，(Entering-tone words of other rhyme-classes were not involved；see Hsueh 1978). Following are some examples of two types of such contrast：

A) 色 /srok̂/ "color" now reads *se* /sə/ or shai /sray/；

白 /pɦak̂/ "white" now reads *bo* /pə/ or bai /pay/；

客 /khak̂/ "guest" now reads *ke* /khə/ or *qie* /khyə/(*/khyay/)

B) 熟 /srɦywɨk/ "cooked" now reads *shu* /srwɨ/ or shou /srɨw/；

角 /kak/ "horn" now reads jue /kywə/ or *jiao* /kyaw/；

藥 /yok/ "drug" now reads *yue* /ywə/ or *yao* /yaw/.

Note that，in Group (A)，the contrast is between syllables with a zero ending (the literary readings) and syllables with a /y/ ending (the colloquial readings)，while in Group (B)，the contrast is between those with a zero ending (the literary readings) and those with a /w/ ending (the colloquial readings). Furthermore，words in Group (A) are from the *Geng-Zeng* rhymes，while those in Group (B) are from the *Tong-Jiang-Dang* rhymes. My phonemicization of the *Dengyun* sound system makes it possible for us to propose the two following rules as the simplest and most logical explanation for the readings of these words in the "colloquial dialect". The rules mean that，at a certain point of time，the palatal ending /k̂/ was replaced by，or changed to，the front semivowel /y/，and the velar ending /k/ was replaced by，or changed to，the back semivowel /w/. (Of course，this is also one of the major reasons why we believe that words of the *Geng-Zeng* rhymes had a palatal ending and words of the *Tong-Jiang-Dang* rhymes had a velar ending at the *Dengyun* time. This makes good sense phonetically，and also makes it possible for us to define a simple vowel system within the frame of the traditional Chinese syllable segmentation.)

$$\hat{k} \longrightarrow y / V\_\_\_ \quad (4)$$

$$k \longrightarrow w / V\_\_\_ \quad (5)$$

The most straightforward explanation for the literary readings of these words is, of course, that they simply lost their ending at a certain time. However, the situation is not really that simple, as we shall see later (see 5.3).

5.1 One question that may be asked about the two rules just proposed: When did the changes they represent take place? Since we know that the loss of the entering tone in the history of the Chinese language is a relatively late event, we might speculate that these changes could not have occurred too early. But internal evidence implies that Rule (4) must have been enforced in Northern Mandarin at least before the change represented by Rule (2') affected that dialect, because words like 白 /pɦak̂/ "white", 宅 /crɦak̂/ "residence", and 麥 /mak̂/ "wheat" couldn't possibly have acquired their present readings of *bai*, *zhai*, and *mai* respectively, if their nuclear vowel had been changed from /a/ to /e/ by Rule (2') earlier. On the other hand, the reading of /srok̂/ "color" as *shai* suggests that Rule (4) could only have taken place after a minor rule had changed its vowel from back to central (o ⟶ a/r ___ k̂), because otherwise the form */sroy/ would have generated a modern reading like *shei* */sriy/ for this dialect, just as the word 黑 /hok̂/ "black" has become *hei* /hɨy/. It could be that the change represented by Rule (4) did not happen very early in Northern Mandarin, but that the influence of the change represented by Rule (2') reached the area rather late. This speculation would imply that the area must be quite far from Loyang and Kaifeng, making Peking an even more attractive candidate.

5.2 Another question may be asked: Did the two changes occur at the same time? There is no clear internal evidence for us to answer this question either way, but external evidence seems to suggest that the answer should be negative. In practically the whole broad area with Loyang and Kaifeng at the center, including ancient cities such as Xi'an, Xuzhou, Qufu, and Jinan, which can be called the "Central Mandarin" area, words like *bai* "white", *ke* "guest", *mai* "wheat", and *se* "color" are pronounced *bei*, *kei*, *mei* and *shei* respectively (Cf. Beida 1962 for some examples). This means that, when the change represented by Rule (4) spread out from the north into this central area, Rule (2') had already been enforced there. On the other hand, former entering-tone words from the *Tong-Jiang-Dang* rhyme-classes, with a few exceptions like 肉(/rywɨk/) *rou* /rɨw/ "meat" and 六(/lywɨk/) *liu* /lyɨw/ "six", are pronounced as syllables with zero ending (i.e., in the "literary" way) in this area. This seems to indicate that Rule (4) occurred much earlier in time, and spread much farther to the south, than Rule(5)did. ①

5.3 As we have said, though the most straightforward explanation for the literary readings of the types of words discussed above seems to be that they simply lost their consonant ending, the real situation is far more complex. This form of reading originally came front the speech of the Loyang-Kaifeng area, or Central Mandarin, which was the most prestigious form of Chinese up to the end of the Song dynasty or the Jin kingdom. Most of the major sound innovations started from this area and spread out to other areas. One change that caused the third division rhymes to merge into those of the fourth division (a ⟶ e/y(w)____) must have occurred quite early. In fact, it must have been before the change effected by Rule (3). Another change that caused most of the first division unrounded words to merge with those of the second division (o ⟶ a/C____E, where E-[-back]) must have occurred fairly late, and definitely occurred after the change effected by Rule (3). (See Hsueh 1975:56—58 for arguments on the order of the rules presented here.) Both changes must have also started from the central area and later spread to all Mandarin areas, creating no cases for the literary/

① Though no documented information is available, my visit to the city of Bangpu a few years ago makes me believe that this form of Mandarin is spoken there, that is, the sound change under discussion has reached that area by now. But it is doubtful that the change had spread that far by the beginning of the Ming dynasty, because otherwise the founder of the Ming dynasty, a native of Fengyang close to Bangpu, might have made Central Mandarin the standard speech.

colloquial contrast. The changes represented by Rule (2') and Rule (1) in effect constitute a restructuring of the sound system, in that they jointly eliminate the phonemic contrast between the palatal and the velar endings (because, as a result of these changes, the former occurs only after the front low vowel, and the latter occurs only after the back low vowel). Phonetically, the palatal endings must have remained for a while and triggered the rising of the front low vowel to join the high vowel, causing the coalescence of some rhymes. Interestingly, after the *Zhongyuan Yinyun*, the merging of the *Gengqing* rhyme was with the 東鍾 *Dongzhong* rhyme in the north, as every Pekingese speaker can verify, but with the 真文 *Zhenwen* rhyme in the south, as is reflected in the rhyming practice of the so-called 'Peking Opera' which we all know originated from eastern Hubei and southern Anhui (see Yu 1972:11). (This can perhaps be taken as a piece of evidence for the argument that the syllable ending of the *Geng-Zeng* rhymes was something between the alveolar and the velar, i.e., the palatal, because when merging with another nasal, it went in either direction.) The rising of the front low vowel before the palatal /$\hat{k}$/ at first occurred in palatalized syllables only (e ⟶ ɨ/y(w)____$\hat{k}$, see Hsueh 1978), for only these types of words were included in the 齊微 *Qiwei* rhyme, while their counterparts in the 山攝 *Shan-she* and the 咸攝 *Xian-she* were included in the 車遮 *Chezhe* rhyme, of the *Zhongyuan Yinyun*. After having served as a conditioning factor for the above change, /$\hat{k}$/ changed to /y/ in Central Mandarin, obviously under the influence of Northern Mandarin, but, in Southern Mandarin, it joined the other three endings /p, t, k/ in becoming a glottal stop (p, t, $\hat{k}$, k ⟶ q/V____), which basically served as a marker for the entering tone. Thus, roughly by the end of the Song dynasty, there existed three major types of Mandarin: Northern Mandarin of the Peking area which was distinctly marked by the features called "colloquial" by later generations, Southern Mandarin of the Nanking-Yangzhou area which was distinguished by its retention of the entering tone and many of the "literary" features, as the later generations called them, and Central Mandarin of the greater Loyang-Kaifeng area which possessed most of the "literary" features and, for a while, maintained the entering tone for those words from the 臻 *Zhen*, 深 *Shen*, *Tong*, *Shan Xian*, and *Jiang-Dang* rhyme-classes (i. e., those syllables originally with /p, t/ or /k/ as ending), but changed those entering-tone words of the *Geng-Zeng* rhymes into syllables with /y/ as ending (see 5.2). Resulting from the split of the standard speech of the Tang dynasty of the Loyang area, the three Mandarin dialects shared the same syllable pattern, the same vowel system, and roughly the same inventory of initials. Therefore, mutual borrowing among them could easily occur and was very common. New innovations, of course, continued to occur within each of them, and they have become perhaps a little more distinct from each other now than they were before. Their differences can perhaps be best illustrated by the following tables to show how the groups of crucial example words in Appendix One have acquired their present readings.

Order of the sound changes in Northern Mandarin that eventually led to the 'colloquial' reading in Modern Pekingese.

例字 / 演化律	木 mwɨk	六 lywɨk	捉 crak	角 kak	各 kok	藥 yok	黑 xok̂	色 srok̂	敕 trhyok̂	力 lyok̂	麥 mak̂	客 khak̂	摘 trak̂	尺 crhyak̂	錫 syek̂	耕 kaɲ	江 kaŋ	
o→a/{r, y}__k̂								srak̂	trhyak̂	lyak̂								
a→e/y(w)__									trhyek̂	lyek̂				crhyek̂				
(3) ø→y/G__a				kyak								khyak̂				kyaɲ	kyaŋ	
(4) k̂→y/v__							xoy	sray	trhyey	lyey	may	khyay	tray	crhyey	syey			
(2') a→e/__ɲ																kyeɲ		
a→o/__{k, ŋ}			crok	kyok												(kyeŋ)	kyoŋ	
k→w/V__	mwɨw	lywɨw	crow	kyow	kow													
(1) t→c/__r									crhyɨy				cray					
(5) w→ø/y__ɨw		lyɨw																
w→ø/wɨ__	mwɨ																	
{o, e}→ɨ__y							xɨy		crhyɨy	lyɨy				crhyɨy	syɨy			
	魚模	尤侯	蕭豪	蕭豪	蕭豪	蕭豪	齊微	皆來	齊微	齊微	皆來	皆來	皆來	齊微	齊微	庚青	江陽	中原音韻
y→ø/yɨ—									crhyɨ	lyɨ				crhyɨ	syɨ			
y→ø/r__									crhɨ					crhɨ				
ay→e/y—												khye				(kyɨŋ)	(kyaŋ)	
	姑蘇	油求	遥條	遙條	遙條	遙條	灰堆	懷來	一七	一七	懷來	乜斜	懷來	一七	一七	東中	江陽	十三轍
拼音音標	mu	liu	zhao	jiao	gao	yao	hei	shai	chi	li	mai	qie	zhai	chi	xi	jing	jiang	
注音符號	ㄇㄨ	ㄌㄧㄡ	ㄓㄠ	ㄐㄧㄠ	ㄍㄠ	ㄧㄠ	ㄏㄟ	ㄕㄞ	ㄔ	ㄌㄧ	ㄇㄞ	ㄑㄧㄝ	ㄓㄞ	ㄔ	ㄒㄧ	ㄐㄧㄥ	ㄐㄧㄤ	

(Table One)

Order of the sound changes in Northern Mandarin that eventually led to the 'literary' reading in Modern Pekingese. Rules above the double line may be those that occurred in the Nanking dialect before the Ming dynasty, but those under the double line are clearly new innovations that occurred after that variation of Southern Mandarin had been incorporated into Northern Mandarin, possibly under the influence of Central Mandarin.

例字 / 演化律	木 mwɨk	六 lywɨk	捉 crak	角 kak	各 kok	藥 yok	黑 xok̂	色 srok̂	敕 trhyok̂	力 lyok̂	麥 mak̂	客 khak̂	摘 trak̂	尺 crhyak̂	錫 syek̂	耕 kaɲ	江 kaŋ	
o→a/{r, y}__k̂								srak̂	trhyak̂	lyak̂								
(2') a→e/__{k̂, ɲ}								srek̂	trhyek̂	lyek̂	mek̂	khek̂	trek̂	crhyek̂				
(3) ø→y/G__a				kyak								khyak̂				keɲ	kyaŋ	
(1) a→o/__{k, ŋ}			crok	kyok												(keŋ)	kyoŋ	
e→ɨ/y__k̂									trhyɨk̂	lyɨk̂				crhyɨk̂	syɨk̂			
t→c/__r									crhyɨk				crek	(crhyɨk)	(syɨk)			
p, t, k→q/V__	mwɨq	lywɨq	croq	kyoq	koq	yoq	xoq	sreq	crhyɨq	lyɨq	meq	kheq	creq	crhyɨq	syɨq			
r→ø/__eq								seq					ceq					
ø→w/{y, C}__o(q) C≠G			crwoq	kywoq		ywoq												相當於洪武正韻時代
q→ø/v__	mwɨ	(lwɨ) lywɨ	crwo	kywo	ko	ywo	xo	se	crhyɨ	lyɨ	me	khe	ce	crhyɨ	syɨ			相當於十三轍時代
y→ø/r__									crhɨ					crhɨ				
{o, e}→ə			crwə	kywə	kə	ywə	xo	sə			mə	khə	cə			(kiŋ)	(kyaŋ)	
拼音音標	mu	(liu) lu	zhuo	jue	ge	yue	hê	sêi	chi	li	mo	ke	ze	chi	xi	geng	jiang	
注音符號	ㄇㄨ	ㄌㄨ	ㄓㄨㄛ	ㄐㄩㄝ	ㄍㄜ	ㄩㄝ	ㄏㄜ	ㄙㄜ	ㄔ	ㄌㄧ	ㄇㄞ	ㄎㄜ	ㄗㄜ	ㄔ	ㄒㄧ	ㄍㄥ	ㄐㄧㄤ	

(Table Two)

Order of the sound changes in Central Mandarin that led to its present-day Xuzou version. Note that this order is identical to that of Southern Mandarin in its earlier stage, showing that Southern Mandarin was a relatively late off-shoot of Central Mandarin.

例字 / 演化律	木 mwɨk	六 lywɨk	捉 crak	角 kak	各 kok	藥 yok	黑 xok̂	色 srok̂	敕 trhyok̂	力 lyok̂	麥 mak̂	客 khak̂	摘 trak̂	尺 crhyak̂	錫 syek̂	耕 kaɲ	江 kaŋ	
o→a/{r, y}__k̂								srak̂	trhyak̂	lyak̂								
(2') a→e/__{k̂, ɲ}								srek̂	trhyek̂	lyek̂	mek̂	khek̂	trek̂	crhyek̂		keɲ		
(3) ø→y/G__a				kyak													kyaŋ	
(1) a→o/__{k, ŋ}			crok	kyok		yok										(keŋ)	kyoŋ	
(4) k̂→y/v__							xoy	srey	trhyey	lyey	mey	lyey	trey	crhyey	syey			
t→c/__r									crhyey				crey					
{o, e}→ɨ/__y							xɨy	srɨy	crhyɨy	lyɨy	mɨy	khɨy	crɨy	crhyɨy	syɨy			
p, t, k→q/V__	mwɨq	lywɨq	croq	kyoq	koq	yoq												相當於《中原音韻》時代
ø→w/{y, C}__o(q) C≠G			crwoq	kywoq		ywoq												
y→ø/yɨ__									crhyɨ	lyɨ				crhyɨ	syɨ			
q→ø/V__	mwɨ	(lwɨ) lywɨ	crwo	kywo	ko	ywo												徐州十三韻 滕縣十三韻
y→ø/r__									crhɨ					crhɨ				
{o, e}→ə			crwə	kywə	kə	ywə										(kɨŋ)	(kyaŋ)	
拼音音標	mu	liu	zhuo	jue	ke	yue	hei	shei	chi	li	mei	kei	zhei	Chi	xi	geng	jiang	
注音符號	ㄇㄨ	ㄌㄧㄡ	ㄓㄨㄛ	ㄐㄩㄝ	ㄍㄜ	ㄩㄝ	ㄏㄟ	ㄕㄟ	ㄔ	ㄌㄧ	ㄇㄟ	ㄎㄟ	ㄓㄟ	ㄔ	ㄒㄧ	ㄍㄥ	ㄐㄧㄤ	

(Table Three)

These tables are adopted from Hsueh 1978, but have been drastically revised to show my present view. For discussions on minor and post-*Zhongyuan Yinyun* changes, please see Hsueh 1975, 1978, 1982, and 1986. A map is included at the end of this paper (Appendix Two) to show roughly the area where Central Mandarin is spoken. More careful field work will have to be done before the border lines can be drawn with any precision①. It seems to me that, together with the eastward movement of the political and economical centers, Mandarin Chinese also began to fan out from Loyang eastwards and then spread out both northwards and southwards.

6. If Chinese history had developed along a somewhat more regular course, Central Mandarin, we can imagine, would have remained as the standard form of the Chinese language. But life has never been that simple. After the Song dynasty and for the first time, China was completely conquered and ruled by a non-Chinese speaking people who did not care much about intellectual life in general, and even less about the Chinese linguistic tradition (at least in the beginning). Kublai Khan chose Peking as his capital, away from the heartland of the Chinese civilization. The new government suspended the civil examinations for many years, to the dismay of the Chinese literati, and even proclaimed that Mongolian was the "National Language". All these factors made it very difficult to sustain the old norms or standards. Meanwhile, Peking, the capital of this new large empire, naturally began to flourish and became the new cultural center. A new vernacular type of poetry, 元曲 *Yuan Qu*, appeared and became popular in this area in the form of the 雜劇 *ZaJu* "theatrical plays". It was naturally

① Admittedly, what I did here is merely guesswork based on my own observation but supplemented by Beida 1962. It is unfortunate that Beida 1962 does not include more key locations in this area, not even Loyang and Kaifeng. (It seems the book merely chooses some big cities at random, without considering their historical and, hence, linguistical significance.)

based upon the local dialect, namely, Northern Mandarin as described above, which helped make it the unofficial but de facto standard Chinese speech which was very carefully recorded by Zhou Deqing in his *Zhongyuan Yinyun*. The always tradition-minded literati did not, of course, give up easily. This is reflected by the many questions they raised about the book, concerning the appropriateness in its classification of the words and rhymes, and the location of its dialect base, as well as by the sometimes self-contradicting concessions Zhou Deqing made to his critics about the language he recorded. (For more information on the book and related issues, see Stimson 1966, 1977, 1978, Hsueh 1975, Yang Naisi 1981, Li 1983, Ning 1985, etc.). It seems that although for a while during the Yuan dynasty, Northern Mandarin almost replaced Central Mandarin as the standard form of Chinese speech, it was never really fully established as such.

6.1. Central Mandarin never regained its status as the standard form of speech, either, even after the Mongols had been driven out. The founder of the Ming dynasty and most of his followers were from the Nanking area and, hence, speakers of Southern Mandarin. Nanking was chosen to be the capital of the new empire and, naturally, Southern Mandarin became the new standard speech form. By the order of the emperor, a new rhyme dictionary, the 洪武正韻 *Hongwu Zhengyun* (1375), was compiled to be the official standard reference (Cf. Ch'oe 1975 and Chou 1989). Even after the capital was moved to Peking about thirty years later, this form of speech continued to be the official standard. Thus, when Matteo Ricci and other missionaries from Europe tried to learn spoken Chinese, even during the later years of the Ming dynasty, they often chose to study it with a native speaker of the Nanking dialect (Cf. Lu 1985 and Yang 1986). Similarly, the Korean textbooks and reference works on the Chinese language of that period of time paid meticulous attention to the *Hongwu Zhengyun*, and only later began to include some Northern Mandarin features (Cf. Kang 1985, Ting 1987 and

Kim 1989). It seems to me that, when this form of speech was transplanted to Peking, it inevitably had to adjust to the local pronunciation and drop its entering tone marker /q/.

6.2. The transplanted and modified form of the Nanking dialect as the standard must have been well received by the educated class, and hence well established, in later Ming, so much so that even the Manchus, who were already speakers of Northen Mandarin before they moved into Peking (Cf. Lin 1987), couldn't, or did not bother to, change that situation. If anything, this Ming practice was further reinforced during the Qing dynasty through the government's emphasis on classical education and civil examination. The readings that originated from Southern Mandarin were considered to be more elegant and 'literary', and they increasingly replaced or obscured their Northern Mandarin counterparts. For example, even the "banner people", the most typical of native Pekingese speakers now, rarely pronounce 竹 *zhu* "bamboo", 錯 *cuo* "incorrect", 國 "state" and 策 *ce* "policy" as *zhou*, *cao*, *gui*, and *chai*, respectively, though sound change rules in Northern Mandarin did generate such readings, and they were recorded as such in the *Zhongyuan Yinyun*.

6.3. What makes this large scale of incorporation of Southern Mandarin readings into Northern Mandarin so easy and smooth is, as we said before, that the two dialects basically share the same sound system, except for the retention of the entering tone by the former. Consequently, the different readings for a certain word generated in the former is often merely an already existing syllable embedded well within the phonological system of the latter, rather than a new phonemic form. In the case of the entering-tone readings in the former, the ending was simply dropped, sometimes with a minor vowel adjustment, when such readings were adapted into the latter. There are, however, quite a few sociolinguistic reasons why the southern forms were preferred. The first was political, at least in the beginning. When the

Hongwu Zhengyun was decreed by the first emperor as the standard for the Ming dynasty, no rulers or ministers after him would even dare to suggest otherwise. Second, aside from the moving of a large number of aristocrats and other officials from Nanking to Peking during the early Ming dynasty, there were also several later occasions of forced population movement from the Central and Southern Mandarin areas to the Peking area (Cf. Chou 1989), in addition to spontaneous migration. This demographical change must have greatly altered the composition of the population in the Peking area, making the Southern or Central way of speaking more acceptable. Third, and perhaps most importantly, the inertia of the tradition was just too powerful. On the surface, it might seem that "standard speech" can change from time to time, and has changed two times after the Song dynasty. But note that these changes were made within the Mandarin Chinese area only. To replace it with the Yue, Min, or even Wu dialect as the standard would definitely be impossible. On the other hand, the entering tone was a most prominent feature in Chinese poetics. Literary scholars simply could not bear the thought that their language no longer had that tone. Some scholars from areas where the entering tone had definitely disappeared insisted nevertheless that they still had it and that their dialect was not 'inferior' to any other for that matter. (See Geng 1988 for many funny examples of this kind.) Among the three Mandarin dialects we discussed above, clearly, only Southern Mandarin had the potential to accomodate this problem. Blessed by the first emperor's decree, scholars earnestly advocated the superiority of that form of speech and forcefully promoted it.

6.4 3 The phenomenon described above may serve as an example of dialectal overlapping. Southern Mandarin was totally put on top of Northern and Central Mandarin to form an "idcalized" literary language. This "artificial" language, as some people might call it, adopted the phonemic forms generated in Southern Mandarin for most of the words by which the three dialects are differentiated, but it allowed alternative readings for many of these words and thus created many cases of literary/colloquial contrast. This was the language that has been taught in school since the Ming dynasty, exerting so great an influence that many of the colloquial readings have been forgotten even by many typical native speakers of Northern Mandarin. In terms of phonetical realization, however, it eventually went along with Pekingese, though, technically, it could have been just about any other Mandarin dialect. Still, this is not the type of language one is likely to hear spoken by "the man on the street" in Peking. More recently, perhaps under the influence of American anthropological linguists who often insist on studying any language (except English, perhaps) the way they did the languages of American Indian or African tribes, questions are occasionally raised about this form of Chinese as to whether it can be considered a "real and living" language. Some Chinese scholars seem to have also begun to feel that they must study the "real" Pekingese and thus regard the language the "banner people" speak as the standard, though it used to be despised even very recently (Cf. Dong 1974). This new trend may possibly lead to a reassertion of the colloquial forms, many of which might be revived and reestablished as, indeed, the standard readings①.

① Personally, I feel the literary form of Modern Chinese is a very real one which continues to be, and should be, the standard form of *Guoyu* or *Putonghua*. Therefore, I call it "Modern Standard Chinese", while using the term "Pekingese" for the local speech of Peking. In a paper I presented less than two years ago (Hsueh 1988), I quoted Professors Lu Guoyao (Lu 1985) and Paul Yang (Yang 1986) as saying that Modern Standard Pekingese originated from Nanking. Professor Yang recently told me in a letter that he means only that the Nanking dialect was the standard form of speech during the Ming dynasty, not that Modern Pekingese came from Nanking. I would like to apologize here to Professor Yang for the misquote, but I also wish to see that he will soon come around to see the corollary I have drawn from his discovery.

REFERENCES

Beida

1962 北京大學中文系:《漢語方音字彙》,文字改革出版社,北京。

Chang, Kun: "Phonological Aspects of Chinese Dialectology",《清華學報》n. s. 9.1, 2 (1971), 192—215.

Ch'oe

1975 崔玲愛:《洪武正韻研究》,臺灣大學中文研究所博士論文。

Chou, Fa-Kao

"On the Structure of Rime Tables in the Yun-ching,"《史語所集刊》54.1 (1983), 169—186.

Chou, Shizhen

Hongwu Zhengyun: Its Relation to the Nanjing Dialect and its Impact on Standard Mandarin, Ph. D. dissertation (1989), The Ohio State University, Columbus, Ohio.

Dong

1974 董同龢:《國語與北平話》,丁邦新編:《董同龢先生語言學論文選集》,臺北,1974,367—369。

Geng

1988 耿振生:《近代漢語等韻學研究》,北京大學博士研究生學位論文。

Hashimoto, Mantaro: Phonology of Ancient Chinese, Tokyo, 1978—79.

Hsueh, F. S.: Phonology of Old Mandarin, The Hague, Mouton, 1975.

1978 薛鳳生:《論入聲字之演化規律》,《屈萬里先生七秩榮慶論文集》,臺北聯經出版社,1978,407—433。

1980a "The Phonemic Structure of Pekingese Finals and their R-Suffixation,"《史語所集刊》51.3 (1980), 491—514.

1980b 《論支思韻的形成與演進》,《中國書目季刊》第十四卷第二期(1980),53—75。

1982 《論音變與音位結構的關係》,《語言研究》1982 年第 2 期,11—17。

1985 《試論等韻學之原理與内外轉之含義》,《語言研究》1985 年第 1

期,38—56。

1986 《北京音系解析》,北京語言學院出版社,1986 年。

1988 《什麽是"標準國語"?》,第二届世界華文教學研討會,臺北,December,1988。

Kang

1985 康寔鎮:《老乞大、樸通事研究》,臺灣師範大學國文研究所博士論文。

Kim, Youngman: Middle Mandarin Phonology: A Study Based on Korean Data, Ph. D. dissertation (1989), The Ohio State University, Columbus, Ohio.

Li

1983 李新魁《〈中原音韻〉音系研究》,中州書畫社,1983。

Lin

1987 林燾:《北京官話溯源》,《中國語文》1987 年第 3 期,161—169。

Lu

1985 魯國堯:《明代官話及其基礎方言問題》,《南京大學學報》1985 年第 4 期。

Ning

1985 寧繼福:《中原音韻表稿》,吉林文史出版社。

Pulleyblank, E. G: *Middle Chinese: A Study in Historical Phonology*, UBC Press, Vancouver, 1984.

Shao

1981 邵榮芬:《中原雅音研究》,齊魯書社。

Stimson, Hugh: *The Jongyuan In Yunn: A Guide to Old Mandarin Pronunciation*, Yale Far Eastern Publications, New Haven, 1966.

"Review of F. S. Hsueh's *Phonology of Old Mandarin*," *Language* 53 (1977), 940 - 944.

"Old Mandarin Dialects, Old Mandarin, Old Pekingese, and the Rhymes of the *Zhongyuan Yinyun*," Proceedings of Symposium on Chinese

Linguistics, 1977 Linguistic Institute of the Linguistic Society of America, Student Book Co., Taipei, 1978, 221 - 232.

Ting

1982 丁邦新:《漢語方言區分的條件》,《慶祝李方桂先生八十歲論文集》,《清華學報》新 14 卷第 1、2 期:257—273。

1987 《論官話方言研究中的幾個問題》,《史語所集刊》58.4, 809—841。

Wang, William S-Y: "Competing Changes as Cause of Residue," *Language* 45 (1969), 9 - 25.

Yang Naisi

1981 楊耐思:《中原音韻音系》,中國社會科學出版社。

Yang, Paul: "A Southern Mandarin Dialect of the Ming Dynasty as Reflected in Matteo Ricci's Portuguese-Chinese Dictionary," paper presented at the 19th International Conference on Sino-Tibetan Languages and Linguistics, Columbus, Ohio, 1986.

Yuan

1960 袁家驊:《漢語方言概要》,文字改革出版社。

Yu

1972 余濱生:《國劇音韻及唱念法研究》,臺北中華書局。

Zhan

1981 詹伯慧:《現代漢語方言》,湖北人民出版社。

Zhou

1943 周祖謨:《宋代汴洛語音考》,《輔仁學志》12:221—285;又見《問學集》581—655。

APPENDIX ONE

Seventeen types of words that have been differently affected by the 'literary' and the 'colloquial' developments.

木:莫卜切;代表通一入聲如"獨、哭、速、禄"等。
六:力竹切;代表通三入聲如"粥、熟、肉、竹"等。
角:古岳切;代表江喉牙入聲如"岳、覺、學、確"等。
捉:側角切;代表江非喉牙入聲如"濁、剥、朔、犖"等。
各:古落切;代表宕一入聲如"莫、鐸、錯、落"等。
藥:以灼切;代表宕三入聲如"著、脚、杓、弱"等。
黑:呼北切;代表曾一入聲如"北、得、賊、國"等。
色:所力切;代表曾照二入聲如"測、仄、嗇、骰"等。
敕:恥力切;代表曾三知照系入聲如"直、陟、食、織"等。
力:林直切;代表曾三其他入聲如"逼、殛、息、憶"等。
摘:陟革切;代表梗二知照系入聲如"窄、宅、策、擇"等。
客:苦格切;代表梗二喉牙入聲如"革、隔、嚇、額"等。
麥:莫獲切;代表梗二其他入聲如"白、百、擲、脉"等。
尺:昌石切;代表梗三知照系入聲如"擲、石、隻、釋"等。
錫:先積切;代表梗三其他及梗四入聲如"狄、覓、昔、績"等。
耕:古莖切;代表梗二喉牙非入聲如"更、行、坑、幸"等。
江:古雙切;代表江喉牙入非聲如"虹、腔、講、巷"等。

APPENDIX TWO

Shady portion in the center represents roughly the area where Central Mandarin is spoken.

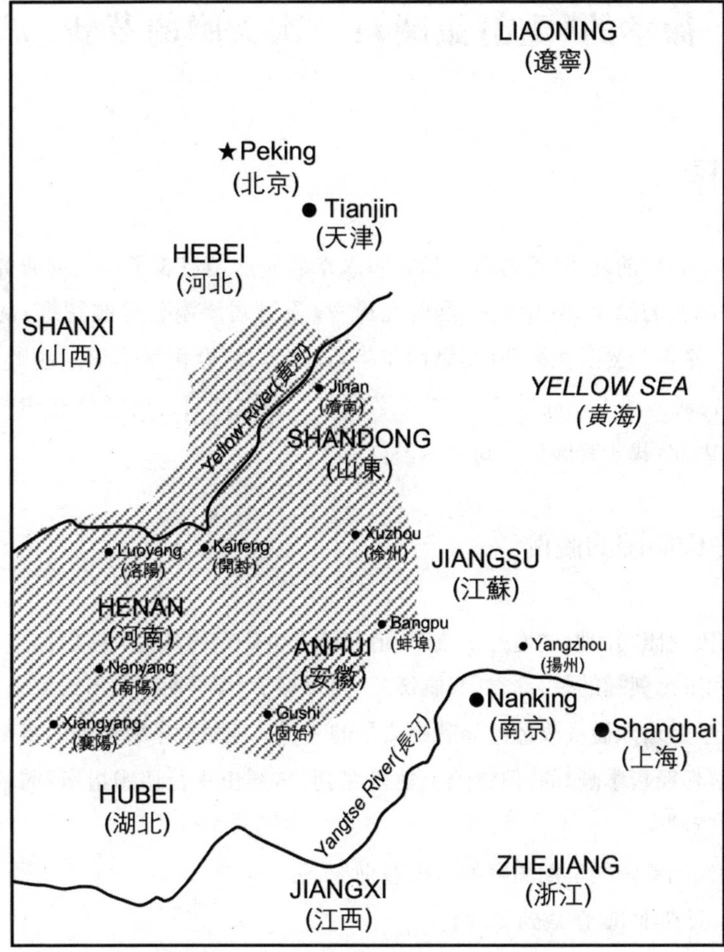

徐孝的《重訂韻圖》:一次大膽的革新*

一、引言

三十多年前,已故著名語言學家陸志韋教授連續發表了一系列研究宋代以後的韻書的論文,其中之一是研究徐孝《重訂司馬温公等韻圖經》的(陸,1947)。徐書刊於明代後期(萬曆丙午年,1606),爲《合併字學篇韻便覽》之一種。此書流傳極少,所以陸先生覺得必須將原書隨同自己的考釋和構擬一起發表。因此,我才有機會見到這本書。

二、徐氏韻圖的體例

徐氏對韻圖的形式進行了改革,這與陸先生研究的其他大多數韻書不同。然而,我最感興趣的是,徐書同《韻鏡》、《四聲等子》等早期韻圖形式完全不同,而且似乎是這類徹底改造的韻圖中最早的一種。雖然徐孝聲稱他的書是依仿司馬光《切韻指掌圖》的,但實際上他是在劉鑒《經史正音切韻指南》的基礎上進行改革的①。

徐氏的韻圖同早期韻圖的重要區别如下:

1) 聲紐從 36 個減到 22 個。

2) 改變傳統的四等爲新的三等,其中中等字極少。

---

* 原載《音韻學研究通訊》1985 年第七期,收入《漢語音韻史十講》。
本文原是提交第十四屆"國際"漢藏語言學術研討會(1983 年,臺北)的論文,題爲 Xu Xiao's Revised Rhyme Tables: a Bold Renovation,俞真譯爲中文。

① 有兩件事使我産生這個想法。第一,同《指南》相同,徐使用"攝"這個術語,但《指掌圖》全然不用。其次,《指掌圖》將 36 個聲母横列一排,而徐却同《指南》一樣,將照組和精組、輕脣和重脣合成一行。

3）將平上去入改爲平上去如,“凡例”説:“設如聲者,謂如平聲也。”①

徐氏還將劉鑒的16攝減爲13攝,其排列如下:

	開口	合口		開口	合口
	平上去如	平上去如		平上去如	平上去如
通:	登等贈能	東董動同	假:	他打納拿	誇把駡麻
止:	資子次慈	居舉句局	拙:	遮者哲宅	靴抽厥掘
祝:		都睹杜獨	臻:	根詪恨痕	昏惛混渾
蟹:	哈海亥孩	乖拐怪槐	山:	干敢炭談	湍疃彖團
壘:	杯壘類雷	灰悔會回	宕:	當黨揚唐	光廣晃黄
效:	蒿好皓豪	包保泡袍	流:	齁吼厚侯	捊剖歆裒
果:	訶啵賀何	多朵惰奪			

現在,我們可以從音位學的角度來討論徐孝的改革,以探討他這樣做的音位學上的理由。這樣,對現代北京話的歷史,我們就能獲得更多的瞭解。

三、聲母系統

徐氏對聲母的縮減和調整,有下列幾點值得注意。

3.1 從邵雍《皇極經世聲音唱和圖》和周德清《中原音韻》等一些宋元資料中,我們可以發現中古全濁聲母消失的痕迹。徐氏的革新韻圖,則非常明確地反映了這個事實。在韻圖中,他采用的聲母代表字,同以前正統的韻圖一樣,但却略去濁聲母並/pɦ/,定/tɦ/,從/cɦ/,牀/crɦ/,邪/sɦ/,群/kɦ/,匣/xɦ/。

3.2 除了標示/s/的心母外,徐氏還列出了另一個白字加框的[心]母,他在凡例中説這個聲母是與“剛”音/s/相配的“柔”音,分别同稔/r/和審/sr/兩個捲舌聲母相配。顯然,[心]母就必須構擬爲/z/。從嚴格的音位學觀點來看,設置這個聲母是完全没有必要的,因爲連徐氏本人也承認這個聲母在他的方言中並不存在,而祇在吴楚等一些南方方言中才有。但是,祇要我們關心方言的比較研究,我們就會承認徐氏的做法不僅是可以理解的,而且是值得稱許的。我

① 徐氏《凡例》説:“復考音義以别剛柔,惟心母脱一柔音,見居吴楚之方,予以□字添心字在内爲母。”徐氏以爲審是剛母,稔是柔母。

們都知道,北京話有兩組噝音聲母[ʦ,ʦʻ,s]和[ʈʂ,ʈʂʻ,ʂ,ʐ],在很多南方方言裹合併了。我曾將這兩組聲母分别歸納音位爲/c,ch,s/和/cr,crh,sr,r/(見薛1980a)。在此基礎上,這種合併就可以很容易地解釋爲捲舌化消失的結果。但是,在我們的音位描寫中還存在一個問題:爲什麽在合併之後,還出現了聲母/r/?在南方方言裹有没有這個聲母的字,如日,人,讓等變成了零聲母字?答案當然是否定的。這些字現在的聲母衹能描寫爲/z/。於是,我們就可以説,早在幾乎四百年以前,徐孝就已經預見到我們現在所面臨的左右爲難的局面,並提出了一種解釋。因此,這個聲母應描寫爲/zr/,而不是單純的/r/。

3.3 徐孝保存了以前的輕脣音非,敷,微(當然,没有濁音奉母),並將這些聲母的字排在"低等",而這個等的字一般都是腭化音節。對於稍具有關古代官話知識的人,這確實是出乎意外的,因爲在《中原音韻》之前很久,非,敷、奉三個聲母已經合併爲/f/,而不出現在腭化韻母之前了(見薛1975,38—40)。將徐氏的韻圖仔細檢查一遍,就會發現他的這一做法完全是隨意的,因爲衹有在非母下才列有一些字,並且他的疏忽也泄露了他原計劃將這些字列在"高等"①。很明顯,他没能完全擺脱傳統的韻圖格式,而且還可能照顧到其他的方言。

3.4 徐孝對脣音聲母的安排最引人注意的,是他將非腭化的脣音字衹列於合口圖裹,唯一的例外是壘攝。他如此有力地推行這個原則,以至僅僅爲此專門在效攝和流攝另增加了兩個圖②。多年來,我一直有一個新的意見,認爲現代北京話聲母的脣音音位衹出現在單純的腭化和單純的脣化韻母之前(即齊齒和合口,見薛1975:38)。在結構的意義上,這是一種最嚴格的規律,但却似乎有一個嚴重的困難:正是爲了這條規律,我們必須承認還存在另兩個韻母/waw/和/wɨw/。從徐孝對效攝和流攝的安排來看,他全然不認爲這是一個困難,在這裹我可以高興地宣稱,我終於在400年前找到了一個"知音"。

3.5 這樣,徐氏韻圖的22個聲母就可以減少爲19個。可以描寫成如下

---

① 在這本書的凡例中,徐氏説:"舊韻圖列字於四等36行下,而我現在衹用三等和18行。"(譯者按,徐氏《凡例》原文爲"舊韻圖四派二十六行,今惟用三派一八行",四派即四等,"二十六"應爲"三十六"之誤)陸志韋先生解釋説實際上,徐氏每圖衹有15行。這衹能説明徐氏開初本想將全部脣音聲母排成一列,但後來改變了主意,把這三個輕脣音和重脣音合排一起。

② 徐氏的效攝和流攝的合口篇裹衹有脣音字,而開口篇相應的位置却没有脣音字。陸志韋認爲這兩個合口圖等於虚設,撮口脣音字應當移開口圖。未解釋徐氏爲何虚設。

的音位:

見	溪	端	透	泥	幫	滂	明	非	曉
k	kh	t	th	n	p	ph	m	f	x
精	清	心	心	照	穿	稔	審	來	影
c	ch	(z)	s	cr	crh	zr	sr	l	ø

這個聲母系統與現代北京話的完全一樣。反過來,我們就可以說,北京方言的聲母系統在明代就已形成,並從那時起,基本完整地保留到現在。

四、韻母系統及韻的含義

徐氏韻圖的最顯著的特點,是他對所謂"等"的革新。他將早期韻圖通常的四等,改成了衹有上、中、下三等。以下是他的新的格局的一些特點。

4.1 徐氏的三等可以很容易地減爲兩等。中等衹有捲舌聲母字,這種做法没有什麽特殊的理由。我們衹能推測徐氏此舉也許有兩個原因。首先精組和照組長期以來發生關係,這種傳統使徐孝不能忽視。其次,更重要的是,因爲到徐孝的時代之前,捲舌聲母已不再出現在腭化韻母之前(參見 4.2),將這些聲母與其他聲母並列一排,就會在衹列腭化韻母的低等留下明顯的空檔。在他勉强地將輕脣聲母同重脣音分成兩排時,這兩種考慮可能也起了作用(參見 3.3)。

4.2 從徐氏的韻圖,我們還可以推出三個關於韻母的次要的變化。

a) 直到《中原音韻》時代,捲舌聲母還既可以出現在腭化韻母之前,也可以出現在非腭化韻母之前,但是到了明代晚期,就不能同腭化韻母相拼了。

我曾經用如下式表示這個變化(薛 1978:45):

$$y \rightarrow ø / r\_\_\_\_$$

問題是,這個變化是什麽時候發生的,並確實是如此地遍及各韻嗎?徐氏的韻圖給我們提供了一些綫索。除了止攝合口圖和祝攝之外,在徐氏所有其他韻圖裏,都可以在中等裏發現以前的二等和三等字混雜一起。看起來這意味着除韻母/ywɨ/外,這裏討論的變化已經影響到了其他所有韻母。對於我所提出的音變是逐步的説法,即在一定時間是經常僅影響一類音節的假説(參見薛

1978和1980b),這是一個很好的例證。

b) 在《中原音韻》時代,用/s/和/l/作聲母的音節中,韻母/wɨŋ/同/ywɨŋ/的對立仍然存在,也就是説松≠鬆和龍≠籠,但在明代晚期這種對立已經消失。徐氏韻圖的通攝表明,到他的時代,雖然龍和籠仍然對立,但鬆和松已成爲同音字了。對於我們上面提到的假説,這又是一個很好的例證。

c) 像雷,壘,内等字,向來是合口字,也就是説,在《中原音韻》時代其韻母是/wɨy/,但在現代漢語裏,這些字全是開口。徐氏韻圖的壘攝表明,早在徐孝的時代之前,這個韻母在/l/和/n/之後,已經失去了介音/w/。

4.3 徐氏的十三攝同清代早期流行的,用作北方地區俗文學押韻標準的十三轍是一致的(見羅1950)。這件事有兩個含義。第一,十三轍所代表的押韻標準,有着比我們迄今所估計的更長得多的歷史,幾乎可以追溯到明代中葉。第二,徐孝所使用的"攝"這個術語,指的是簡單的"韻",而不是傳統意義的"韻的大類"。因而,在每一圖裏,高等(包括中等,但止攝除外)同低等的區别,衹不過是低等字在介音位置有/y/,而高等字則無。在一個韻(或攝)同時具有開口和合口圖時,這意味着這個韻具有全部開,齊,合,撮(或衆所周知的四呼)四種音節類型。徐氏韻圖的基本元音系統顯然保持了《中原音韻》的系統未變(參見薛1975:51—54):

	前	央	後
高		ɨ	
低	e	a	o

韻的總數由《中原音韻》的19個減到徐氏書的13個,意味着在低元音以及有尾韻的對立的進一步消蝕(參見薛1976)。現將我對徐氏13韻的音位構擬,連同陸志韋的音值構擬,以及與其相擬的十三轍的代表字列出以進行比較。

五、結論

通過以上討論,我們可以看到,徐孝的著作給我們提供了一些關於北京方言的歷史的有用的資料,以及對於其代表的語音系統性質的深刻認識。這些資料和認識是以設計很好的圖表的明確的方式發表的,就是因爲這個原因,才不會被人忽視和誤解。由於發生了許多語音變化,韻圖的傳統方式再也不能有效地反映近代北京話的語音系統。因此,徐氏新的韻圖格式的設計,是一個非常有獨創性的符合新時代需要的革新。一件難以理解的事是祝攝和止攝的分立。嚴格地遵守押韻的原則就應將它們合成一韻。但是,十三轍(姑蘇對一七)和北京地區的俗文學的實際押韻習慣,却再一次證實它們需要分立(見羅1950)。我們已經成功地證實了這種分韻並解釋了這兩韻之間的結構關係,但對其分韻的理論性的依據却必須另想辦法解釋①。

徐圖攝名	陸擬	薛擬
通 (東中)	əŋ iŋ uŋ iuŋ	(y)(w)ɨŋ
止 (一七)	ɿ ʅ 'ər' j y(ʉ,iʉ?)	(y)(w)ɨ#
蟹 (懷來)	ai iai uai	$\begin{Bmatrix}y\\w\end{Bmatrix}$ ay
壘 (灰堆)	ei(iei) uei(yei)	(w)ɨy
效 (遥條)	ɒu(?) iɐu(?)	$\begin{Bmatrix}y\\w\end{Bmatrix}$ aw
果 (棱坡)	ɔ iɔ uɔ	(y)(w)o#
假 (發花)	ɑ iɑ uɑ	$\begin{Bmatrix}y\\w\end{Bmatrix}$ a#

徐圖攝名	陸擬	薛擬
祝 (姑蘇)	u,iu	(c)wɨ#
拙 (乜斜)	ɛ iɛ uɛ iuɛ	(y)(w)e#
臻 (人辰)	ən in u(ə)n iun	(y)(w)ɨn
山 (言前)	an iɛn uan iuɛn	(y)(w)an
宕 (江陽)	ɑŋ('ɒŋ'?) iɑŋ uɑŋ(uɒŋ?) (liuɑŋ)	$\begin{Bmatrix}y\\w\end{Bmatrix}$ aŋ
流 (由求)	əu(?) iəu(?)	$\begin{Bmatrix}y\\w\end{Bmatrix}$ ɨw

① 以前,我在兩篇文章裏,曾提出過這種分韻可能有兩個原因:a)韻母/wɨ/的特殊音質,以及b)兒化音節形態變化的一致性。詳細討論見薛1980b。

方言研究

北京音系解析***

序

薛鳳生教授是一位造詣很深,獨樹特色的美國華人漢語歷史語言學專家,長於近代漢語語音和現代漢語語音的綜合研究,能對現代漢語的歷史來源、本質特點和發展趨向等一系列問題作出科學的回答。他在這本《北京音系解析》書裏指出:不論研究漢語音韻史的哪個階段,必須把那個階段與其前後各個階段,尤其現代漢語,儘可能有系統地聯繫起來,絶不能把那個階段作爲孤立的個體來處理。這見解是正確的。"要瞭解本國語言的材料和形式,就必須追溯本國語言的形成和它的逐步發展"(恩格斯《反杜林論》第316頁)。我看薛教授研究北京音系是顯示這種探源析流的精神的。在這書《北京音的歷史背景》一章中所揭示"官話"方言的十條共通性,實際上表述了漢語發展史裏十個重要的音變,而作爲一個方言是否屬於"官話"的檢驗標準。這真知灼見,是他運用新的分析理據,發現音韻系統和規律的新成果。這對我國現代漢語的教學和科研拓寬了視野,給人們横向的具體描寫結合縱向的各個階段的比較以示範。在本書《北京音系的音值律》一章中,在闡述北京音的特有音系後,對説這種話的人的語音所共有的語感作出最合理的解釋,嚴守四條標準原則,足以説明許多語音正變現象,有理有據,剖析精微。特別是觀察北京音系中音位層次以下的發音實踐規律,如韻尾同化韻腹律、韻頭同化韻腹律、韻腹的圓脣化規律、韻腹元音的鬆緊律和高元音的舌尖化律等,生動地描寫了在日常的實際語言交際中,自然的和自由的省略和變動的複雜語音現象。因而所獲得北京

*** 原由北京語言學院出版社出版,1986年。

音系是能够具體地解釋人群所共有的語感。這新穎的觀點和方法,也給人們教學和科研樹立了楷模。總之,這本書無論體系、要素、結構和功能或者説框架結構、觀點和材料上都進行多維型思維的創作。我榮幸地樂於介紹給讀者。

嚴學宭

1985 年 9 月 10 日於武漢市

自 序

有關現代標準漢語音韻的著作,數量已經相當不少,但是有些基本理論方面的問題,似乎猶待探討。這本小册子就代表我對北京音系的看法,算是一個較完整的交代,特别用中文寫出來向國内同行請教。

對於我來説,一個較完整的交代是完全必要的。我的研究重點是漢語音韻史,我對於這種研究的看法是:不管我們研究的是歷史上的哪一個階段,研究者都有義務把那個階段與其前後各階段,尤其是現代漢語,儘可能地有系統地聯繫起來,絶不能滿足於把那個階段作爲一個孤立的個體來處理。這就要求每一個研究者首先確立與説明他對現代漢語的看法。就另一方面説,由於現代漢語是一個大家都熟悉的活語言,討論時不需要涉及許多生僻的文獻,因此討論者的觀點與分析方法才更容易爲大家所理解,並以此爲基礎去瞭解他對歷史音韻的研究。

我對語音的分析,偏重於闡述音位結構與音韻系統。這一系列討論背後的許多理論觀點是經過一段長時間的醖釀於數年前形成的,其中有些片段曾以英文刊布過,另有幾篇也曾在國内外的學術討論會上宣讀過。早在數年前我就有意把這些片段連貫起來,作爲一個整體就教於國内的同好,並曾答應一家書局由他們出版,但由於一直忙於他事,竟一再爽約。這次還是由於得到了全年研究休假的機會,才終於寫了出來。在此不惟要檢討我個人筆頭太懶,更要對我執教的學校美國俄亥俄州立大學(The Ohio State University)以及美中學術交流委員會(CSCPRC)表示謝意。没有他們的支持,這本小册子恐怕一時還是寫不出來的。

除了已發表過的幾個章節以外,這次又加寫了好幾部分,全面地討論了現代標準漢語音系的各方面以及我分析的理論根據。在以前發表過的幾個篇章裏,每次總得先簡略地説明這個音系的大概,然後才在那個基礎上開始討論個别的問題。這次把這許多篇章合在一起,自然就顯得有不少部分重複了,但是我仍決定不加删節。這樣各篇合在一起自然構成了一個有機的整體,但同時又像一個論文集,分開來時各篇多少都還有一些獨立性,可以單獨閱讀。這對那些時間不多的同好來説,也許會提供一些方便的。

在補寫部分章節期間,我在武漢市的華中工學院中國語言研究所停留甚久,並得到該所的尉遲治平先生的多方協助,所長嚴學宭教授也特加照顧,並爲本書作序。書名更承王力先生題署,在此一並致謝。

第一章　緒論:分析的理論基礎與方法

1. 現代標準漢語,在不同的時間與地區,曾有不同的名稱,諸如官話、國語及普通話等,但不論我們管它叫做什麽,它的内涵却是一致的。概括地説,這種語言是在北京話的基礎上逐漸發展起來的。在語音方面,它嚴格遵守北京話的音韻系統。在詞彙方面,則在北京話的基礎上,不斷吸收古語與其他方言的詞彙。在語法方面,它實際上也是嚴守北京話的語法規則的,但是由於它是標準語,自然也就擔任了書面語的角色,因此必須以遠比一般口語更複雜的句式來表達較複雜的意象,這就容易給人造成一種"没有人那麽説話"的印象,其實那些複雜的句式並不違背口語語法的基本規則,而是由這些基本規則推衍出來的。在這本小册子裏,我將不談詞彙與語法的問題,而專門討論語音方面的有關問題。

1.1 語音的研究,大别之,可以分爲兩個方面。一方面我們可以把語音作爲一種物理現象作極細密的分析,另一方面我們則可以把語音在特定語言中的應用方式作極嚴格的分析。前者是物理學中聲學的研究,後者才是語言學中音韻學的研究。對一般人來説,研究某一種語言或方言的語音,當然是記録那種語言中某些字的讀法,也就是要説明那種話是"怎麽説的"。這是一個很自然的想法,早期的西方語言學在觀念上也是這樣的,因此着重在以特定的符號標寫特殊的發音,所謂"國際音標"就是在這一觀念下發展出來的產物。把這一觀念再推進一步,我們自然也可以利用聲學儀器來補救人類耳朵的不足,從而分辨出更多的不同語音,或由發音器官的部位與動態,以及聲波的形態,進一步説明語音構成的方式。這類研究是有許多實用價值的,比如"國際音標"在語言或方言的調查上,以及在語言教學上,都有很大的功用,而語音的聲學分析對合成語音、人機對話以及電訊傳遞等,都可能產生極有效果的功用。但是在另一方面,從純語言學的觀點看,在經過多年的實踐之後,語言學家們終於領悟到,對語音的極細微的分析,不是語言學研究的真正目標,因爲對語音的物理分析,不論如何精微細緻,仍不能表現出語音在實際語言中所擔負的辨别意義的功能。這是因爲在不同的語言或方言中,音值相同或極相近的語音,不一定擔負着相同的辨義功能。一個語音所擔負的辨義功能,衹能由它與跟它在同一個音韻系統中的其他語音所起的對比作用來决定。這種聽覺上的對比,並不完全取决於客觀上的音值差異,而更表現在説話者與聽話者的主觀認識上。語音實質儘管千變萬化,但在個别語言或方言的應用裏,却總是自成簡約而整齊的體系。從語言學的觀點説,音韻學研究的對象不是語言的物理現象,而是語音在語言中的應用方式,也就是語言中的音韻系統。

1.2 在西方的語言學研究中,上述理論觀點到本世紀三十年代才有人提出,即所謂音位(phoneme)學説,音位之間的結構對比關係,經布拉格學派(Prague school)諸學者,以及瑞士學者德·索緒爾(de Saussure)等的宣揚與闡發,遂逐漸爲人接受,並進一步於五十年代發展爲區别性特(distinctive features)的學説,從而更與轉换生成語法理論銜接,形成了目前盛行的"生成音韻學"(generative phonology)説。但是在另一方面,也有一些學者連基本的音位學説也不願接受,比如高本漢(Bernhard Karlgren)先生至死都不願接受這一觀點[①]。另外有一些學者,雖然接受了這一觀點,但是並不徹底。比如有一些人,把音值與音位這兩個觀念衹看作程度上的不同,認爲衹不過前者比較嚴密而後者比較鬆散而已,即所謂嚴式標音(narrow transcription)與寬式標音(broad transcription)之分。另有一些學者則認爲,在研究分析一個語言的時候,兩個或更多的學者可能都采用音位處理法,但可能得到並不完全相同的結論,而這些不同的結論可能都具有類似的良好的效果。趙元任先生的"多能性"(nonuniqueness)學説就代表這一想法(參看 Chao1934)。與上述兩種看法不同的則有以雅可布遜(Roman Jakobson)爲代表的嚴格音位結構説(參看 Jakobson 1951)。依照這一看法,在對一個語言作音位分析時,如果有人得出兩個或更多的結論,不論其間差别多麽微細,我們仍可以根據嚴格的音位分析

① 高本漢先生對於音位學説的批評,最突出的見於所著"Compondium"(Karlgren 1954)。他認爲音位處理法過分簡化,衹不過讓人少用幾個符號而已,並預言這種做法不久將爲語言學者所擯棄。事實證明他這個預言是完全錯誤的。究其原因,這是由於高老先生誤會了音位學的真義,認爲這衹是一種"處理法",别無深義。跟他持同樣態度的迄今仍然大有人在,所以我在本章特别强調:語感(也就是音韻系統的内在結構)才是音位學研究的真正目標。

原理及其他理由,指出其中的某一個結論是理論上較爲妥善的。把這個觀念推到極致,最後所得到的應是獨一無二的妥善結論,也就是該語言所獨具的音位結構。這個看法就把音位觀念與音值觀念作出了本質性的區别,不僅是程度上的差異而已。

1.3 我個人對於漢語音韻的研究是采用最嚴格的音位結構觀點的。我認爲我們研究的目標應該是推論出漢語中某一方言或某一歷史階段所特有的音韻系統。而且我更進一步認爲,由嚴格分析而得出的某一語言的獨特音系,應該能够具體地解釋説該語言的人群所共有的語感,也就是説,它可以作爲這種語感的具體表現。這一終極的目標也許是不容易達到的,但是我們必須把它牢記在心裏,作爲評斷語音分析的尺度。一個語音分析的爲優爲劣,應該取決於它離開這一目標多近或多遠。在這樣的尺度下,即使在最細微的地方僅有毫釐之差,理論上也可以分出高低來。

1.4 我們怎樣才可以知道某一個語言分析是否已經具體表現了(或正確地解釋了)説那種話的人群的語感呢?反過來説,所謂語感表現在什麽地方呢?就漢語説,我們可以用下述幾個現象作爲衡量的標準:

a) 在中國的音韻學研究傳統裏,起初是把字音分成兩個組成部分,即反切法所分的聲母與韻母,後來又把韻母再細分成三個組成部分,即韻頭、韻腹與韻尾。這個分段法具有千餘年的歷史,一直爲本民族的學者所遵從,當然不會是憑空捏造的,而是以民族語的特性與本國人的語感爲依據的。我們説這種分段法表現了語感,還可以用另兩件事作爲證明。其一,歷史上有所謂"射字"的游戲①,即把音節拆散拼合以造成字謎。稍加説明,一般會説漢語的人都可以參加這種游戲,不需要有特殊的音韻學訓練。其二,在不少方言地區,迄今仍有説"隱語"的現象,其法爲拆散字音,按一定的規律增入附加的聲母及韻母(參看 Paul Li 1985)。對這種"話",兒童們最感興趣,而且學得很快,説得很流利,他們並没有音韻學的訓練,祇不過根據他們已養成的語感拆散拼合字

---

① 關於"射字"游戲的較詳細説明,可參看李新魁著《漢語等韻學》第二章第四節(1983:42—43)。有關秘密語的記録與説明,可參看趙 1931 及李 1985。我在此處祇是要借助此類例子來説明,傳統的音節分段法是以漢語音韻内部結構爲依據的,也就是説符合語感,因爲學會做這類游戲的人不可能有(也不需要有)細密的理論知識。

音而已。近代研究漢語的中外學者,除少數例外,一般也都采用這種分段法。我個人認爲,既然這種分段法自《切韻》時代以迄於今都行之有效,而且在許多方面都符合説漢語者的語感,我們就必須嚴格地遵守。反過來説,如果我們能嚴格遵守這種分段法,也就説明我們的分析在這一方面符合了語感。爲了討論時的方便,我一向采用"(C)(M) V(E)"這個簡單的公式來表達這一概念,明確地表示一個音節最多衹能有四個音段。在這四個音段中,C(聲母)、M(韻頭,亦稱介音)、E(韻尾或稱收聲)對音節的構成説,是輔助性的,它們的出現與否以及以何種形態出現,衹發生區别不同音節的功用,對於一個音節之所以成爲一個音節,則是不重要的,所以在上面的公式中,我們把它們都放在括號裏。至於 V(韻腹 nucleus, 亦稱主要元音),則性質完全不同,除了也能以不同的形態出現而區别音節以外,它代表一個音節的高峰(peak), 是我們何以能够聽出一個音節的原因所在,换句話説,也就是一個音節之所以能成爲一個音節的道理。丢了它,一個音節就不成爲一個音節了。

b) 傳統音韻學常把音節作不同的分類。先有所謂"開、合"兩呼之説,後又有"洪、細"兩音之説,其後又把這兩説結合起來,提出了"開、齊、合、撮"的四呼分類法。對於説漢語的人,不需要受特殊的音韻學訓練,衹要多給他們舉些例子,他們就會很自然的把漢語中的音節按上述的分類作適當的歸類了。前文提到的射字與隱語之類的游戲,在音節的拆散與拼合裏,也跟這些分類符合。這説明這些分類法是符合他們的語感的,也是符合這種語言的特性的。另一方面,"韻"也分成若干類,諸如"抵腭、穿鼻、收噫、收嗚"等。正確的分析應該可以合理地説明這些現象。

c) 押韻是最能表現語感的現象。不論什麼語言,押韻的基本道理都是一樣的,一般人也都承認凡是可以互押的音節,必然具有共同的韻基,即相同的主要元音與相同的元音後綴成分(假如有後綴的話)。漢語在這一方而當然也不例外,因此我們的分析是否符合這一原則,也就成爲該分析是否正確的一個檢驗標準。就北京話説,凡是北京人覺得可以押韻的字,我們的分析都必須顯示出它們具有相同的韻基,也就是説,在前述的音節分段裏,所有可以互押的字,都應該含有共同的"V (E)"。需要特别聲明的是,這兒所説的押韻,不是文人詩詞中仿古的押韻現象,而是一個方言區裏的所謂"韻從流水"的押韻現象,也就是出現在民謡民歌裏的自然押韻現象,代表着該地區人們的直感。

d) 雙聲現象,不論是在民歌中或在文學作品中,也是一種語感的表現。在我們分析一個語言或方言時,凡是當地人認爲是雙聲的音節,我們的分析都必須能够清楚地標示它們含有相同的節首輔音,也就是説,必須能够解釋爲什麽當地人覺得它們是雙聲。所謂當地人覺得是雙聲,當然不全指直接詢問他們要他們表示意見,更重要的是由他們説話的方式中作邏輯的推論。

1.5 有關北京語音的著作,可謂已經汗牛充棟,但是迄今還没有一個能够完全滿足上述四個標準的要求的。這就是爲什麽我還要提出一個新分析的道理。當然我們必須充分肯定前人的貢獻。没有他們的開拓性的研究,新的分析是不可能憑空而出的。我們的分析裏,自然包含了許多前人已經提出過的説法,但是我們必須指出,除了增添了一些新説法以外,我們的新的分析頭一次把前人的許多零星片斷的説法連貫起來成爲一個有機的整體。更重要的是,前人提過的一些説法,或則本來就未經充分的論證,或則雖經論證,但是論據是頗有問題的。我們的新分析在吸收這類舊説時,或則爲它們提出新的證據,或則爲它們提出截然不同的理據。但是由於前人有關北京話的著作甚多,逐一評斷是不可能的,因此除了在討論某一論點時必須特別指出某一論著外,我將不注出舊説,而祇説明我的觀點。讀者在自作比較時,便可看出本書與前人論著的差異了。目前音韻學研究的趨勢偏向於以區別性特徵表達音韻的規律,即所謂生成音韻學。我個人的看法是,我們研究的目標是發現音韻的系統與規律,在這個大前提下,表達方式上的差别是次要的。因此我相信,一個用"音位"符號表達的真正準確的分析與一個用"區别性特徵"表達的同樣準確的分析,本質上是没有什麽差别的,因爲在這個意義上所謂"音位"祇不過是"一束區别性特徵"(a bundle of distinctive features)的"概括符號"(cover symbol)而已。因此在討論北京音系時,我將基本上仍以音位符號來表達,祇在確有幫助的個别地方使用區别性特徵的觀念來説明特殊的問題。

1.6 傳統音韻學的主旨是區别字音。起初使用的方法是分韻與標注反切,後來更利用圖表及文字説明來表達不同字音間的韻類與聲類等相互的關係。這種表達方法當然完全是音位性的對比,而不是細微音值的描述,其基本精神與西方晚近的音韻理論是不謀而合的。要想正確地瞭解音韻學的歷史文獻,並從而瞭解漢語在歷代的變遷,我們必須采用、也衹能采用嚴格的音位結構説。我們對於任一歷史階段的音韻的研究,都不能采用“前不見古人,後不見來者”的方式把它作爲一個孤立的個體來處理,而應該把它與現代漢語緊密的統一與聯繫起來。這就要求每一個研究者先確立與説明他對現代漢語的看法。這本小册子中的觀點就代表我對現代漢語的看法,並且是我研究漢語史的基礎。我覺得前文所提出的四條標準原則,可以説是漢語音韻學的公分母。根據這些原則分析出來的音系,不論是方言或某一歷史階段,相互之間才能做有意義的比較。

第二章　北京話的韻母結構

2. 明清以來,中國學者有關北京音韻的著作,爲數甚多①。他們或則用傳統韻書的形式,或則用改良式的韻圖,爲我們提供了許多近代漢語的資料,以及一些頗具新意的見解(當然糟粕也不少),對漢語音節性質上分爲“開、齊、合、撮”四類的確認。就是在這段時間裏達成的。但是限於他們使用的方法,他們衹能間接地暗示出北京話在那個時代的音位對比與音系結構,而北京話其後又發生了一些演變,這就有待於我們的繼續研究與分析了。當然研究當代北京話的音韻系統不需要依賴古人,因爲這是一種活的語言,也是我們大家都會説的語言,衹要采用正確的分析理論與方法,我們的語感就會把我們引向正確的方向,但是前人開拓性的工作顯然給我們提供了許多方便與啓示。把他們研究的成果與現代音韻學理論結合起來,並參考現代中外學者的論著,我們便可以看出北京音系的嚴整結構,並把它清晰地表達出來。

2.1 在分析北京語音時,我采用最嚴格的音位結構説,即認爲這個音系的正確分析衹能有一個,而這個正確的分析恰是説北京話的人的共有語感。具體地説,我們要求這個分析嚴守下列四條原則,因爲他們就是語感的代表。

a) 嚴格遵守傳統的音節分段法,即把一個音節分成聲母、韻頭、韻腹、韻尾四段。我們用(C) (M)V (E)這個簡約的公式來代表這個概念。在音節構成中,衹有 V 是絶對必要的,其他三部分可以不出現。

b) 最嚴格地説明傳統的音節分類法,包括“開、合”兩呼,“洪、細”兩音,“開、齊、合、撮”四呼,以及諸如“穿鼻、抵腭、收噫、收嗚”等韻的分類法。

c) 最嚴格地解釋押韻現象,即把凡是北京人覺得可以押韻的字音分析成

---

① 明清兩代出現了許多韻書,詳細名目可參看趙蔭堂 1957 及李新魁 1983,此處不贅。可以附帶説明的是:在這段時間裏,中國的音韻學家就已開始了理論的探索,頗有百家争鳴之勢。他們各抒己見的精神,與現代語言學家們争相提出新理論的做法也有些類似,尤其是提出了“音有定位定數”的觀念,是與現代音韻理論暗合的。這表示他們都隱約地認識到了漢語的内部音位結構。可惜的是他們没有能够完全從語言的實際出發,反而由於陰陽五行等先入之見,錯誤地把“音有定位定數”的觀念與玄學的術數之説結合起來了。

含有共同的韻基,也就是上面公式中的"V(E)"。

d) 合理地解釋雙聲現象。

在本章裏,我將專門討論北京話的韻母結構,把聲母及聲調留待另外探討,但爲了討論韻母時的需要,我們必須把這兩部分先作一個簡單的交代。

2.1.1 我們認爲北京音系裏祇有十九個聲母(包括零聲母)。它們相互之間的關係可從下表看出來。

方法 部位	不送氣音	送氣音	擦音	鼻音	流音
脣　音	p	ph	f	m	
齦前音	t	th		n	l
齦後音	c	ch	s		
捲舌音	cr	crh	sr		r
舌根音	k	kh	h		ø

需要補充説明的是,上表中每一個方格裏,衹有一個音位,也就是一個聲母,另外我們把腭化音[tɕ,tɕ‘,ɕ]看作舌根音的變體,齦後音與捲舌音這兩組聲母的標音與一般的寫法有所不同,理由都將在第三章"北京話聲母的性質"裏詳細説明。

2.1.2 我們認爲北京話裏有五個聲調音位,即陰平、陽平、上、去及輕聲。在字音單讀時,輕聲是不出現的,但它作爲一個與其他四個聲調構成對比的聲調則是不容否定的。我們對成段音位的分析是以非輕聲音節爲基礎的,這不會造成分析上的問題,因爲輕聲作爲弱化的聲調,並未促成新音位的產生。

2.2 在韻母的三個構成部分中,韻尾(E)所代表的概念是比較單純的,它代表一個音節的收結的方式,但是由於它跟韻腹的關係幾乎密不可分,所以對它的認定比較晚,對不同韻尾的名稱,到明代才出現,而且在某些方面認識尚不够充分。在北京話裏,除了零韻尾以外,我們可以辨別出五個韻尾音位,即/-y、-w、-n、- ŋ、-r/,其中/-r/是一個很特殊的韻尾,除了出現在"兒、耳、二"等字所代表的音節(/ɨr/)裏以外,它衹出現在兒化韻所造成的音節中。這一現象我們將在討論兒化韻的那章裏詳細説明,此處不贅。

2.2.1 與韻頭相比,韻尾跟韻腹的關聯更爲密切,它們共同形成韻基,因此注音符號就干脆用單一的符號代表這兩個音段。在漢語史裏,主要元音的改變,主要是由於韻尾輔音的影響,其次才是韻頭與聲母。另據一些報導,在爲數不少的官話方言裏,鼻音韻尾已經弱化,變成附加在韻腹上的鼻化成分,而一些收[i]與[u]的所謂"複合元音"(diphthong),也變成了單元音,因此可能有人會問:既然如此,我們爲什麽還要承認音節分段中韻尾的存在呢?回答是:北京話裏,這些韻尾仍是清晰可辨的,因此不能否認它們的存在,而承認了它們的存在,可使我們更清晰地看出及説明這個音系的嚴整結構。另外,在漢語史上,根據韻尾區分韻類的做法也是由來已久的。要説明這一現象及詮釋有關的術語,我們也必須接受韻尾的觀念。又有許多人説,作爲韻尾的[i]和[u],是"帶元音性的",因此堅持把這類韻母稱爲"複合元音"。對我們來説,不管它們多麽"帶元音性",它們總不會比作爲韻腹的元音更"帶元音性",所以相對地説,它們衹能是半元音。爲了清晰醒目,我們用/y/和/w/分别代表它們。

2.2.2 傳統音韻學中有幾個關於韻類的術語,在我們所堅持的音節分段法的基礎上,現在可以肯定地説,那是完全以韻尾的形態爲根據的,與韻腹無關。這些術語可以作如下的解釋:

直音(直喉)	收噫(展輔)	收嗚(斂脣)	抵腭	穿鼻
-V ø	-Vy	-Vw	-Vn	-Vŋ

除了這五個韻類術語以外,尚有"閉口、滿口、撮口"等幾個術語。頭一個指收雙脣鼻音/m/的韻類,在現代的北京音裏已經變入抵腭。後兩個則分指"姑蘇"之類的合口直音字及"居魚"之類的撮口直音字,它們被分立出來的原因,一則是前人對以韻尾分韻類的原理尚未能充分掌握,再則也由於明清以來這兩類字在分韻方面始終糾纏不清,許多學者都顯示出舉棋不定的態度。這個問題將留待下文討論押韻問題時再加説明(見 2.4.3 b)。

2.3 把漢語音節分成"開、齊、合、撮"四呼已有數百年的歷史,如果把"開、合"兩呼與"洪、細"兩音的分類法也算在内(因爲四呼實爲後二者的合併),則更可上推近千年。對於一般説漢語的人來説,衹要經過粗略的説明與示例,也不難根據這種分類把漢語的音節作正確的辨認與歸類。可見這類分類法是合乎漢語的特性與説漢語者的語感的。由於受到表達方式的限制,中國學者在過去衹能暗示這種分類是以韻頭爲根據的。現代研究漢語的中外學者,在思想與做法上,大致也都肯定了這一點,但是在少數具有關鍵性的地方,他們却受到他們自認爲是"實際音值"的影響而不能始終如一地堅持這一看法,結果是他們往往給這個分類提出模棱兩可的解釋,使人覺得這不僅是韻頭的問題,而且與韻腹有關。從而給這個分類的真正原理蒙上一層雲翳。更有甚者,有些拼音方式(如"拼音方案")爲了簡便把"東紅"之類的字拼成"dong,hong",把"窮凶"之類的字拼成"qiong,xiong",因而迫使一些語文老師在教學時把前者歸入"開口",後者歸入"齊齒"①。這真是極大的誤解。我們在這兒重申:這個音節分類法的原理純粹是,而且也僅僅是,以韻頭爲根據的,與其他部分毫無關係。我們的分析必須能毫不含糊地表示這完全是音節分段公式中 M 的形態的問題。

2.3.1 在遵守上述原則的基礎上,我們確認所謂"開口"意思就是韻頭爲零"ø","齊齒"韻頭爲"i";"合口"韻頭爲"u","撮口"韻頭爲"ü"。像對韻尾一樣,許多學者都説這些韻頭更像元音或帶元音性,因而堅持用一般的元音符號來代表它們。我們給音節所下的定義確定了它們的附從的性質,因爲不管音值上它們多像元音,音位上與韻腹相比它們就衹能是半元音,所以爲了醒目,我們仍主張用半元音符號來代表它們。當然這衹是符號問題。在實質上是没有多大意義的。我們將用/y/表示齊齒,用/w/表示合口。由於撮口分別與齊齒及合口含有共同的特性,我們將用/yw/這個合體代表它。早在趙元任先生等制定的"國語羅馬字"裏,撮口就以"iu" 的形式出現了,但據説這衹是爲了節約與方便。觀念上把撮口解釋爲齊齒與合口的合體則自美國學者哈特門(Hartman, 1944)開始。我們接受他這一看法但又與他有所不同。他把這個合體中的兩個符號認作兩個音位,而且次序上/y/必須出現在/w/之前。我們

① "四呼"之分顯然是有音韻理論爲依據的。也就是説,漢語中每一音節必然含有某一音韻特性,因此先天地决定了這個音節應屬那一"呼",不是可以隨便改動的。但是有些拼音方式爲了書寫的方便,或者爲了創製者所謂的"語音實際",没能把某些音節的"呼"的屬性標示出來,因此常引起某些人的錯認。比如説,國語羅馬字與漢語拼音方案都把"紅"拼作 hong,把"雄"拼做 shiong 或 xiong),遂使某些人把前者錯認爲"開口",把後者錯認爲"齊齒"。王力先生曾 根據"音韻學這個系統"指出這種做法的不當(王力 1979)。我的分析就是要具體地指出"音韻學這個系統"究竟是個什麽東西。

則認爲這個合體衹代表一個音位,用兩個符號衹是爲了方便,而且它們的順序也不是先後的而是共時的。它們實際上代表兩個正性的區别特徵,/y/代表腭化,/w/代表脣化。采用這個觀念,所謂四呼的真義便可以清楚地界定如下了:

開口 —ø— [−腭化, −脣化](既非腭化又非脣化)

齊齒 —y— [+腭化, −脣化](僅爲腭化而非脣化)

合口 —w— [−腭化, +脣化](僅爲脣化而非腭化)

撮口 —yw— [+腭化, +脣化](既爲腭化又爲脣化)

在這個理論基礎上,要説明"開、合"兩呼與"洪、細"兩音的原理,也就順理成章了。所謂"開、合"實即"脣化"的有無問題,而"洪、細"則爲"腭化"的有無問題。這種解釋顯然是既簡明又合理的。

2.3.2 韻頭又稱介音,是聲母與韻腹結合的媒介。聲母與韻腹可以不需媒介而直接結合,也可以透過三種媒介而結合,因此共得四個不同的結合方式。就語音的性質説,介音是一種滑音(glide),對聲母而言,是一種滑出音(off-glide),對韻腹而言,則爲一種滑入音(on-glide),它與前後兩個音段的關係都是相當密切的。因此也許有人會覺得可以把介音這個音段取消,把它併入聲母。比如把舌根音的腭化變體另立出"j-、q-、x-"三母,就可以把介音中的腭化剔除了。我們認爲這樣做在理論上並不可取。北京話裏聲母與四呼的相配固然不十分完整(比如脣音與齒音都不配撮口),但還是相當系統化的。部分地取消介音這個音段是没有意義的,而全部取消則勢必把聲母的數目增加數倍,這是不合理的,也是違背語感的。另一方面也許有人覺得可以把介音排入韻腹,以便取消韻頭這個音段。這樣做還可以達到把漢語音節解釋爲"CVC"形式的目的。可是這在理論上更不可取。這樣做必須把元音的數目增加數倍,而且還得承認元音不同的音節也可以互相押韻,這就完全違背了我們給押韻現象所下的嚴格定義。另外還有一個需要在此説明的無中生有的糾葛。有些外國學者（Hartman 1944，Hockett 1947）爲了把［tɕ、tɕʻ、ɕ］［ts、tsʻ、s］和［tʂ、tʂʻ、ʂ］這三類聲母解釋爲一類，竟把最後一類聲母中的捲舌成分“r”提出來，硬説它也是介音，這樣四呼就變成五呼了。老實不客氣地説，衹有“洋人的語感”才會使他們有這樣的看法。腭化音聲母在形成與演進中，從來都與捲舌聲母無涉，把它們認作一類是没有意義的。更嚴重的是，新立了一個介音並因此增加了一呼（其實是增加了兩呼，因爲“r”還可以配合口），然後又得説這個介音衹能出現在一種聲母之後，這就是自找麻煩了，道理上也不應該有這樣奇特的介音。

2.4 在詳細地討論過了韻頭與韻尾之後再來討論韻腹，問題就不顯得那麽複雜了。我們衹要堅守着我們訂下的幾條分析原則，尤其是音節的四呼與押韻的原理，便不難推論出北京音系裏應有的元音來。因爲我們大家都會説這種話，所以我們本來就可以憑自己的語感認定這個語言裏字彙的四呼歸屬與押韻現象，所謂“韻從流水”就是指的這種語感。但是爲了保持客觀，我們最好能找出一個公認的標準。現代文人編的韻書諸如《中華新韻》及《現代詩韻》等並不可靠，因爲他們總擺脱不了古代韻書分類的影響以及近代的“音值”觀念。作爲北京地區人們語感的客觀表現，它們倒不如明清以來的一些通俗韻書，而這些通俗韻書又不如那個有韻目而無韻書的“十三轍”。根據羅常培先生的統計分析①，我們知道近代北京地區民歌民謠的押韻完全符合“十三轍”的分韻。其實民歌民謡的作者不可能是查了“十三轍”才作歌的。（本來就無書可查嘛！）他們所作歌詞中的押韻衹不過是一種“順口溜”而已，也就是語感的自然流露。而“十三轍”也不過是這種集體語感的概括歸納而已。當然“十三轍”所表現的是明末清初時代北京話的現象，與現代北京話不可能完全一致，但其間的差别應該是很微小的。我們對現代標準漢語的分析，當然應以現

① 關於“一七”轍與“姑蘇”轍的分界，曾有不同的説法，比如張洵如等認爲它們是以洪細分韻的，即“一七”轍含“支、齊”兩類的字，而“姑蘇”轍則含“魚、模”兩類的字（張洵如 1956）。羅常培在做了客觀的統計分析以後，才發現“一七”轍實含“支、齊、魚”即開、齊、撮三呼的字，“姑蘇”轍僅含“模”即合口一呼的字（羅常培 1950）。其實這種分韻早在徐孝的《等韻圖經》與馬自援的《等音》等書中就已如此。羅先生的發現正説明了他們的分法是“遵循民意”的。

代北京人的語感爲準，但這種語感表現在押韻方面時，應該與“十三轍”是基本一致的。反過來説，能否表達現代北京人的語感以及合理地解釋“十三轍”，對我們的分析將是最大的考驗。

2.4.1 嚴守音節的分段、四呼、與押韻的基本原理，我們就不得不承認：北京音系裏最少有三個元音，而且最多也衹能有三個。説北京音系衹有三個元音已經不是什麽新奇的説法了，在國内可能知道的人尚不太多，但在國外早在1944年就由美國學者哈特門在一篇論文中提出來了（Hartman 1944）。爲北京音系確立一個低元音/a/是大家都能接受的，因爲天[tʻiɛn]、貪[tʻæn]、胎[tʻæi]、他[tʻa]、掏[tʻɔu]、湯[tʻɑŋ]等類的字，雖然分别含有[ɛ、æ、a、ɔ、ɑ]等音值不同的元音，但這些元音都在互補的情况下出現，所以可以看作同一個低元音音位的變體，上面的幾個例子也就可以分别用音位標寫成/thyan、than、thay、tha、thaw、thang/了（“h”表示送氣）。認定一個中元音/ə/則比較困難，因爲很多人仍斤斤計較於音值的差異，認爲諸如姐[tɕie]、哥[kɤ]、果[kuo]、九[tɕiə̯u]、梗[kə̂ŋ]等字都含有不同的元音，最多衹能作部分合併，全部合拼爲一個中元音是不對的。其實前三個例子的主要元音雖然不同，却分别出現在齊齒、開口、與合口三類韻頭之後，構成互補分布，是完全可以合併的。（後兩個例子牽涉到韻尾，容待下文討論）要確認一個高元音/ɨ/，就必須把作爲韻腹的“i、u、ü”等所謂“單元音”分析爲/yɨ、wɨ. ywɨ/等音位合體。這對很多人來説，太違反常規了，簡直是匪夷所思，所以迄今在國外也還有很多人認爲是没有道理的。我們認爲，基於下列三個理由，我們勢必作這樣的音位分析。其一，以這幾個“單元音”爲韻腹的韻母在四呼分類中屬於那一類，一向都是毫無争議的；假如我們堅守四呼的分類（以及“開、合”兩呼與“洪、細”兩音的分類）是以韻頭爲依據的這一原則，我們就必須承認它們都分别含有相應的韻頭。其二，在四呼相配的分布裏，這幾個“單元音”作爲韻腹時與作爲韻頭時相配的方式是完全一致的，這可以看作它們實際上爲韻頭加韻腹之合體的證據。其三，在十三轍的分韻中，衣[i]、屍[ʂi]、居[tɕü]類的字都屬於“一七”轍（羅 1950：35）；假如我們堅守互押的字必須含有相同的韻基這一原則，我們就得承認這些字應該分析成/yɨ、srɨ、kywɨ/，即含有共同的韻基/-ɨø/。哈特門完全遵守了音節分段的原則，也基本上遵守了四呼以韻頭爲依據的原則，所以能够得出北京音系衹有高、中、低三個元音的合理結論。但是他在討論高、中兩個元音的分配時，忽略了押韻的原則；他不瞭解兒化韻的性質，把兒化造成的音節與一般音節相提並論，從而忽略了這個連音變化的規律，並作出了中元音可分長、短的錯誤結論；他又把"r" 也算作介音，從而淆亂了以介音分呼的觀念。這幾點使得他的研究結論顯得美中不足。數年後美國語言學家霍凱特也發表了一篇論北京音系的文章(Hockett 1947)。他大概是看出了北京音系裏元音分配的一個特殊現象(見下文討論)，覺得這個音系連三個元音都没有，其實衹有兩個。爲了支持他這個理論，他不惜打破好幾個原則。第一，語音學一般都把語音分成"元音、半元音、輔音"三類，他則提出應分爲"元音、半元音、半輔音、輔音"四類。第二，他打破音節必須含有元音的原則，認爲元音、半元音、半輔音都可以構成音節。第三，這樣一來，互押的字必有相同的"韻基"這一原則自然也就無法保持了。(他没有直接説，但是大概他覺得没有保持這個原則的必要。)另外，像哈特門一樣，他也認爲捲舌聲母中的"r"成分是一個介音，也把兒化造成的音節同等看待。但是他看出哈特門唯獨把中元音/e/作長、短的區分是不對的，因此提出"根兒"與"歌兒"的區分不是元音長短的問題，而是因爲前者在/r/之前還有一個前半元音韻尾，而後者則没有。這個説法是正確的(請參看論兒化韻部分)，但是他却忽略了另一面，因爲如此一來，他的分析連"兒"字與"蛾兒"的讀音差别都無法區分了，更不用説解釋了。這許多問題都是由於他勉强地减少一個元音造成的。五十年代中期，蘇聯的漢學家龍果夫與龍果娃也發表了他們對北京音系的研究(Dragunov 1958)。據他們自己説，他們在分析時刻意應用中國的傳統方法，而不使用前此歐洲學者研究漢語的模式。基本上他們遵守了音節分段與四呼歸類的原則，並爲北京音的韻母畫出極爲嚴整的幾何圖式。我不知道他們是否曾受到前文提到的那兩位美國語言學家的影響，不過他們的結論與那兩位美國學者的倒很相似。他們不説北京音系有三個元音，而説有三類韻母，即"零"類、"ə" 類，與"a" 類。日本學者藤堂明保亦於 1958 年發表他對北京音系的研究。他對中國的音韻學傳統當然更熟悉。他的結論也是北京音系有三個元音，寫作/ɪ,ɔ,a/。

2.4.2 北京音系中雖然衹有三個元音，但在分配方面却有一個突出的特點。三個元音的音位對比衹在無尾韻(直音韻)中顯示出來。比如宜/yɨ/、爺

/yə́/、牙/yá/三個字,同爲無聲母、無韻尾的齊齒呼第二聲(陽平聲)字,它們相互之間的對比就衹能是韻腹的不同了。因此我們説北京音系裏至少得有三個元音,但也不多於三個,因爲再也没有一個同時含有上列四個共同成分而又與這三個字構成對比的字了。然而在帶尾韻中,不管韻尾是什麽,却衹可能有兩個元音的對比。比如在下列兩兩相對的字組中,每一組的兩個字在聲母、韻頭、韻尾及聲調方面都是相同的,因此使它們構成對比的成分就衹能是韻腹了,而這種對比的字却也没有第三個可能:

雷對來,回對懷,收對燒,有對咬;
深對山,銀對言,本對板,運對院;
燈對當,情對强,碰對胖。

這些對比的性質究竟是什麽呢?當然大家都同意每組對比中的第二個字韻腹都是低元音/a/,那麽與它構成對比的頭一個字的韻腹就有是高元音/ɨ/或中元音/ə/的兩種可能了。不管選擇那一個可能,都可以完全達到區别字音的目的(descriptively adequate),而且衹要我們的選擇始終一致(即把"痕、銀、文、雲"等之類的字解釋成含有相同的元音),也就可以説符合了押韻的原則。在這個問題上,以前的學者們又顯出了分歧。哈特門作了一個混合的選擇。他説由於京[tɕiŋ]與民[min]之類的字顯然含有高元音,所以應把它們的韻腹定爲/i/(我寫作/ɨ/),而更[kə̂ŋ]、門[mə̂n]與九[tɕiə̭u]之類的字與前者在"元音性質上有截然不同的差别"(a clear-cut distinction of vowel quality),所以應該把它們的韻腹定爲中元音/e/(我寫作/ə/)。龍果夫與藤堂明保則把這類字一律定爲含有中元音/ə/。他們没有説明原因,大概是他們的聽覺與哈特門不同吧。當初我也認爲我們這裏所討論的對比是中元音/ə/與低元音/a/的對比,因爲我覺得這個選擇可以讓我們給北京音系的元音分配提出一個概括性的原則,即"在北京音系裏,衹有非高元音([V,-high])才能出現在帶尾韻中。"但是後來的繼續研究使我相信有比這個結構問題更重要的考慮,所以我覺得帶尾韻裏元音的對比必須定爲高元音/ɨ/與低元音/a/的對比,理由如下:

a) 即使在"更、門、黑、頭"等字所代表的音節中,韻腹元音也是很高的。

(連 Wade-Giles 拼音式也給它們帶上小帽子“ê”,表示相當高。)把它們解釋爲高元音完全合理。

b) 爲了合理地解釋兒化韻現象,以及因兒化形成的新音節,我們必須把這類字的元音定爲高元音。(詳細討論請看論兒化韻部分)。

c) 帶尾韻的韻腹元音僅有高低兩度對比這一現象由來已久,而中元音的形成則是較晚近的事,而且形成時並未影響到原含高元音的音節。(見下文論“梭坡、乜斜”兩轍的合併。)所以爲了表明這一歷史性的事實,也應把這類原含高元音的音節保持不變。

2.4.3 在上文討論的基礎上,我們可以用下面這張表來概括北京音系裏韻母的結構,並把“十三轍”的韻目附在下面以供參考。

韻尾 / 韻腹 / 韻頭		ø直音				y收噫		w收嗚		n抵腭		ŋ穿鼻	
		ɨ		ə	a	ɨ	a	ɨ	a	ɨ	a	ɨ	a
開	ø		支	歌	大	黑	來	侯	高	痕	山	亨	唐
齊	y		衣	切	加		(厓)	油	條	銀	先	英	江
合	w	姑		多	花	灰	懷			文	端	翁	王
撮口	yw		居	月						雲	宣	凶	
十三轍		姑蘇	一七	梭乜 坡斜	發花	灰堆	懷來	油求	遙條	人辰	言前	東中	江陽

這張表相當充分地展示了北京音系中韻母的結構。它嚴守了我們所訂的分析規則,因此也就適當地解釋了説這種話的人的語感。現在再把有關的個別問題分條討論如下:

a) 在韻基/-əø/之下,“十三轍”列出了“梭坡、乜斜”兩轍,這似乎違反了押韻的原理,其實不然。我們的分析所顯示的是現代北京音系的結構,而“十三轍”的分韻所表現的則是明清之交的北京音系。在那個音系中,有四個元音,即高元音/ɨ/與三個分前央後的低元音/e、a、ɔ/。其中衹有央元音/ɨ、a/可以出現在帶尾音節裏,這與現代北京話的帶尾韻是一致的,所以“灰堆”以下八轍全合。在無尾韻中,“十三轍”所代表的音系應得四轍,但因/-ɨø/類分作兩轍(見下節討論)故實分五轍,其中“梭坡”的韻基是後元音/-ɔø/而“乜斜”的韻基是前元音/-eø/。所以在這種音系裏,“閣合蛾莫嶽”(梭坡)與另一組“格核額墨月”(乜斜)中兩兩相對的字都不同音。在許多南方官話裏,如湖北、四川等地區,這種對比依然存在,但在現代北京話中,上舉兩兩相對的字已變成同音了,而且原屬“梭坡、乜斜”兩轍的字也完全互押了。我們給這種現象的解釋是:“十三轍”時代以後的某個時期(大概是清代中葉吧),北京音系中的前後兩個低元音合併成爲現代高中低三度元音中的中元音/ə/,所以原來的兩轍就自然合轍了。前後兩個元音的合併並没有影響到/ɨ、a/兩個央元音;尤其是在帶尾韻中,原來的高低對比依然如故。前文討論現代北京音的元音分配時,我們主張把帶尾韻中的元音對比解釋爲高元音/ɨ/對低元音/a/,這就是主要原因之一。

b) 在韻基/-ɨø/之下,“十三轍”也列出兩轍,這顯然是有違押韻原理的。也許有人説,既然“姑蘇”與“一七”分轍,我們就應該爲它們定出不同的韻腹元音。這就等於説,它們的分轍恰可證明我們的分析是錯誤的。我們要説這是不可能的。韻母結構表清楚地顯示出“姑蘇”轍的字實爲“一七”轍的相對合口呼,而“支吉姑居”四個字是四呼相配的這一事實,也是所有説北京話的人都感覺得到的。那麼它們的分轍究竟是什麼原因呢?這確實是一個難題。首先我們必須承認它們的分轍是違反押韻原理的,然後我們才能爲這一現象另找合理的解説。略檢明清以來的韻書,我們便可發現它們在其他各類字的分韻方面大體上都是一致的,有不一致的地方時也可拿語音演變的規律來解釋,但唯獨對韻基爲/-ɨø/的字處置各異①。一方面有人把這類字完全合爲一韻(恰合我們的分析),另一方面則有人把它們按四呼的分别干脆分成四韻。在這兩極端之間,一切可能的分合幾乎是應有盡有。這表示出當時學者的意見分歧,前文(2.2.2節)所説以韻尾分韻類時的錯亂,亦由此起。但大體上説,多數人

① 趙蔭堂的《等韻源流》第258頁之後,附“明清等韻化濁入清系統韻母表”,標名甚怪,但頗有參考價值,所引之書我多半都没有機會見到,但由表的形式看,各書分韻的情形是甚爲相近的,足見它們所依據的必爲各個作者心目中的“標準話”。各書在分韻上的差異多半是由不同歷史階段中的音變造成的,唯獨對“支、齊、模、魚”四類韻母意見分歧。大體説來,最占優勢的分法是與“十三轍”一致的,也有人把這四類韻母合在一起,共得“十二”之數。他們多把這個現象比附於十二律或十二月,分十二韻的人則説於十二月之外復加一閏月云云。這種説法當然是荒誕不經的,因此有人批評他們是爲了凑數才如此分韻的,我的看法則不然。我覺得他們是先看到了這種押韻現象以後,才爲這一現象尋找解釋的。他們深爲這種完整的音韻系統而驚詫不已,自然覺得這是宇宙間的至理,是與道同在的天籟,因而才有玄學式的穿鑿附會。

的分法是與“十三轍”的分法一致的,即把開/ɨ/、齊/yɨ/、撮/ywɨ/三個韻母的字併爲一韻,而把合/wɨ/這一個韻母的字分出來另成一韻。這是什麼道理,我也不敢絶對確定,但可提出兩點解釋:其一,在音位結構上説。這四個韻母雖然同屬高元音,但就音值説,則因受到聲母及介音的影響而分舌前與舌後;“支思衣魚”等字所代表的三個韻母(“一七”轍)在發音上同是利用舌尖或舌前的,“姑蘇”轍的字則顯然爲舌後音,差别甚大,連以北京話爲母語的人也聽得出來,故另成一韻[①]。其二,這種舌前與舌後的差别清楚地顯現在兒化的連音變化中;“一七”轍的三個韻母變化時步調一致,而“姑蘇”轍的字則獨成一格。(詳細討論請看論兒化韻部分。)我猜想這兩轍的分立大概就是由於上述這兩個緣故吧。

c) 我們的韻母表似乎已把北京話中所有的韻母都包攬無遺了,其實不然。細心的讀者應該已經看出其中少了一個,那就是“兒耳二”等字所代表的那個韻母。這是否表示我們對韻母結構的分析有問題呢? 那倒不然,這些字原爲“日”母字,在明代的北京話裏就改讀爲零聲母了(詳細的討論請看論兒化韻部分)。我對這一現象的解釋是:由於音易位(metathesis)的關係,這些字所代表的音節由/rɨ/變成/ɨr/。這就給北京話增添了一個特殊的新韻尾,也就是兒化韻韻尾的來源。但是這個韻尾太特殊了,除了出現在由連音變化所造成的兒化音節裏以外,祇出現在/ɨr/這一個基本音節中。我們的韻母表祇收入基本音節,爲了簡便,没有把/r/這個韻尾包括進去,因此就没有辦法把“兒”等所代表的韻母包括進去了。這是唯一的例外。

---

① 另一個音理性的原因是:漢語中韻腹元音所受的影響主要來自韻尾,其次來自韻頭,所以雖然高元音的性質比較特殊,在有尾韻中四呼仍不分韻,但在無尾韻中,來自韻頭的影響便特别突出,遂使“姑蘇”類的字與其他三個韻母的字迥然有别。

第三章　北京話聲母的性質

3. 一般説來,輔音音位的認定要比元音音位的認定容易得多。北京話裏的聲母一般都説是二十一個,加上零聲母就是二十二個了。這當然已經是初步歸併以後的結果。我們的目標是探求聲母音位系統,因此便可以在這個基礎上作進一步的研究,而不必斤斤計較於它們在音值方面的各種細微變體。這二十一個聲母就是下列二十一個注音符號所代表的輔音:

方法 部位	不送氣音	送氣音	擦音	鼻音	流音
脣　音	ㄅ	ㄆ	ㄈ	ㄇ	
齦前音	ㄉ	ㄊ		ㄋ	ㄌ
齦後音	ㄗ	ㄘ	ㄙ		
捲舌音	ㄓ	ㄔ	ㄕ		ㄖ
舌面音	ㄐ	ㄑ	ㄒ		
舌根音	ㄍ	ㄎ	ㄏ		

這二十一個輔音,一般都用所謂寬式的國際音標標寫如下:

方法 部位	不送氣音	送氣音	擦音	鼻音	流音
脣　音	p	pʻ	f	m	
齦前音	t	tʻ		n	l
齦後音	ʦ	ʦʻ	s		
捲舌音	ʈʂ	ʈʂʻ	ʂ		ʐ
舌面音	ʨ	ʨʻ	ɕ		
舌根音	k	kʻ	h		

3.1 在上列許多聲母中,齦前音、齦後音以及舌根音性質上比較單純,顯然都各自構成單一的音位,因此我們就用不着多費筆墨討論它們了。在此倒有兩個涉及所有聲母的觀念需要先説一下。其一,上面聲母表中,每一方格内

衹可能有一個聲母,這個聲母衹可能是一個音位而不是一個複輔音(consonant cluster),因此除非有特別需要,我們將儘可能衹用單一的符號代表它,基於這一理由,我們將把齦後音的[ʦ] 改寫爲/c/。其二,"送氣"是漢語輔音中的一個極重要的區別性特徵(distinctive feature),送氣與否構成了兩套塞音的對比,在語音史與方言比較的討論中,也是要經常提及的,因此我們覺得有特別需要把它們分標出來,同時爲了使它在音律公式中比較醒目,我們改用"h"作送氣符號,所以齦後音中的[ʦ']就改寫成/ch/了。這樣"h"這個符號就擔當了雙重的任務,一是作爲舌根擦音的單一音位,另一則是作爲"送氣"這個區別性特徵的符號,這兩個功用並不冲突,因爲後者總是出現在另一輔音符號之後的。嚴格地説,上表中的擦音性質上也都是送氣的,但因爲它們衹有一類,未構成對比,所以就用不着標出來了。根據上述的説明,此處討論的三類聲位,就可以寫成/t、th、n、l;c、ch、s;k、kh、h/了。

3.2 我們將把捲舌聲母改寫爲/cr、crh、sr、r/。理由是這類聲母與齦後音聲母的關係,不論是在漢語史上或在現代漢語方言中,都十分密切。我們這樣轉寫就表示我們認定他們的性質是基本相同的,唯一的不同就是前者多了一個"捲舌"成分而後者没有。在許多現代漢語方言中,這兩類聲母的對比已經消失,我們的轉寫方式也爲這種音變提供了最簡便的表達方式,即當捲舌聲母去掉了"r" 這個區別性特徵時,它們自然就跟相對應的齦後音合併了。把"r"這個"捲舌"特徵分標出來,跟上節把"h"這個"送氣"特徵分標出來,其理由與方式是完全一致的,即把前頭的輔音符號當作主體,另加一兩個特殊的區別性特徵而組成一個獨立的音位。所以像/crh/這樣的複合符號,不表示它是三個音位的結合,而衹表示這個音位含有齦後不送氣音/c/所具有的一切區別性特徵,外加"捲舌"與"送氣"兩個特徵。這個做法實質上是一種取巧的手段,即在不必全部采用生成音韻學模式的情况下,充分利用這一新模式的優點以達到顯示音位之間的關係及其轉化的規律。與上節中的"h"一樣,我們在這兒也是讓"r" 這個符號擔任兩種任務的,就北京音系本身説,這同樣也不會造成問題。但在捲舌聲母已變入齦後聲母的方言裏,原讀這個聲母的字並非變爲零聲母字,而是變爲聲母類似[z]的字,可見原聲母的性質較複雜,不僅是一個"捲舌"成分而已。另外需要一提的是,有許多學者把"r"解釋爲韻頭(Hartman

1944, Hockett 1947, Tōdō 1963 等)。我認爲這在理論上是絶對不妥的。增添一個韻頭勢必淆亂了以韻頭分四呼的道理,而含有這個韻頭的韻母又僅能出現在一類聲母之後也是不合理的。

3.3 在我們的書寫方式裏,唇音聲母自然應作/p、ph、f、m/。這些聲母除了/f/以外,都可以與齊齒韻母相配,但全不與撮口韻母相配。在與洪音韻母相配時,它們都顯示出一種不尋常的性向,即開口與合口之對比的消失。這種現象其實並非現代漢語所獨有,研究古音的人早就根據中古的反切系聯提出了所謂"脣音字不分開合"的説法。但所謂不分開合是否能理解爲脣音字的韻母既非開又非合呢?我認爲絶對不可以。如果我們不躲避問題,我們就得在理論上辯證這些韻母到底是開還是合。在現有的絶大多數北京話標寫法裏,讀洪音的脣音字都以開口形式出現,如巴[pa]、忙[man]、夢[mêŋ]、本[pên]、反[fan]、毛[mau]、北[pêi]、白[pai] 等,但却有一個半例外,即韻母爲[u]及韻母爲[uo]者,前者一律都作合口(如布 [pu]、木[mu] 等),後者則有人作合口(如波[puo]、坡[p'uo]等),有人作開口(如波[po]、坡[p'o]等)。但由於這些字都没有開合的對比,我們從音位觀點上就可以把它們解釋做一律爲開口字或一律爲合口字。哪一個選擇都可以達到區别字音的目的,而且都讓我們可以給脣音字的性向作一個概括性的説明,即脣音聲母衹配齊齒與開口韻母,或脣音聲母衹配齊齒與合口韻母。問題是哪一個選擇比較合理。我認爲就音位結構説應把這類字都定性爲合口,理由如下:

a) 説脣音聲母或多或少都有脣化(合口)的現象是一個合理的説法,因此説脣音聲母除配齊齒韻母外衹配合口韻母也就是合理的了。反過來説,要把這類字全解釋爲開口則不可能,把"波"字寫成/pə/([po])而勉强認作開口尚屬似是而非,但把"布"字解釋爲*/pɨ/而認作開口則絶無可能了。這不僅是"讀不出來"或者"聽着不像"而已,這牽涉到了"姑蘇"轍跟"一七"轍分韻的問題,把"布"解釋爲*/pɨ/就等於説這個字跟"四"/sɨ/相押而不跟"素"/swɨ/相押,這是任何説北京話的人都不會同意的。另外就兒化的連音變化説,韻母/ɨ/與韻母/wɨ/的變化迥然不同(參看論兒化韻部分),"布兒"的變化也是與"素兒"相類而不與"四兒"相類的。所以我們必須把"布"之類的字認定爲合口,僅此一端,使我們無法提出前文有關脣音聲母性向的概括説明了。

b）在方言的比較研究中，爲了明白暢達地表現它們之間的對應關係，把這類脣音字解釋爲合口也是較合理的。許多方言中都有以/h/代/f/或者以/f/代/h/的現象，但這種代換衹發生在/h/爲聲母的合口字裏，與開口字無涉，比如下列各例：

風⟶轟，不變“亨”。

非⟷灰，不變“黑”。

飯⟷换，不變“漢”。

房⟷黄，不變“航”。

很顯然，如果我們把這些以/f/爲聲母的字解釋爲合口字，就可以更合理地説明這些對應的現象。

c）即使在兒童學習語言時，以/f/爲聲母的洪音字與以/h/爲聲母的合口字也有互换的現象。我曾經注意到許多孩子（包括我自己的女兒）把“喜歡”説成“喜翻”，但從不把“黑猫”説成“飛猫”。這表示在語音的本質上，脣音聲母的洪音字本來就接近合口字。

3.4 舌面音［tɕ、tɕʻ、ɕ］在北京音系裏的音韻地位是一個相當棘手的問題。這幾個聲母衹能配細音韻母，而齦後音/c、ch、s/，捲舌音/cr、crh、sr、r/，與舌根音/k、kh、h/則都衹配洪音韻母。换句話説，舌面音聲母同時與三類相互構成對比的聲母具有互補的關係。在理論層次上説，把舌面音解釋爲上述三類聲母中某一類的變體是絶對有必要的。如果像注音符號及多數漢語拼音式那樣，把舌面音作爲獨立的聲母音位，自然也不會在實用上造成字音混淆的問題，但在理論層次上，那是一種不表示態度的做法，也就是規避問題。把介音中的“腭化”成分歸併入這些舌面音並從而把它們當作獨立聲母（比如拼音方案就把“居、屈、虚”寫作“ju、qu、xu”）在理論上説也不妥當，因爲這會打亂介音的體系並從而造成對以韻頭分四呼的誤解。所以我們必須把它們解釋爲上述三類聲母中某一類的變體。問題是：到底該是那一類呢？由於三種可能都已經有人提出過（也有采用混合式的，如威妥瑪式、耶魯式及國語羅馬字等拼音方式），我自然不可能提出另一種新的可能。在此我衹能爲我所作的選擇提出一些新的論證。我覺得舌面音應與舌根音歸併爲一類聲母音位，理由如下：

a) 北京話裏有許多部分重叠的半擬聲詞,例如:

劈哩啪啦/phyɨ lyɨ phwa la/[p‘i li p‘a la]

嘀哩嗒啦/tyɨ lyɨ ta la/[ti li ta la]

踢哩趿啦/thyɨ lyɨ tha la/[t‘i li t‘a la]

這些擬聲詞的重叠形式可以歸納爲"C_1i C_2i C_1a C_2a"這樣一個公式,意思是説這種重叠遵循一定的模式,即在四個音節中,頭兩個與後兩個各自互爲叠韻,一三兩個與二四兩個則各自互爲雙聲。在這個模式裏,第二個與第四個音節中互爲雙聲的聲母(C_2)是/l/,但在第一與第三兩個音節中互爲雙聲的聲母。(C_1)則是一個變數。如果我們用諸如/p、ph、m、t、th/等聲母代替公式中的 C_1 自然没有問題,因爲這些聲母都同時可配洪細兩類韻母。但如我們用舌面音代替 C_1,那就有問題了,因爲舌面音衹能配細音而不能配洪音,在這種情況下,第三音節中的聲母應該是什麽呢?下列的例子回答了這個問題,也有力地表明了説北京話者的語感。

嘰哩呱啦(嘰裏旮旯)[tɕi li k(w)a la]

喊哩咵啦[tɕ‘i li k‘(w)a la]

唏哩嘩啦[ɕi li h(w)a la]

這些例子顯示出,在説北京話者的潛意識中,舌面音與舌根音在音位的屬性上應爲一類①。

b) 在漢語史中,舌面音的出現是比較晚的現象,大致在宋代以後。它們是由原出現在細音音節中的舌根音(喉、牙、音)聲母演變出來的。也就是説,舌根音受到細音韻母的同化作用而腭化了。由於腭化的程度逐漸加深,遂使它們似乎變成了不同的聲母。但是這種發音上的改變並没有引起音位系統的重新組合,所以不管它們的讀法聽起來跟舌根音相差多麽大,它們與舌根音仍然是同一類聲母音位的變體。與此同時,齦後音及捲舌音聲母一直都是洪細

① 腭化聲母與舌根聲母的對應關係,也表現在韻腹爲高元音的音節裏。趙元任先生曾引述周法高先生所舉的例子"嘰裏咕嚕"與"唏哩嗯嚕"等,來説明與我們此處所持的相同觀點(趙1968)。李方桂先生曾對我戲舉"吱吱喳喳"[tɕi tɕi tʂa tʂa]作爲反證,好像腭化聲母與捲舌聲母也可以是同位音了。就互補關係説,這當然也可以。我們衹是説,比較而言,把腭化聲母與舌根聲母認作同位音似乎更好一些。比如説,没有人説"嘻嘻吵吵",大家都説"嘻嘻哈哈"。

兩配的(當然它們本身也可能都含有變體,這是我們無法絶對確定的)。這種情況一直延續到清代初期或中葉才有所改變(即“十三轍”形成之後)。首先,捲舌音聲母的細音字變成了洪音,即丟掉了它們介音中的腭化成分,所以原來讀音不同的細音字如“書”/srywɨ/與洪音字如“梳”/srwɨ/就變成同音了,這就造成了一大批京戲傳統上所説的“上口字”(當然所謂“上口字”不限於這一類)。這種轉變是捲舌聲母本身的事,實與舌面音無直接關係,但是如此一來,它們也就有了互補的關係了。其次,不久之後齦後音聲母的細音字也發生了變化。這些聲母也由於受到細音的同化而變爲腭化。這就使它們與原由舌根音變來的舌面音合流了,造成了京戲傳統中所謂的“不分尖團”,原來的尖音如“齊”[ʦʻi]/chyɨ/跟原來的團音如“其”[ʨʻi]/khyɨ/也就變成同音了。這個變化也是齦後音聲母自身的問題,不是原已存在的舌面音聲母的變化,但是音變的結果也使得舌面音與齦後音有了互補的關係。由以上的叙述可知,北京話裏舌面音與三類聲母同時構成互補這一現象,實有層次與順序上的不同,這種層次上的差異仍以不同程度表現在其他方言中。所以如果我們要合理地説明歷史的演進與方言的差異,我們也必須把舌面音與舌根音認作同一類音位的變體。

3.5 綜合以上的討論,我們可以用下面這張聲母表作一個總結。另有一些它們與韻母拼合的細節,將在討論過聲調以後一並説明。在此需要説明的倒有一點,即所謂“零”聲母的問題,在音位結構上説,把這個聲母算作零聲母是完全合理的。但是正如趙元任先生早已指出的,在發音上説,這個零聲母並不全等於零,實爲發聲開始時喉部的收縮,所以在漢語裏,零聲母音節一般都保持獨立而不與前一節的韻尾輔音相結合,就是這個緣故①。我們可以在此指出,在漢語音韻的演變規律裏,“喻” 母字以及“影”母消失以後的字(即零聲母)都是跟隨舌根音以及次濁音聲母字同步轉化的,因此在下面的表裏,我們把零聲母“ø”也標出來,而且放在舌根音與流音的交叉點上。

① 歷史上的音變是與發音方式分不開的。在漢語史中,喻母字(包括由原影母變來者)的演變與喉牙音聲母字是一致的,而與脣舌齒音聲母有别,這也可證它實質上是一個喉音。

方法 部位	不送氣音	送氣音	擦音	鼻音	流音
脣　音	p	ph	f	m	
齦前音	t	th		n	l
齦後音	c	ch	s		
捲舌音	cr	crh	sr	r	
舌根音	k	kh	h		ø

第四章　北京話的聲韻調拼合問題

4. 在我們討論聲韻調的拼合問題之前，自然必須先討論一下調的性質。漢語是以調辨義的語言，這是盡人皆知的事實，但如說到北京話裏究竟有幾個調，以及這些調的性質如何，就往往言人人殊了。比如説，大家都知道調是一種超音段(suprasegmental) 音位，不能獨立存在而必須依附在成段音位上，但依附在哪段音位上呢？這就説法不一了。歸納起來可得四種説法：(1) 調寄附在整個音節上；(2) 調寄附在韻母上；(3) 調從一個音節的頭一個濁音部分開始；(4) 調寄附在韻腹上。我們所堅持的漢語音節的分段方式，即每一音節至多衹能有四個音段而其中衹有韻腹是必須出現的，自然使我們必得承認調是寄附在韻腹上的。這是從嚴格的音位觀點説的，就發音的實際説，正如同成段音位常因受相鄰音位之影響而有變體一樣，調位在發音上自然也可能由於音節構成的不同而擴及韻腹元音之外的部分，但這種現象絶不應使我們對調位是韻腹上超音段音位這一性質發生懷疑。

4.1 北京音系中的調位一般都認爲是四個，這是專就重讀的(stressed)音節而言的。由於漢字是單音節，在一般的情況下我們把單字分讀時。自然也都念成重音，所以才會造成衹有四個調位的説法。其實漢語中有些字，尤其是“語法詞”(syntactic words)，必須是輕讀的。把它們重讀並付與某一聲調是念單字時的不得已的做法，嚴格地説，這就把它們變成另一個音節了，也可以説變成另一個字了，這是不合理的。所以如果我們把輕聲也算作一個調位，那就得説北京音系裏至少有五個調位。這五個調位的實際讀法，根據趙元任先生的五音階標調法，分别應爲：第一聲，陰平，高平調[55]；第二聲，陽平，高升調[35]；第三聲，上聲，低降升調[214]；第四聲，去聲，低降調[51]；輕聲，短調，其音階之高低按一定的規律受其所依附的重讀音調之制約。當然在實際説話時，這些調位的調值不會是那麽固定的，比方説，假如把陰平讀作[44]、陽平讀作[25]、上聲讀作[213]、去聲讀作[31]，對“老北京人”來説，可能會有些“不順耳”，但也不至於發生辨義上的問題。所以純就調位的對比性質而言，北京話的五個聲調可以説是以三個辨别成分來區分的，即重輕[±stress]、高低[±high]與平仄[±level]。(這兒所謂的平仄專指調形的平與不平，與詩韻的所謂"平仄"有别。在連讀中，當上聲出現在其他聲調之前時，上聲的調形是[211]，所以可以看作低平調。)

4.2 不同的調位在音域上有長短之分。這種分别不是音位性的，但却對韻腹元音的性質有相當的影響。音域最寬的是第三聲，常常影響到韻腹元音的音值，使得它聽起來似乎比在别的聲調中要長一些跟低一些。對這種現象，外國人比較敏感，例如哈特門就堅稱"九"字的讀音爲[tɕiə̯u]而"就"的讀音爲[tɕiu]，因此説二者的韻腹元音音位不同，後者爲高元音，前者爲中元音(Hartman 1944)。這種差别甚至表現在經過連音變化的上聲字裏。大家都知道，在北京話裏，當兩個上聲字出現在一起時，頭一個就變爲陽平了。因此"有井"就應該變得跟"油井"完全一樣了。但美國學者霍凱特就不以爲然，他認爲這兩個詞仍然是不同的(Hockett 1950)。我們則認爲上聲使韻腹元音變得相對地低一些是可以肯定的，但那衹是音值的變動，並未改變音位的性質，所以"九、就、油、有"等的元音音位是相同的。

4.3 一般都認爲北京話裏衹有一種輕聲，但也有人指出輕聲實爲兩種(Chen 1984)；因爲原屬輕聲而且衹能是輕聲的字，與本非輕聲但因連讀而變爲輕聲的字，細辨起來仍有一些差别，並且在連音變讀中有不同的結果。我覺得這個觀察是很有見地的，兩類輕聲字的差異也是可以肯定的，因爲像"琢磨着"中輕讀的"磨"字跟"這麽着"中的"麽"字，確有些不同。這類對比詞數目極少，因此不太引起人們的注意，再加上純輕聲詞音量不大，爲了加强語氣，有時就得故意把它們讀響些，遂使這兩類輕聲的差異更不明顯了。然而這種差異是否真是輕聲的問題呢？我倒覺得不一定，因爲輕聲是一種又輕又短的調子，似乎不可能再作更細微的音位性區别了。我覺得這種差别倒可能是韻腹元音的不同。我們已經指出過，北京音系中的高中低三度元音對比衹出現在無尾韻中。高元音的開口無尾韻母/-ɨø/衹能跟齦後音與捲舌音相配，也就是説衹能有"支"與"思"這兩類不同聲母的字，但這衹是就非輕聲音節而説的，輕聲字作爲一個特殊的範疇是否可能不受這個限制呢？我覺得完全有可能。語法詞如"的、了、麽、呢"等，在正常語序中，都代表輕讀的開口無尾音節。一般都認爲它們的韻腹是中元音,我覺得其實可能是高元音。這不惟合理地解釋了爲什麼它們與由連讀造成的輕聲字仍不一樣,而且也較有力地説明了爲什麼它們能與感嘆詞"啊"合組成"d'a、l'a(啦)、m'a、n'a(吶)"等新音節,因爲連讀時高元音比中元音更易丢失。

4.4 爲了具體與全面地顯示出北京話聲韻調拼合的狀態,圖表的方式是最清晰最有效的。下面我們就以"十三轍"爲標目,仿照傳統的等韻圖形式,畫出十一張表,爲北京音系中所有的音節定位。

4.4.1 我們衹需要十一張圖,因爲:(1)"一七"與"姑蘇"兩轍本可合爲一圖;(2)"梭坡"與"乜斜"在現代北京話裏已經合轍;(3)我們以四呼代替四等;所以就不需開合分圖了。聲調方面,因爲輕聲字爲數甚少,所以我們仍衹列"陰、陽、上、去"四聲,而把輕聲另作例外的處置(見下文)。聲母方面,我們儘可能地恢復它們的古稱,即改用"脣、舌、齒頭、正齒、牙"音等名,並把它們平列出來。聲母與韻母的相配自然有些限制。在四呼的基礎上説,可以歸納爲以下幾點:(1)脣音衹配齊齒與合口韻母;(2)齒頭與正齒衹配洪音;(3)舌音中的/t、th/不配撮口韻母;(4)四呼俱配的衹有舌音中的/n、l/及全部牙音(包括零聲母)。在圖表中,凡是聲韻不能相配的交叉點都空着,可以相配的地方,有聲有字的就填入實字,有聲無字的地方就畫上圓圈。

4.4.2 按理説,由於這些韻表是完全依據現代北京音系設計的,不受任何歷史文獻的束縛,所以它們應該是最直接了當的,每一個北京音系中可能有的音節都有一個而且也衹能有一個特定的地位,不需任何門法的補助説明。基本上説,我們做到了這一點,但爲了節省篇幅,我們容許了兩個例外:(1)我們説過,"兒耳二"等字所代表的是三個由音易位形成的特殊音節(/ɨr/);嚴格地説,它們應該自成一轍,但衹爲它們而另立一圖是無此必要的,因此我們把它們寄放在"一七"零聲母下的開口空位上,算是"兒韻寄此",並以括號把它們標示出來。(2)由於我們衹列四個主要調位而省去輕聲,所以那少數幾個衹能讀輕聲的語法詞"的了麼呢"等便無地容身了。我們上文已經討論過,這幾個屬於特殊範疇(輕聲)的音節不受一般聲韻拼合的限制,實以高元音/ɨ/爲韻母,打破了舌音不配韻母/ɨ/與脣音不配開口的通例。我們也把它們放在"一七"轍的開口欄的陰平地位,算是"輕聲寄此",並以括號把它們標示出來,因爲給它們另立一圖是不可能的。另外,根據我們給脣音聲母所下的概括性通則,我們把"油求"與"遥條"兩轍中非齊齒的脣音字統統列在合口欄内,這也是仿徐孝《等韻圖經》的先例(薛 1983)。

一七轍/(y(w))ɨø/姑蘇轍/wɨø/(附:兒、耳、二/ɨr/及純輕聲語法詞)

韻	聲/調	脣音 p	脣音 ph	脣音 f	脣音 m	舌音 t	舌音 th	舌音 n	舌音 l	齒頭 c	齒頭 ch	齒頭 s	正齒 cr	正齒 crh	正齒 sr	正齒 r	牙音 k	牙音 kh	牙音 h	牙音 ø
開 ɨ	陰				(麽)	(的)		(呢)	(了)	兹	刺	思	支	吃	詩	○				
	陽									○	瓷	○	直	持	時	○				(兒)
	上									紫	○	死	止	恥	史	○				(耳)
	去									自	次	四	至	翅	士	日				(二)
齊 yɨø	陰	逼	批		眯	低	梯	妮	哩								吉	七	西	衣
	陽	鼻	皮		迷	敵	提	泥	梨								及	其	習	宜
	上	比	匹		米	底	體	你	李								幾	起	洗	椅
	去	蔽	屁		密	地	剃	逆	栗								季	氣	細	義
合 wɨø	陰	逋	撲	夫	○	都	秃	○	擼	租	粗	蘇	豬	出	書	○	姑	哭	呼	屋
	陽	醭	蒲	扶	模	獨	屠	奴	爐	卒	○	俗	竹	除	孰	如	骨	○	胡	無
	上	補	普	甫	母	賭	土	努	魯	祖	○	○	主	楚	暑	乳	古	苦	虎	五
	去	布	鋪	父	木	杜	兔	怒	路	○	醋	素	住	處	樹	入	故	庫	户	務
撮 ywɨø	陰							○	○								居	屈	虚	遇
	陽							○	驢								菊	渠	徐	於
	上							女	吕								舉	取	許	雨
	去							○	緑								巨	去	叙	玉

坡斜轍/əø/(原梭坡、乜斜)

韻	聲／調	脣音				舌音				齒頭			正齒				牙音			
		p	ph	f	m	t	th	n	l	c	ch	s	cr	crh	sr	r	k	kh	h	ø
開 əø	陰					○	○	○	勒	○	○	○	遮	車	賒	○	歌	科	喝	阿
	陽					德	○	○	○	澤	○	○	哲	○	蛇	○	格	殼	河	蛾
	上					○	○	○	○	○	○	○	者	扯	舍	惹	葛	可	○	噁
	去					○	特	訥	樂	仄	側	色	這	徹	社	熱	個	客	賀	餓
齊 yəø	陰	憋	撇		咩	爹	貼	捏	○								接	切	些	椰
	陽	別	○		○	碟	○	○	○								潔	茄	斜	爺
	上	癟	苤		○	○	鐵	○	咧								姐	且	寫	野
	去	別	○		滅	○	帖	聶	列								借	竊	謝	夜
合 wəø	陰	波	坡	○	摸	多	托	○	啰	撮	搓	梭	桌	戳	說	○	鍋	○	豁	窩
	陽	勃	婆	佛	饃	奪	馱	挪	螺	昨	矬	○	濁	○	○	○	國	○	活	○
	上	跛	叵	○	抹	朵	妥	○	裸	左	○	所	○	○	○	○	果	○	火	我
	去	簸	破	○	沫	剁	唾	糯	落	坐	錯	○	○	綽	朔	若	過	擴	貨	臥
撮 ywəø	陰							○	○								撅	缺	薛	約
	陽							○	○								絕	瘸	學	○
	上							○	○								○	○	雪	○
	去							虐	略								倔	雀	穴	月

發花轍/aø/

韻	聲/調	脣音				舌音				齒頭			正齒				牙音			
		p	ph	f	m	t	th	n	l	c	ch	s	cr	crh	sr	r	k	kh	h	ø
開 aø	陰					搭	他	○	拉	匝	擦	撒	渣	叉	沙	○	旮	咖	哈	啊
	陽					達	○	拿	旯	雜	○	○	紮	茶	○	○	嘎	○	蛤	○
	上					打	塔	哪	喇	○	○	灑	眨	衩	傻	○	生	卡	哈	○
	去					大	踏	那	辣	○	○	卅	詐	詫	煞	○	尬	○	哈	○
齊 yaø	陰								○								加	掐	蝦	丫
	陽								○								夾	○	霞	牙
	上								倆								假	卡	○	雅
	去								○								價	恰	下	亞
合 waø	陰	巴	趴	發	媽								抓	○	刷	○	瓜	誇	花	蛙
	陽	拔	爬	伐	麻								○	○	○	○	○	○	滑	娃
	上	把	○	法	馬								爪	○	耍	○	寡	垮	○	瓦
	去	爸	怕	髮	罵								○	○	○	○	掛	跨	話	襪
撮 ywaø	陰																			
	陽																			
	上																			
	去																			

灰堆轍/ɨy/

韻	聲 調	脣音				舌音				齒頭			正齒				牙音			
		p	ph	f	m	t	th	n	l	c	ch	s	cr	crh	sr	r	k	kh	h	ø
開 ɨy	陰					逮	○	○	勒	○	○	○	○	○	○	○	○	○	黑	○
	陽					○	○	○	雷	賊	○	○	○	○	誰	○	○	○	○	○
	上					得	○	餒	壘	○	○	○	○	○	○	○	給	○	○	○
	去					○	○	內	淚	○	○	○	這	○	○	○	○	○	○	○
齊 yɨy	陰																			
	陽																			
	上																			
	去																			
合 wɨy	陰	悲	胚	飛	○	堆	推			○	崔	雖	追	吹	○	○	歸	虧	灰	威
	陽	○	陪	肥	枚	頹	頹			○	○	隨	○	垂	誰	蕤	○	葵	回	圍
	上	北	○	匪	美	對	腿			咀	○	髓	○	○	水	蕊	詭	傀	悔	委
	去	貝	配	肺	妹	對	退			罪	悴	歲	綴	○	稅	銳	桂	愧	會	胃
撮 ywɨy	陰																			
	陽																			
	上																			
	去																			

懷來轍/ay/

韻	聲/調	脣音				舌音				齒頭			正齒				牙音			
		p	ph	f	m	t	th	n	l	c	ch	s	cr	crh	sr	r	k	kh	h	ø
開 ay	陰					呆	胎	○	○	灾	猜	腮	齋	拆	篩	○	該	開	咳	哀
	陽					○	臺	○	來	○	才	○	宅	柴	○	○	○	○	孩	揺
	上					歹	○	奶	○	宰	采	○	窄	○	骰	○	改	楷	海	矮
	去					代	太	耐	賴	在	菜	賽	債	○	曬	○	蓋	愾	害	愛
齊 yay	陰																			
	陽																			
	上																			
	去																			
合 way	陰	掰	拍	○	○								拽	揣	衰	○	乖	○	○	歪
	陽	白	排	○	埋								○	○	○	○	○	○	懷	○
	上	擺	○	○	買								跩	揣	甩	○	拐	○	○	○
	去	敗	派	○	賣								拽	踹	帥	○	怪	快	壞	外
撮 yway	陰																			
	陽																			
	上																			
	去																			

油求轍/ɨw/

韻	聲／調	脣音				舌音				齒頭			正齒				牙音			
		p	ph	f	m	t	th	n	l	c	ch	s	cr	crh	sr	r	k	kh	h	ø
開 ɨw	陰					兜	偷	○	摟	鄒	○	搜	州	抽	收	○	句	摳	齁	歐
	陽					○	頭	○	樓	○	○	○	軸	愁	熟	柔	○	○	猴	○
	上					抖	○	○	簍	走	○	○	肘	醜	守	○	狗	口	吼	偶
	去					豆	透	耨	漏	奏	湊	嗽	宙	臭	受	肉	購	扣	厚	漚
齊 yɨw	陰				○	丟	○	妞	溜								糾	丘	休	憂
	陽				○	○	○	牛	流								○	求	○	由
	上				○	○	○	扭	柳								久	○	朽	友
	去				謬	○	○	○	六								舊	○	袖	又
合 wɨw	陰	○	剖	○	○															
	陽	○	抔	浮	謀															
	上	○	剖	否	某															
	去	○	○	○	○															
撮 ywɨw	陰																			
	陽																			
	上																			
	去																			

遥條轍/aw/

韻	聲 調	脣音				舌音				齒頭			正齒				牙音			
		p	ph	f	m	t	th	n	l	c	ch	s	cr	crh	sr	r	k	kh	h	ø
開 aw	陰					刀	滔	孬	撈	遭	操	搔	招	抄	稍	○	高	○	蒿	凹
	陽					掏	逃	撓	勞	鑿	曹	○	着	潮	勺	鐃	○	○	豪	敖
	上					島	討	腦	老	早	草	掃	找	吵	少	擾	稿	考	好	襖
	去					道	套	鬧	澇	造	糙	臊	趙	○	邵	繞	告	靠	浩	奥
齊 yaw	陰	標	飄		喵	刁	挑	○	撩								交	敲	消	妖
	陽	○	瓢		苗	○	條	○	遼								嚼	喬	淆	姚
	上	表	漂		秒	屌	窕	鳥	瞭								狡	巧	小	咬
	去	鰾	票		廟	吊	跳	尿	料								叫	竅	效	要
合 waw	陰	包	抛		猫															
	陽	雹	袍		毛															
	上	寶	跑		卯															
	去	報	泡		冒															
撮 ywaw	陰																			
	陽																			
	上																			
	去																			

人辰轍/ɨn/

韻	聲 調	脣音 p	ph	f	m	舌音 t	th	n	l	齒頭 c	ch	s	正齒 cr	crh	sr	r	牙音 k	kh	h	ø
開 ɨn	陰					○	○	○	○	○	參	森	貞	抻	申	○	根	○	○	恩
	陽					○	○	○	○	○	岑	○	○	辰	神	人	哏	○	痕	○
	上					○	○	○	○	怎	○	○	診	磣	審	忍	○	肯	很	○
	去					扽	○	嫩	○	○	○	○	振	趁	慎	刃	艮	裉	恨	摁
齊 yɨn	陰	賓	拼		○	○	○	○	○								巾	欽	欣	因
	陽	○	貧		民	○	○	您	鄰								○	琴	○	寅
	上	○	品		敏	○	○	○	檁								僅	寢	○	引
	去	殯	聘		○	○	○	○	吝								近	沁	信	印
合 wɨn	陰	奔	噴	分	悶	敦	吞	○	掄	尊	村	孫	諄	春	○	○	○	昆	昏	温
	陽	○	盆	墳	門	○	屯	○	輪	○	存	○	○	純	○	○	○	○	魂	文
	上	本	○	粉	○	盹	○	○	○	○	忖	損	准	蠢	吮	○	滾	捆	○	穩
	去	笨	噴	份	悶	頓	褪	○	論	○	寸	○	○	○	順	閏	棍	困	混	問
撮 ywɨn	陰																均	○	勛	暈
	陽																○	群	旬	雲
	上																○	○	○	允
	去																駿	○	訓	運

言前轍/an/

韻	聲／調	脣音 p	ph	f	m	舌音 t	th	n	l	齒頭 c	ch	s	正齒 cr	crh	sr	r	牙音 k	kh	h	ø
開 an	陰					單	貪	○	○	簪	餐	三	沾	攙	山	○	甘	刊	酣	安
	陽					○	談	男	蘭	咱	殘	○	○	蟬	○	然	○	○	含	○
	上					膽	毯	赧	覽	攢	慘	傘	展	産	閃	染	趕	砍	喊	俺
	去					旦	嘆	難	爛	暫	燦	散	戰	儳	善	○	幹	看	旱	暗
齊 yan	陰	邊	偏		○	顛	天	拈	○								肩	千	先	咽
	陽	○	便		棉	○	田	年	連								○	前	咸	延
	上	貶	○		免	點	舐	碾	臉								減	淺	顯	眼
	去	變	騙		面	電	掭	念	戀								件	欠	現	厭
合 wan	陰	般	潘	翻	顢	端	○	○	○	鑽	氽	酸	專	川	拴	○	官	寬	歡	彎
	陽	○	盤	凡	蠻	○	團	○	灤	○	攢	○	○	船	○	○	○	○	環	完
	上	板	○	反	滿	短	○	暖	卵	纂	○	○	轉	喘	○	軟	管	款	緩	碗
	去	半	判	犯	慢	段	彖	○	亂	攥	竄	算	撰	串	涮	○	貫	○	換	萬
撮 ywan	陰																捐	圈	宣	冤
	陽																○	全	玄	元
	上																卷	犬	選	遠
	去																倦	勸	楦	院

東中轍/ɨŋ/

韻	聲／調	脣音				舌音				齒頭			正齒				牙音			
		p	ph	f	m	t	th	n	l	c	ch	s	cr	crh	sr	r	k	kh	h	ø
開 ɨŋ	陰					登	○	○	○	曾	○	僧	征	稱	升	扔	庚	坑	哼	○
	陽					○	疼	能	棱	○	層	○	○	成	繩	仍	○	○	恒	○
	上					等	○	○	冷	○	○	○	整	逞	省	○	梗	○	○	○
	去					鄧	○	○	楞	贈	蹭	○	政	秤	勝	○	更	○	橫	○
齊 yɨŋ	陰	冰	乒		○	丁	聽	○	拎								京	輕	星	英
	陽	○	平		明	○	亭	凝	靈								○	情	行	迎
	上	丙	○		皿	頂	挺	擰	領								井	請	醒	影
	去	並	○		命	定	聽	濘	令								竟	慶	幸	映
合 wɨŋ	陰	崩	烹	峰	朦	東	通	○	○	宗	匆	松	中	充	○	○	工	空	烘	翁
	陽	甭	朋	逢	蒙	○	同	農	龍	○	從	○	○	蟲	○	容	○	○	紅	○
	上	繃	捧	諷	猛	董	桶	○	攏	總	○	聳	腫	寵	○	冗	汞	孔	哄	○
	去	蹦	碰	奉	夢	動	痛	弄	弄	縱	○	送	重	銃	○	○	共	控	訌	甕
撮 ywɨŋ	陰																○	○	兄	擁
	陽																○	窮	雄	喁
	上																迥	○	○	永
	去																○	○	○	用

江陽轍/aŋ/

韻	聲 調	脣音				舌音				齒頭			正齒				牙音			
		p	ph	f	m	t	th	n	l	c	ch	s	cr	crh	sr	r	k	kh	h	ø
開 aŋ	陰					當	湯	○	○	髒	倉	桑	張	昌	傷	嚷	剛	康	夯	肮
	陽					○	唐	囊	狼	○	藏	○	○	常	○	瓤	○	扛	杭	昂
	上					黨	淌	曩	朗	○	○	嗓	掌	廠	賞	壤	港	○	○	○
	去					宕	趟	齉	浪	葬	○	喪	丈	唱	上	讓	杠	抗	巷	盎
齊 yaŋ	陰							○	○								江	腔	鄉	央
	陽							娘	良								○	墻	詳	羊
	上							○	兩								講	搶	享	養
	去							釀	諒								降	嗆	向	樣
合 waŋ	陰	邦	乓	方	○								莊	窗	雙	○	光	筐	荒	汪
	陽	○	旁	防	忙								○	牀	○	○	○	狂	皇	王
	上	榜	榜	仿	莽								奘	闖	爽	○	廣	○	謊	往
	去	謗	胖	放	○								壯	創	○	○	逛	況	晃	忘
撮 ywaŋ	陰																			
	陽																			
	上																			
	去																			

第五章　北京音系的音值律

5. 我們分析北京語音的目標是推論出這個語言的特有音系，也就是想把説這種語言的人群對語音所共有的語感作最合理的解釋。在分析時，我們嚴守四條基本原則，儘可能地把它們推到極限，因爲我們認爲這幾條原則是這種語感的最具體的表徵，可以作爲分析是否正確的檢驗標準。這四條原則是：(1) 漢語音韻學中行之已久而且有效的音節分段法；(2) 歷來漢語音節的各種分類方式，包括"韻類"與"四呼"等觀念；(3) 押韻現象；(4) 雙聲現象。使用這種分析方法所能得到的結論可以説是既具體又抽象的。具體的是：它可以充分説明許多語音現象，簡明整齊，有理有據，對分析結論持不同意見的人也可以根據這些原則據理力爭。抽象的是：音系是語音的深層表現（underlying representation），因此一個音位衹能是一個比較抽象的符號，在不同的情況下，它的實際發音形式（phonetic realization）必然會有所不同，即産生音位變體（allophones），在特殊情況下，也可能會有中和（neutralization）或代换（substitution）等現象。這就使得音位與音值之間的關係顯得不那麽直接，對那些比較重視音值標音或習慣於使用國際音標的人來説，極端的音位標音法就顯得太玄了，因此也許難以接受。其實如果我們的目標不限於記音或制定書寫文字，而更重視語感的理論性解釋，嚴格的音位分析就是絶對有必要的了。在取得了正確的音位分析以後，再由音位結構的觀點看發音方式，其間的關聯就更顯得脉絡分明了。在本章裏，我們將試行説明北京音系的發音規律。

5.1 爲了討論的方便，讓我們先列出北京音系的聲母表及韻母表。這是我們嚴格分析的結果，最大限度地符合了上述四個原則的要求，因此它的性質可以説是絶對的，没有程度上的伸縮變更的餘地。聲母表中的"h"代表送氣，"r"代表捲舌。韻母表清楚地顯示，我們認爲北京音系裏衹有三個元音，以舌位的高低分爲三度，而這種三度區分衹表現在無尾韻中，就帶尾韻母説，實際衹有高低兩度。

脣音	p	ph	f	m	
齦前音	t	th		n	l
齦後音	c	ch	s		
捲舌音	cr	crh	sr		r
舌根音	k	kh	h		ø

韻尾 / 韻基 / 韻頭	ø				y		w		n		ŋ	
	ɨ		ə	a	ɨy	ay	ɨw	aw	ɨn	an	ɨŋ	aŋ
開-ø-		支 ɨ	各 ə	大 a	黑 ɨy	來 ay	斗 ɨw	告 aw	恩 ɨn	干 an	成 ɨŋ	唐 aŋ
齊-y-		吉 yɨ	切 yə	牙 ya		厓 (yay)	尤 yɨw	叫 yaw	因 yɨn	言 yan	丁 yɨŋ	江 yaŋ
合-w-	古 wɨ		多 wə	化 wa	灰 wɨy	外 way			文 wɨn	玩 wan	中 ywɨŋ	壯 waŋ
撮-yw-		玉 ywɨ	月 ywə						雲 ywɨn	元 ywan	用 ywɨŋ	
十三轍	姑蘇	一七	乜梭 斜坡	發花	灰堆	懷來	油求	遙條	人辰	言前	東中	江陽

5.2 爲了討論的方便,我們也得先把代表發音的語音符號作一個概括的説明。由於一般人對北京話的聲母發音方式較少争論,我們就不必列出複雜的輔音表了,但關於韻母的看法則差異甚大,所以我們必須把代表發音方式的元音列舉出來。我們大家都知道,發音的區别本質上是一種程度性的差異,因此對不同的人,由於先天或後天的不同背景,或由於其他的考慮,區别語言時就有多與少的不同。我們無意於作過細的討論,在此衹采用兩個較常見的方式,一個是已在中國廣爲流傳但比較粗略的國際音標。(采自 *The Principles of the International Phonetic Association*, 1949 年倫敦版,1964 年重印本,第六頁。)另一個是在美國比較流行也比較細密的美國語言學會式音標。(采自 B. Bloch and G. L. Trager: *Outline of Linguistic Analysis*, *LSA*, 1942 年版,第 22 頁。)

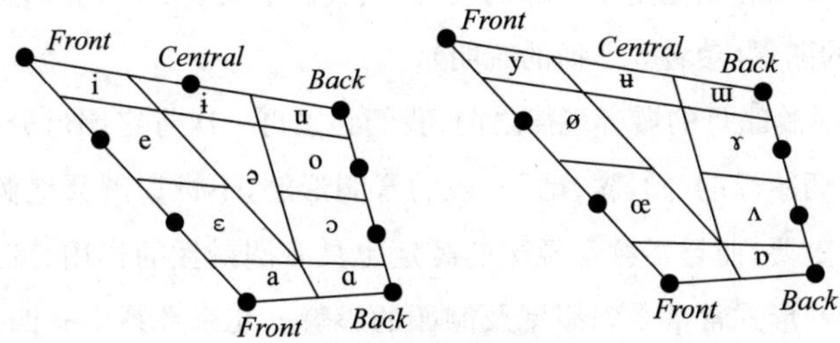

國際音標之元音表

美式音標之元音表	FRONT		CENTRAL		BACK	
	Unr.	Rounded	Unr.	Rounded	Unr.	Rounded
High	i	ü=y	ɨ	u̇	ï= ɯ	u
Lower-high	ɪ	ʊ̈	ᵻ	ʊ̇	ɪ̈	ʊ
Higher-mid	e	ö=ø	ė	ȯ	ë=ɤ	o
Mean-mid	ᴇ	Ω̈	Ė=ə	Ω̇	Ë	Ω
Lower-mid	ɛ	ɔ̈=œ	ɛ̇	ɔ̇	ɛ̈=ʌ	ɔ
Higher-low	æ	ω̈	æ̇	ω̇	æ̈	ω
Low	a	ɒ̈	a	ɒ̇	ä=ɑ	ɒ

這兩種元音標音方式,大致足供我們討論元音發音部位的參考。

5.3 關於北京音聲母的音值,一向爭論不多,因此我們也不必多費唇舌了。需要指出的衹有兩點。其一,由於解釋語感中雙聲現象的需要,我們把舌面腭化音[tɕ、tɕʻ、ɕ]分別與舌根音[k、kʻ、h]合併爲/k、kh、h/三個音位。這合理地説明了音系,但在發音實踐的層次我們就需要一條音律。

$$\begin{bmatrix} C \\ +\text{vel} \end{bmatrix} \longrightarrow [+\text{pal}] / \_\_\_\_ [+\text{pal}]$$

這就是説,在"腭化"成分([+pal],介音中的"y")之前,舌根輔音聲母都受同化而變爲腭化音。其二,爲了説明音系的規律性,我們爲唇音聲母立了一條通則,即唇音聲母衹配齊齒與合口兩類韻母,不與開口及撮口韻母相配。這條通則似與唇音聲母的音值没有關係(其實如用聲譜儀測試,"别"[pie]與

"波"[po]的聲母恐怕還是不一樣的)。但與我們下文要討論的"韻腹圓脣化規律"有直接的關係(參看5.7節的說明)。

5.4 在討論韻母的發音規律之前,我們必須再一次肯定韻母分段的觀念,嚴格確認每個韻母的"頭、腹、尾"三段的音韻形態,不惟對解釋這個韻母的類別歸屬至爲重要,而且對發音規律的認定也具有關鍵性的作用。這是因爲韻腹元音的發音形式常常受到韻尾及韻頭的影響。北京音系中有四個韻尾,即/y、w、n、ŋ/。就發音部位説,/y、n/屬"前音"([+front]),/w、ŋ/屬"後音"([+back]),這種屬性對於韻腹元音發生同化作用。韻頭有三個,即/y、w、yw/。由腭化([±pal])與脣化([±lab])兩個成分組成。它們也影響元音的發音方式。簡言之,腭化使元音移位,脣化使元音變形。這些都留待下文詳論,在此需要指出的是:多數人都説韻頭與韻尾的半元音"帶有元音性",因此堅持用[i、u、ü]等符號標寫,而不用[y、w、ɥ]。我們曾經指出;用什麽符號並不重要,但它們所代表的概念却是重要的。上述這個概念在我們看來就有些模棱(參看5.8.1節),因爲它容易使人混淆韻頭、韻尾與韻腹的界限。有人在接受了上述的概念以後,又加寫一條規律説;當/i u、ü/出現作韻頭時即變爲半元音([-vowel];例如Cheng 1973,Lu Zhiji 1985)。我們的分析一開始就把它們認定爲半元音(與韻腹元音相對而言),所以也就不需要那麽一條音律了。

5.5 就發音方式説,北京音裏到底有多少個元音呢?這個問題也不易回答,因爲元音的認定也往往因人而異。假如我們采納多數人的説法,並參照上文所列的兩種元音表,就大致可列出下面這些元音。

	舌尖	前	央	後	
高	ɿ ʅ	i/ü	ə̂	ï/u	高
半高		e/(ö)		ɤ/o	中
半低		ε/(œ)		ʌ/(ɔ)	低
低		a		ɑ	

表中斜綫的左右兩方分别表示相對應的展脣與圓脣元音,加括號的則表示由於舌位的下降,元音的展圓區别漸趨中和而不顯,所以括號内的符號使用的人

比較少，但它們的存在是可以肯定的①。按照國際音標的習慣，這些元音分屬高低四度，衹有[ə̂]是偏高的央元音，介乎高與半高之間。這些元音也分屬前央後三度，但央元音實際上衹有一個[ə̂]。由於[ə̂]這個元音在高低與前後的分布上地位如此特殊，這就難免令人懷疑它的實質了。在多數報導文獻中，它衹出現在下列幾類音節裏，例如：

黑[hə̂i]　　很[hə̂n]　　亨[hə̂ŋ]

龜[kuə̂i]　　本[pə̂n]　　翁[wə̂ŋ]

如果我們仔細品味這些音節，自然會發現它們的元音比[e]（例如"别"[pie]）、[ɤ]（例如"河"[hɤ]）以及[o]（例如"多"[tuo]）等還要高得多，把[ə̂]與那三個"半高元音"合爲一個元音音位是不合適的。更重要的是：這些韻腹標作[ə̂]的音節所含的元音似乎也不完全一樣。在韻尾爲[i]與[n]的音節裏，元音就顯得靠前，在韻尾爲[ŋ]的音節裏，韻腹元音就顯得靠後。這可以由北京人對英文中 wing 這個字的反應推論出來。儘管這個音節收舌根鼻音，在説北京話的人的聽覺中，這個音節却像"文"字（即似乎與 win 同音），而不像"翁"字。這是因爲 wing 的元音是屬前的，與"文"字的元音同類，而"翁"字的元音則屬後。所以"文"字的發音實爲[wɪn]，"翁" 字的發音應爲[wʊŋ]（其他各字仿此）。因此我們認爲高元音實分兩類，一類爲極高的"緊性"（[+tense]）高元音，即[i、ü、ï、u]（[ï]亦作[ɯ]），另一類爲相對的稍低一些的"鬆性"（[-tense]）高元音，即[ɪ、ö，ï、ʊ]。由此看來，[ə̂]衹是一個概括的（也可以説是"半音位性"的）符號。在我們的音位分析中，我們把這些音節的韻腹都認作高元音，這是理由之一。（當然更重要的理由是這樣可以合理地解釋兒化韻的連音變化。）與此相關的還有"尤、侯"等收嗚字的韻腹問題。許多人都把它們的元音標作[o]，即"尤"作[you]，"侯"作[hou]，但也有人指出，"侯"字中的[o]與"活"[huo] 字中的[o] 相去甚遠，更有人干脆把"尤"類字的韻母衹標作

---

① 爲了遷就國際音標的符號及分度，我們采用[ʌ]代表半低展脣後元音，但就更細微的音值説，也許美式音標的[ӫ]更有代表性，因爲後元音似有相對偏低的現象。我們標出[ö]與[œ]兩個圓脣元音，因爲我們覺得像"月"/ywə/與"元"/ywan/之類的字，韻腹多少有些圓脣成分，但它們的所謂"前音"成分，實際上恐怕衹是相對的"非後"（[-back]），即介乎前與央之間。表右方以虛綫分爲三度，是音位性的分法，將在 5.6 節詳論。

[iu]，表示根本没有[o]音。我們認爲這類字韻尾收嗚是不容置疑的事實，它們的韻腹也是高元音，“侯”爲[hɯw]，“尤”爲[yuw]。

5.6 我們的音位分析衹把北京音系的元音分爲高中低三度。這比前引兩種元音表分爲高低四度或七度都少些。概括地説，我們所立的高元音音位實包括前文所説的“緊”與“鬆”兩類，亦即美式音標所説的高(high)與次高(lower-high)兩度；我們所立的中元音音位則指國際音標中的“半高”元音，亦即美式音標所説的“較高的中元音”(higher-mid vowels)。這説明就發音方式説，北京音的中元音並不很中，實屬偏高，低元音的音域最廣，包括國際音標的“半低”與“低”兩度，也就是美式音標“較低的中元音”(lower-mid vowels)以下各度。這就是説，爲了區分北京音系裏的高中低三度元音，發音時舌位降低的幅度不需要很大，達到“半低”的程度就够用了，當然如果降得更低也不會發生辨義的問題。曾經有些外國朋友問我，爲什麽中國人説話時不張大嘴巴。我總回答説，因爲中國人覺得張大嘴巴不雅觀，所以連唱戲時也得戴上髯口，或用袖子遮住嘴巴。這當然是説笑話，但也可以間接説明北京話裏元音的性質。在每一個高度上，三個元音音位都有好些變體。嚴格地説，由於音位是一個抽象的觀念，就無所謂什麽是正體、什麽是變體。但爲了描述的方便，我們可以把它們單獨出現時的形式看作本體，把其他形式看作變體，並從而討論由正體轉爲變體的規律。我的觀察是：北京元音音位的本體都是偏後的展脣元音，即[ï、ɤ、ʌ]。

5.6.1 由於低元音的舌位甚低，所以國際音標衹分前後，不立央元音，這是可以相信的；同時由於舌位下降，口腔隨着張大，脣部的展圓也就相對的不大明顯了；因此許多記音的人便把低元音一律標作[a]，如“干”作[kan]，“代”作[tai]，“幫”作[paŋ]，“桃”作[tʻaw]，“全”作[tɕʻüan]，“大”作[ta]等，衹把“天”[tʻiɛn]類字的元音標作[ɛ]，其實就發音方式説，更細密的區分是有必要的。比如“大”的元音與“代”的元音就顯有差别，與“瓜”的元音也有不同。所以“大”的發音應爲[tʌ](或作[tɑ])，也就是説它的元音實爲展脣的後低元音，因此我們可以説，[ʌ]是低元音音位/a/的本體，其他的形式是變體。

5.6.2 中元音單獨出現時讀作[ɤ]，即展脣的後元音，這是大家公認的事實，如“蛾”讀[ɤ]，“歌”讀[kɤ]，“車”讀[ʈʂʻɤ]，“色”讀[sɤ]等。所以我們説

[ɤ]是中元音音位/ə/的本體,其他形式是有條件的變體,這是無需多辯的。

5.6.3元音的發音方式變化特别大。更麻煩的是,在標準北京音裏,它從不單獨出現,單獨作韻母時,也衹配齜後音[ʦ、ʦ'、s]與捲舌音[ʈʂ、ʈʂ'、ʂ、ʐ]兩類聲母,分别以所謂"舌尖前元音"[ɿ]與"舌尖後元音"[ʅ]的形式出現。(我倒覺得它們似爲高央元音[ɨ]。)但據一位老先生説,在某些老北京人(旗人?)的土話裏,"去"字念成[k'ɯ]([ɯ]即[ï])。這是一個頗有意思的現象。按"去"字本爲遇攝溪母三等合口字,它的音韻形態一直到現代標準北京話都是/khywɨ/[ʨ'ɥü]。如果這個音節在某個時期丢掉了韻頭中的腭化與脣化,它的音韻形態就衹能是/khɨ/了。我相信北京土話中"去"字念作[k'ɯ]的現象就是這樣形成的,因爲官話方言的歧異有許多都是韻頭成分的增減造成的①。我在武漢停留過一段時間,發現當地人打招呼時常説:"你哪去?"[li la k'ɯ]。有趣的是,他們也像北京土話一樣把"去"説成[k'ɯ]。其變化過程應是相同的,而兩地都把這個高元音韻母念作展脣高元音的,所以我們可以假設這是高元音音位/ɨ/的本體。把這個假設與/a/及/ə/的本體相比對,它們之間的一致性就使得這個假設顯得更有道理了,同時由這個假設推論高元音的其他變體,也是最簡約最合理的,這由下文的討論中可以清楚地看出來。

5.7 在確定了/ɨ、ə、a/的本體爲[ï、ɤ、ʌ]之後,我們就可以用5.5節所列一般人常用的元音符號做基礎,進一步討論北京韻母的發音方式了。由於我們已經把不同形式的[ə̂]細分爲[ɪ、ö、ï、ʊ]等次高鬆性元音,所以常用元音表中就衹有前後兩類而没有央元音了。從這個角度觀察北京音系裏音位層次以下的發音實踐規律(subphonemic rules for phonetic realization),我們將會發現衹有下述幾條簡明的規則而已。

第一條,韻尾同化韻腹律

$$V \longrightarrow [+\text{front}] / \_\_\_ [+\text{front}]$$

---

① 例如"薛"字,原爲山攝心母三等開口入聲,其音位形式爲/syat/,但現在北京音念作撮口[ɕüe],似"學"字(聲調不同),山東滕縣話讀似"索"[suo],則爲合口,而南方官話多讀似"謝"[ɕie]。這種現象可以合理地解釋爲,在三、四等合韻之後,這個字在北方官話裏變爲撮口(即增加脣化介音)。而在南方官話裏則未變。其後在滕縣話(北方官話的一支)裏,這個字丢掉了腭化介音因而變爲合口,並且因爲它已不再是細音,所以它的聲母也没腭化。

這一條規則的意思是,作爲本體的後元音出現在帶尾韻母中時,若韻尾爲“前音”([+front])/y、n/,即受其同化而變爲相應的前元音①,因此下列四個韻基的元音形式變爲:

/ɨy/[iy](賊),/ay/[ɛy](來);
/ɨn/[in](今),/an/[ɛn](天)。

出現在零韻尾及“後音”韻尾之前的元音自然仍保持原形。我們把這條規律列爲頭條,表示它的優越性(primacy)、它的功能高於其他規律。這條規律早已有人指出(例如 Cheng 1973),但值得注意的是,我們的分析使我們可以看出這是一條全面適用的通則,不限於某一些元音。

第二條:韻頭同化規律

$$V \rightarrow [+\text{front}] / [+\text{front}]\_\_\_\ \#$$

這也是適用於所有元音的規律,意思是説,在無尾的細音韻母中,韻腹元音受韻頭中腭化音的影響而變爲前元音,所以下列韻母的發音變爲:

(衣)/yɨ/[yi],(也)/yə/[ye],(牙)/ya/[yɛ](或作[yæ̇]);
(玉)/ywɨ/*[ɥi],(月)/ywə/*[ɥe]。

需要特別指出的是,使元音移位的衹是韻頭中的腭化音/y/,脣化音/w/則没有這種作用。所以撮口韻的“魚、月”等的元音都是前元音,不因有脣化而爲後元音,但單純的合口音如“屋”自然仍保持其後元音。我們在“玉、月”之類的撮口韻母注音前加上星號,表示它們的元音僅因本規則而變爲前元音,然後才因下一條規律而變爲圓脣。

第三條:韻腹的圓脣化規律

$$V \rightarrow [+\text{lab}] / \begin{cases} \_\_\_\ [+\text{lab}] \\ \begin{bmatrix} +\text{pal} \\ +\text{lab} \end{bmatrix} \_\_\_ \\ \begin{bmatrix} -\text{pal} \\ +\text{lab} \end{bmatrix} \_\_\_\ ([+\text{back}]) \end{cases}$$

① 按理説,北京音系中的元音既然衹分爲前後兩類,没有央元音,在用區别特徵符號時,衹需要一個“後音”的正負兩面(〔±back〕)就够了,因爲所謂“前音”就是“非後”(〔-back〕),不必再分前與央。但爲了醒目起見,我在此處仍采用了特定的前音符號〔+front〕。

這一條公式比較複雜,但仍爲適用於一切元音的通律。它指出,在三種特定的情況下,韻腹都受代表脣化的後半元音/w/的影響,因而改變成各自相對應的圓脣元音。這三種情況是:(1) 韻尾爲脣化(收嗚)時,元音一律爲圓脣。故有下列現象:

(歐)/ɨw/[uw],(尤)/yɨw/yuw];

(奥)/aw/[ɔw],(要)/yaw/[yɔw]。

(2) 韻頭既爲脣化又爲腭化(撮口)時,元音也一律爲圓脣。故有下列現象:

(魚)/ywɨ/[ɥü],(月)/ywə/[ɥö];

(雲)/ywɨn/[ɥün],(元)/ywan/[ɥœn];

(永)/ywɨŋ/[ɥuŋ]。

(3) 如果韻頭僅爲脣化而非腭化(合口),則衹有在韻尾爲零或"後音"時,元音才變圓脣。故有下列現象:

(屋)/wɨ/[wu],(我)/wə/[wo],(蛙)/wa/[wɔ];

(翁)/wɨŋ/[wuŋ],(王)/waŋ/[wɔŋ]。

但下列三類韻母的元音仍爲展脣,因爲它們雖爲合口,但韻尾屬"前音",或韻尾雖屬"後音",但韻頭非合口。

(未)/wɨy/[wiy],(文)/wɨn/[win],

(外)/way/[way],(玩)/wan/[wan]。

可以附帶指出的是,由於我們確認脣音聲母/p、ph、f、m/的特性是衹配齊齒與合口兩類韻母(參看 5.3),所以像"波、莫、棒、風、幫、忙"等音節,對我們來說,都屬合口,因此它們的元音都爲本音律所涵蓋而變爲圓脣,實無必要爲它們另立一條規則(參看 Lu Zhiji 1985)。這一事實也有力地支持了我們對脣音聲母之特性的解釋。另有一條值得指出的有趣現象,多年來我一直覺得撮口高元音穿鼻韻母(/ywɨŋ/"用")的元音應爲[ü],頗不同意威妥瑪式拼音把它認作後元音[u](即把該韻母拼作[iung]),然而現在我們的第一條與第三條音律却迫使我不得不承認它應該是[u],看來在區別發音方式的時候,洋人的耳朵是頗有參考價值的,但改變介音則不妥。

第四條:韻腹元音之鬆緊律

$$V \longrightarrow [-\text{tense}]/[-\text{pal}]\_\_\_\ E$$

我們在前文已經指出,就發音方式説,高元音實分爲兩類,即極高與次高,前者性"緊"[+tense],後者性"鬆"[-tense]。現在這一個規律指出,在帶尾的洪音韻母裹,高元音都由緊性的[i、ü、ï、u]分別變爲鬆性的[ɪ、ö, ï、ʊ]也就是説,下列各字中韻腹的念法應爲:(有括號爲一組)

{賊/ciy/[tsɪy], 灰/hwiy/[hwɪy]; {很/hin/[hɪn], 文/win/[wɪn];

{燈/tin/[tïŋ], 翁/win/[wʊŋ]; {侯/hiw/[hʊw], 謀/mwiw/[mʊw]。

有許多人采用寬式注音法,把這些出現在洪音韻母中的鬆元音一律標作[ə̂],(也有人寫作[ə̭]或[ə]),由於這樣也不會造成辨别音讀的問題,所以亦無不可,但却使得發音規律變得籠統了,嚴格説來,並不可取。在帶尾的細音韻母以及所有的無尾韻母裹,高元音自然仍保持緊性。所以:

(思)/ɨ/[ï],(衣)/yɨ/[yi],(夫)/wɨ/[wu];
(女)/ywɨ/[ɥü];(新)/yɨn/[yin],(雲)/ywɨn/[ɥün];
(英)/yɨŋ/[yïŋ],(窮)/ywɨŋ/ɥuŋ];(求)/yɨw/[yuw]。

在這兒有一點值得我們注意:這條元音變鬆律衹能運用於洪音的帶尾韻母,這表示細音韻母的腭化介音有使元音保持其高度的作用。(相對而言,脣化介音可能有使元音變低的傾向。)這使我們認識到,這條規律的功能也許不限於高元音。我們都知道,低元音音位至少也分爲低與半低兩個層次。腭化介音的有無可能使低元音産生類似高元音的緊與鬆的差别。很多人都已注意到,齊齒音的"天"/thyan/[t'yɛn]字與開口音的"灘"/than/[t'an] 字含有不同的元音,一部分人也注意到,撮口音的"元"/ywan/[ɥœn] 與合口音的"玩"/wan/[wan] 也含有不同的元音,但很少人區分"羊"/yaŋ/[yʌŋ] 與"王"/waŋ/[wɑŋ]或"交"/kyaw/[tɕyɔw/與"高"/kaw/[kɑw]的元音。這也許是因爲後元音的低與半低的差距没有前元音的那麽顯著,但稍有差距是可以肯定的[①]。我們把元音的鬆緊律擴大到可以應用於所有的元音,而不限於高元音,上述的這些現象就都得到恰當合理的解釋了,但無尾韻中的低元音,包括細音的/ya/,也都變成鬆性,是這條規律的一個顯著例外。

第五條:高元音的舌尖化

$$/ɨ/ \longrightarrow \begin{cases} [ɿ]/s\_\_\_\# \\ [ʅ]/r\_\_\_\# \end{cases}$$

高元音在單獨作韻母時,由於直接出現在不同的聲母之後而顯出不同的音色。在齦後音/c、ch、s/[ʦ、ʦ‘、s] 之後,發爲"舌尖前元音"[ɿ],在捲舌音/cr、crh、sr、r/[ʈʂ、ʈʂ‘、ʂ、ʐ]之後,發爲"舌尖後元音"[ʅ]。這一條很難説是一個正規的音律,因爲它的性質實在太狹隘特殊了。假如我們認爲這兩種聲母後的高元音韻母根本衹是一個[ï],那就用不着這條規律了。但由於這已成爲漢語標音的長期習慣,我們衹好把它寫成上面這樣的公式,附在最後聊備一格。

5.8 如果我們把上節討論過的五條發音實踐律應用到北京音的韻母系統表上,便可以得出各韻母的發音方式了。但必須再補充兩點,才能使我們的轉寫更合乎一般的標音習慣。這兩點也代表兩個重要的音韻學觀念。

5.8.1 所謂半元音衹能是一個相對的概念,並不指一個特定的音高。它的定義衹能是:(1) 不構成音節[-syllabic]),(2) 較它所依附的元音略高一些。半元音的這種性質早就有人指出過(例如 Bloch 和 Trager 1942, p.23),我們所使用的半元音符號/y、w/就必須如此理解。當它們出現在像"衣"/yɨ/[yi]、"屋"/wɨ/[wu]、"魚"/ywɨ/[ɥü]、"尤"/yɨw/[yuw]等高元音音節中時,性

① 我覺得在北京音裏,後低元音比前低元音的音值似乎更低些,這是爲什麼我在第 631 頁注①裏説,雖然我們用[ʌ]代表後低元音,其實美式的[ӕ̈]可能更妥帖些。就前後低元音的對轉説,它們的關係似乎也不是水平的,而是向後偏低的。如下式:

果如此,後元音的細微差異更難辨認也就可以理解了。

質必然是很高的，但當它們出現於以中元音或低元音爲韻腹的音節中時，就相對地變低了。這大概是一般人標寫漢語時總愛用[i、u、ü]等作介音或韻尾的緣故，其實一旦明白了介音的性質以後，便不必計較什麽"帶元音性"了。在我們轉寫韻母的發音方式時，不妨隨俗，也用[i、u、ü]作半元音符號，而不用[y、w、ɥ]。

5.8.2 音系所要表達的是一個語言的正規而且完整的音韻結構，在這個結構裏，每一個字音都有一個特定的地位。但在日常的實際語言交際中，衹要能達意，總是能省則省的。這是很自然的發音節約(economy in pronunciation)現象，所以有許多字的發音方式，在不違背辨義的原則下，就會有自然的與自由的省略與變動的現象，因此表面看來與音系中的正規念法似乎不一致。但我們必須認識到，省略與變動衹能是以音系爲基礎的，絶不能據之以否定音系的存在。比如説，在北京音中，當"衣"/yɨ/[yi]、"烏"/wɨ/[wu]、"魚"/ywɨ/[ɥü]、"因"/yɨn/[yin]、"君"/kywɨn/[tɕɥün]等的元音，在韻尾與韻頭的影響之下，分別變爲"前、後、展、圓"等特定的元音以後，韻頭介音的辨義功能就爲這些特定的元音包容取代了，因此在發音時是否都把這些介音發出來，也就不那麽重要了。换句話説，把這些字分别衹念作：衣[i]、烏[u]、魚[ü]、因[in]、居[tɕün]，仍可完全達到辨認這些字及其屬性的目的。事實上多數人説話時可能就是這麽説的。但是我們要説，即使有人在録音分析之後，證明在百分之九十的情況下，這些字的念法都没有介音，這一發現也不足以推翻我們的分析結論。因爲這些字的有介音與無介音的念法並不構成對比(英語則不然，如year與ear即構成對比)，而它們在整個音系中的地位，諸如押韻與四呼的歸屬等，都衹能從它們的有介音的念法得到解釋，所以有介音的念法是正規的、全面的，無介音的念法衹能是前者的非正式的代用體(substitute)。許多人對我們把"衣、烏、魚"分析成/yɨ、wɨ、ywɨ/感到茫然不解，堅稱它們："衹是一個單體"，就是因爲他們覺得，在絶大多數情況下，他們都把這幾個音節衹念作[i、u、ü]們而已。但是他們如果能注意到音韻的系統性與全面性，就自然能理解我們爲什麽如此分析了。在轉寫發音方式時，我們仍不妨隨俗，把這些音節衹標作：[i、u、ü]。基於同樣的考慮，我們也用寬式的[ə̂]代替所有的鬆性高元音。

5.8.3 綜合以上幾條音律及補充説明,我們可以用我們的韻母系統表作框架,標出北京韻母的發音方式,另有一些因聲母的有無或調形的長短而形成的細微差别,就不必辭費了。表中有少數幾個韻母另含帶括號的形式,那是因爲有許多人不區分某些元音的展圓形式,或不嚴守韻母分段的原則,遂使我們推衍出來的形式與一般標音的習慣仍不完全相符,所以在此附注出來,以備參考。

韻尾	ø			y		w		n		ŋ	
韻頭 \ 韻基	ɨ	ə	a	ɨy	ay	ɨw	aw	ɨn	an	ɨŋ	aŋ
-ø-	支 ɿ,ʅ	各 ɤ	大 ɑ(ʌ)	黑 ə̂i	來 ai	斗 ə̂u	告 ɑu	恩 ə̂n	干 an	成 ə̂ŋ	唐 ɑŋ
-y-	吉 i	切 ie	牙 ia			尤 iu (yuw)	叫 iɔu	因 in	言 iɛn	丁 iŋ (iïŋ)	江 iʌŋ
-w-	古 u	多 uo	化 uɑ	灰 uə̂i	外 uai			文 uə̂n	玩 uan	中 uə̂ŋ	壯 uɑŋ
-yw-	玉 ü	月 üe (üö)						雲 ün	元 üœn	用 iuŋ (üuŋ)	
十三轍	姑蘇 ¦ 一七	乜梭 斜坡	發花	灰堆	懷來	油求	遙條	人辰	言前	東中	江陽

第六章 關於"兒化韻"

6. 現代標準漢語以北京話爲基準,這是盡人皆知的事,跟其他方言相比,北京話最引人注意的特色,大概就是所謂兒化韻了。在臺灣從事推行國語運動的何容先生,曾經講過一個很有趣的故事,可以引在這兒作爲本章的楔子①:

有一次,一位東北朋友對我嘆息:"什麽國語喲!就是'兒'啊!'兒'啊!……"我跟他顧左右而言他,説:"你們老弟考臺大,要入什麽系呀?"他説:"他喜歡理科兒。"我説:"得罪!得罪!讓您當場出'醜'啦。"

除了甚饒風味以外,這個笑話説明了兩個事實:其一,兒化韻這種現象,並不限於北京話,其他官話方言也有這種現象;其二,這種相當普遍的現象,對一般人顯得很神秘,嘴裏雖然説着,心裏却感覺不到。在這一章裏,我想在音韻學的理論基礎上,談談兒化韻這個問題,找出它的變化規律,從而剥去它的神秘外衣。

6.1 兒化韻起於何時,很難確定,我相信不會早於明朝。這可以從兩方面加以證明。在詩歌方面説,杜甫有兩句詩:"細雨魚兒出,微風燕子斜。"似乎證明早在唐代就有"魚兒"這樣的詞彙了。但這衹能證明"兒"字遠在唐代就被用作詞尾了,絶不能證明唐代已有兒化韻,因爲"兒" 字在這句詩裏顯然自成一個音節,並没有跟"魚"字合併爲一個音節, 也就是説,"魚"字並没有"兒化"。即使晚到元朝,"兒"字用作詞尾已是極普遍的現象,但真正的兒化韻恐怕仍没有形成,例如關漢卿有幾首叫做"一半兒"的小曲兒,其一云:

碧紗窗外静無人,跪在牀前忙要親,駡了個負心回轉身,雖是我話兒嗔,一半兒推辭一半兒肯。

這裏"話兒"跟"一半兒"的用法,與現代的普通話已是完全一樣了。"兒"字顯然用作襯字,所以末句可有九字之多。但這並不一定表示"兒"字與"話"或

---

① 見何先生寫的《〈北平音系小轍編〉再版題記》,載於張洵如 1956,第 8 頁。

“半”合爲一音,很可能它在當時衹讀做輕聲而已。這可以由他的另一首小曲兒證明,“兒”字在此用作韻脚,顯然自成音節:

久客在京師,甚的是閑傳示,心頭眼底,横倘鶯兒。趁西風折桂枝,已遂了青雲志,盼得他一紙音書。却是斷腸詩詞……

(崔張十六事:喜得家書)

另外就韻書及韻圖的演進傳統看,兒化韻也不會早到元代。“兒”在中古韻讀裏是一個“止攝日母”字,在《中原音韻》裏屬“支思”韻。這一韻的字都以高央元音/ɨ/爲韻母,而“日”母到元代已變成/r/了,所以“兒”字在元代的讀法爲/rɨ/,跟我們現在讀“日”字差不多(“日”原屬入聲,演變的方式不同,因此出現在《中原音韻》的“齊微”韻裏,在元代的讀法爲/ryiy/,化入“支思”韻是很晚的事)[①]。到了明代,在徐孝的《重訂司馬温公等韻圖經》裏,“兒”字才跟“耳、二”等字首次出現在“影”母之下(薛 1983)。“影”母在中古代表喉塞音,這個聲母遠在《中原音韻》之前就已經消失(參看薛 1975,33, 45—46)。所以徐孝所謂的“影”母,實際上代表當時的零聲母,原屬“日”母的“兒、耳、二”等字既然出現在“影”母之下,顯然表示它們的聲母早在明代就已經消失了。對於這種現象,我的解釋是:在《中原音韻》以後不久, 代表這些字的那個音節/rɨ/發生了變化,由於音位互换(metathesis)的結果,變成了/ɨr/(參看薛 1980)。這個解釋有兩個好處:其一,它合理地標示出這個音節是如何變成零聲母的,因此也就合理地説明了爲什麽原屬“日”母的“兒、耳、二”現在改屬“影”母了;其二,早期漢語音韻裏本來没有/r/這樣一個韻尾,而現代漢語裏/r/出現作韻尾已是鐵的事實了,那麽這個特殊的韻尾是怎樣產生的呢? 很顯然,我們的解釋也給這個問題找到了合理的答案。這麽説來,/r/出現作韻尾絶不早於明代,而兒化韻的基本要件則爲“兒”字與其所附屬的音節合爲一體,成爲一個以/r/爲韻尾的新音節,所以我們也就可以推斷説,兒化韻的形成也絶不早於明代。至於它確切地發生在哪個年頭,那就不是我們可以推知的了。

6.2 在另一方面,“兒”字作爲詞尾在語義上也有兩點必須説明:其一,

---

① 關於“日”母以及“兒”字跟“日”字的演變,請參閲拙著薛 1975,第 43—44 頁及第 91 頁,以及薛 1980。

“兒”尾的使用是字彙的選擇問題，有的詞兒有“兒”尾，有的詞兒没有，並不是所有的詞兒都可以“兒化” 的，比如下面的幾個例子，“兒”尾的有無不是可以隨便的①。

小便：小辮兒；

打架：打價兒（還價兒）；

郵票：油票兒。

更有一些詞兒，兒化與否，意思就全變了。

一塊（錢）：一塊兒（玩兒）；
火星（五大行星之一）：火星兒（星星之火）；
白麵（小麥粉）：白麵兒（海洛因）；
没跑（没有跑路）；没跑兒（逃不了）。

其次，最常見的兒化詞兒多半兒是名詞，因此有人説“兒”是名詞詞尾，其實兒化不限於名詞；動詞、形容詞、副詞也有兒化的，不過數目比較少而已。例如下面幾句話裏的兒化詞兒都不是名詞：

(1) 請到我們家來玩兒。

(2) 他一聽就火兒啦！

(3) 那孩子長得胖胖兒的。

(4) 你慢慢兒做，别急。

6.3 雖然兒化與否完全是字彙的問題，但是新的兒化詞兒是會不斷出現的，而任何一種讀音的字也都有兒化的可能，兒化了以後，音讀上又都起了許多變化。大家都覺得這些變化似乎是遵循着一定的規律，但是這些規律是什麼呢？認真研究音韻的人是有義務回答這個問題的。有許多西方學者，大概由於不瞭解兒化韻的歷史淵源，在處理上把/r/這個特殊的韻尾與其他韻尾一視同仁，因此也就把兒化音節與其他音節視爲無殊②。我認爲這是不妥的。這樣處理，一則甚不經濟，把漢語的基本音節幾乎增加了一倍，再則也因此忽

---

① 此處及下面的例子，並見於劉澤先 1957。

② 西人多如此處理，可拿 Hartman 1944 跟 Hockett 1947 兩篇文章爲例。

略了漢語音韻在這一方面的特性。兒化韻既是連音變化的結果，那麽在理論分析上，我們就得把這些連音變化的孳生音節(derived syllables)，與一般的基本音節(basic syllables)分開，並進而把這種連音變化的規律發掘出來。

6.4 兒化音節既然是由基本音節加“兒”尾後孳生出來的，我們就必須先瞭解基本音節的音韻形態，然後才能在這個基礎上推繹出兒化的規律，以及兒化音節的形態。兒化現象是韻母的問題，與聲母無關。下面的一張韻母表，代表我對北京音韻的新解釋(薛 1980)，可以拿來做我們討論兒化韻的基礎：

韻尾		ø 直音				y 收噫		w 收嗚		n 抵腭		ŋ 穿鼻	
韻頭 \ 韻基		ɨø		əø	aø	ɨy	ay	ɨw	aw	ɨn	an	ɨŋ	aŋ
開	-ø-		支 ɨ	各 ə	大 a	黑 ɨy	來 ay	斗 ɨw	告 aw	恩 ɨn	干 an	成 ɨŋ	唐 aŋ
齊	-y-		吉 yɨ	切 yə	牙 ya		厓 (yay)	尤 yɨw	叫 yaw	因 yɨn	言 yan	丁 yɨŋ	江 yaŋ
合	-w-	古 wɨ		多 wə	化 wa	灰 wɨy	外 way			文 wɨn	玩 wan	中 ywɨŋ	壯 waŋ
撮	-yw-		玉 ywɨ	月 ywə						雲 ywɨn	元 ywan	用 ywɨŋ	
十三轍兒		姑 蘇	一 七	乜梭 斜坡	發 花	灰 堆	懷 來	油 求	遥 條	人 辰	言 前	東 中	江 陽

6.5 兒化韻之所以顯得如此神秘，主要是由於對許多兒化詞兒的讀法，大家意見不一致，因此争論迭起，似乎没有什麽規律足以解釋這許多雜亂抵牾的現象了。其實這也是一種誤會。問題的真相是：在兒化韻這個問題上，即使是那些説最標準的北京話的人，也分成好幾派。對不同派的人來説，韻母在兒化的時候，變化並不完全一樣。因此有許多單詞兒的讀法，大家就不同意了。要合理地解決這個問題，自然必須就事論事，把各派作個别的處理，然後才能找出各派的獨特規律，並進而比較各派規律間的異同與關係。

在兒化韻這個問題上，説北京話的人究竟分成幾派呢？這個問題也不很容易回答。在“十三轍兒”的傳統裏，有所謂“小轍兒”，就是兒化韻，據説衹包括了“小言前兒”跟“小人辰兒”兩轍兒。這在理論上並没有什麽不可能，連衹有一轍都是可能的。比方説，在四川的成都話裏，“猫兒”讀作[mər]，“米兒”讀作

[miər],“歌兒、梗兒、根兒”都讀作[kər],似乎這種方言就衹有“小人辰兒”一轍兒了(袁 1960,頁 38—39)。但把這兩個小轍兒跟北京的兒化現象一比,就會發現這在實際上是不可能的。因爲北京話的兒化韻,不論是哪一派,都要豐富得多。所以張洵如列了八轍兒,而錢玄同則爲《中華新韻》訂了九韻①。實際上究竟有幾轍兒,這要看我們説的是哪一派。王輔世曾經把“北京音可能有的捲舌韻(母)”逐一列出,並附上例詞兒(王輔世 1963)。我們可以采來作爲討論兒化的起點。我在此把他的“兒”改作“黑兒”,把他的“喔兒”與“窩兒”之分省併了,並把各韻母的次序按我們前面的基本韻母表,重新安排了一下。

以下一組

烏兒:小鋪兒,桶箍兒,羊肚兒,小鼓兒,小豬兒。

鵝兒:唱歌兒,墨盒兒,小河兒,大棵兒,小車兒。

耶兒:臺階兒,小鞋兒,一些兒,小碟兒,爺兒。

窩兒:小説兒,山坡兒,被窩兒,小磨兒,没錯兒。

約兒:木橛兒,賣缺兒,小皮靴兒。

以下一組

啊兒:一把兒,没法兒,打雜兒,出岔兒,找碴兒。

呀兒:小牙兒,豆芽兒,打價兒,一家兒,一下兒。

蛙兒:桃花兒,小褂兒,香瓜兒,牙刷兒,油畫兒。

以下一組.

黑兒:小字兒,墨汁兒,眼淚兒,刀刃兒,二嬸兒。

因兒:鞋底兒,小鷄兒,没信兒,有勁兒,脚印兒。

温兒:土堆兒,墨水兒,小腿兒,冰棍兒,没準兒。

暈兒:金魚兒,驢駒兒,有趣兒,合群兒,彩雲兒。

以下一組

安兒:壺蓋兒,小孩兒,被單兒,門坎兒,杏乾兒。

---

① 參閲《中華新韻》,教育部國語推行委員會編,1941 年 10 月公布。至於“十三轍兒”何以衹有兩個小轍兒,我久思不得其解。1985 年 4 月在北京時與李源敬先生談及此事,得知迄今尚有少數方言,其兒化韻衹發生部分韻類中,如言前轍兒等,另一些韻如遥條等,其兒尾仍自成音節。我乃恍然大悟,原來兒化的過程在歷史上也是分期逐步發生的,所以“十三轍兒”時代僅有兩個小轍兒。

烟兒:靠邊兒,小燕兒,蠶繭兒,抽簽兒,房檐兒。

彎兒:小塊兒,試管兒,鐵罐兒,手腕兒,藥丸兒。

冤兒: 人緣兒, 花卷兒,手絹兒,大雜院兒。

以下一組

歐兒:耍猴兒,紙簍兒,門口兒,種痘兒,紐扣兒。

憂兒:小牛兒,打球兒,抓鬮兒,没救兒,短袖兒。

以下一組

熬兒:小襖兒,黑棗兒,羊腦兒,羊羔兒,草稿兒。

腰兒:麥苗兒,紙條兒,衣料兒,小廟兒,取笑兒。

以下一組

僧兒: 門縫兒,麻繩兒,没棱兒,分層兒,板凳兒。

英兒:甜杏兒,電影兒,眼鏡兒,酒令兒,車鈴兒。

翁兒:小葱兒,小桶兒,酒盅兒,正工兒,没空兒。

雍兒:哭窮兒,小熊兒,没用兒。

以下一組

昂兒:喝湯兒,小缸兒,藥方兒,趕趟兒,聽唱兒。

央兒:小羊兒,雙響兒,没講兒,花腔兒,鞋樣兒。

汪兒:亮光兒,蛋黄兒,小筐兒,村莊兒,小牀兒。

6.5.1 這一列韻母代表着兒化韻在北京音中一切可能有的區别。據王輔世説,在“老北京人”説的“内城話”裏,啊兒(呀兒、蛙兒)與安兒(烟兒、彎兒)的分别已經不存在了,但近二十年來,由於城區的外地人大量增加,區别啊兒與安兒的人反而更多了。史存直更肯定這一區别的必要(史 1957)。我們可以設想這是兒化韻的早期形式,雖然在“内城話”裏已被一種新形式取代了,但在周圍的廣大地區裏還繼續流行着。值得特别注意的是:在這種形式裏,“一七”轍兒的字跟“灰堆”轍兒及“人辰”轍兒的字已經合併了,但“姑蘇”轍兒的字則仍自成一個小轍兒,可見“一七”與“姑蘇”之分不是没有道理的。“梭坡”與“乜斜”的主要元音既早已混同,兒化以後自然也衹有“鵝兒”(“耶兒、窩兒、約兒”)一韻,我們可以管這一韻叫做“小坡斜兒”,這是跟張洵如及錢玄同的説法大不相同的(見 P640 注①及 P649 注①)。此外“言前”轍兒跟“懷來”轍兒經兒化後也合併了(安$_{兒}$類),但仍與"發花"轍$_{兒}$的兒化(啊$_{兒}$類)有别。就詞彙説,我們在這種兒化形式裏,看到以下這些現象:

a) 瓜$_{兒}$ kwa+r≠官$_{兒}$ kwan+r=乖$_{兒}$ kway+r

沙$_{兒}$ sra+r≠山$_{兒}$ sran+r =篩$_{兒}$ sray+r

b) 蝕$_{兒}$ srɨ+r =神$_{兒}$ srɨn+r ≠蛇$_{兒}$ srə+r

枝$_{兒}$ crɨ+r =針$_{兒}$ crɨn+r (跟黑$_{兒}$ hɨy+r 押韻)

根$_{兒}$ kɨn+r≠歌$_{兒}$ kə+r

c) 鷄$_{兒}$ kyɨ+r=今$_{兒}$ kyɨn+r

藝$_{兒}$ yɨ+r=印$_{兒}$ y ɨ n+r≠葉$_{兒}$ yə+r

d) 屋$_{兒}$ wɨ+r≠温$_{兒}$ wɨn+r≠窩$_{兒}$ wə+r

鼓$_{兒}$ kwɨ+r≠滚$_{兒}$ kwɨn+r=鬼$_{兒}$ kwɨy+r≠果$_{兒}$ kwə+r

e) 玉$_{兒}$ ywɨ+r=運$_{兒}$ ywɨn+r≠月$_{兒}$ ywə+r

渠$_{兒}$ khywɨ+r=群$_{兒}$ khywɨn+r≠瘸$_{兒}$ khywə+r

美國的著名語言學家霍凱特曾寫過一篇論北京音韻的文章(Hockett 1947)。顯然他所根據的發音人是能區别,"根$_{兒}$"與"歌$_{兒}$"以及"啊$_{兒}$"與"安$_{兒}$"的。他把這種區别解釋爲有無收噫韻尾的問題。我覺得這個解釋很對。假如采用這個解釋,同時以我們新訂的基本韻母表爲基礎,以上這些兒化現象,便可以用兩條極簡明的規律表示出來了。兒化是韻母加"兒",即(M)V(E)+r,下面兩條公式就是據此推衍的。

$$\text{ø} \longrightarrow \text{y} / (\text{M})\text{ɨ}\_\_\_\text{r} \quad (1)$$
$$\text{M} \neq \text{W}$$

這個公式的意思是:凡韻腹爲高元音/ɨ/而韻尾爲零的韻母,在兒化的時候,韻尾改作"收噫",但韻頭如爲/w/則不在此限。這也就是説,兒化的時候,"一七"轍兒的字改入"灰堆",但"姑蘇"轍$_{兒}$的字則不變。

$$\text{n} \longrightarrow \text{y} / \_\_\_\text{r} \quad (2)$$

這條公式更簡單,意思是説:兒化時,韻尾/n/一律改作/y/。如此一來,原來不同的"官"與"乖"、"三"與"腮"、"回"與"魂"、"鬼"與"滚"等,兒化以後就都變成同音了。兩條規律加起來的結果,連"屍"與"身"、"枝"與"針"、"鷄"與

“今”、“魚”與“雲”等,兒化後也都相同了。總結這兩條規律所引起的變化,我們可以畫出一張兒化韻母表,代表“兒化 第一式”。

韻尾 / 韻腹 / 韻頭	-r			-yr		-wr		- ŋr	
	ɨ	ə	a	ɨ	a	ɨ	a	ɨ	a
ø 開	(兒)	蛾兒	沙兒	枝兒	蓋兒	頭兒	刀兒	燈兒	糖兒
y 齊		姐兒	牙兒	今兒	烟兒	牛兒	條兒	瓶兒	墻兒
w 合	屋兒	果兒	瓜兒	鬼兒	官兒			蟲兒	牀兒
yw 撮		月兒		玉兒	院兒			熊兒	
小轍兒	小姑蘇兒	小坡斜兒	小發花兒	小人辰兒	小言前兒	小油求兒	小遥條兒	小東中兒	小江陽兒

6.5.2 所謂“内城話”,在兒化韻方面,據趙元任先生説,分爲老少兩代(Chao 1968,p51),其他的報導也證實了這一點。我們先説這“老一代”的兒化韻。在這種兒化裏,“啊兒”類與“安兒”類已經不分了,因此“瓜兒”與“官兒”、“瓦兒”與“碗兒”、“把兒”與“板兒”等都變成同音詞兒了。在其他各方面,這一式的兒化,跟前述的“兒化第一式”完全相同。也就是説,它仍然保持着“根兒”與“歌兒”、“黑兒”與“喝兒”、“鬼兒”與“果兒”、“食兒”與“舌兒”、“運兒”與“月兒”等的對立。這個現象把許多外國學者都弄糊塗了,也鬧了許多笑話。美國學者哈特門所據的發音人,説的就是這種話(Hartman 1944)。結果逼得哈氏説,在高、中、低三度元音裏,中元音必須分成長與短兩個音。國内更有人據此直指“三度元音説”爲胡説八道(例如宋 1965)。其實這又是誤解。拿這種兒化現象跟前述第一式比較,便可看出這是早出的第一式進一步演化的結果。演化的方式很簡單,可以用下面的公式表達出來。

$$ø \longrightarrow y/a\_\_\_r \qquad (3)$$

這條公式的意思是:在韻基是低元音/a/的兒化韻母裏,/r/之前增加/y/作爲韻尾。也就是説,上表中的“小發花兒”與“小言前兒”兩轍合併了(合併以後當然仍可稱爲“小言前兒”)。把這條公式加在上節的兩條公式之後,三條公式便是這種較晚出的兒化形式的形成規律了。我們可以管這個叫做“兒化第二式”。王輔世特别强調説,“啊兒”跟“安兒”合併時,是前者變成後者,而不是後者變成前者(李思敬也證實了這一點)。換句話説,是“小發花兒”變入“小言前兒”。但是一般的拼音却把這類兒化韻母寫成[ar],而不寫成[air],可以確知的是,此處的對立已經消失了。

6.5.3 所謂“年輕一代”的兒化韻,顯然也是早期兒化韻的延伸。根據劉澤先的報導(劉 1957),這種兒化形式現在已變成内城話的主流了,説這種話的人自然也不再都是年輕的咯!這種兒化形式與前述第二式極爲接近,仍保持着“根兒”與“歌兒”等的對立,但是却有下列的特殊現象:

第一聲:根兒 kɨn+r≠歌兒 kə+r
鎚兒 crwɨy+r≠桌兒 crwə+r
衣兒 yɨ+r=蔭兒 yɨn+r≠掖兒 yə+r
蛆兒 khywɨ+r≠ 缺兒 khywə+r
第二聲:神兒 srɨn+r≠舌兒 srə+r
輪兒 lwɨn+r≠ 鑼兒 lwə+r
笛兒 tyɨ+r≠碟兒 tyə+r
桔兒 kywɨ+r≠ 橛兒 kywə+r
第三聲:枕兒 crɨn+r≠ 褶兒 crə+r
盹兒 twɨn+r≠ 朵兒 twə+r
几兒 kyɨ+r=姐兒 kyə+r
底兒 tyɨ+r=蝶兒 tyə+r
第四聲:刃兒 rɨn+r≠ 熱兒 rə+r
棍兒 kwɨn+r≠ 過兒 kwə+r
藝兒 yɨ+r=印兒 =yɨn+r=葉兒 yə+r
玉兒 ywɨ+r= 月兒 ywə+r

這些現象顯示出,“小坡斜兒”與“小人辰兒”在這種兒化形式裏,一般還是分開的,但它們的細音字在第三聲與第四聲裏却已混同了。混同的方式如何呢?“几兒”跟“姐兒”合併後,趙元任先生標作“jieel”而不標作“jiee'l”(Chao 1968)。這表示他認爲“小坡斜兒”的三、四聲細音字轉入“小人辰兒”了,但劉澤先則把它們標作“gier”而不標作“gir”(劉 1957),表示他認爲“小人辰兒”的這類字轉入“小坡斜兒”了。我們姑且用下式來表達這種合併,但並不意味我們跟劉澤先完全同意①。

ɨy ⟶ ə/y(w)____r (4)

限於三、四兩聲字

這一派的兒化形式,我們可以稱之爲"兒化第三式",須把以上四個公式連貫起來,才能表示出它的演化規律。

6.6 以上三種漸次蜕變出來的兒化形式,概括了北京話地區的各種兒化現象。將來會如何繼續演化,自然不是我們可以預知的。按常理說,第三式是最晚出的,因此可能代表着演變的一般趨勢;但據前引王輔世的報導看,越來越多的人却在使用第一式了,因此將來的標準音如仍回到第一式,也不是不可能的。日本的著名漢語學者藤堂明保對北京音韻有很深刻的研究。他也認爲北京話衹有三個元音,但他認爲在有韻尾的音節裏,元音的對比是中元音對低元音。在討論到兒化韻時,他首先説這是一個極複雜困難的問題,但緊接着却提出了一個簡單到令人難以置信的解釋。他説在兒化時,原韻母的韻尾/y/或/n/都消失了,别的没有變化。(Tōdō1963)。根據這個説法,兒化韻母應如下表:

韻尾 / 韻腹 / 韻頭	r			wr		ŋr	
	ɨ	ə	a	ə	a	ə	a
ø 開	枝兒	針兒	孩兒	狗兒	套兒	繩兒	張兒
y 齊	鷄兒	今兒	牙兒	油兒	鳥兒	釘兒	羊兒
w 合	屋兒	鍋兒	塊兒			洞兒	胖兒
yw 撮	魚兒	雲兒	園兒			熊兒	

就詞彙説,也應有如下的現象:

① 其實我覺得趙元任先生的觀察,即這類"小坡斜兒"的字轉入"小人辰兒"了,比較可靠。如果我們仔細檢查本文所列舉的兒化規律,就會發現,第一條説/ɨ/與/r/之間增加/y/,第二條説/a/與/r/之間增加/y/作爲韻尾。如此看來,除了/wɨ/以外,韻尾爲零的韻母,兒化時都有增/y/爲韻尾(即舌位略向前上方移動)。那麽,把公式(4)改寫成 ø→y/y(w) ə_r 似乎更合這一趨勢了。我們知道,音段相同的音節,讀作第三聲及第四聲時,其主要元音在音質上總變的較低,而在第一聲與第二聲裏則較高。因此讀作第三聲的"几兒"kyɨyr 跟新形成的"姐兒"kyəyr 也就非常接近了。在音位上説,這少數幾個新形成的韻基爲/əyr/的字,也就加入了"小灰堆兒"(變成/ɨyr/)了。近年來我碰到不少年輕朋友,他們連根兒歌兒,食兒與舌兒,笛兒與碟兒等都不分了。可見對他們來説公式(4)的"細音三、四聲字"這個條件也都用不着了。

食$_{兒}$ srɨ＋r≠ 神$_{兒}$ srən＋r＝蛇$_{兒}$ srə＋r

根$_{兒}$ kən＋r＝歌$_{兒}$ kə＋r

鷄$_{兒}$ kyɨ＋r≠ 今$_{兒}$ kyən＋r

屋$_{兒}$ wɨ＋r≠ 温$_{兒}$ wən＋r＝窩$_{兒}$ wə＋r

玉$_{兒}$ ywɨ＋r≠ 運$_{兒}$ ywən＋r＝月$_{兒}$ ywə＋r

我從來没碰見過説這種話的人,但不敢説絶對没有,因此也不願説藤堂先生的説法是向壁虚造的。

第七章　北京音的歷史背景

7. 現代標準漢語通稱“普通話”或稱“國語”，在海外又稱“華語”。我們一般都説這種話就是北京話，但也有不少人常常强調“國語”或“普通話”並不等於北京話。這個問題可以從三個方面加以分析。首先，就詞彙説，在用這個標準語寫出的文章或演講辭裏，確實有許多詞語是老北京人的言談中聽不到的，因此讀起來不像是北京人在説話，自然就叫人覺得這不是地道的北京話。但是在任何語言裏，詞彙都是最爲變動不居的一部分。由於外在事物的改變，詞彙就必然隨之增減，所以詞彙不可能決定語言的屬性，在語言學界也從來没有人拿詞彙作標準來爲語言或方言分類。其次，就語法説，這個標準語也似乎跟北京口語不大一樣，尤其是文藝或政論性的書面語，這主要表現在許多冗長甚或倒裝的句式裏，使人産生一種“没有人那麽説話”的感覺。其實這也是一種不必要的誤會。由於白話文學的倡導者一再强調“我手寫我口”，遂使一些人真的以爲書面語應該跟口頭語完全一樣。事實上這當然不可能。爲了表達較複雜與較細密的意象，自然就得使用比較複雜與比較長的句式，衹要這些句式符合某一語言的基本語法規則，我們就得承認它們屬於某一語言，没有理由説它們變成了另一種語言。其次，既然是標準語，總比較正規些，因此就不會采用土白中的一些過分特殊的習語與句式，這種使用上的選擇衹是風格的問題，也不可能使它變成另一種語言。最後，就語音説，如果有人能够證明國語或普通話的音系確實與北京話的音系不同，那我們倒真的必須承認它們是兩個不同的語言或方言了。聽説有人在北京城區作過調查，發現不同區段的居民所説的話，確實有不少語音上的差別。這本來並不足怪，像北京市這樣人口衆多的大城，不用調查就可以知道各區居民的口音不可能完全一致，但這却引起了一個問題：所謂“北京話”到底是什麽？很顯然，衹有在回答了這個問題之後，我們才可以説國語或普通話是否就是北京話。我不知道北京居民到底説多少種不同的北京話，但我確知其中有一種最受重視且被公認爲是最標準的，這個“標準北京話”的音系也就是推行普通話時采爲準則的音系。這也就是我們說普通話與北京話音系完全相同的緣故。

7.1 這個標準語是怎麽樣形成的呢？有人說，歷遼金元明清各代七八百年，北京作爲首都自然成爲政教工商的中心，因此北京話也就成爲標準話了。我覺得這話衹說對了一半。這有兩層意義。其一，遼金以異族入侵中原，雖在北方以北京爲首都建立了政權，但當時的北京地區仍較荒凉，不可能成爲主要的文教經濟的中心，因此當時的北京語也不可能取得作爲標準的地位，這種特殊的地位衹有在元代以後才有可能。其二，歷代雖然没有明令規定什麽是"國語"(元朝倒是定了，但指的是蒙古話。)，自然也没有大力推行過"普通話"，但事實上一種所謂"雅音"或"通語"的標準漢語是早已存在了的。當然在不同的朝代，這種"標準漢語"也有不同的内容。但不同時代之間的"標準話"還是脉絡相承的。它們之間的差異主要是由於時代的變化所引起的語言變化，其次才是由於國都遷徙而滲入的方言成分。這是因爲某一地的話(當時的國都)被認作標準話以後，便自然獲得了强大的生命力，在特别重視傳統的文人學士的心目中，便取得了特殊的地位，便會隨着文化經濟的發展與長期大一統的安定局面向四方擴散，所以即使國都後來遷到另一地方，也不會影響到這個標準話的延續。北京話之所以能成爲現代標準漢語，固然因爲北京是元明清三朝大一統時期的國都，但更重要的是因爲"傳統標準漢語"先已擴散到了北京地區。

7.1.1 在中國歷史上，"標準語"的使用可以上溯到什麽時代呢？這個問題可以從兩個角度提出回答。其一，當人類的社會與經濟活動達到一個相當大的高度與範圍時，自然就有必要使用標準語了。因此我們可以想象這在秦漢甚至商周時期，就有某種標準形式的漢語了。其二，上溯現代標準漢語的前身，也就是說把"標準語"這一概念作爲一個連續不斷的整體來看待，我覺得我們至少可以追溯到東漢時期①。東漢建都於洛陽，維持了兩百年的統一局面。

① 我衹把漢語標準語的源頭推溯到東漢時期的洛陽話，這是比較保守謹慎的說法。李新魁等上推到殷周時代，認爲周公治洛，周人承襲了殷人的標準，所以洛陽話早就是標準了(李新魁，《〈中原音韻〉音系研究》1983)。我覺得這有些太渺茫了，難於稽查，不似東漢時代有各種佐證。另外必須强調的是，東漢的洛陽話與現在的洛陽話當然大不相同，而且它們之間的承傳關係也不見得比東漢洛陽話與現代北京話之間的關係更密切。

這個時期特重士風,文人著述漸多,五言詩與樂府歌辭也在這一時期發展起來,反切之學也興起於此時,爲稍後編制韻書創造了有利的條件。這一切都有利於標準語的確立與廣爲流傳,因此首都地區的洛陽話就很自然的成爲標準語了。其作爲標準的地位從此也就不是其他方言可能取代的了。所以東晉雖遷都於南京,復歷宋齊梁陳各代,當時的南京土話也没能變成新的標準話,作爲標準的仍是所謂"洛生咏",而北方亂華的五胡在終於漢化的時候,他們所學的漢語也必然是當時最流行的洛陽話。其時出現了不少韻書,在某種意義上説,這些韻書都可以説是爲了適合當時的需要(學習"普通話")而編寫的正音教科書或參考書,而它們自然又反過來加强了這種標準語的地位。當然這種標準語也隨着時代在改變,而擴散到其他地區以後,也會産生個别地區的特色。例如《切韻》編者們想要綜合進去的"金陵音",實際上就是當時"南京式的洛陽話"。當這類具有某一地方色彩的洛陽話在當地取得了絶對優勢之後,自然也就不再叫做洛陽話而叫做當地話了。宋代的汴梁話,元代的大都話可以説皆屬此類。由於它們本來就是傳統標準的一支,所以在當地成爲國都以後,它們也就成了當時的新標準語。我們可以推斷北京話的"官話"地位大概開始於元代,經明清而益形鞏固。雖然它跟漢魏時代的洛陽話以及宋金時代的開封話都有承傳的關係,但由於時代相去已遠或滲入了一些地方色彩,已經變成了一種不同的方言。因爲有關它的最早的系統化記録見於《中原音韻》,我們將在下文裏略談自《中原音韻》到現代北京話的一些歷史演變問題。

7.2 周德清的《中原音韻》作於元代中葉(1324),其目的是教人如何"正語作詞"。他所謂的詞指的是元代的散曲與雜劇。他認爲這種新興文學所使用的語言應該是當時的"通語",即他心目中的標準語。元曲源於民間文學,所用的語言基本上是口語,因此早期的元代作家在作詞時是用不着查韻書的,也没有曲韻可查,衹憑他們的口耳而已。這些早期作家多半是大都人,或長期活動於大都地區,因此我們猜想他們所用的語言就是當時的大都話,當然這種大都話衹能是"傳統標準語"(尤其是宋金時代的汴梁話)演變流傳到北京地區以後的形式。這些作家的作品顯然極受歡迎,因此有許多作家群起仿效,可惜其中許多人是外地人,説不同的方言,所作之詞就每有"不正"之語,常使説標準語的歌者"拗斷嗓子",這才引起了重申標準的必要,周書便因此而作。多數人(包括我本人)也就認定周書所依據的方言就是當時的大都話。但是也有人以爲不然,比如李新魁就認爲是洛陽話(李新魁 1983, 15—46),邵榮芬則引用陸志韋的話説可能是"河北中南部地區"(邵榮芬 1981,93)。我覺得要解決這個問題,光徵引文獻是不够的,更主要的是比較音韻結構内部的異同。

7.2.1《中原音韻》分韻十九部,每韻之内又分四聲,即平聲陰,平聲陽,上聲及去聲。中古漢語的入聲字分成三類,分别附入平聲陽、上聲及去聲,即所謂"入派三聲"。我曾經嚴格地根據音節分段、音節歸類、押韻原理等原則爲《中原音韻》擬過音(参看薛 1975),此處不能詳細討論,衹把我得出的韻母表列出來,以供下文討論的參考①。

韻尾／韻基／韻頭	ø				y		w		n				m			ŋ		
	ɨ	e	a	ɔ	ɨ	a	ɨ	ɔ	ɨ	e	a	ɔ	ɨ	e	a	ɨ	e	ɔ
開 ø	支		沙	歌	賊	來	侯	豪	根		山		森		三		生	當
齊 y		車	家		齊	皆	尤	蕭	真	天	奸		侵	廉	咸		庚	江
合 w	模		花	戈	微	快	否	郭	文		晚	桓				東	轟	光
撮 yw	魚	靴		嶽					春	川						鍾	兄	
十三轍兒	支思 ┆ 魚模	車遮	家麻	歌戈	齊微	皆來	尤侯	蕭豪	真文	先天	寒山	桓歡	侵尋	廉纖	監咸	東鍾	庚青	江陽

7.2.2 現代的北京話裏有不少破音字。這種一字兩讀的現象通常叫做"讀音"與"語音"的差異,如"色"讀/sə̀/(sè)與/srǎy/(shǎi),"得"讀/tə́/(dé)與/tɨ̌y/(děi),"軸"讀/crwɨ́/(zhú)與/crɨ́w/(zhóu),"落"讀/lwə̀/(luò)與/làw/(lào),"更"讀/kɨ̄ŋ/(gēng)與/kyɨ̄ŋ/(jīng)等等。細查《中原音韻》的收字,這類字都出現在與現代"語音"相對應的韻部("色"在"皆來","得"在"齊微")或小韻("更"與"京"同)裏,衹有"軸"類字互見於"魚模"與"尤侯","落"類字互見於"歌戈"與"蕭豪"。"軸"類字多見於"魚模"(讀音),衹有少數又見於"尤侯"

① 在我的原著(薛 1975)中,我把"東鍾"韻的韻基擬作/oŋ/,"江陽" 韻擬作/aŋ/,"蕭豪"韻則先有三個不同韻基/ow、aw、ew/而後併作/aw/。當時過分重視了音位的對稱性,近些年來的研究使我感到歷史音變的合理連貫性應受到更大的重視,所以我把"東鍾"改擬爲/ɨŋ/,"江陽"改擬爲/ɔŋ/,"蕭豪"改擬爲單一的/ɔw/。改擬的理由散見於薛 1978,1982 及 1985 等文中。

(語音),這是因爲這類入聲字先變同"尤侯",而後又隨着類似的非入聲字如"浮、母、富"等一同變入"魚模"韻(參看薛 1975, 05—107)。"落"類字則絶大多數衹見於"蕭豪"(語音),衹有少數幾個又見於"歌戈"(讀音)。綜觀以上這些現象,我推論説:《中原音韻》所依據的方音是現代北京話中"語音"的祖語。但當時的北方話中,顯然還有一個跟這個"語音"的祖語在作爲標準語的地位方面不相上下的方音,即現代北京話中"讀音"的祖語。這兩個元代的方音,在音韻結構方面,極爲接近,以致當時的人可能還不易分清呢!這兩個方音之間衹有兩個差别。其一,漢語音韻史上有兩個音變,一爲二等開口喉牙音字腭化,一爲梗曾兩攝字合韻,在這兩個方音裏都發生了,衹是時序不同而已。在"語音"的祖語中,先有二等喉牙音字的腭化,故"耕、更"等字變讀爲細音,而後才有梗曾兩攝字的合韻,因此它們就跟原三等的"京"字變爲同音了。在"讀音"的祖語中,恰好相反,先有梗曾的合韻,因而原爲二等的"耕、更"等字就不再是二等了(變爲四等,即韻腹由央低元音變爲前元音),所以後來二等喉舌音字腭化時,它們就未受影響而仍爲供音,所以與"京"字有别(參看薛 1975, 58—59 及薛 1978)。第二個差别是,一部分入聲字在這兩個方音中的演變方式不同。這些入聲字分爲兩類,一類原屬梗曾兩攝,另一類原屬江宕兩攝。這牽涉到《中原音韻》中到底有無入聲的問題,比較複雜,留待下節一並討論。

7.2.3《中原音韻》所依據的方音中是否仍有入聲,迄今仍是一個聚訟的問題,足見統一學術思想實非易事,追根究底,問題還是周德清自己造成的。他一方面把原入聲字分爲三類,派入平(陽)、上、去三聲,另一方面又在序文及起例中説了一些自相矛盾的話。一回説這是"前輩佳作中間備載明白"的,不容置疑,一回又説這是"爲作詞而設耳……呼吸言語之間還有入聲之别。"歷來討論這個問題的人,都喜歡廣徵文獻,用許多外在的資料來支持他們的入聲或有或無的説法。我覺得這類資料雖然能給我們許多啓示,却不一定有論證上的必然性。真正的證明必須來自這個特殊音系的内在結構,而且必須符合一般音理。在討論這個問題之先,我們必須在思想上先有兩個認識。首先,宋、金、元時代是入聲字轉變或消失的時期,這個過程必然是漸次的與緩慢的,而且在不同的地區可能出之以不同的方式(儘管各區都是自有規律的)。所以有的方言可能仍保留入聲,另一些方言則已失掉了入聲,甚或原爲單一的方言區也可能因此而分裂爲幾個次方言區。明乎此就可知道，當我們説《中原音韻》有或無入聲時，我們指的不是當時的北方話，甚至不能説是當時的北京話，而是專指《中原音韻》所依據的那個我們稱之爲“現代北京話中‘語音’之祖語”的特殊方音。其次，一般人，包括周德清在内，常有一種錯覺，即把所記入聲看作一個整體而申論其有無，其實我們應該認識到，入聲字有許多類别，因此在改讀或消失時，可能有先有後，也可能遵循着不同的規律。在上述兩個認識的基礎上，我們可以就“入派三聲”這個問題作以下幾點説明。

a) 説這樣分派祇是“爲作詞而設耳”是絶對不可信的。押韻，真正的押韻，必須有實際的音韻依據，才能使歌者順吻聽者悦耳，這絶不是幾個“欲廣文路”的文人可以隨意决定的。放寬押韻標準也祇能是因爲有某種方言確實允許那麽放寬。

b)《中原音韻》裏的入派三聲，除了“入聲作上聲”這一歸調的方式與現代北京話不盡相合以外，其他各方面，尤其是歸韻的方式，都與現代北京話的“語音”相符，而且演變的規律至爲分明（參看薛 1978）。這是語言本身的客觀演變，不可能是“廣其押韻”的文人代爲預擬的。語言學發展迄今，雖然對音理已有不少突破性的發現，仍不可能預測出未來的音變。假如在《中原音韻》所依據的方言中，入聲字果真仍爲入聲，而幾個文士竟能預料到它們的未來發展並據以“廣其押韻”，那未免太神奇了，即使像關鄭馬白般的偉大作家恐怕也做不到，説他們不約而同地碰巧了也不合理，所以祇能是因爲在他們使用的那種方音中入聲字的確已經如此演變過來了。

c) 現代北京話中“語音”與“讀音”的差異突出地表現在兩類入聲字的讀法上。一類原屬梗曾兩攝，在“語音”中都改讀“收噫”，如“色”/srǎy/（shǎi），“白”/pwāy/（bɑ́i），“黑”/hɨ̄y/（hēi），“宅”/cráy/（zhɑ́i）等，另一類原屬江宕兩攝，在“語音”中都改讀“收嗚”，如“落”/làw/（lɑ̀o），“薄”/pwáw/（bɑ́o），“學”/hyáw/（xiɑ́o），“杓”/sráw/（shɑ́o）等，這些字在“讀音”中都屬直音韻（即收零韻尾）。在《中原音韻》裏，原屬梗曾的入聲字都分别出現在“皆來”韻與“齊微”韻中，與“語音”的方式完全相合，如果按照“讀音”的方式歸韻，它們都應該出現在“車遮”韻中，但“車遮”韻没收。原屬江宕的入聲字都出現在“蕭豪”韻中，正與“語音”相符，但其中一小部分又見於“歌戈”韻，倒是符合“讀音”的方式的。根據這些現象,我推論《中原音韻》所依據的方音是現代北京話中“語音”的祖語,而把“歌戈”韻中的入聲字解釋爲是這個方音(“語音”的祖語)從另一方音(“讀音”的祖語)借來的讀法,並據而推測這個“讀音”的祖語在當時一定也有很强的標準代表性。至於其他各類入聲字的演變,這兩個方音倒是完全一致的,如山咸兩攝的入聲字即按一定的規律出現在“歌戈、家麻、車遮”等“直音”韻中(參看薛 1978),與現代北京話中的音讀全合,没有破讀的現象。這兩個元代的方音到底是否仍有入聲呢?就音理説,我以爲“語音”的祖語不可能仍有入聲,因爲入聲字的特色是具有塞音韻尾。當這些塞音分别變爲“收噫”或“收嗚”時,它們的位置已被這個新音段占據了,不可能再加一個塞音韻尾,那是違反中古以來漢語的音節構造的。但在“讀音”的祖語裏,我相信入聲仍然存在,原來不同的塞音韻尾在這個方音裏可能已經合併爲一個喉塞音,但衹要這個喉塞音仍然占着韻尾的位置,入聲也就依然存在。

7.3 元代享祚甚短,而且當時的政府也没有故意地要樹立一個標準的漢語(他們的興趣是推行“國語”,即蒙古話),所以那個自然形成的新標準音,即《中原音韻》所依據的那個“語音”方音,並没有能够確立不可移易的標準地位。降及明代,這個標準地位就讓那個“讀音”方音所取代了。這有好幾層原因,最重要的當然是這個所謂“讀音”的方音本來就流行甚廣。它與那個所謂“語音”的方音本來就相差無幾,就音系説,幾乎全同,衹多了一個喉塞音韻尾,就字彙説,除了上文所討論過的差别以外,其餘完全相同,因此對一般人説,這種標準的更代在語言的交際中是毫無困難的。其次,明朝的皇親國戚以及達官貴人多來自南京地區,明代初期又屢次遷徙南方的居民以充實北京地區。這些人所説的話或則仍有入聲,或則雖無入聲但入聲字變化的方式較近前文所説的“讀音”形式,因此當他們在北京地區接觸到“讀音”與“語音”兩種不同的念法時,自然便覺得前者較順耳,後者難接受了。再次,讀書人較保守,“平、上、去、入”四聲之説早已深入骨髓,加以國初在南京時所頒布的《洪武正韻》已經成爲“祖宗之成規”,自然不敢妄議,因此當他們受命(或自動)審定音切時,面對着“讀音”與“語音”兩個可能的選擇,前者自然就被視爲正音而後者衹能是俗音了。一旦如此定性以後,通過科舉與學校的推廣,“讀音”的正統地位便確定下來了,歷清迄今而不變,也不能再變了,因爲“語音”中這類字的特殊讀法,除了幾個常用字以外,都已廢而不用了①。有人說近代官話史中這段轉變是北京音系受了南方話(尤其是南京話)的影響而造成的。我覺得似不盡然,因爲由《中原音韻》可以看出,"讀音"這個系統早已存在,明朝時遷到北京的南方人衹是幫助促成了它取代"語音"作爲正音的地位而已,没有影響到它的音系。北京話此後的轉變衹是語音的自然演化而已。

明代有幾本目的在教人學標準話的韻書,例如蘭茂的《韻略易通》與畢拱辰的《韻略匯通》,自然都以北京音爲依歸,而且都分列入聲,甚至保守到以入聲字分别配屬陽聲韻。我們曾推論説在"讀音"音系中,入聲韻尾已合併爲一個喉塞音,當然不能再分别與不同的陽聲韻相配了。蘭、畢的做法似乎證明我們的設想不對,但如仔細檢查他們分列的入聲字,就可發現他們的做法衹是因循舊章而已,在許多地方都露出了馬脚。其實元明時代北京話中的"讀音"音系最多衹能保留一個以喉塞音爲韻尾的入聲,而且連這個入聲也在日趨式微,所以當明末的徐孝編制《司馬温公等韻圖經》時,韻圖的嚴格形式便明白地顯示出當時的北京話已經没有入聲了(參看薛 1983)。徐孝的十三攝與後來民間流傳的所謂"十三轍"完全符合,可以推斷出其韻母的音位結構如下表:

韻尾	ø直音					y收噫		W收嗚		n抵腭		ŋ穿鼻	
介音 \ 元音	ɨ		e	a	ɔ	ɨ	a	ɨ	a	ɨ	a	ɨ	a
ø開	支		格	大	歌	黑	來	侯	豪	跟	山	生	唐
y齊	一		切	加			厓	油	遥	因	言	京	江
w合		古	拙	花	果	灰	懷				晚	東	王
yw撮	玉		月		嶽					君	全		
十三轍	一七	姑蘇	乜斜	發花	梭坡	灰堆	懷來	油求	遥條	人辰	言前	東中	江陽
徐孝	止	祝	拙	假	果	壘	蟹	流	效	臻	山	通	宕

這個韻母系統與現代北京話的韻母系統至爲相似,不同的衹是原"梭坡"(果攝)與"乜斜"(拙攝)兩轍現在已經合併了。

① 由於"讀音"早在明代就取得了正統標準的地位,説"語音"方言的人自然也深受影響,許多字的"語音"念法也都早被忘記了,因此再改以"語音"爲標準已是絶不可能的了。比如"錯、索"等字見於《中原音韻》的"蕭豪"韻,表示它們的"語音"念法應爲 cao 與 sao,用這種念法來代替它們的現讀 cuo 與 suo 將會造成很多混亂。

7.4 由以《中原音韻》爲代表的早期官話到以今天的北京話爲代表的現代標準漢話,當然已經發生了不少音變。我們可以先舉出那幾個影響到分韻的音變並簡略地討論一下,這些音變所造成的後果可以由比照上文的兩個韻母表看出來。我們將按音韻結構的内在關係並參考有關文獻來推斷它們發生的先後,並按這個次序討論它們。

$$m \longrightarrow n / V\_\_\_ \qquad (1)$$

這個公式所代表的是北方話中閉口韻的消失,有關的字都改讀爲"抵腭"了,因此原來的"侵尋"韻即併入"真文","監咸"併入"寒山","廉纖"併入"先天"。即使早在周德清的時代,某些方言中閉口韻就已經消失了,但在他所記録的那個"正語"裏,顯然仍舊存在,所以他在起例中特别指出"針有真,金有斤,南有難,兼有堅"等等。在明代的標準音中,閉口韻似乎到蘭茂時代仍然存在,但不會晚於我們要討論的下一個音變。

$$\left.\begin{matrix} ɔ \\ e \end{matrix}\right\} \longrightarrow a / \_\_\_ n \qquad (2)$$

《中原音韻》中"寒山、桓歡、先天"三韻之字因韻腹不同而分押,這是天經地義的,有人以爲它們是因介音的不同而分韻,那是誤解。這幾韻的差别到蘭茂時仍舊存在,但其後不久就合韻了,成爲"十三轍"的"言前"轍,畢拱辰的《韻略匯通》雖然把這類字分爲"先全"與"山寒"兩韻,其實衹是洪細之分。這一合韻的過程當然包括了原來"監咸"與"廉纖"兩韻的字,音韻内部的簡約原則(rule of simplicity)使我們相信這個音變比上個音變要晚一些。

$$y \longrightarrow ø / yɨ\_\_\_ \qquad (3)$$

原來的"齊微"韻中包含了兩個韻母,即/yɨy/齊類字與/wɨy/微類字(還有一個由幾個入聲字如"賊"等演變出來的韻母/ɨy/)。這些字晚至蘭茂的時代仍以含有相同的韻基/ɨy/而互押①,但稍後就不再互押了。畢拱辰把原來"魚

① 我爲《中原音前》的"齊微"韻擬了兩個韻母,即"微"類字的/wɨy/與"齊"類字的/yɨy/。前者一般人較易接受,因爲他們的擬音多作[uei],後者他們覺得"衹是一個[i]",因此難免感到我的擬法"太形式化"了(參看丁邦新 1981)。我的理由是:(1)"齊"類字與"微"類字同屬"止"攝,所以必然具有相同的韻尾;(2)它們在《中原音韻》時代同屬一韻,所以必然具有相 (轉下頁)

模”韻中的字按合口與撮口之别而分爲“呼模”與“居魚”兩韻，又把原“齊微”韻中的“齊”類字併入“居魚”。徐孝更把“齊”類字分出，讓它們跟“支思”類及“居魚”類的字共同構成一個“止”攝。“十三轍”的做法與徐孝完全一致，即把這三類字合成一個“一七”轍。這幾家的做法表面看來非常奇怪，因此歷來備遭訴病，其實他們的處置是不得不然的，羅常培先生已經發現民歌中就是這麽押韻的嘛（羅 1950）！此處的公式所代表的音變是：“齊”類字的韻母由/yɨy/變爲/yɨ/，即丢掉了韻尾。假如我們牢記住押韻的基本原理，自然就會明白爲什麽它們轉而與“思、魚”之類的字相押了。

$$\text{e} \longrightarrow \text{ɨ} / \underline{\quad\quad} \ \text{ŋ} \qquad (4)$$

《中原音韻》的“庚青”與“東鍾”韻之分，在明代的標準語最少保持到《易通》成書之時（1442），其後就合併了。《匯通》仍分兩韻，但那衹是洪細之别。徐孝的《等韻圖經》就把它們合爲一個“通”攝。此處的公式就代表這個音變，即“庚青”韻的韻腹由前元音上升而變爲高元音，因此就與“東鍾”互押了，成爲“十三轍”的“東中”轍。“庚青”韻的字絶大多數都屬開口（廣義的），合口字極少。早在《中原音韻》裏，這些合口字（如“崩、肱”等）就已重見於“東鍾”韻，而“東鍾”韻裏與它們相對應的字却不重見於“庚青”韻，足證兩韻合併的過程是“庚青”變入“東鍾”。在所謂“京戲”的傳統裏，原“庚青”韻的字，合口歸“東鍾”，開口却歸“人辰”，這一看似特殊的現象當然與標準話無關，而是京戲（即皮黄戲）發源地的方音造成的。

（接上頁）同的韻基；（3）“齊”類字後來不再跟“微”類字互押了，轉而與“支、魚”兩類字合爲一韻（“一七”轍），最合理的解釋是：它們丢掉了韻尾，因此變得與後兩類字具有共同韻基/iø/而與“微”類字不再具有相同的韻基了。有人説“齊”與“微”兩類字可以互押的原因是它們都含有[i]。這是講不通的，因爲此説（1）自相矛盾。（既如此，爲什麽現在不互押了？）（2）違背押韻原理。（“來”[lai]也含有[i]，爲什麽不跟它們押韻？）這兒牽涉到的是一個音韻學的觀念問題。我們一再説過，一個語言的音位分析，目的是解釋説那種語言的人的語感，亦即它們對語音的聽覺反應。這種反應跟實際的發音並不完全一致。比如英語中 fit 與 feat 兩個字的元音讀法完全不同，但對衹會説漢語的人來説，聽起來却是一樣的，因爲漢語音系中没有這兩種對比的元音。我們可以推論，在《中原音韻》的音系中，没有/yɨy/與/yɨ/[i]這兩個韻母的音位性對比，因此儘管發音時可能有[i]的存在，但在聽覺反應中，當時人還是把它當作/yɨy/的，即認爲這個韻母是齊齒性的，並且可與“微”類字（/wɨy/）押韻。後來音系起了變化，韻母/yɨ/産生了，因此韻母發音方式爲[i]的字就不再與“微雷賊”一類的字押韻了。

$$ay \longrightarrow e / y\_\_\_ \qquad (5)$$

《中原音韻》的“皆來”韻裏有少數讀齊齒音的字，都是由二等韻喉牙音的腭化造成的，例如“街、楷、鞋”等字，因此它們的韻母衹能是/yay/，但現在的北京話裏，它們的韻母已變爲/yə/了，即與“接、斜”一類字相同，此處的公式就是表示這個音變的。我相信這個音變發生的時間相當晚，應在“十三轍”的音系形成之後，但不可能晚於下節要討論的“梭坡”與“乜斜”的合轍。這有兩層道理。頭一個是外證。在許多普通話方言中，這類字仍屬“懷來”轍，在所謂“京戲”的押韻中，也是如此的，可知這一音變發生的時間不會太早，應爲晚近北京話中特有現象。第二個道理是内證。這個公式雖然簡明地標出了韻母/yay/改讀以後變爲/ye/，但嚴格説來音理上是相當含混的。它表示原來的韻腹與韻尾的合體/ay/變成了一個單一的韻腹/e/，没有標明到底是那一個音位在改變，更没有標明改變的音理。（在極少數情况下，以音位符號爲單位來表達音變會有困難，此即一例。如采用“區别性特徵”表示法，這種困難就比較容易解決。）這個音變的原因實際上是語音的異化現象。就音位的形態説，韻母/yay/的韻腹元音是央低元音/a/，但就實際發音説，因受韻頭與韻尾兩個前半元音的雙重影響，/a/在此處必然是一個較前與較高的同位音[ε]或[e]。由於這個韻母含有相同的韻頭與韻尾，後來便因異化作用而丢掉了韻尾，也就是我們此處討論的音變，其變化過程實爲/yay/＝[yey]⟶[ye]＝/ye/，因此變入了“乜斜”轍而不變入“發花”，後來又因“乜斜”與“梭坡”合轍而變爲今讀/yə/。我們説這個音變應早於下節公式(6)所代表的音變，因爲其時尚有一個前元音音位可以供它認同，若晚於公式(6)，則無前元音可以歸附了。（假如我們可以找到一個方言，在那兒“皆楷介”等已改押“乜斜”而“乜斜”與“梭坡”尚未合轍，便可證明我們此處的推論是完全正確的了。）

$$\left.\begin{matrix} ɔ \\ e \end{matrix}\right\} \longrightarrow ə / \_\_\_ \# \qquad (6)$$

這個公式所代表的是一個很晚的音變，即“十三轍”裏的“乜斜”與“梭坡”兩轍在現代北京話中的合轍。近古漢語的元音系統包含四個音位，逐漸演變成現代北京話的三音位元音系統。試比較一下《中原音韻》的韻母表與“十三轍”的韻母表,我們便可看出,元音對比的簡化是由帶尾韻開始而逐步進行的。在《中原音韻》之前,“收噫”韻即首先受到影響,其次是“收嗚”韻(參看薛1975,66—67),所以在中原音韻的韻母表上,這兩類韻母衹有高低兩度對比。《中原音韻》之後,公式(2)與(4)所代表的音變相繼發生,遂使“抵腭”韻(“人辰”對“言前”)與“穿鼻”韻(“東中”對“江陽”)也衹剩下兩度對比了,所以在“十三轍”的韻母表裏,衹有無尾韻才保持了四個元音的對比。公式(6)所代表的音變發生在“十三轍”形成以後的北京話裏,至此便形成了現代標準漢語的高中低三音位元音系統。但這最後一個音變在許多南方官話裏却没有發生,所以許多湖北與四川的方言迄今尚分押“梭坡”與“乜斜”兩類字,更不用説皮黄戲的押韻了。

以上各節所討論到的幾個音變,羅常培先生在他的“京劇中的幾個音韻問題”(羅 1963)也討論到了。他的解説在許多方面與我們頗不相同,爲節省篇幅,在此不擬一一比較,有興趣的讀者可以對照閲讀。羅先生還舉了許多别的“上口字”問題,都是牽涉到聲母或介音的,如果一一説明,勢將太費篇幅。在此我衹擬指出,假如立足於我們的分析並以音變的時序觀念來看這些現象,它們將顯得井然有序、順理成章,表明它們所依據的方音與北京話實屬近親,衹是在語音的發展中晚了幾步而已。我們可以再舉兩個例子來説明這種現象。

a) 捲舌聲母/cr. crh、sr、r/(ㄓ、ㄔ、ㄕ、ㄖ)晚至明末仍是洪細兩配的。例如在《匯通》中,“枝”讀/crɨ/(ㄓ)入“支辭”韻,“知”讀/cryɨ/(ㄓㄧ)入“居魚”韻,京劇的讀法與此相同;又如“梳”讀/srwɨ/(ㄕㄨ)入“姑蘇”韻,“書”讀/srywɨ/(ㄕㄩ)入“居魚”(“一七”)韻,京劇的押韻與此亦同。但在北京話裏,由於這類聲母後的/y/消失了,故原來因此分讀的字也就變成同音字了,這個音變(y→ø/r____)顯然是晚出的。

b) 舌尖塞擦音與擦音聲母/c、ch、s/(ㄗ、ㄘ、ㄙ),晚至明末清初也是洪細兩配的,配細音時並不腭化,因此與原喉牙音的ㄐ、ㄑ、ㄒ仍然有别,而後者晚至畢拱辰時仍被認爲是與ㄍ、ㄎ、ㄏ同類的,這可由他用來代表聲母的早梅詩看出來。例如“西”讀/syi/(ㄙㄧ),“希”則讀/hyi/(ㄒㄧ)。京戲及許多方言都保持這種區别,叫做“尖音”字對“團音”字。但在今北京話中,前一類聲母高度腭化,因此與後一類合併了,造成了所謂“尖團不分”的局面,這也是晚近的現象。

上述各種所謂“上口字”現象,顯示出北京話與皮黃戲所依據的方言,原來相差並不太多,祇不過北京地區的新音變没有影響到那些方言,遂使它們跟新的“標準語”(今北京話)有了距離。

第八章 “官話”的特性

8.“中國話”或“漢語”所代表的概念是甚爲寬泛的。習慣上我們把所有漢族人民説的話都叫做漢語，而把不同形態的漢語叫做方言。但是漢族人民具有悠久的歷史文化，居住在極爲廣闊的土地上，因此他們所説的“方言”也就往往有極大的差異。王力先生把漢語方言分爲五類，即官話、吴語、閩語、粵語及客家話。趙元任先生則分爲九大類，即廣州方言、客贛方言、厦門汕頭方言、福州方言、吴方言、湘方言、北方官話、南方官話及西南官話。其後又有許多不同的分法，在此無須列舉[①]，但有一點須在此指出。語言學中所謂的 language 與 dialect 兩詞，一般譯爲“語言”與“方言”，它們的區别是：當人們所説的兩種不同的話仍可互通時，它們就仍然是同一個語言的兩種方言，否則就變成兩個不同的語言了。當然所謂可通性（intelligibility）並不是一個絶對的概念，而是有程度性的，衹不過相差的程度不能太大而已。用這個定義來看趙、王兩先生所劃分的漢語方言，我們就得説，他們所謂的“方言”實在都是不同的語言，因爲除了趙先生所分的三個官話方言之間容或可通之外，其餘的都自成一系，與别的“方言”是不能相通的，甚至他們各自包含的次方言之間，如閩南與閩北話，也是無法相通的。由此可見，中國學者所謂的“方言”是由“漢語”（漢族人民説的話）這一概念派生出來的，它的定義衹能是“漢話的幾個大類”。用這個特有的定義來評斷，趙先生把官話分爲三種，並把它們與其他幾個方言並列，就不如王先生把它們合而爲一來得妥當合理了。在本章裏，我們想着重地討論一下“官話”這個概念的含義，也就是官話作爲“漢話的一個大類”與其他幾大類的不同之處。其次我們也將討論一下官話内部次方言之間的差異。

8.1 在漢語的幾個大方言類别中，官話無疑是最大最重要的。這固然由於説這類話的人分布最廣數目最多，但更由於它所代表的政治與文化的歷史

① 有關漢語大方言區劃分的許多説法，請參看詹伯慧 1982。詹氏自己主張應分爲六個大區，即北方方言、吴方言、湘方言、客贛方言、粵方言和閩方言。我覺得就中國學者的“方言”定義來説，這是比較合情理合邏輯的。

背景。它直接上承漢民族文化中的“雅言”與“通語”的傳統,作爲官方使用的標準語,也是晚近七八百年間一切重要的文化活動與文學創作所使用的語言。反過來説,也正因爲它有這樣特殊的歷史背景,所以它的分布地區才會如此之廣,使用人數才會如此之多。然而官話的特性究竟是什麼呢?也就是説,官話與非官話的漢語方言究竟有哪些差别呢?多年前在我研究河南林縣臨淇方言(Wang and Hsueh 1973)與山東平度方言(薛 1973)時,就感到有回答上述問題的必要,因爲我們必須指出這些方言的隸屬。當然直覺上我們都可以推測説它們一定是官話方言。“是北方話嘛!”但是以地理的緣故來決定方言的分類顯然是不合理的,正確的做法應該是從語言本身的特性着眼。這就必須首先確定什麼是官話了。當時我草擬了十條“測驗條例”,也就是我認爲的官話方言的共通性。後來在討論“支思”韻的形成時(薛 1980),曾把這十條共通性譯述出來,但始終未及逐條討論,現將這十個條例略加修訂,列舉於後,作爲討論官話特性的基礎。

(甲) 全獨上聲字之改讀去聲。

(乙) 全濁聲母之化清。

(丙) 二等韻喉牙音之腭化。

(丁)“梗、曾”兩攝陽聲字之合韻。

(戊)“支思”韻之形成。

(己) 閉口韻之變爲抵腭。

(庚) 入聲變讀與消失。

(辛) 兒化韻之出現。

(壬) 捲舌音聲母後腭化介音之消失。

(癸) 尖團音之混合。

這十個條例實際上代表漢語史中十個重要的音變。音變自然是有時間性的,有先有後。由歷史文獻的記録以及音韻的内部邏輯,我們推論。上述十個條例的排列就代表這些音變在歷史上發生的順序。作爲一個方言是否屬於官話的檢驗標準,這些條例的重要性大概可以説是由上向下遞減的。也就是説,爲了確定某一方言是否算是官話,也許前五條或六條就够了,餘下的幾條也許可以作爲官話次方言的分類標準。

8.2 所有的漢語方言都源自同一個祖語，這是理論上必須如此假定的。由這個祖語孳生出不同的方言，這些方言又各自孳生出自己的次方言。我們一般都用樹狀圖式來表達這種語言的分支狀態，即所謂樹狀理論（tree theory）。但是由於標準語觀念的確立，我們可以把其中一支視爲主幹，其他各支作爲旁出。從這個觀點看，我們自然可以説官話是漢語演進的主幹，非官話方言是旁支。一個語言分化成許多不同方言的原因，自然是在不同的地點或社區發生了不同的音變，使得個别地區的話産生了與其他地區不同的特色，因此嚴格地説，樹狀圖式的每一分叉都代表一個重要的音變，標示着由此分支出去的方言與其他方言的不同。實際情况如果真是這樣單純，我們就應該可以用一條音變規則便把官話的特性標示出來了，但是這不可能。因爲人類的社會活動是複雜多端的，當一個地區發生了獨特的音變而形成方言時，該地區的人民與其他地區的人民仍會有或多或少的接觸，因此該方言的特色可能漸次波及其他方言，其他方言的特色也可能波及這一方言，方言學中的所謂波浪式理論（wave theory）就是根據這個現象提出來的。因此在討論官話與非官話的不同時，就不可能衹用一條規律把它們區分開來，而必然涉及好幾條規律，用這幾條規律的總和而不是其中的某一條作爲官話的特性。换句話説，這幾條規律中的某一兩條可能也影響到了某些非官話方言，但衹有官話才包含這些規律的全部。反過來説，衹有在完全符合了這幾條規律之後，一個方言才可以算作一種官話方言。這些規律是什麽？有多少？我個人覺得應包含前文所列的十個條例中的前六條，約略討論如下。

（甲）全濁上聲字之改讀去聲。

這一現象研究宋詞的人早就注意到了。宋代的“官話”應該是當時汴梁地區的方音，因此我們可以推想這個音變至少早在北宋時期就在中原地區發生了。現代官話上承宋代的中原雅音，自然具有這一特性。

（乙）全獨聲母之化清。

中古漢語裏全濁聲母與全清及次清聲母構成音位對比。這種現象現在僅保持在吴湘兩種方言裏，官話及其他方言則已失去此一對比。我們一般管這種改變叫做全濁化清。其實在某些地區當地人説話很“重”，他們口中的“全清”聲母就音值説還是相當“濁”的,所以我們這兒所説的現象,主要是全濁音與清音已失去了音位的對比性。全濁音化清之前,至少有兩個音變是以全濁音爲條件的,一個是上文討論的全濁上聲字改讀去聲,另一個是多數官話方言中的平聲分爲陰平與陽平。因此可以推論説,全濁化清這個音變在官話歷史上不會早於宋代中葉,甚至可能晚到金代,但在元代的《中原音韻》成書之前就已完成了。在閩粤等非官話方言中,全濁音也都變爲清音了,但在多數情況下是以聲調的陰陽對比代替聲母的清濁對比。這與官話中全濁化清的性質與方式都是不同的,所以不可能是同一個音變的結果。在官話方言中,全濁聲母化清後以聲調爲條件歸入不同的聲類,比如在《中原音韻》及現代北京音的音系中,原爲平聲的全濁字都改讀爲陽平次清,原爲入聲的全濁字都改讀爲陽平全清,而原爲上聲及去聲的全濁字都一律讀爲去聲全清。但在有些方言裏,全濁聲母的化清並未造成平分陰陽,比如在河南林縣的臨淇方言(Wang and 薛 1973)以及另外某些西北官話系的方音裏,就衹有一個平聲。可見平分陰陽不是官話的定性標準,但可作爲官話的分類條件。

(丙)二等韻喉牙音字之腭化。

“家、街、交、間、江”等原二等喉牙音聲母字,本來都没有介音,但在現代官話中都讀齊齒呼了。這在官話方言中是一個極普遍的現象,似乎很少例外,而在非官話方言中,這類字仍無介音,聲母自然也没有腭化。這條官話中特有的音變早在《中原音韻》之前就已發生了,但據有關文獻推論,似乎也不會太早。

(丁)“梗、曾”兩攝陽聲字之合韻。

早期等韻圖把“梗、曾”兩攝各韻分爲兩攝,但稍後的韻圖就把它們合爲一攝,名爲“混等”,這自然是音變造成的,其時間不會早於宋代[①]。其後這一攝的陽聲字合爲一韻,即《中原音韻》的“庚青”韻。這是官話方言中的普遍現象。元代以後,這一個新韻部的字在官話方言中分向兩途發展。在北方官話中,它們的韻腹元音上升,因而合併於“東鍾”韻。在江淮官話中,它們的韻腹元音也

① 我對等韻的看法見於拙著《試論等韻學之原理與内外轉之含義》。該文提出於 1984 年在桂林舉行之音韻學討論會,將刊出於《語言研究》1985 年第 1 期。

上升了，但却合併於“真文”韻，這是爲什麽在皮黄戲裏，原“庚青”韻的開口字改押“人辰”轍的道理。原屬“梗、曾”兩攝的入聲字，也有不同的發展，同樣造成了官話方言的分歧。在所謂“讀書音”裏，它們也合韻了，讀入十三轍的“乜斜”轍，但在所謂“口語音”裏，則改讀收噫，並且由於原不同“等”的關係，分别讀入《中原音韻》的“皆來”韻與“齊微”韻。以上這些現象都是官話方言内部的問題，非官話方言則不然。

（戊）“支思”韻之形成。

“支思”等所謂“零韻母”（zero syllabic）的字，顯然也是官話方言特有的現象，非官話方言似乎没有這種字音。關於這個問題的較詳細的討論，請參看拙著“論支思韻的形成與演進”（薛 1980）。

（己）閉口韻之變爲抵腭。

所謂“閉口韻”就是原以雙脣鼻音/m/爲韻尾的韻部。在等韻音系裏屬“深、咸”兩攝，晚到明代中葉蘭茂的《韻略易通》裏，它們仍自成韻部。但早在《中原音韻》的“正語作詞起例”裏，周德清就特别指出要注意“侵尋”韻與“真文”韻的區分（“真有針”）以及“監咸、廉纖”等韻與“寒山、先天”等韻的區分，表明當時已有一些方言不再保持閉口韻了，即韻尾由/m/變爲/n/了。這一音變後來顯然普及到所有的官話方言。就我所知，除了由連讀形成的少數音節以外（如“他們”讀爲/ta・m/）官話方言都没有閉口韻了。吴語中也没有閉口韻（連抵腭韻都没有），但似乎不是同一個音變形成的，其他如閩粤等非官話方言則多半仍保持着閉口韻。

8.3 上面討論的六個條例，似乎可以概括出官話的特性。爲了認定某一方音是否屬於官話系統，也許不需要這麽多，這祇是我個人的意見。在官話範圍之内，趙元任先生區分出北方官話、南方官話及西南官話三大次方言。近年來多數學者傾向於把他的北方官話分爲北方官話與西北官話兩種，我覺得這是比較合適的。這幾個次方言之間的差别自然也不能純以地域爲準，而必須作語言本身特性的詮解。上文所列的十個條例中的最後四條似乎就可能含有這一功能。比方説，入聲之存在與否便可以把南方官話及西北官話的一部分跟北方官話及西南官話區分開。現代標準漢語以北京音系爲準，這十個條例基本上也就是根據這個觀念設計的,因此一個方言符合這些條例之多寡,也標示着它與北京話之遠近。另外還有一些語音現象,比如:(一)聲母/n/與/l/之分合,(二)韻尾/n/與/ŋ/之分合,(三)"讀音"與"語音"之差别等,都是區分官話方言的具體標準,此處不再詳論。一般人常喜歡强調官話内部的一致性,並以黑龍江人與雲南人可以互相通話來説明這一事實。其實這一説法頗有點似是而非。這兩個邊遠省份都是近代的新開發區,當地人所説的漢語一致性自然比較大。中部古老地區的方言便較多歧異,比方説,許多山西土話我就完全聽不懂①。由此可見,官話内部的歧異性,雖然也許没有吴語或閩話内部那麼複雜,顯然也是相當可觀的。

① 最近聽説有人主張把"晉方言"分出來,獨立於"官話"之外。我覺得似乎頗有道理,因爲像臨淇方言那樣(Wang and Hsueh 1973),既有入聲,平聲又不分陰陽,與别的官話方言相差着實很大。果如此分類,我們就可以説西北官話也是没有保留入聲的次方言了。

第九章　注音符號的本質

9. 研究音韻學的目的

記得許多年前當我還在大學讀書的時候，一位音韻學老教授在講完了如何用國際音標標寫國音之後，回過頭來附帶講一講注音符號。他在盛贊國際音標如何精確之外，不免感慨系之地説："注音符號作爲標音工具實在是没有多少道理可講的，衹不過是一種簡便的實用工具而已。"我重述這個小故事，絶無輕蔑前賢的意思，衹不過想藉此説明一般人常常誤解注音符號的性質，連飽學的老宿也在所難免。當時我們都懾於國際音標的博大精深，自然不敢妄議，但私底下總不免有些疑問：假如説注音符號作爲標音工具果真是没有多少道理可講的，爲什麽應用起來那麽簡便與準確呢？爲什麽連小學生學習與使用起來也是那麽得心應手呢？到美國以後，開始教美國學生説中國話，發現有些美國學生一旦學會了注音符號以後，也運用自如，愛不忍釋。這一切都使我感到注音符號一定是大有道理的，但道理究竟在什麽地方呢？這個問題一直到我進一步研習了音韻學理論以後才得到解答。音韻學理論中比較晚出的音位學(phonemics) 與"區別性特徵"(distinctive features) 等學説，把語音研究的重點從語音的描寫(phonetic description) 轉移到音位的對比(phonemic contrast)上來。這類學説使我們認識到，音韻學研究的真正目標不是個别語音的細微的描寫，更不是用多不勝數的符號逐個地區别它們，而是確認某一特定語言中的音韻系統以及這一系統中各個音位的對比關係。我國傳統音韻學的主旨是區别字音以及標明不同字音間的韻類與聲類等關係，其基本精神與上述晚近的音韻理論可以説是不謀而合的。注音符號是由傳統音韻學演變出來的，也可以説是傳統音韻學現代化的初步，因此我們也就可以肯定它是很有道理的。

9.1 北京音系

爲了進一步而且更具體地説明注音符號的道理，讓我們先從純理論的觀點上看一看北京話的音韻結構,下面就簡介我對北京音的分析[①]。必須先在此聲明的是:我采用的是極嚴格的音位分析法。對於我來説,我們對任何一個語言作最嚴密的音位分析時,衹能有一個最妥當的結論[②],這個結論就是該語言所獨具的音韻結構,而這個音韻結構所表現的也就是説這種語言的"原鄉人"[③]對於語音的感受(native speakers' feeling of, or reaction to, phonetic sounds)。

我們怎麽樣才能知道我們的分析真正地體現了(亦即正確地解釋了)原鄉人的語感呢?就中國話來説,可以由以下幾點得到驗證:

a) 精當地解釋押韻的現象。不論是什麽語言,押韻的基本道理都是一樣的,一般也都承認,凡是可以互押的音節,必然具有相同的主要元音以及相同的後加成分。中國話在這一方面自然也不例外,因此是否符合這一原則,也就成爲分析是否準確的一種檢驗標準。换句話説,凡是北京人覺得可以押韻的字,都必須被分析成具有相同的元音及相同的韻尾(假如有韻尾的話)。

b) 明確地説明雙聲現象。原鄉人覺得是雙聲的音節,正確的分析必須把它們標明爲含有相同的節首輔音,也就是説,必須可以解釋爲什麽原鄉人覺得它們是雙聲。

c) 中國傳統音韻學把字音分析成四個組成部分,即聲母、韻頭、韻腹與韻尾。這個具有近千年歷史的傳統,當然不是憑空揑造的。它也表現出作爲原鄉人的本國學者的語感。正確的分析不能對這個現象視而不見,而應爲它提出合理的解釋。

d) 傳統音韻學有把字音區别爲"開、齊、合、撮"的所謂"四呼"分類法,又有所謂"洪、細"的兩分法,以及廣義的"開、合"兩分法。稍具音韻學知識的人,

---

① 這兒介紹的是我個人對北京話音韻的音位分析,較詳細的討論見於薛 1980。

② 趙元任先生曾有一篇文章討論音位標音法。他認爲:標寫一個語言時,同樣合適可用的標寫法可能不止一個(趙 1934)。我認爲如果衹是爲了書寫方便,趙先生當然是對的,但目的如果在瞭解嚴格的音韻結構,我們就必須承認每一個語言都衹有一個特有的音位結構。

③ 英文中 native speaker 一詞,指的是以某一種語言爲母語的人,因此討論語感時,應以他們的感受爲準。這個詞一直没有適合的中文譯名,譯爲"本地人"或"土著"都不妥帖,也不典雅,我在本文裏姑且借用鍾理和的"原鄉人"作爲該詞的新譯,是否妥帖也不敢説,但衹要讀者明白我給這個詞下的定義就行了。

憑着他們的直感，都可以把個別字音在這些分類法中作正確的歸類，但對於這些分類法的原理，却往往説不清楚，或説得前後不一致。我覺得這些分類法也是原鄉人語感的具體表現。正確的分析也必須能爲這些現象提出嚴格的與一貫的理論解釋。

我們給北京音所作的分析，把以上這幾點完全照顧到了，這可以由下文的簡介中看出來：

9.1.1 傳統音韻學把字音分析成聲母加韻母，又把韻母分析成韻頭（介音）、韻腹（主要元音）與韻尾。聲母、韻頭、與韻尾可以是零，但韻腹是不可少的。我用(C)(M)V(E)這個公式來代表這種音節結構的分析。一個音節最多衹能有這個公式裏所包含的四個組成單位。爲了特殊的考慮，有時候我們也可以用兩個或更多的字母代表一個單位，但須記住它們衹屬於一個音位。

9.1.2 這個公式中的C所代表的是聲母。北京音中可能有的聲母及其相互關係如下表：

p	ph	f	m	
t	th		n	l
c	ch	s		
cr	crh	sr		r
k	kh	h		ø

關於這張聲母表，我們須作兩點說明：

a) 表中似乎没有[tɕ、tɕʻ、ɕ]這三個聲母，其實已經包括在其中了。這一組聲母同時與/c、ch、s/[ʦ、ʦʻ、s]，/cr、crh、sr/[ʈʂ、ʈʂʻ、ʂ]和/k、kh、h/[k、kʻ、h]三組聲母形成互補，因此拼寫時可以與其中任一組合併。如何取决，容待下文詳論。

b)"h、r"這兩個符號個别出現時與跟其他符號共同組成一個單位時，性質有所不同。作爲音位的一部分，"h"代表"送氣"成分（也就是傳統所謂的"次清"），"r"代表"捲舌"成分。

9.1.3 韻母(M)V(E)的實際分配形態，可以從下表看出來。

關於這張韻母表，我們也須作幾點説明：

韻尾 / 韻基 / 韻頭	ø			y		w		n		ŋ	
	ɨ	ə	a	ɨy	ay	ɨw	aw	ɨn	an	ɨŋ	aŋ
-ø-	支 ɨ	各 ə	大 a	黑 ɨy	來 ay	斗 ɨw	告 aw	恩 ɨn	干 an	成 ɨŋ	唐 aŋ
-y-	吉 yɨ	切 yə	牙 ya		(厓) (yay)	尤 yɨw	叫 yaw	因 yɨn	言 yan	丁 yɨŋ	江 yaŋ
-w-	古 wɨ	多 wə	化 wa	灰 wɨy	外 way			文 wɨn	玩 wan	中 wɨŋ	壯 waŋ
-yw-	玉 ywɨ	月 ywə						雲 ywɨn	元 ywɨn	用 ywɨŋ	
十三轍	姑蘇 ¦ 一七	乜梭 斜坡	發花	灰堆	懷來	油求	遥條	人辰	言前	東中	江陽

a) 傳統音韻學所謂的“開、齊、合、撮”四呼,在如此嚴格的分析之後,便有了理論上的着落。這種音節分類法顯然是以韻頭爲唯一依據的,與主要元音無關。廣義的“開”(韻頭不含 w)與“合”(韻頭含 w),以及“洪”(韻頭不含 y)與“細”(韻頭含 y)等觀念,因此也很容易解釋了。這種分類法成功地表現了漢語音韻的特性。

b) 押韻的原理是:韻基(即“V(E)”)相同的字才可以互押,這是大家公認的,但却常被忽略。我們把韻頭、韻腹及韻尾嚴格分開以後,就給北京音中的押韻現象找到了清晰的理論根據。

c)“各、切、多、月”等字在現代北京話裏是押韻的,所以必須解釋爲含有相同的元音。這一解釋也清楚地標示了一項歷史音變,即十三轍的“梭坡”與“乜斜”兩轍在北京話裏已經合併了。“一七”與“姑蘇”兩轍的分立則比較特殊。根據羅常培先生的歸納研究(羅 1950),我們知道“一七”包含/-ɨ、-yɨ、-ywɨ/三個韻母的字,而“姑蘇”衹包含/-wɨ/這一個韻母的字,這與押韻原理相違,但對兒化韻的解釋則甚有幫助(參見 8.2.4 節)。

d) /ɨ,ə,a/高中低三度元音的對比突出地表現在無尾韻中。但在有尾韻中,却衹有兩度對比。爲瞭解釋歷史的演變,更爲瞭解釋兒化韻現象,我們必須把這個兩度對比解釋爲/ɨ/與/a/的對比。

9.1.4 兒化現象一直是一個很令人困惑的問題,如何拼寫更成了難題。

但我個人研究的結果却顯示兒化本身並不十分複雜。造成問題的是:北京地區裏至少有三種不同的兒化方式,一般人未加分辨,因此覺得高深莫測,實在是一種錯覺。在我的韻母分析基礎上,根據許多前人的報導,我用四條音律把三種不同的兒化方式解釋爲三個連續的歷史演變階段。

a) 兒化第一式:

我相信這代表兒化韻初期狀況,最早出現於明代的北京話裏,雖然在北京城區已被後起的形式代替,却已流傳到廣大的官話區裏,所以至今仍爲多數人所使用。這一種兒化形式造成兩種韻母上的改變,其一爲:韻腹爲高元音,而韻尾爲零的韻母,兒化的時候,韻尾變爲"收噫",但韻頭爲/w/的韻母不變。也就是説,兒化的時候,"一七"轍的字變得跟"灰堆"一樣,但"姑蘇"轍的字不變。我用下面的公式表達這一改變:

$$ø \longrightarrow y/(M)\ ɨ \_\_\_\_ r \quad M \neq w \tag{1}$$

另一改變爲:兒化時,韻尾/n/一律變爲/y/,也就是説,"言前"轍的字變同"懷來","人辰"轍的字變同"灰堆"。

$$n \longrightarrow y/\_\_\_\_r \tag{2}$$

b) 兒化第二式:

這種兒化形式顯然是由第一式演變出來的,爲現在北京城裏的"老北京人"所使用。這種形式跟第一式不同之處爲:兒化以後"懷來"轍跟"言前"轍的字與"發花"轍的字也都不再區分了①。如果我們把下面的公式加列在(1)、(2)兩條公式之後,三條音律所造成的結果就是兒化第二式了。

$$ø \longrightarrow y/a\_\_\_\_r \tag{3}$$

c) 兒化第三式:

這是北京"内城話"中新起的發展,趙元任先生説這是"年輕一代"的兒化

① 關於兒化第二式,報導的人較多,可參看:Chao 1968,第 46—52 頁;王輔世 1963;美國人 Lawton Hartman III 分析北京音時(1944),所根據的發音人顯然是説兒化第二式的,但當 Charles F. Hockett 寫他的"Peiping Phonology"(1947)時,他所根據的發音人則顯然是説兒化第一式的。

形式(Chao 1968),但趙先生所説的年輕人現在當然也不再年輕了。這種形式的特點是:兒化以後,“坡斜”轍(“梭坡”與“乜斜”的合併)的字基本上仍與“小人辰兒”(“灰堆”、“人辰”與“一七”兒化後的合稱)的字區分,但在第三聲與第四聲裏,它們的細音字却都混同了,如几兒與姐兒同音,玉兒與月兒同音等。其他各方面與第二式全同。顯然這種形式是由第二式繼續演變出來的。如果我們在前述三條音律之後增加一條,四條連貫的音律就會産生出兒化第三式的現象。

ɨy→ə/y(w)____ r(限於第三聲及第四聲) (4)

上述三種兒化形式是漸次蜕變出來的。最晚出的第三式可能代表演變的趨勢,但就人數説,迄今説第一式的人仍是絶大多數。據近年的報導,由於人口移動的結果,現在連在北京市内説第一式的人也是多數了。

9.2 上文簡介了我對北京話音韻結構的分析。從這個分析的基礎上看注音符號,便可明白它的奥妙了,也就可以明白,爲什麼稍事學習之後,連洋人孺子也能運用自如了。很顯然,注音符號的設計是相當符合原鄉人的語感的。這當然並不足怪,因爲它本來就是由作爲原鄉人的學者根據千百年來的傳統而設計出來的。我們可以用上文提出的驗證條件來檢查一下。

9.2.1 先就押韻説,注音符號是跟原鄉人的語感完全一致的。這種語感就是所謂“韻從流水”,具體表現在明清以來自然形成的“十三轍”裏。上文説過,押韻的條件是:韻基“V(E)”完全相同的字。注音符號在這兒采用了一個取巧的辦法,即衹用一個單一的符號代表這兩個音位。其實連這種取巧的辦法也是語感的表現,在中國話的音節中,這兩個音位的關係特别密切。韻腹元音的實際發音(phonetic realization),總是首先受到韻尾的影響的,其次才是韻頭,再其次才是聲母;在一些方言中,作爲韻基的兩個音位,甚至已經合而爲一(比方説,收鼻音韻尾的韻基,變成了一個單一的鼻化元音);因此我們可以説,用一個單一的符號代表韻基是一個符合語感的巧妙辦法。代表韻基的注音符號與“十三轍”的關係可以由下表看出:

韻基	wɨ	øɨ yɨ ywɨ	ə		a	ɨy	ay	ɨw	aw	ɨn	an	ɨŋ	aŋ
十三轍	姑蘇	一七	梭坡	乜斜	發花	灰堆	懷來	油求	遙條	人辰	言前	東中	江陽
注音符號	ㄨ	(ø) ㄧㄩ	ㄛㄜㄝ		ㄚ	ㄟ	ㄞ	ㄡ	ㄠ	ㄣ	ㄢ	ㄥ	ㄤ

上表清晰地顯示出自“發花”以下九轍,注音符號的標音與原鄉人的押韻感完全一致,這是它比許多拉丁拼音式高明的地方。“梭坡”與“乜斜”兩類字分轍是有歷史根據的。“梭坡”是一個以後元音爲韻基的轍,“乜斜”則是以前元音爲韻基的轍。在北京話裏,這兩個元音已經合併爲中元音/ə/,原來的兩轍自然也就合轍了。因此“閣合蛾莫”與“格核額墨”等字的讀音差别也就不存在了。但一些南方官話仍保持着舊音(參看 Chao 1968,52)。注音符號爲了照顧方音,便用“ㄝ”注“乜斜”類字,用“ㄜ” 注“梭坡”類字,同時又用一個“ㄛ”來注“梭坡”類的合口字,這是很牽强的。實際使用上也做不到,因此現在國語注音中,“ㄝ” 與“ㄜ”(含“ㄛ”)的真正區分已變爲分注細音與洪音了,與原來兩轍之分無關。另一方面,“姑蘇” 與“一七”分轍的現象,我們在前文已有説明,這是一個與通例不合,因此相當令人困惑的問題。對這樣的問題,一般人最容易采用“視而不見”的辦法。注音符號采用了“不標出元音”的辦法,也就把這個問題撇開了。(假如我們説注音符號是以“零”標注作爲韻基的高元音的,那麽它就與我們的分析完全相同了。)

9.2.2 注音符號對聲母的處理也很簡潔明快,衹有對ㄐㄑㄒ這三個聲母的處置稍有商榷的餘地。上文已經提到,這三個聲母同時與ㄍㄎㄏ、ㄓㄔㄕ、ㄗㄘㄙ三組聲母互補,因爲它們衹能配細音韻母而後三組則衹能配洪音韻母。那麽它們究竟應該跟哪一組合併爲一組音位呢?各種拼寫方式都見仁見智,各采不同的選擇。我的看法是,爲瞭解釋北京話中的雙聲現象,我們應該把它們跟ㄍㄎㄏ合拼。國語中有一類擬聲詞(onomatopoeia),諸如ㄆㄧ ㄌㄧ ㄆㄚ ㄌㄚ(劈哩啪啦)、ㄉㄧ ㄌㄧ ㄉㄚ ㄌㄚ(嘀哩嗒啦)等,其中的第一音節與第三音節的聲母總是相同的(即雙聲)。但是在同型的擬聲詞ㄐㄧ ㄌㄧ ㄍ(ㄨ)ㄚ ㄌㄚ(嘰哩呱啦)、ㄑㄧ ㄌㄧ ㄎ(ㄨ)ㄚ ㄌㄚ(喊哩咵啦)和ㄒㄧ ㄌㄧ ㄏ(ㄨ)ㄚ ㄌㄚ(唏哩嘩啦)裏面,第一音節與第三音節的聲母是ㄐㄑㄒ對ㄍㄎㄏ,這表示在原鄉人的語感中,這兩組實爲一類,故能構成雙聲關係①。注音符號在這個問題上又采用了“不表示態度”的辦法。這雖然未能妥善的説明問題。而且浪費了三個符號,但就標音説,倒未造成任何困難。

9.2.3 注音符號嚴格地用ㄧ、ㄨ、ㄩ做韻頭,因此給音節的四呼分類法提供了明顯的解釋與標注,同時也給“洪、細”與“開、合”的兩分法提供了簡潔的説明。這是許多别的拼音法不及它的地方。

9.2.4 大概由於兒化韻的性質相當神秘吧,注音符號的設計者當初未曾碰這塊“熱山芋”,後來雖有錢玄同及張洵如等編制兒化韻及小轍編,這個問題却始終未能得到妥善地解决。我們上文的討論已把這個問題廓清了。根據這個討論,用注音符號來標注兒化韻,倒也簡單明了。這是因爲兒化時某些韻母雖然變了形態,但衹是變成另一個已有的韻母,而没有産生出新韻母。如何標寫,容待下文舉例。

9.3 由以上的討論,我們已經可以看出,注音符號在教學上是有很多優點的。學習一種語言時,最重要的是認知與熟諳那種語言的語感。注音符號是建立在語感的基礎上的,因此用它來教本國的或外國的兒童,都有事半功倍之效。在理論的説明上,注音符號當然有一些弱點,主要由於它的標寫方式有時不能抓住問題的核心與原理,但在實用於教學時,這少數缺點倒不致於造成問題。即以兒化韻爲例,由於説第一式的人數最多,在做普及教育時,也許應該以這一式爲標準。我們已經指出,這一式實在衹是由兩條韻母變化的規律造成的,但在用注音符號表達時,却必須用下列五條公式。

原韻基		兒化後	説　明		例　字
1 ø	⟶	ㄟㄦ	支、思類字	“一七”變同“灰堆”	ㄓㄟㄦ(枝兒)
2 ㄧ	⟶	ㄧㄟㄦ	衣、鷄類字		ㄐㄧㄟㄦ(鷄兒)
3 ㄩ	⟶	ㄩㄟㄦ	居、魚類字		ㄩㄟㄦ(魚兒)

① 在“嘰哩呱啦”及“唏哩嘩啦”等詞裏,第三音節都是合口(ㄍㄨㄚ及ㄏㄨㄚ)。這是受到文字的影響。由於北京話裏ㄍㄚ、ㄎㄚ、ㄏㄚ三個音節有聲無字,故衹能借用相對的合口字充數,但也因而可以把他們讀爲合口了,在實際説話中,這些詞的第三音節讀作開或合都可以。

續表

原韻基		兒化後	説　明	例　字
4 ㄣ	⟶	ㄟㄦ	"人辰"變同"灰堆"	ㄓㄟㄦ(針兒) ㄐ丨ㄟㄦ(今兒) ㄩㄟㄦ(雲兒) ㄍㄨㄟㄦ(滚兒=鬼兒)
5 ㄢ	⟶	ㄞㄦ	"言前"變同"懷來"	ㄍㄞㄦ(干兒) ㄨㄞㄦ(玩兒) ㄐ丨ㄞㄦ(尖兒) ㄩㄞㄦ(院兒)

這主要是由於注音符號衹用一個符號標示韻基,因此没有辦法標示韻基内部的變化,也就無法表達變化的正確性質。在實際教學上,這一理論問題可以暫時不管。上列五條規則非常具體,因此在教學時,不需用太多時間解釋,就可收到相當良好的效果。

第十章　漢語的拼音化問題

10. 爲了適應現代生活的需要,漢語的書寫方式確有改革的必要。改革的方式之一是用拼音文字代替傳統的方塊字。這在理論上是極淺顯的道理,但在感情上及實際應用上都造成了許多糾葛。反對的人大聲疾呼,說什麽如此一改,中國文化將淪喪殆盡,中國語言也將完全消滅。提倡的人也態度偏激,說什麽把一切古籍都付之一炬或“丢在毛厠坑裏”。雙方的態度既然如此,理性的討論自然也就非常困難了。但經過半個多世紀的實踐,現在多數人都已明白漢語拼寫無損於中國語言也無損於中國文化,而且爲了生活的需要也是勢在必行的。另一方面大家也都覺悟到,推行拼音並不就是“徹底廢除漢字”,二者是可以而且應該並存的。

有了這樣的共同認識以後,我們就可以進一步討論拼音化中的一些實際問題了。從馬可波羅時代起(其實還更早些),就有人用拉丁字母書寫漢語中的詞彙。起初當然是片斷的,漫無章法的,但逐漸形成了諸如威妥瑪式、拉丁化等各式各樣的較有系統的寫法,後來還分别頒布了“國語羅馬字”及“漢語拼音方案”。每一個較有系統的寫法都代表創製人對漢語音韻性質的理解與分析,同時也代表他們創製的動機與目的。由於各人的理解不一定全面,分析也不一定妥善,因此,現有的各式拼寫法也就難免有不同程度的缺陷。“拼音方案”當然是比較好的,但也不是至善至美的。我個人對現代漢語的音韻系統特别有興趣,因此形成了一套自己的看法。多年來,很想在這個基礎上提出我對漢語拼寫的一些意見,但由於中國政府已於前幾年明令公布以漢語拼音方案爲標準,形成了“定於一”的局面,就覺得不便“再唱反調”了,因此迄今未曾把我的意見寫出來。1982 年 3、4 月間,中國漢語教授代表團應邀訪美,我受美中關係委員會之托,陪同他們在各地參觀訪問,因此有機會跟張志公先生討論及請教這個問題。張先生告訴我說:“采用拼音方案爲標準是因爲大家覺得現在必須有一個標準,但我們仍然可以繼續討論。”這對我是一大鼓勵,因此我現在就效野人之獻曝,把一己的意見說出來供大家參考。

10.1 普通話的音韻既然是與北京音系一致的，我們現在就可以在前文所描述的基礎上，討論應如何標寫的問題了。標寫時，首先我們應該注意到下列幾個問題。

a) 聲調是漢語音韻的必要組成部分，北京話的成段音位數目很少，聲調在這一方面可以説起了補償的作用，因此拼寫時絶不應省略。現有的許多拼寫法都采用上加標號，但寫時往往省去。另一方面，有的拼寫法，如國語羅馬字，采用拼入式，結果又把音節拼法弄得過於複雜，似乎也不是好辦法。我覺得上加標號並非不可用，如法文中就有 accent acute(v́)與 accent grave(v̀)，漢語拼寫可以采爲第二聲與第四聲之標號。上聲字數目少音量長，可用重寫元音法表示，如陝西作"Shaanxi"之類，輕聲可仍用音節前加點或分節號，不加標號的自然就是第一聲了，情形如下式：

八 bɑ，拔 bɑ́，把 bɑɑ，罷 bɑ̀，吧 .bɑ

b) 過去大家談拼寫時，常常過分注意如何節省符號，因而把拼寫規則弄得複雜了，其實無此必要。漢語詞彙雖然有多音節化(polysyllabic)的趨勢，單音節詞仍居多數，拼寫時多寫一兩個字母不惟不算浪費，反而可以避免誤認，增加美觀，同時更可以借此照顧到音韻結構及拼寫規則的一致性。比如説，四呼之別是漢語音節的特質，對一般説漢語的人自然也是一説就懂，拼寫時應該保持。與其把"知"寫作 zhi，"梯"也寫作 ti，倒不如把後者寫作 tyi。

c) 音節可以按照詞彙的性質分寫或連寫在一起，這是拼寫法的優點之一，是方塊字做不到的，但這個優點也會産生問題，那就是：如何才能使讀者正確地辨認出原來的音節而不致錯認。這與聲母及韻母的寫法有直接關係，最容易造成問題的是零聲母的音節，以及韻尾爲"n"與"ng"的音節。這些問題是可以在聲母與韻母的符號選擇上得到解决的。選擇符號時，如果衹注意漢語音位的對比分辨，問題是不大的，但如果要同時照顧到這些符號在國際音標中或歐洲語文中的習慣用法，那就有些困難了。我個人的看法是：應以前者爲主而同時儘可能兼顧後者。

10.2 聲母符號的選擇是比較容易的，衹要在已通用的拼音方案基礎上稍作改動就行了，可用下表説明。

b	p	f	m	
d	t		n	l
z	c	s		
zh	ch	sh		r
g	k	h		

這張表完全遵循拼音方案,衹删除了"j、q、x"三個符號。就音節分辨的需要説,浪費這三個符號是没有必要的,同時它們也與歐洲語文的習慣用法相差太遠。我們知道[tɕ、tɕ'、ɕ]這三個聲母同時分别與/z/組、/zh/組及/g/組的聲母構成互補;就歷史演變及普通話地區人們的直感説,它們與/g/組最有關係,其次跟/z/組,但對歐洲人的聽覺説,它們似乎跟/zh/組最接近。衹要我們在韻母的介音部位把洪細分清,用上述任何一組同時代表[tɕ、tɕ'、ɕ]都可以達到辨音的目的。如"知、吃、詩"作/zhi、chi、shi/,所以"鷄、妻、西"就可以作/zhyi、chyi、shyi/,但我以爲仍該用/g/組,這既合乎本國人的語感,同時與歐洲語文的習慣寫法相去也不遠,比如 g 在英文的 giant 與 wage 中,就很像我們的[tɕ]。

省下來的"j、q、x"三個符號,可以移作他用。比方説,漢語中的叠詞越來越多,尤其是副詞與形容詞的重叠,用"x"代表重複的音節是一個簡約的辦法,比如"漂漂亮亮"可寫成 pyaoxlyangx,複合動詞的重叠也可以采用這個辦法,如"商量商量"可寫作 shanglyangxx。這辦法既節約又幫助了音節的辨認,但對名詞不適用,因爲它代表的是一種語法現象。

"j"與"q"在特定的情况下也可用來幫助音節的正確辨認,容待下一節討論韻母時再詳細説明。

10.3 韻母的處理要複雜得多。在選擇符號時,我認爲應該注意幾個原則。

a) 四呼的分辨。這樣做既照顧了漢語音韻系統,也便利了語文教學(參看王力 1979)。

b) 押韻現象的反映。凡是互押的字,拼寫時都應標爲含有共同韻基,即"V(E)"相同,這也有助於語文教學。

c) 音節的辨認。如何在不用附加符號的情况下,使讀者能够正確地而且輕易地辨認出連寫的音節,這是拼音化的一項重要課題。

在上述三個原則的基礎上,並且儘可能照應拼音方案的既成事實,我覺得韻母的標寫可如下表。

韻尾 韻頭	ø				y		w		n		ng	
開口 ø	i		o	a	ei	ai	ou	ao	en	an	ing	ang
齊齒 y	yi		yo	ya			you	yao	yen	yan	ying	yang
合口 w	wi		wo	wa	wei	wai			wen	wan	wing	wang
撮口 yw	ywi		ywo						ywen	ywan	ywing	
十三轍	一七	姑蘇	坡斜	發花	灰堆	懷來	油求	遙條	人辰	言前	東中	江陽

表中韻母的寫法,除了少數幾個如/ywi(玉)、yo(夜)、yen(因)、ing(亨 hing)/以外,絶大多數是跟一般的習慣相吻合的。這少數的改動,使我們達到好幾個目的:其一,押韻現象得到明確的標示;其二,連寫時如何區分音節也得到了相當適應的解決;其三,兒化時的連音變化也可以得到簡明的處理;其四,漢語的特性,如洪、細、四呼等,都得到了照應。

以上四點,第一點及第四點是至爲明顯的,二、三兩點也許需要舉例説明,我們可以列出以下幾條音節區分的規則。

a) 字母 u 標示音節的終止。

b) 除了出現在 u 之前以外,字母 o 也表示音節的終止。

c) 除了出現在韻尾 ng 之前以外,字母 i 也代表音節的終止。[因此 Hyian(西安), ziao(自傲), gyinan(濟南) 等就很容易分節了。]

d) 我們把韻尾 n 與 ng 之前的高元音分寫作 e 與 i,自然幫助解决了許多困難的分節問題。[這樣就解决了 Shyen-gan (心肝)與 Shyingan (興安)等的分節問題,其中前者 g 屬後節,後者 g 屬前節,因爲 e 不出現在韻尾 ng 之前,i 不出現在韻尾 n 之前,而 ng 不作聲母。]

e) 由於 n 既可以作聲母又可作韻尾,同樣地, g 既作聲母,又作韻尾 ng 的一部分,這樣便給低元音音節的連寫造成了問題,尤其是發花、言前與江陽三轍字的連寫。[如 yanan (延安? 亞南?)、Gyanan (建安? 嘉南?)、nanyi (難易? 納逆?)、Danyang(丹陽? 大娘?)等等。]要解决這個問題,當然可以使用分節號,但是如果我們想避免使用分節號:(附加符號太多了!),我們也可以采用改换字母的辦法,也很容易,就是用 o 代表江陽轍的主要元音,另加一條附則:“連寫時,收 a 的音節(發花轍的字),改以 q 做韻尾”。我没采用後者,主要是遷就拼音方案,怕這個辦法太“警世駭俗”。其實以 o 爲江陽轍的主要元音,對説英語的人更合適些。(如 long 似“郎”, young 似“楊”, wong 似“王”等。)

10.4 兒化韻如何拼寫,一直是一個令人頭痛的問題。上文的分析(9.4 節)已經證明兒化韻本身並不是太複雜的。如果以我們擬訂的韻母拼寫表爲基礎,兒化韻的拼寫法就更顯得異常簡單了。爲了表示兒化第一式,也衹要兩條簡則就够了,即“增寫兒尾時,(1) 以 i 爲韻腹的音節(一七轍)於 i 前增加 e;(2) 原韻尾 n(“人辰”轍與“言前”轍)變爲 i”。至於第二式或第三式,也衹要在第一式的基礎上增添一條或兩條規則就是了。r 既作聲母又作韻尾可能造成問題,但情況不多。如想避免這個困難,可以仿威妥瑪式用 j 代表“日”母。

10.5 作爲結語,我想再次聲明,上面所説的意見衹代表我個人的看法,聊供有心人參考而已。同時我還想提出一個有關基本觀念的看法。在設計拼寫方案時,我們自然必須注意到它的系統化與一致性,但是如果拼寫的漢語將來能成爲通用的文字,顯然不可能也不應該把所有的詞語都按這個拼法寫出。英文中凡是遇到外國的人名或地名時,都一律照抄,衹在必要時用括號在後面加注讀法。寫法不能改動,因爲那會造成文書檔案的雜亂與視覺上的誤認。中國的文字如果改爲拼寫,顯然也必須走同樣的道路,也就是説,必須在拼音方案的系統化與一致性的基礎上,允許例外。這可以分兩方面説。其一是外語人名地名在漢語中的拼寫。不惟 Moscow、Paris、Marx 等等要照寫,連本國少數民族的人名地名如 Urumqi, Lhasa 等也得照寫。其次是漢語人名地名在外語中的書寫。由於一向没有標準拼寫法,所以有少數本國的人名與地名在外文中已有了習慣的寫法,成爲外語的一部分,諸如 China、Peking、Canton、Confucius、Chou Enlai 等,皆已舉世聞名,假如衹爲了系統化而改寫它們,並堅持在外語文字中使用,就得不償失了。在這類情況下,不妨承認這些名詞有兩個名字或兩種寫法,一種用在外語裏,一種用在本國的拼寫文字中。

參考文獻

中文部分

陳治文 《關於北京話裏兒化的來源》,《中國語文》1965 年 5 月,第 369—370,412 頁。

程祥徽 《關於普通話音位》,《中國語文》1957 年 6 月,第 25—26 頁。

丁邦新 《與〈中原音韻〉相關的幾種方言現象》,《史語所集刊》第五十二本第四分(1981),第 619—650 頁。

董同龢 《漢語音韻學》,學生書局,1968 年。

傅懋勣 《北京話的音位和拼音字母》,《中國語文》1956 年 5 月。

胡雙寶 《談京劇現代戲的字音和韻轍》,《中國語文》1965 年 2 月,第 139—143 頁。

李方桂 《上古音研究》,《清華學報》新九卷第一第二期合刊(1971),第 1—16 頁。

李　榮 《漢語方言調查手册》,科學出版社,1963 年。

李新魁 《〈中原音韻〉音系研究》,中州書畫社,1983 年。

劉澤先 《北京話裏究竟有多少音節》,《中國語文》1957 年 2 月,1—8, 3 月份,第 17—23 頁。

龍果夫、龍果娃 《漢語普通話的音節結構》(高祖舜譯),《中國語文》1958 年 11 月,第 513—521 頁。

羅常培 《北京俗曲百種摘韻》,來薰閣重校本,1950 年。

《京劇中的幾個音韻問題》,《羅常培語言學論文集》,中華書局,1963 年。

羅季光 《北京話 i 和 ɿ(ʅ)的音位問題》,《中國語文》1961 年 1 月,第 33—34,40頁。

尚　静 《〈關於北京話裏兒化的來源〉小議》,《中國語文》1966 年 1 月,第 67—68 頁。

邵榮芬 《〈中原雅音〉研究》,齊魯書社,1981 年。

沈乘麐 《韻學驪珠》(一稱《曲韻驪珠》,收入汪經昌編《曲韻五書》),廣文書局影印,1965 年。

史存直 《北京話音位問題商榷》,《中國語文》1957 年 2 月,第 9—12 頁。

宋元嘉 《評哈特門 (Hartman) 和霍凱特(Hockett)對北京語音的分析》,《中國語文》1965 年 3 月,第 167—178 頁。

唐　虞 《兒(er)音的演變》,《史語所集刊》第二本第四分(1932),第 457—467 頁。

陶蔭培、尹潤鄉 《略談兒化》,《語文學習》1957 年 10 月,第 31—32 頁。

王輔世 《北京話韻母的幾個問題》,《中國語文》1963 年 2 月,第 115—124 頁。

王　力 《現代漢語語音分析中的幾個問題》,《中國語文》1979 年 4 月,第 281—286 頁。

徐世榮 《北京語音音位簡述》,《語文學習》1957 年 8 月,第 22—24 頁。

《兒化韻的基本變化規律》,《語文學習》1960 年第 1 期,第 18 頁。

薛鳳生 《論入聲字之演化規律》,《屈萬里先生七秩榮慶論文集》,臺北聯經出版社,1978 年。

《論支思韻的形成與演進》,《中國書目季刊》第十四卷第三期(1980),第 53—75 頁。

《論音變與音位結構的關係》,《語言研究》1982 年第 2 期,第 11—17 頁。

《試論等韻學之原理與内外轉之含義》,《語言研究》,1985 年第 1 期,第 38—56 頁。

楊耐思 《周德清的〈中原音韻〉》,《中國語文》1957 年 11 月號。

尹仲賢 《漢語的聲調在音位系統中的地位》,《中國語文》1957 年 6 月,第 27—28,30 頁。

袁家驊 《漢語方言概要》,語文出版社。

詹伯慧 《現代漢語方言》,湖北人民出版社,1981 年。

《談談漢語方言的調查研究》,日本亞非語言文化研究所 CAAAL19 (1982),第 51—73 頁。

張　静 《談北京話的音位》,《中國語文》1957 年 2 月,第 13—15 頁。

張洵如 《北平音系十三轍》(魏建功校),中國大辭典編纂處,1937 年。

《國語裏捲舌韻之功用》,《國文月刊》54 (1947),第 12—16,30 頁。

《北平音系小轍編》,開明書店,1972 年。

趙蔭棠 《等韻源流》,商務印書館,1957 年。

趙元任 《反切語八種》,《中央研究院歷史語言研究所集刊》第二本第三分(1931),第 312—354 頁。

英文部分

Chao, Yuen Ren: "The Non-uniqueness of Phonemic Solution of Phonetic Systems", *Bulletin of the Institute of History ond Philology* (BIHP), Vol.4, No.4 (1 934),363 - 398.

——: *A Grammar of Spoken Chinese*, Berkeley, California,1968.

Chen, Chung-yu: "Neutral Tone in Mandarin: Phonotactic Description and issue of the Norm". *Journal of Chinese Linguistics* (JCL),Vol.12,No.2 (1984).

Cheng, Chin-chuan: *A Synchronic Phonology of Mandarin Chinese*, The Hague, 1973.

Cheng, Robert L.: " Mandarin Phonological Structure ", *Journal of Linguistics*, Vol.2. No. 2 (1966),135 - 158.

Hartman, Lawton M. III: "The Segmental Phonemes of the Peiping Dialect", *Language* 20 (1944),28 - 42.

Hashimoto, Mantaro J.: "Notes on Mandarin Phonology", R. Jakobson and S. Kawamoto (ed): *Studies in General and Oriental Linguistics*, Tokyo, 1970.

Hockett, Charles F.: "Peiping Phonology", *Journal of American Oriental Society* (JAOS)67

(1947)253 - 267.: "Peiping Morphophonemics", *Language* 26(1950), 63 - 85.

Hsueh, F. S.: "The P'ingtu Dialect as a Variant of Mandarin", *Tsinghua Journal of Chinese Studies*, n.s.10 (1973),74 - 89.

____: *Phonology of Old Mandarin*, The Hague, 1975.

____：“The Phonemic Structure of Pekingese Finalsand Their R-Suffixation”, *BIHP*, Vol. 51, Part 3 (1980), 491 - 514.

____：“Xu Xiao's RevisedRhyme-Tables：a BoldRenovation”, Chu, Coblin, and Tsao (ed)：*Papers from the 14th International Conference on Sino-Tibetan Languages and Lin guistics*, Taipei, 1983, 153 - 170.

R. Jakobson, C. Fant, and M. Halle：*Preliminaries to Speech Analysis*, The MIT Press, Boston, 1951.

Karlgren, Bernhard：*Compendium of Phonetics in Ancient and Archaic Chinese*, Goteborg, 1963.

Li, Fang-kuei：“The Zero Initial and the Zero Syllabic”, *Language* 42 (1966), 300 - 302.

Li, Paul Jen-Kuei：“A Secret Language in Taiwanese”, *JCL*, Vol, 13, No. 1 (1985), 91 - 121.

Light, Timothy：*The Chinese Syllabic Final: Phonological Relativity and Constituent Analysis*, Ithaca, New York, 1976.

Lu, Zhiji：“Notes on the Structure of Finals and the Vowel System of Mandarin Chinese”, *Journal of the Chinese Language Teachers Association*, Vol. XX, No. 2 (May, 1985).

Martin, Samuel E.：“Problems of Hierarchy and Indeterminacy in Mandarin Phonology”, *BIHP* 29 (1957), 209 - 229.

Stimson, Hugh M.：*The Jongruan In Yunn*, New Haven, Conn., 1966.

____：“Review on F. S. Hsueh's Phonology of Old Mandarin”, *Language*, Vol. 53, No. 4 (1977), 940 - 944.

____：“Old Mandarin Dialects, Old Pekingese, and the Rhymes of the Zhongyuan Yinyun”, Cheng, Li, and Tang (ed)：*Proceedings of Symposium, on Chinese Linguistics*, 1977 Linguistic Institute of the Linguistic Society of America, Taipei, 1978, 223 - 231.

Ting, Pang-hsin：“Review on F. S. Hsueh's Phonology of Old Mandarin”, *Journal of American Oriental Society*, Vol. 100, No. 1 (1980), 94.

Todo, Akiyasu: "The Phonemes of the Peiping Dialect", *Project on Linguistic Analysis* 4 (1963), 1-18.

Walton, A. Ronald: *Tone*, *Segment*, and *Syllable in Chinese: A Polydimensional Approach to Surface Phonetic Structure*, Ithaca, New York, 1983.

Wang, John C. and Hsueh, F. S.: "The Lin-ch'i Dialect and its Relation to Mandarin". *JAOS* 93.2 (1973), 136-145.

The Phonemic Structure of Pekingese Finals and Their R-suffixation**

0. ABSTRACT

This article is aimed at a special audience, namely, the scholars who are already very familiar with the details of Pekingese phonetics but are nevertheless still keenly interested in its theoretical interpretation. The purpose of this study is to present, through examining some previous studies on Pekingese phonology, a new analytical interpretation of the phonemic structure of the Pekingese syllable finals. In this process, it tries to demonstrate that classical studies on this subject, such as Hartman 1944 and Hockett 1947, are either descriptively inadequate or theoretically unsound, or both. The basic premise of this study is its author's conviction that the truly phonemic study of a language must always be an accurate reflexion of, or a logical explanation for, the feeling of its native speakers, in particular, their habit of rhyming. It concludes that Pekingese has indeed three vowel phonemes, but proposes a new theory to account for their distribution. On this basis, a very simple and logical specification of the morphophonemic process of r-suffixation in Pekingese phonology is presented.

1. INTRODUCTION

The sound system of Modern Pekingese (MP) and its immediate earlier

---

** 中文題爲《北京話韻母的音位結構與兒化》,原刊《史語所集刊》第 51 本 3 分,1980 年。

forms had been the subject of numerous and intensive studies by Chinese scholars long before Western linguistic technology was introduced into China. Since Chinese scholars in the past used Chinese graphs instead of phonetic symbols as the means of representation, their works represent, in effect, an effort to specify the contrasts, and the relationship thereof, in the sound system of their language. They did this by classifying the words (or graphs) in their language into various classes and subclasses as determined by the different ways these words were read, or by using some ingeniously designed charts (or tables) to show the relationships among these words in their reading. In other words, although the Chinese did not know, and therefore, never used the term "phoneme", they were actually doing phonemic study on their own language long before this concept was understood in the West. The introduction of Western linguistics in its prephonemic form into China is, I would say, a mixed blessing. On the one hand, it gave the Chinese a set of phonetic signs as a simple and effective tool, but, on the other hand, it so impressed and awed some Chinese scholars that it made them forget the beauty of their own tradition. With the rising of phonemic theory, the study of the Chinese language in the West also entered its phonemic phase. First we saw Hartman's "The Segmental Phonemes" (1944). Though still containing a number of errors and misconceptions, Hartman's article marks, in my opinion, a remarkable beginning in the theoretical interpretation of the MP sound system. It carries a potential, though its author did not seem to be aware of it, to hook up modern phonological theory with traditional Chinese phonological study and, thereby, to make us understand and appreciate the latter better. The hook-up, however, did not take place. Instead, we saw a few years later Hockett's "Peiping Phonology" (1947) which, though winning wide attention after its publication, is actually not even descriptively adequate (see 7.1). Many more studies on MP have appeared since then, not only in the West, but also in Russia and Japan. In Mainland China, under the influence of Western phonemic theory, the social and functional nature of speech sounds was reaffirmed, and a lively debate about the phonemes in Pekingese was carried on from the late 50's to the early 60's, until it was presumably interrupted by the "Great Cultural Revolution", before a general consensus could be reached (see Bibliography). When generative phonology became the fashion, studies on Pekingese phonology cast in this new mode also appeared, and we hear complaints that for too long the study of Chinese phonology has stayed on the phoneme level.

It might seem rather strange that, after so many people have worked on this subject for so long, I should want to do it again. However, with due respect to all those who have worked on this subject, and acknowledging that, in different degrees, they have all contributed something to the understanding of this subject, I must say that I still have a few ideas to add to this discussion.

1.1. Since it will take too much time and space to comment on all the previous writings on this subject, I shall, in this paper, reluctantly restrict myself to merely expressing my own ideas, except in those cases when I have to criticize somebody to make a point. The differences between my interpretation of the MP sound system and all the other interpretations perhaps come from a conceptual difference between myself and the others. To me, phonemic study represents primarily an effort *to understand*, *as well as to explain*, *the feeling of the native speakers*. Other considerations, such as phonetic similarity and economy in transcription, are only secondary by principle. The ultimate test of a successful analysis of a sound system will be whether it can best explain the spontaneous reactions of the native speakers to speech sounds, for example, rhyming. Therefore, we shall *not* accept alternative (or non-unique, see Chao 1934) solutions, because, by applying vigorously the criterion we have set for ourselves, one of the "alternatives" eventually will have to be judged as the right one for being explanatorily better than the others. In order to achieve this goal, the style or format in which an analysis is presented will have no substantial bearing. I believe there is no fundamental difference between a truly accurate analysis expressed in terms of "phonemes" and an equally accurate analysis expressed in terms of "distinctive features". It is true that an analysis in terms of phonemes will have to be supplemented by remarks about the phonetic realization of these phonemes and this can perhaps be better done in generative terms, but it is also true that generative phonology can do this better if it can start with a set of accurately induced phonemes, because in this sense a "phoneme" is nothing but a "cover symbol" for "a bundle of distinctive features".

1.2. Since there have been so many studies on this subject, it might seem that some of the ideas the present paper presents have been proposed by one or another of the previous studies. However, it should be noted that the present paper is the first one to incorporate these many piecemeal proposals into an intergrated body. More importantly, many of these previous proposals have been made either without sufficient justification or on grounds that are theoretically questionable. They are now reintroduced either with completely different justification or with additional new evidence in their support.

2. SYLLABLE PATTERNS IN CHINESE

Phonological study in China has always been focused on the analysis of "monosyllables". This is, of course, dictated by that fact that Chinese is by and large a monosyllabic language (see Chao 1968: 139). It is true that a few disyllabic or polysyllabic morphemes did exist in the language even in the very ancient time and the number of such morphemes has been steadily on the increase ever since, but even in Modern Chinese their number is still very limited in the total vocabulary. Moreover, the overwhelming tendency among the native speakers of Chinese to identify any single syllable with a meaning reflects their subconscious feeling about their language in this respect. Thus, we can see that the traditional practice is really a very pragmatic and ingenious approach. Practically, all modern scholars have adopted this traditional approach as a general frame in their study of the Chinese language, though some, especially those in the West, often added a somewhat apologetic note to the effect that they did so only for convenience or that there were other ways which might be equally effective. However, we believe that the traditional way is the most effective way predetermined by the nature of the language①.

2.1. As we all know, this tradition specifies that a syllable in Chinese consists of three parts, *shēng* 聲(or 聲母, the syllable initial), *yùn* 韻(or 韻母, the syllable final), and *tiào* 調(or 聲調, the tone of the syllable). Of these, the final has been further analyzed into three subparts, *yùn-t'óu* 韻頭(or 介音, the medial), *yùn-fù* 韻腹(or 主要元音, the nucleus), and *yùn-wěi* 韻尾(or 收聲, the ending). Furthermore, the practice of rhyming requires (and this has been widely acknowledged) that words can rhyme only when the syllables that represent them share the same vowel and the same ending. For many years, I have been using the following formula as a way to sum up this traditional description. This formula can, of course, be easily justified synchronically in MP, but the fact that it is based on a tradition of more than ten centuries implies that it has the most far-reaching potential for the study of the Chinese language. Indeed, I believe historical studies of the Chinese language and comparative studies of Chinese dialects will be more successful, when they are executed on this basis.

＃(C)(M)V(E)＃

---

① It may be noted here that this traditional Chinese approach has been applied with apparent success to some other languages. See, for example, Hu Tan's "The Tonal System of Modern Tibetan (Lhasa Dialect)" and Wang Fushi's "The Comparison of Initials and Finals of Miao Dialects", two papers presented at the 12th International Conference on Sino-Tibetan Languages and Linguistics, October, 1979, Paris.

The four letters in the formula represent respectively the initial consonant, the medial, the nuclear vowel, and the ending. Of these, only V appears without parentheses. This is our way to state that *a syllable by definition must have a vowel*. Other parts are important for their syllable-differentiating function, but "V", besides differentiating syllables on its own, represents the peak of a syllable, the part that is responsible for a syllable to be a syllable. This definition of "syllable" implies immediately that we reject such notions as "vowel-less syllables" and "syllabic consonants". As mentioned above, the generally accepted definition for rhyming is that syllables can rhyme when and only when they share the same vowel and the same ending, namely, "V (E)" in our formula which I have labeled "rhyme base" (*yùn-chī* 韻基). Quite obviously, adherence to this definition of rhyming is possible only when we adopt the definition for "syllable" mentioned above. This does not mean that we would admit no exception to this definition of rhyming, but it means that exception or exceptions must be very marginal and must be supported by highly convincing non-phonological explanations.

2.2 There has been controversy about the nature of the tone. The following opinions have been expressed: (1) it goes with the whole syllable; (2) it starts with the first voiced element in the syllable; (3) it covers the whole final; and (4) it goes with the vowel. A direct corollary of our definition of "syllable" is that the tone goes with the "V". Just as a vowel phoneme can be phonetically realized in different ways as a result of the influence of its neighbouring elements, a toneme can also be extended phonetically beyond a vowel to cover other compatible-elements in the syllable, and this fact should not be allowed to confuse its phonemic status as a suprasegmental element of the vowel. We have to recognize five tones in Pekingese, the four regular tones in stressed syllables and the neutral tone in unstressed syllables. The present study will concentrate on the three segmental units in the final with tone mentioned only when it is relevant to the discussion of these segmental elements.

2.3 In order to keep this paper within a reasonable length, but, more importantly, for the sake of directing undivided attention to the main issues in the finals, we are not going to discuss the initial consonants here. Instead, we shall let our view be represented by the following chart, together with a few clarifying remarks.

Manner / Point	Unasp. Stops	Asp. Stops	Fr.	Nas.	Liq.
Labials	p	ph	f	m	
Dentals	t	th		n	l
Alveolars	c	ch	s		
Retroflexes	cr	crh	sr		r
Velars	k	kh	h		(ø)

a) Each occupied box in the chart stands for one phonemic unit of that description, i.e., one "phoneme", whether represented by a single letter or a cluster.

b) When "h" and "r" appear together with another letter, they each represent a "feature", rather than a separate "phoneme". For example, the phonemic unit /ph/ means "the bundle of features represented by the cover symbol /p/ plus aspiration". Similarly, /crh/ means "/c/ plus retroflexion and aspiration/."

c) We interpret [tɕ, tɕʻ, ɕ] as allophones of /k, kh, h/ respectively.

3. MEDIALS

For several centuries, syllables in Chinese have been classified into four types, namely, *k'āi-k'ǒu* (開口), *ch'í-ch'ǐh* (齊齒), *hó-k'ǒu* (合口), and *ts'ō-k'ǒu* (撮口). Due to the technique they employed, Chinese scholars in the past could only imply that this classification was based on the medial of a syllable. Modern studies on Chinese have generally confirmed this, though, in some limited but crucial cases, many scholars have been confused by what they conceived to be the "real phonetic value". Consequently, their conclusions have somewhat clouded the true meaning of this traditional classification by misleading people to believe that this may be a matter of the main vowel, too(e.g., Tung 1968: 21). We would like to reiterate here that the classification is based *purely and solely on the syllable medial* and nothing more①. Thus, to us, *k'āi-k'ǒu* means simply zero medial, *ch'í-ch'ǐh* means [i] as medial, *hó-k'ǒu* means [u] as medial, and *ts'ō-k'ǒu* means [ü] as medial.

3.1. Some scholars say the medials are "more vowel-like", and thus insist that they be represented by normal vowel symbols. Our definition for syllable, however, forces us to say that phonemically they must be semi-vowels, because no matter how vowel-like they may be phonetically, they cannot be more vowel-like than the vowel (V). To mark clearly their subordinate status, we shall use /y/ for *ch'í-ch'ǐh* and /w/ for *hó-k'ǒu*. Since *ts'ō-k'ǒu* shares a common characteristic with each of them, we shall, following Hartman, represent it by the compound /yw/. For descriptive convenience, we shall always write "y" before "w", but unlike Hartman, we do not recognize them as separate phonemes. They are rather "features" representing jointly a single phoneme. As features, "y" stands for palatalization, and "w" stands for labialization. In this way, the four-way classification can be defined in a clearcut manner as follows:

---

① Though Wang Li also defines this classification improperly (Wang 1979: 284 - 285), he shows sound understanding of this issue, when he, in an effort to correct some common misidentifications caused by the Pinyin transcription, refers repeatedly to a certain vague "phonological system" ("音韻學", "這個系統"). The fact is every Chinese syllable bears a special property which qualifies it as a member of one of the four classes, regardless of how it might have been transcribed. A strict phonological interpretation must reveal this fact overtly and properly.

開口	K'āi-k'ǒu	-ø-	$\begin{pmatrix}-\ \text{pal}\\-\ \text{lab}\end{pmatrix}$
齊齒	Ch'í-ch'ǐh	-y-	$\begin{pmatrix}+\ \text{pal}\\-\ \text{lab}\end{pmatrix}$
合口	Hó-k'ǒu	-w-	$\begin{pmatrix}-\ \text{pal}\\+\ \text{lab}\end{pmatrix}$
撮口	Ts'ō-k'ǒu	-yw-	$\begin{pmatrix}+\ \text{pal}\\+\ \text{lab}\end{pmatrix}$

3.2. This definition also explains two sets of contrastive terms in traditional Chinese phonology, namely, *k'āi* vs. *hó* (both in a broader sense) and *húng* (洪) vs. *hsì* (細). We can see now that the former represents a contrast between the absence and the presence of labialization, while the latter represents a contrast between the absence and the presence of palatalization. A further but unnecessary complication about the medials comes from the fact that quite a few scholars interpret the "r" in the retroflex initials as a medial (e. g. Hartman 1944 and Hockett 1947). Their purpose for doing so is to justify their grouping of [tɕ, tɕ', ɕ] [ʦ, ʦ', s] together as one series of initial phonemes. Since we interpret [tɕ, tɕ', ɕ] differently, treating "r" as a medial becomes purposeless, but more importantly, it is undesirable to establish a medial which can occur only after one single series of initial phonemes.

4. ENDINGS

Syllable endings, when compared with syllable medials, seem to be more closely tied to the vowels that occur before them, so much so that the National Phonetic Letters (注音符號) always represents the two elements, "V(E)" in our formula, with a single symbol. Moreover, it has been reported that in a number of Mandarin dialects, diphthongs representing "VE" such as [ai] and [au] (or [ao]) have become single vowels, with [i] or

[u] merging into the preceding vowel, and nasals as ending have been replaced by nasalization superimposed on the vowel (Dragunov and Dragunova, 1955: 516). It may be asked, then, why we have to recognize the existence of "E". The answer is that in MP it is still recognizable and its recognition greatly clarifies the vowel system. Moreover, classification of syllables into different types according to syllable ending is also a time-honored practice in the Chinese tradition, with a number of technical terms to be defined in this way.

4.1. We recognize altogether five endings: [-i, -u, -n, -ŋ, -r]. Of these, "r" is a peculiar one. Except in the syllable representing such words as 兒耳二, its occurrence as a syllable ending is the result of a morphophonemic process. So we shall discuss this peculiar ending later (see Section 6). It has been suggested that [i] and [u] as endings are even more vowel-like, but, again, our definition of "syllable" allows them only a subordinate role. To mark this fact, we shall also represent them with /y/ and /w/ respectively. The traditional classification of syllables on this basis can thus be defined as follows[①]:

Chíh-yīn	(直音)	-Vø
Shōu-yi	(收噫)	-Vy
Shōu-wū	(收嗚)	-Vw
Tĭ-ò	(抵腭)	-Vn
Ch'uān-pí	(穿鼻)	-Vŋ

4.2. Both medial and ending can exert. strong influence on the phonetic realization of the vowel phoneme that occurs between them, but it has been observed that primary assimilating force on the vowel always comes from the

① Terms for syllables classified according to the ending are adopted mainly from Shen Ch'eng-lin's (沈乘麐) Yùn-hsuéh Lí-chū (韻學驪珠). Other sources may vary somewhat. Shen uses simply Pí-yīn(鼻音) for Ch'uān-pí, and includes other terms like Măn- k'ǒu (滿口), Ts'ō-k'ǒu(撮口)(in addition to Chíh-yīn) and Pì-k'ǒu(閉口)(for rhymes with /m/ as ending).

ending. That is why the vowel and its ending in a syllable are almost inseparable.

5. THE VOWEL

One of the main concerns in traditional Chinese phonology is rhyming which, as mentioned before, has been defined as a matter of the nuclear vowel and the ending of a syllable. This means that all words represented by syllables with identical "V(E)" can and must rhyme as a group. If we take this definition of rhyming seriously, as I think we should, we will be forced to say that any analysis of the MP sound system which cannot explain its general practice of rhyming (hence, the native speakers' feeling in this regard) in terms of "V(E)" is unsatisfactory. By the same token, the success of the reconstruction of any historical period should be measured with the same yardstick. As we said before, this does not mean that no exception from the definition will be permitted. But exception, if any, must be very few, and each of them must be given an explanation. However, in practically all previous studies on MP, rhyming as a factor has hardly been considered, and in most historical reconstructions which are based on old rhyme dictionaries, its logical definition has often been ignored.

5.1. By following this definition of rhyming, I have come to the conclusion that we must recognize at least three and no more than three vowel phonemes in MP. That MP can be phonenucized as having only three vowels is hardly anything new by now. It was first proposed by Hartman in 1944. To establish a low vowel phoneme /a/ and a mid vowel phoneme /ə/ (Hartman's /e/) is relatively easy, but to establish a single high vowel phoneme /ɨ/(Hartman's /i/) almost contradicts "common sense". It can be done only by recognizing that vowels like [i, u, ü] in this language represent the phonemic compounds /yɨ, wɨ, ywɨ/ respectively. Even today, there are many people who can see no justification for further analyzing these "single vowels" into phonemic compounds (e. g. Cheng 1973: 12 – 13). We say this is absolutely necessary for two reasons: (1) to understand that the classification of syllables into *K'āi-k'ǒu*, *Ch'í-ch'ǐh*, *hó-k'ǒu*, *ts'ō-k'ǒu* and the two binary contrasts *k'āi* vs. *hó* and *húng* vs. *hsì* are practices based *exclusively* on medial (see Section 3); (2) to explain the native speakers' feeling in rhyming words like 衣([i] =/yɨ/), 屍([ʂ̩] =/srɨ/), 居([tɕü] = /kywɨ/) together. (In the "Thirteen Tracks" 十三轍 tradition, they all belong to the *yīch'ī*—七 Rhyme. Cf. Lo Ch'ang-p'ei 1950: 35. In our interpretation, *yīch'ī* has /-ɨø/ as its rhyme base.) However, Hartman did not seem to be aware of these justifications. For he did not *mention* the first, and he clearly violated the principle of rhyming in his conclusion (see 5.2). This deviation and a few others from the Chinese tradition somewhat spoiled his otherwise very remarkable paper. It would seem that Hartman's paper could be greatly improved by making it conform more to the Chinese tradition. Instead, it was followed by Hockett's "Peiping Phonology" (1947) which, in trying to further simplify the already very simple MP vowel system, moved even farther away from the Chinese tradition. In Russia, Dragunov and Dragunova published their research on MP in 1955. By their own confession, they delibrately followed the Chinese way, instead of using the European model as studies on MP before theirs did. We do not know, whether they were aware of (and hence, influenced by) Hartman's and Hockett's works or not, but their conclusion is very similar to the American's, perhaps more so to Hockett's. Instead of saying there are three vowel phonemes in MP, they say there are three "types" of syllable finals: the zero type, the "ə" type, and the "a" type. In 1958, Tōdō Akiyasu, the Japanese expert on the Chinese language, also published his research on the MP sound system. Needless to say, he was more familiar with the Chinese tradition than the Russians. His conclusion is also that there are three vowel phonemes in MP, /ɪ, ə, a/.

5.2. One peculiar thing in the MP sound system is that only syllables without ending show a three-way contrast in vowel height (e. g. ,宜 /yɨø/, 爺 /yəø/,牙 /yaø/, while syllables with ending show a two-way contrast in vowel height (e. g. ,今[tɕin] vs. 奸[tɕiɛn]). Since words like 元 /ywan/,江 /kyaŋ/, 怪 /kway/,桃 /thaw/, etc. have obviously the low vowel /a/, their counterparts 雲[yün],京[tɕiŋ],貴[kuêi],頭[t'ou] can be interpreted as having either the high vowel /ɨ/ or the mid vowel /ə/. Either choice, if consistent, would be not only descriptively adequate, but also good enough to explain the native speakers' habit in rhyming. Hartman, however, made a mixed choice, for the sake of "a clear-cut distinction of vowel quality" (Hartman 1944: 41). He argued that since words like 京[tɕiŋ],民[min] etc. have clearly a high vowel, the high vowel phoneme /ɨ/ should be assigned to them, but words like 更[kəŋ],門[mən], 九[tɕiə̯u] etc., must have the mid vowel phoneme /ə/, because they are phonetically lower. Both Tōdō and Dragunov assigned the mid vowel to all these words. They did not explain why, but presumably what were clearly high to Hartman's ears were mid to theirs. As far as I know, Stimson seems to be the first and only one who once chose to use the high vowel phoneme /ɨ/ consistently though he did not specify his reason for doing so (Stimson 1966: 15-16). I once criticized him for this choice on the structural ground (Hsueh 1973: 80, 1975: 135). To me, the generalization that "In MP only [V, -high] can occur before syllable ending" was simple, logical, and, therefore, better. My recent research has, however, convinced me that two other considerations should be given priority before the consideration for structure. These considerations are:

a) The choice of the high vowel /ɨ/ will better explain (and highly faciliatate our description of) the morphophonemic process for r suffixation. This will become self-evident when we deal with that process in Section 6.3.

b) This choice can better reflect the real nature of the sound system in terms of historical developments. The vowel system of the Chinese language from the T'ang dynasty to the beginning of the Ch'ing dynasty had four vowels distributed in the following manner (Hsueh 1975 and 1976):

	front	central	back
high		ɨ	
low	e	a	ɔ

Due to the gradual but steady erosion of the contrast among the low vowels, there eventually appeared the three-vowel system in MP. The situation before the last erosion was clearly registered in the famous "Thirteen Tracks". This product of the early Ch'ing dynasty showed a two-way contrast in vowel height in all syllables with ending, but included the three rhymes *miēh-hsiéh* (乜斜), *fāh-huā* (發花), and *sō-p'ō* (梭坡) which can only be reconstructed as /-eø/, /-aø/ and /-ɔø/ respectively. The last step of the erosion took place sometime before the middle of the Ch'ing dynasty, when *miēh-hsiéh* and *sō-p'ō* coalesced in sharing the mid vowel /ə/ ({ɔ, e} → ə/__ ♯), and the transition from the four-vowel system to the three-vowel system was finally completed. Thus, we can see the two-way contrast between the high vowel and the low vowel in syllables with ending has been there in the language for a long time and has not been affected by the merging of the *miēh-hsiéh* and the *sō-p'ō* rhymes.

5.3. The following chart of syllable finals is given here as a summing up of our discussion on the total final system. Labels for rhymes from the "Thirteen Tracks" are attached at the bottom for easy reference.

M \ E / V	ø			y		w		n		ŋ	
	ɨ	ə	a	ɨ	a	ɨ	a	ɨ	a	ɨ	a
ø	支	歌	大	黑	來	侯	豪	跟	山	生	唐
y	衣	切	加		厓	油	遥	因	言	京	江

續表

M \ V \ E	ø				y		w		n		ŋ	
	ɨ		ə	a	ɨ	a	ɨ	a	ɨ	a	ɨ	a
w	姑		説	花	灰	懷			文	晚	東	王
yw		居	嶽						君	全		
十三轍	姑蘇	一七	梭乜坡斜	發花	灰堆	懷來	油求	遙條	人辰	言前	東中	江陽

The reason why there are two rhyme labels under rhyme base /əø/ has been explained in 5.2b, but the separation of *kū-sū*（姑蘇）from the *yī-ch'ī*（一七）under the rhyme base /ɨø/ is obviously a violation of the difinition for rhyming. To interpret as a rhyme with a different vowel is clearly out of question from the phonemic point of view. What, then, is the cause for its separation from the *yī-ch'ī*? This is indeed a problem for which no completely satisfactory answer can be found. One can only speculate that, to the native speakers of this dialect, the phonetic quality of the final /wiø/ (*kū-sū*) must have been somewhat noticeably different from the three finals in the *yī-ch'ī* rhyme, namely, /øɨø, yɨø, ywɨø/, which shared some common acoustic effect. This speculation is strongly supported by the fact that, in the morphophonemic process of r-suffixation, words of the *kū-sū* rhyme stand out prominently as a unique group, while all three types of words in the *yī-ch'ī* rhyme follow the same change, and, as a result, join those of the *huī-tuī*（灰堆）and the *jén-ch'én*（人辰）rhymes (see 6.3).

6. R-SUFFIXATION

Mandarin Chinese, particularly MP, is unique when compared with other forms of Chinese in that it possesses a new syllable ending /r/ which did not exist in Ancient Chinese and is most definitely a different thing from the Archaic Chinese ending /r/, if it did exist there (see Fang-kuei Li 1971: 27).

Where did this ending come from? My own research shows that at the time of *Chūng-yuán Yīn-yùn*（中原音韻，1342），words like 兒耳二 had the reading /rɨ/（plus tone），but by Hsú hsiào's（徐孝）time（1606），a metathetical change must have rendered this syllable into /ɨr/（Hsueh 1975：91 and 1975b），and this unique ending thereby came into existence. But since this was the only *basic* syllable that had this unique ending，the few words of this reading never formed a separate rhyme，though theoretically they should（they were still put together with words like（支思 etc.）. When the word 兒 that had this reading became a diminutive noun suffix，[①] it lost its vowel through phonetical fusion. Consequently，a large number of *derived* syllables with /r/ as ending appeared. The process through which these r-suffixed syllables are derived will be fully described but before we do that，we have to decide how the syllable represented by words like 兒耳二 should be phonemically represented in MP.

6.1. Practically all previous studies transcribe words like 兒耳二 as /er/（or /ər/），i. e.，having the mid vowel. This is explanatorily inappropriate and descriptively inadequate. As explained above，these words had the reading /ɨr/ as late as the beginning of the Ch'ing dynasty when the former four-vowel system was not yet replaced by the three-vowel system of MP. There is no reason to say the change of the vowel system in this case has affected this syllable（see 5.2 and Hsueh 1976）. More importantly，when we take the r-suffixed syllables into consideration，it becomes necessary to interpret this particular syllable as one with the high vowel /ɨ/. Words like 蛾鵝 etc. are represented by the syllable /ə/，that is，the mid vowel alone. When they are suffixed with /r/，naturally they should be transcribed /ər/.

① This is only a convenient oversimplification. Actually，suffix "r" came etymologically from several different sources，such as 裏（那兒），日（今兒），and 兒（see Chao 1968：46，Ch'en 1965，Hockett 1950，Shang 1966）. Moreover，it may also occur after verbs（e. g.，玩兒）and adverbs（e.g.，慢慢兒地）.

Since this r-suffixed syllable is in clear contrast with the syllable representing 兒耳二 etc., to transcribe the latter also as /ər/(or /er/) should be out of question, but both Hartman and Hockett transcribe 兒 as /er/. Since Hartman proposed that 歌兒 be transcribed as /keer/(i. e., with a *long* mid vowel; hence, 蛾兒 as /eer/), he succeeded in differentiating the two syllables in question by this strange and arbitrary, means, though he did not seem to be aware of the crucial problem we are now discussing. On the other hand, since Hockett proposed a two-vowel system by eliminating the high vowel, and he correctly insisted that 歌兒 must be transcribed as /ker/(hence, 蛾兒 as /er/), he simply had no means to mark the phonemic contrast between 兒 and 蛾兒 (he transcribed 日 as /r/). In other words, he committed the mistake of "underdifferentiation" which is unacceptable in phonemicization. This is why I say his system is not even descriptively adequate, though his interpretation of the contrast between 歌兒 (/ker/) and 根兒 (/keir/) is much more credible than Hartman's (see 6. 3). I do not know if Tōdō Akiyasu was aware of this problem or not, when he interpreted 兒 as /rr/, that is, "a syllabic r"(he interpreted 日 as /rrɪ/). He succeeded in marking the contrast by this ad hoc means which, perhaps, Hockett could have used, too; but we cannot accept this solution, both because it is ad hoc, and because it violates the definition of syllable which he observed everywhere else.

6.2. The occurrence of the suffix "r" in MP is basically a lexical matter, that is, it does not occur after a clearly definable class of forms, but occurs rather by choice or convention①. Wherever it occurs, however, it merges with its preceding syllable, apparently by following some morphophonemic rules. Exactly what are these rules, if they do exist? For decades, different scholars have responded with different and often contradicting answers.

① The conventional nature of this suffix can be seen from the fact that it may drastically change the meaning of the term to which it is attached; for example, 火星"Mars" vs. 火星兒 "sparks", 白麵"white flour" vs. 白麵兒"heroin". For more examples, see Liu 1957:(3)19.

Those who do not accept the three-vowel system for MP often argue that, for r-suffixed syllables, there should be at least two or more mid vowels (e.g., Sung 1965 and Wang 1963). Among those who do accept the three-vowel system, some propose rather fantastic solutions. For example, Hartman allows the contrast "long vs. short" for MP, but restricts it to the mid vowel alone①, and Hashimoto recommends three rules which will "render it unnecessary to mark the contrast in question on the phonemic level" (Hashimoto 1970: 215). It seems to me that the controversy arises from a misunderstanding of the nature of the problem. The fact is, for this matter, native speakers of MP split into different groups, each following a different set of rules. Dr. Y. R. Chao seems to be the first one to point out that there is a difference in this matter between the "old generation" and the "new generation" (Chao 1968: 51). My own investigation indicates that among the speakers of both the new and the old generations, there are different versions. The situation is very much comparable to that when entering tone words changed in different ways in different dialects. (Hsueh 1975: 91-133, and 1978). In cases like these, precise specification will be possible only when we deal with the different versions separately. When we adopt this approach, and use the system of finals given above (see 5.3) as the basis for specification, we shall find the morphophonemic process for this matter is almost unbelievably simple.

6.3. The so-called old generation seems to consist of two groups. In the speech of the first and possibly older group to which Hockett's informant obviously belongs (see also Shih 1957: 11), we notice the following

① The derivational nature of r-suffixed syllables was obviously overlooked by scholars like Hartman and Hockett who treated them just as other types of syllables. So, strictly speaking, as far as these scholars are concerned, no morphophonemic process is involved here, i.e., no r-suffixation. Nevertheless, in his "Peiping Morphophonemics" (1950), Hockett did include a brief discussion on alternations caused by "the suffixes /r/", which is basically an enumeration.

phenomena：

a) 瓜兒 kwa +r≠ 官兒 kwan +r= 乖兒 kway+r.
沙兒 sra +r≠ 山兒 sran +r= 篩兒 sray+r.
b) 蝕兒 srɨ +r= 神兒 srɨn +r≠ 蛇兒 sre +r.
枝兒 crɨ +r= 針兒 crɨn +r，(rhyming with 黑兒 hɨy+r.)
根兒 kɨn +r≠ 歌兒 kə +r.
c) 鷄兒 kyɨ +r= 今兒 kyɨn +r.
藝兒 yɨ +r= 印兒 yɨn +r≠ 葉兒 yə +r.
d) 屋兒 wɨ +r≠ 温兒 wɨn +r≠ 窩兒 wə +r.
鼓兒 kwɨ +r≠ 滚兒 kwɨn +r= 鬼兒 kwɨy+r ≠ 菓兒 kwə+r
e) 玉兒 ywɨ +r= 運兒 ywɨn +r≠ 月兒 ywə +r.
渠兒 khywɨ +r= 群兒 khywɨn +r≠ 瘸兒 khyuə +r.

Hockett interprets the contrasts like the above as a result of the presence or the absence of syllable ending /y/ before suffix /r/, and the lack of contrast as a result of ending /n/ changing to /y/ before /r/. I think he is right, though we have to add that, in some cases, /y/ is added before /r/ is attached (Rule A below). On the basis of our proposal that, in syllables with ending, the vocalic contrast 5.2), we can now describe the morphophonemic changes that are responsible for the above phenomena by two simple rules as follows. The note to the first rule means that this rule does not apply to the pure labialized final /wɨø/, i.e., words of the *Kū-sū* rhyme.

A. ø→ y/(M)ɨ____r

M ≠w

B. n→ y/____r

A chart of the r-suffixed finals in this version is given below. It can be seen that words of the *Kū-sū* rhyme stand prominently apart from those of the *yī-ch'ī* rhyme which has merged with the *huī-tuī* and the *jén-ch'én* rhymes.

E / V / M	-r			-yr		-wr		-ŋr	
	ɨ	e	a	ɨ	a	ɨ	a	ɨ	a
ø開	(兒)	蛾兒	沙兒	枝兒	蓋兒	頭兒	刀兒	燈兒	糖兒
y齊		姐兒	牙兒	今兒	烟兒	牛兒	條兒	瓶兒	墻兒
w合	屋兒	葉兒	瓜兒	鬼兒	官兒			蟲兒	牀兒
yw撮		月兒		玉兒	院兒			熊兒	

6.4. The second version of r-suffixed syllables in the speech of the so-called "old generation" is reflected by a further erosion of contrast among syllables with the low vowel /a/. For example, words in each of the two groups under (a) in the last section have become homophones, so have 瓦兒 (wa+r) and 碗兒 (wan+r). In other aspects, it is exactly the same as the first version, (Obviously, Hartman's informant speaks this form of Pekingese,) We, therefore, can interpret this phenomenon as the result of a further development of the version described above by adding one simple rule to the two above.

C. y →ø/a____r

This version is supported by Wang Fu-shih's report (Wang 1963). However, Wang asserted that it is 啊兒, 呀兒, and 蛙兒 that joined 安兒, 烟兒, and 彎兒 respectively (Wang 1963: 117). If he is right, the rule will have to be rewritten as ø→y/a____r. I have some reservation about his interpretation, though the lack of contrast in these cases as he reported is beyond any doubt. Moreover, Wang says his report is based on the speech of the old Peking residents (老北京人), particularly those of the inner city (内城話), though since the "liberation", because of the great inflow of population from other areas, the first version that maintains the contrast between 啊兒 and 安兒 etc. has become more popular. There is no need to draw a chart for the r-suffixed syllables in this version. We may have one by simply removing the /-ayr/ column from the above chart (and filling the slot for /ywar/ with 院兒).

6.5. There also seem to be two groups in the "new generation". One of these versions can be inferred from Liu Tse-hsiei's report (Liu 1957: 21 - 22). In his version of Pekingese, though palatalized pairs of the first and the second tones like the following are still in contrast, their counterparts in the third and the fourth tones have become homophones①.

1st tone:	衣兒	yɨ	+r =	蔭兒	yɨn	+r≠掖兒 yə+r.
	蛆兒	khywɨ	+r ≠	缺兒	khywə	+r.
2nd tone:	笛兒	tyɨ	+r ≠	碟兒	tyə	+r.
	橘兒	kywɨ	+r≠	撅兒	kywə	+r.
3rd tone:	幾兒	kyɨ	+r =	姐兒	kyə	+r.
	底兒	tyɨ	+r =	蝶兒	tyə	+
4th tone:	藝兒	yɨ	+r =	印兒	yɨn	+r =葉兒 yə+r.
	玉兒	ywɨ	+r =	月兒	ywə	+r.

Strict formulation for this version is rather difficult, because it involves tone which has not been included in our discussion. However, we can add verbally "For syllables of the third and the fourth tones, apply the following rule".

D. ɨy →ə/y(w) ____r

Since Liu's version is identical with Wang's (see 6.4) in every other

① Liu's report is in agreement with Chao's remark on palatalized syllables with the third or the fourth tone (Chao 1968:51). However, Liu still differentiates the non-palatalized pair of the third tone 鬼兒 vs. 菓兒 which, according to Chao, have become homophones for the "new generation". On the other hand, Liu's transcription shows that, when 幾兒[gi+r] and 姐兒 [gie+r] became homophones, it is the former that changed to the latter ([gier]), but Chao's transcription shows that it is the other way around (both are /jieel/, instead of /jiee'l/). Moreover, after saying that 小鷄兒 sheau-jiel ≠小街兒 sheau-jie'l. but 幾兒 jieel and 姐兒 jieel are homophones, he adds: "It should be noted in passing that the distinction as represented by the 根兒: 歌兒 gel: ge'l contrast and the 鷄兒: 街兒 jiel: jie'l contrast is disappearing fast." Here Dr. Chao seems to be predicting that rhyme base /ɨyr/(小人兒辰兒, 根兒, 鷄兒, 鬼兒, 笛兒) and rhyme base /ər/(小坡兒斜兒: 歌兒, 街兒, 菓兒, 碟兒) will coalesce in the future. It must be pointed out that both the two contrasts he mentioned exist in Liu's speech as he emphatically stated, and in Tōdō's version (see 6.6), only the contrast 根兒:歌兒 disappeared, while 鷄兒 is still in contrast with 街兒(even with 今兒).

aspect（including 根$_{兒}$≠歌$_{兒}$），we can now explain his by adding the above rule to the three needed for Wang's. In this way，we are really claiming that Wang's version represents the first step of moving away from the oldest version；while Liu's version represents the second step.

6.6. The fourth version implied by the solution proposed by Tōdō Akiyasu（1958：16－18）is drastically different from the three already discussed. It seems to indicate that a restructuring of the MP sound system has taken place. As we do，Tōdō recognizes three vowel phonemes /ɪ，ə，a/，but unlike us，he interprets the vocalic contrast in syllables with ending as one between the mid and the low vowels. On this basis，while admitting that phonemic symbolization for the r-suffixed syllables is very difficult，he proposes an incredibly simple（I'm temted to say "simplistic"）solution，namely，"When suffix 'r' is added to the basic syllables，/n/ and /y/ as syllable ending are dropped."（This is my summing up of his solution. Tōdō actually resorts to enumeration.）This implies that，in the Pekingese he knows，we should see the following phenomena：

a）瓜$_{兒}$ kwa ＋r ＝ 官$_{兒}$ kwan ＋r ＝ 乖$_{兒}$ kway＋r.
b）蝕$_{兒}$ srɪ ＋r ≠ 神$_{兒}$ srən ＋r ＝ 蛇$_{兒}$ sre ＋r.
根$_{兒}$ kən ＋r ＝ 歌$_{兒}$ kə ＋r.
c）鷄$_{兒}$ kyɪ ＋r ≠ 今$_{兒}$ kyən ＋r，Rhyming with 歌$_{兒}$.
d）屋$_{兒}$ wɪ ＋r ≠ 温$_{兒}$ wən ＋r ＝ 窩$_{兒}$ wə ＋r.
e）玉$_{兒}$ ywɪ ＋r ≠ 運$_{兒}$ ywən ＋r ＝ 月$_{兒}$ ywə ＋r.

Rhyming of r-suffixed syllables in this version would be like the following chart.

E / V / M	-r			wr		-ŋr	
	ɪ	ə	a	ə	a	ə	a
-ø	枝兒	針兒	孩兒	狗兒	套兒	繩兒	張兒
-j-	鷄兒	今兒	牙兒	油兒	鳥兒	釘兒	羊兒

續表

E / V / M	-r			wr		-ŋr	
	ɪ	ə	a	ə	a	ə	a
-w-	屋兒	鍋兒	塊兒			洞兒	胖兒
-jw-	魚兒	雲兒	園兒			熊兒	

Viewed on the basis of the sound system we have proposed for the basic syllables in MP. Tōdō's solution implies two fundamental changes which can be represented by the following rules:

$$1)\ ɨ \rightarrow ə / \_\_\_ E \quad E \neq r$$

$$2)\ \begin{Bmatrix} y \\ n \end{Bmatrix} \rightarrow \emptyset / \_\_\_ r$$

These two rules are quite different from the four rules discussed above (6.3 – 6.5). The first may be regarded as a symbolization of the final victory of the internal structural pressure over the external historical holding back (see 5.2). The second seems to be a symbolization of a subconscious effort in trying to conform to the basic phonemic patterns of Chinese syllables which allow only one single ending. To be frank, I have some misgivings about Tōdō's proposal, though I have no intention to dispute the truthfulness of his report by suggesting that be tailored the language to suit his theory. So I assume his report is probably true, and speculate that the dialectal version he reported might possibly have pointed out the direction to which the MP sound system in general is moving.

REFERENCES

Chao, Yuen Ren: "The Non-uniqueness of Phonemic Solution of Phonetic Systems", *Bulletin of the Institute of History and Philology (BIHP)*, Vol. 4, No. 4 (1934), 363 – 398.

____：*A Grammar of Spoken Chinese*, Berkeley, California, 1968.

Cheng, Chin-chuan: *A Synchronic Phonology of Mandarin Chinese*, The Hague, 1973.

Cheng, Robert L.: "Mandarin Phonological Structure", *Journal of Linguistics*, Vol. 2, No. 2 (1966), 135-158.

Hartman, Lawton M., III: "The Segmental Phonemes of the Peiping Dialect", *Language* 20 (1944), 28-42.

Hashimoto, Mantaro J.: "Notes on Mandarin Phonology", R. Jakobson and S. Kawamoto (ed.): *Studies in General and Oriental Linguistics*, Tokyo, 1970.

Hockett, Charles F.: "Peiping Phonology", *Journal of American Oriental Society (JAOS)* 67 (1947), 253-267.

____: "Peiping Morphophonemics", *Language* 26 (1950), 63-85.

Hsueh, F. S.: "The P'ingtu Dialect as a Variant of Mandarin", *Tsinghua Journal of Chinese Studies*, n. s. 10 (1973), 74-89.

____: *Phonology of Old Mandarin*, The Hague, 1975.

____: "The Emergence and Development of the Chīh-szū Rhyme", paper presented at the 8th International Conference on Sino-Tibetan Linguistics, October, 1975, Berkeley, Calif.

____: "Seven Centuries of Rhyming in Chinese Poetry: a Linguistic Interpretation", paper presented at the annual meeting of the American Council of Teachers of Foreign Languages, November, 1976, New Orleans.

Li, Fang-kuei: "The Zero Initial and the Zero Syllabic", *Language* 42 (1966), 300-302.

Martin, Samuel E.: "Problems of Hierarchy and Indterminacy in Mandarin Phonology", *BIHP* 29 (1957), 209-229.

Stimson, Hugh M.: *The Jongyuan In Yunn*, New Haven, Conn., 1966.

Tōdō, Akiyasu: "The Phonemes of the Peiping Dialect", Project on Linguistic

Analysis 4 (1963), 1 - 18.

Wang, John C. and Hsueh, F. S.: "The Lin-ch'i Dialect and its Relation to Mandarin" *JAOS* 93.2 (1973), 136 - 145.

Wong, Helen: "Outline of the Mandarin Phonemic System", *Word* 9 (1953), 268 - 276, and 10 (1954), 71 - 72.

Chang 1937 張洵如:《北平音系十三轍》,中國大辭典編纂處。

____ 1947《國語裏捲舌韻之功用》,國文月刊 54 (1947),12—16,30。

____ 1956 北平音系小轍編,開明書店影印。

Chang 1957 張　静:《談北京話的音位》,《中國語文》1957 年 2 月,13—15。

Chao1957 趙蔭棠:《等韻源流》,商務印書館。

Ch'en 1965 陳治文:《關於北京話裏兒化的來源》,《中國語文》1965 年 5 月,369—370,412。

Ch'eng 1956 程祥徽:《關於普通話音位》,《中國語文》1957 年 6 月,25—26。

Dragunov 1955 龍果夫、龍果娃:《漢語普通話的音節結構》(高祖舜譯),《中國語文》1958 年 11 月,513—521。

Fu1956 傅懋績:《北京話的音位和拼音字母》,《中國語文》1958 年 5 月。

Hsu1957 徐世榮:《北京語音音位簡述》,《語文學習》1957 年 8 月,22—24。

____1960《兒化韻的基本變化規律》,《語文學習》1960 年第 1 期,18。

Hsueh 1978 薛鳳生:《論入聲字之演化規律》,《屈萬里先生七秩榮慶論文集》,臺北聯經出版社,1978,407—433。

Hu1965 胡雙寶:《談京劇現代戲的字音和韻轍》,《中國語文》1965 年 2 月,139—143。

Li 1971 李方桂:《上古音研究》,清華學報,新九卷第一第二期合刊(1971),1—16。

Li 1963 李　榮:《漢語方言調查手册》,科學出版社。

Liu 1957 劉澤先:《北京話裏究竟有多少音節》,《中國語文》1957 年 2 月,1—8;3 月份,17—23。

Lo1950 羅常培:《北京俗曲百種摘韻》,來薰閣重校本。

____1963《京劇中的幾個音韻問題》,《羅常培語言學論文集》,中華書局,1963。

Lo 1961 羅季光:《北京話 i 和 ɿ(ʅ)的音位問題》,《中國語文》1961 年 1 月,頁 33—34,40。

Shang 1966 尚　静:《〈關於北京話裏兒化的來源〉小議》,《中國語文》1966 年 1 月,頁 67—68。

Shen1965 沈乘麐:《韻學驪珠》(一稱《曲韻驪珠》,收入汪經昌編:《曲韻五書》),臺北廣文書局影印,1965。

Shih1957 史存直:《北京話音位問題商榷》,《中國語文》1957 年 2 月,頁 9—12。

Sung 1965 宋元嘉:《評哈忒門(Hartman)和霍凱特(Hockett)對北京語音的分析》,《中國語文》1965 年 3 月,頁 167—178。

T'ang1932 唐　虞:《兒(ər)音的演變》,《史語所集刊》,第二本第四分(1932),頁 457—467。

T'ao1957 陶蓙培、尹潤薌:《略談兒化》,《語文學習》1957 年 10 月,頁 31—32。

Tung 1968 董同龢:《漢語音韻學》,臺北學生書局。

Wang1963 王輔世:《北京話韻母的幾個問題》,《中國語文》1963 年 2 月,頁 115—124。

Wang1979 王　力:《現代漢語語音分析中的幾個問題》,《中國語文》1979 年 4 月,頁 281—286。

Yin1957 尹仲賢:《漢語的聲調在音位系統中的地位》,《中國語文》1957 年 6 月,頁 27—28,30。

Historical Phonology and Dialect Study:

Some Examples from the Pingdu Dialect**

—1—

In reconstructing the historical forms of a language, we naturally have to rely on its modern dialects. In cases where written documents from the past are not available, our dependence on the modern dialects or languages would be total, but in cases where historical documents are available, as it is for Chinese, this dependence may sometimes be reduced to a relatively low degree, in proportion to the abundance or paucity of such documents. There are quite a few fairly comprehensive rhyme dictionaries in Chinese, each presumably representing a certain historical period of the language. One of them is the Zhongyuan Yinyun (ZYYY, 中原音韻) of the Yuan dynasty①. It is of special importance to us, not just because it includes a large number of entries (5876 characters), but, more importantly, because we have reasons to believe it is a careful and objective recording of the Chinese language of its day. Insofar as a rhyme dictionary of this kind has maintained all the existing distinctions in the language of the period for which the book was compiled, we may safely assume that the phonemic system of the language of that period underlies the book. Our job is then to reconstruct or decode this underlying system in modem phonological terms. However, there are occasions when we

---

** 中文題爲《音韻史與方言研究:平度話中的幾個例子》,原載香港中國語文學會編《王力先生紀念論文集》,三聯書店香港分店,1987 年。

① For this rhyme dictionary, I used primarily Zhao 1936. For a detailed analysis of the book in phonological terms, see Hsueh 1975.

may encounter some uncertainty in our reconstruction, mainly due to the insufficiency of the data we have. Such uncertainty may sometimes be resolved by the study of modern dialects. In this paper, I shall try to show how one such uncertainty in our study of Old Mandarin (OM, i. e. ZYYY) can be eliminated with the help of the Pingdu 平度 dialect (PD). In addition, I will present another case in which this dialect seems to suggest something in the development from Old Mandarin to Modern Pekingese, and I am going to show how some of the differences between this dialect and Old Mandarin or Modern Pekingese can be best understood when we look at them from a strictly phonemic angle.

—2—

The Pingdu dialect is spoken in a small area of the Shandong 山東 peninsula. The various dialects of the peninsula have been regarded as subdialects of one large dialect area called the Jiaodong 膠東 dialect which showed, according to Yuan Jiahua, author of *Hanyu Fangyan Gaiyao* 漢語方言概要, a number of unusual characteristics, when compared with Pekingese (Yuan 1960:24). This is one of the reasons why I became interested in the dialects of this area and chose PD for a close analysis. As a result of my own study, the phonological structure of PD can be summarized as follows①.

—2.1—

Syllables in PD can be analyzed in the same model as that for Pekingese and other Chinese dialects, namely, each syllable consists of three parts: the

---

① See Hsueh 1973. The present summary is, however, a revised version. Most important of all, I have reinterpretated the vowel contrast in syllables with ending (E) as a contrast between the high and the low vowels, instead of one between the mid and the low. This revision is necessary because of my new study on Pekingese phonology (see Hsueh 1977). For romanization, I have also shifted from Wade-Giles to the Pinyin system.

tone, the syllable initial, and the syllable final. As in Pekingese, there are four tones in PD. They are labeled here in such a way as to show their one-to-one corresponding relationship to those in Pekingese, though their phonetic realization is often drastically different from that of their Pekingese counterparts[①].

1st tone:	low level	(11)
2nd tone:	high falling	(53)
3rd tone:	mid level	(33)
4th tone:	low falling	(31)

—2.2—

There are twenty-one syllable initials (C) in PD, including the so-called zero initial.

	S(h) (stops)		Fr (fricatives)	R (resonants)
B(labial)	p	ph	f	m
Ds(dental)	ť	ťh	θ	
D(alveolar)	t	th		n
Gi(gingival)	c	ch	s	l
P(retroflex)	cr	crh	sr	
G(guttural)	k	kh	h	ø

All of these initials are phonemically unit sound (in contrast to clusters). /r/ is to be recognized as a symbol for "retroflexion" pertaining to its preceding consonant. Similarly, /h/ represents the feature "aspiration" as a part of its preceding consonant, but when it occurs alone in the initial position, it stands for a full consonantal phoneme. It is merely for convenience, especially for historical and comparative studies, that the two features are separated from the bundle of distinctive features wherein they are each a member (Cf. Hsueh 1975:29).

① The phonetic value of the tones is represented here numerically, following Chao 1930.

—2.3—

The final is analyzed into three components: the medial (M), the nuclear vowel (V), and the syllable ending (E). There are two semivowels in PD, /y, w/, which may occur in the medial position either separately or jointly in the order /yw/. Syllables can thus be classified into four types according to the medial: those with zero medial, those with medial /y/, those with medial /w/, and those with medial /yw/①. The two semivowels can also occur in the syllable ending position, in addition to the two nasals /n/ and /ŋ/. The slot of nuclear vowel is the only one which, by definition, must be filled for every syllable. As in Pekingese, there are only three vowel phonemes in PD: the high /ɨ/, the mid /ə/, and the low /a/. Altogether, there are thirty-five syllable finals in PD, which may be presented in a chart. The four rows represent the four types of finals according to the medial, while the five columns represent the five classes of fianls according to the syllable ending. Blanks in the chart indicate that possible finals of such descriptions do not exist in the dialect.

Chart 1

E / V / M	ø			y		w		n		ŋ	
	ɨ	ə	a	ɨ	a	ɨ	a	ɨ	a	ɨ	a
ø	ɨ	ə	a	ɨy	ay	ɨw	aw	ɨn	an	ɨŋ	aŋ
y	yɨ	yə	ya		yay	yɨw	yaw	yɨn	yan	yɨŋ	yaŋ
w	wɨ	wə	wa	wɨy	way			wɨn	wan	wɨŋ	waŋ
yw	ywɨ	ywə						ywɨn	ywan	ywɨŋ	

① In terms of distinctive features, the four types of medial can be represented by [−lab, −pal], [−lab, +pal], [+lab, −pal], and [+lab, +pal], where lab = labialization, pal = palatalization. In such a treatment, the question of order of the two semivowels in the compound /yw/ will be irrelevant.

—3—

We may begin our discussion on this dialect from its initial system which shows two prominent differences when compared with that of Pekingese.

—3.1—

The most peculiar feature in PD is obviously the existence or the dental sibilants /t̆，t̆h，θ/. These initials were never recorded in any rhyme book (i.e.，no rhyme book has been given a reconstructed system with them)，and to my knowledge，nor is it reported in other Chinese dialects. The question is when and how they came into existence. Common sense may suggest that they came from a period even before Ancient Chinese (AC) as represented by *Qieyun* 切韻①，but upon closer scrutiny，we find the deep phonological structure of the dialect reveals unmistakably that they have a rather recent origin. To illustrate this point，we have to discuss this series of initials together with the gingivals and retroflexes，and with frequent references to Ancient Chinese and Old Mandarin.

—3.1.1 —

The situation in PD can be summarized as follows：

(a) With no exception，all the words with /t̆，t̆h，θ/ as initials in PD have /c，ch，s/ respectively in Pekingese. They belong to the so-called "apical sibilant" series (chitou. 齒頭) in AC，namely，[ʦ, ʦʻ，dzʻ，s，z]②.

(b) Words with retroflex initials in PD have the same initials in their Pekingese reading. Most of them appear in the second division under the

① Lu Fayan：*Qieyun*，A.D. 601，more widely known through its Song edition，*Guangyun* 廣韻.

② These five initials are represented by 精清從心邪 among the "thirty-six initials" appearing in books of rhyme tables. The phonetic transcription for these initials，and for Acient Chinese in general in this paper，it based on Karlgren 1954.

retroflex sibilants [ṭs, ṭs‘, ḍz‘, ṣ] and the palatal stops [ȋ, ȋ‘, ȡ‘] in the rhyme tables①. The exceptions concentrate in syllables with the finals /ɨ/(e. g., zhi 枝, "branch," AC [tśjie̯], PD /crɨ/), /wɨy/(e. g., shui 水, "water," AC [śjwi], PD /srwɨy/), and /wɨŋ/(e. g., zhong 鍾, "bell," AC [tśi̯woŋ], PD /crwɨŋ/). These exceptions are all third division words in the rhyme tables.

(c) Words with the initials /c, ch, s/ and nonpalatalized finals in PD have /cr. crh, sr/ respectively in their Pekingese reading. They are *third division* words under the palatal stops [ȋ, ȋ‘, ȡ‘] and sibilants [tś, tś‘, dź‘, ś, ź] in the rhyme tables (see Note 7), including such words as *zhi* 知, "to know, (AC [ȋjie̯], PD /cɨ/) and *chi* 尺," yardstick, "(AC [tś'iäk], PD /chɨ/)".

—3.1.2—

The above phenomena can be best explained with reference to the phonology of Old Mandarin as recorded in ZYYY. Viewed in this light, even the "exceptions" mentioned above (3.1.1b) are no longer exceptions but logical consequences in the development of this dialect. The AC distinction between the two series of initials [ṭs, ṭs‘, ḍz‘, ṣ] and [tś, tś‘, dź‘, ś, ź] disappeared quite early, as a result of the loss of medial /y/ in syllables with the former initials. With the latter occurring before /y/ only, the two series became thus allophones of one single series of initials which were represented

---

① The five retroflex initials 照穿牀審禪 of the thirty-six initials occur in both the second and the third divisions of the rhyme tables. Critical Studies of *Qieyun* have revealed that there existed two series of initials in the language represented by the book, which correspond to the single retroflex series mentioned above. They have been labeled 莊初崇生[ṭs, ṭs‘, ḍz‘, ṣ] which occur in words of the second division of the rhyme tables only, and 章昌船書常[tś, tś‘, dź‘, ś, ź] which occur in words of the third division only (Cf. Li 1956). The three initials 知徹澄 which occur only in words of the second and the third divisions have been reconstracted [ȋ, ȋ‘, ȡ‘] by Karlgren. Lo Changpei, however, has quite convincingly demonstrated that they are retroflexed [ṭ, ṭ‘, ḍ‘] when they occur in the second division(Lo. 1931).

among the thirty-six initials of the rhyme tables by 照穿牀審禪(see Note 7). To be sure, there must still have been some phonetic difference between the two AC series, but whatever that difference might be, it was now only allophonic. If the /y/ in the medial position of a syllable with this type of initial should be lost, we normally would expect no change in the part of the initial phonemically, though it must undergo phonetically an automatic shift, possibly from palatalization to retroflexion. This has been proved to be true in numerous Mandarin dialects, including Pekingese. To a lesser degree, this was also proved to be true in ZYYY. In this rhyme dictionary, the coalescence of the palatal sibilants and the retroflex sibilants mentioned above had clearly occurred. Moreover, the palatal (or retroflex) stops [ṭ, ṭ', ḍ'](/tr, trh, trɦ/) had already been affricated and thus joined the above newly formed retroflex series.

$$t \rightarrow c / \_\_\_ r \qquad (1)$$

So for OM, only one series of initials /cr, crh, sr, r/ is needed for the three AC series (Hsueh 1975: 41 - 44). AC syllables of the third division with palatal stop or sibilant initials (see Note 7) must now be reconstructed in OM with /y/ in the medial position, except in the following cases:

(a) The unrounded syllables of the *Zhishe* 止攝 with these initials, namely, syllables having these initials and the final /yɨy/, lost medial /y/ (Hsueh 1975:43).

$$y \rightarrow \emptyset / Pr \_\_\_ ɨy \qquad (2)$$

This process must have taken place *before* the AC palatal stops joined the newly formed retroflex series (Rule 1) and *before* the fourth division words of the *Xieshe* 蟹攝 joined the *Zhishe* (Hsueh 1975: 66 - 69), for words like *zhi* "to know" and *chi* "yard-stick" were found in the fourth rhyme of ZYYY (i.e., *Qiwei* 齊微) Instead of as homophones with such words like *zhi* "branch" and *chi* 齒 "tooth" (AC [tś'ji], PD /crhɨ/) respectively in the third rhyme (i. e., *Zhisi* 支思).

(b) Words that could have been reconstructed with the final */ywɨy/ are always found to be homophones with those which have comparable initials but should be reconstructed with the final /wɨy/. I interpret this phenomenon by postulating that the final /ywɨy/ lost the /y/ in its medial position sometime before ZYYY (Hsueh 1975:69–70).

$$y \rightarrow \varnothing / \_\_\_ w\text{ɨ}y \quad (3)$$

This includes, of course, words of this kind with retroflex initials (i. e., those originated from the palatalsibilants and stops in AC), such as *zhui* 追, "to pursue," and *shui*, "water," (sec Column B in Chart 2).

(c) Words with retroflex initials that could have been reconstructed with the final /ywɨŋ/ in one case were also listed at homophones with a word (*chong* 崇 "to worship" AC [dẓʻi̯uŋ]) which should be reconstructed with the final /wɨŋ/①. This fact seems to suggest that the final /ywɨŋ/ had also lost its medial /y/ in syllables with retroflex initials sometimes before ZYYY.

$$y \rightarrow \varnothing / Pr \_\_\_ w\text{ɨ}\text{ŋ} \quad (4)$$

If so, words like*zhong*, "bell," and *chong* 充, "to fill up," (AC [tśʻiwoŋ]) should then be reconstructed as /crwɨŋ/ and /crhwɨŋ/ respectively. But here is the problem. Since *chong*, "to worship," is the only word of its kind included in ZYYY, we really cannot be too sure that the loss of the contrast between /wɨŋ/ and /ywɨŋ/ after retroflex initials was so early in time. To make matter worse, the same homonym group also includes two graphs representing different initials which regularly would have to be reconstructed

---

① The nuclear vowel of The *Dongzhong* rhyme in ZYYY was formerly reconstructed as /o/ (Cf. Hsueh 1975: 54–55), but I have changed my mind and now believe it should be /ɨ/ (Cf. Hsueh 1979 & 1980). This revision makes it possible for us to avoid some unnecessary complications and thereby simplify our discussion here. 崇 appears in Homonym Group No. 27 of the *Dongzhong* rhyme.

as /sr/ and zero initial[1]. This is why in my study of ZYYY I still transcribed the few homonym groups involved here with the final /ywɨŋ/, though I established a rule to specify the change (Hsueh 1975:55 & 84). I was afraid at the time that the only example might be the result of irregular development or simply a mistake made by the compiler himself or the editors of the book in later times.

—3.1.3—

The seemingly drastic difference between Pekingese and PD described above are obviously the result of separate post-ZYYY developments in the two dialects. These developments can be summarized in the following manner.

(a) Initial /r/ remains the same in Pekingese, but in PD it first changed to /l/ before the final /ɨ/, and then disappeared unconditionally.

(b) The loss of medial /y/ after all retroflex initials then took place in both Pekingese and PD. In Pekingese, the process is very simple. After the loss of medial /y/, words formerly differentiated this way became automatically homophones, for example, *shu* 梳, "comb," (AC [ṣi̯wo], OM /srwɨ/, Pk /srwɨ/) vs. *shu* 書 "book," (AC [śi̯wo], OM /srywɨ/, Pk /srwɨ/). The process in PD is more complex. When the medial /y/ was lost, the initials in these syllables became instead gingivals /c, ch, s/. They caused a chain reaction, so to speak, by forcing the original gingivals to move further forward to become dental sibilants.

$$\begin{bmatrix} \text{c} \\ \text{ch} \\ \text{s} \end{bmatrix} \rightarrow \begin{bmatrix} \check{\text{t}} \\ \check{\text{t}}\text{l}_1 \\ \theta \end{bmatrix} / \_\_\_ \text{(w)V} \qquad (5)$$

$$\text{ry} \rightarrow \varnothing \qquad (6)$$

Not affected by theserules are, of course, the gingivals in palatalized

---

① The two words are *yong* "lazy" (慵 AC [źi̯woŋ], Pk /ywɨŋ/ and *yong* "tench" (鱅 AC [źi̯woŋ] and [î̯woŋ], Pk /ywɨŋ/).

syllables.

(c) Retroflex initials /cr, crh, sr/ in all nonpalatalized syllables in OM remain unchanged in PD. Those *third division* words with palatal stop or sibilant initials in AC but depalatalized before ZYYY discussed above (Rules 2, 3, 4) naturally retain their retroflex initials, including words like *zhong*, "bell," *chong*, "to fill up," and *chong*, "worm." This fact indicates that the change /ywɨŋ/ to /wɨŋ/ after retroflex initials, of which we are not quite sure, definitely took place before ZYYY. We can thus be released from our doubt.

Chart 2

Qieyun	(A)			(B)		(C)	
	支	知	齒	追	水	蟲	崇
	tsjie̯	t̂jie̯	tś'ji'	t̂jwi	śjwi	d̂'iuŋ	dz'iuŋ
Rhyme Table	cryɨy	tryɨy	crhyɨy	trywɨy	srywɨy	trɦywɨŋ	crɦwɨŋ
y→ø/Pr___ɨy y→ø/Cɨ___ t→c/___r y→ø/___wɨy y→ø/Pr___wɨy	crɨy crɨ	cryɨy	crhɨy crhɨ	crywɨy crwɨy	srwɨy	crɦywɨŋ crɦwɨŋ	
ZYYY	RG03	RG04	RG03	RG04	RG04	RG01	RG01
y→ø/yɨ___ ry→ø		cryɨ cɨ					
Pingdu	crɨ	cɨ	crhɨ	crwɨy	srwɨy	crhwiŋ	crhwɨŋ
Pekingese	crɨ	crɨ	crhɨ	crwɨy	srwɨy	crhwiŋ	crhwɨŋ

—3.2—

The contrast between the gingivals /c, ch, s/ and the gutturals /k, kh, h/([tɕ, tɕ', ɕ]) in palatalized syllables has been lost in Pekingese but still kept in PD. However, in at least one case, the contrast has also been lost in PD, namely, in syllables with the final /yɨ/. For example, *qi* 七, "seven," (AC [tś'iĕt], Pk /khyɨ/) and *xi* 西, "west," (AC [siei], Pk /hyɨ/) have the reading /khyɨ/ and /hyɨ/ respectively in PD. In other words, syllables like

*/cyɨ/, */chyɨ/, and */syɨ/ do not exist in PD.

$$\begin{bmatrix} c \\ ch \\ s \end{bmatrix} \rightarrow \begin{bmatrix} k \\ kh \\ h \end{bmatrix} / \_\_\_ yi \# \qquad (7)$$

This is seemingly a very simple matter, but it raises one serious question about one basic concept in linguistic theory. Is the coalescence of /c, ch, s/ and /k, kh, h/ in palatalized syllables in Pekingese a one-step process, or is it rather a gradual process with intermediate stages, e. g., first before the final /yɨ/, as in PD, and then before other finals one or several at a time? it seems unlikely that we can ever answer this question one way or the other with absolute confidence. There are two fundamental concepts in modern linguistic theory, namely, simplicity and generality which are often regarded as two aspects of the same thing. When there are two ways to account for a certain observed linguistic phenomenon satisfactorily, it is assumed that the simpler one is the better one which is also the one making a more general claim. Applying this concept of simplicity to the coalescence of /c, ch, s/ and /k, kh, h/ in Pekingese, we would be forced to admit that it is a one-step process, but as we noted, there is actually no absolute guarantee that this conclusion is closer to the truth. I do not mean to say that the concept of simplicity or generality is invalid or illogical. On the contrary, I believe it is a necessity in methodology and it is one of the most important principles to be observed in the diachronic study of any language, but we should also remember that it is not an absolutism and we should be ready to revise our rules whenever new evidence is found which makes the revision necessary.

—4—

The entering tone words of AC developed in different ways in different dialects. (To put it differently, the divergence in the development of the entering tone words is one of the most important criteria for setting up different dialect groups.) Following are three peculiar developments of the entering tone words observed in PD, which partly account for its difference from Pekingese and OM.

—4.1—

As we have said, the four tones of this dialect hold a one-to-one corresponding relationship to those of Pekingese (see 2.1). However, the entering tone words of AC, after losing their entering tone status, were redistributed among the other tones in PD quite differently from the way they were in OM and Pekingese. For OM, the following rule has been formulated (Hsueh 1975:32-33).

$$F^5 \rightarrow \left\{ \begin{array}{l} F^4 / R\_\_ \\ F^2 / \text{ɦ}\_\_ \\ F^3 \end{array} \right\} \qquad (8)$$

This means that finals (F) with the entering tone (5) developed into three different tones according to the initials before them: those occurring in syllables with resonant (nasal, lateral, or zero) initials acquired the fourth tone (i.e., *qusheng* 去聲, those after voiced obstruants (stops, affricates, and fricatives) acquired the second tone (i.e., *yangping* 陽平), and those with voiceless initials acquired the third tone (i.e., *shangsheng* 上聲). Pekingese agrees with OM in the first two cases (e.g., mu 木, "wood," AC [muk], OM /mwɨ⁴/, Pk /mwɨ⁴/; and *she* 舌, "tongue," AC (dź'iät], OM /srye²/, Pk /srə²/), but differs in the third, for AC entering tone words with voiceless initials may have any one of the four tones in Pekingese (Stimson 1962). PD agrees with OM only in the second case (e.g., she, "tongue," PD /sə²/). Syllables of the other two types all belong to the first tone (e.g., mu, "wood," PD /mwɨ¹/, and ke 客, "guest," AC (k'ɐk), Pk /khə⁴/, PD /khɨy¹/). So the rule for PD is as follows:

$$F^5 \rightarrow \begin{Bmatrix} F^2/\text{ɦ}\_\_\_ \\ F^1 \end{Bmatrix} \tag{9}$$

In this respect, PD is different from the dialects of both Qingdao 青島 and Jinan 濟南, two big cities close by, but similar to those Mandarin dialects in central China, e.g., the Zhengzhou 鄭州 dialect①.

—4.2—

Words like *ge* 割, "to cut," (AC (kât), OM /ko/, Pk /kə/) and *he* 合, "to combine," (AC [ɣap̣], OM /ho/, Pk /hə/) have the low vowel in PD as their final, instead of the mid vowel as in Pekingese. These are entering tone words of the first division in the *Shanshe* 山攝 and the *Xianshe* 咸攝. In this regard, Pekingese and OM are in agreement. In ZYYY, we find that words representing unrounded syllables of the first division appear for the most part in the same rhyme as their counterparts in the second division. I interpreted this phenomenon by postulating that when the nuclear vowel of the first division was not preceded by /w/ or followed by zero ending (i.e., syllable boundary), it became the same as the nuclear vowel of the second division, under two minor conditions: first, the syllable ending (E) must not be /w/; second, if the initial (C) is a guttural (G), the ending must not be a stop consonant (S, i.e., /p, t, k/). In other words, entering tone words of the first division with guttural initials were not affected by this vowel shift rule (Hsueh 1975: 112-113).

$$o \rightarrow a/C\_\_\_E \tag{10}$$

(i) E≠w;

(ii) if C = G, then E≠S.

It is most interesting to note here that if we eliminate the second of the two conditions to the vowel shift rule, the reading of *ge*, "to cut," and *he*, "to combine," as /ka/ and /ha/ in PD will be explained automatically. I relate

① For Jinan and Qingdao, see Li 1963: 84. For Zhengzhou, see Yuan 1960.29.

this case here as an illustration to show how differences between dialects can often be explicitly and yet easily specified, if we adopt a strictly phonemic approach.

—4.3—

The AC rhymes in the *zengshe* 曾攝 and *Gengshe* 梗攝 have merged in all modern Mandarin dialects. This has also been observed in ZYYY, for words of these two classes of rhymes are found together in its fifteenth rhyme (*Gengqing* 庚青). The entering tone words of these two classes of rhymes, however, show great divergence in their development in different dialects, —a matter which we can, it seems to me, explain by reordering the diachronic rules for each dialect. For ZYYY whence came the so-called "colloquial reading" in Pekingese (Hsueh 1975:124 - 125), I have postulated a development of four stages for the words of these two classes of rhymes:

(a) *Zengshe* joined *Gengshe* in forming a single class of rhymes of the so-called "outer series" (*waizhuan* 外轉), with rhymes in all four divisions①.

(b) Unrounded syllables of the second division with guttural initials in all classes of rhymes were palatalized, including, naturally, those in the *Gengshe* (Hsueh 1975:44 - 45).

$$ø \rightarrow y/G\_\_\_a \qquad (11)$$

This explains why words like*geng* 耕, "to plow," (AC [kɛŋ], OM /kyeŋ/) and *jia* 家, "home," (AC [ka], OM /kya/) had a reading with medial /y/.

(c) The entering tone words of this kind had their syllable ending changed from /k̂/ to /y/ (Hsueh 1979 & 1980).

$$\hat{k} \rightarrow y \qquad (12)$$

① My view on the rhyme tables has changed quite drastically since the completion of Hsueh 1975. I now interpret both the *Zengshe* and the *Gengshe* as rhyme classes with palatal endings /ɲ, k̂/ (Cf. Hashimto 1970) in contrast to the three rhyme classes, *Jiang*, *Dang* and *Tong*, which have velar endings /n, k/. For more detailed discussion, see Hsueh 1979.

So the entering tone words of the second division had now the finals /ay/, /way/, and /yay/, and were consequently entered into the sixth rhyme (*Jielai* 皆來) in ZYYY (Hsueh 1975:103 - 104).

(d) Words of the first and the second divisions in the *Geng-Zeng* combination joined the fourth division in sharing the same vowel.

$$\begin{Bmatrix} o \\ a \end{Bmatrix} \rightarrow e/\_\_\_\_\text{ɲ} \qquad (13)$$

Consequently, words like *geng*, "to plow," and jing 京, "capital," at this Point became homophones (Hsueh 1975:58 - 59). This process, of course, did not affect the entering tone words of these two classes of rhymes, because after the change specified by Rule 12, they were no longer entering tone word, and hence did not belong to this category any longer.

Qieyun	耕 kɛŋ	京 kieŋ	麥 mɛk	墨 mək	額 ŋɛk		客 k'ək		色 ṣiək		
Rhyme Table	kaɲ	kyaɲ	mak̂	mok̂	ŋak̂		khak̂		srak̂		
a→e/y____ ŋ→ø/#____		kyeɲ			ak̂						
ø→y/G____a k̂→y {o, a}→e/____ɲ	kyaɲ kyeɲ		may	moy	yak yay		khyak khyay		sray	k̂—q /____{k̂, ɲ}	/____{k̂, ɲ}
{o, e}→ɨ/____y ay→e/____y (opt.)				mɨy	yay	ye	khyay	khye			
ZYYY Pk—coll.	RG15 kyɨŋ	RG15 kyɨŋ	RG06 may	RG04 mɨy	RG06	RG14 ye	RG06	RG14 khye	RG06 sray		
	kɨŋ	kyɨŋ	mə	mə	ə		khə		sa	Pk—lit.	
	kɨŋ	kyɨŋ	mɨy	mɨy	ɨy		khɨy		srɨy		PD

For PD, as well as for the Pekingese "literary reading," all of these changes occurred, too. But we have to change the order of the rules somewhat. Obviously, Rule 13, which affected both the entering and the non-entering tone words in PD and Literary Pekingese, occurred first. Rule

12 then came into operation for PD. but in Literary Pekingese, syllable ending /k̂/, together with /p, t, k/, became a glottal stop which was eventually lost (Hsueh 1980). Rule 1 is now irrelevant for words of this category, because by this time, as a result of Rule 13, there were no longer second division words among them. Thus, by partially reordering the rules, we have explained how words of this kind developed in PD and in Literary Pekingese, and we have now a better understanding of the differences between these two dialects and Colloquial Pekingese or Old Mandarin.

—5—

In our discussions on the development of the initial system and the entering lone words, we have already, by necessity, elabo rated on most of the changes involving the final system of this dialect. Following are a few more changes not yet discussed. They partly account for the differences between this dialect and Pekingese.

—5.1—

The change of the final /o/ to /wo/ observed in ZYYY and in Pekingese (Hsueh 1975:109－110) has one condition, viz., the initial of the syllable must not be a guttural, e.g., *duo* 多, "many," (AC [tâ], OM /two/, Pk /twə/), but *he* 何, "what," (AC [ɣâ], OM /ho/, Pk /hə/).

$$\emptyset \rightarrow w/C\_\_\_o\# \qquad (14)$$
$$C \neq G$$

The condition is obviously unnecessary for PD, for words like *ke* 哥, "elder brother," (AC [kâ], OM /ko/, Pk /kə/) and *e* 餓, "hungry," (AC [ŋâ], OM /ŋo/, Pk/wə/), as well as *he*, "what," given above, have the final /wə/ in PD. In fact, /ə/ alone as a final, which came from the OM /o/ and /e/, is not possible for PD except after gingivals. There are two possible explanations for this. One is to establish a two-stage development for words of this kind in PD, namely, they first developed in the same way as in OM, then, after ZYYY, those with guttural initials also acquired /w/ in the medial position. The other, which I believe is better, is to treat it as the result of a one-stage pre-ZYYY change, namely, Rule 14 without the condition. Syllables with the final /ə/ and gingival initials in PD are, of course, the consequence of the depalatalization of syllables with retroflex initials (Rule 6) which took place much later. Incidentally, the irregular reading of the first person pronoun (*wo* 我, AC [ŋâ] OM /ŋo/, Pk /wə/) in Pekingese may perhaps be regarded as the result of influence from dialects like PD, though not necessarily PD itself.

—5.2—

One post-ZYYY change observed in Pekingese is the loss of medial /w/ in the final /wɨy/ after initials /l/ and /n/ (e. g., *lei* 雷, "thunder," AC [luậi], OM /lwɨy/, Pk /lɨy/; *nei* 内, "inside," AC [nuậi], OM /nwɨy/, Pk /nɨy/). In fact, the two syllables */lwɨy/ and */nwɨy/ do not exist in Pekingese. The same change is also observed in PD, only to a much broader extent, because it is not restricted to syllables with initials /l/ and /n/. It took place in all syllables except those with retroflex and guttural initials. In other words, syllables with the final /wɨy/ but non-retroflex or non-guttural initials do not exist in PD. So words like *tui* 推, "to push," (AC [t'uậi], OM /thwɨy/, Pk /thwɨy/) and *cui* 脆, "crispy," (AC [ts'i̯wäi], OM /chwɨy/, Pk /chwɨy/) are pronounced /thɨy/ and /ťhɨy/ respectively in PD.

—5.3—

The same process of delabialization under the same restrictions discussed above obviously also affected the two finals /wɨn/ and /wan/ in PD (though not in Pekingese), for words like *luan* 亂, "disorder," (AC [luân], OM /lwon/, Pk /lwan/), *suan* 蒜, "garlic," (AC [suân], OM /swon/, Pk /swan/), *sun* 孫, "grandson," (AC [suən], OM /swɨn/, Pk /swɨn/), and *dun* 頓，“pause，”（AC［tuən］，OM /twɨn/，Pk /twɨn/）are all without medial /w/ in PD. This process to so widespread in PD that it seems the only restraining force other than retroflex and guttural initials is the velar nasal and zero ending. This may perhaps justify the following highly general rule which is more than enough to cover the process discussed in this section and the last.

$$w \rightarrow \emptyset / C\_\_\_ VE \qquad (15)$$

i）C≠ Pr，G；

ii）E ≠ ŋ.

This process must have taken place before the depalatalization of syllables with retroflex initials after ZYYY discussed earlier（Rule 6），for only under the initials /c，ch，s/ are there a few words with the finals /win/ and /wan/.

—6—

The major events of phonological development which mark off PD from other Mandarin dialects，particularly Pekingese，have been discussed. In one case at least，we find this dialect helps us dispel one uncertainty in our reconstruction of OM. In another，it raises one question about a post-ZYYY change in Pekingese which we cannot readily answer. But even in those cases which do not make us feel obligated to revise or reconsider our inter-pretation of OM and Pekingese，the highly systematic way with which we have accounted for them certainly reinforces our confidence in the conclusions reached in our study. It must now be rather self-evident that the best way to show explicitly the phonemic correspondences among the Chinese dialects is the systematic way we have demonstrated here. As a summing up，we may list the phonological rules we have discovered in their proper historical order. For the pre-ZYYY rules，we shall list only the few which are relevant to PD， but all the post-ZYYY rules will be listed, that is, including a few observed in both PD and Pekingese but not discussed in this paper①, as there are not too many anyway.

Pre-ZYYY development:

$$\text{(i) } F^5 \rightarrow \left\{ \begin{matrix} F^2/\text{ɦ}\_\_\_ \\ F^1 \end{matrix} \right\} \qquad (9)$$

$$\text{(ii) } \left\{ \begin{matrix} \text{o} \\ \text{a} \end{matrix} \right\} \rightarrow \text{e}/\left\{ \begin{matrix} \hat{\text{k}} \\ \text{ɲ} \end{matrix} \right\} \qquad (13)$$

$$\text{(iii) } \hat{\text{k}} \rightarrow \text{y} \qquad (12)$$

$$\text{(iv) } \text{ø} \rightarrow \text{y/G\_\_\_a} \qquad (11)$$

$$\text{(v) } \text{o} \rightarrow \text{a/C\_\_\_E} \qquad (10)$$

$$\text{(vi) } \text{ø} \rightarrow \text{w/C\_\_\_o\#} \qquad (14)$$

Post-ZYYY development:

$$\text{(i) } \left\{ \begin{matrix} \text{ŋ} \\ \text{v} \end{matrix} \right\} \rightarrow \text{ø/\#\_\_\_}$$

$$\text{(ii) } \text{m} \rightarrow \text{n/\_\_\_\#}$$

$$\text{(iii) } \left\{ \begin{matrix} \text{e} \\ \text{o} \end{matrix} \right\} \rightarrow \text{a/\_\_\_}\left\{ \begin{matrix} \text{n} \\ \text{w} \end{matrix} \right\}$$

$$\text{(iv) } \text{y} \rightarrow \text{ø/yɨ\_\_\_}$$

$$\text{(v) } \left\{ \begin{matrix} \text{e} \\ \text{o} \end{matrix} \right\} \rightarrow \text{ə}$$

$$\text{(vi) } \left\{ \begin{matrix} \text{c} \\ \text{ch} \\ \text{s} \end{matrix} \right\} \rightarrow \left\{ \begin{matrix} \breve{\text{t}} \\ \breve{\text{t}}\text{h} \\ \theta \end{matrix} \right\} \text{/\_\_\_(w)V} \qquad (5)$$

$$\text{(vii) } \text{ry} \rightarrow \text{ø} \qquad (6)$$

$$\text{(viii) } \text{w} \rightarrow \text{ø/C\_\_\_VE} \qquad (15)$$

1) $C \neq$ Pr, G;

2) $E \neq$ ŋ.

① For post-ZYYY changes in Pekingese, much remains to be done. The ten simple rules listed at the end of my study of ZYYY without explanation (Hsueh 1975: 135 - 136) may be of some interest for comparison with the ten post-ZYYY rules in PD.

$$\text{(ix)}\ \begin{Bmatrix} c \\ ch \\ s \end{Bmatrix} \rightarrow \begin{Bmatrix} k \\ kh \\ h \end{Bmatrix} /\_\_\_\,\text{yɨ}\# \qquad (7)$$

References

Chao, Yuan Ren. 1930. "A System of Tone Letters." in *Le Maitre Phonetique XLV*. 1930. 24 - 27.

Hashimoto, Mantaro Joseph. 1970. "Internal Evidence for Ancient Chinese Palatal Endings," *Language* 46.2 1970, Part 1, 336 - 365.

Hsueh. F.S. 1973. "The P'ing-tu Dialect as a Variant of Mandarin," in the *Tsing Hua Journal of Chinese Studies*, n.s. X, No. 1. 1973, 74 - 89.

——. 1975. *Phonology of Old Mandarin*, The Hague.

——. 1977. "Pekingese Phonology Revisited," *paper presented at the Symposium on Chinese Linguistics*, Honolulu. Kawaii. 1977.

——. 1979. "A New Interpretation of the Inner/Outer Contrast in the Rhyme Tables and its Implication of Middle Chinese Phonology," *paper presented at the 12th International Conference on Sino-Tibetan Linguistics*, Paris, 1979.

——. 1980. *Lun rushengzi zhi yanhua guilu* 論入聲字之演化規律, *Papers Presented to Qu Wanli on His Seventieth Birthday* 屈萬里先生七秩榮慶記文集. Taipei. 407 - 433.

Karlgren, Bernhard. 1954. "Compendium of Phonetics in Ancient and Archai Chinese," in the *Bulletin of the Museum of Far Eastern Antiquitie*. 1954. Reprint, 1963.

Li, Rong 李榮. 1956. *Qieyun yinxi*. 切韻音系, Beijing.

——. 1963. *Hanyu fangyan diaocha shouce* 漢語方言調查手册 Beijing.

Luo, Changpei 羅常培, 1931. "Zhi che cheng niang yizhi kao" 知徹澄娘音值考, *shi yu suo jikan* 史語所集刊. Vol. 3. 121 - 157.

Stimson, Hugh M. 1962. "Ancient Chinese -p, -t, -k Endings in the Peking

Dialect," *Language* 38.376 - 384.

Yuan, Jiahua 袁家驊. 1960. *Hanyu fangyan gaiyao* 漢語方言概要 Beijing.

Zhao, Yintang 趙蔭棠. 1936. *Zhongyuanyinyun yanjiu* 中原音韻研究 Shanghai.

音韻史與方言研究:平度話中的幾個例子*

一、緒論

在探索一個語言的音韻史時,我們自然得依賴其後代的各種方言。如果這個語言缺少文獻記載。我們就得全靠其後代的方言,但如果是有文獻記録的(例如漢語),這種對方言的依賴,視文獻記録的多寡,就相對地減少了。漢語史上有好幾本相當完整可靠的韻書,分别代表某一特定的歷史時期,其中一本是元代的《中原音韻》[①]。這本書對於我們特别重要,不僅因爲所記的字數甚多,更關鍵的是,我們有許多理由相信,這是當時漢語"通語"的忠實記録。類似這樣的一本韻書,衹要是全面地記述了該語言當時的字讀差别,我們就可以説,該語言當時的音系就隱含在這本書裏,因此我們的任務就該是,如何用現代音韻學的理論與方法,構擬(更確切地説是"破解")那個隱藏着的音系。然而在構擬時,如果資料不够充分,我們也可能會遇到一些不易確定的情况,這就得靠研析當代方言來幫助解决了。在給《中原音韻》的構擬中,就有這樣一個難以確定的情况。我就在本文裏嘗試説明,這個問題可以借平度話之助,得到合理的解决,另外也將説明,對於早期官話(即《中原音韻》)到現代標準漢語的演變過程,平度話也有助於我們選擇較合理的解釋。至於平度話與《中原音韻》及現代標準漢語之間的差異,本文也將舉例説明,衹有從嚴格的音系角度觀察,才能得到最合理的解釋。

---

* 原載《漢語音韻史十講》,華語教學出版社,1999 年。
本文原爲英文,題爲 Historical Phonology and Dialect Study: Some Examples from the Pingdu Dialect.

① 有關《中原音韻》音系的分析,請參看薛 1975。當時所根據的是趙蔭棠的《中原音韻研究》(商務印書館,1936)。

二、平度音系簡介

平度話是膠東方言的一支。多年前看到袁家驊先生説(袁 1960:24),膠東方言有不少特點,而當時我有一位同學好友恰是平度人,他的口音確實比較特殊,因此引起了我的興趣,便以他爲“發音人”,作了一些頗深入的分析,推證出其音系結構,撮要簡述如下①:

2.1. 平度話的音節也由聲韻調三部分構成。調分爲四,與北京話的四聲相對應,但調值大異,如下述:

第一聲　低平[11]

第二聲　高降[53]

第三聲　中平[33]

第四聲　低降[31]

2.2. 平度話有 21 個聲母(含零聲母),如下表。表内方格中的符號都代表單一聲母,雖然有的是由兩個或三個字母代表的,但不是音位的組合,而是共同代表一個單獨的音位。“r”代表[+捲舌]成分,附屬於其前之輔音;同樣地,“h”代表[+送氣]成分,附屬於其前之輔音,二者都衹在單獨作聲母時代表獨立的音位。我們把這兩個成分由其所屬的“一束區别性特徵”(a bundle of distinctive features)中分離出來,衹是爲了討論歷史音變時的方便而已(參看 Hsueh 1975:29)。

	塞(擦)音(S)		擦音(F)	響音(R)
脣音(B)	p	ph	f	m
舌齒音(Ds)	ť	ťh	θ	
齦前音(D)	t	th		n
齦後音(Gi)	c	ch	s	l
捲舌音(Pr)	cr	crh	sr	
舌根音(G)	k	kh	h	ø

(按:舌齒音 ṫ、ṫh、θ 即國際音標的 tθ、tθ‘、θ)

① 平度話音系的詳細分析,請參看薛 1973,發音人是于宗先博士。

2.3. 平度話的韻母也分爲個三音段(M)V(E),即韻頭(M)、韻腹 V、韻尾(E)。根據韻頭的形態韻母可分爲“開、齊、合、撮”四類,韻腹分别爲高/ɨ/、中/ə/、低/a/三個元音,韻尾分爲五類,除零韻尾外,分别爲/-y,-w,-n,-ŋ/,這都是與北京話一致的,可見平度話與北京話同屬官話,衹是腔調差别很大而已。其 35 個韻母的分布,可按韻頭(直行)及韻尾(横列)列表如下:

E / V / M	ø			y		w		n		ŋ	
	ɨ	ə	a	ɨ	a	ɨ	a	ɨ	a	ɨ	a
ø 開	ɨ	ə	a	ɨy	ay	ɨw	aw	ɨn	an	ɨŋ	yaŋ
y 齊	yɨ	yə	ya		yay	yɨw	yaw	yɨn	yan	yɨŋ	yaŋ
w 合	wɨ	wə	wa	wɨy	way			wɨn	wan	wɨŋ	waŋ
yw 撮	ywɨ	ywə						ywɨn	yawn	ywɨŋ	

三、平度話聲母之特色

平度話的聲母系統與北京話相比,有兩個顯著的差别,分别討論如下:

3.1. 舌齒塞擦音/t̆、t̆h、θ/顯然是平度話最突出的特色。據我所知,未見有人爲哪本韻書作過這樣的構擬,也未見其他方言的報導。因此我們可能直覺地認爲其來源早於“三十六字母”時代。但進一步的觀察可以看出,這個方言的深層音韻結構清楚地顯示,這三個聲母的出現是相當晚近的事。要説明這一點,必須把這一組聲母與齦後音(精系)及捲舌音(照系)一併討論,而且必須隨時提到《切韻》及《中原音韻》。

3.1.1. 這三組聲母在平度話裏的情況,可以概括説明如下:

(a) 聲母爲/t̆、t̆h、θ/的字在北京話裏都分别以/c、ch、s/(即“z、c、s”)爲聲母,在中古音裏都屬精系,即[ʦ、ʦ‘、dz‘、s、z]。

(b) 以捲舌音爲聲母的字,在北京話裏也都以捲舌音爲聲母。在韻圖中這些字多屬二等,聲母屬莊或知組;少數例外屬三等,韻母分别爲/ɨ/(例如:枝 AC [tśjie̯]、DY /cryɨy/、PD /crɨ/),或者是/wɨy/(例如:水 AC [śjwi]、DY

/srwɨy/、PD /srwɨy)，或者是/wɨŋ/(例如：鍾 AC [tśi̯woŋ]、DY /crywɨŋ/、PD /crwɨŋ/)①。

(c) 原屬三等的知系及照系(章組)字，在北京話及平度話裏，都變爲洪音(即丢掉了顎化介音)。但在北京話裏仍讀捲舌，而在平度話裏，聲母分别改讀爲/c、ch、s/(即變入了精系)，例如：知(AC [t̂ji̯e]、DY /tryɨy/、PK /crɨ/、PD /cɨ/)，尺(AC [tś'iäk]、DY /crhyak̂、PK /crhɨ/，PD /chɨ/)。

3.1.2. 上述幾種現象，可以在跟《中原音韻》音系的對應中，得到最合理的解釋。從這個角度看，連 3.1.1b 節中的"例外"，也顯然是平度話自身演變的必然結果了。《切韻》音系中的莊組與章組聲母，很早就合爲一系了，故等韻僅以"照穿牀審禪"代表這兩組聲母。這是由於莊組聲母的細音字變爲洪音(丢掉顎化介音)，而章組聲母原來就衹配細音，所以這兩組就變成"同位音"了。二者容或仍有些發音上的差異，但如果這類細音字(原章類字)後來也變爲洪音，在一般情況下，其聲母所屬的音位應保持不變。這一點可在多數方言中(包括北京話)，得到證明，在稍欠明朗的情况下，也在《中原音韻》中得到證實。在該書所代表的音系中，莊章兩組並爲照系是顯而易見的，而且更進一步，連舌上音"知徹澄"(/tr、trh、trɦ/也已經塞擦化，也已經塞擦化，因而分别併入"照穿牀"(/cr、crh、crɦ/)了。

$$t \rightarrow c/\_\_\_\_r \qquad (1)$$

所以《中原音韻》的/cr、crh、sr、r/四個聲母，涵蓋了《切韻》的知莊章(含日母)三組，原知章兩類聲母的三等字，仍爲細音，但有下述幾項例外：

(a) 原止攝開口字的韻母爲/yɨy/，其照三類字後來丢掉了顎化介音(參看 Hsueh 1975：43)。

$$y \rightarrow ø/pr\_\_\_\_ɨy \qquad (2)$$

這個音變必然發生在公式(1)所代表的音變之前，也必然發生在蟹攝四等字變同止攝字之前(看參 Hsueh 1975：66－69)，因爲"知、尺"(注音見 3.1.1c)這兩

① 本文中所有聲韻母及例字的標音：中古時期(AC，即《切韻》)，采用高本漢的擬音(Karlgren 1954)；等韻時期(DY)，根據薛 1985；《中原音韻》時期(OM)，根據薛 1975；北京音(PK)，根據薛 1986；平度音(PD)，根據薛 1973。

類字，都出現在“齊微”韻裏，而非與“枝”（見3.1.1b）及“齒”（AC［tś‘ji］、DY /crhyɨy/、PK&PD /crhɨ/）等一同出現於“支思”韻中。

（b）原止攝三等合口字的韻母爲/ywɨy/，但在《中原音韻》裏，已與韻母應爲/wɨy/的字（來自蟹攝一等）合流，因此我們相信，這類字在《中原音韻》之前，就變爲洪音了（參看 Hsueh 1975：69－70）。

$$y \rightarrow \varnothing / \_\_\_\_ w\text{ɨ}y \qquad (3)$$

這個變化遍及各類聲母字，自然也包括捲舌音，如“追、水”等（見表二B行）。

（c）通攝三等照系及知系字，韻母本爲/ywɨŋ/，列於二等的照系字，韻母已變爲/wɨŋ/，但在《中原音韻》裏卻列在一起，例如東鍾韻平聲陽内，蟲（DY /trɦywɨŋ/）與崇（DY /crɦwɨŋ/）即同屬一個小韻。這似乎顯示，在捲舌聲母之後，韻母/ywɨŋ/也丢掉了顎化介音①。

$$y \rightarrow \varnothing / pr \_\_\_\_ w\text{ɨ}ŋ \qquad (4)$$

假如這個推論是對的，那麽像“種充戎”等照三聲母字，也都得擬爲洪音了。但是我們實在不敢確定，因爲上例是個孤證。通攝照二系字本來就不多，在《中原音韻》裏，與照三系字收入同一小韻的，就衹有一個“崇”字；更糟的是，同一小韻中，還有“慵、墉”兩個字，其聲母按理應擬爲/sr/或零聲母。要解決這樣的問題，就得參考方言了；平度話在這個問題上，給我們提供了答案。

3.1.3. 舌齒音聲母是平度音系最突出的特點（3.1.1節），現在看來，可以相當肯定地説，是較晚近的音變造成的，可能尚晚於《中原音韻》時代。相關的一些音變可以概括地説明如下：

（a）北京話仍保留着日母/r/，平度話則不然；首先，在韻母爲/ɨ/的音節裏，/r/變爲/l/，然後，在其他音節裏，完全消失。例如：“二”讀爲/lɨ/，“日本人”則讀爲/yɨ、pɨn、yɨn/。

（b）捲舌聲母的細音字變洪音。這個晚於《中原音韻》的音變，在北京話與平度話裏都發生了，但在北京話裏，這個過程很簡單，原來僅以洪細區分的

---

① “東鍾”韻的韻腹，我原擬爲後低母音/o/，但在分析了等韻音系以後，發現原擬不妥，應改爲高母音/ɨ/。（較詳細的説明，可參看魯譯 p.110，追注［3］。）

字,就自然變爲同音字了,而在平度話裏,則較爲複雜。首先,由於聲母/r/已經消失,原日母字因此不受影響,而仍爲細音;其次,當這個音變發生時,聲母中的捲舌成分也隨着介音/y/同時消失,因而變爲精系聲母了;其三,雖然這類字變爲精系字了,但卻未與原精系洪音字合流,而是引起一個連鎖反應,造成原精系洪音字的聲母前移而變爲齒擦塞音/ť、ťh、θ/,這就是平度話中這幾個聲母的來源。

$$\begin{Bmatrix} c \\ ch \\ s \end{Bmatrix} \rightarrow \begin{Bmatrix} \check{t} \\ \check{t}h \\ \theta \end{Bmatrix} / \_\_\_\_ (w)V \qquad (5)$$

$$ry \rightarrow \emptyset \qquad (6)$$

這個連鎖變化當然未影響到原精系細音字。

(c) 聲母原爲照二系的洪音字,在平度話裏仍爲捲舌,這是意料中事,但有些照三聲母字也仍爲捲舌,就是前文公式(2)(3)(4)所討論的幾類字。因爲這幾類字早在《中原音韻》之前就丟掉了顎化介音,所以在平度話裏,不應像其他照三系字一樣讀爲精系字。但公式(4)在《中原音韻》裏衹有一條孤證,那個音變是否早已發生,我們實在不敢確定。現在發現"蟲充鍾"等字,在平度話裏都是捲舌音,而不變爲精系字,可見這類字先已變爲洪音,故不受公式(6)所代表的那個後期音變的影響,因此也就證明在《中原音韻》之前,公式(4)所代表的音變就已發生過了。

(表二)

切韻音	(A)			(B)		(C)	
	枝	知	齒	追	水	蟲	崇
	tśjie̯	t̂jie̯	tś'jï'	t̂jwi	śjwı	d̂'iu̯ŋ	dẓ'iu̯ŋ
等韻音	cryɨy	tryɨy	crhyɨy	trywɨy	srywɨy	trɦywɨŋ	crɦwɨŋ
y→ø/pr____ɨy	crɨy		crhɨy				
y→ø/Cɨ____	crɨ		crhɨ				
t→c/____r		cryɨy		crywɨy		crɦwɨŋ	
y→ø/__wɨy				crwɨy	srwɨy		
y→ø/pr____wɨŋ						crɦwɨŋ	

續表

切韻音	(A)			(B)		(C)	
	枝	知	齒	追	水	蟲	崇
	tśjie̯	t̂jie̯	tś'ji'	t̂jwi	śjwi	d̂'i̯uŋ	dź'i̯uŋ
ZYYY	RG03	RG04	RG03	RG04	RG04	RG01	RG01
y→ø/yɨ____		cryɨ					
rv→ø		crɨ					
Pingdu	crɨ	cɨ	crhɨ	crwɨy	srwɨy	crhwɨŋ	crhwɨŋ
pekingese	crɨ	crɨ	crhɨ	crwɨy	srwɨy	crhwɨŋ	crhwɨŋ

3.2. 所謂"尖音"(聲母屬精系的細音字)與"團音"(聲母爲喉牙音的細音字),在北京話裏已經混同,但在平度話裏仍然分立,衹在韻母爲/yɨ/的音節裏不再區分,例如:"七"(AC [ts'i̯ĕt],DY /chyɨt/)讀/khyɨ/([tɕ'i],與"欺"同),"西"(AC [siei]、DY /syey/)讀/hyi/([ɕi],與"希"同),可見在這個韻母之前,"尖"已變爲"團"了。

$$\begin{Bmatrix} c \\ ch \\ s \end{Bmatrix} \longrightarrow \begin{Bmatrix} k \\ kh \\ h \end{Bmatrix} / \_\_\_ yi\# \qquad (7)$$

表面看來,這衹是一個小問題,但卻牽涉到一個音韻學基本概念的問題:北京話細音字的"尖團混合"究竟是一步達成的呢?還是一個分階段的逐步擴散過程呢?比如説,先在韻母/yɨ/之前混同(像平度話那樣),然後在其他韻母之前逐個地相混。對這個問題,恐怕很難絶對地説是這樣或那樣。當代語言學有兩個基本概念,即所謂"概括性"(generality)與"簡約性"(simplicity),而二者常爲一體之兩面,其意爲:當我們能爲某種語言現象提出兩個都相當圓滿的解釋時,我們就假定那個較簡單的解釋是較妥善的解釋,概括性通常也比較大。由這個觀點看北京話的尖團混合,就不得不説那是個一步完成的過程,但正如適才所説,我們實在不敢斷言這個結論是較爲符合事實的。我不是説,簡約性和概括性是不正確或不必要的,恰恰相反,我認爲在作任何語言的歷時研究時,這兩個概念都是方法學上極重要的原則,是必須遵守的。但我們也必須認識到,這也不是一成不變的,因此在推論音變規律時,如果發現有新材料證明某一規律過寬,就必須隨時作適當的修正。

四、入聲字在平度話裏的演變

中古音的入聲字，在不同的方言中演變也不相同；反過來説，入聲字的不同演變方式正是方言區分的一條極重要的標準。平度話裏，入聲字有下述三個較特殊的演變，是與北京話和《中原音韻》不同的部分原因。

4.1. 前文已經提到(2.1 節)，平度話的四個聲調與北京話的四聲相對應，但入聲改讀爲舒聲後，其聲調分配，與北京話及《中原音韻》都不相同。《中原音韻》裏入聲字的分配如下式(參看薛 1975:32－33)：

$$F^5 \rightarrow \begin{Bmatrix} F^4 / R\_\_\_ \\ F^2 / ɦ\_\_\_ \\ F^3 \end{Bmatrix} \qquad (8)$$

此式意爲：入聲韻母(F)，依聲母的性質“派入三聲”，其條件爲，聲母爲次濁音的(R：鼻音邊音及零聲母)，改讀去聲(F^4)，聲母爲全濁的(含“ɦ”成分者)，改讀陽平(F^2)，其餘皆讀上聲(F^3)。北京話裏前兩類的分配，與此完全相同，例如“木目緑月”等皆讀去聲，“舌”(AC [dźʻiät]，DY /crɦyat/)讀陽平等，但在第三類方面，似乎没有規律，改讀任何一聲的都有。平度話衹在第二類方面，與《中原音韻》及北京話相同，如“舌”讀/se^2/，另兩類則全讀爲陰平，其演變規律顯然比較簡單。

$$F^5 \rightarrow \begin{Bmatrix} F^2 / ɦ\_\_\_ \\ F^1 \end{Bmatrix} \qquad (9)$$

這個演變方式，與其鄰近的青島及濟南話都不一樣(參看李榮 1963:84)，卻與鄭州及徐州等地的中原官話相同(參看袁 1960:29)，頗爲奇特。

4.2. 原屬一等的喉牙音開口入聲字，如“割”(AC [kât]，DY /kot/，OM /ko/，PK /kə/)及“合”(AC [ɣap]，DY /xɦop/，OM /ho/，PK /hə/)等，在平度話裏，韻母皆爲低元音，如“割”讀/ka/，“合”讀/ha/。這是與《中原音韻》和北京話都不一樣的。在《中原音韻》裏，原一等開口字，包括入聲字，絶大多數都與二等字同韻。我曾把這個音變歸納爲下列公式(參看薛 1975:112－3)：

$$o \rightarrow a/C\_\_\_E \qquad (10)$$

(i) $E \neq w$

(ii) 若 $C=G$,則 $E \neq S$.

其意爲:當其前没有/w/介音(即合口字除外)或其後帶有韻(即果攝除外)時,一等字的主要元音變同二等,但另有兩個補充條件:(1) 韻尾不得爲/w/(即效攝除外);(2) 如果聲母是喉牙音,則韻尾不得爲塞音(即喉牙音入聲字除外)。有趣的是,要解釋平度話裏"割合"等入聲字的讀法,祇要把第二條補充條件删去就行了。我特别舉出這個有趣的現象,意在説明,祇要采用嚴格的音系觀點,方言之間的差異,就能很明確地解説清楚。

4.3. 曾梗兩攝各等的陽聲字,在官話方言中已經合韻;這個現象早已反映在《中原音韻》裏,即"庚青"韻,但其入聲字改讀舒聲的方式,卻在不同的方言之間有相當大的差别。要合理地解釋這些差别,也許可以采用音變先後的觀點,即同樣的一組音變規律,以不同的順序發生在不同的方言中。《中原音韻》所反映的是北京話"口語音"的祖語(參看 Hsueh 1975:124-25),爲了解釋這類入聲字在口語音中的演變,我曾提出四個與此有關的音變,其時序爲:

(a) 首先,曾梗兩攝合併爲一個四等俱全的"外轉"攝,即所謂"内外混等",記録在《四聲等子》裏(參看薛 1985)。

$$o \rightarrow a/y\_\_\_ \qquad (11)$$

即曾攝三等字變同梗攝三等,因其韻腹/o/受介音/y/之同化而前移變爲/a/。

(b) 喉牙音二等開口字顎化。這在口語音裏先發生,遍及各攝,自然包括梗攝。

$$o \rightarrow y/G\_\_\_a \qquad (12)$$

因此在口語音裏,"更耕行家江鞋巧"等等,都變爲細音。

(c) 兩攝的入聲字,變爲收噫的舒聲字。

$$\hat{k} \rightarrow y \qquad (13)$$

因此梗攝二等入聲字的韻母,分别變爲/-ay,-way,-yay/,這類字如"麥額客色"等等,就都出現在"皆來"韻裏了。

(d) 兩攝各韻完全混同,構成後來的“庚青”韻,這是受顎化鼻音韻尾同化的結果。

$$\begin{Bmatrix}o\\a\end{Bmatrix} \rightarrow e/\underline{\quad\quad} ɲ \qquad (14)$$

因此“更耕京”等字就變成同音字了。這個變化衹限於陽聲字,因爲相應的入聲字先已變同“蟹攝”,所以後來的這個音變就跟那些字没有關係了。

上述四個音變,在平度話及“讀書音”的歷史上,也都發生過,但發生的時序卻不一樣。公式(14)所代表的音變,顯然早於(12)所代表的音變,先使得梗攝二等字變同四等了,所以當後者發生時,就没能影響到這類字,這是“耕額克”等字在平度話和讀書音裏未變細音的緣故。公式(13)所代表的音變,在平度話裏發生的時代也晚於(14),故“麥白色”之類的二等字,雖也變爲“收噫”,其韻腹則已不是低元音/a/了。在讀書音裏(源自南京話),這類入聲字都未變爲“收噫”,而是與别的入聲字一樣,丢掉了韻尾變爲“直喉”音,可見音變(13)在該方言裏未曾發生過。這幾個音變在這三種話裏所造成的錯綜現象,可由[表三]窺其梗概。有趣的是,衹要把這幾個音變的相對時序作部分更動,就可成功地説明這類字在不同的方言裏的演變過程,也成功地説明了這些方言之間的親疏關係。

切韻音	耕 kɛŋ	京 kiwŋ	麥 mɛk	墨 mək	額 ŋɛk		客 k‘ək		色 ṣiək		
等韻音	kaɲ	kyaɲ	mak̂	mok̂	ŋak̂		khak̂		srak̂		
a→e/y___ ŋ→ø/#___		kyeɲ			ak̂						
ø→y/G___a k̂→y $\begin{Bmatrix}o\\a\end{Bmatrix}$→e/___ɲ	kyaɲ kyeɲ		may	moy	yak yay		khyak khyay		sray	k̂—q /___$\begin{Bmatrix}\hat{k}\\ ɲ\end{Bmatrix}$	/___$\begin{Bmatrix}\hat{k}\\ ɲ\end{Bmatrix}$
$\begin{Bmatrix}o\\e\end{Bmatrix}$→ɨ/___y ay→e/___y (opt.)				mɨy	yay	ye	khyay	khye			
中原音韻	RG15	RG15	RG06	RG04	RG06	RG14	RG06	RG14	RG06		
北京口語音	kyɨŋ	kyɨŋ	may	mɨy		ye		khye	sray		
北京讀書音	kɨŋ	kyɨŋ	mə	mə	ə		khə		sa	Pk—lit.	
平度音	kɨŋ	kyɨŋ	mɨy	mɨy	ɨy		khɨy		srɨy		PD

五、造成平度話與北京話差異的另三個音變

這三個音變都與韻母的差別有關,分條簡述如下:

5.1. 原果攝開口字變爲合口,早在《中原音韻》中已很明顯(參看薛 1975:109－110)。根據該書的記録,可以看出這個音變受限於一個條件,即;聲母爲喉牙音的不變;例如"多"爲 AC [tâ],DY /to/,OM /two/,PK /twɔ/,而"何"則爲 AC [ɣa],DY /xɦo/,OM /ho/,PK /hə/。

$$o \rightarrow w / C\_\_\_ o\# \qquad C \neq G \tag{15}$$

對平度話來說,這個限制條件顯然是不必要的,因爲像"何哥餓"之類的字,都讀合口。事實上,除了在精系聲母之後以外,/ə/(來自早期官話的/o/和/e/)是不能單獨作爲韻母的。我們可以給這個現象提出兩個不同的解釋。一個是假定這是兩步音變的結果,即認爲平度話先亦有(15)式那樣的音變,《中原音韻》時代以後,這類喉牙音字才也變爲合口;另一個是假定這是個一步達成的音變,即認爲早期平度話就發生過這樣一個没有聲母條件的音變,這似乎是較妥善的解釋。至於那些個韻母爲/ə/的精系字,當然跟這條音變無關,而是原捲舌聲母字在更晚的時期改配洪音的結果〔音變公式(6)〕。

5.2. 北京話裏有一個晚近的音變,即與聲母/l-,n-/搭配的韻母/wɨy/,丢掉了介音/w/,例如"雷"(AC [luậi],DY /jwoy/,OM /lwɨy/,PK /lɨy/)及"内"(AC [nuậi],DY /nuoy/,OM /nwɨy/,PK /nɨy/)。這個音變也發生於平度話中,所涉範圍更廣,不限於這兩個聲母,而是除了捲舌音與喉牙音之外的所有聲母,所以"推"(AC [t'uậi],DY /thwoy/,OM /thwɨy/,PK /thwɨy/)讀/thɨy/,"脆"(AC [ts'i̯wäi],DY /chyway/,OM /chwɨy/,PK /chwɨy/)讀/ťhɨy/,餘類推。

5.3. 上節所説的合口字變開口現象,在同樣的條件下,也在平度話裏波及/wɨn/和/wan/這兩個韻母。例如,亂(AC [luân],DY /lwon/,OM /lwon/,PK /lwan/),蒜(AC [suân],DY /swon/,OM /swon/,PK /swan/),孫(AC [suən], DY /swɨn/, OM /swɨn/, PK /swɨn/), 頓(AC [tuən], DY /twɨn/, OM /twɨn/, PK /twɨn/)之類的字,在平度話裏都讀開口。如此看來,這個音變涵蓋的範圍甚廣,即在非捲舌和非喉牙聲母之後,除了韻尾爲舌根音或没有韻尾之外,所有合口韻母都變爲開口。因此我們可以爲平度話建立下面這樣一條功能寬廣的音變規律。

$$w \rightarrow \emptyset / C\_\_\_VE \quad (16)$$

(i) C≠Pr, G;

(ii) E≠ŋ

這個音變發生的時間雖然不會太早,但至少應在公式(6)所代表的音變之前(見3.1.3節),因爲衹有在精系聲母之後,才有幾個韻母爲/wɨn/或/wan/的字,而這些字原來都是因公式(6)由照系字變來的。

六、結論

平度話與其他官話方言之間,尤其是北京話,有不少差異。本文從音韻史的觀點,討論了造成這些差異的主要音變。我們發現,至少在一個情況下,這個方言説明我們解決了一個構擬《中原音韻》時無法確定的難題,在另一個情況下,提出了一個北京話音變過程的疑問。另幾個平度話的音變,雖未因而使我們覺得有改擬《中原音韻》的必要,但其高度的系統規律性,卻增强了我們對前此研究的信心。通過本文的研究,我們可以看出,如果想具體明確地顯示方言間的親疏關係和音位對應規律,本文所使用的系統化推論,應爲一個相當可行的方法。作爲本文的總結,我們可以把相關的音變,按其歷時順序排列出來。《中原音韻》以前的音變,將衹列出與平度話有關的幾條,但《中原音韻》以後的音變,包括在平度話和北京話裏都曾發生而本文未加討論的幾條(即前五條)①,都將一併列出。

《中原音韻》時代以前的音變

① 由《中原音韻》時期到現代北京話的音變,猶待作更深入的探討;在拙著薛1975裏(pp. 135–136),我曾粗略地列出十五條,或可以拿來跟此處變入平度話的九條音變相比較。

（一）$F5 \rightarrow \begin{Bmatrix} F^2/\text{ɦ}\_\_\_ \\ F^1 \end{Bmatrix}$ (9)

（二）$\begin{Bmatrix} o \\ a \end{Bmatrix} \rightarrow e/\begin{Bmatrix} \hat{k} \\ \text{ɲ} \end{Bmatrix}$ (14)

（三）$\hat{k} \rightarrow y$ (13)

（四）$ø \rightarrow y/G\_\_\_a$ (12)

（五）$o \rightarrow a/C\_\_\_E$ (10)

（七）$ø \rightarrow w/C\_\_\_o\#$ (15)

《中原音韻》時代以後平度話的演變

（一）$\begin{Bmatrix} \text{ŋ} \\ v \end{Bmatrix} \rightarrow ø/\#\_\_\_$

（二）$m \rightarrow n/\_\_\_\#$

（三）$\begin{Bmatrix} e \\ o \end{Bmatrix} \rightarrow a/\_\_\_\begin{Bmatrix} n \\ w \end{Bmatrix}$

（四）$y \rightarrow ø/y\text{ɨ}\_\_\_$

（五）$\begin{Bmatrix} e \\ o \end{Bmatrix} \rightarrow \text{ɔ}/\#\_\_\_$

（六）$w \rightarrow ø/C\_\_\_VE$ (16)

1）$C \neq Pr, G$；

2）$E \neq \text{ŋ}$.

（七）$\begin{Bmatrix} c \\ ch \\ s \end{Bmatrix} \rightarrow \begin{Bmatrix} \breve{t} \\ \breve{t}h \\ \theta \end{Bmatrix} /\_\_\_(w)V$ (5)

（八）$ry \rightarrow ø$ (6)

（九）$\begin{Bmatrix} c \\ ch \\ s \end{Bmatrix} \rightarrow \begin{Bmatrix} k \\ kh \\ h \end{Bmatrix} /\_\_\_y\text{ɨ}\#$ (7)

The Ping-tu Dialect as a Variant of Mandarin **

0.1. In the most comprehensive work on Chinese dialectology published so far, *Hanyu Fangyan Gaiyao*, its author said, concerning North Mandarin, that of the numerous subdialects of this dialect area, those of the Shantung peninsula and the coastal areas of the Liaotung peninsula show a number of peculiar characteristics (when compared with Pekingese, the standard speech)①. However, to my knowledge, very few investigations on the dialects spoken in this densely populated area have been published either in China or in the West②. Consequently, it is not yet clear to what extent the dialects of this area are different from (or similar to) Pekingese Mandarin, nor do we know what justification there may be for grouping them together as variants of the same dialect area generally called the Chiāo-tūng dialect. A study of any dialect of this area is thus not unwarranted.

0.2. In addition to the reason given above, there are at least two others which are more directly responsible for arousing my interest in this group of dialects. When I first met my informant, I was immediately drawn by the amusingly peculiar nature of his speech. It is clearly different from Pekingese, and yet it seems to be fairly intelligible to speakers of Pekingese

---

** 中文題爲《論平度方音中之官話成分》,原刊《清華學報》1973 年第十卷第一期。
本文寫作得到美國俄亥俄州立大學發展基金的資助。

① Yüán Chiā-huá: *Hanyu Fangyan Gaiyao*, 1960, Peking, p. 24.

② Yüán Chiā-huá mentioned a study on the P'éng-lái dialect by Pào Míng-wěi (op. cit., p. 31). He also mentioned some aspects of the I-hsièn dialect (p. 40) and the Wén-tēng dialect (p. 41) without giving the sources of the information. There is also one report in English on a subdialect of this area. Gerty Kallgren: "Notes on the Kiaohsien Dialect", *Bulletin of the Museum of Far Eastern Antiquities* 27(1955), pp. 11-40.

who have had a fair exposure to other forms of Mandarin. It also happened that at the time of our meeting. I was studying a late Ming dynasty rime dictionary, *Yǜn-lüèh Huì-t'ūng*① which contains some peculiar features not readily explainable to me at that time. Since the compiler of the dictonary, Pì Kŭngch'en, was from I-hsièn of the Shan-tung peninsula, and since it has been a common habit for some modern scholars in their study of historical Chinese to blame the compiler of any rime dictionary, whenever there appears something seemingly inexplicable, for carelessly or subconsciously entering some features of his own non-standard dialect into his book, I felt then that a study of the dialect of P'íng-tù which is not far from I-hsièn may help us to solve some of the puzzles in the above-mentioned rime dictionary, or it least to clarify the matter.

0.3. The present study of the P'íng-tù dialect (PT) is based almost entirely on the Speech of Dr. Yǘ Tzūng-shiān, a research fellow of the Institute of Economics, Academia Sinica (Taipei), though I have also made some random checks with one person from Chū-ch'éng and another from Jìh-chào, both to the southwest of P'íng-tù. I was told by these people that PT is fairly close to the Tsingtao dialect, but clearly distinct from that of Wén-tēng to the east and that of wéi-hsièn to the west. Obviously, a great deal of research will have to be done before we know how to classify dialects of this area②. As to the dialect or dialects of the Liaotung peninsula, I know practically nothing, nor have I read any report about them, though presumably they must be fairly closely related to those of the Shan-tung peninsula, thanks to large scale migration.

---

① Pì Kŭng-ch'én: *Yǜn-lüèh Huì-t'ūng*, A. D. 1642. Reprint 1963, Taipei.

② My informants suggest that the peninsula should be divided into at least four subdialectal areas: the east, with Yēn-t'ái as its center; the central, which includes P'íng-tù and Tsingtao; the northwest, with Wéi-hsièn as its center; and the southwest, including Chu-ch'éng and Jìh-chào. However, judging by the fragmentary knowledge we have (see 5.1), I am rather skeptical of this suggestion.

0.4. In this study, I shall follow as much as possible the tradition of phonological study in China, partly because, for all practical purposes, the approach has worked unusually well, but more importantly, because this approach will make the present study more usable when it is compared with studies of other Chinese dialects done by other scholars. This means that the present study will concentrate on the three essential components in a Chinese monosyllable: the tone, the initial consonant, and the syllabic final. Intonations and morphophonemic changes will by and large be left untouched.

1. The tones

In dealing with the problems of tones in the numerous Chinese dialects, the five-degree scale designed by Dr. Y.R. Chao has been widely adopted.① The scale has four intervals divided by five points represented each by a numeral: [1] for low, [2] for lower-mid, [3] for mid, [4] for higher-mid, and [5] for high. Any tone can thus be sufficiently identified, if not precisely described, by mentioning its starting and ending pitches, or, in the case of a circumflex tone, its turning point, too. Like Pekingese, PT has also four tones which can be described as follows:

1st tone: low level	[11]	[in^{11}] "cause"
2nd tone: high falling	[53]	[in^{53}] "a person"
3rd tone: mid level	[33]	[in^{33}] "to drink"
4th tone: low falling	[31]	[in^{31}] "to print"

1.1. The first tone has a variant form which can be represented by [112]. It occurs when a first tone syllable receives extra stress, either when it appears in a sequence of syllables or in isolation. The second tone has

① Y R Chao: "A System of Tone Letters," *Le Maitre Phonétique* XLV (1930), pp. 24 - 27.

clearly a sandhi form which can be identified as [55]. It occurs to any second tone word when it appears before another second tone word, provided that the syllable sequence is uttered with a reasonably fast tempo; for example, the first syllable in the term *jén min* [in^{55} min^{53}] "people". However, unlike the case in Pekingese, neither of the two sandhi forms will cause any misidentification, as they do not constitute a change from one toneme to another. The other two tones seem to be fairly stable in all instances where they occur. In addition to the four tones, one more may be needed. It occurs with unstressed syllables and can thus be called "unstressed" or "weak" tone. A word belonging to any one of the four tonal categories mentioned above can be realized in this way when it receives weak stress.

1.2. The correspondence between the tones of this dialect and those of Pekingese is very neat. In fact, this is why we have chosen to label the tones of PT the way we do. So the first tone in PT will also be the first tone in Pekingese, etc. However, two things must be kept in mind. First, though labeled in the same way and corresponding to each other, a tone in PT may be phonetically realized in a drastically different way from its counterpart in Pekingese. For example, the first tone is realized as [11] in PT but [55] in Pekingese. Secondly, though words of a certain tone in one dialect belong for the most part to the corresponding tone in the other dialect, there does exist a sizable number of exceptions, especially with regard to the so-called entering tone words in Ancient Chinese.

2. The initials

Following the traditional practice, the segmental elements of a syllable can be divided first into two parts, the initial, that is, the consonantal segment (not including semivowels) which initiates a syllable, and the final which is the rest of the syllable after the initial. When a syllable starts with a vowel or a semivowel, technically it will be said to have a "zero initial," and the whole syllable will thus be identical to its final. Altogether twenty-five consonantal units in the initial position (except the "zero initial") are found in PT.①

Labials:	p	pʻ	f	m	
Dental sibilants:	tθ	tθʻ	θ		
Dental stops:	t	tʻ			
Alveolars:	ʦ	ʦʻ	s		l
Retroflexes:	ṭṣ	ṭṣʻ	ṣ		
Palatals:	ʨ	ʨʻ	ɕ	ȵ	
Velars:	k	kʻ	x	ŋ	

2.1. The labials [p, pʻ, m, f] and the dental stops [t, tʻ] are roughly the same both in quality and in behavior as their counterparts in Pekingese. When they occur before [i], they show a slight tendency of palatalization. Though the tendency is somewhat stronger in PT than in Pekingese, it does not consist of a phonemic distinction. We thus have to recognize only six distinctive initials.

2.2. [n] and [ȵ] should be treated as allophones as the same phoneme, because the latter occurs only before [i] and [y] while the former never occurs before them. Both for being phonetically similar and for being in complementary distribution, they stand for a single phoneme which shall be written as /n/. Since [ŋ], like [n], does not occur before [i] and [y] either, and is thus also in complementary distribution with [ȵ], it may seem that it is equally desirable to group [ŋ] and [ȵ] together as members of one

① The phonetic symbols used in this paper are those of the IPA system taken from Yuan Chiāhuá (op. cit., p. 7), except that, for typographical convenience, I use [ṭṣ, ṭṣʻ, ṣ] for the retroflex sibilants.

phoneme①. However, the feeling of the native speakers works strongly against this alternative solution. When comparing PT with other dialects where [ȵ] does not exist, for example, Pekingese, we find that words with [n] as their initial in PT correspond only to words with the initial [n] in the other dialects. Hence, for a meaningful comparative study, it is also obligatory to group [n] and [ȵ] together. [ŋ] as an initial in PT is actually very limited in its distribution. It occurs only immediately before a relatively low vowel in a stressed syllable. Such syllables always correspond to syllables with a comparable final but with zero initial in Pekingese, for example, the word *an* "peace"(PK [æn]) is pronounced [ŋæn] in PT. Indeed, speakers of PT are often not aware of the existence of this initial. Given syllables like [ei] or [ɑu], they would reproduce them automatically with [ŋ] as the initial. However, in one case at least, [ŋ] as an initial does contrast with zero initial. The word *ēn* "favor"(PK [ən]) is pronounced [ŋən] in PT, while [ən] as an interjection meaning "yes" also exists in the dialect. The same interjection can also occur in the form [əŋ], but because [ŋəŋ] is not a syllable with meaning, the constrast is accidentally lost there. It may seem that [ŋ] and zero are thus not in complementary distribution in the initial position, and therefore cannot be phonemicized as members of one unit, but both because interjections sometimes exist beyond the limits of the phonemic system of a language, and because the contrast is so marginal, I still think it reasonable to treat the two elements as allophones of one phoneme, i.e., to leave out the [ŋ] unmarked in a phonemic transcription, though this will create a unique case where "zero phoneme" has a non-zero allophone.

2.3. The three sibilant series [tθ, tθ‘, θ], [ʦ, ʦ‘, s], and [tṣ, tṣ‘, ṣ] are clearly distinct from one another phonemically, as can be seen from the

① There is nothing unusual in grouping [ȵ] and [ŋ] together as allophones of one phoneme. For example, in Hakka, this is exactly what has to be done. Cf. Yüán, op. cit., p. 150.

following contrast：

a) *tzū* "wealth" [tθɿ] vs. *chīh* "to know" [tsɿ] vs. *chīh* "branch" [tṣʅ].

b) *ts'án* "cruel" [tθ'æn] vs. *ch'án* "to wrap" [ts'æn] vs，*ch'án* "greedy" [tṣ'æn].

c) *sāo* "bewitching" [θɑu] vs. *shāo* "to burn" [sɑu] vs *shāo* "top (of a tree)" [ʂɑu].

Consequently，they should all be established as separate phonemes. In order to stress the fact that phonemically all initials are unit sounds (in contrast to clusters)，as well as for typographical convenience，they shall be rewritten as follows respectively：/ť，ť'，θ/，/c，c'，s/，and /č，č'，š/①. The dental series is a very unique one，because，as far as I know，it has never been reported for any Chinese dialect. But since the series also exists in the speech of the person from Chū-Ch'éng and the one from Jìh-chào，I suspect it may be one of the common characteristics of the Chiaotung group of dialects. Of these three series of sibilants /c，c'，s/ is the only one which can occur before [i] and [y]. /l/，clearly a separate phoneme，is listed here with /c，c'，s/，instead of with /t，t'，n/ as is done in most studies of Pekingese phonology，because，(a) like the sibilants，it occurs before the so-called "apical vowel" (e.g.，*èr* "two" [lɿ]，but see also Note 12 in 3.1)，and (b) like /c，c'，s/ in particular，it also occurs before [i] and [y].

2.4. As in Pekingese，the palatals [tɕ，tɕ'，ɕ] in PT occur only before [i] and [y]，while the velars (or gutturals) do not occur there②. It is thus

---

① We may also follow Hartman (Lawton M. Hartman Ⅲ："Segmental Phonemes of the Peiping Dialect，" *Language* 20 (1944)，pp. 28 - 12. Also in Martin Joos' *Readings in Linguistics*. pp. 116 - 23) in analyzing /č，č'，š/ as /c，c'，s/ followed by /r/，but we must keep in mind that /r/ in such a treatment can only be regarded as a symbol for the distinctive feature "retroflexion，" instead of a separate phoneme. (Cf. F. S. Hsueh：*Phonology of Old Mandarin：a Structuralistic Approach*，Ph. D. dissertation，Indiana University，1968，p. 38) Moreover，the desirability of such a treatment for PT where /r/ is not needed as an initial is even more questionable than for Pekingese.

② Cf. Hartman，op. cit..

possible and reasonable to regard them as allophones of a single series of phonemes, especially when, unlike the case in Pekingese, /c, c', s/ also occur before [i] and [y] and are thus in contrast with [tɕ, tɕ', ɕ]. However, the situation is somewhat confounded by the fact that both the dental sibilants and the retroflexes are also in complementary distribution with the palatals, as they do not occur before [i] and [y] either. Consequently, no matter which one of the three possible series we choose to group together with the palatals, we must give our reasons to support our choice. I think the choice should be the velars, because (a) in point of articulation, the dental sibilants and the palatals are separated by several intermediate series and hence show very little phonetic similarity to each other, (b) to the native speakers, the palatals are closer to the velars than to the retroflexes, though foreign speakers may feel the opposite, and (c) in historical development, the palatals came almost exclusively from the same source as the velars, with practically noing to do with the retroflexes. We shall denote this series of phonemes /k, k', h/.

2.5. To sum up our discussion on the initials, we can now rewrite them phonemically as follows. For typographical convenience, we shall use /h/ to replace the aspiration mark. No confusion will arise, as it stands for an independent initial phoneme only when it is not preceded by another consonant.

Labials:	p	ph	f	m
Dental sibilants:	ť	ťh	θ	
Dental stops:	t	th		n
Alveolars:	c	ch	s	l
Retroflexes:	č	čh	š	
Gutturals:	k	kh	h	(ø)

3. The finals.

There are thirty-six distinctive syllabic finals in PT. They are listed here in five groups corresponding approximately to the height of tongue with which they are pronounced.

Ⅰ. [-ɿ, -ʅ, -i, -u, -y, -in, -yn, -iŋ, -yuŋ]

Ⅱ. [-ei, -uei, -ou, -iou, -ən, -uən, -əŋ, -uəŋ]

Ⅲ. [-ʌ, -uʌ, -iᴇ, -yᴇ]

Ⅳ. [-æi, -iɛi, uæi, -æn, -iɛn, -uæn, -yæn]

Ⅴ. [-a, ia, -ua, -au, -iau, -ɑŋ, -iɑŋ, -uɑŋ]

In analyzing these finals into phonemic elements, we shall again follow the traditional approach. This approach recognizes a nuclear vowel (*yǜn-fù*) for each final. In addition to the nucleus, a final may or may not have a syllabic ending (*yǜn-wěi*) which follows the nucleus and/or a medial (*chièh-yīn* or *yǜn-t'óu*) which precedes the nucleus. The medial, as can be seen from the transcription of the finals given above, appears in one of the three forms [-i-,-u-,-y-] These elements are by nature a kind of on-glide and represent respectively palatalization, labialization and palato-labialization. Since the last element [y] shows the characteristics of both palatalization and labialization, it can be analyzed into the combination [iu][1]. To emphasize the fact that they are by nature different from the nuclear vowels, we shall use /j/ for [i], /w/ for [u], and /jw/ for [iu](i. e., [y]). Depending on what form the medial assumes, or the absence of it, finals (hence, syllables) have been categorized into four types, called "four exhalations" (*szù-hū*) in

---

[1] Cf. Y. R. Chao: *Mandarin Primer*, Cambridge, Mass., 1948, p. 24, and Hartman, op. cit. p. 118.

Chinese[①]. As to the syllabic ending in this dialect, clearly four elements can occur in that position, namely, [-i, -u, -n, -ŋ]. Phonemically, they will be transcribed /-j, -w, -n, - ŋ/.

3.1. Applying the above-mentioned analysis to the five finals [ɿ, ʅ, i, u, y] in the first group will lead us to the same conclusion as Hartman did in his study of Pekingese. Since [ɿ] occurs only after /ť, ťh, θ/ and /c, ch, s, l/[②], while [ʅ] occurs only after /č, čh, š/, they can be recognized as members of a high vowel phoneme /ɨ/. [i, u, y] can then be phonemicized /jɨ, wɨ, jwɨ/ respectively. For convenience, the four finals with nasal endings in the first group will be discussed in the following section.

3.2. There are three vowels in the finals of the second group, namely, [e, o, ə]. They are obviously in complementary distribution, with [e] occuring before [i] (/j/), [o] before [u] (/w/) and [ə] before the nasals. We can thus establish a phoneme /e/. The two vowels [ʌ] and [E] in the third group are also in complementary distribution with each other, as the latter occurs after [i] (/j/) and [y] (/jw/) while the former does not. Furthermore, they can be recognized as members of the same phoneme with the three vowels of the second group, because the latter only occur before a syllable ending while the former do not. The four finals with nasal endings in the first group can apparently be phonemicized with the high vowel /ɨ/ as their nucleus. But our suspicion will be aroused when we notice that they are, as far as the medial is concerned, in complementary distribution with their

① In terms of distinctive features, the four types can be represented as [−pal, −lab], [+pal, −lab], [−pal, +lab], and [+pal, +lab], where pal = palatalization and lab = labialization.

② Following the Karlgren tradition, I recognize two "apical vowels" here, the front one [ɿ] occurring after/c, ch, s/and the back one [ʅ] occurring after /č, č‘, š/. I have marked the apical vowel after /ť, ťh, θ/ and that after /l/ as being also [ɿ], but frankly, I am not sure of this. To those with ultrasensitive ears, perhaps a different symbol will be needed after each different type of initials.

counterparts in the second group, namely, [ən, uən] and [əŋ, uəŋ]. The strict structural pattern requires that the four finals [ən, in, uən, yn] must share the same nucleus. The same saying is also true with the four finals [əŋ, iŋ, uəŋ, yuŋ]. Indeed, this is how the native speakers of this language feel, for they always rime words like *lín* "woods"[lin^{53}] and *lún* "wheel" [luən^{53}] together and words like *yìng* "hard" [iŋ^{51}] and *tùng* "to move" [tuəŋ^{51}] together. The question is whether we are going to identify their nucleus as /ɨ/ or as /e/, or to put it differently, whether we are going to associate the finals of the second group with those of the third group or with those of the first group as having the same nucleus. This is not an easy question to answer at this moment, but one thing is clear that it is obligatory to interpret the finals [ən, uən, in, yn] or [əŋ, uəŋ, iŋ, yuŋ] as sharing the same nucleus①.

3.3. Finals in Group Ⅳ and Group Ⅴ can be easily phonemicized as sharing the same nucleus which we may call the low vowel /a/. The distribution of its allophones is as follows: [ɛ] after /j/ and before /j/ or /n/, /æ/ before /j/ or /n/ but not immediately preceded by /j/, [ɑ] before /w/ or /ŋ/, [a] before zero ending (or syllable boundary). It is now clear that the vowel system of PT as we set up here is identical to that of Pekingese. There are only three vowels: /ɨ/, /e/, and /a/, differentiated by the sole feature of tongue-height, though in phonetic realization, they may appear to be either front or back, under the assimilating influence primarily of the syllable ending, but sometimes of the medial, too. The question

① The same problem exists in Pekingese, too. Hartman argues that two different vowel should be recognized for the four finals in each set discussed here, because "there is a clear-cut distinction of vowel quality."(Hartman, op. cit., p. 122). Studies after his have generally come to the agreement that only one vowel can be recognized for such finals, though whether such a vowel is high or middle is still in dispute. See, for example, Mantaro J. Hashimoto: "Notes on Mandarin Phonology," in R. Jakobson and S. Kawamoto's (ed.) *Studies in General and Oriental Linguistics*, Tokyo, 1970, pp. 207 - 220, and Hugh M. Stimson: *The Jongyuan In Yunn*, New Haven, Conn., 1966, pp. 15 - 16.

whether the nuclear vowel of the finals [ən, uən, in, yn] and that of [əŋ, uəŋ, iŋ, yuŋ] should be interpreted as high vowel /ɨ/ or middle vowel /e/ can now be answered. As we have said in the last secton, either choice will be descriptively (or rather transcriptively) adequate. The question is thus purely theoretical in nature, and as such, we would propose to choose /e/. The reason is that since there are only three vowel phonemes differentiated by tongue-height, the choice we propose will make better sense structurally. By so doing, we shall be able to make a strong generalization that /e/ and /a/ as a group ([-high]) can combine with all syllable endings while /ɨ/([+high]) does not with any. The peculiar nature of the high vowel will thus be unequivocally specified. The other choice would make the middle vowel the one that does not combine with syllable endings, and consequently the above claim would be lost.

3.4. To sum up our discussion on the syllabic finals, we may restate the following points.

a) There are two semivowels, /j/ and /w/, which can occur both in the medial and in the ending positions.

b) In addition to the two semivowels, the two nasals /n/ and /ŋ/ can also occur in the ending slot.

c) There are only three nuclear vowels, high /ɨ/, mid /e/, and low /a/.

d) The finals in their phonemic form may be rearranged in a chart as follows.

E / V / M	ø			j		w		n		ŋ	
	ɨ	e	a	e	a	e	a	e	a	e	a
ø	ɨ	e	a	ej	aj	ew	aw	en	an	eŋ	aŋ
j	jɨ	je	ja		jaj	jew	jaw	jen	jan	jeŋ	jaŋ
w	wɨ	we	wa	wej	waj			wen	wan	weŋ	waŋ
jw	jwɨ	jwe						jwen	jwan	jweŋ	

In addition to the finals already discussed, there are, as in Pekingese, a number of "retroflexed finals," i. e., finals with [r] as their ending. The best way to handle this [r] in PT, a noun suffix, is, I believe, to treat it as an allophone of the phoneme /l/. I have not included these finals in our discussion for two reasons. First, I have not, frankly, spent enough time on this aspect of the dialect. Secondly but more importantly, since practically all the retroflexed finals can be derived from the ordinary finals we have discussed by a set of simple rules, I think they should be treated as a phenomenon on the morphophonemic level, so that the basic phonological analysis will not have to be unduely complicated. The derivational rules in this dialect are for the most part comparable to those in Pekingese, for example, syllable ending /n/ will disappear when the suffix [r] is added. However, two differences have been noticed. First, unlike Pekingese, where the ending /r/ often appears phonetically as nothing but a simultaneous retroflexion with the nuclear vowel, PT shows clearly an additional [r] at the end of a retroflexed syllable which may even appear as a rolling [r]. Second, when a palatalized final (i. e., a final with /j/ in the medial position) takes the suffix [r], it loses its palatalization. For example, *tièn* "shop" /tjan/, when taking the suffix [r], becomes [tɛrr^{31}]. Consequently, [t'ɑurr^{53}] may mean "a note"(*t'iáo-er* /thjaw+l/) or "peach"(*t'áo-er* /thaw+l/).

In PT, as in Pekingese and Old Mandarin, the labial initials also behave in a peculiar way. It may be said that they phonemically combine only with finals which have either /j/ or nothing in the medial position, or it may be said that they combine only with finals which must have either /w/ or /j/, but not both, as their medial. My argument that structurally the latter alternative is better also suits PT very well①.

① Cf. Hsueh, op., cit., pp. 78 - 79.

4.

After we have determined the phonemic structure of the dialect, it is now possible to discuss the various aspects of its historical development and to compare it with other Chinese dialects, particularly, Pekingese. First of all, the question whether PT is a Mandarin dialect ought to be answered. A proper answer to this question should, of course, be in terms of the linguistic structure of the dialect, rather than its geographical location. Purely for the purpose of classifying the numerous Chinese dialects, I have drafted a check list of ten points. It is my hope that this check list can help us determine explicitly in linguistic terms if a Chinese dialect is a form of Mandarin, and, if so, which subgroup of Mandarin dialects it belongs to. The following is the list with its ten points arranged in what I believe to be an historical order①. It must be remembered that this list is still tentative in nature. I shall not attempt to explain here how such a list is arrived at, as it involves too many things to be discussed within the scope of the present paper.

i. The change of the rising tone syllables with voiced stop or fricative initials to the going tone.

ii. The split of the even tone into two and the subsequent devoicing of the initial stops and sibilants.

iii. The acquisition of medial /j/ by the unrounded syllables of the second division with guttural initials.

iv. The complete coalescence of the *kěng-shè* and the *tsēng-shè*.

v. The emergence of the final (C) ɨ#. (i.e, the *chīh-szū* rime.)

vi. The disappearing of the entering tone.

---

① Cf. Hsueh, op., pp. 234 - 36 and 249. The list has also been briefly discussed and applied in my (co-authored with Professor John C. Wang) "The Lin-ch'i Dialect and its Relation to Mandarin." (To appear *in the Journal of American Oriental Society*.)

vii. The merging of /m/ with /n/ as syllable ending.

viii. The loss of medial /j/ in finals after all retroflex initials.

ix. The emergence of syllables with /r/(or /l/) as their ending.

x. The merger of /c, ch, s/ with /k, kh, h/ respectively before palatalized finals.

When we examine PT with the above list, we shall find it passes all the checks there except the last one (x). Nothing has to be said about its passing (ii), (v), (vi), (vii), (viii), and (ix), as these points are already clear from our description of the dialect. However, a few examples are perhaps needed to illustrate that it passes (i), (iii), and (iv), too. We believe it passes (i), because rising tone words in Ancient Chinese like *hàn* "drought" (AC [ɣân], PT /han/)[①] and *chìng* "quiet" (AC [dz' iäŋ], PT /cjeŋ/) are now pronounced with the fourth tone in PT. It passes (iii), for words like *chiēn* "disloyal" (AC [kan], PT /kjan/) and *hsiáng* "to surrender" (AC [ɣâŋ], PT /hjaŋ/) are now pronounced with medial /j/. As in Pekingese, the *kēng-shè* and the *tsēng-shè* have not only coalesced, but have been joined by the *t'ūng-shè* in forming a single rime group, as is evident from the reading of the following words: *kēng* "to plow" (AC [kɛŋ], PT /keŋ/), *sēng* "a monk" (AC [səŋ], PT /θeŋ/), and *tūng* "winter" (AC [tuoŋ], PT /tweŋ/). The fact that PT passes easily nine out of the ten checks and fails at only one which is probably the least relevant of them all should be taken as evidence that it is closely related to such a typical Mandarin dialect as Pekingese. In other words, it not only qualifies as a Mandarin dialect, but belongs to the same subgroup of dialects as Pekingese does, namely, North Mandarin. This does not mean, however, that PT is very similar to Pekingese. In fact, there are so many differences as to make the two dialects almost mutually

① Phonetic transcriptions for Ancient Chinese (AC) used in this paper are based on Bernhard Karlgren's *Compendium of Phonetics in Ancient and Archaic Chinese*, *BMFEA* 1954. Reprint, 1963.

unintelligible. A detailed discussion of these differences and their historical implications does not seem to be quite proper here, as it would make the present article somewhat too lengthy. I, therefore, shall do this in a separate paper①. Suffice it to say here, perhaps, that most of the differences between PT and Pekingese can be traced back to the near past, well after the formation of the so-called Mandarin language as recorded in the rime dictionary *Chūng-yüán Yīn-yün*.

5. A few remarks can be added here as a summing up to our study of this dialect.

5.1. I started with the belief that PT is only a subform of a Mandarin dialect called "The Chiaotung Dialect" which is spoken in the Shantung peninsula and part of the Liaotung peninsula. For the various forms of speech of this area to be grouped together as one dialect, there certainly must be some clear signs of internal and systematic features shared by them all. This, however, does not seem to be the case. Studies on the dialects of this area are still too few to give us a clear picture. Following are some fragmentary information available to us.

a) The I-hsien dialect to the north of PT is reported to have surprisingly only three tones: the first (yīn-p'íng), the second (yáng-p'íng), and the third (shǎng-shēng). It is said that words having the going tone (ch'ǜ-shēng) in Ancient Chinese (presumably the entering tone words, too) are now distributed among the three existing tones②.

---

① The problems mentioned here have been dealt with in a paper under the title "Impact of Dialect Study on Historical Linguistics: Some Examples from the P'ing-tu Dialect" which was presented in the 4th International Conference of Sino-Tibetan Linguistics (held at Indiana University, Oct., 1971).

② Cf. Yüán, op. cit., p. 40. Yüán, however, failed to mention how the information was obtained.

b) The Kiaohsièn dialect is reported to have also only three tones which are, however, quite different from those of the I-hsièn dialect. Its "even tone" corresponds to the first tone (yīn-p'íng) of PT, its "rising tone" comprises words with the second (yáng-p'íng) or the third tone (shǎng-shēng) in PT, and its "falling tone" corresponds to the fourth tone (ch'ǜ-shēng) of PT. Words with the entering tone in Ancient Chinese are distributed among the three tones in more or less the same way as they are in Pekingese①.

c) The speech of P'éng-lái, a coast town to the northeast of P'íng-tù, is reported to show a unique characteristics in its initial system. In most modern dialects, the contrast between the initials /c, ch, s/ and /k, kh, h/ in palatalized syllables is either maintained (as in PT) or lost (as in Pekingese), but in the P'éng-lái dialect, the former has joined the retroflex series in the form [tʃ, tʃ', ʃ], contrasting to [c, c', ç] (i.e., /k, kh, h/) in palatalized syllables②.

In light of these reports, one cannot but wonder what common ground there might be for grouping these dialects together as subdialects of the so-called Chiaotung dialect. Clearly, more research will have to be conducted before we can justify this categorization.

5.2. As I have said at the outset of this paper that one of the reasons to choose this particular dialect for study is to see whether the rime dictionary *Yǜn-lüèh Huì-t'ūng* was indeed influenced in any significant way by the native tongue of its compiler, if not intended to represent it exclusively. A detailed discussion cannot be given here, but for those who have some knowledge of the book, it must now be pretty clear that the phonological

---

① Cf. Kallgren, op. cit, pp. 30-32. Quite uncharacteristically, Kallgren said nothing about the phonetic value of the three tones.

② Cf. Yüán, op. cit., p. 31. The information is obtained from a study of the dialect by Pào Míng-wěi.

system represented by the book is quite different from that of PT. From the fragmentary information we have about the dialect of I-hsièn where the compiler was born, it seems that the relation between the book and that dialect is even farther apart, as the latter has only three tones (see 5.1b). A good lesson we can draw from this is that when we study any rime dictionary, we should never brush aside prematurely any facts contained in that book, no matter how unlikely they may seem to be. Only by trying to explain in phonological terms all these facts can we ever hope to gain some meaningful knowledge about the historical development of the Chinese language.

5.3. It has been said that a Mandarin speaker from Manchuria and Mandarin speaker from Yünnan can converse freely, each in his own dialect①. While this remark is true, it is also somewhat misleading, if it is intended to show the uniformity of the numerous Mandarin dialects. In the first place, the two areas mentioned above were developed rather late in Chinese history, and hence tend to have a more uniform language. The Mandarin dialects spoken in areas between these two extremes often differ from one another much more drastically. Secondly, the close relationship among the numerous Mandarin dialects seems to be a matter of phonemic correspondence, rather than close phonetic similarity. This can be seen from the fact that speakers of different Mandarin dialects often have difficulty in understanding each other at the beginning but improve their mutual intelligibility marvelously fast. It may be argued that this is mostly because they have gradually grasped the corresponding rules between their dialects, often unconsciously, not because they have succeeded in imitating each other's speech.

Only when two modern dialects have been analyzed in a strictly

---

① Cf. Y.R. Chao: *Mandarin Primer*, Cambridge, Mass., 1948, p.7; and Yüán, op. cit, p.23. (Charts of Sylables with nonpalatalized and palatalized finals, on pp. 15, 16)

structural model can we possibly display in a meaningful way the phonemic correspondence between them and state in unequivocal terms how these dialects are related to each other, and in what specific ways they differ from each other. The quasiphonetic approach has not proved itself sound enough to achieve this goal. It is to be hoped that the day will come soon when a reasonably large number of Chinese dialects have been analyzed in this model so that the foundation of systematic dialectology can be firmly established.

The Ohio State University

Glossary of Romanized Terms

ān 安
ch'án 纏,饞
Chiao-tung 膠東
chièh-yīn 介音
chiēn 奸
chīh 知,支
jén-mín 人民
Jìh-chào 日照
kēng 耕
kēng-shè 梗攝
Kiaohsien 膠縣
Liaotung 遼東
chīh-szū 支思
chìng 静
Chū-ch'éng 諸城
ch'ù-shēng 去聲
Chūng-yüán Yin yǜn 中原音韻
ēn 恩,嗯
èr 二
hàn 旱
Hanyu Fangyan Gaiyao 漢語方言概要
Hsiáng 降
I-hsièn 掖縣
lín 林
lún 輪
p'éng-lái 蓬萊
pì kǔng-ch'én 畢拱辰
P'íng-tù 平度
sāo 騷
sēng 僧
shǎng-shēng 上聲
Shangtung 山東
shāo 燒,梢
szù-hū 四呼
t'áo-er 桃兒
t'iáo-er 條兒
tièn 店
tūng 冬

t'ūng-shè 通攝

tùng 動

tsēng-shè 曾攝

Tsingtao 青島

tzū 資

Wéi-hsièn 濰縣

Wén-tēng 文登

yáng-p'íng 陽平

Yēn-tái 烟臺

yīn-p'íng 陰平

yìng 硬

Yu Tzung-shian 于宗先

Yüán Chiā-huá 袁家驊

yǜn-fù 韻腹

yǜn-lüèh Huì-tūng 韻略匯通

Yünnan 雲南

yǜn-t'óu 韻頭

yǜn-wĕi 韻尾

Chart of syllables with nonpalatalized finals.

I \ F	ɨ	e	a	ej	aj	ew	aw	en	an	eŋ	aŋ	wɨ	we	wa	wej	waj	wen	wan	weŋ	waŋ
p			把	北	敗		包	本	搬	蹦	幫	不	薄							
ph			怕	拍	派		泡	盆	盤	碰	胖	鋪	破							
f			法	飛			否	墳	反	風	方	父	佛							
m			馬	妹	埋		帽	門	慢	夢	忙	木	磨							
ť	資		雜	賊	再	走	燥	尊	攢	曾	葬	租	作						宗	
ťh	此		擦	脆	菜	凑	草	存	殘	層	藏	粗	搓						葱	
θ	死		撒	塞	腮	叟	騷	孫	散	僧	喪	酥	鎖						鬆	
t			打	得	帶	斗	到	頓	擔	燈	當	都	奪						東	
th			他	特	太	偷	桃	吞	攤	疼	湯	秃	駝						通	
n			拿	内	奶		鬧	△	暖	能	囊	奴	糯						濃	
c	知	這	△			咒	招	針	展	蒸	賬	煮	拙				準	磚		
ch	尺	扯				臭	超	陳	纏	稱	長	出	綽				春	川		
s	濕	舌	傻	誰		受	燒	神	閃	升	上	熟	説				順			
l	二		拉	勒	來	樓	老	嫩	懶	冷	狼	爐	落						聾	
č	支		炸	摘	齋	皺	罩	箴	斬	争		獨	桌	抓	追	△			鍾	莊
čh	齒		差	拆	踩	愁	炒	襯	饞	撑		鋤	戳	△	吹	揣			冲	牀
š	是		殺	骰	篩	瘦	梢	參	山	生		贖	所	耍	水	衰		栓		霜
k			割	格	該	够	高	根	幹	更	剛	姑	哥	瓜	鬼	怪	棍	關	公	光
kh			渴	客	開	扣	烤	肯	看	坑	糠	褲	可	誇	虧	快	困	寬	空	框
h			喝	黑	害	後	好	狠	旱	横	行	户	火	花	灰	壞	混	換	紅	黄
ø			阿	扼	礙	嘔	襖	恩	安	△	骯	屋	餓	瓦	爲	外	問	萬	翁	王

Chart of syllables with palatalized finals.

F / I	jɨ	je	ja	jaj	jew	jaw	jen	jan	jeŋ	jaŋ	jwɨ	jwe	jwen	jwan	jweŋ
p	鼻	别				表	賓	邊	兵						
ph	皮	撤				嫖	貪	偏	平						
m	泥	咩				苗	民	面	明						
t	地	爹	嗲		丢	掉		店	釘						
th	剃	鐵				條		田	聽						
n	尼	滅			牛	鳥		年	擰	娘	女				
c		姐			酒	焦	晉	賤	精	將	足	絶	俊	△	蹤
ch		切			秋	悄	秦	錢	清	搶	娶	雀	殘	全	
s		寫			羞	簫	新	綫	星	像	宿	雪	荀	宣	松
l	梨	獵	倆		留	了	林	連	鈴	良	緑	略			龍
k	鷄	接	假	皆	久	澆	近	見	驚	江	鋸	脚	均	捐	窘
kh	七	茄	恰	△	球	敲	勤	欠	輕	腔	去	缺	群	拳	窮
h	西	血	吓	蟹	休	曉	欣	縣	行	香	許	學	訓	險	兇
ø	日	惹	牙	挨	肉	饒	人	眼	英	羊	于	月	雲	圓	用

△Indicates local expressions for which no standard character representation has been generally accepted.

The Lin-ch'i Dialect and Its Relation to Mandarin**

A unique dialect of North China is chosen here for analysis in strictly structural terms, with a view to displaying how divergent dialects can be, even within such a limited concept as "Mandarin Chinese." The phonemic system of the dialect is set up, and it is found that its tone and vowel systems are drastically different from those of the Peking dialect, while the two dialects share practically the same set of initial consonants. The question "What is Mandarin?" is raised. A tentative list of essential characteristics for Mandarin dialects is then suggested for the purpose of testing if a Chinese dialect can be classified as a Mandarin dialect or not, and if so, which subgroup of Mandarin dialects it belongs to. The Lin-ch'i dialect is thus determined in formal terms to be a Mandarin dialect (perhaps of the Northwestern group). Finally, a systematic comparison between this dialect and Pekingese is made, with frequent reference to Ancient Chinese and Old Mandarin.

0. Introduction

The Lin-ch'i dialect (LC) is spoken by a relatively small number of people in a secluded area in the northwestern tip of Honan Province. If we regard Lin-Ch'i as the center of the dialect area, the total area covers just

---

** 中文題爲《臨淇方言及其與官話之間的關係》,原刊美國《東方學會會刊》(JAOS)1973 年第 93 卷第 2 期。

本文初稿曾在康奈爾大學包擬古(Nicholas Bodman)教授主持的漢語語言學研討會上發表,感謝包擬古教授的意見。

about a hundred square Chinese miles. The reason for choosing this dialect for a linguistic study is twofold: First, one of us (John Wang) was born and raised there until the age of eleven, and is thus able to serve as a native informant. Secondly, though geographically it is surrounded by some well-known North Mandarin dialects, it yet offers many interesting contrasts to those dialects and to Pekingese, the most striking difference being the existence of the so-called entering tone.

A complete phonological study of a Chinese dialect should at least include such items as juncture, stress, tones, initials and finals. But since the phonetic data are furnished largely through childhood memory, it seems best for the present study to concentrate only on features we can be fairly sure of, i. e., tones, initials and finals. In dealing with each of these three items, we shall first give a phonetic description to the best of our knowledge, and then attempt a phonemic analysis. As a working principle, we shall adopt the definition of a phoneme given by Bloch and Trager as "a class of phonetically similar sounds, contrasting and mutually exclusive with all similar classes in the language."①

Throughout the paper constant reference to the Peking dialect will be made for purposes of elucidation and comparison. Examples from Ancient Chinese (AC., i. e., *Ch'ièh-yǜn*, A. D. 601) and Old Mandarin (i. e., *Chūng-yüán Yīn-yǜn*, A. D. 1324) will also be cited toward the end of the paper for purposes of historical explanation.

1. Tones

There are four phonetically distinct tones in the dialect. Following the

① B. Bloch and G. L. Trager, *Outline of Linguistic Analysis*, *Baltimore*, 1942, p. 40.

practice of Dr. Y. R. Chao①, we shall divide the average range of the speaker's voice into four equal intervals separated by five points:

5 High

4 Lower-high

3 Middle

2 Higher-low

1 Low

The four tones in LC can then be represented conveniently as follows:

Tone 1: [21] ˨˩

Tone 2: [41] ˦˩

Tone 3: [55] ˥

Tone 4: [2] ˨

Tone 4 is numerically represented by just one figure because of the noticeable shortness of the vowel in producing it. It can be characterized as starting on the higher-low pitch, and then immediately brought to an end. It is invariably followed by a glottal stop.

Although phonetically there are four distinct tones in the dialect, phonemically, Tone 1 [21] and Tone 4 [2] can be grouped together, because Tone 4 only occurs with the glottal stop, while Tone 1 occurs everywhere else, and they share similar tonal quality.

Phonemically, then, there are only three tones in the dialect:

Tone 1: { [2] when followed by a glottal stop
[21] elsewhere }

Tone 2: [41]

Tone 3: [55]

It may be interesting to note at this point that there are no tones with rising contour in LC, while the Peking dialect has two (Tone 2 [35] and Tone

① Y. R. Chao, "A System of Tone Letters" *Le Maitre Phonétique*, XLV (1930), 24-27.

3[214]).

2. Initial Consonants

In the study of the Chinese language, it has been a standard practice to analyze a syllable as consisting of two parts: an initial and a final. An initial is that consonantal part of the syllable which starts the sound of the whole syllable. Just as in the Peking dialect, the initial in LC, when there is one, is always a single consonantal segment. The final is the rest of the syllable which comes after the initial. If there is no initial consonant, technically called zero initial, the final corresponds to the entire syllable.

Altogether 21 initial consonantal segments are found in the dialect①:

p	t	k	ʦ	tʂ	ʨ
P‘	t‘	k‘	ʦ‘	tʂ‘	ʨ‘
f		x	s	ʂ	ɕ
			l	ʐ	
m	n				

2.1. As far as the number and phonetic quality of these initial consonants are concerned, they are roughly identical with those in the Peking dialect. This does not, however, mean that the initial consonants in the two dialects can be phonemicized in the same way. In the Peking dialect, for example, the palatal series [ʨ, ʨ‘, ɕ] and the alveolar series [ʦ, ʦ‘, s] can be readily identified as allophones of the same phonemes respectively, the palatalization of the former being merely conditioned by the following [i]②. But LC in this respect is a different case altogether. Here both the alveolars

① Unless noted otherwise, all the phonetic symbols used throughout the paper are based on the IPA system, taken from Yuán Chiā-huá's *han-yu fang-yan gai-yao*, Peking, 1960, p. 7.

② See Lawton M. Hartman III, "Segmental Phonemes of the Peiping Dialect," *Language*, 20 (1944), 38.

and the palatals can be followed by [i], and when so followed, they remain distinct from each other. Thus in LC, chì [ʦi] "to make sacrifice to," ch'i [ʦ'i] "even," and hsī [si] "west" are kept distinct from chì [ʨi] "season," ch'i [ʨ'i] "his," and hsī [ɕi] "to hope" respectively. It is clear that in LC these two series will have to be handled differently.

2.2. In LC, the palatals [ʨ, ʨ', ɕ] are in complementary distribution with both the retroflexes [ʦ̢, ʦ̢', ʂ] and the velars (or gutturals) [k, k', x]. The palatals always occur before the high front vowels [i, y], while the retroflexes and velars only occur before vowels other than these two. From the viewpoint of phonetic similarity, the palatals might be thought to be closer to the retroflexes, but from the viewpoint of the intuitive reaction of the native speakers as well as historical development, the palatals are more easily identifiable with the velars. One is seemingly left with an optional decision here. For a purely descriptive study, it may seem that there is not much difference between the two options, because either choice can satisfactorily keep apart this type of syllables from those with [ʦ, ʦ', s] as their initials. But if we intend to make a meaningful analysis for further historical and comparative studies (as will become clear in later discussions) as well as to explain some other phenomena①, we have actually no choice but to group [ʨ, ʨ', ɕ] and [k, k', x] as one series of phonemes. We may for the moment write them as /k, k', x/.

2.3. [p] is phonetically similar to [p'], the only difference being the presence of the element of aspiration in the second. If, following Hartman as mentioned before, we set up an /h/ for aspiration, [p'] can then be phonemically denoted as /ph/. The same analysis may be applied to the other pairs [t, t'], [k, k'], [ʦ, ʦ'], [ʦ̢, ʦ̢'] and [ʨ, ʨ']. Excluding [k, k']

① For example, the matching of palatals with velars in the onomatopoetic expressions and the reaction of the native speakers to foreign words with velars before [i].

and [tɕ, tɕ‘], five phonemes may now be established: /p, t, ʦ, ʈʂ, h/. The three phomenes /k, k‘, x/ established one paragraph above can now be rewritten as /k, kh, h/. We may replace /x/ with /h/ because velar fricative and aspiration are similar in nature and are in complementary distribution in this dialect.

2.4. As for the rest of the initials, no further grouping is possible based on either the principle of phonetic similarity or that of complementary distribution. They will be considered separate phomenes, each having only one allophone: /f, m, n, s, ʂ, ʐ, l/.

2.5. Altogether, then, there are 13 initial consonantal phonemes in this dialect. In order to indicate the fact that initials are all unit sounds, we shall replace /ʦ/ with /c/, and /ʈʂ/ with /č/. To be consistent, /ʂ/ will be replaced by /š/, and /ʐ/ by /ž/[①]. The table of initials in § 2 can thus be rewritten phonemically as follows:

p	t	k	c	č	(k)
ph	th	kh	ch	čh	(kh)
f		h	s	š	(h)
m	n				
			l	ž	

3. Syllabic Finals

39 syllabic finals are found in LC, which can be arranged into four groups corresponding roughly to the positions of their articulation: high, mid-

① We may also follow Hartman (op. cit.) in analyzing the retroflex initials as alveolars followed by /r/, but we must remember that /r/, just like the sign of aspiration /h/, is not a separate phoneme but one of the distinctive features pertaining to the initial consonants. Cf. F. S. Hsueh: *Phonology of Old Mandarin: a Structuralistic Approach*, Ph. D. dissertation, Indiana Univ., 1968, p. 38.

high, mid-low, and low.

a) [ɿ, ʅ, i, u, y, iŋ, yŋ]

b) [əʔ, iəʔ, uəʔ, yəʔ, ei, uei, ou, iou, əŋ, uəŋ]

c) [ɛ, iɛ, uɛ, yɛ, ɔ, iɔ, uɔ, ʌʔ, iʌʔ, uʌʔ, yʌʔ]

d) [a, ia, ua, ya, ai, uai, ɑu, iɑu, ɑŋ, iɑŋ, uɑŋ]

3.1. Traditionally, the final has been analyzed, where feasible, into three constituents: the medial, the nucleus, and the ending. This approach has proved to be a very fruitful one with Ancient Chinese①, Old Mandarin, Modern Pekingese, and many other Mandarin dialects. Naturally, we want to try to apply this approach to the Lin-ch'i dialect, which we have many reasons to believe was developed from Ancient Chinese and is quite closely related to Pekingese. At the same time, a successful application of this approach to LC will by itself prove that its relation to Ancient Chinese and Pekingese is indeed what we suspect it to be. The medial, when it exists in a final, is a kind of on-glide, to be realized in the form of a semivowel. It can be realized in three possible ways, represented in the above transcription by [i-, u-, y-]. The last one can be analyzed as the combination [iu]②. To show that they are categorically different from the nucleus of a syllable (the vowel), we shall follow Hartman in using /j/ for [i] and /w/ for [u]. Depending upon what form the medial assumes, or the absence of it, syllables can be classified into four types, called "the four exhalations" (szù-hū) in Chinese. These are as follows: those with zero medial, those with medial /j/, those with medial /w/, and those with medial /jw/③. When we apply this analysis to the five finals [ɿ,ʅ, i, u, y] in the first group listed above, we

① Cf. Samuel E. Martin, *The Phonemes of Ancient Chinese*. JAOS, 16 (1953), supplement, 20 - 23.

② Cf. Y. R. Chao, *Mandarin Primer*, Cambridge, Mass., 1948 and Hartman, op. cit.

③ In terms of distinctive features, the four possible types of medial can be represented [-lab, -pal], [-lab, +pal], [+lab, -pal], and [+lab, +pal], where lab = labialization(w), pal = palatalization (j).

shall come to the same conclusion as Hartman did in his analysis of the Pekingese dialect. In LC, [ɿ] occurs only after /c，ch，s，l/ while [ʅ] only occurs after /č，čh，š，ž/. They can thus be treated as allophones of a high vowel /ɨ/，which functions in these cases as a final without medial and ending，[i] can then be analyzed into /jɨ/，[u] into /wɨ/，and [y] into /jwɨ/.

The two semivowel phonemes /j，w/ can also be used in the ending slot to represent the two types of off-glide. In addition，two consonants [ŋ，ʔ] can also occur as syllable ending，as is clear from the above transcription of finals. We thus have to add two consonantal phonemes /ŋ，ʔ/，specifying that they can only appear in the ending position①.

3.2. Finals of the second group are peculiar in one respect，viz.，there is not even one which does not have a syllable ending. The three vowels [ə，e，o] are clearly allophones of one phoneme，because [o] occurs only before [u] (/w/)，[e] only before [i] (/j/)，and [ə] before /ŋ/ and /ʔ/. When we check the distribution of the medial in these finals，we find there are only two with ending /ŋ/ in this group，one with zero medial ([əŋ])，the other with medial /w/([uəŋ]). There is nothing unusual about this uneven distribution until we notice that there are two finals with ending /ŋ/ in the first group，[iŋ] and [yŋ]，which so far as the medial is concerned are in complementary distribution with the two in the second group. Upon closer scrutiny，we find that [i] in [iŋ] and [y] in [yŋ] are somewhat lower than when they occur before zero ending. The two finals can perhaps be more realistically represented by [iɨŋ] and [yɨŋ]. Thus it is not unreasonable to move them down to the second group to form a quartet with [əŋ]and [uəŋ]. After having done so，it becomes increasingly clear that finals of the first

① An alternative is to identify ending /ŋ/ with initial /n/ and ending /ʔ/ with initial /k/. However，this seemingly economical alternative will cause some unnecessary confusion in historical studies.

group and those of the second group can be combined, since we can say they share the same nuclear vowel /ɨ/.

A sweeping generalization can now be made: the tongue position of the high vowel phoneme /ɨ/ is somewhat lower when it is followed by an ending than when it is followed by nothing, and its phonetic realization as to being central, front, or back is conditioned primarily by its ending and secondarily by its medial.

3.3. Finals of the third group cannot possibly be phonemicized as having one and the same nuclear vowel, [ɛ] and [ɔ] are clearly in contrast in that they both occur with no ending and both combine with the same types of medial. Two more vowel phonemes are thus needed. For typographical convenience, we shall represent [ɛ] with /e/ and [ɔ] with /o/. It seems that [ʌ] may be grouped together with either of the two, since it only occurs before /ʔ/, and is thus in complementary distribution with both. The question is with which it should be grouped. Unless we can bring forth some convincing argument, a decision made either way would only be arbitrary. The principle of phonetic similarity does not help us here, for while [ʌ] is similar to [ɔ] in being relatively back ([+grave]), it shares: the same quality of unroundedness ([-flat]) with [ɛ]. We shall, therefore, delay our decision for the moment.

3.4. There are two vowels in the fourth group which are in complementary distribution: [ɑ] before /w/ and /ŋ/, [a] before /j/ and zero ending. They are thus allophones of a low vowel phoneme which will be denoted by /a/. There remains the problem of the finals with the vowel [ʌ] in the third group. We notice that it is also in complementary distribution with both [ɑ] and [a], because the latter do not occur before /ʔ/. So it is also possible to treat [ʌ] as an allophone of the phoneme /a/. When we take the whole vowel system into consideration, we shall notice that the decision to make [ʌ] an allophone of /a/ is much more attractive than to make it an allophone of either /e/ or /o/. Several reasons can be advanced. In the first place, /a/ is to be differentiated from /e/ for being non-front ([+grave]), and from /o/ for being unrounded ([−flat]). The two qualities are just what [ʌ] possesses (see 3.3), though phonetically its tongue position in height is closer to /e/ and /o/. Secondly, if we should assign [ʌ] to either /e/ or /o/, the glottal stop would be the only syllable ending possible to that vowel phoneme. We would then be obliged to account for this unusual situation. Thirdly, like the high vowel /ɨ/, the low vowel /a/ can take various types of endings. If we did not assign [ʌ] to /a/, we would create a skew case to the effect that /a/ can occur before any type of ending except /ʔ/—an unnecessary exception. Fourthly, by assigning [ʌ] to /a/, we can make a strong generalization by saying that of all the vowel phonemes, only the central ([+grave, −flat]) can take an ending, while the front ([−grave, −flat]) and the back ([+grave, +flat]) cannot.

3.5. As a summary to our discussion of the vowel system, a chart of the phonemicized syllabic finals may be presented as follows:

V	ɨ					e	a					o
M \ E	ø	j	w	ŋ	ʔ	ø	ø	j	w	ŋ	ʔ	ø
ø	ɨ	ɨj	ɨw	ɨŋ	ɨʔ	e	a	aj	aw	aŋ	aʔ	o
j	jɨ		jɨw	jɨŋ	jɨʔ	je	ja		jaw	jaŋ	jaʔ	jo
w	wɨ	wɨj		wɨŋ	wɨʔ	we	wa	waj		waŋ	waʔ	wo
jw	jwɨ			jwɨŋ	jwɨʔ	jwe	jwa				jwaʔ	

4. Phonemic inventory

The LC phonemic inventory can be summarized as follows, together with a few clarifying remarks.

3 tones: 1st tone ([2] before glottal stop; [21] elsewhere),

2nd tone ([41]), 3rd tone ([55]).

15 consonants:

	labial	dental	alveolar	retroflex	guttural	
stops	p	t	c	č	k	ʔ
Fricatives	f		s	š	h	
resonants	m	n	l	ž	ŋ	

2 semivowels: j w

4 vowels:

	front	central	back
high		ɨ	
low	e	a	o

4.1. We have come to the conclusion that there are three tones in LC, with the first tone having two allotones. This is because we have taken the term "tone" in its strict sense, namely, the pitch of the voice. If the term is to be treated as an equivalent of the term shēng in traditional Chinese phonology, we shall have to keep the two allotones apart. From the viewpoint of historical study, this is better, as we shall then be able to say that LC has maintained the tonemic system of Ancient Chinese with practically no change.

4.2. In LC, as in Pekingese and Old Mandarin, the labial initials also behave in a peculiar way. It may be said that they phonemically combine only with finals which have either /j/ or nothing in the medial position, or it may be said that they combine only with finals which must have either /w/ or /j/, but not both, as their medial. F. S. Hsueh's argument that structurally the latter alternative is better also suits LC very well①.

4.3. [r] does occur as syllable ending in LC, in such common

① Cf. Hsueh, op. cit., pp. 78-79.

expressions as [tɕiər] "today," [miər] "tomorrow," etc. But not enough examples of this kind are remembered to include it in the phonemic analysis above. However, we believe this [r] can perhaps be treated as an allophone of /l/, comparable to the so-called "dark l" when it occurs after the nuclear vowel.

5 LC as a Mandarin dialect

The question whether LC is a Mandarin dialect or not can hardly be answered indisputably unless we define first what we mean by "Mandarin." However, an *explicit* linguistic definition of this term by which we can test any Chinese dialect is yet to be worked out①. The following is a highly tentative list of criteria with reference to Ancient Chinese, which we hope can help to determine in formal terms if any Chinese dialect can pass as a Mandarin dialect. The ten points are arranged here in what is believed to be an historical order, and hence, an order of decreasing relevance②.

i. The change of the rising tone syllables with voiced stop or fricative initials to the going tone.

ii. The split of the even tone into two and the subsequent devoicing of the initial stops and fricatives.

iii. The acquisition of medial /j/ (i.e., palatalization) by the unrounded syllables of the second division with guttural initials.

iv. The complete coalescence of the *kěng-shè* and *tsēng-shè*.

v. The emergence of the final (C)ɨ#. (i.e., the *Chih-szŭ* rime).

vi. The disappearing of the entering tone.

---

① To our knowledge, Yuán Chiā-huá's work (op. cit., pp. 23-41 and 315-21) seems to be the best effort in this direction, though it still falls short of what we would like to call "an explicit linguistic definition."

② Cf. Hsueh, op. cit., pp. 234-36.

vii. The merging of /m/ with /n/ as syllable ending.

viii. The loss of medial /j/ in finals after all retroflex initials (i. e., depalatalization).

ix. The emergence of syllables with /r/(or/l/) as their ending.

x. The coalescence of /k-, kh-, h-/ and /c-, ch-, s-/ respectively before palatalized finals (i. e., finals with /j/ in the medial position).

A typical Mandarin dialect like Pekingese will of course pass all the checks, while a non-Mandarin dialect (or language) like Cantonese may fail on all ten counts. But between these two extremes, there are many dialects which can pass some but not all. For example, even *Chūng-yüán Yīn-yǜn* cannot pass (vii), (viii) and (x), while there is no way to check it with regard to (ix). We do not know how to make the calculation yet, i.e., how much a dialect has to score in order to pass as a Mandarin dialect. Perhaps a simple majority is enough①.

5.1. When we subject LC to this test, we find it can indeed pass eminently as a Mandarin dialect, even though it fails at three important points. It cannot pass the second one, because its first tone ([21]) corresponds to the even tone in Ancient Chinese without a split, though the voicing feature in some of the initials has been lost (having become aspiration after stops in the even tone and disappeared otherwise). It also fails at (vi) and (x), for it still retains its entering tone in the form of a terminal glottal stop and it maintains the contrast between /k, kh, h/ and /c, ch, s/ before /j/(see 2.1.). But it passes all the others. Nothing has to be said with regard to (v), (viii), and (ix), as they are already clear from our description of the

① Two alternatives can be suggested here. First, each of these ten points (perhaps more will be needed) can be assigned a value of relevance, for example, (i) may receive a value of ten units, while (x) is given only one. Second, the ten points may perhaps be divided into two sets: one set (e.g., the first five) to determine if a certain dialect is Mandarin, the other to determine which subgroup of Mandarin dialects it belongs to, if it is a Mandarin dialect.

dialect. However, a few words are needed to prove that it passes (i), (iii), (iv) and (vii) as well. We believe it passes (i) because rising tone words in Ancient Chinese like *chìn* "near"(AC [g'iən], LC /kjɨŋ/)[①] and *hòu* "thick" (AC [ɣəu], LC /hɨw/) belong to the third tone ([55]) in LC, which corresponds to the going tone in Ancient Chinese and the fourth tone in Pekingese. It passes (iii) because words like *chiā* "home" (AC [ka]) and *ch'ià* "just right" (AC [k'ap]) now have the reading /kjo/ and /khjaʔ/ respectively in LC, both with medial /j/. Words of the *kěng-shè* and the *tsēng-shè* have not only merged, but furthermore, as in Pekingese, have joined the *t'ūng-shè* in forming one rime. For example, *t'úng* "identical" (AC [d'uŋ], LC /thwɨŋ/), *hèng* "unreasonable" (AC [ɣωɐŋ], LC /hwɨŋ/), and *těng* "to wait" (AC [təŋ], LC /tɨŋ/) now share the same nuclear vowel. At first sight, there seems to be no way to tell whether LC can pass (vii) or not, as it has neither /n/ nor /m/ as syllable ending, but its deep structure indicates it passes that, too (see 5.2).

5.2. The fact that the even tone in Ancient Chinese did not split into two in LC seems to suggest that the dialect might have been separated from most Northern Mandarin dialects, including Pekingese, even before *Chūng-yüán Yīn-yùn*[②]. The puzzle is that even after the split, it has not taken a completely different course of development. On the contrary, it shares with Pekingese quite a few post-*Chūng-yüán Yīn-yùn* changes, some obvious,

---

① The transcription for Ancient Chinese (AC) used in this paper is based on Bernhard Karlgren's *Grammata Serica Recensa*, Stockholm, 1957.

② A different interpretation is that formerly there were also two even tones in LC which later merged unconditionally. Within the limits of the data we have, either decision is obviously tentative in nature. Structurally, it might be strongly argued that LC is a branch of the dialect from which came the so-called literary pronunciation in Pekingese (cf. Hsueh, op. cit., pp. 179 - 81). It may also be added here that the tonal categories, and even their phonetic realization, in LC are very close to those of the T'ài-yüán dialect (cf. Yuán Chiā-huá, op. cit., p.29). Indeed, it is said, so John Wang remembers, that the people of Lin-ch'i migrated from some place in Shansi Province.

others discernible only in its deep structure. The obvious ones are:

a) The loss of /ŋ/ and /v/ as initials.

b) The loss of medial /j/ after retroflex initials.

c) The change of the final /jaj/ to /je/.

Those obscured by later developments are:

a) Ending /m/ must have first changed to /n/, as in Pekingese, before being changed to [ŋ] (*yīn* "sound" AC [ʔiəm]LC /jɨŋ/) or lost (*t'án* "talk" AC [d'âm], LC /tha/).

b) Finals of the first division and the fourth division in the *shān-shè* (including *hsién-shè*) must have first joined those of the second division before syllable ending /n/ was lost (e. g., *kuān* "official" AC [kuân], LC /kwa/; *hsiēn* "former" AC [sien], LC /sja/; *tièn* "shop" AC [tiem], LC /tja/).

5.3. The vowel system of LC as set up here is identical with that of Old Mandarin①. This, however, should not be taken as a sign suggesting a closer relationship between LC and Old Mandarin than that between Pekingese and Old Mandarin. Actually, the phonological makeup of most morphemes in LC is distinctly different from that in *Chūng-yüán Yīn-yǜn*. Aside from the changes mentioned in the last section which LC shares with Pekingese, the following are some of its unique developments which account for its difference from both Old Mandarin and Pekingese.

a) The change of /n/ to /ŋ/ after the high vowel /ɨ/(e. g., *fēn* "to divide" AC [pi̯uən], LC /fɨŋ/; *chìn* "to enter" AC [tsi̯ən], LC /cjɨŋ/).

b) The change of the low back vowel /o/ to join the low front vowel /e/ in syllables with zero ending (e. g., *kē* "older brother" AC [kâ], LC /ke/; *hé* "river" AC [ɣâ], LC /he/).

c) The move of the central low vowel /a/ in syllables with zero ending to

---

① Cf. Hsueh, op. cit., p. 88.

the back /o/ (e. g., *ch'á* "tea" AC [d'a], LC /čho/; *chiā* "home" AC [ka], LC /kjo/).

d) The loss of ending /n/ after the central low vowel /a/, which took place after the two obscured changes mentioned in the last section, and of course (c).

e) The move of both the front and the back low vowels to join the central low vowel in the entering tone syllables (just as when they occur before /n/). The result is that words like *chiă* "armor" (AC [kap]) and *chiéh* "to knit" (AC [kiet]) become homophones (LC /kjaʔ/).

Two changes observed in Pekingese obviously did not take place in LC:

a) The coalescence of /c, ch, s/ and /k, kh, h/ respectively when they occur before /j/ (see section 2).

b) The loss of medial /j/ in the final /jwɨŋ/ when it occurs after initials other than the gutturals. Consequently, words like *lúng* "dragon" (AC [liwoŋ], LC /ljwɨŋ/) and *lúng* "cage" (AC [luŋ], LC /lwɨŋ/) are still pronounced differently, while they have become homophones in Pekingese.

5.4. The entering tone in Ancient Chinese is preserved in LC. However, not all the words of this category survive as entering tone words in this dialect. How did this happen? Any attempt to lay down strict rules to account for the loss of glottalization of certain entering tone words in LC is bound to fail in view of the following list of pairs of words:

i) *tú* "solitary" AC [d'uk], LC /twɨʔ/;
tú "poison" AC [d'uok], LC /twɨ/.

ii) *fá* "to conquer" AC [b'i̯wɐt], LC /faʔ/;
fá "to punish" AC [b'i̯wɐt], LC /fo/.

iii) *sù* "sleep" AC [si̯uk], LC /sjwɨʔ/;
sú "vulgar" AC [zi̯wok], LC /sjwɨ/.

iv) *shú* "virtuous" AC [ẑi̯uk], LC /šwɨʔ/;
shú "cooked" AC [ẑiuk], LC /šwɨ/.

v) *yù* "desire" AC [i̯wok], LC /jwɨʔ/;

yù "jade" AC [ngi̯wok], LC /jwɨ/.

Obviously, the retention or loss of the glottal stop in LC is not to be explained in terms of the nature of the initials or the vowels in Ancient Chinese, as has been done for Old Mandarin and Pekingese. The explanation lies perhaps in interdialectal borrowing. As we have noted, LC is spoken by a small community in a somewhat secluded area. This is perhaps why it has been able to preserve its entering tone to some extent. But since LC is like a small island surrounded on all sides by more prestigious Mandarin dialects in which the entering tone has been lost, it is almost unimaginable that speakers of this dialect would not be influenced by its neighbouring dialects. The irregular status of the former entering tone words in this dialect can thus be viewed as a manifestation of this inevitable situation. Fortunately, the problem of rendering the existing entering tone words into their Pekingese reading is a rather simple one for the native speakers of this dialect. All that they have to do is to drop the glottal stop when it occurs after the high vowel /ɨ/, and to change its low vowel /a/ to the Pekingese middle vowel /e/ before dropping the glottal stop, except in two types of syllables: /(C)aʔ/(C ≠ gutturals) and /(C)jaʔ/(C= gutturals), where LC /a/ should be rendered either as Pekingese /a/ or /e/, depending upon the origin of the entering tone words in which it appears (see the syllabary charts).

Chart of syllables with unpalatalized finals.

I \ F	ɨ	e	a	o	ɨj	aj	ɨw	aw	ɨŋ	aŋ	ɨʔ	aʔ	wɨ	we	wa	wo	wɨj	waj	wɨŋ	waŋ	wɨʔ	waʔ
p			半	把	杯	白		包	崩	邦	不	八	布	波								
ph			扮	爬	陪	排		跑	碰	胖	撲	拍	普	破								
f			飯	罰	飛				分	方	福	發	父									
m			慢	馬	妹	買		毛	門	忙	没	莫	母	磨								
t			蛋	打		代	斗	倒	等	當		得	度	多	短		堆		動		獨	△
th			談	他		太	頭	討	疼	湯		特	土	拖	團		推		同		突	托
n			南	拿		乃		鬧	能	囊		納	奴	挪	暖		閃		弄			△
c	自		暫	雜		再	走	早	增	髒		則	租	坐	鑽		最		總		族	作
ch	次		參			才	凑	草	層	藏		擦	粗	錯	△		催		從		促	銼
s	思		三	洒		賽		掃	僧	喪		塞	素	鎖	算		歲		送		速	索
l	二		藍	拉		來	漏	老	冷	朗		獵	路	羅	亂		累		籠		録	落
č	知	遮	站	詐		齋	周	找	真	張	直	窄	住	著	專	抓	追	跩	種	莊	竹	捉
čh	池	車	産	茶		柴	愁	吵	成	常	吃	插	處	△	川		吹	揣	充	窗	出	綽
š	詩	蛇	山	沙		晒	受	少	生	上	十	殺	書	所	拴	耍	睡	帥	順	雙	束	説
ž	日	惹	然				肉	繞	認	讓	△	熱	如		軟		鋭		容		入	若
k		哥	敢		給	該	够	高	更	剛		各	古	過	官	寡	貴	拐	公	光	谷	國
kh		可	看			開	口	考	肯	抗		渴	苦	科	寬	誇	愧	快	空	狂	哭	括
h		河	汗			海	後	好	很	航		黑	胡	火	换	花	會	壞	紅	黄	忽	或
ø		餓	安	啊		愛	牛	傲	恩	昂		惡	五	我	玩	蛙	味	外	問	汪	屋	握

Chart of syllables with palatalized finals.

F / I	jɨ	je	ja	jo	jɨw	jaw	jɨŋ	jaŋ	jɨʔ	jaʔ	jwɨ	jwe	jwa	jwɨŋ	jwɨʔ	jwaʔ
p	比	别	便			表	兵		必	鱉						
ph	皮	△	片			票	平		劈	撇						
m	米		面			妙	明		蜜	滅						
t	地	爹	店		丢	掉	定		的	跌						
th	替		田			跳	停		踢	鐵						
n	你		年		妞	鳥	寧	娘		捏	女					
c	祭	姐	剪		酒	焦	進	將	即	接	聚				足	絶
ch	妻	且	前		秋	瞧	請	搶	七	切	取		全		漆	雀
s	洗	寫	先		修	小	信	想	息		序		選	松	宿	雪
l	利		連	倆	留	了			力	列	旅	△	練	龍	律	
k	己	街	見	家	久	叫	景	江	及	甲	居	△	卷	君	菊	脚
kh	氣	茄	欠	卡	丘	橋	輕	强	乞	恰	去	瘸	拳	窮	曲	缺
h	喜	鞋	限	下	休	校	行	向	吸	歇	虚	學	玄	凶	畜	
ø	衣	爺	烟	呀	油	要	音	央	一	業	雨		元	暈	欲	藥

Indicates a meaningful syllable for which we have failed to find a representing charater.

Glossary of Romanized Terms

ch'á 茶

chì 祭,季

ch'í 齊,其

chiā 家

chiǎ 甲

ch'ià 恰

chiéh 結

Ch'iè-yǜn 切韻

chī-szū 支思

kěng-shè 梗攝

kuān 官

lín-ch'í 臨淇

lúng 龍,籠

shān-shè 山攝

shansi 山西

shēng 聲

shú 淑,熟

sú 俗

chìn 近,進
Chūng-yüán Yīn-yǜn 中原音韻
fá 伐,罰
fēn 分
Hanyu Fangyan Gaiyao 漢語方言概要
hé 河
hèng 横
Honan 河南
hòu 厚
hsī 西,希
hsiēn 先
hsién-shè 咸攝
Hsueh 薛
kē 哥
sù 宿
szù-hū 四呼
T'àiyüán 太原
t'án 談
tēng 等
tièn 店
tsēng-shè 曾攝
tú 獨,毒
t'ūng-shè 通攝
t'úng 同
Wang 王
yīn 音
yüán Chiā-huá 袁家驊
yǜ 欲,玉

唐詩格律

唐詩聲律之本質*

1. 唐詩的格律,已得到廣泛的研究①,除非有了新的發現,似乎没有必要再加以討論。我們對這一古老的課題進行新的探討,不過希望能得到一些新的解釋。

1.1. 首先必須澄清的是,本文所使用的“唐詩”這一術語,與一般的含義不同。衆所周知,唐代詩人寫詩有兩種不同的形式,即“古體”和“今體”(或“近體”)。我所説的“唐詩”這一術語,僅指“今體”,因爲衹有今體才是唐代所獨創;而“古體”,顧名思義,則是古代的體裁,唐代和後代的詩人用古體所寫的詩,不過是仿古之作。看起來,本文所謂“唐詩”似乎範圍太窄,實際上它不僅包括唐代用今體寫的詩,而且也包括唐朝以後所有朝代、所有國家的詩人所寫的今體詩,而今後用這種形式寫的詩,仍會叫做“唐詩”,因此相反有着更廣泛的代表性。

1.2. 根據對仗和格律,我們可以將唐詩同古體區别開來。對仗是句法形式上的特點,而格律則是音韻形式上的特點。雖然二者在唐詩中經常並用,但却是互不相關的兩種特徵。對仗指的是相對的兩句中對應的字嚴格對偶,雖然唐詩普遍運用對仗,但嚴格説來,對仗並不是唐詩獨有的特徵,在前代的所謂“古律”和“古絶”中就已經存在了。作爲唐詩,唯一的必須而充分的特徵,是其具有的特殊的聲調模式,這是貫穿全詩,每句每聯都必須遵循的模式。這正是本文所要討論的特徵。事實上,甚至在一些有名的唐詩中,我們都可以發現有一兩句不合於所要求的聲調模式,但這並不能否定構成這些模式的基本法

---

* 原載《音韻學研究通訊》1986年第10期,收入《漢語音韻史十講》。
本文原題 Elements in the Metrics of T'ang Poetry,刊於《史語所集刊》1971年第42本3分。杜平譯爲中文。

① 參考文獻中僅收了少量當代學者的研究成果,大多數著作並未列入。其中最爲詳贍的權威著作無疑首推 Wang1963,筆者受益甚多。王力教授根據一些基本原理,清楚地闡述了詩律的系統,本文不過對其提出新的解釋,並没有超出其範圍。

則。正如人們常説,萬事都有例外,而才華横溢的詩人,往往有意違背常規,以追求所要表達的某種效果。

1.3. 詩歌格律系統的形成可以有不同的方式。John. Lotz(Lotz1960)的格律類型(Metric Typlogy)首先分成簡單型(simple)和複雜型(Complex)兩大類,又將複雜型的聲律分成三種型式,即聲調型(tonal)、動力型(dynamic)和延續型(durational)。一種語言爲什麽選擇這種型式而不選擇另一型式,在很大程度上取决於其語言特徵,雖然嚴格説來,任何特定的選擇都没有什麽邏輯上的必然性。漢語可能從來就是一種聲調語言,因此,選擇聲調作爲詩律法則的基礎是很自然的。這就使漢語詩律系統完全不同於英語和古希臘語的詩律。英語詩律是動力型的,建立在音節重音(syllable stress)的基礎之上;而古希臘語的詩律則是延續型的,建立在音節長音(syllable length)的基礎之上。重音和長音顯然是一種穩定的特點,特别是在詩律中加以運用時。對立總是二項的,重對輕、長對短①。具體的重音和長音,多不會有誤解的問題。一般説來,古人所説的重輕和長短,今人也認爲是重輕和長短,將來也不會改變。因此,可以認爲動力型和延續型的格律基礎是不變的,現在仍然可以像從前那樣加以運用。但是,聲調型格律就不是如此。我們知道,唐代的漢語有四個調類,現在衹能作爲一種語音術語來理解,其具體調值我們所知有限。事實上,甚至在唐代之前,四聲調值在不同的方言中就存在着很大的差别②,此後,一定又經過多次的、不同方向的變化。由此可見,以四聲爲基礎的唐詩格律系統的實際含義,對唐代的人遠比對我們更有意義。

1.4. 上述結論,使我們和傳統的觀念發生直接冲突。傳統的觀念認爲唐詩的格律系統同音樂有着特别密切的關係,這個觀點我發現很難接受。如果從儘可能廣泛的意義上理解"音樂"這一術語,即聲音、包括語音的序列的有規則的出現,那麽所有的格律系統都同音樂發生緊密的關係,因爲構成所有格律

---

① 當然,這並不意味有重音和音長特徵的語言裏不存在更多等級的音位差别。這裏指的是詩律中衹能有這些特徵的二項對點。正如 Samuel R. Levin 所指出的(Levin 1962:43 脚注):"分析詩律時,如果在'重讀'(stress)和'非重讀'(absence of stress)之外,包含更多的項目,諸如'次重音'(minor)或'半重音'(half-stress)等附加項目,就會使得詩律系統和語言超音段系統(suprasegmental system)混淆不清。"

② 陸法言《切韻序》:"秦隴則去聲爲入,梁益則平聲似去。"

系統基礎的根本法則,就是在規則模式裏語音的變化。唐詩的格律系統和上述意義上的音樂之間,似乎並没有什麽特别的關係。但是,如果將"音樂"的含義限制在更爲專門的意義上,即按一定格律系統寫的詩往往較符合音樂的旋律,那麽在我看起來,唐詩的格律剛好可能比起其他的格律形式,更不合於這種觀念,因爲這個系統是建立在聲調的變化格式之上的。Arthur Waley曾經説漢語的曲折調(deflected tone,即非平聲)帶有比較强的語勢,因而同英語的重讀音節有點類似(Waley 1919:23)。我覺得這種類比相當可疑,但是,我們還是暫時接受這個觀點,以便進行另一個類比。如果有一句詩,平聲同一種非平聲相間出現,這一句就會同英語的一句抑揚格(iambic meter)的詩句類似。如果有人相信,這一詩句同一定的音樂旋律類型特别相合,那麽它的對句,因爲是揚抑格(trochaic meter),就會對同樣的旋律顯得極不協調。古代漢語的情况極爲特殊,據《切韻》的編輯者陸法言所述,《切韻》方言的平聲近似於四川方言的去聲(參見上頁脚注②),所以,標準方言的抑揚格的詩句,到四川方言裏可能變成揚抑格,或者甚至没有任何韻律可言,因爲非平聲實際上有三種,衹有一種可能同標準方言的平聲相似,這將意味着衹有在平聲確實是平調的方言裏,並且衹有在那個方言的調值尚未發生變化的時候,本文所研究的格律系統才有意義。换句話説,在其他方言裏,在唐代以後的近代漢語裏,就其對音樂的關係而言,這個格律系統幾乎不可能存在。但是,所有證據都表明,在唐朝以及以後的朝代的各種方言裏,這個格律系統都被很好地運用着,而在現代北京話裏,也仍然有一些意義,即使不可能像以前那樣充分。因此,我們能够引出的必然結論是,這個系統同音樂衹有一種不確定的中性關係。正如其他的格律系統一樣,漢語的格律系統也僅僅是一種構成某些語音規則格式的手段,對於音樂家來説,其作用也僅限於此。

2. 通過以上分析之後,我們可以轉到對唐詩格律系統本身的討論。正如我們剛才所説,古代漢語有四個聲調。這四個聲調可以分成兩種互爲對比的格律基礎。平聲字比其他任何一種聲調的字都多兩倍,單獨形成一種基礎。其他三種聲調,即上聲、去聲和入聲一起形成另一基礎。所謂"仄聲",有多種譯法,如曲折調(deflected tone)、傾斜調(oblique tone)、變化調(changing tone)或者非平聲(uneven tone)。本文使用非平聲這一術語,因爲非平聲清楚地表現了同平聲的對比。

2.1. 八句的律詩和四句的絶句的詩律格式,是漢語詩歌的普通知識,在每一種詩的選本中都有實用性的記載,過去每個學生都能背誦。在一些發表漢語詩歌的英語出版物裏,也包含着這些格式,例如 Bynner 和 Kiang 的 The Jade Mountain。我們可以列出這些格式,以便展開下文的討論,其中○表示平聲,×表示非平聲:

	A 式	**A' 式**
1、	××○○×	○○××○○×
2、	○○××○	××○○××○
3、	○○○××	××○○○××
4、	×××○○	○○×××○○
5、	××○○×	○○××○○×
6、	○○××○	××○○××○
7、	○○○××	××○○○××
8、	×××○○	○○×××○○

	B 式	**B' 式**
1、	○○○××	××○○○××
2、	×××○○	○○×××○○
3、	××○○×	○○××○○×
4、	○○××○	××○○××○
5、	○○○××	××○○○××
6、	×××○○	○○×××○○
7、	××○○×	○○××○○×
8、	○○××○	××○○××○

	C 式	**C' 式**
1、	×××○○	○○×××○○
2、	○○××○	××○○××○
3、	○○○××	××○○○××
4、	×××○○	○○×××○○

5、	××○○×	○○××○○×
6、	○○××○	××○○××○
7、	○○○××	××○○○××
8、	×××○○	○○×××○○

	D式	D'式
1、	○○××○	××○○××○
2、	×××○○	○○×××○○
3、	××○○×	○○××○○×
4、	○○××○	××○○××○
5、	○○○××	××○○○××
6、	×××○○	○○×××○○
7、	××○○×	○○××○○×
8、	○○××○	××○○××○

人們總是用一句著名的口訣“一三五不論,二四六分明”來對上表加以補充,正如 Downer 和 Graham 所指出的,這句口訣的意思是説“1、3 和 5 字允許破例,2、4 和 6 字則嚴格”(Downer and Graham 1963:146)。其確切的意思,是指除了末字,一句中所有單數字都可改用平仄相反的字,但雙數字必須是格式中規定的聲調的字。江亢虎曾用符號“丄”表示那些能用平聲字代替的非平聲字,用符號“丅”表示可以用非平聲字代替的平聲字,這樣就解決了冗長地描寫大量可供選擇的格式的麻煩。但是,衹要加以分析思考,便能立刻發現表的數目可以進一步縮減。在 A(或 A')式和 B(或 B')式的第一句下加一個注語,大意爲當要求押韻時,這一句可以分别被 C(或 C')式和 D(或 D')式的第一句所代替。因此,王力先生(Wang 1963:72—73)和劉若愚(Liu 1962:26—27)都發現有四個表已足够了。王力先生還注意到,七字句實際上是五字句的延長,即在句首加上兩個字,這兩個字同下面兩個字的平仄相反(Wang 1963:75—76),由此他就可以把表縮減爲衹有兩個,雖然他没有這樣做。至於絶句,傳統的解釋是截取八句律詩的任四句而成,這是 種不合實際的推想,但大多數學者似乎都相信這種説法,包括像王力先生這樣的當代權威學者(Wang 1963:34)。清代學者趙執信曾論及這個問題,提出絶句産生於律詩之前,而律詩則由絶句

擴展而成(參見 Wang 1963:34),但是很少有人接受這一觀點。下面我將試圖進一步論證這一論點。

2.2. 在 John Lotz 的一篇文章中,我們可以找到一個非常巧妙的處理方法,來解決下面所要研究的問題。由於采用了一個相當抽象的方式,他成功地僅列了兩個表。如果我們把七字句的頭兩個字放在括號裏,表示其出現是隨意的,這兩個表就很容易壓縮爲一個。下面是修訂後的表,×表示兩個聲調基礎(即平仄)之一,圓圈表示相反的聲調基礎,黑點表示没有明確規定的聲調,括號裏的 r 表示這句末字押韻(rhyme)(Lotz 1960:145)。

(·○)·×·○·	(r)
(·×)·○·×·	(r)
(·×)·○·×·	(–)
(·○)·×·○·	(r)

這種方式比傳統的方法更好,因爲它清楚地表現了一聯中上下句的對比和相鄰兩聯同樣的互相對比。但是,它仍然不能令人滿意。其一是,它會使人誤以爲一句的末字聲調没有規定,而事實上它們的聲調却是最嚴格的,另一點是,它未能概括所有可能的格式。

2.3. 唐詩格律系統的傳統表示方法在許多方面都不能令人滿意,它既不精密,也不完善。事實上,這種方法是一種編排或者列舉一系列表的嘗試,而這些表却無法編排或列舉。同許多其他情況類似,當我們充分地列舉表面現象時,我們却失去了任何機會去發現基本的普遍原則。當然,就其所涵蓋的内容而言,編排的表是正確的,但也僅此而已。有些學者聲稱可從以上的表中,清楚地看出這一格律系統的基本原則①,我相當懷疑。在我看來,這類表無論多少,也不可能明確地告訴我們這些原則是什麽。上面所列的表,甚至加上文字説明一些位置上的聲調是可變的,也不能概括必須包含的所有現象。正如我們在後面的討論中將要看到的那樣,在一些特有的條件下,至少有兩種違背這些表的做法是允許的(見 § 3.5 和 § 3.6)。另外一方面,這些表僅僅顯示了

① 例如 James Liu 教授(Liu 1962:27)在這四個格式之後推論説:"從以上的表,可以清楚地看到句中聲調變化的原則和全詩裏聲調序列的重複和對比。"

律詩和絶句這兩種特殊形式的格律,而格律詩還有其他形式,例如:一聯可以單獨存在,即所謂"對聯"或"對子";三聯也可以作爲一個單位,叫做"三韻小律";五聯或者更多聯的詩叫做"排律",衹要詩人能够或者願意寫多長就可以寫多長。爲了包括所有這些格律形式,也爲了表示出詩律的一般原則,製表顯然不是一個理想的方法。像 Arthur Waley 和 Hans H. Frankel 那樣衹作一點印象派式的説明(Waley 1919:25 和 Frankel 1963:261—63),也達不到這個目的。爲了適應這一需要,我們應該尋求建立一系列嚴格的法則,這些法則應能産生所有可能的格式。

3. 在律句裏最重要的音節顯然是最後一字,但靠近末字的那些音節,顯然也是重要的。從以下事實我們可以看出這一點。首先,末字的聲調永遠必須合於平仄。其次,倒數第三字雖然可用平仄相反的字,但最好還是要符合平仄規定(參見 Wang 1963:90)。第三,正如王力先生所正確闡述的(Wang 1963:75—76),五字句延長爲七字句時,這一擴展衹是頭上加頂,而原句的平仄格式不受影響。第四,雖然偶數字的平仄無論在何位置都不能改變,但有證據説明,比起離句末較近的字,詩人們往往不太注意離句末較遠的字的平仄①。在討論某句的聲調格式時,我發現需要從句尾開始,而不是從句首開始。在我看來,上面陳述的事實可以爲這一做法提供根據。無論如何,這樣就可以用同樣的方法處理五字句和七字句,這將簡化我們的討論②。

3.1. 一旦采用這種可稱爲"倒序"的方法,衹要稍加想象,我們就會看出建立詩句韻律格式的基本原則。這個原則是一個鏡式反映程序,按照或此或彼的順序,重叠兩個對比成分③。如果用 a 表示一個平聲或非平聲,用 b 表示

① 例如李白《黄鶴樓送孟浩然之廣陵》的首句"故人西辭黄鶴樓","人"字是平聲字,而按規定應爲仄聲(參見 Bishop1955:55)。

② 作爲一個明顯的反例,可看 Wang 1963:108,在那裏,他不得不重複這樣一些冗長的句子:"五言句的第三字,和七言句的第五字。"對我們來説,當從句末算起時,這兒説的實際上是同一個字。

③ 我從 Bishop1955 中獲悉吉川幸次郎的 Some Remarks on Meter in Chinese Poetry(遠東學會六届年會論文,1954 年 4 月)一文。他的引文是:"在傳統的西方詩律中,一個格式一再重複,衹有微小的變化,傳統的漢語詩律與此不同,是建築在一聯内聲調對比原則的基礎上的,就好像漢語聲調調高的自然結果。借用音樂的術語,與其説是模擬式擴展,倒不如説是使用鏡式對比。"因爲没有機會看到這篇文章,不知道他所説的"鏡式對比"是什麽意思,但是我懷疑他説的可能同本文中所説的意思相近。

平仄相反的對立成分，我們就可以用公式表達如下：

（Ⅰ）$_{m}$[ab]＝[……baabbaabbaab]

上面的公式裹，寫在下角的 m 指方括號裹的序列按鏡象對映（mirror image）程序，並按照 m 所在的方向擴展。從理論上説，這個程序一個人願意運用多少次就運用多少次。换句話説，此公式能産生任何長度的詩句。事實上，唐詩的句長是有限制的，衹有五字或七字，但這决不能否認上述原則的正確性。借用 Chomsky 的觀念，我們認爲這個原則代表了詩人組織這類詩句的能力。實際上詩人不寫九字、十九字或一千○一字的句子，衹不過是受到實踐的限制。我們知道，從歷史上看，五言句産生幾百年後，七言句才開始使用。我們可以想象得到，在此之前，很多人可能認爲七言句不能接受，正如我們現在幾乎不能接受九字句一樣，但是七言句還是産生了。值得注意的是，對聯作爲律詩的一種特殊形式，上下聯都必須遵循這裹所討論的詩律格式，而字數却可以多於七言[①]。無論如何，如果需要，我們就能够很容易地規定一句可以有多少音節。我們提出的這個公式，可以産生任何長度的詩句，有力地表現了它的能産性，這絶不是一個缺點。

3.2. 由上節所建立的公式，可以産生兩個基本句型。當 a 代表平聲、b 代表非平聲時，有下列型式，可以稱之爲 α 式句：

[……×○○××○○××○○×]

其最後七字或五字爲：

[(○○)××○○×]

當 a 代表非平聲、b 代表平聲時，則有下列型式，可以稱之爲 β 式句：

[……○××○○××○○××○]

而最後七字或五字爲：

[(××)○○××○]

---

① 例如有名的對聯"寄寓客家寤寐寒窗空寂寞，迷途遐遠退還蓮徑返逍遥"（×××○××○○○××，○○○××○○××○○），除了幾個例外，即是遵循本文所討論的這些法則（參見§3.4）。

將這兩個基本句型同§2.1的八個表加以比較,如果我們暫時不管一句中最後三字,這三個位置我們將在後面(§3.3)討論,我們就會極爲驚奇地看到,唐詩詩句排次嚴格遵循的原則,跟句中音節排次的原則竟然完全相同。不同之處僅在於,在句中鏡象程序是從句尾向前或向上發生作用,但在詩句之間,則是從詩首開始發生作用。如果用A表示α式句或β式句,用B表示相對立的句型,我們可以用下面的公式表示這個程序:

(Ⅱ){AB}m={ABBAABBAABBA……}

這裏我們可以又一次指出,這一公式具有極大的能産性,可以按照詩人的願望使用多少次。幸運的是,這一次我們有證據支持這一主張,因爲我們可以找到不同長度的這種類型的詩。正如前面所指出的,我們有對聯(兩句)、絶句(四句)、三韻小律(六句)、律詩(八句)和排律(十句以上)。有相當多的排律有兩百句,這一長度似乎是在實踐中的上限,但我們仍相信這僅僅是在實際寫作中的界限。衹要有人願意寫,就没有理由説這種類型的詩不能有一萬句。

3.3. 和英語一樣(Levin 1962:42),漢語詩歌特别是唐詩遵循的兩個最重要的音韻規則,是格律和押韻。當然,這兩個特徵總是交織在一起的。在唐詩裏,押韻的規則是衹有雙數句入韻,韻字必須全是平聲字①。除首句外,單數句不押韻,並且末字必須全部用仄聲字。首句是否入韻是隨意的,但當不入韻時,末字必須用仄聲字。這些限制顯然與上節公式發生冲突,上節公式規定的詩句的排次,α式句和β式句二者都可作爲雙數句或單數句出現。顯然,我們還必須再作些工作。我們又一次發現了一個有效的基本法則,以便進行所有需要的調整。這一法則可以用文字非常簡潔地表達出來,儘管並不十分精密,即"在要求押韻時,末字的聲調須同倒數第三字的聲調交换"。其意思是説,α式句是單數句時,仍然是[(○○)××○○×],但當它是雙數句時,則必須修正爲[(○○)×××○○];β式句是雙數句時,仍然是[(××)○○××○],但當它是單數句時,則必須修正爲[(××)○○○××]。當它們作爲詩的首句時,根據是否需要押韻而加以變化。上述的程序,可以用下面的法則表達出

① 這個主張建立在大多數格律詩押平聲韻的基礎之上,顯然,這衹是一種約定俗成,看不出律詩不能押仄聲韻的理由。事實上,我們發現了有些律詩是押仄聲韻的(見§4.2),但這主要是五言絶句,這是它所謂古絶影響的明顯標志。

來,這個法則帶有一種數學式的精密性,雖然由於必須補充不少注釋,從而看起來有點笨拙。

(Ⅲ) [X+a+S+b]Nth→[X+b+S+a]Nth

注釋:1. 當 N=1 時爲非强制性(Optional)

2. 當① N=2n,a=○,b=×,

② N=2n+1,a=×,b=○時爲强制性(Obligatory)

3. S 爲一個單字(single syllable)

4. n 爲除零外的任何整數

以上法則加上前面兩個公式,就可以推演出所有可能的聲調格式的基本形式,包括§2.1 節裏的八個表。這是些最嚴格的形式,實際上極少有詩是完全按這些形式寫成的,它們實際上都要加上更進一步的變化。在著名的詩選《唐詩三百首》中[①],全部這種類型的律詩裏,衹有兩首絶句同這些基本格式的兩種完全相符(但我必須聲明,我没有極爲細緻地查檢)。下面就是這兩首詩。

聽彈箏

李端

鳴箏金粟柱　素手玉房前

○○○××　××××○○

欲得周郎顧　時時誤拂弦

××○○×　○○××○

征人怨

柳中庸

歲歲金河復玉關　朝朝馬策與刀環

××○○××○　○○×××○○

三春白雪歸青冢　萬里黄河繞黑山

○○××○○×　××○○××○

3.4. 這些基本的格律格式,對現實的語言説來,顯然是很嚴苛的。例如,正如王力先生指出的(Wang 1963:112),在數目字裏,衹有“三”和“千”是平聲

① 這本詩選,我選用的是喻守真的注釋本(Yu 1957)。

字。這樣詩人要想按這些最嚴格的格式寫作，選擇符合規定的字往往會一籌莫展，因此，需要放寬尺度來給人們以更大的創作自由，這就產生了著名的歌訣“一三五不論，二四六分明”，即從句末算起，所有的雙數字必須符合平仄規定，但單數字，除了末字外，可以換用平仄相反的字。我們可以再提出一個法則來表示這種任意性的變化：

(Ⅳ)［X＋a＜SS＞n］→［X＋b＜SS＞n］

注釋：1. S爲一個單字

2. n爲除零外的任何整數，表示＜SS＞出現的次數

3. a，b＝○，×；但a≠b.

對這條法則還必須補充兩點：

1）可能有人會問，爲什麼這個格律系統對雙數字這樣嚴格？在我看來，這個問題很不容易説清，没有完全令人滿意的答案。一個合理的解釋是，漢語似乎有向雙音節詞發展的趨勢，並且第二字一般重讀，上舉法則衹不過是這種語言現象的反映[①]。無論如何，我們更爲關心的是這個格律系統是什麼，而不是它爲什麼是這樣。上述現象是我們觀察到的，而這條法則闡述的就是這個現象。

2）根據上述法則，倒數第三字可以改變平仄，但實際寫詩往往没這樣做。這種句子叫做“拗句”，最好是予以避免或加以補救。對拗句的補救稱爲“拗救”，指的是如果倒數第三字不用規定的平仄，那麼最好倒數第五字也用平仄相反的字從而取得平衡。在我看來，拗句的“救”和避免都有着音韻學上的動機，雖然我們很難用嚴密的術語加以闡述。十分遺憾的是，這一韻律特徵幾乎不能納入這個格律系統，因爲它不嚴密，也不十分明確，所以無法看作這個系統的基本法則的組成部分。但是，它常常表現爲一些獨特作家的獨特的風格。例如晚唐著名詩人許渾就是一個善於寫拗體詩的老手（Wang 1963：94），宋代著名詩人黄庭堅也常常特意寫拗句。采用法則Ⅳ所支配的格式寫的詩是很常

① 李方桂博士在一次私下談話中對筆者語，句中停頓的位置（在五言句第二字或七言句第四字之後），可能同這裏討論的事實有點關係。我個人覺得這個意見也許可以稍加引申，即在每一個雙數字之後都有可能產生一個節奏停頓，這個節奏點使得此處的聲調規定得相當嚴格。傳統的吟詩方法，每個雙數字都可以曼聲拉長，可以爲這種説法提供一些支持。

見的,這裏我們可以引用一首詩作爲例子,平仄改變的地方畫綫於下。

同鄉偶書

賀知章

少小離家老大回　　鄉音無改鬢毛衰

××○○××○　　○○○××○○

兒童相見不相識　　笑問客從何處來

○○○××○×　　×××○○×○

3.5. 修正了的β式句可以進一步從[(××)○○○××]式變爲[(××)○○×○×]式,這一新的格式連科舉考試都正式接受,根據王力先生所説(Wang 1963:103—8 和 823—25),比起它本來的格式,甚至在詩人中更爲流行。這一可以任意選擇的改變意味着,當連續三個平聲字的序列直接發生在最後兩個非平聲字之前時,相鄰的平聲和非平聲可以互换。用公式表達爲如下法則:

(Ⅴ)[X+○○○××]→[X+○○×○×]

包含這種格式句子的詩相當普遍,這裏可以引兩首作爲例子。這兩首詩幾乎每一句都符合基本格式,但根據這一新法則變化的兩句却除外,因此顯得更爲引人注目。

宿建德江

孟浩然

移舟泊烟渚　　日暮客愁新

○○×○×　　×××○○

野曠天低樹　　江清月近人

××○○×　　○○××○

送僧歸日本

錢起

上國隨緣住　　來途若夢行

××○○×　　○○××○

浮天滄海遠　　去世法舟輕

○○○××　　×××○○

水月通禪寂　　魚龍聽梵聲

××○○×　　　　○○××○

惟憐一燈影　　　　萬里眼中明

○○×○×　　　　×××○○

這條新法則顯然違背了著名的口訣“一三五不論,二四六分明”,因爲不僅倒數第二字從仄聲變成了平聲,而且倒數第三個字也必須嚴格用仄聲。因此,王力先生曾再三批評這個著名的口訣(如 Wang 1963:83、100),他還告誡,實行以上法則,衹限於這些修正過的 β 式句,而 β 式句倒數第五字平仄不變(即未受法則Ⅳ影響)。在我們看來,這個批評和告誡可能並不需要,由此我們可以清楚地看到我們的方法比傳統方法的優越處。王力先生指出的困難並不存在,因爲對我們説來,這個由來已久的口訣代表一個稍高層次的機制,它的正確性是不容懷疑的。我們必須作的是在排次這些法則時,將法則Ⅴ排在法則Ⅳ之後,以使規律Ⅴ衹能在仍有連續三個平聲字的句子中起作用,它所産生的句子不再服從法則Ⅳ所決定的變化。

我們可以試着解釋爲什麽法則Ⅴ所決定的變化受到大多數詩人的歡迎,以及爲什麽這個變化僅限於平聲字的連續序列。在我看來,這種做法有音韻上的有力動機。正如我們所看到的,我們的法則産生的同一聲調的字的連續序列,最長是三個音節,現在法則Ⅴ説的是連續三個非平聲字是允許的,而連續三個平聲字雖然尚可,但最好變成兩個。如果我們記得,所謂仄聲實際由三個不同的聲調組成,但平聲則衹有一個,我們就能理解其原因了。一個連續三個或更多非平聲字的序列,如果不限於衹是三個仄聲(上聲、去聲、入聲)中的同一個,就仍然可以有一些變化,但是,一個連續三個或更多的平聲字的序列發音則不免有些單調。

3.6. 現在我們可以注意到另一法則,這一法則將使以上解釋更爲可信。這一法則在科舉考試中未取得合法地位,雖然如此,仍有許多詩人運用這一法則(Wang 196:111)。這一法則説的是,在一聯裏出句是 α 式句,而對句是 β 式句時,如果 β 式句的倒數第三字已從非平聲變成平聲(即受到法則Ⅳ作用),那麽 α 式句的倒數第二字可以從平聲變成仄聲(Wang 1963:108)。這 程序可用以下公式表達。

(Ⅵ) [X+○×]→[X+××]/ ____ [X+○×○]

我們可以引用一首絶句作爲例子。

聽彈琴

劉長卿

泠泠七弦上　　静聽松風寒

○○×○×　　××○○○

古調雖自愛　　今人多不彈

××○××　　○○○×○

根據我們的解釋,這首詩的格律形式,源自其基礎形式,首先由於法則Ⅳ的運用,影響第二和第四句,然後由於法則Ⅴ的作用使第一句變形,最後將第四句作爲其條件,由於現在這條法則的作用,修正第三句。因爲現在的法則是將法則Ⅳ作用的結果作爲條件,我們必須説明這條法則是在法則Ⅳ之後起作用。事實上,這條法則影響的那一句可能已經受到法則Ⅳ的作用,這就是我們没有在法則中規定這一句最後兩個字之前的字的原因。由此可以允許一個連續四個甚至五個非平聲字序列存在,我們曾指出三個或更多的非平聲字連用詩人通常並不有意避免,這是對我們這一説法的有力而直接的支持。當這條法則作用於一個"拗"而"救"的α式句時,就會産生一個連續四個非平聲字的序列(○××○× →○××××)。例如下舉詩的第一句。

登峴山

孟浩然

人事有代謝　　往來成古今

○××××　　×○○×○

江山留勝迹　　我輩復登臨

○○○××　　×××○○

水落魚梁淺　　天寒夢澤深

××○○×　　○○××○

羊公碑尚在　　讀罷淚沾襟

○○○××　　×××○○

如果這條法則作用於一個"拗"而未"救"的α式句,就會産生一個連續五個非平聲字的序列(××××○×→×××××),下舉詩裏的第一句就是如此。這種句式,在唐詩裏不太有代表性,但仍然被采用①。

登樂游原

李商隱

向晚意不適　　驅車登古原

×××××　　○○○×○

夕陽無限好　　只是近黄昏

×○○××　　×××○○

3.7. 我們已經詳盡無遺地討論了對唐詩的全部基本的格律限制。下面是這些法則的集合及其次序,這些法則按照這個次序運用,就可以有希望描寫這一系統的結構。由於一些技術上的困難,我們必須稍微修改前面提出的一些法則的形式,但它們在實質上仍是代表前面討論已經闡述的原則。

TP #(TP 爲唐詩的聲調格式 tonal patterns)

1. $TP \rightarrow \begin{Bmatrix}\alpha+\beta \\ \beta+\alpha\end{Bmatrix} m$

2. $\begin{Bmatrix}\alpha \\ \beta\end{Bmatrix} \rightarrow m\begin{Bmatrix}○X \\ X○\end{Bmatrix}$

3. [X+a+S+b]Nth→[X+b+S+a]Nth

  1) 當 N=1 時爲非强制性

  2) 當① N=2n,a=○,b=×;

    ② N=2n+1,a=×,b=○時爲强制性

  3) S 爲一個單字

  4) n 爲除零外的任何整數

4. [X+a<SS>n]→[X+b<SS>n]

  1) 非强制性

  2) S 爲一個單字

① Arthur Waley 曾説(Waley 1919:25):“唐代以前的詩歌中可以發現這樣的句子,其中接連出現五個曲折調(deflected tone)。這種詩句,對唐代詩人的耳將十分刺耳。”這裏舉出的例子顯示,這種句子對唐代詩人不一定太刺耳。

3）n 爲除零外的任何整數，表示＜SS＞出現的次數

4）a，b=○，×；但 a≠b

5. [**X**+○○○××]→[**X**+○○×○×]

非强制性

6. [**X**+○×]→[**X**+××]/____[**X**+○×○]

非强制性

4. 以上這些法則並非同等重要，根據一個人希望的嚴格程度，一些非强制性的法則可以不用，例如最後一個法則，正如我們曾指出的，在各朝的科舉考試中從來未曾被接受過。另一方面，又可以再加上一些法則以使這個格律系統更加不能通融，上述的法則中没有包括的一點，就是所謂“犯孤平”，照字面講其意思是“犯衹有一個平聲字的錯誤”，它真正的意思，如用我們的術語表達則是，法則Ⅳ不能作用於β式句（○○××○）的倒數第五個字，除非它同時作用於該句的倒數第三個字。換句話説，[×○××○]式句不是一個好形式，但[×○○×○]式句則可以接受。我没有把這條限制納入以上的法則中，不僅因爲它似乎有點任意性，也就是説缺乏音韻上的理據，而且因爲它很早以來就已被人們忽略了（Wang 1963：88）。

4.1. 上述集合中强制性的必須遵守的法則中，法則 1 規定了一首詩裏句子的安排，法則Ⅱ則描寫了一句中字的安排，前者似乎没有後者重要，因爲有時我們會發現一些詩遵循法則Ⅱ而不采用法則Ⅰ。杜牧的《贈别》可以作爲一個例子。

贈别

杜牧

娉娉裊裊十三餘	豆蔻梢頭二月初
○○×××○○（α）	××○○××○（β）
春風十里揚州路	卷上珠簾總不如
○○××○○×（α）	××○○××○（β）

違犯法則Ⅰ可以用不同的方式，擴展一首詩時，如果鏡象程序被忽略，其結果就會使前面一聯的對句和後面一聯的出句未能共用同樣的格式，這叫做“失

黏”,剛才引用的那首詩就是一個例子。在寫某一聯的兩句時,如果選用的都是α式句或β式句同一形式,這就會產生“失對”。在唐詩中,失對極爲少見,而失黏則相對説來較爲常見。這或許不太難理解,可以想象,一聯裏的語音對比,比上下聯的對比更重要。或許可以將同樣的理由引申來解釋,爲什麽法則Ⅱ和法則Ⅲ幾乎總是被小心地遵守,但法則Ⅰ却會偶然被忽視,因爲相較於一聯中兩句中的對比和各聯間的對比,一句内的語音對比無疑更爲重要。

4.2. 一般認爲唐詩僅押平聲韻,我們接受這一主張,是因爲我們發現絶大多數律詩用平聲字作韻脚。但是,不難發現有些五言絶句押的韻是某一非平聲。下面就是一個很好的例子。

送上人

劉長卿

孤雲將野鶴	豈向人間住
○○○××	××○○×
莫買沃洲山	時人已知處
×××○○	○○×○×

當盛唐詩人用某個仄聲韻寫律詩時,他們總是嘗試着將不入韻句的末字選用其他三個聲調的字,以表現出儘可能的變化(Wang1963:80—82)。舉例説,上面那首詩首句和第三句不押韻,但第一句末字是入聲,第三句末字是平聲,而入韻字是去聲。但是請注意,每句的格式和排次,都嚴格地遵循着我們已經發現的法則。如果所有不入韻的句子都用平聲字結尾,我們就可以很容易地標定其形式。我們要做的,就是像下面那樣,對法則Ⅲ的條件稍加修改:

(對仄韻詩)

當1) N=2n,a=×,b=○;

2) N=2n+1,a=○,b=×時,爲强制性。

稍後的詩人寫仄韻詩時,不入韻句的末字果真衹用平聲字(Wang 1963:81),這或許毫不足奇,他們正是遵循着這條修改的法則。

從語言學角度看七百年來中國詩歌的押韻*

研究一種語言的歷史，一般説來就是研究這種語言的語音演變的歷史。對於具有傳統音韻學的中國來説尤其如此。研究漢語音韻學以産生於不同時代的韻書爲主要依據。現存最早的一部韻書是隋代的《切韻》(公元 601 年)。研究《切韻》以前的語音，衹能借助於古典文獻中的韻文和諧聲字。由於在唐代以後産生了各種韻書，似乎唐以後的文學作品對於我們研究語音變化幾乎没有什麽價值。事實上，這種看法是極其錯誤的。一方面，所有的韻書，即使是那些按照客觀語音實際編纂的，也衹能反映它們那個時期語音系統静止的方面。如果我們企圖説明這一歷史時期與下一歷史時期之間的語音變化，那麽産生於這兩個時期之間的文學作品，尤其是作品中互相押韻的字，對於我們確定發生在這兩個時期之間的語音變化過程，或者對於我們驗證先前用其他方法確定的這個過程，具有不可估量的作用。因此，研究唐代之後的文學作品，的確具有語言學的意義。另一方面，就研究文學本身來説，這也是一項重要任務。任何形式的文學作品，特别是詩歌，如果我們不能解釋它的韻律，就不能算是深入、透徹的研究。我認爲衹有通過對語言的精準研究，運用嚴格的形式，才可能獲得這種解釋。

一、幾種主要形式的中國詩歌的押韻標準

本文的目的主要在於説明大約從十三世紀到當代中國詩歌押韻的一般情況。我們都知道，英語單詞“Poetry”在漢語中還没有一個詞能準確對譯。它的意思包括漢語的詩、詞、曲和其他形式的民歌。在這七百年中，所有這些形

---

* 原載陝西省語言學會編《語言研究與教學》1982 年總 4 號。收入《漢語音韻史十講》。
本文原是提交美國中文教師協會 1976 年年會(路易斯安納州新奥爾良市)的論文，題爲 Seven Centuries of Rhyming in Chinese Poetry: a Linguistic Interpretation，劉静譯爲中文。

式都得到了發展。因此,我將先略述它們的押韻情況,儘可能地從語言學的角度,説明其道理何在,儘管有時可能衹是一般的概述。

1.1 毋庸置疑,詩是詩歌中最受崇尚的形式。從唐代到清代,它一直是科舉考試中規定的項目。這樣一來,制定一個官方認可的押韻標準,自然也就成爲迫切的需要了。首先,隋代陸法言編纂的《切韻》,受到官方的認可,滿足了這一需要。但是,時有古今,音有轉移。逐漸地,《切韻》所分的一百九十三韻就不合實際了。因此,我們發現,早在武則天時期,許敬宗就上疏請求允許某些韻可以同用。例如,"東鍾"合韻,"支脂之"合韻①。在整個唐代,都使用這個補救的辦法,而《切韻》的基本形式得以保存。到了宋代,出現了官修韻書《禮部韻略》。這部書的收字數目和韻部數目都大大減化了。先前被稱爲"同用"的韻部合併爲一個韻部②。這種合併韻部的做法一直持續到元代,韻部數目逐漸減少,直到《平水韻》的106韻(或107韻),這一結果後來衹因被陰時夫的《韻府群玉》采用才聞名於世。這部書爲後來編纂《佩文韻府》奠定了基礎。《佩文韻府》産生於清代,是中國最著名的一部詩歌用詞的百科全書。詩的押韻標準就這樣早在元初或更早的時代,硬性地固定下來了,直到現在,如果我們希望自己成爲一個懂得怎樣寫詩的人,也必須嚴格遵循這一規範。

1.2 和詩比較起來,詞没有自己傳統的押韻標準,但這並不意味着詞可以不押韻,或者押韻不像詩那樣重要。事實恰恰相反,詞也講究押韻,衹是詞没有詩那樣的官方制定的押的標準。衆所周知,詞最早出現在唐代,被稱爲"詩餘"。因此,人們覺得詞也許根本没有必要制定一個與詩不同的押韻標準。當時,詞和詩的押韻所依據的語言基本上是相同的。但是,當語言變化之後,由於詞從未有幸(或説"不幸")得到一個官方制定的押韻標準,詞家就覺得没有必要去遵循特别的標準。他們衹依據自己的方言押韻,正如《四庫全書總目提要》所説的那樣③:

"三百年間,作者如云,亦無詞韻,間或參以方音,但取歌者順吻,聽者悦耳而已矣。"

---

① 參看唐封演《聞見記》;又見於張世禄1938,第96頁、第103頁所引。

② 《禮部韻略》的産生有一段相當複雜的歷史。詳細情況請參看張世禄1938,第104—114頁。

③ 參看《中原音韻提要》;又見於王力1963,第536頁所引。

然而，尋找一個可以遵循的標準似乎是人類的通性。於是，晚至明代，沈謙才編著一部詞韻字典，後經清初學者仲恒修訂，即今所見之《詞韻》，平、上、去聲各分十四個韻，再加上入聲的五個韻。較之平水韻，它顯得過於簡單了，在詞家中從來未得到廣泛承認。

1.3 元代，戲曲藝術形成高潮。元曲起於民間，因此，它的押韻也是根據當時的北京方言，而不是傳統的書面語言。1324 年，周德清編纂《中原音韻》，忠實地記録了按實際語音押韻的情況。這部書立即成爲包括散曲和雜劇在内的北曲押韻的標準。但是，隨着時間的推移，戲曲藝術中心從北方移向南方，這本最有威望的韻書也因過時而不合實用了。到了明代，官修韻書《洪武正韻》問世。它極力要使語言規範化。由於它是根據南方官話編纂，它比《中原音韻》更適合南戲，這便出現了"南從洪武，北宗中原"的口號。後來，另外一些爲戲曲創作而編纂的韻書也相繼出現了，但都采用《中原音韻》和《洪武正韻》的模式①。

1.4 明代的藝術中心雖然移到了南方，但是北京很快恢復了作爲國家的政治中心的地位。由於是國家首都，北京地區的語言，自然也就成爲官方語言，也就成爲其他地區人民努力學習的對象。明清兩個朝代，一批類似教科書的韻書産生了。其中有雲南蘭茂的《韻略易通》，山東畢拱辰的《韻略匯通》，朝鮮的《老乞大》、《朴通事》(作者不詳)等。另一方面，北京地區的押韻也由當地人民的藝術活動反映出來，如那些京戲、彈詞、京韻大鼓以及其他民間文學形式。著名的十三轍對這些地方藝術押韻做了很好的概括。

二、各種押韻標準的語音背景

面對這種情況，有一項雙重任務有待於完成。一方面，我們必須爲這些不同的押韻標準做出最符合邏輯，最富於系統性的解釋；另一方面，我們有機會利用大量的這類文學作品去解決漢語音韻學史的某些難題。顯然，僅僅這些民間文學作品是無法擔當這第二項任務的。

---

① 参看張世禄 1938，圖 7，第三部分；趙蔭棠 1936，第一部分。

2.1 平水韻作爲詩的押韻標準已被詩人采用,仲恒的詞韻由於太寬泛而未能得到詞家承認。但在反映從元代到現代這段相當長的歷史時期中,漢語語音系統的發展變化方面,它們都同樣幾乎不能給予我們什麼啓示。“平水韻”據説是根據金王朝政府的敕令而制定的,因此,也衹能反映中國北方從唐代到金代語音變化的一般趨勢①。但是,要説明所根據的時間和地點是不可能的。毫無疑問,它揭示了唐以後漢語語音發展的主流,由於這些變化都發生在十三世紀之前,本文就不討論了。

2.2 雖然元代初期還没有一個官方認可的曲韻,但早期元曲作家諸如關漢卿、馬致遠、白仁甫都是根據北京方言進行創作的。因此,他們作品的押韻反映了那一時期的語音實際。周德清作了精湛的總結,將它們記録在他的不朽的著作中。《中原音韻》建立十九個韻部,每個韻部都有四個聲調(不算所謂的入聲)。這種新的分韻方法與傳統分韻方法不同,所有早期韻書在給漢字分韻時,首先劃分聲調,在同聲調中按韻分類。《中原音韻》顯示了不計聲調直接劃分韻部的新趨向。當然一個字(音節)能與另一個字押韻是因爲它們發音時有一個相同的主要元音(韻腹)和音節末尾(韻尾)。這個簡單但又是根本的原則,得到了廣泛的承認。然而,令人驚訝的是,幾乎没有一個學者在構擬某一歷史時期的語音時,能嚴格遵循這一原則。我堅決遵守這一原則,重建一個可以圓滿解釋《中原音韻》韻部分類的語音系統。這個語音系統有四個元音音位。列表於下②:

	前	中	後
高		ɨ	
低	e	a	o

當這四個元音與六個可能存在的韻尾(包括零韻尾)結合時,理論上可以組成二十四個韻基。但事實上當時的語言中衹有十八個,這十八個韻基非常整齊地與《中原音韻》除支思韻和魚模韻以外所有的韻部相對應。按照我們的

① 參看張世禄 1938,第 124 頁、第 127—130 頁。106 韻與 107 韻的區別在於迥、拯兩部,拯部後來併入迥部。

② 參看薛 1975,圖 5。

理論,支思和魚模應該合併爲一個韻部。因爲它們共有一個韻基/iø/。也許由於語音上的區別和歷史沿革,它們一直是分立的(明代的藝術中心從北方移向南方,南戲的押韻顯然也就受到南方官話的影響。因此,《洪武正韻》被認爲是適應這種新情况的較好的韻書)。許多曲韻書顯示,這種偏差僅限於齊微韻和魚模韻。究其原因,歷史的傳統與方言的差異都起着重要的作用。在對蕭豪韻和"寒山、桓歡"二韻分立的處理上,較之《洪武正韻》,曲韻書的著者們似乎更遵循《中原音韻》。這是不值得驚奇的。我們知道,漢語音韻的變革常常起源於北方,然後慢慢擴展到南方。在《中原音韻》時代,許多語音變化被周德清記録在他的著作中,後來這些音變逐漸擴散到南方,使得南方方言在許多方面與周德清時代的北京方言相像,儘管這時新的北京方言已經産生。如果我們想徹底搞清楚南戲的押韻,那還有待於掌握更多的與南戲有關的知識和材料。例如,爲了探明周昂爲什麽設立一個"知如"韻,我們必須懂得蘇州方言[①]。

2.3 清代小學派的韻書揭示了漢語語音變化的主流。這些韻書的作者大部分不是北京人。一般地説,他們著書的目的也是企圖讓非北京地區的人學説他們認爲是正確的官話。這些韻書産生於明代及其後的不同時期,因此,認真研究這些韻書可以揭示《中原音韻》以後北京方言的演變規律。本文的旨趣在押韻,下面我們將直接討論涉及韻腹和韻尾的那些語音變化。

三、宋以後影響押韻的語音變化

我們爲《中原音韻》推證出的元音系統,大概也是唐宋等韻圖所依據的元音系統[②]。關於北京話的押韻,顯然由哈特姆(Hartman)首先提出的三元音系統,最能圓滿説明現代北京地區講本地話的人的感覺[③]。韻圖時期的四元音系統向三元音系統的轉化引起了一些主要元音循序漸進的變化,這些變化反映在産生於不同時期的韻書中。

---

① 參看薛1968,第74頁。

② 參看薛1975,圖3;第3、6章。

③ 參看哈特曼(Hartman)1944。我不完全同意哈特曼的觀點。不同的見解請參看薛《北京音系解析》。

3.1 第一個變化發生在蟹攝，即帶有低元音和/j/韻尾的韻攝。我們發現《中原音韻》的齊微韻中有許多一等字，實際上所有的三、四等字，例如計(/kjej/蟹攝)寄(/kjɨj/止攝)都已經變爲同音字。我們用下面這個公式表示這個元音變化。

$$\begin{Bmatrix} e \\ o \end{Bmatrix} \longrightarrow \text{ɨ}/\_\_\_\text{j} \qquad (1)$$

這説明在平水韻的齊、佳、灰三韻中，衹有佳韻一直約略地與《中原音韻》的皆來韻對應，齊灰二韻所含之字都已合併到齊微韻中，齊灰兩韻因而消失。同時也説明了《中原音韻》衹有兩個韻部帶有/j/韻尾的原因。

3.2 第二個元音變化發生在效攝，即帶有低元音和/w/韻尾的韻攝。在《中原音韻》中，我們發現衹有一個蕭豪韻與這個韻攝相對應，這似乎表示平水韻中的蕭、肴、豪三韻在《中原音韻》以前已經合併成一個韻了。但進一步分析就會發現事實並非如此，因爲“交”和“嬌”出現在不同的小韻中，這種情況衹能被認爲是/kjaw/和/kjew/的對立。“保”和“飽”也被分派到不同的小韻中，因此，我們衹得分别構擬它們的音值/pow/和/paw/。這兩對字在蘭茂的《韻略易通》中却作爲同音字處理了，因此，下面這個公式嚴格地説，在《中原音韻》所依據的那個方言裏，尚未完成。

$$\begin{Bmatrix} e \\ o \end{Bmatrix} \longrightarrow \text{a}/\_\_\_\text{w} \qquad (2)$$

如果《中原音韻》時代真有/ow，aw，ew/三個不同的韻基，那麽我們不禁要問，爲什麽周德清没有像爲寒山，桓歡和先天那樣，建立三個韻部呢？對於這個問題，我的回答是，在周德清所依據的方言(或次方言)中，這三個韻基顯然是對立的。但是，在元代偉大的戲曲家諸如關漢卿、鄭光祖、馬致遠、白樸等所處的方言區中，這種對立已經消失了。因此，周德清衹好遵從大作家而承認一個韻部。但同時他又按照自己所依據的方言謹慎而明確地將這一韻部的字分派到不同的同音字組中去了。换句話説，他在這裏使用了雙重標準，儘管也算是合理的①。

---

① 詳細的討論請參看薛 1975，圖 5，第 10 章。

3.3 蘭茂之後,明代又出現了兩本重要的韻書。一本是1606年出版的徐孝的《重訂司馬溫公等韻圖經》,這本書大膽地改訂傳統的韻圖結構,以便適合那一時期的語音實際。另一本書是畢拱辰的《韻略匯通》,產生於明末(1642年,作者死於一次對清戰鬥中)。另一方面,在清代之前,作爲北京地區民間文學和京劇押韻標準的十三轍,大概已被普遍采用了。從這三種材料中我們發現了北京方言語音系統的一些變化,這些變化導致了重建韻部,我們將在下文着重討論這個問題。這一時期出現的語音變化的順序還不能全部解釋清楚,所以我必須繼續發掘更多的歷史材料。我們希望在蘭茂的《易通》和徐孝的《等韻圖經》之間,能找到一些我們未知的材料。

3.3.1 閉口韻的消失肯定發生在很早的時期。我們在徐孝的書中發現傳統的咸攝字諸如"琰、三"等和山攝中的字諸如"閑,千"等排列在一起。同樣,傳統的深攝中的"林、心"等字和臻攝中的"真、根"等字也排列在一起。在畢拱辰的書中,我們發現了同樣的現象。此外,畢拱辰在《韻略匯通》的序言中,明確指出了音韻學前輩的"錯誤"。認爲他們不該將真文韻從侵尋韻中分出,先全韻從廉纖韻中分出,山寒韻從緘咸韻中分出。我們還發現十三轍中先前的一些以/m/爲韻尾的字與那些以/n/爲韻尾的字混到一起了,我們列出下面的公式,説明這個變化:

$$m \longrightarrow n/V\_\_\_ \qquad (3)$$

3.3.2 我們在3.1和3.2中討論的那個元音的重要變化,這時也發生在以/n/爲韻尾的字中。我們相信它發生在3.3.1討論的那一變化之後,所以可用下面公式表示:

$$\begin{Bmatrix} e \\ o \end{Bmatrix} \longrightarrow a/\_\_\_n \qquad (4)$$

這個音變肯定發生在這一時期,因爲它最圓滿地説明了《中原音韻》和《韻略易通》中的寒山/-an/、桓歡/-on/和先天/-en/三韻已經合併成十三轍的"言前"轍的原因。但是,在畢拱辰的《韻略匯通》中,我們看到仍存在山寒和先全二韻,似乎它們一直是分立的。但進一步考察就會發現事實不是那樣,我們發現原來分別屬於寒山韻和監咸韻的間/kjan/和監/kjam/現在與堅/kjen/和兼

/kjem/作爲同音字一起出現在畢拱辰的先全韻中。這説明畢拱辰不是根據主要元音劃分他的山寒和先全二韻的，而是根據介音位置上有 j(先全)或無 j(山寒)來劃分的。我們正在討論的這個元音變化當然發生在畢拱辰之前。

3.3.3 這個元音變化也發生在以後鼻音/ŋ/爲韻尾的韻中。但是，在這種情況下，我們發現帶有前低元音的韻(庚青/-eŋ/)和帶有高元音的韻(東鍾/-ɨŋ/)在十三轍中合併成了一個帶有高元音轍(中東/-ɨŋ/)，而没有歸入央低元音。

$$e \longrightarrow ɨ/\_\_\_ŋ \qquad (5)$$

許多韻書都記録了這個變化的結果，但是，畢拱辰的《韻略匯通》仍然把東洪和庚晴分立。進一步分析，我們發現畢拱辰書中這兩韻的分立不是主要元音的問題，而是介音位置上存/w/(東洪)或無/w/(庚晴)的問題。因此，我們認爲這個元音變化一定是在畢拱辰時期之前，甚至在徐孝之前就已完成，因爲我們發現徐孝把東鍾和庚青二韻中的字合併到通攝中去了，畢拱辰把東鍾和庚晴作爲通攝的合口呼與開口呼處理了。

3.3.4 下一個變化涉及《中原音韻》齊微韻中以/jɨj/爲韻母的字，例如“齊、西、一、吉”等。這個變化没有産生任何新韻，但却引起了許多音韻學家做出一些看似奇怪但理論上符合邏輯的事情。首先，我們發現徐孝把“鷄、西、皮”等字作爲他的止攝齊齒呼和支思韻中的字放在同一圖中，而把“居、魚、女”等字作爲撮口呼從魚模韻中分出，也放進了止攝。我們還發現，畢拱辰把“希、虚、衣、餘、朱”等字併入同一韻(居魚韻)。在十三轍中，有個“一七”轍，它不僅包括了畢拱辰居魚韻中的全部字，而且還包括了他的支辭韻全部的字①。這些重組的韻部似乎無法解釋，實際上，通過下面這個公式就看得很清楚了。

$$j \longrightarrow ø/jɨ\_\_\_ \qquad (6)$$

這個變化的結果使得像“齊、皮、西”等字不可能再與“灰、微、堆”之類的字押韻了，因此，應該把它們從含有/-ɨj/韻基的齊微韻中分出來。當它們的韻尾失去之後，這些字便和原來屬於支思韻/-iø/的字和魚模韻/-wɨø/的字同具一個韻基/-iø/，因此，它們和原來屬於支思韻和魚模韻的字現在同屬一個韻部。這

① 參看羅常培 1950，第 35 頁。

是合乎語音理論的,也是符合邏輯的。但是,在十三轍和同時代其他韻書中,以及民間文學的實際押韻中,我們發現合口呼(/Cwiø/)的字單獨形成一個轍(姑蘇轍),而其他三呼的字,開口呼(/Ciø/)、齊齒呼(/Cjiø/)、撮口呼(/Cjwiø/)合併起來形成一個轍(一七轍)。雖然現在我們的分析還不能揭示姑蘇轍和一七轍分離的原因,但我們至少能够説明爲什麽開口、齊齒、撮口三呼併爲一轍,這個秘密便解開了[①]。

四、北京地區十三轍以後的語音變化

對於現代的北京語音,我們確知還有兩個變化影響了當代的押韻。由於這兩個變化没有記録在清初的十三轍中,因此,我們肯定這種變化一定發生在離現在不太遠的時期内,大概是清代中葉。

4.1 梭坡轍和乜斜轍在十三轍中是分立的。就我們的觀點來説,這是由於它們的韻基是對立的/-oø/和/-eø/。這就説明岳/ywo/和月/ywe/的分立,不僅是因爲音節不同,甚至韻也不同。現代北京話中,它們已成爲同音字。現代北京人可能不明白爲什麽梭坡和乜斜要分爲兩轍,這當然是下面公式所顯示的變化的結果。

$$\begin{Bmatrix} e \\ o \end{Bmatrix} \rightarrow ə/\_\_\_\_ \# \qquad (7)$$

這個結果表明,十三轍四元音系統中的前、後、低元音併入了現代北京話三元音系統中的央元音/ə/,這是元音大變移的最後一步。至此,北京話新的元音系統得以最後完成。

4.2 第二個語音變化涉及十三轍懷來轍中少部分字。這個轍中的一些字像"街、介、鞋"等原來以/jaj/爲韻母,現在以/je/爲韻母,因此和梭坡轍和乜斜轍的字也能押韻了。這個變化顯然在零聲母字中没有發生,因爲像"崖、挨(矮?)"等仍讀/ja/或/aj/。所以我們必須再加上一個公式:

$$aj \longrightarrow ə/Cj\_\_\_\_ \qquad (8)$$

① 詳細的討論請參看薛 1975。

4.3 最後一點，在十三轍之後還有兩個重要的變化。嚴格説來，它們不屬於這篇論文討論的範圍，因爲它們不涉及押韻的問題。但是，它們在京劇傳統中又顯得非常重要，所以我還是決定在這裏談一談。第一個變化是“分尖團”。所謂“分尖團”就是在十三轍時代，聲母[ʦ、ʦ‘、s](/c、ch、s/)仍然可以出現在介音/j/之前，因此就和也能出現在/j/之前的聲母[ʨ、ʨ‘、ɕ(/k、kh、h/)形成對立，以[ʦ、ʦ‘、s]爲聲母的字叫做尖音，以[ʨ、ʨ‘、ɕ]爲聲母的字叫做團音。十三轍之後，發生了下面這個變化：

$$\begin{Bmatrix} c \\ ch \\ s \end{Bmatrix} \rightarrow \begin{Bmatrix} k \\ kh \\ h \end{Bmatrix} / \underline{\quad\quad} j \qquad (9)$$

變化的結果是尖團不分。十三轍時代相互對立的字變成了同音字，例如，須/sjwɨ/與虚/hjwɨ/；津/cjɨn/與巾/kjɨn/；青/chjɨŋ/與輕/khjɨŋ/等等，但京劇一直是分尖團音的。另一個語音變化與“上口字”有些關係。“上口字”這一術語説明了某些字在京劇中的發音與現代北京音是不同的。造成這種現象的原因很多(而這些原因常常互不相涉)①，其中之一是，帶有捲舌音聲母的音節發生了變化，像“書”和“知”在京劇中一定要讀作/srjwɨ/和/crjɨ/，它們分别不同於梳/srwɨ/和支/crɨ/，這是因爲十三轍時代京劇還保存這種對立。十三轍之後下面公式所顯示的變化將這種對立消除了。

$$j \rightarrow ø / r\underline{\quad\quad} \qquad (10)$$

五、結語

作爲這篇論文的大綱，我把上面的公式總列於此，一並注出由於這些語音變化而形成的新韻部。

$$(1)\ \begin{Bmatrix} e \\ o \end{Bmatrix} \rightarrow ɨ / \underline{\quad\quad} j$$

① 關於上口字參看羅常培 1963，第 172—174 頁。京劇另一類上口字涉及庚青韻與真文韻的關係，這顯然是南方官話的變化結果，對北京音没有影響。

平水韻的齊、灰等韻併入《中原音韻》的齊微韻。

(2) $\begin{Bmatrix} e \\ o \end{Bmatrix} \rightarrow a / \_\_\_ w$

平水韻的蕭、肴、豪等併入蘭茂《韻略易通》的蕭豪韻。

(3) $m \longrightarrow n / v \_\_\_$

侵尋韻歸入真文韻，監咸韻併入寒山，廉纖韻併入先天韻。

(4) $\begin{Bmatrix} e \\ o \end{Bmatrix} \rightarrow a / \_\_\_ n$

蘭茂《韻略易通》中的山寒、端桓、先全三韻併入十三轍的言前轍。

(5) $e \rightarrow ɨ / \_\_\_ ŋ$

蘭茂《韻略易通》中的東洪、庚晴二韻併入十三轍的中東轍。

(6) $j \rightarrow ø / ji \_\_\_$

《中原音韻》齊微韻中齊齒呼的字併入十三轍的一七轍。

(7) $\begin{Bmatrix} e \\ o \end{Bmatrix} \rightarrow ə / \_\_\_ \#$

十三轍梭坡、乜斜二轍合併。

(8) $aj \rightarrow ə / Cj \_\_\_$

懷來轍中此類字混入乜斜轍。

(9) $\begin{Bmatrix} c \\ ch \\ s \end{Bmatrix} \rightarrow \begin{Bmatrix} k \\ kh \\ h \end{Bmatrix} / \_\_\_ j$

尖團不分。

(10) $j \longrightarrow ø / r \_\_\_$

部分上口字。

縱觀整個文學史，押韻在任何形式的詩歌中一直是一個基本而顯著的特色。近半個世紀來，由於受西方詩歌的影響，我們的詩失去了這個特色。許多詩人學做無韻"自由詩"，但最近出版的中國刊物説明，工農兵詩人還是喜歡押韻。然而由於缺少一個官定的押韻標準①，當代詩人多按照自己的語感押韻，

① 民國政府教育部在1941年爲編製新的押韻標準做了極大的努力，十月出版了《中華新韻》，但現代作家根本不理會這本韻書。

即按照他們所説的方言押韻,就像劉半農的"教我如何不想她"那首詩的押韻一樣。這類作品的押韻,使得用押韻這個工具去揭示語音變化的規律愈來愈困難。

參考文獻

羅常培　1963　《羅常培語言學論文集》,中華書局。

王　力　1963　《中國音韻學》,商務印書館。

薛鳳生　1986　《北京音系解析》,北京語言學院出版社。

張世禄　1938　《中國音韻學史》,商務印書館。

趙蔭棠　1936　《中原音韻研究》,商務印書館。

Hsueh,F.S.　1975　*Phonology of Old Mandarin*, The Hague.

Hartman,Lawton M., Ⅲ　1944　"The Segmental Phonemes of the Peiping Dialect, *Language* 20:28-42.

薛鳳生 著

薛鳳生文集

鳳凰出版社

語法探索

試論漢語句式特色與語法分析**

前言

八十年代初我到國内時，就聽許多朋友説，漢語研究應從漢語特點出發。我覺得很有道理，但究竟是誰先提出這個想法的，我倒没弄清楚，後來才看到有人説，王力先生早在三十年代，就主張"在注重漢語自身特點的基礎上，吸收國外語言學科學或有用的成果"(《王力語言學詞典》前言)。這是很令人敬佩的，然而漢語到底有哪些特點，仍然未見有人具體清楚地説明過。近十年來，我的興趣漸次轉移到漢語語法，尤其是古代漢語語法。因此更迫切地感覺到，必須把這個問題作較明確的交代，否則對個别問題的討論，就會令人有虚空無憑的感覺，所以在我近幾年所寫的幾篇古文文法研究中，就試着列舉出幾條相關的漢語句法特點。但這個問題絶非那麽簡單，前此所列自然不够完備，説明也不够清楚，因此擬在本文裏作一較完整的解説，顯然這也衹是進一步的嘗試而已，期能産生抛磚引玉的作用。必須聲明的是，我認爲所謂"漢語的特點"，並不是説漢語作爲一種語言，本質上與其他語言特别不同，因而不能使用一般語言學理論解析詮釋，而是説在風格上，古今漢語的句式都有某些特色，因此在分析當代口語或古代文獻時，就必須充分掌握這些特色，才能正確地認定其語法結構及語意指向。换句話説，是要先認清語料的性質，然後才據以建立或套用某種語法理論，也是在八十年代初，我曾聽説有某位前輩批評某些年輕理論家的做法是"空對空"。起初我頗不以爲然，一則不解其意，再則認爲可能"傷害青年學者的積極性"，但後來猜想他的意思可能是説，某些青年學者没有真正對漢語下過工夫(此一空也)，衹學了點外國語法，便施施然宣稱采用某種語法理論分析漢語，而實則對該理論的真意可能尚未摸透(此又一空也)。果

** 原刊《古漢語研究》1998 年第 4 期。

爾,名之曰“空對空”不亦宜乎?本文的目的是釐定漢語句式的這些特色,强調在研究句法時,必須充分考慮到這些特色,否則就會誤解例句的性質,並因而造成語法分析的錯誤。由於我的興趣偏重古文,所以將多舉些古代漢語的例子。

一、漢語句式的特色

1. 高度的“口語風格”。

就其目的而言,先秦的傳世文獻,如諸子書及《左傳》《國語》《國策》等,大致可分爲“説教、游説、講古”等類;其語言上的共同特點則爲講説式的,且常出之以對話的形式。這些著作對後世影響極大,成爲摹仿的藍本,故其口語風格遂成典範。所以古文用詞雖日趨典雅,其句式則常較簡短,句中成分之間的關係亦較鬆散,這些正是口語的表現,白話文的發展過程也是這樣的。六朝以下的佛經與變文、唐宋時期的各式語録、宋代的話本、元明時代的講唱文學,都是口語式的;其後雖有專供閲讀的個人創作,如《紅樓夢》與《金瓶梅》等,仍皆不脱口語風格。這些作品也成爲後來白話文的範本,所以胡適之提倡白話文時,即以“我手寫我口”爲口號。這一現象,衹要把前述作品與現代的文藝作品作一比較,就可以看出來了。後者是所謂“歐化”的結果,但所謂“歐化”的含義,應爲“脱離了口語風格”,而非“完全不合中文文法”,故趙元任先生特名其書曰《中國話的文法》(A Grammar of Spoken Chinese),用以表明其性質。本文所舉之“特色”,因此同樣合於“文言文”和“正宗白話文”,而下文所及之其他特色也多與此項特色有關。

2. 主謂之含意爲話題與説明。

從印歐語言的語法角度看,漢語常有一些“莫明其妙”的句子;例如:“美國駐華大使换了司徒雷登了!”(借用吕叔湘先生的例子)。類似的句子在漢語中是極常見的,這究竟是漢語語法很奇怪呢?還是觀察的角度有問題呢?趙元任先生顯然認爲是後者。所以他把主語和謂語這兩個語法單位在漢語中的關係,重新界定爲話題對説明。這是一個極重要的發現;從這個角度來看,當“駐華大使”這個話題提出來了以後,用“换了司徒雷登了”加以説明,非常自然,實在没有什麼好奇怪的。爲什麼漢語的主謂關係需要作這樣的特殊界定呢?我過去一直不大明白，現在意識到，這其實也是口語風格的一種反映。衹要謂語可以説明主語是什麽，就算合格，至於這個謂語是不是一個動詞組合，就不一定了。這類句子在古文中也是常見的。例如："貨，惡其棄於地也，（不必藏於己）。"（《禮記·禮運》）趙先生提出的這一觀點，足以解釋漢語的一切句式，不限於上述例句。他這個説法廣爲語法學者所引用，也受到高度贊揚，本應對漢語句式結構的分析與認定，有極大的影響，但却未得到充分的發揮，這是很令人惋惜的。本文所提出來的幾個看法，雖然有不少與趙先生不同的地方（見下文討論），但可以説都是從趙先生的理論觀點（特别是 Chao 1968，Chapter 2）推演發揮出來的。

3．語氣詞特别豐富。

早期白話文與現代日常口語中，語氣詞甚多而且常見，這是不用多説的，其實連古文也是這樣的。古文獻中的所謂發語詞如："蓋、夫、且"等，收尾詞如："也、乎、哉"等，都是常見的（參看：郭錫良 1988/9 文）。語氣詞的含意往往不易捉摸，這在其他語言中亦然（例如英語中的"Well，well，..."等），但比較少見於書面語。漢語中語氣詞數目之多，當亦爲"口語風格"的表現。語氣詞多半與句調有關，大有益於句子結構的認定，所以在作語法分析時，要特别留意。

4．語法詞（"虚詞"）常有省略。

在各種語言的非正式用語中，都有省略語法詞的現象；例如美國餐館的門上常貼着"No shirt，no shoes，no service"，意思不是説他們没有（或不賣）這三種東西，而是説："假如你没穿上衣，没穿鞋，我們就不提供服務！"不同的是，這個現象在漢語中更爲普遍，且常見於正式文字中。例如："橘生()淮南則爲橘，生於淮北則爲枳"（《晏子春秋》），首句顯然省掉"於"字。又如《戰國策·齊策》，有兩組結構相同的對照句，(a)"是其爲人也，……是助王養民()也"；(b)"是其爲人()，……是助王息其民者也"；可以看出，前一組中次句省"者"字，後一組中首句省"也"字。上兩例是明顯的省略，但在多數情況下，可能不會那麽明顯，尤其是連詞"而、則"等的省略，衹能從語境中推證出來，這個現象當亦爲"口語風格"之反映。由於講話時有"現場"（immediate situation）的幫助，省略幾個語法詞也許不會造成誤解，但脱離了"現場"或上下文以後，就可能産生歧義。對語法分析來説，要想正確地認定一個句子的語法結構，就得隨時記着這個句式特色,不能衹看表面,從而推論出一個句子的正確結構與語意。

5. 詞類活用。

所謂"詞類活用",也許應正名爲"實詞活用",因爲"虚詞"是不能活用的。詞以類分並常帶標記,不同的詞類擔任不同的語法功能,這是歐語的常例,但漢語則不然,其"詞類"(我也認爲詞是可以分類的,參看劉承慧 1995,否則就無所謂活用了)與"語法功能"之間的關係並不固定,所以在標示一個句子中的成分時,不應先入爲主地徑指其爲某類。漢語的這個特性,早已盡人皆知了,不必多説,但在許多討論漢語語法的著作中,却又常見"詞類"與"語法功能"這兩個概念糾纏不清。我們認爲,如果不把這兩個概念嚴格分開,並且隨時留意"詞類活用"這個漢語句法特色,就一定會造成語法分析的困擾與錯誤(見下文討論)。可喜的是,國内有許多學者已經想出辦法來這樣區分了,即爲語法功能另立一套與"詞"相對的術語,如"主語,賓語,謂語,述語,定語,狀語,補語"等,但似乎迄今尚未普及和嚴格地應用。

6. 詞序極爲重要。

漢語的構詞法及語法機制,在極大程度上依賴"詞序"(嚴格地説,也許應改稱"語序"),其含意之一爲:修飾語必須置於被修飾語(中心語)之前,這也是衆所周知的。在作語法分析時,這條特色自然應受到優先考慮,詞彙的類别是次要的,用以解説何以"黄牛"爲"牛","牛黄"爲"黄",又如古文中的"以"字,在多數情況下都出現在述語("主要動詞")之前,其功能類似英語的"前置詞"(preposition),但此字亦能出現在其他動詞之後,比如《孟子》中既有"易之以羊",也有"以羊易之"(梁惠王上),我們相信這肯定是有所謂的,因此如果不論其出現的先後,都把"以"認作"前置詞"(或"介詞"),是不妥當的(參看:薛 1996);再如所謂"動補結構",目前流行的看法也與詞序原則不合(見下文討論)。

7. 謂語形式不拘一格。

由於漢語語句的"謂語"是"説明語",所以衹要有説明意味的詞或詞組都可充任,因而謂語能以不同的形式出現,這常讓習慣於歐語的人感到不解。最常見的形式大概是動詞組(我没統計過),這是與歐語一致的,但漢語還有幾種别的形式;例如:(1) 直接以形容詞(組)作謂語,這迫使語法學家説形容詞也是一種動詞,即所謂“静動詞”(stative verb)。(2) 名詞(組)直接作判斷句的謂語,這在古代漢語中較爲常見,因爲古文没有像“是”之類的“連系動詞”,衹把作謂語的名詞放在主語之後就算了。(3) 以名詞作描述句的謂語,這在白話與文言中都有,但比較不常見;例如:“那個姑娘大眼睛小嘴巴”(借用趙元任先生的例子);古典詩詞中也有這種句式,例如:“浮雲游子意,落日故人情”(李白),“深秋簾幕千家雨,落日樓臺一笛風”(杜牧),“鷄聲茅店月,人迹板橋霜”(温庭筠)等。研究詩詞的人常在這類地方大作文章,對研究語法的人來説,這並不太特殊,重要的是,在看到一個名詞或名詞組時,不要先入爲主地認爲那不可能是謂語。(4) 謂語本身可以是一個句子,既“主謂結構作謂語”。據趙元任先生説,早在二十年代,陳承澤就提出“得以句爲説明語”這個看法了。這當然也是“謂語爲説明語”的反映,白話與文言裏都有這種句式,其出現頻率可能遠超過語法學家們的認知。這有兩層原因:其一,現代漢語通常省略作爲賓語的代名詞,因此像“這件事我知道”這樣的句子,受歐語影響的人可能説是“賓語提前”,而不認爲是“主謂結構作謂語”,但古代漢語裏有個“之”字作賓語,碰到“夏禮吾能言之”(《論語·八佾》)這類句子時,其爲“主謂結構作謂語”明矣!是賴不掉的!其次,當作爲謂語的那個句子省略了主語時,可能就會被誤作一般的“動詞句”,例如,當我們説“冰水爲之”(《荀子·勸學》)是以句爲謂語時,大概持異議者不會太多,但説“青取之於藍”也是以句爲謂語時,可能就有人反對了;究其實,衹不過後一例的謂語句没有主語而已。

8.“無主句”極爲常見。

没有主語的句子各種語言都有,不限於漢語。不同的是,歐語如英法等,句子都以主謂俱全爲常,即使在不能或不必指明主語時,其語法也要求有一個虚泛的形式主語;例如英語的所謂填補代詞“it”和法語的無定代名詞“on”,漢語則不然,例如在説到風雨等自然現象時,其語法並不要求必須有主語,衹説“下雨了,起風了”就可以了;但在歐式語法的影響之下,我們常有一種先入爲主的想法,一説到“句子”,就直覺地想到主謂俱全的“整句”,立刻想找出主語,連上例中的“風、雨”都得説成是“倒裝的主語”,衹有在實在找不到的時候,才説是“無主句”,其實古今漢語中,都有大量的“無主句”,甚至可以説“無主句”

是漢語的主流(參看 Chao 1968,第二章中的論“零句”)。這一方面是漢語的特定主謂關係造成的,因爲主語既是話題,故當在語境裏已屬明顯時,就不必重複了;另一方面也是由於漢語語法不要求形式上主語必須出現,所以在説到難以指名的現象時,就乾脆免了。在詮釋古文獻及分析語法時,必須充分掌握這一特色,才能正確地認清句子結構與真意。

二、漢語句式之特色與語法分析

在爲漢語的各種句子作語法分析時,我們似乎應該立下兩個目標。其一,這種分析必須符合漢語造句的一般原則,包括上文所提的幾個特色;其次,這種分析必須能够合理地説明那些句子的含意,即把語法結構與語意詮釋結合起來。這對古漢語的研究尤爲重要,因爲這種研究是以古代文獻爲依據的,其目的主要爲“訓詁”,既爲如何正確地詮釋古文獻提出理論性的根據。正確的語法分析當然有待於對語料的正確認定。由於過去分析漢語時,未能充分掌握上述的某些特色。因而對某些語法詞的功能,或某些例句的結構,作出不盡適當的解説。或根本無法提出任何解説。略舉數例如下:

1. 語氣詞在句式上的重要性,尚未受到充分的認識,例如句末語氣詞“啊、嗎、呢、嘔”等,雖然各含有不同的語意,但却有一個相同的功能,既表示句調,可以説是“句子”的標志(特色 3),這一看法也許有人不以爲然,因爲我們常看到像“張三啊,還没來!”或“李四呢,我也没看見!”之類的句子,所以有人説,這類語氣詞也“出現於主語和謂語之間”;連趙元任先生都這麽説,從而得出“主語謂語作爲一問一答”的結論,這個看法有兩個問題:(1) 説這類語氣詞既可出現於句末又可出現於主謂之間,是將其語法功能一分爲二,這是不必要的;(2) 説這類詞出現於主謂之間,就等於説“句法結構未變所以語意也基本未變”,但這是不確的,有没有這類語氣詞,各句的意思是很不一樣的。(如果把“李四”看作“賓語提前”,那就更離譜了!)爲什麽很多人會有這種看法呢?我猜想有兩個原因:其一,雖然大家都知道“無主句”是漢語中的常例(特色 8),但在歐西語法的影響之下,都不自覺地忙着找主語;其二,雖然大家都知道漢語的謂語常以多樣化的形式出現(特色 7),但受到歐西語法的影響,仍覺得

“張三、李四”這樣的名詞，不可能是謂語，假如我們能够充分地認識到上述三個特色的重要性，就會認識到“張三啊?”（意爲“你問張三啊?”）和“李四呢?”（意爲“至於李四呢?”）都是没有主語的句子。這樣分析就消除了上文所說的兩個問題。古代漢語的“也、歟、哉”等句末語氣詞亦當作如是觀；如：“而某也東西南北之人也!”（《禮記·檀弓》），就應該分析爲兩個無主的單句，“某”不是語法意義上的主語。

2. 如果没有充分注意到“謂語多樣化”（特色 7）和“無主句”（特色 8）這兩個現象，也會給語法詞的詮釋造成困擾，從而作出不適當的語法分析。例如，“而、則”是古文中兩個常用的連詞，但如何界定其語法功能及語意指向，却一直是一個問題。多數語法學家都説，它們連接“動詞組，形容詞組，句子”等語法結構，含意爲“順接，逆接，平接”等，但在碰到“人而無儀”（《詩·鄘風》）、“士而懷居”（《論語·憲問》）、“此則寡人之罪也”（《孟子·公孫丑》）之類的句子時，又説“還能連接主語和謂語”，至於含意，就不解釋了。如果我們考慮到上述兩個特色，就可以看出，這兩個連詞是連接子句以構成複合句的，其前爲狀語性的子句，其後爲核心子句，正合漢語的“詞序”（特色 6）原則（參看薛 1991）。這樣解析可達到雙重目的，一則爲這兩個語法詞找到了簡明的定義，再則爲各該句作出了妥當的分析；更重要的是，我們也因此能爲古代文獻作出正確的詮釋；例如：“士而懷居”絶不等於單純的“士懷居”。當孔子對他的學生説“士而懷居，不足以爲士矣!”的時候，是有針對性的，是告誡他們説，“（你們）作爲士，假如還想安居，就不够資格作士了!”同樣地，“此則寡人之罪也!”絶不衹是説：“這是我的錯!”而是説“説到這件事嘛，那（我承認）是我的錯!”現代漢語裏的“就”字是與“則”相對應的連詞，其語法功能亦然。例如“老張是好人，老李就難説了!”例中的“老李”絶不可能是該句的主語，“就”這個語法詞更幫助我們確認了這個事實。

3. 歐語大都有所謂“被動態”（passive voice），因此西方學者自然想找出漢語中與之相應的“被動式”（passive construction）；在西洋語法影響下，很多中國學者也在找被動式，中外合作的結果收穫頗豐，找到了好幾個，諸如：“爲（N）（所）V”，“見 V”，“V 於 N”，“被（N）V”等。麻煩的是，雖然這類句式通常確有被動意，但也並不一定；例如現代漢語中的“老張被（他愛人）哭得心煩意亂”,另一方面,不能用“被”字的句子倒可能有被動意;例如:“要打的電話都打了”,更令人不解的是,有了這麽多“被動式”(英語好像衹有一個 passive voice),似乎還不够用,結果還得説多數動詞都可能有“主/被”兩解,因爲還有很多像“票已經買了”的句子。古文裏也有很多像“昔者龍逢斬,比干剖,萇弘胣,子胥靡”(《莊子·胠篋》)之類的句子,説漢語有那麽多被動式而其動詞本身尚含“主/被”兩解,未免把漢語説得太奇怪了;所以我覺得較合理的解釋也許還是語法結構,動詞的所謂“主/被”兩解也許是“主語省略”造成的,即在一個以“主謂結構爲謂語”的句子裏,謂語句的主語没出現,是特色 7、8 合併造成的語法現象。至於那幾個所謂“被動式”,我們可以很輕易地證明,都不是表被動意的特定形式,而爲“述賓”結構(“爲、被”等是動詞而非語法詞),衹是慣用於表示被動意而已(參看薛 1997)。

4. 漢語有一個常見的語法結構,即所謂“動補結構”(叫“述補”似乎更合理)。其表面形式爲“動詞+形容詞”;例如“打敗”和“擊破”。把這一形式叫做“動補”,自然是説動詞是中心形容詞是補充。這樣分析似乎頗可商榷,因爲:(1) 這一組合是所謂“向心結構”(endocentric construction,亦稱“偏正結構”),向心結構是一個語法術語,不是詞彙術語,所以在爲其内部成分定性時,不應執着於各成分的詞類歸屬,而應着重於其語法功能,從而認定何者爲中心語,何者爲修飾語。(2) 所謂“動補結構”的整體語法屬性與“及物動詞”同,其含意却是與後面的“形容詞”一致的。在語法層次上,形容詞可以活用爲“述語”,動詞可以活用爲“狀語”,這是漢語句法特色所允許的(特色 5),所以這一結構的“補”才是中心,是個“使動動詞”(causative verb),其“動”實爲修飾語,是活用爲狀語的(動詞作狀語並不稀奇,例如“飛快、猜想、搶救、出賣”等的頭一個字)。(3) 把“動”看作中心語,把其後的“形容詞”看作“補充語”。是違背了漢語的“詞序”原則(特色 6)。(4) 由於把“動”看作中心,就迫使一些人説,在“把字句”中,“把”字後邊的名詞是“賓語提前”;這就給如何分析“把字句”造成許多困擾,無法解釋像“你可把我想死咯!”之類的句子(參看薛 1994)。(5) 把“動”看作中心語,還會發現“補”的語意指向相當紛歧;正如陸儉明(1997)所指出的,“砍光”的“光”指向受事,“砍累”的“累”指向施事,“砍鈍”的“鈍”指向工具等等,因此還得用“語意指向分析法”來説明這個問題。但如果我們把“補”改釋爲“狀述”,就可看出那個“述”(原來所謂的“補”)的指向,永遠是其前之主語(或“把”的“賓語”,實亦主語也;參看薛 1994),指向有紛歧的,正如同别的狀語一樣,倒可能是那個作狀語的“動”。當然,以語意指向爲依歸的研究法是我完全贊成的,因爲形式與意義的結合是語法研究的終極目標,也祇有在結合了以後,形式(或“公式”)才會簡明合理。上面指出的幾個所謂“動補結構”的問題,是忽略了三個漢語特色(5,6,7)的結果,一旦改釋爲“狀述”以後,這些問題也就不存在了。

5. 漢語句子的主語通常是有定指的人或物,這也是“主語爲話題”(特色2)的必然推論;但有時候又似不然,例如我們常説的“人不能没有良心”,或“父母要以身作則”等。古文中也有“人誰不死”(《左傳·昭二》)和“士不可以不弘毅”(《論語·泰伯》)之類的句子。上例中的“人,父母,士”等,顯然都不屬定指,這種現象如何解釋呢?在不否定“主語有定”的原則下,有人提出在定指與不定指之外,還有一種“泛指”,指與其他類别相對比的某類事物,而“泛指”也含有相當的“有定性”,因此可以作主語,這個説法誠然不無道理,但其定義似不十分具體,用於語法分析時,也有泛用之虞。我覺得在許多情況下,上述現象還可作另一解釋,即把上例中的所謂“主語”分析爲根本不是主語,而是代表“無主句”的謂語(特色 7、8),因爲在這些所謂“主語”之後,通常都得作停頓,而停頓具有與句末語氣詞類似的功能(特色 3),也可以説是句末語氣詞省略的結果(特色 4),更重要的是,祇有這樣分析才能反映各該句的真正含意。上例都含有規勸之意,在語用上説,是有針對性的,所以其意應分别爲:“作爲人,咱們不能没有良心”“作爲父母,應當以身作則!”“既然是人,誰能不死?”“作爲士,不可以不弘毅!”。假如按照“找主語”的習慣,把上例中的“人,父母,士”都分析爲主語,各該句的意思就太死板了,也失掉了原意;就語法分析説,這個提議縱不能取消“泛指”這一格,也可以減少其泛用。

三、漢語句式之特色與訓詁

詮釋古文獻時,正確的語法分析當然是必要的條件,但不是充分的條件,因爲我們還必須考慮到作品的歷史背景,作者寫作或講話的特定目的,以及他當時心中的預設情境。祇有在充分考慮過語法結構和語用因素以後，才能給某一古文獻提出較可靠的詮解。試以《老子》首章爲例，我們可以提出下面這樣的綜合性解説。

《老子》的性質顯然是"説教"式的，目的在傳播一種深奥不可名狀的哲理。據説其成書的情境是：老子出關時，應關尹之請，留下了"五千言"。不論這個傳説是否屬實，却頗能表現作者的心境：面對着要求他解説"那個東西到底是什麽"的人（實際的或想象中的），他開始宣講。在這種情況下，他按理不會立刻説出那個"不可名狀"的東西的名字的。我們可以引一段類似的文字作比較。基督教的《新約·約翰福音》是這樣開頭的。

"In the beginning, there was the Word, and the Word was with God, and the Word was God..."（中譯："太初有道，道與神同在，道即是神……"）

從文學的觀點看，中譯極好。用"道"字譯"the Word"，可以立刻引起中國讀者的共鳴，正如佛教初入中土時的"以道解佛"；但却不合原意，因爲原文祇是一個中性的"Word"，不含特别的意義，祇在後來幫助引出一個"名可名，非常名"的"God"。

有了上述的語用觀點，我們就可以給《老子》的首章做語法分析了。通行本《老子》甚少虚詞，而古文又例無標點，所以歷來各家注本的點讀，常有歧異。近年發現的西漢帛書本虚詞較多，似乎可以幫助解決不少句讀問題，因此有人説這是真本，虚詞是後人删去"以實五千言之數"的。但此説似乎亦未必，也許原本虚詞不多，帛本書的虚詞是西漢人憑自己的解讀加上去的呢！下文的討論將仍以通行本爲據。

(1)"道可道，非常道；名可名，非常名。"

這兩句的點讀，各注本皆同。帛書本於停頓處加"也"字，用意亦然。至於解讀，各家亦多相同；各注本於首句三"道"，字皆作兩解，即以第二個"道"字爲"言説"義，另兩個爲"神道"義，於次句三"名"字，則作一解，俞正燮的看法大爲不同，他説："老子此二語道名，與他語道名異，此言道者，言詞也，名者，文字也。"至於句法，各家都説頭一個"道"字和"名"字是主語，王雱更説："可道之道，……"James Legge 的英譯作"The Tao that can be trodden..."對句式的看法與王氏同。我對通俗的解釋相當懷疑，理由是：(一）這兩句是對稱的，三

“名”字既爲一解,則三“道”字亦應爲一解,否則即不對稱,故俞説甚有見地;(二)把“道可道,名可名”解釋爲“可道之道,可名之名”,是改變詞序以爲説;(三)要解説一個不可名狀的東西時,一開口就説出名字來(“道”),似乎不合常理。所以我覺得,頭一個“道”與頭一個“名”之後也應有逗讀,每一逗讀都是一個謂語,亦即没有主語的分句,因爲問者(關尹)與講者(老子)的心中,同有一個“不可名狀”的話題,故不用説出來。所以這兩句話(兩個“複句”),就可以解讀爲:“要解説嘛,可以解説,(但將)不是尋常的解説;要命名嘛,可以命名,(但將)不是尋常的名稱。”由此開端,引出下文。(“常”字依《休休庵老子解》,“可以説也,非尋常之道。”)

(2)“無名天地之始;有名萬物之母。”

各本對這樣分成兩句,皆無異議,帛書本句末有“也”字,顯然也是這樣分讀的。但對句中的逗讀,則意見分歧。《史記·日者列傳》引首句作“無名者萬物之始也”,與帛書同而多“者”字,可見西漢人是把“無名”連讀爲一詞的,當然也是把“有名”看作一詞的,許多注本都采這一看法,但漢人的解讀也不一定可信。另一些注本則將“無、有”單讀,而以“名”爲述語;例如王安石説:“無所以名天地之始;有所以名萬物之母。”我認爲後一看法是正確的,符合上下文的邏輯性。作者一開始先交代説,他要講的“話題”是難以名狀的,故先不點出,至此才勉强地給它提出兩個名稱,並説明這兩個名稱的分别所指,下文更專就“有、無”兩名爲説,指出連它們也衹是一體的兩面。(這個解釋更可反證,篇首的“道”字不可能是作爲“話題”的名詞。遲至第二十五章,作者才説出那個東西叫做“道”的緣故。)

(3)“故常無欲以觀其妙;常有欲以觀其徼。”

這兩句的形式各本差異甚大,有的没有“故”字,有的没有兩“以”字,有的連兩“欲”字都没有。帛書本“欲”字後有“也”字,是以“無欲、有欲”分别相連爲詞,許多注本都采此説,另一些注本則於“無、有”之後作逗。我認爲後者是正確的。上節已論定“有、無”爲兩名號,此當亦然。就文意説,若在此處忽然提出“有/無欲望”,似乎也有些突兀;就語法説,那樣解釋就等於把“無欲/有欲”看作謂語中心,而把“以”字短語看作補語了(參看薛 1996)。這恐怕也有本末倒置之嫌。

(4)“此兩者同出而異名,同謂之玄;玄之又玄,衆妙之門。”

這一段的文字與點讀,通行本的名注本均同,帛書本則爲:“兩者同出,異名同謂,玄之又玄,衆妙之門”,含意與通行本無別,文句則更簡潔。各注本給這一段的解讀基本相同,衹是對“兩者”的所指,頗有差異。主張“無名/有名”連讀的人,自然認爲“兩者”指的是“無名/有名”,甚至有説是指“無欲/有欲”的(河上公本注)。這在文意與語法兩方面,都頗難説得通;根據前文各段的解讀,我們當然同意,這裏的“兩者”,顯然是指“無/有”的。

綜合以上的解讀,我們可以把《老子》的這一章譯成白話。這會相對地減少其神秘性,好玄之士或將不以爲然,但這是考慮到語用和語法兩方面以後,所得到的結論。

“要解説嘛,可以解説,(但)不是尋常的解説;要命名嘛,可以命名,(但)不是尋常的命名。(可以叫做)‘無’,指的是天地未分時的狀態;(也可以叫做)‘有’,指的是萬物出現時的過程。所以(我)常常(把它看做)‘無’,借以觀察它的本質;(也)常常(把它看做)‘有’,借以觀察它的表相。兩者來自同源。名稱雖然不同,指的是一回事,比一切神秘的東西都更神秘,是通往所有奧妙的門户。”

參考文獻

王　力　《中國現代語法》香港(重印本),1971 年。

——　《漢語語法史》,《王力文集》第十一卷,濟南,1990 年。

吕叔湘　《中國文法要略》,香港,1942 年。

朱謙之　《老子集釋》,香港,1962 年。

郭錫良　《先秦語氣詞新探》,《古漢語研究》1988 年第 1 期,第 50—55 頁;1989 年第 1 期,第 74—82 頁。

陸儉明　《關於語義指向分析》,《中國語言學論叢》第一輯,1997 年,第 34—48 頁。

趙元任　《漢語口語語法》(吕叔湘譯),北京,1979 年。(原書刊於 1968 年)

《中國話的文法》(丁邦新譯),香港,1982 年。

劉承慧　《先秦漢語實詞的分類問題》,《國科會計劃期末報告》,臺北,1995

年,第19—45頁。

薛鳳生 《試論"把"字句的語義特性》,《語言教學與研究》1987年第1期,第4—22頁。

——— 《試論連詞"而"字的語意與語法功能》,《語言研究》1991年第1期,第55—62頁。

——— 《"把"字句和"被"字句的結構意義》(沈家煊譯),《功能主義與漢語語法》,北京,1994年,第3—59頁(原作刊於1989年)。

——— 《古代漢語的動補結構和"以"字短語的語法功能》(耿振生譯),《古漢語研究》1996年第2期,第14—20頁(原作寫於1995年,後刊於1997年)。

——— 《古漢語中的主語省略與所謂的被動句型》(馮勝利譯),《中國語言學論叢》第一輯,1997年,第105—117頁(原作刊於1994年)。

嚴靈峰 《老子宋注叢殘》,臺北,1979年。

漢語句式特色之成因

——趙元任先生給古文句法研究之啓示**

一、爲何分析古文句法？

所謂“注意漢語的特點”，意思是在分析漢語句子時，應優先考慮漢語構句的某些特色。歐語的構句當然也有某些特色，我們不應把那些特色强加於漢語的分析上。怎樣才能認定漢語的特點，或擺脱印歐語的眼光呢？我覺得這基本上是一個語意的問題，即先認清語法分析的目的。分析古文的目的當然是闡明語意，但要隨時記住這個目的却也不太容易。語法是很有系統性的，雖然不完全等於邏輯，却與之有相當的重叠，很容易使人迷於其形式而忘其目的。這在介紹或試圖提出某種“新理論”時，最容易發生，因爲我們往往會不自覺地挑選一些“合適”的例句來介紹某一理論，指證某句合法或不合法，從而忽略了説明爲什麽某句話衹能含有某種語意。所以我覺得要認清“漢語的特點”，我們必須再次肯定分析的目的，即句子的結構分析，必須與其語意相吻合，因此一個表面形式相同的句子(例如“他來了”，參看薛 1982)，在不同的情況下，可能必須分析爲含有幾個不同的結構，以説明其不同的含義。要瞭解下文的討論，這一點是必須强調的。爲了避免讓人誤會，以爲我説漢語跟别的語言有什麽根本的差異，因而不能用一般的理論加以分析，我不用“漢語特點”這一説法，改稱“漢語句式特色”，用以説明在古代漢語和近代“白話”(早期白話文及現在的日常口語)裏，句子的表面形式有一些特色，是印歐語所不常見的(並非絶對没有)，因此在作語法分析時，必須隨時考慮到這些特色，以免誤認句子的結構和語意。

** 原刊《語言科學》2004 年第 6 期。

二、漢語的句式有哪些特色?

在前文提到的那篇短文(薛鳳生 2000)裏,我曾嘗試着歸納出八條漢語句式的特色,謹再列舉於下,進一步深入討論。

1. 高度的“口語風格”。

這一條與其説是一個“原則”,倒不如説是一種“現象”。古代漢語和早期白話文,都是以對話或講故事的形式出現的,自然都有這種風格。趙先生堅持用“中國話的文法”作他的書名,可見他早已注意到了這一點。這種風格對句式的構成影響甚大;下面所舉的句式特色,有好幾條可以説都是這一風格造成的。所謂“歐化”的現代漢語,實爲脱離了口語風格的“書面語”,自然不屬此類。

2. 主語和謂語的含義爲話題與説明。

這是趙先生的一個重要發現(趙 1968:69—78),是口語風格的一種展現。從這個角度看,許多看似“奇怪”句子就不奇怪了,因爲謂語既爲説明語,衹要有説明的功用就合格了,不必拘於其詞類。忽略了漢語句子的主謂關係,就容易落入印歐語的窠臼,錯以爲謂語必須含有某種動詞。例如形容詞在漢語裏可以直接作謂語,這是典型的説明語,再自然不過了,用不着説形容詞也是“動詞”。但囿於歐式語法,不少人都説漢語的形容詞也是一種動詞,即所謂“静動詞”(static verb),而漢語名詞也可以直接作謂語,却未見有人説名詞也是某種動詞。

3. 語氣詞具有標示句式的功能。

這也是口語風格的一種表現。古今漢語中語氣詞都很多,皆與句調有關,可以幫助認定句子的結構,尤其是句末語氣詞。作爲一個句末語氣詞,“也”字就有這種功能。例如:“斯人也,而有斯疾也!”,以及“今也,則亡。”(並見《論語》“雍也”);這兩例中的“也”字都告訴我們,“斯人”和“今”都不是其所在句的主語或狀語,而是分别代表一個句子的(連詞“而、則”也幫助我們認清這種結構)。又如《莊子》中也有“父邪?母邪?天乎?人乎?……命也夫!”(《大宗師》末段);這裏的“邪,乎,也,夫”等字也都告訴我們例中的“父,母,天,人,命”

都分别代表以名詞作謂語的句子。我這個看法與趙先生有别,但却都是受到他的啓示。這裏牽涉到的一個問題是"句子"的定義。歐式語法恒以"主語加謂語"(即"NP＋VP")爲其基本定義;趙先生則從現代語言學的角度,把句子定義爲"前後皆有(有意的)停頓的話語",因此句子有"零句"(minor sentence,或稱"小句")與"整句"(full sentence)之别,而整句可以説是由零句組合而成的。(Chao 1968:57—68)趙先生特别强調"零句"這一概念在漢語語法分析中的重要性。這給我們此處的討論奠定了基礎。

4. 語法詞常有省略。

這個現象古今漢語都很常見。尤以"而,則,於"等爲然,這恐怕也是口語風格的遺風。按理説,省略語法詞會造成語意的錯亂,但在語境的制約下,引起誤解的情况並不太多;例如《國語·晉語一》"優施教驪姬"段,"夫豈惠其民而不惠於其父乎?"不會因前一"惠"字之後没有"於"字而造成誤會。就修辭來説,這種省略有時還是必要的,例如李白的"三山半落青天外",假如不省掉"青天"之前的"於"字及其後的"之"字,就没法跟"二水中分白鷺洲"對仗了。當然過分省略語氣詞有時也會造成太大的想象空間,給解讀古籍太多自由;例如朱熹的《周易本義》(其他注本也有同樣的情况)。試舉一例如此下:晉卦(坤下離上),初六:"晉如摧如,貞吉。罔孚,裕無咎。"朱子解曰:"(以陰居下,應不中正),欲進見摧之象。占者如是而能守正則吉。設不爲人所信,亦當處以寬裕,則無咎也。"朱子在這裏利用"而、則、設、亦、以"等語法詞,總算給極爲難解的初六爻辭一個説法,但恐怕也衹是聊備一説。總之,我要説的是:古文時有省略語法詞的現象,在面對古籍時,如能隨時考慮到這一特色,將極有益於確認其句法結構。

5. 所謂"詞類活用"。

這個説法是提醒習慣於歐語的人,不要用"印歐語的眼光"看漢語,其意爲:大異於歐式語法,漢語的詞類與其語法功能無固定的關係。但有兩個與此相關的問題:其一,對不認爲漢語詞彙可以分類的人來説,此説豈非等於白説?其二,對認爲漢語詞彙可以分類的人來説,問題是漢語有哪些詞類?這的確是一個難解的問題。認爲應該分類的人,包括趙先生,似乎迄今也未能提出一個完全令人滿意的説法。我有兩個想法:其一,我們也許可以采用傳統的二分法,即“實詞”與“虛詞”,把這個特色改稱爲較明確的“實詞活用”,因爲作爲語法詞的“虛詞”通常是不能活用的;其二,爲了撇開這個棘手的問題,可以遵守時下逐漸流行的做法,即嚴格地采用“主語,謂語,述語,賓語,定語,狀語”等術語,把語法功能與詞彙分類區別開來,這樣在碰到“爾欲吴王我乎?”(《左傳》定公十年),和“(是故先王制諸侯)使五年四王、一相朝”(《國語·魯語上》“莊公如齊觀社”段)之類的句子時,就不用説名詞“王”在此活用爲“動詞”,衹説實詞“王”擔任述語的角色就够了。當然要瞭解更基層的語法機制,“實詞”還是要分類的,以便認定哪些可以活用,活用時的語意轉化,及與其他詞條之間的搭配關係。

6.“詞序”決定詞類之語法功能。

在構詞法和造句法裏,詞與詞之間出現的相對順序,常決定其語法功能。這已是一個公認的現象了。問題是:在試圖分析漢語句子的結構時,我們是否充分考慮到這一現象?還是常受到歐語詞類決定語法功能的影響,而忽略漢語的這一現象呢?常見的做法多屬後者;例如“以”字,常見的説法是將之定性爲“介詞”,或稱“前置詞”,想到的是 preposition,但“以”字有時也出現在“動詞(組)”之後,例如,既有“以羊易之”,又有“易之以羊”(《孟子》“梁惠王”章),有時還出現在兩個“動詞(組)”之間,例如“樂以忘憂”(《論語》“述而”),因此又有“後置詞”和“中置詞”之説。這樣做不唯太煩瑣,而且有違其所在句之語意。假如我們考慮到“詞序”的重要,以及“詞類活用”的現象,這裏的問題就可以解決了。(參看薛 1997)在構詞法方面,兩個成分出現的先後秩序,決定前者爲輔後者爲主,古今漢語皆如此要求。如果嚴格遵守這個原則,所謂“動補結構”就必須改析爲“狀述結構”。(參看薛 2000)但在造句法方面,由於古文的句子通常都很簡短,複句之間的關係,也都遵守上述原則,而現代漢語的複句漸趨冗長(尤以所謂“歐化”句爲然),再加上“如果”之類連詞的使用,上述原則就可能放寬了。

7.謂語形式多樣。

趙先生將謂語定義爲“説明語”,是對這一現象的最深入的觀察。不似印歐語那樣要求謂語必須爲動詞(組),漢語句的謂語可以是名詞、動詞、形容詞等,甚至數詞及句子(即所謂“主謂結構”作謂語),衹要該成分有説明的功能就合格了。這個現象也是廣爲人知的,但也常遭忽略。例如當我們説“吾三十而立”中的“三十”是謂語,可能就有人覺得奇怪,如果再説“人而無信”(兩例並見《論語》“爲政”)中的“人”字也是謂語,不以爲然的人可能就更多了,但如能撇開印歐語的眼光,充分考慮到此處討論的謂語形式問題,以及連詞“而”的功能,上述的結論是理所當然的。(參看薛鳳生 1991)

8.“零句”極普遍。

這一現象在古今漢語中都極普遍,是人所共知的所謂“無主句”,但在分析古文時,却也是最容易受到忽略的。大概也是印歐語的影響,我們不自覺地都有先找主語的傾向,看到句首是名詞,往往就認定是主語了。例如:“相鼠有皮,人而無儀;人而無儀,不死何爲?”(《詩·鄘風》),其中的“人而無儀”(正如前舉“人而無信”一例),一般都説“人”是主語,“而”是連接主語和謂語的連詞,亦爲“假若”。這樣解讀顯然很有問題:(1)“而”本身没有假設的意思,這可由該句頭一次出現時看出來;(2)主語和謂語之間是不需要有連詞的,漢語不會那麽特殊;(3)把“人”看作主語,既違背漢語主語“定指”的一般原則,更誤解了這句話的含義,因爲作者是在咒駡某一個特定的人,説他“作爲一個人却没有人格。”假如我們能認識到名詞“人”可以是謂語,代表一個没有主語的句子,這些問題就都可以解决了。趙先生把漢語句子分爲“零句”和“整句”兩類;所謂“零句”就是没有主語的句子,因爲句子可以没有主語,但却不能没有謂語。他還説“零句”是漢語口語的常態。這是一個極重要的觀察,由於古文含有極强的“口語風格”,所以“零句”也就特别多;認清這一點且隨時留意,是正確解讀古代文獻和論證古文文法體系的必要條件。(歐化的現代漢語書面語,常用“它、人們”之類的詞充數作主語,可見歐式語法影響之大,但這在口語中是極不尋常的,古文更没有這類充數的主語。)

三、漢語句式特色的綜合表現

上列八條是我受到趙先生的啓示後歸納出來的。這些都是漢語中常見的現象,多數都已早爲人知,不是什麽新發現。問題是:分析漢語句法時,是充分考慮過這些特色,還是常常不自覺地使用歐語模式。當數條特色同時存在於一個句子中的時候,仔細分析就更必要了。略舉數例以説明這類綜合性特色的影響。

其一,《論語》中的名句“君君,臣臣,父父,子子”(“顔淵”章),一般的注釋都説,頭一個“君、臣、父、子”是主語,第二個是名詞活用爲動詞的;其否定式“君不君,臣不臣,父不父,子不子”自然也是這樣注釋的。準此,像“花非花,霧非霧”(白居易詩)這類句子的結構也是這樣的了!用歐語的眼光看,這樣分析似乎是理所當然的,但這樣分析,對我們解讀上述各句的含意有什麽幫助呢?我們已經説過,漢語中主要子句的主語含有定指性;上述各例的所謂“主語”顯然都非定指。説這些“主語”是所謂“泛指”,也不恰當。這就要求我們提出另一種分析。所以我覺得,這個例子裏的“君、臣、父、子”所擔任的語法角色,都是謂語,分别代表没有主語的子句。這樣分析是完全符合漢語句式特色的,即名詞可作謂語(特色7)和無主句極爲常見(特色8),同時這也解決了“主語定指”的問題,當然更重要的是,我們相信這樣分析才符合這幾句話的真意。我們相信,當孔老夫子説這話的時候,他的意思是説:“做皇帝要像皇帝,做臣要像臣,做父親要像父親,做兒子要像兒子。”這是符合他的倫理觀念的,因爲他認爲,人生在世都無可避免地要擔任某種角色,如果人人都適當地擔任各自的角色(所謂“倫常”),天下太平了。這種觀念似乎在孔子之前即已流行,《國語·周語中》“劉康公聘於魯”段,即有“臣聞之:爲臣必臣,爲君必君。”又如,《齊語》“葵丘之會”段,也有“爲君不君,爲臣不臣,亂之始也。”孔子衹不過簡化了文字擴大了範圍而已;其實這樣簡化也不始於孔子,《晉語四》“寺人勃鞮求見”段,即有“君君,臣臣,是謂明訓。”至於“花非花,霧非霧”的語法結構,當然亦同上例,那個没説出來的主語顯然是詩人心目中的某人或某種東西,正如同蘇東坡咏楊花時所説的“似花還似非花”,如此而已。現代漢語仍保留着這種句式,例如看到不順眼的人,我們可能會説他是“男不男,女不女!”,或者“中不中,西不西!”

其二,流行的説法有所謂“動補結構”(或稱“述補結構”),指的是“擊敗”“攻破”之類的複合詞;從漢語句式特色的角度看,也值得商榷(參看薛鳳生2000),因爲這不但違背“詞序”原則(特色6),也忽略了“詞類活用”現象(特色5),給句式結構分析造成一些不必要的問題;例如“把”字句中常含有這類複合詞，所謂“動補”就給如何分析“把”字句造成許多困擾，從而誤解了“把”字句的性質；（參看薛 1989）根據這類誤解去找“把”字句的歷史源頭自然就會“造成歷史的誤會了”。當然在找“動補”的源頭時，最好也先確認其性質。

其三，漢語有沒有特定的“被動式”？這個問題從未有人提出過，自然也就沒有人回答過。由於印歐語有一種叫做“被動態”（passive voice）的格式，很多人就想當然地認爲漢語語法也該有所謂“被動式”，因此就在古今漢語中找出許多個“被動式”，但同時又説漢語動詞本身都有“主被兩解”。這難免令人驚異，不禁要問“天底下真有如此奇怪的語法嗎？”我曾爲文（薛 1994）指出過此説之欠當，因爲那些所謂的“被動式”都不是專爲“被動意念”而設的，也不一定衹能有被動意念，而動詞爲什麼會有“主被兩解”，我們也必須爲之提出理論上的説明。我的觀察是，純就語法結構説，漢語没有專設的被動形式，而是采用一種間接的方式表達被動意念的。最常見的方式是由漢語句式的兩個特色造成的，即主謂結構作謂語（特色 7）和省略主語（特色 8）。當作爲謂語的那個子句没有主語時，被動意念也就自然表達出來了。這就是爲什麼漢語動詞好像含有主被兩解的道理。“烹、藏”這兩個字，在“狡兔死，良狗烹；高鳥盡，良弓藏”（《史記》“淮陰侯列傳”）裏，都含有被動意，就是這個道理。又如：“孔文子何以謂之文也？”（《論語》“公冶長”），以謂語句中的“謂之”表達被動意，就更明顯了，因爲“之”字是“謂”字的賓語，清楚地説明“謂”是主動詞。現代漢語没有“之”這樣的代名詞作賓語，因此像“鷄我吃了”這樣的句子，常被誤會爲賓語提前的“倒裝句”，實則不然。這個句子有兩個重點：一個是“吃的人是誰？”，這時候“我”字絶不能省，另一個是“鷄怎麼了？”，這時候作爲謂語句主語的“我”字就不那麼重要了，可以省掉，結果“鷄吃了”就含有被動意了。當然我們也可以説：“鷄被（我）吃了”，但與前者相較，這個説法恰可證明“被”字是與被動意念無關的，因爲被動意在前句中已經存在了，不必再用“被”字作“標記”（marker）。嚴格地説，有没有“被”字，意思是不一樣的，因爲“被”字的原意是强調主語遭遇到某種不太好的事故，所以我認爲“被”字是一個含有這種特定意義的動詞，是以“（我）吃了”這類句子作賓語的。更進一步説，“被”字後面那個所謂的“VP”（即作賓語的那個無主句），也不一定含有被動意念，例如：“在那場大火裏，他被燒了兩棟房子”，燒的顯然不是“他”，意思衹是説“他”遇到了

那種不幸。(參看薛 1989)

其四,掌握語法詞的功能與用法,可以說是正確認證漢語句子結構的關鍵,但受到歐式語法的影響,我們常會誤解漢語的語法詞。這主要是由於我們常不自覺地先找"主語"(忽視特色 8),和不自覺地把此詞類與句法功用固定起來(忽視特色 5)。例如連詞"而"字的核心語意與用法,歷來都未能說清楚,我曾爲文詳論(薛 1991),玆不贅述,僅再就另一個連詞"則"字略舉數例。這個連詞的基本功用也是連接子句以構成複句的,例如"名不正則言不順"(《論語》"子路"章);但當其前爲一名詞時,就常引起誤解。例如:"此則寡人之罪也!"(《孟子》"公孫丑"章),"此"字在此意爲"至於這個";又如:"我則既言之矣!"(《禮記》"檀弓下"章),"我"字意爲"至於我自己"。"此、我"兩個字,都必須解作分別代表一個没有主語的謂語句。啓蒙讀本《三字經》中的"兄則友,弟則恭",也應解爲:"(假如你)是哥哥,(你)就要友愛;(假如你)是弟弟,(你)就要恭敬",不是單純的"哥哥友愛;弟弟恭敬",唯有這樣分析,才能正確地掌握住"則"字的核心語法功能。連詞"而、則"之前的名詞有時帶有語氣詞"也"字,這就更突顯了那個名詞的謂語角色了,因爲"也"字基本上是一個句末語氣詞;例如前引的"斯人也,而有斯疾也!",和"今也,則亡!"。把"以、與"這兩個詞固定爲"介詞",也是忽略了"特色 5"和"特色 6"。(參看薛 1997)

四、結語

中國古無專門研究語法的傳統,直到近代才出現馬建忠的《文通》。作爲一本創始之作,自然就以拉丁文法爲藍本了,其前幾位歐洲學者的著作也都是這樣的。這樣做是完全可以理解的,但很多學者都已認識到這會造成許多牽强附會的說法。然而要改變這種做法也不太容易。時下國外學者討論漢語語法時,常見的做法仍是:先列出例句,注出拼音,然後逐字標示其詞性,諸如"N, V, Adj, Adv, Conj, Prep"等,或其假定的語法功能,諸如"Subj, Obj, V, Asp, Complement, Passive"等。這樣做當然有不得已的道理,因爲這類論文是寫給不諳漢語的人看的,人類學家在調查土著的語言時,都是這樣做的。但這些符號所代表的觀念都源自歐式語法,應用於漢語時,就很容易不自覺地受到歐式語法的影響。要"擺脱印歐語的眼光",自然就得"采用漢語的眼光"。趙元任先生顯然早就注意到而且設法解决這些問題了。他首先根據"句子"的新定義,提出漢語句式以"零句"爲最常見,而"整句"可以説是"零句"的組合;再提出"整句"中主語和謂語的關係是"話題"與"説明",用來解釋那些所謂"不合文法"但中國人却常説的句子。這是一種實事求是的態度,先接受中國人説話的方式,再討論"中國話的文法",所以他特别重視口語。這給了我莫大的啓示,所以數年來我就開始歸納漢語句式的特色,並將之應用於古漢語語法的研究,因爲古文原是古代的口語(世豈有歐化文言文乎?!)。我發現充分考慮到這些特色,對我們解讀古文獻的語意及其句子結構大有裨益,其效果有些是連趙先生都没提到的,例如我們對所謂"動補結構"和所謂"被動式"的討論。這種分析法當然跟一般語法理論並不冲突,而是相輔相成的,因爲衹有在正確的解讀了例句之後,所謂句法的機制和詞類的配價才是有根有據的,也就是吕叔湘先生所説的:"才能實現西方的語言理論與漢語研究的結合。"

參考文獻

陸儉明　1997　《關於語義指向分析》,《中國語言學論叢》第一輯,第34—48頁,北京語言文化大學出版社。

吕叔湘　1977　《漢語語法分析問題》,商務印書館。

王　力　1990　《漢語語法史》,載《王力文集》第十一卷,山東教育出版社。

薛鳳生　1982　The Role of Semantics in Teaching Syntax: Some Examples from Mandarin Chinese, *Journal of the Chinese Language Teachers Association* Vol. 17, No. 1(February), 1-13.

薛鳳生　1989　"The Structural Meaning of BA and BEI Constructions in Mandarin Chinese," in Tai&Hsueh(ed.): *Functionalism and Chinese Grammar*, 95-125.

薛鳳生　1991　《試論連詞"而"字的語意與語法功能》,《語言研究》第1期,第55—62頁。

薛鳳生　1994　Subject Deletion and "Passive Constructions" in Classical Chinese, in Gassmann & He(ed.): *Papers of the First International*

Congress on Pre-Qin Chinese Grammar, 383 - 419.

薛鳳生　1997　Verb Complement in Classical Chinese and its Implications as Revealed by the Particle 以, in Chaofen Sun (ed.): *Studies on the History of Chinese Syntax*, 27 - 48.

薛鳳生　2000　《試論漢語句式特色與語法分析》,載《文化的饋贈・語言文學卷》(漢學研究國際會議論文集),第381—397頁,北京大學出版社。

趙元任　1980　《中國話的文法》,丁邦新譯,香港中文大學出版社。

Yuen Ren Chao　1968　*A grammar of spoken Chinese*. Berkeley: University of California Press.

試説如何“擺脱印歐語的眼光”**

前言

研究漢語語法時,必須注意到“漢語的特點”,這是前修早已提出的觀點;我完全同意這一看法,所以不久前曾寫過一篇《試論漢語句式特色與語法分析》(薛 2000)。試圖具體指出漢語到底有哪些“特點”。在北京宣讀該文時(1998),有人對我説,吕叔湘先生曾提出另一説法:“必須擺脱印歐語的眼光,才能實現西方的語言理論與漢語研究的結合。”我覺得這個説法極好,因此引起了再寫一篇短文的念頭,談談如何“擺脱”那種眼光。稍加思考以後,我覺得“提脱印歐語的眼光”這一説法,實際上和“注意漢語的特點”説的是一回事;後者從正面説,漢語有某些特點必須注意到;前者從反面説,印歐語也有某些特點。我們不應把那些特點强加於漢語的分析上。换句話説,在分析漢語時,能優先考慮到漢語的特點,自然提脱印歐語的眼光了。但常會影響漢語分析的有哪些印歐語的特點呢?

一、漢語句式的特色

爲了下文討論的方便,有必要重述一下我以前提出的八條漢語句式的特色(薛 2000),並稍加説明。

1. 高度的“口語風格”。

古代漢語、早期白話文以及日常口語都屬此類;但不包括“歐化”的漢語。

2. 主謂的關係爲話題與説明。

這是趙元任先生的發現,應爲口語風格的一種表現。

** 第十八届 ICCL 會議論文,新加坡,2000 年,未刊稿,據會議論文打印稿編輯。

3. 語氣詞非常多。

語氣詞與句調有關,可以幫助認定句子的結構。

4. 語法詞(虚詞)常有省略。

這個現象古今漢語都有,尤以連詞爲然。

5.“詞類活用”。

指“實詞”而言;其意爲詞類與語法功能無固定關聯。

6.“詞序”極重要。

詞彙間出現的相對順序,決定其語法功能。

7. 謂語形式多樣。

這是謂語爲“説明語”的必然現象,能説明即合格。

8.“無主句”(或曰“零句”)極爲常見。

或曰“零句”“小句”,古今漢語中都極普遍。

上列八條可能不够全面,也可能需要修正。説這些是漢語的“特色”,也是受到“印歐語眼光”的影響,這些都是漢語中常見的現象,一點兒也不“特”,但在印歐語中,却是較少見的。印歐語當然也可以是口語式的,但我們常聽到和常讀到的多爲較正規的形式,因而形成了我們的印歐語眼光;西方學者用印歐語眼光看漢語,自然就更可理解了。

二、常影響漢語句分析的印歐語特點

上列八條漢語句式特色,是分析漢語句子結構時必須考慮到的。但由於“印歐語的眼光”,却常遭忽視,因爲這些特色的反面,幾乎可以説都是印歐語的特色,其中最關鍵的是第二條。所謂“subject”(“主語”),其本意原爲 subject matter(話題),而所謂“predicate”(“謂語”),也衹意爲作出 predication(論斷)。從這個角度看,趙元任先生説漢語句主語與謂語的關係是“話題”與“説明”,是理所當然的事;這也就解釋了爲什麽漢語的造句方式含有(7)(8)兩個特色。但歐語句的主語與謂語的含義則比較狹窄,分别意爲“行爲者”(actor)與其“行爲”(action)。(參看趙 1968:69—70)由於這個緣故,反映在歐語句式上的,就有兩個突出的特色。其一,除了祈使句之類少數例外,一般都要求句子必須帶主語，即使在没有明確的主語時，也要求用一個虛設的主語，例如英語的所謂“填充主語”it，和法語的所謂“無定代名詞”on。其二，要求謂語中必須含有一個 verb（“動詞”，包括 be 這樣不會動的詞），缺少 verb 就不成句子了；其重要性還可以從另一件事看出，即 verb 一詞既指詞類又指語法功用，而其他詞類則不然，例如 noun（“名詞”）就衹指詞類。這兩條歐語的特色，與漢語的（7）（8）兩條特色直接冲突，所以用印歐語眼光看漢語，造成的誤解也就特別多。在這兩條歐語特色的影響之下，許多想分析漢語句子結構的人，往往連漢語的“詞類活用”，以及“詞序特別重要”都忘記了；同樣也因此常常忘記漢語語法詞的特定功能或其省略。

三、“印歐語眼光”所造成的誤解

如何“擺脱印歐語的眼光”？最簡單的回答就是“采用漢語的眼光”，更具體地説，就是放棄由歐語語法引起的某些偏見，重新認識漢語句式的特色。在歐語語法的影響之下，我們常會不自覺地用其語法模式分析漢語。下列諸例可以説明常見的欠妥分析。

1. 把詞類與語法功能的關係固定化，因而難以看出在像“三十而立”（《論語·爲政》）這樣的句子裏，“三十”不是什麽“時間副詞”，而是謂語。在通俗古文讀本《三字經》裏，也有“一而十，十而百，百而千，千而萬”這樣的句子，其中的數字也都是謂語，分别代表一個没有主語的句子。（有人説“主、謂”是兩個相對的術語，因此“無主句”這個説法是“不科學”的；這更是歐式語法“主，謂”俱全的影響。）現代口語也可以説，“都已經三十了，還不結婚呢！”這裏的“三十”之前還有兩個狀語，其爲謂語核心，更可知矣。

2. 忽視詞序的重要性，因而把“以羊易之”和“易之以羊”（並見《孟子·梁惠王上》）兩句話中的“以”字，都看作“介詞”，這不僅違背了詞序原則（特色6），也違背了詞類活用原則（特色6）。所謂“動補結構”（“狀補結構”）的説法，也是違背了這兩個原則（Cf. 薛 1997）。

3. 由於歐式語法要求謂語必須含有某種動詞，因此像“他大嘴巴”（指人不能保密），或“他牛脾氣”（指人固執）之類的句子，用印歐語的眼光看，就都

"很奇怪"了。但如瞭解漢語謂語的定義(特色2),就會明白這些都是很自然的句子。在古代漢語中,名詞直接作判斷句的謂語本爲常例,其前還可以直接加狀語,例如:"若乃梁,則吾乃梁人也!"(《戰國策·趙策》)。可見狀語的出現是以"謂語"爲條件的,與作爲謂語的那個詞或詞組的詞類屬性無關。

4. 像"這件事我知道",或"那個人我認識"之類的句子,用印歐語的眼光看,當然是"賓語提前"了,但從漢語句式特色的觀點看,却不盡然。這可從兩個角度看。其一,根據漢語主語的定義(特色2),在主謂俱全的句子("整句")中,出現在句首的名詞就是主語,因此無所謂"提前"。其二,由於現代漢語不用指代事物的代名詞作賓語,因此頭一個例子没有代名詞作賓語,第二個例子説的是"人",當然可以帶"他"字,但通常都省去,這樣上舉的例句看起來就好像是"賓語提前"了;但古代漢語的代名詞"之"字是可以作賓語的,例如"夏禮吾能言之"(《論語·八佾》),這就證明上舉的例子都是以"主謂結構"作賓語的。

5. 句子主謂俱全,是印歐語的常例;用這種眼光看漢語,常使我們忙着找主語,因而可能對句子的結構作出錯誤的分析。例如:"民無信不立"(《論語·顔淵》),很容易讓人覺得"民"是全句的主語;有人引用時,甚至把"民"改作"人",意思變成了"人不講信用是不會成功的"。這是違背原意的,可從兩方面證明;其一,就語法講,由漢語的主語爲話題,所以常常是"定指"的,把上例中的"民"字認定爲全句的主語,是不符合這條通則的("主語定指"這條原則,我認爲衹限於主要子句,附屬子句應不受此限);其次,要瞭解古文,必須瞭解詞條在古語中的原義,也必須瞭解古代的社會背景:"民"在古語中絶不等於"人",指的是"被統治者"即《管子》所説的"士、農、工、商,謂之四民",是與"王、公、卿、大夫"等統治者相對而言的,"立"的意思是"保持住政權",這是與平民百姓無關的,所以"不立"衹能是個無主句,其主語是没説出來的"爲政者"。此類例子甚多,必須隨時留意。

6. 漢語的所謂"詞類活用",可以説是盡人皆知的了;但在分析語法時,是否人人都能隨時考慮到這個因素,就很難説了,有人把"看看、説説"(例如:"讓我看看","請你説説")之類的短語看作"動詞重複"(verb copying)。這顯然是印歐語的眼光("明明是verb麽!")但重複一般都表示加强語氣,爲什麽漢語的“動詞重複”反而減弱了語氣呢？這不是太奇怪了嗎？假如我們能擺脱印歐語的眼光，就可以理解爲什麼第二個動詞不必看作頭一個動詞的重複，而是活用指賓語的，前述語意上的困難，就可以得到解決了。在漢語中，如果作爲賓語的名詞或量詞所帶的數次是“一”，總是可以省略的；例如：“買本書”，“吃點兒東西”，“撒個謊”等。正因爲所省的是“一”而非多數，所以各該句都含有“少許”的意思；以此類推，就可以知道“説説、看看”實爲“説一説、看一看”的省略，也就用不着再去找“重複”的規律了。又如：很多人都把“打破、吃飽、立正”之類的短語分析爲“動補結構”（或稱“述補結構”），也是咬定衹有動詞才能作述語；這不有點兒像“膠柱鼓瑟”嗎？（參看薛 1997）。

7. “我頭疼”之類的句子，似乎也可以從“詞類活用”的角度再多考慮，囿於印歐語的習慣，當初很多人都將之分析爲“我的頭，疼”，即以“頭”爲主語，以“我”爲領屬格。當然在漢語語法中，這也是允許的，但却與語意（或“語感”）不合，因此趙先生將之重新分析爲“我，頭疼”，即把“頭疼”看作子句，是“以句爲説明語”的。這完全合乎語感，也符合漢語“謂語多樣化”的現象（特色 7），所以比前一個（印歐式的）分析合理得多。我是非常服膺這個看法的，但覺得似乎還不够周全。這類短語相當多（另如：“心疼、口渴、眼尖、嘴快”等），其前還可以加“很，真、非常，别”之類的狀語，其中一些還可以帶賓語（例如：“我非常頭疼這個人”“你别心疼花錢”），因此將之看作小句，就不太合理了：所以需要補充説，當這類短語變爲習用的單詞（idiomatized）以後，就不再是句子了，其中頭一個字應當分析爲“名詞作狀語”；這似乎較爲合理。基於同理，我們更可以説，“張三人好極了！”裏的“人”字，也是“名詞作狀語”的。

8. 多年前，在美國中文教師學會的一次討論會中，有人問如何解釋“男不男，女不女”這樣的句子；與會學者議論紛紛，莫衷一是；但他們却有一個共同的看法，都認爲兩句話中的頭一個“男、女”是主語，第二個“男、女”是動詞，因爲其前有“不”字。同樣的解釋也出現在古文的注釋裏，例如一般注解都説，在“君君，臣臣，父父，子子”（《論語·顔淵》）中，頭一個“君、臣、父、子”是主語，第二個是活用爲動詞的；其否定式“君不君，臣不臣，父不父，子不子”也是這樣注釋的。用印歐語的眼光看，這樣分析似乎是理所當然的，但這樣分析，對我們瞭解上述各句的含意却没有什麼幫助。我們已經説過，漢語中主要子句的主語含有定指性;上述各例的所謂“主語”顯然都非定指。有人説,代表某類特定事物的統名也可以作主語,即所謂“泛指”,那麽“男不男,女不女”的意思,就應該是“男人都不是男人,女人都不是女人”了! 恐怕不是吧? 當我們駡某(些)人“男不男,女不女”的時候,我們的意思不是“説他是男人他不是男人,説他是女人他不是女人”嗎? 假如這個解釋是正確的話,那就要求我們提出另一種分析了,所以我覺得,這個例子裹的兩個“男”字和兩個“女”字所擔任的語法角色,都是謂語,分别代表没有主語的子句。這樣分析是完全符合漢語句式特色的,即名詞可作謂語(特色 7)和無主句極爲常見(特色 8),同時這也解决了“主語定指”的問題,當然更重要的是,我們相信這樣分析才符合這句話的真意。同理,我們相信“君君,臣臣,父父,子子”的語法結構亦當作如是解。

9. 不同的語言,如何用不同的方法表示“被動語意”,是語法研究的一個重要課題。由於歐式語法的影響,很多人就認爲漢語語法也該有“被動式”,並在古今語中找出許多個句式充數,但仍不得不承認,那些“被動式”有時候不一定表示“被動”。而漢語動詞通常都有“主被兩解”。我曾爲文(薛 1994)批評這種做法,認爲那些所謂的“被動式”都不是專爲“被動語意”而設的,而動詞爲什麽會有“主被兩解”才是必須研究的核心。我認爲純就語法結構説,漢語是采用一些間接的方式表達被動語意的,即以主謂結構作一個“整句”的謂語(特色 7)和省略那個主謂結構的主語(特色 8),這樣被動語意就間接表示出來。這種説話方式是漢語表達被動語意的常態,但是在歐語的影響下,“被字句”竟變成了所謂 passive construction,大量地出現於書面語中,幾乎可以説泛濫成灾,其實這類“被”字多半應該劃掉,但由於“被”字的原意已經消失了,新的“被動句”越看越像“被動式”,這恐怕已經成了無法挽回的趨勢。但在較常規的漢語裹,我們仍可看到許多利用無主句表達被動意念的説法,例如:“可以(這麽)説……”,“應當注意到……”,“必須指出……”等。這類説法在印英語中都是以被動形式出現的(必須順序譯爲: 1. It may be said that... 2. It should be noted that... 3. It must be pointed out that...),因爲“施事”爲誰是不必指明的。

四、結語

印歐語的構句有一些常見的方式，習於印歐語的人自然很容易將之視爲句式的常態，並用這種眼光看待漢語句，因而忽略漢語句式的一些常態，即本文所謂的"特色"("特"乃相對於印歐語而言)。我們認爲，衹有在充分考慮到這類特色以後，才能正確地看出漢語句子的語法結構；因此，"擺脱印歐語的眼光"，其實就是重新認識漢語句式的"特色"。正如吕叔湘先生所説，衹有這樣，"才能實現西方的語言理論與漢語研究的結合"，也才能讓我們超脱語言的表像而求得其真義。這個問題觸及漢語的本質，所以文中古今漢語的例子並舉，不限於哪一種。

本文試圖列舉出漢語的句式"特色"，事屬草創，自然難謂完備。必須再一次聲明的是，這樣的分析法不僅僅在於説明句子的合法或不合法，而是以正確的語意詮釋爲主要考慮的，因爲我們認爲，真正有意義的語法分析必須能妥當地反映語意。這種分析法最易招致的批評是"增字求解"；甚至可能有人會説："如果隨便加字，怎麽解釋或分析都可以。"對這樣的批評，我們必須作出響應。先説"隨便"吧！讓我們仍以"民無信不立"爲例；我們説，"不立"不是以"民"爲主語的，而是有一個未出現的主語(特色 8)；同時我們也説，條件子句"民無信"之後有一個省略了的連詞"則"(特色 4、6)。這樣説是"隨便"加字嗎？絶對不是，因爲衹有這樣才能説明爲什麽這句話衹能是這個意思("如果老百姓失掉信心，統治者就站不住了")，所以這絶不是"隨便"説的。再説"加字"吧！其實也不是，因爲那些所謂加上去的字，衹是爲了説明或翻譯時的方便而加的，實際上都早已隱含於原文的句中了；這是因爲既然"民"不是謂語"不立"的主語，這個謂語自然就是一個隱含着主語的"無主句"，而當這因句子作爲主要子句出現於條件子句"民無信"之後時，也就意謂其前隱含着連詞"則"字，不是我們加的。這些現象都是漢語造句機制的自然産物，是完全合乎漢語語法規則的，不是亂加的。

參考文獻

王　力:《漢語語法史》,《王力文集》(第十一卷),山東教育出版社,1990 年。

吕叔湘:《漢語語法分析問題》,商務印書館,1977 年。

陸儉明:《關於語義指向分析》,《中國語言學論叢》第一輯,1997 年,第 34—38 頁。

趙元任:《中國話的文法》(A Grammar of Spoken Chinese,1968),丁邦新譯,香港,1982 年。

薛鳳生:“The Role of Semantics in Teaching Syntax: Some Examples from Mandarin Chinese.” *Journal of the Chinese Language Teachers Association* Vol. 17. No. 1 (February), 1982, 1 - 13.

——— “The Structural Meaning of BA and EEI Constructions in Mandarin Chinese,” in Tai & Hsueh (ed.): Functionalism and Chinese Grammar, 1989, 95 - 125. (沈家煊譯:《“把”字句和“被”字句的結構意義》,《功能主義與漢語語法》,北京. 1994,第 35—59 頁)

——— 《試論連詞“而”字的語意與語法功能》,《語言研究》1991 年第 1 期,第 55—62 頁。

——— “Subject Deletion and ‘Passive Constructions’ in Classical Chinese.” in Gassmann & He (ed.): *Papers of the First International Congress on Pre-Qin Chinese Grammar*, 1994, 383 - 419. (馮勝利譯:《古漢語中的主語省略與所謂被動句型》,《中國語言學論叢》第一輯,1997,第 105—117 頁。)

——— “Verb Complement in Classical Chinese and its Implications as Revealed by the Particle 以,” in Chaofen Sun (ed.): *Studies on the History of Chinese Syntax*, 1997, 27 - 48. (耿振生譯:《古代漢語的動補結構和“以”字短語的語法功能》.《古漢語研究》1996 年第 2 期,第 14—20 頁。)

——— 《試論漢語句式特色與語法分析》,《古漢語研究》1998 年第 4 期,第 67—74 頁。又見《文化的饋贈:或言文學卷》(漢學研究國際會議論文集),北京大學出版社,2000 年,第 381—397 頁。

古漢語中的主語省略與所謂的被動句型[**]

一、漢語句式的某些特徵

“古代漢語”這個詞,對不同的人有時指的是不同的東西。主張先秦文言文(如《左傳》《孟子》)跟後代文言文不同的人認爲,衹有前者堪稱“古代漢語”,後者不過是一種“文學語言”。這裏我們不作區分,因爲我下面所要作的是比較概括性的句法分析。事實上,我們所要討論的都是漢語中非常一般的基本問題,甚至現代漢語也不例外①。因此在例句的選擇上,我們也不僅僅囿於先秦典籍。此外,像許多中國國内的學者一樣,我也認爲研究漢語的語法必須“從漢語的特性出發”。問題是漢語的特性到底是什麽? 顯然,這不是一個簡單的問題,不同的人有不同的答案。就個人而言,儘管我不敢説漢語到底有多少特性,但是我以爲下面幾點應該包括在内。

1.1. 主語跟謂語相當於(語意上的)主題與評論

在中國話裏,主語和謂語的含意相當於主題跟評論。這是趙元任先生研究漢語“口語”時最重要的發現(趙 1968:69—87)。儘管也許(實際上也的確)有人反對趙先生所説的“普遍的中文語法”,我想没有人會懷疑這條發現同樣適用於古代漢語。下面這個簡單的例子就足以打消一切懷疑。

(1) 夫戰,勇氣也。(《左傳·莊公十年》)

** 原載《中國語言學論叢》(第一輯),北京語言學院出版社,1997 年。
本文曾在瑞士蘇黎世大學召開的“古代漢語語法研討會”上宣讀。

① 趙元任先生提出的“一個共通的中文語法”,跟他對文言文的評述,即“文言文的語法結構不僅跟北京方言,而且跟其他任何方言,本質上都是一樣的(趙 1968:13)”,曾經引起一些反對意見(見雅 1986:115)。我覺得問題是如何理解“本質上一樣”這句話。無疑,就詞彙跟句法來講,古今確有很多不同,然而就趙先生所强調的最基本的語法原則來説,我同意他的意見。可以肯定地説,我們這裏討論的句法原則就可以看做是“普遍”的,對所有的各式各樣的中國語言都適用。

1.2. 詞彙在句法功能上的靈活性

漢語中"詞類活用"這一特點早已衆所周知。最奇怪、最極端的要算下面這類例子了：

(2) 爾欲吴王我乎？(《左傳・定公十年》)

因爲這類活用在漢語中大量存在，有些學者如高名凱(1956)、Dobson(1959)便走向極端，否認漢語詞彙有詞性，這實際上就等於主張漢語的語法衹包括句法(syntax)。其他學者如王力(1956)、Cikoski(1978a)則堅決反對走這條路。最近，中國的學者逐漸采用了兩套術語來處理這一問題。其一是"詞"，如"名詞""動詞""形容詞""副詞"等；其二用句法功能來表述，如"主語""謂語""賓語""述語""定語""狀語"等。這種做法也許更切合實際，因爲這爲我們提供了一種鑒定和解釋某些特殊語彙的基礎。如上例所示，當我們在處理詞彙語義改變以及它們在語境限定下所表現出的特殊用法時，這種方法尤其有效(Liu 1991)。

1.3. 句法上，句子的主語不一定必須出現

印歐語言的句法對句子的主語有嚴格的限定，即使在不明主語所指時，主語位置也要有一個明確詞來充填(如英文裏的空指主語"it"以及法語的代詞"on")。漢語與印歐語不同，基本没有那種對主語的句法限定。因此無主句在現代漢語跟古代漢語中比比皆是。下文我們將集中討論這種現象及其在句法上的意義。

1.4. 判斷句無係詞

這是古漢語的一個特點。衆所皆知，這個特點意味着：名詞短語不用係詞就可以直接用作謂語，來表達它跟主語的某種對等關係。多數情況下，表肯定語氣的"也"常常出現在這個名詞謂語之後。如：

(3) 宋，先代之後也；(於周爲客)。(《左傳・僖公二十四年》)

其實"也"的作用不過是表達發話者的某種態度，不能誤解是這類句子必須的句法標志，因爲很多這類句子並不需要"也"。如：

(4) 荀卿，趙人。(《史記・荀卿列傳》)

(5) 子非魚，安知魚之樂？(《莊子・秋水》)

一般説來，這類句子分析起來並不成問題。可是當主語不出現時，就會常

常引起誤解以至錯誤的分析(參看 2.2、2.3 跟 2.4)。

1.5. 缺乏被動語意的特定句法結構

漢語這方面的特徵尚未引起足够的重視。對這種現象的解釋,我們將在第三節中提出,與此相關的其他句法現象將在第四節裏討論。

二、主語省略及其對句法分析的影響

在本文裏,我使用"主語省略"這個短語來説明漢語的句子並不是非有主語不可,儘管這一術語也許並不十分恰當。我個人認爲,"主語省略"是趙元任先生有關漢語主語定義的一個重要的、必然的引申。因爲"主語"的意思在漢語裏是"主題",如果説話者覺得他要説明的主題已經是聽者所知道或理解的,那麽他就没有必要再指出或重複,這就導致了所謂的"無主句"。

2.1. 當然主語省略這個現象人們早已注意到,但是我覺得漢語這一特點以及他在漢語句法分析上的深刻意義,尚未得到人們充分的理解。根據吕叔湘先生的分析(1955:95 注 2),漢語有兩種不同的"成分短缺"的句法形式。一是"省略",就是按規則該有的而没有;一是"隱藏",就是按規則本來就不該有的。這種分析也許能運用到我這裏談的主語省略的現象中來。就是説,有的無主句是"省略",因爲主語前見,所以可承上而省。如:

(6) 吾日三省吾身:(吾)爲人謀而(吾)不忠乎?(《論語·學而》)

有的是"隱藏"(或"不言而喻"),因爲太一般,無勞指出。如:

(7) (任何人)有朋自遠方來,(此)不亦樂乎?(《論語·學而》)

2.2. 無論"省略"的原因是什麽,重要的是,當我們讀古文作句法分析時,我們必須對無主句或無主分句時常保持警覺。忽略這一點就會造成對原文的誤解,以至錯誤地分析句子的語法結構和其中虚詞的功能。譬如,下例句中的"中壽",如果我們忘記名詞經常充當謂語這一現象,就極易誤解爲衹是個名詞。事實上,"中壽"正是謂語,不過它的主語已經省略了。

(8) 爾何知?(若)中壽,爾墓之木拱矣!(《左傳·僖公三十二年》)

2.3. 在虚詞的分析上,忽視漢語的這一特點曾經引起過更嚴重的混淆。譬如:

(9) 相鼠有皮,人而無儀!(《詩經·鄘風·相鼠》)

(10) 人而無信,不知其可也。(《論語·爲政》)

(11) 子產而死,誰其嗣之?(《左傳·襄公三十三年》)

這裏的"而"字,王力(1982:445)跟周法高(1959:218)兩位先生都主張:它的作用是連接主語"人"跟謂語"無儀"等。如果這樣、我們不禁要問:主語跟謂語之間爲什麼要用一個連詞?他們(以及我所知道的其他學者)都未能對"而"字的句法和語義功能給出一個前後一致,自圓其説的定義。這都是由於對"而"字以及其他語法現象的誤解造成的。如果我們能看到(9)、(10)中的"人",還有(11)中的"子產"的句法作用都衹是不帶主語的謂語,那麼這三句便可以根據這一新的分析,準確地翻譯成:

(9) 瞧!連老鼠都有一層皮,(他)是個人,可是(他)却没有一點風度。

(10) (不管誰)衹要是個人可又不講信用,(我)真不知道那怎麽行!

(11) (説到)子產,(他)要是死了,那誰來接替他呢?

據此,我們可以得出下面的結論:在句法上,虚詞"而"總是連接兩個分句(clauses);在語義上,它的作用是讓前面的分句從屬於其後的分句(詳見薛1991)。

2.4. 除了"而"以外,對虚詞"則"的誤解也是由於同樣的錯誤造成的。"則"也是一個連詞,同樣衹連接兩個分句(薛1994)。然而,在我所知道的學者裏面(例如:韓1984:577—579)都把它定爲"副詞",並且認爲下列句中出現在"則"之前的名詞都是該句的主語:

(12) 此則寡人之罪也。　　　　(《孟子·公孫丑上》)

*這當然是我的罪過。

(13) 豈人主之子孫則必不善哉?　　　　(《戰國策·趙策四》)

*難道人主的子孫一定不好嗎?

(14) 彼則肆然而爲帝。　　　　(《戰國策·趙策三》)

*他放肆地做起帝王來了。

根據我們的分析,"則"前的名詞性成分都是省略了主語的謂語。因此上述諸句都應該譯爲①：

(12) 關於這件事,(那)就是我的罪過了。

(13) 難道(任何人)是人主的子孫,(他)就一定不好嗎?

(14) 輪到他自己,(他)却放肆要作世界領袖。②

爲什麼學者們會誤解上述句子呢?很可能是每一句話的兩個分句都没有了主語。否則的話,誤解的機會將會大大減少。例如:

(15) 子女玉帛,則君有之,羽毛齒革,則君地生焉。(《左傳·僖公二十三年》)

要論女人和玉帛,那麼您早就有了;要論鳥獸毛革,那麼您這兒也出産。

(16) 若乃梁,則吾乃梁人也!(《戰國策·趙策三》)

要論梁,那麼我正是梁人啊!

例(16)尤其是我們有力的證據。"梁"在這裏毫無疑問是用作謂語,不然它不可能被副詞"若乃"來修飾。

三、中文爲什麼没有純"被動"句型?

中文的動詞即使没有任何標記,却常常兼有主動跟被動的雙重功能。這一點很多人都注意到了。(例如:趙 1968:72—75)。譬如:

(17) 鷄吃,魚不吃。

a. 鷄吃(東西),魚不吃(東西)。

b. 鷄(被)吃,魚不(被)吃。

同樣,下面兩句古文根據純句法分析,也可以有如下兩種解釋,儘管上下文告

---

① 何樂士教授在她對"有主句"跟"無主句"的統計研究中附帶説明:"由於無主句幾乎都出現在動詞謂語句,統計的全是動詞謂語句。"(何 1982:242)很明顯,我們這裏没有同意她的説法。我不明白爲什麼她認爲名詞性的謂語句不能省略主語,我相信一定會有非常之多的這類"無主句"。

② 這裏的原文是:"權使其士,虜使其民"接着才是"彼則肆然而爲帝。"所以整體的意思是:"(秦王)用欺騙的手段對待知識分子,把老百姓當做奴隸一樣使用,可是輪到他自己呢,(他)却厚着臉皮要作天下的帝王!"

訴我們衹有第一種解釋正確。

(18) 令尹誅而楚奸不上聞。仲尼賞而魯民易降北。(《韓非子·五蠹》)

a. 令尹殺了(一個舉報自己父親的人)以後,楚國的罪犯就不再被人向上級告發了。仲尼賞賜了(一個孝順的逃兵)以後,魯國的人民就輕易的向敵人投降。

b. 令尹被殺了以後,楚國的罪犯没有向君王匯報。仲尼被賞賜了以後,魯國的人民就很容易被征服。

不難想象,通過不同的搭配組合,上述兩句還可以有很多種不同的解釋。爲什麽他們可以有不同的解釋呢?原因就是其中的動詞“誅”“聞”“賞”“降”既可以理解爲主動,也可以理解爲被動。下面的句子可以充分證明這一點:

(19) “誅”作被動:彼竊鉤者誅,竊國者爲諸侯。(《莊子·胠篋》)

那些偷鉤子的人被處决了,可是偷國家的人却成了諸侯。

(20) “聞”作主動:公聞其期,曰:可矣!(《左傳·隱公元年》)

鄭莊公聽説了日期以後説:可以行動了。

(21) “賞”作被動:受賞者甘利,未賞者慕業。(《韓非子·六反》)

受到賞賜的人得到甜頭,還没有被賞的人覬覦創業。

(22) “降”作主動:晋降彭城而歸諸宋。(《左傳·襄公二十六年》)

晋國征服了彭城以後把它給了宋國。

就我所知,没有哪個學者稱這類句子爲“被動句型”,當然它們確實不是。然而這種奇特的現象一定要得到合理的解釋。國内有些學者稱之爲“意念上的被動”,並説這是由“動詞本身”的性質决定的。這似乎不是一種十分嚴肅的解釋。另有一種比較嚴肅而巧妙的解釋就是 Cikoski 的處理辦法。他將中文的動詞分作兩類:一類叫“中性動詞”;一類叫“唯被動詞(ergative)”(Cikoski 1978B:135)。這種分法所遇到的難處是,這兩類之間的區别並不容易確定。同時在歷史上,有的詞在這兩類中游移不定,彼此轉换。這裏我想提出的一個新説法是:這類現象也許是由於主語省略所造成的,並且這也許正是中文爲什麽没有,也不必有“特定的被動句型”的原因。

3.1. 如果仔細觀察一下那些含有“被動”意念的句子,我們可能會懷疑它們所謂"被動"的真正的性質。以(17)爲例,如果一個人對飯店的女服務員説"鷄吃,魚不吃",難道他真在説"鷄被吃了,魚不被吃"嗎?更切近情理的,難道不是(23)中的意思嗎?

(23) 鷄(我)吃;魚(我)不吃。

也就是説,上述兩個句子中各含一個謂語分句,在語境中十分清楚的情况下,分句的主語可以删除。這是漢語主題跟評論直接作爲句法意義上的主語跟謂語的必然結果。當主語被删除以後,動詞所表示的行爲指向就出現"兩可"的可能(趙 1968:72)。從這個角度看,我要大膽地提出:漢語動詞的這種表現,正是由其句法結構所决定的,並非其自身所固有的。

3.2. 上面的論證是建立在現代漢語句法分析的基礎上的。當然我們也可以將它運用到古漢語句法分析中來。我們不妨仍以(19)爲例。前半部分可以重新分析爲:

(24) 彼竊鈎者,(主語)誅。

至於那些偷鈎子的人,(有人)殺死(他們)。

"誅"是該句的謂語,但省去了主語。這就是説,所謂"誅"的被動意義實際上是從主語省略而來。其實所謂被動句,總是意味着它的主語是"受事者",是"施事者"所發出的動作的接受者。不管"施事"出現不出現。在某些語言裏,主語跟謂語的關係通常是施事者及其行動,因此當施事者跟受事者的詞序相反時,就需要特定的句法形式來標識。但是在主語跟謂語的關係是主題跟評論的語言裏,這種句法標志就有點多餘。因爲要是發話者想强調表達這類概念時,衹要把受事者推向主題的位置,然後用一個不帶主語的句子來評論它就行了。例句(24)正是如此。

3.3. 上述表達被動意念的方式是用來强調的一種手段。這種方式很多學者已經注意到了,然而學者們大都忽略了下面的另一種方式:被動意念也可以用一種不那麽强調的手段來表達。要達到這一目的很簡單,那就是直接删除主語(施事者)。當然這衹有在整個語境允許的情况下才能如此。通常,這種含有被動意義的句子的賓語或受事者是用代詞"之"來表達的。例如:

(25) 請京,使居之,謂之京城大叔。(《左傳·隱公元年》)

(姜氏)要京城,(莊公)讓(叔段)住在那裏。因此(人們)叫他(亦即他被叫做)京城大叔(參 Legge 的譯文:"and(he) came to be styled T'ae-shuh" Vol. V. p. 5)。

(26) 將立之而卒。(《左傳・襄公三年》)

(公)剛要任命他(亦即他剛要被任命),(他)就死了。(參 Legge 的譯文:"Hoo, however, died, as he was about to be appointed." Vol. V. p. 420)

(27) 兵者不祥之器,……不得已而用之。(《老子・道經》)

武器這個玩藝,是不祥的東西,……祇在没辦法的時候(人)才用它(亦即;它才被用)

(28) 不違農時,穀不可勝食也。(《孟子・梁惠王上》)

(統治者)要是不違背農時(亦即農時不被違背),那麽粮食就吃不完。

(參 Legge 的譯文:"If the seasons of husbandry be not interfered with,..." Vol. II. p. 130)

(29) 寶玉而題之以石;貞士而名之以誑。(《乾非子・和氏》)

(這)是一塊寶玉,但是(他們)却叫它(亦即它被叫作)石頭;(這)是一個忠貞之上,可是(他們)却説他(亦即他被説成)是騙子。

當一種語言具備上述的句法手段以後,語意上的被動便可以間接地而又恰當地表達出來。這一點,我敢大膽地説,就是漢語爲什麽不需要,因此也没有"特定的被動句的句法結構"的原因。當然,漢語也像其他語言一樣,可以通過一套間接的、修辭上的手段來表達被動概念。這一點我們將在下文討論。

四、幾個所謂"被動句型"的實質

一個語言裏,除特定的被動句法形式以外,利用修辭手段也可以表達被動概念。譬如英文可以説;

(30) He met his death in thc hand of an assassin.

他 遇到 他的 死亡 在 這 手 所屬格 一個 刺客

"他死在一個刺客的手裏。"

(31) He was the victim of an assassin.

他 是 這 犧牲品 所屬格 一個 刺客

“他成了刺客的犧牲品。”

(32) He lost his life in an accident.

他 丢了 他的 生命 在 一個 事故

“他出事死了。”

上述各句都意爲“He was killed(他被殺了)”,但是没有一句可以算作被動句型。古代漢語裏也有幾個慣用形式,經常表達被動的語意概念。在大多的語法著作中,它們都被列爲被動句型。有些學者甚至以它們爲基礎,來研究被動句句型的歷時發展。在我看來,這些學者都有意或無意地忽略了語意概念跟句法形式之間的區别。我們將在這一節專門檢驗這些慣用形式,看他們是否真的可以叫做“特殊被動句法結構”①。

4.1. 古代漢語中的一個最常見的成語慣用形式是用“見”構成的,亦即“見+行爲動詞”的句子。如果用形式來表達,就是(N=名詞,V=動詞):N-見-V,例如:

(33) 隨之見伐,不量力也。(《左傳·僖公二十年》)

隨國被攻打是因爲(他)自不量力的結果。

(34) 盆成括見殺於齊。(《孟子·盡心下》)

盆成括在齊國被殺死了。

(35) 説行而有功則見忘,説不行而有敗則見疑。(《韓非子·説難》)

要是一個人的游説行得通因而有功,那麽(他)就會被忘記;要是一個人的游説行不通因而失敗,那麽(他)就會被懷疑。

毫無疑問,短語“見-V”包含被動的意義。問題是這是否就能代表句法意義上的“被動結構”。衆所周知,“見”本身是一個動詞,通常以名詞作賓語。譬如:

(36) 民不見德。(《左傳·僖公二十二年》)

---

① 我所見到的對古漢語被動句研究最有啓發性的論述,要屬 John S. Cikoski 1978B 那篇文章。雖然我對他的有些結論仍持存疑態度,但是我頗得益於此文而且甚爲欽佩他高度的分析推理。這可以從比較該文與本文中清楚地看出。

人民看不到(統治者的)道德。

Cikoski(1978B)認爲:由於跟這類句子的類比關係;"中性"的動詞也被用來代替像"德"這樣的抽象名詞作爲賓語(P-148)。他接着指出中性動詞"見"很快變成了一個構成被動式的附着語(passive-forming affix),同時"見-V"短語也便由句法性質一變而成構詞性質。他進而指出,第一步,從《詩經》時代到《孟子》時代,這一變化過程衹限定在"中性"動詞範圍内。到了《荀子》時代才擴大到"唯被動動詞(ergative verbs)"。我覺得他的研究令人十分欽佩,其論證也頗有説服力。然而他上述的結論却不能讓我完全接受。我覺得難以確信的理由有三。第一,詞彙的靈活性是漢語的一大特點。動詞充當句法上的賓語是一件再自然不過的事。因此(34)可以非常自然地分析成:"盆成括在齊國遇害。"這就如同前面所引的英文一樣(30—32),它們無疑涵隱"被動的意義",但却不能視爲"被動句型"。第二,要是"見-V"的確發展成爲了一個句法上的,或者詞法上的被動句型,在如此漫長的歷史演化中,它也早應該發展成熟了,因此勢必會有很强的生命力。然而,正如吕叔湘先生所發現的(吕,1955:46),漢朝剛過(或當漢之際),"見-V"之"見"便發展出了一個嶄新的意義,具有間接指代功能,代表句子的賓語而不是主語。例如:

(37) 布有何過,君前見攻之甚也。(《後漢書·張布傳》)

我有什麽錯讓你以前那麽厲害地攻擊我(不是"*你被攻擊")。

這一新功能竟成了文學語言中的標準用法。譬如,要是我覺得我得罪了誰,我也許會説(寫作中更是如此)"敬祈見恕",意思是,"我恭敬地祈求(您)原諒我"。而根據早期的句法規則,則應該是"*我恭敬地祈求您被原諒",這顯然是説不通的。第三,正如吕指出的(1955:50),在文學語言裏,上述"見"字結構的"見"在有的句子裏可以既指主語又指賓語。兩種理解絲毫不影響句子的意義。例如:

(38) 失愛於叔父,故見罔耳。(《三國志·魏志·武帝紀》)

a. (我)失去了叔父對我的愛,所以(他)欺罔我。

b. (我)失去了叔父對我的愛,所以(我)被他欺罔。

很明顯,後半句的句法可以根據設想的主語的不同而有不同的分析。這都是由於主語的省略,以及"見"在語境中的不同的功能造成的。在早期古漢語中,

“見”就其一般意義而言,是一個動詞,意思是“看見”、“遇見”。但是到了晚期古漢語,它可以用使動詞,意思是“讓人看”。在我看來,這清楚地表明無論“見”的兩種不同的功能怎樣使用,説或者寫古漢語的人總是把他當做一個地道的動詞,而不是一個附着語(affix)。

4.2. 另一個句型也常常被看做是“被動句結構”的代表,這就是“被(N)V”。比較而言,這一形式在漢語史上算是比較新的。可是它對後代的影響却遠非其他形式所能比,以至於外文的被動語態“passive voice”(被動式)就是用它來翻譯的[①]。事實上,正如我以前指出的(薛,1989),從嚴格的意義上講,我們甚至不應該把現代漢語的被動式,跟印歐語系的被動語態等同起來,衹有所謂的“歐化句”可以除外。古代漢語裏的被動表達法肯定就更没有資格作“被動結構”了。例如:

(39) 國一日被攻,雖欲事秦不可得也。(《戰國策·齊策一》)

一旦你的國家被攻打,即使想事奉秦國也晚了。

(40) 信而見疑,忠而被謗。(《史記·屈原列傳》)

(他)是可信的,可是(他)却被懷疑,(他)很忠誠可是(他)却被誹謗。

這裏“被攻”跟“被謗”很明顯都是[動—賓]結構。就是説,儘管“攻”跟“謗”都是動詞,它們都是前面動詞的賓語。因而,這兩句字而上都可以分析爲:“遭受—攻擊”跟“遭受—誹謗”。而“見疑”,如第三節所論,則應理解爲:“他遭到懷疑。”下面三例可以進一步證明我們關於“被”的分析。

(41) 身被二十餘創。(《漢書·趙充國列傳》)

身上受了二十多處傷。

(42) 亮子被蘇峻害。(《世説新語·方正》)

庾亮的兒子受到蘇峻的迫害。

(43) 常被元帝所使。(《顔氏家訓·雜藝》)

(他)常常受元帝的指使。

(41)中的“被”顯然是主要動詞,它的賓語是一個名詞,這没有什麽疑問。

---

① 王力先生雖然使用了“被動式”這一術語,但是他解釋説:這不等於被動語態(passive voice),而且跟印歐語言比較,它的用法在漢語裏也非常有限。(王 1984:124,128)然而,這個術語在學界(包括王先生在内)一般性的大量使用中,已經變得跟英文的被動語態幾乎没有什麽不同了。

然而,當它的賓語是一個動詞時,比如(42)中的"害",那就會帶來一些混淆。這個充當賓語的動詞也許就會被誤解爲主要動詞,同時"被"也就因此而誤爲一個被動句的標志了。這個賓語動詞看來即使對古人來説似乎也不大自然。於是他們有時候就把一個名詞化的語素"所"加在第二個動詞前邊,因而有(43)這類句子。在我看來,這個"所"字清楚地表明:説母語的人感覺到"被"是個主要動詞,而跟在它後面的東西衹能是名詞化的成分。因此第二個動詞之前的名詞[如(42)中的"蘇峻"],或者"所"前的名詞[如(43)中的"元帝"]都具有附加語(adjunctive)的性質,就是説它們都是所屬格成分。

4.3. 很多語法學家也把"V-於-N"叫做"被動句型"。這又是一個没有區分語意概念跟句法形式的例子。無可否認,在下例中,出現在"於"字之前的動詞如"治""食""傷"等,都含有被動的意義。

(44) 治於人者食人,治人者食於人。(《孟子·滕文公上》)

被人統治的人奉養别人,統治人的人被别人奉養。

(45) 克傷於矢。(《左傳·成公二年》)

克被箭射傷。

問題在於他們的被動意義是否就是因爲有了後面的"於-N"短語。對這種主張最有力的反證就是Cikoski提供的例子(1978B:198—202)。

(46) 管夷吾治於高傒。(《左傳·莊公九年》)

管夷吾比高傒更會治理。

(不是:"*管夷吾被高傒統治")

我們還可以加上一條。

(47) 當仁,不讓於師。(《論語·衛靈公》)

面對"仁"的問題,就是對老師(你)也不能謙讓。

(不是;"*對待'仁'的問題,(你)不會被老師責讓")

(46)跟(47)清楚地表明,附加的"於-N"短語並不一定能使前而的動詞變成被動,甚至不一定能使同樣的一個動詞變成被動。由此我們可以得出結論,"V-於-N"不可能是句法意義上的被動句型。

4.4. "爲(N)(所)V"句式也同樣被認作"被動結構"。分析至此,我們不禁要問:爲什麽漢語需要如此之多的不同的被動結構?答案很簡單,它們都不

是真正的“被動結構”。這個“爲(N)(所)V”句式實際上是兩個句式的合成。第一個是不帶“所”字的,如:

(48) 自今無有代其君任患者！有一於此,將爲戮乎?(《左傳·成公二年》)

從今以後不會再有替國君赴湯蹈火的人啦！現在有一個,難道還非要殺了他不可?

(49) 吾屬今爲之虜矣。(《史記·項羽本紀》)

我們現在要被他俘虜了。

第二個是帶所字的,如:

(50) 不者,若屬皆且爲所虜。(《史記·項羽本紀》)

要不然,你們都會被俘虜。

(51) 及爲匈奴所敗,乃遠去。(《史記·大宛傳》)

當(他們)被匈奴打敗以後,(他們)跑遠了。

然而,正如Cikoski所指出的(Cikoski 1978B:136),第一式並不是從第二式省減而來。更接近事實的也許倒是相反的情況。這一點,我將在下文討論。爲什麽會把“爲”字句看做被動句型的一個原因,恐怕是由於對“爲”這個動詞的誤解而造成的。在很多情况下,這個詞雖然有點像系詞,但是絶不能認爲它就是一個系詞,或者把它跟英文的“be”(是)等同起來。事實上,它是一個及物動詞,意思是“做、作爲、當、承當”;其引申義爲“變成”。因此,作爲一個動詞,它總携帶一個賓語。從發話者的主觀認知來説,要是他認爲A跟B兩個事物之間的關係是固定的,恒常的,那麽相當於英文中的一句“A is B”(A是B),用古漢語來説,就是“A,B也”。要是他覺得二者的關係是暫時的,相對的,那麽他就用“A爲B”的形式。請看下面諸例。

(52) 爾爲爾,我爲我。(《孟子·萬章下》)

你作爲你,我作爲我。

(53) 遂爲母子如初。(《左傳·隱公元年》)

於是又跟當初一樣,母親像母親,兒子像兒子了。

(54) 知之爲知之,不知爲不知,是知也。(《論語·爲政》)

知道就承認知道,不知道就承認不知道,這才是所謂的“知道”。

粗略而言,“爲”在上述句子中無疑可以用英文的“be”(是)來對譯,然而,正如

(54)和前文例(3)所示,這裹的"be"(爲)跟在對等句裹真正的係詞"be"(是)是不一樣的。如果我們忽略了這種不同,那麽"爲"所負載的微妙的語義涵藴,就會喪失無造①。我們一旦充分瞭解了"爲"字的語意涵藴及其句法要求,那就很容易看到,當語彙動詞(lexical verb)充當"爲"的賓語時,這個賓語動詞的作用便不是"動詞",其功能衹相當一個名詞性的成分。因此,要想真實地反映它們的句法結構,那麽(48)中的最後一部分"將爲戮乎"就要理解爲:"他將會變成殺戮的對象嗎?"(49)則要分析爲:"我們現在要給他做俘虜了"。拿(49)跟下面的句子比較,更可以證明我們這裹的分析。

(55) 吾不忍爲之民也。(《戰國策·趙策三》)

我不能忍受給他做臣民。

然而,用"動詞"來充當"爲"的賓語似乎總有一點不一般,似乎對古人也是如此。這也許正好説明爲什麽他們有時候在這個"動詞"之前加一個"所"字來使它名詞化。例(50)跟(51)便是其證。不難看出,這裹跟在4.2.中的例(43)所用的方法是完全一樣的。前者是用"所"來使"被"後面的動詞名詞化;這裹用"所"來使"爲"後的動詞名詞化,其用意實出一轍。對我們來説,這裹所顯示的最重要的信息是:"爲"跟"被"一樣,都是這類句子的主要動詞。它不是一個附着成分(affix),或者一個被動標志(marker)。我們這裹所看到的衹是一個簡單的動賓結構,而不是一個"被動結構"②。

---

① 有意思的是,這兩種不同類型的"be"(是)在語意跟句法上的對立仍然可以在現代漢語裹看到,當然詞彙形式不同了。譬如,要是一個男人説:"I'm a man but I want to be a woman."用中國話就得説成:"我是男人,可是我想做(或"當")女人。"也許正是這種深深根植於漢語古今的對應關係,使得趙元任先生撇開表層上的不同形式,提出"普遍的中文語法"這一概念。

② 在上述所討論的幾種句式中,"見殺"不能説成"*見王殺"。可是"被害"可以説成"被蘇峻害"。同時,"爲虜"可以説成"爲之虜",但是"被蘇峻害"不能説成"被之害",爲什麽呢?根據我們的解釋,上述三種句式中的"殺""害""虜"都是賓語。但是[見-V]是較固定的成語式,所以中間一般不能插入施動者。[被-N-V]中的N爲領屬格(其後可以增"之"字)。而"爲之虜"是雙賓語結構,"之"是"爲"的賓語。所以"爲之虜"最好譯成"給他作俘虜"(或奴隸);而不是"做他的俘虜(或奴隸)"。"爲之民"譯成"給他作臣民"而不是"做他的臣民"。至於爲什麽"治於人"可以表示被動,而"治於高傒"則表示比較,亦即爲什麽同是[V於N]形式,而其語義表達不同呢?我初步認爲(更深入的研究有待另文專述):行爲動詞的用法可以轉化成爲表示"静態"的動詞,轉化以後就跟形容詞一樣,是所謂的Stative Verbs(静態動詞)。當它們以"静態動詞"的身份出現時,句子含有比較的意思就不足奇怪了。

五、結語

作爲結語,我想重複一下我在這篇文章裏試圖説明的幾個觀點。第一,我希望通過本文能説明這一點:無論對哪種語言,任何有意義的研究必須首先以該語言自身固有的特性爲基礎,而不盲目的“應用”某種先驗的理論。以這些特性爲起點,邏輯分析才是最有效的。第二,我相信,要談句法分析的話,漢語最重要的特點就是趙元任先生所發現的規律:句子的主語跟謂語之間的語意關係就是主題跟評論之間的語意關係。這一發現具有很多含意,有些,即使是趙先生本人,也没有完全意識到。第三,上述規律所導致的必然結果之一就是:主語在漢語的句子中不一定必須出現。這也是漢語的一個主要特點。第四,忽視“主語省略”(一時没有更好的術語)常常造成句法研究上的混淆和誤解,就是有些著名的學者也很難避免。最説明問題的一個例子就是不能給連詞“而”跟“則”下一個令人滿意的定義。我在以前的一篇文章裏曾證明(薛1991),衹要我們把“主語省略”考慮進去,這些虚詞是可以通過一個簡單而又清楚的定義來概括的。第五,漢語究竟是怎樣通過句法來表現被動觀念的,這仍然是一個謎。已發表的大多數的文章似乎都未能清楚地區分什麼是語義意念上的被動,什麼是特定句法形式上的被動句型。然而衹有後者才可以確鑿地叫做“被動句型”。不能區分意念被動跟形式被動的結果,往往衹是根據句子的含意拉出一個任意性的清單。有的學者甚至還試圖將這些所謂“被動句”從古至今的歷時發展畫出一個模式。在這篇文章裏,我試圖説明這些所謂的“被動句型”根本就不是特定的被動句式。它們都是“主動句型”,衹不過在成語和修辭法的意義上,它們可以間接地用來表這“被動”而已,因此也就帶有一定程度上的强調意味。因爲主語省略是漢語最突出的一個特點,我於是大膽地主張這個語言不需要給被動句專門設置一個特定的句法形式。换言之,正是由於這一特點,漢語才没有發展出來一個專門的被動句型。道理很簡單,因爲一個句子中的及物動詞,衹要它的主語被省略或者不出現,它就自然而然地意味着被動(見3.3)。總之,我是試圖從句法特點的角度來解漢語的這個謎,而其他采用邏輯分析法的學者如Cikoski,則試圖通過對語素内在特徵或性質的發掘來解决這個問題。問題很可能不是誰對誰錯,也許(起碼我們希望)這兩種方法都可以對這方面的研究提供一些新的啓迪,從而幫助我們加深對漢語的認識。

參考文獻

編寫組　1979,《古代漢語常用字字典》,北京:商務印書館。

高名凱　1956,《三論漢語的詞類分别》,《漢語的詞類問題》,上海:中華書局。

韓峥嶸　1984,《古漢語虚詞手册》,長春:吉林人民出版社。

何樂士　1982,《〈左傳〉的單句跟複句初探》,《先秦漢語研究》(程湘清主編),濟南:山東教育出版社,第143—271頁。

黄六平　1974,《漢語文言語法綱要》,香港:中華書局。

廖序東　1981,《文言語法分析》,上海:上海教育出版社。

劉景農　1965,《漢語文言語法》,北京:中華書局。

吕叔湘　1955,《漢語語法論文集》,北京:科學出版社。

太田辰夫　1987,《中國語歷史文法》(蔣紹愚、徐昌華譯),北京:北京大學出版社。

王　力　1984,《中國語法理論》,《王力文集》,第一卷,濟南:山東教育出版社(1944年版重印)。

——　1956,《關於漢語有無詞類的問題》,《漢語的詞類問題》,上海:中華書局。

王　力　1981,《古代漢語》(王力主編,修訂本),北京:中華書局。

謝紀鋒　1992,《虚詞詁林》,哈爾濱:黑龍江人民出版社。

薛鳳生　1991,《試論連詞而字的語意與語法功能》,《語言研究》(武漢)總第二十期,第55—62頁。

——　1993,《論古文中的主語省略及其對文法研究的影響》,《語文建設通訊》(香港)第四期,第33—34頁。

楊伯峻　1963,《文言語法》,北京:中華書局。

楊樹達　1972,《高等國文法》,臺北:鼎文書局影印。

雅洪托夫　1986,《漢語史論集》(唐作藩、胡雙寶編選),北京:北京大學出版社。

周法高 1986,《中國古代語法·造句篇(上)》,臺北:"中央研究院"歷史語言研究所。

Chao, Yuen Ren (1968). *A Grammar of Spoken Chinese*. Berkeley, CA.

Chu. Chaunccy C. (1987). *Historical Syntax*: *Thoery and Application* to Chinese The Crane Publishing Co., Taipei.

Cikoski John S. (1978a), "An outline sketch of sentence structures and ward classes in Classical Chinese" *Camputational Analyses of Asian & African Languages*, (Tokyo), Na. 8. pp. 17 - 152.

Cikoski. John S. (1978b). "An analysis of some idioms commonly called 'passive' in Classical Chinese." *CAAAL*, *No*. 9, pp. 133 - 208.

Dobson, W. A. C. H. (1959). *Late Archaic Chinese*. University of Toronto Press, London.

Harbsmeier, Christoph (1981), *Aspects of Classical chinese Syntax*, Curzon Press, London.

Hsueh. F. S. (1991), "The Structural Meaning of BA adn BEI Constructions in Mandarin Chinese: Do they really mean DISPOSAL and PASSIVE?" In Tai&Hsueh (eds.): *Functionalism and Chinese Grammar*, CLTA Monograph No. 1, pp. 95 - 125.

Legge, James (1982). *The Chinese Classics*. Third edition. (Five volume, reprinted from the last editions of the Oxford U. Press.)

Liu, Cheng-hui (1991). *Nouns*, *Nominalization and Denominalization in Classical Chinese*: *A Study Based on Mencius and Zuozhuan*. Ph. D. Dissertation, The Ohio State University.

Norman, Jerry (1988). *Chinese*, Cambridge University Press.

試論“把”字句的語義特性[**]

緒論

漢語裏的“把”字是一個常用詞,用這個字構成的句式自然也是極常見的。以現代漢語爲母語的人都能運用自如,毫無困難。所以就語言的實際應用來説,這種句式不是一個困難的問題。但是就語言的理論解釋(以及漢語對外教學)來説,這却是一個大問題。因此多年來在語言學界的討論中,這種句式,也就是王力先生所説的“處置式”,一直是一個頗有争議的中心論題,國内外的學者也發表了不少論述這種句式的文章。我是一個極不喜歡争議的人,但腦子裏偏偏常有一些頗有争議性的想法,對“把”字句也是如此。所以總是閉口不言,更不用説寫文章了。可是這次由於一個巧合引起了我的興趣,便實在忍不住了。這個巧合是:北京語言學院的王還教授今年應邀來我校(俄亥俄州立大學)訪問,於三月間作了一個學術報告,題目是“把”字句。四月間臺灣大學的梅廣教授也應邀來我校參加一個漢語討論會,報告題目也是“把”字句。兩次討論,我都“語焉不詳”地發表了一些“謬論”,自然未能引起多少“共鳴”,成了“反派” 角色,心中難免有點兒“被誤解了”的感覺,這才覺得非多説幾句不行。因此把心一横,姑且“大發謬論”,希望能找到幾個“臭味”相投的知音①。

“把”字句的基本形式爲:“某人(或某事)把某人(或某事)怎麽樣”。這可以概括成下面這樣的公式:

** 原刊《語言教學與研究》1987 年第 1 期。

① 本文撰寫期間,王還教授仍在我校訪問,因此我有機會數度向她請教。雖然我們的意見差距甚大,我仍由她的辯難中獲益甚多,對本文作了不少補充,謹在此向她表示謝意。本文中的例句,有許多是抄自她的演講稿。這倒不是由於我愛抄襲,而是因爲對某些“把”字句的合法性。我們有時看法不同,所以我就乾脆抄她的例句,好讓她没話説。她與王力先生一樣,非常謹慎,常從文學作品中找例句(我也照抄),其實我覺得大可不必,因爲我相信他們對漢語的理解與語感,絶不比那些作家低,可能還高很多。

A 把 B+VP

這個公式裏的 A 和 B 都代表一個名詞性的語段,VP 則代表動詞性的語段,作爲句子的謂語。討論"把"字句的論著已經相當不少,這些研究的結論大致可以歸納爲以下數點:

1)"把"字句有許多種,含義各不相同。

2)句中的 A 以某種行動"處置"B。

3)VP 内表示行動的詞是主要動詞。

4)A 是那個"動詞"的主語(或施事者,agent)。

5)B 是那個"動詞"的賓語(或受事者,patient),即所謂"賓語提前"。

6)B 必須是一個定指性的名詞。

在本文裏,我們采用一個不同的理論觀點,希望能給所有的"把"字句提出一個綜合性的"一體化詮釋"(an integrated interpretation),並從而證明上述關於"把"字句的六點看法,都是些似是而非的皮相之論,未能觸及"把"字句結構的基本性質。下面我們就在"把"字句公式的基礎上給"把"字句定性。

定性(一):"把"字句中的"把"祇能是一個單一的語素(morp-heme)。

這是一個最基本的原則,因此聽起來好像是廢話,但其實不然。在中文裏,用一個方塊字代表好幾個不同的語素並不稀奇。比如説,"吃了一把花生"裏的"把"字,"百把個人"裏的"把"字,以及"把花生吃了"裏的"把"字,就不可能代表相同的語素。所謂"處置式"中的"把"是代表一個語素還是幾個不同的語素呢?表面上大家似乎都把它看作一個語素,没有什麽争議。但是在許多討論"把"字句的論著中,我們却常看到作者列舉"把"字的"第一種用法、第二種用法、第三種用法、……",而未見説明這許多種用法的共通性(common property)。這就等於説,這些用法是互不相干的,衹不過是語法形式的偶然巧合而已;也就等於説,這些用法裏的"把"字含義不同,分别代表不同的語素。也許有人不承認這一説法,那麽我們要問,除非你能指出這些用法的共通性,你憑什麽能説"把"字在這些不同用法裏的語義或語法功能是一致的呢?也就是説它代表同一個語素呢？現在我們既然肯定地説“把”字句中的“把”字是一個單一的語素，那就等於承認我們有義務找出它那些不同用法的共通性，也就是它的基本定義，否則我們的研究就没有理論性的意義了①。這是一個很困難的問題，但我們願意接受這一挑戰。下文的討論就是我們的應戰。

定性(二)：“把”字句中的 VP 必須是一個説明由於某一行動而造成 B 的某一狀態的描述語段(a descriptive statement about B's condition as a result of a certain action)

凡是“把”字句都必須符合這一原則。當然 VP 可能以許多不同的形式出現，但衹要它含有這種描述性，並以 B 的狀態(state)爲對象，也就是説以 B 爲其主題，就算合格。與“把”字句的這一性質相關的，有以下幾點需要加以説明。

(1) 這一特性説明，“把”字句中的 VP，在語法結構上説，是與 B 直接發生關係的，與 A 衹間接發生關係。過去常有人誤以爲 VP 是以 A 爲主語以 B 爲賓語的，所以便覺得以下這類句子頗爲費解：

a) 他把黑板(上)寫滿了字。

b) 他把花瓶(裏)插了一把花。

c) 他把墻(上)釘了一根釘。

d) 他把那隻狗打斷了兩條腿。

其實這些都是很自然的句子，因爲它們完全符合了定性(二)所説的條件限制，也就是説用“寫滿了字”描寫“黑板(上)”是極自然的，用“插了一把花”描寫“花瓶(裏)”，用“釘了一根釘”描寫“墻(上)”也同樣是自然的。説“那隻狗打斷了兩條腿”似乎不太自然，因爲我們平常衹説“那隻狗斷了兩條腿”。但前者並非絶不可以。在此需要特别强調的是，這幾句話裏的 VP 是描述性的，重點在説明 B 的狀態，而不在説明動作或動作者。漢語中又有所謂“得以句爲謂

① 這句話當然是專就理論性説的。從另一角度看，爲了教學上的實用，尤其是對外漢語教學，如果有人能把“把”字句歸納成幾種不同的用法，並給以明確的解釋，那自然也是很大的貢獻。

語”的一種結構。衹要那個作爲謂語的句子是描述性的,它自然也就可以作爲“把”字句的謂語,這是毫不足怪的。例如:

e) 他把那幾個學生每人駡一頓。

f) 快把那隻鷄毛拔下來。

(2) 既然 VP 描述的是某種特定行動使 B 變成某種特定狀態,那麽我們就衹能把 B 的狀態作明確的説明,不能空泛地説它不處於某一狀態。因爲那樣就等於説某一特定行動的結果使 B 變成不定的狀態,這顯然是不合常理的。所以“把”字句的 VP 是不能直接加以否定的,必須把否定詞放在“把”之前。例如:

a) *他把錢不還給我。

b) 他不把錢還給我。

但是有少數習慣用的否定詞却可以作“把”字句的 VP。這是因爲它們形式上雖爲否定,而實質上却是積極性的,所以並不算違規。例如:

c) 他把我差點兒没氣死。

d) 他們把我的提議否决了。

可是如果 VP 是一個由動作詞加“得”引領的語段,則不在此限(參看下文第 6 節),因爲這時的否定詞也是積極性的。

(3) 漢語中的所謂“動補”結構,是由一個表示動作的詞後加一個表示結果或趨向的詞構成的,諸如:“打破、殺死、搶走、買來、送去、扔進來、踢出去”等等。這類複合詞都是及物動詞,可以帶有賓語。因此一般人都很直覺地把表示動作的部分看做“動詞”(verb),而把其後表示結果或趨向的部分叫做“補語”(complement)。在這個問題上,我的想法又是頗有争議的。我認爲假如我們給“動詞”下的定義不是表面上的“動作”(action),而是本質性的“謂語的核心”(center,or head of VP),我們就得承認所謂“動補”結構中的“補語”實爲真正的動詞,而其前的所謂“動詞”實爲狀語。這個説法初看起來似乎有點兒“離經叛道”,但就近代語言學理論來説,這才是最“正統的説法”。所謂“動補”結構,就其詞性來説,都是所謂“向心結構”(endocentric construction),也就是説,其中的某一成分是整個結構的核心或“首詞”(head),而整個結構的詞性與“首詞”的詞性是一致的。當我們説“推開門”或者“把門推開”的時候,意思是説“以推而使門開”,語義的重心是“使門開”,而不是“推”。由此可見複合動詞“推開”的詞性與“開”的詞性是一致的,“推”衹是達成“開”的一個手段而已。(别的手段尚有:“打、踢、撞、叫、擠”等。)在現代漢語中,作爲“動補”結構中所謂“補語”的詞多爲形容詞,單獨出現時,絶大部分衹能用作修飾語或狀態動詞(stative verb),而不能用作及物動詞。但在古代漢語中,把這類詞用作及物動詞是極平常的,即所謂“使動用法”。我覺得現代漢語中的所謂“動補”結構中的“補語”,實際上都是“使役動詞”(causative verb),是從古代漢語的“使動用法”沿襲出來的。衹不過在現代漢語中這種用法所受的限制特别嚴而已。它的條件是:必須與表示手段的“動作狀語”(action adverb) 同時應用。例如:我們衹能説“打死他!”, 不能説“*死他!”:衹能説“做完功課”,不能説“*完功課”等①。“把”字句用所謂“動補”結構做 VP 是常見的。在我們正確地認識了“動補”結構的性質以後,下列這類“把”字句的性質也就很明顯了:

a) 他把頭發剃光了。

b) 我把朋友送走了。

c) 你快把我想死嘍!

d) 春風又把江南吹緑了。

在這些句子裏,VP 的核心是“光、走、死、緑”,其前的“剃、送、想、吹”衹是達成那些狀態的手段與途徑而已。更重要的是,這些 VP,正如它們的核心詞一樣,都是直接描述 B 的狀態的,不與 A 直接發生關係,因此完全符合定性(二)的要求。

(4) 在上一節裏,我們給“動補”結構的詞性提出了一個新的解釋。這個結論,很自然地產生了一個有趣的系論(corollary):既然所謂“補語”才是真正的動詞,而所謂“動詞”衹不過是表示手段或途徑的動作狀語而已,那麼在以“動補”結構爲謂語的句子裏,動作狀語的語義深層的施事者(agent)就不一定非是全句的主語(A)不可了。當然在絶大多數的情况下,A 也就是那個動作

---

① 在現代漢語裏,仍有少數形容詞可作“使動用法”的及物動詞。例如,開(門)、累(人)、滿(一杯酒)、臭(他兩句)等。所謂“趨向補語”也有這種用法。例如。來(一杯茶)、去(你的)、進(一批貨)、出(個主意)等。但總的來説,數目甚少,而且多用於習語中,不似在古代漢語裏那樣完全自由。

狀語的施事者,所以下面這類句子是最常見的:

a) 他説破了嘴。

b) 他把嘴説破了。

但是就語法的規則來説,衹要動作狀語能合理地表達某一狀態是如何形成的,就算合格了。至於施事者是誰,倒是没有限制的,也就是説這兒並没有一個施事者非是A不可的語法限制(syntactic constraint)。例如,在下列的句子裹,動作狀語的施事者不是A而是B:

c)"喲,四爺,可想死我嘍!"(老舍《茶館》)

d) 你可把我想死嘍!

e) 那出戲把他唱累了。

f) 那班學生把王老師教慘啦!

g) 這件事差點兒把他惱死了。

有時候連動作者到底是誰都用不着標出來,例如:

h) 這一番話終於把他説服了。

i) 一百塊錢就能把那個警察買通。

這些都是正常的句子,因爲VP的重心是那些個所謂的"補語",是描寫B的,不違背定性(二)的規定。

(5)"把"字句的VP,也可能衹含有一個表示行動的詞,而没有所謂"補語"。(當然這個詞的後面必須加"了",前面也是可以加狀語的。)例如:

a) 我把汽車賣了。　　(試比較:汽車賣了。)

b) 他把鷄殺了。　　(試比較:鷄殺了。)

c) 别把錢丢啦!　　(試比較:錢丢了。)

d) 把桌子一拍……　　(試比較:桌子一拍……)

在這類句子裹,它們的動詞是否真的代表動作,而且直接與A發生關係呢?我以爲不然。漢語裹的許多動詞除了代表動作以外,還可以代表由該動作産生出來的結果。這是它們既可用於主動語態(active voice),又可用於被動語態(passive voice)的緣故。被動語態的被動分詞形容詞(passive participial)基本上是静態的(stative),有描述的性質,所以在"把"字句中,能以B爲主題而直接描述它。不僅上述各例爲然,就是像"我把他打了"這句話裹的"打"字也屬這種性質。這一特性還可以從另外三個方面加以證明：

其一，這些動詞的施事者，不一定是A。例如：

e）他把頭髮剪了。

這句話的重點是：“頭髮剪了”，至於是他自己剪的還是別人替他剪的却無關宏旨。

其次，這類動詞前而可加數量副詞（adverb of quantity）。例如：

f）我把花生全吃了。

“全”字在這兒使我們知道，VP“全吃了”衹能是以“花生”（B）爲依歸的，不與“我”（A）發生直接關係。

其三，這類動詞前，可以加“給”字。例如：

g）我把他給忘了。

動詞前的“給”字有使動詞變成被動語態的作用，這是我們都知道的。其實我們不僅必須把這類“把”字句中的動詞認作“被動語態”，就是上兩節裏討論列的“使役動詞”（即所謂“動補”結構中的“補語”），出現在“把”字句中作VP時，也都屬於被動語態，因爲衹有那樣它們才有資格作爲B的描述語。

（6）“把”字句中的VP，除了以上討論到的形式以外，還有一種常見的形式，即在一個動作之後加上“得”（或“的”）字，用以引導一個較長的描述語。例如：

a）他把我説得一文不值。

b）他把我氣得糊裏糊塗的。

c）老李把老張駡得抬不起頭來。

這些例子，進一步證明了我們給VP所下的定義是正確的。“得”字有把動詞轉化爲修飾語的功能，這是大家都知道的。這説明“得”字之前的“動詞”不可能是VP的核心，它的核心衹能是後面的描述語。正如同“動補”結構中的所謂“動詞”一樣，“得”字之前的“動詞”也不一定是以A爲其施事者（agent）的。例如：

d）辣椒把我吃得舌頭都麻了。

e）那些衣服把他洗得直不起腰來。

f）那班學生把王老師教得心灰意懶。

g）哀怨的笛聲把我們吹得心酸淚落。

h）她把我想得神魂顛倒。

我們説“把”字句中的VP必須是一個描述性的語段,這當然是就標準性的“把”字句説的。語言是一種社會活動,在個别人的使用中,有時候就不一定全按標準出牌。比如説,鼓詞中就有“我兒在家把書攻”這樣的句子,而阿Q也曾高唱“我手舉鋼鞭將你打”(“將”字性質同“把”)。這樣的句子總讓我們覺得有點兒不大對勁,似乎話還没有説完。究其原因,我覺得就是因爲它們的VP(攻、打)仍表示動作,而不是描述性的,因此破了格。如果改成“我兒在家把書攻得滚瓜爛熟”,以及“我手舉鋼鞭將你打翻在地”,就顯得更爲自然了①。另一方面,當我們説“某一行動造成B的某一狀態”時,也許會引起一些誤會,因爲有人可能會説,像“他把你看了一眼”這句話裏,“你”的狀態並没有什麼變化呀!就事物的實際情況(physical condition)説,這種説法當然是對的,但就説話人所投射的心理狀態(psychological condition)説,却不盡然。“把他打一頓”固然明顯地影響到了“他”,“把他駡一頓”,或者“在背後把他議論一番”,也同樣可以説是影響到了“他”。就“把”字句的本質説,衹要是説話人心理上認爲某人或某事受到某一行動的影響,就可以用“把”字句來表達他的這種想法或感覺,不一定非是明確的實際影響不可。因此假如我覺得“她偷看了你一眼”可能對“你”有某種影響或後果,我就可以對“你”説:“她把你偷看了一眼。”

定性(三):“把”字句中的B必須是句子的首要主題(main topic)

我們已經説過,“把”字句的VP是描述性的,是以B爲主語的。有許多人

① 由於“把”字句的這一特性未經及早確認,因此有些關於“把”字句的論著便作出了不很適當的結論。比如説,大家對“把”字句的起源都很感興趣,有人引用杜甫的詩句“醉把茱萸仔細看”,説這種句式早在唐代就已經形成了(Cheung 1976)。我不知道“把”字句究竟起於何時,但根據這句杜詩説它起於唐代,顯然論據不足。因爲這句話的VP“仔細看”指主語(省略了)的行動,而不是對“茱萸”的描述,所以與真正的“把”字句貌合神離。(如果改成“醉把茱萸看仔細”就比較合格了。)另一方面,也曾有人試圖爲“把”字句的本質下一概括性的定義(Y. C. Li 1974),用意極佳,但所得的結論却是:對於特定事物的特定行動(a specific action upon a specific object),並進而推論説,那個“動詞”標示着“賓語”的某種定指性(The verb indicates a certain definiteness in the object)。這個結論顯得過於煩瑣,也不能概括所有的“把”字句。究其原因,還是誤解了“把”字句VP的特性,錯把“動詞”看作VP的核心。

把B解釋爲“賓語提前”,這種説法雖然完全誤解了B與VP之間的語義語法關係,却也暗示了B是被突出作爲主題的。在漢語語法中,“主題”是一個極爲重要的觀念,但是除了“出現在句首”這個不十分明確的定義以外,它還有什麼特徵呢?有些人説它必須是“定指的”。這是一個頗有見地的説法,不幸的是有許多人又把此處所謂的“定指”等同於英語的“the”(definite/indefinite之區别)。在多數情況下,這樣畫等號似乎相當合適,但是碰到下列這類句子時就會感到莫名其妙了。

1)書到用時方恨少,事非經過不知難。

2)一人做事一人當。

3)山外有山,人外有人。

這些句子裏的主題,顯然都不是英講語法中的所謂“definite”能够解釋的。似乎漢語的所謂“定指”與英語的“definite”含義不同,但是其不同究在何處呢?這是一個很不容易回答的問題,多年來我也搜索枯腸而不得其解,直到最近才豁然有會於心,又有了個頗有“争議”的想法。這個問題的答案,説穿了真似羚羊挂角,不着痕迹,但如果我們猛一抬頭,就會發現它正挂在我們的眼前。我現在覺得:所謂“定指”(邏輯性的definite,不限於英語)這個概念,基本上是客觀性的(objective),它標示一個特定的事物,因此比較容易界説。但“主題”這個概念則不然,它完全是主觀性的(subjective)。人世間的事物何止億萬,衹要是出於説者的主觀選擇,任何一件事物都可以成爲他的話題,不必待其成爲“定指”而後可。當然在語言的實際應用中,這兩個概念所涵蓋的事物常常是重叠的(overlapping),也就是説“主題”在絶大多數的情况下,同時也是“定指”的。但那衹是表面現象,若從而得出一個它們是“一而二,二而一的”的結論,那就完全錯了。因爲它們是屬於不同範疇(different categories)的概念。我没聽人説過英語裏的“主題”必須是定指的,爲什麼漢語裏的“主題”非是定指不可呢?這個問題正如同“把”字句中A與“動詞”(即“動作狀語”)的關係一樣。在絶大多數的情况裏,A都是那個“動詞”的施事者,但這也衹是表面現象。假如從而得出結論説:那個“動詞”的施事者一定是A,所以A是那個“動詞”的主語,B是它的“賓語提前”云云,那也就錯了。我們現在要重新闡明,“定指”不是“主題”的必然屬性,而且“主題”也不一定要出現在句首。“把”字句的特性之一是:B 必須是 VP 的主語,而且在語義語法的關係上,是比 A 更重要的主題。從這個觀點看,B 不僅不是什麽“賓語提前”,反而是“主題移後”了。這也就是“把”字的一個特有的語法功能①。以明顯的定指名詞作爲主題(B)的“把”字句實在太普通了,用不着舉例。下面衹略舉幾個主題(B)不是定指名詞的例子,並稍加説明。

4) 現在有人把書法講得未免太死板了。

5) 真正把書讀進去了,就越讀越有意思。

6) 美洲没有馬,後來西班牙人才把馬運到美洲去。(以上見鄧拓《燕山夜話》)

7) 這家伙不把人當人看。

在這幾個例子裏,出現在 B 的位置上的名詞,顯然都不是定指的,但却都是説者要評述的話題,也可以説“把”字使它們獲得了主題性(topicality)。這樣的“把”字句當然是完全合格的了。“把”字的這種功能,從下列的對比句中,更可以清楚地看出來:

8) a) 他買重了一本書。

b) 他把一本書買重了。

9) a) 他寫了一個劇本。

b) 他把一個劇本寫得像小説一樣。

10) a) 他説了幾句客氣話。

b) 他把幾句客氣話説得非常得體。

11) a) 他遞給我一雙筷子。

b) 它把一雙筷子遞給我。

---

① 國外有許多學者非常勇於立説。曾經有人提出漢語的句式已由“動賓”變爲“賓動”了(Li and Thompson 1975),更有人説,這種詞序的轉變始於北方漢語而不見於南方漢語,是受到阿爾泰(Altaic)語的影響(M. Hashimoto 1976, A. Hashimoto 1975, So 1976)云云。持這種看法的人,自然也都以“把”字句中所謂“賓語提前”的現象作爲證據。我的同事黎天睦曾爲文指出此説的不妥(Light 1979)。同時也有人指出,傣語裏也有類似“把”字句的“賓語提前”的句式(Jagacinski 1986)。對於這類頗有争議性的問題,我一向不願置身,在此衹想指出,假如我們給 B 所作的定性是正確的話(B 是 VP 的主語,不是 VP 裏那個“動詞”的“賓語提前”),就不能用“把”字句來證明漢語已經變爲“賓動”語了,持此説法的人最好另找證據。

由以上這四組對比句,可以清楚地看出,這些個普通句中不定指的名詞,出現在“把”字句中時,都仍然是不定指的,但却變成了説者要强調的話題。有時候經由這種過程變來的主題,也可能會同時由不定指變爲定指。例如:

12) a) 他攢起錢來了。

b) 他把錢攢起來了。

13) a) 我想給她介紹一個朋友。

b) 我想把一個朋友介紹給她。

爲什麽不定指的名詞因“把”而變爲主題時,有的仍爲不定指而有的却變爲定指呢? 坦白地説,我還没想通。這可能不是語法的問題,而是由於詞彙本身的含義變動不居。

定性(四):“把”字句中的A衹能是句子的次要主題(secondary topic)

“把”字句中的A出現在句首,當然是主題無疑。但就其語義功能來説,它是次要的,B才是主要的。這可以從兩方面看出來。其一,VP直接描述B,關係密切,與A的關係則隔了一層;其次,省略了A的“把”字句,仍然是一個很好的原意不改的“把”字句,但如省掉B,就不成話了。例如

1) a) 糟糕,我把這件事忘了!

b) 糟糕,把這件事忘了!

c) *糟糕,我把忘了!

在日常生活中,省略A的“把”字句是常見的,有時候連A到底是什麽都不容易説清楚。例如:

2) 看,把他累得(成了這個樣子)!

3) 真要把我急死了!

4) 把小李跑得上氣不接下氣。

5) “我編的,我還不怕,就把你怕成那樣!”(趙樹理《李有才板話》)

A在“把”字句中究竟擔任什麽角色呢? 我覺得可以這麽説:“通過‘把’字的聯繫,表示B之所以成爲VP所描寫的狀態,是與它有相當關係的。”在這個定義

裏,我們僅僅説"與它有相當關係",這是因爲衹有這樣才能涵蓋所有合乎文法的"把"字句。這種關係當然可以有許多程度上的差別,最直接也是最常見的,就是由A親手造成B的某種狀態。例如:

6)猫把老鼠咬死了。

7)他把汽車開走了。

可是有時候,這種關係可能不那麽直接,衹能説B的某種狀態是由A引發或促成的而已。例如:

8)喲,你怎麽把頭髮燙得那麽漂亮呀?

9)你要把我想死嘍!

10)洗冷水澡把他洗病了。

11)那首歌把人家唱得情緒激昂起來。

更有甚時,這種關係可能顯得相當疏遠,衹能説B的狀態跟A多少有點兒關聯,因而説話人覺得A可能負有點兒道義責任而已。例如:

12)三年困難時期,他把一個獨生兒子餓死了。

13)他失業才不久,又把兩間房子失火燒了。

14)他衹顧搞販運,結果把個老婆也跑丢了。

這類"把"字句不常見,但絶不能説不合文法。可見就"把"字句的合法性(grammaticality)來説,衹要B的狀態與A有相當的關係,也就够了,不一定是由A一手造成的。

結論

綜合以上各節的討論,我們對"把"字句的基本性質可以説已經有了一個相當明確的認識①。概括地説,這種句子的定義是:

---

① 王力先生把"把"字句分爲"處置式"與"繼事式"等類,而有些人認爲"把"字句的含義不一定是"處置",因此不同意這樣的命名。但是多年來也未見有人提出更妥善的新名,多數人仍使用"處置式"之名,或者籠統地叫做"把"字句。我覺得如果我給"把"字句所作的詮釋是正確的話,稱作"導致式"也許更有概括性。但是名可名非常名,既然"處置式"沿用已久,實在用不着再改了,重要的是如何確認這種句式的真正含義。對於某些"把"字句的"合法性",有時候大家的意見也不容易一致。比方説,像"他已經把你(送)的禮物收到了",這樣的句子,(轉下頁)

語法結構:A 把 B+VP

語義詮釋:由於 A 的關係,B 變成了 VP 所描述的狀態。

"把"字句的討論至此似乎可以結束了,但我想附帶說一說"被"字句。這兩種句式是有關聯的,這早已有人指出來了。(王還教授就曾寫過一本《"把"字句與"被"字句》。)在上文討論"把"字句的基礎上,我們現在可以明確地看出,這兩種句式是一正一反,互爲倒影(mirror image)的。所以"被"字句的定義可以概括爲:

語法結構:A 被 B+VP

語義詮釋:由於 B 的關係,A 變成了 VP 所描述的狀態。

也就是説,與"把"字句恰恰相反,在"被"字句裏,A 是首要主題,B 是次要主題,但是這兩種句式的 VP 都必須是描述性的語段。因此上文所説"把"字句中 VP 的屬性,也都適用與"被"字句的 VP。這衹要看下面兩個例子就可以明白了

1) a) 茅臺把我吃醉了。

b) 我被茅臺吃醉了。

2) a) 丢東西把他丢怕了。

b) 他被丢東西丢怕了。

這兩種句式的關係,還可以用下面的圖式説明:

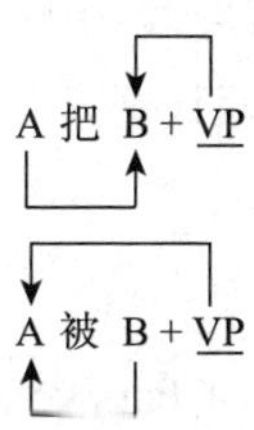

在這兩個圖式裏,箭頭所指的是首要主題,也就是説話的人要用 VP 描述的話

(接上頁)有人就認爲不合文法,因此把"動詞"或者"補語"加以分類,説某些類不能用於"把"字句云云。但是另一些人,包括我在内,就覺得上面的例句是可以接受的。關於這類有争論的句子,顯然都是文法結構中低層次的問題,本文旨在闡明"把"字句的最基本的含義,對低層次上的問題就略而不論了。

題,不能省略;次要主題不與VP發生直接關係,是可以省略的[①]。

參考文獻

一、中文部分

王　力　《中國現代語法》,中華書局,1954年。

王　還　《"把"字句與"被"字句》,上海教育出版社,1984年。

王　還　《"把"字句中"把"字的賓語》,《中國語文》,1985年第1期,第48—51頁。

吕叔湘　《"把"字用法的研究》,《漢語語法論文集》,科學出版社,1955年,第125—144頁。

宋玉柱　《關於"把"字句的兩個問題》,《語文研究》,1981年第2期。

陳初生　《早期處置式略論》,《中國語文》,1983年第3期,第201—206頁。

胡附、文煉　《現代漢語語法探索》,上海新知識出版社,1956年。

張志公　《漢語語法常識》,上海新知識出版社,1956年。

湯廷池　《國語變形語法研究》,臺北,1979年修訂本。

詹開第　《"把"字句謂語中動作的方向》,《中國語文》,1983年第2期,第93—96頁。

潘允中　《漢語動補結構的發展》,《中國語文》,1980年第3期,第53—60頁。

葛　毅　《"把"字句(處置式)的起源》,《中國語文》69(1958)第117—118頁。

梅　廣　《"把"字句》,《文史哲學報》(臺灣大學),1978年,第145—180頁。

二、英文部分

Bennett. Paul A.:"The Evolution of Passive and Disposal Sentences", *Journal of Chinese Linguistics* (JCL) 9.1(1981),61-90.

Chao, Yuen Ren: *A Grammar of Spoken Chinese*, *Berkely*, U.C. Press,1968.

---

① 這裏所謂的可以省略或不能省略,是綜合"把"字句和"被"字句兩種句式的説法。兩相比較,B在"把"字句中絶不能省略,但在"被"字句則可以省略,因此可知B在前式中爲首要主題,在後式中爲次要主題。而A的主題地位則恰好相反。A在"被"字句裏雖爲首要主題,有時候也可以省略,但這種省略是主題已經完全明顯時的一般性省略,不限於"被"字句。

Chen, G. T.: "The Ba Construction: A Topic and Comment Approach", *Journal of the Chinese Language Teachers Association* (JCLTA) 18-1 (1983). 17-29.

Chen, Chung-yu: "On Predicative complements", *JCL* 7.1 (1979), 41-64.

Cheung, Hung-min Samuel: "A Comparative Study in Chinese Grammars: The ba-construction", *JCL* 1.3(1973)343-382.

Cheung. Yat-shing: "Word Order change in Chinese: Some contribuying factors and implication", U. Microfilms international, 1976, Ann Arbor, Mich. 183-216.

Chu, Chauncey C: "'Conceptual Wholeness' and the 'Retained' Object", *JCL*. 4.1 (1976). 14-23.

Hashimoto, Anne Oikan Yue: "Southern Chinese Dialects-the Tai Connection", *paper read at the Eighth International Conference on Sino-Tibetan Linguistics*, 1975.

Hashimoto, Mautaro J.: "Language Diffusion on the Asian Continent Problems of Typological Diversity in Sino-Tibetan", *Computational Analysis of Asian and African Languages* (CAAAL) 3(1976), 49-65.

Huang, C. T. James: "Phrase Structure Lexical Integrity, and Chinese Compounds", *JCLTA* 19. 2(1984), 53-78.

Huang, shuan-fan.: "Historical Change of Prepositions and Emergence of SOV Order", *JCL* 62(1978), 212-242

——"The History of the Disposal Construction Revisited Evidence from Zen Dialogucs in the Tang Dynasty", *JCL* 14-1(1986), 43-52.

Ngampit Jagacinski: Lue of Xishuangbanna: a Study of the reversed OV order in the Taii au-Construction, Ph. D, dissertation, The Ohio State University, 1986.

Li, Charles N., and Thompson, Sandra A.: "An Explanation of Word Order Change SVO-SOV", *Foundations of Languages* 12(1974), 201-214.

——"A Linguistic Discussion of the 'Co-Verb' in Chinese Grammar",

JCLTA 9.3(1974),109－119.

—— Mandarin Chinese: a Functional Reference Grammar. UC Press,1981.

Li, Y. C.:"what Does 'Disposal' Mean? Features of the Verb and Noun in Chinese", *JCL* 2.2(1974),200－218.

Light, Timothy:"Word Order and Word Order Change in Madarin Chinese", *JCL* 7.2(1979),149－180.

Lin, Shuang-fu:"Locatial Construction and ba-construction in Madarin", *JCLTA* 9.2(1974). 66－83.

Lu, John H-T.: "Resultative Verb Compounds Vs. Directional Verb compounds in Madarin", *JCL*. 5.2(1977),276－313.

So, Chung: "The ba-construction and Verb final Drift in Chinese", *CAAAL* 3.

Tai, James H-Y.:"Chinese SOV Language", *Papers from the Ninth Regional Meeting of the Chicago Linguistic Society*, 1973.

——"On the Change from SVO to SOV in Chinese", Papers from the Parasession on Diachonic Syntax, Chicago Linguistic Society, 1976, 291－304.

——"Word Order in Chinese and the X Theory", *JCLTA* 19. 2(1984). 23－35.

Teng, Shou-hsin:"Subject and Theme, in Chinese: a Critique of the SOV Hypothesis", *Paper read at the Eighth Sino-Tibetan Conference*, 1975.

——"A Grammar of Verb-Particles in Chinese", *JCL*. 5.1(1977),1－25.

Thompson, Saudra:"Transitivity and Some Problem with the BA Construction in Mandarin Chinese", *JCL* 1.2(1973). 208－221.

Thompson, Saudra A.:"Resultative Verb Compounds in Mandarin Chinese: a Case for Lexical Rules.", *Language* 49.2(1973),361－379.

“把”字句和“被”字句的結構意義

——真的表示“處置”和“被動”?**

一、引言

“把”和“被”屬於漢語普通話裏最常用的小詞,它們參與構成的“把”字句和“被”字句一直是當代從事漢語研究的語言學家討論的課題和衆多研究的對象(見參考文獻)。以往的研究對我們瞭解這兩種句式的句法結構和歷史演變頗多貢獻,但是(在我看來)它們的語義特性還没有被正確地認識和定義,其結果是,以往對這兩種句式的結構和來源的研究所得出的許多結論是很值得懷疑的。本文采取一種全然不同的理論觀點,對這兩種句式的語義特性重新加以定義①。

我相信,衹有在正確定義這兩種句式的語義特性後,對它們的句法説明和教學上的解釋才會更有依據和更加合理。重新定性的出發點是我對語言研究的一些總的基本的信念,它們可簡述如下。

1.1 語言系統的局限性

語言系統是人類心靈試圖描繪外部世界時的主觀和任意的產物。操不同語言的人用不同的系統來描繪外部世界。這些系統都各有自己内在的邏輯,可以對它們作出具體説明和闡述。然而,這些系統永遠不足以對它們所要描繪的外部世界作出完整的、確實的描繪,例如,操任何一種語言的人一般總是

** 原載《功能主義與漢語語法》,戴浩一、薛鳳生主編,北京語言學院出版社,1994年。

① 本文的基本思想形成於三年之前,當時北京語言學院的王還教授在俄亥俄州立大學的東亞語言文學系當客座教授。主要在她的鼓勵下我開始思考“把”字句。雖然我們有許多觀點不一致。但我從她富有啓發性的論點中獲益匪淺,我願在此表示感謝。我最初的想法後來用中文寫成“試論把字句的語義特性”一文,發表在《語言教學與研究》1987年第1期上。本文在該文基礎上作了較大的修改和補充,增加了“被”字句的討論和我對語言研究的一些觀點。對此我要感謝我的同事戴浩一,他看來很喜歡這樣的思路,在過去兩年内一直敦促我撰寫成文。

下意識地按照這種語言的音位系統來解釋各種自然聲，也一般總是下意識地按這種語言的詞彙系統來給各種事物分類。但是現實世界與用來描繪現實世界的語言系統之間完全重合或者一致的情形極少。因此，在語言描繪的任何一個層面上一般都有某些東西是語言系統無法完全描繪出來的。

1.2 語言研究的目標

如果上述觀點是正確的，那就意味着我們可以爲語言研究確立不同的目標。一方面，我們可以選擇在語言系統本身的範圍内進行研究，也就是去發現和説明某種自然語言特有的語言系統的内在邏輯和結構。我們因此就有可能建立一些高度抽象和高度形式化的規則來定義語言系統和解釋説話人對本族語的直覺，這實際上是同一件事情的兩面。另一方面，我們可以超越語言系統本身的範圍，試圖描寫語言系統與外部世界之間的交互作用，也就是研究語言系統如何在物質的、文化的、社會的條件下和各種情景中實際起作用。這就是語用學和功能主義的路子。確實，要想瞭解爲什麽在某個特定場合我們使用這個詞語而不是那個詞語，爲什麽某個詞語在一定條件下喪失它通常的字面意義而獲得某種特定的含義，我們衹能求助於語用學。我們可以，也許還應該使語用研究儘可能地形式化，但是十有八九我們的研究衹能得出一些傾向性的規律而不是嚴格的規則，因爲形式化也許衹適用於語言系統本身，不適用於語言系統與對應的外部實體之間的聯繫。

1.3 嚴格形式化和語用解釋

從以上觀點必然得出這樣一個推論：語言系統反映説話人對本族語的語言直覺；雖然嚴格的形式化是定義這個語言系統的理想方式或必要方式，但在解釋詞語在現實世界中的各種實際用法方面，其能力是極其有限的，這是由它的本性所決定的。爲了做到後一點，我們不得不求助語用學。另一方面，形式化即便有許多嚴格的、具體的限制，它仍然可能容許許多從未實際用過的詞語存在（或生成），也就是容許在某些人看來不合語法的詞語存在，因爲這樣的詞語這些人“不説（或從來没聽説過）”。我的觀點是這不應該被視爲形式化的一個缺陷，因爲我們有理由認爲，這種形式化所容許的“未曾聽説過的”詞語，其可接受的程度（或合乎語法的程度）肯定比形式化所排除的詞語來得高。

1.4 本文的研究範圍

本文的目標很有限,衹是想揭示"把"字句和"被"字句的語義特性,並不想詳細討論這兩種句式的句法結構或這兩種句式實際體現的句子使用當中的語用特點。但是,本文要强調的是:這兩種句式獨有的語義特性是對其句法結構作出説明的主要依據。不然的話,對句法結構的説明衹不過是某種有趣但是人爲的游戲,不管這種説明可能多麽嚴整或"能産"。

二、以往研究的結論

雖然這兩種句式都是當代從事漢語語言學研究的學者熱衷討論的問題,"把"字句比"被"字句更受人注意,也許是因爲"把"字句更爲特殊,類似句式在其他語言中極少發現,而"被"字句可以而且已經跟大多數歐洲語言裏的"被動語態"對等起來。這兩種句式的基本結構可分别用兩個公式抽象地表示如下:

A把B+C

A被B+C

這兩個公式中,A和B代表名詞性成分,C充當句子謂語[大多爲動詞短語(VP),但不盡然]。按照這兩個公式,以往對"把"字句研究得出的結論可歸納如下:

1) 有幾種不同的"把"字句,含義各不相同。

2) A通過某種動作處置B。

3) C裏的"動作動詞"是主要動詞。

4) A是那個"動詞"的主語和施事。

5) B是那個"動詞"的提前賓語和受事。

6) B是一個定指(或專指、通指)名詞。

同樣,對"被"字句的研究結論可歸納如下:

1) "被"字句也有不同種類,大多是被動句,但有的不一定是。

2) A被B以某種方式所處置。

3) C裏的"動作動詞"是主要動詞。

4) A是句子的主語而又是那個"動詞"的受事。

5) B是"被"字的賓語而又是那個"動詞"的施事。

這兩種描寫都已經是老生常談,爲大家所接受,但在我看來却都是錯誤的引導。下面我將試圖證明這兩種描寫都是基於膚淺的觀察,結論是生硬的。我先從"把"字句談起,但是這兩種句式又密切相關,而且以同樣的方式跟許多其他句式相關,所以我對"把"字句的論述大多也適用於"被"字句。

三、"把"字句的定性

要重新定性"把"字句,第一步必須承認它是一種有特殊結構意義的特殊句式。這就是説,必須把"把"字看作一個單一的語素,它是這種句式中存在於各成分間的一種特殊關係的標記。换句話説,列數"把"字句的"不同種類"在理論上是没有意義的,除非我們能定義這些不同種類的"把"字句的共通性①。衹有這樣,我們才能對各種可能的"把"字句作出統一的解釋,從而證明衹有一種獨特的"把"字句式的主張是合理的。所有"把"字句的共通性於是就成爲"把"這個獨特語素的定義。基於這一理解並按"A把B+C"的公式,我們可以着手給這一特殊句式定性。

3.1 "把"字句最突出的語義特性也許是這樣一種限制:上述公式中的C必須是對某種動作造成的B的狀態的描述性詞語。"描述性詞語"這個名稱不是簡單指形容詞或修飾語,而是指一個陳説,它充當句子的謂語,描寫在某一時刻B所處的狀態或情形,而不是描寫對B采取的行動或處置過程。這種描述性詞語可以各種不同的句法形式出現,但衹要它具有描述的性質,它就有資格充當"把"字句公式裏的C。否則,具體的"把"字句是否合乎語法就成問題。對"把"字句中C的這一限制會因此産生好幾個推論,不妨依次論述如下。

3.1.1 推論一

這一限制表示,就句法結構而言,C直接與B相關,衹是間接與A相關。

---

① 這種説法當然完全是出於我們對理論解釋的關心。從教學的角度看,特别是外語教學,將"把"字句分出幾種不同的類型並對每一種作出明確的説明,顯然是很有幫助的。

由於以往的研究没有看到"把"字句的這一方面,而是把A看作主語,把B看作C中"動詞"的"賓語提前",很自然遇到下面這種帶有所謂"保留賓語"的"把"字句就會迷惑不解[①]:

a) 他把黑板(上)寫滿了字。

b) 他把花瓶(裹)插了一把花。

c) 他把那個桔子剥了皮。

這樣的"把"字句很常見,從我們對"把"字句的新解釋來看,它們没有什麽不尋常的地方,因爲這些句子中的C顯然是描述B的狀態,而且B和C能一起構成意思基本相同的自然句子,例如:

a') 黑板(上)寫滿了字。

b') 花瓶(裹)插了一把花。

c') 那個桔子剥了皮。

3.1.2 推論二

由於"把"字句中的C描述的是某一特定動作造成的B的一個特定狀態,那就意味着C衹能明確肯定地描述那個狀態,而不能模糊地説B不處於某一特定狀態,因爲那就等於説某一特定動作的結果是B處於一種不確定的狀態——這是有悖於常理的。因此,"把"字句的一個句法限制是謂語C不能被直接否定。否定詞衹能出現於"把"字或它前面的任何一個助動詞之前,用來表示B還没有或不會變成某個特定狀態。例如:

a) *他想把錢不還給我。

b) 他不想把錢還給我。

但是,如果一個否定詞出現在有肯定含義的慣用語裹,這個慣用語自然能充當"把"字句裹的C。例如:

c) 這件事把他差點兒没氣死。

---

① 爲了儘可能避免在合不合乎語法問題上的争論,本文引用的例句大多抄自王還(1984)、李臨定(1980)和吕文華的未發表稿"被字句的語義分析"。跟大多數中國語言學家一樣,這些學者都十分謹慎,經常從現、當代作家如魯迅、老舍、巴金、王蒙的文學作品中尋找例句,雖然我個人並不認爲有必要這麽做(因爲我覺得他們對漢語的感覺和理解應該比那些作家還要好,至少是不相上下),我還是采納了好些這樣的例子,特别是那些聽上去不太"正常"的例子,如5.1節中的例句(a)(b)(c)。

3.1.3 推論三

漢語的一個衆所周知的事實是没有句法標記區分主動語態和被動語態。(參看 Chao 1968:702—706)。所以下面這個著名的例子可以有主動和被動兩種理解。

a) 鷄吃,魚不吃。

有被動意思的動作動詞〔或被動分詞,有如英語句"My heart is broken"(我的心碎了)中的"broken"(碎了)〕基本上是屬於情狀描寫性質的,而不是表示過程或動作。因此它們有資格在"把"字句中充當描述 B 的 C。有許多"把"字句的謂語 C 是由一個動作動詞加上"了"構成的,例如:

b) 我把汽車賣了。

c) 他把鷄殺了。

d) 别把錢丢了!

這些句子裏,動詞"賣"、"殺"、"丢"都有被動的意思,跟以下句子相比較就看得更清楚:

b') 汽車賣了。

c') 鷄殺了。

d') 錢丢了。

這個特殊的句法性質可以從另外三個不同的方面看出來。第一,動作動詞的施事不一定就是 A,例如:

e) 他把頭髮剪了。

這句話的主要意思是他的頭髮剪了,至於是他自己剪的(不大可能)還是别人剪的(可能性大),句子没有明確。第二,動作動詞前可以加一個數量副詞,例如:

f) 他們把花生全吃了。

將這個句子與"花生全吃了"相比較,可以看出副詞"全"表明動詞短語"全吃了"直接跟"花生"(B)相關而不是跟"他們"(A)相關。第三,動作動詞前可以任意加上"給"字,例如:

g) 我把他給忘了。

我們知道動詞前的"給"表示被動。

3.1.4 推論四

漢語普通話裏常見的一種句法格式是所謂的"動補"式,它由一個動作動詞加上一個表示結果或趨向的詞構成,如"打破"、"殺死"、"搶走"、"拿來"、"送去"等等。這些動補複合詞都充當及物動詞,大多數人幾乎憑直覺就認爲動作動詞是"主要動詞",並把後面表示結果或趨向的詞看作"補語"。但是,如果我們對"主要動詞"不是簡單地定義爲"表示動作的詞",而是從實質上定義爲"動詞短語的中心語",我們就不得不説那個"補語"實際上是動詞,而那個"動詞"實際上是動作狀語,因爲從内部結構看,所謂的動補式全都是向心結構,"補語"是它的中心語①。例如,當我們説"推開門"或"把門推開"時,中心意思是"開","推"衹是一個動作狀語,表示實現"開"的方式。(有許多其他方式,如"踢""叫""罵""哭"等。)所謂的動補式中的所謂"補語"大多是形容詞。在現代漢語,它們單獨出現時衹能充當修飾語或狀態動詞,不能充當及物動詞。但是,它們在古代漢語裏經常充當及物動詞,也就是所謂的"使動用法"。因此,當它們在現代漢語的動補式中充當所謂的"補語"時,把它們看作"使役動詞"並不是没有道理的。唯一的差别在於,它們充當使役動詞在古代漢語幾乎是完全自由的,而在現代漢語則受到很大限制,這個限制就是它們必須與一個動作狀語同現②。例如,我們衹能説"吃完飯""打破一隻杯子",不能説"*完飯"或"*破一隻杯子"。在我們正確定義所謂的動補式的真實性質後,以下"把"字句的性質也就清楚了。

a) 他把頭髮剃光了。

b) 你快把我想死咯!

c) 我剛把一朋友送走。

這些句子中,C(或動詞短語)的中心語顯然是"光"、"死"、"走",而前面的"剃"

---

① 事實上,這樣來看待"動補式"的人絶不止我一個。例如,我的同事戴浩一在未發表的一篇文章"論漢語動補結構中謂話的中心語"(1973 年美國語言學會年會上提交的論文)中就存有基本相似的觀點。

② 事實上,這個限制在現代漢語也不太嚴格,我們仍能發現許多一般叫做"形容詞"的詞用作及物動詞表示使動。例如除了"開"之外,我們可以説"紅臉兒"(使臉變紅),"乾杯""喜人""完了一件事"等。甚至某些所謂"趨向補語"也還能這麼用,例如,可以説"上菜""下酒""來一杯茶""出個主意"等。不過,這樣的用法數量有限,一般衹用在慣用語中。

“想”“送”是修飾語，表示形成這些狀態的方式。更重要的是這些短語都直接描述B的狀態，與A没有直接關係。此外，跟上一節討論的“把”字句中單一的動作動詞一樣，出現在“把”字句中的使役動詞（即“補語”）也表示被動，用來描述B的狀態。

3.1.5 推論五

這個推論實際上是上一節剛討論的那個推論的推論。既然我們已經證明所謂“動補式”裏的“動”其實不是動詞而是動作狀語，而“補”是真正的動詞，那就意味着在“動補式”作謂語的句子裏，動作狀語的施事不一定是句子的主語（A）（即不存在這樣的句法制約）。唯一相關的是那個動作狀語是否能合理地表達B的狀態得以實現的方式。誠然，在大多數這樣的句子裏，A實際上是動作狀語的施事，如以下句子極爲常見：

a）他説破了嘴。

b）他把嘴説破了。

但是，在以下例句中，動作狀語的施事顯然不是A而是B：

c）你可想死我咯！

d）你可把我想死咯！

e）那出戲把他唱累了。

f）那班學生把王老師教慘啦！

有時候，動作狀語的施事究竟是誰没有也不必明確説出，例如：

g）這一番話終於把他説服了。

h）一百塊錢就能把那個警察買通。

上述例子都是正常的句子，因爲所謂的“補語”實際上是謂語C的中心語，它依照我們已經指出的句法限制描述B的狀態。在句法上，動作狀語的施事是誰無關緊要。

3.1.6 推論六

當“把”字句裏的C是一個較長的描述性短語時，它通常由一個動作詞加上“得”（或“的”）字起頭，例如：

a）他把我氣得糊裏糊塗的。

b）老李把老張罵得抬不起頭來。

這樣的例子進一步證明我們對"把"字句中C的性質的說明是準確的。一個廣爲人知的事實是,"得"字可以將它前面的那個詞語變成修飾語,不管那個詞語原來是什麽。顯而易見,"得"字前的那個"動詞"不可能真是動詞,即不可能是謂語的中心語。謂語的中心語衹能是"得"字後面的描述性詞語。跟所謂"動補式"裏的"動詞"一樣,"得"字前的那個"動詞",其施事不一定是A;它也可以是B或某個未知實體。例如:

c) 辣椒把我吃得舌頭都麻了。

d) 那些衣服把她洗得直不起腰來。

e) 哀怨的笛聲把我們吹得心酸淚落。

3.1.7 當我們説"把"字句裏的C必須是一個狀態描述性詞語時,當然衹是指的標準"把"字句。然而,語言使用是一種社會現象,有些人説話有時不認真按標準説。例如在一種民間文藝形式"鼓詞"中,我們能發現如下句子:

a) 我兒在家把書攻。

同樣,魯迅小説《阿Q正傳》中的主人公也喜歡哼哼:

b) 我手舉鋼鞭將你打。

這樣的句子在生來操普通話的人聽起來總有點兒"不對勁"。其原因我認爲是這些句子中的C,即(a)句的"攻"和(b)句的"打",是表示動作而不是狀態,因而違背我們所述的C的限制。如果後頭再加上一個描述性詞語,它們就聽上去完全正常了[①]:

a') 我兒在家把書攻得滚瓜爛熟。

b') 我手舉鋼鞭將你打翻在地。

另一方面,當我們説C是對某個動作造成的B的狀態的描述性詞語時,有人可能過於機械地理解這句話並提出異議。他們可能舉出如下的句子,

---

① 有許多研究"把"字句的論文,由於對謂語C有不正確的解釋而得出不正確的結論。例如,曾有人提出"把"字句最早見於唐代,因爲杜甫詩中有一句"醉把茱萸仔細看"(Cheung 1976)。"把"字句是否出現這麽早是另一個問題,這個詩句顯然不足爲據(如果我們的解釋是正確的話),因爲它的C"仔細看"表示A(未出現)的動作,而不是描述B(茱萸)的狀態。如果不是"仔細看"而是"看仔細",那就好得多。李英哲曾試圖一舉解決"把"字句的定性(Li 1974),他的結論是"把"字句表示"對一個特定事物的特定動作""動詞表明賓語有一定程度的定指性"。這個定義不能涵蓋所有的"把"字句,顯然,他也誤把"動作動詞"當作C的中心語。

c) 她把你看了一眼。

並指出“你”的狀態並没有受什麽影響。這當然不錯,但衹是就“你”的實際狀態而言。如果考慮到説話人在説話時想象中投射的心理狀態,他們的説法就不對了。就語言學的解釋而言,歸根結蒂是以説話人想些什麽爲準。例如,如果説話人想象一個男人由於被某個女人看了一眼而狀態受到影響,他就可以對那個男人説“她把你看了一眼”,意思是“她在注意你”或“你受到她的注意”。因此,“把”字句要合乎語法,B的狀態不一定要受看得見的影響,主要以説話人的設想爲準,有時B還可以是一個未知因素。

3.2 以上對“把”字句裏C的定性實際上也同時澄清了B的性質,也就是説B既是話題又是謂語C的主語。這裏我們重申和强調這樣的觀點:“把”字句的特性之一是,句法上B是謂語C的主語,語義上B是全句的主要話題。這一觀點與以往大多數研究的觀點相背,那些研究認爲B是定指(或專指、通指)名詞,充當C裏“動詞”的“提前賓語”。從我們的這一新觀點也可得出幾個推論如下。

3.2.1 推論一

作爲句子的主要話題,B任何時候不能省略。例如,以下句子不合語法且没有意義:

a) *他們把看得太簡單了。

必須説成像(b)這樣才行:

b) 他們把他看得太簡單了。

3.2.2 推論二

B是一個後置話題和謂語C的真正主語,從以下例句可以看出,B確定無疑不是“賓語提前”。過去大多數人却都這麽認爲,有人甚至以此爲“據”來論證漢語已從“主動賓”(SVO)型語言演變爲“主賓動”(SOV)型語言①。

---

① 有人提出漢語已從SVO演變爲SOV型語言的觀點(如Li&Thompson1974,Tai 1973&1976),還有人甚至把它解釋爲受阿爾泰系語言影響的結果(如Hashimoto 1975)。他們自然都以“把”字句裏所謂的“賓語提前”爲證據。黎天睦曾撰文提出異議(Light 1979)。我並不想介入這場論爭,但想指出我對B的定義取消了它作爲“提前賓語”的資格。那些主張SOV説的人應從其他地方尋找證據。

a) 把我笑得肚子都疼了。

b) 一瓶茅臺把他喝得爛醉如泥。

3.2.3 推論三

雖然我們跟有些學者(如 Tsao 1987)一樣把 B 看作話題(而且是主要話題),我們並不認爲 B 必須是定指的(或專指、通指)。定指性和話題性是名詞性詞語的兩個互不相關的語義特徵,屬於不同的範疇。它們互不爲對方的必要成分,儘管在語用平面上它們經常重合。因此,"把"字句裏的主要話題 B 不一定非得是定指名詞,雖然大多數是定指的。B 是定指名詞的"把"字句極爲常見,無需舉例,這裏衹舉兩個 B 不是定指,也不是"專指""通指"名詞的例子:

a) 一顆流彈把一個路人打傷了。

b) 什麼槍都能把人打死。

"把"字句裏的 B 不一定非得是定指的,這一事實可以從以下成對句子的比較中看得更清楚。非"把"字句裏的無定指名詞在對應的"把"字句裏充當 B 時仍然是無定指的。唯一的區別是,在"把"字句裏,那個名詞變成説話人意欲强調的話題。

c) 他買重了一本書。

c') 他把一本書買重了。

d) 他遞給我一雙筷子。

d') 他把一雙筷子遞給我。

但是在有些場合,非"把"字句變換成"把"字句時,無定指賓語不知怎麼變成了定指的。例如:

e) 他攢起錢來了。

e') 他把錢攢起來了。

f) 我想給她介紹一個朋友。

f') 我想把一個朋友介紹給她。

坦率地説,我還不明白這種變化是什麼原因,但我猜想這可能是因爲詞彙的意義有時隨不同的語境而有所搖擺①。

3.3 由於A出現在“把”字句的開頭，按趙元任的定義，A也是話題。但是B是“把”字句的語義重點；A跟B不一樣，衹能叫做句子的次要話題。這樣説明A的性質也會得出兩個推論。

3.3.1 推論一

A與謂語C的關係，在語義和句法上都是間接的。如以下例句所示：

a) 這班學生把王老師教得心灰意冷。

b) 這段路把小李跑得上氣不接下氣。

3.3.2 推論二

不帶A的“把”字句仍然是一個完好的“把”字句，意思基本不變，但“把”字句却不能没有B。事實上，有時很難確定開頭省略的A到底是什麼，如果它確實存在的話。

a) 看，把他累得……

b) 真要把我急死了！

c) 我編的。我還不怕，就把你怕成那樣？(《李有才板話》)

A在“把”字句中所承擔的角色也許可以定義如下：“通過‘把’字的聯繫，表示B之所以成爲C所描寫的狀態，是與它有關係的。”當然，“有關係”的程度可能不一樣，但是就“把”字句是否合乎語法而言，A爲了有資格擔當這樣的角色，它“有關係”的程度可以但不一定很深很直接。當A直接造成B的狀態時，A有關係當然最爲明顯，例如：

d) 猫把老鼠咬死了。

但有時A與B的狀態變化衹有疏遠的關係，或衹是充當工具，例如：

e) 你快把我想死咯！

f) 洗冷水澡把他洗病了。

還有，A有時衹是使B發生變化的一個不經心的因素，但衹要説話人覺得它多

① 除了個别的詞彙可能隨語境而改變詞義外，我還想指出，這兩對句子(都引自王還)中(f)和(f')這一對作爲例子可能不合適，因爲“給”字的相對位置有變化。在我看來，(f')對應的是“我想介紹一個朋友給她”而不是(f)。“給她”的相對位置變化造成句子意思上的細微差别，這一點常常爲人所忽視，可參看薛1983的有關討論。

少負有一點責任,就可以讓它充當那個角色。例如:

g) 他衹顧搞販運,結果把個老婆也跑丢了。

h) 他失業才不久,又把房子失火燒了。

i) 三年困難時期,他把一個獨生兒子餓死了。

注意,以上三個句子裏的所謂"動詞"(跑,燒,餓)很難説是以A(他)作爲施事。很明顯,A没有主動也無意造成B的狀態。然而,説這些句子的人似乎在暗示,每一句裏的A至少要對發生的事情部分負責,因爲可以想象A本來可以阻止這樣的事情發生。

3.4 以上對"把"字句的定性可歸納如下:

句法結構:A把B+C

語義詮釋:由於A的關係,B變成C所描述的狀態。

這一定性既具體又精確,足以説明這種獨特句式的結構意義;另一方面,它又很寬泛,足以涵蓋所有的"把"字句。要作出任何有意義的句法説明,這個定性是基礎。很難在其他語言中找到語義詮釋相似的句式,但在我看來,英語中"A+have+B+過去分詞"的句式(如"John has his car repaired",(約翰[讓人]把汽車給修好了)與"把"字句很相近。差别在於,這個英語句式含有A讓别人對B做某事的意思,而"把"字句大多表示A自己做的意思。但這一差别也不是絶對的。例如,當有人説"I promise I'll have the job done tomorrow"(我答應明天一定把那活兒幹了)時,我們一般不會理解爲他要找别人幹那活兒,而是理解爲他自己動手幹。同樣,英語句子"John has his car repaired"可以極爲自然地翻譯成漢語"約翰把車修好了",後者可以但一般不表示約翰自己修理的意思。因此,我們不妨説,這兩種句式雖然在語義上很相近,在語用平面上則相去甚遠。另一個語用上的差别是,"把"字句在漢語裏用得非常多,能産性高,而那個英語句式在英語裏遠非如此。

四、"被"字句的定性

普通話裏的"被"字句長期以來一直被認同於"被動語態"。由"被動"這個詞所體現的這一錯誤觀念還進入了常用詞彙,例如,現在經常聽説"這件事使我們很被動”這樣的話。因此,要想對“被”字句的性質作出任何有意義的説明,必須首先消除這種錯誤的認同。這可以從兩方面來論證。首先,我們可以證明不是所有的“被”字句都有被動的意思;其次,不是所有表示被動意思的句子都用“被”字。這就是説,這種特殊的句法結構必定有自己特殊的語義詮釋。

4.1 我們已用大量證據證明,漢語的動詞,無需形態變化,既能表示主動也能表示被動(見以上 3.1.3 節。有人稱漢語爲“作格”語言,但既然漢語動詞缺乏形態標記,我不敢説這是個合適的名稱)。以下的一些例子表明,有時候表示被動意思的句子根本不能用“被”字(也不能用“叫”“讓”“給”):

a) 電話已經打了。

a') *電話已經被打了。

b) 那節課衹上了三十分鐘。

b') *那節課衹被(我們)上了三十分鐘。

c) 他升級了没有?

c') *他被升級了没有?

另一方面,有的“被”字句没有被動意思,例如:

d) 老張被他太太哭得没了主意。

e) 我讓他那麽一説,倒不知道該怎麽辦了。

f) 她被那首歌唱得流眼淚。

上面這樣的例子清楚地表明,“被”字句和被動語態雖然大部分重合,但分別是兩個不同的概念,决不應該把它們等同起來。因此,有必要找出“被”字句的更爲確切的結構意義。

4.2 “把”字句和“被”字句之間有不同尋常的相似之處,這一點已爲許多學者所注意。爲瞭解釋這種相似,也偶有一些對這兩種句式某些方面的説明,但是至今還缺乏專門的、全面的合理解釋。本文試圖提供這樣的解釋,我們的基本觀點是,就基本成分而言,這兩種句式除標記字(見以上第 2 節)外完全一致,但在成分與成分的相互關係方面,兩者有重大差别。這就是説,“把”字句裏描述性謂語 C 是以 B 爲主語,並且衹是通過 B 與 A 發生間接聯繫;“被”字句裏的關係正好相反,C 雖然也是描述性謂語,但以 A 爲主語,並且衹通過 A 與 B 發生聯繫。因此,我們對“把”字句裏 C 施加的句法和語義上的限制也完全適用於"被"字句裏的C,而我們對"把"字句裏B的定性則適用於"被"字句裏的A,對"把"字句裏A的定性則適用於"被"字句裏的B。

4.3 既然"被"字句裏的C與"把"字句裏的C性質相同,我們對"把"字句裏C的定性以及由此得出的六條推論(見以上3.1.1至3.1.6節)也同樣適用於"被"字句裏的C。其實,衹需交换一下先前引用的"把"字句裏A和B的位置,我們等於有了足够的例子來證明我們對"被"字句的觀點。但爲了强調起見,我們又增加了以下例子。

推論一(C可以帶一個"保留賓語")

a) 阿Q……被人揪住了黄辮子。

推論二(否定詞位於"被"字前)

b) *我被他没罵過。

b') 我没被他罵過。

推論三(單一的"動詞"有被動義)

這一點十分明顯,無須舉例。

推論四("補語"是有被動義的使役動詞)

c) 他們的房子被人霸占了。

推論五(B不一定就是"動詞"的施事)

d) 他們被爛米吃病了。

推論六(A不一定是較長的C裏帶"得"字標記的"動詞"的受事)

e) 老張被大蒜吃得滿嘴臭氣。

4.4 既然"被"字句裏A的角色相當於"把"字句裏B的角色,我們對後者的定性以及由此得出的三個推論也同樣適用於前者,如以下例於所示:

推論一(A不能省略)①

a) *??? 被塗上了紅色。

a') (雕像)嘴唇被塗上了紅色。

① 我們説A不能省略,這是指與可以輕易省略並經常省略的B相比,A在"被"字句中不可或缺,就像"把"字句中B不可或缺一樣,但是漢語句法的一個普遍現象是:句子的話題,通常位於句首,常被省略,衹要語境已將其指明的話。因此,"被"字句的A也能省略,不過這是另一種類型的省略。

推論二(A不一定就是C裏"動作動詞"的受事)

b) 他被武俠小説看得着了迷。

推論三(A不一定是定指的)

c) "文革"期間什麽人都被整過。

4.5 跟"把"字句裏的A一樣,"被"字句裏的B是次要話題,它不一定像許多人認爲的那樣就是C裏"動作動詞"的施事。因此對"把"字句裏A的定性以及由此得出的兩個推論也同樣適用於"被"字句裏的B,如以下例子所示:

推論一(B祇與C發生間接聯繫)

a) 他被那本小説看得出了神。

推論二(作爲次要話題,B可以省略)

b) 因爲以權謀私,他被開除了黨籍。

4.6 根據以上例句,我們可將"被"字句的定性歸納如下:

句法結構:A被B+C

語義詮釋:由於B的關係,A變成C所描述的狀態。

這一定性足以涵蓋所有合乎語法的"被"字句,它還能明確解釋爲什麽大家都覺得"把"字句和"被"字句在形式和意義上都十分相像。確實,如果這一解釋是正確的,這兩個句式可以看作互爲鏡像,差别衹在A和B之間强調重點的變换。

五、"把"字句和"被"字句的相互聯繫

語言的各種結構式總是協同起作用,構成一個完整的系統;在這個系統裏不同的組成部分互相聯繫,互相作用。"把"字句和"被"字句當然也是如此。這兩種句式之間的相互聯繫可以敘述如下。

5.1 我們對這兩種句式的定性意味着它們很容易互相變换。從理論上講這是絶對正確的,雖然存在一些語用上的限制。大多數"簡單"句(即不帶"把"和"被"的句子)都很容易變换成"把"字句或"被"字句,反過來也一樣。有些"簡單"句不能這麽變换。然而"把"字句和"被"字句之間總是可以較爲容易和自然地互相變换。這兩個方面可從以下例子中看出。

a) 我緊張的心情頓時被他的笑容一掃而光。

a') 他的笑容頓時把我緊張的心情一掃而光。

a'') *他的笑容頓時一掃而光我緊張的心情。

b) 那塊布被他做了一條褲子。

b') 他把那塊布做了一條褲子。

(比較英語“I made him a coward”(我把他變成一個懦夫))

b'') *他做了那塊布一條褲子。

c) 她的花布衫被雨水緊緊地裹在身上。

c') 雨水把她的花布衫緊緊地裹在身上。

c'') *雨水緊緊地裹她的花布衫在身上。

5.2 這兩種句式可以很自然地出現在同一句子裏。這時候,在形式和意義上都是“被”優先於“把”,雖然可能有一些邊緣的(含胡的)例外。以下例子可説明這層關係。

a) 她把嘴脣咬破了。

a') 1. 我被她把嘴脣咬破了。

2. 她被我把嘴脣咬破了。

a'') 1. *我把嘴脣被她咬破了。

2. ? 我把嘴脣讓(叫)她給咬破了。

b) 賊把錢偷光了。

b') 1. 我被賊把錢偷光了。

2. 賊被我把錢偷光了。

b'') 1. *我把錢被賊偷光了。

2. ? 他把幾塊錢都讓(叫)賊給偷光了。

還可舉出更多的例子,但看來没有必要。這些例子已足以説明以下幾點。第一,“把”字短語位於“被”字短語前的句子顯然不可接受,但如果把“被”換成較爲口語化的“讓”或“叫”,可接受的程度就會增加。第二,在“把”字句裏,當B所指的事物歸屬於誰没有具體説明時,一般認爲它歸屬於A,同樣,我們一般認爲C裏“動作動詞”的施事是A。但是這兩點也許衹是語用平面上的假設而已。往深裏講,事實不一定如此,因爲這些成分在句法上並没有什麽標記。第三,我們説同時帶"把"和"被"的句子裏"被"字優先於"把",意思是説"被"必須位於"把"字前,而且謂語C描述的是"被"字前而不是"把"字前那個名詞性詞語的狀態,但是也可以認爲這樣的句子基本上是"把"字句,"被"字短語是後插入的。插入的目的也許是爲了説明"把"字後名詞的歸屬,以及C裏"動作動詞"的施事。已有人指出,如果去掉"把"字和後面的名詞,句子的結構和意義都不受影響(王還 1984:56)。以上例子似乎表明事實不完全如此,有一個限制條件是"把"字後面的名詞性詞語必須是一個與"被"字前的名詞性詞語同指的代詞,如下例所示。

c)(他)叫人家廣聚把他攆走了。

5.3 "被"字句和"把"字句最根本的區别在於説話人想把聽話人的注意吸引到A和B身上。這一點可以用以下成對的例句來説明:

a) 茅臺把我吃醉了。

a') 我被茅臺吃醉了。

b) 丢東西把他丢怕了。

b') 他被丢東西丢怕了。

c) 他把花盆絆倒了。

c') 他被花盆絆倒了。

六、結論

本文的唯一目的是正確定義"把"字句和"被"字句的結構意義。我們認爲,如不真正掌握它們結構意義的本質就忙於作出具體的句法説明,那是在浪費時間,並且衹會把這樣的努力變成一種迷人但是空洞的學術練習。我們希望本文的討論已有助於揭示這種本質。然而,在試圖給基本要素定性時,有許多低層次上涉及的問題以及實際應用的問題經常會無可避免地被棄而不顧。自然,我們對這兩種句式的定性也没有觸及許多其他的重要的特性。其中有一些可在這裏簡要評説,詳細的討論不屬本文的範圍。

1) 已有人指出,典型的"被"字句總是表示不如意、不愉快的事情(從A的角度而言)。這多半是古漢語裏作動詞的"被"(表示"覆蓋""遭受"等意思)本義的反映。但是,隨着將"被"字句與被動語態等同起來的傾向不斷發展,這一使用限制已在逐漸消失。類似的限制似乎也適用"把"字句,但適用的程度要低得多。

2) "把"字句一直是,而且還將繼續是極爲常用的句式,而"被"字句的使用率過去一般很低,現在倒有明顯的增長,特別是書面語,也許也是誤將其與被動語態等同起來的結果。

3) "被"字常用於較正式的口語和書面語,它的兩個變體"讓"和"叫"則多用於口頭的日常交談。還有一個"給"字現在也這麽用,但地道的北京人不怎麽用。"把"也有一個變體"將",似乎是個方言詞,一般給句子增添一些正式的味道。

4) "被"字可以略去後頭的名詞,直接出現在 C 裏的"動作動詞"前,但它的變體"讓"和"叫"不可以,至少要加上個假位名詞"人"或"人家",即使説話人並不想具體指誰。地道的北京人説話,"給"字衹能直接用在"動作動詞"前。

5) 雖然在使用率上"把"字句比"被"字句更常用,但"把"字句似乎要受一些"被"字句不受的限制。例如,有些類型的動詞如"看見""得到"等據説不能用"把"字句(參看王還 1984:16),如不能説"我把飛機看見了",而"被"字句被認爲是可以用的,如可以説"飛機被我看見了"。另外,像"到""贊成"這類動詞兩種句式都不能用。

6) 已有人指出,"把"字句可以有命令句形式,如可説"把車開過來!",而"被"字句没有命令句形成(參看王還 1984:55)。顯然,從簡單的道理上講,用"被"字句發出命令很别扭。但是還應該指出,否定的"被"字句可以是命令句,表示禁止的意思,例如"别讓人騙了!"。

關於這兩種句式,顯然還有許許多多其他問題有待解釋,但我覺得這些問題可能大多屬於語用平面,或者是與語義有關的較低層次上的句法問題,例如根據是否適用於這兩種句式而對"動詞"的再分類問題。總之,我們根本不可能在這樣一篇不算長的文章内一一討論這些問題。本項研究與以往大多數研究的一個重要差别有必要再重申一下。以往的研究毫無例外都把注意力完全集中在謂語(C)的所謂"動詞"上,而本文則一貫將這個謂語看作一個單一的、自足的單位,其中的"動詞"起動作狀語的作用。這就使我們得以説明 A、B、C

三個基本成分之間的邏輯關係。從這樣一個目標出發，也爲了避免可能出現但不必要的複雜化，我們決定使用這些完全中性的符號，而不使用比較常用但有過多内涵的NP(名詞短語)和VP(動詞短語)。我們還力圖把主語、謂語、話題、評述、介詞、副動詞這類語法術語的使用減低到最小限度，但是不太成功。這些術語有豐富的約定俗成的含義，就我們的研究方法和目的而言，它們即便不是毫不相干也不是絶對必需的；對有些人而言它們甚至可能證明是在制造混亂。

參考文獻

中文部分

陳初生　1983　《早期處置式略論》,《中國語文》1983年第3期,第201—206頁。

葛　毅　1958《把字句(處置式)的起源》,《中國語文》69(1956),第117—118頁。

龔千炎　1980　《現代漢語裏的受事主語句》,《中國語文》1980年第5期。

———　1986,《論'把'字兼語句》,宣讀於第十九届國際漢藏語言和語言學年會,1986年9月,美國哥倫布市。

薛鳳生　1987　《試論'把'字句的語義特性》,《語言教學與研究》1987年第1期,第4—22頁。

胡附,文煉　1956《現代漢語語法探索》,上海新知識出版社,1956年。

李臨定　1980　《被字句》,《中國語文》1980年第6期,第401—402頁。

劉世儒　1956　《被動式的起源》,《語文學習》59(1956),第32—33頁。

陸儉明,馬真　1985　《現代漢語虚詞散論》,北京大學出版社,1985年。

吕文華　1987　《"被"字句的語義分析》,北京語言學院油印本,1987年。

吕叔湘　1955　《把字句用法的研究》,《漢語句法論文集》,科學出版社,1958年,第125—144頁。

———　1986　《漢語句法的靈活性》,《中國語文》1986年第1期,第1—9頁。

梅　廣　1978　《'把'字句》,《文史哲學報》(臺灣大學)1978年,第145—180頁。

潘允中　1981　《漢語動補結構的發展》,《中國語文》1980 年第 3 期,第 53—60 頁。

宋玉柱　1981　《關於把字句的兩個問題》,《語文研究》1981 年第 2 期。

湯廷池　1979　《國語變形語法研究》,臺北,1979 年修訂本。

王　還　1984　《"把"字句與"被"字句》,上海教育出版社,1984 年。

王　力　1954　《中國現代語法》,中華書局,1954 年。

詹開第　1983　"'把'字句謂語中動作的方向",《中國語文》1983 年第 2 期,第 93—96 頁。

張志公　1956　《漢語語法常識》,新知識出版社,1956 年。

朱德熙　1982　《語法講義》,商務印書館,1982 年。

英文部分

Bennett, Paul A. 1981. 'The Evolution of Passive and Disposal Sentences', *Journal of Chinese Linguistics*(JCL)9. 1:61 - 69.

Chao Yuen Ren. 1968. *A Grammar of Spoken Chinese*, Berkeley, U. C. Press.

Chen, G. T. 1983. 'The Ba Construction: A Topic and Comment Approach'. Journal of *the Chinese Language Teachers Association* (JCLTA) 18. 1: 17 - 29.

Chen, Chung-yu. 1979. 'On Predicative Complements', *JCL* 7. 1:44 - 46.

Cheung, Hung nin Samuel. 1973. 'A Comparative Study in Chinese Grammars: The Ba-construction.' *JCL* 1. 3:343 - 382.

Cheung, Yat-shing. 1976. 'Word Order Change in Chinese: Some Contribuying factors and implications,' U, *Microfilms International*, *Ann Arbor*. Mich. 186 - 16.

Chu, Chauncey C. 1976. "Conceptual Wholeness and the 'Retained' Object," *JCL* 4.1:14 - 23.

Hashimoto, Anne Oikan Yue. 1975. 'Southern Chinese Dialects—the Tai Connection', paper read at the Eighth International Conference on sino-Tibetan Linguistics.

Hashimoto, Mantaro j. (1976). 'Language Diffusion on the Asian Continent: Problems of Typological Diversity in Sino-*Tibetan*', *Computational Analysis of Asian and Africa Languages* (CAAAL) 3:19－65.

Hsueh, F. S. 1982. 'The Role of Semantics in Teaching Syntax: Some Examples from Mandarin Chinese', *JCLTA 17*. 1:1－13.

——. 1983. 'A Note on the Grammatical Functions of Gei,' *JCLTA* 18. 3: 81－85.

Huang, C. T. James. 1984. 'Phrase Structure, Lexical Integrity, and Chinese Compound,' *JCLTA*. 19.2: 53－78.

Huang, Shuang-fan. 1978. 'Historical Change of Prepositions and Emergence of SOV Order,' *JCL* 6.2:212－242.

——. 1986. 'The History of the Disposal Construction Revisited—Evidence from Zen Dialogues in the Tang Dynasty', *JCL* 14.1:43－52.

Ngampit Jagacinski. 1986. *Lue of Xishuanglanna: A Study of the Reversed OV Order in the Tai? -au-Construction*, ph. D. dissertation, The Ohio State University.

Li, Charles N., and Thompson, Sandra A. 1974. 'An Explanation of Word Order Change SVO-SOV', *Foundation of Languages* 12:201－214.

——. 1974. A Linguistic Discussion of the 'Co-Verb' in Chinese Grammar. *JCLTA* 9.3:109－119.

——. 1981. *Mandarin Chinese: A Functional Reference Grammar*, UC Press.

Li, Y. C. 1974. 'What Does "Disposal" Mean? Features of the Verb and Noun in Chinese'. *JCL* 2.2:200－218.

Light, Timothy. 1979. 'Word Order and Word Order Change in Mandarin Chinese', JCL 7.2. 149－180.

Lin, Shuang -fu, 1974. 'Locatial Construction and ba-construction in Mandarin', JCLTA 9. 2:66－83.

Lu, John H-T. 1977. 'Resultative Verb Compounds Vs. Directional Verb Compounds in Mandarin', *JCL* 5. 2:276－313.

So, Chung: 'The ba-construction and Verb Final Drift in Chinese', *CAAAL*. 3.

Mangione, Louis Stephen. 1982. *The Syntax, Semantics and Pragmatics of Causative, Passive, and Ba Construction in Mandarin*, Ph. D. dissertation, Cornell U.

Tai, James H-Y. 1973. 'Chinese SOV Language', *Papers from the Ninth Regional Meeting of the Chicago Linguistic Society*.

——. 1976. 'On the Change from SVO to SOV in Chinese', *Papers from the Parasession on Diachronic Syntax*, Chicago Linguistic Society: 291-304.

——. 1984. 'Word Order in Chinese and the X Theory', *JCLTA* 19. 2: 23-35.

Teng, Shou-hsin. 1975. 'Subject and Theme in Chinese: a Critique of the SOV Hypothesis'. Paper read at the Eighth Sino-Tibetan Conference.

——. 1977. 'A Grammar of Verb-Particles in Chinese', *JCL* 5. I : I-25.

Thompson, Sandra. 1973. 'Transitivity and Some Problems with the Ba Construction in Mandarin Chinese'. *JCL* 1.2:208 221.

——1973. 'Resultative Verb Compounds In Mandarin Chinese: a Case for Lexical Rules', *Language* 49.2: 361-379.

Tsao, Feng-fu. 1987. 'A Topic-Comment Approach to the Ba Construction', *JCL* 15.1:1-53.

Verb Complement in Classical Chinese and Its Implications as Revealed by the Particle 以 **

1. INTRODUCTION

It has long been noticed that "word order" plays a crucial role in Chinese syntax, both modern and classical. Its syntactic implication is that, in an endocentric construction, the modifier always precedes the modified, while on the sentence level, the subject precedes the predicate and the verb or co-verb precedes the object①. When we consistently and vigorously apply this fundamental principle in our analysis of the ancient texts, we often have a better chance of getting the correct, or at least a more appropriate, interpretation for a certain text in question, and acquiring subsequently a better understanding of the nature of Classical Chinese syntax in general. There are, however, some cases in Classical Chinese where the above principle seems to have been violated, particularly in connection with the particle 以 *yi*. In this paper, I choose to argue that this seeming violation is a phenomenon on a lower level by reevaluating the concept of "verb complement" in its syntax. I shall further argue that, once we accept this type of construction as a verb complement in Classical Chinese syntax, we shall be able to not only provide a reasonable explanation for the seeming

---

** 中文題爲《古代漢語的動補結構和"以"字短語的句法功能》,原載《中國語言學報》(JCL)單刊第 10 卷"漢語句法理論研究",1997 年。

① There has been some talk that word order in Chinese sentences has changed from SVO to SOV (see, for example, Tai 1973, Li and Thompson 1974). I doubt very much that this is true even for Modern Chinese. For Classical Chinese, I think everybody agrees that the order is definitely SVO.

violation of the word order principle, but also rectify two misconceptions held by most scholars of Classical Chinese grammar: first, regarding the co-verb 以, the particle of instrumentality, as a conjunction on the same level as 而 *er* and 則 *ze* and, second, calling such syntactic patterns as 可 *ke*-V, 足 *zu*-V, 難 *nan*-V and 易 *yi*-V passive constructions.

2. SOME CRUCIAL FEATURES OF CLASSICAL CHINESE

For the study of Classical Chinese syntax, different people may have different goals. My primary goal is to find correct interpretations for the ancient texts by proposing some general syntactic principles. This approach may have theoretical implications, but they are only the by-products, so to speak. In other words, I believe we must have accurate understanding of the data before we rush to theorize about them. Western linguistic theories, ancient or modern, started mostly and understandably from the study of European languages. And it is only natural that many modern linguists, Chinese or non-Chinese, have tried to apply one or another of such theories in their analysis of the Classical Chinese texts. There is, of course, nothing wrong with that. It is actually very beneficial. But there must be one precondition, namely, proper understanding of the Chinese data. It happens that, when compared with most Indo-European languages, Classical Chinese shows some rather "special" features which are rarely seen and hence are overlooked in the former①. If

① This idea was actually raised by some scholars in China when they said the study of the Chinese language "must start from the special characteristics of the language" (從漢語的特性出發). However, as far as I am aware, no one has ever said what these characteristics are. In my earlier article on passivity (Hsueh 1994), I tentatively listed and discussed some features which I thought might be called special for CC syntax. Among the five discussed in this current paper, three are from the former list and two are new. Note that the word "special" here does not mean "unique." Quite possibly, some other non-Indo-European languages have some of these features, too.

these features are not taken into consideration, misunderstanding of the data will inevitably occur and, consequently, we will have difficulty discerning the true nature of the grammatical particles and the syntactic structures. In the following, some of the special features relevant to our present study will be briefly discussed. Note that I am not trying to propose any new theory, but am merely pointing out some crucial facts about the language upon which some theory can be firmly grounded.

2.1 Style Is Conversational

When early European scholars first encountered the Chinese language, they reached the ridiculous conclusion that Chinese has no grammar. If that is somewhat understandable, the more recent claim by some that Classical Chinese was not even a language (or was merely an "artificial language" at best) but "a system of code symbols"[①] would seem to be inexcusable. One may simply ask: How could, or why should, Confucius choose an artificial code system as the vehicle for his teaching, instead of his own spoken language? Even if this were possible, Confucius probably would have been unwilling to waste time training his disciples to use that artificial system! Contrary to the above speculation, I would argue that Classical Chinese not only started as a natural spoken language but has also remained very conversational (or colloquial) in style ever since. All the so-called Confucian Classics before Confucius, as well as 論語(*Analects*),孟子(*Mencius*),左傳(*Tso-Chuan*)[②], etc., were in dialogues or in a story-telling mode. Even argumentative or philosophical works of later times, such as 莊子(*Chuang-Tzu*),荀子(*Hsün-Tzu*),韓非子(*Han-Fei-Tzu*), etc., were cast in the same

① A typical example is the article "On Representing Abstractions in Archaic Chinese" by Rosemont (1974:71 - 88), which Cikoski has severely criticized(1978a:18).

② For the romanization of Chinese characters in this paper, we use the Pinyin system. However, since the titles of most Chinese classics have been widely known by their Wade-Giles romanization, they will be referred to by such forms.

conversational mode. With all the great model works of this type, being conversational in style became an inseparable and essential characteristic of Classical Chinese. The result is that, though highly polished and elegant ("literary") lexically, Classical Chinese remains rather loose syntactically, as colloquial speech in all languages usually is, and it does not allow elaborately long sentences, as all experienced writers of Classical Chinese can tell us. This characteristic of the language has many implications. The other features discussed below are all related to, or implied by, this feature.

2.2 Subject and Predicate Can Be Viewed as Topic and Comment

This is Y. R. Chao's great discovery for Modern Spoken Chinese (Chao 1968:69—78), and I believe it applies to Classical Chinese equally well. Note that Chao did not propose a new syntactic theory, but only defined somewhat more broadly the two syntactic concepts of "subject" and "predicate" within the framework of sentence grammar. This discovery explains most convincingly the logic behind various types of Chinese sentences, some of which often seem to be illogical or ungrammatical when we look at them from the viewpoint of Latin grammar. Accurate analysis of many Classical Chinese sentences can be made only when we keep Chao's proposal in mind. For quite some time, I have been puzzled by the question of why "subject" and "predicate" in Chinese must be defined this way. Now, I feel the answer is probably that both Modern Spoken Chinese and Classical Chinese are spoken or conversational in style①.

2.3 Subject Is Not Always Required

Subjectless sentences are abundant in Classical Chinese (cf. 何 He 1982). Sometimes the missing subject may be said to have been deleted or omitted, since it can be restored easily by the context, but there are times when the

① This seems to be true for colloquial speech even in the English language. Mark Haney, a graduate student and native English speaker in my class, told me that, when referring to the turn of duty, people often say "I'm Monday; you're Tuesday; he's Wednesday."

reference is so general and broad that it cannot be easily specified. Given this fact, we may conclude that, unlike many European languages (at least in their relatively more formal speech) which always require an overt subject for sentences, Chinese does not seem to have such a syntactic requirement①. This seems to be a logical corollary of Chao's proposal that subject in Chinese sentences means "topic." Thus a speaker naturally feels free to omit the topic when he feels it is already known to the people to whom he speaks. This phenomenon, of course, is also a natural consequence of the spoken or conversational style of the language②.

2.4 A Sentence Can Function as a Predicate

This rather unusual feature of Chinese syntax was noted long ago by some Chinese grammarians when they claimed 得以句爲説明語"(A sentence) can have another sentence [i. e., a clause] as its predicate."③ Viewed from the angle of the new definitions for subject and predicate in Chinese, we can again see that this is just another corollary of Chao's discovery. Note that this is different from normal topicalization in that the subject often is not part of the predicative clause. For example④.

---

① When my paper on passivity (Hsueh 1994) was presented in Zurich, Professor Heo Pyog (許壁) of Yonsei University pointed out to me that subjectless sentences are also extremely common in Korean.

② Highly colloquial speech in English seems to have this tendency, too. A gardener once said to me: "Don't know will rain or not," which sounds to me like 不知將雨否 in Classical Chinese. Note also the folk saying "Easy come, easy go."

③ According to Y. R. Chao, 陳承澤 was the first to point out this fact. (See Chao 1968:95, footnote.)

④ For the convenience of those who do not read CC, the format of this paper follows the LSA/JCL style. However, I personally feel that the use of romanization and glosses in the data examples is unimportant, Romanizations that provide a Modern Chinese reading are irrelevant, while the many "reconstructed" readings for Archaic Chinese are neither quite reliable nor really important for our discussion. Moreover, form-class labels such as NP, NOM, VP, Vb, Prep, Asp, etc, in the example sentences are confusing, or even misleading, unless first elaborately defined for Classical Chinese, which is exactly what the present paper is trying to do.

(1) 夏禮,吾能言之,杞不足徵也。(論語:八佾)

xia li, wu neng yan zhi, qi bu zu zheng ye

NAME ritual, 1st can talk 3rd, NAME NEG enough testify PART

"Xia's rituals, I can describe them, Qi is not good enough to testify."

(2) 回也,其心三月不違仁。(論語:雍也)

hui ye, qi xin san yue bu wei ren

NAME PART, POSS heart three month NEG against benevolence

"Hui, his mind for three months won't go against REN."

The subject of the embedded sentence can, of course, be absent, as explained in 2.3. For example:

(3) 貨,惡其棄於地也,不必藏於己。(禮記:禮運)

huo, wu qi qi yu di ye, bu bi cang yu ji

goods, hate POSS discard on ground PART, NEG must store with self

"Valuables, (one) would hate that they are discarded on the ground, though (they) need not be possessed by oneself."

2.5 Grammatical Particles Are Sometimes Omitted

For a non-inflectional language like Classical Chinese, we would expect to see that it relies heavily on its grammatical particles to indicate the syntactic relations among the individual words in a sentence. To a very great extent, this is quite true. It is, therefore, rather puzzling to see that some particles which are expected to be present are often simply omitted. This can be seen by contrast in the following examples.

(4) 橘生[於]淮南則爲橘,生<u>於</u>淮北則爲枳。(晏子春秋:内篇雜下第六)

ju sheng [yu] huai nan ze wei ju, sheng <u>yu</u> huai bei ze wei zhi

orange grow [in] NAME south then be orange, grow <u>in</u> NAME north then be bramble

"(When an) orange grows [in] the south of Huai it becomes an orange,(when it) grows in the north of Huai, it becomes a bramble."

(5) [鍾離子]是其爲人也……是助王養其民[者]也;[葉陽子]是其爲人[也]…是助王息其民者也。(戰國策:齊策四)

[zhonglizi] shi qi wei ren ye...shi zhu wang yang qi min [zhe] ye; [yeyangzi] shi qi wei ren [ye]...shi zhu wang xi qi min zhe ye

[NAME] DEM POSS be person PART... DEM help king support POSS people [one] PART; [NAME] DEM POSS be person [PART]...DEM help king increase POSS people one PART

"[Zhong Lizi] as a person...is [one who] helps the king take care of his people; [Ye Yangzi] as a person...is one who helps the king increase his population."

(6) 子夏子張子游以有若似聖人,欲以所[以]事孔子事之。(孟子:滕文公上)

zixia zizhang ziyou yi youruo si shengren, yu yi suo [yi] shi kongzi shi zhi

NAME NAME NAME because NAME resemble sage, want yi what [yi] serve KONGZI serve 3rd

"Because You-Ruo looked like the Sage, Zi-Xia, Zi-Zhang and ZiYou wanted to serve him the way (they) served Confucius."

In many cases, however, the omission may not be so obvious but can only be determined from the broader context. This is particularly true in the case of conjunctions, especially 而 and 則. In most cases, thanks to the context, the omission of some particles may not seriously hinder proper interpretation. This is perhaps why they were called "empty words" 虛字 by early grammarians. But, without the help of the context, omission of grammatical particles will likely cause some ambiguity. We may even speculate that some authors, Lao-tzu for example, might have deliberately omitted some grammatical particles, so that their rather terse sayings or writings might be subjected to various possible interpretations and thus acquire a mysterious colour[①]. Syntactically, I think it is the spoken or conversational character of the language which permits such omissions, because the immediate situation often helps reduce or eliminate most of the ambiguities. Conversely, we may perhaps say that, since the context has made some of the grammatical relations among the individual words clear, specific indicators for such become relatively unnecessary and, hence, are omitted.

3. THE WORD ORDER PRINCIPLE AND 以 AS A FULL VERB

The special syntactic features listed above for Classical Chinese are, of course, not exhaustive, but they are the ones which are most often overlooked or not fully appreciated. For our discussion in the following, they must be constantly kept in mind. Other important features of the language which are already well-known include the role word order plays and the flexible use of lexemes for different syntactic functions without marking.

3.1 Why 以 Is Not Always a Preposition

As we have said, Classical Chinese, being a non-inflectional language, depends heavily on word order as a way to indicate syntactic relations. The claim that in an endocentric construction modifiers always precede the modified is, of course, based upon semantic interpretation for such phrases. Vigorous application of this rule means that, when two such phrases consist of exactly the same words but in different order, the words play different syntactic roles and the phrases must have different meanings. For logical and consistent syntactic theorization, the difference is of utmost importance, no

① Professor Feng Youlan (馮友蘭), the well-known scholar of Chinese philosophy, once said: "The sayings and writings of the Chinese philosophers are so inarticulate that their suggestiveness is almost boundless." (Fung Yu-lan: A Short History of Chinese Philosophy, 1966, p.11). It seems he was talking about the same thing I am here. The difference is that, while he attributes this to inarticulateness ("terseness" as I call it), I think it is more due to the omission of grammatical particles.

matter how subtle it may be semantically. For example, we find both 以羊易之 and 易之以羊 in *Mencius* (see Examples 9 and 10 below). It seems they both mean the same thing, roughly "replace it with a goat." Many scholars call 以 a preposition or co-verb and claim that the prepositional phrase (hence, the modifier) can occur either before or after the verb phrase, though they admit that when it occurs after the verb phrase as a complement it seems to receive more emphasis①. Two theoretical objections can be raised here. First, how can the prepositional phrase, a modifier, occur after the verb phrase which it modifies? That would be a violation of the word order principle. Second, if it is truly a complement, why should it receive greater emphasis than the main verb phrase? That would be a contradiction by definition (for more detailed discussion, see Wu 1994:19.24).

3.2 The Grammatical Roles of 以 Redefined

The so-called prepositions or co-verbs, including 以, do not have to be labeled as such in all their occurrences. They sometimes function for other syntactic roles, as other types of lexemes in Classical Chinese do. They are all verbs by origin and occasionally still occur by themselves as main verbs in addition to their co-verbal use. For example:

(7) 以吾一日長乎爾,毋吾以也。居則曰:"不吾知也!"如或知爾,則何以哉?(論語:先進)

yi wu yi ri chang hu er, wu wu yi ye. ju ze yue: bu wu zhi ye! ru huo zhi er, ze he yi zai

because 1st one day old than 2nd, NEG 1st regard. now then say: NEG 1st know PART! suppose some know 2nd, then what do PART

---

① See, for example, 劉景農 Liu Jing-nong 1956:198—201. Another interesting example is Lu Guoyao's article (魯國堯 1982), in which he argues against Liu's idea that the 以 phrase as a complement carries more emphasis. He thinks whether the 以 phrase is put before or after the verb phrase is purely a stylistic matter and makes no difference in meaning. I don't quite agree with him. It seems he did not differentiate between syntactic and pragmatic considerations.

"Don't take me too seriously just because I'm a few days older than you. Now you often say: 'Nobody understands me!' Suppose somebody did understand you, what would you do?"

(8) 桓公九合諸侯,不以兵車。(論語:憲問)

huan kong jiu he zhuhou, bu yi bing che

NAME lord nine assemble princes, NEG use weapon chariot

"Lord Huan summoned the vassal lords together many times, (in doing that, he) did not use military force."

Clearly, at least the second and the third 以 in (7) serve as the main verb where they occur, though there have been different opinions as to what they mean. Equally clearly, the only 以 in (8) is also the main verb. On the other hand, when a speaker (King Xuan of Qi, for example) deliberately changes the word order in his speech, he must mean to convey a special message. Therefore, the two sentences must have different meanings, as in my translations of the following.

(9) [何可廢也?!]以羊易之!(孟子:梁惠王上)

[he ke fei ye?!] yi yang yi zhi

[how can abolish PART] with goat replace 3rd

[How can (that) be abolished?!] Replace it with a goat!"

(10) 我非愛其財而易之以羊也。(孟子:梁惠王上)

wo fei ai qi cai er yi zhi yi yang ye

1st NEG love POSS cost and replace 3rd use goat PART

"It is not true that, because I cared about the cost, (I) used a goat to replace it."

In other words, I believe in (9) 以羊 functions as an adverbial modifier and 易之 is the modified verb phrase, but in (10) they switch their roles. This syntactic change is directly responsible for the change in meaning, and it is dictated by the principle of word order in the language as well as by the tendency in the language to have the logical predicate located on the center of the grammatical predicate (cf. Chao 1968: 78 - 80). Following are some more examples in which the 以 phrase was deliberately put after the other verb phrase to show that it is the semantic focus and, hence, the main verb phrase[①].

(11) 五畝之宅，樹之以桑。(孟子:梁惠王上)

wu mou zhi zhai, shu zhi yi sang

five CL REL home plant it use mulberry

"(When) planting on a 5-mou home lot, use mulberry trees."

(12) [子南]執戈逐之，及衝，擊之以戈[②]。(左傳:昭公元年)

[zinan] zhi ge zhu zhi, ji chong, ji zhi yi ge

[NAME] hold spear pursue 3rd arrive crossroad hit 3rd use spear

"[Zi-Nan] with a spear in hand, pursued him, and used the spear to hit him at the intersection."

(13) 何不試之以足?(韓非子:外儲説左上)

he bu shi zhi yi zu

why NEG try 3rd use foot

"Why didn't (you) use (your own) feet to try them?"

(14) 載我以其車，衣我以其衣。(史記:淮陰侯列傳)

zai wo yi qi che, yi wo yi qi yi

---

① Other co-verbs (or prepositions), particularly 於, seem to behave in a similar manner, though not as clearly. The real question is: Given the fact that lexemes in Classical Chinese are quite flexible in playing different syntactic roles, is it logical to establish a lexical class such as "co-verb" or "preposition" and to treat its members always as such? To put it differently, should we use such a term as a label for a lexical class or for a syntactic function? The issue is too big for me to handle in this paper.

② This example is particularly noteworthy for our argument. The focus of the first clause is clearly that Zi-Nan pursued his opponent, not that he held a spear. So 逐之 functions as the main verb phrase, while the other verb phrase 執戈 appears before it as an adverbial modifier. In the second clause, the main point is that he used a spear, not that he attacked the other person. Thus 以戈 was deliberately made the main verb phrase, while the other verb phrase 擊之 was put in front of it as an adverbial modifier, We know this for sure, because the larger context tells us Zi-Nan was later charged with unwarrantable use of a dangerous weapon and exiled.

carry 1st use POSS carriage, clothe 1st use POSS clothes
"(He) used his own carriage to carry me, and used his own clothes to clothe me."

4. VERB COMPLEMENT (VC) CONSTRUCTION AND 以 AS A CO-VERB

The above argument is not meant to deny the existence of verb complement construction in Classical Chinese. Actually, the main purpose of this paper is to redefine that concept and thereby rectify some serious misunderstandings about Classical Chinese syntax.

4.1 Verb Complement Construction

The term "verb complement construction" 動補結構 has been used for some syntactic constructions in both Modern Chinese and Classical Chinese. In Modern Chinese, the most prominent form referred to as "complement" 補語 is the second element in the so-called resultative compounds, such as 打破, 吃光, 灌醉, etc. In an earlier paper (Hsueh 1989), I argued that the so-called verb in such compounds actually functions as an adverbial modifier, while the so-called complement is the real verb in the causative sense. The causative use of various kinds of lexemes as transitive verbs is very common and context-free in Classical Chinese. This feature survived into Modern Chinese but became context restricted, in that such a causative verb must have an action verb as its adverbial modifier①. The logic for this conclusion is

① According to 王力 Wang Li (1990:368), the practice of adding an action verb before the causative verb started from the Han dynasty. It steadily spread until the causative verb became context-restricted in Modern Chinese. The question is whether this added restriction has altered its nature so much that it is no longer a verb but a complement to its former modifier. My answer is obviously negative. Actually, there are still some causative verbs without such restriction in Modern Chinese, though they tend to appear in idiomatic expressions, for example, 出錢, 盡力, 上菜, 下酒.

the same as when we discussed the word 以 in the last section, namely, consideration for the matching of syntactic focus with semantic focus. For the same reason, we now have to accept a different type of syntactic form in Classical Chinese as the complement to its preceding verb phrase. This seems to be a violation of the word order principle, but I would argue that this is a phenomenon on a lower level, that is, the verb and the complement form a unit which then follows that principle.

4.2 The 以 Phrase and Verb Complement Construction

Let us take a look at the following examples.

(15) 命子封帥車二百乘以伐京。(左傳:隱公元年)

ming zifeng shuai che erbai sheng yi fa jing

order NAME command chariot 200 CL to attack NAME

"(The lord) ordered Zi-Feng to lead 200 chariots to attack Jing."

(16) 晉侯復假道於虞以伐虢。(左傳:僖公五年)

jin hou fu jia dao yu yu yi fa guo

NAME marquis ask path through NAME to attack NAME

"The marquis of Jin once again asked for permission to pass through Yu in order to attack Guo."

(17) 焉用亡鄭以陪鄰?(左傳:僖公三十年)

yan yong wang zheng yi pei lin

why use destroy NAME to benefit neighbor

"Why do (you) have to destroy Zheng just to benefit your neighbor?"

(18) 我聞忠善以損怨,不聞作威以防怨。(左傳:襄公三十一年)

wo wen zhong shan yi sun yuan, bu wen zuo wei yi fang yuan

1st hear loyal good to reduce complaint NEG hear do menace to guard complaint

"I heard that (one) should take loyal and generous actions to reduce complaints, (I) did not hear that (one) should use intimidating force to shut up complaints."

(19) 今逐客以資敵國，損民以益仇。(李斯：諫逐客書)

jin zhu ke yi zi di guo, sun min yi yi chou

now expel guest to benefit enemy state reduce people to augment enemy

"Now (you) expel immigrants to benefit (your) rival states, and reduce (your) population to augment that of (your) opponents."

When we compare the above examples with those from (10) to (14) in 3.2, we may feel that they all share a common feature, namely, the 以 phrase occurs after the verb phrase. Then, according to the principle of word order, the 以 phrase would have to be accepted as the main verb phrase, while the verb phrase before it could only be an adverbial modifier. But we know this is not right, because the semantic focus in the examples above is clearly on the verb phrase before the 以 phrase. Therefore, syntactically, the 以 phrase should be analyzed as being complementary to the verb phrase, even though it seems to be a violation of the word order principle. If we take a closer look at the examples above, we can see that they are really quite different from those in 3.2, The 以 phrases here are far more complex. The word 以 here is not followed by a nominal as its object but by a verb phrase for which it serves as an adverbial modifier. In other words, 以 is here playing its normal prepositional role, with the action represented by the preceding verb phrase as its understood object. It is thus closely connected to the preceding verb phrase and marks the following verb phrase as a complement to the former. The VC construction so formed becomes thus a tight unit within which the word order rule does not apply.

4.3 Problems with Identifying a VC Construction

The VC construction as described above might seem fairly straightforward and simple. However, Classical Chinese texts sometimes cannot be judged simplistically on the surface. This is due to the incomplete nature of the recording, particularly the occasional omission of grammatical particles discussed in 2.5. Therefore, when 以 occurs between two verb phrases, as it does in the examples in 4.2, it is not necessarily a sure sign for a VC construction. There are two reasons why it may not be such. First, the verb phrase after 以 may represent, together with 以, a separate clause. The whole sentence would have to be read with a pause after the first verb phrase to indicate two separate events, as in the following examples.

(20) 孤違蹇叔,以辱二三子;孤之過也。(左傳:僖公三十三年)

gu wei jianshu, yi ru er san zi; gu zhi guo ye

1st violate NAME for humiliate two three man 1st REL fault PART

"I acted against Jian-shu's (advice), and thereby humiliated you gentlemen; (this is) my fault."

(21) 回也聞一,以知十;賜也聞一,以知二。(論語:公冶長)

hui ye wen yi, yi zhi shi; ci ye wen yi, yi zhi er

NAME PART hear one with know ten CI PART hear one with know two

"After Hui learns one (lesson), (he can) thereby infer ten; after I learn one, (I can only) thereby infer two."

Second, when the two verb phrases stand for separate events, the conjunction 而 can be used between them. For example:

(22) 首其請於寡君而以戮於宗。(左傳:成公三年)

shou qi qing yu gua jun er yi lu yu zong

NAME probably ask from POSS ruler and with execute in temple

"Shou would probably ask for permission from our ruler first and therewith execute (me) in (our) clan temple."

But normally, unless the understood object of 以 is spelled out in the form of the pronoun 之, the conjunction is omitted, as in the following examples.

(23) 大人世及以爲禮,城郭溝池以爲固。(禮記:禮運)

da ren shi ji yi wei li, chenghuo gouchi yi wei gu

big man generation reach by make norm castle moat take for security

"The big men kept successions in the family, and thereby made it a norm; (they) built castles and moats, and relied on such for their security."

(24) 以舅犯之謀與楚人戰以敗之。(韓非子:難一)

yi jiufan zhi mou yu chu ren zhan yi bai zhi

follow NAME REL advice with NAME people fight by defeat 3rd

"Following Jiu-fan's advice, (he) fought with the Chu people and thereby defeated them."

For the reasons given above, VC constructions cannot be identified mechanically on surface structure only and there may be times when we cannot be absolutely sure.

5. VC CONSTRUCTION AND ITS IMPLICATIONS

The VC construction as defined above naturally has some quite important implications for Classical Chinese syntax. In addition to its seeming violation of the word order principle which we have already discussed, two other equally important implications must be pointed out.

5.1 Conjunction

All grammarians of Classical Chinese of whom I am aware (see Bibliography) do not see the distinction between the type of sentences exemplified in 4.2 and the other type in 4.3. They regard both types as compound sentences and, therefore, call 以 in these sentences a conjunction (e.g., 周 Zhou 1961:267). Many of them even say 以 in this use is just the same as 而. This, I venture to say, is really a very superficial observation. Note that 而 cannot be substituted for 以 in any of the sentences in 4.2, either because it will be ungrammatical or the meaning will change. For those in 4.

3，it is indeed possible（i. e.，grammatical）to replace 以 with 而 without causing any serious change in meaning. But this should by no means be used as evidence to conclude that they are the same. As can be seen in (22)，they can Co-occur with each playing its own role. It is only a matter of rhetorical style that usually one is included while the other is omitted（or implied，cf. 2.5). Sometimes both are omitted. Therefore，we can say 以 is most definitely not a conjunction①.

5.2 Passivity

Passivization as a syntactic process has been a controversial issue in the study of Classical Chinese. Simply put，the question is whether there are any genuine passive constructions in Classical Chinese. Most scholars accept unquestioningly such patterns as 見-V，爲(N)(所)V，V-於-N and 被(N)V as passive constructions，in addition to acknowledging the conceptual passiveness（意念上的被動）in the verb itself（see，for example，李 Li 1983:374). These assertions have been forcefully questioned by Cikoski in his article "An Analysis of Some Idioms Commonly Called 'Passive' in Classical Chinese" (1978b: 133 - 208). Since his study is limited to the texts of the Warring States period，he did not talk about the 被 passive which appeared only in the Han dynasty. He flatly refuted the 於 passive as passive at all，and he acknowledged only half of the 爲 passive（i. e.，the earlier pattern without 所）as passive，but only in the first two-thirds of the CC period. On the other hand，he argued that the 見 passive represents a genuine passive construction，and claimed that the four "ergative verbs"可難易足 can make any CC verb passive when prefixed to it to form the 可 passive construction，In my article on the same topic（Hsueh 1994)，I chose to argue that Classical Chinese has

① It seems the misidentification did not start with the grammarians，but with some post-Han writers of Classical Chinese prose. See，for example，the two lines "木欣欣以向榮，泉涓涓而始流"from Tao Yuan-ming's（陶淵明）famous essay，歸去來辭，where 以 and 而 were indeed used interchangeably.

no passive construction at all in a strictly syntactic sense by demonstrating that none of the above so-called passive constructions are specifically and exclusively for the representation of the passive meaning, but are only idiomatic forms often used for such. I did not discuss the so-called 可 passive in that article. But unless we can prove that phrases so formed do not represent a syntactic pattern for passivity, we won't be able to defend the sweeping claim that Classical Chinese has no passive construction. Now we can do that, with the notion of VC construction as I defined it. Let us take a look at the following examples.

(25) 子犯請擊之,公曰:"不可。"(左傳:僖公三十年)

zifan qing ji zhi, gong yue:"bu ke"

NAME ask attack 3rd lord say NEG okay

"(When) Zi-Fan asked to attack them, the lord said:'(It's) not okay'."

(26) 若寡人者,可以保民乎哉?!(孟子:梁惠王上)

ruo guaren zhe, ke yi bao min hu zai

like 1st one okay with protect people PARTPART

"One like me is okay to therewith protect the people?!"

(27) 朽木不可雕也。(論語:公冶長)

xiu mu bu ke diao ye

rotten wood NEG okay carve PART

"A piece of rotten wood is not okay to carve."

The word 可 is very difficult to translate. For consistency, I used the colloquial term "okay," though it would be far better to render it "possible; acceptable; right," depending on the context. The point here is that 可 may occur alone, or before a verb phrase with 以, or before a verb phrase without 以, as we can see from the three examples above. It is, therefore, a full verb and it can naturally have a complement, The 以 phrase in (26) is just that, because the semantic focus is clearly on 可. A verb complement does not need to have a co-verb like 以 as its modifier. So, by the same logic, I claim that in (27)可 is the main verb with 雕 as its complement. Note that, while (26) does not imply the passive meaning, (27) seems to be passive semantically. But syntactically, neither can be said to be in passive construction. This can perhaps be compared with English sentences with an infinitive phrase after the verb or adjective such as "An understanding person is hard to find" (which can be rendered 知音難). Though "to find" implies the passive sense, syntactically, it is not in passive form. The other three verbs 難易足 are just like 可. So the 可 passive also does not represent a passive construction. My claim that Classical Chinese has no passive construction still stands.

6. SUMMARY

In this paper, I have chosen to make a careful study of the word 以, with the hope that some important mechanisms of Classical Chinese syntax can thereby be revealed. It seems fairly clear that the word is a verb by origin and the basic notion it represents can be said to be "instrumentality," that is, "to engage (somebody or something) as an instrument." Syntactically, aside from serving as a verb by itself, it can also serve as a preposition or co-verb, with overt or understood object, to modify the verb phrase that follows it in the sense that "by means of" or "because of" its object, some event takes place. When 以 occurs with an overt object after another verb phrase, it has been mistakenly called a complement by many grammarians, but it is actually the main verb, while its preceding verb phrase functions as an adverbial modifier(see 3.2). When it occurs by itself between two other verb phrases, 以 is definitely not a conjunction, as many grammarians have mistakenly called it, In reality, it is still a co-verb with the preceding verb phrase as its understood object and serving as an adverbial modifier to the following verb phrase. The two verb phrases may represent two separate events with the first as background and the second as focus (see 4.3), or the second may be the complement to the first to form a VC construction (see 4.2). The test is whether the conjunction 而 can be inserted between them (see 5.1). Through this study, we now fully recognize that VC construction is part of CC syntax, and we can thereby prove that such phrases as 可知,難求,易忘,and 足誠 do not really represent passive construction in a syntactic sense. But co-verbs and VC constructions are very complex issues. They, particularly the "Co-verb" 於,will have to be studied more carefully and more thoroughly.

BIBLIOGRAPHY

Chinese:

編寫組　《古代漢語常用字字典》, 商務印書館, 1979 年。

韓峥嶸　《古漢語虚詞手册》, 吉林人民出版社, 1984 年。

何樂士　《〈左傳〉的單句和複句初探》,《先秦漢語研究》(程湘清主編),山東教育出版社,1982, pp. 143—271.

黄六平　《漢語文言語法綱要》, 中華書局,1974 年。

李新魁　《漢語文言語法》, 廣東人民出版社, 1983 年。

廖序東　《文言語法分析》,上海教育出版社, 1981 年。

劉承慧　"左傳裏的名詞與動詞化現象,"第一届國際漢語語言學會議, 新加坡, 1992 年。

劉景農　《漢語文言語法》, 中華書局, 1956 年。

吕叔湘　《漢語語法論文集》, 科學出版社, 1955 年。

魯國堯　《〈孟子〉'以羊易之','易之以羊'兩種結構類型的對比研究》,《先秦漢語研究》(程湘清主編),山東教育出版社,1982, pp. 272—90.

太田辰夫　《中國語歷史文法》(蔣紹愚、徐昌華譯),北京大學出版社, 1987 年。

王　力　《中國語法理論》,《王力文集》第一卷, 山東教育出版社, 1984 年。(Reprint of the 1944 edition.)

——　《漢語語法史》,《王力文集》第十一卷,山東教育出版社, 1990 年。

謝紀峰　《虛詞詁林》，黑龍江人民出版社，1992 年。

薛鳳生　“試論連詞而字的語意與語法功能，”《語言研究》No. 1，1991，pp. 55—62.

——　“論古文中的主語省略及其對文法研究的影響，”《語文建設通訊》(Chinese Language Review. Special issue in honor of Lu Shuxiang) 42(1993)，pp. 33—34.

楊伯峻　《文言文法》，中華書局，1963 年。

楊樹達　《高等國文法》，鼎文書局影印，1972 年。

雅洪托夫　《漢語史論集》(唐作藩、胡雙寶編選)，北京大學出版社，1986 年。

周法高　《中國古代語法—造句編(上)》，“中央研究院”歷史語言研究所，1961 年。

English：

CHAO，Yuen Ren. 1968. *A Grammar of Spoken Chinese*，Berkeley：University of California Press.

CHU，Chauncey C. 1987. *Historical Syntax：Theory and Applicalion to Chinese*. Taipei：Crane Publishing Co.

CIKOSKI，John S. 1978a. An outline sketch of sentence structures and word classes in Classical Chinese. *Computational Analysis of Asian and African Languages* 8:17 - 152.

——. 1978b. An analysis of some idioms commonly called Passive' in Classical Chinese. *CAAAL* 9:133 - 208.

DOBSON，W. A. C. H. 1959. *Late Archaic Chinese*. Toronto：U. of Toronto Press.

FENG，Roxana Suk-Yee. 1994. On ‘Comparative Constructions’ in the History of the Chinese Language. Paper presented at *the Third International Conference on Chinese Linguistics*，Hong Kong，July 14 - 16.

HARBSMEIER，Christoph. 1981. *Aspects of Classical Chinese Syntax*. London：

Curzon Press.

HASHIMOTO, Mantaro J. 1976. Language Diffusion on the Asian Continent: Problems of Typological Diversity in Sino-Tibetan. *Computational Analysis of Asian and African Languages* 3:49 – 65.

HSUEH, F S. 1989. The Structural Meaning of BA and BEI constructions in Mandarin Chinese: Do they really mean 'disposal' and 'passive'? In Tai and Hsueh (eds.), *Functionalism and Chinese Grammar*, CLTA Monograph 1:95 – 125.

——. 1994. Subject Deletion and 'Passive Constructions' in Classical Chinese. Paper presented in *the Symposium on Ancient Chinese Grammar held at University of Zurich*, Switzerland, Feb, 21 – 25.

LEGGE. James. *The Chinese Classics*. 3rd ed. 5 vols. (Reprinted from the last editions of the Oxford University Press, 1885.)

LI, Charles N, and Sandra A. Thompson. 1974. An Explanation of Word Order Change: SVO-SOV, *Foundation of Language* 12:201 – 14.

LIU, Cheng-hui. 1991. *Nouns, Nominalization and Denominalization in Classical Chinese: A Study Based on Mencius and Zuozhuan*. Ph. D. dissertation, The Ohio State University.

LIGHT, Timothy. 1979. Word Order and Word Order Change in Mandarin Chinese. *Journal of Chinese Linguistics* 7.2: 149 – 80.

NORMAN, Jerry. 1988. *Chinese*. Cambridge: Cambridge University Press.

PEYRAUBE, Alain. 1989. History of Passive Constructions in Chinese until the 10th Century. *Journal of Chinese Linguistics* 17.2:335 – 71.

ROSEMONT, Henry, Jr. 1974. On Representing Abstractions in Archaic Chinese. *Philosophy East and West* 24.1:71 – 88.

SUN, Chaofen. 1991. The Adposition yi and word order in Classical Chinese. *Journal of Chinese Linguistics* 19.2:202 – 20.

TAI, James H.-Y. 1973. On the Change from SVO to SOV in Chinese. Paper from the Parasession on Diachronic Syntax, Chicago Linguistic Society.

Pp. 291－304.

WU，Sue-mei. 1994. *Instrumentality in Classical Chinese: A Study of the Function Word Yi 以 with Special References to the Confucian Analects*. M.A. thesis，The Ohio State University.

試論連詞"而"字的語意與語法功能**

1. 多年來在國外從事古代漢語的教學工作,使我體認到嚴密解析其語法的重要性。學生的母語不是漢語,而且學習的目標主要是閱讀,這就要求我們多作教材的分析,特别要把句式及語法詞(即使是最常見的)解釋清楚。可惜我們這方面的知識仍嫌不足,因此有許多古文選本在注釋虛詞時,就經常有一些模棱兩可的説法。比如説,如何解釋複句的形成,以及如何界定虛詞"而"字的功能與含義,就是我在教學中經常碰到的問題。本文旨在通過這個問題的討論,在這方面發生一點兒抛磚引玉的作用。

2. 在討論一個"字"(尤其是"虛字")的意義時,我覺得我們應該堅守兩條基本原則。首先,我們必須確定這個字是代表一個語素(morpheme),還是代表幾個不同的語素。一旦認定它祇代表一個語素以後,就應該嚴格地界定這個語素的基本語意成分與語法功能。不能祇一二三四地列舉它的"不同"含義與功能,而要指明這些不同的含義與功能之間的共通處,否則就是理論上自相矛盾。其次,在爲某一語素提出其基本含義與功能的定義時,我們必須能够充分地證明這個定義具有最大的周遍性,即適用於這個語素所能出現的一切句式,並且祇有采用這個定義,才能最精確地解釋這類句子的含義。用這兩條原則來檢驗前人給"而"字所作的解説,我們便可看出很多不足之處。

3. 早期學者如王引之及馬建忠等,常作一些"隨文注釋"式的解説。例如,在説到"人而無儀"及"子産而死"之類的句子時,王引之就説:"而猶若也。"(《經傳釋詞》卷七),還進一步想在音韻學的基礎上,證明爲什麽它們是相通的。但稍後,他又説:"而猶則也。"這種解説是片面的,業已有人指出其

** 原刊《語言研究》1991 年第 1 期。
本文曾於 1989 年底在"新加坡世界華文教學研討會"上宣讀。現稍加改定,發表於此,以就教於國内同行,並祝賀《語言研究》創刊十周年。

不妥[①]。又如馬建忠説:"兩動字意平而不相承者,則間以而字連之。兩意相反者亦如之。"(《馬氏文通》卷五)這不等於没説嗎?早期的學者志在解經,不在系統性地研究古文的文法理論,因此我們實在不必苛責;同時由於他們的許多正確而寶貴的意見,都已爲後來的學者吸納引用,所以在本文的討論中,我們將不直接批駁他們的説法。現代學者的目標是語法系統與理論,所以在下文中,我們衹把他們的説法提出來稍加評論。

3.1. 關於"而"字,王力先生的説法是(引自他主編的《古代漢語》修訂本):

a) 連詞"而"字的作用是連接形容詞、動詞、或動詞性的詞組,表示兩種性質或兩種行爲的聯繫。(P.444)

b)"而"字還可以連接兩個句子,表示兩件事情的聯繫。(P.444)

c)"而"字可以用於順接,也可以用於逆接。(P.445)

d) 有時候,"而"字用在一句話的主語和謂語之間,……有時候,"而"字用在主語和謂語之間,含有假設的意思。(P.445)[②]

e)"而"字還可以用在狀語和動詞之間。(p.446)

3.2. 周法高《中國古代語法·造句編》則按他自己的系統,綜合各家的説法,把"而"字分别在不同的章節裏加以説明:

a) 聯詞(connectives):聯結兩個平行的子句,如"而";聯結副語和述語,如"而"。(P.52)

b) 有時"而"字聯結兩組成份,在"而"前面的成份好像是修飾"而"後面的成份似的。(論副語,P.149)

c) 加於條件子句之記號。

---

① 吕叔湘先生説:"前人往往説這個'而'字等於'若',其實這衹是一種方便的説法。這個'而'字雖然有表示條件的作用,可不必當作與常見的"而"字不相干涉的另一關係詞。"(1942:下册152)按:吕氏以爲不必把這個"而"字當作另一關係詞,是非常正確的説法,可惜他没有從語法的角度解釋爲什麽。又:他説這個"而"字有表示條件的作用,則不確。請參看下文 5.4.3 節的討論。

② 王力先生雖然説:"有時候,'而'字用在一句話的主語與謂語之間。"但他又説:"細玩文意,實際上也是一種逆接。"(1982:445)可見這類句子的結構不是簡單的主謂關係可以解釋的。好在大家對這類句子的真意都能"細玩文意"而"心裏有數"。本文的目的,就是要給我們共有的語感,提出一個具體的解釋(詳見下文 5.4.3.節)。王先生説:"所謂順接與逆接,衹是從具體的上下文的意思看的,並不是説'而'字有兩種性質。"(p.446)這是很正確的看法。

通常“如、若”放在主語的前後均可，但“而”衹能放在主語之後。……

主語＋而＋謂語。……（論假設句，P.218）

d）“而”的用途很廣，可以作平行、轉折的記號，但也可以作表先後的記號。（論時間句，P.277）

3.3. 其他學者，如楊伯峻、劉景農、黄六平、李新魁等（見參考文獻），對“而”字的看法，亦率多雷同。西方學者之治古文者，近年來也多沿舊説。例如 Jerry Norman 在其著 *Chinese* 中，一則稱“而”爲 verbal conjunctive particle（p.105），但稍後又説：It is more usual to find clauses joined by the two connectives ér and zé（P.107）。倒是數年前 Dawson 説的話頗有可采。他認爲“而”是純語法詞，而且是連接子句的，但他又説有許多例子是跟這個説法不符的，因此我們不應把這個説法看得太死板太教條（PP51—52）①。綜合這些説法，可以看出他們都認爲：在語法方面，“而”字可以連接（a）形容詞，（b）動詞，（c）動詞性的詞組，（d）主語和謂語，（e）狀語和動詞；在語意方面，“而”字表示（a）並列，（b）順接，（c）逆接，（d）假設等。我們不禁要問，到底“而”字所代表的是一個還是好幾個不同的語法詞呢？他們的説法是與我們在上文所提出的基本原則冲突的。顯然我們必須先回答這個問題，然後才能作有意義的討論。

4. 我猜想多數人都承認語法詞“而”代表一個單一的詞素，這也就是我的

---

① Dawson 的原文是：“The conjunction *erh* 而 has been a very controversial word in Chinese grammatical studies. Attempts to reach too precise a definition of its meaning rather than its function are misguided, because its importance lies in the part it plays in the structure of sentences. What is clear about *erh* is that it usually separates two clauses and that, for translation purposes, it works best not simply to render it as ‘and’ or ‘but’ but to take it as subordinating the clause which precedes it to the clause which follows it. But we should not apply this rule too dogmatically-since there are cases where we find that we have to regard the clause preceding the *erh* as the main clause and the clause succeeding the *erh* as a purpose or consequence clause. There are also difficulties which arise from the fact that the *erh* is sometimes preceded, not by a clause, but by a word or phrase.”（Dawson 1968：51－52.）他這段話前半甚有見地，但後半則不够嚴謹。其實在提出一個語法規律時，我們應儘可能地把它在理論上推衍下去。這才是對該規律的最佳考驗，不是什麽教條不教條的問題，更不是翻譯的問題。下文的討論可以證明，衹要堅守本文提出的觀點，那些令 Dawson 不解的困難，都會得到理所當然的解釋。

看法。這就要求我們給這個語法詞提出新的詮釋。我覺得我們可以綜合它的用法,給它下一個這樣的定義:“而”字的基本定義:(a) 語法功能:連接子句以構成複句;(b) 語意功能:表示其前之子句爲副(subordinate clause),即副詞性的描述語(adverbial modifier),其後之子句爲主(main clause),即語意焦點(focus)。這個簡明的定義可以概括住“而”字的衆多不同用法,更重要的是,衹有這樣的定義才能讓我們合理地解釋那些不同用法的真正含義。

5. 把“而”字定爲一個“衹能連接子句”的連詞,就等於説,它所連接的兩個成分都分別代表一個單句。直覺上我們也許會感到這與事實不符,因爲我們總覺得句子必須是主語與謂語俱全的,而“而”字所連的却常常衹是“形容詞、動詞、或動詞性的詞組”,甚或衹是兩個名詞。其實這都是一些表面現象?一個句子不必主謂俱全。當主語爲何已甚明顯時(由於上文已提出,或由於其性質極廣泛,類似法文的“on”),通常是把主語省略的。這是漢語的特性之一。但謂語則絶不能省略,因爲那樣就不成句子了。在這個基礎上,我們可以順理成章地説,當“而”字所連的成份不似句子時,那些成份都是謂語,代表省略了主語的子句。下面讓我們舉例分條説明。

5.1. “而”字連接兩個主謂俱全的子句。例如:

1) 任重而道遠。(《論語·泰伯》)

2) 昔者瓠巴鼓瑟而沉魚出聽,伯牙鼓琴而六馬仰秣。(《荀子·勸學》)

3) 兔不可復得而身爲宋國笑。(《韓非子·五蠹》)

這類句子結構甚爲明晰,語意上也都是重點在後,是“而”字句的最基本形式,用不着多作解説。可以指出的是,衹有在前後兩個子句的主語不同而且都不能省略時,才會有這種形式。

5.2. “而”字所連的子句,其一主謂俱全,其一主語省略。

5.2.1. 就連詞“而”的性質説,語法上並不限定它前後的子句必須具有相同的主語,但事實上這種情況特别多。這樣就没有重複主語的必要了,因此“而”後子句省略主語的例子最常見。略舉兩例以備一格:

4) 小子鳴鼓而攻之可也。(《論語·先進》)

5) 臣以神遇而不以目視。(《莊子·養生主》)

但在全篇的行文中,衹要某一主語已屬明顯無疑,就可以省略。所以“而”後子

句所省略的主語,倒不一定跟“而”前子句的主語相同。例如:

6) 人不知而(己)不愠,不亦君子乎?(《論語·學而》)

7) 日出而(吾)作,日入而(吾)息。(《古擊壤歌》)

8) 宋無罪而(楚)攻之,不可謂仁。(《墨子·公輸般》)

5.2.2. 也有些例子,是省略“而”前子句的主語但保留“而”後子句的主語的。道理已如前述,但這種情況衹有在兩個子句的主語不相同,而前一子句的主語已屬明顯時,才會發生,因此古書中這類例子較少。例如:

9) 取之而燕民悦則取之……取之而燕民不悦則勿取。(《孟子·梁惠王》)

10) 建一官而三物成,能舉善也。(《左傳·襄公三年》)

由習用語如“既而”“已而”“俄而”等引領的句子,如果後跟的子句是帶有主語的,也屬於此類。因爲這類習用語多半是表示時間的,而漢語中單純表示時間的句子,往往省略(或“根本没有”,參看劉景農 1958:84)主語。例如:

11) 既而齊人來讓。(《左傳·襄公二十八年》)

12) 俄而子輿有病。(《莊子·大宗師》)

5.3. “而”字連接的兩個子句,也可能都省略了主語。這種情形常給人造成一種錯覺,以爲“而”字是動詞或動詞性詞組的連詞。這類句子很多。例如:

13) 學而時習之,不亦説乎?(《論語·學而》)

14) 怒而飛,其翼若垂天之雲。(《莊子·逍遥游》)

15) 棄甲曳兵而走。(《孟子·梁惠王》)

上面的例句裏,前後子句所省略的主語是相同的。但文法規則並無非如此不可的要求,因此在這類完全省略主語的複句裏,所省略的主語也可能代表不同的人或事物。例如:

16) 危而不持,顛而不扶。(《論語·季氏》)

17) 三進及溜而後視之。(《左傳·宣公二年》)

18) 今又内圍邯鄲而不能去。(《戰國策·趙策》)

習用語“然而”、“既而”、“已而”等所引領的子句。如果没有主語,本質上也屬於這一類。例如:

19) 然而不王者,未之有也。(《孟子·梁惠王》)

5.4. “而”字連接的成份,有些表面看來似乎衹是單純的形容詞、數詞、時間詞、方位詞、名詞(甚或專有名詞)。這種現象最容易引起誤會。結果把"而"字説成可以連接狀語和述語,還可以連接主語和謂語等。我們不禁要問:(1)爲什麽這個連詞有這麽多不同的功用?(2)狀語和述語之間爲什麽需要連詞?(3)主語和謂語之間怎麽也需要連詞了呢?這類説法頗使我感到不解。因爲我們知道"而"字是一個語法詞。它是在特定的語法結構中發生作用的。也就是説,它所連接的不是某些詞類中的個别詞彙,而是這些詞彙在語法結構中所擔任的角色(The role a lexeme plays in a syntactic construction)。另一方面,我們也都知道,古代漢語中"詞類活用"是一個極爲普遍的現象。以形容詞、數詞、名詞等作謂語是毫不足怪的。所以我們説,"而"字所連接的數詞、時間詞、方位詞、名詞等,實際上都是以謂語的角色出現的。也就是説,"而"字所連接的是包含這些謂語的子句,衹不過這些子句的主語已經省略掉罷了。我們可以分類舉例説明。

5.4.1. 以形容詞作謂語的"而"前子句。例如:

20)秦師輕而無禮。(《左傳·僖公三十三年》)

21)夫子莞爾而笑。(《論語·陽貨》)

22)我怫然而怒……廢然而反。(《莊子·德充符》)

作爲個别詞彙,"輕、莞爾、怫然"等,當然都可以作狀語,而且直接出現在動詞之前。但這些形容詞也可以作謂語。我認爲當它們出現在"而"字前面時,它們在語法結構上説,都是形容詞用作謂語的。"而"前子句是描述"而"後子句的。假如兩個子句的主語相同,因而省略了"而"後子句的主語,那麽"而"前子句的那個作爲謂語的形容詞,就很像狀語了,但這種功能並非來自它本身,而是來自"而"前子句。

5.4.2. 以數詞、時間詞和方位詞作謂語的"而"前子句。例如:

23)三十而立,四十而不惑,……(《論語·爲政》)

24)日鑿一竅,七日而渾沌死。(《莊子·應帝王》)

25)長驅到齊,晨而求見。(《戰國策·齊策》)

26)北而攻齊……東而攻越……(《墨子·非攻》)

以上各例中,"而"字前面的數詞、時間詞及方位詞,絶非單純的狀語,而是謂語。"三十"意爲"到了三十歲"。"七日"意爲"過了七天"。"晨"意爲"還是一大早”。“北、東”則爲動詞,意爲“往北(或往東)行進”,這可由《左傳》中“秦師遂東”句(僖公三十二年)得到證明。如果把這些例句中的“而”字省掉,上述各詞就變爲狀語了,各句的意思也就跟着變動了。

5.4.3. 以一般名詞或專有名詞作謂語的“而”前子句。例如:

27) 相鼠有皮,人而無儀!

人而無儀,不死何爲?(《詩·鄘風·相鼠》)

28) 人而無信,不知其可也。(《論語·爲政》)

29) 士而懷居,不足以爲士矣。(《論語·憲問》)

30) 管氏而知禮,孰不知禮?(《論語·八佾》)

31) 子產而死,誰其嗣之?(《左傳·襄公三十年》)

32) 十人而從一人者,寧力不勝智不若耶? 畏之也!(《戰國策·趙策》)

這類帶“而”字的句子,表面上看來相當奇特,也造成了許多誤解。最常見的説法是,“而”字連接主語和謂語,又説它含有假設的意思。其實如果我們抓住“而”字的本義,就會看出它在這些例句裏的用法,並無特異之處,也跟假設毫無關係。試看“相鼠”第二句“人而無儀”,以及《趙策》的“十人而從一人”,哪裏有什麽假設的意思呢?① 這類句子,衹有出現在表示結果的子句之前時,才會有假設的意思。那是由於出現的地位使然,跟“而”字没有關係。“而”字的作用仍然是指明它前面的那個名詞用作謂語,代表一個没有主語的子句。名詞作謂語,一般衹出現於判斷句或述語是“爲”或“有”的句子裏。所謂 copular verb(“to be”,是)existential verb(“to have”有),在各種語言裏都是比較特殊的“動詞”,在古代漢語裏尤其特殊。古文中根本連一個有形的 copular verb 都没有。判斷句是完全以字序的方式表達的。在判斷句的主語省略了以後,剩下來的謂語就衹能是一個名詞了。以上諸例就是這樣形成的。“而”字前面的“人、士、管氏、子產、十人”,絶不是各該句中的主語,而是没有主語的謂語。它們的意思分别是:“作爲一個人”,“作爲一個士”,“説到管氏那樣的人”,“有個子產這樣的官”,“(他們)有十個人”。這樣解析,不僅讓我們可以給“而”字

① 後代古文家對“而”字的這種用法,掌握得非常成功。比如蘇東坡有句云:“匹夫而爲百世師”(潮州韓文公廟碑),當然不是直指韓愈爲匹夫,而是説“(他)原來衹是一個普通人,而(他)後來却成爲歷代尊崇的大宗師”。這句話顯然没有任何假設的意思。

下一個統一而完整的定義,而且可以抓住各句的真意與精神。把那些名詞解作主語,就完全不對頭了①。

6. 在上文裏,我們給"而"字提出了一個統一與全面的新詮釋。可以看出,衹有采用這樣的詮解,才能正確地理解"而"字的真意。當然複句的形成並不一定非有連詞不可,但是有了像"而"這樣的連詞,我們就可以完全肯定,那些構成複句的子句,不是作爲單句而存在的。而且這些子句之間的關係不是平等的,而是前者爲副後者爲主的。也可以説,"而"字幫助把語意重心集中在後面的子句上。反過來説,它標示出前面的子句是説明那個語意焦點的背景的。背景當然可以是多方面的,包括時間的先後,事物的對比,事件的起因,假設的條件,行爲的手段與工具等。"而"前子句的功能很寬,可以涵蓋這些不同的語意差别。例如:

a) 先後:公入而賦,…姜出而賦。(《左傳·隱公元年》)

b) 對比:敏於事而慎於言。(《論語·學而》)

c) 起因:令尹誅而楚奸不上聞,仲尼賞而魯民易降北。(《韓非子·五蠹》)

d) 假設:凡天下强國,非秦而楚,非楚而秦。(《戰國策·楚策》)

e) 手段:天之道,損有餘而補不足。(《老子》)

就"而"字的功能説,上面最後兩種用法(d與e)比較不尋常。前者接近"則"字,後者接近"以"字。這兩個語法詞跟複句的形成也是大有關係的。由於篇幅所限,不擬在此詳論,但可以指出,跟"而"字一樣,"則"也是一個衹能連接子句的連詞②。不過它的含意比較窄而具體,是專指較明顯而特定的假設

---

① 如果"而"後子句也是一個省略了主語的判斷句,或者是衹有一個用作動詞的名詞,就會産生一個表面看來極不尋常的現象,即"而"字連接兩個名詞。例如:

(蟹)六跪而二螯。(《荀子·勸學》)

夷狄而中國,則中國之,中國而夷狄,則夷狄之。(韓愈)

其實這類句子並非例外。由本文所提出的觀點看,"而"字前後的名詞都是謂語,分别代表一個子句。

② 由於前人未能充分掌握"而"字與"則"字的這種特性,在注解古書時,有時就會造成一些頗可商榷的問題。例如《古代漢語》中《魯仲連義不帝秦》的標點與注釋有這樣一段:"(秦王)權使其士,虜使其民;彼則肆然而爲帝[8],過而遂正於天下[9],則連有赴東海而死耳,吾不忍爲之民也!"(P.117)注釋者在"彼則肆然而爲帝"之前用分號";"表示與上文分開,又在其後用逗號","表示與下文連成一句。另外在注(8)裏説:"則,假如,假設連詞。"又在注(9)裏説:"這句話不好懂,疑有誤字。"(p.118)我覺得如果我們充分地掌握"則"與"而"的本義,就會(轉下頁)

關係的①。“以”字本是表示手段或工具的介詞，不是連詞。但它有一種較特殊的用法，可以幫助我們認定複句。這兩個語法詞，在各自不同的含意上，都跟“而”有某種程度的重叠(Overlapping)，但本質上三者各有專司，把它們互換，在多數情況下，就會造成語句含意的轉變。

參考文獻

王　力　《古代漢語》(修訂本)，1982 年。

吕叔湘　《中國文法要略》，1942 年。

劉景農　《漢語文言語法》，1958 年。

黄六平　《漢語文言語法綱要》，1974 年。

李新魁　《漢語文言語法》，1983 年。

周法高　《中國古代語法·造句編》，1959 年。

楊伯峻　《文言文法》，1963 年。

韓峥嶸　《古漢語虛詞手册》，1984 年。

Cikoski，J. S.：*Three Essays on Classical Chinese Grammar*，in *Computational Analysis of Asian and African Languages*，8：17 - 151；9：77 - 208，Tokyo：1978.

Dawson，Raymond. *Introduction to Classical Chinese*，Oxford. 1968.

Dobson，W. A. C. H.：*Late Archaic Chinese*，Toronto，1959.

Harbs meier，Christoph：*Aspects of Classical Chinese Syntax*，London，1981.

Norman，Jerry：*Chinese*，Cambridge，1988.

(接上頁)發現這段話並不難懂。因爲這樣我們就可以確定，“則”字前面的“彼”和“而”字前面的“過”，在此都用作謂語，意思分别是“至於他自已”和“犯了過錯以後”。同時我們應該把“彼則肆然而爲帝”與上文連作一意，並到此斷句。全句的意思是：“(秦王)不把自己的人民當人看，至於他自己，反倒老着臉皮要做世界領袖！”“過”字以下另成一句，意思是：“(假如在他)犯了這樣的過錯以後，接着倒成了全世界的標準與正統，那我就衹有……。”

① 關於“而”字與“則”字的差别，吕叔湘先生説：“‘而’字的基本作用是平行的聯絡，是粘合，是無情的連係；‘則’字的基本作用是上下承接，是配合，是有情的連係。”(《要略》下，P. 93)周法高先生説：“按‘而’、‘則’義近，未嘗没有通作的地方；……‘而’、‘則’不同之處，如《孟子》‘可以速則速’，語彙較急；‘可以速而速’，語彙較緩。未嘗不可兩存，不必歸於一解。”(《造句編》上，p. 279)他們都認爲“而”與“則”的含意不同，這是完全正確的，但是他們的解釋却未免“玄”了一點兒。老實説，我是似懂非懂的。

說“呢(呐、哩)”:兼談句末語氣詞[**]

一、引子

80年代初期,美國一家名爲 Wendy’s 的快餐連鎖店,推出了一個甚有創意的電視廣告。廣告裏有三位老太太,面前放着一個大號的漢堡包,但衹有一片很小的牛肉餅放在中心。其中兩位老太太注視着漢堡包,不停地誇贊面包真好,又大又鬆軟,第三位却板着臉一再追問:“Where’s the beef?”這個廣告立刻引起了全民的興趣,到處都可以聽到這句問話,後來總統競選時,連孟岱爾(Mondle)副總統也采用來質問對手,意謂“除了好聽的空談以外,到底有什麼真材實料?”許多年輕人都穿着印有這句話的T恤衫,而且也出現了不同的中文版:寫着“牛肉在哪兒?”,或者,“牛肉在什麼地方?”。這也引起了我的興趣,不由得思考這句話到底該如何譯爲中文。上述兩種譯法實在太死板了,絶不足以表達這句話在那個場合裏所含有的特殊風味。我覺得最妥帖的譯法應該是極簡單的“牛肉呢?”這就牽涉到“呢”的語意與語法功能了。

二、“呢”的核心語意

由上例可以看出,“呢”是一個至爲生動且富於表情的語氣詞。説“呢”是一個語氣詞大概没有人反對,問題是它跟别的語氣詞在含意與用法上有什麼不同。談語法當然離不開語意,我覺得這個語氣詞表達的是“對某一出乎意料的事件的反應”(a reaction to a certain unexpected event)。當然這指的是其最基本的含義,即所謂“核心語意”(core meaning),由此可以産生出許多相關但不完全相同的引伸義;例如對出乎意料的事,我們的反應可能是因迷惑而産

** 未刊稿,據作者打印稿编辑。
本文據薛鳳生1983年和1985年文改訂增寫。

生“震驚”甚或“憤怒”,也可能因迷惑而感到“驚”或者“覺得很有趣”;但不管是哪一種反應,因爲都是由“感到意外”而來,所以都可以用“呢”來表達。“Where's the beef?”這句話到底該怎麼翻譯,有人的看法跟我完全相同,但對我給“呢”所下的定義却不以爲然(例如 Chu 1984)。他們往往强調“呢”的多義性,認爲“呢”含有三或四種不同的意思或功能,在篇章分析(discourse analysis)或語用(pragmatic)層面上互生作用。這些都是可能的,但本文的目的是在句法(sentence grammar)範圍内,給“呢”下一個核心定義,並據以説明與之有關的語法現象。我們不認爲“呢”代表好幾個獨立的語意,否則就很難解釋爲什麽同一個語氣詞會代表那麽多不同的含義。需要補充説明的是:所謂出乎意料的事件,可能是真實的(説者的實際感受),也可能是假裝的(故作吃驚的),還可能是設想的(猜測聽者會有意外的感受),而所謂對意外的反應,可能是相當强烈的,也可能是很輕微的,但不管是哪一種,都符合“呢”的定義,所以都可以用“呢”來表達那種語氣。(待下文討論用法時再舉例説明。)

三、有關“呢”字的誤解

關於“呢”字的語法功能,常見有下述兩種誤解:

(1) 認爲“呢”表達持續的狀態(continuance),甚至有人説是表達“進行式”(progressive tense)的。這顯然是受到印歐語法的影響。其實漢語没有特定的表達“時態”的語法形式,有必要時,一般祇用副詞(包括時間詞)表達事件發生的時間。像“他正在吃飯呢!”,或“我們等着你呢!”,這類句子,即使去掉“呢”,表達的仍然是持續狀態,可見“持續”實與“呢”字無關,加上“呢”祇是爲了表達説話的語氣;在頭一個例子裏表示“我没想到!”,或“你没想到吧!”;在後一個例子裏,僅表示“你可能没想到吧!”。

(2) 認爲“呢”是一個疑問詞,幫助造成問句。這也祇是表面的看法,恐怕也是受到印歐語的影響,直覺地認爲疑問句一定要有一個特定的形式或標號;其實漢語不是這樣的,上面舉出的兩個例了,都含有“呢”,但都不是問句,已足證明“呢”不是疑問詞。可以帶“呢”的疑問句祇有四種,而這四種句式本身都足以構成問句,用不着“呢”的幫助。頭一種句式是在一個名詞性的謂語後面加“呢”;這種問句可以説都是反問句,即在發現情况有異後的反問;例如,本以爲在某時某地可以見到張三,届時却未見到,就可能問:“張三呢?”(假如不以爲怪,當然就不用問了!)又如,聽見某人説張三是個大好人,我們可能感到他别有所指,就可能反問:“(那)李四呢?”,也可能開玩笑地説:“(那)我呢?”。我們説這種句式是在名詞性謂語後加“呢”字,意思是説,不管那個詞或短語原來的屬性爲何,在這種情况下,都是以一個整體作爲名詞性謂語出現的;例如某甲説:“喝酒不好!”,某乙就可能反問:“抽烟呢?”。第二種句式是在條件小句之後加“呢”字;例如某甲説:“我會跟老張一塊去。”,某乙如果覺得他話中有話,就可能會反問:“(如果)老張不去呢?”當然也可以用複句“(如果)老張不去,你去不去呢?”,可見祇含條件小句的“呢”字句,是複句的簡化。上述兩種帶“呢”的問句,祇要有語調(intonation)的配合,即使不帶“呢”字,也可以構成問句,足見“呢”不是構成問句的必要條件,而是表達反問的語氣詞。第三種帶“呢”的問句更足以充分證明我們的觀點;這類句子本身就是疑問句,例如:“老張什麽時候來呢?”,“老張怎麽没來呢?”,“老張來不來呢?”等等;可見“呢”與問句之所以成爲問句無關。第四種帶“呢”的句子,是以副詞“還”聯繫的選擇問句,例如:“老張(是)來還是不來呢?”在這種句式裏,“還”所連結的兩個小句可以分别都帶“呢”,例如:“老張(是)來呢? 還是不來呢?”;又如:“是老張呢?還是老李呢?”。當然這些都是疑問句,跟帶不帶“呢”字不相干。最明顯的證據,當然還是“呢”經常出現在非問句中,而所表達的語氣是與在問句中一致的。

四、“呢”字句結構上的限制

就句式的結構説,能帶“呢”字的疑問句可分爲上述四類,但在出現於非問句中時,却多了一個限制,即“呢”所依附的,不能祇是一個名詞性的謂語,而必須是一個整句,或没有主語但含有述語(動詞或形容詞)的謂語句;例如,我們可以説“老張呢?”這樣的問句,但不能説“*老張呢!”這樣的非問句,而祇能説“(没想到)是老張呢!”,或“(老張)相當厲害呢!”;在特殊情况下,如果有副詞“還”,或句末語氣詞“了”,名詞性的謂語也可能帶“呢”,例如有人叫我“富翁!",我就可以説:"還富翁呢!(都快破産咯!)",又如突然發覺已經晚了,就可以説:"(已經)十二點了呢!"在這樣的句子中,"還"與"了"清楚地標明,"富翁"與"十二點"所擔任的角色實爲"動詞化"了的謂語。

在嚴格的語法意義上説,"呢"衹能是一個句末"語氣詞"。這個定義自然會引起兩個問題:何謂"句"? 何謂"句末"? 像"老張呢?"和"十二點了!"這樣的句子,有人就可能不認爲"呢、了"之前的部分是句子;這就牽涉到漢語的句式問題了。漢語的構句有一些特色,省略主語就是一個常見的特色,所以成句與否關鍵在謂語,而漢語句的謂語形式是多樣化的,不像印歐語那樣必須含有"動詞",因此"老張"和"十二點",像在上兩例中一樣,都可作"謂語",也就構成"句子"了,所以即使在這樣的句子裏,我們仍有理由説"呢"是句末語氣詞("了"當然也是)。另一方面,也許有人會説,"呢"不一定衹出現於句末,認爲在像"老張呢,也不願意!"這樣的句子裏,"呢"是出現於主語和謂語之間的,表示停頓。這個看法很值得商榷;就"呢"的功能説,這等於把它一分爲二,不能説明它的核心語意;就語法結構説,這是把"老張"看作句子的主語,也不恰當。(語意上,"老張"當然是"也不願意"的施事。)這句話的結構跟"老張呢,恐怕還得找他談談!"是一致的,是説話人的自問自答,因此實爲兩個句子,都是無主句。這樣就解開了上述的兩個難題:"呢"仍是一個句末語氣詞,但由於是自問自答,"老張呢"這個問句的强度就大爲減弱了。

五、"呢"字句解讀舉例

把"呢"字定位爲"句末語氣詞",並將其含義定爲"表達對意外的反應",我覺得不但可以正確地解説"呢"字句的語意,也可以正確地分析出"呢"字句的結構。趙元任先生是最善於從漢語特色的角度討論漢語語法的前輩,給我們許多寶貴的啓示。他對語氣詞("助詞")的討論也比較全面。對於我們所説的"呢"字句(他以"呐"爲主要形式,另指出"哩"源自方言,但讀音都是一樣的),他似乎分爲兩類,即"P6 呐＝呢",與"P7 呐＝哩"(Chao 1968:801—83),並分條舉例説明其含義。這對學習漢語的外國學生顯然是極有幫助的,但也許有些好奇的外國人會問:"爲什麽中文用一個語氣詞表達那麽多不同的語氣呢?"

這就必須指出“呢”字的核心語意了，我們可以試用本文給“呢”提出的定義，重新檢視趙先生舉出的那些例句，以確認“呢”這個語氣詞的核心語意。（采用吕叔湘先生的翻譯，吕 1979：357—358；例句編號爲本文作者所加，便於討論。）

P6 呐＝呢

（1）有上下文的問話（比較 P8 啊）：

（a）那麽他呢？他來不來呐？

（b）現在咱們幹點什麽啊？

“呢”的基本定義就決定了“呢”字句必然是前有所承的。例（a）含有兩個“呢”字句；頭一句是一個簡化句；簡化了的句子通常都可能有歧義，所以説者緊接着説第二句，表示他原以爲“他”會來，但此時却感到有些意外，因此追問。例（b）亦然，説者本來以爲要做某事，但此時却不知道要做什麽了，因此反問。

（2）有特指點的問話：

（a）你懂了，“他懂不懂呐？”

（b）他會拉提琴，你呐？

兩句都是反問句；説者因見某人或某事有某種情況，而感到另一人或另一事（特指點）有可能也是那樣的，但又覺得可能不然，因而追問。

（3）有意停頓：

（a）將來的問題呐，他就等到將來再説。

（b）錢呐，錢用光了；事情呐，事情没做。

兩例都是自問自答。我們給“呢”下的定義，自然就决定了例（a）是兩個句子，例（b）則是四個句子。例中承接“呢”字句的句子（答話），都各帶主語，可見“呢”前的名詞不是主語，而是謂語；説者覺得聽者（包括他自己）可能會對某事提出問題，因而自問自答。既然是問與答，當然就是兩個句子了。（就語法説，各例中承接句的主語都可以省略；這就會給人造成一個錯誤的印象，以爲自問自答是一個句子，即認爲“呢”前的那個名詞是一句的主語。）

（4）温和的警告：

（a）這倒很危險呐！

（b）那不是玩兒的呐！

兩例都表示,説者發現聽者對某事的危險性似乎昧然不知,自然感到意外而提醒他。

P7 呐=哩(都音 ne),“哩”字見於舊小説,li 音見於某些方言(在那裏,P6“呢”音 ni 或 nyi)

(1) 繼續著的狀態:

(a) 還没到時候呐。

(b) 説着話呐。

這個“呐”有個特别的用法是帶諷刺的駁回,含有“你還認爲是這個狀態,實際已經超過這個狀態了”的意思。

(c) 真好玩兒……還“好玩兒”呐!

(d) 老朋友啊!……還“老朋友呐!”

例(a)中的“還”與例(b)中的“著”,才是兩例表達“繼續著的狀態”的真正原因,所以“呢”實與持續狀態無關(參見 3.1 節),“呢”表達的仍然是“没想到”的意思。在這兩例中,可能是説者自己没想到,也可能是説者以爲聽者可能没想到,但在例(c)與例(d)中,就衹能是説者發現聽者竟然没想到,因此感到不可思議,所以帶有諷刺的意味。副詞狀語“還”字清楚地表明“老朋友”這個名詞在此處是作爲“謂語”出現的。

(2) 肯定到達什麽程度:

有一百尺呐,深的很呐。

這個例子説的是一件事,但語法上則是兩句話,加上“呐”衹爲表示“没想到”,因而有點兒吃驚的意思。

(3) 對進一步的信息的興趣:

(a) 他們還賣古琴呐。

(b) 後院還有個金魚池呐。

(e) 他還會扯謊呐。

這三例都表示説者對他發現的事感到有點兒意外,但意外所帶來的是驚奇與興趣。這都符合“呢”的核心語意,因爲“呢”衹表達某種或强或弱的意外之感。對“意外”的反應可能因人因事而異,因此像“詫異、恐懼、疑慮、憤怒、感嘆、諷刺、喜悦”等等反應,都是有可能的。但這都是“呢”的副作用,是“呢”的延伸而非其核心語意。

六、結語

本文的主旨是要解決兩個問題:其一,語氣詞“呢”(吶、哩)的核心語意究竟是什麼?答案是:表達説者心目中的“意外感”及因之而起的反應;其二,這個詞在語法結構上有什麼特殊功能?答案是:它是一個“句末”語氣詞,即衹能出現在句末;也就是説,它的出現能幫助我們認定它前面的那個詞或詞組,不管其原來的屬性爲何,都是代表一個句子的,這對正確地分析句子的結構是非常重要的。表達語氣的詞當然不一定都出現在句末,副詞“還、又、再”等在重讀時,都能表達相當强烈的語氣;但有一類語氣詞却衹能出現於句末,“呢”是其中之一,他如表示語氣的“了”(句末“了”)和“啊”亦然。這些詞除了表達不同的語氣以外,在句法上,有時也會受到不同的制約,例如“呢”衹能出現於四種不同的問句中(見3.2節),而“啊”則不受這個限制。趙元任先生曾提出一個極有啓發性的説法,他認爲“整句”的主語和謂語是一問一答的關係,舉出“(1)兩人對話;(2)自問自答;(3)把問和答合成一個整句,中間没有停頓”三種形態,説明其間的共通性(Chao 1968:81—83;吕譯50—51)。這是一個很有趣的想法,但我覺得真正的主謂關係恐怕不能説是一問一答,因爲如果真是一問一答,就成了兩個句子了。所以主謂好像是問答,恐怕衹是形式上的偶合。在主謂之間加入語氣詞或停頓,是別有用意的,這就改變了句子的結構和含義,使得原來的主語不再是主語了,原來的整句也不再是整句了,這個看法是與漢語句式的特色相符合的(薛2000),因爲漢語的句子經常省略主語,以“零句”的形式出現。正確地認識“呢”及其他句末語氣詞的性質,既能幫助我們認清句子的結構,也能讓我們看出其用法的一致性。

參考文獻:

趙元任(吕叔湘譯)　《漢語口語語法》,商務印書館,1979年。

薛鳳生　《試論漢語句式特色與語法分析》,《文化的饋贈·語言文學卷》,北京大學出版社,2000年,第389—397頁。

Chao, Yuen ren: *A Grammar of Spoken Chinese*, UC Press, Berkeley, 1968.

Chu, Chauncey: "Beef it up with Ne", *Journal of the Chinese Language Teachers Association (JCLTA)*, Vol. XIX, No. 3 (Oct., 1984).

(Hsueh, F. S.): "Beef with Ne", *JCLTA*, Vol. XVIII, No. 3 (oct., 1983), pp. 81 - 85.

"We're still cooking Ne ne!", *JCLTA*, Vol. XX, No. 1 (Feb., 1985), pp. 95 - 97.

“得”字後邊是補語嗎?**

“他漢語説得很好。”這種句子在漢語中是很常見的句式。現在語法界認爲“説”是謂語動詞,“很好”是補語,“説得很好”被稱作動補結構。其根據,仿佛衹是因爲“很好”在動詞後邊。動詞後邊除了賓語,剩下的一概都是補語。我認爲這樣的劃法是欠科學性的,特别在對外漢語教學中很缺乏説服力。對於中國人來説,怎樣劃分也許顯得並不很重要。可是對於學習漢語的外國人來説,語法劃分得不清,便會生出許多問題來。外國學生的許多誤用,不僅僅是外國人母語的影響,有些正是由於國内語法劃分上不够科學而引起的。“説得很好”句式便是一例。現在所説的程度補語和結果補語對外國學生是很難講清楚的句式,給對外漢語教學帶來很大麻煩。

在實際教學中,我曾把這種句式作爲動詞謂語句講授過。外國學生根據對動詞句的理解,常把句子説成“他很好地説了漢語”或“老師很早地來了”。當我向他們解釋這種句式不是在説“怎麽樣行爲了”,而是在説“行爲怎麽樣”,所以不應用動詞過去式叙述,而應用形容詞描述。這時學生們很自然地對此種動詞謂語句提出了質疑。因爲日語中這種句子是用主謂結構形式來表達的。爲此我將日語和漢語進行了諸多比較,發現漢語的這種“得”字表現方法很複雜,不是日語的主謂結構形式所能完全表達得了的。雖然這樣,我仍認爲“説得很好”這種句式還是不要視爲動補結構,視爲主謂結構較好些。

1990年8月在北京舉行的第三届國際漢語教學討論會上,我曾就此觀點發表了自己的看法。我很同意德國柯彼得先生的意見,他認爲“漢語作爲外語教學的語法體系是在漢語作爲母語教學語法體系的基礎上早已於50年代定型的,這不符合漢語作爲外語教學已發展成一門獨立學科的要求”。現行的語法體系其目的主要是爲了讓已會説漢語的中國人如何正確理解和正確使用自

** 原載《語文分析》A19第1—8頁。

己的語言,换句話説目的是對内的。我們不能否定現行語法所起到的重大作用。根據當前形勢發展的要求,現在需要一個對外的,以教授非漢語爲母語的外國成年學生爲目的的語法。當然這裏所説的語法絶對不會是全新的,不過是在現行語法的基礎上進行補充、改進,使其利於對外教學。比如"補語"這一定義就很含糊,將動詞後很多詞性、用法都完全不同的成分都籠統地稱作"補語",這也許對國内不同看法的争義起到了緩解作用,但衹是爲了叫法更合理,却根本没考慮對外教學。特别是將表示程度的"得"字句與表示可能的"得"字句都稱爲動補結構更容易引起混亂。而且至今對"得"字也没一個很清楚的解釋,給教學帶來不少麻煩。所以我認爲將表示程度的"得"字句視爲主謂結構更妥當,下面就此觀點談談我的理由。

一、主語部分

要説明"説得很好"是主謂結構,首先要説明"説得"能否充當主語。

主語一般是由名詞充任的。可形容詞或動詞後邊加"的",便可構成一個名詞概念,從而可去充任主語。這在名詞謂語句中是很常見的。如:"這次參加的是李老師"。"參加的"代指人,充任主語。由於句子用了"是",是名詞謂語句,人們很好理解。所以在以後的説明中我要常常用名詞謂語句做比較。下面我們把"參加的"這一名詞概念放到形容詞謂語句中看一看。

1. 這次會議參加的不多。(人數)

2. 這種會議參加得不多。(次數)

按現在的語法規定,例 1 與例 2 要分别用"的"與"得"。句子中的"的"與"得"都是結構助詞,都是在起代指或概括作用,都是將動詞變成了一個明細概念。不同的衹是"的"指行爲的人數,"得"指行爲本身的次數。再如:

3. 他買的不好看。(物)

4. 他買得不合算。(事)

這兩句的"的"與"得"也衹不過是"具體的東西"和"買東西這件事"的區别而已。上 4 例可以看出"的"一般是代指行爲以外的一個物,或是行爲的主體,或是行爲的客體。而"得"則是指行爲本身這件事。例 1 的主語是"參加的人”,是一個修飾關係的名詞結機。而例 2 的主語可以理解爲,將“人”提前,成爲“人參加的”,是一個主述關係的名詞結構。例 3 是“買的東西”,例 4 是“東西買得”。它們都是名詞結構,因爲結機關係不同,所强調的内容不同罷了。

我們再把“説得很好”做一下比較。

5. 他説的(中文)很好。

6. 他(中文)説得很好。

例 5 和例 6 如果不省略“中文”二字,語意上好像還稍有些區别。省略了“中文”,可以説就變成了一句話,起碼口語中聽着不會有什麽區别。其實兩句話所説的意思是一樣的,衹是强調的重點有些不同罷了。我們可以把“説中文”這一動賓詞組單拿出來分析一下。“説中文了”是强調賓語“中文”,一旦把賓語提前,“中文説了”則是强調謂語“説”了。“中文説的(得)”也一樣,我們可以看成是把“説的中文”的賓語提前了,是在强調“説”的。再如:

7. 他説故事(説得)很好。

8. 他(説)故事説得很好。

例 7,例 8 兩句不做省略的話,是完全一樣的句子,意思實際是在説“他説故事很好”,這裏“説故事”這一動賓詞組作主語。爲了强調“説”而將賓語提前,再加“得”將其名詞化,構成了“故事説的(得)”作“很好”的主語。其實例句 8 中的“説得”和例句 7 中的“説故事”完全是同一内容,是句中的主語。

在漢民族下意識的口語實踐中,在漫長的文字使用上,人們是將“的”與“得”相同對待的。這不僅是因爲它們發音相同,而是因爲它們用法相同,語意相同,都是在起概括,代指、引申作用。即使我們現代人,當説到“他剛才説的……”時,你能分辨出這句話應該是“的”還是“得”嗎! 不能。可是,因爲有“de”這個音,我們就可以知道,下面要對“説的”進行闡述了。無論是“説的是誰”,還是“説得怎麽樣”,“説的”這個發音在我們意識中已完全不是一個動詞概念,而是一個用“de”結出的名詞概念了。所以它完全有資格充當主語。

另外“的”有表示已然的功能,把它放在動詞後表示行爲已經發生。如:

我騎車去。(未去) 我騎車去的。(已去過)

爲什麽“的”能表示已然呢! 這是因爲“的”把動詞變成了名詞概念,把動詞句變成了一個名詞句。“我是騎車去的”與“我騎車去了”不同,“騎車去的”

不表示行爲,衹表示一種方法,是很典型的“什麽是什麽”的名詞謂語句。而名詞是指一個實際存在的東西,所以“的”把行爲變成一個已經發生的既成事實。

將它用在主語時也相同,如:

玩是我的愛好。

玩的是騙人把戲。(已然)

“得”字句也同樣表示已然的行爲,如:

玩很有意思。

玩得很有意思。(已然)

“玩”可以作主語,“玩的”可以作主語,“玩得”這一即成事實爲什麽不可以作主語呢?其實“得”與“的”在説話人心裏是根本没有區别的。

在一九九一年第一期《世界漢語教學》雜志上,登載了一篇王還先生對我的觀點進行評論的文章。王先生不同意我的觀點,並舉出了幾個實例説明。下面我也想就這幾個實例談談我的看法。實例如下:

1. 小姑娘長得很好看。

2. 我們笑得腰都直不起來了。

3. 他氣得三天没吃飯。

4. 他嚷嚷得四鄰不安。

例1中“長得”乍看不像主語,可我們如果把“長得”换成“長相”,“小姑娘長相很好看”中“長相”不是當然的主語嗎?而“長得”不可看作“長的(得)相貌”的略語嗎?王先生也説“例1是説明長得怎麽樣的句子,句子的重點是‘小姑娘很好看’,有形容詞謂語句的性質。‘長’這個動詞簡直不起什麽作用。翻成外語,至少英語,根本翻不出來。”在日語中也一樣,翻譯時衹能略去不管。問題也正在這裏。漢語中可以省掉、翻譯時可以略去的這一部分到底是什麽成分?大家知道,謂語是句子的重點,没有謂語便不能表達意思。而主語不過衹是陳述的對象,是可以而且是常常被省略掉的。“長得”被略去也是順理成章的事,毫不奇怪。衹是如果把它當成謂語動詞,就無理可講了。王先生也説“在對外漢語教學中,把它(“得”後面的部分)解釋爲謂語,外國學生容易接受,因而有些外語,至少英語,没有這種補語。”我想問題不是没有這種補語,被稱作補語的“很好看”英語不是也有嗎。恐怕是因爲没有中國這種解釋的謂語吧,“長得”作了謂語,真的謂語如何處置呢?

下面三個例句中“我們笑得”“他氣得”“他嚷嚷得”,王先生用我的話説“在漢民族下意議的口語使用中”都不像是名詞概念。對於知規識矩的漢語學者,也許是這樣,他們也許已經不去下意識地使用語言。可是如果换一個目不識丁的農夫,當他説到“我們笑 de……”時,“de”這個發音在他頭腦中肯定已形成了一個固定的語意,而且話一出口,到此爲止的語意是不會改變,不能收回的。如果他接下去説的是“(我們笑 de)是他,笑 de 没道理嗎?”。這裏的“de”不是一個非常清楚的名詞概念嗎?同樣“他氣的是你不聽話”“他嚷嚷的(是)什麽”不是可以作主語嗎?。我們知道在“de”後邊是可以停頓的,接下去説什麽有很大的隨意性。如果説帶“是”的名詞謂語句,人們便無争議了。如果後邊用形容詞謂語或一句話,人們便生出許多非義。其實這不是人們想用“的”還是“得”來決定的,而是“de”這一發音在漢民族人們頭腦中固定下來的語法功能在起作用。“de”可以將一個動詞變成名詞,將一個動詞句變成已成事實的名詞概念。放在主語後可同“是”一起構成名詞謂語句,放在謂語前可獨立充當主語。我估計王先生所不能認同的實際並非它像不像名詞概念,而是它能否充當主語這一點上。我也想用實例論證論證。

我們笑不行嗎?

他氣關你什麽事。

他嚷嚷怎麽没完没了?

上邊的“我們笑”“他氣”“他嚷嚷”無可争議是主謂結構成分作主語,主語説的是一種行爲。在這一行爲後加“de”,將其變成一個即成的事實,由這個事實去充當主語爲什麽不行呢?也許有人覺得這幾句話的主語關係不太搭配,那些動詞嚴格説都是表示原因的。可是漢語中,表示原因的成分並非不可作主語,如:

牙疼真難受。

這次考試把他搞得一蹶不振。

這次長跑累死我了。

這幾句的主語都不是謂語的直接叙述對象,而是表示原因的。這點很像“得”字句。細看,這些句子都可以變成“得”字句。

這個牙疼得真難受。

這次考得他一蹶不振。

跑得要累死我了。

根據以上理由,我認爲“得”同“的”一樣,可以把動詞化爲名詞概念作主語。

二、謂語部分

句子的結構性質是由謂語中心詞的詞性決定的。句子的各種變化、時態表現等都是在謂語部分進行的。根據謂語的成分,句子可分爲三種形式:

1. 名詞謂語句:名詞＋是＋名詞。表示什麽是什麽。

2. 形容詞謂語句:名詞＋形容詞。表示什麽怎麽樣。

3. 動詞謂語句:名詞＋動詞。表示什麽幹什麽。

這三種形式可以説是各種語言都通用的,所以我認爲首先應視此爲大法——任何語言都須遵從的國際法,是一切地方法規制定時的依據。漢語語法當然也不能與此三原則背馳,否則一時也許通了,但會越走越窄。中國人或許不感覺怎樣,外國人會百思不得其解。

爲了證明“得”後邊是形容詞謂語,我想從以下幾方面進行論述:

1. “得”字句的中心詞

如果“得”字後是補語,句子的中心詞應是動詞,句子是動詞謂語句。動詞謂語句應是叙述“誰幹什麽”的句子。從任何角度看,這類句子也不是在説“誰幹什麽”或“誰幹了什麽”。而是在説這一發生了的行爲,或説幹了的事“怎麽樣”的。回答“怎麽樣”的形容詞才是句子的中心詞,句子理所當然應是形容詞謂語句。“説得”不過是與“寫得”“看得”等相比較,在提出其某一方面讓形容詞去描述。這不是很典型的主謂結構的形容詞謂語句嗎?

2. “得”字句的否定表現

分析一個句子不應衹看它的肯定表現,也應看它的其他表現用法和語法特徵。特别是對外漢語教學,一個句子的各種用法常是同時教授的。否定表現和肯定表現是一對孿生兄弟,應同時出現。句子不會因否定而改變其性質。

任何句子的否定表現都應是否定謂語部分的。主語因其衹是一句話的主題,是叙述的對象,不應被否定。老師向學生講“動詞後帶補語、賓語時,否定句要否定動詞。衹能説‘不去兩天’,不能説‘去不兩天’”。没想到又一種動補結構“得”字句隨後出現了。“我不説得很好”,學生們這樣説了,説得有理有據,理直氣壯。他們有法可依,因爲老師剛剛説過這是動詞謂語句。誰在理呢?理不是,自生非。法不正,自生亂。否定謂語動詞是没錯的,錯在它否定了主語。動詞後邊不一定都是補語,像“你去不好,我去好些”。動詞後面不是還有謂語嗎?何况中間還有一個“得”字呢。這個“得”字不給中國人講他也用不錯,可不給外國人講清楚他肯定不會用。

3. 疑問表現

漢語的疑問表現有幾種方法,謂語中心詞的肯定否定重迭法便是其一。任何一本基礎漢語教科書上都會有此解釋。這適用於“得”字句嗎?按動補結構的説法便不行,不能説成“他説不説得好”。衹能按形容詞謂語句的説法説成“説得好不好”。

4. 過去式表現

句子過去式表現各種語言都有,也是基礎課教學的一個内容。動詞謂語句過去式表現用“了、過”,形容詞謂語句用時間名詞表示。“得”字句一般是表示過去式含意的句子,如“説得很好”“吃得很多”都是對已發生的行爲做出的描述。如果“得”字句是動詞謂語句,此句就應該説成“你説了很好”,如同“去了一天”一樣。可是不,此句不能。衹能按形容詞謂語句那樣,或前邊加個“剛才”啦、“昨天”啦什麼的時間名詞,或根本什麼也不用,這是漢語形容詞謂語句的特點。

5. 變化的表現

“得”字句中並非不能加“了”,衹是加在什麼地方,表示什麼意思。動詞謂語句加“了”表示過去,形容詞謂語句句尾也可加“了”,但表示變化。如“天氣越來越冷了”。這也正好符合“得”字句,“你説得越來越好了”。

6. 比較句的表現

比較句多是將兩個或幾個名詞或名詞概念的句子進行比較,换句話説是將兩個句子的主語進行比較,謂語用形容詞表示。如“你高還是他高?我比他高。”“去好還是不去好?去比不去好”。同樣“説得好還是寫得好?説得比寫得好"。這裏比較的也是兩個名詞概念、兩個主語。

7. 接續的表現

比如"也"字,"中國地也大物也博"不能説成"中國也地大也物博"。"也"衹能放在主語後去强調主語。"他説得也好,寫得也好"這句話外國學生常説成"他也説得好,也寫得好",不知何故。

"又"字是强調謂語時用的,要求放在謂語前。"他説得又好,寫得又好。"學生也常説成"又説得好,又寫得好"。他們是相信"説"和"寫"都是謂語動詞,"又説又笑"就可以説嘛。所以法不清,行便無準則。

根據以上理由,我認爲"得"字句還是作爲主語結構較利於外語教學。這樣也許會出現另一個問題,即如何解釋語意。當謂語部分是形容詞時,因表示一個行爲怎麽樣,語意較好理解。當謂語部分是動詞或較長的句子時,作爲主謂關係有時好像顯得語意上有點不搭配。我認爲這是由於語言邏輯造成的。説一個行爲怎麽樣了還可以,説一個行爲幹什麽這從語言邏輯上也講不通。但我發現"得"字後面的動詞句往往不是表示幹什麽的行爲,而是表示一種狀態,或結果的。如

累得爬不起來了。

高興得不知怎麽辦好。

學得頭腦發昏。

細看,後邊的動詞句都是表示某種狀態或結果的。它們的主語嚴格講都應該是一個人稱代詞,我們可以説成"累的他""高興的他""學的他"。而"他"並不是所要叙述的主要對象,要説的是"他的行爲"怎麽樣了。所以將"他"提前,説成"他累的""他高興的""他學的"。這樣理解主謂關係就搭配了。這同前邊説的"買東西""説中文"一樣,衹是那些是動賓結構的賓語提前,這些是主謂結構的主語拖後吧。

自己本人也曉得提出這個論點有些膽大包天,衹有包天的膽子,没有包天的能力。"得"字句還牽涉到許多别的語法現象,如形容詞後邊的"得"字如何解釋等,有牽一髮動全身的感覺。教學的需要使我急切地拿出了這便不成熟的論文,僅供大家商討。

“了”是何物?**

一、前言

在現代漢語中,“了”是一個極常見的語法詞,真可以説連三歲小孩都會使用;但理論上如何詮釋起語法規律及語意功能,却是不容易的。這在對外漢語教學時,尤其是一個難點。多年前爲了教美國學生,我曾寫過一篇短文,涉及這個問題。在那篇短文裏,我强調語法分析應以語意詮釋爲依據。從語意角度觀察,許多複雜的語法形式可能就變得容易理解了。這當然不是説語法形式的描述不重要,而是説形式的描述必須能够符合語意詮釋。爲了這個目的,任何有幫助的語法理論,都可采用,而不必拘泥於某一特定理論家的學説。套用一位名人的話説,我們也許應該“少談些理論,多解决問題”;所以本文的目的不在介紹“新理論”,而是以解决“了”這個問題爲主。

二、“了”字的性質

研究“了”字的論文已經相當多了。大致説來,有兩種不同的意見:一方面有人認爲“了”字衹代表一個單獨的語法詞,不可分割;另一方面有人認爲“了”字其實代表兩個不同的語法詞,即所謂“Verb・le”(動詞後綴“了”)與“Sentence・le”(句子後綴“了”)。我基本上是同意後一看法的,但我覺得我們最好先説明,這兒牽涉到的是兩個語意概念,也就是兩個不同的語法成分,然後再説分别代表它們的是什麽樣的符號(什麽“字”),頭一個語意概念直接與

** 未刊稿,據作者打印稿編輯。
我曾從對外漢語教學的觀點,寫過一篇題爲 The Role of Semantics in Teaching Syntax:Some Examples from Mandarin Chinese(美國《中文教師學會學報》1982 年第 17 卷第 1 期)的短文。本文即據該文論及“了”字的部分增改而成,對“對内漢語教學”也許有點兒用處。

句子的述語(“動詞”)有關,是一個“情貌詞”(可以用 Asp 作代號),表達那個“述語”所代表的事件是否已先“發生”,在肯定句裏,這個概念是以“了”的形式出現在述語之後的,但在否定句裏則以“有”的形式出現在述語之前。另一個概念則與整句有關,是一個“語氣詞”(可以 Md 爲代號),表達在説話人的思維中,該句所述的是一種跟以前不同的“新情況”。這兩個概念當然是會相互影響的,因而造成許多錯綜複雜的現象。具體地説,一句話可能完全不含這兩個成分,也可能同時含有兩者或祇含其一,以簡化的單句爲例,可以公式化爲:Subj(Neg)(Asp)V(Obj)(Md)。根據這兩個成分在句中是否出現,自然就可以區别四類句子,其情形恰如漢語音節由於是否含有“腭化”與“脣化”而分爲“四呼”一樣。再加上“肯定”與“否定”的差别,更可以分爲八類句子;這可以用下表顯示出來。

句式	– Neg(肯定句)		+ Neg(否定句)	
– Asp – Md	1a	李白喝(酒)。	1b	李白不喝(酒)。
+ Asp – Md	2a	*李白有喝(酒)。	2b	*李白不有喝(酒)。
– Asp + Md	3a	李白喝(酒)了。	3b	李白不喝(酒)了。
+ Asp + Md	4a	*李白有喝(酒)了。	4b	**李白不有喝(酒)了。

表中部分句子帶有星號(*),俟下文説明(見 3.4. 節)。

三、“了”字複雜的緣故

由上節的説明可以看出,在相關句類的基本結構(或曰“深層結構”)中,我們所討論的那兩個語法成分,是非常清楚的;它們是否出現,直接決定一句話的含義,可以説是條理分明,没有什麽複雜理解的地方;但在低層次的語法變化中,却把它們弄混了,往往造成一些歧義句,也就造成了對它們的誤解。在上表的基礎上,我們可以較具體地説明這兩個語法成分的變化與互動。

3.1. 1a 與 1b 是單純事實的陳述,跟這兩個語法成分無關,也無所謂“時態”(tense)的問題,這是跟英語不同的。3a 與 3b 則增加了語氣成分(+Md),表達説話人認爲李白原不喝酒,此時却改而喝酒了(3a),或原來喝酒,此時却改而不喝了(3b)。這兩類句子也與時態無關;四類句子都已經是正常合法的漢語句子了。

3.2. 2a 與 4a 兩類肯定句都含有情貌成分(+Asp),表達事件的實際“發生”,或相對於另一事件,可能較早“發生”。這也與時態無關,與“完成”與否也無直接關係。標準漢語要求這類句子的[+Asp](“有”)從述語之前移到述語之後,並改以“了”爲代表,但許多方言却不改動,可見這是一條較低層次的規律,也是造成“了”字含意混淆的主要原因。另有一個仍有争議的問題,即 2a 是否可以獨立成句,抑或衹能作輔助句;例如單説“李白喝了酒”,似乎没有把話説完,而説“李白喝了酒就作詩”,就很圓滿了。但是如果賓語帶有數量詞,例如“李白喝了五斗酒”,就又很自然了。爲什麼會有這樣的限制呢?我猜想仍是語意的問題。因爲“了”在此處表達的是事件的“發生”,如果是獨立句,自然就要求必須説得具體些,所以在賓語“具體化”以後,就可以接受了,例如説“走了路”,不大完滿,説“走了十里路”,就很順當了;相對於“説了話”,“説了三句話”也更自然;這都是“具體化”使然。

3.3. 現代漢語有一條很特殊的規定,“有”字(不論其爲動詞或語法詞)之前的否定詞必須是“没”,不能是“不”(古代漢語似無此一規定,例如:“不有博弈者乎?”《論語·陽貨》)。所以 2b 與 4b 中的否定詞“不”都得改作“没”,由於“没”字作爲否定詞衹出現在“有”之前,“有”字是否還得出現就不那麼重要了,因此可以省略。

3.4. 我們給 2a,2b,4a,4b 都加上星號(*),表示其原型尚非正常的説話方式。在經過上述兩條改寫規則之後,2a,2b 及 4a 就都變爲正常的形式了,而 4b 則仍有問題;但這是語意的問題,因爲“没有”既然表示某事件未曾發生,却在句末加上“了”字表示那個未曾發生的事件造成了“新情況”,這在邏輯上是相互矛盾的,所以單純的 4b 句是站不住的;但如加上一個時間詞,例如“李白三天没(有)喝(酒)了”,這類句子就變爲合法了;這是什麼緣故,容待下文討論複句時再加説明。

3.5. 4a 含有兩個“了”字,各有所司,因此顯然與 3a 有别;但在通常説話及行文中，往往把頭一個"了"字省略掉，這就使得 4a 與 3a 表面看來没有分别了，因而容易引起誤解；更麻煩的是如果句中没有賓語（由於省略，或由於述語是不及物動詞），兩個"了"字就會出現在一塊兒了，語法上也就要求把它們合二爲一了。這就使得 4a 在表面上不僅與 3a 無别，而且與 2a 也相同了；所以"李白喝了"（或者"張三來了"）這樣的句子，都有是 2a 或 3a 或 4a 的可能。這是爲什麽"了"字顯得如此神秘的緣故，衹能靠語境或某些狀語（例如："早，已經；快，馬上"等）幫助區别了。

四、"有/了"(+Asp)與"了"(+Md)在複句中的互動

在複句中，這兩個語法成分的出現及其互動，也有許多值得注意的地方，試舉幾個例子説明如下：

4.1. 疑問句有一種所謂"A-not-A"的形式。在一般的情況下，這個公式當然没有什麽大問題；例如："李白喝（酒）不喝（酒）？"或"李白喝（酒）不喝？"，或者"李白喝不喝（酒）？"，或"李白喝（酒）不？"；在衹含情貌詞"有/了"的時候，也没有問題；例如"李白喝了（酒）没有？"（亦有作"李白有没有喝（酒）？"等形式者）；但在牽涉到語氣詞"了"時，情況就比較複雜了，因爲其正反兩面衹能是：一個含語氣詞"了"，另一個不含語氣詞"了"。例如："李白喝（酒）不喝（酒）了？"就衹能解讀爲"1a-not-3b"的形式，而非"3a-not-3b"的形式，因爲給這個問題的回答衹可能是"喝，還喝"，或"不喝了"。又如："張三來了没有？"也必須解讀爲"4a-not-2b"，因爲衹能回答説"（已經）來了"，或"（還）没來"。這都是語意使然，自然就影響到語法了；死守着"A-not-A"的公式是不妥當的。

4.2. 前文（見 3.4. 節）曾説到，單獨的 4b 式句子是不合邏輯的，但在加上時間詞以後，就可變爲合法句式了。我們現在可以嘗試着解釋其原因。時間詞可以分爲好幾種，一種標明一個時段（duration，例如"三天"），另一種衹指明起點（starting point，例如"（從）上個月起"）。這兩種形式都能使 4b 式的句子合法（其他形式與此處的討論無涉，姑不論）。

4.2.1. 像"李白三天没喝（酒）了"這樣的句子，要瞭解其結構，必須先"擺脱印歐語的眼光"，即不可把"三天"這樣的時段詞直覺地看作"時間副詞"，而

要考慮到“漢語句式的特色”,認識到“三天”在語法結構上有可能是一個謂語,代表一個没有主語的輔助句。説“三天”是一個謂語,也許有人會覺得不可思議,但考慮到漢語句式的特色,這是毫不足怪的。這個例子的詞序可以改爲“李白没喝(酒)三天了”,其含意與原句相同,衹是更凸顯出“三天”的謂語性及其與“了”字的關係,其結構與古文句“不食三日矣”(《左傳·宣公二年》)完全相同,足見“了”所代表的語意概念是以“三天”爲依據的,也就是説,“了”在上例中與“没”不屬於同一個小句,所以我們可以推論説,這是時段詞能使貌似4b類的句子合法的緣故;實際上,這樣的句子所包涵的不是真正的4b類句子,而是2b類句子。

4.2.2. 表示起點的時間詞也能使貌似4b的句子合法,例如:“李白五十以後就没喝(酒)了”。這類句子通常都帶有“就”字,而“就”字與古文的“則”字相似,含有連詞性,標示其前爲一輔助句,試比較“我明天來”與“我明天就來”,就可感覺到後者意爲“我一到明天就來”;更值得注意的是,起點詞都隱含着某種動詞性的所謂“介詞”,如“從、自”等,而且以過去時間爲起點的時間詞,都隱指“直到現在(説話時)”(以將來時間爲起點的時間詞,顯然不可能與4b式的句子結合);這都證明,含起點時間詞的4b句不是一個單句,而是複句,“了”不是與“没喝(酒)”直接發生關係的,而是通過“就”與整個複句發生關係的。

4.2.3. 在4b式句子的“没”與述語之間,如果插入“再”字,也可以使之變爲合法句,例如:“李白没再喝(酒)了”;這樣的句子顯然有“預設”(presupposition),即先認定前此發生過的某一事件已先“終止”,而後指出其是否再度“發生”;這正是“再”的性質與功能(另見文專論);如果説話人覺得,某事的再或不再或没再發生,是一種“新情況”,自然就會在句末加上“了”。在前兩節所舉的例句中,也都可以在其“没”字與述語之間插入“再”字;這就增强了語氣,但就語法説,由於有了時間詞,“再”字就可有可無了。(如果有人認爲獨立的“李白没喝(酒)了”也是合法的句子,那也可以説是省略“再”字的結果。)

五、“了”字句解讀舉例

把上文所作的解析應用在實例上,更可以清楚地看出“了”字句的複雜性。

試以趙元任先生所列舉的七種"句末'了'"的含義爲例(Chao 1968. pp. 798—800),分析其深層的語法結構如下(借用吕叔湘先生的譯文,吕 1979,pp. 354—356;例句編號爲本文作者所加)。

P2 了

(1) 表示事情開始:(a)"糟了!"(b)"下雨了!"或者是一種新出現的情况……這種新情况可能等於已經達到了某一數量或程度,如(c)"哎呀,十一點半了!",(d)"你今年四十歲了,都!"。用在形容詞之後,可以含有過度的意思:(e)"湯鹹了",(f)"這鞋小了",(g)"你寫重(chong)了"。

這些例句都是表達"新情况"的。"了"前若爲名詞性的謂語,如(c)(d),或爲形容詞性的謂語,如(a)(e)(f),這個"了"字可以説是個單純的[+Md];但其前若爲動詞性的謂語,就很可能有歧義,例如(b)就可能有兩種含義,一爲"(要)下雨了!",這是單純的Ⅲa式句子,另一爲"(已經開始)下雨了!",這就是涉附屬條件(見3.5節)而簡化了的Ⅳa式句子了。(g)的謂語是一個所謂"動補結構"詞;我曾一再指出,所謂"動補"實爲"狀述"(薛 1989、1997),所以此處的"重"實爲"使動動詞",與(a)(e)(f)中的形容詞作謂語不同,因此"寫重"後面的"了"可以是[+Md](例如"(别)寫重了!"衹能是個Ⅲa式的句子),也可能是[+Md]與[+Asp]的複合體(例如"(又)寫重了!"顯然是個Ⅳa式的句子)。

(2) 適應新的情况的命令:

(a) 吃飯了! (b) 請了! (c) 咱們坐了!

這三例中的"了"當然都代表[+Md],因爲説者衹是敦促聽者作某種行動,而該行動尚未發生,故不涉及[+Asp],所以這三例都是Ⅲa式的句子。但在不同的語境裏,這些句子也可能是Ⅳa式的句子,例如説到請了些什麽人,就可以説"(張三)請了!(李四還没請呢!)"。

(3) 情節的一個進展[也是一種新情况]:

(a) 後來天就晴了。(b) 那房子就塌了。(c) 他就説了:……

例(a)的"晴"與例(b)的"塌"有點兒像是形容詞,但其實還是動詞,這可由這兩句話的否定式看出來;我們衹能説"後來天没晴",不能説"*後來天不晴了”,衹能説“那房子没塌”,不能説“*那房子不塌了”。(此處所謂的“不能説”,是因爲這幾個例子説的都是過去發生的事情;其實這也衹是相對而言,在特定的語境裏,這類句子還是可以説的。)這與(1)類中的例(e)和例(f)不同;那兩句話的否定式可以是“湯不鹹了”(因爲加了水),以及“這鞋不小了”(因爲楦過);所以本節的(a)與(b)都是簡化後的Ⅳa式句子。例(c)則有點兒特殊;趙先生在“説了”之後加上引號,其意當爲“他説了下述的話”,但我覺得句末“了”([+Md])似乎不能出現於直接引語之前;恐怕連後綴“了”([+Asp])也不能;例如像“? 他就説了:你不懂”這樣的句子,即使可以接受,其中的“了”也衹能是後綴“了”,而“你不懂”也必須是一個間接引語,即以一個整體作爲“説”的賓語,例如:“他就説了你不懂,没説别的”。

(4) 過去的一個孤立的事實:

(a)我昨兒到張家吃飯了。(b)那天我也去聽了。

(c)是的,昨天他真的哭了。

三個句子説的都是過去發生的事件,自然都含有[+Asp],所以都是簡化後的Ⅳa式句子,即“了”同時代表[+Asp]和[+Md](參看3.5節);因此這些句子的否定式就衹能是“没(有)VP”,而不是“不 VP 了”。説這些事件是“孤立的”,也許不太恰當,因爲“了”([+Md]所代表的“新情況”是相對於“舊情況”而言的。

(5) 截至現在爲止已經完成的動作:

(a) 我回來了。(b) 我今兒早晨寫了三封信。(c) 我教書教了四十年了。(下略)

由(b)和(c)兩例,可以清楚地看出[+Asp]和[+Md]的分工互動;這是最明顯的Ⅳa式句子。例(a)雖然衹有一個“了”,但既然説的是“已經完成”的事,就説明也是Ⅳa型的句子,衹是經過簡化而已,與單純的Ⅲa型句子(例如:“我(要)回來了”)不同。

(6) 用在後果小句裏表示一種情況:

(a) 那我就不走了。(b) 你一摁門鈴兒,他就來開門了。

條件或其他從屬小句裏邊也會有一個“了”。它跟句末的助詞“了”的不同,可以從句中位置辨别:(下略),(也)可以從方言裏看出來:(下略)。

例(a)中的"了"顯然是單純的句末"了",否則就不能用"不"爲否定詞,所以這是一個Ⅲa型的句子。例(b)的"了"也是一個句末"了",但這句話究竟是單純的Ⅲa型句字,還是省略了後綴"了"的Ⅳa型句子(參看3.5節),就得看語境了。如果説者是向"你"保證"你"不會吃閉門羹,那就是前者,如果是向"你"保證"你"未遭怠慢,那就是後者。至於從屬小句裏的"了"是什麽? 趙先生舉了好些例子,包括上海話及廣州話的例子,説明後綴"了"與句末"了"不同。那些例子當然都是正確的,但可能會造成一個錯誤的印象,讓人以爲他説從屬小句裏的"了"不可能是句末"了"。我猜想這大概不是他的意思,因爲句末"了"也可以出現在從屬小句裏;例如甲乙兩人約定同往某地,後來甲决定不去了,乙就可能説:"(既然)你不去了,我也不去了。"句中的兩個"了"都是句末"了",所以都用"不"爲否定詞。

(7) 表示顯而易見:

(a) 這個你當然懂了。(b) 再好沒有了。

這個用法的"了"有時候説成"咯"。

兩例中的"了"當然是單純的句末"了",構成IIIa式句子。兩句所説的"新情況"都是説者一厢情願的設想,因此不涉及[+Asp]。例(b)中的"有"是動詞,不是[+Asp],所以"沒有"之後才會出現句末"了"。

六、結語

語法詞"了"字之所以難解,一方面是由於一字兩用,既代表語法成分[+Asp],又代表語法成分[+Md],而在代表[+Asp]時,却又有一個變體"有"字;另一方面是由於這兩個語法成分之間的相互牽制與糾纏,造成了許多貌合神離的歧義句,讓人弄不清楚"了"字到底代表什麽意思。本文的分析,也許可以説,大致上把這個語法詞的性質及功能交代清楚了;與之相關的問題當然還很多,需要更深入的研究,非本文之所能盡;在此衹能再略舉幾條,作爲上文的補充。

6.1. 説"了"[+Md]是一個句末語氣詞,衹是一個簡便的説法,實則這個詞與句子的内部結構密不可分,是與其他句末語氣詞,諸如"啊、嗎、呢、嘔"等,大不相同的,所以必須出現在那些語氣詞之前,但常與之結合,諸如"啦、啰、嘍"等,那是語音的問題。

6.2. 表示"經歷"的情貌詞"過",與表示"發生"的情貌詞"有/了"關係密切;"過"祇能在含"有/了"的句子中出現,這是淺顯的語意道理,自然也就是語法的要求。這在否定句中可以很清楚地看出來,例如:"他没(有)見過鬼";但在肯定句中,却得省掉"了"字,因此祇能説"他見過鬼",不能説"*他見了過鬼"。當然可以説"他見過鬼了",但這個"了"是句末語氣詞[+Md]。也可以説"他見過了鬼",但這是一個 2a 式輔助句(例如:"他見過了小鬼,然後才去見閻王"),其中的"了"字確實是情貌詞[+Asp],但正如"吃過了飯",其中的"過"字是所謂"動補結構"中的"補語"(姑從俗稱),不是我們此處所討論的表"經歷"的"過"。

6.3. 在解讀古文時,我們常説"矣"字相當於白話文的"了";這基本上是正確的,但失諸籠統;與"矣"相當的祇能是那個代表語氣詞的"了",與那個代表情貌詞的"了"無關。

6.4. 要認清"了"字到底代表哪一個語法成分,除了根據語境判斷以外,某些助動詞及副詞也能給我們很多幫助。例如,表示"可能發生"的助動詞,諸如"要、能、會、可以"等,語意上是與作情貌詞的"了"字不兼容的,所以像"他會走了"句中的"了"字,就祇能是作語氣詞的"了"。另一方面,表示"情況如舊或如預料"的副詞,如"才、還"等(見另文專論),則與作語氣詞的"了"不兼容,所以像"才走了一忽兒"句中的"了",就祇能是作情貌詞的"了"。

A Note on the Grammatical Function of Gei **

The review article on Li and Thompson's Mandarin Chinese by Zhang Zhanyi（1983）raises several interesting questions. I would like to comment on one of them，namely，the usages of gěi 給. Basically，I agree with Zhang when he says that the sentence wǒ sòng-le yì-běn shū gěi tā and the sentence wǒ gěi tā sòng-le yì-běn shū，contrary to Li and Thompson's claim（1981：387，'I gave him/her a book'），do not mean the same thing. Zhang merely translated them in different ways to show that they indeed do not mean the same（Zhang 1983：106）without trying to explain why they do not mean the same. I think the semantic difference can be explained in terms of syntactic difference. Reversely，no syntactic analysis can be said to be correct unless it can properly account for the semantic interpretation. The two sentences can possibly share the same meaning，but only under one specific and limited condition. The semantic difference between the two sentences will become evident，if we add something to them like the following：

S_1）Wǒ gěi nǐ sòng-le yì-běn shū gěi tā.

'I gave a book to him for you.'

S_2）Wǒ gěi tā sòng-le yì-běn shū gěi nǐ.

'I gave a book to you for him'

The gěi nǐ phrase can be omitted in both sentences（i. e.，syntactically unspecified），but that does not change their respective syntactic structure and semantic interpretation. Without the phrase gěi nǐ，S_1 would mean '（For somebody）I gave a book to him，' and S_2 would mean '（To somebody）I gave

---

** 中文題爲《"給"字的語法功能》，原刊美國《中文教師學會學报》(JCLTA)1983 年第 18 卷第 3 期。

a book for him.' The 'somebody' can, of course, be anybody, including 'myself' (wǒ zì jǐ, the giver). S_2 can possibly mean the same as S_1 only when their unspecified but implied 'somebody' has a co-referential relationship with the tā in their gěi tā phrase.

Apparently, gěi is a very troublesome word. Misunderstanding/misinterpretation is thus not surprising. If anyone has any doubt about its complexity, he needs only be referred to Professor Zhu Dexi's two articles which appear in Fangyan (No. 2, 1979, pp. 81-87) and Zhongguo Yuwen (No. 3, 1983, pp. 161-66). While I find zhu's articles very fascinating and inspiring, I also feel they are too technical for pedagogical purpose. (Just imagine what would happen, it we try to teach our first-year students how to use gěi by summarizing the articles to them! But to be fair, we must remember pedagogical need is probably not Zhu's concern) As a teacher, I am more concerned with how to transmit to our student, in the most straightforward way, the essential meanings and usages of this 'word'. I would like to share my own approach with my colleagues, and would like to hear theirs.

Quite obviously, gěi must be syntactically defined as two words, the co-verb (preposition) gěi and the main verb gěi, though they may be etymologically and semantically related. As a co-verb, gěi always occurs before the main verb of the sentence (gěi + N + VP) and it may indicate either of the two following meanings.

a) As a marker of the agent in a sentence of the so-called 'passive voice' in colloquial style. For example:

   Wǒ gěi (rén) piàn-le.

   'I was cheated (by somebody).'

b) As a marker of the benefactor. For example:

   wǒ gěi tā mǎi-le yì-běn shū.

   'I bought a book for him.'

Generally, it is quite easy to determine whether the co-verb gěi means

(a) or (b), but in some marginal cases, ambiguity may arise. For example:

wǒ gěi tā piàn-le liǎng- wàn-kuài qián.

'I was cheated of $20,000 by him.' or

'I got $20,000 through cheating for him.'

As the main verb of a sentence, gěi 'to give' may be the only verb in a sentence as in (c), or the last verb in a sentence, after other 'verb(s)' or 'verb phrase(s)' as in (d) and (e).

(c) Tā gěi wǒ liǎng-wàn-kuài qián.

'He gave me $20,000.'

(d) Tā qiǎng gěi wǒ liǎng-wàn-kuài qián.

'He gave me $20,000 by robbing it (from somebody).'

(e) Tā qiǎng-le liǎng-wàn-kuài qián gěi wǒ.

'He gave me $20,000 after having robbed it (from somebody).'

This interpretation of gěi as the main verb (indeed the only real verb) of the sentence is in line with two general principles in Chinese syntax. First, lexical items in Chinese are not marked as to 'form class' (or 'parts of speech'). They are so flexible that their syntactic role can mostly be defined only within a syntactic structure. There is, therefore, nothing unusual for a 'verb' (i.e., a lexeme which in common sense denotes an action) to function syntactically as an adverb, like qiǎng in above. Second, 'word order' is the most important syntactic feature in Chinese syntax, and the general rule is that modifiers always precede the modified. The 'verbs' before gěi are thus actually adverbial modifiers specifying the manner of giving or tsansferring. Practially, all 'verbs' can occur adverbially before the verb gěi, if only a conceivable situation, no matter how far-fetched, permits that. For example:

Wèn 'ask,'

wǒ yě bù zhī dào; děng yìhuír wǒ wèn gěi nǐ.

'I don't know that either; I'll get it for you by asking somebody after a little while.'

Xué 'imitate, repeat,'

Bǎ Zhāngsānde huà xué gěi Lǐsì.

'Give to Lisi what Zhangsan said by repeating him.'

tōu 'steal.'

Tōu gěi wǒ liǎng-wàn-kuài qián.

'Give me $20,000 by stealing it (from somewhere).'

Of course, 'verbs' that occur most often as adverbs before the verb gěi are those which have a built-in semantic component of 'giving, transferring' such as sòng 'send, present,' mài 'sell,' huán 'return', shǎng 'reward,' etc. ('v' in Zhu's classification). Because of this built-in semantic of 'giving/transferring' without the help of the word gěi, though it is perfectly alright to add gěi after them, without any change in meaning.

REFERENCES

Chao, Yuen Ren. 1968. *A Grammar of Spoken Chinese*, Berkeley.

Chappell, Hilary. 1982. 'A Semantic Solution to Syntactic Constructions with Gěi,' paper presented at *the 15th International Conference on Sino-Tibetan Language and Linguistics*, Peking.

Li, Charles N. and Sandra A. Thompson. 1981. *Mandarin Chinese: A Function Reference Grammar*, Berkeley.

Paris, Marie-Claude. 1982. 'Gěi in Mandarin Chinese', *paper presented at the ACTFL-CLTA annual meeting*, New York.

Zhang, Zhanyi. 1983. 'Review on Li and Thompson's Mandarin Chinese' in *JCLTA*, Vol. XVIII, No. 2, pp. 93-107.

Zhu, Dexi. 1979. 'yǔ Dòngcí Gěi xiāngguānde jùfǎ wèntí, (Syntactic problems Related to the verb Gěi), in *Fangyan*, No. 2, pp. 81-87.

Zhu, Dexi. 1983. 'Bāohán Dòngcí Gěi de Fùzá jùshì, (Complex sentences containing the verb Gěi), in *Zhongguo Yuwen*, No. 3, pp. 161-66.

The Chinese Numerical System and Its Implications**

0. In studying a foreign language which is drastically different from one's own native tongue, both in a linguistic and in a cultural sense, one of the most difficult problems is the numerical system of the target language. Normally it is by no means a matter of unsurmountable complexity of the foreign numerical system that bars us from acquiring a native-like competence in our handling of it. The difficulty arises rather from the preconcept about numerals which has been planted in our mind since our childhood. The problem is then mainly how to "think" in the new system, somewhat comparable to the difficulty one will encounter when one tries to transfer from the Anglo-Saxon measurement to the metrical system. Many Chinese students of English (this author included), even after decades of studying and using the language, still have difficulty in handling large numerical figures in normal conversations. Very often they have to stop a speaker and ask him to repeat a large figure slowly while they do some silent mental translation. Those of us who have had some experience in teaching Chinese to American students certainly remember how difficult it seems to be for our students to master the Chinese numerical system, even though it is, when compared with that of the European languages, almost ridiculously simple, as we shall see in later discussion (see Sections 1.1 and 1.2).

In this short paper, I am going to try to show the simplicity of the Chinese numerical system and its contrastive aspects with the English system by a

** 中文題爲《漢語的數字系統及其啓示》,原刊美國《中文教師学會学報》(JCLTA)1974 年第 9 卷第 3 期。

notion which I shall label "psychological maximum sum." It is my hope that this notion will help us understand some of the problems arising from the use of numerals in literary or figurative expressions. I shall also try to show how the proper usages of the two "twos"（èr 二 and lyǎng 兩）in modern Chinese can be unequivocally stated when we adopt this notion as a base for specification.

1. In each language or group of languages with the same cultural background, there is often a large unit of number which seems to be the maximum in a psychological sense. There are, of course, larger numbers than this in a mathematical sense, but larger numbers are merely multiples of this unit and bigger units of number are nothing but the self-multiplications of this base unit. This unit is what I have called the "psychological maximum sum." Take English（or any other European language）as an example, such a "maximum sum" is obviously the number "thousand." Any number above this unit will have to be rendered in this language as a certain number of this base unit, or the self-multiplications of this base unit such as millions, billions, trillions, etc. The practice of pointing off a large sum into groups of three digits from right to left is only a direct and logical reflection of this fact in the language. Chinese, on the other hand, is different. Its "psychological maximum sum" is not chyān 千 "thousand" but wàn 萬 "ten-thousand." This fact has been somewhat vaguely recognized for some time, though not its full implications. For example. M. Gardner Tewksbury wrote years ago in his Speak Chinese[①]:

> The next units above the chyān（1,000）group are not millions and billions as in English, but wàn（10, 000）and wànwàn（100, 000, 000）. This makes the transfer of larger sums into Chinese quite difficult for the Westerner. One way to make this transfer is to point off these higher sums into groups of four digits, rather than the familiar three.

① M. Gardner Tewksbury: Speak Chinese, New Haven, 1948, p. 29. Cf. also Y. R. Chao: A Grammar of Spoken Chinese, Berkeley, 1968, pp. 573 - 374. It may be noted here that the romanizations in this paper are of the Yale system.

Actually, the way Mr. Tewksbury suggested for the transfer is not just one way to do it; it is really the only way to do it. We may add here a very large sum as an illustration to show that larger units above wàn such as yì 億 (100,000,000) and jàu 兆 (1,000, 000,000,000) are merely the self-multiplications of the base unit wàn①:

3,132, 213,221,322 would be in the Chinese way

3,1322,1322,1322 (verbally sān jàu, yì-chyān sān-bǎi èr-shŕ èr yì, yì-chyān sān-bǎi èr-shŕ èr wàn, yì-chyān sān-bǎi èr-shŕ èr).

It is quite clear that wàn in Chinese performs the same psychological function as "thousand" does in English. However. this simple fact of the language is often overlooked even by the Chinese themselves. We often find large sums in Chinese writings marked off into groups of three digits, clearly a blind acceptance of European practice②.

1.1. The Chinese numerical system is probably the simplest of all. The principle of decimal numeration is strictly and precisely reflected in the language. After the establishment of four basic positional terms for powers of ten, gè 個 "one,"③ shŕ 十 "tens," bǎi 百 "hundreds," and chyān 千 "thousands," the language requires that all numbers must be verbally stated

---

① Both yì and jàu have two different definitions. In their narrow sense, yì is said to be ten wàn (10, 0000) and jàu is ten yì(i.e., a hundred wàn: 100,0000), but in their broad sense, yì means wànwàn (1,0000, 0000) while jàu means or wàn-yì or wànwànwàn(1,0000,0000,0000). I have adopted their broad definitions, because they have been so standardized in modern spoken Chinese when they do occur, though rarely. For the definitions of these terms and those of even higher order, see Tsź-hǎi 辭海 and Chao. op. cit., p. 573.

② According to Dr. Y. R. Chao (op. cit., p. 573), large figures were once indeed marked off by fours in Chinese writing, but foreign influence has changed that. However, as we can see now, the foreign influence, even with official blessings, has had no effect whatsoever on the Chinese system, perhaps because it is an intrinsic part of the spoken language.

③ Strictly speaking, we cannot count gè as a numerical positional term. It is actually a general measure word which is not an essential part of a pure number. Here I am simply following the general practice of the Chinese schoolteachers in using it as a label for the "ones" position.

strictly in accordance with these positional terms. For example, 1234 must be yì-chyān èr-bǎi sān-shŕ sż (-gè). Numbers above the "thousand" will be a repetition of these terms with gè replaced by wàn or its self-multiplications such as yì and jàu. Not only is such an expression as "quatre-vingt-sept," which finds its way into English in the form of "four score and seven," absolutely impossible in Chinese (it must be bā-shŕ chī 八十七), but terms like "eleven" and "twenty-five hundred" are not found in Chinese, either. They have to be respectively (yì-)shŕ yì① and èr-chyān wǔ-bǎi.

1.2. There are seemingly a few exceptions to the rule just stated. They can be listed and explained as follows.

a) A logical corrollary of the strict rule given above is that once a certain positional term has been mentioned, the following positional term will be predictable and, therefore, does not have to be mentioned, if a speaker wants to save his breath. Thus, yì-chyān wǔ-bǎi "1500" can be shortened to yì-chyān wǔ and yì-chyān wǔ-bǎi lyòu-shŕ "1560" may be simply yì-chyān wǔ-bǎi lyòu.

b) When a position or several consecutive positions in a group of four digits (pointed off in the Chinese way) except the last position are filled with zeroes, the gap filler líng 零 will be used, if the following position is filled with a non-zero digit, e. g., 305 is sān-bǎi líng wǔ, and 4,0006 is sż-wàn líng lyòu. If two zeroes in a group of four digits are separated and both are followed by non-zero digits, verbally only the second one must be mentioned as líng, while the zero or zeroes not followed by a non-zero digit will not be mentioned②; for

① For the reason why yī before shŕ is parenthesized, see 1.2c.

② The term líng with its basic meaning of "dripping of raindrops" implies that what follows it is only a fragment to the round figure that precedes it. This explains why any figure following líng will be automatically taken to be of the lowest rank, namely, in the ones position, unless a higher positional term is specifically added. For example, sān-wàn líng èr can only mean 3,0002. while 3,0020 must be sān-wàn líng èr-shŕ. For the same reason, only one líng is needed, no matter how many consecutive intermediate zeroes there may be. This is why the practice of repeating líng as many times as there are zeroes never had a chance to stick (cf. Chao, op. cit., P. 575).

example, 300, 0604, 0870 is verbally sān-bǎi yì (líng) lyòu-bǎi líng sż wàn líng bā-bǎi chī-shŕ.

c) In ordinary speech, if the tens position in a group of four digits (pointed off in the Chinese way) is filled by "one" while the hundreds position is occupied by zero or by boundary marker, the yī for the tens position is generally omitted, though it can be retained. Thus, ten, eleven, twelve, etc. are verbally shŕ, shŕ yī, shŕ èr, etc. respectively, instead of (yī-shŕ, yī-shŕ yī, yī-shŕ èr etc., though the latter forms are also acceptable. Similarly, 10, 0013, 1019 will be shŕ yì líng shŕ sān wàn yì chyān líng shŕ jyǒu. This is seemingly a violation to the general rule stated in Section 1.1, but actually it is not. Syntactically, numerical positional terms form in modern Chinese a special subclass within the form-class which has been generally labeled measure words①. As a general rule, a measure word must be preceded by a numeral②, but if the numeral happens to be yī "one" and the measure word is a numerical positional terms, the yī can be optionally omitted. So bǎi wǔ-shŕ means yì-bǎi wǔ-shŕ "150" and wàn sān-chyān is to be understood as yí-wàn sān-chyān "1, 3000." Consequently, yī-shŕ, yī-shŕ yī, yī-shŕ èr etc. can be simply shŕ, shŕ yī, shŕ èr etc.. The only difference between shŕ and other positional terms is that for the former the short form is favored, while for the latter the long form is preferred.

---

① Many scholars, though accepting numerical positional terms as measure words, do not treat them as a special kind exclusively. For example, Chao treats shŕ, bǎi, chyān, etc., together with dwèi and shwāng "pair," as "group measure." while differentiating their "determinative" function from their "measures" function (op. cit., pp. 595 - S96). I personally feel it is perhaps syntactically justifiable to treat them as a special subclass of measure words, because among all the measure words only they can occur between a numeral and another measure word. This treatment also makes it possible for me to make such a simple statement as the one in 2.2c.

② This is obviously a very strict way to put it. It presupposes that jè běn shū is a shortened form for jè yì-běn shū "this book," and hē bēi chá is derived from hē yì-bēi chá "have a cup of tea." Cf. Chao, op. cit., p. 554 and p. 565.

2. The Chinese numerical system, as described above naturally has implications in the spoken language. Two may be discussed in the following.

2.1. Since the "psychological maximum sum" in Chinese is wàn, the term occurs frequently in both speech and writing in the sense of "a very large countless number." just as the word "thousand" is often used in English. Consequently, in literary and figurative speeches, the Chinese word wàn should be equated with the English word "thousand." regardless of their difference in the mathematical sense. Thus the English phrase "hundreds and thousands" (of things or people). when translated into Chinese, should be upgraded to chyān-chyān wàn-wàn de 千千萬萬的, or chéng-chyān chéng-wàn de 成千成萬的, and vice versa. In order to achieve the desired psychoiogical effect, it will be only proper to translate the two lines chyān shān nyǎu fēi jywé 千山鳥飛絶, wàn jìng rén dzūng myè 萬徑人蹤滅 in Lyǒus Dzūng-ywán's (柳宗元) famous poem as "Over the hundred hills, no trail of a flying bird; Along the thousand paths, no trace of a moving soul;" instead of a so-called literal or word-by-word translation, as many translators often do to show "how the Chinese say it." More often than not, a literal translation is only misleading. The notion of "psychological maximum sum" also helps explain why the word wàn appears so frequently in Chinese as, may be exemplified by such expressions as wà-yī 萬一 "by any chance," chyān-wàn 千萬 "by all means," wàn-swèi 萬歲 "long life," wàn-chwán 萬全 "perfect," etc.

2.2. The puzzling question of how to use the two "two's" in modern colloquial Chinese can also be better answered with the notion of "psychological maximum sum." though this must be supplemented by another notion, the use of measure words. Simply stated, the concept (or sememe) "two" in modern Chinese (Pekingese in particular) can be represented either by èr or lyǎng. However, the two terms are not in free variation, nor are they in clearly defined complementary distribution. The grammar of the language requires that in some cases one or the other must be specifically used while in other cases either may occur. How to define these cases has been quite a challenge to scholars of the language①. Without bothering about the morphemic status of these two terms②, I shall try to specify here the ways they are used in the language.

a) The problem we have now does not exist m Classical Chinese where lyǎng means "a pair" and èr means "two." But many compounds and idiomatic expressions made with two terms in their classical sense appear frequently in Modern Chinese. The èr and lyǎng in such expressions as tyān wú èr r̀, mín wú èr jǔ, 天無二日，民無二主 "There are not two suns in the sky. (and so) there cannot be two masters for the people." and yì dāu lyǎng duàn 一刀兩斷 "cut into two with one stroke: resolute separation." are idiomatic and have to be memorized as such③.

b) The term lyǎng is inherently to be used only in a quantitative sense, that is, when two objects (persons or things) are involved simultaneously and collectively. This means that when we count one by one, and when we give a

① In addition to all the textbooks on Mandarin Chinese where a discussion on this problem is always included, the following special treatments can be given here as examples: Chao, op. cit., pp. 568 - 571; Eugene Ching: "The Difference between Two and Two in Mandarin Chinese," Papers of the CIC Far Eastern Language Institute 1966 and 1967, Ann Arbor, 1968, pp. 57 - 76; Shen Sha: "èr he lyǎng de yùngfā yánjyōu." Jūngguó Yǔwén Ywèkān, Vol. 17, No. 1 (July, 1965), pp. 35 - 38; and Earl Wieman: "Quantitative Expressions in Mandarin Chinese." Journal of the Chinese Language Teacher Association. Voo. VIII, No. 3 (Nov., 1973), pp. 150 - 166 (discussion of èr and lyǎng on p. 153).

② Some people have argued that èr and lyǎng may be treated as two allomorphs of a single morpheme; see, for example. Section 10 in Charles F. Hockett's "Problems of Morphemic Analysis." Language 23 (1947), pp. 321 - 343. Though it is not my intention to determine the morphemic status of these two terms, the way I define their usages seems to lend some support to Hockett's argument.

③ For some more examples, see Ching, op. cit., p. 61 and p. 65.

number in the telephone style, the "two" there can only be èr①. It also means that in any ordinal number, if "two" is the only figure there, or happens to be the last digit, it also must be èr. Thus, we have the following expressions with èr which cannot be replaced by lyǎng: dì ér 第二"No. 2," ér ywè 二月"the second month: February," syīng chī ér 星期二"weekday No. 2: Tuesday." ér jyě 二姐"second elder sister." wǔ-bǎi yì-shŕ ér hàu 五百一十二號"No. 512," etc.. However, when a cardinal number of multiple digits is turned into an ordinal number, the "two" that occupies the hundreds position or above can be either ér or lyǎng, following the specifications to be given in (e). For example, No. 2200 can be lyǎng-chyān lyǎng-bǎi hàu 兩千兩百號 èr-chyān èr-bǎi hàu 二千二百號 etc.

c) Closely related to the quantitative sense of the term lyǎng is the fact that it can only occur with a measure word②. With the exception of the subclass of measure words which consists of numerical positional terms, when "two" alone appears before any measure word (#2-M#). lyǎng is always used to represent it. unless the measure word happens to be lyǎng 兩 "ounce" a homophone but a completely unrelated word③. Thus, in the following examples, èr and lyǎng are not interchangeable: lyǎng-běn (shū) 兩本(書) "two (books)," lyǎng-bēi (shwěi) 兩杯(水) "two cups of (of waters)," but

① We are here concerned, of course, only with normal colloquial Chinese, but It has been reported that, as an effort to avoid possible difficulties in communication, a set of noise-resistant forms in which two is always represented by lyǎng have been in use, especially by the military people (cf. Chao, op. cit., p. 567).

② This is apparently a very strong way to put it, for there are a few cases where lyǎng does not occur immediately before a measure word. e. g., lyǎng-sān-ge "two or three." and sān-sān lyǎng-lyǎng de "in two's and three's." I take these examples as cases in which the measure word after lyǎng has been deleted.

③ The statement that before a measure word lyǎng is always used may seem to be too strong. By saying this, it is implied here that terms like èr-jīn yán "two catties of salt." èr-chéng "two tenths," and èr-máu wǔ "two dimes and five (cents)" (see Chao, op. cit., p. 569), though occurring in speech, are not typical modern colloquial forms but rather expressions formed under literary influence.

èr-lyǎng (jīndz) 二两(金子)“two ounces of gold.”

d) When “two” is not followed by a measure word (including positional terms), it must always be èr. Thus, #502# must be wǔ-bǎi líng èr, and the abbreviated way of saying yí-wàn lyǎng-chyān “12000” (see 1.2a) can only be yí-wàn èr.

e) The concept of “psychological maximum sum” is very crucial in defining the usages of èr and lyǎng in large sums. Suppose we have the following number pointed off into groups of four digits in the Chinese way. #2, 2022, 2202, 2222#, several rules governing the choice of èr and lyǎng can be put down:

i. The “two” that occupies the tens position in any group of four digits must always be èr.

ii. The “two” occupying the ones position (including wàn, yì, jàu, etc.) must always be èr, unless it is preceded by zero in the tens position or by boundary marker. In these two exceptional cases, it can be either èr or lyǎng, if it is followed by a measure word(including positional terms).

iii. The “two” that appears in the hundreds or the thousands position in any group of four can be either èr or lyǎng optionally.

Consequently, the above example can be rendered verbally as:

{lyǎng / èr} jàu {lyǎng / èr} chyān líng èr-shŕ èr yì {lyǎng / èr} chyān {lyǎng / èr} bǎi líng {lyǎng / èr} wàn {lyǎng / èr} chyān {lyǎng / èr} bǎi èr-shŕ èr(ge).

The Role of Semantics in Teaching Syntax: Some Examples from Mandarin Chinese** ①

1. This paper aims at drawing some attention to a simple but fundamental concept, namely, as far as pedagogical need is concerned, elaborate syntactic specification may not be as effective (and hence as useful), as well-focused(or at least fairly close)semantic definition. I will try to illustrate this point with some examples drawn my own experience in teaching Mandarin Chinese.

2. The above suggestion might possibly cause some misunderstanding which I would like to disperse. Some of our colleagues might think that I am trying to belittle pure syntactic Study, If so, I must violently deny it, I certainly agree that elaborate and precise syntactic specification is an essential part of both theoretical and applied linguistics, and should, therefore, be pursued vigorously. What I mean here is merely that, for practical teaching, we should perhaps pay some more attention than we did before to the semantic definition of grammatical particles. The reason is very simple. In a classroom, we are dealing with a group of intelligent human beings who, nevertheless, may be very naive about linguistic theories. They are used to thinking in terms of 'meaning,' and often feel overwhelmed by logical but dry abstractions of the underlying system of syntactic structure.

** 中文題爲《語義學在句法教學中的作用:普通話的幾個例子》,原刊美國《中文教師学會学報》(JCLTA)1982 年第 17 卷第 1 期。

① In addition to the more traditional studies on this subject, we have wang 1965, Teng 1973, and Lu 1975, It may be noted here that my interpretation is not exactly the same as theirs. For example, Wang discusses the verb *-le* (Asp) only, and indentifies yǒu-guo as a single morpheme, while Teng regard s yǒu as a 'higher verb.'

Moreover, syntactic specification, no matter how precise, is no substitute for accurate semantic definition. For beginning students, the opposite may be closer to the truth; that is, through deliberate and careful definition, they may gradually and more easily grasp the subtlety of syntactic constraints.

3. I shall try to give support to the above claim by redefining three different sets of grammatical terms in Mandarin Chinese. They are grouped together because they are related in 'meaning,' at least in English translation.

3.1. The confusing *le*（了）

One of the most perplexing questions to the students of the Chinese language is how to correctly interpret and use the particle *le* This issue has drawn a great deal of attention from scholars①. Consequently, its basic meaning has become fairly clear. I have hardly anything semantically new to offer, except restating that there are actually two function words involved here. One is *an aspect marker of the verb (Asp)* which assumes the form of a post-verbial *le* in affirmative verb phrases but a pre-verbial *yǒu*（有）in negative verb phrases. Semantically, its inclusion indicates that the notion of occurrence is involved. The other is *a mood marker for the whole sentence (Md)* which Always occurs as *le* at the end of the sentence②. *Asp* indicates the actual or projected occurrence of an action represented by the verb it modifies, while Md indicates the speaker's mood in thinking that the situation described by the sentence represents a new phase of the affair. But how to convey these ideas to our students may be a serious problem. Like many

① To be more specific, we have to say that Md (sentence -*le*) occurs at the end of a sentence but before other sentence particles such as（啊，嗎，吧，呢，etc.）

② It may be interesting to note here that the classification of simple (or basic) Chinese sentences into the following four patterns on the basis of the two semantic elements, Asp and Md, is very much comparable to the classification of Chinese syllables into four types（開，齊，合，撮）in terms of the two phonological features, palatalization and labialization. Indeed, my interpretation of the particle *le* is directly inspired by my own phonological study (see Hsueh 1975: 26－30).

others, I once also composed a set of simplified transformational rules for this problem and tried them in class. I must admit it was a great failure. Most of the students seemed to be no less confused than they were before, if not more. I now feel that a 'semantic presentation' of this problem and its solution Maybe better for our students. First of all, we must make it absolutely clear to them that this problem has nothing to do with *tense*. (Indeed, we have to say that tense does not exist in Chinese syntax, though it is always present in English syntax.) Then, we can show them a table like the following, revealing a four-way contrast as a result of the inclusion or the exclusion of the two semantic elements, *Asp* and *Md*①.

	Affirmative		Negative
—Asp —Md Ia	Ta hē(jiú). 他喝(酒) 'He drank/drinks/will drink (wine).'	Ib	Ta bù hē (jiǔ). 他不喝(酒)。 He did/does/will not drink (wine).
+Asp —Md IIa	Ta hē le (jiǔ). ② 他 喝 了 (酒)。	IIb	Ta méi yǒu hē (jiǔ). 他 没 有 喝 (酒)。
—Asp +Md IIIa	Ta hē (jiǔ) le. 他 喝 (酒) 了。	IIIb	Ta bù hē (jiǔ) le. 他 不 喝 (酒) 了。
+Asp +Md IVa	Ta hē le (jiǔ) le 他 喝 了 (酒) 了。	IVb	* Ta méi yǒu hē (jiǔ) le. * 他 没 有 喝 (酒) 了。

① As to whether pattern IIa can form an independent sentence or merely an adverbial clause as a point of reference for the relatively later incident (e.g., 他喝了酒就罵人), there are still different opinions. Personally, I feel it cannot form an independent sentence unless its object is qualified by numeral and classifier (e.g., 三杯酒), though in publications from People's China we do find such expressions as(周總理在大會上講了話。)

② Naturally, we are talking about simple sentences here. In terms of generative grammar, we are claiming that, in the deep structure, *Neg*, *Asp*, and *Md* cannot altogether exist under the same node 's.' On the other hand, there do seem to exist some counterexamples to, this claim; for example: a) 他三天没喝了。b) 上個月起,他就没喝了。c) 我勸了他以後,他就没喝了。Note that all these examples contain a time expression which indicates a duration of time immediately before the time of the main clause. and all may have zài(再) added before their main verb hē without any change in meaning. I suspect that examples like these are possible because of the word *zài* which may be optionally deleted due to the time expression. In view of both its semantic nature and its syntactic distribution (see 3.2.4b and Note 8), *Zài* should perhaps be recognized as a special kind of anxiliary verb, rather than a mood marker. (Cf, 青春不再).

On the basisof the above table, we can easily specify the following syntactic constraints.

a) *Asp* and *Md* cannot both be present in a negative sentence①. If they did, it would be tantamount to saying that a new situation has been created by something that did not occur, an obvious contradiction. Therefore, pattern IIb by itself is ungrammatical.

b) In Pattern IVa where *Asp* and *Md* are separated by the object of the verb, the first *le* (*Asp*) can be optionally deleted. But if the two *le*'s are not separated, either because the object is transposed or because the verb happens to be intransitive, they must be condensed into one. Consequently, transformed Pattern IVa may on the surface look exactly like Pattern IIIa or even Pattern IIa. This is how ambiguity and confusion are created.

c) Auxiliary verbs indicating possible incidents(要、能、會、可以、etc.)are semantically incompatible with the aspect marker *le*. Therefore, in simple sentences which include an auxiliary verb of this kind and a *le*, the *le* can only be *Md*.

d) *Guo* (過), another aspect marker which indicates experience, presupposes the doing or non-doing of something. Therefore, it can occur only in sentences with Asp (i.e., Patterns IIA, IIB, IVa). It always occurs after the verb, and it replaces aspect marker *le*.

e) The *bù* that occurs immediately before *yǒu* must be replaced with *méi*. *Yǒu* then becomes optional.

3.2. *Zài*(再), *yòu*(又), and *hái*(還)——the different 'agains.'

In all dictionaries and textbooks, zài and yòu are defined as 'again,'

---

① In my thinking, guò is a homophonous form for two different morphemes. It can be a verb complement meaning, 'finish doing something' as in Chīguòle zǎofàn(吃過了早飯), or it can be an aspect marker meaning 'have the experience of doing something' as in chīguo shéròu (吃過蛇肉). Aspect guo replaces Asp-le, but Complement guò does not. Phonologically, complement guò is always stressed, but Aspect guo normally is not.

while *hái* is often defined as 'still,' but it can also be translated 'again,' as in the following sentences: *Nǐ hái lái ma*?(你還來嗎?)

Will you come again?' In what way or ways do they differ? They are all the so-called 'fixed adverbs' and behave quite similarly (but see 3.2.4.b). The answer, therefore, must be semantic in nature. In order to differentiate them, many people evoked the syntactic concept of *tense*. For example, M. G. Tewksbury(1948:98)defines *Zài* as 'again(in future)' and *yòu* as 'again (in part).' This definition is obviously not acceptable. As it has been pointed out (see 3.1), Chinese syntax does not include *tense*. More seriously for teaching, this will confuse our students to no end when they encounter sentences like thefollowing.

a) yòu yɑo xiɑ̀ yǔ le.

又 要 下 雨 了

'It's going to rain again.'

b) zuótiɑn tā jiɑ̀o wǒ zɑ̀i lɑ́i, jīntiān tā yòu jiɑ̀o wǒ bú yɑ̀o lɑ́i le.

昨天 他叫 我再來,今天 他又 叫 我 不要 來了。

'Yesterday he told me to come again, but today he told me not to come.'

These words, therefore, must be redefined. I hereby suggest that they be recognized as function words which purely represent mood. Their inclusion in a sentence indicates only the feeling (or 'mood') of their speaker, not that of the subject of the sentence. (Unless the subject and the speaker are identical.) Their semantic functions can be described as follows.

3.2.1. *Zài* indicates *the reactivation of an actual or projected action which is/was about to be, or has/had been, cancelled*. Its occurrence presupposes the *cancellation* of such an action in the thinking of the speaker. This definition can explain why native speakers feel the different occurrences of *Zài* in the following examples are semantically identical, that is, they represent the same morpheme.[①]

a) Zài jiàn!

再　見!

'(Our meeting is over, but I wish I may) see you again!'

b) Zài mǎi liǎng ge.

再　買　兩　個。

'(After having bought some,) buy two more.'

c) Děng yihuir Zài gàosù tā

等　一會兒再　告訴　他。

'(Not now;)let's tell him after a little while.'

d) Ta méi zài yào.

他　没再　要。

'(After the last time he asked,) he hasn't asked for it again.'

e) Wǒ míng tiān zài lái.

我　明　天　再來。

i) '(I have to leave now, but) I'll be back tomorrow.'

ii) '(I have to cancel my plan, but) I'll come tomorrow.'

f) Wǒ bù néng zài hē le.

我　不能　再喝了。

'(I've stopped;)I can't drink any more.'

g) Nǐ zài bù lái, wǒ jiù zǒu le.

你再不來,我就走了。

'If you still don't come, I'll be leaving.'

3.2.2. *Yòu* represents the aggravating effect on one incident after another in the feeling of the speaker. The incidents may be of the same kind, or seemingly unrelated, or even contradictory, but they may be connected by

---

① Examples in this paper have been deliberately translation in an unusual way, but due to the nature of the issues discussed here, translations are indeed merely 'necessary evils,' and tend to mislead. For this reason, sometimes they are not translated at all.

yòu, if only the speaker feels the second one somehow aggravates his feeling or impression caused by the one. For example:

a) Tā (gang bìngguò, xiànzai) yòu bìng le.

他（剛　病過，　現在）又　病了。

'He (being sick recently) is sick again.'

b) Tā shuōle yòu xiào, xiàole yòu shuō.

他　說了又　笑，　笑了又　說。

'He laughed after talking, talked after laughing.'

c) Tā zuótian méilái, jīntian yòu lái le.

他　昨天没來，今天　又　來了。

'He didn't come yesterday, but came today.'

If the two incidents somehow intensify each other in the speaker's feeling, *yòu* can appear with both, For example, *yòu shuō yòu xiào*(又說又笑), *yòu kū yòu tiào*(又哭又跳), *yòu bùdong yòu bù wèn*(又不懂又不問), *yòu shuō yào yòu shuō bú yào* (又說要又說不要), *yòu bù shuō yào yòu bù shuō bú yào*(又不說要,又不說不要), Note that most of the example may seem to indicate that the intensification is undesirable in the thinking of the speaker, but accually this is not quite true. We can also say for instance, *yòu cōngming yòu piàoliang*(又聰明又漂亮) *yòu piányi yòu nài yòng*(又便宜又耐用)

3.2.3. *Hái* emphasizes the continuing effect of an incident or the continuation of a state, affirmative or negative, in the feeling of the speaker, It is thus in sharp contrast with *Zài* which implies diacontinuction. For example, the simple English sentence 'I'll come again, tomorrow.' can be correctly translated as either *Wǒ míngtian Zài lái* (我明天再來), or *wǒ míngtian hái lái* (我明天還來), but the two Chinese sentence are quite different in meaning, as can be seen from the following contrastive pair which one may hear from a debt collector.

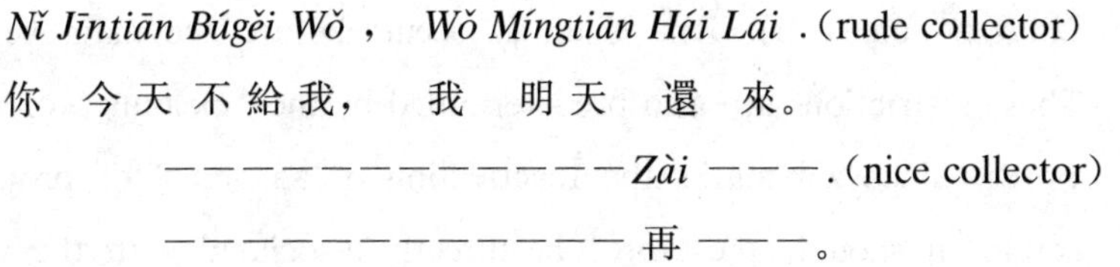

Nǐ Jīntiān Búgěi Wǒ， *Wǒ Míngtiān Hái Lái* .（rude collector）

你 今天不給我， 我 明天 還 來。

——————————————*Zài* ———.（nice collector）

—————————————— 再 ———。

Other seemingly diversified usages of *Hái* can also be easily justified on the basis of this definition. For example：

a）Nǐ míng nián hái lái kāi huì ma?

你 明 年 還來 開 會 嗎?

‘will you come to this meeting again，next year?’

b）Tā hái chī yào.

他 還 吃 藥。

‘He's still on drugs.’

c）Tā bǐ nǐ hái gāo.

他 比 你 還 高。

‘He's even taller than you.’

d）Tā hái méi lái.

他 還 没 來。

‘He hasn't come yet.’

3.2.4. The new definition given to these function words also help us understand the rationality of some of the syntactic restriction or at least make it easier for our students to remember them. I can mention two here.

a）*Hái*，the marker for continuation，and the ‘sentence *le*’（*Md*），which indicates a change of status，are mutally exclusive in a simple sentence. The logic is so clear that I think no explanation is necessary.

b）*Yòu* and *hái* occur before the whole verb phrase they modify，including the negative（*bù* or *méi*）and any auxiliary verb（想，能，可

以，願意，etc），but *Zài* generally occurs before the main verb.[①] These restrictions are also predetermined by the 'meaning' of these words. Since zài marks the reactivation of an actual or projected action，it should，therefore，be directly associated with the verb，while *yòu* and *hái* mark respectively the aggravating effect and the continuing effect of an incident represented by the whole verb phrase (negative or affirmative)，and should，naturally，precede the entire phrase.

3.3. *Cái*（才）and *jiù*（就）——'just，only，merely'? Compared with the three particles discussed above，*cái* and *jiù* are relatively simple. They are also markers of mood，representing obviously two opposing views in the thinking of the speaker. This fact，however，is often obscured by the various confusing translations they are given for their different occurrences. But if we redefine *jiù* as a *marker of positive/conforming mood*，and redefine *cái* as a *marker of negative/defyinig mood*，in the thinking of the speaker，we shall be able to see the common semantic feature their seemingly diversified usages share. This can be seen from the following pairs of sentences.

a) Tāmen jiù(yǒu) yíge háizi.

他 們　就(有)　一個孩子。

'They have only one child (and that's that).'

Tamen cái (yǒu)yíge haizi.

他 們　才（有）一個孩子。

'They have only one child(and that's not enough).'

b) Tā míngtian jiù lái.

他　明　天就來。

---

① Actually，zài may also occur before the negative bù，as in Example (g) in 3.2.1. It is thus syntactically similar to an auxiliary verb.(Compare 不可以去，可以不去). This is one reason why I also suspect that it may have to be recognized as a special kind of auxillary verb (see Note 5).

'He'll come (as early as) tomorrow.'

Tā míngtian cái lái.

他 明 天 才 來。

'He won't come until tomorrow.'

c) Nǐ qǐng wǒ, wǒ jiù lái.

你 請 我，我 就 來。

'I'll come, if you invite me.'

Nǐ qǐng wǒ, wǒ cái lái.

你 請 我，我 才 來。

'I won't come, unless you invite me.'

d) Bú xiàyǔ, wǒ jiù qù.

不 下 雨，我 就 去。

'I'll go, if it doesn't rain.'

Bú xiàyǔ, wǒ cái qù.

不 下 雨，我 才 去。

'I won't go, unless it doesn't rain.'

e) Xià yǔ, wǒ jiù bú qù.

下 雨 我 就 不 去。

'I won't go, if it rains'

xiàyǔ, wǒ cái bú qù.

下雨 我 才 不 去。

'I'll definitely go, unless it rains.'

Syntactically, *jiù* may co-occur with 'sentence *le*' (*Md*), but *cái* never does, This can also be made easier for our students to understand by appealing to 'meaning.' Being a marker of *negative/defying* mood, implies that the incident represented by the verb phrase it modifies is a belated realization or an unlikely hypothesis. It is thus semantically incompatible with the change-of-status marker (*Md*).

4. I hope I have succeeded to showing that, for practical teaching, an

appeal to 'meaning' can be an effective approach. Even in cases where meaning has been fairly clear a *semantic presentation* may still carry us a long way, language are different in syntactic structure, just as they are different in phonemic structure, and the syntactic structure of a language is closely related to, or conditioned by, its semantic categorization. Trying to explain the syntax of one language by employing the syntactic framework of another language is often futile, especially when the two languages are not genetically related. Although I am not much given to speculation, sometimes I cannot resist its temptation. It seems to me that Chinese syntax is primarily mood-oriented, while English syntax is basically *tense*-oriented. Not that English syntax does not have elements of mood (e. g., subjunctive mood) or aspect (e. g., the so-called 'perfect tense'), but that these elements can be incorporated into a broader frame of tense, so that a somewhat systematic though loose. presencation is available for pedagogical, need. I envision, therefore, the possibility that someday we may have a better organized presentation of Chinese syntax based on mood into which other features such as the completive *le* and the experiential *guo* will be incorporated.

REFERENCES

Chao, Y. R. 1968, *A Grammar of Spoken Chinese*. Berkeley.

Hsueh, F. S. 1975. *Phonology of Old Mandarin*. The Hague.

Tai. John H-T. 'The Grammatical Item "le" in Mandarin,' *JCLTA* VOL. X, No. 2. (1975), 53-62.

Teng, shou-hsin. 'Negation and Aspects in Chinese,' *Journal of Chinese Linguistics*, Vol. I, No. 1. (1973), 14-37.

Tewksbury, N, G, 1948. *speak chinese*. New Haven.

Wang, william S-Y, 'Two Aspect Markers in Mandarin,' *Language* 41 (1965), 457-470.

語文建設

什麽是“標準國語”**

在國語的推行工作中,何謂“標準國語”顯然是一個最基本的問題。不少學者已就此發表了意見。討論的重點多爲“國語”與“北平話”是否相同,結論往往是見仁見智、莫衷一是。本文以爲要回答這一問題,首先要把“北平話”和“國語”這兩個概念的定義弄清楚,然後才有互相比較的可能。北平市面積廣闊人口衆多,一些學者的調查已經證明,不同地區的居民所説的話並不完全一致。因此我們有必要清楚地指出,作爲標準語的“北平話”究竟是哪一種以及其内涵爲何。另一方面,我們必須認清,國語的“標準性”並不是絶對的,而是有程度性的。因爲我們可以有標準程度最大的“國語”,即與“標準北平話”極爲接近或完全相同的國語,也可以有標準程度相當低的“國語”,即與“標準北平話”相差頗大但可以互通的“國語”。在推行國語時,可以在這兩極之間選定某一個程度作爲教學時的取舍標準。根據上述的觀念,本文的結論是:理想的“標準國語”在音系方面應該跟“標準北平話”完全一致,但對後者所特有的某些邊緣性讀音現象(peripheral features). 則往往可以忽視。在本文裏,我們將舉例説明下述幾個方面:(a) 輕重音及語調的讀法(stress and intonation);(b) 調值與連讀變調 (tone value and tone sandhi);(c) 兒化的規律(rules for r-suffixation)等。在詞彙方面,國語多采用書面語中規範化的詞語,少用北平話裏的土詞,這一方面且已影響北平話向國語看齊。在語法方面,國語也放鬆了北平話中某些低層次的規則(relaxation of minor syntactic restrictions)。以上的現象在本文一一舉例説明。至於不太標準“國語”可以在哪些方面放寬,文中亦分條説明。

** 未刊稿,據作者打印稿編輯。
第二届世界華文教學探討會論文,1988 年 12 月。

一、緒論

在日常生活中,有些概念,例如"詩、詞、愛情"等,似乎人人都懂得,但在追問之下,却又很少有人能説清它們的定義,所謂"標準國語"似乎亦屬此類。我們常説,某人會説標準國語,或者自謙地説:"我的國語不標準。"但是要是有人問:"標準"到底是什麽?究竟有多少?恐怕就不太容易回答出來了。然而這又不能説是一個抽象的問題,不能置之不論,因爲在推行國語時,這顯然是一個最基本而且無法迴避的問題。這直接牽涉到某些字的讀法,某些詞的用法,以及某些句法是否合乎文法等問題。由於"標準"未曾得到明確的界説,所以歷來每有争論,給國語的推行以及對外華語教學造成一些困難。比如説,有人因爲苦於無法掌握具體的標準,就乾脆堅持説:"衹有北平話才算國語。"一切都以他們所習知的北平話爲準,結果就造成了諸如臺灣小學生把"我和你"中的"和"字説成ㄏㄢ的一類怪現象。在國外的華語教學中,也曾出現過類似的情況。趙元任先生編的國語入門(趙 1948)就收入了許多北平土話,John DeFrancis 編的教科書(1966),也用了好些北平土話,以致有人評爲"北京奶媽説的話"。對於這類現象,當然也有人頗不以爲然。如董同龢先生,多年前就寫過一篇短文,題爲"國語與北平話"(董 1974),重申國語決不等於北平話這個意思。我跟董先生完全同意,但是我覺得問題不那麽簡單。衹説國語不等於北平話並不能解決問題。當我們説甲是否等於乙時,首先得把甲乙的内涵弄清楚,儘可能地減少含混的成分,才不致引起誤會與争議。在下文的討論中,我們將着重地説明國語與北平話的性質,並從而説明二者的關係,以及與之相關的一些教學上的問題。

二、北平話與"標準北平話"

北平市面積相富廣闊,人口也相當多,居住在内城、外城及郊區的人口,也各有其不同的歷史與社會(甚至民族)的背景。他們説的話也就會有相當差異,這可以想見。近年來一些學者的調查更證實了這一現象。可見北平話有許多種，據説圓明園附近與香山地區的話就有差别(俞 1987)，甚至同在市中心區的前門與牛街的話也不全同(沈 1987)。這就産生了到底哪種話是"標準北平話"的問題。衹有在回答了這個問題以後，才有可能説明國語與北平話的關係。《國音常用字彙》序文特别指出："係用其音系，而非字字悉從其土音。"這一説明是完全正確的，但似嫌簡略，仍難免引起誤會。在下文裏，我們將具體説明這個"音系"是什麽樣子的，以及哪類"土音"是我們不能遵從的。

2.1 北平音系

北平音系的性質，我在拙作《國語音系解析》(薛 1986)中已經詳細論述，在此無法細説，也不必重複，爲了本文討論的方便，衹需摘録出其聲母表及韻母表就够了。

北平音系聲母表

p	ph	f	m	
t	th		n	l
c	ch	s		
cr	crh	sr		r
k	kh	h		ø

北平音系韻母表

<table>
<tr><td>韻尾 / 韻基 / 韻頭</td><td colspan="5">ø</td><td colspan="2">y</td><td colspan="2">w</td><td colspan="2">n</td><td colspan="2">ŋ</td></tr>
<tr><td></td><td colspan="2">ɨ</td><td colspan="2">ə</td><td>a</td><td>ɨy</td><td>ay</td><td>ɨw</td><td>aw</td><td>ɨn</td><td>an</td><td>ɨŋ</td><td>aŋ</td></tr>
<tr><td>開口-ø-</td><td colspan="2">支
ɨ</td><td colspan="2">各
ə</td><td>大
a</td><td>黑
ɨy</td><td>來
ay</td><td>斗
ɨw</td><td>告
aw</td><td>恩
ɨn</td><td>干
an</td><td>成
ɨŋ</td><td>唐
aŋ</td></tr>
<tr><td>齊齒-y-</td><td colspan="2">吉
yɨ</td><td colspan="2">切
yə</td><td>牙
ya</td><td></td><td>厓
(yay)</td><td>尤
yɨw</td><td>叫
yaw</td><td>因
yɨn</td><td>言
yan.</td><td>丁
yɨŋ</td><td>江
yaŋ</td></tr>
<tr><td>合口-w-</td><td colspan="2">古
wɨ</td><td colspan="2">多
wə</td><td>化
wa</td><td>灰
wɨy</td><td>外
way</td><td></td><td></td><td>文
wɨn</td><td>玩
wan</td><td>中
ywɨŋ</td><td>壯
waŋ</td></tr>
<tr><td>撮口-yw-</td><td colspan="2">玉
ywɨ</td><td colspan="2">月
ywə</td><td></td><td></td><td></td><td></td><td></td><td>雲
ywɨn</td><td>元
ywan</td><td>用
ywɨŋ</td><td></td></tr>
<tr><td>十三轍</td><td>姑蘇</td><td>一七</td><td>乜斜</td><td>梭坡</td><td>發花</td><td>灰堆</td><td>懷來</td><td>油求</td><td>遙條</td><td>人辰</td><td>言前</td><td>東中</td><td>江陽</td></tr>
</table>

由上表可以看出，北平音是一個由高、中、低三度對比元音構成的語音系統。它上承"十三轍"的音系，但又不完全相同。其間的差别是，後者代表一個

由高、低、前、後形成對比的四度元音系統,但這種差别衹具體表現在韻尾爲零的音節("直喉")裏,在所有的帶尾韻中,它們是完全一致的,即衹有高、低兩度對比。我們管這個音系叫做"北平音系",衹是一種較具代表性的説法,其實並不全面,因爲使用這一音系的並不限於北平話。許多别的官話方言也用這個音系辨别音讀。概括地説,官話方言中的"北方官話"都使用這個三度元音的音系,而"南方官話"(或稱"下江官話")及"西南官話"則仍沿用以前的四度元音系統。由於各種官話方言的音系相同或相近,方言之間的借讀現象就非富自然而且極爲普遍,這是因爲借來的讀法雖與本方言的讀法不一樣,却未跳出本方言的音系。記得趙元任先生在一次談話中曾經説過,當初創製國音符號是爲了推廣北平話。但想不到許多方言地區的人却用當地發音的方式讀這些符號,因此他們的"國語"也就走了樣。趙先生没有説是哪些方言,我猜想這種想象在官話方言區裏一定特别突出。造成這種現象的基本原因是兩方面的,其一爲這些方言的音系相同或相似,其二爲國音符號本身就是音位性的(薛 1985),所以能很自然地跟其他官話方言的音讀對上號。關於這一點,下文討論國語與北平話的關係時,將再仔細申述(參看 3.1 節)。

2.2 北平話的語音

北平音系雖與許多其他官話方言的音系相同,其實際的發音方式(Phonetic realization)却不相同。這一現象不僅出現在北平話與其他官話方言的比較裏,而且北平當地人説的話也在不同程度上顯示出來。前文曾提到北平話似乎有許多種,所指的就是這種現象。根據一些學者的調查(參看林 1987,沈 1987,俞 1987 等),我們可以舉出下面幾個例子。

(a) 相當多的北平人把合口呼的零聲母字讀作帶[v]聲母。例如:"晚"讀[van],"外"讀[vai]等。

(b) 有些北平人把出現在開口呼裏的[ʦ,ʦ‘,s]等聲母(/c、ch、s/)讀爲舌齒音[tθ、tθ’、θ]。例如:"四"讀[θɿ],"咱"讀[tθan]等。

(c) 部分北京人把開口呼的零聲母字讀爲帶喉塞音[ʔ]。例如:"安"讀[ʔan]、"傲" 讀 [ʔan]等。

(d) 北京地區的兒化韻讀法,至少有三種不同的形式。(參看薛 1986,並見下文討論)。

以上所舉衹是幾個比較顯著的例子,當然還有許多更細微的差别。這些差别最容易引起初學華語的外國學生或學者的注意,他們在做了所謂"田野調查"以後,有的會驚訝地説:"原來我們學了好幾年的北京話,其實不是真正的北京話呀!"這顯然是一種以偏概全的誤會。上面的例子,除了最後一條,都是些發音變體,與音位系統無關,而且大多數的北平人,尤其是北平的知識分子,並不那麽説話。我們所教的華語,自然應該是多數知識分子説的具有代表性的"標準北平話",而不是隨便哪一個生長在北平的人所説的話。關於這種標準話的細節,將在下文詳論。

三、國語與北平話

上文已經交代,當我們用"北平話"這一名詞時,我們通常指的是那種多數知識分子説的具有代表性的"標準北平話",而非那種帶有沉重鼻音與特殊變體的當地土音。當我們説"國語就是北平話"時,基本上也是這個意思,往往把每個生長在北平的人都當做權威,問他們"該怎麽説?"那是誤解。董先生就曾指出,促使北平話變成全國標準語的人並非全都是在北平土生土長的,而最"地道"的北平人是旗人,但即使在當地,他們的話也不是一般人願意模仿的(董 1974)。另一方面,"國語"這個名詞,還具有其他的内涵,也不是單純的"北平話"一詞可以涵蓋的。首先,作爲"標準語",就可能有程度上的差别,既然可能有"最標準"的國語,也可能有標準性相當低的"國語",類似人們常説的"臺灣國語"或"廣東官話"。其次,在詞彙與語法方面,"國語"一詞更不是"北平話"可以概括的。在下文裏,我們將分條討論國語的"標準性"問題。

3.1 國語與北平話的密切關係,顯然是在語音方面,即《國音常用字彙》序所説的:"係用其音系,而非字字悉從其土音。"但這話説的不够精確。對非官話區的人來説,如臺、浙、閩、粤等地,要學國語當然首先要掌握國語的音系,但對北方官話區的人來説,由於他們的音系跟北平話的音系是一致的,學國語的重點就是學北平人的發音腔調。較具體地説,這包括下列四個方面。

(A) 國音四聲的調值是不能馬虎的。北平話裏第一聲爲高平調〔55〕,第二聲爲高升調[35],第三聲爲低平調[211]或低升調[214],第四聲爲低降調

[51](參看趙 1948:25)。標準國音完全采用,因此學國語時必須遵守,使四聲的讀法儘可能與北平話接近,否則就可能被譏爲説天津話或山東話了。但如放寬標準,衹要能保持四聲的對比,並保持字彙的四聲歸屬與北平話相對應,也就可以達到辨音與交際的目的了。另一方面,北平話裏有許多特殊的連讀變調(tone sandhi),爲外國學者所津津樂道。這類變調往往是北平人都不自覺的語音自動調節,因此在教學國語時,實在不必多花時間,能學會固然好,學不到也無損於國語的標準性。

(B) 複合詞的輕重音模式,在多數官話裏,包括北平話,都是先輕後重的。例如,"飛機"的重音在"機"字上,"飛機好"的重音就跑到"好"字上了。他如"旅行、圖書館、特別高興"等,重音也都在末節,衹有少數習語,如"胡塗、眼睛、嘴巴"等,才把第二音節讀作輕聲。跟其他方言相比,北平話裏的"重輕"甚至"重輕輕(輕)"式的讀法特別多(孟 1987)。例如把"西瓜"的重音念在"西"字上。又如"金魚"與"乾魚"的念法是正常的,即重音在"魚"字上,"胡同兒"的念法也是正常的,重音在"同"字上(讀第四聲,加兒化),但是"金魚胡同"與"乾魚胡同"的念法却變爲"重輕輕(輕)"了,而且"同"字不許兒化①。這一類的變讀都是個別詞彙的問題,並無規律可尋,學會了固然很有"北京味兒",没學會也對"標準國語"無損,教學時自然也用不着特別强調。

(C) 兒化韻是官話方言的一個特色。國語以官話爲本,自然不能撇開這問題。但兒化與否是一個詞彙熟習程度的問題,很難絶對説定哪些詞必須兒化,那些詞絶不該兒化。更糟的是,連兒化的方式北平當地人也不一致②。因此有人主張教國語時不教兒化韻。如果我們放寬標準,這自然並無不可。但如要説相當標準的國語,兒化韻就非教不可了。據我個人的研究(薛 1986),兒化有三種方式,來自其發展中的三個歷史階段。不久前北平城區裏多數人説的是第二式,衹有内城的少數人説第三式。近些年由於城區擴大,而且外地移入的人口大量增加,説第一式的人占多數了。由於第三式是晚起的,影響有

① 據説爲了典雅,"乾魚胡同"已改稱"甘雨胡同"了。有趣的是,由於此處"魚、雨"兩字在北平土話裏都讀輕聲,因此在念法上,這個改動對北平人説等於没改,但對外地人就不同了。

② 據原在臺灣推行國語,現任北師大教授的俞敏先生説,原籍西郊香山的齊鐵恨先生,説話時兒化特別多,而圓明園區的一位老太太説的話,兒化較少,而且形態也不一樣。參看俞 1987。

限,自然不宜采作標準,頭兩式倒都有可能,而且也不複雜,它們的形態如下表。

韻基	wɨ	øɨ yɨ ywɨ	ə		a	ɨy	ay	ɨw	aw	ɨn	an	ɨŋ	aŋ
十三轍	姑蘇	一七	梭坡	乜斜	發花	灰堆	懷來	油求	遙條	人辰	言前	東中	江陽
注音符號	ㄨ	(ø) ㄧㄩ	ㄛㄜ	ㄝ	ㄚ	ㄟ	ㄞ	ㄡ	ㄠ	ㄣ	ㄢ	ㄥ	ㄤ
兒化轍	ㄨㄦ	ㄟㄦ	ㄜㄦ		ㄚㄦ	ㄟㄦ	ㄞㄦ	ㄡㄦ	ㄠㄦ	ㄟㄦ	ㄞㄦ	ㄥㄦ	ㄤㄦ

ㄟㄦ 小人辰兒　　ㄞㄦ 小言前兒

由上表可以看出,兒化以後,“一七、灰堆、人辰”三轍的字歸併。形成“小人辰兒”轍,第一與第二式都是這樣的,但在第一式中,衹有“言前”轍與“懷來”轍的字歸併成“小言前兒”轍,而在第二式中,“發花”轍的字加入了“小言前兒”(用虚綫表示第二式)。作爲國音的依據,兩式都有可能,但如考慮到多數官話方言的情況,用第一式作標準似乎比較實際些。

(D)自宋、元以來,官話方言的歷史演化,大致可分爲南北兩個系統。其間的差别最突出地表現在幾類入聲字的改讀方式裏。北式的演變可以拿《中原音韻》作代表。原“梗、曾”攝的入聲字改讀“收噫”,因而進入“齊微”與“皆來”兩韻,如“賊、國、白、客”等。原“通、宕、江”攝的入聲字改讀“收嗚”,因此進入“尤侯”(後復改入“魚模”)與“蕭豪”兩韻,如“熟、竹”與“學、藥”等字(hsueh 1975)。南式的演變可以拿《洪武正韻》作代表。前述各攝的入聲繼續保持甚久,反而先是“梗、曾”兩攝合爲一韻,“江、宕”兩攝也合爲一韻,其後入聲韻尾才脱落;原“梗、曾”攝的入聲字因而讀入十三轍的“乜斜”轍、如“澤、勒、或”等;原“江、宕”攝的入聲字改讀入“梭坡”轍,如“捉、各、錯”等;原“通”攝的入聲字,則以洪、細之分而改讀入“姑蘇”或“一七”轍、如“逐、宿”(姑蘇)與“局、玉”(一七)等,這兩種演變雖然造成這類字的不同讀法,但都未超出原有的音系,因此可以很自然地互借,在相對的方言裏構成“又讀”。由於歷史上的許多因素,自明代起,南式演變的結果被確定爲標準讀法,即我們現在所説的“讀音”,少數常用字的北式讀法得以保留下來,即我們現在所謂的“俗音”(Chou 1988)、這個現象在教學上本不成問題，衹要查閱一下國音字典就可以知道哪個讀法是標準的了。但對那些喜歡“田野調查”的人却可能造成困惑。當他們碰到幾個“真正的北京人”時，可能會發現那些人仍然使用未被采作標準的讀法，例如把“學校”說成ㄒㄧㄠˊㄒㄧㄠˋ，把“覺得”說成ㄐㄧㄠˊㄉㄜˊ，這可能會使他們感到：“原來我們學的不是真正的北京話呀！”因此有必要把這個問題在此重加說明。另一方面，關於北平話的來源，近年來學術界頗有争論。有些學者，如南京大學的魯國堯教授（魯 1985）與喬治敦大學的楊福綿教授（Yang 1986）認爲現代標準北京話源自明代的南京話。另有一些學者，如北京大學的林燾教授（林 1987），則認爲現代的北京話源自東北地區，是隨旗人入關進京的。這兩種說法各有各的道理。由我們在本文中的討論可以知道，就字彙的標準讀法說，作爲南方官話代表的南京音，確實似乎掩蓋了北京音，而構成一種新的標準語，但就語調及發音方式說，現代北京話與東北地區的方言極爲近似，而與其他官話方言相去較遠，說它源自東北是有道理的。比較全面的說法也許應該是：標準國語是用北平話的發音方式，讀由南京方言形成的標準音。從嚴格的語言學觀點說過，標準國語當然仍是北京話，衹不過從南方官話大量借讀而已。

3.2 標準國語或標準北平話與北平土話的差異，也明顯地表現在詞彙方面。嚴格地說，用詞彙區分方言是很不可靠的，因爲個别詞彙的使用是習慣的問題，變動的也特别快。不同的方言或語言之間互相借字的現象也是常有的，一旦約定俗成以後，就會變爲己有。官話的形成是有歷史淵源的，是數百年來政治、經濟與文化的活動，尤其是文學作品的流傳，逐漸形成的。這些活動與文學創作，並不限於北京地區，因而吸取各地的詞語，形成了一套較有規範的詞彙。標準國語自然應該使用這一類詞彙。這個道理至爲淺顯，本來不成問題，但是由於有些人誤解了“國語就是北平話”的含義，認爲衹有北平土話才是正宗。正如董先生指出的，有些人故意把“頭”說成“腦袋”甚或“腦袋瓜子”，就是故意賣弄了。作家老舍當初最喜歡用北平土話，認爲衹有那樣才有勁，後來也有所覺悟，承認那不是正途（老舍 1959）。近三四十年來，由於政治的隔離以及新事物的不斷出現，臺灣地區的文學作品裏，就出現了許多新詞彙，是大陸不使用的。反之，大陸也出來了許多臺灣不使用的詞彙。黄國營教授曾注意到這個問題，收集了許多有差異的詞彙（黄 1988），並把在臺灣使用的國語稱爲“漢語在這孤島上的一種變體”。其實就詞彙説,我看倒也不見得,説不定臺灣的用詞將來會變爲“正體”的。比如“空中小姐”大陸上叫“飛機乘務員”,“斑馬綫”大陸上叫“横道綫”,“三字經”大陸上説“駡人話”,我覺得臺灣的説法就比較乾净利落,很有取代大陸説法的可能。總而言之,詞彙的標準化,不純粹是語言的問題,也很難硬性規定,但標準國語的詞彙决不等於北平的土語,這是毫無疑問的。反之,在這一方面説,是北平土話必須向國語靠攏的。記得許多年前,美國的一本華文教科書上仍用“洋胰子”這個土詞,一位北平朋友看了大笑着説:“現在都叫肥皂了嘛!”當然像“取燈兒”或“洋火兒”一類的詞兒,也已經被“火柴”取代了。於此可見一斑。

3.3 與詞彙相比,語法是穩定得多的。漢語的基本語法特性,不僅在官話方言區裏相當一致,連在非官話方言裏也相差不多,衹在低層次的少數規則上略有差異。所以我們可以説,標準國語的語法系統是與北平話完全一致的,衹在個别的地方略有鬆動。我們可以舉出下面三點爲例。

(A) 作爲標準語,國語的句式自然要正規些,而口語裏則常有一些破碎片斷的句式,教國語時,自然應該避免。董先生説的好,北平土話裏類似“張三他爸爸”,以及“他没來呢,還!”在標準國語裏是不允許的,應該改爲“張三的爸爸”及“他還没來呢!”(董 1974)

(B) 北平人説話,不用像“昨天晚上有没有下雨?”這樣的正反問句,必須説成“昨天晚上下雨了没有?”但在多數官話方言裏,頭一個説法是允許的,因此在教國語時,就不妨把規則放寬些,不必斤斤計較這樣的細節。

(C) 北平人不用“去美國”這樣的説法,必須説“到美國去”,但是前者已經流行開了,國語就不妨接受。與此相比,我曾聽到一個播音員説“去到上海的旅客”這樣的句子,這種説法似仍不應算作標準。

上舉三例旨在説明,雖然國語的語法與北平話相同,不能説北平人的任何説法都是無上權威。國語的句法是經過規範的,而且要照顧到普遍性。

四、結論

我們的討論已經比較具體地界定了標準國語的性質。概括地説,這個標

準語是跟北平話關係至深的,但絶不能説跟北平土話完全一致。標準國語的性質可以從三個方面再總結如下:

(A) 就語音説,它采用北方官話(包括北平話)的音系,大量吸納由南方官話形成的所謂"讀音",而以北平的知識分子説話的聲調與腔調發音,但排除北平土話裏的許多發音變體。

(B) 就詞彙説,國語的詞彙是數百年來,官話方言區裏的文化活動促成與規範的,其中北平話的貢獻衹是一部分,因此在這一方面,更不能説國語就是北平話,反之,北平人跟其他方言區的人一樣,也得"學習國語"。

(C) 就語法説,標準國語采用的是官話方言語法的基本規律。這些規律爲許多方言所共有,因此在這一方面,更無理由説"國語就是北平話"。反之,北平土話裏的一些比較特殊與散漫的句式,都在排除之列,因爲"標準語"必須是正規的。

在推行國語時,我們的目標自然是推廣"標準國語",所以必須嚴守上文提到的規範。但是我們也説過,"標準"是有程度性的(陳 1983),適當地降低一些,仍然可以達到對話交際的目的。爲了盡速推廣"大衆國語",下列的幾個方面,似可略作通融。以便節約時間,加强與加速詞彙的教學。

(a) 掌握北方話的音系,但不一定以北平話的方式發音。

(b) 不堅持捲舌聲母與相對應的非捲舌聲母之分。

(c) 不堅持聲母/n/與/l/的區分,以及/f/與/h/在合口呼裏的區分。

(d) 忽視兒化韻。

(e) 不堅持韻尾/n/與/ng/的區分。

參考文獻

董同龢:《國語與北平話》,丁邦新編:《董同龢先生語言學論文選集》,臺北,1974 年,第 367—369 頁。

老　舍:《土話與普通話》,《中國語文》,1959 年 9 月號。

林　燾:《北京官話溯源》,《中國語文》,1987 年第 3 期。

魯國堯:《明代官話及其基礎方言問題》,《南京大學學報》1985 年第 4 期。

孟　琮:《北京胡同兒名兒裏的語音問題》,1987 年 10 月在美國俄亥俄州立大學的演講稿。

臺灣“‘國語’推行委員會”:《國音標準匯編》,臺北,1952 年。

薛鳳生:《國語音系解析》,臺北,1986 年。

———《注音符號之理論基礎與教學實踐》,《第一屆世界華文教學研討會論文集》,臺北,1985 年,第 427—436 頁。

俞　敏:《駐防旗人和方言的兒化韻》,《中國語文》,1987 年第 5 期。

陳章太:《略論漢語口語的規範》,《中國語文》,1983 年 9 月號。

黄國營:《臺灣當代小説的詞彙語法特點》,《中國語文》,1988 年第 3 期。

沈　炯:《北京話合口呼零聲母的語音分歧》,《中國語文》,1987 年第 5 期。

Chao, Yuen Ren: *Mandarin Primer*, Harvard university Press, 1948.

DeFrancis, John: *Advanced chinese*, Yale University Press, 1966.

Hsueh, F. S.: *Phonology of Old mandarin*, Mouton, The Hague, 1975.

Chou, Shizhen: Hong Wu Zheng Yun: its relation to the Nanjing dialect and its impact on Standard Mandarin, Ph. D. Dissertation, The Ohio State University, 1988.

Yang, Paul Fu-mien: “A Southern Mandarin Dialect of the Ming Dynasty as Reflected in Matteo Ricci's Portuguese-Chinese Dictionary.” Paper presented at the *19th annual meeting of the International Conference on Sino-Tibetan Languages and Linguistics*, The Ohio State University, Columbus, Ohio, December 12-14, 1986.

國語與北平話**

我寫這篇短文，提出這兩個大家常見的名詞，目的在闡明一件事，就是國語不等於北平話。其實這是一件顯而易見，而且大家都早已知道的事。不過是近來許多人偏偏把它忘記了，漸有異乎此的言論或行動發生，我就不得不重新提醒大家一句。

世界各國，無論大小，都不免有方言存在；同時，爲補救語言的隔閡，各國又都有流行全境的標準語。在中國，幾百年來，北平知識階級的語言一直是所謂的"官話"；民國以來，更經政府正式規定爲全國的標準語，並封以"國語"的尊號。

那麽請記住：國語的形成固然有它的地域基礎，同時却也有它的社會基礎。所以，你如把"張三的爸爸"説成"張三他爸爸"，或者你不説"他還没來呢？"而説"他没來呢，還"；那固然够北平味兒，却不合國語語法的通例。如有人以爲"頭"非説作"腦袋"甚或"腦袋瓜子"不可，那是他要故意賣弄北平土話的字眼兒，國語並不如此。又如現時臺灣小學教科書上不把連詞"和"注作"ㄏㄜˊ"而注作"ㄏㄢˋ"，"暖和"也不注作"ㄋㄢˇ""ㄏㄨㄛ"而注作"ㄋㄤˇㄏㄨㄜˊ"①。那也太遷就北平土音了，許多從内地來的老北平教育界人士都覺得奇怪。

上面那些話你不信嗎？請看教育部頒布的"國音常用字彙"。在序文裏，國語推行委員會的主編人一再説："係用其音系（指北平），而非字字悉從其土

** 未刊稿，據作者打印稿編輯。

① 其實把"暖和"的"暖"徑注作"ㄋㄤˇ"還是不明白注音的道理。一部分北平人所以把"暖"説作"ㄋㄤˇ"完全是受後面"和"的影響。"和"的聲母"ㄏ"是舌根音，它會使 "暖（ㄋㄨㄢˇ）"的韻尾同 化作"ㄤ"，而北平話又没有"ㄋㄨㄤ"的音，因此"ㄨ"又消失了。這是一種語音的自動調節。如果要管，真是管不清，事實上也盡可以不管。"老虎"的"老"不讀"上聲"而讀"陽平"（與"勞"同），"小姐"的"小"不讀"上聲"而讀"陽平"（與"肴"同），其理爲一，不是從來没有人每處都注出來嗎？"爸爸"的第二個字的聲母往往變濁音，注音符號不是根本没給它預備一個特別的符號嗎？

音。”關於字音,國語與北平話的關係如此。詞彙與語法自然可想而知。

我們還可以想一想,北平知識分子的語言之所以能變成全國的標準語,是因爲幾百年來,以那些人爲基幹而發揚的文化影響及於全國。然而那些人乃是社會上的領導階級與活文學的作家,却不是所有在北平土生土養的人。再反過來看,現在最“地道”的北平人是旗人,而旗人的話,即在北平本地,也不是一般人願意模仿的。

一種語言是屬於一群人的,不是由某地生長出來的。我們常借地名爲語言名,衹是習慣如此,其實並不是很恰當。舉例來説:現在世界上説英語的人,在英倫三島以外的,數目比三島本土多好幾倍:三島本土,除英語外,仍有其他土語存在;再追根究底,英語也不過是五世紀後才由歐洲大陸搬上三島的呢。我們的國語從前是“官話”,現在是標準語,它並非與北平這個地方不可分,就不待多言了。北平與國語發生關係,衹是説國語的人一向以那個地方作活動的中心而已。抗戰八年,社會上的領導階級與文化人紛紛遷入西南各省。他們受西南方言的影響,口語與作品中自然而然的加入西南方言的成分。那些成分,如“要得”等,由他們來傳播,就變成國語的常用詞了。然而北平話裏有這些嗎?“尷尬”與“揩(ㄎㄚ)油”本來不是上海話嗎?至於“摩登”,“幽默”……,更是舶來品了。

没有哪一國的標準語就是它的某地土語。羅馬方言發展爲意大利的標準語,但丁(Dante)等人的文學作品有奠基之功;倫敦方言發展爲英國的標準語,則喬叟(Chaucer)等的影響很大。同樣的,如胡適之先生所説,我們的國語是以關漢卿、施耐庵、曹雪芹等所用的語言爲基礎的。由此看來,高喊“衹有北平話才是國語”的人可以罷休了。

我覺得,就國語之爲全中國的標準語而言,我們實在應該多多的看重它的社會性,如果忽略了它的社會性,就會消減它的實用範圍,使它失去“標準”的資格,結果衹可以供少數懂得北平土話的人或研究方言的人欣賞。所以我們向大家介紹國語時,凡音讀、詞彙、語法,都應該選取約定俗成的標準去介紹。所以“約定俗成”,就是指那些標準所以形成的文化背景,有無比的力量可以讓大衆接受。反之,如果你衹注重“北平味兒”,一意的把你所知道的北平音,北平字眼兒,北平説法往外搬,以爲那才是國語,那麽你試試看,久而久之,看你的貨究竟能賣去多少？

但是請不要誤會，我並不主張用文縐縐的國語。我幾次提到“文化”，它也是廣義的搬“凡人所做的”。國語一直是活的語言，那就是説，它是幾百年來許多人天天在説的話。就問，誰每説一句話都要咬文嚼字或引經據典呢？人活着，需要飲食；語言活着，也會不斷地由外面吸取新分子。但是請注意，國語吸收新分子的源泉是多方面的，不是衹有北平話。如果衹有北平話，國語怕早就患營養不良症死去了。

儘量把方言裏的成分介紹進入國語是我們充實國語的一個好途徑。可是我們要弄清楚，那件事和向大衆介紹國語完全是兩回事。第一，方言成分要成爲國語，必由廣義的文化力來推進，單單編入教科書是不行的。第二，我們要忠於國語，忠於學國語的人，就一定要向大衆介紹已經約定俗成了的國語；還没有稱爲約定俗成的國語的方言分子，縱然自己有偏愛，也衹好耐着性兒等一等再説。

末了，我還想奉告學國語的人幾句話。没有到過北平的人一樣的可以學會説一口好的國語。生於北平長於北平的人要説好的國語也需要學。他們學國語衹有近水樓臺之便；但如不學，他們説的話永遠衹是北平話，絶不是國語。

現代漢語閲讀課中的“假借字”問題**

與世界上其他語言相比，漢語的書寫方式是相當特殊的。在造型上説，這種文字雖然經過多次轉變，基本上仍保持着本民族所創製的圖象文字的性質，因此看起來跟各種拼音文字顯然有别。這就給一般人造成一種錯覺，以爲這種書寫方式是直接表達意義的，也就是有些人所常説的："英文是表音的文字，中文是表義的文字。"這一概念自然就讓人産生一種不自覺的想法與做法，即在閲讀中文時，總是"就字論字"，想從每個方塊字的本義中推衍出一個詞彙的意義。不知是出於自然還是由於漢語老師的影響，上述的想法與做法在學習漢語的外國學生中也相當普遍，每當在閲讀中碰見一個新詞條時，便逐字查檢，但有時仍找不到正確的解釋。要解決這類問題，首先我們必須認清，漢字在造型上當初雖有"表義"的主觀願望，但在實際應用上，自始就是以"表音"爲主的。這有兩層含義。其一，"文字"這一概念的定義衹能是"代表特定語言中特定的字彙符號"，而這些字衹能以特定的語音形式而存在（參看 Y. R. Chao: Language and Symbolic Systems，1968，第 8 章）。其二，人世間的事物，包括實際的與構想的，數目幾乎是無限大的，所以任何語言中的詞彙都是隨時增減變動不居的，爲每一個含有特定意義的字造一個特定的符號，顯然不可能。反之，用表音的符號就簡明得多了。漢字雖然未演變成一套純粹的拼音系統，但每個漢字都可以作爲一個表音的符號來使用，這是自古已然的事實。古籍中大量使用"假借字"的現象，便是這一事實的最好注脚。如何辨認與解釋假借字是訓詁學上的一門專門學問。明清以來的經學大師們早已看出，假借字的關鍵是讀音，因此提出由音以求義的主張，甚至於有"音同義亦同"的説法，此説雖嫌過於武斷，却也是頗有見地的。

由上文所論可知，假借字是漢語書寫方式的一種特有現象。這種現象是

** 原載《第二届國際漢語教學討論會論文選》，1987 年 8 月。

發乎自然的,絶不限於先秦的古代漢語,在歷代以及現代漢語中也是常見的。不同的是,由於去古已遠,我們對上古的音系所知不多,當時的假借字便成了問題,也就引起了我們的注意。反之,由於現代漢語是我們日常使用的語言,對其中的一些假借字,衹要不是太顯眼的"别字"(或"白字"),我們就往往習而不察地視爲當然了。在對外漢語教學中,也就常常忽略了這個問題。其實,正如同古籍中的假借字對我們一樣,現代漢語中的假借字,對母語不是漢語的學生來説,也是一個相當突出的問題,在輔導他們閲讀時,需要特别留意。如能説明其成因以消除學生的困惑,將會增强他們的理解與記憶。

"錯别字"是語言使用中的一種普遍現象,各種語言裏都有,心理語言學中有一個專門名詞,叫做"malapropism",所指的就是這種現象。有些心理學家認爲,通過對錯别字的研究,也許可以增進我們對人類大腦活動的瞭解,從而得知大腦是如何分類儲存語言資料,以及在必要時如何分别提取這些資料的。本文的目的不是從心理語言學的角度研究錯别字,而是爲了閲讀教學的實際需要來討論這個問題。因此我們衹討論那些常見的似是而非的(也可以説是"是非不分"的)"錯别字",亦即"假借字"。我們的目的也不是甄别與糾正這些假借字,而衹是把它們當作客觀存在的事實,分别討論其構成的原因,希望能對閲讀教學有所幫助。這個問題引起我的注意,是前幾年的事。當時我來國内講學,有朋友送了我幾本文學作品,包括 1980 與 1981 年的《短篇小説選》以及《喬廠長上任記》等,我發現這些作品甚爲優美,是現代漢語閲讀課的好教材。但我同時也注意到,在用詞遣字方面,許多作家有時候都有不太正常的地方,因此我便隨手摘録了一些。後來發現這種現象絶不限於這一些作家,報紙雜志上也所在皆有,雖然這些假借字的用法已被普遍接受了。下文分類討論的例子,都是這樣隨手摘録來的,並非我的臆造,衹是注明出處實在太麻煩,也似乎没有必要,所以概從略。

上文已經指出,假借字的使用主要是由讀音决定的,古代漢語中大半如此。但在現代漢語中,則多數同時含有若即若離的語義成分。這麼一來,含有假借字的詞條與本詞之間,從字面上看,就可能意義不全相同了。但在實際應用上,則是毫無區别的。這也就是我們需要特别提醒外國學生的地方。有一些假借字也牽涉到字形,不過爲數極少。下面我們就分類舉例説明這些現象,並把假借字與本字分别畫綫標出。

一、純由讀音造成的假借現象

1. 烟花＝烟火＝焰花＝焰火
2. 爆竹＝爆仗＝炮仗
3. 歪打正着＝歪打正招
4. 暈了過去＝昏了過去
5. 參與＝參預
6. 急欲知道＝急於知道
7. 温文爾雅＝温文而雅
8. 偶爾看到＝偶而看到

上例第一條中,正假兩方的讀音似不相同,但其實非常相近。因爲烟花之"花",正如棉花之"花",北京人是把它説成"火"的。當然爲了假借,衹要近似也就够了。第五條以下都是由於對古文的用字不甚瞭解而造成的,嚴格地説,用了代字以後,意思也就不同了,但在實際使用上,意思絲毫未變。

二、由讀音造成並含有語義成分的假借現象

這一類含有假借字的詞條特别多,多半是由"聞音生義"而杜撰出來的,是一種語言學上所謂的"folk etymology"現象。當然用了假借字以後,嚴格地説,含義也就有了相當的變動,但實際的用途則完全相同。

1. 直截了當＝直接了當
2. 絶不可能＝决不可能
3. 折本生意＝蝕本生意
4. 妨礙＝妨害
5. 欺侮＝欺負
6. 大多没來＝大都没來
7. 統統走了＝通通走了

8. 勢利眼＝勢力眼
9. 各人有各人的命＝個人有個人的命
10. 個別＝各別
11. 抓住一點不計其餘＝抓住一點不及其餘
12. 可望而不可及＝可望而不可即
13. 包涵＝包含
14. 相悖＝相背
15. 按部就班＝按步就班
16. 津津計較＝斤斤計較
17. 其醜無比＝奇醜無比
18. 躬與其盛＝恭與其盛＝恭於其盛＝躬於其盛
19. 邪魔外道＝邪門外道＝斜門外道＝斜門歪道
20. 莫名其妙＝莫明其妙＝莫名奇妙＝莫明奇妙
21. 聽天由命＝聽天有命
22. 死生有命＝死生由命

由以上的許多例子可以看出，有時爲了遷就近似的語義，往往可以放寬讀音相似的要求，如 3，4，5，6 等條。但是因爲有語義成分的幫助，這類假借字特别容易被接受。同時也可以看出，要正確瞭解這些假借現象，相當程度的古文修養是必要的，12 條以下都是好例子。

三、由讀音、語義及字形共同形成的假借現象

1. 即使＝既使
2. 吸取教訓＝汲取教訓
3. 截至八月八號＝截止八月八號

這類例子不多，有時候也不易判定它們是否真與字形有關，但像頭一個例子裏的“即”與“既”，原意可以説是恰恰相反的，按理不能互代，此處以“即”代“既”，除了讀音近似以外，當與字形類似有關。

四、由方言讀音造成的假借現象

由於漢語方言的分歧相當大，因此這類例子也相當多，其實這些假借的形成原理，仍不出前述三種方式，衹是因方言的讀音而異罷了。這些方言多半是與北京話比較接近的其他官話方言，由於它們的音系相當接近，系統化的對比才有可能。我們可以把這些假借字按方言與普通話的讀音差別，分成下列數類：

A. 由缺乏捲舌聲母的方言形成的假借現象

許多官話方言裏，齒音聲母的捲舌與非捲舌之分已經消失了，因此造成了許多互代的例子，説北京話的人自然會覺得不太自然。

1. 金戒指＝金戒子
2. 衹想自己＝自想自己
3. 心裏琢磨著＝心裏捉摸著
4. 涸轍之魚＝涸澤之魚
5. 崇山峻嶺＝叢山峻嶺

B. 由缺乏鼻音韻尾對比的方言形成的假借現象

許多官話方言，尤其是長江流域的，都已經不再區分舌根鼻音韻尾-ng與舌尖鼻音韻尾-n了，因此形成了許多"分，風"之類的同音字，這也表現在同音互用的假借裏。

1. 終身大事＝終生大事
2. 低聲下氣＝低身下氣
3. 隱隱約約＝影影約約
4. 貧民窟＝平民窟

這類例子似乎不多，我衹看到上面幾條。但在簡化字的聲符裏却是常見的，比如以"井"爲"進"(进)的聲符，以"兵"爲"賓"(宾)的聲符等。另外，有些杜撰文字學家也常利用這種現象而瞎説。另外還有一些較特殊的方言歧異現象，也在假借字的選用上反應出來，例如有的方言不分聲母"l"與"n"，因此我們看到有人把"非常惱火"寫成"非常老火"，有時連"日"母字(原爲鼻音)也受到影響，例如"花蕊"又可寫作"花蕾"。由於這類例子不多,我們就不再細論了。

語言中的詞彙總是與時推移的,其轉變的原因很多,有純語言性的,也有非語言性的,本文討論的假借字現象,就是詞彙轉變的原因之一,是純語言性的。因爲經過長期與普遍的使用以後,所謂假借字就可能取正字而代之,變成正常的寫法了。所以本文的目的不在"改錯字",而是想通過這一研究,能更有效地輔導外國學生閱讀中文。爲了達到這一目的,我們顯然必須提醒他們增强普通話音系與方言對比的認識,以及增强古代漢語的訓練。至於其他方面的詞彙轉變,多非語言本身的問題,而多出於社會的與政治的考慮,因此不太可能找出一般性的規律,便衹好個别處理了。例如"服務員"一詞,在構詞法上説,與英文的 servant[serv(e)加 ant]完全一致,按理説不是一個很光彩的稱呼,但現在却極爲流行,而"工友"一詞,雖含有"工人階級"與"朋友"兩重意義,一般却認爲含有貶意,就語言本身説,這真是奇哉怪也。但這種現象自有其特定的社會背景,學習的人别無他法,衹好逐條記憶。一般説來,詞彙的流傳是約定俗成的,往往不以個人的意志爲轉移,但是對於新生事物的命名,創始者如能謹慎地考慮,還是會有積極的作用的。這使我想到國内最近使用的兩個名詞,私意頗不以爲然。一個是"方便面"(instant noodle),這三個字聲母全是脣音,韻母也類似("便,面"更屬叠韻),因此説起來甚爲拗口。這種食品將來大概會廣爲流行,如果不改名,吃起來固然方便,説起來就不大方便咯!(臺灣叫做"即食面",也不高明,令人聯想到"鷄食"或"鷄屎"。)另一個是"數據庫"(data bank),似乎更糟,三個字聲調雷同,又屬叠韻,因此念起來像繞口令似的,真是自找麻煩(臺灣叫做"資料庫",似乎比較好些)。如在命名之初,能够考慮到讀音的問題,就可以避免這類麻煩了。

中國語文建設之我見**

做好漢字規範化、詞語規範化，還有漢語拼音化的工作，都是非常重要的，但是，最基本的還是推廣普通話。

臺灣推行"國語"，新加坡推行華語（"國語"、華語就是普通話），儘管工作中還存在一些枝枝節節的問題，但基本上是成功的。當地人絶大多數可以聽得懂，而且可以交談。如果大陸能先把這項工作做好，再做其他語文改革工作時，就可以收到事半功倍的效果。

漢字簡化是爲了方便書寫，這很需要。但似乎太注意一筆兩筆的多少問題，而没注意整個字形的系統化。比如"专"字，寫起來就很不順手。一味地簡化漢字也不是個辦法。現在，在很多情况下，掌握一個漢字要學兩個符號。我認爲，漢字簡化工作可以適可而止。

詞彙規範問題，就是調查、統計詞語的使用地區和使用頻率。在這個大前提下，可以對個别詞語加以斟酌。比如有的詞語，使用頻率很高，但使用過程中容易造成誤會或者不雅，就可以用頻率較低的詞語來代替，加以適當的調整。語言是社會交際工具，是約定俗成的，可以引導，但硬性規範是很難的。

有人認爲，推廣普通話，就是要禁止方言，推行拼音化，就是要廢止漢字。這是錯誤的。二者是可以並行的。推行拼音化以後，漢字並不就被廢止了。有人説，到那時候，漢字衹能成爲學者研究的東西了，我看也不見得。

我再三强調要推廣普通話，是因爲中華人民共和國成立快 40 周年了，而推廣普通話的工作做得很不理想。很多地方似乎並不重視這件事情。廣播、電視這樣的大衆傳播工具多得很，影響也大，因此，現在是推廣普通話十分有利的時機。

** 原刊《語文建設》1987 年第 6 期。

文學風雅

文學周報

The Languages of the Sages and the Poets: Some Aspects of the Chinese Linguistic Tradition**

The first part of the subject of my talk tonight was originally only "The language of the sages." I didn't realize it at that time, but, apparently, it is somewhat ambiguous, because some kind people have said to me: "I am eager to hear what kind of a language it is," While some other people have said to me, jokingly perhaps, "You mean only Chinese is the language of the sages? bull-!" No, I didn't mean that. So let me make it clear now that I am not going to talk about the Chinese language itself at all, but the traditional linguistic scholarship about that language. What I actually meant by that part of the title is merely that, as far as the Chinese linguists of the past were concerned, only the language of the ancient sages could be a worthy subject of study. Actually, they also accepted another form of language as a worthy subject of their efforts, the language of the poets. So I have changed that part of the title to "The Languages of the Sages and the Poets." These are the two concerns of the Chinese linguists of the past, and, as I will explain later, two distinctly different approaches for linguistic study eventually emerged because of these two concerns.

As we all know, Chinese is one of the languages first recorded in human history. Fragmentary recordings dated back more than 4000 years ago, but real comprehensive recordings came about only in the writings of the ancient sages, particularly the so-called Confucian Classics that appeared 3,000 to

** 中文題爲《哲人和聖人的語言:漢語語言學傳統的幾個方面》,原載美國《俄亥俄州立大學人文學院就職演説》(Inaugural Lectures 1985—1987),1987 年,第 29—35 頁。

2,500 years ago, which were followed by the even more extensive writings of the philosophers, or latter-day sages, during the so-called Warring States period of twenty-five to twenty-two hundred years ago. The Confucian classics, together with the writings of some of the philosophers, played a most important role in the formation of the Chinese civilization, perhaps a much greater role than that of the Bible for the European civilization. Naturally, they became the focus of scholars' attention from the very ancient time. The need to interpret these classics correctly, which at times could be a matter of life or death, thus gave birth to an early form of linguistic study. As early as the second century B. C., glossaries of words from the classics and other forms of reading aids for them appeared. The most famous collection was a book titled Erya(爾雅) which immediately became a classic itself and was mistakenly thought to be a work by a famous ancient sage, the Duke of Zhou, This used to the compilation of the first comprehensive dictionary in the Chinese history, namely the Shuowen Jiezi(説文解字) by Xu Shen(許慎) of the 1st century A. D. This dictionary attempts to classify and define more than 10,000 words or characters, not only about what they meant, but, more importantly, why they were drawn, or written, in a certain particular form. This book has thus become the foundation of paleography, a branch of linguistic study which is often neglected in the West but has always been very popular, and commanding great respect, in China. Another book which is not so well-known but is perhaps far more interesting to linguists of the modern time appeared soon after Xu's dictionary, namely, the Shiming(釋名), or "On Defining Names", by Liu Xi(劉熙) of the second century A. D. This book is interesting in a metalinguistic sense. The author tried to define the meaning of words by their pronunciation. Of course, most of the definitions are nothing but arbitrary speculations, but the concept behind is a very interesting one. It is what has been called "sound symbolism" and it reminds us of the debate between the Naturalists and the Conventionalists in ancient Greece. Did the Greek Naturalists influenced him? Probably not. More likely, he got the idea from Confucius who once defined a few words in this manner. For example, when he was asked by his disciples what he meant by humanity, he answered: "Humanity means (how) to be a human being" (Ren zhe ren ye 仁者人也). Another important linguistic work that I may mention is the Fang Yen (方言) by Yang Xiong (揚雄) who lived in the same age as Jesus Christ. As a result of the expansion of the Han empire, and the improvement of communication, linguistic diversity became too obvious to be ignored, and the study of dialects in the Chinese linguistic tradition thus started at this time with this book. Linguistic works of this kind, though each assuming a different form, share one feature in common, i. e., the concern for the lexicography of the writings of the ancient sages. Throughout Chinese history down to the very pre-modern time, Chinese scholars not only tried to read but to write the classical language of the sages, which they stubbornly believed to be the only acceptable form for formal expression. Traditional education meant almost nothing more than the mastering of this language. Linguistic scholars classified the lexicon into two categories, the substantive words vs. the empty words, and concentrated on the former. They did little about the so-called "empty words", i. e, the function words in the grammar of the language, and they did practically nothing about the phonology of that language, presumably because they couldn't see how they could be benefitted by these two branches of linguistics in their understanding of the language of the ancient sages. The study of these two branches had to wait until a much later date, as late 15th century in the Ming dynasty, when linguistic changes had made the language of the ancient sages an almost totally different one from the language of that time, both in syntactic structure and especially in pronunciation. It was also at this point that Chinese linguists finally realized and accepted the fact that all languages change in time. This realization is also partially the result of the influence of a different methodology which had been developed in the study of the language of the poets, as I will explain soon. Equipped with this new method and motivated by an even greater enthusiasm for the writings of the sages than their predecessors, the great scholars of the Ming and the Qing dynasties began to reconstruct the language of the ancient sages. The concern for that language thus eventually led to historical reconstruction in the Chinese linguistic tradition. This is quite different from how comparative-historical linguistics started in Europe, which, as we know, grew primarily out of a fascination with the genetic relationship among different languages, and, in some cases, a concern for national identity.

Long before the Ming and the Qing scholars began reconstructing the sound system of the "Archaic Chinese", i. e., the language of the sages, a different concern occurred, namely, the study of the language of the poets. Poetry has consistently played a very crucial role in the Chinese life, and there are many different forms of poetry, each springing up from a form of folk song of a certain historical period. It seems that it is easier to imitate the prose of an ancient period than its poetry. Perhaps, the best poetic expressions are possible only when they are uttered spontaneously in the language one knows the best, normally one's own native tongue. At any rate, imitations of the ancient Shijing(詩經), or "The Confucian Odes", as Erza Pound called it, and imitations of the Chuci(楚辭), or "The Songs of the South," as Arthur Waley translated it, are rather rare. Best poetic creations were made mostly in the language of the poets' time. A new form of poetry appeared toward the end of the Han dynasty, i. e., the end of the second century A. D., flourished and culminated by the Tang dynasty, also known as the Golden Age of Poetry. The desire to understand this form of poetry, and the magic of poetry in general, was very high in the mind of the scholars and the poets. It also happened that Buddhism was introduced into China and flourished during this period of time. As we all know, the ancient Indians were excellent linguists. They put great emphasis on properly reciting and chanting the sacred sutras of their religions, and thus developed some highly refined techniques for linguistic analysis. This Parnini tradition, so to speak, was inherited by the Buddhists and eventually brought to China. Under this influence, Chinese scholars for the first time realized that a syllable, or a character in their writing, was not the smallest unit, but could be broken down into smaller units, and, more interestingly, theirs was a tone language, with as many as four different tones. The excitement that followed these discoveries was almost unbelievable. They, particularly the leading scholar-poet Shen Yue(沈約), claimed thereupon that the secrets of poetry, and literary creation in general, that had remained a great mystery to the humans since the beginning of the world, was now finally uncovered by them, and they began to formulate a number of rules of DO's and DON'T's on linguistic ground for what they asserted to be proper ways of poetic composition. Poetry is, of course, not that mechanical, but rhythmic and rhyming patterns are obvious important elements of poetics. Due to the advocation of these literary scholars, the need for the study of the phonology of the spoken language became an absolute necessity and was hotly pursued. Many rhyme dictionaries were compiled during this period, which were eventually summed up in an authoritative and enlarged edition entitled Qieyun (切韻) by Lu Fayan(陸法言)in 601 A.D. These rhyme dictionaries served a useful function in standardizing the then official spoken language. Linguistically, however, what is more significant is that they adopted a new method for the notation of pronunciation. This method, known as fanqie (反切), is really quite simple, but, also effective and precise. A syllable represented by a character was first analyzed into two components, the initial consonant, also called simply the "initial"(shengmu 聲母), and the rest of the syllable, technically called the "final"(yunmu 韻母). Then, two different characters would be chosen to form a notational compound, with its first character representing a syllable having an identical initial but a different final, while the second standing for a syllable with a different initial but an identical final. In this way, the reading of every existing word, or character, in the language could now have a precise written representation, something the Chinese never knew how to do until then. It was, therefore, a clever solution for the frustrating old problem of how to accurately indicate the pronunciation of words on paper—a problem inherited from the unique writing system which the Chinese invented for their own language. We could legitimately ask: Since these ancient Chinese linguists were under the influence of the ancient Indians, why didn't they simply adopt the Sanskrit alphabet to mark the reading of the Chinese characters, in the same way as modern Chinese linguists use the IPA symbols for that purpose? Well, when it comes to humanities, simple logic sometimes does not work. It almost never worked for the Chinese, anyway. As with most foreign things, including Buddhism and Marxism, foreign linguistic ideas also must be first transformed into something Chinese before they were absorbed. This is not necessarily a bad thing, though. Actually, I would argue, as a matter of fact, I have argued for a number of years, that this might have been the best possible thing that ever happened to Chinese linguistics, because it pre-determined, from the very start, that Chinese phonological study was to be highly abstract in nature, i. e. , strictly problem, due to this unique manner of representation and its single-minded concern with phonemic contrast.

The Chinese linguists were not satisfied with just marking the readings of words accurately. They were also interested in the overall sound system and its internal structure. Starting from the middle of the. Tang dynasty, i. e. , roughly in the 9th century, they began to draw rhyme tables, or charts, to show the unique structure of every possible syllable, and the relationship among the numerous syllables and rhyme classes of the language. They were so ingeniously designed that every phonologically possible syllable in the language had one and only one particular slot in a particular table. Furthermore, all syllables were defined as having four possible segments arranged in a specific canonical pattern, and these segments were further defined as being qing(清) 'clear/voiceless' or zhuo(濁) 'muddy/voiced', kai(開) 'open/unrounded' or he(合) 'close/rounded', and belonging to a certain yin(音) 'sound-type', or belonging to a certain deng(等) 'rank', etc., etc.. Concepts like these make me feel that this Chinese approach is really very much in agreement with the theory of "distinctive features" in modern linguistics. It seems quite amazing to me that human mind, East and West, separated so far apart both in time and in space, could have worked in such an almost identical way, and it is, I would say, a great pity that this approach developed in China more than a thousand years ago was not known to the linguists in the West. Otherwise, we perhaps would not have to wait until the beginning of the 20th century for the concept of "phoneme", and until the middle of the century for the concept of "distinctive features."

As time went on, the language changed with it, and various forms of poetry appeared. In the Song dynasty, it was the ci(詞) poetry that flourished; in the Yuan dynasty it was the qu(曲) poetry; and after that it was a few different forms of folk literature in verse, including Peking opera. Naturally, new rhyme dictionaries for each period had to be and were compiled. Rhyme dictionaries from as early as the fifth century to the nineteenth century were always referred to as the jinyun(今韻)"modern phonology", in contrast to the guyun(古韻)"ancient phonology", a term referring to the reconstruction of the language of the sages. Many people have been puzzled by these terms. How on earth can you call the study of a language more than a thousand years ago a modern phonological study? Well, it is actually not that confusing, if we do not take the term jin "the present day" too literally. When we take a closer look at these two branches of study in Chinese linguistics, we will notice that they represent two conceptually different approaches. In one case, the concern is the histerical reconstruction of the language of the sages; in the other, it is a synchronical analysis of the language of the poets. In other words, they represent the contrast of diachronical vs. synchronical studies. This is again a seemingly very modern concept, but it had been in practice for many centuries in China.

If, as I have claimed so far, the ancient Chinese linguists had indeed adopted a strictly phonemic approach, moved very close to the distinctive feature approach, and observed the contrast between synchronic and diachronic studies, many centuries before their Western colleagues got these ideas in the 20th century, a logical question can perhaps be raised as to how it could have been possible to keep these ideas from being known to the Western scholars, because, after all, communications between the East and the West, though difficult at first, have been going on fairly regularly at least since the time of Marco Polo. There is no sure answer for such a question, but two plausible explanations might perhaps be offered. The first is that, unlike other forms of scientific or technological inventions such as gunpowder, navigation compass, printing and paper, which are obvious for anybody to see, linguistic discoveries are very much dependent on specific languages. One can hardly understand, and less to appreciate, a linguistic discovery without a keen interest for linguistic theory and a very high level of proficiency in the language where a certain discovery was made. This may perhaps also explain why, even in this modern time of ours, the famous British scholar Joseph Needham didn't include a chapter on Chinese linguistic discoveries in his Science and Civilization in China. I believe he would, if he knew that the Chinese were leading in linguistic studies not merely up to the 14th century, as he claimed they were in most other fields, but up to the beginning of the present century. The second cause for this rather unfortunate lack of communication is a creation of the Chinese themselves. They buried their theories under a pile of technical jargon and fancy names.

For some highly technical and theoretical studies, a certain amount of technical jarson is certainly necessary, but they can also create a barrier for proper understanding. When linguists of the Tang dynasty designed their rhyme-tables, they naturally used a number of technical terms. Since they were talking about their own spoken language, the terms they used must have been fairly clear to their fellow native speakers and linguists, and, therefore, required no elaborate defining, but after several hundred years, sound changes often clouded the meaning of these terms, while misinterpretations of these terms by later linguists, as well as the new terms they added, often tend to aggravate the problem. Furthermore, starting from the Song dynasty, especially since the time of the mysticist-philosopher Shao Yong(邵雍)of the 11th century, and culminating by the Ming-Qing period, a kind of mysticism prevailed in linguistic studies in China. Many Chinese scholars who were more oriented toward abstract theoretical interpretation began to explain phonological matters in terms of ancient Chinese musicology which was hard for the laymen to understand, as well as in terms of Chinese cosmology or astrology, using such terms as yin(陰), yang(陽), the five basic elements of the universe (wuxing 五行), etc., which are even more mysterious to us. Quite obviously, it seems to me, these linguists must have been astonished and mystified by what seemed to them to be an incredibly symmetrical sound system underlying their language, which they could somewhat intuitively recognize but could not clearly describe. This must have led them to believe that nothing short of God's wish could have brought something so marvelously systematic into existence, and it, therefore, must be a universal and heavenly phenomenon, instead of something for the Chinese language alone, and thus could only be described in cosmological terms. As a consequence, while the works of these scholars are highly valuable for us to understand the various stages in the development of the Chinese language, they are wrapped up in thick layers and layers of mystery which are almost impossible to penetrate.

How to cut through these layers and reach the core is a hard but also very intriguing question which has bewitched me for the past 20 years.

The seemingly confusing nature and the highly technical aspects of traditional Chinese linguistics can be quite awesome and discouraging to a beginner. Moreover, many of the works on this subject by modern scholars are rather vague and, therefore, equally confusing. But if one is curious enough to pick up this challenging subject, it may eventually become a most interesting one, as it has turned out to be to me. In my pursuit of this subject, I was greatly inspired by my study of modern linguistic theories, especially phonemics and the distinctive feature theory. I found a strictly phonemic interpretation of the historical data often helped us explain why the ancient Chinese linguists classified the data the way they did in the rhyme dictionaries or the rhyme-table books which they compiled, and the seemingly inscrutable technical terms used by them then, more often than not, turned out to be easier to understand and entirely logical when really understood. There are, of course, many difficult problems and frequent frustrations in this decoding process, and that's why so far I have merely succeeded in moving backward from the modern time to roughly the 8th century A. D., just about half way in the long recorded history of the Chinese language, but there are also great satisfactions and joys whenever I succeeded in cracking a seemingly insoluble enigma, and so I plan to continue my search into the past, hopefully to the beginning of the Chinese civilization and beyond, if I can live long enough. (I figured I need only about one hundred years.) To decipher the enigmatic problems in the Chinese linguistic tradition is, of course, only one aspect of our research. Somewhat more importantly, we shall be able to acquire, through this process, good and solid knowledge about the Chinese language itself in its many historical periods, and this will, I believe, help us explain all other aspects of the Chinese civilization. The research can be, therefore, both entertaining to ourselves and enlightening to others. Upon looking back at my own career, I often found naturally quite a few disappointing occasions, but in general it is a feeling of satisfaction. Sometimes I feel very lucky when I realize that my type of research and teaching often gives me a wonderful opportunity to read and reflect on the teachings of the ancient sages, and to enjoy the beautiful poems of the numerous great poets in history. Reading their books is, as one sage puts it, the best way to make friends with the brightest minds in human history.

元微之年譜***

序

文學欣賞固應側重一流作家，然就文學史之研究而言，如欲明瞭某一時代之特色，於該時代之次要作家，匪唯不當忽視，且應加以研究。蓋文學描寫之對象，乃人類天性之本然，喜怒哀樂之情，古今咸同。故偉大之文學作品，雖千古而常新，力足以超越時代之羈絆而直迫人性之根本者，唯一流作家爲能，然亦因是之故，其作品縱不乏時代特色，而該等特色則往往相形之下隱晦不顯；反之，二流作家每難脱其時代之樊圄，因之其作品常帶明顯與强烈之時代色調，我們若就該等作家着手研析，必然更易把握各時代之特色與精神。

詩至唐而極盛，老杜之後，白得其正、韓得其變，此前修之確論也。與白傅關係最深者，厥爲元相。就文學成就言，微之誠非樂天之匹，是以歷來宗白詩者，代不乏人，而研習元詩者，幾於不聞，而元和一代之文學特色，亦歷千年而不彰，雖飽學之老宿，猶或不能詳知，陳寅恪氏於此論之詳矣，然其故安在？寧非困於不明前説之故歟？余有鑒及此，因纂斯編，期在發明元和詩體之本質與夫當日文壇之梗概。（拙論大要見於"元和十五年"條。）竊以爲微之個性務進，乃倡運動立新説之能手，是以不僅爲當日詩壇之盟主、新體詩文理論與創作之先導，且爲當日政壇一小集團之領袖。世有識者苟不以我説爲妄，則斯編之作或不無抛磚之效；爲老元辯冤白謗，搜微發奇，固又在其次矣。

一九六〇年於臺灣大學中國文學研究所

*** 原由學生書局出版，1977 年。

世系親屬暨幼年時代之家境略考

元稹字微之,河南人。

新、舊《唐書》本傳,《白氏長慶集》六一《元稹墓志》並同。

《元氏長慶集》五八《陸翰妻河南元氏墓志》云:

"始祖有魏昭成皇帝,後失國,今稱河南洛陽人焉。"故知河南乃稹之郡望也。《全唐詩》元稹條小傳作"河南河内人"。

魏昭成皇帝之裔。

《舊唐書》一六六本傳云:"後魏昭成皇帝,稹十代祖也。兵部尚書、昌平公巖,六代祖也。曾祖延景,岐州參軍。祖悱,南頓丞。父寬,比部郎中、舒王府長史。"

《新唐書》七五下《世系表》云:"元氏出自拓拔氏……什翼犍,昭成皇帝也,始號代王,至道武皇帝改號魏,至孝文帝更爲元氏。"

"什翼犍第六子力真。力真二子:意烈、意勁。意勁,彭城公,五世孫敷州刺史禎。禎二子巖、成。"巖字君山,隋兵部尚書、平昌公。巖生弘,隋北平太守。弘生義端,魏州刺史。義端生延景,岐州參軍。延景生悱,南頓丞。悱生寬,北(當作比)部郎中、舒王長史。寬生稹,相穆宗。

又《元和姓纂》四云:"昭成生力真。力真生意烈、勃……勃元孫植,生巖、成。巖,隋兵部尚書、平昌公,生琳。琳生義恭、義端。……義端,魏州刺史,生……延景。……延景生俳……俳生寬、宵。寬比部郎中,生秬、稹。"

又《白氏長慶集》六一《河南元公墓志》云:"公即……後魏昭成皇帝十五代孫也。"

又《元氏長慶集》五七《河陰留後元君(秬)墓志》云:"有魏昭成皇帝十一代而生我隋朝兵部尚書府君諱某,後五代而生我比部郎中、舒王府長史府君諱某,君即府君之第二子也。"

案微之世系,諸説紛紜,《舊書》以昭成爲十世祖,《新書》以爲十四世,《姓纂》以爲十三世,白撰稹志以爲十五世,而微之自作仲兄墓志則以爲十七世,當以微之自言爲可信。至於微之本出元魏,乃絶無可疑者。

六世祖巖仕隋爲兵部尚書,自後其族日蹙。

本集五九《告贈皇祖祖妣文》云:"始兵部賜第於靖安里,下及天寶,五世其居。冕昇駢比,羅列省寺……冠冕之盛,重於一時。燕寇突來,人士駭散,蔭籍朘削,龜繩用稀。我曾我祖,仍世不偶。"

父寬,嘗總集群言成書,抄以傳子,以宗人之累,官不得進。

本集五七《河陰留後元君墓志》云:"先府君叢集群言,裁成百葉書抄,君懼不得授,乃日一食以齋其心者一月。先太君憐而請焉,由是盡付其書。"

又同書五八《陸翰妻河南元氏墓志銘》云:"府君諱某,以四教垂子孫:孝先之,儉次之,學次之,政成之。當乾元、廣德之間,郡國多事,由雲陽昭應尉馮翊猗氏長遷于殿中侍殿史,或未環歲,或未浹時,而五命自天。非夫公不來則人不蘇,公不遷則善不聳,何是之速也。董芳書奏議者凡八人。其在比部郎中也,宗人得罪有不察。夫玉與珉類而不雜□屈,我府君爲虢州别駕,累遷舒王府長史,至則懸車息□宴如也。嘗著百葉書要,以萃群言。"

母鄭氏,滎陽人,睦州刺史濟之次女,賢而文,親授其子以書學。

《白氏長慶集》二五《河南元府君夫人滎陽墓志銘》云:"父諱濟,睦州刺史。夫人,睦州次女也。……夫人爲婦時,元氏世食貧……夫人爲母時,府君既歿,稹與方齠齓,家貧,無師以受業。夫人親執書,誨而不倦,四五年間,二子皆以通經入仕。"

又《舊唐書》一六六《稹傳》云:"稹八歲喪父。其母鄭夫人,賢明婦人也,家貧,爲稹自授書,教之書學。"

案微之亦自云(本集三十三《同州刺史謝上表》):"幼學之年,不蒙師訓,因感鄰里兒稚有父兄爲開學校,涕咽發憤,願知詩書。慈母哀臣,親爲教授。"則鄭夫人之賢明知書可知矣,宜乎白樂天盛稱其德行也。

兄沂、秬、積。

《白氏長慶集》二五《河南元府君夫人滎陽鄭氏墓志》云:“夫人有四子二女,長曰沂,蔡州汝陽尉。次曰秬,京兆府萬年縣尉。次曰積,同州韋城尉。次曰稹,河南尉。”

又本集五八《陸翰妻河南元氏墓志》云:“夫人兄沂、兄秬、弟積、弟稹,或遠游,或守官,或歸養,皆不克會葬。”

按微之長兄沂,長於稹當在三十歲左右。(秬長於稹二十六歲,則沂之年可從而推知之。)當其父之喪也,阻官於蔡,未克奔喪(見秬志)。及其母歿,又逾二十年(稹父卒於貞元二年,母卒於元和元年,皆見後考),而白居易撰稹母墓志,仍謂沂爲蔡州汝陽尉,則其宦途不達也可知。微之平素詩文亦少及之,其後亦不可考。次兄秬(白居易撰稹母墓志、《元和姓纂》皆作拒,並見前引;稹撰陸翰妻元氏墓志,《新唐書》世系表皆作秬,亦見前引。疑當以秬爲是,蓋積、稹皆從禾也。)字玄度,長於微之二十有六。其爲人也,恭慎誠篤,父歿之後,即獨力持家,微之稱其“四十年事親,無一日之怠,三十年養下,無一詞之倦。撫諸弟無正色之訓而亦不至於不恭,教諸子無鞭笞之責,而亦不至於不令。以閑處劇,而吏不忍欺;以直立誠,而忤不及物。”其與微之,幾於嚴父,從可知也。官至侍御史、河陰留後。(《新唐書》世系表謂爲萬年尉,蓋據白撰稹母墓志,不知秬後復有升遷也。)後去官從稹,卒於虢州。《元氏長慶集》五七有墓志。次兄積,與稹年相若,官至司農少卿。稹歿時尚在,且董稹之喪。(見白撰稹志、《新唐書》世系表。)

(按白居易撰稹志謂爲“仲兄”,頗不可解。本集二有《三兄遺白角巾》詩一首,以文意推之,當指秬言,唐人排行,常以從兄並計,如稹爲第四子而呼爲元九。今但曰次兄。)

姊二人,長適陸翰,次爲比丘尼。

《白氏長慶集》二五《河南元府君夫人鄭氏墓志》云:“夫人有四子二女……長女適吴郡陸翰,翰爲監察御史。次爲比丘尼,名真一,二女不幸皆先夫人歿。”

按微之長姊適陸翰,其事迹見於本集五八《陸翰妻河南元氏墓志》。志云:

"生十四年遂歸於吴郡陸翰……翰少孤,事親以至行立,釋褐太平主簿,我姊由是而歸之。逮陸君之宰夏陽也,事姑垂二十年矣。"又云:"享年三十有□,歿世於夏陽縣之私第,是唐之貞元二十五年(按貞元僅有二十一年,而二十一年八月即改元,此云二十五,'五'字當是衍文。)十二月初五日矣。冬十月十有四日,歸葬於河南洛陽之清風郡……永貞之元年歲乙酉,朔旦景申,辰在己酉,須時順也。"以是考之,翰妻卒於貞元二十年,其時三十四五歲,長於稹約八九齡;其歸於陸氏,當在興元元年前後,即稹六七齡時,父寬歿前之二三年也。

次姊比丘尼,名真一,僅見於白撰稹母墓志,以時間約略計之,疑長於微之。(按微之伯兄沂長於微之二十六歲以上,已見前考,然則微之生時,其母之年當在四十以上,可無疑矣。其母卒時,微之已二十八,是其卒年必不少於七十,而白居易所撰墓志云:"年六十寢疾,歿於萬年縣安里私第。"如無誤,似不可解,否則沂、秬當非其所出,則鄭氏爲繼室矣。此就秬志觀之,固甚少可能者,姑存此以待續考。)

前妻韋叢,字成之,京兆人,太子少保韋夏卿之幼女。生未盈月而喪母,依繼母段氏以長,賢淑有聞,無禄早世。

《韓昌黎集》二四《監察御史元君妻京兆韋氏墓志》(又見《全唐文》五六五)云:"夫人諱叢,字茂之,姓韋氏……王考夏卿,以太子少保卒,贈左僕射。僕射娶裴氏皋女,皋爲給事中,皋父宰相耀卿。夫人於僕射爲季女,愛之。選婿得今御史河南元稹,稹時始以選校書秘書省中。……年二十七,以元和四年七月九日卒。"又《元氏長慶集》五八《唐左千牛韋佩母段氏墓志》云:"予亡妻生不盈月而先夫人歿,免水火之灾,成習柔之性,用至於妝櫛針組書誡琴瑟之事,無遺訓,誠有以賴焉。"按昌黎《韋氏志》云韋叢字茂之,茂當爲成之誤,稹有"夢成之"(本集九)詩,足證。昌黎又云韋氏卒年二十七。按成之歸微之時,爲貞元十九年,微之二十五歲(前人皆以微之婚於韋氏,在貞元十八年,竊疑其誤,説見後考),則其時成之應爲二十歲。《元氏長慶集》六《祭亡妻韋氏文》云:"況夫人之生也,選甘而味,借光而衣,順耳而聲,便心而使,親戚驕其意,父兄可其求,將二十年矣。"是韋氏嫁時,尚未及二十。祭文又云:"逮歸於我,始知貧賤,食亦不飽,衣亦不温。然而不悔於色,不戚於言,他人以我爲拙,夫人以我爲尊。”又本集九《遣悲懷》一云:“謝公最小偏憐女,自嫁黔婁百事乖。”韋氏之賢淑,於此可知。

《舊唐書》一六五《韋夏卿傳》云:“韋夏卿,字雲客,杜陵人。……大曆中與弟正卿俱應制舉,同時策入高等。……深於儒術,所至招禮通經之士。……貞元末……徵夏卿爲吏部侍郎,轉京兆尹、太子賓客,檢校工部尚書、東都留守,遷太子少保。卒時年六十四,贈左僕射。夏卿有風韻,善談讌,與人同處終年,而喜愠不形於色。撫孤侄,恩逾己子,早有時稱。其所與游辟之賓佐,皆一時名士。爲政務通適,不喜改作。始在東都,傾心辟士,頗得才彦,其後多至卿相,世謂之知人。”按夏卿以女妻微之,足證其知人,而微之之交游,與此亦大有關係。(如友於方群、李景儉等。)

繼室裴淑,字柔之,河東人。

《白氏長慶集》六一《河南元公墓志銘》云:“今夫人河東裴氏,賢明有禮,有輔佐君子之勞,封河東郡君。”《元氏長慶集》一二《酬樂天東南行詩一百韻序》云:“通之人莫可與言詩者,唯妻淑在旁,知狀。”又同書二一有《黄草峽聽柔之琴二首》,皆謂裴氏也。按裴氏之出身門第與夫婚於微之之原委,今皆莫可詳考,意其出身必不若韋叢之高貴,至其婚期疑爲元和十一年夏微之守通時(見後考)。又陳寅恪先生《元白詩箋證稿》四“艷詩及悼亡詩”條云:“若更取其(稹)繼配裴氏以較韋氏,則裴氏稍知文墨。”按陳氏此説甚諦,於此亦可稍稍推出二女婚時之狀況。何以言之?韋叢依其繼母而成立,未及二十即歸微之,宜其受教之少也。《元氏長慶集》五八《韋佩母段氏墓志》云:“是以予妻之言於予曰:‘離則思,思則夢,夢則悲,疾則泣,戀戀然予不知其異所親矣。’”由是觀之,成之嫁後,尚屬稚氣未泯也。至於裴淑與微之結縭時之年齡,雖不可知,然必不若韋叢嫁時之幼,殆可斷言。

子道護。女保子、小迎、道衛、道扶。

《白氏長慶集》六一《河南元公墓志銘》云:“前夫人京兆韋氏……生一女曰保子,適校書韋絢。今夫人河東裴氏……生三女,曰:小迎,未笄;道衛、道扶,齠齓。一子,曰道護,三歲。”按微之在江陵時,曾納妾安氏,生一子,名荆。(本集五八葬安氏志。)集九有《哭子十首》,注云:"翰林學士時作。"疑此子即荆也(見後考)。同卷復有哭女樊、哭小女降真等詩,明積先更有二女,皆不幸夭折(二女所出與夫微之美妾之關係,詳見後考)。又《全唐詩》白居易三五《夢微之》云:"夜來携手夢同游,晨起盈巾淚莫收。漳浦老身三度病,咸陽宿草八回秋。君埋泉下泥銷骨,我寄人間雪滿頭。阿衛韓郎相次去,夜臺茫昧得知不。"自注云:"阿衛,微之小男;韓郎,微之愛婿。"(詩又見《白氏長慶集》六八,無注。)是微之卒後,其子又復夭折也。

侄易簡、從簡、行簡、弘簡。侄女四。

本集五七《河陰留後元君(秬)墓志銘》云:"諱某,字玄度,娶清河崔鄰女,生四子:長曰易簡,滎陽尉;次從簡,曲沃尉;次行簡,太樂丞;幼弘簡。長女適劉中孚,中孚早卒。次嬰疾室居,次適蘇京,舉進士。次適李殊,殊妻早夭。"又本集九有《誨侄等書》,尋翻其文意,似屬秬子,所指侖鄭等,意皆易簡等之乳名。又按沂、積等必亦皆有子,然已不可考矣。

附世系表

昭成皇帝（什翼犍，始號代王）—力真—意勁（彭城公）（注一）

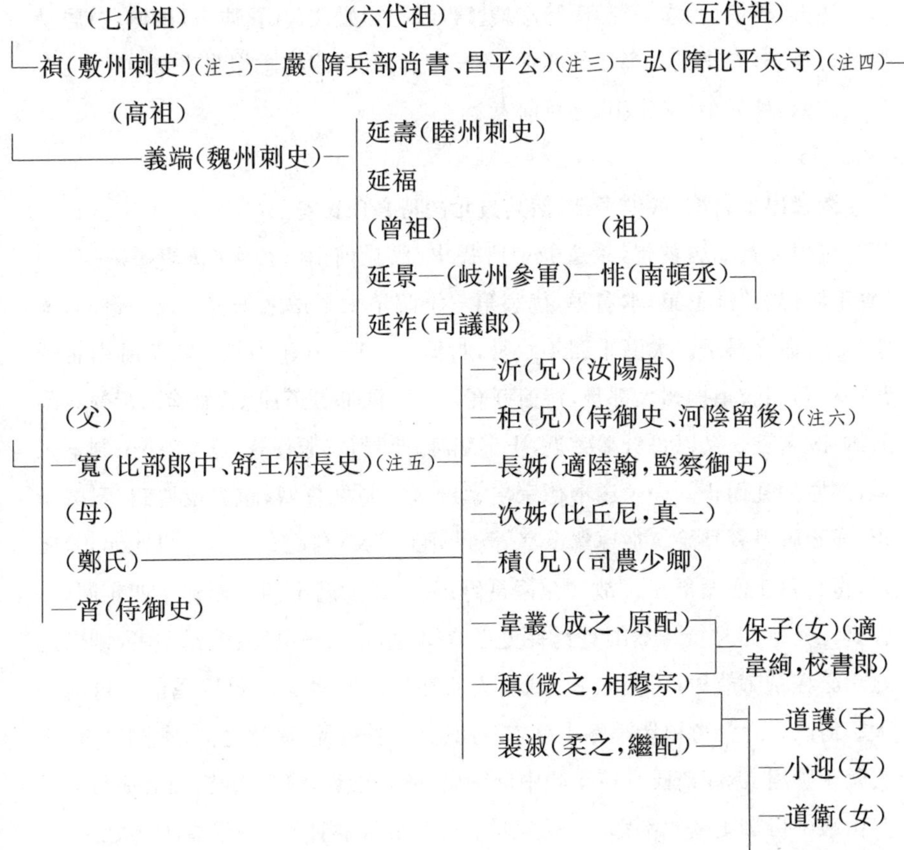

注一：《新唐書》世系表謂力真二子意烈、意勁。《元和姓纂》云力真生意烈、勃。

注二：《新唐書》世系表云意勁五世孫名禎，禎生巖成，《元和姓纂》云勃元孫生巖成。

注三：六代祖諸書皆作巖，唯稹撰《陸翰妻元氏墓志》（本集五八）作嚴，仍以巖爲是。又巖之封號，《舊唐書》稹傳、白居易《元稹墓志》暨微之《陸翰妻元氏墓志》皆作昌平公。《新表》暨《元和姓纂》皆作平昌公。考《隋書》六二、《北史》七五巖傳，皆作昌平公。

注四:《新表》、《積志》俱云五代祖弘。《元和姓纂》云巖生琳,琳生義恭、義端。

注五:稹撰《秬志》、《陸氏姊志》暨《告贈皇祖妣文》,《舊唐書》稹傳,白居易撰稹母墓志,皆謂其父爲比部郎中。唯《新表》既白撰稹志作北部郎中。

注六:稹兄秬,又作拒,已見前考。

微之出生之地,頗難考知,然其貞元初時必在長安。

按稹父寬謫居虢州,累遷舒王府長史,已見前引。復考《舊唐書》一五〇《舒王誼傳》:"舒王誼,本名謨,代宗第三子昭靖太子邈之子也。以其最幼,德宗憐之,命之爲子。大曆十四年六月,封舒王。……(建中)三年,蔡帥李希烈叛……乃詔誼爲揚州大都督,持節荆襄、江西、沔鄂等道節度,兼諸軍行營兵馬元帥,改名誼。又以哥舒翰聲近,士卒竊議,改封晉(原作普,誤)王……制下未行,涇原兵亂而止。……遂奉德宗出幸奉天。賊之攻城,誼晝夜傳詔,慰勞諸軍,僅不解帶者月餘。從車駕還宫,復封舒王。"又《舊紀》一二:"(貞元元年)四月,復封晉王誼爲舒王。"故知誼兩爲舒王:一在大曆十四年至建中四年間,一在貞元元年四月後。然則寬爲長史之時間,亦有二種可能:若爲前者,則微之之生必在京師故居;若爲後者,則爲寬所在地之官舍矣。竊以爲前一可能較大。何以言之?考稹撰陸翰妻墓志,言其父:"當乾元、廣德之間,郡國多事,由雲陽昭應尉、馮翊猗氏長遷于殿中侍御史,或未環歲,或未浹時,而五命自天。"其由殿中侍御史遷比部郎中,疑至遲不得晚於大曆四年,則謫棄十年之後,十四年歸爲舒王府長史,實不爲速。復考《秬志》:"貞元初,蝗且儉,我先太君白府君貨女奴以足食。"其所以一貧至此者,頗疑寬於兵亂之後,失其官守,益以蝗灾,誠所謂"時難年荒世業空"者,遂至貧窶困頓以終,亦云悲矣。

又按《舊紀》一二:"(貞元元年正月)戊戌,大風雪,寒,去秋螟蝗,冬旱,至是雪,寒甚,民饑凍死者踣於路。"取此與前引秬志相印證,知興元元年及貞元元年,寬與其家人皆寓長安。秬志又云:"先府君棄養之歲,前累月而季父侍御史府君捐館……遺其家唯環堵之宫耳。皆曰:'貨是以襄二事,可也。'君跪言於先太君曰:'斯宇也,尚書府君受賜於隋氏,乃今傳七代矣,敢有失守,以貽太夫人憂。'按此所謂"受賜於隋氏"之宇,即《告贈皇祖祖妣文》(本集五九)所謂之'始兵部賜第於靖安里下'之宅第,亦即稹詩常及之"靖安里故居"也。稹父卒於貞元二年(見後考),是該年稹仍在長安。(《元和郡縣圖志》一萬年縣條云:"周明帝二年……始於長安城中置萬年縣。隋開皇三年遷都,改爲大興縣,理宣陽坊。武德元年復爲萬年。乾封元年分置明堂縣,理永樂坊。長安三年廢。天寶七年改爲咸寧。乾元元年復爲萬年縣。")

父卒後,無以爲生,乃隨母兄徙鳳翔。

按稹父卒於貞元二年,則其家徙岐之日,可能是在歲末,亦可能爲次年。本集一一《答姨兄胡靈之見寄五十一韻》序云:"九歲解賦詩……時方依倚舅族。"詩云:"憶昔鳳翔城,齠年是事榮。理家煩伯舅,相宅盡吾兄。詩律蒙親授,朋游忝自迎。"同書卷六《寄吴士矩端公五十韻》云:"昔在鳳翔日,十歲即相識。"卷三十《誨侄等書》云:"吾幼乏岐嶷,十歲知方,嚴毅之訓不聞,師友之資盡廢,憶得初讀書時,感慈旨一言之嘆,遂志於學。是時尚在鳳翔,每借書於齊倉曹家,徒步執卷,就陸姊夫師授。"因知微之九歲十歲,亦即貞元三四年時,皆在鳳翔,"依倚舅族,分張外姻"(本集五九《告贈皇考皇妣文》)。亦即《同州謝上表》所云"母兄乞丐以供資養"者也。(陳寅恪先生《元白詩箋證稿》四"艷詩及悼忘詩"條云:"微之幼時,依其姊婿陸翰,居於西北邊境荒殘之地。"就前引"理家煩伯舅"及"徒步執卷,就陸姊夫師授"觀之,其所依者乃伯舅而非翰。然翰於稹家必多所濟助,自屬無疑。)

微之幼時所依之舅族,必屬近親。按稹父卒時,鄭雲逵爲作墓志。(《白氏長慶集》二五《稹母墓志》云:"比部府君世禄官政文行,有故京兆尹鄭雲逵之志在。"今《全唐文》所收鄭雲逵文不見此志,蓋已佚失。)

而微之《叙詩寄樂天書》(本集三〇):"故鄭京兆於僕爲外諸翁,深賜憐奬,因以所賦(寄思玄子詩)呈獻,京兆翁深相駭異。"微之寄思玄子詩作於十五歲前後(見後考),則其爲雲逵所"深賜憐奬",自屬更早。《新唐書》一六一《鄭雲逵傳》(《舊書》一三七《雲逵傳》略同)云:"鄭雲逵系本滎陽……誕譎敢言,已登進士第,去客燕朔,朱泚善之,表爲掌書記,妻以滔女。……滔助田悦,雲逵諫,不從,遂棄室自歸。德宗悦,擢諫議大夫。帝在梁,雲逵依李晟,晟表以禮部侍郎爲軍司馬,時時咨逮戎略。元和初,爲京兆尹,卒。"而李晟貞元三年前後爲鳳翔隴右節度使(見《舊紀》一二及《晟傳》),則其時雲逵極可能在鳳翔,積之伯舅或從雲逵官於其地,而積家復往倚之也。此説雖難免穿鑿之譏,然微之與雲逵關係之深厚,於此乃略可窺知。竊嘗以爲,少年時代於微之影響最大者,一爲其父寬,另一即爲雲逵。寬雖不必果如積所稱之"盛德大業",要亦不失爲篤學慎行之士,早歲登朝頗速,一經謫棄,遂至奄頓下寮,終不復起。至若雲逵則不然,史稱其"誕譎敢言",觀其行事,誠果決進取之士,故終爲顯宦。此二人遭遇之强烈對比,於微之幼小之心理意識中所造成之影響爲何如哉! 微之一生之仕宦行徑,其心理背景固已形成於其童年矣。

年　譜

唐代宗大曆十四年己未(七七九)。一歲。

案微之生年,諸書皆不載。唯《舊唐書》一六六本傳云:"二十八應制舉才識兼茂、明於體用科,登第者十八人,稹爲第一,元和元年四月也。"又云:"(大和)五年七月二十二日暴疾,一日而卒于鎮,時年五十三。"《白氏長慶集》六一《河南元公墓志》亦云:"大和五年七月二十二日遇暴疾,一日薨於位,春秋五十三。"又《元氏長慶集》三十《叙詩寄樂天書》云:"又不幸三十二時有罪譴棄。"(指元和五年貶江陵言。見後考。)綜合諸説推之,稹之生必在本年。王性之《傳奇辨正論鶯鶯傳》(見趙德麟《侯鯖録》)亦云:"(稹)當以大曆十四年己未生。"

五月,代宗薨,皇太子適即位,是爲德宗。

李白已卒十七年〔肅宗寶應元年(七六二)卒〕。

杜甫已卒九年〔大曆五年(七七〇)卒〕。

孟郊二十九歲〔玄宗天寶十載(七五一)生〕。

韓愈十二歲〔大曆三年(七六八)生〕。

柳宗元七歲〔大曆八年(七七三)生〕。

白居易、劉禹錫、吕温皆已八歲〔同爲大曆七年(七七二)生〕。

賈島亦生於本年。(據李嘉言氏《賈島年譜》)

建中四年癸亥(七八三)。五歲。

十月,涇原節度使姚令言反,犯京師,德宗奔奉天。朱泚反,僭號秦王,改元應天。(《舊紀》一二,《新紀》七)

武元衡、韋純(即貫之,後避憲宗諱,因以字行)等登進士第。(《登科記考》一一)

德宗興元元年甲子(七八四)。六歲。

五月,李晟復京師。六月,姚令言、朱泚並伏誅。七月,德宗自興元還京師。(《新紀》七)

德宗貞元元年乙丑(七八五)。七歲。居長安(見前考)。

家至貧,至貨女奴以自給。(見前考)

七月,關中蝗食草木都盡,旱甚。八月,新除中書侍郎、同平章事張延賞罷位,以與李晟隙,晟自鳳翔上表論之也。

韋執誼、韋純登賢良方正、直言極諫科。(《登科記考》一二)

白樂天十四歲,旅居蘇、杭二郡。時韋應物刺蘇州。

貞元二年丙寅(七八六)。八歲。居長安。

六月,淮西兵馬使吴少誠殺其節度使陳仙奇,自稱留後。

八月,吐蕃寇汾寧涇隴四州。九月,寇好畤,京師戒嚴,復寇鳳翔,李晟出師禦之,一夕而退。(《舊紀》一二)

季父侍御史宵卒,後累月,父舒王府長史寬亦卒,家貧幾無以治喪,因有鬻宅之議,以兄秬之諫乃止。

本集三三《同州刺史謝上表》云:"臣八歲喪父,家貧無業,母兄乞丐以供資養,衣不布體,食不充腸。"同書五七《故河陰留後元君墓志》云:"先府君棄養之歲,前累月而季父侍御史府君捐館。予伯兄由官阻於蔡,叔季皆十年而下,遺其家唯環堵之宫耳。皆曰:'貨是以襄二事可也。'君跪言於先太君曰:'斯宇也,尚書府君受賜於隋氏,乃今傳七代矣,敢有失守,以貽太夫人憂,死無以見先人於地下。'由是匍匐乞,以終其喪。"新、舊《唐書》稹傳皆云稹八歲喪父。又鄭雲逵爲稹父作墓志,已見前考。

家貧無師以受業、母鄭氏親教以書學。

《舊唐書》一六六本傳云:"稹八歲喪父,其母鄭夫人賢明婦人也,家貧爲稹自授書,教之書學。"又本集三三《同州刺史謝上表》云:"幼學之年,不蒙師訓,因感鄰里兒稚有父兄爲開學校,涕咽發憤,願知詩書,慈母哀臣,親爲教授。"則稹之早慧好學可知矣。

韓退之十九歲,至長安。(據宋洪興祖《韓子年譜》)

白樂天十五歲,避難於越中。

貞元三年丁卯(七八七)。九歲。徙居鳳翔。(見前考)

三月,鳳翔隴右涇原四鎮北庭管内兵馬副元帥李晟罷爲太尉。

閏五月,渾瑊及吐蕃盟於平凉,吐蕃執會盟副使崔漢衡,瑊逃歸。六月,吐

蕃寇鹽、夏二州。九月,寇汧陽。(《新紀》七)

家貧無以爲生,乃隨母兄徙鳳翔,往依伯舅,時已能賦詩。與姨兄胡靈之等游從。

本集一一《答姨兄胡靈之見寄五十韻》序云:"九歲解賦詩,飲酒至斗餘乃醉,時方依倚舅族。舅憐,不以禮數檢,故得與姨兄胡靈之之輩十數人爲晝夜游。"詩云:"憶昔鳳翔城,齠年是事榮。"同書三〇《叙詩寄樂天書》云:"稹九歲學賦詩,長者往往驚其可教。"《舊唐書》本傳亦云:"稹九歲能屬文。"《元和郡縣圖志》二"鳳翔府"條:"武德元年復(扶風郡)爲岐州,至德元年改爲鳳翔郡,乾元元年改爲鳳翔府。"又:"東至上都三百一十里。"

白樂天十六歲,至長安,以詩謁顧況,大爲况所推奬。

李德裕生。

貞元四年戊辰(七八八)。十歲。在鳳翔。

正月,劉玄佐爲四鎮北庭行營涇原節度副元帥。五月,吐蕃寇涇邠寧慶鄜五州。

始從姊夫陸翰受學,又從姨兄吴士矩、士則等游。

本集三〇《誨侄等書》云:"吾幼乏岐嶷,十歲……遂志於學,是時尚在鳳翔,每借書於齊倉曹家,徒步執卷,就陸姊夫師授。"同書卷六《吴士矩端公五十韻》云:"昔在鳳翔日,十歲即相識。……西州戎馬地,賢豪事雄特。……予時最年少,專務酒中職。未能愧生獰,偏矜任狂直。"又卷十一《答姨兄胡靈之見寄五十韻》云:"傳盞加分數,横波擲目成。華奴歌《淅淅》,媚子舞卿卿。閂設狂爲好,誰憂飲敗名。"凡此皆足徵微之在鳳翔時之生活。按胡靈之、吴士矩,兩《唐書》皆無傳。(《新唐書》一五九有吴士矩,乃開成間人,非與微之游者。)吴既稱端公,明其曾官至侍御史也。(端公爲侍御史之别稱,見李肇《國史補》及洪邁《容齋四筆》。)又集一九有《贈吴渠州從姨兄士則詩》。

貞元五年己巳(七八九)。十一歲。

夏,吐蕃寇長武城,韓全義敗之。

裴度登進士第。

柳子厚十七歲,至長安求進士。(《柳河東集》三三《與楊誨之書》)

貞元七年辛未(七九一)。十三歲。

劉禹錫二十歲,至長安,應進士舉,中試,聲名大噪。(據羅聯添《劉夢得年譜》)

令狐楚登進士第。

白樂天二十歲,在徐州符離。

貞元八年壬申(七九二)。十四歲。在長安。

兄秬調興平、長安、萬年尉,因隨歸京師。

本集五七《河陰留後元君墓志銘》云:“丁比部府君憂。服闋,調興平、長安、萬年尉。”同書五九《告贈皇考皇妣文》云:“始□兄集得尉興平,然後衣服飲食之具粗有准,而猶卑薄儉貧,給不假足。”按積父寬卒於貞元二年,除服當在貞元四年以後,秬之調萬年尉,縱不必即在除服之始,諒亦不致太久。考積於九年擢明經,即在長安,今爲謹慎計,姑定其歸長安於是年。又集六《寄呈士矩詩》云:“岐路各營營,别離長惻惻。行看二十載,萬事紛何極。”集一一《答胡靈之詩序》:“日月跳擲,於今餘二十年矣。”詩云:“岐下尋時别,京師觸處行。”集三〇《誨侄等書》云:“吾竊見吾兄自二十年來,以下士之禄,持窘絶之家。”二詩並書皆作於元和五年(見後考),逆推二十年,當在貞元八年之前。

韓愈、崔群、李絳、王涯等同第進士。

裴度登博學宏辭科。

柳子厚二十歲。冬,貢於京師。

貞元九年癸酉(七九三)。十五歲。居長安。

二月,復築鹽州城,既成之後,邊患乃息。四月,韋皋奏破吐蕃於西川。七月,西川六蠻内附,以韋皋之導,皆來朝貢。(《舊紀》一三)

始擢明經及第。

本集三〇《誨侄等書》云:“至年十五,得明經及第,因捧先人舊書於西窗下鑽仰沉吟,僅於不窺園井矣。”同書三三《同州刺史謝上表》云:“年十有五,得明經出身,自是苦心爲文,夙夜强學。”《白氏長慶集》六一《河南元公墓志銘》云:“十五明經及第。”皆是其證。案《新唐書》四四《選舉志》云:“而明經之别,有五經,有三經,有二經,有學究一經”。而《舊唐書》一六六《積傳》云:“十五兩經擢第。”故知微之所擢乃二經也。復按唐代風尚重進士而輕明經,如《新書》四四

《選舉志》云:"大抵衆科之目,進士尤爲貴。"《唐摭言》一云:"縉紳雖位極人臣,不由進士者,終不爲美。"又云:"其艱難謂之'三十老明經,五十少進士'。"《東觀奏記》上云:"李珏,趙郡贊皇人,早孤,居淮陰,舉明經。李絳爲華州刺史,一見謂之曰:'日角珠庭,非常人也。當掇進士科,明經碌碌,非子發迹之路。'"今微之掇明經而不由進士,其以家境貧寒,急於入仕耶?兄積亦擢明經(見白撰積志),疑在同年。

又《唐語林》六《補遺類》云:"李賀爲韓文公所知,名聞縉紳。時元相稹以明經擢第,亦善詩,願與賀交。詣賀,賀還刺,曰:'明經及第,何事看李賀。'元恨之。制策登科,及爲禮部郎中,因議賀父名'晉肅',不合應進士。竟以輕薄爲衆所排。文公惜之,爲著諱辯,竟不得上。"(參康駢《劇談録》)考李賀生於貞元六年(據朱自清《李賀年譜》),幼於稹十二歲,賀得名時,微之久已名滿天下,似無元和中往詣賀而見拒之理;且微之元和元年已以首選登制科,豈有一爲明經而終生貽羞者乎?而微之未嘗爲禮部郎中,自亦無排賀之事。此説之妄,無俟詳辨。

於詩已識聲病。得陳子昂感遇詩,因作《寄思玄子》詩二十首。

按本集三〇《叙詩寄樂天書》,自言"年十五六粗識聲病"。目睹朝廷之苟安、豪勢之跋扈、宫市之擾民,因云:"僕時孩騃,不慣聞見,獨於書傳中初習,理亂萌漸,心體悸震,若不可活,思欲發之久矣。適有人以陳子昂《感遇》詩相示,吟玩激烈,即日爲《寄思玄子》詩二十首。故鄭京兆於僕爲外諸翁,深賜憐奬。因以所賦呈獻,京兆翁深相駭異,秘書少監王表在座,顧謂表曰:'使此兒五十不死,其志義何如哉!惜吾輩不見其成就。'因召諸子,訓責泣下。僕亦竊不自得,由是勇於爲文。又久之,得杜甫詩數百首,愛其浩蕩津涯,處處臻到,始病沈、宋之不存寄興,而訝子昂之未暇旁備矣。不數年,與詩人楊巨源友善,日課爲詩。"微之與楊巨源相友善,疑不得晚於貞元十一年,即微之十七歲時,集五有詩七首,自注云:"並年十六至十八時作。"其中一首爲《春晚寄楊十二》,楊十二即巨源,知該詩之作不得遲於貞元十二年春也。今書云:"得杜甫詩……不數年,與詩人楊巨源友善。"而得陳子昂詩更在得甫詩之前,故以最保留之態度,訂於貞元九年,實則可能更早。唯《寄樂天書》有"時貞元十年已後"之句,疑微之追憶稍誤,而微之不以《寄思玄子》詩入年十六至三十七時所作之列,别云:"貴其起予之始。"更爲一有力佐證也。今本《元氏長慶集》及《全唐詩》皆不載《寄思玄子》詩。

又《舊書》一三七《鄭雲逵傳》云:"奉天之難,雲逵奔赴行在,李晟以爲行軍司馬,戎略多以咨之。歷秘書少監、給事中,尋拜大理卿,遷刑部、兵部二侍郎。"按貞元三年,李晟罷爲太尉(見前引)。貞元二十年,鄭雲逵在刑部侍郎任(見嚴耕望《唐僕尚丞郎表》),其間雲逵必歷官於長安,故得於微之多所獎譽也。

柳宗元、劉禹錫、武儒衡、穆員、盧景亮、陳佑等同登進士第。

貞元十年甲戌(七九四)。十六歲。居長安。

得杜甫詩數百首,愛之,有《代曲江老人百韻》。

按上引微之自云得杜甫詩,在得陳子昂詩後,今繫在本年,或不至甚誤。本集一〇有《代曲江老人百韻》,題下注云:"年十六時作。"當爲得老杜詩後之仿製。微之一生心儀子美,殆自兹始。微之與樂天皆愛杜詩,然頗有不同。樂天多就其諷咏時事之作着眼(見《與元九書》),而微之則"愛其浩蕩津涯,處處臻到",所撰《杜工部墓志銘》(本集五六)亦稱其"盡得古今之體勢,而兼人人之所獨專"。《上令狐相公詩啓》(《舊書》本傳)云:"或希構厦之餘,一賜觀覽,知小生於章句中欒櫨榱桷之材,盡曾量度,則十餘年之邅迴,不爲無所用矣。"蓋學杜之結果也。

又本集三〇《誨侄等書》云:"吾生長京城,朋從不少,然而未嘗識倡優之門,不曾於喧嘩縱觀,汝信之乎?"然觀其投吴端公崔院長(本集五)及答胡靈之詩(本集一一)所言,知微之此時期正少年遨游縱酒之際,《誨侄書》云云,未可信也。

李逢吉、王播等登進士第。

裴度、崔群、王播登賢良方正直言極諫科。

白居易丁父憂,在襄陽。

貞元十一年乙亥(七九五)。十七歲。在長安。

與楊巨源相游從,日課爲詩。

微之與楊巨源相友善,已見前引《叙詩寄樂天書》,其與巨源定交,似在本年。本集五有《清都夜境》《春晚寄楊十二》《永壽寺看牡丹》《春餘遣興》《憶雲之》《別李三》《秋夕遠懷》等七詩，題下注云："並年十六至十八時作。"因繫於此。楊十二，即巨源也，字景山，蒲州人，累官國子司業，以詩名於時。見《全唐詩》小傳，新、舊《書》皆不載其事迹。李三，疑即卷七《遣病》所云"李三三十九，登朝有清聲"之李三，名顧言，字仲遠，卒於元和九年，元、白二公皆有詩悼之。雲之，未詳。

劉禹錫登博學宏詞科，授太子校書官。

崔玄亮。韓泰登進士第。

貞元十二年丙子(七九六)。十八歲。在長安。

寄寓開元觀，始習道術，親符籙藥物之事。

本集一〇《開元觀閑居酬吴士矩侍御四十韻》，題下注云："中有問行藏求藥物之意，十八時作。"是微之年十八時居開元觀之證也。然始居之時間，可能更在作此詩之前，以無可考訂，姑繫於本年。又本集五《臺中鞫獄憶開元觀舊事呈損之兼贈周兄四十韻》云："憶在開元觀，食柏練玉顏。疏慵日高臥，自謂輕人寰。"疑亦指此時期事。按微之自言"性不近道"(見《叙詩寄樂天書》)，此所以有符籙藥物之求者，蓋年少喜奇，且受當日風尚之影響也。

柳子厚二十四歲，登博學宏詞科。

孟郊四十六歲，第進士。

貞元十四年戊寅(七九八)。二十歲。

吕温、王起第進士。

柳子厚二十六歲，授集賢殿正字。

貞元十五年己卯(七九九)。二十一歲。

游於浦州，寓普救寺。所謂"崔氏孀婦"者，亦挈家止於該寺。

按《太平廣記》四八八有元稹撰《鶯鶯傳》，其爲微之之自述，前人辨之已詳，且證據確鑿，無俟再考。其文云："無幾何，張生游於蒲，蒲之東十餘里，有僧舍曰普救寺，張生寓焉。適有崔氏孀婦將歸長安，路出於蒲，亦止兹寺。……是歲，渾瑊薨於蒲，有中人丁文雅不善於軍，軍人因喪而擾，大掠蒲人。崔氏之家，財産甚厚，多奴僕，旅寓惶駭，不知所托。先是，張與蒲將之黨有善，請吏護之，遂不及於難。十餘日，廉使杜確將天子命，以總戎節，令於軍，軍由是戢。"是微之游蒲時，乃渾瑊之卒年也。考《舊紀》一三云："(貞元十五年）十二月庚午，朔方等道副元帥、河中絳州節度使、檢校司徒、兼奉朔中書令渾瑊薨。……丁酉，以同州刺史杜確爲河中尹、河中絳州觀察使。”則其爲貞元十五年必矣。（其年微之僅二十一歲）而傳云：“以是年二十三，未嘗近女色。”蓋小説家言，未足深究。又王性之《傳奇辨正》（見趙德麟《侯鯖録》，又見《全唐文紀事》一百四引）及陳寅恪先生《元白詩箋證稿·四》“艷詩及悼亡詩”條，引傳文皆云“年二十二，未嘗近女色”。愚所見二本皆作“二十三”，未詳何故？存此以待續考。

蒲州（今山西永濟）即河中府，見《元和郡縣圖志》一二。其屬有解縣，本集一〇《黄明府詩》序云：“小年曾於解縣連月飲酒。”疑亦在本年。

張籍、李景儉登進士第。

吕温登博學宏詞科。

白樂天二十八歲，自宣城鄉貢入京。

貞元十六年庚辰（八〇〇）。二十二歲。

春，始會雙文。夏，去，之長安。秋，復會雙文於蒲。冬，又去之。

諸事皆見《鶯鶯傳》，其時間可約略推之如上。按傳載初會鶯鶯時，其母云：“終於庚辰，生年十七矣。”明微之初見雙文在本年也。

有《贈雙文》《春詞》《恨妝成》《月暗》《新秋》《會真詩三十韻》等詩，皆咏與雙文之戀者。又有《古决絶詞》三首，訣雙文之詞也。

按諸詩本集皆不載，今見於韋縠《才調集》及《全唐詩》元稹二七。《决絶詞》又見於《樂府詩集》四一。就詩意觀之，微之之别雙文似在春季，果爾，則爲次年春矣。又陳寅恪先生《元白詩箋證稿·四》“艷詩及悼亡詩”條，謂微之幼居於鳳翔西北邊境荒殘之地，及弱冠游於繁盛殷闐之蒲州，因謂微之“鳳翔之誘惑力不及河中，因得以自持。而以守禮誇詡，欺人之言也”。夫微之是否果爲“内秉孤堅，非禮不可入”，乃屬另一問題；然陳氏之説，亦似有未的，蓋據前考，可知微之“長於京師”，豈蒲州之誘惑力反大於長安耶？

白樂天二十九歲，登進士第。中書舍人高郢知貢舉。

韓退之三十三歲。春，赴徐州，旋歸洛陽。冬，往長安。

孟郊五十歲，在洛陽應銓選爲溧陽尉。

貞元十七年辛巳(八〇一)。二十三歲。在長安。

應試不第,因止於京師,與雙文有書札往還。

按《鶯鶯傳》云:"明年,文戰不勝,張遂止於京,因貽書於崔,以廣其意,崔氏緘報之。"云云。微之試而不第者,疑即爲吏部之銓選。或以《决絶詞》之物候斷之,定微之、雙文之别在本年春,是冬應試,明年春選畢(選制以十一月始集,次年三月畢事。見後辨)。因謂"明年文戰不勝",則諸事當屬十八年,即微之二十四歲時,於理亦頗可通。

有《魚中素》《雜憶》等詩,疑作於本年,念雙文之作也。

柳子厚二十九歲。調藍田尉。

白樂天三十歲。在徐州符離。

韋夏卿自吏部侍郎改授京兆尹。

貞元十八年壬午(八〇二)。二十四歲。在長安。

冬,復應吏部試。

按本集三三《同州刺史謝上表》、《舊書》本傳,暨《白氏長慶集》六一稹志,皆云微之二十四判入等,授校書郎。實則微之以本年冬應試,登科及授官皆在明年(説見十九年考)。諸書皆約而言之,後人不察,因謂微之授官亦在本年(如王性之《傳奇辨正》及陳寅恪先生《元白詩箋證稿·一》"論《長恨歌》"條),並推論微之與韋叢結縭亦在本年,均誤。

王涯登博學宏辭科,中書舍人權德輿知貢舉。

韓退之三十五歲,調授國子監四門博士。

劉禹錫三十一歲,調補京兆渭南主簿。

竇群以韋夏卿之薦,徵拜左拾遺。

按《舊書》一五五《竇群傳》云:"字丹列……群兄常、牟,弟鞏,皆登進士第,唯群獨爲處士,隱居毗陵,以節操聞。……著書三十四卷,號《史記名臣疏》。貞元中,蘇州刺史韋夏卿以丘園茂異薦,兼獻其書,不報。及夏卿入爲吏部侍郎,改京兆尹,中謝日,因對復薦群,徵拜左拾遺。"微之後與群及鞏相友善,蓋亦由其丈人之關係歟?

貞元十九年癸未(八〇三)。二十五歲。在長安。

春,吏部試畢,以平判入第四等,授秘書省校書郎。同第者有吕炅、王起、白居易、李復禮、吕頻、哥舒頒、崔玄亮等。

《白氏長慶集》六一《河南元公墓志銘》云："二十四，試判入四等，署秘省校書。"(《舊書》本傳及微之《同州刺史謝上表》皆同)是以微之之拜校書郎，爲二十四歲，即貞元十八年也，後人多因此而致誤。今據《白氏長慶集》二六《養竹記》云："貞元十九年春，居易已拔萃選及第，授校書郎。"故陳振孫《白文公年譜》，謂樂天貞元十九年以拔萃選登科，按《新書》四五《選舉志》，吏部以十一月爲選始，至翌年春三月而畢。知元白諸公實以十八年冬應試，至本年春始登科而授官也。陳氏此説甚是。又按本集五《酬樂天詩》乃元和元年作，詩云："昔作芸香侶，三載不暫離。"本集三〇《誨侄等書》云："至年十五得明經，及第，因捧先人舊書於西窗下鑽仰沉吟，僅於不窺園井矣。如是者十年，然後粗霑一命，粗成一名。"以詩及文反正推之，皆可證微之授官實爲本年。

又本集一六《酬哥舒大少府寄同年科第》云："前年科第偏年少……八人同看彩衣裳。"注云："同年科第，宏詞：吕二炅、王十一起。拔萃：白二十二居易。平判：李十一復禮、吕四頻、哥舒大頒、崔十八玄亮，逮不肖八人，皆奉榮養。"

《新書》四七《百官志》云："(秘書省)校書郎十人，正九品上……掌讎校典籍，刊正文章。"

時鄭珣瑜領選部，裴垍爲考功員外郎，主考詞判。微之後日多爲垍所引拔，深分當自玆始。

《白氏長慶集》二一《泛渭賦序》云："左丞相鄭公之領選部也，予以書判拔萃登科。"鄭公即珣瑜也。又《舊書》一四八《裴垍傳》云："字弘中，河東聞喜人……弱冠舉進士。貞元中，制舉賢良極諫，對策第一，授美原縣尉。秩滿……拜監察御史，轉殿中侍御史、尚書禮部考功二員外郎。時吏部侍郎鄭珣瑜請垍考詞判，垍守正不受請托，考覈皆務才實。"微之與裴垍之關係，可自本集《七感夢》一詩見之。

始與白居易、李建、崔玄亮等定交。

本集五四《李公(建)墓志銘》云："公始校秘書時，與同省郎白居易、元稹定死生分。"又《白氏長慶集》二一三《寄微之百韻》云："憶在貞元歲，初登典校司。身名同日授，心事一言知。"注云："貞元中與微之同登科，俱授校書郎，始相識。"按李建字杓直，傳見《舊書》一五五、《新書》一六二，與元、白交契最厚，《舊書》本傳云:"家素清貧無舊業,與兄造、遜於荆南躬耕致養,嗜學力文。舉進士選,授秘書省校書郎。"又云:"以廉儉自處,家不理垣屋,士友推之。"故白樂天以善人名之。崔玄亮,字晦叔,傳見《舊書》一六五、《新書》一六四,史稱其"性雅澹,好道術,不樂趨競""每一遷秩,謙讓輒形於色"。白樂天詩:"平生定交取人窄,屈指相數唯五人。"所謂五人者,元、白、李、崔之外,更益以劉夢得。然夢得晚年與樂天過從始密,論平生交分、死生不渝者,四人而已。

夏,娶韋夏卿之女韋叢,叢字成之。

《韓昌黎集》二四《監察御史元君妻京兆韋氏墓志銘》云:"夫人於僕射爲季女,愛之,選婿得今御史河南元稹。稹時始以選校書秘書省中。"既云"始以選校書秘書省中",疑即在本年夏。韋穀《才調集》五《微之夢游春七十韻》(又見《全唐詩》元稹二七)云:"一夢何足云,良時事婚娶。當年二紀初,佳節三星度。朝蕣玉佩迎,高松女蘿附。韋門正全盛,出入多歡裕。"所謂"二紀初"者,殆謂年滿二紀之初,若必釋爲二十四,則泥矣。又《鶯鶯傳》云:"後歲餘,崔已委身於人,張亦有所娶。"所謂"後歲餘",亦謂張生得鶯鶯書且發於其朋游後之"後歲餘"也,與微之二十五歲始婚於成之之事實亦不相抵牾。

夏卿時已自京兆尹遷太子賓客,冬,復改爲東都留守。

按夏卿何時去京兆尹任,史無明文,唯《舊紀》一三云:"(十九年三月)乙亥以司農卿李實爲京兆尹。"疑實即代夏卿者。又去:"冬十月乙未,以太子賓客韋夏卿爲東都留守、東都畿汝都防禦使。"可證三月至十月之間,夏卿猶爲太子賓客也。

杜佑以二月自淮南入朝,三月拜相。

劉禹錫三十二歲。自渭南主簿拜監察御史。

柳子厚三十一歲。自藍田尉擢監察御史裏行。

韓退之自四門傳士遷監察御史。十二月,貶爲陽山令。

杜牧之生。

貞元二十年甲申(八〇四)。二十六歲。在長安。

在校書郎任。時韋夏卿爲東都留守,故微之每往來於京、洛之間。史稱夏卿在東都時,"傾心群士,頗得才彦"。微之此際游於韋門,因得多結時彦。

本集一六《華嶽寺》,題下注云:"貞元二十年正月二十五日,自洛之京。二月三日春社，至華嶽寺，憩實師院。曾未逾月，又復徂東，再謁實師，因題四韻而已。"又同卷有"與太白之東洛，至櫟陽，太白染疾駐行，予九月二十五日至華嶽寺，雪後望山。"疑亦本年作。太白劉姓，與微之、樂天相善，餘不詳。

五月，曾夜宿天壇，有詩還贈馬逢。

本集一六《天壇上境》，題下自注："貞元二十年五月十四日，夜宿天壇石幢側。十五日得盩厔馬逢少府書，知予遠上天壇，因以長句見贈。"篇末仍云："靈溪試爲訪金丹。"因於壇上還贈。馬逢，生平不詳，既稱少府，明其時正攝盩厔尉也（見《容齋四筆》一五"官稱别名"條）。後從辟東川爲侍御史，微之在荆時有詩送之。

又集五《韋氏館與周隱客杜歸和泛月》《劉氏館集隱客歸和子元及之子蒙晦之》等詩並集一六之大部分篇什，疑皆本年前後之作。詩中所及之周隱客、吕子元、庾及之、杜歸和、竇晦之、張弘、辛丘度等，今皆不可考。盧子蒙即盧十九經濟，與微之贈答頗多。

《舊書》一七一《李景儉傳》云："字寬中……性俊朗，博聞强記，頗閲前史，詳其成敗。自負王霸之略，於士大夫間無所屈降。……韋夏卿留守東都，辟爲從事。竇群爲御史中丞，引爲監察御史。群以罪左遷，景儉坐貶江陵户曹。"群爲夏卿所薦，已見前引。疑微之得與竇群、竇鞏、李景儉等相交游，皆在本年前後。

九月，有《崔鶯鶯傳》。李紳爲作《鶯鶯詩》，合叙與雙文之戀者也。

《太平廣記》四八八元稹撰《鶯鶯傳》云："貞元歲九月，執事李公垂宿於予靖安里第，語及於是。公垂卓然稱異，遂爲《鶯鶯歌》以傳之。"今從陳寅恪先生考（《元白詩箋證稿》一"《長恨歌》"條），繫於本年。《新書》一八一《紳傳》云："字公垂。……六歲而孤，哀等成人。母盧，躬授之學。爲人短小精悍，於詩最有名，時號'短李'。蘇州刺史韋夏卿數稱之。……元和初，擢進士第。"疑紳以本年舉進士貢於京師，其與微之之游或亦由夏卿之故也。

十二月，長姊陸翰妻卒於夏陽（今陝西韓城市境），時翰宰其地。

本集五八《陸翰妻河南元氏墓志銘》云："享年三十有□，殁世於夏陽縣之私第，是歲唐之貞元二十五年十二月之初五日矣。"按貞元曆僅得二十一年，而二十一年之八月即改元永貞。《志》又云："冬十月十有四日，葬於河南洛陽之清風郡平樂里之北邙……永貞之元年,歲乙酉。”是陸氏以永貞元年十月葬,其卒當在本年十二月,《志》云“二十五年”,於理不合。

李賀十五歲,以樂府歌詩名動於時。

吕温三十二歲。冬,副張薦使於吐蕃。

德宗貞元二十一年(一月—七月),順宗永貞元年(八月—十二月)乙酉(八〇五)。二十七歲。在長安。

正月,德宗崩,皇太子誦即位,是爲順宗。二月,韋執誼爲相。先是,順宗爲太子時,王伾、王叔文同以書棋得幸。時韋執誼爲翰林學士,乃傾心結附叔文,因成所謂王韋黨者。迨順宗即位,以風疾久不能言,叔文乃得暗中决事,引韋執誼、劉禹錫、陳諫、韓曄、韓泰、柳宗元、房啓、凌準等所謂‘八司馬’者,互爲倡和,至是乃相執誼,而劉、柳等皆遷官。七月,皇太子淳以宦者之力,勾當國事。八月,皇太子即位,是爲憲宗。順宗自稱太上皇,改元永貞,叔文黨皆坐貶。(《通鑒》唐紀二三六及《順宗實録》)微之以官卑,不預政事,仍與同省校書郎白樂天、李杓直等日夜宴游。

《白氏長慶集》四五《策林序》云:“元和初,予罷校書郎,與元微之將應制舉。”是元、白二公永貞元年仍爲校書郎也。又本集一〇《酬翰林白學士代書一百韻》,注云:“予與樂天、杓直、拒非輩多於月燈閣閑游,又嘗與秘省同官醵宴昆明池。”“本弦才一舉,下口已三遲。逃席衝門出,歸倡借馬騎。狂歌繁節亂,醉舞半衫垂。……幾遭朝士笑,兼任巷童隨。”可見此際正微之少年狂歌縱酒之時也。拒非與元、白二公游從頗密,餘待考。

有《貞元曆》《恭王故太妃挽歌詞》二首,《病减逢春期白二十二辛大不至十韻》等詩。

按是年八月改元,故有《貞元曆》詩。後二詩下並注:“校書郎時作。”微之以貞元十九年三月後始授校書郎,二十年春正往來於京、洛之間(已見前考),其能病减逢春,疑非本年莫屬。白二十二即樂天。辛大,未詳。

十月,姊陸翰妻葬於洛陽。有《夏陽縣令陸翰妻河南元氏墓志銘》(見前考)。

十二月,韋夏卿自東都留守轉太子少保。有《贈韋氏兄弟及大隱洞》等詩,當作於十二月前。

本集一七有《陪韋尚書丈歸履信宅因贈韋氏兄弟》《韋居守晚歲常言退休之志因署其居曰大隱洞命予賦詩因贈絶句》二詩。按履信宅大隱洞,皆夏卿在洛之居第,然則微之本年或復有洛陽之行也。

柳宗元三十三歲。貶永州(今湖南零陵境)司馬。

劉禹錫三十四歲。貶朗州(今湖南常德境)司馬。

李景儉、吕温皆黨於叔文。景儉以丁母憂,温以使於吐蕃,因免於譴謫。

李宗閔、牛僧孺、楊嗣復等登進士第。

憲宗元和元年丙戌(八〇六)。二十八歲。在長安。

正月丁卯,大赦改元。有與李公垂、庾順之閑行曲江詩。

本集一七有詩目云:"永貞二年正月二日,上御丹鳳樓,赦天下。予與李公垂、庾順之閑行曲江,不及盛觀。"李公垂即李紳,已見前引。庾順之名敬休,《舊書》一八七下(《新書》一六一略同)本傳云:"庾敬休,字順之……舉進士,以宏詞登科,授秘書省校書郎。……姿容温雅,襟抱夷曠,不飲酒茹葷,不邇聲色。著《諭善録》七卷。"蓋與微之同官校書郎也。

丁卯,韋夏卿卒。甲申,順宗崩。

西川劉闢反,從宰臣杜黄裳奏,以高崇文率軍進討(九月平之)。

罷校書郎,與白樂天退居華陽觀,閉門勤讀,將應制舉也。

《白氏長慶集》四五《策林》序云:"元和初,予罷校書郎,與元微之將應制舉。退居於上都華陽觀。閉户累月,揣磨當代之事,構成策目七十五門。及微之首登科,予次焉。"是微之罷校書之任在本年初,然究爲何月何日,則莫可考究矣。

二月,鄭雲逵自金吾大將軍徙爲京兆尹。四月,命宰臣監試制舉人,是時順宗未葬,憲宗不便親試。

應制舉才識兼茂明於體用科,以首選登第,拜左拾遺。

本集三三《同州刺史謝上表》云:"年二十八,制舉首選,授左拾遺。"《白氏長慶集》六一《河南元公墓志銘》:"二十八應制策,入三等,拜左拾遺。"《舊書》一六六本傳云:"二十八應制舉才識兼茂明於體用科,登第者十八人,稹爲第一,元和元年四月也。制下,除右拾遺。"案諸本皆作左拾遺,《舊書》作"右",誤。考《全唐文》紀事二六"正直條"引《册府元龜》云:"韋貫之爲右補闕,憲宗元和元年與中書舍人張宏靖考制策,第其名者十八人,其後多以文稱遷。"知本年實主制策者乃韋、張也。又宋敏求《唐大詔令集》一〇六《才識兼茂明於體用科策問》,注云:"四月二十八日。"其下乃有放制舉人敕,然則制下除官,當在五月,諸書多作四月,疑誤。敕云:"才識兼茂明於體用科人,第三次等:元稹、韋惇。第四等:獨孤郁、白居易、曹景伯、韋慶復;第四次等:崔韶、羅讓、元修、薛存慶、韋珩。第五上等:蕭俛、李蟠、沈傳師、柴宿。達於吏理可使從政科第五上等:陳岵等。"(又見《唐會要》七六)知微之所登實第三次等也。

附:王讜《唐語林》八"補遺"條云:"唐制:常舉人之外,又有制科,搜揚拔擢,名目甚衆。則天廣收才彦,起家或拜中書舍人、員外郎,次拾遺、補闕;明皇尤加精選,下無滯才。然制舉出身,名望雖美,猶居進士之下。"

《容齋續筆》云:"唐世制舉,科目猥多,徒異其名耳,其實與諸科等也。"

《新書》四七《百官志》云:"(門下省)左拾遺六人,從八品上,掌供奉諷諫,大事廷議,小則上封事。"

微之《才識兼茂明於體用策》一道,載本集二八。

既除拾遺,遇事輒諷,有《論教本書》《獻事表》《論追制表》《論諫職表》《論討賊表》《論西戎表》《遷廟議狀》等奏。

本集三二《叙奏》云:"元和初,章武皇帝新即位,臣下未有以言刮視聽者,予始以對詔在拾遺中供奉,由是《獻教本書》《諫職》《論事》等表十數通,仍爲裴度、李正辭、韋纁訟所言當行,而宰相曲道上語,上頗悟,召見問狀。宰相大惡之,不一月,出爲河南尉。"《舊書》本傳云:"稹性鋒鋭,見事風生,既居諫垣,不欲碌碌自滯,事無不言,即日上疏論諫職。……乃獻《教本書》……又論西北邊事,皆朝政之大者。"(參《通鑒》二三七《唐紀》)

七月,順宗葬於豐陵。有《順宗挽歌詞》三首。又有《含風夕》《秋堂夕》《酬樂天》《楊子華畫》等詩,皆拾遺時作也。

按《秋堂夕》詩有句云:"啼兒屢哑咽。"此時微之或已有所育矣。

八月,憲宗召問於延英,大爲宰相所疑忌。九月,貶爲河南尉。時裴度適自監察御史出爲河南府功曹,乃相偕之洛。旋以太夫人鄭氏之喪復歸長安。

本集一〇《酬翰林白學士代書一百韻》云:"佞存真妾婦,諫死是男兒。便殿承偏召,權臣懼撓私……敢嗟身暫黜,所恨政無毗。"注云:"予元和元年任拾遺，八十三日延英對，九月十日貶授河南尉。”案“八十三日”不可通，當作“八月十三日”，《叙奏》云：“上頗悟，召見問狀，宰相大惡之，不一月，出爲河南尉。”可爲佐證。墓志云：“憲宗召對，言及時政，執政者疑忌，出公爲河南尉。”《舊書》本傳云：“憲宗召對問方略，爲執政者所忌，出爲河南尉。”按元和元年八、九月間在相位者，爲杜黄裳、杜佑、鄭餘慶及鄭絪等（見《新書》六二宰相表中），皆有直名，忌貶微之者爲誰，頗難推斷。竊以爲少年氣盛，好議是非，姑不論其言之當否，恒不爲老成所喜，此古今一理也。微之登朝於王、韋黨人初貶之後，進取喜事，屢議朝政，其不爲宰執所樂，可想而知，固不必遭巧者佞者而後始見屈抑也。

本集一九《西歸絶句》十二首之一云：“共貶河南亞大夫。”注云：“裴中丞度。”同書三十《上門下裴相公書》云：“昔者相公之掾洛也，稹護陪侍道途，不以妄庸，語及章句，則固竊聞。”又《舊書》一七〇《裴度傳》云：“字中立……貞元五年進士擢第，登宏辭科，應制舉賢良方正、能直言極諫科，對策高等，授河陰縣尉。遷監察御史，密疏論權倖，語切忤旨，出爲河南府功曹。”是知元、裴此時同貶河南也。本集二五有《華之巫》《廟之神》二詩，皆本年作，疑皆貶洛途次所寫，蓋有感於浮雲蔽日之作也。《白氏長慶集》二五《唐河南元府君夫人滎陽鄭氏墓志銘》云：“有唐元和元年九月十六日，故中散大夫、尚書比部郎中、舒王府長史河南元府君諱寬，夫人滎陽縣太君鄭氏，年六十寢疾，殁於萬年縣靖安里私第。”又本集三〇《誨侄等書》云：“蓋以往歲忝職諫官，不忍小見，妄干朝聽，謫棄河南，泣血西歸，生死無告。”

可知微之貶河南後，不旋踵而復歸長安矣。

白樂天登制舉，授盩厔縣尉，作《長恨歌》。

韓退之三十九歲。六月，召爲國子博士。

吕温三十五歲。自吐蕃使還，轉户部員外郎。

李紳登進士第，除國子助教。

元和二年丁亥（八〇七）。二十九歲。在長安。

二月，葬母，白樂天爲作墓志銘。

《白氏長慶集》二五《滎陽縣太君鄭氏志》云：“越明年二月十五日，權祔於咸陽縣奉賢鄉洪瀆原，從先姑之塋也。”又云：“稹泣血孺慕，哀動他人，托爲談述,書於墓石。"

李紳赴潤州,從辟李錡幕。旋錡反,紳被囚。十月,錡伏誅,紳乃得出。

韓退之四十歲。知國子博士,分司東都。

白樂天三十六歲。罷盩厔尉,試進士。事畢,爲集賢校理。十一月,授翰林學士。

李賀十八歲,至洛陽,以詩謁韓退之。

李吉甫以正月自中書舍人拜中書侍郎、同平章事。

元和三年戊子(八〇八)。三十歲。在長安。

仍在母服中。

皇甫湜、牛僧孺、李宗閔等以四月共登賢良方正科。因策語過切,爲李吉甫所訴,考策官韋貫之、楊於陵、鄭敬、李益等皆貶官。王涯亦以親累貶。

白樂天以四月二十八日授左拾遺。有《論制科人狀》。

裴垍以九月自户部侍郎拜中書侍郎、同平章事,代李吉甫也。吉甫出爲淮南節度使。

竇群自御史中丞貶黔中觀察使,以與吕温等圖傾吉甫也。温亦坐貶道州刺史,李景儉坐貶江陵户曹。

元和四年己丑(八〇九)。三十一歲。

二月起拜監察御史,宰相裴垍之所薦拔也。

本集五《臺中鞫獄憶開元觀舊事呈損之兼贈周兄四十韻》云:"二月除御史。"《墓志》云:"服除之明年,剛授監察御史。"《舊書》本傳云:"服除,拜監察御使。"皆證微之以本年二月起復。又本集三一《上門下裴相公書》云:"獨憶得近日故裴兵部之爲人也,堅辨清净,號爲名流。及其爲相也……秉政不累月,閣下(裴度)白外寮爲起居郎,韋相(貫之)自巴州知制誥,張河南自邕幕爲御史,李西川(夷簡)自饒州爲雜端,密勿建梁之地,半得其人。如故韋簡州勛及稹等,拔於疑礙、置之朝行者,又十數。"明微之之復起,垍力爲多,且其後日與李夷簡之關係或亦由垍之故也。

附:《新書》四八《百官志》云:"御史臺,大夫一人,正三品;中丞三人,正四品下。其屬有三:一曰臺院,侍御史隸焉;二曰殿院,殿中侍御史隸焉;三曰察院,監察御史隸焉。"又云:"監察御史十五人,正八品下,掌分察百寮,巡按州縣。"

有《和李紳新題樂府十二首》,疑作於本年。

本集二四《和李校書新題樂府十二首》序云:"予友李公垂貺予《樂府新題二十首》,雅有所謂,不虛爲文。予取其病時之尤急者,列而和之,蓋十二而已。"惜乎未言作詩之時間。今公垂原詩已不可見,其作成之時間亦難考訂,所可知者,白樂天就李、元之作改進擴充,亦有《新樂府五十首》(《白氏長慶集》三),序云:"元和四年爲左拾遺時作。"則微之所作,必亦在四年或四年以前,自不待言。今考《舊書》一七三、《新書》八一《紳傳》,皆云紳以元和元年去國子助教,從辟浙西李錡幕。錡誅後,復從事山南觀察府,未有爲校書之記載。陳寅恪先生定微之《新樂府》作於本年(見《元白詩箋證稿》五"《新樂府》"條),未詳所據,今姑從之。然竊以爲微之再度登朝後,官務繫身(見後考),似未有時間作此諸詩之可能,疑或作於本年初,或在本年以前。

三月,奉使巴蜀。劾奏故節度使嚴礪等違制擅賦,又平塗山甫吏民之冤,名動一時,然爲嚴礪黨所厚怒。微之一生坎坷乏遇,蓋種因於兹矣。

本集一〇《黃明府詩》序云:"元和四年三月,予奉使東川,十六日至褒城東數里。"同書一四《褒城驛》云:"四年三月半,新筍晚花時。悵望東川去,等閑題此詩。"同書一七《使東川》序云:"元和四年三月七日,予以監察御史使川。"《墓志》云:"使于蜀,按任敬仲獄,得獄情。又劾奏東川帥違詔條過籍税。又奏平塗山甫等八十八家冤事,名動三川。"《舊書》本傳云:"四年奉使東蜀,劾奏故劍南東川節度使嚴礪……時礪已死,七州刺史皆責罰,稹雖舉職,而執政有與礪厚者惡之。"

《收暨閑談》云:"稹聞西蜀薛濤有辭辯,及爲監察使蜀,以御史推鞫,難得見焉。嚴司空潜知其意,每遣薛往。洎登翰林,以詩寄之。(按,指《寄贈薛濤》七律、又見《全唐詩》元稹二八。)"今考微之所使乃東川,去濤所居之成都甚遥,"難得見焉",自屬必然,何來"嚴司空"竟得"潜知其意"而"每遣薛往"?此誠牧豎野語,未足深辯也。

五月,使竟歸朝。川行詩篇頗多,白行簡代寫爲東川卷。旋受分務東臺之命,乃之洛。

本集五《臺中鞫獄憶開元觀舊事》云:"二月除御史,三月使巴蠻。蠻民詀諵訴,囓指明痛瘝。憐蠻不解語,爲發昏師姦。歸來五六月,旱色天地殷。分司别兄弟,各各泪潸潸。哀哉劇部職,唯數贓罪鍰。"知微之歸朝在五、六月間。新、舊《書》本傳暨《墓志》並云微之使還分務東臺,然均未及其歸朝與分司之時間。又本集一七《使東川》序云:"元和四年三月七日,予以監察御史使川。往來鞍馬間,賦詩凡三十二章,秘書省校書郎白行簡爲予手寫爲東川卷。今所録者,但七言絶句長句耳,起《駱口驛》、盡《望驛臺》二十二首云。"按此二十二首今全載於本集十七。另卷五《西州院》、卷十《黄明府詩》、卷一四《褒城驛》,當皆《使東川》之詩,然仍不足微之所云三十二章之數。白行簡,字知退,樂天之弟,新、舊《書》皆附《白居易傳》。又就《使東川》詩觀之,知微之在長安數年間,與白居易、白行簡、李建、庾敬休、崔韶暨拒非(?)等過從甚密。又按《舊紀》一四,李夷簡以本年四月末遷御史中丞(《夷簡傳》見《新書》一三一),微之之舉職分司,或與夷簡不無關係,本集三四有《代李中丞謝官表》一則,觀其文意,知非夷簡莫屬,然就時間言之,則有可疑,容待續考。

七月,夫人韋氏卒,有祭文。

《韓昌黎集》二四《監察御史元君妻京兆韋氏墓志銘》云:"(夫人)以元和四年七月九日卒。"按微之以五、六月之際使還,旋分務東臺,其確切之時間不可考。故韋氏卒時,微之在長安抑在洛陽,亦不得而知。

八月,在洛陽。有《與吕靈同宿話舊》詩。

本集一七《贈吕三校書》,注云:"與吕校書同年科第,後爲别七年。元和己丑歲八月,偶於陶化坊會宿。"按吕三當作吕二,見貞元十九年考。又《白氏長慶集》一四和詩亦作吕二,皆是其證。

十月,韋夫人葬於咸陽,微之以官滯洛,未克親臨窀穸,有詩悼之。

《韋氏墓志》云:"其年十月十三日葬咸陽。"本集九《空屋題》自注云:"十月十四日夜。"詩云:"更想咸陽道,魂車昨夜回。"《白氏長慶集》一四《答騎馬入空臺》云:"鰥夫仍繫職,稚女未勝哀。寂寞咸陽道,家人覆墓迴。"可證韋氏之葬咸陽,微之未克躬與其事也(參陳寅恪先生《艷詩及悼亡詩箋證》)。按微之悼亡詩之作乃千古絶唱,其約略可考知作於本年者有:《夜閑》《感小株夜合》《追昔游》《空屋題》《初寒夜寄盧子蒙》《城外回謝子蒙見諭》《旅眠》《除夜》等。

分司東臺日,奉法唯謹,不避權貴,因多所忤犯,遂種遠貶之因。

本集三二《叙奏》云:"無何,外莅東都臺,天子久不在都,都下多不法,百司皆牢獄,有栽接吏械人逾歲而臺府不得而知之者。予因飛奏絶百司專禁錮。河南尉判官,予劾之,忤宰相旨……類是數十事,或移或奏,皆主之。貞元以來,不慣用文法,内外寵臣皆喑嗚。"《墓志》暨新、舊《書》本傳略同,而《志》云:"凡此者數十事,或奏或劾或移,歲餘皆舉正之。"則不無小誤,蓋微之分務東臺爲時僅半載,未及歲餘也。

在洛日,所與游者有盧子蒙、李仁風暨劉頗等。頗以氣俠聞於時,自是與微之爲終生交。

盧子蒙已見前考。李仁風見本集一七《仁風李著作園醉後寄李十》,事迹有待續考。劉頗字保極,事迹見本集五六《萬州刺史劉君墓志銘》,其末云:"予爲監察御史時,始與君更相許爲將相。"本集一四《劉頗詩》,疑即本年所作,時頗或在壽安主簿任也。又本集一八《寄劉頗二首》,其二云:"前年碣石烟塵起,共看官軍過洛城。"蓋本年成德節度使王承宗反,内官吐突承璀率軍征討,以十一月經洛陽也。

白樂天、李杓直皆在長安,爲翰林學士。

韓退之四十二歲。六月,改都官員外郎、守東都。

李賀二十歲。在洛陽,從韓退之、皇甫湜游。

元和五年庚寅(八一〇)。三十二歲。

正月,劾奏浙西觀察使韓皋有違典章,皋因罰俸。

《舊紀》一四云:"(元和)五年春正月,浙西觀察使韓皋以杖决安吉令孫澥致死,有乖典法,罰一月俸料。"參《新唐書》本傳暨《墓志》,知爲微之所奏。論奏見本集三八。

二月,有《辛夷花》詩,寄問韓退之。退之時爲都官員外郎,亦在東都。

本集二六《辛夷花》,題下注云:"問韓員外。"據洪祖興《韓子年譜》,愈以去歲六月改都官員外郎、守東都;而微之本月末即奉召西歸(見後),復以花候考之,則此詩之作,惟有本月爲可能,且證韓元此際亦間有過從也。

河南尹房式爲不法事,因急攝之,且擅停其務,式雖罰俸,微之亦因而去官。

《舊紀》一四云:"(元和五年二月)東臺監察御史元稹攝河南尹房式於臺,

擅令停務,貶江陵府士曹參軍。"《舊書》本傳云:"河南尹房式爲不法事,稹欲追攝,擅令停務,既飛表聞奏。罰式一月俸,仍召稹還京。"本集五詩目云:"元和五年,予官不了,罰俸西歸。"知微之以攝房式事過急,因奉召去官,歸長安,時在二月;然其時尚無遠貶之詔,《舊紀》即以貶江陵繫本月,蓋約而言之。汪立名《白香山年譜》謂稹以正月貶江陵,則誤矣。

三月,御史中丞李夷簡徙户部侍郎,兵部侍郎王播遷御史中丞。微之月初上道,三日,至三泉驛,有詩。六日,至陝府,會吴士矩及崔韶,有詩五十韻。次敷水驛,中官後至而争廳,致爲其所厚辱,因復有貶江陵士曹參軍之詔。李絳、崔群、白居易共上疏論其枉,皆不報。

李夷簡及王播之改官,見《舊紀》一四。

本集二六《三泉驛》詩云:"三泉驛内逢上巳。"觀詩意,知爲微之去洛時,因其友好送别而作。同書五詩目云:"元和五年,予官不了,罰俸西歸。三月六日至陝府,與吴十一兄端公、崔二十二院長思愴曩游,因投五十韻。"吴十一即士矩,微之姨兄;崔二十二名韶,與微之同登制舉,皆見前考。詩云:"分司在東洛,所職尤不易。罰俸得西歸,心知受朝庇。"可證此際尚無遠貶之詔。《舊書》本傳云:"仍召稹還京,宿敷水驛,内官劉士元後至,争廳,士元怒,排其户,稹襪而走廳後。士元追之後,以箠擊稹,傷面。執政以祺少年後輩,務作威福,貶爲江陵府士曹參軍。"《白氏長慶集》四二《論元稹第三狀》,亦作"中使劉士元"。然《新書》本傳則云:"召稹還。次敷水驛,中人仇士良夜至,稹不讓,中人怒,擊稹,敗面。宰相以稹年少輕樹威,失憲臣體,貶江陵士曹參軍。"同書二〇七《仇士良傳》亦同。二説莫知孰是,今但依《通鑒》例,稱中官而已。《白氏長慶集》四三《論元稹第三狀》云:"右伏緣元稹左降事宜,李絳、崔群等再已奏聞。"知絳、群、樂天等皆曾一再奏聞微之之枉,時諸公皆在翰林。又微之貶官之原因,頗爲複雜,今請分條略陳於後。

一、奉使東川時,劾奏嚴礪、裴玢等,已先樹敵。本集三二《叙奏》云:"予自東川而還,朋礪者潛切齒矣。"《舊書》本傳云:"執政有與礪厚者惡之。"

二、分務東臺時,持法不苟,因多結怨黨。《叙奏》又云:"無何,外莅東都臺,天子久不在都,都下多不法,百司皆牢獄……予因飛奏絶百司專禁錮。河南尉判官,予劾之,忤宰相旨……類是數十事,或移或奏,皆主之。貞元以來,不慣用文法，内外寵臣皆喑嗚。會河南尹房式詐諼事發，奏攝之。前所喑嗚者皆叫噪。宰相素以劾判官事相銜，乘是黜予江陵掾。”《墓志》及新、舊《書》本傳所云皆略同。可知微之貶官，乃由其早樹怨黨，奏攝房式，並非最重要之原因。本集二一《酬樂天聞李尚書拜相以詩見賀》注云：“予爲監察御史，劾奏故東川節度使嚴礪……由是操權者大怒。分司東臺日，又劾奏宰相親，因緣遂貶江陵士曹耳。”皆可證微之遭貶，與劾奏河南尉而忤宰相旨，大有關聯。唯劾奏河南尉狀詞已不存，難稽其詳。今考白樂天《論元稹第三狀》，内云：“元稹守官正直，人所共知。自授御史已來，舉奏不避權勢，只如奏李公佐等事（《舊書》白傳引作李佐公），多是朝廷親情。人誰無私？因以挾恨，或假公議，將報私嫌。”疑此李公佐，即微之所劾之河南尉。按四年三月至五年三月，始終在相位者，唯杜佑、于頔、裴垍、李藩四人（見《新書》六二《宰相表中》），杜、于皆不負實際政務，裴垍與微之關係極深，集七《感夢》且云：“前時予掾荆，公在期復起。自從裴公無，吾道甘已矣。”其非爲垍所黜，自不待言。然則貶抑微之者，似舍李藩莫屬矣；然藩與李公佐之關係，則已難考。

三、與内侍争廳，因觸憲宗之怒。

《通鑒》二三八《唐紀》五四云：“河南尹房式有不法事，東臺監察御史元稹奏攝之，擅令停務。朝廷以爲不可，罰一季俸，召還西京。至敷水驛，有内侍後至，破驛門，呼罵而入，以馬鞭擊稹，傷面。上復引稹前過，貶江陵士曹。翰林學士李絳、崔群言稹無罪，白居易上言：‘中使陵辱朝士，中使不問而稹先貶，恐自今中使外出益暴横，人無敢言者。……’上不聽。”胡三省注云：“前過，謂擅令河南尹停務，上知曲在中官，故引前過以貶稹。”《新書》二〇七《仇士良傳》云：“嘗次敷水驛，與御史元稹争舍上廳，擊傷稹。中丞王播奏御史、中使以先後至得正寢，請如舊章。帝不直稹，斥其官。”白樂天《論元稹第三狀》云：“昨元稹所追勘房式之事，心雖徇公，事稍過當，既從重罰，足以懲違。況經謝恩，旋又左降，雖引前事以爲責辭，然外議喧喧，皆以爲稹與中使劉士元争廳，因此獲罪。至於争廳事理，已具前狀奏陳……今中官有罪，未聞處置；御史無過，却先貶官。遠近聞知，實損聖德。”則是微之之貶，似又主由與内侍争廳觸憲宗之怒者。憲宗雖號明主，然就其因五坊小使而罪裴寰（見《舊書》一七〇《裴度傳》）及因神策小將而怒柳公綽（《通鑒》卷二三九《唐紀》五五）諸事觀之，因内侍而貶稹，自極可能，其所以不似前二人之遭遇者，蓋以微之官卑不得專達，又早樹怨於内外寵臣，故終不得直而遭遠謫也。

月之下旬，即就江陵道。白樂天以詩二十章奉行。途中有《思歸樂》等詩。

本集六詩目云："三月二十四日《宿曾峰館，夜對桐花寄樂天》。"同書一九《桐花》詩序云："元和五年，予貶掾江陵，三月二十四日，宿曾峰館。山月曉時，見桐花滿地，因有八韻寄白翰林詩。"然則微之離長安必在三月二十四日之前也。《白氏長慶集》二《和答詩十首》序云："五年春，微之從東臺來，不數日又左轉爲江陵士曹掾。詔下日，會予下内直歸，而微之已即路。邂逅相遇於衢中，自永壽寺南抵新昌里北，得馬上話别……是夕足下次於山北寺，僕職役不得去，命季弟送行，且奉新詩一軸致於執事，凡二十章，率有比興……及足下到江陵，寄在路所爲詩十七章，凡五六千言，言有爲章有旨……僕思牛僧孺戒，不能示他人，唯與杓直、拒非及樊宗師輩三四人時一吟讀，心甚貴重。然竊思之，豈僕所奉者二十章遽能開足下聰明，使之然耶？抑又不知是行也，天將屈足下之道、激足下之心，使感時發憤而臻於此耶？若兩不然者，何立意措辭與足下前時詩如此之相遠也？"按微之赴江陵途次所作，今集一《思歸樂》以下全卷十四首及集二《青雲驛》《陽城驛》等皆是，率以諷興立意，其亦微之胸臆不平之氣之發抒歟？然元、白二公相互觀摩改進，自亦爲重要原因之一。又有《曾峰館寄樂天》《商山館感夢》《途中寄樂天》《渡漢江》等詩。

六月，抵江陵，晤李景儉等。時景儉貶守江陵府户曹參軍，有《泛江玩月十二韻》《紀懷贈李六户曹崔二十功曹五十韻》，又以《思歸樂》等十七章、《夢游春七十韻》寄白樂天。

本集一一《泛江玩月十二韻》序云："予以元和五年自監察御史貶授江陵士曹掾。六月十四日，張季友、李景儉二侍御，王文仲同録、王衆仲判官兩昆季，爲予載酒炙、選聲音，自府城之南淮攀月泛舟，窮竟一夕，予賦詩以紀之。"蓋微之初抵江陵，李等邀游之作。張季友並二王皆不詳，集九《獨夜傷懷贈呈張侍御》，當亦指季友。同卷《紀懷贈李六户曹崔二十功曹》云："甲科崔並騖，柱史李齊升……他鄉元易感，同病轉相矜。"疑亦微之抵江陵不久作。李六即景儉。崔二十未詳，考微之試判同入等者有崔十八玄亮，同登制科者有崔二十二韶，此崔二十或屬微之擢明經時之同科，然已無可考矣。《白氏長慶集》一二和《夢游春詩一百韻》序云:"微之既到江陵,又以《夢游春詩七十韻》寄予。"可證微之《夢游春》詩作於初抵江陵時,該詩今本不録,見於《才調集》五及《全唐詩》元稹二七,又有《夢昔游》詩,亦憶與雙文之戀者,疑亦作於本年。

白樂天以五月除京兆户曹參軍。有和《樂天初授户曹喜而言志》詩,又有《和樂天贈樊著作》《酬翰林白學士代書一百韻》《和樂天贈吴丹》《酬樂天書懷見寄》《酬樂天登樂游園見憶》等詩,二公詩篇往還,多本年。不勝考,以上諸作,略可考訂,皆作於①

《寄吴士矩端公五十韻》《寄隱客》《答姨兄胡靈之見寄五十韻》,皆抵江陵後寄故舊之作。《聽庾及之彈烏夜啼引》《江陵三夢》,皆抵江陵後悼亡韋氏之作。

本集九《烏夜啼引》云:"四五年前作拾遺,諫書不密丞相知。"故知當作於江陵,然則微之少年之友庾及之此時亦在江陵耶?待考。《江陵三夢》其一云:"悲君所嬌女,棄置不我隨。"疑微之隻身遠赴江陵,韋氏所遺之女未克隨行,至六年春始隨往江陵,故其時有"身將稚女帳前啼"之句。

《誨侄等書》亦作於本年。《書》云:"我謫竄方始。"可以證之。

《琵琶歌》《桂花晚》《種竹》等詩,皆作於本年。

裴垍以十一月罷相,改授兵部侍郎,以中風久病故也。

韓退之四十三歲。拜河南縣令。

李賀二十一歲。應河南府試獲選。

元和六年辛卯(八一一)。三十三歲。在江陵。

春,有《遣懷》八首,悼韋夫人也。時幼女保子已至江陵。

本集九詩目云:"六年春,《遣懷》八首。"其六云:"我隨楚澤波中水,君作咸陽泉下泥。百事無心值寒食,身將稚女帳前啼。"知其時微之幼女已在江陵,然其抵荆究在本年初抑在去年末,則不可知矣。三月,右僕射嚴綬改江陵尹、荆南節度使,封鄭國公。微之自兹多爲綬所知賞。

《舊紀》一四云:"(元和六年三月)丁未,以檢校右僕射嚴綬爲江陵尹、荆南節度使。"《舊書》一四六《綬傳》(《新書》一二九《綬傳》略同)云:"(元和)四年,

① 編者注:原稿如此,疑有缺文。

(白河東節度使)入拜尚書右僕射。綬雖名家子,爲吏有方略,然鋭於勢利,不存名節,人士以此薄之。……尋出鎮荆南,進封鄭國公。"微之之得入綬幕,疑在綬鎮荆之後,本集五五《贈太保嚴公行狀》云:"其所行事,由荆而下,皆所經見,由荆而上,莫非傳信。"明綬鎮荆之前,與微之尚無關係也。本集七《遣病十首》之二云:"棄置何所任,鄭公憐我病,……身賤殺何益,恩深報難罄。公其千萬年?世有天之鄭。"足見微之於綬感德之深。

官爲修宅於江干,因作《江邊四十韻》《有鳥二十章》。

本集一三《江邊四十韻》自注云:"官爲修宅,卒然有作,因招李六侍御。"同書六《酬樂天早夏見懷》云:"君詩夏方早,我嘆秋已徂。……荒草滿田地,近移江上居。"以是知微之移居江邊,必在秋前。《有鳥二十章》,載於卷二五,題下注"庚寅"二字,似屬元和五年之作。考本集四《蟲豸》詩序云:"始辛卯年,予掾荆州之地……予所舍又荆州樹木洲渚處,晝夜常有羽翅百族鬧心,不得閒静,因爲《有鳥二十章》以自達。"明該詩乃微之本年移居江邊以後所作,題注非是。

始納妾安氏,且舉一子,名荆。

本集五八《葬安氏志》云:"予稚男荆,母曰安氏,字仙嬪,卒於江陵之金隈鄉莊敬坊沙橋外二里嫗樂之地焉。始辛卯歲,予友致用憫予愁,爲予卜姓而授之,四年矣……稚子荆,方四歲。"是微之以本年納妾,且當年即舉一子也。頗疑微之自幼女赴荆之後,乃有移居納妾、自立門户之舉,特未得更明確之證耳。致用,姓氏不詳。數考未得。本集三有《訓别致用》,一三有《飲致用神麴酒三十韻》。一七有《哀病驄呈致用》,一八有《送致用》,一九有《留呈夢得子厚致用》,《安氏志》更云微之納妾乃致用爲之"卜姓而授",其人必爲微之之密友,自不待言。觀諸詩並文之内容,似致用乃微之之舊交,其時亦貶於江陵,後復遠徙,至元和十年乃與微之、夢得、子厚諸貶官同奉詔入朝,其人與微之一生大有關係,容待續考。

四月,白樂天母陳太夫人卒,訃聞七月始達江陵。有《祭翰林白學士太夫人文》,遣侄某代祭。樂天去歲已自翰林學士改授京兆户曹,至是丁母憂,乃退居渭上。

樂天丁母憂及退居渭上,並見陳、汪二譜。本集六《祭翰林白學士太夫人文》云:"維元和六年七月某日,文林郎守江陵府士曹參軍元稹,謹遣弟某侄男,祇酌奉饌,敢昭告于白氏太夫人之靈。"是微之七月始悉白母之卒而遣侄往祭也。祭文又云:"視惟幼女在側,無處言情。"益證其時微之幼女已在江陵也。

八月,吕聞卒,有《哭吕衡州六首》(本集八)。

《舊書》一三七《吕渭傳附温傳》云:"温字化光……(元和)三年……貶道州刺史。五年,轉衡州。秩滿歸京,不得意,發疾卒。"考《柳河東集》九《衡州刺史吕君誄》,知温以六年八月卒。微之悼詩自更後,其三云:"勢激三千壯,年應四十無。"温是年恰四十歲也。

有《寄劉頗一》一首(本集一八)。

其二云:"前年碣石烟塵起,共看官軍過洛城。"蓋指四年王承宗反,憲宗命内侍吐突承璀率神策軍往討而言。其時微之爲御史,分務東臺,故知寄詩作於本年。

李夷簡以四月自户部侍郎出爲山南東道節度使、檢校禮部尚書。

裴垍以七月自太子賓客轉太子少傅。

韓退之四十四歲。遷尚書職方員外郎。

柳子厚三十九歲。守永州司馬。

劉禹錫四十歲。守朗州司馬。

元和七年壬辰(八一二)。三十四歲。在江陵。

春,竇鞏來會,有《酬竇校書二十韻》《酬友封話舊叙懷十二韻》《酬友封見贈》等詩。旋鞏去荆,復有《送友封》三首。

本集一一《酬竇校書二十韻》云:"哪知暮江上,俱會落花前。"同卷《酬友封話舊叙懷十二韻》云:"風波千里别,書信二年稀。……春深鄉路遠,老去宦情微。魏闕何由到,荆州且共依。"明鞏來荆時在春季。本集一八《送友封二首》,其二云:"鵬翼張風期萬里,馬頭無角已三年。"微之以五年貶荆,至是已三年矣。末二句云:"若見中丞忽相問,爲言腰折氣衝天。"中丞謂竇群也,時在開州刺史任。同卷《送友封》又云:"斗柄未回猶帶閏,江痕潜上已生春。"考微之在荆日,唯六年十二月閏、九年八月閏,詩所指之閏,必指六年十二月無疑,益證鞏以本年春到荆,疑鞏赴開州訪其兄群,途出於荆也。《舊書》一五五《竇群傳附鞏傳》云:"鞏字友封,元和二年登進士第……能五言詩,昆仲之間,與牟詩俱爲時所賞重。性温雅,多不能持論,士友言議之際,吻動而不發,白居易等目爲

‘囁嚅翁’。”

《遣興十首》(本集三),蓋本年之作。

末首云:“河清諒嘉瑞。”注云:“是歲黄河清。”然遍揀《新書》志及新、舊《書》憲宗紀,此數年中皆無河清之説。同首末二句云:“一到江陵郡,三年成去塵。”微之以五年貶荆,則該詩作於本年,可無疑矣。

自編詩集,類分十體,得二十卷,八百餘首。

本集三〇《敘詩寄樂天書》云:“適值河東李明府景儉在江陵時,僻好僕詩章,謂爲能解,欲得盡取觀覽。僕因撰成卷軸……自十六時至是元和七年,有詩八百餘首,色類相從,共成十體,凡二十卷。”按微之謫棄江陵,適在壯盛之年,自謂:“性不近道,未能淡然忘懷,又復懶於他欲。全盛之氣,注射語言,雜糅精粗,遂成多大。”知微之此數年間,篇章特盛,今本所録,江陵歌咏獨多,除少數可考其確切之年月者外,餘多昧然,勉强考之,徒覺無味,特從略。爲欣賞計,但知其爲在荆之作足矣。

白樂天四十一歲,丁母憂,居渭村,與微之時有篇章往來。

李商隱生(據張采田《玉溪生年譜會箋》)。

元和八年癸巳(八一三)。三十五歲。在江陵。

四月,竇群自開州刺史移容州刺史、邕管經略使。有《奉和竇容州七律》一首。

《舊書》一五五《群傳》云:“(元和),六年九月貶開州刺史。在郡二年,改容州刺史。”《舊紀》一五“元和八年”條云:“夏四月……以開州刺史竇群爲邕管經略使。”本集一八《奉和竇容州》云:“明公莫訝容州遠,一路瀟湘景氣濃。……自嘆風波去無極,不知何日又相逢。”就詩意觀之,疑群自開州赴容州任,途次江陵,會於微之,因而有酬和之作也。考《劉賓客文集》一八有《代竇中丞謝上表》,題下注云:“群時在朗州相逢,因以見托。”其時群兄常爲朗州刺史(見《舊書》一五五《群傳附常傳》)。禹錫仍守朗州司馬,群赴任經其地,因倩禹錫代作謝表。由是觀之,則群自離開州任後,自峽而下,過江陵、轉朗州、溯瀟湘、趨容桂,乃極自然之路綫。然則微之和詩作於本年夏,似屬無疑矣。

秋,染疾,有《遣病》十首(本集七)。

其一云:“服藥備江瘴,四年方一癘。”其五云:“壯年等閑過,過壯年已五。”

微之自五年貶荆,至是四載,且其年恰爲三十五也。其八云:"檐宇夜來曠,暗知秋已生。"其九云:"秋依静處多。"可證其時在本年秋。

冬,朗州劉禹錫有詩來贈。

《劉賓客集外集》五詩目云:"《酬竇員外郡齋宴客,偶命拓技,因見寄,兼呈張十一院長、元九侍御》。"自注云:"員外時兼節度判官,佐平蠻之略,張初罷任,元方從事。"員外謂竇常也,時爲武陵(朗州)守。平蠻之略,謂本年秋溆州蠻酋張伯靖等,因嚴綬曉諭而歸降也(參羅聯添《劉夢得年譜》)。按微之、夢得,同遭貶棄,天涯淪落,當不無惺惺相惜之感;而荆、朗相去匪遥,贈答之作,似不應少,今考元集,除卷一八《酬劉二十八贈石枕》一篇爲在通時之作外(見後考),餘不得見,其佚失歟?

杜甫孫嗣業,以甫柩歸葬於襄陽,途經江陵,因其請作《唐故工部員外郎杜君墓系銘》。

本集五六《杜君墓系銘序》云:"適子美之子子嗣業,啓子美之柩,襄祔事於偃師,次於荆,雅知予愛言其大父爲文,拜予爲志。辭不可絶,予因係其官閥而銘其卒葬云。"銘曰:"維元和之癸巳,粤某月某日之佳辰,合窆我杜子美於首陽之前山。"知杜甫之歸葬,時在本年。按甫卒於耒陽,初葬其地。後世有因見耒陽有甫墓而偃師無之(趙德麟《侯鯖録》、宋敏求《春明退朝録》並有此記)。而疑子美未嘗歸葬者。歷來賞子美者多矣,然能不徒嘆其偉大且能道其所以偉大者,微之之前,似尚無其人。微之謂子美"盡得古今之體勢,而兼人人之所獨專",又謂:"苟以爲能所不能,無可不可,則詩人以來,未有如子美者。"其論子美之偉大,可謂卓識。以是知微之匪唯爲天才之創作家,亦且爲天才之批評家也。

與甄濟之子逢游善,逢每痛其父之節行不書於史,因爲作書致史館修撰韓退之以明之。

本集二九有《與史館韓侍郎書》,侍郎謂退之也。考退之以本年春改尚書比部郎中、史館修撰,《書》稱侍郎,未解其故。退之《答元侍御書》,據宋洪興祖《韓子年譜》及清方成珪《昌黎先生詩文年譜》,皆繫於九年,韓書有"去歲得書"句,知微之致韓書當作於本年末。按濟之事略,後復得襄州刺史袁滋之表奏,因編得載於史。傳見《舊書》一八七下、《新書》一九四。

李夷簡自山南東道節度使改授檢校户部尚書、成都尹、充劍南西川節度使。

袁滋自户部尚書出爲襄州刺史、山南東道節度使。竇鞏從辟爲掌書記。

白樂天四十二歲，退居渭村。聞微之病瘴，寄以大通中散碧腴垂雲膏，且贈以詩。(《白氏長慶集》一四)

元和九年甲午(八一四)。三十六歲。

春，於役潭州。有《夢成之》《陪張湖南宴望岳樓》《何滿子歌》《盧頭陀詩》《醉别盧頭陀》《湖南登臨湘樓》等作。

本集一八《盧頭陀詩序》云："元和九年，張中丞領潭之歲，予拜張公於潭。"同書二六《何滿子歌》題下注云："張湖南座爲唐有熊作。"詩云："我來湖外拜君侯，正值灰飛仲春琯。"比對而觀，知微之湖南之行在本年春。

張中丞，謂張正甫也。《舊紀》一五云："(元和八年冬十月)以蘇州刺史張正甫爲湖南觀察使。"可證。本集九《夢成之》云："燭暗船風獨夜驚，夢君頻問向南行。……一夜洞庭江水聲。"知爲微之南行途中夢韋夫人之作。陪《張湖南宴望岳樓》《河滿子歌》《盧頭陀詩》《醉别盧頭陀》等詩，由前引可知皆爲在潭時所作。卷一四《湖南登臨湘樓》云："歲閏覺春長。"知該詩亦必是年作，以本年閏八月故也。另有《岳陽樓》《寄庾敬休》《鹿角鎮》《晚宴湘亭》《洞庭湖》《花栽二首》《宿石磯》《遭風二十韻》等詩，觀詩意知皆爲往來荆湘間之作，疑皆爲本年春作。

三月，歸江陵。妾安氏卒，作葬安氏志。

本集五八《葬安氏志》云："予稚男荆母，曰安氏，字仙嬪，卒於江陵之金隈鄉莊敬坊沙橋外二里嫗樂之地焉。始辛卯歲，予友致用憫予愁，爲予卜姓而授之，四年矣。……近歲嬰疾，秋方綿痼。適予與信友約浙行，不敢私廢。及還，果不克見。"辛卯爲元和六年，下推四載，知安氏以本年終。微之以本年秋去荆(見後考)，《志語》所云"近歲嬰疾，秋方綿痼"，乃指去歲而言。唯"予與信友約浙行"一語，甚不可解。頗疑"浙"乃"湘"之誤，然則安氏以去秋染疾，歷冬至春而卒，時微之適有湘行，故歸而已不及見矣。至定其時爲二月者，則以微之三月終已在江陵故也。

月終，杜元穎歸京，有餞别及送行詩。

《全唐詩》元稹二八詩目云:"《三月三十日程氏館餞杜十四歸京》。"

本集一九《送杜元穎》云:"江上五年同送客,與君長羨北歸人。"

知元穎北歸在本年。《舊書》一六三《杜元穎傳》(《新書》九六《附如晦傳》)云:"貞元末進士登第,再辟使府,元和中爲左拾遺。"未言其所辟爲何府,其或亦在嚴綬幕耶?

九月,荆南節度使嚴綬,改檢校司空、襄州刺史、山南東道節度使。微之以從事隨之任。有《和嚴司空重陽日》《游三寺》《過襄陽樓》等詩。

《舊紀》一五"元和九年"條云:"(九月丙戌)以山南東道節度使袁滋檢校兵部尚書、兼江陵尹、荆南節度使,以荆南節度使嚴綬檢校司空、襄州刺史、山南東道節度使。"

按微之從綬移襄,並無直接證據,然綬鎮荆時,爲檢校右僕射、封鄭國公(見前考)。至是乃晉位檢校司空,而本集一八有《奉和嚴司空重陽日同崔常侍崔郎中及諸公登龍山落帽臺佳宴》《游三寺回呈上府主嚴司空》《過襄陽樓呈上府主嚴司空》諸詩,可證皆作於綬改官之後,而其時微之亦在襄陽也。依制貶官不得擅離本所,微之隨任必爲綬之力,亦見綬於微之依重之深也。《過襄陽樓》詩題下復云:"樓在江陵節,度使宅北隅。"頗不可解,待續考。

十月,詔以嚴綬兼充申光蔡等州招撫使。時淮西節度使吴少陽新卒,其子元濟拒受朝命,故命綬統諸軍討之。

微之爲綬作《謝招討使表》,旋隨之赴唐州,有《代諭淮西書》。

《舊紀》一五"元和九年"下:"(十月甲子制)宜以山南東道節度使嚴綬兼充申光蔡等州招撫使,仍命内常侍崔潭峻爲監軍。"本集三四《爲嚴司空謝招討使表》云:"伏奉今月十九日敕,以臣兼充申光蔡等州招撫使……臣先奉恩詔,令臣發赴唐州。"明綬以十月下旬得詔,旋即赴唐。又本集一二《酬樂天東南行百韻》云:"重喜登賢苑,方日佐伍符。"下注云:"九年,樂天除太子贊善,予從事唐州也。"《代諭淮西書》(卷三一),當爲赴唐後作,則其時應在十一月矣。

《舊書》一六六本傳云:"荆南監軍崔潭峻甚禮接稹,不以掾吏遇之。常徵其詩什諷誦之。長慶初,潭峻歸朝,出稹《連昌辭》等百餘篇奏御。"《新書》一七四本傳云:"稹之謫江陵,善監軍崔潭峻。長慶初,潭峻方親幸,以稹歌詞數十百篇奏御。"二説均以微之在荆時即識崔潭峻,然潭峻之名,始見於本年十月詔，前此未見。本集一八《奉和嚴司空重陽日》所云之“崔常侍”，就詩語“貴重近臣光綺席”觀之，或即指潭峻，然該詩之作疑不早於綬移襄之前。豈嚴綬鎮荆時，潭峻已監於其軍耶？然微之究以何時始交於潭峻，終不可考矣。

《通鑑》二三九《唐紀》五五云：“初，上以嚴綬在河東，所遣裨將多立功，故使鎮襄陽，且督諸軍討吴元濟。綬無他材能，到軍之日，傾府庫賚士卒，累年之積，一朝而盡。又厚賂宦官，以結聲援，擁八州之衆萬餘人，屯境上，閉壁經年，無尺寸功。”則綬之才俱可知也。

十二月，有《祭淮瀆文》（本集六〇）。

西川從事韋臧文以本年來會，及其歸，有《貽蜀五首》以問舊好。

本集一九《貽蜀五首》序云：“元和九年，蜀從事韋臧文告别。蜀多朋舊，稹性懶爲寒温書，因賦代懷五章，而贈行亦在其數。”臧文之來，當稹在荆之時抑爲移襄之後，已難考定。詩所及之五人，張元夫、韋臧文史並無傳，不可考。盧子蒙，乃微之幼年友，已前見。贈詩云：“唯公兩弟閑相訪，往往潸然一望公。”未詳所指，本集一四有《誚盧戡》，二〇有《送盧戡》，觀詩意知皆在荆襄時之作，戡或即子蒙之弟？李尚書，謂夷簡、時爲檢校户部尚書、西川節度使，傳見《新書》一三一。李中丞表臣，即李程，傳見《舊書》一六七、《新書》一三一，時在夷簡幕爲行軍司馬成都少尹。贈詩云：“韋門同是舊親賓，獨恨潘郎簟有塵。”觀此微之與表臣或屬誼在連襟也。

韓退之四十七歲。十月，轉考功郎中、兼史館修撰、知制誥。

白樂天四十三歲。冬，入朝拜太子左贊善大夫。

孟郊六十四歲。八月，暴卒於河南閿鄉。

元和十年乙未（八一五）。三十七歲。

正月，奉召歸京，途次有《桐花詩》《西歸絶句十二首》《藍橋驛留呈夢得、子厚、致用》等詩。月終抵京。

本集一二《酬樂天東南行百韻》云：“駟騎來千里，天書下九衢。因教罷飛檄，便許到皇都。”注云：“十年春，自唐州詔予召入京。”同書一九《桐花詩》序云：“元和五年，予貶江陵……及今六年，詔許西歸……元和十年正月題。”知微之自唐州從事任，奉詔入京，本年正月已在道中。案《劉賓客集》四或有詩目云：“元和甲午歲，詔書盡徵江湘逐客，余自武陵赴京，宿於都亭，有懷續來諸君子。”可證召貶官之詔乃去歲末所下，唯不見本紀，以理推之，知其必然，惜史失載耳。又《柳河東集》四二有《詔追赴都，二月至灞亭上》一詩。陳寅恪先生《連昌宫詞箋證》云：“是微之略前行，而子厚後隨，子厚於二月達灞亭，即長安近傍，時微之已到長安。故綜合推計之，謂微之元和十年到長安之時，約在正月下旬或二月初旬。”案子厚自永州歸京，二月抵達。禹錫發自朗州，故先於子厚，微之自唐而來，因又早於禹錫，故謂微之以正月下旬抵京，亦可以無疑矣。

《西歸絶句》乃途次隨感而發，似非一地之作。其三云：“同歸諫院韋丞相，共貶河南亞大夫。”注云：“韋丞相貫之，裴中丞度。”案度以去歲十一月自中書舍人拜御史中丞，元和元年與微之同貶河南，已見前考。貫之去冬臘月以尚書右丞守本官拜相，元和元年微之爲拾遺時，貫之爲右補闕，故曰‘同歸諫院’也。微之先以詩投於韋、裴，殆亦冀其念舊交而有所引拔歟？

又本集一四有《歸田詩》，題下注云：“時三十七。”詩云：“我亦今年去，商山淅岸村。”同書一九《西歸絶句》之九云：“今朝西渡丹河水，心寄丹河無限愁。若到莊前竹園下，殷勤爲遶故山流。”注云：“丹淅，莊之東流。”似微之曾於丹水側置産，有歸田之意，旋奉詔入京而棄去之也。然以時間計之，頗爲不協，容待續考。

既抵京，有《酬盧秘書》詩。

本集一二《酬盧秘書》序云：“予自唐歸京之歲，秘書郎盧拱作《喜遇白贊善學士二十韻》，兼以見貽，白時酬和先出，予草蹙未暇皇，頻有致師之挑，故篇末不無憤辭。其次用本韻，習然也。”知該詩乃微之抵京不久之作，樂天《酬盧》詩題下注云：“時初奉詔除贊善大夫。”則似作於去歲末。盧拱，史無傳。

嘗與樂天等春游城南，馬上唱和。又有編次《元白往還集》之議，旋以再貶而廢。

本集二二詩目云：“爲樂天自勘詩集，因思頃年城南醉歸，馬上遞唱艷曲，十餘里不絶。”《白氏長慶集》二八《與元九書》云：“如今年春游城南時，與足下馬上相戲，因各誦新艷小律，不雜他篇，自皇子陂歸昭國里，迭吟遞唱，不絶聲者二十里餘，樊、李在傍無所措口。……時足下興有餘力，且欲與僕悉索還往中詩，取其尤長者，如《張十八古樂府》《李二十新歌行》《盧楊二秘書律詩》《竇七元八絶句》，博搜精掇，編而次之，號爲《元白往還集》。衆君子得擬議於此者,莫不踊躍欣喜,以爲盛事。嗟乎!言未終而足下左轉,不數月而僕又繼行,心期索然,何日成就,又可爲之太息矣。”微之與樂天游城南時,“在傍無所措口”之“樊、李”,初疑即《澧西餞别微之之樊宗憲與李景信》(見後),後見《白氏長慶集》一五有《游城南留元九李二十晚歸》一首,又有《初授贊善大夫早朝寄李二十助教》一首,知公垂本年亦在京師,且復爲國子助教也。則同游城南者,亦可能爲樊宗師、李公垂矣,未詳孰是。張十八即張籍,《白氏長慶集》一七《江樓夜吟元九律詩》云:“老張知定伏,短李愛應顛。”注云:“張十八籍、李二十紳皆攻律詩,故云。”可證。盧謂盧拱,已前見。楊謂楊巨源,《白氏長慶集》一五有《贈楊秘書巨源》一首,微之有《和樂天贈楊秘書》(本集二〇)詩云:“舊與楊郎在帝城,搜天斡地覓詩情。”皆證其爲巨源無疑。元八名宗簡,字居敬,以詩名於時,史無傳,事略見於《白氏長慶集》《元少尹文集》。竇七,疑即竇鞏,《白氏長慶集》一六《東南行百韻》,所及者有竇七校書,詩云:“論笑杓胡硉,談憐鞏囁嚅。”似竇七非鞏莫屬。然新、舊《書》鞏傳皆謂袁滋鎮襄荆時,鞏皆從辟於其幕,而滋本年恰在荆南節度任,頗爲費解。意者,鞏斯時或已去袁幕而歸京師,因得躬與此一時之盛也。

三月,奉詔復出爲通州司馬,因以三十四歲以前詩二十卷貽樂天。月終,别樂天等於鄠東蒲池村,遂赴通州(今四川達州)。

本集一二《酬樂天東南行百韻》序云:“元和十年三月二十五日,予司馬通州,二十九日與樂天於鄠東蒲池村别,各賦一絶。”同書一九詩目云:“《澧西别樂天博載樊宗憲李景信兩秀才侄谷三月三十日相餞送》。”《白氏長慶集》一七詩目亦有“十年三月三十日别微之於澧上”一語,知微之於三月下旬奉詔,月終即匆匆就道。本集三〇《叙詩寄樂天書》云:“自十六時至是元和七年矣,有詩八百餘首,色類相從,共成十體,凡二十卷。自笑冗亂,亦不復置之於行李。昨來京師,偶在筐篋,及通行,盡置足下。”又《通鑒》二三九《唐紀》“元和十年”條云:“王叔文之黨坐謫官,凡十年不量移,執政憐其才,欲漸進之者。悉召至京師,諫官争言其不可,上與武元衡亦惡之。三月,皆以爲遠郡刺史,官雖進而地益遠。”微之初與王黨同被召歸,及王黨復黜,而微之亦隨之再貶,蓋微之以年少務進而遭忌,其情形正同於劉、柳故也。

途次褒城驛,追懷昔游,有詩二首。過青山驛,作《紫躑躅》《山枇杷》等詩。

本集八《褒城驛二首》之二云:“梨枯竹盡黄令死,今日再來衰病身。”蓋追懷元和四年春奉使東川泄黄明府事也。同書二六《紫躑躅》云:“去年春别湘水頭,今年夏見青山曲。”又云:“爾躑躅,我向通川,爾幽獨,可憐今夜宿青山,何年却向青山宿。”《山枇杷》云:“左降通州十日遲,又與幽花一年别。”可知諸詩皆本年貶通途次所作。

閏六月,抵通州,有《見樂天詩》及《叙詩寄樂天書》。旋罹重疾,有《遣病長篇》一首。

本集一二《酬樂天東南行百韻詩》内注云:“元和十年閏六月至通州,染瘴危重。”知微之以閏六月抵通,不久即染重病。本集二〇《見樂天詩》云:“通州到日日平西……見君詩在柱心題。”《白氏長慶集》一五詩目云:“微之到通州日,授館未安,見塵壁間有數行字,讀之即僕舊詩。”知該詩乃微之甫抵通之作。本集三〇《叙詩寄樂天書》云:“又不幸年三十二時有罪譴棄,今三十七矣。”又云:“昨來巴南道中,又有詩五十一首。……僕少時授吹嘘之術於鄭先生,病懶未就。今在閑處,思欲怡神保和,以求其病,異日亦不復費詞於無用之文矣。”明該書作於本年抵通之後。書中未及患瘴事,頗疑乃微之抵通後與染疾前之作,未知然否。要之,微之是書必先於樂天《與元九書》,亦不待證。此點頗爲重要,蓋由此可以略窺二公文學思想之後先也。

本集七《遣病》題下注云:“自此通州後作。”詩云:“今年京城内,死者老少并。”而其所及者如獨孤郁、趙昌等,皆卒於元和九年,雖行文之際不可過泥,然亦足證該詩乃微之抵通後不久之作也。

八月,病益痼,而樂天謫潯之信適至,有《聞樂天授江州司馬七絶》一首。

《舊書》一六六《白居易傳》云:“十年七月,盗殺宰相武元衡,居易首上疏論其冤,急請捕賊,以雪國耻。宰相以宫官非諫職,不當先諫官言事。會有素惡居易者,掎摭居易,言浮華無行,其母因看花墮井而死,而居易作《賞花》及《新井》詩,甚傷名教,不宜置彼周行。執政方惡其言事,奏貶爲江表刺史。詔出,中書舍人王涯上疏論之,言居易所犯狀迹,不宜治郡,追詔授江州司馬。”然考《舊紀》一五“元和十年”下:“六月辛丑朔,癸卯,鎮州節度使王承宗遣盗夜伏於靖安坊,刺宰相武元衡,死之。”是元衡以六月初遇害,樂天上疏不當逾六月,疑傳誤。本集一二《酬樂天東南行百韻》自注云:“元和十年閏六月,至通州,染瘴危重。八月,聞樂天司馬江州。"又云:"三月,稹之通川。八月,樂天之江州。"蓋樂天貶信八月始聞於通也。《白氏長慶集》二八《與微之書》云:"又睹所寄聞僕左降詩云:'殘燈無焰影憧憧,此夕聞君謫九江。垂死病中驚起坐,暗風吹雨入寒窗。'此句他人尚不可聞,況僕心哉! 至今每吟,猶惻惻耳。"按此詩見於本集二〇,唯第三句作"垂死病中仍悵望",略有不同。《容齋隨筆》二"長歌之哀"條云:"元微之在江陵,病中聞白樂天左降江州,作絶句云:'殘燈無焰影憧憧,此夕聞君謫九江。垂死病中驚起坐,暗風吹雨入寒窗。'樂天以爲'此句他人尚不可聞,況僕心哉'。微之集作'垂死病中起悵望',此三字既不佳,又不題爲病中作,失其意矣。"案洪氏之説,不無見地,唯謂微之此詩作於江陵,則失考矣。

《感夢五古》一首,乃敘夢及裴垍之作,疑在本年十月。

本集七《感夢》題下注云:"夢故兵部裴尚書相公。"詩云:"十月初二日,我行蓬州西。……我病百日餘,肌體顧若刲。"微之以閏六月抵通,旋即染疾,至十月初恰爲百餘日,故疑該詩作於本年。然微之何爲以重病之身離通西行,遠及蓬州(今四川儀隴境),則不可考矣。本集二〇《新政縣》一首,疑亦同時所作。

劉禹錫四十四歲。春,自朗州徵還,旋出爲連州刺史。

柳子厚四十二歲。二月抵長安,三月改柳州刺史。

白樂天四十四歲。冬初抵江州,臘月有《與元九書》。

韓退之四十八歲。夏,進《順宗實録》。

元和十一年丙申(八一六)。三十八歲。

春,逢故人熊士登,有贈詩。旋熊之嶺南,有《别嶺南熊判官詩》,並以一札托遺江州。先是,疾篤時,曾自封平生詩文,預囑他日以遺樂天,故白書云云。

本集二一《酬樂天得微之詩知通州事因成四首》,其二云:"此中愁殺須甘分,惟惜平生舊著書。"注云:予病甚,將平生所爲文自題云:"異日送白二十二郎也。"案樂天原詩作於貶謫江州之前,微之酬詩作於何時,則頗爲難知。病篤封詩之時間,自更難考,然必在本年春以前。何以言之?《白氏長慶集》二八《與微之書》云:"僕初到潯陽時,有熊萬(作孺,微之贈詩作士)登來,得足下前年病甚時一札,上報疾狀,次序病心,終論平生交分,且云:'危惙之際,不暇及他。唯收數帙文章,封題其上曰:他日送達白二十二郎,便請以代書。'悲哉!

微之於我也，其若是乎！”按樂天此書作於元和十三年四月，則獲微之書時，自屬本年。本集一五《贈熊士登》云：“今日梅花下，他鄉逢故人。”知熊乃微之故交，餘則無考。《别嶺南熊判官》云：“况復三巴外，仍逢萬里行。桐花新雨氣，梨葉晚春晴。”明熊去岭南，時值春暮。微之或以其途過江州，因托遺札於樂天也。

五月，始納裴淑爲繼室。淑字柔之，其出身亡考。

案微之與裴夫人之婚，諸書皆未明言其時間。今考《白氏長慶集》一六《寄蘄州簟與元九因題六韻》，題下注云：“時元九鰥居。”樂天此詩作於江州，其時間當在十年末。微之《酬樂天寄蘄州簟》（本集一五）云：“蘄簟未經春，君先拭翠筠。”可爲佐證。然以通江相去之遥，微之得樂天所寄之簟，當已在本年春，而其時微之尚屬“驚卧老龍身”，則微之移貶通州時尚未續娶，從可知矣。然本集一五《景申秋八首》即本年秋所作，其四云：“婢報樵蘇竭，妻愁院落通。”似其時微之已有婦，然則謂元、裴之婚在本年春秋之間，當不甚誤。本集二二《初除浙東妻有阻色因以四韻曉之》云：“嫁時五月歸巴地。”其所指乃本年五月，可無多疑。然今復有一問題，即微之婚時究在通州抑在興元，又不可考矣。

秋，在興元（今陝西南鄭）。有《獻滎陽公五十韻》《奉和滎陽公離筵作》《寄獻滎陽公》等詩。滎陽公，謂鄭餘慶也，時在山南西道節度使任。

本集一二《獻滎陽公詩五十韻》云：“自傷魂慘沮，何暇思幽玄。”注云：“稹病瘧二年，求醫在此，滎陽公不忍歸之瘴鄉。”《舊書》一五八《鄭餘慶傳》云：“（元和）九年檢校右僕射、兼興元尹、充山南西道節度觀察使。三歲受代，十二年除太子少師。”知本年餘慶駐節興元，而微之正求醫於其地也。本集一五《滎陽鄭公以稹寓居嚴茅有池塘之勝寄詩四首因有意獻》云：“暫停隨梗浪，猶閲敗霜荷。”其時似屬暮秋。取此與前引注語比觀，知微之居興元之時間必不甚短，且頗爲餘慶所眷顧也。然微之究以何時至興元，則不甚可考。竊疑微之去冬之適蓬州，即爲求醫，稍後即來興元，以餘慶故，因得留居其地。若此説不誤，則别熊士登、婚裴柔之，皆在興元矣。

十月，權德輿代餘慶爲山南西道節度使。有《奉和權相公行次臨闕驛十四韻》。

《舊紀》一五“元和十一年”下：“冬十月丁巳，以刑部尚書權德輿檢校吏部尚書、兼興元尹、充山南西道節度使。"本集一二有《奉和權相公行次臨闕驛，逢鄭僕射相公歸朝，俄頃分途，因以奉贈詩十四韻》，末二句云："公方先二虜，何暇進愚儒。"時正用兵討伐淮西吴元濟、河北王承宗，故詩語及之。德輿字載之，傳見《舊書》一四八、《新書》一六五。

白樂天四十五歲，在江州。秋，作《琵琶行》。

韓退之四十九歲，春，遷中書舍人。夏，改太子右庶子。

李賀二十七歲，卒於昌谷（今河南宜陽境）。

姚合登進士第。

元和十二年丁酉（八一七）。三十九歲。

春，作《生春二十章》。

本集一五《生春》題下注云："丁酉歲，凡二十章。"知詩作於本年春，疑其時微之仍寄寓興元。

進士劉猛、李餘以古樂府數十首投獻，因選而和之，作《古題樂府十九首》，並以長序明其原委。

本集二三《樂府古題序》，題下注"丁酉"二字，知必作於本年。《序》云："昨梁州見進士劉猛、李餘，各賦古樂府詩數十首，其中一二十章咸有新意，予因選而和之。"觀此知微之見劉猛、李餘當在本年微之寓興元之時；然其確定之時日則頗難知，愚謂必在本年秋以前，蓋本年秋微之已歸通州（見後考）。又本集八有《酬劉猛見送》一首，疑亦作於本年，即微之去梁歸通之時。

案元、白詩文，以鋪陳直叙、明白曉暢見長，然其弊則在繁蕪露骨，少委婉之致。此點二公亦自知之。《白氏長慶集》二《和答詩十首》序云："頃者在科試間，常與足下同筆硯。每下筆時，輒相顧語，共患其意太切而理太周。故理太周則辭繁，意太切則言激，然與足下爲文，所長在此，所病亦在此。足下來序，果有辭犯文繁之説。今僕所和者，猶前病也。"然微之《古題樂府》之作，可謂一掃前弊，若《織婦田家》等篇，結語委婉曲折，尤屬可愛。其用辭之簡練、立意之含蓄，均爲元、白二公前此所未嘗及者。陳寅恪先生有《古題樂府箋證》論之，説極精當。

九月，在通州，權知州務。有《報三陽神文》。

本集五九《報三陽神文》云："維元和十二年九月十五日，文林郎、守通州司馬、權知州務元稹，謹遣攝録事参軍元叔則以清酒庶羞之奠，以報於三陽神之靈。"知微之九月間已在通州，何時歸來，則不可知。微之移通時刺史爲誰，考之未得，誠一憾事。至於微之何以權知州務，頗疑因其州守以疾廢事之故。同書同卷《告畬三陽神文》乃十三年十一月所作，中有"自喪守侯，月環其七"之語可證，微之之歸通或亦以是故也。

同月，李逢吉罷相，出爲劍南東川節度使。微之有《和東川李相公慈竹十二韻及酬東川李相公十六韻》，疑皆作於本年。

《舊紀》一五"元和十二年"下："（九月丁未）以朝議大夫、門下侍郎、同平章事李逢吉檢校兵部尚書、使持節梓州諸軍事、梓州刺史，充劍南東川節度副大使、知節度事。"逢吉字虚舟，以本年四月拜相，傳見《舊書》一六七、《新書》一七四。《舊傳》云："逢吉天與奸回，妒賢傷善。時用兵討淮蔡，憲宗以兵機委裴度，逢吉慮其成功，密沮之，繇是相惡。及裴親征，學士令狐楚爲度制辭，言不合旨。楚與逢吉相善，帝皆黜之，罷楚學士，罷逢吉政事，出爲劍南東川節度使。"按逢吉乃唐代朋黨之關鍵人物，微之後與裴度之交惡，多因逢吉而起。他如韓愈、李紳之争，李德裕、牛僧孺之争，推本溯源，皆逢吉使然。本集七《和東川李相公慈竹十二韻》，自屬作於逢吉莅川之後，其時間稽前於同書八《酬東川李相公十六韻》，後詩有"臘月巴地雨，瘴江愁浪翻"之句，明作於臘月，其有可能者，唯本年冬與明年冬。蓋十四年春，微之即去通之虢矣。（見後考）

十月，淮蔡平。十一月，吴元濟伏誅於長安。有《賀誅吴元濟表》。

《舊書》一五《憲紀》云："（元和十二年十月）己卯，隨唐節度使李愬率師入蔡州，執吴元濟以獻，淮西平。……十一月丙戌朔，御興安門受淮西之俘，以吴元濟徇兩市，斬於獨柳樹。"本集三四《賀誅吴元濟表》，以理推之，疑作於十二月。微之以佐貳之官而有賀表，或亦由其權知州務之故歟？

又《白氏長慶集》一七《題詩屏風序》云："十二年冬，微之猶滯通州，予亦未離湓上，相去萬里，不見三年。"案微之本年冬誠在通州，然樂天之語則未足證。蓋通江懸邈，二公本年書札酬唱幾至斷絶故也（前引《與微之書》有"不得足下書欲二年矣"之語）。

白樂天四十六歲。在江州。於香爐峰下築草堂。冬，題微之詩於屏風，又有《東南行百韻寄微之杓直》等。

韓退之五十歲。七月,以彰義行軍司馬隨宰相裴度出征淮蔡。十二月,歸朝,拜刑部侍郎。

元和十三年戊戌(八一八)。四十歲。在通州。

春,有《上門下裴相公書》。時裴度已歸朝復相,故以書干之,冀其拔録。

本集三一《上門下裴相公書》云:"今陛下當晉武平吴之後,閣下即東征而還。……碣石餘沴,束身之款未堅。"又云:"况當今陛下,在宥四海,與人爲天。"案度以去歲十二月歸朝復相,本年正月詔赦天下,四月始詔復王承宗,故疑微之上書在本年春。

《連昌宫詞》,或作於本年春。

陳寅恪先生有《連昌宫詞箋證》一篇,於該詩寫作之時間反復考辯,文繁不及具引,今略述其梗概。陳氏先作二種假定,一爲經過行宫感時撫事之作,一爲閉門伏案依題懸擬之作。若爲前者,則其時間必爲暮春,其有可能者唯元和十年至十四年間之五年耳。陳氏皆證其絶無可能,因謂該詩必爲閉門伏案依題懸擬之作。復次,陳氏以微之集一二有《見人咏韓舍人新律詩因有戲贈》一詩,謂微之在通時曾有機緣見昌黎之詩,而昌黎於十一二年冬淮西平後,有《和李正甫過連昌宫七絶》一首,"頗疑李氏原詩或韓公和作,遠道流傳,至次年即十三年春間,遂爲微之所見,因依題懸擬,亦賦一篇"。愚意以爲,陳氏之所否定者,至爲精賅,然其所肯定者,推理仍有未周,且未見其必然。蓋既非睹物興懷而爲閉門懸想之作,則其作成之時間不必限於暮春,至於因微之曾見韓之新律,而謂其亦曾見及韓之七絶,且時在十三年春,則更非愚敢知矣。然陳氏既以如是長之篇幅,用如是大之氣力,考定此詩作成之時間,末學淺見,於未獲有力證據之前,實不敢妄議其是非,今但從陳氏繫於本年春云爾。(竊疑若以該詩繫於十四年微之抵虢時,或較妥當,蓋微之舊地重游,因有所感,雖時不當春,亦於無礙懸想也。)

獲崔韶《轉達樂天來書暨東南行百韻》《送客游嶺南二十韻》等詩二十四章,乃並其舊寄八首盡和之,得三十二章。適李景信自忠州來訪,有《喜李十一景信到》《與李十一夜飲》《贈李十一》等詩。及李去,復有《别李十一七絶五首》《通州丁溪館夜别李景信三首》。

本集一二《酬樂天東南行百韻》序云:"十三年予以赦當遷,簡省書籍,得是八篇(元和十年樂天所寄)。吟嘆方極,適崔果州使至,爲予致樂天去年十二月二日書。書中寄予百韻至兩韻凡二十四章。屬李景信校書自忠州訪予,連牀遞飲之間,悲咤使酒,不三兩日盡和去年已來三十二章,皆異。李生視草而去。四月十三日,予手寫爲上下卷,仍依次重用本韻。亦不知何時得見樂天,因人或寄去。通之人莫可與言詩者,唯妻淑在旁,知狀。”景信去後,微之乃編寫其詩,時在四月,疑其來訪,當在三月間。崔果州,謂崔韶。韶以十一年九月貶爲果州(今四川南充)刺史。李景信,景儉之弟,時景儉在忠州(今重慶忠縣)刺史任(見《舊書》一七一《景儉傳》)。微之又有《憑李忠州寄書樂天》一首(本集二〇),疑亦本年或稍前作。《喜李十一景信》等詩,分見本集二〇及二六。

三月,劍南西川節度使李夷簡入朝爲御史大大,復改拜門下侍郎、同平章事。樂天意微之行將歸朝,乃以詩來賀,因有酬作。旋夷簡復出爲淮南節度,微之入朝之望又成泡影。

《舊紀》一五《元和十三年下》:“三月庚寅,以劍南西川節度使李夷簡爲御史大夫。……庚子,以御史大夫李夷簡爲門下侍郎、同平章事。”又云:“(七月)辛丑,以門下侍郎、同平章事李夷簡檢校左僕射、同平章事、揚州大都督府長史、淮南節度使。”《白氏長慶集》一七《聞李尚書拜相因以長句見賀微之》云:“憐君不久在通川,知已新提造化權。”夷簡以三月拜相,七月罷去,樂天此作自必在三月至七月間。本集二一《酬樂天聞李尚書拜相以詩見賀》云:“尚書入用雖旬月,司馬銜冤已十年。若待更遭秋瘴後,便愁平地有重泉。”似微之此詩亦作於本年秋以前。然此點愚頗疑之。元、白二公斯時相去甚遥,故微之嘗有“遠來書信來年聞”之語(本集二一《酬樂天嘆窮愁見寄》),雖不無誇張之嫌,然動盈數月,自屬必然。今夷簡以三月拜相,樂天於江州獲悉其事,當在相當時日之後,然後爲詩以寄微之。迨詩達微之之手,意其時至早當已逢秋矣。又元、白酬唱之作,往往有數年後始補和者,前引《酬樂天東南行百韻》序已足略證,今請更以一證以明之。《白氏長慶集》六〇《因繼集重》序云:“去年微之取予《長慶集》中詩未對答者五十七首追和之,合一百一十四首寄來,題爲‘因繼集卷之一’。”觀此,可知元白酬和之作,若但就其原詩而定其作成之時間,乃相當可疑之事,今以微之《酬樂天賀詩》姑繫於此。

十一月,有《告畬三陽神文》《告畬竹山神文》。

二文並見本集五九。《告畬竹山神文》云:“今天子斬三叛之明年,通民畢賦,用其閑餘,夾津而南,開山三十里,爲來年農種張本。自十月季旬,周甲癸而功半就。”故知亦作於十一月。觀二文,知微之權知州務以來屢有興廢,嘉惠通民至多。

《三兄以白角巾寄遣髮不勝冠因有感嘆》一首,疑作於本年。

詩載本集二〇,末云:“我身四十猶如此,何況吾兄六十身。”微之本年恰爲四十。唐人排行乃以從兄弟合計,此云三兄,以年齡考之,必不爲積,而可能爲秬,時秬當在河陰留後任(見本集五七《秬志》)。

劉禹錫以文石枕來贈,並題以詩,因以壁州鞭報之,亦附以詩。

本集一八詩目云:《劉二十八以文石枕見贈,仍題絶句以將厚意,因持壁州鞭酬謝,兼廣爲四韻》。”壁州(今四川通江)地近通州,知該詩當爲微之守通時所作,今姑繫於本年。蓋本年終微之受詔,明年春即去任之號也。劉二十八即禹錫,時在連州刺史任。《劉夢得外集》五有《贈元九侍御文石枕以詩獎之》及《酬元九侍御贈壁州鞭長句》二詩。

十二月,奉詔移授虢州長史。

《白氏長慶集》二六三《游洞》序云:“平淮西之明年,久,予自江州司馬授忠州刺史,微之自通州司馬授虢州長史。”同書《忠州刺史謝表》云:“臣以去年十二月二十日伏奉敕旨,授臣忠州刺史。”樂天既以本年終奉詔,明年春赴任,微之亦以明年春赴任,疑其奉詔當亦在本年終。本傳及墓志皆過爲簡略。

柳子厚四十六歲。守柳州,作《平淮西雅》。

韓退之五十一歲。撰《平淮西碑》,以多叙裴度事,爲李愬妻所訴,詔廢去,命段文昌重撰。

元和十四年己亥(八一九)。四十一歲。

二月,李師道伏誅,淄青平。

春,離通州。沿江而下,過涪州,有《黄草峽聽柔之琴》二首。三月,與樂天、知退會於夷陵(今湖北宜昌),三宿而别。四月,抵虢州(今河南三門峽市陝州區境)。

《白氏長慶集》二六三《游洞》序云:“平淮西之明年,予自江州司馬授忠州刺史,微之自通州司馬授虢長史。又明年春,各祗命之郡,與知退偕行。三月十日參會於夷陵，翌日，微之返櫂送予至下牢戍。又翌日，將别未忍，引舟上下者久之。"同書一七詩目云："《十四年三月十一日，夜遇微之於峽中，停舟夷陵，三宿而别》。"以是知微之自通之虢，乃沿嘉陵下長江，轉襄洛，而後至虢之一途也。本集一二《酬樂天東南行百韻》序附注云："其本卷（和樂天詩所成之上下卷）尋時於峽州面付樂天。"當亦指夷陵之會事。同書二一《黄草峽聽柔之琴二首》，其二云："憐君伴我涪州宿。"當爲微之途經涪州時所作。同書二〇《寒食日》云："莫將心道是涪州。"疑亦同時所作。然《全唐詩》於此詩"涪"字下注云："一作通。"故未敢必。微之三月中旬尚在夷陵，以其地去虢州之距離約略推之，疑其抵虢已在四月。

秋，女樊卒，有《哭女樊》七絶及《哭女樊四十韻》各一首。

本集九《哭女樊四十韻》題下注云："虢州長史時作。"《哭女樊》云："秋天净緑月分明。"故知樊之殤在本年秋，以微之在虢僅及一秋也。《哭女樊四十韻》云："去伴投遐徼，來隨夢險程。四年巴養育，萬里硤回縈。"知此女卒時至少已五歲，其非裴夫人之出，自屬必然。疑此女乃微之妾安氏所出。同詩又云："最憐貪栗妹，頻救懶書兄。"其妹疑即"小女降真"，其兄或即安氏所産之子名荆者。

九月，兄秬卒於虢。十一月，葬秬於咸陽，有《河陰留後元君墓志銘》。

本集五七《故河陰留後元君墓志》云："元和十四年，以疾去職，九月二十六日，殁於季弟虢州長史積之官舍。"銘云："唐元和之己亥，惟孟年十一月十六日仲月之辰，合葬我元君于咸陽縣之洪瀆川。"秬卒時，微之必仍在虢州長史任，然其葬時，微之在虢抑在長安，在長史任抑已歸朝，則不甚可考矣。

冬，奉召入朝，拜膳部員外郎。

本集三三《同州刺史謝上表》云："元和十四年，憲宗皇帝開釋有罪，始授臣膳部員外郎。"《舊書》本傳亦云："十四年，自虢州長史徵還，爲膳部員外郎。"（《新書》本傳云元和末）。然微之奉召，不當前於九月，故云在本年冬。《墓志》云："長慶初，穆宗嗣位，舊聞公名，以膳部員外郎徵用，既至轉祠部郎中。"大誤。樂天與微之爲終生交，所爲墓志謬訛甚多，誠不可解。

柳子厚四十七歲。十一月，卒於柳州。

韓退之五十二歲。正月，以諫迎佛骨貶潮州刺史，十月，移袁州刺史。

令狐楚以七月入朝拜相。

元和十五年庚子(八二〇)。四十二歲。在長安。

正月,内侍陳弘志弑憲宗於中和殿。太子恒即位,是爲穆宗。貶皇甫鎛爲崖州司户。段文昌拜中書侍郎同平章事。監察御史李德裕右拾遺李紳禮部員外郎庾敬休並守本官充翰林學士。貶諫議大夫李景儉爲建州刺史,以其凌蔑宰輔故也(《舊紀》一五、一六)。

令狐楚時在相位,嘗徵其詩,因以詩五卷獻之,並爲文自叙,於元和詩體多所闡發。

《舊書》一六六本傳云:"十四年自虢州長史徵還,爲膳部員外郎。宰相令狐楚一代文宗,雅知稹之辭學,謂稹曰:'嘗覽足下製作,所恨不多,遲之久矣,請出其所有,以豁予懷。'稹因獻其文,自叙曰:……楚甚稱賞,以爲今代之鮑謝也。"按微之以去歲末還朝爲膳部員外郎,本年夏,遷授祠部郎中、知制誥。楚亦以本年七月罷相(見後),微之獻詩在膳部員外郎任,故知必在去歲末至本年五月間。自叙又載於集外文章,附本集後,當爲後人所益,而題下注云"時爲膳部郎中"則誤矣,蓋微之未嘗一爲膳部郎中也。

又微之之詩,據其自序,可分三類,今請略述於後:

一、感物寓意可備矇瞽之風者。

二、杯酒光景間之小碎篇章。

三、戲排舊韻、别創新辭之次韻相酬。

實則此種分類不獨可用於微之之作,即用於樂天之作亦至爲妥切。其作爲第一類之代表者,即樂天之《新樂府五十首》、微之之《新舊題樂府》及《赴江陵道中十七章》。皆以諷諭立意,欲以文濟世者。然此並非元、白之所獨專,同時之張文昌、李公垂,較早之陳子昂、杜子美,皆已及之,且多有佳構。實則此乃傳統文學實用思想之産物,亦可謂爲士大夫政治思想之延伸。元、白之特殊貢獻,乃確立此類創作之理論。

其製作雖足以"作唐一經"(參陳寅恪先生《新樂府箋證》),然在當日,却未能如其所期望之蔚爲風氣,造成輿論(參胡適之先生《白話文學史》)。《白氏長慶集》二八《與元九書》云:"今僕之詩,人所愛者,悉不過《雜律詩》與《長恨歌》已下耳。時之所重,僕之所輕。至於諷諭者,意激而言質;閑適者,思淡而辭迂。以質合迂，宜人之不愛也。”微之自叙亦云：“辭直氣粗，罪尤是懼，固不敢陳露於人。”皆是其證。

其第二類與第三類，乃所謂之“元和詩體”。杜牧之《樊川文集》九《李戡墓志銘》引李戡語云：“嘗痛自元和以來，有元白詩者，纖艷不逞。非莊士雅人，多爲其所破壞，流於民間，疏於屏壁，子父女母，交口教授，淫言媟語，冬寒夏熱，入人肌骨，不可除去。吾無位，不得用法以治之。”乃指此二類詩之末流而言。後人多不了此意，因妄以第一類諷諭詩當之，陳寅恪先生之《論“元和體詩”》一文，可謂發百世之秘。然愚於此欲更有説者，其第二類所謂小碎篇章，當以艷曲爲主（參本譜“元和五年”條）。夫唐世文人，率多狎妓，艷異之作，由來已久，其所以能蔚爲元和一代之風氣者，疑皆受微之艷詩之影響也。

其第三類之次韻相酬，特色不在“驅駕文字，窮極聲韻”，而在“戲排舊韻，別創新辭”。本集二二《酬樂天餘思不盡加爲六韻》自注云：“樂天曾寄予千字律詩數首，予皆次用本韻酬和，後來遂以成風耳。”《白氏長慶集》五二《和微之詩二十三首》序云：“大凡依次用韻，韻同而意殊；約體爲文，文成而理勝。此足下所長者，僕何有焉？”可知此類次韻酬和，亦創自微之，且爲其所獨擅也。然則“元和體者”，直可謂爲“元微之體”矣。觀微之自叙所云：“司文者考變雅之由，往往歸咎于稹。”更可瞭然。愚作此語，絶非有意抑樂天而揚微之，第以就歷史觀點作客觀研究，固不得不特爲標出耳。况元和詩體一詞，並非美名，當微之之世即已歷遭詬病者乎？

五月，轉祠部郎中、知制誥，得内侍崔潭峻之引薦也。朝廷以是多鄙之。然一變詔書之體，純厚明切，與古爲侔，遂盛傳於代。

《通鑒》三四一《唐紀》五七云：“初，膳部員外郎元稹爲江陵士曹，與監軍崔潭峻善。上在東宫，聞宫人誦稹歌詩而善之，及即位，潭峻歸朝，獻稹歌詩百餘篇。上問稹安在，對曰：‘今爲散郎。’（元和十五年）夏五月庚戌，以稹爲祠部郎中、知制誥，朝論鄙之。”本集四〇《制誥》序云：“元和十五年，余始以祠部郎中、知制誥。”同書三二《叙奏》云：“穆宗初，宰相更用事。丞相段公一日獨得對，因請亟用兵部郎中薛存慶、考功員外郎牛僧孺，予亦在請中。上然之。不十數日，次用爲給舍。”按微之入翰林，乃得潭峻之引薦，新、舊《書》本傳暨《通鑒》皆明言之，自屬無疑。雖詭稱爲文昌之請，未足信也。本集三三《同州刺史謝上表》云:“元和十四年,憲宗皇帝開釋有罪,始授臣膳部員外郎。與臣同省署者,多是臣初登朝時舉人,任卿相者半是臣同諫院時遺闕。愚臣既不能低心曲就,輩流亦以望風怒臣。不料陛下天聽過卑,知臣薄藝,朱書授臣制誥,延英召臣賜緋。宰相惡臣不出其門,由是百計侵毁。”此不啻爲微之之自供。緣微之出身寒微,中經久貶;歸朝之後,復自負其才,不同流俗,遂召衆忌。然性本務進,不甘下寮,終而誤入交結内侍之一途,亦云悲矣。

《舊書》本傳云:“辭誥所出,夐然與古爲侔,遂盛傳於代。”《白氏長慶集》五六《酬微之整集舊詩長句加爲六韻》云:“制從長慶詞高古。”自注云:“微之長慶初知制誥,文格高古,始變俗體,繼者效之也。”以是知微之匪唯爲當日歌詩之盟主,亦且爲文體變革之領袖也。

時李德裕、李紳並在翰林,才名相類,情意款洽,號爲“三俊”。

《舊書》一七三《李紳傳》(一七四《德裕傳》略同)云:“穆宗召爲翰林學士,與李德裕、元稹同在禁署,時稱三俊,情意相善。”《全唐詩》元稹二八《奉和浙西大夫李德裕述夢四十韻述翰苑舊游》云:“分阻杯盤會,閑隨寺觀遨。”注云:“學士無過從聚會之例,大夫與稹,時時期於寺觀閑行而已矣。”可證其時微之與德裕交情之厚,而公垂乃微之舊交更勿論矣。

六月,貶史館修撰李翺爲朗州刺史,坐與李景儉相善。七月,令狐楚出爲宣歙觀察使。八月,崔植拜相。令狐楚再貶爲衡州刺史(《舊紀》一六)。

《舊書》一七二《令狐楚傳》云:“楚再貶衡州刺史。時元稹初得幸爲學士,素惡楚與(皇甫)鎛膠固希寵,稹草楚衡州制略曰:‘楚早以文藝,得踐班資,憲宗念才,擢居禁近,異端斯害,獨見不明,密隳討伐之謀,潛附奸邪之黨,因緣得地,進取多門,遂忝臺階,實妨賢路。’楚深恨稹。”按微之拜祠部郎中、知制誥時,楚尚爲相,或即微之所謂於其“百計侵毁”之一人,至是乃借機泄憤歟?楚與李逢吉友善,微之後日多爲逢吉所排,此際似已有朋黨之徵兆矣。

八月,始蒙穆宗召見,自是數度召對,自謂多言天下事,而流言寖多。

本集三二《叙奏》云:“始元和十五年八月得見上。”又云:“他相忿恨者日夜構飛語,予懼罪比,上書自明。上憐之,三召與語,語及兵賦泊西北邊。因命經紀之。是後書奏及進見,皆言天下事,外間不知多臆度,陛下益憐其不漏省中語。”

嘗爲《長慶宫辭》數十百篇,今皆不傳。

《舊書》本傳云:"即日轉祠部郎中、知制誥……由是極承恩顧。嘗爲《長慶宫辭》數十百篇,京師競相傳唱。"按今本《元氏長慶集》無《長慶宫辭》,《全唐詩》亦無。

十月,成德軍節度使王承宗卒,其弟承元上表請朝廷命帥。因以魏博節度使田弘正移鎮鎮州,遷王承元爲義成軍節度,以李愬鎮魏州(《舊紀》一六)。

十一月,穆宗欲幸華清宫,群臣多諫,不聽,卒行。

《舊紀》一六"元和十五年"下:"(十一月)戊午詔曰:'朕來日暫往華清宫,至暮却還。'御史大夫李絳、常侍崔元略以下伏延英門切諫。上曰:'朕以成行,不煩章疏。'諫官再三論列。……己未,上由複道出城幸華清宫……至晚還宫。"本集三四《兩省供奉官諫駕幸温湯狀》末注曰:"元和十五年十二月二十日,兩省三十人同狀。"疑注誤。又微之自知制誥後,制狀甚多,不遑備考,今從略。

冬,白樂天自忠州刺史入拜司門員外郎,微之有《内狀詩寄楊白二員外》。

本集二一《内狀詩寄楊白二員外》題下注云:"時知制誥。"按樂天以本年冬入朝拜司門員外郎(並見陳、汪二譜),十二月改授主客郎中、知制誥,則微之此詩作於本年冬明矣。楊謂巨源也,同卷有《贈别楊員外巨源》,可證。

韓退之五十三歲。九月,自袁州召還爲國子祭酒。

張籍自校書郎除國子博士。

賈島四十二歲,在長安,有詩投於微之。(説見李嘉言《賈島年譜》,然《微之集》未嘗一及賈島。)

穆宗長慶元年辛丑(八二一)。四十三歲。在長安。

正月,蕭俛罷相,改尚書右僕射。二月,段文昌亦罷,出爲劍南西川節度使。杜元穎拜相。刑部侍郎李建卒。三月,幽州盧龍軍節度使劉總請罷,以張弘靖繼任。李德裕遷考功郎中,李紳遷司勛員外郎,並依舊知制誥。錢徽下進士及第鄭朗等十四人,衆議以爲不公,詔王起、白居易等覆試。四月,覆試畢,十一人復落下,錢徽、李宗閔、楊汝士皆坐貶。五月,皇妹太和公主出降回紇。七月,群臣上尊號曰文武孝德皇帝。幽州軍亂,囚節度使張弘靖,立朱克融爲留後。八月,鎮州監軍奏田弘正遇害,王廷凑自稱留後。詔以涇原節度使田布爲魏博節度使。以深州刺史牛元冀充深冀節度使。以河東節度使裴度充幽鎮兩道招撫使。李景儉復入爲諫議大夫。十月,王播拜相。以裴度充鎮州四面行營都招討使。白居易徙授中書舍人。裴度上疏論元稹與内官魏弘簡交通,罷稹學士,出爲工部侍郎。十一月,朱克融寇定州,節度使陳楚敗之。十二月,貶諫議大夫李景儉爲楚州刺史,以其乘醉辱罵宰臣也。獨孤朗等並坐貶。赦朱克融,專討王廷凑(《舊紀》一六)。

本年微之在翰林,專司内命,所爲辭誥多涉當朝大政,以其過多,不遑細考,僅以有關史實簡列如右,略備參考而已。

春,奉召入禁内,爲中書舍人、承旨學士。與内官多有往來,而與樞密使魏弘簡尤爲相善。

本集三五《謝恩賜告身衣服並借馬狀》云:"去年陛下擢自郎吏,命掌書詞。……感恩深切,頻獻封章,遂遭分外侵誣……豈謂恩光轉至……拔令承旨,不顧班資。"《白氏長慶集》三三《元稹除中書舍人翰林學士賜紫金魚袋制》云:"去年夏拔自祠曹員外。"凡此皆證微之以本年拜中書舍人、承旨學士,然究在何月,頗不易考。據《白氏長慶集》二三《祭李侍郎文》,知本年五月微之已爲"中散大夫、除中書舍人、翰林學士、上柱國、賜紫金魚袋"。今姑定其時在本年春,當不甚誤。《舊書》本傳謂其拜祠部郎中、知制誥後,"居無何,召入翰林爲中書舍人、承旨學士。中人以潭峻之故,争與稹交,而知樞密魏弘簡尤與稹相善"。

三月,禮部侍郎錢徽下進士及第,登榜者皆權近子第。段文昌以請托不行,訴於帝,李德裕、李紳與微之亦連横上言其不公。因詔王起、白居易共覆試,於是錢徽、李宗閔等皆貶官。旋有詔戒百寮勿爲朋黨。文出微之,朋比之徒因多牽怒。

《舊書》一六八《錢徽傳》云:"長慶元年,爲禮部侍郎。時宰相段文昌出鎮蜀川……將發,面托錢徽,繼以私書保薦(楊渾之)。翰林學士李紳亦托舉子周漢賓於徽。及榜出,渾之、漢賓皆不中選。李宗閔與元稹素相厚善,初,稹以直道譴逐久之,及得還朝,大改前志,由逕以徼進達,宗閔亦急於進取,二人遂有嫌隙。楊汝士與徽有舊,是歲,宗閔子婿蘇巢及汝士季弟殷士俱及第。故文昌、李紳大怒。文昌赴鎮,辭日,内殿面奏,言徽所放進士鄭朗等十四人,皆子弟藝薄,不當在選中。穆宗以其事訪於學士元稹、李紳,二人對與文昌同。遂命中書舍人王起、主客郎中知制誥白居易於子亭重試,内出題目《孤竹管賦》《鳥散餘花落詩》,而十人不中選。……尋貶徽爲江州刺史,中書舍人李宗閔劍州刺史,右補闕楊汝士開江令。……既而穆宗知其朋比之端,乃下詔曰:'……'元稹之辭也。制出,朋比之徒,如撻於市,咸睚眦於紳、稹。"(詔即本集四〇《戒勵風俗德音》)同書一六四《王播傳附起傳》云:"先是,貢舉猥濫,勢門子弟,交相酬酬,寒門俊逸,十棄六七。及元稹、李紳在翰林,深怒其事,故有覆試之科。"同書一七六《李宗閔傳》云:"時李吉甫子德裕爲翰林學士,錢徽榜出,德裕與同職李紳、元稹連衡言於上前。"觀上引,可知微之《戒風俗德音》乃作於本年四月覆試之後,然《新書》一七四本傳則云:"擢祠部郎中、知制誥……進非公議,爲士類訾薄。稹内不平,因誡風俗詔,歷詆群有司,以逞其憾。俄遷中書舍人、翰林承旨學士。"似該文之作,乃微之除祠部郎中後不久,其説與《舊書》徽傳大異,未詳孰是。

五月,葬李建(建卒於二月),爲撰墓志,有《與樂天同葬杓直五絶》一首。又有《與樂天同祭杓直文》,則樂天筆也。

《贈工部尚書李公墓志銘》載本集五四,詩見本集八。

《白氏長慶集》二三有《祭李侍郎文》。

嘗與樂天同直,夜宿南郊齋宫,夜後對吟,達旦不寐,學士卒吏皆群觀之。

本集二二《爲樂天自勘詩集》序云:"長慶初,俱以制誥侍宿南郊齋宫,夜後偶吟數十篇。兩掖諸公洎翰林學士三十餘人,驚起就聽,逮至卒吏,莫不衆觀。群公直至侍從行禮之時,不復聚寐,予與樂天吟哦竟亦不絶。"詩云:"齋宫潛咏萬人驚。"觀此,可知元、白二公果如樂天所云幾如"詩魔"也。

《哭子十首》,疑亦本年所作,至遲不得逾十月。

本集九《哭子十首》題下注云:"翰林學士時作。"微之以本年十月罷内職,則諸詩之作必在十月前可知也。此子之名不詳,疑即《哭女樊四十韻》所云"頻救懶書兄"之兄,與妾安氏所出之子名荆者。然其三云:"爾母溺情連夜哭。"其八云:"消遣又來緣爾母,夜深和淚有經聲。"似其母尚在。然觀諸詩之意,此子已不甚小,絶不可能爲裴夫人所出。同卷又有《哭小女降真》一首,未詳其時。

十月,罷學士,改授工部侍郎,爲河東節度使裴度所訴也。有《感事三首》,

疑即咏爲流言所傷事。

《舊紀》一六"長慶元年十月"下:"河東節度使裴度三上章,論翰林學士元稹與中官知樞密魏弘簡交通,傾亂朝政。以稹爲工部侍郎,罷學士,弘簡爲弓箭庫使。"《通鑒》卷二四二《唐紀》五八云:"翰林學士元稹與知樞密魏弘簡深相結,求爲宰相,由是有寵於上,每事咨問焉。稹無怨於裴度,但以度先達重望,恐其復有功大用,妨己進取,故度所奏畫軍事,多與弘簡從中沮壞之。度乃上表,極陳其朋比奸蠹之狀。……表三上,上雖不悦,以度大臣,不得已,以弘簡爲弓箭庫使,稹爲工部侍郎。"(參《舊書》一七〇《度傳》)。本集三二《叙奏》云:"是後書奏及進見(知制誥後)皆言天下事,外間不知多臆度,陛下益憐其不漏省中語,召入禁司,且欲亟任爲宰相。是時裴太原亦有宰相望,巧者謀欲俱廢之,乃以予所無,構於裴,裴奏至,驗之,皆失實。上以裴方擁兵,不欲校曲直,出予爲工部侍郎,而相裴之期亦衰矣。"按微之此説,佐以次年逢吉離間元、裴之事,頗足采信。宫省事密,本多不爲外間所知,况裴度復在外藩,道路傳聞,不無失實之可能,《通鑒》所作微之嫉度之解説,亦似不成理由。竊以爲就微之先此之言行及此際之交游觀之,謂其由徑以求達則可,謂其嫉賢害能則似有未然。本集四《感事三首》題下注云:"此後並是學士時作。"疑皆屬遭裴度所奏時所爲,其内心之痛苦由此三詩可見一斑。其三云:"白頭方見絶,遥爲一霑衣。"蓋專爲裴度而作也。

十二月,諫議大夫李景儉乘醉入中書,面疏宰相之失,因貶漳州刺史。時微之已罷學士職,欲救不得,有《别毅郎二首》以傷之,亦自傷也。

《舊書》一七一《李景儉傳》云:"未幾,元稹用事,自郡(建州)召還,復爲諫議大夫。其年十二月,景儉朝退,與兵部郎中知制誥馮宿、庫部郎中知制誥楊嗣復、起居舍人温造、司勛員外郎李肇、刑部員外郎王鎰等,同謁史官獨孤朗,乃於史館飲酒。景儉乘醉詣中書謁宰相,呼王播、崔植、杜元穎名,面疏其失,辭頗悖慢,宰相遜言止之,旋奏貶漳州刺史。是日同飲於史館者皆貶逐。景儉未至漳州,而元稹作相,改授楚州刺史。議者以景儉使酒,凌忽宰臣,詔令纔行,遽還大郡。稹懼其物議,追還,授少府少監。從坐者皆召還。而景儉竟以忤物不得志而卒。"按穆宗承憲宗之後,河朔悉平,四海偃安,徒以性好宸游,而所任宰輔復乏遠見,不二年間,河朔再叛,此固衆所痛惜,况自負"王霸之略"之景儉乎？今特廣徵其傳文，以明其與微之之密切關係。且由景儉之使酒，亦足反映微之對當日輔政者之態度。本集二一《别毅郎二首》，題下注云："工部侍郎時詩。"其一云："爾爺衹爲一杯酒，此行那知死與生。"知毅郎必爲景儉之子。其二云："愛惜爾爺唯有我，我今顧頷望何人。傷心自比籠中鶴，剪盡翅翎愁到身。"悲景儉亦復自悲也。

韓退之五十四。七月，自國子祭酒轉拜兵部侍郎。

李商隱十歲。喪父，奉母歸鄭州。

長慶二年壬寅（八二二）。四十四歲。

正月，魏博節度使田布爲史憲誠所迫，因自克，詔以史憲誠爲節度使。二月，詔雪王廷凑，令兵部侍郎韓愈往宣諭。考功郎中李德裕遷中書舍人。崔植罷相。元稹守工部侍郎、同平章事。李德裕再遷御史中丞。李紳遷中書舍人。裴度罷河東節度，改東都留守。三月，李逢吉入爲兵部尚書。左饒衛上將軍張奉國卒。裴度入朝，因留相。王播罷相。牛元翼率十餘騎突圍出深州。太子少傅嚴綬卒。六月，裴度、元稹同罷相，李逢吉拜相。七月，白居易出爲杭州刺史。刺史李岕叛於汴，八月，李岕伏誅，汴州平。九月，李德裕出爲浙西觀察使。十一月，穆宗風眩就牀。十二月，穆宗於紫宸殿御大繩牀見百官（《舊紀》一六）。

二月，始拜相。時已赦朱克融、王廷凑。旋裴度罷節度，改東都留守。史謂微之怨度，因解其兵。

《舊書》一七〇《裴度傳》云："及元稹爲相，請上罷兵，洗雪廷凑、克融，解深州之圍，蓋欲罷度兵柄故也。"按詔雪廷凑、克融，皆在微之拜相之前，《舊書》誤。《通鑒》卷二四二《唐紀》五八長慶二年二月下："崔植、杜元穎爲相，皆庸才無遠略，史憲誠既逼殺田布，朝廷不能討，遂并朱克融、王廷凑以節授之。由是再失河朔，迄於唐亡，不能復取。"書於微之拜相之前，似較妥。以是知河北之罷討，乃當時事勢所迫，决非微之爲解裴度之兵權而請罷，况其時微之尚不在其位乎。然微之既相之後，或以既赦廷凑、克融，因以舊憾而罷度兵柄，則似有可能。

五月，有李賞者上變，告和王傅于方爲元稹結客欲刺裴度。詔令三司按驗，無狀。六月，度與稹並罷相，度改拜尚書右僕射，稹出爲同州刺史，後以諫官言責稹太輕,因復削其長春宫使。李逢吉繼爲相。史謂“稹度之争”,皆爲逢吉所巧中。

《通鑒》卷二四二《唐紀》五八長慶二年五月下:“王庭凑之圍牛元翼也,和王傅於方欲以奇策干進,言於元稹,請遣客王昭於友明閑説賊黨,使出元翼,仍賂兵吏部令史僞出告身二十通,令以便宜給賜。稹皆然之。有李賞者知其謀,乃告裴度云方爲稹結客刺度。度隱而不發。賞詣左神策告其事。詔左僕射韓臯等鞫之。三司按于方刺裴度事皆無驗。六月,度及元稹皆罷相,度爲右僕射,稹爲同州刺史,以兵部尚書李逢吉爲門下侍郎、同平章事。”按微之以二月拜相,元翼三月突圍來朝,則微之謀出元翼當屬二、三月間事,其事至五月始發耳。《舊書》本傳云:“詔三司使韓臯等訊鞫,而害裴事無驗,而前事盡露,遂俱罷稹、度平章事。乃出稹爲同州刺史,度守僕射。諫官上疏言責度太重、稹太輕,上心憐稹,止削長春宫使。”《新書》一七四《李逢吉傳》云:“長慶二年,召入爲兵部尚書。時度與元稹知政。度嘗條稹憸佞,逢吉以爲其隙易乘,遂并中之,遣人上變,言:和王傅于方結客,欲爲稹刺度。帝命尚書左僕射韓臯、給事中鄭覃與逢吉參鞫方,無狀,稹、度坐是皆罷,逢吉代爲門下侍郎、平章事。”

至同州,有《同州刺史謝上表》(本集三三)。

八月,汴州平。有《賀汴州誅李夵表》(本集三三)。

太子少傅嚴綬以五月卒,微之爲撰行狀,當在謫同州後不久。

本集五五《嚴公行狀》云:“稹燮贊無狀,孤負明恩,天付郡符,官未稱責。”可證。

十二月,穆宗於紫宸殿御大繩牀見百官。微之有《賀聖體平復表》(本集三四)。

韓退之五十五歲。二月,奉使宣慰鎮州。九月,還拜吏部侍郎。

白樂天五十一歲。七月,自中書舍人出爲杭州刺史。

劉禹錫五十一歲。改拜夔州刺史,正月至任。

賈島四十四歲。舉進士,以才瀧遭貶。

長慶三年癸卯(八二三)。四十五歲。

春,楊巨源來會,有《第三歲日咏春風憑楊員外寄長安柳及贈别楊員外巨源》等詩。

本集八《酬楊司業十二兄早秋述情見寄》題下注云:"今春與楊兄會於馮翊,數日而别。此詩同州作。"微之以去歲六月守同,本年冬即改官,中經一春,故知必在本年初。巨源於微之拜相前已爲員外郎,然未詳隸於何部。早秋述情詩已稱司業,是其時巨源已改拜國子司業矣。《贈巨源詩》載本集二一,其前更有二首,一爲《送公度之福建》,一爲《喜五兄自泗州至》,注云:"並同州刺史時作。"疑皆在去歲。公度、五兄並不詳。《喜五兄自泗州至》云:"慚愧臨淮李常侍。"李常侍亦不詳,其微之在翰林時所交結之内侍歟?

四月,有《和王侍郎酬廣宣上人觀發榜後相賀詩》。

《舊紀》一六"長慶三年"下:"(正月)禮部侍郎王起奏當司所試貢舉人,試訖申送中書,候覆訖,下當司,然後大字發榜。從之。"同書一六四《王播傳附起傳》云:"長慶元年,錢徽掌貢士,爲朝臣請托,人以爲濫。……徽貶官,起遂代徽爲禮部侍郎。掌貢二年,得士尤精。"知王起拜禮部侍郎後,唯掌二年及三年貢,而本年始有大字放榜之奏,故知和詩必作於本年,而選制以三月畢,則酬和之詩作於四月亦從可知也。《全唐詩》三〇云:"廣宣姓廖氏,蜀中人。……元和、長慶初爲内供奉,賜居安國寺紅樓院。有《紅樓集》。"

五月,劉頗喪訃至,以墓志相托,因撰《故萬州刺史劉君墓志銘》。

本集五六《劉君墓志》云:"歲長慶之癸卯,五月,日乙亥,處士禄汾以予友保極喪訃於予,且告保極遺意,欲予志卒葬。"頗誠可謂爲微之生死之交矣。又本集五三有《田弘正墓志銘》、本集五四有《崔倰墓志銘》,皆長慶二、三年間所爲,知微之在同時,諛墓之作特多。

秋,有《旱災自咎貽七縣宰》五古長詩。又有《祈雨九龍神文》《報雨九龍神文》。

本集五九《祈雨九龍神文》云:"積始長慶二年夏六月相天子無狀,降居於同。……涉歲於兹。"同書卷四《旱災有咎貽七縣宰》,題下注"同州"二字,詩云:"臘雪不滿地,膏雨不降春。……六月天不雨,秋孟亦既旬。"故知本年同州苦旱,上述詩文皆本年秋所作。

改授越州刺史、兼御史大夫、浙東觀察使,疑在暮秋。裴夫人以遠去京畿,頗有難色,因有詩曉之。

《舊書》本傳云:"在郡(同州)二年,改授越州刺史、兼御史大夫、浙東觀察使。”本集五一《永福寺石壁法華經記》云:“予始以長慶二年相先帝無狀,譴於同。又明年徙會稽。”皆明微之以本年徙越。而微之以十月抵任,則改官之詔必不晚於九月。本集二二詩目云:“《初除浙東,妻有阻色,因以四韻曉之》。”自爲初奉詔時所作。

途經姑蘇,會李穰。十月中,抵杭州,與樂天並牀話舊,三宿而後别。既抵越(今浙江紹興)有《酬樂天喜鄰郡》《再酬復言和前篇》《以州宅誇於樂天》等詩。自後杭、越之間,詩篇往來,幾不間旬。

《白氏長慶集》五三《除官赴闕偶贈微之》云:“去年十月半,君來過浙東。今年五月盡,我發向闕中。”樂天以四年歸朝,故知微之以本年十月中抵杭也。同書同卷《答微之咏懷見寄》云:“閣中同直前春事,船裏相逢昨日情。分袂二年勞夢寐,並牀三宿話平生。”本集五一《永福寺石壁法華經記》云:“徙會稽,路出於杭,杭民競相觀睹。刺史白怪,問之,皆曰:非欲觀宰相,蓋欲觀曩所聞之元、白耳。”同書二二《再酬復言和前篇(樂天喜鄰郡)》云:“經過二郡逢賢牧,聚集諸郎宴老身。”二郡,謂蘇杭也。《唐語林》二“文學”條云:“白居易長慶二年以中書舍人爲杭州刺史……時吴興守錢徽、吴郡守李穰皆文學士,悉生平交,日以詩酒寄興。官妓高玲瓏、謝好好巧於應對,從元稹鎮會稽,參其酬唱,每以簡竹盛詩來往。”汪立名本《白香山詩後集》一詩目云:“《蘇州李中丞以元日郡齋感懷詩寄微之及予,輒依來篇七言八韻,走筆奉答,兼呈微之》。”而微之本集二二復有《酬復言長慶四年元日郡齋感懷見寄》一篇,知復言即李穰,時在蘇州判史任。按微之《元和十年西歸十二絶》(本集一九)之二云:“兩紙京書臨水讀,小桃花樹滿商山。”注云:“得復言樂天書。”知穰亦微之舊交。

又張君房《脞説》云(引見陳振孫《白文公年譜》寶曆元年下):“高玲瓏,餘杭歌者。樂天作郡日,賦歌與之……元微之在越,厚幣邀至,月餘,使盡歌所唱之曲,作詩送行,兼寄樂天云:‘休遣玲瓏唱我詞,我詞多是送君詩。’”按《脞説》所引,即本集二二重贈詩,辭微不同。以《脞説》與《語林》比觀,疑玲瓏赴越即微之過杭莅任時,然亦未可過必,今姑繫於此。

時明州歲貢海物,萬里傳遞,民以爲苦。微之既至郡,因奏罷之。

《白氏長慶集》六一《元公墓志銘》云:“先是,明州歲進海物,其淡蚶非禮之味尤速壞,課其程,日馳數百里。公至越,未下車,移奏罷。自越抵京師,郵夫獲息肩者萬計,道路歌舞之。”《舊紀》一六“長慶三年十一月”下:“停浙東貢甜菜、海蚶。”可證奏罷進貢海味果爲抵越之初。狀載本集三九。

李餘登進士第,及歸蜀,張籍、姚合、賈島等皆有贈詩。韓退之五十六歲。六月,除京兆尹、御史大夫,敕放其臺參,因與御史中丞李紳相忤。十月,退之改授吏部侍郎,紳改授户部侍郎。

二氏之争,乃宰相李逢吉所間(《舊紀》一六、《舊書》一六七《逢吉傳》)。按李逢吉是時在朝,廣結朋黨,勢傾朝野。微之本集二六有《樹上烏》一篇,題下注“癸卯”二字,知爲本年作,疑即歌諷其事。

長慶四年甲辰(八二四)。四十六歲,在越州。

正月,穆宗崩,太子湛即位,是爲敬宗。

春,有《酬李穰元日郡齋感懷見寄》和《樂天早春見寄》等詩。

本集二二詩目云:“《酬復言長慶四年元日郡齋感懷見寄》。”李詩作於元日,酬詩自必稍後。又樂天以本年夏去杭,其早春詩當屬本年春無疑。

崔玄亮刺湖州,當在本年春。

《白氏長慶集》五三詩目云:“《得湖州十八使君書,喜與杭越鄰郡,因成長句代賀,兼寄微之》。”詩云:“湖州最小君應屈,爲是蓬萊最後仙。”明玄亮之刺湖在微之守越後、樂天去杭前。玄亮與微之交契至深,理當有詩,然今本不見,疑已佚。

四月,作《永福寺石壁法華經記》(本集五一)。寺在杭州。

《和樂天示楊瓊》《酬樂天吟張員外詩見寄》等,疑皆本年樂天去杭以前之作。

《全唐詩》元稹二七《和樂天示楊瓊》,其末注云:“楊瓊本名播,少爲江陵酒妓。去年姑蘇遇瓊叙舊,及今見樂天此篇,因走筆追書此曲。”微之赴越時,曾過姑蘇,已見前考,故知該詩作於本年,疑瓊是年由蘇之杭,樂天因有贈詩,微之復從而和之。汪立名本《白香山詩後集》一《問楊瓊》後按語引微之和詩注,謂白詩作於蘇州,今考微之無再游蘇州之記載,疑汪説誤。又本集二二詩目云:“《酬樂天吟張員外詩見寄,因思上京每與樂天於居敬兄升平里咏新詩》。”詩云:“四人一爲泉路客,三人兩咏浙江詩。”案居敬謂元宗簡,卒於去歲(見《白氏長慶集》五九《元少尹文集序》)。張員外疑謂張籍,籍有《祭韓退之詩》(見洪興祖《韓子年譜》),自謂本年夏罷國子博士,兩月後始除新官,則其拜禮部員外郎不得早於夏秋之交。微之和樂天詩有"三人兩咏浙江詩",似該詩之作乃樂天去杭之前,與籍之除官時間頗不協,容續考。

五月,樂天秩滿去杭,入朝爲左庶子,分司東都。微之有《代杭民答樂天》《代杭民作使君一朝去》《酬樂天重寄别》《和樂天重題别東樓》等詩。

樂天去杭事並見汪、陳二譜暨前引《白氏長慶集》五三《除官赴闕偶贈微之》詩。微之所作《代杭民答樂天》等詩分見本集卷八、一五、二二。

劉禹錫自夔州刺史改和州刺史(今安徽和縣),十月抵任。時李德裕在潤州(今江蘇鎮江),守浙西觀察使。微之與之皆間有篇什往來。

《劉賓客文集·外集七》詩目云:"《和浙西李大夫晚下北固山喜徑松成蔭悵然懷古偶題臨江亭,並浙東元相公所和,依本韻》。"案浙西李大夫即謂德裕,二年九月自御史中丞出爲浙西觀察使。禹錫和詩疑作於本年(見羅譜),然微之和詩則已不見。本集一五有《酬李浙西先因從事見寄之作》一首,同書二二有《寄浙西李大夫四首》,疑皆本年前所作(見後説)。以微之與德裕在翰林時之款密,其往來篇什自不應少。

冬,爲樂天編集詩文,亦自整比舊作。以長慶將終於是歲,固並名《長慶集》。今本《元氏長慶集》乖訛頗多,然細審諸篇,類皆長慶四年以前作,以是知其爲微之自編文集之殘本也。四年以後之作,十不存一,其未嘗手自編集之故歟?

本集五一《白氏長慶集》序云:"長慶四年,樂天自杭州刺史以右(他書皆作左)庶子詔還。予時刺會稽,因得盡徵其文,手自排纘,成五十卷,凡二千一百九十首。前輩多以前集、中集爲名,予以爲陛下明年秋(?)當改元,長慶迄於是,因號曰《白氏長慶集》。……長慶四年冬十二月十日,微之序。"以是知微之本年夏已着手編集,至冬始成耳。然微之本集何時何人所編,彼未嘗自言,亦未見他人言及。今考《舊書》本傳云:"稹長慶末因編删其文藁,自叙曰……"(案即本集三二《叙奏》)。明微之於長慶末曾自編其文。本集二二詩目云:"《郡務稍簡,因得整比舊詩,并連綴焚削封章繁委篋笥,僅逾百軸,偶成自嘆,因寄樂天》。"知微之在越時,亦曾手自整比其舊詩,其時間當與編删文稿相同。竊疑微之爲樂天編集詩文之同時,因亦編次己作。甚或因先編己作,而後乃有代樂天編集之舉。復以今本《元氏長慶集》觀之,其有時間可考者,無一不在長慶四年前;此後之作,除少數散見他書者外多已散佚,僅間可由樂天和詩中知其名目,則今本《元氏長慶集》乃微之長慶四年所自纂之殘本,亦從可知矣。

又今本《元氏長慶集》僅六十卷,與《新書·藝文志》著録不合,其始末可參宋劉麐《禮序》、明馬元調刻本《婁堅序》(《學古緒言》)、及清《欽定四庫全書提要》,玆不復贅。

韓退之五十七歲。八月,疾罷吏部侍郎。十二月卒,謚曰文。

敬宗寶曆元年乙巳(八二五)。四十七歲,在越州。

三月,白樂天除蘇州刺史,五月抵任。微之嘗取《白氏長慶集》中未和之詩五十七首追和之,題爲"因繼集卷之一",疑在本年。

樂天刺蘇事,並見陳、汪二譜。除官及抵任之初,皆有寄微之詩,然今本《元氏長慶集》無一及之者,蓋以本集所收詩文迄於長慶四年故也(見前考)。《白氏長慶集》六〇《因繼集》重序云:"去年微之取予《長慶集》中詩未對答者五十七首追和之,合一百一十四首寄來,題爲"因繼集卷之一"。今年復予以近詩五十首寄去,微之不逾月依韻盡和,合一百首又寄來,題爲"因繼集卷之二",卷末批云:'更揀好者寄來。'蓋示餘勇,磨礪以須我耳。……二年十月十五日,樂天重序。"案樂天此序不繫年號,其有可能者唯寶曆二年、大和二年而已。考微之爲樂天勘詩,時在長慶四年,追和之念當起於集成後不久,而本年樂天刺蘇,蘇越相去匪遥,篇什往還必多,因繼集之作,疑即在此一二年間。至若大和元年及二年,樂天已歸京而微之仍滯越,因繼酬和之作可能似較少。

冬,有《酬樂天初冬早寒見寄》。

《全唐詩》元稹二八《酬樂天初冬早寒見寄》云:"洛水碧雲曉,吴宫黄葉時。兩傳千里意,書札不如詩。"樂天去歲分司東都,本年刺蘇,明年秋復去(見陳譜),則樂天寄詩之作,唯本年冬爲有可能。

奏除竇鞏爲副使,疑最早不前於本年。史稱微之所辟皆文士,鏡湖秦望之咏極多,號《蘭亭絶唱》,惜今皆不傳。

《舊書》一五五《竇群傳附鞏傳》云:"元稹觀察浙東,奏爲副使,檢校秘書少監、兼御史中丞、賜金紫。"同書一六六《稹傳》云:"會稽山水奇秀,稹所辟幕職皆當時文士,而鏡湖秦望之游,月三四焉,而諷咏篇什,動盈卷帙。副使竇鞏,海内詩名,與稹酬唱最多,至今稱《蘭亭絶唱》。”按今本《元氏長慶集》有關浙東之詩,無一及鞏者,明長慶四年前鞏尚未從辟爲副使。鞏究以何時至浙東,已不可考,然必不早於本年則可無疑。

微之守越六年,乃其一生最爲安定豐裕之時期,此數年間,詩作必夥,所謂《蘭亭絶唱》及《白樂天後集》酬和詩目,皆可證之,惜乎多已散佚,幾成絶響。《全唐詩》元稹二八有《戲酬副使中丞(竇鞏)見示四韻》,未詳作於何時,今姑繫此,以爲元、竇酬唱之一證耳。

劉禹錫五十四歲。在和州,有《陋室銘》《金陵五題》等作。

杜牧之二十三歲。作《阿房宫賦》。

寶曆二年丙午(八二六)。四十八歲。在越州。

十二月,敬宗遇弑,江王涵立,是爲文宗。

白樂天以新作五十首寄來,因盡和之,題爲“因繼集卷之二”(見元年考)。

李德裕以《觱篥歌》及《述夢四十韻》相次見寄,因並和之。今前詩和篇已佚。

《全唐詩》元稹二八《奉和浙西大夫李德裕述夢四十韻》云:“近酬新樂録,仍寄續《離騷》。”注云:“近蒙大夫寄《觱篥歌》,酬和才畢,此篇續至。”明二篇之作,爲時相去不遠。又汪立名本《白香山詩後集》一《小童薛陽陶吹〈觱栗歌〉(和浙西李大夫)》,篇後汪氏案語云:“李德裕有《霜夜對月聽小童陽陶吹〈觱栗歌〉》。羅隱詩云:‘平泉上相東征日,曾爲陽陶吹《觱栗》。吴江太守會稽侯,相次三篇皆俊逸。’太守謂公,會稽侯謂元也,然元相集中已失此詩。”可證《觱栗歌》之作,乃樂天刺蘇時。樂天以去年五月抵蘇,本年秋冬之交罷郡職。則微之酬和德裕二詩不得晚於本年,亦從可知矣。

劉禹錫五十五歲。秋,罷和州刺史。

白行簡卒。

文宗大和元年丁未(八二七)。四十九歲。在越州。

春,有《酬白樂天杏花園詩》。

《全唐詩》元稹二八《酬白樂天杏花園》云:“算得貞元舊朝士,幾人同見太和春。”樂天去歲離蘇,本年三月除秘書監。微之和詩當不出本年。

九月,與浙西視察李德裕同加檢校禮部尚書。

《舊紀》一七上“大和元年九月”下：“丁丑，浙西觀察使李德裕、浙東觀察使元稹，就加檢校禮部尚書。”按樂天撰《微之墓志》，盛稱其在越之政，謂其政成課高，故就加禮部尚書。而《舊書》本傳云：“稹既放意娱游，稍不修邊幅，以瀆貨聞於時。”《新書》本傳云：“晚節彌沮喪，加廉節不飾云。”《墓志》雖不無溢美之嫌，本傳亦皆以傳聞爲説，似皆未可過信，兹並録於此以備參。

劉禹錫五十六歲。歸洛陽，八月，代張籍爲主客郎中，分司東都。

杜牧之二十五歲。登進士第。

大和二年戊申（八二八）。五十歲，在越州。

以新作二十三首寄樂天求和。諸詩今皆不傳。

《白氏長慶集》五二《和微之詩二十三首》序：“微之又以近作二十三首寄來，命僕繼和，其間瘀絮四百字，車斜二十篇者流，皆韻劇辭殫，瓌奇怪譎。又題云：‘奉煩只此一度，乞不見辭。’意欲定霸取威，置僕於窮地耳。……況曩昔唱酬，近來因繼，已十六卷，凡千餘首矣。其爲敵也，當今不見，其爲多也，從古未聞，所謂‘天下英雄唯使君與操耳’。”其首篇和《晨霞》題下注云：“此後在上都作。”《和我年三首》云：“我年五十七。”案樂天以去歲除秘書監，本年二月拜刑部侍郎（《舊紀》一七上），其年恰爲五十七，皆證獲微之寄詩在本年。然微之原詩固不必皆爲本年作，如和詩有《和寄問劉白》一首，題下注云：“時夢得與樂天方舟西上。”知微之原詩必爲去年或前年所作。

白樂天五十七歲。秋，自編《續集》。

劉禹錫五十七歲。至長安，拜主客郎中、充集賢學士。

杜牧之二十六歲。閏三月，登制科，授校書郎。

大和三年己酉（八二九）。五十一歲。

《醉題東武詩》（一作《題東武亭》），當作於本年。

詩見《全唐詩》元稹二八，其辭云：“功夫兩衙盡，留滯七年餘。病痛梅天發，親情海岸疏。”微之以長慶三年鎮越，至是恰爲七年也。

又有《贈毛仙翁》《贈劉采春》等詩，皆在越之作，最晚不得逾本年九月。

《全唐詩》元稹二八《贈毛仙翁》序云：“余廉問浙東歲，毛仙翁惠然來顧，越之人士識之者相與言曰：‘仙翁嘗與葉法善、吴筠游於稽山，迨兹多歷年所，而風貌愈少，蓋神仙者也。’余因得執弟子之禮，師其道焉。”案毛仙翁名于姫，以能察人窮通修短著於時，《唐詩紀事》八一載當時名士如裴度、牛僧孺、李翺、李程、王起、李益、白居易、劉禹錫、令狐楚等，莫不與之游。

《贈劉采春詩》，亦見《全唐詩》元稹二八。《雲溪友議》云："稹廉問浙東，有優人周姓妻劉采春者，自淮甸而來，善歌，容華莫比。稹愛之，以藁砧在不可奪。盧侍郎簡求讀此詩，戲曰：'丞相雖不好鱸魚，爲好鏡湖春色耳。'謂采春也。"

九月，奉召入京，拜尚書左丞。

《舊紀》一七上"大和三年九月"下："戊戌，以前睦州刺史陸亘爲越州刺史、浙東觀察使，代元稹。以稹爲尚書左丞，代韋弘景。"

途經洛陽，會白樂天，有詩二首。樂天本年春以病免刑部侍郎，以太子賓客分司東都。

《白氏長慶集》六〇《祭元相微之文》云："唯近者公拜左丞，自越過洛，醉别悲吒，投我二詩云：'君應怪我留連久，我欲與君辭别難。白頭徒侶漸稀少，明日恐君無此歡。'又曰：'自識君來三度别，這回白盡老髭須。戀君不去君須會，知得後回相見無。'吟罷涕零，執手而去。"

既拜左丞，出郎官頗乖公議者七人，然不爲人情所服。

《舊書》本傳云："三年九月，入爲尚書左丞，振舉紀綱，出郎官頗乖公議者七人。然以稹素無檢操，人情不厭服。"《新書》本傳略同。

冬，喜護一子，即道護。

《白氏長慶集》五八詩目云："《予與微之老而無子……今年冬各有一子，戲作二什》。"其二自謂云："五十八翁方有後。"樂天本年適爲五十八歲，故知微之舉子亦在本年。又微之卒時，道護始三歲，故知此子即道護。

劉禹錫五十八歲。轉禮部郎中，仍充集賢學士。與白樂天屢有唱和，三月，樂天編《劉白唱和集》。

李商隱十八歲。十二月，從天平軍節度使令狐楚辟，爲節度巡官。

大和四年庚戌（八三〇）。五十二歲。

正月，宰相王播卒。微之謀復輔政，不遂。旋出爲鄂州刺史、武昌軍節度使。有《贈裴夫人詩》。

《舊紀》一七下"大和四年正月"下："甲午，守左僕射、同平章事、諸道鹽鐵使王播卒。”同書《稹傳》云：“會宰相王播倉卒而卒，稹大爲路岐，經營相位。四年正月，檢校户部尚書、兼鄂州刺史、御史大夫、武昌軍節度使。”然《舊紀》一七下“大和四年正月”下：“辛丑，以尚書左丞杜元穎檢校户部尚書、充武昌軍節度、鄂岳鄆黄安申等州觀察使。”案元穎以長慶三年鎮蜀，大和三年十二月貶爲循州司馬，本年正月未得爲尚書左丞甚明，《舊紀》大誤。

又《唐詩紀事》云：“稹自會稽拜尚書左丞，到京未逾月，出鎮武昌，裴夫人柔之難之曰：‘歲杪到家鄉，先春又赴任邪？’稹贈詩云：‘窮冬到鄉國，正歲别京琴。……嫁得浮雲婿，相隨即是家。’”

途次藍橋驛，作《藍橋懷舊寄劉禹錫》等。唯該詩今已不傳。

《劉賓客文集·外集六》詩目云：“《微之鎮武昌，中路見寄〈藍橋懷舊〉之作，凄然繼和，兼寄安平（韓泰）》。”是知微之過藍橋時曾有懷舊詩篇，然今已不得見矣。

至鄂州，仍辟竇鞏爲副使。

《舊書》一五五《竇群傳附鞏傳》云：“稹移鎮武昌，鞏又從之。”知微之在鄂復辟鞏爲副使，意其時必有酬和之作，然已無一篇傳於今。《太平廣記》“異器類”有微之在鄂得寶説，荒誕不經，兹不録。

杜牧之二十八歲。在江西觀察使沈傳師幕，九月，從徙宣歙。

張籍卒於本年前後，賈島有悼詩（見李嘉言《賈島年譜》）。

大和五年辛亥（八三一）。五十三歲。在鄂州。

七月，暴疾，卒於位。臨終，以墓志托樂天。

《舊書》本傳云：“五年七月二十二日，暴疾，一日而卒於鎮，時年五十三。贈尚書右僕射。有子曰道護，年三歲。”《白氏長慶集》六一《元公墓志銘》云：“大和五年七月二十二日，遇暴疾，一日薨於位，春秋五十三。”同書《修香山寺記》云：“予與元微之定交於生死之間。微之將薨，以其志文見托。”是知微之卒於本年七月。《舊紀》一七下“大和五年八月”下：“庚午，武昌軍節度使、檢校户部尚書元稹卒。”蓋微之卒訊，八月始聞於朝也。

《墓志》又云：“以六年七月十二日附葬於咸陽奉賢鄉洪瀆原，從先兆也。”是知微之本年卒於鄂，次年始歸葬於咸陽。

後　記

兹編爲余肄業於臺灣大學中國文學研究所時所作之碩士論文,得蒙業師臺静農教授多方指導,寫畢於一九六〇年。既爲"少作",錯漏難免,而敝帚自珍,常在篋笥。每思重加釐訂,更擬增寫專文數篇,詳論元和詩體之本質與夫元氏之政治生涯、文學思想及其詩文之創作藝術。然十餘年來,栖栖遑遑,爲謀枝栖,奔走於新舊大陸之間,雖初衷猶在,終竟未能補綴一字,心常憾焉。學長羅聯添教授,治唐詩之佼佼者也,所著《劉夢得年譜》於我啓迪尤多,頃接來書云:"近年常有學者詢及大著,或莅臨本系要求借閲。"因囑以該編刊布於其所主編之《書目季刊》,並慨允代爲校對。勝情高誼,敢不應命。因書數語,明其本末,且於師友之謬愛,略志感銘之忱。然余增訂是編之日,又復不知將在何年矣。

一九七六年九月,薛鳳生識於美國之哥倫布市

詩·魏風[**]

一

《詩經》是我國最早的一部純文學作品,除了雅頌中的部分廟堂文學之外,其中大部分是情思深永的歌謡,爲一般民衆的情感流露。唯其出自一般民衆,故其形式造語均極自然,亦唯其所歌咏的多爲民衆的親身感受,故其情感真摯動人,令千載而後的我們讀之,亦每隨作者的悲喜而改容。此種真摯情感的自然流露,可以説是《詩經》最成功的地方,也是最值得我們珍視的地方。

我國人是最重藝文的民族,可是歷代之重視藝文,幾乎完全是自實用觀點出發的。孔子曾説:"《詩》可以興,可以觀,可以群,可以怨。邇之事父,遠之事君,多識於鳥獸草木之名。"這段話簡直就鑄定了我們兩千多年的文學觀。《詩》之所以能爲國人普遍傳誦,而且完整地保存了兩千多年,一大部分是由於它變成了"經"的結果。它被當作"經夫婦、成孝敬、厚人倫、美教化、移風俗"的工具,至於它的本來面目,却似乎没有多少人去注意。

由於這一"實用文學觀"的推演,《詩經》中的每一首詩幾乎都沾染上了政治或教化的色彩,於是國風之風也就被解釋成了諷諫之諷,結果遂使許多原很明顯的詩篇,經過解釋以後反而更爲晦澀難解了。

説文學是時代的反映,我想是不會有多少人反對的。Taine 就認爲時代、環境與種族是文學的三大要素。本來一個作者秉其特有之遺傳,生長在一個特有的時代與社會環境中,要説不受時代的影響,那簡直是不可思議的;因此,一般説來,"治世之音安以樂,其政和;亂世之音怨以怒,其政乖;亡國之音哀以思,其民困",自也是必然的現象。但是我們却不能忘記,詩這種東西是緣情而生的,先要有"情動於中",而後才能有形之於外的言;它雖然往往同時反映出

** 原刊臺灣《文學雜志》六卷五期,1959 年。

了它所由而出的時代,但却是“無爲而自發”的,因此,如果我們説“文學是時代的反映”,或者説得更精確一點,“我們可以由文學作品看出其作成時代的精神”,自然是不差的,但如果我們説“文學必須反映時代”,或者説“作者在創作之先都存有某種實際的動機”。(這樣的例子當然並非絶對没有,都不免言之過當,我們至多衹能説他是因某事有感而發的。)用這段話來説《詩經》,尤爲允當,因爲《詩經》是一部上古的作品,古代的詩歌十之八九都是隨感而生的自然流露,很少是有所爲而爲的用心刻畫。

我們現在如果要把《詩經》當作一部文學作品來欣賞,就必須把它從一切偏見中解脱出來,還其本來面目;不把它看作其作者爲了達到某項實用目的的工具,更不把它當作我們自己爲了達到某些實用目的的工具,而把它當作一首一首純文學作品來閲讀,參照歷史的記載,就詩的本文來探求它的意義,更進而“悟”出它的情趣。

二

用現代的眼光看,《詩經》的菁華當然在國風。所謂國風,自然如朱子所説的是諸侯國中的民俗歌謡,毛傳的那一套説法已是歷史的陳迹了。

在十五國風之中,魏風是比較特殊的,它一共衹有短短的七首詩,就内容看,大致可以説是一意貫串的,正所謂“亂世之音怨以怒”,都是些貧苦小民的不平之鳴、籲天之聲,也唯其如此,差不多每一首詩都表現出很强烈的個性。

襄公二十九年《左傳》有這樣一段話:“叔侯曰:虞、虢、焦、滑、霍、揚、韓、魏,皆姬姓也。”據此可知原來的魏國是姬姓諸侯,大概受封於西周初年,至於始封的是什麽人則不可考知了。這個姬姓魏國,到魯閔公二年,亦即周惠王十七年,就被晉獻公滅掉了,獻公把這塊地方作爲大夫畢萬的采邑,到後來三家分晉,畢萬的後人就在這裏建起國來,也名之爲魏,這就是戰國七雄之魏,《詩經》的成書遠在七國之魏立國之前,當然與它没有什些關係。

魏風究竟是什麽時代的作品呢?鄭康成《詩譜》云:“當周平、桓之世,魏之變風始作”。這就是説魏風作於姬魏被滅之前。朱子《詩集傳》則引蘇氏語云:“魏地入晉久矣,其詩疑皆爲晉而作,故列於唐風之前,猶邶墉之於衛也。”接着他自己又説:“今案篇中公行、公路、公族皆晉官,疑實晉詩,又恐魏亦嘗有此官,蓋不可考矣。”大體説來,國風之作成遲於雅頌,而魏風的文辭也比較平易,因此朱子的懷疑不是没有理由的。但我們若就魏風的内容看,其中多爲怨怒之詞,分明是所謂“亂世之音”,以畢萬受封到季札觀樂(襄公二十九年《左傳》,魯爲季札歌魏)百餘年間的史實看,其時正是晉國强盛之時,似乎不應該有詩中所歌咏的現象,所以仍以鄭康成的説法爲妥,果如此,即魏風乃作於東周之初,在國風中算是相當早的了。

姬魏之封地在晉國之南,南枕河曲,北逾汾水,也就是現在的山西省南部。魏之國土不廣,地瘠民貧,西面與秦國接壤,北面與晉國爲鄰,弱國强鄰,其處境是可以想見的,桓公四年《左傳》有秦師圍魏之記載,而其國終爲晉國所滅,以常理推測,秦晉之侵魏必不止一次,故詩語云:“日見侵削,國人憂之。”魏國之政治如何,雖乏直接史料可資參證,然以其屢受侵伐而終無以自立的事實,以及魏風中所歌咏的情形看,貪污腐化等亡國之象,必普遍流行於上下官吏之間,賦税徭役之繁重,自亦爲必然之結果。小民生於此種社會之中,呼天不應,投告無門,不得已而發爲憤怒之詞、哀怨之歌,其事可嘆、其情可憫,我們今日閲讀這些動人肺腑的詩篇時,實不應忘記這都是古人的血淚結晶啊!

歷來之説詩者,多以魏爲虞夏之故地,因而説其國人尚儉,有聖賢之化,更推説魏君儉而至於嗇,不中禮度,因而發了許多妙論,以朱子説《詩》之通達,猶不免此累。清馬瑞辰《毛詩傳箋通釋》更大事發揮云:“奢者,惡之大也,儉者,德之基也,奢之極者必貪……儉之極者亦必貪,非重斂不足以濟之,故魏風首《葛屨》,《汾沮洳》以刺儉,而終以《伐檀》《碩鼠》刺貪鄙也。”又説:“魏惟《園有桃》之薄税,乃有《碩鼠》之重斂。”馬氏在字句訓釋方面的成就,是我們所佩服的,至於這裏所引的話,簡直叫人有點不知從何説起。這都由於讀詩之先,胸中先存成見所使然。其實國土狹隘,土地貧瘠的結果,固然曾使得“民貧俗儉”,却不見得就是“聖賢之遺風”;再則老百姓貧苦節儉,王公貴人却不見得也貧苦節儉,反之,古今中外的史例都可以證明,越是國小民貧瀕於覆亡的國家,其主持政柄者越曾窮侈極奢,唯其如此,才會激起民衆的不平之鳴,促成國家的滅亡。我們就魏風的詩文看,其情形也正是這樣的。

三

魏風一共包括七首詩，題旨與文字都相當顯明，它們的順序是《葛屨》《汾沮洳》《園有桃》《陟岵》《十畝之間》《伐檀》《碩鼠》。但爲了討論方便起見，我在本文中將不依照這個順序，好在這衹不過是采詩或編詩的人任意安排的結果，並不見得就是它們產生的先後秩序，因此也就不是不可變動的。

《葛屨》一詩，明言刺褊，然此所謂褊心當指器量狹小而言，無論如何是與國君之儉嗇没有什麽關係的。

《十畝之間》一首，毛傳以其言十畝而不言百畝，便認爲是"其國削小，民無所居"，説得不客氣一點，簡直是"匪夷所思"。朱子所云："政亂國危，賢者不樂仕於朝，而思與其友歸於農圃，故其詞如此。"恐亦不免囿於預設的"政亂國危"之成見，單就詩文説，是看不出這種意思的。就詩而求意，這首詩似不可能有那麽一番道理存在背後，試問如果把它放在魏風之外，誰還會發這些奇思妙想？我們必須知道，文學固可反映時代，却不必一定反映時代。就心理方面説，不管一個人的環境如何窘困，他也不可能時時刻刻都滿懷憂愁，少不得也有一些輕鬆的時間，當此之際，目接山林美景、田園風光，於是心曠神怡而有悠然之思，也是人之常情，更何况在苦難的大環境中，也還會有些並不苦難的人呢？總之，我願再强調一句，在非常的時代中，產生一些並不非常的作品，也並非不可能的事。對於這首詩，我們也當作如是觀。

《詩經》中有關行役之怨辭極夥，《陟岵》一詩即屬其類。魏國屢受侵伐，當然少不了戰争，再則王公貴人愛好虚飾排場，也必然有許多工程要做，這些都是老百姓的負擔。《陟岵》所表現的就是徭役重壓下的民衆的痛苦。然此類作品屢見於小雅、國風之中，就魏風而言，這首詩似乎不算太特殊。可喜的是作者以其親身的感受，托之於想象，發爲歌咏，於質樸的言詞中，表現出凄惋的情調，所以頗爲動人。試想居家的父母兄長思我尚且如是，身受此苦楚的我，心情該是怎樣的呢？

以上三首詩，或因其含意較爲隱晦，或因其題材較爲普泛，在魏風之中，都比較缺乏個性，因此我們在這裏也不再多討論它們了。

四

當一個國家日趨衰弱,政治漸次腐化之時,一般國民儘管昧然無知,甚至部分尚且醉生夢死,但也必然不乏少數遠見之士,欲救危亡而不能得,於是將其憤時憂國之心,發爲感喟之詞。《園有桃》一詩很可能就是在這種心情下寫成的。詩人不以當道者之設施爲然,苦於己意不爲所容,又不爲人所諒解,反因其先見而備受冷嘲熱刺。然而已既明察此危,雖不欲思,又不能得,遂至鬱結於心,終於吐而爲詩。"心之憂矣,其誰知之?其誰知之,蓋亦勿思!"這樣的詩真可謂其辭委婉,其情凄切了。

假如我們把《園有桃》看作亂象初萌時期的作品,則《汾沮洳》與《伐檀》可以説是作成於國事日非之後。這兩篇的題旨大致是相同的,祇是所表現的情感在程度上有深淺的不同。在《汾沮洳》中,祇是一種不以爲然而又莫可奈何的慨嘆,但在《伐檀》中,則出之以憤激的詛咒了。

《汾沮洳》一詩,向來説者多以爲是"刺"儉不中禮的。之所以如此,無非由於他們先存了一個"魏君尚儉"的觀念,儉是一種美德,於是"美無度"便成了"儉不中禮"了。這一看法之不可靠,我們在前面已經説過,因此這裏的屈裏拐彎的解釋自然也不足信。其實在一個貧弱的國家,官吏如能勤儉自勵,在老百姓看來是再自然也没有的了。唯其不然,才會引起批評之聲。我們相信《汾沮洳》就是這樣的作品。所以"美無度"實在是説愛尚虚飾、漫無節度的。這篇詩也分爲三章,但不同於其他各篇的是它的句式,每句都很簡短而字數又參差不齊,其三字句之複迭使用,尤使通篇文字活潑流暢,充分表現出歌謡之特色。就含意説,這首詩並不算太深刻,但也表現了部分民隱。

更深刻的民隱表現在《伐檀》裏。要明瞭這首詩的真精神,我們也必須從一個新的角度去看它。首先讓我們看看前人的説法。我仍舉毛傳與朱傳爲例,因爲這兩部書的影響最深也最廣。毛傳説:"《伐檀》,刺貪也,在位貪鄙無功而受禄,句子不得進仕爾。"説這首詩乃因有感於"在位貪鄙無功而受禄"而作,當然絶無問題,至於"君子不得進仕爾"一句,可以作兩方面的解釋,如果説政治之腐敗、國家之衰危是由於"君子不得進仕",自是千古不易之理;但如果説由於“君子不得進仕”,才作了這麽一首詩去“刺”那些“在位”的,一則不無争飯碗之嫌,再則就詩本文而言,也看不出這個意思。朱傳説這首詩是“比也”,又説:“詩人言有人於此用力伐檀,將以爲車以行陸也,今乃置之河干,則河水清漣而無所用,雖欲自食其力而不可得矣。然其志則自以爲不耕則不可以得禾,是以甘心窮餓而不悔也。詩人述其事而嘆之,以爲是真能不空食者。”這一段話真是新鮮有味,於詩人之外,又出來了這麽一位一介不苟的大賢人。如果真有這麽一位“甘心窮餓”、非其力不食的伐木工人,我們雖非詩人,也必爲之贊嘆不已。可惜我們於此説實在找不到堅强的根據。伐木而置之河干,不見得就是不用啊!

我覺得毛傳與朱傳之失,又都是蔽於成見。在他們的心目中,《詩經》裏所有的篇章,都是“君子”“賢人”所作,尋常百姓是作不出來的。司馬遷説:“《詩》三百篇,大抵賢聖發憤之所爲作也。”正代表了兩千多年來一般文人對《詩經》的看法。這是由於後人對《詩經》的崇拜,於是把《詩經》的創作過程也神秘化了。其實國風既是“民俗歌謡”,它的創作者自然也就是一般平民,用不着扯不上君子賢人的,如果後人因爲他們作出這些不朽的詩篇而崇拜他們,那自然是另一回事。

從這一觀點來看《伐檀》,我們可以毫不猶豫地相信這是勞苦的農民在伐木之時所作的歌唱。由於他終日操勞,猶然貧困不堪,而自己工作的成果却被那些“不稼不穡”“不狩不獵”的人輕輕地剥奪去了,於是在工作疲憊之時,仰望蒼天,俯覽河水,悲憤不平之念不禁油然而生,因而發爲詛咒之詞,以消胸頭不平之恨。唯其發自淳樸的農民,故這首詩裏所表現平等觀也是異常單純率直的。他們的思想看法很直接,要吃飯就得種田,要食肉就得打獵。當他們發現事實恰恰相反,自己力田狩獵反而不得温飽時,當然難免其憤憤。所以這位作者不禁要詰問那些剥削他的人,終於狠狠地駡道:“有人格的人是不白吃飯的啊!”這種平等觀在以“勞心”自任的士大夫是不會有的。正因爲這樣自然懇切的情感,由淳樸質直的鄉民發出,才更能給人以凄凉悲切之感。像這樣偉大的社會詩,與漢魏樂府及唐代杜、張、元、白等的擬古或新樂府中的社會詩,真是前後輝映,同爲中國文學中不朽的成就。

五

當一個人處於窘窮困厄的環境時,"感物吟志",初則有不滿之詞,繼則有怨怒之聲。在這時候,作者心中總還存有一個希望,希望有一天這種混亂的現象將成過去,而後便可安適地生活了。但如果此種禍亂並不戢止,反而日益亟迫,則長期生活於苦難中的民衆,必對現實感到失望乃至絶望,自然地在想象中求滿足;幻想中的滿足究竟並非實在,而現實的壓迫又無時或已,到頭來填胸滿臆的便祇有一種極度空虚的幻滅之感了。我們要欣賞《碩鼠》一詩,必須先有這一瞭解。因爲我太喜歡這首詩了,禁不住要把它抄下來:

碩鼠碩鼠,無食我黍;三歲貫女,莫我肯顧;
逝將去女,適彼樂土。樂土樂土,爰得我所。

碩鼠碩鼠,無食我麥;三歲貫女,莫我肯德;
逝將去女,適彼樂國。樂國樂國,爰將我直。

碩鼠碩鼠,無食我苗;三歲貫女,莫我肯勞;
逝將去女,適彼樂郊。樂郊樂郊,誰之永號!

就字句説,這首詩是相當淺顯的,自來之注釋者於一二句字句之間,容或略有差異,比如"碩鼠"一詞,朱子説:"比也。……民困於貪殘之政,故托言大鼠害己而去之也。"毛傳則説:"國人刺其君重斂,蠶食於民,不修其政,貪而畏人,若大鼠也。"既然説"若大鼠也",當然也是"比"的意思,但除"貪"以外,又扯出"畏人"一事來,則不免蛇足,因爲在詩文中,比類聯誼是少不了的,兩件事物儘管毫不相干,但衹要有某一地方有點類似,便可因詩人的慧眼而聯想比附在一起,這時所着重的是其相似之處,其各别的其他性質就不必管了。殘削小民以肥己的官吏與盜食坐享不勞而獲的老鼠有些相像,至於老鼠的其他性質(四條腿、有尾巴、畏人等),當然用不着計較(如果由於聯想的引伸而有價值的判斷,那又不純是"比"的問題了)。所以我們以爲,還是以朱子的説法爲簡明。但這對於詩的整體意境是没有太大影響的。

説到本詩的整體意境,筆者淺陋,所見到的諸家説詩之作不多,然就所見者而言,幾乎没有一家的説法足以令人完全滿意。他們幾乎毫無異議地認爲,這是民衆困於貪殘之政,托言大鼠而遷往“有道之國”,因而作的“與之訣别”之詞。我想,這首詩的含意是不會這麽簡單的,我之特别喜愛它,也因我在其中看出一種新的意藴。我在前面説過,要欣賞本詩,必須先明白,民衆在經過長期痛苦之後,對現實必然失望,於是在幻想中求滿足,本詩所歌咏的正是這種心情。詩人自言他在貪婪如碩鼠的官吏之治下,經過長期的容忍,仍不得安生,因而憤言即將離而遷往康樂之鄉,然後又自己安慰自己説:“如果我能到達那個地方,我就有了安身之所了。”然而這裏所説的“樂土”“樂園”與“樂郊”,是否真有其地呢?我想這不過是詩人假設之詞,其作用正如“烏托邦”一樣,衹是人類不滿現狀時在想象中臆造的世界,不必實有其地,因此泛名之曰“樂土”。再退一步説,縱然在作者的心目之中真有這麽一個“有德之國”,他是否能够前往呢?恐怕也不會那麽容易,否則他就去了,何必長期忍受這種痛苦呢?(古代人並没有十分强烈的國家觀念)我們要知道,貧苦無力的小民,雖然備受不平的待遇與殘酷的剥削,往往迫於窘窮的環境,除了發出一點怨怒之音以外,是無力反抗的,也是無法逃避的。這一點《碩鼠》一詩的作者必然是身受心知。明乎此,我們才能够真切地領略到這首詩所含藴的深邃的意義,也才能真正欣賞這首詩。

這首詩也與《詩經》中其他許多篇一樣,分爲三章,但本詩除了也具有一唱三嘆的情味之外;却在平穩中寓有變化,這也就是它特别可貴之處。前兩章是由於感受到暴政的壓迫,自然而然地想到逃避,因而悠然神往於想象中、或傳聞中的安全之鄉,反復歌咏,聊以自慰,然而“桃源望斷無覓處”,幻想究竟是虚空的,想象的滿足代替不了現實的痛苦,在第三章裏,作者又意識到現實之無可逃避,因而在結尾語意一轉,“樂郊樂郊,誰之永號!”在這個世界上,如果真有這樣的干净土,而我又能前往的話,誰還會在這裏作此徒然無補的哭喊叫號呢!這是多麽沉痛的話啊!這是滿懷辛酸的無辜小民力竭望絶之後,心頭所發出的最後一聲啊!

六

欣賞詩,也和欣賞其他藝術一樣,必須以作品爲媒介,憑想象在自己的心中創造出一個含蘊着原作者的情感的意象。這一意象的造成,固然有待於想象,但也絶對離不開經驗,也可以説想象是憑經驗而生的。詩的欣賞更有賴於社會生活的經驗,因爲它不像音樂與造型藝術那樣直接,它的傳達媒介是語言,而語言的音與義是隨着時代變動不居的,它所描寫的也多關涉到人事;但是時移世易之後,人事冥滅,若無足够的文獻以資徵考,便無法知道它所述説的事迹,它所含蘊的情感自然也就隔着一層了;再則縱有相當的史料,我們是否能完全明瞭古人的生活情況,也還是問題。古代作品之難於欣賞,就因爲在欣賞之先,我們必須作一番極爲艱難的瞭解工夫。讀《詩經》的苦楚也就在這裏,因爲它的時代離我們太遠了,文字上既有聲韻與訓詁的困難,有關的史料又是那麽簡略,所以首先瞭解的工夫就難做得令人十分滿意。這麽説,難道我們就無法欣賞古代的詩歌了嗎?那也未必,因爲時代雖然改變了,人類所禀賦的情感却没有多大改變;再則歷史固然不會重演,但在歷史演進的過程中,在某些階段裏,相互之間必然會有一些類似之處,有這一點類似也就够了。我們生活在自己的時代裏,有了相當的生活經驗以後,便可用這點經驗作爲想象的憑借,再根據可以獲得的一切有關的歷史資料,然後以自己的情感去領悟古人的情感。惟有如此才不致祇見原作的表面意思,而忽略了它們含蘊的意境的深度。這種心領神悟就是欣賞,用 Croce 的話説,也就是創造。我欣賞魏風是基於我自己對它的瞭解,也許難免過當之處,如蒙識者指正,使我對它有更深刻的理解,自是我所衷心感激的。

大賦淺説**

在文學裏一提到"賦"字,我們立即會把它與馬、揚、班、左之類的名字連起來,或者更進一步,馬上聯想到諸如《上林》《羽獵》《兩京》《三都》之類的篇目。這説明了一個事實:所謂"賦"的代表作,就是那些長篇大幅、佶屈聱牙的怪文章。

然而除此之外,以賦名篇的還有較晚出的小賦與散文賦。在此我衹想討論早期以叙事咏物爲主的長篇賦作,爲了避免混淆,我采用一般習用的"大賦"一詞,但在下文裏,除了特別説明,爲了省事起見,衹用一個"賦"的,而與南方的騷體詩也有嫡傳關係,不過由於字面與用詞的偶有類似,因此弄得糾纏不清。其實"大賦"之名以爲賦,與詩六義中所謂的"賦",以及《楚辭》末流之所謂的"賦",在邏輯上説,衹不過是幾種同名異義的東西而已。"賦"在這個地方,是一個多義名言(equivoal term),而論者不察,乃昧於字面之相同而視其爲一物,甚至許多賦的作家也都信之不疑,更進而仿古,遂使它們之間愈來愈不清晰,愈來愈像大有關係了。這一事實,由賦作家先後時代的比照是很容易看得出來的。司馬相如的賦都没有序(《長門賦》是一個例外,有人懷疑這篇不是他寫的,但序非出其手當無問題),他似乎是不爲賦的來路及功用而煩惱的,衹注力於寫作而已,及至揚子雲,他以一代鴻儒自居,作賦的時候就不免要與詩騷拉關係了;班固在《兩都賦》序裏也説"賦者,古時之流也",而左太冲的《三都賦》序,可謂是這派思想的集成宣言了。

就内容來説,我覺得與其説大賦是"雅頌之流亞",倒不如説它是《史籀》《三蒼》的變形,不同的是它不再是那麽固定的四字成句、隔句一韻的千字文式的東西,而是一種長短不拘、分别物類、排比湊韻的玩意。這樣變化就比較地多了一點,因此也比較地稍不枯燥。

** 原載《大學生活》第四卷第一期,1958年。

再就其表現方法來看,我們可舉先後兩大作家爲例。在司馬長卿的《子虛賦》裏,楚使對齊王説:“臣聞楚有七澤,嘗見其一,未睹其餘也。臣之所見蓋特其小者耳,名曰雲夢。雲夢者方九百里,其中有山焉,其山則……其土則……其石則……其東則有……其南則有……其高燥則生……其埤濕則生……其中則有……其北則有……”

讓我們再看看左太沖的《蜀都賦》。西屬公子對東吴王孫大吹他的老家:

“夫蜀都者……於前則……其間則有……於後則……其樹則有……於東則……其中則有……於西則……”

很明顯,在結構上,這祇是一種物名分類細目表,一種賬目式的東西,當中多加一些形容詞而已。對於這種記録式的東西,我們又何苦爲它硬找來歷呢?

這樣一種奇形怪狀的東西,竟然能够形成,並且高度發展,自然也並不偶然,它有特殊的時代與社會背景,在它存在的社會裏,具有其特殊的功用,我們可以根據它的社會功用的轉變,而分期研究。

一、諂諛期

中國文學經過一段漫長時期的發展,再經過秦代的統一,字數愈來愈多,也愈趨完備,於是文字游戲與文字魔術便成爲可能的了。這時候可謂適逢其運,正碰上漢朝大一統的局面,國力富强,疆域廣袤,社會既安定又富庶,再加上帝王威權的高漲以及王公貴族之養尊處優,文字游戲便被他們視爲消遣的妙品而特加愛尚了,因此便促成了賦的畸形發展。這一時期的作者,多是些純文士型的人物,他們從未想到什麽治國安邦、立德立言的問題,他們祇知道有人用高官厚禄鼓勵這種作品,而他們又有制作此種作品的能力,於是就一手去博取個人的榮華富貴了。這一派最適當的代表當然是司馬相如,他是一個標準的浪子型文人,既然王公貴族欣賞他的文字游戲,他自然就孜孜於此,博求功名利禄。我們可以假想到,如果没有功名利禄的引誘,同時它的酒店又是生意興隆可以致他於巨富的話,説不定他會開一輩子的酒店的。其他作者如枚乘、東方朔、吾丘壽之流,他們的境遇容或各有不同,然其利用此一“手藝”,以達到博取富貴的目的,則莫不如出一轍。至於那些王公貴族以及大皇帝呢?

他們對聲色犬馬之樂都已感到不稀奇以後,玩玩這種把戲自然也不失爲調劑口味之一助,因之對於供給他們此種娱樂的人,也像對於供給他們其他娱樂的人一樣,不免要"倡優蓄之"了。

這一時期的賦雖然也有諷諫的説法,實則不過是羊頭狗肉、欺瞞天下人耳目的勾當而已。我們衹要看每篇賦的末段多麽像一條與上文極不相稱的猪尾巴,就可以明白。作者既爲時勢所迫(其時儒家已入於一尊的地位),不得不加上那麽一套僞裝,而讀者也各取所欲,對這條尾巴毫不重視,而當有人攻擊賦的時候,也會坦率地代爲辯護(當然更爲自己辯護),説什麽"賢於倡優博弈者遠矣!"由此可知,賦在這一時期,都是極盡吹嘘之能事,其目的在討好君王、阿諛時主,其功用也就僅止於此了。

二、諷諫期

在文士們迎合着大皇帝的口味,大量創作那種極端誇張的文章,而一個個都獲得了高官厚禄之後,另外一些"學而優則仕"的儒者,原來把它視爲"淫靡不急",此時爲了遷就現實,也不得不改變他們入仕的策略了,於是模仿制作,以求接近帝王的機會。然而他們名爲儒者,意在致君堯舜的,當然不好意思僅憑這一手去撈上一官半職,因此他們就想提高賦的身份,死抓住"源自詩騷、志在諷諫"兩點不放。因爲詩是儒家的重要經典,而騷在漢代也有其特受重視的地位,詩騷既然是那麽神聖,導源於時騷的東西自然也不可等閑視之了。

賦的形式,在司馬相如時代,已由他一手造成;《子虚》《上林》便是最好的藍本。他説的"合纂粗以成文,列錦綉而爲質,一經一緯,一宫一商,此賦之迹也",已經把賦的性質説得很清楚了,此後的作者也多遵照着他的軌範。但本期的作者,往往過分重視了歷史發展,有時難免就變了格。班固雖然説"賦者,古詩之流也",他的《兩都賦》,體制還依長卿之舊。揚子雲的賦,也多用長卿體,但如《甘泉賦》一篇,則全仿《楚辭》體,不免是拘於歷史成見了。這篇東西可以説是僅有的變調,内容是咏物叙事,但形式上却兮呵兮的,叫人讀了特别感到難受。

至於諷諫問題,更是儒家作者津津樂道的。賦的功用既在諷諫,自然便與治國安邦等經國大計有了關係,不能説是"壯夫不爲"的"雕蟲小技"了。(揚子雲晚年的覺悟,那是後來的事。)有了這一點作護符,他們才放膽地寫作。這一期可以揚雄爲代表。差不多在每篇賦之前,他都要加上或長或短的一段序,説明他是爲什麽事情"奏賦以風"的。我們可以拿短短的《長楊賦》序爲例。

"明年(作《羽獵賦》的明年),上將大誇胡人以多禽獸,秋命右扶風發民入南山,西自褒斜,東至弘農,南毆漢中,張羅網置罘,捕熊羆豪猪,虎豹狖玃,狐兔麋鹿,載以檻車,輸長楊射熊館,以網爲周袪,縱禽獸其中,令胡人手搏之,自取其獲,上親臨觀焉。是時農民不得收斂,雄從至射熊館,還上《長楊賦》,聊因筆墨之成文章,故藉翰林以爲主人,子墨爲客卿以風。"

這意思是够明顯的了,作者看見大皇帝爲逞一時之快,不顧百姓的死活,强驅之去爲他逮捕野獸,因此他才感念蒼生疾苦,上賦迄求大皇帝的哀憐。單就序看,其用心可謂良苦,但當我們讀了賦的本文以後,我們真不禁要驚得目瞪口呆。在這篇賦裏,開頭是子墨客卿提出的一段疑問,可以説就是作者序裏的意思,然後翰林主人便好好地把他訓了一頓,千言萬語不外乎一句話:大皇帝德配天地,要做的事多着哩,此特不過其小焉者而已!"客徒愛胡人之獲我禽獸,曾不知我亦已獲其王侯。"似乎子墨所問的衹是爲了幾隻老虎了!奇怪的是,"言未卒,墨客降席再拜稽首,曰:'大哉體呼!允非小人之所能及也。'"這簡直是爲大皇帝做辯護,哪裏説得上什麽諷,什麽諫呢?

在司馬相如的賦裏,那條諷諫的尾巴是拖在後面的,多多少少還正面地説了幾句話,大體上還理有可通;至於楊雄,則把那條尾巴裝到額頭上去了,看起來當然更爲不倫不類,"言之者無罪"的作用可謂已發揮到了極點。這也是他們不得不然之處,上之所好好之,上之所是是之,雖則一肚子的不贊成,也不容説出口來,但在字裏行間,又時刻不忘諷諫,不敢痛快地吹一陣。我們可以説,正因爲司馬相如不滿意賦的所謂諷諫之用,他的作品還有點文味;至於揚雄,則真把諷諫(其實是歌功頌德)當作兩回事,因而他的作品,現在讀起來就更覺其索然無味了。

我把這一期名之爲"諷諫期",與其説是就賦的社會功用而言,毋寧説是根據作者的意識,就骨子裏看,這一期的賦與前一期的是没有太大差别的,不過是依類葫蘆的玩意,其作用仍在阿諛時主以邀君寵;但因作者身份不同,思想稍别,結果對於賦也不無影響。

三、誇詡期

西漢富庶的社會漸漸衰微了,愛好文字游戲的帝王也改换了口味。在這種客觀情勢之下,賦似乎已失去它賴以存在的背景,理應衰微了。但由於數百年的積習,賦在文人的心目中已建立起其崇高的地位,幾乎成爲文人品評的標準了。雖則無實利(直接的)可獲,却也有虚名可圖,因此寫賦的還時有人在,已知拖到西晉,才由那位《三都賦》的作者做了一個驚人的結束。

這一時期的賦可以説已經擺脱了所謂諷諫的羈絆,至多也不過是"先王采焉以觀士風"而已。如果還有人强調賦與詩騷的關係以及他的諷諫功用,那不是有意地抬高賦的身價,就是迂腐不堪。無論如何,這種强調對於賦的創作是没有什麽重要影響的。我們衹要看《三都賦》中那三位先生各爲其本鄉本土大事吹嘘,而末了西蜀公子與東吴王孫竟那麽俯首帖耳地對魏國先生甘拜下風,便會知道這種結局法比之揚、馬還更爲牽强不近情理,我想作者本人也不會相信那兩位鄉土觀念如是之重的人,會那般輕易服輸。其所以要安排這樣一個結局,衹不過他的文字寫完了,依例需要一個結束而已。這就説明了作者更認清了賦的唯一需要即在事物的鋪叙,也衹有在這一部分才有機會炫耀個人的辭章,獲得同儕的重視。

最足代表這一時代的當然是那位苦幹的左太冲。據説他轉爲寫《三都賦》就"構思十年,門庭藩溷皆着紙筆,過一句即疏之",結果皇天不負苦心人,"都邑豪貴,鼓相傳寫",弄得"洛陽爲之紙貴",文名大噪,可以説完全達到作者的目的了。

左氏在序裏表示了他對賦的意見。這篇序向來極受重視,他的意見也被普遍地接受,幾乎成了評賦的準則。但我的意見則稍有不同。我們可以把它分成三段加以討論。

> 蓋詩有六義焉,其二曰賦。揚雄曰:"詩人之賦麗以則。"班固曰:"賦者,古詩之流也。"先王采焉,以觀土風。見"緑竹猗猗",則知衛地淇澳之産;見"在其坂屋",則知秦野西戎之宅。故能居然而辨八方。

表面看這一段是説賦的歷史及功用，其實説來説去衹是説詩而已，至於賦到底怎麽樣，等於一個字也未提。這不得已衹有把它硬跟古詩拉上點關係而説説詩了。其實此賦非彼賦，那關係是非常牽强的。

然相如賦《上林》而引“盧橘夏熟”，揚雄賦《甘泉》而陳“玉樹青葱”，班固賦《西都》而嘆以出比目，張衡賦《西京》而述以游海若。假稱珍怪，以爲潤色，若斯之類，匪啻于兹。考之果木，則生非其壤；校之神物，則出非其所。於辭則易爲藻飾，於義則虚而無徵。且夫玉巵無當，雖寶非用；侈言無驗，雖麗非經。而論者莫不詆訐其研精，作者大氐舉爲憲章。積習生常，有自來矣。

這一段批評前人作賦之失，但也衹集中在“不信不實”一點上。其實就賦的性質而言，這一批評也不太有力。賦本來就是一種游戲之作，衹要能寫得光怪陸離，讓讀者看得眼花繚亂而有一種目不暇接的快感就成，它的目的在争取讀者的驚異感嘆，根本説不上信實的問題，至多也衹能求其大概而已。如果真要死板地據實報道，結果可能更是味同嚼蠟。今以不信不實責於司馬相如，這位風流才子，豈能心服？老實説，由此正可看出，司馬相如究不愧爲賦的最大作手，唯有他最能把握賦的本質，左氏之責難，未免有點書生氣了。

左氏既不贊成這種做法，他自己怎麽辦呢？

余既思摹《二京》而賦《三都》，其山川城邑則稽之地圖，其鳥獸草木則驗之方志。風謡歌舞，各附其俗；魁梧長者，莫非其舊。何則？發言爲詩者，咏其所志也；升高能賦者，頌其所見也。美物者貴以其本，贊事者宜本其實。匪本匪實，覽者奚信？且夫任土作貢，《虞書》所著；辯物居方，《周易》所慎。聊舉其一隅，攝其體統，歸諸詁訓焉。

但是問題又來了。你所依據的那些地圖方志，又敢保其完全可靠嗎？否則你能追求的信實又在哪裏呢？像《蜀都賦》裏的“孔雀群翔，犀象競馳，白雉朝雊，猩猩夜啼。金馬騁光而絶景，碧鷄儵忽而曜儀”就很難叫人全部相信。但這似乎並無損於《三都賦》，反而使它生色不少。此類大賦根本就不是實用的東西，又何必過分求其信實？

也許有人認爲以上面的分析太過分了。不錯，單就序的推理來説，可謂順理成章，無奈賦這東西是不能講這些道理的，因此儘管作者如此説，而做起來還是與前人無大差别。

賦本身以離奇取勝，在文學史裏它也是最離奇的東西。它全在那一種"門庭藩溷，皆着紙筆"的地方，見其特長，一種苦幹的硬功夫，使人讀了都震於它的艱難晦澀，而覺得它博深偉大。曹子建曾說："揚馬之作，趣幽旨深，讀者非師傅不能析其詞，非博學不能綜其理，匪唯才懸，抑亦字隱。"但也許他所真正感到的困難，還是頭痛的"字隱"吧？

然而文學究竟並非全屬文字的雕琢與堆砌，而主在情感與靈性的抒發，自然與本色的表現，苦幹對於文學，衹能作爲一種手段，以達到一種更爲高尚的目的。從這一觀點看，我們真懷疑賦是否屬於文學的領域。因此有些人把它摒棄與文學史之外，雖然略録大膽，却也並非全無理由。

A Comparative Study of Three English Translations of Chang Chi's "Chieh-fu Yin", or "The Song of a Virtuous Wife"**

節婦吟　　　　　　寄東平李司空師道

Chieh-fu Yin　　（A poem written as a message to General Li.）

君　知　妾　有夫

Chün^{1} chih^{1} ch'ieh^{4} yü^{3} fu^{1},

贈　妾　雙　明　珠

Tseng^{4} ch'teh^{4} shuang^{1} ming^{2} chu^{1};

感　君　纏　綿　意

Kan^{3} chün^{1} ch'an^{2} mien^{2} yi^{4},

繫　在　紅　羅襦

Hsi^{4} tsai^{4} hung^{2} lo^{2} ju^{2}.

* * * * * * *

妾　家　高　樓　連　苑　起

Ch'ieh^{4} chia^{1} kao^{1} lou^{2} lien^{2} yüan^{4} ch'i^{3},

良　人　執　戟　明　光　裏

Liang^{2} jen^{2} chih^{1} chi^{1} ming^{2} kuang^{1} li^{3};

知　君　用　心　如　日　月

Chih^{1} chün^{1} yung^{4} hsin^{1} ju^{2} jih^{4} yüeh^{4},

事　夫　誓　擬　同　生　死

Shih^{4} fu^{1} shih^{4} ni^{3} t'ung^{2} sheng^{1} szu^{3}.

* * * * * * *

** 未刊稿，中文題爲《張籍〈節婦吟：寄東平李司空師道〉三個英文譯本之比較研究》，據作者打印稿編輯。

還　　君　明　　珠　雙　　淚　垂

Huan^{2} chün^{1} ming^{2} chu^{1} shuang^{1} lei^{4} ch'ui^{2},

何(恨)不 相　　逢 未　嫁　　時

Ho^{2} pu^{1} hsiang^{1} feng^{2} wei^{4} chia^{4} shih^{2}.

——from《全唐詩》六百六册張籍試卷一頁四①

The poem quoted above was written by Chang Chi, a poet of the eighth century in the T'ang Dynasty②. The dividing of this short poem into three stanzas as shown here is my own idea, because I feel it is quite reasonable to do so with regard both to its meaning and to its form. Each stanza is thus, so to speak, "a unit of meaning," marked off by the use of a different rhyme. A romanized version of the poem in modern reading is given here as a reference, but in order to show approximately the original rhyme scheme; a tentative reconstruction of each rhyme-word is also added after its modern form③.

Before discussing the translations, I think it is necessary to make clear, whenever possible, the controversial parts in the original poem and to mention something about its historical background, but to make the matter simple, let me first give a literal translation of it. The sole aim here is faithfulness in meaning; therefore, any word the equivalent of which cannot be found in the original poem will be put in parentheses.

You know I have (a) husband,

(Yet you) give me two shining pearls,

Moved (by) your binding (and) lingeringlove(affection),

(I) fasten (them) to (my) red silky coat.

* * * * * * *

---

① Adopted from the phonographed edition by I-wen Booksore 藝文印書館 Taipei, 1961.

② The dates of birth and death of the poet are both unknown, but according to《全唐詩》(All the Poem of the T'ang Dynasty) he got his Chin-shih degree in the fifteenth year of Cheng-Yüan (799).

③ All the reconstructions here are based upon the rules set by Prof. Tung in his《中國語言史》(History of Chinese Phonology).

My family's high building by (the imperial) garden stands,

My husband serves (as a) guard in (the) Ming-kuang (palace).

(I) know your intention is like (the) sun (and the) moon,

(Yet for) serving (my) husband, (I have) sworn (that I) shall live (and) die together (with him).

* * * * * * *

(I) return (to) you (now these) luminous pearls, (with) two tears (on my cheeks),

Why didn't we meet when (I was) not married?

The beauty of the poem can perhaps be fully appreciated only when we read it with a knowledge of its historical background, and this in turn can be seen from two aspects. First, in form, the poem, as is shown by its title "yin," belongs to what is called yüeh-fu (樂府), or "verse for music," a form first developed in the Han Dynasty and characterized by its relatively loose rules. It was a favorite to the T'ang poets, but by that time, it had lost its musical function and become nothing but a kind of "free verse." For this reason, many poets of that age started to invent some new forms for themselves within this broad framework, and one which is, in my opinion, related to the poem we are now discussing is Tu Fu's "Chang-jen Shan" (丈人山)① Tu's poem has only eight lines, the first four of which have each five characters and are in one rhyme, while the last four have each seven characters and in a different rhyme. The result of this arrangement is that the poem has thus a melodious touch and reads very lively. The first two stanzas of Chang's poem obviously bear a strong resemblance to Tu's poem, and have also the same effect. Whether Chang was under Tu's influence when he wrote this poem is very hard to prove, though it is very likely. What

① 《杜工部集》(The Complete Works of Tu Fu.) vol. 4, p. 5. It seems to me that Tu Fu once invented several new poetic forms, such as《秋雨嘆》〔卷一,頁五(2首)〕and《曲江》三章章五句(卷一,頁九). But few of these forms have been followed by the poets?

is more important here is that Chang did something more than Tu had done. By adding two lines in a third rhyme, he had achieved a greater varialion moreover, since these two lines carry the main idea of the poem, and the rhyme is in even-tone, in contrast to the uneven tone of the preceding stanza, when a reader reaches this part, he almost has to slow down, somewhat unconsciously, as if with a sigh. Such is Chang's magic. It is quite doubtful whether content and form can be linked in a still happier way.

Then, in contact, the poem has even a richer tradition behind it. As the subtitle shows, the poem was actually a reply to a warlord who tried to enlist the service of the poet, then a poor and low official in the central government, though well-known. This kind of symbolistic writing had its origin in Ch'u Ts'u, a book second in importance only to Shih Ching in the history of the Chinese poetry, and was hence quite familiar to the Chinese mind. On the other hand, the comparison of a loyal official to a virtuous wife was also a common one, because they were both supposed, according to the Chinese traditional moral code, to serve only one master in their life. The use of "pearls" as an image undoubtedly reminds one of the common saying "to throw pearls into darkness"(明珠暗投), meaning to use one's talents in the wrong place. The second stanza was obviously influenced by a famous Han poem "The Sun Rises from the South-east Corner"(日出東南隅) in which a modest woman refused the flirtation made to her by telling the man that she already had a husband who was in no way inferior to him, All these elements join forces in making the poem so beautiful and so dear to the Chinese mind that the poem, especially the last two lines, has become a part of their language. But taken simply as a love song, the poem is already a masterpiece. Thus even Dr. Hu Shih, a renowned antagonist of the allusive style, has to admit that it is a beautiful "riddle", the answer of which does not have to be known[①]

① Hu shih: 白話文學史(History of the Vernacular Literature.)p. 387.

It is well-known that there is often some ambiguity in a piece of Chinese poetic work, because connectives and other particles are often omitted. This poem, smple as it is in its selection of words and phrases, is no exception. One word or phrase, though having been narrowed by its context, can still be interpreted in several different ways, and it is up to the reader to make the best choice. The mysterious thing is that even those interpretations which one discards may work there in one's subconscious and thus enrich the interpretation one chooses, or help to erase any possible incongruity. The following is some of the confusing points in this poem, and they all in a way illustrate the mystery mentioned above.

The sixth character of the fifth line means originally "a garden," but since the word does not mean an ordinary garden but a big one, and it frequently appears in the compound 御苑 (the imperial garden) so in the course of time, it alone may mean "the imperial garden." This derived meaning apparently suits this context better and should be adopted, because a family which has a high building and lives near the palace is, needless to say, a noble one, but the first definition is also possible and perhaps underlies here, hinting that the family has also a big garden of its own. The phrase 執戟 in the next line has also a two-fold functions. Literally, the phrase means "to hold a halberd" that is, to serve as a guard (in the court); however, the term had long been used in a used in a metaphorical sense, meaning only to serve as a court official"①. Again, I personally feel, the derived meaning fits here much better, while at the same time, the original meaning will suggest that the official was a strong, wellbuilt and handsome man. "Like the sun and the moon" in the following line functions in an even subtler way. It may mean (your intention is) "as clear to me as the sun and the moon," but it may also mean (it is) "as pure as the sun and the moon," because an innocent

① 《文選》卷四二《曹植與楊德祖書》:"昔揚子雲,先朝執戟之臣耳。"

heart is always said to be bright, with nothing concealed. (光明正大) The first interpretation seems to be more in accordance with the next line than the second, but it is often thought to be rather shallow, and all the annotators adopt the latter while ignoring the incongruity. It is quite possible, in my opinion, that the first interpretation, though not adopted, may have contributed something in this respect. In a like manner, the phrase 誓擬 in the next line is also a very subtle one. Many people interpret it as "having sworn" (to be faithful), and thus give it a strong passive mood, as if the woman were virtuous only reluctantly, while actually she deserves to be trusted with more initiative spirit, because the word "swear" here can also be interpreted in the sense of "being determined to," as the second character of the phrase obviously indicates. Of course, the best way would be to leave the meaning of this phrase somewhere in between these two interpretations, as major be the intention of the poet, so that use the first as an excuse for the refusal, while showing the speaker's dignity with the second. Finally, the first character of the last is 何(why) in some editions of Chang's work, that 恨(regret) in others. Both seem to be very good.

I have perhaps said too much about the original poem, but it is my wish that, by so doing, the result of comparison may come out without actually comparing, or at least, a solid ground for comparison may have been formed. We may now try to measure how far or how close a translation is from the model, though this may be unfair to the intrinsic value of the former as an individual poetic work①.

There may be already quite e few English translations of this poem, but so far I have seen only three. They are quoted here as follows,

① Jachson Mathews: "Verse translations should not be printed facing their models. The life is knocked out of translated poems by the kind of misleading they get under these dircumstances." On Translation, p. 77.

Song of a Modest Woman

My lord, you know that I am married and have a husband,
Yet you still give me this pair of crystal pearls.
I am moved by your lingering passion,
I conceal the pearls in my coat of red silk.
There in the high towers adjoining the palace,
My husband holds the gold sword of a king's guard;
I know your heart shines like the sun and moon,
But you must know that I have sworn constancy whether I live or die.
I return your crystal pearls, while tears fall from my eyes,
Regretting that we did not meet when I was unmarried

—Robert payne: The White Pony (1949), p. 243

The Virtuous Wife

Two perfect pearls you give to me;
　　I clasp them light.
My dress is crimson; they reflect
　　The rosy light.

But I am true. My lord has gone
　　To fight the foe;
What Tartar horde he meets tonight
　　I may not know.

You come too late; your charger turn
　　upon his track,

Two perfect tears, to match your pearls,
　　I give you back.

—Mable Lorenz Ives: Chinese Love Songs (1949), P-47

A Letter

Pearls:
Twin pearls,
Bright gems of ocean,
To me, a married woman,
You have sent!

Yet you know I have husband
In attendance, in the palace,
On the Lord of Light, the Emperor—
May he live ten thousand years!

But the thought that prompted you
I cherish
In my bosom with the jewels.
There they've lain hidden till this hour,
In the soft, enfolding silk.

I know—you need not tell me—
That your thoughts are pure as moonlight,
Or as the glowing sun at midday
Over head.

My home lies noble in its gardens.

There the marriage oath I've taken,
And I ever shall be faithful,
Even past the gates of death.

So! —
The twin pearls are in this letter.
I send them back to you in sadness
With a sigh.

If you look closely, you'll find with them
Two other twin gems lying,
Twin tears fallen from my eyelids,
Telling of a breaking heart.
Alas, that perverse life so willed it
That we met too late, after
I had crossed my husband's threshold
on that fateful wedding day!

—Henry H. Hart: The Hundred Names (1938), pp. 86 - 87

Whether a poet, as Mr. Jackson Mathews says, "must be at least an amateur philologist,"① I am not sure, but I am fully convinced that a reader of Chinese classical poems must have some philological training, if he wants to fully appreciate them. However, we must feel satisfied here, when all the translators assume this poem as a simple love song, and ignore all its rich and colorful historical background, since it is impossible for a single translation to carry such a heavy burden. I shall, therefore, first check a little their fidelity in meaning to the original, then measure them by the standards set by the translators themselves, and finally, I shall try, as far as I can, to see which one is better not only as a translation but as a piece of poetic work, too.

At one glance, anybody can tell that Mr. Payne's translation is the most "faithful," and indeed such is his sole aim. In his "Method of Translation,"

① Ibid. p. 70.

he writes: "It has seemed best to translate the poems as simply and literally as possible, and to avoid foot-notes wherever possible. The Chinese has therefore been translated line by line —without rhyme, for to have succeeded in rhyme would have necessitated padding out the lines or so changing their forms that they would have become unrecognisable." We must admit here that he has roughly reached the standard set by himself. Doubtless there is full recognition, but the problem is: where is the poem? To me, the translation does not read much better than the low-class prose version I gave above, and almost all the elements that make the poem a poem are gone. It is quite legal and very wise to translate a Chinese poem into English without rhyme, because while it is almost an essential in the former language, it is not required in the letter①. But in throwing it away, "a translator has to express a phrase, an event, a situation as it should be said in his own language."② He must try to find some other device in his own language to convey approximately the original feeling; otherwise, it would be a kind of evasion of one's responsibility in one's note a translator. He tries to avoid the difficulty without justifying his own work. The greatest problem lies perhaps in the principle of literalness set here by the translator. It has long been proved unworkable anywhere③, especially between two languages widely different in linguistic origin, in grammar, and in turns of expression derived from historical episodes. Let's take the seventh line as an example. Mr. Payne gives here approximately an exactly literal translation, (though strictly speaking, "your heart shines" is still questionable.) but does the sentence convey the same meaning as the Chinese? I don't know what the English sentence exactly means, but I doubt it can produce the above-mentioned subtle effects of the Chinese sentence. (The secondary meaning of "bright" is

---

① Wang Chi-chen: "Chinese Poetry" in Dictionary of World Literature, p. 53.

② Horst Frenz: "The Art of Translation" in Comparative Literature, p. 94.

③ Ibid. p. 83.

"clever" in English, but that of its Chinese equivalent, 明, a combination of the sun and the moon, is "honest.") Thus to be verbally faithful is often to be semantically misleading and esthetically. It should never be taken as a principle in translating poetry.

But even merely using the measure or faithfulness, I find Mr. Payne's translation is not without fault. To use the verb "conceal" (line 4) for the Chinese verb 繫 (to fasten to) is clearly not "faithful," but this may be a clever twist of the translator, and hence should not be counted as a mistake, but in the next two lines, there is an unforgivable mistake. While it doesn't matter too much whether the husband holds a "gold sword" or a halberd, the place where he holds it, if he really does, is certainly not "the high towers adjoining the palace" It is hardly credible that with the help or several I famous Chinese scholars and poets, he should still make such a mistake, but we must give him credits for the phrase "adjoining the palace." He seems to be the only one of the three, who really understands the original phrase, though he deprives the family of the "high towers" by mistaking them to be parts of the palace. In the eighth line, by putting "I have sworn constancy," he makes a choice between the two possible interpretations, as one must in translating, but it would be better, in my opinion, to choose the other one. Finally, simple and literal as Mr. Payne tries to be, he finds "more often than we have wished, it has been necessary to translate the Chinese by far more words than there are in the original"[①], a confession of the unfeasibility of strict literalism.

When I read Miss Ives' translation, I have a feeling that we are now in the other extreme of the world. At first glance, it is almost unrecognizable as a translation of this poem, but for the two pearls. However, after reading it several times, I feel it is, compared with Mr. Payne's, closer to the original

① Robert Payne: The White Pony, p, 21.

in spirit. The three stanzas more or less correspond both in spirit and in order with those of the model, though they are all drastically modified. The first stanza is the most successful. With the clever omission of the line "You know I have a husband, the lively and cheerful air of the whole stanza, as the young woman must be in at receiving the gift, is intensified. But the second stanza is almost a joke. It is totally an unhappy invention, perhaps through the misunderstanding of the two phrases "to hold a halberd" and "to live and die." The blunder is, however, somewhat by the simple sentence "but I am true," which is the key tune of its corresponding stanza. The last stanza was perhaps deliberately enlarged so as to match the preceding two. The addition of a "charger" may not be a good idea, but the sending of the two tears is no doubt a remarkable elaboration. The whole poem reads, as it should, more like a Western lyric song, but I feel, with some revision and correction, it may become an ideal translation of the Chinese poem.

In "The Problems of Translation" printed at the beginning of his book, Mr. Hart writes:

> "The translator must divorce himself from the Western response to experience. He must approach his work subjectively, as a Chinese, seeing life through Chinese eyes,... otherwise he will fail, his work will be a distorted presentation of the original. The translation must be a faithful rendition of the poet's own words,... Nothing must be read into them, and nothing left out. When translations can not meet this test, they are not translations."(p.31)

It must be quite surprising to see that a translator with such a conviction should have produce such a work as we quoied above. The ideas represented here are all quite admirable, but the problem is how we can carry them into practice. Obviously, the translator is not very successful at this, because though he has seemingly left out nothing, he has read into the poem quite a lot, and it is doubtful that he has seen "through Chinese eyes." Many people have noticed that, in translating a Chinese poem, it is often necessary to add some words not found in the model, and this, I think, is a legitimate practice, because, as a famous Chinese critic puts it, "the Chinese poetic language is an extremely intense one…… sometimes a line may consist of nothing else but a series of nouns which are left there to work out the effects by themselves, just as a post-impressionistic painter puts several different colours side by side and lets them work out the harmony by themselves."① This naturally does not mean we may add as much as we like. It means rather that we should not add anything unless it is strictly required, otherwise, the beauty of simplicity and implication will be completely damaged. It is true that, with a few exceptions, most of the things Mr. Hart supplemented in his translation are implied in the original work, but isn't it better to imply them also as far as possible in the translation. To the Chinese mind, nothing can be more unpoetic than to speak out everything with no reservation, To translate a poem of ten short lines with eight stanzas is really rather too much. It means almost every line has been enlarged into a stanza and new elements have been called in to enforce it. The result does not seem to be quite desirable, as is shown particularly by the second and the fourth stanzas. The order of the lines in the original poem was also rearranged, but since the order of the three original stanzes has been roughly kept, no serious damage has been made.

According to the translator, his method is as follows:

> The poem is carefully studied in the original. The text is restored to its original form as far as possible. A rough literal translation is then made, the meanings of each word and phrase being noted. After a few readings of this translation, the words and phrases fall into a pattern which, to the translator, appears to convey the proper meaning of the

① 聞一多《唐詩雜論》p. 162.

poem. The words and their meanings thus approximate the Chinese syllables and their connotations, as far as the differences in the two languages permit. This final translation should be in metrical English. The pattern may vary; invariable however, is fidelity to the original text." (p. 30)

This is indeed a marvelous method, and should certainly produce wonderful result, if it can be carried through. It apparontly requires more strictly that the translator must understand the original poem thoroughly. But unfortunately, Mr. Hart has not fulfilled this requirement as is shown by the misinterpretations "the Lord of Light" in the second stanza, and "My home lies noble in its gardens,/There the marriage oath I've taken," though we must notice that his understanding of the original poem is far better than that of the other two, as can be seen from the second line of the second stanza and the second line of the fourth stanza. But his translation is indeed in good metrical English as he wished it would be, and as such, it deserves great admiration.

It is perhaps useless for a translator to try to satisfy the native readers of the poem he is translationg, because they can never be satisfied as it has been said that even FitzGerald faild to satisfy the Persians, I am afraid that, in the above evaluations, I may have been rather too strict in the problem of faithfulness, and hence have not done justice to the translators. But I have deliberately tried to put more emplasis on the poetic quality of the translations and tried to see how close they have come to the model, that is, how successful they have been in their "continuous subconscious association with the original."① Thus I feel Mr. Hart's translation, though long-winded, is the best of the three, Miss Ives', though careless and too simple, still keeps part of the original mood, while Mr. Payne's can hardly be called a poem,

① Horst Frenz: op. cit., p. 94.

because by translating literally, he lost completely the formal beauty of the model without inventing any "normal effects in his ovn language that give a sense of those produced by the original in its own."①

BIBILIOBRAPHY

In English:

Fang, Achilles: "Some Reflections on the Defficulty of Translation" in On Translation (ed, Brower.), Cambridge, 1959. pp. 111-33.

Frenz, Horst: "The Art of Translation" in Comparative Literative (ed. Stalknecht and Frenz.) Carbondale, 1961, pp. 72-95.

Henry H. Hart: The Hundred Names: a Short Introduction to the study of Chinese Poetry, Berkeley, 1938.

Ives, Mabel Lorenz (tr. & ed.): Chinese Love Songs, New Jersey, 1949.

Kiang, Kang-hu: "Chinese Poetry" (Intro. II) in The Jade Mountain, New York, 1929, pp. xxi-xxxvii.

Mathews, Jeckson: "Third Thoughts on Translating Poetry" in On Translation. (ed. Brower.) Cambridge, 1959, pp. 67-77.

Payne, Robert: The White Pony, London, 1949.

Wang, Chi-chen: "Chinese Poetry" in Dictionary of World Literature (ed. Shipley.) New York, 1943.

In Chinese:

張籍詩,《全唐詩》六百六册,中華書局,1960 年。

胡　適:《白話文學史》,樂天出版社,1974 年。

杜　甫:《杜工部集》,《四部備要》本。

董同龢:《中國語音史》,華崗出版有限公司,1967 年。

聞一多:《唐詩雜論》,中華書局,1959 年。

① J. Mathews: op. cit., p. 67.

石夫吟草***

咏曇花

一九五九年十月，時在臺大

奇花當夜發，月下散清芬。
莫道良宵短，須憐艷質純。
能成一夕好，其貴百年身。
脉脉情何限，知音有幾人。

歲暮感懷兼遣大華静波

一九六〇年，時於役三重

古邳有拙夫，秉性近痴頑。
生逢喪亂世，每感立身難。
少小多狂念，有志勒燕然。
立功期萬里，心儀張與班。
乾坤中道改，中原遍烽烟。
神州居不易，蓬島少得閑。
持危恨無力，感時淚常漣。
迷途何所事，埋首入簡編。
蟹文孜孜讀，經史矻矻研。
孔孟修齊訓，莊老《養生》篇。
誦久間成病，思深偶入玄。

*** 薛鳳生教授將歷年詩作結集爲《石夫吟草》，未刊，據作者打印稿編輯。

始悟生生理，唯在性所安。
混世貴無名，雲月何須攀。
客心驚歲晚，憂思忽如泉。
日月亦云邁，行届而立年。
步兵哭歧路，夫子嘆逝川。
大化爐不熄，陰陽輪未懸。
功名猶塵土，二毛初上顛。
豈有多情笑，但感世媸妍。
應召入軍伍，干戈勉力肩。
風雨感舊交，袍澤結新緣。
荆楚多豪傑，齊魯出俊賢。
二子同臭味，杯酒談笑間。
志高薄青雲，才美勝瑚璉。
每發匡濟論，使我開心顔。
僕非惜力也，才微何用焉。
以子相知深，敢爲披肺肝。
願隨二子後，亦著祖生鞭。
且待承平歲，再買泛洋船。
放歌四海外，陶然作地仙。

送乃長之汶萊 并序

一九六一年十二月，乃長兄與余為臺大外文系同窗，後同任助教半載，因得朝夕相處，杯酒之歡，幾於無日無之。俄而去之汶萊，因作長歌以贈之。

與君相識早，歡會長恨少。
纔獲朝夕親，又送君遠道。
遠道迢迢何處尋，南海森森闊且深。
知君生有擒龍手，遥望天涯俟好音。
感君友愛難爲報，短句豈足明我心。

婚後戲題寄靖宇

一九六五年春,時余在印大,靖宇在康大

去夏君方娶，今春我亦婚。
莫謂時地殊，且喜歲月新。
從此天涯不寂寞，各有生死同命人。
昔年猶如無繮馬，今日皆成有覊身。
兒女情代英雄氣，擾擾濁世不復聞。
自兹無多願，願與君爲鄰。
咫尺兩家常聚首，晨昏一堂共論文。
君有彩筆干氣象，我吟拙句亦自珍。
貧富窮通渾皆忘，唯樂身前酒滿樽。

戲題《西風瘦馬圖》寄東邪

一九六八年六月

昔飲長城窟，水寒傷我骨。
失蹄白登道，愧對戍邊卒。
傷骨未傷腦，葉落知機早。
本無千里足，不恨伯樂少。
駑軀隨風發，因緣到天涯。
蹇步逐水草，倦伏偶思家。
家山歸無路，浮雲雜塵霧。
宵露濡我鬃，明朝何處去。
去去念舊知，隔洋相憶時。
路遥力難報，舉首獨長嘶。
澌嘶聲漸哀，悲風從天來。
勉起陟高崗，猶恐壯心衰。

偶成

一九六八年七月

艱難困苦劫餘身，偶憶前塵偶失神。
舉措失儀君莫怪，須憐癡態無心人。

接文憑口號一首

一九六九年二月

六年甘苦一張紙，萬里鄉心半白頭。
了卻人間兒女事，明朝跨鶴向滄州。

偶作贈端端同學

一九七〇年六月

幽并少年早別家，狂歌單騎走天涯。
客中偶念鄉關遠，對酒獨吟《天净沙》。

題贈義成同學

臨留莫長嘆，逝者本如斯。
寄語少年友，立身須及時。

離臺後有感　奉和以仁、邦新

一九七〇年夏

用世無方自笑癡，明時難俟轉增悲。
空懷越鳥巢南意，終似鷦鷯棲一枝。

喜獲嵩叔信 并序

一九七六年三月。余於一九七三年春,試以一札寄傑叔,久無回音。漸感絶望。不意三年後突獲嵩叔來信,悲喜交集。歷久不減,因題一律

如身蓬轉久辭根，每立斜陽望浮雲。
親友時思空有淚，鄉關夢返了無痕。
崎嶇世路八千里，羈旅生涯三十春。
喜獲家書來故土，又憑魚雁接親人。

答元亮表弟

一九七六年八月

別來廿八年，回首總鼻酸。
垂髫同游伴，今皆兩鬢班。
傷心大母逝，額手親朋安。
一紙珍重意，憑郵寄邯鄲。

悼林洙

一九七七年

生僅三紀半，病及二十年。
書法王逸少，詞宗辛稼軒。
多才何所用，力學亦徒然。
恰似幽憂子，古今人共憐。
故交萬里外，無語問蒼天。
悵望漢家樹，茫茫盡是烟。

游凡爾賽宫

一九七九年作，寄邦新、以仁

霸業已同塵土盡，空餘帝闕自巍峨。
龍廷太液今猶在，御苑繁花依昔多。
大匠千秋耀金粉，風霜百代蝕銅駝。
游人盡道凡宫美，誰憶梁公《五噫歌》。

附以仁和詩

吊古何人愁不盡，欲從篇咏想巍峨。
秦宫已共重瞳化，漢苑空餘瓦礫多。
碧浪一舲杳西子，黄沙千里失明駝。
興亡中外尋常事，莊缶誰爲發一歌。

四言以復邦新改字之見[①]

邦新來函云腹聯"蝕"字宜改作"泣"字，因作四言以調侃之

異哉邦新，素稱解人。
偶失禪機，乃發謬論。
銅駝未泣，觀者傷神。
悠悠大化，不辨古今。

首度返鄉有感[②]

余於一九八一年二月首度返鄉，途經西雅圖，飛機凌空後有感而作

塵埃野馬蔽山崗，滄溟無涯映夕陽。

---

① 原詩無題，爲索引之方便，特擬此題。
② 原詩無題，爲索引之方便，特擬此題。

鐵翼御風歸去也，浮雲盡處是吾鄉。

歸徐二咏

莫遣兒童唱《大風》，重瞳隆準已無蹤。
江山空自换新色，父老何曾醉太平。
吕雉專權幾傾國，蕭何忍辱僅全生。
可憐九里山頭月，還照滄桑彭祖城。

莫遣兒童唱《大風》，余哀歷代總傷情。
河山百戰誰爲主，功過千秋孰作評。
劫後黄樓無片瓦，舊時燕子但餘名。
巍巍淮海新碑館，又伴徐民話廢興。

附邦新所和前詩

莫遣兒童唱《大風》，漢家威武愧無蹤。
東鄰鼠子恨方雪，北鄙豺狼難未平。
一海中分悲故國，千山阻隔哭蒼生。
可憐最是舊時月，猶照受降塞外城。

碾莊即事

鄉導聒聒道今古，老農默默事耘耕。
只緣生長龍争地，慣見臨淮落大星。

去徐抒懷

風歌聽罷只心傷，三十三年始返鄉。

漫道虛名傳海外，須憐形骸在他邦。
田園廬舍覓無處，姨舅叔姑鬢染霜。
拼把離愁寄杯酒，彭城夜色正茫茫。

贈靖宇

一九八一年春，靖宇率海外華人作家訪華，途次武漢，因得晤談於璇宫飯店

江城三月故人來，岸上春花猶未開。
黄鶴樓平笛聲杳，璇宫夜語有餘哀。

游黄州赤壁

一九八一年夏

大江東去憶坡仙，拍岸驚濤去不還。
千載沈沙埋赤壁，獨留辭賦在人間。

麻將室

八一年初，得返故國。其夏，往游廬山參觀所謂“青年文化中心”者，據云其地原爲某幹行館，諸多設施之外，麻將室赫然在焉，感而作打油詩一首

方城之戲惡名傳，革命來時不許玩。
孰料洶洶十年裏，匡廬山頂伴高官。

答復旦吴歡章教授

八二年春，中國漢語教授代表團應美國教育部之邀，來美訪問。余受美中友協之托，陪往各地參觀，朝夕相處，友好日增。由芝加哥赴夏威夷途中，長途飛行頗多餘暇，因有贈和之作

久作天涯淪落人，忽聞古調欲沾巾。
相逢意氣敢辭醉，再起爲君盡一樽。

附吴君贈詩

一口家鄉話，滿腔故國情。
千里邀明月，萬家共舉樽。

和張志公教授

性弱不耐酒，體頑堪泛船。
逐波無定止，何處是家園。

附志老贈詩

共持一杯酒，同登萬里船。
飄泊四海外，時念舊家園。

贈别志老

志老嘉名久已聞，天涯邂逅始相親。
同游但恨爲時少，煮酒京華再論文。

機中贈代表團諸君

九霄雲海莽蒼蒼，故國遥看總斷腸。
何幸得陪諸君子，壯游十日似還鄉。

游黄山寄臺島友好

一九八二年夏

知君最愛山，攝取畫圖寄君看。
若問在何處，錢塘揚子間。
名不列五岳，是以後世無傳焉。
一自霞客品題後，遂教世人競來攀。
我亦有所思，長在大江南。
寄身每恨鄉關遠，欲登靈山苦無緣。
悲莫悲兮長別離，樂莫樂兮終來還。
終來還，相見歡，斜陽仍照舊山川。
排雲殿前雲似海，百丈泉頭飛瀑懸。
仙女凌波處，潺潺流温泉。
迎客送客松不老，羅漢拱立在雲端。
玉屏樓上望，蓮華分外妍。
何年天竺飛來石，化作猴王踞峰巔。
爲赴王母蟠桃宴，來經人間一綫天。
一綫天，行路難，仰望天都坐長嘆。
千尋石級卻我步，仙人指路我其還。
噫吁嚱！松奇石怪，所在皆有，對此可以開心顔。
七十二峰盡靈秀，匆匆三日看不完。
登高極目望東海，有美人兮海東邊。
知君亦有煙霞癖，盍興乎來，盍興乎來！再偕子同觀。

附以仁回贈

世上誰人不愛山，試從圖照想奇觀。
故鄉風物何由夢，七十峰棲雲霧間。

過明孝陵

祭殿已夷，唯紅墻半堵耳

紅墻半堵證滄桑，不見當時紀念堂。
獨賸鳳陽花鼓調，流民歲歲唱年荒。

偶　成

頃見學者數輩以英文侈談詩律，因戲作短句。一九八四年

李杜文章格律深，法傳百代少知音。
痴兒不識個中苦，也捧唐詩逐字吟。

自題小照

神游故國髮華早，斗室獨吟馬齒增。
感念邦家無限事，還持黄卷向青燈。

步韻奉和邦新見寄二首①

八四年暮春，邦新夫婦自密州來訪，歡叙兩日，歸後以見寄，因步韻奉和

其一

與君早定文字交，唯恨不常共酒肴。
海外相逢同把盞，放懷　笑百憂消。

附原詩

細雨春寒訪舊交，家家美酒與珍肴。

① 原詩無題，爲索引之方便，特擬此題。

故鄉新事憑君問，折却梅花恨怎消。

其二

每感年華傷逝水，幾回搔破老頭皮。
故交遠問何由對，空有園蔬傍竹籬。

附原詩

平生未見象噴水，異域奇觀蛇蜕皮。
恰是哥城驚日變，輕車訪舊過東籬。

戲應邦新次詩[①]

邦新次詩以皮爲韻，所謂險韻也，其欲以相難乎！且以蛇象入詩，筆法尤奇，因戲作動物詩以應之

吹牛無地藏狐尾，蒙馬何方覓虎皮。
我每嘆人蛇畫足，人常嫌我狗穿籬。
鴟鴞豈解鯤鵬運，燕雀敢隨鴻雁飛。
狡兔多疑三築窟，黔驢無技一揚蹄。

觀莊因詩畫[②]

觀莊因詩畫，以詩討之。一九九〇年冬

莊生屎入畫，皮某屁填詞。
二豎芒唐日，斯文掃地時。

---

① 原詩無題，爲索引之方便，特擬此題。
② 原詩無題，爲索引之方便，特擬此題。

羞煞豐子愷，氣死胡適之。
宜即斷生指，再圖鞭某尸。
釋家謂有文字孽，特向君説君須知。

莊因回辯

莊生屎入畫，皮某屁填詞。
二子皆才美，豈可消遣之。
豐老撫髯笑，胡適豎姆指。
斯文千古事，鳳生何嗤嗤。

贈莊因

一九九〇年春於莊宅歡宴，步邦新原韻，其時余與莊因相識已逾三十年，而莊君之婚適爲二十年

卅載風雲彈指間[①]，賸將白髮伴紅顔。
故人重聚莫辭醉，酒蟹詩圖豈等閒。

客中感懷

一九九〇年夏返國機中作

憶昔避亂狐兔走，竄逃荆棘不知醜。
終去故國豈我願，寄寓他邦聊餬口。
年少不識愁滋味，更結新交競賭酒。
酒酣高歌驚番佬，酒醒夜闌淚沾手。
故園西望路漫漫，不見京華見北斗。
可憐浮雲游子意，覓機還歸訪戚友。

① 或作：廿載雨雲牀笫間。

太平洋上去復回，俯看白雲變蒼狗。
白雲蒼狗空悠悠，家山遥看點點愁。
年華行將客中盡，惆悵月明獨倚樓。
日日思君令人老，魂夢何夕不神州。
鄉關望斷無覓處，空自天涯待首丘。

和心恒兄元旦見寄[①]

心恒兄以其一九九〇年元旦之作見寄，接獲時已屬春暮矣，因步原韻而和之

春盡天涯獨閉門，鄉心萬里對空樽。
多情喜有知交在，遠寄新詞慰客魂。

戲贈靖宇留意性命之學兼呈邦新伉儷[②]

聞靖宇亦康，近者頗留意於性命之學，因戲贈一律，兼呈邦新伉儷。一九九〇年二月

莊叟有名言，死生如往還。
是非一指辯，毁譽衆人傳。
有用同無用，無絃即有絃。
勸君齊物我，隱几法天然。

戲贈邦新兼呈靖宇

一九九〇年春

半百男兒頭半秃，歌殘紅袖憶當初。

---

① 原詩無題，爲索引之方便，特擬此題。
② 原詩無題，爲索引之方便，特擬此題。

金山重遇笑相問，還有前時需要無。

附邦新和詩

鬢自成霜頭自禿，男兒未許説當初。
拼將此身酬師友，不問王喬有與無。

和紹愚兄庚午歲除見贈

一九九一年一月

不余知者斥余狂，君見我狂謂我臧。
自古賢豪重收斂，都緣人世忌鋒芒。
蠖伸匡俗吾無術，龍隱立言子有方。
歲暮天寒吟白雪，暫忘佳節在他鄉。

附原詩

駐車握手披肝膽，恥效阮生不否臧。
辨析音聲分秒忽，推敲字句到毫芒。
已有文章驚海内，更栽桃李遍遐方。
屢度滄波傳學術，此心耿耿向家鄉。

聞國堯兄東瀛歸來戲寄一律

一九九一年三月

學劍無成改學書，分聲析韻聊自娱。
索居海外知音少，歷劫中原我道孤。
斯學克傳其在魯，方輪獨造空嗟余。
東鄰説法歸來後，又有新論饗我無。

游揚川偶題

一九九一年

星映如琴勝有聲，玉屏日暖雨初晴。
江湖人老十年後，又倚橋欄看月明。

和延煊之《遣悶》①

延煊以近作《遣悶》見示，因戲效魯迅打油體以和之。一九九一年初冬

混世無方不入流，藏身鬧市畏人稠。
常羞阿堵囊中少，敢爲蒼生天下憂。
飯飽即憑高枕卧，酒酣偶索香菸抽。
望洋興嘆緣何事，海客有心隨海鷗。

附延煊原詩

又當涇水匯清流，曉夢東山翠竹稠。
未必子雲尋字苦，何如文正覽濤憂。
新醅緑螘樽徐酌，舊擁青箱卷漫抽。
媧角小園枝著蕾，沉吟斗室喟群鷗。

和耀東《窗外有棵相思》二首②

閱耀東兄《窗外有棵相思》，因效仿某氏《少女情懷總是詩》句以戲之二首

一九九二年一月

士子情懷亦似詩，窗前獨坐聽蟬嘶。

---

① 原詩無題，爲索引之方便，特擬此題。

② 原詩無題，爲索引之方便，特擬此題。

壯心漸歇禪心起，方是静觀萬物時。

士子情懷亦可哀，聽風聽雨自徘徊。
遥看窗外相思樹，忽悟蟬鳴歸去來。

附延煊和詩

支離漂泊敢言詩，賸水殘山任雨嘶。
明鏡豈堪勤拂拭，邇來無復羡楊時。

處士佳篇盡我哀，神州域外兩徘徊。
何當手植堂前柳，三徑榛蕪歸去來。

附陳穎和詩

清腴小品似吟詩，十載歸心待馬嘶。
猶憶海疆曾一聚，長宵客館劇談時。

秋蔭鳴蟬自引哀，琴書裝就復低徊。
浮生不盡相思意，隔水青山送雨來。

咏　曇

同事陳穎兄以咏曇四絶見示，勉和二首，聊博一笑。一九九二夏

一朵優曇獨占枝，含羞默默故來遲。
天生尤物易憔悴，須看初開未放時。

良宵對酒且歡歌，莫道芳菲但霎那。
花落花開自成趣，世人何必嘆蹉跎。

附原作

鹿苑仙葩葉作枝，含苞展瓣漏遲遲。
禪心不待窺全貌，已愛佛花初放時。

静觀花發暫清歌，絶世容顔一霎那。
秉燭夜游良有以，曉來人事任蹉砣。

游威海即興二首

一九九二年八月

早聞海上花園城，心嚮往之恨未能。
今日來游償夙願，青山緑水看分明。

少讀《齊諧》愛鵬運，老來北海觀蜃樓。
雲烟變幻人間世，海外何曾更九州。

贈威海大學許玉琪校長

齊魯由來出俊賢，文風又到威海邊。
白墻紅瓦青山下，不輟弦歌似昔年。

種苦瓜

一九九三年夏

兩度當轅豈足誇，心爲形役實堪嗟。
仔肩卸後風光好，重把鋤頭種苦瓜。

懷嚴老 并序

余於八一年返國，首至武漢即拜識嚴老。時先生已年七十，每來共余慷慨論學論世且及音韻學會之策劃。余嘗戲謂曰：“嚴老人届七十，例多告退以頤養天年，先生何爲自苦若此？”乃正色對曰：“十載浩劫，百廢待興，第恐時不我與，豈敢浪擲？假我十年，或可重振斯學，爲前賢繼耳。”嗚呼！壯矣！哲人已逝，緊余懷之，因書短句，以寄永思。一九九三年二月，時次新加坡。

七十老翁何所求，心傷劫火噬神州。
音聲絶學憑誰繼，一叟曾呼立楚丘。

重讀前作，感慨至多，因憶嚴老歿時實已八十整壽，因改前作，增爲四韻。時甫返哥倫布市

八十老翁何所求，心傷劫火噬神州。
白雲黄鶴人終去，血雨腥風恨亦休。
猿嘯洞庭哀國士，霧迷江渚送歸舟。
音聲絶學憑誰繼，一叟曾呼在楚丘。

奉答心恒

心恒兄雅好詩，日前以《初夏晚晴小雨後西風斜陽凉初透》見寄，云爲散步偶得，命爲補足，乃鼓勇戲題數句。豈敢云補，亦所謂續貂云爾。一九九三年十一月二十日古邳石夫謹志

遥想詩人小溪畔，悠然遠見南山秀。
何不門前多種菊，秋來更賞黄花瘦。

自雷諾下山偶成

冷月無聲照岡巒，寒光映雪萬重山。
冰清世界疑瓊宇，人在虛空飄渺間。

贈孔昭順先生

讀其《南海雀飛瀛臺》，深佩其爲人，因寄一律

南海鴻飛天外天，瀛臺棲隱幾多年。
鋭錐不是囊中物，利劍豈徒壁上懸。
高節常爲友朋道，藝名終獲世人傳。
芎林佳勝君須會，心遠正宜居地偏。

寄亞濤 并序

余與亞濤少小同窗，童稚相親，情同手足。爾後分散，音訊遂絶，雖歷年所未嘗忘懷，八一年後數度返鄉，查訪再三，終無消息。乃今春忽由友人轉來一信，言現居宜賓，且已兒孫繞膝矣。故人無恙，喜何如之，因寄四韻，以慰遥思。一九九四年春

别來消息兩茫然，童稚親情久益堅。
驚獲音書滿眼淚，試從圖照認當年。
休嗟白髮盈顛上，且喜兒孫繞膝前。
夜雨巴山重聚日，五糧液熟醉同眠。

鷗湖夜泛 并序

九四年夏，愚夫婦偕必松、英貝同訪天睦、志欣於密州鷗湖，月夜泛舟，因有戲作

碧空如水水連天，明月照人人在船。
同泛鷗湖六仙侶，輕舟夜話蓬萊邊。

戲贈靖宇、邦新

時晏集於靖宇宅中。末句以丁爲韻，邦新讓余出韻矣，余則曰："此中華新韻也。"一九九四年冬

同學同行志趣同，同膺讓座喜重逢。
老王獨獲高高椅，端坐揚眉傲薛丁。

戲和邦新〈堪校〉

時余方擬提早退休，故邦新譏之。九四年十二月

我愛陶公飲必醺，醉看富貴若浮雲。
悠然采菊東籬下，半畝荒園自理勤。

附邦新原作 并序

聞鳳生兄嫂提早退休，有意來加州長住，賦此打油詩以贈之，中有失粘之處，未暇細細推敲也

我效陶公亦偶醺，自吟拙句半閑雲。
昨來方定歸田計，誰共爾曹説懶勤。

答心恒兄再度來美見示[①]

心恒兄於九五年再度訪美，自杜克大學來示，言及鄉情，重提同隱雲龍

① 原詩無題，爲索引之方便，特擬此題。

山之約，且戲以《番邦賦詩亦大難 山水人情兩不干》相贈。因竊取其意，足成一絶以答之

久居異域我知難，風土人情兩不干。
望斷鄉關何處是，雲龍山下霧漫漫。

賀漢泉年登七秩①

作藩教授年登七秩，門生祝嘏徵詞於余。素仰高賢，因作短句以爲壽。末句竊師了一先生八十自壽詩之意

承先啓後傳聲韻，化雨春風四十年。
莫道古稀精力少，還祈鼓勇寫千篇。

偕子還鄉題徐州師院②

九六年春偕子還鄉，訪問徐州師院（時尚未改爲大學），樂見莘莘學子，因應鳴皋院長之囑，喜而題詞

天涯爲客久，長憶古彭城。
喜看雄豪地，英才輩輩生。

留别亞濤 并序

九六年春偕明遠兒返鄉，乃專程訪亞濤於宜賓，相見之時，悲喜交集。坡公有句云"相逢握手一大笑，白髮蒼顔略相似"，庶或近之。各述别後之情，多有不忍言者。盤桓數日，依依而别

四十餘年憶舊游，重逢今在古戎州。

① 原詩無題，爲索引之方便，特擬此題。
② 原詩無題，爲索引之方便，特擬此題。

鄉音雖改人猶健，莫嘆年華似水流。

晨赴加大途中打油戲贈邦新、洪年兩兄

一九九七年十月

戴月披星巴克萊，惺忪睡眼未全開。
黎明即起忙啥事，再爲斯文走一回。

赴戴維斯途中大霧戲作

九七年十一月

車行如矢路茫茫，唯賴燈光作導航。
漫道加州天氣好，入冬晨霧倍猖狂。

庭中茶花冬放

九七年十二月

縱無點點臘梅香，麗質耐寒性亦强。
吹落紅顔入泥土，北加風雨忒輕狂。

戲贈以仁 并序

二〇〇一年。余於今夏割除前列腺，以仁聞之，來函慰問，且云彼稍前亦因肝疾而動手術，現已完全康復。函中並附其近作詩詞數十首，余才力已竭，弗克奉和，乃爲四韻打油以報之，語稍近謔，以互勵也

吾因前列痛開膛，色即是空方自傷。
足下生來富肝膽，割除少許又何妨。
君詩高妙人争誦，我首低垂誰短長。

宋玉詞章今復見，巫山仰止拜周張。

與同好共游西藏有感[①]

徐州師大與拉薩師院合辦語言學討論會，余亦在邀，因得游覽西藏。同行友好多以余高齡而擔憂，乃戲化短句以谢之。二〇〇四年六月

莫笑七旬加二翁，登山涉水猛如龍。
高原缺氧何須道，待上中華第一峰。

① 原詩無題，爲索引之方便，特擬此題。

編後記

一

薛鳳生先生 1931 年 10 月 9 日出生於江蘇徐州邳縣(今邳州市),2015 年 9 月 6 日在美國内華達州逝世,享年 85 歲。薛先生長期致力於漢語音韻學、語法學、詩律學和古代文學等研究,主張從漢語自身特點分析漢語,在國際漢語語言學界産生了重要的影響。薛先生的等韻學研究自成一家,其中有關"内外轉"的解釋,得到王力先生的重視和肯定。

薛先生少年時代曾在徐州中學讀書,1949 年隨父母到臺灣,在新竹中學就讀。旋考入臺灣大學外文系,1957 年畢業,同年復入本校中文研究所,師從臺靜農先生專攻古代文學,並跟董同龢先生學習聲韻學,1960 獲碩士學位。1962 年在好友王靖宇先生推薦下入美國明尼蘇達大學做助教,1963 年入印第安那大學學習比較文學,一個學期之後轉入語言學系師從豪斯侯德爾(Fred W. Householder)博士學習理論語言學,1968 年獲博士學位。薛先生 1966 年開始在愛荷華大學任教,1969 年在臺灣大學訪問,1970 年開始任教於俄亥俄州立大學東亞系,1995 年退休,後又在斯坦福大學和加州大學伯克利校區短期任教。

在俄亥俄州立大學任教期間,薛先生於 1983—1989 年擔任《中文教師學會學報》主編;於 1986—1988 年、1991—1993 年,兩度擔任東亞系主任;1993 年任 Bliss M. & Mildred A. Wiant 傑出講席教授。

薛先生特别重視海内外語言學家的交流。從 20 世紀 80 年代開始,薛先生積極推動世界各地的漢語語言學家開展學術交流,在俄亥俄州立大學建立中國學者訪問項目,有力地促進了中美學者之間的交流。北京大學的唐作藩、蔣紹愚、陸儉明等先生,中國社科院語言所的吴宗濟、侯精一等先生,北京語言大學的王還、吕必松等先生和南京大學的魯國堯、卞覺非先生等一大批中國學者,曾在薛先生的幫助下赴美交流訪問,薛先生還曾受美中友協之托負責接待美國教育部邀請的中國教授代表團在美訪問行程,代表團的張志公先生曾贈詩一首以謝之:"共持一杯酒,同登萬里船。飄泊四海外,時念舊家園。"薛先生在《贈別志老》中回曰:"志老嘉名久已聞,天涯邂逅始相親。同游但恨爲時少,煮酒京華再論文。"在薛鳳生先生的不懈努力下,俄亥俄州立大學東亞系成爲美國最著名的中文教育與研究中心之一。

二

我對薛先生的瞭解是從學術之外開始的。改革開放之後,薛先生和師母薛陳慕勤教授是有心回國服務和定居的,所以,1981 年中美之間剛剛有所鬆動,薛先生就受俄亥俄州立大學和美中學術交流委員會的資助隻身一人第一批回國工作,擔任華中工學院英文系教授和中國語言研究所客座教授,與嚴學窘先生朝夕相處,"論學論世"。1982 年參加在西安召開的中國音韻學研究會第二届年會,1983 年之後就經常往返中美兩國,並在中國各大名校講學和訪問。我那時先在徐州師範學院(即今江蘇師範大學)讀本科,後讀研究生,對當代語言學理論,包括結構主義語言學、轉换生成語言學等很感興趣,大有"外國的月亮也比中國的要圓"的感覺;對當代華人學者並不太關注,是一個妥妥的井底之蛙。因此從老師口中聽説有個邳州的美籍華人學者薛鳳生教授甚是了得,但我其时对其不甚了了。薛先生當時也還没有在徐州講過他的學術成果,估計當時薛先生回國,一方面確實是學術交流太忙,武漢、西安、上海、北京等地,排程很緊,但更多的也是尋親訪友吧,離開故土三十多年,能不思鄉思親?後來才知道薛先生那不是一般地思鄉思親,他對故土有着濃郁的家國情懷,有詩爲證:"莫遣兒童唱《大風》,重瞳降準已無蹤。江山空自换新色,父老何曾醉太平。吕雉專權幾傾國,蕭何忍辱僅全身。可憐九里山頭月,還照滄桑彭祖城。"(《歸徐二咏》之一)而對親人,薛先生更是一個都不能少,一一找到,叙舊言歡,每談及找到了一個新的親戚,薛先生的眼圈都是紅紅的,正如薛先生《去徐抒懷》所言:"風歌聽罷只心傷,三十三年始返鄉。漫道虚名傳海外,須憐形骸在他邦。田園廬舍無覓處,姨舅叔姑鬢染霜。拼把離愁寄杯酒,彭城夜色正茫茫。"説來也巧,在他的"姨舅叔姑"中,還真有一位與我也有關聯的。薛先生有一個舅舅"文革"前在我讀中學的學校——贛榆中學擔任過教導主任,他姓高,十年動亂時也在打倒之列,薛先生找到他雖已是改革開放之時了,但既作爲"臭老九"又是"走資派",他心靈的扭曲和心有餘悸還是顯而易見的,薛先生心疼不已。我認識這位高主任,他的孩子跟我是髮小,更巧的是髮小的母親跟我母親還是中學(板浦中學)時很要好的同學,現在又在同一個地方工作。由於這層關係,我當時似乎在對薛先生的學術貢獻還不怎麽瞭解的情况下,就對薛先生淳樸真摯的爲人有了相當親近的感覺,我還替他們相互帶過東西。

真正與薛先生在學術上的接觸,是在1985年3月,我和同届的研究生同學專程到南大聽薛先生的講座,然後回徐州又聽了兩場講座。薛先生講座伊始就提出一個問題:漢語普通话有幾個元音?他接着回答説用三個元音就可以應付了。我一聽就來了興趣,這是嚴格的音位學説,按現代漢語元音的音值來看,簡直不可思議,不過從關係對比來看,其實也就是高、中、低三個元音,每個元音有不同的變異。不僅是對共時音系的描寫,對歷時音系的分析也是一個原則到底。薛先生不沿襲高本漢的傳統,根據方音和域外對音等構擬出一個"靠譜"的擬音來,而是看其在語音系統中的關係,特别是對古代韻書、韻圖的研究,主要的工作是詮釋其關係,整理出内在的音系,而不是着重於重新構擬。對於傳統韻書和韻圖中的"内外轉"和"等"這些概念的研究,薛先生也是强調立足音位的角度來進行,薛先生認爲這些古代的韻書韻圖不是簡單地記某個地點或個人的發音的,而是記録音位對比的音系,韻書記音本質上是音位性的。甚至薛先生説過"所有韻書(不僅《中原音韻》)在語音上没有告訴我們任何東西,它們僅僅展示了一個潛在的音位系統的'代數'結構",可能薛先生在嚴格音位學的道路上走得有點遠,但其觀點的核心思想的確如此。這其實就是歷史比較法與結構主義的區别。

我對這樣的思想是完全贊同的,當時我正在撰寫畢業論文《李氏音鑒音系研究》,就是先根據韻書本身的材料,運用透視分離法給出一個語音系統,然後再考慮給這個語音系統一個恰當的擬音,擬音當然要有根據,但主要是爲了説明音系的建立是科學的,是與左鄰右舍相對比而給出的,不一定是真實的讀音

(也不可能是真實的讀音)。中古和上古的擬音更不能當真,但語音系統必須是科學的,每個音之間必須有音位區别特徵,反映語音系統的面貌。具體操作上也學着薛先生的辦法用了些生成音系學表述方式。

就這樣,我和薛先生成了學術上的"知音"(後來薛先生在其《漢語音韻史十講》序中説過我們早就"互通聲氣",引爲"知音"),我把薛先生當老師,薛先生把我當忘年交,不僅對我愛護有加,而且對我的學生也是關懷備至。我1990年做副教授開始指導研究生,1994年做了教授,擔任副系主任,1995年又擔任了語言研究所所長,1996年擔任副校長,分管科研、學科建設、研究生和圖書館等。這期間,薛先生經常來徐州,在學校小住,跟我和我的學生們一起討論學術和爲文爲人之道,幫我指導研究生,對我和我的學生幫助甚多。

1993年和1995年,薛先生正值盛年,但是他先後主動辭去了俄亥俄州立大學東亞系主任和教職,他的想法是以後可以有更多的時間回到中國,回到徐州,做自己想做的事情。1996年,薛先生處理完在俄亥俄州立大學的退休手續以及斯坦福大學和伯克利加州大學短期教學工作之後,基本上以徐州爲其學術活動中心了。薛先生在江蘇師範大學做了三件事。第一件事是薛先生和師母一起在江蘇師範大學設帳授徒,薛先生講音韻學、語法學,師母講英文學術寫作,師母因是圖書館學專業的專家,還對我校圖書館建設提出了很好的建議,我1999年去美國訪問,師母也帶我去看了一些美國頂尖高校的圖書館建設。第二件事是薛先生將其在美國使用的英文語言學原版書籍悉數捐給了江蘇師範大學語言研究所,包括喬姆斯基、布龍菲爾德等大家的英文學術專著和一些語言學英文原版教材,這些英文原著滋養了一代學者,江蘇師範大學後來走出了一批頗有語言學理論素養的學者,與此有密切關係。這些原版書在上世紀八九十年代殊爲難得,記得那時候要買英文原版書須申請"世行貸款"。第三件事是設立"薛叙齋語言學獎勵基金"支持江蘇師範大學語言研究所學生的學業,當時語言所的研究生,不管是音韻學專業的,語法學專業的,英漢比較專業的,還是神經語言學專業的,許多都曾得到這個基金的獎勵和支持,他們之中許多人已經成爲教授,甚至是國家級領軍人才和長江學者等。

薛先生學術造詣很深,是一位嚴謹和嚴厲的學者和教師,但不是書呆子,運動和娛樂都在行,很有生活情趣。我上世紀80年代第一次見到薛先生,他給我的印象是典型的現代美國西部牛仔模樣,頭戴鴨舌帽,身穿粗呢方格休閑西裝和牛仔褲,腳蹬運動鞋,體格健壯,意氣風發,俠肝義膽,就缺一把標配的柯爾特左輪手槍了,喝可樂而不喝水;我跟薛先生説,我喝可樂衹能是當飲料喝幾口,要解渴必須喝水才行,薛先生説,那衹是習慣問題,喝可樂完全可以解渴。與薛先生西化的物質生活習慣相比,他的精神生活卻很中國,他尊師重教,因爲本科和碩士班受教於董同龢先生,因此稱王力先生爲太老師;他也曾專程帶着學眼科的兒子來徐州認祖歸宗;和唐作藩先生、楊耐思先生等打麻將時,認真的勁頭不亞於學術討論;他晚年英文和普通話都忘記了,卻還能説一口流利的徐州話。薛先生古道熱腸,不僅是對家人、同學和同事,甚至對我們這些晚輩也非常關心,不僅他自己,他還請他在斯坦福和伯克利加大的好友也邀請我們去美國訪學。我在美國開會和做研究,去薩克拉門托看望薛先生,也是先生親自開着車去機場接送,吃住都在先生家,師母每天忙着下厨。天氣好的時候薛先生還和師母一起帶我去西海岸好多個高校參訪,從加州大學伯克利校區、三藩市校區,一路往南到戴維斯校區等,還去了雷諾等地,讓我一試身手。薛先生和師母在徐州生活時,最開心的就是與研究生們一起春游和秋游,我們一起去過雲龍山、皇藏峪、拔劍泉等地。讓我至今記憶猶新的是 2004 年夏天,我們第二屆海外中國語言學者論壇第二階段在拉薩師範學校舉行,西藏自治區教育廳安排專家去納木錯考察,路過念青唐古拉山口,海拔 6000 米以上,72 歲的薛先生全程没有任何反應,更不用任何吸氧工具,爲打消大家的擔憂,還戲作七絶一首贈與會學者:“莫笑七旬加二翁,登山涉水猛如龍。高原缺氧何須道,待上中華第一峰。

三

薛鳳生先生逝世之後,薛先生的弟子和晚輩們曾多次動議編輯全集之事,我也參與了一些討論,凡我參加的,我都表示堅決支持,需要我做什麽就做什麽。2016 年 6 月的一天,離薛先生逝世還不到一年,師母就遠渡重洋來到徐州——因薛先生生前有遺願,逝世之後在徐州設立衣冠冢——我們陪同師母去徐州漢王公墓拜謁了薛先生的衣冠冢,期間也跟師母言及薛先生的學生、後輩準備編輯薛先生的全集,我們徐州的同仁會全力配合的,師母聽聞後很是寬慰。

2020 年 1 月 30 日,我突然收到師母從美國發來的電郵,其中主要内容是有關薛先生著作整理出版授權問題。師母説:“現在有一事想徵求你的意見。關於替老伴出文集之事,爲了在收集、編輯和排版技術上的問題更容易統一意見,及方便與出版社溝通,我想委托江蘇師範大學語言研究院辦理。熟識老伴的好友們都清楚他對祖國的關心和對家鄉濃厚的情結。在他最後失憶的日子裏,什麽事都忘卻了,在連我和孩子們是誰都忘记的情况下,他唯一念念不忘的是,‘回老家!’。加上這麽多年來對師大的深厚感情,他的著作應該屬於他的‘老家’。因此,我希望將他所有在學術上的論著編輯出版權留給江蘇師範大學語言研究院,你認爲可以嗎?很抱歉在你百忙中打擾。我希望儘快解决授權的問題,以便加快出版工作的進展。”收到郵件,我立即回復師母説:“感謝您授權我們來編輯出版薛先生文集,這是對我們極大的信任,我們完全同意,也深感榮幸。薛先生對徐州和江蘇師範大學有着深厚的感情,曾多次來學校弘播學術,捐贈學術書籍,對江蘇師範大學語言學學科的發展有着巨大的貢獻,同時還在江蘇師範大學設立了薛叙齋獎助學金,傾情資助後學,培養了一批青年才俊,我們永志不忘,深表感謝!現在您决定由薛先生故鄉的語言學同仁和江蘇師範大學語言科學與藝術學院來承擔薛先生所有論著的編輯出版,我們一定做好工作,不辜負您的期望,也不辜負薛先生的在天之靈。”

很快,師母發來了《薛鳳生教授著作集委托授權書》,提出“將薛鳳生教授生前撰寫的所有著作及手稿(包括已經出版文章著作和未曾出版的手稿)交由中國江蘇師範大學語言科學與藝術學院搜集、整理出版”,“由江蘇師範大學語言科學與藝術學院院長楊亦鳴教授全權負責”。師母將此事授權於我,作爲薛先生的家鄉人和後學,我義不容辭,深感這是一種信任,一種責任,也是一種擔當。

其實薛先生在世時,有三本與薛先生有關的著作的出版,我也參與了其事。一本是 1999 年出版的《漢語音韻史十講》,薛鳳生著,耿振生、楊亦鳴選編。薛先生在序中説,“由他們兩位編校這本書,再理想不過了,因爲本書所討論的是漢語音系由中古到現代的流變,這也正是他們多年來研究的課題,且各有專著,例如耿教授的《明清等韻學通論》,楊教授的《李氏音鑒音系研究》,所以我們早就‘互通聲氣’,更由於他們甚能領會我的一些‘不太尋常’的觀點,我常把他們引爲知音。”其實該書編輯的實際工作主要是耿振生兄做的,薛先生也説道:“這次能結集成册,全得歸功於耿振生和楊亦鳴兩位教授,尤其是耿教授;由於他能體諒到楊教授新近擔任了繁重的行政任務,便主動承擔了大部分的編校工作……”實際上,不是大部分,差不多是全部。第二本是 2011 年出版的《基於本體特色的漢語研究——慶祝薛鳳生教授八十華誕文集》,侍建國、耿振生、楊亦鳴主編。這本書主要是侍建國兄和耿振生兄兩位操持的。第三本是擬議中的《薛鳳生語法論集》,這本書是薛先生晚年委托我負責整理編輯的,我們商議好的出版範圍是薛先生語法方面的所有論文,包括中英文,全部結集出版,薛先生考慮到對年輕人英文寫作的培養,英文論著中有中文譯本的,也都全數收入,中英文對照出版。薛先生爲此還陸續從美國寄來一些文稿,可是萬萬没想到,薛先生突然病逝,離開了我們,許多在徵集中的文稿也暫時中斷了。

現在,逝者已逝,生者如斯,我們的想法是按照師母的願望,立即開展工作,争取在 2024 年迎來薛先生與師母鑽石婚紀念的日子裏刊出這部文集,既是對逝者的追憶,也是對生者的慰藉,更是爲後輩學者和學術史留下薛先生較爲完整的著述。

爲了做好工作,按照師母的委托,我們以江蘇省和江蘇師範大學的力量爲主成立了編委會,所有的成員都是曾受教於薛先生的晚生和後輩或者是親屬代表,大家分工合作。其中執行主編之一王爲民教授出力最多,從搜集薛先生的著述到排版校訂,親力親爲,付出了大量的時間和精力。王爲民教授在江蘇師範大學讀書期間曾受薛先生親炙,深得真傳,也算是“有事弟子服其勞”矣。

四

《薛鳳生文集》收文範圍和編輯思路、編輯體例,需要作一説明。

薛先生一生,著述頗豐,除了專著和論文,還有一些手稿尚待收集,特别是薛先生主持編纂或者是參與編輯的、面向外國人的、以現代漢語和古代漢語爲内容的漢語二語教材多部,影響很大,因爲時間關係,一時也難以搜集齊備,就都没有收入這部文集。其他著述目前也還没有搜集完整,故本集題爲《薛鳳生文集》。

本集編纂的基本思路是:第一,保持論文或著作的完整性。凡是由於各種原因,有所删節的論文或著作,本次結集暫未收録。比如,魯國堯、侍建國於1990年曾將薛先生的博士論文"Phonology of Old Mandarin"翻譯成中文,以《〈中原音韻〉音位系統》爲名在北京語言學院出版社出版。這個中文譯本將原著例字所標馬丁的中古漢語擬音删除了。再如耿振生於1991年將"On Dialectal Overlapping as a Cause for the Literary/Colloquial Contrast in Standard Chinese"翻譯成中文,以《方音重迭與普通話文白異讀之形成》爲題刊登在《紀念王力先生九十誕辰文集》中,亦收録在《漢語音韻史十講》中,題爲《方音重疊與標準漢語文白異讀之形成》。這個中文譯本將原作的附録Ⅱ删除了。因此上述兩個中文譯本本集都未收録。

第二,嘗試部分實現薛先生生前曾經希望的將其所撰寫的英文論著與中譯本(或翻譯成中文),以中英文形式一併出版的願望,本集挑選在音韻學研究史上有重大學術影響的一部著作和一篇論文作爲嘗試。著作是前面提到的薛先生的博士論文"Phonology of Old Mandarin",這本書1975年由Mouton出版社出版,在學術界産生了重要的影響,至今仍然是有關《中原音韻》研究的代表作,充分展示了薛先生"嚴格的音位學理論"和"内外轉學説"。我們編輯團隊中的執行主編之一王爲民教授對原著進行了重新翻譯,最大程度恢復原著的面貌,且保留薛先生在前一个中文譯本中的的所有追注。至於例字的標音,則在標注原著中馬丁的中古漢語擬音之後,再輔以"攝、呼、等、調、韻、聲"顯示例字的中古音韻地位,以方便國内讀者的閱讀習慣。我們將原著"Phonology of Old Mandarin"和新的中文譯本(此譯本書名根據原名直接譯爲《古官話音系》)前後排列,從而實現中英文對照閱讀。論文是《音韻史與方言研究——平度話中的幾個例子》,這篇文章原題爲"Historical Phonology and Dialect Study: Some Example from the Pingdu Dialect",發表在1987年香港中國語文學會編《王力先生紀念論文集》。這篇論文是方言音韻史研究的代表作,同時也以平度方言的例子解决了《中原音韻》知莊章三組聲母字演變的"孤證"問題。我們亦將原作“Historical Phonology and Dialect Study：Some Example from the Pingdu Dialect”與中文譯本前後排列。

第三，在内容上有包含關係的多篇論文衹收録内容最完整的篇目。比如《論古文中的主語省略及其對文法研究的影響》這篇論文曾刊登在《語文建設通訊》1993年第4期，但其内容包含在《古漢語的主語省略與所謂的被動句型》一文中，本集衹收録後者。

本集共收録薛先生的論文和著作52篇(部)，其中論文48篇，著作4部，有8篇論文和1部詩集爲未刊稿，共分爲“音韻理論”“方言研究”“唐詩格律”“語法探索”“語文建設”和“文學風雅”六類，作爲一級目録。

在目録編排中，爲了醒目起見，論文均爲二級目録，衹顯示論文題目所對應頁碼；曾單獨出版或結集的著作或詩集則出現三級目録，顯示“章”或“詩題”所對應頁碼。凡之前薛先生結集出版過的論文在題注時以“＊”爲標記，説明首發原刊何處，後收録於何文集，首發時薛先生的原題注轉行另起迻録；其他首次在此結集的論文在題注時以“＊＊”爲標記，注明出處和刊載詳情，首發時薛先生的原題注轉行另起迻録；曾單獨出版的論著或結集的詩集在題注時以“＊＊＊”爲標記，注明出版詳情或結集緣由。

2024年5月12日